THE HUMANITIES IN WESTERN CULTURE

BRIEF VERSION

THE HUMANITIES IN WESTERN CULTURE

A Search for Human Values

FOURTH EDITION

BRIEF VERSION

ROBERT C. LAMM
ARIZONA STATE UNIVERSITY, RETIRED

Brown & Benchmark
PUBLISHERS

Madison   Dubuque, IA   Guilford, CT   Chicago   Toronto   London
Caracas   Mexico City   Buenos Aires   Madrid   Bogota   Sydney

Book Team

Publisher   *Rosemary Bradley*
Senior Developmental Editor   *Deborah Daniel*
Associate Marketing Manager   *Kirk Moen*

President and Chief Executive Officer   *Thomas E. Doran*
Vice President of Production and Business Development   *Vickie Putman*
Vice President of Sales and Marketing   *Bob McLaughlin*
Director of Marketing   *John Finn*

Times Mirror
Higher Education Group

Chairman and Chief Executive Officer   *G. Franklin Lewis*
Executive Vice President and Chief Operations Officer   *James H. Higby*
President of Manufacturing and Senior Vice President   *Roger Meyer*
Senior Vice President and Chief Financial Officer   *Robert Chesterman*

The credits section for this book begins on page 569 and is considered an extension of the copyright page.

This book was designed and produced by
CALMANN & KING LTD
71 Great Russell Street, London WC1B 3BN

Editor   *Ursula Sadie*
Designers   *Barbara Mercer and Richard Foenander*
Picture researcher   *Carrie Haines*
Maps by Oxford Illustrators
Typeset by 𝆑 Tek Art, Croydon, U.K.
Printed in Hong Kong

10 9 8 7 6 5 4 3 2

Front cover   Pierre Auguste Renoir, *Le Moulin de la Galette*, detail. 1876. Oil on canvas, full painting 4' 3½" × 5' 9" (1.31 × 1.75 m). Musée d'Orsay, Paris. Photo: R.M.N., Paris.

Spine   *Snake Goddess*, from Knossos Labyrinth, Crete. Ca. 1600 BC. Faience, height 17½" (44.5 cm). Archaeological Museum, Heraklion, Crete. Photo: Dagli Orti, Paris.

Back cover   The Standard of Ur, from Iraq. Sumerian, Early Dynastic II. Ca. 2600–2400 BC. Bitumen base inlaid with shell, red limestone, and lapis lazuli, height 8" (20.3 cm). British Museum, London.

Half-title   Rhyton in the Form of a Lion-Griffin. Persian. 5th century BC. Gold, height 6¾" (17.1 cm). Metropolitan Museum of Art, New York (Fletcher Fund, 1954).

Frontispiece   Jan Vermeer, *Woman Holding a Balance*, detail. Ca. 1664. Oil on canvas, full painting 16¾ × 15" (42.5 × 38.1 cm). National Gallery of Art, Washington, D.C. (Widener Collection).

Preface   Tutankhamen's treasure, detail of a large wooden coffin showing Isis. New Kingdom. Ca. 1350 BC. Gilded wood. Egyptian Museum, Cairo. Photo: Dagli Orti, Paris.

Prologue   Constance Marie Charpentier, *Mlle. Charlotte du Val d'Ognes*, detail. 1785. Oil on canvas, full painting 5' 3½" × 4' 2⅝" (1.61 × 1.29 m). Formerly attributed to David. Metropolitan Museum of Art, New York (Mr. and Mrs. Isaac D. Fletcher Collection; bequest of Isaac D. Fletcher, 1917.17.120.204).

Unit Opener Illustrations

Unit 1   Queen Hatshepsut, architectural detail of the Mortuary Temple of Queen Hatshepsut, Deir-el-Bahri (Thebes), Egypt. New Kingdom, 18th dynasty. Ca. 1480 BC. Photo: Spectrum, London.

Unit 2   Statuette of a youth, "Mantiklos dedicated me. . . ." Ca. 700–680 BC. Bronze, height 8" (20.3 cm). Museum of Fine Arts, Boston (Francis Bartlett Donation).

Unit 3   Pont du Gard, near Nîmes, France. Ca. 20–10 BC. Height 180' (275 m). Photo: Spectrum, London.

Unit 4   *St. Michael*, St. Mark's, Venice. 10th century. Enameled gold plaque. Photo: Werner Forman, London.

Unit 5   Duccio, *Rucellai Madonna*, detail, after restoration, 1989. 1285. Tempera on wood, 14' 9" × 9' 6" (4.5 × 2.9 m). Galleria degli Uffizi, Florence. Photo: Dagli Orti, Paris.

Unit 6   Giotto, detail of campanile, Florence. 1334–50s. Photo: Scala, Florence.

Unit 7   Louis le Vau and Jules Hardouin Mansart, Palace of Versailles, part of central section of garden facade. 1669–85. Photo: Robert Harding, London.

Unit 8   Pierre Auguste Renoir, *Le Moulin de la Galette*, detail. 1876. Oil on canvas, full painting 4' 3½" × 5' 9" (1.31 × 1.25 m). Musée d'Orsay, Paris. Photo: R.M.N., Paris.

Unit 9   Gerhard Richter, *Vase*, detail. 1984. Oil on canvas, full painting 7' 4½" × 6' 6¾" (2.25 × 2 m). Museum of Fine Arts, Boston (Juliana Cheney Edwards Collection).

Contents

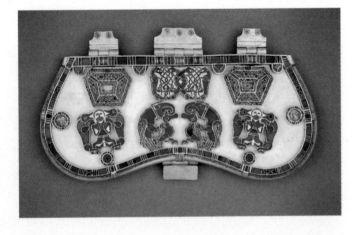

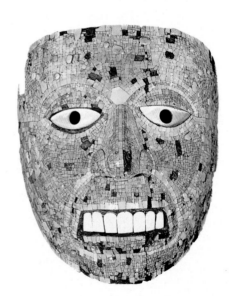

UNIT 9
The Twentieth Century   453

Listening Examples

Maps

Preface

Welcome to the tenth edition of a text that first appeared over forty years ago with multiple authors and entitled *The Search for Personal Freedom*. The original title continued through the seventh edition, after which the undersigned became the sole author of what is now *The Humanities in Western Culture*.

This brief one-volume version of the two-volume text is for the integrated humanities: the arts of literature, painting, music, sculpture, photography, architecture, and film, and the discipline of philosophy. Although philosophy is not an "art" in the strictest sense, the major philosophical ideas so consistently permeate each of the arts that they are, of necessity, interwoven throughout the book. The components of the humanities—philosophy and the arts—are presented not as separate technical disciplines but as interrelated manifestations of human creativity. Moreover, they are studied within the context of important developments in science, technology, economics, and politics. This is, in sum, a book about people and about "art's eternal victory over the human condition" (André Malraux).

In order to understand better why we are the way we are, our studies are centered on our cultural legacy—from Mesopotamia, Egypt, Greece, and Rome to the present day. Throughout the book the accomplishments of the past are considered not as museum pieces but as living evidence of enduring responses to the perplexities of life. These achievements have become, in our day, a basic part of our attempts to make sense of the universe.

The text is arranged chronologically and divided into nine major units. Because artists naturally respond to the issues of their own time, each unit is prefaced by an overview of the social, scientific, religious, and philosophical climate of the period. Forming the core of this text are the primary sources, the art works themselves: extracts from plays, poetry, short stories, sections of large works, hundreds of art illustrations, and numerous musical examples. Introduced with appropriate commentary, the selections are followed by practical exercises and questions. Additionally, there are maps, time charts, and a glossary of important terms in philosophy and the arts. There is more than enough material for a one-semester course based entirely on the text; alternatively, the book can be used as a central text embellished by additional primary sources.

Because each major culture is distinct and merits its own special study, this is an examination of the evolution of Western civilization and its place in American culture. It is perhaps more multicultural than any other civilization because it has been more open to outside influences and ideas. Western culture—the humanities in particular—derives not just from the Mesopotamian, Egyptian, Graeco-Roman, and Germanic heritage. It has been influenced, altered, and/or enlarged over thousands of years by virtually every culture in the world. With its diverse origins Western humanities is an especially rewarding study in what is undoubtedly the most multicultural nation on earth. From colonial times onward, the United States has been a gathering of immigrants. Whether political refugees or seekers after a better life, people from all parts of the globe have been coming here for over three centuries, and will continue coming. What was once dubbed a "melting pot" culture is actually a rich and unique civilization. Whatever one's ancestry, there is something singular and special about being an American and, to cite only one example, we see it writ large at every session of the Olympic Games.

The presence of numerous non-Western immigrants in a rapidly changing population strongly reinforces the necessity of studying the cultural heritage of the West. Many immigrants are, after all, attracted to Western civilization because of the educational and vocational opportunities and the high standard of living, all of which have derived from the economic, political, and scientific development of Western nations. This does not imply, however, that newer citizens must leave their culture behind: far from it. It is most important to go on to study other major cultures plus what is currently called "global humanities," for global considerations are among the conspicuous realities of the late twentieth century. However, the author is convinced that most students, whether native-born or recent arrivals, would derive greater benefits from studying other cultures after they have acquired a better understanding of the Western heritage. Establishing a frame of reference seems the most practical and efficient way of comprehending cultural developments around the globe, most of which have been influenced by Western civilization.

In this new edition there are many changes in both content and style; a humanities textbook is, or should be,

a living document that adjusts to the ever-changing world. New facts about the past are continually emerging, while today's world changes so rapidly as to leave us grasping for comprehension, not to mention gasping for breath.

The biggest change in this book is the addition of many feature boxes that, variously, focus on interesting ideas, other cultural influences, and significant events. There are more and better color illustrations and improved maps. The chapter on Greek music has been integrated into the chapters on art and philosophy. Added to the art chapters are descriptions and color illustrations of the art and craft of jewelry. The unit on the Middle Ages includes additional material on Islamic arts plus a selection from Christine de Pisan, an important writer and early feminist. There is, in fact, increased coverage throughout of some notable contributions of women, especially in art and literature. The Literary Selections in the final chapter now include poems and short stories from Argentina, France, Greece, and Israel. Other additions in the second half of the book include consideration of the religions other than Christianity, Judaism, and Islam that have become increasingly important in American life. These include Hinduism, Buddhism, and Zen Buddhism. The multiplicity of religious beliefs has, of course, added to the multiplicity of American life and culture.

What has not changed is the reading level of the text. After abundant input from users, reviewers, editors, and other interested parties, the author has concluded that writing down to students benefits no one. A watered-down text is manifestly unfair not only to students, but to teachers and higher education in general. Textual clarifications have been added as deemed necessary and the glossary has been substantially enlarged to better support the meaningful utilization of technical terminology. Much of the book has been reorganized with more precise heads and subheads that should contribute to the clarity of the text. The spelling of a number of the Greek proper names has been altered to reflect the most common usage, although a twenty-four-letter alphabet in which thirteen letters differ from the Latin ones can never be totally standardized. Overall, the author has endeavored to compose lucid material that is both accurate and consistently interesting, even entertaining, bearing in mind that the Greeks demanded of their dramas both enlightenment and entertainment. It should surprise no one that much of the content is challenging, for it concerns difficult and abstract concepts. What is most important, however, is that this material represents an essential aspect of what it means to be prepared to live and even flourish in a complex world of ceaseless change.

Robert C. Lamm

ACKNOWLEDGMENTS

This book could not have been written without the expertise and diligence of a reference librarian, photographic associate, and in-house editor, namely Katy Lamm.

I wish to thank the team at Calmann & King for their expertise during production: editor Ursula Sadie, designers Barbara Mercer and Richard Foenander, and picture researcher Carrie Haines.

I also wish to thank the following professors whose careful reading of the manuscript proved invaluable for this tenth edition: Kurt A. Canow, Longview College; Barbara Kramer, Santa Fe Community College; David L. Matson, Cedarville College; David C. Pinnix, Benett College; Alice Gates Schwehm, Pensacola Junior College; Richard C. Tubbs, Community College of Aurora; and Robert A. Whisnant, Jr., Eastfield College. Thanks to Nanette Kelly of Imperial Valley College for her contributions to the new material on women in the humanities.

SUPPLEMENTS FOR THE INSTRUCTOR

The integrated teaching package of ancillary materials is available to instructors using *The Humanities in Western Culture*. Please contact your Brown & Benchmark sales representative or call 800–338–5371 to obtain these supplements, or to ask for further details.

Instructor's Resource Manual and Test Item File

The Instructor's Resource Manual is designed to assist instructors as they plan and prepare for classes. Included are chapter summaries, learning goals, lists of key terms, discussion topics, essay questions, and ideas for optional activities. The revised test item file appears at the end of the Instructor's Manual and contains chapter specific objective-type test questions that may be photocopied and used for quizzes or tests. Also included is a list of videotapes, recordings, videodiscs, and their suppliers.

MicroTest III

The questions in the test item file are available on MicroTest III, a powerful yet easy-to-use test generating software available for DOS, Windows, and Macintosh. MicroTest III allows instructors to generate tests and quizzes, and customize questions, headings, and instructions.

Call-in/Mail-in/Fax Service

Instructors may use Brown & Benchmark's convenient call-in/mail-in/fax service to generate tests. Select questions from the test item file at the end of the Instructor's Manual. Then call 800–338–5371, or mail your selections to Educational Resources at Brown & Benchmark Publishers, 25 Kessel Ct., Madison, WI 53711, or fax your request to

Educational Resources at 608–277–7351. Within two working days of receiving your order, Brown & Benchmark will send by first-class mail (or fax) a test master, a student answer sheet, and an answer key for fast and easy grading.

Three Audiocassettes

Two sixty-minute cassettes (one each for Volumes 1 and 2) and one ninety-minute cassette (for Brief) contain the core Listening Examples from the text, a total of thirty-eight musical selections. Instructors may obtain copies of the cassettes for classroom use by calling 800–338–5371. Individual cassettes may be purchased separately, or, upon request, cassettes can be packaged with corresponding texts.

Instructor's Set of Compact Discs

This is from *Listener's Guide to Musical Understanding*, seventh edition, by Leon Dallin. An instructor's set of four CDs includes thirty-seven of the Listening Examples in the text as well as additional musical selections.

Slides

A set of fifty high-quality color slides correlated to Volumes 1 and 2, or a museum-specific videodisc, is available free to qualifying adopters.

Videos

Qualifying adopters may select video(s) from the Brown & Benchmark video catalog.

Humanities Transparencies Set

A set of seventy-three acetate transparencies is available with *The Humanities in Western Culture*. The set includes illustrations of art elements and principles; architectural styles; media; maps; musical forms, instruments, and selected musical scores.

Technology Products

Culture 2.0

Developed by Cultural Resources, Inc., Culture 2.0 © takes interdisciplinary humanities students on a fascinating journey into humanity's cultural achievements via Hypercard © software. Available for purchase in either IBM PC or MAC formats, this seven-disk program gives students access to essays, almanacs, and visual and musical examples. For each time period, categories include history, politics, religion, philosophy, art, and music, which provides an interactive Socratic method of learning for students. Culture 2.0 also features note-taking capabilities, report capabilities, and a student workbook for more guided learning. Contact your Brown & Benchmark sales representative or call Educational Resources at 800–338–5371 for ordering and purchase information.

Explore the Humanities!

Currently under development by Brown & Benchmark, this CD-ROM series will soon be available for purchase. *Explore the Humanities!* provides you and your students with a fully interactive exploration of many of the arts, ideas, and societies discussed in *The Humanities in Western Culture*. For further details, call your local Brown & Benchmark sales representative.

An Introduction to Integrated Humanities

Each of the [artistic] masterpieces is a purification of the world, but their common message is that of their existence and the victory of each individual artist over his servitude, spreading like ripples on the sea of time, implementing art's eternal victory over the human situation.

André Malraux

Everyone is capable of living a more rewarding life, which is reason enough for studying the humanities. From cave art to the present, the arts and ideas of human beings are beacons of hope, truth, and beauty for a world that needs to pay far more attention to the humanities, to the arts that teach us "nothing except the significance of life," in the words of twentieth-century American author Henry Miller. In our integrated approach to the humanities, we examine literature, painting, music, sculpture, philosophy, and architecture not as separate disciplines but as marvelous varieties of human creativity. Nor do we study the arts and artists in isolation. Artists are individuals, coping with the stress and strain of everyday life and, perhaps more than other people, influenced by the ideas and values of their society. "Artists are," observed composer Ned Rorem, "like everyone else, only more so."

The focus of our study of the humanities is the belief that the quality of life can be enhanced and that this enrichment is available to all. Unlike Middle East oil reserves, the reservoir of Western (or any other) culture is limitless; the more we draw from it the more there is to draw upon. The only deposits necessary are time and effort. The process amounts to addition or even multiplication; no one has to discard a collection of rock records to listen to Beethoven nor exchange Cowboy Art for Rembrandt.

This prologue is an introduction to the significance of the artist as an individual, the necessity of art, and the primacy of human values. Fundamental to cultural development are values such as truth, beauty, love, justice, and faith. Our investigation of how other cultures developed their value systems is chronological, a "return to the past" to see how the Egyptians, Greeks, and later civilizations handled their problems. What questions did they ask? What solutions did they try? We explore earlier cultures from the vantage point of our own world, studying earlier

achievements not as museum pieces but as living evidence of enduring responses to life's perplexities. This priceless legacy is central to our attempts to make sense of the world and of our lives. Some will ask why we look to the past to prepare for the future. Where else can we look?

WHY STUDY THE HUMANITIES?

We explore the humanities not just to acquire facts about past eras but to try to understand those cultures: their questions, answers, and values. We can see the qualities they prized in their art and philosophy, and in their social and political institutions. We examine all of these areas to learn what they did; more importantly, we are concerned with why and how their cultures evolved in certain unique ways. Culture can be defined as what remains after a particular society has vanished. What is left behind is much more than artifacts. The creations of other cultures reveal their visions, their hopes, their dreams.

This is a text for the integrated or interdisciplinary humanities, the interrelationships of the arts, philosophy, and social and political ideas and institutions. Life is itself interdisciplinary. Using the interdisciplinary approach we study the "lives" of other civilizations to see how their values are manifested in just about everything they did, made, or thought. Whatever we learn from other cultures leads inevitably to a fuller understanding of civilization in general and of our own culture in particular.

Each of us has the option of accepting value systems from institutions or other persons, or we can generate a personal set of beliefs and values. The acquisition of an informed set of personal values is, of course, a lifelong project. The knowledge and understanding of other cultures and of ourselves are certainly their own reward, but there are additional advantages. If "the unexamined life is not worth living," as Socrates said, then self-knowledge would seem to be an acquired virtue. The greater our understanding of what is going on in our lives, the more likely we are to be aware of our options and thus of opportunities to improve the quality of life.

We can achieve the freedom objectively to examine alternatives and possibly make better choices. This freedom is not conditioned absolutely by political, social, and

economic considerations, although these factors can help or hinder. One can imagine a political prisoner of a totalitarian state whose knowledge and informed personal values allow a free and independent spirit in the most squalid of surroundings. The prisoner's goals, in this case, are not those of going somewhere or of acquiring material things, but of being a particular person. Those who, in the phrase of American essayist and poet Thoreau, "lead lives of quiet desperation" are at the mercy—intellectually and spiritually—of unknown forces over which they have no control. With no knowledge, no understanding, there is no way to determine whether there are one, two, or more viable choices. All of us have to accept the "slings and arrows of outrageous fortune" (Shakespeare) when we have no alternative. The trick is to be so aware of what is going on in our society and in our lives that we can, at least some of the time, select viable options that will help improve the quality of life. It is worth our while—worth our lives in fact—to study cultures of the past and present, and to make conscious cultural choices.

Western Civilization

As proclaimed by the title, this book is primarily—but not exclusively—concerned with Western civilization and its monumental contributions to world culture: its art, literature, performing arts, philosophy, science, and technology. Because it has had great complexity and influence and because it is our very own heritage, Western civilization commands our full attention. Light years from being monolithic, Western civilization is multicultural, having assimilated elements of every advanced culture in the world from ancient Mesopotamia and Egypt to modern India and China.

> All important cultures have ingenuities of their own. They are all marvelous manifestations of the power of the mind. But our own culture—Western civilization— is the most intellectual of all. More than the others, it is the product of systematic thought. The whole world uses its inventions. Its [science and] scientific methods . . . have been adopted by other civilizations and are transforming them.[1]

That the preeminence of Western culture is the result of systematic thought is only part of the equation. By asking, "systematic thought about what?" we can find the key to Western dominance in science.

> Dear Sir
> Development of Western Science is based on two great achievements; the invention of the formal logical

system (in Euclidean geometry) by the Greek philosophers, and the discovery of the possibility to find out causal relationship by systematic experiment (Renaissance). In my opinion one has not to be astonished that the Chinese sages have not made these steps. The astonishing thing is that these discoveries were made at all.[2]

Yes, these discoveries are astonishing, for they led to the preeminence of the West in empirical science and technological advances. But there is more. The social and political values of the West have also had worldwide influence, ranging from the thought of Solon, Plato, and Aristotle to Cicero, Dante, Voltaire, John Locke, Thomas Jefferson, and Martin Luther King, Jr. Though immigrants from Asia, and Africa, for example, cannot readily perceive Western culture as "theirs," the fact is that their own cultures have adopted much of Western culture, and only partly because of colonialism. The adoption in various degrees of Western technology, science, political, and economic systems by the rest of the world speaks for itself. The further fact that Western civilization was, in general, created by what some have called "dead white men" alters nothing for we cannot rewrite history. The Greeks invented democracy, speculative philosophy, and formal logic, and Renaissance innovators invented and developed the experimental scientific method. The list of Western inventions is virtually endless: the incandescent light bulb, telephone, automobile, airplane, computer, space flight, and, yes, nuclear fission and fusion. The power eventually attained from nuclear-fusion power plants may even save the world from its manifold excesses.

The Culture-Epoch Theory

One begins to understand a culture by learning how that culture developed and what it means to us. We consider the past using a simplified version of the culture-epoch theory of cultural formation. Except for a smattering of political-military history, many of us are neither concerned nor knowledgeable about our cultural heritage. The culture-epoch theory helps overcome that deficiency: it stresses the critical fact of ceaseless change; it weaves cultural and intellectual history into a historic tapestry; and it emphasizes evolutionary processes in the course of history. The theory is neither more nor less "true" than other concepts of cultural evolution; for our purpose, in an interdisciplinary context, the theory works.

According to the culture-epoch theory, a culture is founded upon whatever conception of reality is held by the great majority of its people over a considerable period of time. Most people may not be aware of any concept of reality or, more likely, take it so much for granted that they don't know it is a human idea, held on faith. Thus, for most people at the time this is written, a typewriter is real, a physical tree is real, and all things that can be seen, heard, smelled, felt, or tasted are real.

1. Gilbert Highet, *Man's Unconquerable Mind* (New York: Columbia University Press, 1954), p.14.
2. Albert Einstein, Letter to J. E. Switzer, 23 April 1953. In D. J. de S. Price, *Science Since Babylon* (New Haven: Yale University Press, 1962), p.15n.

Scientists, philosophers, and theologians have given us different concepts of reality that have, at various times in history, come to be widely held. These thinkers contemplated the millions of forms of life, many of them similar yet each one different; they examined the forms of earth, air, fire, and water; they wondered about the processes of change by which a tree today may, at some time in the future, disintegrate into earth and reappear in some totally alien form. They watched such non-tangible things as sunlight and air becoming leaf and branch. Pondering these things, they came inevitably to the ultimate question: "What is the nature of reality?"

To reach an answer, they usually focus on a few profound inquiries, some of which may be given here. For example, they might say, "We see change all around us. We see grass eaten and turn into cow. We see cow eaten and turn into human. We see humans disintegrate and become earth. If all these changes can take place, what are the universal elements of which all things are composed?" Or they might say, "We see an individual human, Jane Doe, as baby, as youth, as adult, as frail old woman, as corpse. From one moment to the next, she is never the same, yet she is always the same, Jane Doe, a distinct being. Can it be that nothing is permanent, that reality is a process rather than a thing or group of things? If we have change, then, how does the process take place? And more to the point, we know that we live in a world of constant change, but what force directs the process?"

"Nonsense," retorts another group of thinkers. "Anything in a constant state of flux cannot be real. Only that which is permanent and unchanging is real. What, then, in the universe is permanent, unchanging in itself, yet can transform itself, manifest itself, or produce from itself the countless forms we see around us?" The responses to basic questions such as these are various concepts of reality.

Based on the idea of reality accepted as "true," specialized thinkers build different thought-structures that underlie visible institutions. These include a philosophy of justice from which particular forms of law and government spring; a philosophy of education that dictates the nature and curriculum of our schools; a religious philosophy that becomes apparent in churches and creeds, in synagogues, mosques, and temples; and an economic philosophy that is manifested in the production and distribution of goods and services. There are, of course, other philosophies and institutions, but these are some that affect our daily living.

A culture may be said to be "complete" and "balanced" when its underlying philosophies and its institutions are in harmony with its concept of reality, but by the time such a pattern is established, there are new forces already at work to undermine it. The wreckers are new critics who note inconsistencies within the idea of reality itself, who question postulates and detect contradictions.

From these innovative thinkers (philosophers, scientists, theologians) emerges a new idea of reality so convincing that it cannot be brushed aside. Once the new reality is generally accepted, the whole cultural structure finds itself without foundation. Law and justice of the old culture are no longer appropriate; educational philosophies are unsatisfactory; religious beliefs must be adjusted or even discarded; old ways of making and distributing things no longer suffice. Over a stretch of time, the culture is plunged into a period of chaos, the first step in the formation of a new epoch.

Periods of Chaos

A notable example of a chaotic period is the Early Middle Ages (ca. 400–800), once called the Dark Ages. The relative stability of the Graeco-Roman era of 480 BC to AD 180 began to disintegrate following the reign of Marcus Aurelius, though the Greek ideal of the individual as reality was superseded by the Roman view that reality was the state without seriously disturbing the cultural balance. Both the Greek and the Roman were secular societies with a general respect for law and justice, a stable social order, and reasonably effective government. Rome's decline was very gradual. Government, the economy, and the rule of law began to unravel and both the rise of Christianity and the barbarian invasions helped finish off a weary and decadent civilization. Most of western Europe soon found itself deep in a period of chaos. Graeco-Roman civilization was not totally destroyed—as demonstrated by the classically inspired Renaissance—but the stage was set for a new idea of reality through which order would be restored.

Periods of Adjustment

Out of the turmoil and confusion of chaotic periods of past cultures emerge periods of adjustment. At these times innovative artists and thinkers—whether painters, scientists, writers, composers, or philosophers—make important contributions that can suggest innovative lines, shapes, or patterns for a new culture.

No one needs to know all about new ideas of reality. In our own time, for example, artists (in particular) may or may not understand Einstein's theories of relativity. As sensitive persons, they generally feel the tensions caused by Einstein's work and its implications. Because they are creators, artists feel compelled to explore the impact that theories, ideas, and events have on their society and to examine or invent new experiences and relationships.

Many people experience the tension and turmoil in periods of chaos and adjustment, but artists tend actively to respond to the chaos and confusion. They explore conflicts within their culture and create new structures and designs; they synthesize the elements of dissension and give fresh meaning to experience. Some works of art are so outstanding that they become symbols of the new age. The Parthenon, for example (see fig. 7.26), still symbolizes the Golden Age of Athens.

At some point another element of the population—we may call them intellectuals—enters the picture. They are people like ourselves, college students and faculty, government officials, business executives, and others who have been troubled by the tensions and conflicts of the time. Still laboring in the period of adjustment, they become aware of fresh meanings and patterns produced by artists and other innovators. They begin reshaping these designs into new philosophies of government, justice, education, economics, and the like. Through their work, order slowly emerges out of chaos. Based on the idea of the Christian God as the ultimate reality, the period of adjustment of the medieval world saw the expansion of the power of the Church of Rome, the rise of universities, and the growth of cities (plus other factors) that coalesced in the thirteenth century into the period of balance of the High Middle Ages.

Periods of Balance

Order is the hallmark of periods of balance. At this point the idea of reality, the philosophies underlying the basic institutions, and the institutions themselves are all in harmony. Life must be very satisfying early in a period of balance with everything tidy and orderly. But new and challenging ideas are already stirring. Probably no one in thirteenth-century Europe perceived the era as a period of balance. Certainly no one foresaw that the balance would be upended by forces leading to stronger national states, the revival of humanism, and the rediscovery of Greek philosophy.

But change is the only constant. At the beginning of this century, for example, some physicists were convinced that the ultimate discoveries had been made with little left to do but some tidying-up. Yet Albert Einstein was just then formulating theories that would overthrow previous knowledge in physics. Exactly when people become certain of virtually everything during a period of balance, new ideas are already fermenting that will dump the apple cart into a new period of chaos.

A word of caution is needed here. This systematic description of an epoch makes it appear that artists function only in a time of chaos or adjustment, or that philosophers quit philosophizing until their proper time comes around. Of course this is not true. While any epoch can be divided roughly into the three periods described above, all functions occur with greater or lesser impact throughout the entire time period.

A COMMON BASIS FOR UNDERSTANDING THE ARTS

In the humanities we take art seriously. As Aristotle observed, "Art is a higher type of knowledge than experience." As previously indicated in the description of a culture-epoch, eminent artists help to create patterns for a way of life. "The object of art is to give life a shape," said the twentieth-century French dramatist Jean Anouilh. The Parthenon, Chartres cathedral, Augustine's *The City of God*, Beethoven's Ninth Symphony, Michelangelo's *David* and

Sistine Chapel ceiling are only a few examples of art works that have affected life in the Western world.

One might ask what area of the universe is the darkest, the most unknown. The universe itself? Einstein once said that the most incomprehensible fact about the universe is that it is so comprehensible. No, the most bewildering portion of the universe is yourself. As a member of the human race you are (or should be) asking yourself such questions as "Who am I?", "What am I?", "Why am I here?" It is the artist who persists in reacting to these questions, who seeks answers from within, and who discovers answers that strike responsive chords in the rest of us. As Henry Miller said, "art teaches nothing, except the significance of life."

A Shakespearean scholar once remarked that Shakespeare, in his plays, had made discoveries as important as those made by a scientist. Such an assertion seems, at first, to be an overreaction to the dominance of science in today's world. Consider, however, the playwright's treatment of love and hate in *Romeo and Juliet*, good and evil in *King Lear*, and murder and revenge in *Macbeth*. As enacted on stage, these aspects of the human condition constitute artistic truths. This idea of discoveries by Shakespeare or any other artist can provide a basis for a better understanding of the arts. In this respect, as the French poet and playwright Jean Cocteau observed, "art is science in the flesh."

The physical world is explored by the sciences; the social sciences make discoveries about the behavior and activities of people in various groups; the arts and humanities probe the inner meaning: humanity's hopes, fears, loves, delights as individuals act and react within a social context. "All art is social," historian James Adams noted, "because it is the result of a relationship between an artist and his time." Art is also exploration, and the discoveries made can be expressed as concepts and percepts. Concepts are intangible ideas such as friendship, beauty, truth, and justice. What we perceive with our senses are percepts: line, taste, color, aroma, volume, pitch, and so forth. Artists express concepts by the unique manner in which they choose to arrange the percepts, that is, the sense-apparent objects and materials. Obviously this kind of vivid creativity can never be done by committee. "Art is the most intense mode of individualism that the world has known," said nineteenth-century Irish writer Oscar Wilde.

Differences and Similarities

Because of variations in media and modes of expression, the arts differ from one another in a variety of ways. Certainly a time-art such as music, which exists only as long as it is heard, differs from a space-art such as painting, which uses visual symbols as its means of expression. Both arts are separated from literature, a word-art that depends upon fully developed literacy. The differences between Beethoven's Fifth Symphony, the *Mona Lisa*, and *Hamlet* are obvious; not so obvious are their similarities. "Painting," wrote nineteenth-century American poet and essayist Emerson, "was called silent poetry, and poetry speaking painting. The laws of each art are convertible into the laws of any other." As early as the fourteenth century Dante called sculpture "visible speech." The common basis of all the arts is the exploration, by means of sensory percepts, of the emotions, mind, and personality of human beings; their common goal is to speak directly to our inner being. As Emerson also wrote: "Raphael paints wisdom; Handel sings it; Pheidias carves it; Shakespeare writes it."

The artist deals subjectively with all materials while drawing upon a singular store of personal experience. Artistic production depends as much on the background and personality of the artist as it does upon the raw material of experience. It therefore follows that each artist is unique and that the artist's production is necessarily unique. To illustrate, let us examine the treatment two literary artists make of the same theme: the emptiness of the life of a woman who, herself, is virtually a complete blank, but who moves from man to man, living only as a reflection of each man. Read Dorothy Parker's "Big Blonde" and Anton Chekhov's "The Darling," both short stories. Though the experience is very similar in the two stories, the end result is quite dissimilar and the reader's experience is also different. The reader might protest: "But one of them must be right about this woman and one must be wrong." Actually, both Parker and Chekhov are right—both stories have the ring of truth—and any other artist treating the same material with a different insight would also be right. The discovery of multiple truths is a personal matter and the corollary is that the realm of truth in personality, that prime area where the arts are focused, is inexhaustible. Anyone who understands any work of art grows with each facet of experience shared with the artist. Our boundaries are expanded as we add the artist's experiences to our own.

> Thanks to art, instead of seeing one world, our own, we see it multiplied and, as many original artists as there are, so many worlds are at our disposal.
>
> André Malraux

SUMMARY

The humanities include, but are not limited to, the arts of literature, painting, music, sculpture, architecture, and dance, and the discipline of philosophy that permeates all the arts and finally unites them all. The arts, taken together, are a separate field of human knowledge with their own area of exploration and discovery, and with a method of their own. So these volumes will concentrate on some of the most significant artistic productions of each of the major periods of Western civilization. Each unit begins with an overview of the social, scientific, religious, and philosophic climate of the period in which the artists were working, for artists usually accept the scientific and social worldpicture of their time. Following these introductory discussions, attention turns to the arts themselves to reveal answers to the great questions of humankind—the new patterns, structures, and meaning that artists found for life in their time. This procedure enables the student to trace the development and changes of the problems that plague us so sorely in our own time. Equipped with knowledge of the great answers found in the past that still shape the way we live today, having come to know the exalted expressions of humanity revealed at their fullest, each individual can work to develop an informed set of values and a freedom to be the person he or she would like to be.

Not everyone will derive the same kind or degree of satisfaction from a particular art form, but the educated person is obliged to know that "there is something in it," even if that "something" is not deeply moving. And perhaps, with deeper acquaintance and wider knowledge, that "something" will become clearer and of greater value. "I don't get it" is no refutation of either Einstein or Bach.

We have made the assertion that the artist is an explorer and discoverer in the realm of the human personality. The artist uses the methods of intuition and composition. The artist's raw material lies in the human personality and in human experience, with their vast and unknown reaches, their disrupting conflicts. The artist gives form to the component elements of personality and experience, and in so doing generates an artistic truth. No matter whether we speak of literature, painting, sculpture, music, or any of the other arts, this concept of creating form out of chaos is the common basis and foundation for all aesthetics.

Ancient River-Valley Civilizations

Prehistory

(most dates approximate)

PALEOLITHIC AGE
40,000 BC
18,000 BC

30,000–20,000 *Venus of Willendorf*, Austria
18,000–15,000 Last Ice Age
13,000 Lascaux cave paintings, France

MESOLITHIC AGE
10,000 BC

10,000 Invention of bow and arrow, first domestication of wheat and barley

NEOLITHIC AGE
8000 BC

8000 Domestication of animals, development of agriculture, pottery, weaving, permanent houses, settlements, fortifications, warfare

Mesopotamia   Egypt

5000 BC

5000 Infiltration of Semites from west and north, non-Semites from east; fusion
3500–3000 Sumerian Protoliterate Period. Infiltration of Sumerians (origin?) and fusion with resident population; invention of written language

5000–3100 Pre-Dynastic Period
4200 Invention of solar calendar
3500 Development of religion: sun worship
3100–2700 Dynasties I and II. Development of hieroglyphics and central administration

BRONZE AGE
3000 BC

3000–2350 Sumerian dynasties
2700 Reign of Gilgamesh, king of Uruk
2500 First dynasty of Ur
2350–2100 Akkadian Period
2350 Sargon the Great
2050–1900 Third dynasty of Ur (Neo-Sumerian Period), Gudea of Lagash

2686–2181 Old Kingdom, dynasties III–VI. Highly centralized political theocracy; strong artistic development
2590–2514 Pyramid Age
2260–2130 First Intermediate Period, dynasties VII–X
2134–1786 Middle Kingdom, dynasties XI–XII. Expansion and prosperity; refinement of arts

2000 BC

2000 *The Epic of Gilgamesh*
1900–1500 First dynasty of Babylonia
1792–1750 Hammurabi and Law Code
1500–1100 Kassite Period, status quo
1076–612 Assyrian Empire
884–859 Assurnasirpal II, capital of Nimrud
722–709 Sargon II, capital of Khorsabad
669–626 Assurbanipal, capital at Nineveh

1780–1550 Second Intermediate Period: Hyksos, dynasties XIII–XVII
1570–1085 New Kingdom (Empire), dynasties XVII–XX
1379–1362 Akhenaton (Amarna Period)
1085–664 Post-Empire Period, dynasties XXI–XXV

IRON AGE
1000 BC

625–539 Chaldean (Neo-Babylonian) Empire
604–562 Nebuchadnezzar II
586–539 Babylonian Captivity of Israelites
539–331 Persian Empire
539–530 Cyrus the Great
521–485 Darius I
(490–479 Persian invasions of Greece)
485–465 Xerxes I
331 Alexander the Great conquers Persian Empire

670 Assyrian conquest of Egypt
663–525 Saite Period, dynasty XXVI; cultural renaissance
525 Persia conquers Egypt
525–343 Persian kings, Egyptian dynasties XXVII–XXX
343–332 Persian kings
332 Alexander the Great conquers Egypt
332–311 Macedonian kings
311–30 The Ptolemies
51–30 Cleopatra VII

1 BC

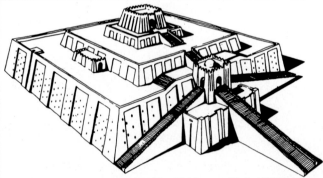

Reconstruction of the ziggurat at Ur. Sumerian, Third Dynasty of Ur. Ca. 2150–2050 BC. Height ca. 90' (27.4 m).

Egyptian columns. From left to right: bud, foliated, palm leaf, papyrus blossom, reed bundle, lotus.

CHAPTER 1

The Emergence of Early Culture

PREHISTORY

Archaeologists have prosaically labeled the periods before the invention of writing according to weapons or tools used, thus the Stone Age, Bronze Age, Iron Age. There are three phases of the extended Stone Age: the Paleolithic (Gk., *paleos*, "old"; *lithos*, "stone"), the Mesolithic ("middle stone"), and Neolithic ("new stone"). The Paleolithic era began about 40,000 BC at about the time that *Homo sapiens* ("the one who knows," meaning "who thinks") had evolved from proto-humans while also deposing Neanderthals.

Human history began with *Homo sapiens*, who invented art during the Paleolithic, domesticated wheat and barley during the Mesolithic, and developed written language and civilization during the Neolithic. Most of what we would call Paleolithic art is today found in the caves at Altamira in Spain and at Lascaux and other caves in southern France. Permanently closed to the public twenty-one years after their discovery in 1940, the Lascaux caves contain paintings that are still remarkably fresh today because there are no visitors bringing in outside contaminants. The spectacular Hall of Running Bulls (fig. 1.1) is filled with art but no one knows why these artists decided to paint all these images. They made no attempt to highlight or frame any of the animals nor, apparently, were they concerned about overpainting earlier work. Standing in this hall is an uncanny experience; while studying the paintings one feels the presence of creative forces applied to those walls many thousands of years ago.

Considerably older than the Lascaux paintings is the so-called Venus of Willendorf (fig. 1.2), at present the first

---

1.1 Hall of Running Bulls, Lascaux, near Montignac, France. Ca. 13,000 BC. Paint on limestone rock walls, individual bulls ca. 13'–16' (4–5 m) long. Archiv für Kunst und Geschichte, Berlin.

1.2 Venus of Willendorf, from Lower Austria.
Ca. 30,000–20,000 BC. Limestone, height 4½"
(11.4 cm). Naturhistorisches Museum, Vienna.

1.3 *Below*   Stonehenge, Salisbury Plain, England.
Ca. 2200–1400 BC. Stone, diameter of circle 97' (29.6 m),
height of tallest monoliths 13'6" (4.1 m). Photo: Skyscan
Balloon Photography, Cheltenham.

known portrayal of a human being. Very likely a fertility symbol, this ancient statuette has exaggerated female characteristics but no face, possibly indicating a general statement about childbearing and motherhood. Several hundred female figures have been found but no male figures, thus confirming the fertility thesis. Calling what is possibly an early representative of the goddess religion "Venus" is, of course, a misnomer but the label makes a certain amount of sense in today's world.

Trying to learn anything at all about the history of humankind during the prehistoric period is a difficult, complex, and frustrating endeavor. Although archaeologists and anthropologists, among others, can discover objects and unearth ruins all are hard pressed to determine "Why?" Why did artists paint in caves? Why did artists carve representations of nude women? Why was Stonehenge built and why did the people living there continue building for hundreds of years (fig. 1.3)? Stonehenge was probably a Neolithic shrine, but for what purpose? For what gods? It is positioned to align with the summer solstice, indicating that its designers possessed certain astronomical and mathematical skills. How extensive were these skills? Were they exercised by a priesthood? Was there a priesthood?

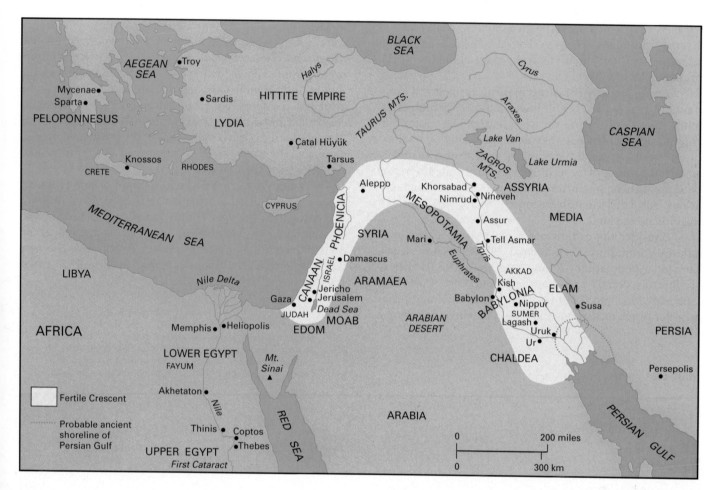

Map 1.1   Ancient Near East and the Fertile Crescent.

The questions raised by these ancient art works are endless, but so is the fascination of exploring them. Not until we advance to the Neolithic Age and the invention of writing and civilization do we begin to get some answers and, even then, so many explanations are incomplete and subject to speculation.

MESOPOTAMIA: THE LAND BETWEEN THE RIVERS

The roots of Western civilization are found in the Near and Middle East in such widely separated sites as Jericho in Palestine, Çatal Hüyük in southern Turkey, and the Sumer area in southern Mesopotamia (Gk., "land between the rivers"). A new way of life evolved in all these locales but we shall concentrate on Sumer, which has been studied longer and in greater depth than other Neolithic cultures. Beginning around 8000 BC in the fertile valleys of the Tigris and Euphrates rivers (map 1.1), there gradually appeared a series of innovations: pottery, weaving, permanent houses (rather than tents), organized communities, the buying and selling of crops and goods, calendar fashioning, mathematics, and, most important, writing. What prompted this startling surge of new ideas?

Culture: Cultivation

The answer, in a word, is agriculture. For millennia, nomadic tribes had followed the seasons as they hunted game and gathered edible plants and fruit. At some point the puzzle of propagation was solved and the connection made between seeds and germination, mating and gestation. The resulting planting, harvesting, and animal husbandry enabled tribes to produce more food than was needed, a surplus that normally freed them from the precarious existence common to all hunting/gathering societies. Drought, floods, and storms have always plagued farmers but nomadic hunters are totally at the mercy of a capricious nature.

Stone Age people apparently continued to hunt and gather while cultivating some crops. In about 8000 BC, however, some Mesopotamian tribes settled into permanent villages, where they became wholly dependent on their animals and crops. The innovations that had freed nomads from famine now actually imprisoned agricultural societies. However, returning to the previous existence was never an option. Whatever the endeavor, advancing technology takes

12   **Chapter 1**

a society in one direction only. In today's world a retreat to a horse and buggy, 78 r.p.m. records, or black-and-white television with a 9-inch (23-cm) screen is, quite simply, unthinkable for most of us.

The establishment of permanent agricultural communities marked the beginning of "culture," which originally meant cultivating the soil. As the Mesopotamian communities flourished, they developed a higher civilization than that of Neolithic nomads, a culture as we understand the meaning of the term: socially transmitted behavior patterns, beliefs, institutions, arts, and other human creations.[1] All of this was a direct consequence of settling down to cultivate the land.

Consider the ramifications of creating a new agricultural community. Permanent dwellings become necessary for a population no longer on the move (domestic architecture, pottery, and other household items). Cultivated land is divided into "your land" and "my land," and properly identified, measured, and recorded (surveying, maps,

mathematics, and writing). Because privately owned lands were now at stake, villages organized for defense against those who chose to steal rather than plant (community organization, village fortification and defense). The spring floods upon which most agriculture depended must be anticipated, measured, recorded and, in time, somehow controlled and exploited (development of a calendar, study of the heavens to learn the wishes of the gods, invention of dams and the water wheel, development of irrigation, and ever more writing and recording).

Inevitably, farmers grew too much of one crop and not enough of another; this led to the bartering of grain and, later, to full-fledged commerce as crops, animals, and household goods were bought and sold. This commercial activity necessitated a legal system to stabilize the new world of agriculture, manufacturing, and trade. Further,

1. The concept of culture was first explicitly defined in 1871 by British anthropologist Edward B. Tyler as "that complex whole which includes knowledge, belief, art, morals, law, custom and any other capabilities and habits acquired by man as a member of society." As opposed to genetically endowed behavior, culture always entails learned behavior.

Map 1.2   Early Mesopotamia.

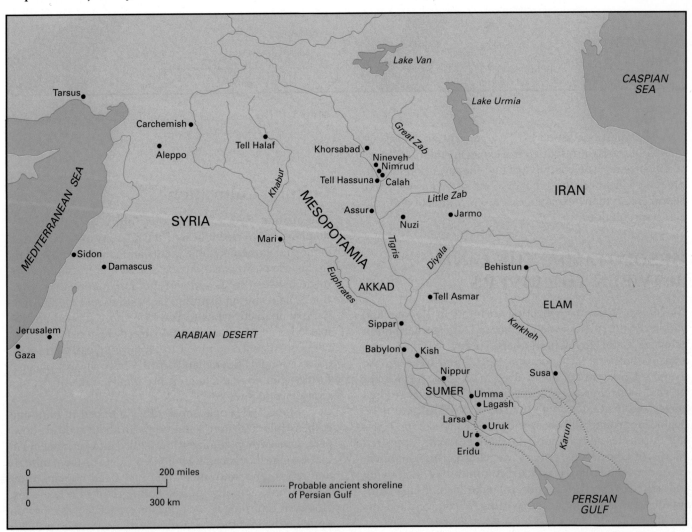

the buying and selling of goods worked most efficiently when concentrated in financial centers, stimulating the development of commercial hubs. This, in turn, helped promote commerce. As commerce increased, villages grew into towns that became cities and then city-states as urban developments interacted with the surrounding countryside.

It was in Sumer that a loose confederation of city-states consolidated political and economic power into one of history's earliest ruling dynasties. Sumer lay in the eastern arc of the Fertile Crescent, that broad belt of productive land extending north-westward from the Persian Gulf and curving down the Mediterranean coast almost to Egypt (map 1.1). This was a settlement zone but also one of transit in which the ebb and flow of people and ideas enriched—and disrupted—the growth of civilization.

SUMERIAN PERIOD, 3000–2350 BC

No one knows why a high civilization began in Sumer and, at about the same time, in Egypt. In prehistoric times both centers formed part of a larger cultural region: Mesopotamia was at first indistinguishable from northern Syria, and southern Mesopotamia (Sumer) was linked with Persia (map 1.2). Similarly, Egypt shared its early predynastic culture with neighboring Libya, Nubia, and possibly the Sudan. And then came the cultural burst that detached Sumer and Egypt from their surroundings, as it established their place in history.

The mystery is compounded because the origin of the Sumerians is also unknown. Migrating into the river valley around 4500 BC, they amalgamated with the resident population and by about 3000 BC had established themselves as the dominant class. They (or the neighboring Subarians) have been credited with inventing the first written language, a system called **cuneiform** (KYOO-nay-uh-form, "wedge") writing. Cuneiform was used initially to record the behavior of the rivers and the astronomical events that provided clues to the return of the life-giving floods.

Early Religion

Predicting annual inundations was only one of the reasons for studying the stars. Primitive religions characteristically attribute natural phenomena—floods, storms, earthquakes—to unseen gods; more advanced cultures study the heavens for clues to superhuman powers involved with the creation and governance of the universe. Sumerian beliefs reflected the abundant concerns of everyday life: storms, catastrophic floods, earthquakes, and endless raids by hostile neighbors. Their religion, consequently, was quite self-centered and practical, emphasizing sheer survival in a hostile world.

Mesopotamian gods were considered powerful and immortal but otherwise much like human beings writ large:

frivolous, selfish, quarrelsome, sometimes petty, often childish. The gods were arranged in a hierarchy, making this the first systematic **polytheistic** religion. An (or Anu) was a sky god and head of the pantheon (Gk., "all the gods"). Enlil was "Lord Breath," god of the atmosphere. Inanna (or Inini) was "Queen of Heaven," the planet Venus, daughter of the moon god, and spouse of Anu; her name was subsequently changed to the more familiar Ishtar.

All these gods were derived from the deities of nomadic societies in which men were the dominant sex, mainly because of their greater size and strength. Men maintained their dominance as nomadic life evolved into agricultural communities, even though one would expect the goddess of fertility to be the prime deity. By contrast, the fertility goddess was dominant in a Minoan agricultural society that had no nomadic prehistory (see p. 44).

Ascertaining the will of these fractious gods was an overriding concern of the believers and thus was born astrology, later transformed into the science of astronomy. Through prayer, incantations, and magic, the Sumerians attempted to keep the gods happy or at least tolerant and forgiving. The gods would help individuals in distress but never at the time of death. Male-dominated societies have generally accepted this death orientation, unlike life-affirming cultures such as Minoan civilization, in which the sexes are virtually equal in cooperation and responsibilities. In Sumer, pleasing the gods was more desirable than leading a good life—a pragmatic point of view that did little to promote or improve ethical behavior.

The king was chief servant of the gods and their earthly representative; his government presumed that the gods were in charge and that they occupied large areas set aside as sacred communities. Collective labor was employed on temple lands but the rest of the city was divided into private properties. Because sky gods made up the pantheon,

ANCIENT BREW

A Sumerian tablet of ca. 3500 BC is inscribed in cuneiform with a recipe for "wine of the grain." No one knows who invented beer but the Sumerians (or Egyptians?) were apparently the first (ca. 6000 BC) to make barley better for brewing by germinating barley grains, thus developing enzymes that change starch into fermentable sugars, a process called malting. Because beer turns up so often in Sumerian and Babylonian tablets we can assume that Mesopotamians liked their beer and also liked variety, as attested to by a list of nineteen different kinds of beer. We know also that Ninkasi was the goddess of intoxicating drink but, in these strongly male-dominant societies, we don't know why a mere goddess ruled over beverages as important as beer and wine.

their worship should be from temples atop hills or mountains; the closer to the gods the more likely were the deities to be content—and less likely to torment helpless humans.

Sumerian Art and Architecture

With no hills, much less mountains, in the vast and level deserts surrounding the river valleys, the Sumerians had no natural temple sites nor were there any practical building stones. They solved the problem by erecting massive artificial hills made of sun-dried mud bricks. These **ziggurats** were towers constructed as terraced pyramids with inclined walkways connecting each terrace. The ziggurat at Ur (see time chart on p. 8) dates from the Neo-Sumerian Period. It is a refined version of the earliest known ziggurat, which was built a thousand years before at Uruk, reputedly the oldest city in the world. The Ur ziggurat has three stairways, 100 steps each, that converge on the first platform; other stairways ascended to the second and then to a third level on which stood the temple of the god.

The elegant bull-headed lyre of the Queen of Ur suggests a splendid, luxurious court (fig. 1.4). Only the wood

---

1.4 Bull-headed lyre, from the Tomb of Queen Puabi, Ur, Iraq. Sumerian. Ca. 2685 BC. Wood inlaid with gold, lapis lazuli, and shell, height ca. 17" (43.2 cm). University Museum, University of Pennsylvania, Philadelphia (Neg. T4–29c2).

1.5 *He-Goat and Flowering Tree* (offering stand for fertility god), from Ur, Iraq. Sumerian. Ca. 2500 BC. Wood overlaid with gold, silver, lapis lazuli, shell, and red limestone, height 20" (50.8 cm). British Museum, London.

---

and strings have been restored; all else is original: gold-decorated posts, bull's head with **lapis lazuli** beard, and four narrative scenes. A consistent symbol of Mesopotamian royal power, the bearded bull is intensely alert as if straining to hear the music of the lyre.

The strange and fascinating *He-Goat and Flowering Tree* (fig. 1.5) is a masterful example of sculpture created by adding elements instead of cutting them away. As alive and alert as the bearded bull, the goat peers intently through the decorative branches of a symbolic tree. An age-old emblem of male sexuality, this is undoubtedly a fertility symbol.

In addition to their distinctive art and architecture, the Sumerians made important contributions to writing, law, and religion. They also established the foundations of mathematics, science, and engineering. In arithmetic they created multiplication, division, and square and cube roots. They used a 10-base (decimal) system of mathematics plus a 60-base system from which they were the first to derive 60 seconds to a minute and 60 minutes to an hour. In geometry they used the 60-base system to mark out a circle of 360 degrees.

The Epic of Gilgamesh

The most significant Sumerian literary work was *The Epic of Gilgamesh*, the first story in world literature to have a protagonist with a name and personality. This is also the earliest written record of the discovery of death, which Gilgamesh strongly suspects means total extinction but which his contemporaries, still rooted in simple notions, assume to be another form of existence. Originally sketched by the Sumerians, reworked by the Akkadians, and shaped into final form by the Babylonians, *The Epic of Gilgamesh* is the story of a debauched half-historical, half-legendary king whom the gods propose to chastise. To humble the arrogant monarch they create a foil: Enkidu of the strong limbs and simple heart. Before he encounters Gilgamesh, the gods civilize Enkidu by providing him with a courtesan to instruct him in the erotic arts. This humanizing process enables Enkidu to overcome his brutish nature and gain worldly wisdom. As the gods intended, Enkidu and Gilgamesh meet in combat, ending in a draw, as a chastened Gilgamesh joins his new-found comrade in a string of exciting adventures. Inevitably, a misadventure provokes the wrath of the gods and Enkidu dies in the arms of a bereft Gilgamesh, who is left alone to face the meaning of life—and death.

But the story does not end there. Learning that the great flood's legendary hero, Utnapishtim, possesses the secret of eternal life, Gilgamesh tracks him down and finds the thorny plant that guarantees immortality, exactly as revealed to him by the hero. Ecstatic over his precious discovery, Gilgamesh celebrates by bathing in a nearby pool. At that moment "a serpent snuffed [put out] the fragrance of the plant; it came up from the water and carried off the plant. Going back it shed its slough." Considered immortal because of its annual sloughing off of skin, the snake steals immortality from Gilgamesh. "Thereupon Gilgamesh sits down and weeps, His tears running down over his face." This is the truly final loss, confirming the dark Mesopotamian suspicion that life only seems to be hopeful, happy, and bright. Ultimately the truth is learned, usually the hard way: life ends in nothingness.

The following selections tell of a great flood. This may have been the famous deluge that inundated Mesopotamia around 2900 BC, or, it may be a creation **myth**. Whatever the intention, there are interesting parallels with the flood described in Genesis, chapters 6–8. This is understandable for "The biblical accounts are themselves based on some form of the Gilgamesh epic: Sumerian, Babylonian, or Assyrian, either brought in by Abraham from Ur of the Chaldees or experienced in Jewish exile in Babylonia."[2]

LITERARY SELECTION 1

The Epic of Gilgamesh
From Tablet XI

The story is told to Gilgamesh by Utnapishtim, who relates how he was instructed by the gods.

Tear down this house, build a ship!
Give up possessions, seek thou life.
Forswear worldly goods and keep the soul alive!
Aboard the ship take thou the seed of all living things.
The ship that thou shalt build,
Her dimensions shall be to measure.
Equal shall be her width and length.
On the fifth day I laid her framework.
One whole acre was her floor space,
Ten dozen cubits the height of each of her walls,   10
Ten dozen cubits each edge of the square deck.
I laid out the contours and joined her together.
I provided her with six decks,
Dividing her thus into seven parts.
Her floor plan I divided into nine parts.
I hammered water-plugs into her.
I saw to the punting poles and laid in supplies.
Bullocks I slaughtered for the people,
And I killed sheep every day.
Must, red wine, oil, and white wine   20
I gave the workmen to drink, as though river water,
That they might feast as on New Year's Day.
On the seventh day the ship was completed.
The launching was very difficult,
So that they had to shift the floor planks above and
     below,
Until two-thirds of the structure had gone into the water.
Whatever I had I laded upon her:
Whatever I had of silver I laded upon her;
Whatever I had of gold I laded upon her;
Whatever I had of all the living things I laded upon her.   30
All my family and kin I made go aboard the ship.
The beasts of the field, the wild creatures of the field,
     All the craftsmen I made go aboard.
I watched the appearance of the weather.
The weather was awesome to behold.
I boarded the ship and battened up the entrance.
With the first glow of dawn,
A black cloud rose up from the horizon.
For one day the south-storm blew,
Gathering speed as it blew, submerging the
     mountains,   40
Overtaking the people like a battle.

2. Philip R. Wiener, editor in chief, *Dictionary of the History of Ideas*, Volume III (New York: Charles Scribner's Sons, 1973, pp. 279–80). Source: James B. Pritchard, ed., *Ancient Near Eastern Texts Relating to the Old Testament* (Princeton: Princeton University Press, 1950), pp. 42, 72, 109.

No one can see his fellow,
Nor can the people be recognized from heaven.
The gods were frightened by the deluge,
And, shrinking back, they ascended to the heaven of
   Anu.[3]
The gods cowered like dogs
   Crouched against the outer wall.
Ishtar cried out like a woman in travail,
The sweet-voiced mistress of the gods moans aloud:
"The olden days are alas turned to clay,   50
Because I bespoke evil in the Assembly of the gods.
How could I bespeak evil in the Assembly of the gods,
Ordering battle for the destruction of my people,
When it is I myself who give birth to my people!"
Six days and six nights
Blows the flood wind, as the south-storm sweeps the
   land.
When the seventh day arrived,
   The flood-carrying south-storm subsided in the battle,
Which it had fought like an army.
The sea grew quiet, the tempest was still, the flood
   ceased.   60
I looked at the weather: stillness had set in,

And all of mankind had returned to clay.
The landscape was as level as a flat roof.
I opened a hatch, and light fell upon my face.
Bowing low, I sat and wept,
Tears running down my face.
I looked about for coast lines in the expanse of the sea:
In each of fourteen regions
   There emerged a region-mountain.
On Mount Nisir the ship came to a halt.   70
Mount Nisir held the ship fast,
   Allowing no motion.
One day, a second day, Mount Nisir held the ship fast,
   Allowing no motion.
A third day, a fourth day, Mount Nisir held the ship fast,
   Allowing no motion.
A fifth, and a sixth day, Mount Nisir held the ship fast,
   Allowing no motion.
When the seventh day arrived,
I sent forth and set free a dove.   80

3. The highest heaven in the Mesopotamian conception of the cosmos.

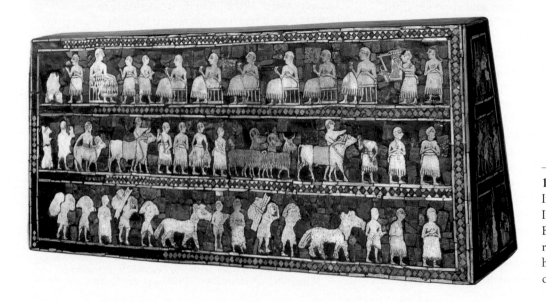

1.6 The Standard of Ur, from Iraq. Sumerian, Early Dynastic II. Ca. 2600–2400 BC. Bitumen base inlaid with shell, red limestone, and lapis lazuli, height of each panel 8" (20.3 cm). British Museum, London.

The dove went forth, but came back;
Since no resting-place for it was visible, she turned
    round.
Then I sent forth and set free a swallow.
The swallow went forth, but came back;
Since no resting-place for it was visible, she turned
    round.
Then I sent forth and set free a raven.
The raven went forth and, seeing that the waters had
    diminished,
He eats, circles, caws, and turns not round.
Then I let out all to the four winds
    And offered a sacrifice.   90
I poured out a libation on the top of the mountain.

The "Standard of Ur"

The so-called "Standard of Ur" was found in a tomb in the royal cemetery at Ur (fig. 1.6). Though these two panels form the front and back of a musical instrument, they are described as they appear in the figure, i.e., as upper and lower panels. The upper "war" plate shows, in the top register, the king alighting from his carriage to receive captives. In the center a line of lancers in heavy cloaks faces vanquished enemies on the right. The four chariots in the bottom register drive across the bodies of fallen warriors.

The lower "peace" panel highlights a banquet scene: the court drinks with the king to the sound of apparently stirring music (judging from the far right figure). In the center row servants are leading animals and holding fish, which may be a depiction of food preparation in a lower part of the palace. The bottom register probably illustrates the spoils of war.

STUDY QUESTIONS

1. **a.** Imagine living with a tribe of nomads with all edibles either gathered or hunted. As you follow the seasons in search of food, what would you carry with you? What would constitute "excess baggage," i.e., things neither useful nor needed?
   b. Now, imagine that you are raising crops and breeding animals. In what ways would your life differ from that of the nomads? What possessions would you have that were previously impractical? How different would your relationships be with your neighbors and with your community?
2. What were the lasting contributions that the Sumerians made to civilization?

AKKADIAN PERIOD, 2350–2150 BC

The first Sumerian period ended when the city-states fell to Semitic barbarians from the north, the Akkadians, some of whom had probably served the Sumerians as mercenaries. The Akkadians introduced the new concept of a divine monarchy supported by force of arms, which eventually caused the collapse of the Sumerian social order that had, among other things, protected the free peasants. In time, competition with, and the expansion of, large estates reduced the by then debt-ridden peasants to serfdom: the perennial battle of haves and have-nots. New rulers then settle down into the same pattern of inequalities; peasants are crushed and the whole process restarts, leading to takeovers by the Babylonians, the Assyrians, and the Persians.

The dynamic ruler of the Akkadians was Sargon the Great, the first notable military conqueror in history. The bronze head from Nineveh (fig. 1.7), very likely representing Sargon, expresses a new idea in sculpture: a dignified and powerful monarch. Bound in the Sumerian fashion, the hair is plaited, wound around the head, and gathered in a tight bun. This is a ruler in absolute control.

The Akkadians refined Sumerian art and the quality of life but could not convince the Sumerians that they were kinfolk rather than rank outsiders. Sargon and his successors even called themselves kings of Sumer and Akkad, but the Sumerians continued to fume under "foreign" domination and eventually regained political control. A major factor in the fall of Akkad was a volcanic eruption followed

---

1.7 Head, from Nineveh, Iraq. Akkadian. Ca. 2350–2150 BC. Bronze, height 12" (30.5 cm). Iraq Museum, Baghdad. Photo: Hirmer, Munich.

1.8 Gudea of Lagash, from Iraq. Neo-Sumerian.
Ca. 2050 BC. Diorite, height 29" (73.7 cm). British Museum,
London.

by centuries of a drought that turned their verdant land
into a desert, from Egypt and Akkad all the way to India.

NEO-SUMERIAN PERIOD,
2050–1900 BC

After the fall of the Akkad dynasty in about 2100 BC, Gudea,
ruler of the city of Lagash, united the Sumerians in a renaissance of Sumerian culture. About twenty statues of Gudea
have survived, possibly indicating a popular king or an
expert in public relations—or both. For Gudea's statues
(fig. 1.8) Sumerian sculptors used **diorite**, an exceptionally hard stone, which may also account for the large number of surviving statues. All the statues are similar to this
one, portraying the ruler as both devout and wise, a carefully crafted image of composed serenity.

At some time during the waning of this period, according to the Bible, Abraham led the Hebrews from the Sumerian
city of Ur of the Chaldees toward an eventual occupation of
the Land of Canaan, later called Palestine. The emigration
of the Hebrews (see pp. 165–9) may have been prompted by
the Babylonian invasion of Sumer.

OLD BABYLONIA, 1900–1500 BC

Although the Sumerians and Akkadians had coexisted
through the Sumerian revival, the invading Babylonians
(originally called Amorites) found a divided land so exhausted from constant friction that opposition was nonexistent.
The Sumerians and Akkadians couldn't even get together
long enough to fight off a truly foreign invader. Nomads
from the Arabian desert, the Babylonians established a powerful state centered on their royal city of Babylon. Excavations

1.9 **Stele** of Hammurabi (upper portion), from Iraq.
Babylonian. Ca. 1760 BC. Basalt, height of entire stele 7'4"
(2.24 m). Louvre, Paris. Photo: R.M.N., Paris.
The Code of Law is inscribed on the lower portion of the
stele. Above it the king is standing before a divinity who is
probably Shamash, the sun god, regarded as the lawgiver.

at Mari, in the middle Euphrates valley, have revealed an enormous palace of nearly 300 rooms containing thousands of tablets from the royal archives. Chief among the royal correspondents was Hammurabi (ca. 1792–1750 BC), who consolidated the territories of Sumer and Akkad into a powerful Babylonian kingdom.[4]

A striking characteristic of all Mesopotamian cultures was the large number of land-owning merchants and farmers. With its potential for chaos this situation needed a structure that regulated private property, trade, and other business affairs. Legal standards had been developed in the past but none so practical as Hammurabi's Code of Laws that established the rule of law from the Persian Gulf to the Mediterranean Sea (fig. 1.9). Consisting of a rather poetic prologue and epilogue, the code has a central section that lists 282 regulations dealing with perjury, theft, land tenure, licensed drinking, commerce, marriage and divorce, inheritance, adoption, medical treatment, construction, and the hire of livestock, laborers, and slaves. Oddly enough there is no reference to taxation. In common with earlier codes, the basic principle was "retaliation in kind" or, as expressed by the Hebrews, "an eye for an eye, a tooth for a tooth." As a combination of contemporary tribal practices and of more enlightened provisions for justice, the code did replace some (not all) "retaliation in kind" with fines and money compensation to aggrieved parties. Most important, it worked.

Hammurabi summarized, in the code's prologue, his contribution to the people after he "pronounced the majestic name of Babylon and decreed the extension of its power over the whole universe" so that "I might bring order to my people and so that I might free them from evil and wicked men, that I should defend the weak from the oppression of the mighty." Although self-serving and verging on purple prose, these words do have a noble intent. Establishing order, protecting society, and making all equal before the law are worthy goals in any society.

STUDY QUESTIONS

1. Compare the portraits in figures 1.7 and 1.8. How do they differ and how are they similar? Considering the visual evidence, what can you deduce about the two rulers?
2. Why was Hammurabi's Code of Law so significant? Before responding to the question, try to imagine what life would be like if you lived in an area in which each community had its own laws. How might this situation affect commerce, trade, and other activities?

4. The reference to Old Babylonia is modern hindsight; there was a later kingdom called Neo-Babylonia.
5. These and subsequent royal dates are reigning periods.

THE ASSYRIAN EMPIRE, 1076–612 BC

After lackluster nomads (Kassites from Iran) had ruled Babylonia in a reasonably benign manner from ca. 1500 to 1100 BC, a far more warlike power emerged in the north. The first militaristic state in history, Assyria was to become, in the words of one of its kings, "Lord of the World," the most powerful and ruthless of all Near Eastern empires.

Assyrian art and architecture served the king, glorifying the monarch as a mighty hunter and implacable warrior (fig. 1.10). The intent was to intimidate any foes foolish enough to resist Assyrian military might. The enormous palace of Assurnasirpal II (uh-soor-NAS-ir-pall; 883–859 BC)[5] at Nimrud (ancient Kalkho), was the administrative center of a garrison state that extended from the Tigris to the Nile and from the Persian Gulf to Turkey (map 1.3, p. 21). Erected in the Mesopotamian tradition of clusters of rooms surrounding courtyards, the palace walls were covered with elaborate reliefs of warring, hunting kings (much like the scene in fig. 1.10), which were veritable symphonies of violence and death. The palace entrance was flanked by huge figures of human-headed, winged bulls carved both in relief and in the round (fig. 1.11). Designed to ward off evil spirits, the bulls are depicted at rest (frontal view) and in motion (side view), an illusion furthered by the fifth leg. This combination of fine attention to detail, sweeping wings, and sheer size communicates an awesome vigor symbolizing the invincibility of Assyrian might. Assurnasirpal II's standard policy guaranteed fear of him and his army. Upon capturing an enemy town his soldiers rounded up surviving inhabitants, cut off their hands and feet, and piled them in the town square to bleed to death.

During the reign of Sargon II (721–705 BC) innovative Assyrian sculptors created immensely powerful solitary figures of divinities, kings, and heroes. The "genius" (person of great influence) illustrated in figure 1.12, thought to be Gilgamesh himself, is a huge model of massive strength, impressive and intimidating. This is how con-

1.10 Lion Hunt of Assurbanipal (uh-soor-BAH-nee-pall), from the Palace of Assurbanipal, Nineveh, Iraq. Assyrian. Ca. 668–630 BC. Gypsum, height ca. 23" (58.4 cm). British Museum, London.

1.11 Winged human-headed bull from Nimrud, Iraq. Assyrian period of Assurnasirpal II. 883–859 BC. Alabaster, height 10'4" (3.15 m). British Museum, London.

quered enemies were supposed to view their new masters.[6]

The Assyrian Empire reached the pinnacle of its power during the reign of Sargon II. Because mass murder frequently stiffened enemy resistance, the Assyrians initiated an alternative policy: control dissent by removing entire populations from their homes and scattering them throughout the empire. It was Sargon II who dispersed the population of Israel—the "ten lost tribes of Israel."

Assyrian power gradually waned shortly after the conquest of Israel. Sennacherib's (sen-NAC-ur-ib) sack of Babylon in 689 BC and the conquest of Egypt in 670 BC were the last major successes of the Assyrian juggernaut. A coordinated effort of Babylonians, Medes (from northern Persia), and Palestinians decisively defeated the Assyrians in 612 BC, resulting in the destruction of all their major cities, especially the royal city of Nineveh. The end was spectacular. No other ancient empire collapsed so swiftly nor was devastated so completely. The empire simply disappeared, confirming the biblical saying that those who live by the sword shall perish by the sword.

6. "The Assyrians were fierce, well-disciplined and cruel. Their cruelty was calculated, at least in part, to terrorize real and potential enemies, for the Assyrians boasted of their brutality." Donald Kagan, et al., *The Western Heritage* (New York: Macmillan, 1979), p. 22.

1.12 *Propitiatory Genius of a Hero* (Gilgamesh), from Iraq. Assyrian. Reign of Sargon II. 722–705 BC. Alabaster, height 13'10½" (4.23 m). Louvre, Paris. Photo: R.M.N., Paris.

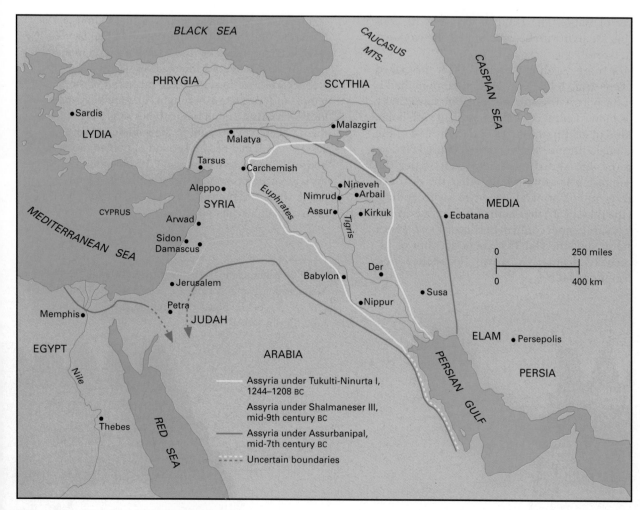

Map 1.3 The Assyrian Empire.

THE CHALDEAN (NEO-BABYLONIAN) EMPIRE, 625–539 BC

The Chaldeans were a Semitic desert race from, perhaps, the Syrian area. They had settled in and around Babylon even before forming the alliance with the Medes that helped destroy Assyria. As the last upholder of Mesopotamian culture, the newly rebuilt Babylon was little more than a sumptuous museum in which older traditions, mostly Sumerian, were collected and preserved. Innovation was virtually unknown in a Babylonia that had shut itself off from the outside world as it contemplated past glories.

With the accession of Nebuchadnezzar II (neb-oo-kud-NEZ-ar, also spelled Nebuchadrezzar; 605–562 BC) to the throne, the legendary might of Sumer and Assyria was recalled in a monumental architecture and in a series of military expeditions that consolidated Babylonian power. A vigorous and brilliant commander, Nebuchadnezzar drove the Egyptians from Palestine, conquered Jerusalem in 586 BC, and exiled many Jews to Babylon. Jeremiah had advised cooperation with Babylon, reasoning that it was better to yield to a Semite foe than join a weak and faithless Egypt. The Jews ignored his sensible counsel and revolted, with predictable results. The king of Judah was blinded, his children and nobles killed and

> ¹²Nebuzaradan, the captain of the bodyguard who served the king of Babylon, entered Jerusalem. ¹³And he burned the house of the Lord and the king's house and all the houses of Jerusalem.
>
> Jeremiah 52:12–13

According to Jeremiah (52:27–30) 4,600 Jews were carried into what they called their **Babylonian Captivity** (586–538 BC). Though Jeremiah stated that "Judah was carried captive out of its land," it was mostly artisans and other skilled workers who were carted off. Many of the poorer class were left behind to continue the traditions of their people as best they could.

Nebuchadnezzar continued to build in Babylon in the grand manner, including an enormous ziggurat 295 feet (90 m) high and named Entemenanki ("Temple of the Foundation of Heaven and Earth") that may have been the biblical Tower of Babel. The Hanging Gardens he constructed for his Median wife became one of the wonders of the ancient world.

One of the more dazzling designs was for the glazed brick Ishtar Gate (fig. 1.13). The Mesopotamians had a special talent for portraying animals, an ability especially evident in this monumental work. Embellished with lions, bulls, and a kind of griffin, the gate stood at the end of the main processional entrance to the opulent capital city.

Despite the size and the splendor of its cities the Babylonian Empire was quite fragile. After the death of Nebuchadnezzar in 562 BC its decline was swift, ending, according to the Bible, with the death of Belshazzar in 539 BC. Biblical scholars cannot confirm Belshazzar's existence or even his name, but the Old Testament account of his demise effectively dramatizes royal decadence and Babylon's precipitous fall.

[1]King Belshazzar made a great feast for a thousand of his lords, and drank wine in front of the thousand.
[2]Belshazzar, when he tasted the wine, commanded that the vessels of gold and of silver which Nebuchadnezzar his father had taken out of the temple in Jerusalem be brought, that the king and his lords, his wives, and his concubines might drink from them. [3]Then they brought in the golden and silver vessels which had been taken out of the temple, the house of God in Jerusalem; and the king and his lords, his wives, and his concubines drank from them. [4]They drank wine, and praised the gods of gold and silver, bronze, iron, wood, and stone.

1.13   The Ishtar Gate (restored), from Babylon, Iraq. Reign of Nebuchadnezzar II. Chaldean. 604–562 BC. Glazed brick, height 48' (14.6 m). Staatliche Museen, Berlin. Photo: B.P.K., Berlin (Klaus Göken).

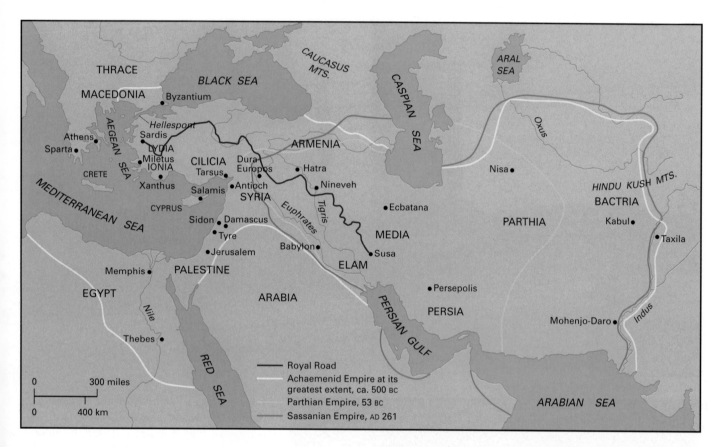

Map 1.4   The Empires of Persia.

⁵Immediately the fingers of a man's hand appeared and wrote on the plaster of the wall of the king's palace. ⁶Then the king's color changed and his thoughts alarmed him; his limbs gave way and his knees knocked together.

¹³Then Daniel was brought in . . . [and] ¹⁷answered before the king "I will read the writing to the king and make known to him the interpretation.

²⁵"And this is the writing that was inscribed: MENE, MENE, TEKEL, and PARSIN. ²⁶This is the interpretation of the matter: MENE, God has numbered the days of your kingdom and brought it to an end; ²⁷TEKEL, you have been weighed in the balance and found wanting; ²⁸PERES, your kingdom is divided and given to the Medes and Persians."

³⁰That very night Belshazzar the Chaldean king was slain.

Daniel 5:1–6, 13, 17, 25–28, 30

Internal strife, decadence, and degeneracy took their toll, leaving no opposition to the conquering Persians. The Assyrian Empire had gone down fighting; Babylon, the last of twenty-five centuries of Mesopotamian kingdoms, expired with scarcely a whimper.

THE PERSIAN EMPIRE, 539–331 BC⁷

The Persians migrated from somewhere east of the Caspian Sea into the high plateau country north and east of the Persian Gulf. Apparently closely related to the Medes who lived farther north, they spoke an Indo-Iranian language, as did the Medes.⁸ Under the remarkable leadership of Cyrus the Great (539–530 BC), the Persians first absorbed the Medes and then moved against the Lydian kingdom ruled by the legendary Croesus (KREE-sus). Croesus had already formed alliances with Egypt and Sparta in anticipation of a preventive war against Persia, but he was uncertain about success until he consulted the Delphic Oracle. According to the Greek historian Herodotos (484–425 BC), the oracle predicted that a Lydian attack would destroy a great army. That did indeed ensue—but the vanquished army was commanded by Croesus.

7. As the successor to a long progression of Middle Eastern civilizations, the Persian Empire is considered both here and on pp. 61–2, where a discussion of the empire's conflict with Greek civilization is included.
8. With only a few exceptions, all inhabitants of modern Europe speak languages derived from ancient tongues brought from Eurasia (Ukraine or east of there) by Bronze Age conquerors. The term Indo-Iranian identifies various language branches as spoken in Europe, Iran, and northern India. These include Greek, Latin, Sanskrit, Persian, Celtic, and the Germanic languages. The name Iran (used after AD 600) means "land of the Aryan."

1.14 *Above* East staircase of the Audience Hall of Darius and Xerxes, Great Palace, Persepolis, Iran. Persian. Ca. 500 BC. Stone. Photo: Rainbird/Robert Harding, London.

1.15 Rhyton in the Form of a Lion-Griffin. Persian. 5th century BC. Gold, height 6¾″ (17.1 cm). Metropolitan Museum of Art, New York (Fletcher Fund, 1954).

With the conquest of Egypt in 525 BC by Cyrus's son Cambyses (kam-BYE-sez), the Persian Empire expanded rapidly, eventually extending from Greece to the Himalayas and from southern Russia to the Indian Ocean, the greatest empire the world had yet seen (map 1.4). Like the later Romans, the Persians allowed subjugated peoples to retain their own customs, laws, and religion. The Hebrews, for example, were allowed to worship Jahweh (or Yahweh) and those in Babylon were encouraged to return to Jerusalem, though few chose to do so. For the pragmatic Persians such tolerance was eminently sensible, enabling the government to collect tribute from the far-flung empire without unduly annoying the populace.

One of the major Persian achievements was an elaborate network of imperial roads that formed the best highway system prior to Roman roads. The Royal Road extended some 1,600 miles (2,580 km) from the Persian Gulf to Asia Minor, connecting the empire's principal cities of Susa and Sardis. By using a series of relay riders the "king's messengers" could travel the entire Royal Road in a week. According to Herodotos, "Nothing mortal travels as fast as these Persian messengers. Not snow, nor rain, nor heat, nor gloom of night stays these couriers from the swift completion of their appointed rounds" (*Histories*, VIII).[9]

Although the Persian king did not employ Assyrian terrorist tactics, he was still an absolute monarch whose authority was tempered only by some power sharing with his nobles. From the admittedly biased Greek point of view, Cyrus, Darius, and Xerxes were oriental despots and the Persian army a mighty but mindless machine. Some claim that the Persian Empire was quite liberal and humane, but the many insurrections throughout its history testify to the heavy yoke of the man called the King of Kings.

Persian culture was as derivative and eclectic as that of their Roman contemporaries. With nothing original to contribute they adapted their art and architecture from Mesopotamian, Egyptian, Lydian, Palestinian, and Greek models. Probably the most characteristic expression of their culture was their architecture. They copied the raised platform and terraced building style of Babylon and Assyria, adding winged Assyrian bulls and glazed Babylonian bricks. They chose forests of **columns** in the Egyptian manner but with Greek **fluting** and **capitals**. Most importantly, their architecture was wholly secular. Because their new religion of Zoroastrianism (see below) required no priests, rituals, statues, or temples, they concentrated instead on building elaborate palaces.

The Great Palace of Darius and Xerxes at Persepolis (fig. 1.14) was destroyed by Alexander the Great but enough remains of this enormous complex to give some idea of its magnitude. The view shown is of the eastern stairway in front of the Audience Hall, with the Gate of Xerxes on the left. The Great Hall was 250 feet square (23.2 m²) . It could

9. From which the U.S. Postal Service derived its motto.

PERSIAN MAGIC

The English word "magic" is derived from Magi, the priestly hierarchy of Zoroastrianism. Like the Brahmans of India the Magi were members of the highest caste and keepers of the cult. Supposedly "wise in the things of God," a **Magus** probably functioned as both priest and scribe. A branch of the clan moved to Babylon where they specialized in casting horoscopes, telling fortunes, and interpreting dreams, which qualified them as practitioners of magic, to use the word in its modern meaning. Three Persian Magi appear in the **Gospel** of Matthew as the "wise men from the East" who came to worship the infant Christ.

hold 10,000 people and originally had 100 stone columns, each 40 feet (12.2 m) high and all brightly painted. This was the first use of interior columns in the Mesopotamian world. Though influenced by Egyptian examples, these columns are more closely patterned after Greek models and were probably designed and constructed by Greek artisans. They are topped by a series of complicated capitals composed of the forequarters of lions, bulls, or human-headed bulls. The low reliefs show Persian guards standing at attention—a security guard in stone. The influence here is clearly Assyrian but nowhere in the palace are there kings slaughtering enemies or helpless animals. Persian kings preferred tidy and efficient administration of their vast empire without blatant intimidation in the Assyrian manner.

Persian culture was highly refined. An example of the luxury enjoyed by the upper class is a drinking horn ingeniously combined with a fantastic lion-griffin (fig. 1.15). The details are sharp and precise: tongue, teeth, sharp claws, tiny tufts of hair. Characteristic of the Persian style are such stylistic conventions as the figure-eight shoulder-muscle and the tulip-shaped muscle on the foreleg.

Zoroastrianism

Perhaps the most important contribution of the illustrious Persian culture was a new religion. A prophet named Zoroaster (Gk.; Zarathustra in Persian) was both a reformer of traditional folk religion and the creator of a new faith. Born sometime in the seventh century BC (660?), he was the first exponent, according to some scholars, of an ethical, **monotheistic** religion. Other scholars contend that Zoroastrianism was a **dualistic** religion, albeit ethical. Which is it? Examining the evidence may supply some answers, but, as in all religions, final explication rests with each interpreter.

In the *Gathas,* his only surviving authentic work, Zoroaster declares that Ahura Mazda (also called Ormazd) is the principle of truth and also the Holy Spirit, the Creating Word that existed before the world was born, the Word that brought all forms of life into being, boding good for all species, particularly the human race. In order that people might, through struggle, appreciate the true meaning of goodness, a twin of the Holy Spirit—Ahriman the Evil One—was created. It is unclear whether Ahriman was invented by Ahura Mazda (Ormazd) or created simultaneously as the evil twin of Ormazd, and thus the scholarly disagreement about monism and dualism. In any event, all life became a contest between good and evil, truth and error, light and darkness.

In its original form Zoroastrianism was a personal religion with no place for rituals, priests or temples. The emphasis was on practical moral living without extremes such as celibacy or cloistered seclusion; anyone could seek the good and the true. The ethical life was dedicated to the active realization of a just society finally freed from evil.

An elaborate **eschatology** looked forward to the coming of the Saoshyans or Savior, who would resurrect the dead for judgment. The righteous would then pass to heaven and the wicked to hell to suffer physically for their sins. In another passage Zoroaster described the just as residing in the House of Song while the unjust are doomed to the House of the Lie.

According to Zoroastrianism the conflict between good and evil would not last forever. Ultimately Ahura Mazda would overcome Ahriman. Not even those condemned to the House of the Lie would stay there forever. The final victory of Ahura Mazda and the destruction of Ahriman would usher in the *Fraskart,* the ultimate "making excellent" or rehabilitation of Ahriman's followers.

The new faith was so far beyond the capacity of the common people that, over time, its abstractions were minimized and emphasis placed on sacrifice, liturgy, and priestly mediation—the very paraphernalia Zoroastrianism had tried to eradicate. Ishtar, the ancient Mesopotamian fertility goddess, returned to the pantheon where she was joined by Mithra, god of light and new Persian deity. Thus, in time, a religion that had protested against polytheism and empty formalism took on some of the characteristics of the old beliefs it had sought to supplant. Having readily gained the support of the Persian rulers, the new faith later became influential in Mesopotamia, Asia Minor, and Egypt. Much that was new and vital in Zoroastrianism can be detected in subsequent religious movements.

Zoroastrianism languished after the destructive invasion of the Middle East by Alexander the Great and nearly foundered 1,000 years later during the seventh-century Muslim conquest of Persia. Preserved by a mass migration to India and subsequently revived through scholarly Parsee leadership, Parsism (Zoroastrianism) is still practiced in India by the descendants of Persian exiles.

STUDY QUESTIONS

1. Compare Persian Zoroastrianism with the polytheism of Mesopotamia. What changed? Why?
2. What are the elements in Zoroastrianism that seem to have influenced Judaism, Christianity, and Islam?

SUMMARY

Part of the history of Western civilization begins in Mesopotamia with the early agricultural settlements there. When nomads settled down to farm, everything changed, with one invention following upon another: animal husbandry, pottery, weaving, permanent houses, communities, fortifications, mathematics, a calendar, and writing. In due course came trade, manufacturing, law, and all the other complexities of civilization—including warfare.

The Sumerian Period (3000–2350 BC) saw the development of organized polytheism and ziggurats with temples on top; advances in mathematics, writing, and astronomy; and the first major literary work, *The Epic of Gilgamesh.*

Under Sargon the Great the Akkadians assumed political control of Sumerian culture (2350–2150 BC) and refined and improved their art forms. Continually unhappy under Akkadian domination, the Sumerians regained control under Gudea of Lagash (Neo-Sumerian Period, 2050–1900 BC).

The incessant internecine strife of Sumerians and Akkadians left them vulnerable to the Amorites, opportunistic nomads from the Arabian desert, who established the Babylonian Empire (1900–1500 BC), centered on the royal city of Babylon. Chief among the royal rulers was Hammurabi, whose legal code confirmed the rule of law throughout the empire.

Other desert nomads, the Kassites, established a rather benign rule in Babylon (1500–1100 BC), maintaining the culture but doing little to improve life or art. The Kassites were conquered in turn by Assyria, the first militaristic state in history (1076–612 BC). Entirely at the service of the king, Assyrian art had essentially two themes: power and conquest. Ruthless in their warring and ruling, the Assyrians stressed their brutality as a warning to potential dissidents. Assyria's enemies were equally pitiless when the end came, destroying everything Assyrian.

The Assyrians were demolished mainly by the Medes and the Chaldeans, the latter a Semitic desert tribe that reestablished the Babylonian Empire, known today as the Chaldean (Neo-Babylonian) Empire (625–539 BC). Under Nebuchadnezzar II Babylon bloomed briefly as a kind of museum of past glories, the final flowering of a Mesopotamian culture that had begun 2,500 years before.

Last of the ancient Near Eastern powers, the Persian Empire (539–331 BC) was also the greatest that the world had yet seen. Persian culture was eclectic: it incorporated a variety of ideas and styles in art and architecture from other civilizations. This was a highly sophisticated society with an efficiently governed empire that had a truly "international" concern for the diverse cultures it embraced. The Persians' strikingly original contribution, Zoroastrianism, was arguably one of the great world religions.

A culture that began in the Land between the Rivers in about 3000 BC succumbed, finally, to a European power in 331 BC. Not until the expansion of Islam, 1,000 years later, would the Near or Middle East again figure prominently in world affairs.

CULTURE AND HUMAN VALUES

For the average Mesopotamian life was a matter of survival in the here and now. There was some personal freedom but, on the whole, people were at the mercy of forces beyond their control, from raging rivers to warring kings. The gods were believed to be fractious and enemies seemed always at the gates. Ultimate reality was understood as nothing more than the visible world with its constant imperfections and occasional terrors.

None of the Mesopotamian cultures seems to have achieved any appreciable period of balance. Each historical era was mainly one of adjustment, from Sumerians to Akkadians, to Sumerians, Babylonians, and all the rest. There was a chronic proclivity to stagger from one crisis to another without falling totally into chaos but also without rising to a plateau of stability.

If we are to believe ancient Egyptian and Greek writers, Mesopotamia's long and troubled history reveals little concern about ideals such as the true, the good, or the beautiful. We are told that neither its polytheistic religions nor its authoritarian governments inspired any urge toward personal excellence. Pleasing the gods was supposedly more important than living a good life. To a certain extent the ancient writers were probably right, but that is not the whole story. The extant art and architecture alone testify to the notable accomplishments of the several cultures, as do their contributions to writing, law, religion, mathematics, and astronomy—all of this in the face of drought, floods, war, and other disasters. Moreover, there is nothing in Egyptian literature, for example, that compares with *The Epic of Gilgamesh*. Theirs is a remarkable record of human resilience, ingenuity, and creativity, an abiding confirmation of the hardiness of the human spirit.

Egypt: Land of the Pharaohs

ONE PEOPLE, ONE LANGUAGE

As the first truly national state (one people, one language), Egypt had a far more consistent and unified development than did the quarreling, warring city-states of Mesopotamia. Egypt was, in fact, virtually the antithesis of Mesopotamia, largely because of its geography and climate. Mesopotamian cities lay exposed on the broad plain between the rivers with no naturally defensible sites. Egypt was protected on the north by the Mediterranean, by cataracts and mountains on the south, and on the east and west by the trackless Sahara. A 750-mile (1,200-km) strip of richly fertile land averaging 10 miles (16 km) in width, this was the "gift of the Nile." No wonder Greek writer Herodotos defined Egypt as "all the country covered by inundations of the Nile" and Egyptians as "all men who drink Nile water" (*Histories*, II; map 2.1).

The Nile valley produced two crops a year, an agricultural prosperity unmatched in the ancient world. How could a land that was 97 percent desert outproduce all other regions? The answer is supplied by the mighty river that flowed from south to north carrying the mingled waters of the White and Blue Niles. Originating in the African lakes far to the south, the White Nile bore a generous supply of decayed vegetable matter. The Blue Nile flowed from the Abyssinian (Ethiopian) Plateau, carrying soil rich in potash. The fortuitous combination formed a nearly perfect organic fertilizer. Herodotos marveled, "They obtain the fruit of the field with less trouble than any other people in the world." The climate was dry and consistently sunny, with little likelihood of such natural catastrophes as the earthquakes, fierce storms, and raging floods that so bedeviled the people of Mesopotamia. No other area was so sedately stable as the land of the mighty Nile, with its life-giving and predictable patterns of flood and retreat. Naturally enough, Egyptians viewed nature's laws and those of their living god, the king (later called pharaoh), as immutable, and the afterlife as a continuation of the good life in their splendidly affluent valley (see chapter opener opposite).

Opposite Banquet, from the tomb of Netamun, Thebes, detail. Ca. 1400 BC. Painted stucco, height of full figures ca. 25" (63.5 cm). British Museum, London. Photo: E.T. Archive, London.

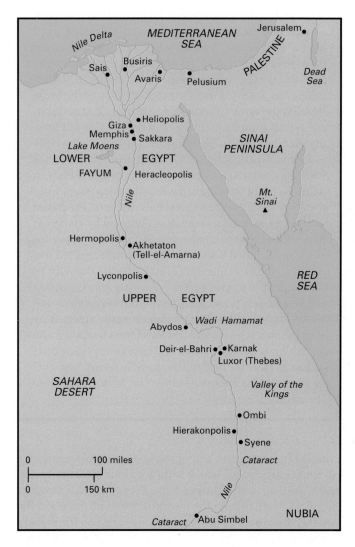

Map 2.1   Ancient Egypt.

THE GOD-KINGS

Egypt was a **theocracy** throughout its long history. Considered the genesis of all, the pharaoh was, to his people, a living god on whom life, safety, and prosperity depended. He was, after all, the source of the good life because he controlled the Nile. The best kind of life included not only affluence and safety but also right actions. This

MUMMIFICATION

Egyptian preoccupation with embalming was based on the premise of the *ka*, the indestructible vital principle of each person. The ka was believed to leave the body at death, but it could return at any time once the body was properly mummified and ready for a hereafter even finer than the previous life. Herodotos was the earliest writer to discuss embalming but it is also mentioned in the Bible in the Book of Genesis. The word "mummy" is derived from *mumiai* (or *mummia*), the Persian word for tar or bitumen, probably because New Kingdom mummies were frequently coated with a black resin resembling tar. Fully developed embalming, or mummification, followed these steps: (1) extracting the brain through the nose; (2) removing the lungs and abdominal organs through an incision in the left side but leaving the heart and kidneys in place; (3) soaking the body in natron, a salty solution; (4) filling the bodily cavities with spices and Arabic gums and wrapping the body in many layers of bandages that incorporated pages from the *Book of the Dead* and good luck amulets. The entire process took about seventy days, followed by elaborate funeral ceremonies confirming the magical properties of the mummified bodies. It was the magic that led to a unique prescription for every disease known to humankind. Up until several centuries ago European physicians were prescribing powdered mummy as a universal cure-all. Egyptian mummies were imported by pharmacists, who ground them up (linen wrapping and all) for eager patients, inspiring some enterprising merchants to meet the demand by manufacturing "ancient" mummies. This bizarre practice was finally banned in the sixteenth century.

entailed following the will of the gods as symbolized by a principle called *maat*, which embraced four qualities: order, truth, justice, and righteousness. Proper ethical conduct prepared every citizen for a continuation of the good life beyond the grave. Death, embalming, and the tomb were fundamental concerns for every Egyptian. This suggests a morbid preoccupation with death, but the exact opposite was true. Security, prosperity, a benign climate, with pharaoh on his throne and all right with the world, made Egyptian life zestful and endlessly rewarding. Egyptians were concerned about death because they loved life and wished it to continue in a similar form after death.[1]

Life was far more uncertain in Mesopotamia, with the emphasis on living for the present with dim hopes for anything beyond the grave. An afterlife seemed intimidating (more problems) rather than hope for anything better. By contrast, Egyptian life and religion were inseparable, with genuine concern about love and social equality plus a strong element of monotheism. Herodotos, a secular-minded Greek, wryly rated the Egyptians as "religious to excess, far beyond any other race of men." Mesopotamia's polytheistic religion was different: pragmatic and self-serving. This resulted in part from polytheism's built-in problem: Which god is mad at me and how can I satisfy one god without offending the others? Almost inevitably ethical conduct becomes secondary and self-interest primary. Mesopotamian culture was therefore essentially legalistic whereas Egyptian culture was basically ethical. A law code, such as Hammurabi's, was a natural consequence in a legalistic society. Egypt's structured theocracy needed no code of law. There were, however, more opportunities in Mesopotamian kingdoms for social and economic mobility.

Mesopotamians built their ziggurats, temples, and palaces of sun-dried mud bricks and generally used art in the service of royalty. Egyptian tombs, temples, and sculptures of their god-kings were fashioned of stone: readily available and imperishable, thus symbolizing the timeless perfection of the Egyptian world. Adherence to traditional beliefs, politics, and culture was believed necessary to maintain perfection and prevent the collapse of the universe. Pharaoh was thus the living god and the kingdom an extension of royalty: unchanging, eternal. Humans changed constantly whereas animals, such as the cat, were objects of worship because they were part of the changeless natural world. Art was massive and solemn because it was mainly sacramental, as were many of the rituals that undergirded everyday life. The essentials of Egyptian religious beliefs remained constant for 3,000 years; the arts established principles of style and form that also endured down those long corridors of time.

No other people in the ancient world were as steadfastly consistent in their common traits, especially their good-natured equanimity. Herodotos noted that they "adhere to their own national customs and adopt no foreign usages." Their sense of themselves and of their land was exact and certain, for they were, said the Greek historian, "the best skilled in history of any men that I have ever met."

They were no less certain about their religion. The exalted sun god, giver of life, was Re (or Ra), called Amon or Amon-Re. The gods who personified the vegetative powers of nature were fused into the deity Osiris, who was originally god of the Nile and later of the underworld. The cult of Osiris began as a nature religion. According to the story, Osiris, a benevolent ruler, was murdered by his wicked brother Set, who chopped his body to bits. Isis, his wife and

---

1. Early Egyptians were desert nomads and thus a male-dominant society with the usual concerns about survival and the reality of death. It appears, however, that the relative ease and affluence of their later agricultural society led them into a more life-affirming way of living. Men maintained their authority but, by the time of the New Kingdom, women could own and bequeath property, initiate divorce, and be deputies for husbands who served as officials.

2.1   Palette of King Narmer: *The Victory of King Narmer over the Delta,* from Hierakonpolis. Pre-Dynastic period. Ca. 3100 BC. Slate, height 25" (63.5 cm). Egyptian Museum, Cairo. Photo: Hirmer, Munich.

sister, reassembled the pieces and restored him to life. The risen god regained his kingdom but eventually descended to the nether world as judge of the dead. The falcon-headed Horus, his posthumous son, grew to manhood and avenged his father's murder by killing Set.

The myth accounting for the Nile's spring floods was later deepened to convert Osiris's death and resurrection into a promise of personal immortality; as the god had risen, so people could triumph over the grave. Finally, the victory of Horus, god of kingship, over Set represented the triumph of good over evil and the pharaoh's supremacy.

These and associated legends instructed each generation through "sacred carvings," a combination of pictographs and sound signs that the Greeks termed hieroglyphs. The ability to read these sacred carvings was the key to the exalted position of the priestly class (see the hieroglyphs in fig. 2.6).

With no central government, Egyptian culture evolved very slowly during the Pre-Dynastic Period of ca. 5000–3100 BC. In about 3100 BC, with the first dynasty,[2] the two kingdoms of Lower Egypt (Nile delta) and Upper Egypt (700 miles [1130 km] of Nile valley to the first cataract) were united by King Narmer (fig. 2.1). Narmer means "catfish"

but his subjects called him Menes, the first king of *tawy* ("two lands"). Found in ancient Hierakonpolis (Gk., "city of the falcon"), the palette shows Menes holding a fallen enemy by the hair, about to dispatch him to join his two comrades depicted below. At the upper right a falcon (Horus; representing Upper Egypt) appears above a papyrus clump, holding a rope connected to a human head apparently growing out of the soil. The soil, head, and papyrus symbolize agriculture and represent Lower Egypt; the connecting rope symbolizes the joining of the two lands by Menes. Even at this early date the basic conventions of Egyptian art have been set: the face and legs in profile but the eyes and torso as if viewed from the front.

OLD KINGDOM, 2686–2181 BC, DYNASTIES III–VI

Little is known of the first two Egyptian dynasties, but the third dynasty is so well documented that scholars have dated the Old Kingdom, the first major division of Egyptian history, from that time. It was, however, the fourth dynasty that invented the enormous tombs that launched the brief but monumental Pyramid Age of the Old Kingdom.

In the fifth century BC, when Herodotos beheld the 2,000-year-old Sphinx and the great pyramids he was as awed by their antiquity as by their overwhelming size (fig. 2.2). The **Sphinx**, which combines the body of a lion with the head of the Pharaoh Khafre (fl. 2869 BC?), is the largest surviving colossus and a majestic symbol of royal power. It was not built but carved out of the sedimentary bedrock. The prodigious amount of excess stone was presumably used to build a solar temple under the paws of the beast, with the remainder going into Khafre's pyramid. The Sphinx is believed to represent Khafre as Horus, protector of kingship, while the solar temple is early evidence of a transition from Horus the sky god to Amon-Re the sun god.

The Great Pyramid of Khufu occupies over 13 acres (5.27 ha); 756 feet square (231 m²), it has a volume of 91 million cubic feet (27,700,000 m³). The largest of the three major pyramids,[3] it contains about 250,000 stones, each weighing over 2 tons. Consisting of pyramid, temple, and imitation palace, the pyramid complex represented a funerary cult place and an eternal palace. With a shape pointing heavenward, the pyramid linked kingship and the cosmos, while also representing the primeval mound upon which the universe had supposedly been created.

The massiveness of the pyramids was intended, in part, to foil grave robbers searching for the treasure that accompanied each king to the afterlife. They were,

2. In about 300 BC Egyptian priest-historian Manetho of Sebennytos divided Egyptian history into thirty dynasties or periods of ruling houses. Though later information has shown some of his facts to be incorrect, Egyptologists still follow Manetho's scheme.
3. There is a total of eighty pyramids.

2.2   Sphinx, Giza, oblique view. Old Kingdom, 4th
Dynasty. Ca. 2540–2514 BC. Length 840' (256 m), original
height 75' (23 m). Top of the Great Pyramid of Khufu,
Giza. Old Kingdom, 4th Dynasty. Ca. 2590–2568 BC.
Original height 482' (147 m). Photo: Spectrum, London.

2.3 *Above   Portrait of the Court Official Hesira,* from the tomb
of Hesira at Sakkara. Old Kingdom, 3rd Dynasty. Ca. 2750
BC. Wood, height 3'9" (1.15 m). Egyptian Museum, Cairo.
Photo: Marburg.

however, conspicuous targets, to put it mildly, and all
were robbed. Later attempts to hide, disguise, or otherwise protect pharaonic tombs were equally futile; only
Tutankhamen's treasure survived relatively intact. The
Pyramid Age lasted less than four centuries, a brief period
by Egyptian standards. By contrast, other forms of Egyptian
art and architecture followed conventions of style and form
that endured throughout Egypt's long history.

The bodily proportions used in the Palette of Narmer
(fig. 2.1) were refined in the *Portrait of the Court Official
Hesira* (fig. 2.3). There is more subtlety here and the proportions are made more heroic with broad shoulders, narrow hips, and noble raised head. The stylized frontal view
of body and eyes with face and legs in profile has been
developed into a classical model which was to remain valid
for literally millennia. The proportions may change over
the centuries but the conventions remain. This arrangement shows key body parts in their most telling and easily understood view, the way artists know (in their mind's
eye) rather than how they actually see the parts. Further,
by avoiding specific settings and placing boldly two-dimensional figures on a frontal plane, artists emphasized the
timeless character of Egyptian art.

When depicting royalty Egyptian sculpture displayed
an impassive calm and enduring serenity that suggested
their eternal existence. The statue of *Mycerinus and His
Queen* (fig. 2.4) shares qualities (conventions) common to

2.4   *Mycerinus and His
Queen,* from Giza. Old
Kingdom, 4th Dynasty. Ca.
2599–2571 BC. Slate schist,
height 4'6½" (1.38 m).
Museum of Fine Arts,
Boston (Shaw Collection,
Neg. C.13249).

every Egyptian sculpture of human figures. Egyptian statuary has a monumental frozen quality best observed from directly in front or squarely from each side. Symbolizing the total control of the god-ruler, this immobility is a visual counterpart of Egyptian belief in immutable laws that govern people and nature. Also characteristic of Egyptian portraiture is the rectangularity of the figures, as if they were standing within a rectangular box that reinforces the impression of composed immobility. The rigidity of the figures is heightened by leaving as much stone intact as possible, e.g., in the webbing that binds the tense arms and clenched fists to the figure. In this example, the queen, conveyor of property through the female line, clasps her husband's waist and touches his left arm to symbolize the transfer of power to the pharaoh.

Egyptian portraiture conventions required formal depictions of high-ranking persons such as the pharaoh but less exalted personages were portrayed more realistically. The celebrated statue of an unnamed scribe (fig. 2.5) clearly follows three-dimensional conventions but lacks the air of a pharaoh's divine authority. It is therefore more realistic, particularly in the steady gaze of the polished stone eyes. The artist accepted the conventions but moved beyond the formula to create this powerful image.

MIDDLE KINGDOM, 2135–1786 BC, DYNASTIES XI–XII

Between the Old and Middle Kingdoms there was a hiatus later called the First Intermediate Period (2260–2130 BC; dynasties VII–X). Apparently not even stable, conservative Egypt could sustain more than five centuries of peace and prosperity. A constantly expanding bureaucracy, the growing power of priests, and rebellious local officials all weakened the central authority. For over a century there was civil unrest, political instability (historian Manetho facetiously remarked that the seventh dynasty consisted of seventy kings in seventy days), and invasions by desert barbarians.[4] However, the next four dynasties stabilized the political situation and led Egypt to renewed peace and prosperity. Politically there was considerable local authority that, when coupled with a strong middle class and a weaker but stable central government, made the twelfth dynasty the closest to a democratic state that the Egyptians ever achieved. This was the affluent society of the Middle Kingdom with the highest standard of living yet achieved in the ancient world.

The major art forms of the age followed the canons of the Old Kingdom but with a new refinement and mastery of the material that carried over into the New Kingdom,

---

4. Neither the First nor even the Second Intermediate Period was as chaotic and disruptive as most of the political upheavals in Mesopotamia. They were more like ripples on a calm sea but seemed, to the Egyptians, to be very troublesome just because the sea was usually so serene.

2.5 *Seated Scribe*, from Sakkara. Old Kingdom, 5th Dynasty. Ca. 2500 BC. Painted limestone, height 21" (53.3 cm). Louvre, Paris. Photo: R.M.N., Paris.

---

the last splendid period of Egyptian power and influence. In the scene from the Sarcophagus of Queen Kawyt (fig. 2.6), the queen is seated on a throne holding a cup to her lips with her right hand and a mirror in her left. A maid ties the curls of her wig while a manservant pours her a drink. His words wishing her well appear in the hieroglyphs between them. The composition is spacious, uncluttered, and incised with elegant lines, as in the adroit hands of the woman dressing the wig. Note the convention of ignoring **perspective** and scaling figures according to importance.

The decorative arts, too, flourished in this era. Jewelry is one of the oldest of these, dating back more than 7,000 years to the earliest civilizations in Mesopotamia and Egypt. Making fine jewelry was long an Egyptian specialty but the jewelers of the Middle Kingdom surpassed their predecessors (fig. 2.7). The exquisite necklace is made of gold, lapis lazuli (purple with gold specks), carnelian (red), and turquoise (light blue to darker greenish blue). The pectoral is primarily of gold-inlaid green feldspar and lapis lazuli

2.6 Sarcophagus of Queen Kawyt, detail, from Deir-el-Bahri (Thebes). Middle Kingdom, 11th Dynasty. Ca. 2100 BC. White limestone, life-size. Egyptian Museum, Cairo. Photo: Hirmer, Munich.

BEAUTIFICATION

All the Middle Eastern cultures used cosmetics but the Egyptians also exported cosmetics throughout the ancient world. Egyptian women painted their lashes, eyelids, and eyebrows black with kohl, a paste made with soot and antimony. This was standard practice in the Middle East; kohl not only beautified eyes but also protected them from flies and the fiery sun. (The palettes on which eye makeup was ground inspired ceremonial palettes—see fig. 2.1—that were decorated with reliefs.) Henna was used to dye hair, nails, palms, and the soles of the feet. The Egyptians compounded various raw materials (some imported) to produce perfumes, creams, and lotions. Rouges and lipsticks (red ochre), bath oils, and teeth-cleaning abrasives were used by the upper classes of both sexes. Among these materials were almond, olive, and sesame oils, thyme, oregano, rosewater, saffron, myrrh, frankincense, and spikenard, an aromatic plant imported from India. The ancient Egyptian word for the scent of a perfume was always combined in a form meaning "fragrance of the gods," implying a religious function. Many cosmetic materials used throughout the Middle East began as adjuncts to religious rites before becoming, so to speak, secularized.

2.7 Necklace of drop and ball beads, from the Treasure of Lahun. Middle Kingdom, 12th Dynasty. Ca. 1880 BC. Gold, carnelian, lapis lazuli, turquoise, green feldspar, amethyst, and garnet, length 32" (80 cm). Metropolitan Museum of Art, New York (Rogers Fund and Henry Walters Gift, 1916, 16.1.3.)

with carnelian highlights. The facing falcons symbolize Horus the sky god while the kneeling girl presumably represents the recipient of "one of the supreme masterpieces of Egyptian jewelry" (Metropolitan Museum of Art). The necklace was presented to Princess Sit-Hathor-Yunet by her royal father, Sesistris II (reigned ca. 1897–1878 BC).

STUDY QUESTIONS

1. What is a theocracy? Explain how Egyptian government functioned. Why was the Nile so crucial to the concept of a theocratic state?
2. What does jewelry tell us about a culture? Using supplemental sources, consider several pieces of jewelry from the Old, Middle, and New Kingdoms. How do they differ? What do they have in common?

2.8 Avenue of the Rams and Temple of Amon, Karnak. New Kingdom, dating from the 20th century BC but constructed mainly from the 16th to 12th centuries BC. Photo: Spectrum, London.

NEW KINGDOM (EMPIRE), 1570–1085 BC, DYNASTIES XVIII–XX

The disruption that ended the Middle Kingdom was more serious and more protracted than that of the earlier Intermediate Period. This was the Second Intermediate Period (1780–1550 BC, dynasties XIII–XVII), marked by the invasion of the Hyksos (Egyptian, "rulers of foreign lands"). These Syro-Palestinians unwittingly set the stage for the emergence of the Egyptian Empire. Though little is known about Hyksos domination, it appears that they introduced the horse and war chariot to their hostile hosts and that the culture was stable despite the belligerent Egyptian reaction. The greatest damage was psychological because the Hyksos were barbarian intruders who wounded Egyptian pride, but who acted also as a catalyst, spurring eighteenth-dynasty rulers to imperial conquests.

At first the New Kingdom pharaohs were neither land-hungry nor bound for glory. Detesting anything foreign, especially alien domination, they first occupied adjoining areas in order to create buffers against hostile incursions. Later—human nature being what it is—conquest became

an end in itself, enlarging pharaonic power and glory and producing a bonanza of additional taxes.

Government in the New Kingdom was even more autocratic than it had been in the Old Kingdom. Military might rather than national unity formed the basis for the rule of the pharaoh, a title now associated with the ruler's person. ("Pharaoh" means "great house," a term originally applied to the king's court and residence.) Local authority declined to its lowest level, leaving the pharaoh with consolidated control over an expanding empire.

Temples and Worship

Egyptian temples were the first structures in the ancient world to be built entirely of stone and the first to exploit the **post and lintel construction** that other cultures had used on a small scale. Their imposing, thickly columned temples were visual symbols of the wealth of the pharaohs and the power of the gods, not to mention the authority of the priests who served the gods. The Temple of Amon at Karnak (fig. 2.8) was the seat of the throne of Amon and the center of religious administration. The view is of the main entrance, which was approached from the Nile and then through the avenue of ram-headed sphinxes to Pylon I, thus following the solar path of Amon-Re. With 134 massive columns in the Great Hall alone, this was the most extensive temple in Egypt and one of the largest sanctuaries in the ancient world.

As symbols of divine and royal authority, Egyptian temples were usually built on the flat banks of the Nile, the eternal source of Egyptian power. Constructed below limestone cliffs at Thebes on the west bank of the Nile, the mortuary temple of Queen Hatshepsut (fig. 2.9 and p. 7) is a brilliantly conceived complex and possibly the only Egyptian temple that was designed without a Nile backdrop. It was planned as a memorial to the first woman to rule Egypt of whom we have any firm record (there may have been one or two before her). To make the structure more imposing, given the immensity of the setting, the architect, Senmet, thrust the upper courtyard into the cliff face so that the towering mass of rock appears as a kind of natural pyramid. This temple is unique, as was Hatshepsut. Married to Thutmose II, who died prematurely, she became regent for Thutmose III, her son-in-law, whom she relegated to a secondary role as she ruled firmly and effectively for twenty-two years. It was only after her death that Thutmose III, known today as the Napoleon of ancient Egypt, became the greatest of Egypt's warrior kings.

Even in its ruined condition, the Temple of Amon-Mut-Khonsu (fig. 2.10) clearly illustrates the nature of Egyptian religious architecture. Temples were designed as a succession of spaces of increasing holiness entered through a main portal (number 1 in fig. 2.11) flanked by ponderous masses of stone called pylons which led to the first court (2, fig. 2.11). After passing through the 74- foot (22.6 m) columns of the Great Hall (4, fig. 2.11), ordinary worshipers assembled in the sequestered second court (5, fig. 2.11) but could go no farther. They could only marvel at the mysterious forest of columns that darkened the inner sanctuaries, the

2.9 Senmet, Mortuary Temple of Queen Hatshepsut, Deir-el-Bahri (Thebes). New Kingdom, 18th Dynasty. Ca. 1480 BC. Photo: Hirmer, Munich.

2.10 Temple of Amon-Mut-Khonsu, Luxor, Great Court of Ramesses II. New Kingdom, 18th Dynasty. Ca. 1390–1260 BC. Sandstone, column height 30' (9.1 m). Photo: Robert Harding, London (Philip Craven).

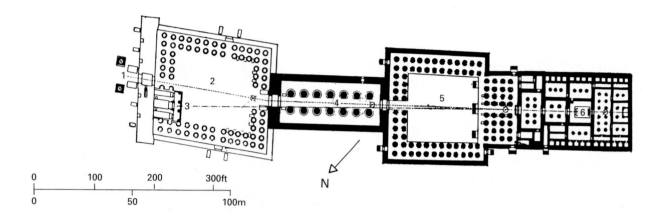

0 100 200 300ft

0   50   100m

N

exclusive preserve of the priesthood (6, fig. 2.11). There, the all-powerful clergy administered the temple of Amon, his wife Mut, and their son Khonsu.

Amenhotep IV

The power of the priesthood was a grave concern of Amenhotep IV (reigned 1379–1362 BC, later known as Akhenaten), who had ample reason for anxiety. Egyptian religion had reached its highest ethical level near the end of the Middle Kingdom and the beginning of the New Kingdom. By Amenhotep's time it had become seriously debased, its ethical foundation reduced as superstition and magic gained ascendancy. The result was a marked increase in the power of the priesthood, who preyed on the fears of the masses. Or, was debasing the religion a means of increasing priestly power? In either case, priests began selling magical charms that were alleged to prevent the heart of the deceased from alerting Osiris to his or her true character. The priests also sold formulas that supposedly facilitated the passage of the dead to celestial realms. The aggregate of these purchased prayers constituted the *Book of the Dead*. Good deeds and a clear conscience had too often become passé.

Amenhotep IV met the problem head on. He drove the priests from their temples, confiscated their property and possessions, and ordered the names of the traditional gods removed throughout the land. The pharaoh then commanded his people to worship a new god called Aten, an ancient designation for the sun. The pharaoh further stipulated that all worship must be directed to him personally, for only he could communicate with the Aten. Changing his name from Amenhotep ("Amon is satisfied") to Akhenaten (ah-kun-AH-tun; "beneficial to the Aten"), he ordered the construction of his capital, Akhetaton ("the horizon of Aten"), on a virgin site at Tell el-Amarna (see map 2.1). The traditional artistic style was temporarily replaced by a new lightness and naturalism known as the Amarna style. Perhaps the best-known Egyptian sculpture, the portrait head of Akhenaten's wife, Queen Nefretete (fig. 2.12), portrays an elegantly beautiful young woman. Though

2.11 *Above* Floor plan of Temple of Amon-Mut-Khonsu, Luxor: (1) entrance, (2) first court, (3) earlier sanctuaries, (4) great hall, (5) second court, and (6) sanctuaries of Amon, Mut, and Khonsu.

2.12 Portrait head of Queen Nefretete. New Kingdom, 18th Dynasty. Ca. 1370 BC. Painted limestone, height 20" (50.8 cm). Staatliche Museen, Berlin. Photo: Hirmer, Munich.

possibly an idealized portrait, it is certainly an excellent example of the Amarna style.

Was the worship of Aten the world's first monotheistic religion? Aten was indeed its only god but it should be emphasized that Amon-Re was already regarded as the god of the whole earth, a belief that was well-established during the reign of Akhenaten's father, Amenhotep III. This makes Akhenaten's reform less drastic than his enemies claimed.

What were Akhenaten's motives? Was he trying to establish a new religion or attempting to regain religious control of the country? He certainly put the priests of Amon-Re out of business and exercised total control through his claim that only he spoke for and to the Aten. All prayers had to be directed to the pharaoh, "the beautiful child of the Aten." All contemporary depictions of the sun disk show the rays descending to the pharaoh and his queen and to no one else. This was, in effect, a return to the Old Kingdom idea that the king was identified with the sun god, the only difference being the name change.

> The customary Egyptian fiscal system that had divided income between local shrines, the larger temples, and the needs of the palace without being too burdensome now gave way to the all-powerful pharaoh, his new religion, and his new city. Designed for shrines to the

2.14   The Golden Coffin of Tutankhamen, from the Valley of the Kings. New Kingdom, 18th Dynasty, Late Amarna period. Ca. 1352 BC. Gold inlaid with carnelian, lapis lazuli, and turquoise. Egyptian Museum, Cairo. Photo: Robert C. Lamm, Scottsdale.

2.13   Throne with Tutankhamen and Queen, from the Valley of the Kings, detail of the back. New Kingdom, 18th Dynasty, Late Amarna period. Ca. 1352 BC. Wood plated with gold and silver, inlays of glass paste, ca. 12 × 12" (30.5 × 30.5 cm). Egyptian Museum, Cairo. Photo: Robert Harding, London (Richard Ashworth).

> Aten and for the royal court, Akhetaten was built with incredible haste, not to mention expense. Financing was made possible only by pouring all the nation's resources into the coffers of the king and his god.[5]

Akhenaten's death signaled a sea change. What prompted this to happen so rapidly

> was doubtless the chaos caused by the economic consequences of Akhenaten's religious reforms that brought about a complete reversal to the old order as

5. I. E. S. Edwards et al, ed., *The Cambridge Ancient History*, 3rd ed., vol. II, part 2 (London: Cambridge University Press, 1970), p. 53.

soon as he was dead. The recollection of the misery of such times was strong enough to bring upon him the odium of later generations.[6]

The naturalistic Amarna style ended with the reign of Akhenaten's son-in-law Tutankhamen (toot-ahng-KAH-mun; 1347–1338 BC). Though he was a minor king, ruling for only nine years, his tomb contained a marvelous array of treasures. Discovered in 1922, the collection was relatively intact, making "King Tut" a household name. Figure 2.13 reveals a richly colored scene of the young king and his wife. The loose-limbed figures are portrayed in an intimate setting with a certain sweetness that was unusual in the Amarna style. The presence of the sun disk at the top is puzzling; Amon-Re was supposedly restored by this time.

The Golden Coffin of Tutankhamen (fig. 2.14) is perhaps the most famous and justly acclaimed creation of the art of goldsmithing, one of an ensemble of coffins that totaled about 450 pounds (204 kg) of gold. The cover of the coffin is a sensitive portrait of a youthful king who was about nineteen when he died. In figures 2.12, 2.13, and 2.14 one sees clear evidence of the grace and beauty so characteristic of the Amarna style.

The artistic backlash against the Amarna Period was strong and, given Akhenaten's unpopularity, predictable. The reaction skipped the New Kingdom's ornamental style and the Middle Kingdom classic style, moving back twelve centuries to the static formal style of the Old Kingdom. The style then remained about the same until the gradual decline of Egyptian power after 1085 BC. Falling, in succession, to the Cushites, Assyria, Persia, and Alexander the Great, Egypt became, in 30 BC, an important Roman province. The fall from power, however, cannot diminish Egypt's magnificent achievements over an incredible span of 1,600 years. No other people have had a longer or more distinguished record.

STUDY QUESTION

Explain the forces that impel a military state to ever more conquests. You should expand your discussion beyond the army and officer corps to include merchants, contractors, those who needed workers, patriots, and so on.

THE RECENT PAST

Civilizations dating back to 3000 or 4000 BC may seem alien, even peculiar, and not relevant to our world. This apparent remoteness is lessened, however, if we reflect on what we share with the past. Consider, for example, an invention that, given the tens of thousands of years that *Homo sapiens* has roamed this planet, occurred a very short time ago—less than 6,000 years. This is the creation of written language as independently invented by the Mesopotamians, Egyptians, Chinese, and Maya of Central America. Written translatable languages are the common thread connecting such disparate personalities as Hammurabi, Hatshepsut, Confucius, the Buddha, Julius Caesar, Cleopatra, Muhammad, Queen Elizabeth I, William Shakespeare, Abraham Lincoln, and Margaret Thatcher. All use one or more versions of written communication that connects literate cultures throughout recorded history and around the world.

SUMMARY

Egypt was the first national state, the ancient world's most homogeneous society. With only two significant interruptions, her history extended from the first dynasty of about 3100 BC until a final slow decline after the fall of the New Kingdom in 1085 BC. This power, prosperity, and continuity were a direct result of the relative security and consistent agricultural affluence of this "gift of the Nile." Artistic styles evolved a bit but the basic conventions remained the same throughout Egyptian history, prompting Plato to remark that Egyptian art had not changed "in ten thousand years" (*Laws*, 656D–E).

The artistic conventions were perfected during the Old Kingdom (2686–2181 BC): a cubic view of standing or seated rulers that conveyed immutability. This was an expression of the theology that the pharaoh and the state were one: divine and indivisible.

After an era of instability (First Intermediate Period, 2260–2130 BC) the eleventh dynasty established the less autocratic Middle Kingdom (2135–1786 BC). This was the classical period of Egyptian civilization, reflecting new levels of affluence and corresponding artistic achievement, possibly indicating that achievement and affluence are interrelated. Artists continued and refined the creation of fine jewelry, furniture, pottery, and other household items.

The invasion of the Syro-Palestinian Hyksos was a serious and long-lasting blow to Egyptian pride (Second Intermediate Period, 1780–1550 BC). After the seventeenth dynasty expelled the invaders, the eighteenth dynasty of

6. Ibid., p. 54.

the New Kingdom (1570–1085 BC) began the imperial period with a series of military campaigns designed to prevent any subsequent foreign menace.

Some of the famous surviving buildings were constructed during the imperial (New Kingdom) period. These include the mortuary temple of Queen Hatshepsut, the Temple of Amon at Karnak, and the Temple of Amon-Mut-Khonsu at Luxor.

A daring pharaoh of the eighteenth dynasty introduced a new religion while attempting to eradicate the old religion and depose its priests. Egyptologists still debate the motives of Amenhotep IV, who changed his name to Akhenaten and decreed that the nation would worship one God, Aten the sun disk, whose sole earthly representative was the pharaoh himself. This was the Amarna period, when artistic styles became more naturalistic than at any other time in Egyptian history.

With all revenues funneled into the royal treasury for maintaining the pharaoh and his god and for the new capital of Akhetaten at Tell-el-Amarna, the economic consequences were disastrous. Following his death, the new city was immediately abandoned as the nation returned to its traditional religion. Attempts to eradicate Akhenaten and Aten from Egyptian history had no more success than Akhenaten had had in trying to erase Amon-Re's religion.

The years of declining power after 1085 BC put an end, finally, to several millennia of Egyptian civilization —a record of accomplishments that remains unique in the annals of humankind.

CULTURE AND HUMAN VALUES

Each of the Three Kingdoms can be seen as an extended period of balance. There seem to be just two periods of adjustment: between the Old and Middle Kingdoms and between the Middle and New Kingdoms. Once the nation had a central government, the society was so structured and stable that it could weather almost any disruption, at least until after 1085 BC with the sporadic civil wars and, later, the arrival of foreign invaders.

Egyptian life was generally safer and more pleasant than life in Mesopotamia but the great mass of people functioned as cogs in the splendid state machine. A rigid class structure allowed virtually no social mobility, although under the law there was some equality of treatment despite differences in class. This, however, was the most stable society in the ancient Mediterranean world; people knew exactly where they stood in the scheme of things. Further, because of their extensive trade throughout the then known world, the Egyptians knew how much better off they were than any other people.

One aspect of Egyptian culture that is of particular interest today is its indifference to the color of a person's skin. There is still some speculation about whether Queen Nefretete, Cleopatra or any other Egyptian was white, brown, or black. We do know that Cleopatra was Greek but, as Egyptologists have repeatedly asserted, there is no way of knowing about the others because skin pigmentation was not a major consideration in that ancient world.

Egyptian cultural achievements were truly monumental and influenced Minoan, Mycenaean, Greek, and Roman civilizations. Further, Egyptian religion had a significant ethical component called *maat*, which translates as a synthesis of four ideas: order, truth, justice, and righteousness. A quality not of people but of the world, *maat* symbolized the established moral order of the universe that functioned as a kind of natural law. Acting in accordance with that natural order encouraged harmony with the gods. For peasants this entailed working hard and honestly; for officials it suggested dealing justly. A concern for *maat* coupled with the highest standard of living in the ancient world helped make Egyptian life cheerful and confident for all and— for the wealthy—wonderfully elegant.

Greece: Birthplace of Western Civilization

Greece

(most dates approximate)

	People and Events	Art and Architecture	Literature	Philosophy and Science
BRONZE AGE 3000–1100 BC	3000–2000 Early Helladic (mainland) culture; Early Cycladic culture in Aegean 2000–1700 Mycenaeans enter Greece 2000–1100 Minoan civilization on Crete 1550–1100 Mycenaean civilization 1260–1150 Trojan War	3000–2000 Helladic and Cycladic figurines 1700–1380 Minoan Late Palace Period: frescoes, pottery, jewelry	1750–1600 Minoan Linear A script 1600–1100 Minoan-Mycenaean Linear B script	
DARK AGE 1100–900 BC	1100–800 Dorian invasions of mainland 1100–950 Ionian migrations to Asia Minor 900– Dorian migrations to Aegean islands and Asia Minor	1100–900 Loss of writing		
GEOMETRIC PERIOD 900–700 BC	800 Aristocracies begin to replace kingships 776 First Olympic Games	900–750 Furniture, textiles, glassware, figurines, but mostly pottery	750–700 Homer: *Iliad* and *Odyssey*	
ARCHAIC PERIOD 700–480 BC	750–550 Colonization by city-states 621 Draco's law code, Athens 600 Coinage introduced 594 Constitutional and economic reforms by Solon of Athens 546–527 Pisistratos: third great reformer in Athens 546 Persian conquest of Greeks in Asia Minor 507 Democratic constitution of Cleisthenes 490 First Persian invasion; Battle of Marathon	660 First life-size statues 620–500 Attic black-figure pottery 600 Early Doric temples 580–500 *Kouros* and *kore* figures 530–400 Attic red-figure pottery	700 Hesiod: *Theogony* 600 Sappho: lyric poetry; Aesop: *Fables*	**Thales** 636–546 Ionian philosopher **Anaximander** 610–546 Ionian philosopher **Pythagoras** 582–507 philosopher and mathematician **Herakleitos of Ephesos** 535–475 Ionian philosopher
CLASSICAL PERIOD 480–400 BC	480–479 Second Persian invasion; Battles of Thermopylai, Salamis, and Plataea 460–430 Golden Age of Athens (Age of Pericles) 431–404 Peloponnesian War	490–430 Pheidias, sculptor: Parthenon frieze and metopes 480–470 Severe Style of early classicism: *Critios Boy* and *Delphi Charioteer* 480–407 Myron: *Discobolus* 460 Bronze sculpture of *Poseidon* 447–405 Buildings on Acropolis, Athens: Parthenon, Propylaea, Temple of Athena Nike, Erechtheion fl. 430 Polykleitos: sculptor and initiator of the "canon"	**Aeschylus** 525–456 dramatist: *Oresteia* **Sophocles** 496–406 dramatist: *Antigone, Oedipus* **Herodotos** 484–425 "father of history" **Euripides** 480–406 dramatist: *Medea, Trojan Women* **Thucydides** 471–399 *History of the Peloponnesian War* **Aristophanes** 450–380 dramatist (Old Comedy): *Lysistrata*	**Empedocles** 495–435 philosopher and scientist **Protagoras** 481–411 sophist **Socrates** 469–399 philosopher and "gadfly of Athens" **Hippocrates** 460–377 physician **Democritos** 460–362 atomic theory **Plato** 427–347 philosopher, writer, and teacher
LATE CLASSICAL PERIOD 400–323 BC	395–340 Warfare among Greek leagues 384–322 Demosthenes: Athenian orator and statesman 338 Battle of Chaeronea; Philip of Macedon controls city-states 336–323 Reign and conquests of Alexander the Great	350 Theatre at Epidauros by Polykleitos the Younger fl. 340 Praxiteles of Athens, sculptor: *Aphrodite of Knidos* 4th c. Lysippus, sculptor: *Apoxyomenos*	**Xenophon** 434–355 historian and general	399 Trial and death of Socrates 387 Plato founds Academy near Athens **Aristotle** 384–322 philosopher and teacher, founded Lyceum in Athens in 335
HELLENISTIC AGE 323–30 BC	323–30 Despotism dominant form of government 148 Macedonia becomes Roman province 146 Romans level Corinth 86 Sulla sacks Athens	230–220 *The Dying Gaul* 190 *Nike of Samothrace* 180 Atlar of Zeus, Pergamon 174 Work begins on Temple of the Olympian Zeus, Athens 120 *Aphrodite of Melos*	**Menander** 342–291 New Comedy dramatist 300 Founding of library at Alexandria	**Epicurus** 342–270 philosopher **Zeno the Stoic** 335–263 **Euclid** fl. 300 mathematician and physicist **Archimedes** 289–212 mathematician **Eratosthenes** 276–195 mathematician and astronomer

The Citadel, Mycenae, plan.

CHAPTER 3

The Aegean Heritage, ca. 3000–1100 BC

Historians sometimes refer to the great leap that propelled Western culture forward as the "miracle of Greece." Miracle implies something that can't be explained, but, by examining what these people valued, we can begin to understand their spectacular achievements. They prized individualism, rationalism, justice, beauty, and the pursuit of excellence and thereby created a remarkable civilization.

As we have seen in Egypt and Mesopotamia, climate, topography, and geography shape cultures in particular

ways and Greece is no exception. The early Aegean cultures, while important in and of themselves, were also crucial preludes to the rise of Greece. There were three Aegean cultures: the Cycladic (KYE-kla-deek) of the Aegean Islands; the Minoan (mi-NO-un) of Crete; and the Late Helladic of the Mycenaeans (my-se-NEE-uns) on the Greek mainland.

Map 3.1   Ancient Greece.

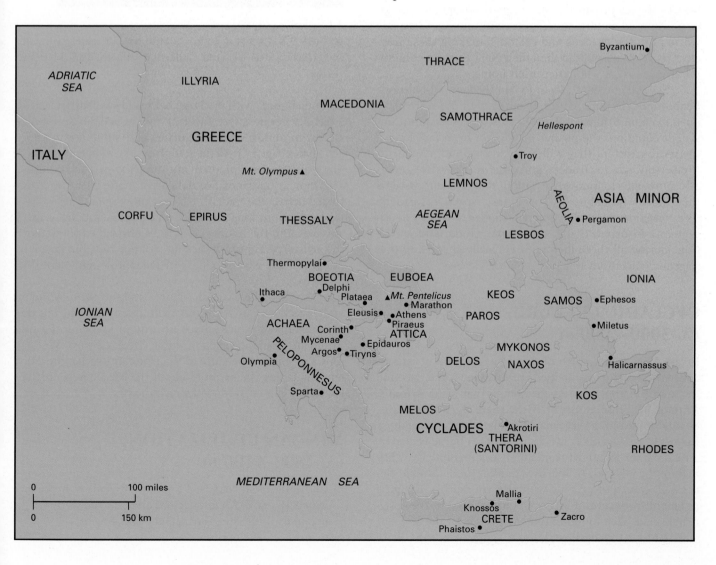

All three cultures enjoyed a maritime climate that was apparently more energizing than that of the landlocked agricultural lands of the Middle East. Whether living on the islands or the mainland, the Aegean peoples had solid assets that included sufficient agricultural resources, a temperate maritime climate, and, most important, ready access to the sea. With about 1,000 islands dotting the Aegean, sailors were never out of sight of land (a vital factor in the days of rudimentary navigation); even on the mainland no one was more than a few hours' ride from the sea. Homer's "wine-dark sea" helped shape the destinies of the Aegean cultures and, later, that of classical Greece (map 3.1).

The Greek lands consisted of narrow valleys guarded by steep mountains, slender coastal plains, and the multitude of islands studding the Aegean Sea. There was no single land mass to be controlled, as pharaoh ruled the Nile valley; nor were the Aegean lands subject to the extremes of continental weather that so frequently afflicted Mesopotamia. The sea, for the Aegean people, was a kind of golden bowl that nourished the development of their civilizations. A temperate climate, security against invasion, rich fishing grounds, and multiple highways for trade and travel—the sea provided it all. Frequent voyages to foreign ports exposed sailors, merchants, and tourists to a wide world of different ideas and customs, making these travelers more cosmopolitan than their Near Eastern contemporaries, most of whom never left home.

Several constants seem to run through all cultures. Seaports are, by their nature, urban centers, cities are more open to change than rural areas. This leads to a quite consistent equation: the farther people are from a seacoast, the more resistant they will be to change and new ideas. Conversely, sailors, traders, and other travelers are generally more open to innovative notions and unusual customs than those who habitually stay home, especially farmers. As a consequence, civilizations are shaped mostly by developments in urban living, commerce, trade, and travel. Considering all these factors, it is hardly surprising that Aegean civilizations reached such high levels.

CYCLADIC CULTURE,
CA. 3000–2000 BC

In the Aegean Sea north of Crete lies a group of islands called the Cyclades, so-named because they "cycle" around the sacred birthplace of Apollo and his twin sister Artemis. A minor Neolithic culture flourished here, but little remains beyond some remarkable marble idols, if that is what these figures were. Strangely modern, they are characterized by a rectangular angularity and an abstract simplicity. They include heads and, primarily, standing nude female figures, all carved of pristine white Parian marble. Ranging in height from several inches to nearly life-size, these figurines have been found in tombs throughout the Aegean.

Unlike the earliest known sculptures that were

3.1   Cycladic figurine. Ca. 2500 BC. Marble, 22 × 5¼" × 3¼" (55.9 × 13.3 × 8.3 cm). Seattle Art Museum (Norman and Amelia Davis Classical Collection). Photo: Paul Macapia.

bulbous figures with the large belly and swollen breasts of a fertility goddess (see fig. 1.2), most Cycladic sculptures were slim, almost virginal figurines with subtle sexual characteristics (fig. 3.1). All the sculptures have sharply defined noses and traces of pigment outlining the eyes and mouths. The female figurines are delicately made with the arms folded across the midriff. No one knows what these artistic conventions mean because no trace of Cycladic writing survives. But the figures seem to be abstracted versions of the artists' perceptions; they are not portraits but possibly images of the earth goddess of Paleolithic and Neolithic cultures.

Because the Cycladic figures and the entire Minoan and Mycenaean civilizations were discovered during the past century or so, we have no way of knowing the full extent of their influence on later Greek culture. We can only suggest that because of their proximity, the intensely curious Greeks knew more about the earlier Aegean civilizations than current evidence indicates.

MINOAN CIVILIZATION,
CA. 2600–1100 BC

One of the great islands of the world in midsea, in the
winedark sea, is Krete: spacious and rich and
populous, with ninety cities and a mingling of
tongues . . . and one among their ninety towns is

Knossos. Here lived King Minos whom great Zeus received every ninth year in private council.

Homer, *Odyssey*, Book XIX[1]

The first people who dwelt in Greek lands about whom we have much information were the Minoans, named after the fabled King Minos (MY-nus) who supposedly lived and ruled on the island of Crete. They were probably not truly "Greek"; their language, so far as one can tell, does not seem related to the Indo-Iranian family. (Existing clay tablets in the "Linear A" Minoan script remain deciphered.) Agrarian people colonized Crete around 6000 BC, very possibly from the culture that produced Çatal Hüyük in Turkey. Minoan culture itself existed from about 2600 till about 1100 BC, and approached its peak around the period 2000 to 1800 BC with the building of the splendid temples at Knossos (KNAWS-us), Phaistos (FEST-os), Mallia (MAH-ya), and Zacro (ZAH-kro).

Although Linear A script remains a mystery we do have considerable knowledge of this culture because of excavations by British archaeologist Arthur Evans (1851–1941) and others. (Active excavations continue at the four temples and other promising sites on Crete and on the island of Thera.) Evans' excavations and reconstructions at Knossos reveal a rich and sophisticated culture that prospered because of a semitropical maritime climate, productive agricultural areas, and, remarkably, an absence of warfare. The Minoans had no traditional enemies and apparently viewed warfare as neither necessary nor desirable. Their trade empire was far more productive than the trophies and territories secured by military aggression. Their ships carried agricultural and manufactured products throughout the eastern Mediterranean and returned to Crete bearing products from many cultures, making them the greatest Mediterranean traders before the Greeks and Phoenicians.

MINOAN WOMEN

According to the available evidence there were no laws or customs in Minoan society that relegated women to subordinate positions. A Minoan wife retained full control of her dowry, which her husband could not use without her permission. Divorce was a right available equally to husband and wife. Further, a wife who proved her husband at fault could reclaim any property given him during the marriage. However, the uniqueness of gender equality in the ancient world is not fully explained by the dominance of the earth goddess. The Minoans were sailors and sailors are usually away from home for long periods of time. What better person to look after their mutual property than the mariner's wife?

Religion

Minoan religion centered on nature worship, especially the cycle of birth, death, and regeneration that lay at the heart of agricultural societies. The chief deity was an earth goddess derived from peaceful Neolithic societies[2] that lived in what has been characterized as Old Europe.[3] The essential power lay with the queen as the earthly representative of the goddess, the incarnation of the earth mother. Neither a matriarchy nor a patriarchy, this exceptional society is best described as shared responsibilities in a partnership government.

A noted architectural historian[4] believes that the consistency of temple orientations and settings confirms the worship of the earth goddess in Minoan society. All major temples are set in enclosed valleys with the north–south axis pointing toward a nearby conical or mounded hill and a more distant notched cleft (saddleback) or a set of double peaks. The paired mountains can be seen as breasts and the saddleback as the female cleft. Visible at all sites, this orientation is particularly noticeable at Knossos and Mallia.

Temples

Until recently archaeologists agreed, more or less, with Sir Arthur Evans, prime excavator at Knossos, that he had uncovered a royal palace and that major buildings at other sites were also palaces. Current best evidence suggests that these buildings were temples and that Evans had made his initial mistake by believing what Homer had to say about King Minos in Book XIX of the *Odyssey*, which is quoted above. Schliemann had found Troy by studying Homer but the poet (and persistent Greek legends) laid a false trail to ancient Crete. There may have been a king, or a king and a queen, but no one knows for sure. No palaces have yet been found but some rooms in the huge temples could have been royal residences.

Unlike, say, Egyptian sanctuaries, Minoan temples were three- to five-story structures that had hundreds of small rooms, rambling corridors and staircases, walls gaily decorated with colorful **murals**, running water, bathtubs, flush toilets, sewage systems, terraces, open galleries, and many light wells that conveyed natural illumination to lower levels. The temples may have functioned not only

1. Robert Fitzgerald, trans. (Garden City, N.Y.: Anchor Books, 1963).
2. Riane Eisler, *The Chalice and the Blade: Our History, Our Future* (San Francisco: Harper & Row, 1987).
3. Marja Gimbutas, *Goddesses and Gods of Old Europe* (Berkeley: University of California Press, 1982). There are about 3,000 Neolithic sites in southeastern Europe and islands of the Aegean and Adriatic seas, some dating back to around 7500 BC. These peaceful agricultural societies apparently influenced Aegean civilizations in the Cyclades, Crete, and Lesbos.
4. Vincent Scully, *The Earth, The Temple, and the Gods* (New Haven, Conn.: Yale University Press, 1979).

3.2 Customs House, Knossos Labyrinth, Crete. Labyrinth first constructed in 1930 BC. Abandoned after a fire in 1380 BC. Photo: Scala, Florence.

3.3 Floor plan of the Knossos Labyrinth, Crete (after Reynold Higgins).

as religious centers but also as administrative centers for the far-flung trade empire.

Probably the most important temple was the Knossos Labyrinth (fig. 3.2), the vastness of which can only be hinted at in Evans' partial reconstruction. The building illustrated stands at the northern end of the palace; Evans called it the Customs House because it was possibly the main checkpoint for visitors arriving by sea 4 miles (6.4 km) to the north. The flaring columns are of wood and apparently symbolized tree trunks. The multiple levels, wandering corridors, and countless rooms (fig. 3.3) possibly inspired the Greek legend of the labyrinth of Minos that was guarded by the fearful Minotaur (half man, half bull—the result of the queen's impregnation by a bull). After Queen Pasiphaë (pus-i-FAH-ee) gave birth to the monster, Minos had it imprisoned in the basement of the palace. The earth-shaking roars attributed to the awesome beast were caused, of course, by the earthquakes that periodically racked Crete.

What Evans called the Throne Room of Minos (fig. 3.4) is a small chamber at ground level containing a simple, high-backed alabaster throne with stone benches

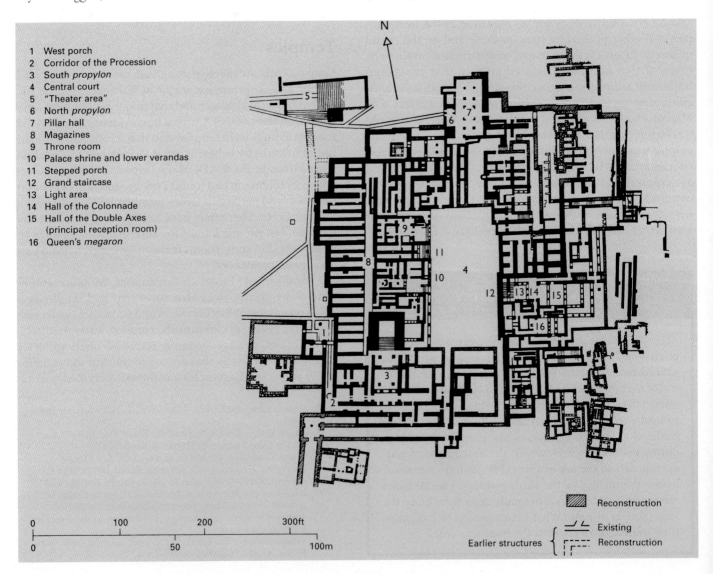

1 West porch
2 Corridor of the Procession
3 South *propylon*
4 Central court
5 "Theater area"
6 North *propylon*
7 Pillar hall
8 Magazines
9 Throne room
10 Palace shrine and lower verandas
11 Stepped porch
12 Grand staircase
13 Light area
14 Hall of the Colonnade
15 Hall of the Double Axes
   (principal reception room)
16 Queen's *megaron*

N

0   100   200   300ft

0   50   100m

▨ Reconstruction

Earlier structures { ⌐⌐ Existing
                     ⌐⌐ Reconstruction

3.4 Throne Room, Knossos Labyrinth, Crete. Photo: Ancient Art & Architecture, London.

3.5 Queen's Megaron (reconstruction), Knossos Labyrinth, Crete. Ca. 1600–1400 BC. Photo: Ancient Art & Architecture, London.

around three walls (including the wall with the throne). The fanciful griffin mural is a modern reconstruction based on fragments found in the ruins. A **colonnade** opposite the throne separates this room from an open **atrium** that adds fresh air and light to the intimate and unpretentious setting. Given the female orientation of the religion and the relative equality of the sexes, it is far from certain that a king occupied the throne; it might have been a queen. Perhaps they alternated, or conceivably a head priestess or priest was the occupant.

The wall decorations in what Evans called the Queen's Megaron are especially elegant. Legendary friends to all sailors, five dolphins frolic contentedly in a seascape mural (fig. 3.5) painted on wet plaster (**fresco**). Brightly illuminated by a light well, the apartment also features bright blue floral designs on the door frames and an adjoining bathroom complete with a bathtub.

Minoan Art

Remarkably different from the arts of Mesopotamia and Egypt, Minoan art emphasizes aspects of agriculture and such reflections of the natural world as representations of animals and insects. The warfare and hunting themes that

CIVILIZED LIVING IN INDIA

From about 2500 BC, the Indus city of Mohenjo-Daro had the first known main sewage system to which every house in the city was connected. Brick-lined pipes carried sewage from each home into covered channels that ran along the centers of the main streets to disposal points well away from the city. The sewers took waste from kitchens and bathrooms with indoor toilets. The main drains even had removable covers at crucial inspection points where efficient operation of the system was monitored. The later Minoans and Romans had efficient sewers but not until the seventeenth century (thousands of years later!) did European cities begin using comparable sewage systems.

3.6 *Snake Goddess,* from Knossos Labyrinth, Crete. Ca. 1600 BC. Faience, height 17½" (44.5 cm). Archaeological Museum, Heraklion, Crete. Photo: Dagli Orti, Paris.

3.7 *Below* Gold Bee Pendant, from the Khrysolakkos tomb at the Temple of Mallia, Crete. Ca. 1600 BC. Height 1¾" (4.5 cm). Archaeological Museum, Heraklion, Crete. Photo: Ekdotike Athenon.

preoccupied the eastern male-dominant cultures are noticeably absent. The playful themes and depictions of the joys of Minoan life also differ from the generally solemn and often fierce art of the other civilizations. One should remember that the eastern cultures emerged from nomadic forebears who struggled to survive, whereas Minoan culture apparently emerged from a comfortable agrarian base with no evidence of a previous nomadic existence.

A culture without a divine monarch has no compelling need for monumental sculpture and indeed none has been found. But typical of diminutive Minoan sculpture is the so-called *Snake Goddess* (fig. 3.6), whether she was a priestess, goddess, or queen. The statue probably relates to goddess worship, for the serpent is a major image in Minoan religion, symbolizing regeneration. Though the rigid frontal pose of this miniature figure suggests an Egyptian influence, the raised arms and the animal on her head (a panther?) help make the mood light and playful. Characteristic of feminine attire at the time, the colorful tiered skirt, tight bodice, and bared breasts appear, to our eyes, very worldly for what is apparently a cult figure.

By about 2400 BC the Minoans had mastered the art of goldsmithing. Gold had always been used in making jewelry because it does not oxidize nor can fire consume it. Further, it is rare (therefore precious), malleable, and, above

3.8 *Antelopes*, from Thera, Greece. Ca. 1500 BC. Fresco, height 8'2½" (2.5 m). National Archaeological Museum, Athens.

all, beautiful. One of the most celebrated Minoan creations is the Gold Bee Pendant (fig. 3.7). Two bees are symmetrically placed on opposite sides of a circular honeycomb, leaving a drop of honey on it. Particularly notable is the delicate granulation: minute spherical grains of gold soldered to the gold background. The ancient method left no visible solder between the grains and the gold surface, a sophisticated technology that was not rediscovered until this century. It should be noted that Minoan artisans used magnifying glasses to achieve the fine details in their jewelry and intricate seal stones.

Another Minoan site, Akrotiri, on the island of Thera, was first explored in the 1860s while pumice was being quarried for use in building the Suez Canal and has been extensively excavated since 1967. Buried under ash from a volcanic eruption, this is the Minoan equivalent of Pompeii, a wealthy city with a high standard of living comparable to anything in Crete. The fresco of the *Antelopes* (fig. 3.8), for example, is similar in style and quality to frescoes found at Knossos.[6] The broad sinuous ribbons that outline the bodies give the illusion of being enameled areas in an elegant cloisonné. The contrast of rhythmic curves with open

A KILLER VOLCANO

Seventy-five miles (120 km) north of Crete on the island of Thera, a large volcano about 10 miles (16 km) in diameter and possibly 4,500 feet (1,372 m) high erupted violently, covering the island with pumice to a depth of 13 feet (4 m). After minor activity for thirty years, the volcano erupted again in an explosion that was undoubtedly heard throughout the Mediterranean and that buried Akrotiri and the rest of the island under ash over 200 feet (61 m) deep. During this final eruption such massive quantities of pumice, ash, and rocks were ejected that the volcano's cone collapsed into the exhausted magma chamber below. The sea rushed into the fiercely hot caldera, leading to the final calamity, the tsunami that raced outward from the caldera at a probable height of 300 to 400 feet (90–120 m). Because most Minoan settlements were on Crete's northern and eastern shores, virtually the entire culture was washed away by the massive wave. Thera's destruction has traditionally been dated at around 1500 BC but recent studies contradict this. Information from radiocarbon dating of plant remains on Thera, aberrations in the world dendrochronological (tree ring) record, and volcanic debris buried in Greenland's ice suggest that 1628 BC is a more accurate date.[5]

5. According to the *New Grolier Multimedia Encyclopedia*, a 1995 CD-ROM. The earlier date requires reevaluations of all Minoan and Mycenaean chronology. That some of Thera's ash was found in Greenland attests to the magnitude of an eruption that may have been greater than the Krakatoa explosion on 27 August 1883.
6. The ongoing excavations at Akrotiri confirm to a considerable degree what some critics called the "highly speculative" nature of the reconstructions of Sir Arthur Evans at Knossos.

interior space sets up a masterful mobile tension that is both fluid and artful.

The excavations on Thera also contribute to the much-debated theory that this was the legendary Atlantis. According to Plato, the end came with "violent earthquakes and floods; in a single day and night of misfortune . . . the island of Atlantis disappeared in the depths of the sea."[7]

The Minoans rebuilt after the Thera disaster but possibly around 1450 BC the Mycenaeans, a rugged warrior race from the mainland, invaded Crete. With the power of Crete broken the Mycenaean Greeks became the overlords of the Aegean world.

MYCENAEAN CIVILIZATION, CA. 1600–1110 BC

From about 1900 BC on tribes from northern Europe had slowly been infiltrating Greece. By about 1600 the invaders had occupied all of the Greek mainland, including the large land mass known as the Peloponnesus (pel-uh-puh-NEES-us) where, at Mycenae, their Great King established his fortified palace. These were warlike people who inevitably came into contact with the Minoans. Their conquest of Crete, however, was more like an occupation in which the invader absorbed much of Minoan culture, though it did replace the Linear A Minoan script with Linear B. In 1953 archaeologist Michael Ventris deciphered the clay tablets in Linear B, proving that the Mycenaeans were true Greeks who spoke a Greek language and worshiped the Greek pantheon of sky gods. The Minoan earth goddess was de-emphasized but continued in Greek mythology as Demeter (de-MEE-ter) and Persephone (per-SEPH-o-nee), enduring symbols of the cyclical regeneration of nature. This male-dominant society created the heritage that was to unite the Hellenes (HEL-uh-neez), as the Greeks called themselves, for it was the Mycenaeans who fought the Trojan War that centuries later became the subject of the Homeric epic poems and the core of the Hellenic tradition.

Homeric Poems

Before them now arose Lord Agamemnon, holding the staff Hephaistos fashioned once and took pains fashioning: it was a gift from him to the son of Kronos, lordly Zeus, who gave it to the bright pathfinder, Hermes. Hermes handed it on in turn to Pelops, famous charioteer, Pelops to Atreus, and Atreus gave it to the sheepherder Thyestes, he to Agamemnon, king and lord of many islands, of all Argos.

Homer, *Iliad*, Book II[8]

Until little more than a century ago much of what anyone knew of the Aegean world was contained in some Greek

myths and in Homer's supposedly fictional *Iliad* and *Odyssey*. Helen of Troy, Achilles (ah-KILL-eez), Agamemnon (ag-a-MEM-non), Mycenae, and Troy itself were, according to the experts, figments of Homer's fertile imagination. Then, in 1871, Heinrich Schliemann (1822–90), a wealthy German merchant-cum-archaeologist, startled the world when he announced the discovery of Troy in northwest Turkey, just where his meticulous study of the *Iliad* indicated it should be. He later located what he thought was the palace of Agamemnon at Mycenae and uncovered a wealth of art treasures in and around Mycenae.

The Mycenaeans established themselves in small independent kingdoms with each king occupying a strongly fortified but richly decorated palace. Each ruled through officials who supervised the farmlands, collected taxes in produce, managed religious celebrations, and otherwise acted as the king's deputy. Although all kings were equal they did owe some allegiance to the Great King at Mycenae. As seen in the *Iliad*, a local ruler could challenge the high king—as Achilles did with Agamemnon—and not be disciplined or forced to follow the ruler.

Mycenaean trade was mainly between the Greek islands and Asia Minor though Mycenaean influence extended throughout the Mediterranean world. Gold, ivory, textiles, and spices were bartered for the local products; the numerous gold ornaments and cups found in the royal tombs at Mycenae and other palaces attest to substantial royal wealth. Though not as rigid as cultures to the east, this was a male-dominant society that esteemed honor and courage, as evidenced in the Homeric poems. For these Greeks, human worth and dignity lay in total self-fulfillment, usually on the battlefield, where their exploits would bring death, perhaps, but instant fame and renown for generations to come as bards recounted their deeds in song and story.

Another much admired aspect of the Greek character (then and now) was the exercise of a cunning and crafty intelligence. The wily Odysseus (o-DIS-ee-us) is the supreme example of this quality. Thus, when Odysseus finally won his way home to his kingdom of Ithaca, he put ashore disguised as a beggar. Here Athena (uh-THEE-nuh; see box 4.1) heard his lying tale. Her response was typical of the Greek attitude:

"What a cunning knave it would take," she said, "to beat you at your tricks! Even a god would be hard put to it.

"And so my stubborn friend, Odysseus the arch-deceiver, with his craving for intrigue, does not propose even in his own country to drop his sharp

---

7. Most of Thera vanished into the sea leaving behind three very small island remnants.
8. Robert Fitzgerald, trans. (Garden City, N.Y.: Anchor Books, 1975).

practice and the lying tales that he loves from the bottom of his heart. But no more of this: we are both adept at chicane. For in the world of men you have no rival as a statesman and orator, while I am preeminent among the gods for invention and resource."

And a few lines later:

"How like you to be so wary!" said Athena. "And this is why I cannot desert you in your misfortunes: you are so civilized, so intelligent, so self-possessed."

Perhaps in our time we cannot readily admire a man who was so smoothly deceitful in gaining his own ends; even in classical Greece the playwright Sophocles (SOF-o-kleez) detested these qualities, as he pictured a despicable Odysseus in the drama *Philoctetes* (fil-OK-ti-teez). For the Greeks of the heroic age, however, this was just one more example of self-fulfillment. Odysseus would have been a fool not to have exploited his keen intelligence, not to mention his cunning.

3.10 Funeral mask from the royal tombs, Mycenae, Greece. Ca. 1500 BC. Beaten gold, height ca. 12" (30.5 cm). National Archaeological Museum, Athens. Photo: Hirmer, Munich.

3.9 Lion Gate, citadel at Mycenae, Greece. Ca. 1250 BC. Limestone, height of relief 9'6" (2.9 m). Photo: Hirmer, Munich.

The King's Citadel

The ruined citadel of the Great King at Mycenae was originally a massive structure whose gigantic stones were placed, according to legend, by a mythical race of one-eyed giants called cyclopes (KY-klo-peas). Located on a broad hilltop site backed by a rugged mountain, what remains of the palace is immediately below the mountain peak. Recurring waves of invading Dorians made fortress architecture a necessity on the Greek mainland. This highly efficient citadel has a ceremonial entrance protected by high walls on three sides (fig. 3.9). The lintel of the ponderous gate is topped by a stone relief of two lions, now headless, flanking a Minoan column symbolizing Mycenaean hegemony in Crete.[9]

After astounding archaeologists with his discovery of Mycenaean civilization, Schliemann continued to amaze everyone as he excavated the royal tombs at Mycenae. They were full of precious jewelry, elaborately decorated weapons, and gold death masks, one of which Schliemann attributed to Agamemnon himself (fig. 3.10). It was soon determined, however, that this Mycenaean had predated

9. Though Mycenae ruled the Minoans there was so much cultural interchange that it is impossible to determine exactly how each culture influenced the development of Greek classical civilization.

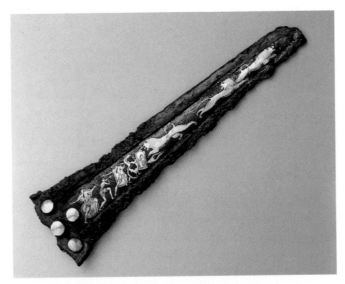

3.11 Dagger: *Archers and Hoplites Hunting Lions*, from Mycenae. 16th century BC. Bronze with gold, silver, and niello incrustations, length 9⅜" (23.8 cm). National Archaeological Museum, Athens.

the Homeric king by several centuries. Realizing that argument was futile, the undaunted German jokingly renamed his Agamemnon "Schulze." Whatever the appropriate name, the mask from Mycenae is a superb example of the highly developed metal craftsmanship called **toreutics** (tuh-RUE-tiks), the hammering of metals into representational form. The death mask (plus weapons and jewelry) represents a Mycenaean adaptation of the Egyptian funeral practice of burying the illustrious dead with items commensurate with their status in life.

The bronze daggers (fig. 3.11) that Schliemann found in the tombs at Mycenae are striking examples of Minoan metalworking technology as used by Mycenaean artisans. One can immediately see how time has corroded the bronze while scarcely affecting the gold, silver, and niello (a black compound of silver, lead, copper, and sulfur). The gold and silver figures were inlaid in a strip of niello and then engraved to make them sharp and crisp. Note how the figures are adapted to the diminishing space.

Mycenaean dominance ended sometime around 1200 to 1000 BC but no one knows what brought about the downfall of the Mycenaean world. Whatever happened, the Mycenaean heroes had completed their turn on the stage of history but were later immortalized in the Homeric sagas of the *Iliad* and the *Odyssey*, probably the two greatest epic poems in Western history.

STUDY QUESTIONS

1. **a.** Consider the cultures that developed in ancient Mesopotamia, Egypt, and the Greek lands in the Aegean area. (1) In what ways did climate, topography, and geography affect or condition cultural development in each major area? (2) How and why did people in rural areas react differently from those in urban areas? (3) How and why did seaports differ from inland cities? (4) What conclusions can you draw about the three cultures?
   b. Consider the cultures that developed in New England and in the Deep South during the eighteenth and nineteenth centuries. Then, answer questions (1) to (4) as posed above. What are the similarities between American cultural development and that in the ancient world? Are there any differences? Why or why not?
2. Assume that our world has miraculously grown so peaceful that no nation need maintain any armed forces. What might the total Pentagon budget be spent on and how might this affect American society? Be sure also to consider the short- and long-term effects of the elimination of defense contracts.
3. Using supplemental art books, describe the level of sophistication of Minoan jewelry. Now, consider the technology involved in making the Gold Bee Pendant (fig. 3.7) and other pieces. What does their jewelry tell us about Minoan culture? As a comparison, consider current fashions in American jewelry and what they seem to say about our culture.

SUMMARY

The Greeks absorbed much of the cultural heritage of Mesopotamia and Egypt while also drawing upon the indigenous cultures of the Aegean civilizations: the Cycladic, Minoan, and Mycenaean. Little is known about the Cycladic civilization except for the abstract sculptures that have survived and imply a form of goddess worship. The Minoans, however, have been extensively documented as a prosperous and enterprising people who operated the greatest trade empire of their age. Elegant and refined, their culture formed a firm basis for the flowering of Western culture.

The Mycenaeans, conquerors of the Minoans, were a warrior race descended from migrating Dorian tribes that infiltrated from the north. The apex of their civilization was reached with the Trojan expedition of about 1260 BC. Whatever brought down the Great King and his subordinate rulers, posterity inherited the remains of Mycenaean culture and their heroic age as immortalized by Homer.

CULTURE AND HUMAN VALUES

Not enough is known of Cycladic culture to justify any speculation about its cultural evolution but the Minoans have been studied in great detail for over a century. The period of balance of their high civilization lasted, it would appear, from about 2000 to about 1628 BC, when a volcanic eruption devastated their civilization. They may have rebuilt but the Mycenaean invasion of 1450 BC (?) finished it off. There followed a period of adjustment as the Minoans tried to adapt to Mycenaean rule.

The predominant characteristic of Minoan culture was that a good life of security, peace, and possessions was available to much of the population. The economy supported a high standard of living. Vigorous trade helped in the development of a middle class of artisans and merchants, thus reinforcing political and economic stability. Perhaps most importantly, Minoan civilization flowered because of the earth goddess religion and the resulting relative equality of the sexes. Rather than emphasizing such nomadic virtues as strength and courage, the Minoans created a peaceful, joyous, and elegant culture celebrating the pleasures of gracious living.

The period of balance of Mycenaean civilization seems to have begun shortly after the occupation of Crete in about 1450 BC. This was both the high point of Mycenaean culture and, ironically, the beginning of its decline and fall. They had compromised their integrity and honor (the Trojan horse) in the quest for victory at Troy. The price was too high.

For the inhabitants of the Mycenaean city-states ultimate reality was the heroic life—and death—of the noble warrior. An ethical man told the truth, was as good as his word, and kept the faith with king and comrades. First and foremost, he was always prepared to make the ultimate sacrifice, to die fighting for a noble cause, as did Achilles, Hector, and many another warrior.

One can examine the heroic age in several different ways: the actual time period; the Homeric epics; and the view from Athens of the Golden Age. The heroic ideal was something espoused by a noble warrior-aristocrat; Achilles, with all his faults, was the personification of the heroic ideal.

Homer composed the *Iliad* between 750 and 700 BC, nearly four centuries after the Trojan campaign. As with many events of the distant past, time heals, and violence is often romanticized as necessary in the service of a noble cause. (American Civil War buffs, for example, seem to revel in romantic fantasies about Bull Run, Shiloh, and other bloody battlegrounds.) The pain and horror of the Trojan War had faded away; only the heroic ideals were left and no one could better celebrate the valiant heroes of a fabled past than the blind poet.

By the time of the Athenian Golden Age—ca. 460–430 BC—another four centuries had passed and the Trojan adventure was twice removed. Homer and the *Iliad* had become romanticized. (Small wonder that nineteenth-century scholars considered the Trojan campaign the stuff of dreams.) The Athenians accorded the Mycenaean heroes their just due without, however, endorsing war (Ares, the god of war, was never treated as anything other than an inhuman outcast). Odysseus and his comrades were seen as imposing figures of the Hellenic past; they had earned admiration but no one expected emulation.

CHAPTER 4

Early Greece: Preparation for the Good Life

Life in the Greece of the fifth century BC, particularly in Athens, developed a quality that has seldom if ever been equaled. For the first time—and most gloriously—citizens flourished in a political system that allowed individuals the greatest possible freedom compatible with the coherence of the social group. Here, too, there was enough wealth and leisure to allow individuals to develop their capabilities to the fullest. Further, this was a highly competitive society that challenged its people to pursue excellence and willingly honored superior accomplishments.

This chapter traces the development of Greek society from its beginnings to around 480 BC. The focus is necessarily on Athens, where the highest achievements took place and where ideas generated throughout Greece were vigorously discussed and disputed in the marketplace. This was a lively, highly verbal, even brawling culture in which flourished some of the finest flowers of Western civilization.

Let it be said at the outset that there never was, in the ancient world, a nation called Greece. But the people who called themselves Hellenes were united by a common language, religion, and heritage. They lived in independent city-states, each with its own form of government. These states, unlike Mesopotamia or Egypt, were not confined to one geographical location. The mainland of Greece (see map 3.1, p. 43) forms the tip of the Balkan Peninsula and is joined by a narrow isthmus to a large land mass known as the Peloponnesus. This is the Greek heartland. When Dorian tribes invaded from the north between about 1100 and 800 BC, many mainland Ionians fled to the Aegean Sea's Asian coast and the coastal islands to form a flourishing Greek cultural center. This became known as the Ionian coast that eventually caused the Persian Empire so much grief. Later, in the seventh and sixth centuries BC, land poverty on the mainland encouraged many city-states to send out colonists to develop new lands. As a result, Greek cities were formed from Byzantium (bi-ZANT-e-um; then Constantinople; now Istanbul), to western Mediterranean

shores. Important cities included Syracuse in Sicily, Sybaris and Paestum in Italy, and Marseilles in France. Although widely dispersed and frequently at war with each other, the people of these cities shared a common culture (heritage, religion, language) that gave them a sense of kinship as Hellenes. The Hellenes felt that they were different from and better than the "barbarians" (which means non-Greeks), a belief that created unity amid the vast diversity and a pride that helped lead to the remarkable accomplishments of the people known as the Greeks.

THE GEOGRAPHY OF MAINLAND GREECE

The Aegean islands had a relatively benign climate but the mainland was a harder country in which to live. Mountain ranges divided the area, making communication across the countryside extremely difficult; further, the mountains were so eroded that little farmland was available. There were broad and fertile plains in the north but a shorter growing season than in the warmer, sunnier south, where sheep and goats grazed on the mountain slopes and bee-culture was common. The valleys between the mountains offered small plots of arable land on which grew the chief crops of olives and grapes. It was in these valleys that the first villages appeared that would later merge to become city-states.

The climate was milder than that of Mesopotamia but it was not conducive to easy living. Great winter storms roared down from the north bringing torrential rains and, on the mountain peaks, a good deal of snow. Summers were hot and dry but tempered by the ever present sea, which was basic to Greek life. Major cities such as Athens, Argos, and Corinth were seaports and no city, not even Sparta, was far from the sea.

All these factors contributed to the Greek character. People in a hard land must be ingenious and clever to survive. When nature yields little, people must manufacture objects to make a living. Unlike other civilizations, Greek city-states had more artisans and artists than peasants. Finally, the proximity of the sea offered a livelihood for sailors and traders (and pirates). Commerce always broadens horizons because traders barter not only goods and services but

---

Opposite Cossutius, Temple of the Olympian Zeus, Athens. Ca. 174 BC–AD 131. Pentelic marble. Photo: Spectrum, London.

ideas they can carry home. One cannot attribute the character of people to geography and climate alone, yet these factors certainly contributed to the Hellenic personality.

GREEK RELIGION IN THE HEROIC AGE

The worship of the Olympian gods was a complex and fascinating religion. At its most straightforward the religion used mythical gods and goddesses to explain natural forces—for example Poseidon (po-SIDE-on), who controlled the storms that stirred the seas and the quakes that shook the land. At a higher level the Olympians symbolized the most complex of human drives and aspirations—for example Athena, goddess of wisdom and civilized living who represented life lived as an art form.

Their religion illustrates a prime Greek characteristic: a special ability to deal with information on both a literal and an abstract level. Zeus was as abstract as the power principle he represented, but he was also the irrepressible seducer of mortal women. Aphrodite symbolized all of love's aspects from love of beauty to maternal love to the joys of erotic love, but her amorous adventures competed with those of Zeus.

This religion had no "revealer," divine or mortal: no Christ, Muhammad, or Buddha. Nor was there a sacred book such as the Talmud, Bible, or Koran. The religion evolved primarily as a collection of myths honored in various ways throughout the Greek world. Consistently imaginative, the myths varied greatly, so that no single version of the history and nature of the gods exists. Hesiod

BOX 4.1   THE GREEK PANTHEON

Zeus and his two brothers seized power from Kronos (Saturn) to originate "The Twelve," the Olympians who figure most prominently in Greek life. (The names in parentheses are Roman but these are only approximations since Greeks and Romans had entirely different attitudes toward their respective gods, and toward most everything else for that matter.)

Zeus (Jupiter, Jove). Leader, god of the thunderbolt, representative of the power principle and womanizer.

Hera (Juno). Long-suffering wife of Zeus, goddess of marriage and domestic stability.

Poseidon (Neptune). God of the sea and earthshaker (earthquakes).

Demeter (Ceres). Sister of Zeus and goddess of agriculture. Mother of Persephone and fertility symbol.

Hades (Pluto, Dis). God of the underworld. Connected with nature myth by his marriage to Persephone who spends half her time on earth (the growing season) and half in the underworld (fall and winter). Thanatos represents death itself.

Pallas Athena (Minerva). Goddess of wisdom, warfare, arts and crafts. Sprang fully-armed from the brow of Zeus. Patron goddess of Athens, representing the art of civilized living.

Phoibos Apollo (Sol). Son of Zeus and Leto, daughter of the Titans Krios and Phoebe. Sun god, archer, musician, god of truth, light, and healing. Represents principle of intellectual beauty.

Artemis (Diana, Cynthia). Sister of Apollo; virgin goddess of the moon and the hunt.

Aphrodite (Venus). Goddess of love and physical beauty. According to one version she was the daughter of Zeus and Dione; an alternate mythic version has her rising from the waves à la Botticelli.

Hephaistos (Vulcan). Lame blacksmith god who made armor for heroes, forged the thunderbolts of Zeus. Much-deceived husband of Aphrodite.

Hermes (Mercury). Son of Zeus and Maia, daughter of Atlas. Messenger and general handyman of Zeus. God of commerce, traders, travelers, and thieves.

Ares (Mars). Son of Zeus and Hera. God of war.

Hestia (Vesta). Virgin sister of Zeus and goddess of hearth and home. Later replaced among the Twelve by Dionysos.

Dionysos (Bacchus). Son of Zeus and mortal woman Semele. Connected, like Demeter, with the principle of fertility and, like Persephone, represented the nature myth by dying in the autumn and being reborn in the spring. The Eleusinian Mysteries were dedicated to all three fertility deities and the festivals of Dionysos were periods of wild, Bacchic rejoicing: scheduled orgies so to speak. Since plays were usually performed at these festivals Dionysos also became god of the **theatre.** He embodies the ecstatic principle as contrasted with the intellectual principle represented by Apollo.

LESSER OLYMPIANS

Eros (Cupid). Eternal child of Aphrodite and Hephaistos. Spirit of love with darts.

Pan (Pan). Son of Hermes, woodland god with goatlike horns and hoofs. Player of the pipes (panpipes).

(HEE-see-ud; fl. 8th century BC) in his *Theogony* (thee-OG-uh-nee) had limited success in systematizing the story of the gods. The truth is, Greek religion—all Greek mythology—was probably the most creative collection of mythic literature that the world has ever known.

Vastly simplified, the genealogy is as follows:

In the beginning was Chaos, composed of void, mass, and darkness. From Chaos emerged a god, Ouranos (YOOR-uh-noss), representing the heavens, and Gaea (JEE–ah), a goddess who represented earth. Among their offspring were the Titans, who personified earthquakes and other earthly cataclysms. Kronos (KRO-nos), a Titan, led a revolt that overthrew his father and took his sister Rhea (REE-uh), also an

earth goddess, as his wife. From this union, though not without difficulty, emerged the Olympian gods. The difficulty was that Kronos knew of a prophecy that one of his children would overthrow him; to prevent this, he swallowed all his progeny at birth (Kronos may be thought of as Time that swallows all things). Rhea saved Zeus from being ingested and spirited him away to Crete where he grew to manhood. Zeus then led the prophesied revolt and, aided by some Titans, imprisoned his father in the dark cave of Tartarus, but not before Kronos had regurgitated the other children: Demeter (di-MEET-er), Hera (HAY-ra), Hades (also called Pluto), Poseidon, and Hestia. Zeus then took Hera as his wife and from this union arose such gods and goddesses as Apollo, Aphrodite, and Artemis (box 4.1).

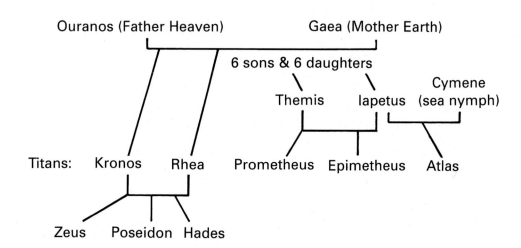

Nemesis. Avenging goddess, the principle of retribution.

Hebe. Goddess of youth and cupbearer to the gods.

Iris. Goddess of the rainbow and sometimes messenger of the gods.

Hymen. Son of Aphrodite and Dionysos; god of the marriage festival.

The Three Graces: Aglaia (Splendor), *Euphrosyne* (Mirth), and *Thalia* (Good Cheer). Embodied the principle of the happy life and always represented as a unit, which is a clear indication of the Greek version of the happy life.

The Nine Muses. Spirits of learning and of the arts. *Clio* (History), *Ourania* (Astronomy), *Melpomene* (Tragedy), *Thalia* (Comedy), *Terpsichore* (Dance), *Calliope* (Epic Poetry), *Erato* (Love Poetry), *Polyhymnia* (Sacred Poetry), and *Euterpe* (Lyric Poetry).

The Erinyes (Furies): *Tisiphone, Megaera* and *Alecto.* Represented pangs of conscience; relentlessly hounded wrongdoers.

The Three Fates allotted to each his/her destiny. *Clotho* spun the thread of life. *Lachesis* wove it into a pattern that determined the kind of life that would be led. *Atropos* cut the thread, terminating existence.

Stories about the immortals offer a fascinating range of subjects. We see Zeus pursuing an infinite variety of mortal women; some gods drank copiously and all quarreled constantly among themselves; they had favorites among the mortals, as we saw Athena protecting Odysseus; and everyone used dirty tricks to foil each other's designs for the success of their favorites. How could one revere such an assembly?

Understanding this religion is the key to understanding the Greek character, and particularly their passion for living life to the fullest. Significantly, the Greeks created the gods in their own image. Emphasizing this, Xenophanes of Colophon (zuh-NOFF-uh-neas; 6th century BC) maintained that if oxen, horses, and lions had hands and could paint like men, they would paint their gods as, respectively, oxen, horses, and lions. Black people would worship black gods and Thracians would believe in gods with blue eyes and red hair.

The gods were regarded as a race infinitely superior to human beings in that they were completely powerful, immortal, and always young and beautiful; they had the same characteristics as humans, but in a higher category. If people sometimes showed wisdom and nobility, so did Athena or Apollo (uh-POL-o), but to a vastly superior degree. If mortals were sometimes lustful, Zeus was much more so and, with his power, far more successful. If people were skilled artisans, so was Hephaistos (hay-FYCE-toss); if humans were crafty and skillful, so was Prometheus (pro-MEE-thee-us)—but the skill, wisdom, lust, or whatever quality one may choose of the gods was infinitely beyond that of mortals. Death was a dark oblivion for the Greeks but the gods had life forever, and life in boundless beauty, vigorous youth, and absolute power.

The Gods' Symbolic Roles

Before reviewing actual religious practices, we should consider the symbolic roles of the gods. Representing the power principle, Zeus is amoral, just as power is amoral. At the opposite extreme is Hera, goddess of marriage and domestic order, constantly striving to control and civilize a force that deals in thunderbolts. Athena and Apollo represent the Greek ideals of the arts of civilization and the beauty of intellect. Aphrodite was enthusiastically worshiped by a civilization that viewed the erotic arts as a healthy component of the good life. Superior craftsmanship was also highly valued as attested to by the importance of Hephaistos, an artisan elevated to the status of a god. The Greeks even had a god—Hermes—for their peripatetic world of travel, commerce, and trade (and thievery).

Throughout Greek history Ares never received a kind word. He represented violence and destruction and thus had no redeeming virtues. Dionysos, the god of ecstasy, is particularly important and peculiarly Greek. Espousing the virtues of rationality and the life of reason, the Greeks

were acutely aware and deeply respectful of the non-rational aspect of humankind. These deep, surging drives had to be understood, acknowledged, and treated with deference.

The Greeks did not distinguish between nature and human nature, believing that nature's laws governed both the physical universe and the moral universe. All mortals and even the gods were subject to what the Greeks called *ananke* (uh-NAHN-key; "what has to be"). This idea of a universal power that is also personal has both a scientific and a religious quality.

The worship of these gods during Mycenaean times and later may help clarify these religious practices, for the formal ceremonies were always feasts. Animals were sacrificed, and part of the meat was burnt upon the fire. The rest was roasted and eaten by those performing the sacrifice. Wine was drunk, with a certain amount poured out first as a libation to the gods. Then the feast proceeded, with the assumption that the god was present as a guest at the meal, and that he or she enjoyed such things as much as mortals.

A Humanistic Culture

There is one further aspect of this religion that was critical in the development of human values; there was no permanent priesthood nor even a priestly class. The Hellenes, unlike the Egyptians, were never subject to priestly dos and don'ts. To us their religious practices seem unstructured, almost casual; there was certainly room for freedom of thought. We will see later that in political organization the Greeks were not oppressed by despots, or at least not for very long. Thus in both religion and politics the Greeks maintained the widest possible latitude for thought, questioning, and experimentation, which, though turbulent and unstable, produced superb humanistic values.

The local variants were many but the general principles of the Olympian religion were practiced throughout ancient Greece. There were always some doubts among the intellectuals but the common people believed in the gods and in the oracles that were consulted for important state decisions. That Apollo's priestess at Delphi or another seer's answers were riddles subject to several interpretations did not shake people's faith in the oracles themselves.

In this bewildering interrelationship of gods and people, what determined an individual's fate? As before, we must rely on Homer, who wrote centuries after the Heroic Age and was himself none too certain of the answer. It was vaguely believed that each person, each hero, had his own *moira* (MOY-ruh), or pattern of life, which he would fulfill. This may be seen as a jigsaw puzzle that the hero's life would piece together, with this complication: the individual never knew what the finished picture would be nor even when it was completed.

Within each person's life there were the three forces

of free will, accident, and divine intervention. These worked together—or sometimes in opposition—to determine the course of a person's life, and nothing was ever certain until death finished the picture. (This problem is considered in detail in Sophocles' *Oedipus the King*; see pp. 95–6.) The gods frequently punished anyone whose overweening pride led them to exceed human limits and aim for the realm of the gods. Such *hubris* (HOO-bris) almost certainly brought doom. The gods were not omnipotent, however, because there was a force even more powerful than the gods called *ananke*, "what has to be," or natural law.

For the most part, in the Heroic Age, a person's character was his or her fate. The people accepted the consequences of what they did because of the kind of person they were. Thus Achilles, despite attempts to outwit his predicted fate, lived his brief life gloriously because he valued personal honor and fame. Odysseus, on the other hand, enjoyed a long and productive life as a daring warrior and as a shrewd and wily Greek with the wit to talk, deceive, and survive.

THE ARCHAIC PERIOD, CA. 750–500 BC

As discussed in the preceding chapter, Mycenaean culture began its decline in the twelfth century BC with the arrival of Dorian invaders from the north. Of the same racial stock as the Mycenaeans, the Dorians were forced south to the Greek mainland because of invasions of their own homeland. The invasions upset everything and produced a long "dark ages" with little cultural development. By the eighth century BC these dark ages moved almost imperceptibly into the Archaic (ar-KAY-ic) times of historic Greece, a period quite well known through Hesiod's poems, *Works and Days*. A farmer in Boeotia, Hesiod once won a poetry contest but apparently knew little else but bad luck. He describes a life of endless tasks with little reward and no future plus a landed aristocracy whose chief occupation was squeezing the small farmer. Justice, so called, was dispensed by these **patricians**, who generally rendered decisions based on the largest bribe. Always reverent toward the gods, Hesiod neither expected nor received either reward or justice, and his plight was the common lot of most of his compatriots.

Homer, too, composed his epic poems during the latter part of the eighth century. Hesiod described his own life and times but Homer's work celebrated the distant glories of the heroic Mycenaeans. We know little about Homer the poet and even less about the man himself. Computer analysis confirms that a single poet, whom we call Homer, was the *Iliad*'s composer. Analysis of the adventure tale that is the *Odyssey* is less conclusive, though Homer is the probable poet. Authorship, however, is not the issue. These poems are at the very heart of the Greek heritage. Greek ideals, the idea of superiority over the barbarians,

and the overwhelming desire for personal honor were embodied in these works, which came as close to a central religious text as the Greeks ever possessed. Memorized by every student, they were sung and recited at the festivals and games throughout the Hellenic world. The stories were not Homer's inventions but a collection of legends that originated in the songs and recitations of generations of bards and were brought together and transformed into epic tales by the sure hand of a literary genius. The *Iliad* and the *Odyssey* would invigorate and inspire the Greek mind.

Economic and Political Changes

But to return to Hesiod's troubled times. The first problem was the landed aristocracy who, by force and guile, appropriated land from the poor farmers. Lending the farmer money was the most efficient way of acquiring land because the farmer had to use his own person to secure the loan. Failure to pay the debt forfeited his land and the farmer became a slave. But the greatest problem was land poverty, meaning not enough land to support the population.

The inspired solution to land poverty was colonization, with city-states exporting bands of adventurers to found Greek colonies throughout the Mediterranean. The ensuing expansion of the Greek world led to increasing trade among all the Hellenic cities and a swelling flow of wealth into the mother cities. A key factor in the vertical ascent of the lower classes was the large surplus of goods created by Greek artisans. By producing far more goods than they needed the Greeks enlarged their economy and gained leisure time for other pursuits: gymnastics, education, philosophic-scientific investigations, discussions in the **agora**. Trade and manufacturing enabled a prosperous and influential commercial class to emerge as a major factor in urban life. In a city controlled by the aristocracy, farmers were powerless but the new commercial class became a political force to reckon with.

The rise of *tyrants* marked the first of a series of political changes. For us the term suggests a harsh military dictator but among the Hellenes it was just another word for "king." The tyrant seized power and established himself as absolute ruler as long as he could hold office. Maintaining authority required the support of a majority of the population, which he gained with political, judicial, or economic reforms that ensured his continuing popularity. (Unpopular tyrants were sometimes murdered or exiled.) Tyrannical rule thus led, paradoxically, to the early reforms that eventually steered Athens and other cities toward democracy.

THE RISE OF ATHENS

From here on we focus on political developments in Athens, destined to become the most glorious of Greek cities, and where the most significant changes were made under four reformers. Sixth-century Athens had a curious power structure. Determined largely by economic status, three factions waged an unequal battle for power. In descending order of influence, they were the landed aristocracy, the growing commercial class, and the poor farmers eking out a living on marginal land. The political mix was made more complex by four family-clans, originally of the aristocracy, who controlled the individual lives of their members and dominated the city's politics. So long as these four tribes remained powerful their traditions would govern political and economic affairs.

The Reformers

The legendary Draco (DRAY-ko; fl. 621 BC) was the first of the reformers, an early tyrant and publisher of a monumental step toward freedom: the first Greek code of laws. Hesiod and others had complained that only the aristocratic judges knew the laws and that they seemed to make up the rules as they went along. An ordinary citizen involved in litigation was at the mercy of the judges, who generally rendered decisions according to the litigant's economic status, family connections, and the size of the proffered bribe. Draco's Code, though very severe (many crimes were punishable by death), did offer a single standard of justice for all people and, because the law was published, people could know their legal rights. No matter how harsh the laws, their publication was a momentous step toward the development of a rational system of justice devoid of class and privilege.

The second reformer was Solon (SO-lon; ca. 640–558 BC) whose name has become a synonym for a wise lawgiver. A member of the nobility, like Draco, he had traveled extensively and was, moreover, intensely interested in the commercial ventures of the rising middle class. Painfully aware of land distribution injustices and the cruelty of debt-slavery, his first reform freed all slaves who had failed to redeem their land. A man who sought moderation in all things, he was pressured to break up the great estates and distribute the land to the farmers, but he didn't have enough faith in the uneducated masses to take this drastic step. He did, however, encourage everyone to become involved in political affairs. He limited the important governmental offices to the upper classes of aristocrats and merchants but allowed members of the lower class to serve as jurors. Though not as glamorous as public office, jury duty helped educate people in the mechanism of social action. He greatly broadened civic responsibilities by establishing an administrative Council of Four Hundred. Shrewdly anticipating conservative resistance to change and liberal proclivities for tinkering, Solon stipulated that all reforms must remain unchanged and in force for ten years.

Solon encouraged trade and commerce by adopting a much lighter coinage. He also imported skilled artisans, particularly potters, since pottery manufacture was a major industry and a prime export. With his reforms Athens broke away from an economic dependence upon agriculture and evolved into a city whose wealth was generated by manufactured objects independent of natural forces.

Pisistratos (pi-SIS-truh-toss; ca. 605–527 BC), who governed Athens from 546 till his death, was the third reformer. Surpassing Solon's economic reforms, he dismembered the large estates and distributed land to the almost landless peasants. Because economic status usually decided voting privileges and government participation, this single reform broadened the political base and allowed people already involved in social action by Solon's changes to assume a larger role in governing the state. He and his sons further increased employment by initiating some great public works, but Pisistratos' most important contribution was his advancement of artistic life. He imported Simonides and Anacreon, two of the finest Hellenic poet-musicians of the time, and commissioned the first scholarly edition of Homer's poems, which may have been the reformer's single greatest contribution. As citizens learned these poems and heard them recited at public functions they gained a sense of common heritage and a feeling of unity *as citizens of Athens*, not as members of a particular family clan. The tyrants of Athens, consciously or unconsciously, were leading the people toward democracy and, by educating them through increased responsibility, making them ready for active participation in a democratic society.

A Democratic Government

Democracy became a reality with the reforms of Cleisthenes (KLICE-the-neez; fl. 507 BC), who sharply curtailed the influence of the four aristocratic tribes who had long dominated Athenian politics. He created ten new "tribes" with membership based on place of residence rather than heredity. First dividing the city into *demes* (neighborhoods), he created artificial units as the basis of a new political structure. Selected at random, the demes were composed of neighborhoods of the shore (people connected with shipping and seafaring trades), the city itself, and the outlying rural areas. No tribe was dominated by any one economic group because the ten tribes that comprised the city-state were themselves a product of the new demes.

With fifty members representing each of the new political tribes, Cleisthenes replaced Solon's Council of Four Hundred with a Council of Five Hundred. The old council had become the voice of the four traditional tribes and Cleisthenes was determined to break their grip on government. Each artificial tribe in the new government nominated a large slate of candidates for the Council from which fifty were then selected by lot, on the theory that any citizen who was nominated —the nomination process eliminated the obviously unfit—was as capable as any other citizen of administering affairs of state. The executive branch of the government consisted of a committee of ten

HERODOTOS, THE "FATHER OF HISTORY"

Much of what we know about the Mediterranean area and the Persian wars is derived from the *Histories* of Greek historian Herodotos. Concerned primarily with the enmity between East and West from about 550 to 479 BC, he wrote in lively detail about the lands, peoples, religions, customs, geography, and history of the Persian Empire and of the Mediterranean peoples. He interviewed witnesses to historic events (and their descendants, as necessary), combining these with extensive visits to many lands to produce a work of insight and wit. His fascinating narrative ends with the Greek victories over the Persians at Salamis and Plataea in 480 and 479 BC that ensured the survival of freedom in the Western world.

generals elected yearly by the Council and headed by a commander-in-chief, also elected for one year.

Political freedom was something the Athenians had to get used to. When ruled by a despot most people adjust, turn inward, just survive. One of the greatest defects of any tyranny (out of a very long list) is that it stifles not only dissent but productivity and creativity as well. Freedom offers challenge and opportunity; despotism is denial. Herodotos succinctly described what happened in a democratic Athens:

> And it is plain enough that freedom is an excellent thing; since even the Athenians, who, while they continued under the rule of tyrants, were not a whit more valiant than any of their neighbors, no sooner shook off the yoke than they became decidedly the first of all.
>
> *Histories*, V

Persian Invasions

While Athens was developing its political institutions the mighty Persian Empire was becoming increasingly irritated with the rebellious Greek cities in Asia Minor. Athens supported the Ionian Greeks in their refusal to pay tribute to Darius (da-RYE-us), the Persian king, which gave him all the excuse a despot needs to give rebels a lesson in power and the upstart Athenian democracy some instruction in humility. A pivotal date for the future of Western culture, 490 BC was when the Persians invaded mainland Greece. North of Athens, on the plain of Marathon, the mighty army of a totalitarian state faced a badly outnumbered Athenian force. Led by General Miltiades (mil-TIE-uh-deez), the Greeks, like the wily Odysseus, outwitted the Persians and in a stunning dawn attack drove the humiliated Persians back into their ships. Herodotos reported that the Persians

lost more than 6,000 men with only minimal Greek casualties. Free people had turned back the Asian hordes and changed the course of history. Phidippides (fi-DIP-i-deez), the messenger who ran the 22 plus miles (35 km) from Marathon to Athens, symbolized more than news of an incredible victory. Greek pride in Hellenism, in the superiority of their culture over that of the "barbarians," was fully corroborated.

While the vengeful Persians prepared a second invasion the Athenians mined the newly discovered silver deposits at Mount Laurium in Attica that greatly enriched the treasury. Themistocles (the-MIS-tuh-kleez), the Athenian commander-in-chief, sent a delegation to Delphi to ask the Oracle how to combat the Persians and was told by the priestess that they should protect themselves with "wooden walls." Themistocles felt that Athens must defend itself with a strong navy, so, about as wily as Odysseus, he convinced his compatriots that the "wooden walls" were ships. Consequently, the rich silver mines helped build a strong Athenian navy, which became a triumphant military force and the catalyst that turned Athens into a mighty commercial center.

The Persian invasion of 480 was massive. Herodotos estimated the Persian forces at 5,000,000 men—an obvious exaggeration but indicative of the awesome size of the invading horde. Closely attended by a huge navy, the Persian army marched south to the first great engagement, the battle at the pass of Thermopylai (Ther-MOP-a-lye), a Persian victory, but a glorious episode in Greek history. Here, at a narrow pass between the mountains and the sea, 300 soldiers from Sparta (a military state by then allied with Athens) under their king, Leonidas (lee-ON-uh-dus), faced the entire Persian army and fought magnificently. When the Spartans were told to surrender or archers would darken the sky with arrows, Leonidas calmly replied that the Spartans would therefore fight in the shade. As often happened in Greek wars, they were betrayed by a traitor who showed the Persians an alternative route through the mountains. The Spartans were surrounded, but, even in the face of such odds, they fought on until all were killed. The inscription later carved on the tomb of the heroic Spartans, in tremendous understatement and compression of meaning, testifies to the spirit of the encounter:

> Go tell the Spartans, thou that passest by,
> That here, obedient to their laws, we lie.
>
> Simonides of Keos

Meanwhile, the Persian fleet sailing down the coast in support of the army had suffered defeats from both Greeks and storms, but it still overwhelmingly outnumbered the ships of Athens and its allies. The Persians sailed to the Bay of Salamis (SAL-a-mise) near Athens while the army moved inexorably toward its goal of sacking that city. Themistocles abandoned the city and all of Attica, moved everyone to the island of Salamis, and gambled everything on a single naval battle. By trickery he enticed the Persian fleet into the Bay of Salamis, where the fleet's very size was a disadvantage; narrow waters made it impossible to maneuver so many ships. Superior Greek sailors in their faster ships taught the Persians a lesson in naval warfare they would never forget. The victory was total. The land war dragged on for another year, ending with a decisive Spartan victory at the Battle of Plataea (pla-TEE-uh), and the Persian threat was no more.

Greek pride in these victories cannot be overstated. At the time, Persia controlled Egypt, the entire eastern end of the Mediterranean Sea, and all the land as far east as India. Yet a relatively few Greek men, poverty-stricken in comparison to the Persians, had beaten off the totalitarian enemy. The Greeks rightly felt that their cherished freedom, the glory of their honor, and the love they felt for their cities had been decisive factors, as indeed they were. Although the old aristocratic, **oligarchical** party continued to be a force in Athens, the years following the Persian wars marked the complete triumph of democracy in Athens. Suddenly the idea of freedom had worked.

For us in the Western world those ancient wars are monumental landmarks, because the Greek tradition —principally the concept of the worth of the individual— flourished, giving form and substance to the ideas we now hold as of greatest significance. If the Greeks had failed, today's Western world might be a very different place.

GREEK THOUGHT

Systematic speculation about the nature of the universe was a Greek innovation. The Egyptians had made astronomical observations to predict such events as the spring floods upon which their agriculture depended. Babylonian astrologers had studied the stars and made pseudo-scientific predictions about earthly affairs. But pure thought about the nature of things was uniquely Greek. The freedom to think was due, in part, to the loose and relatively non-authoritarian character of a religion that had no mandatory creeds or dogmas and no priestly class.

It was the Greeks who first conceived a universe something like that we envision today. Their ideas were characterized by a lively skepticism. Once, for example, when Herodotos made a tour of Egypt, he was shown a temple in which priests put out food for the god every night. The food was always gone in the morning, a fact which they presented to Herodotos as proof of the god's existence. "I saw no god," he commented, "but I saw many rats around the base of the statue." It's hard not to like someone who thinks like him.[1]

Further, philosophy is a rational and very personal activity that is perhaps best accomplished in a clearheaded society that cherishes such values as individualism, justice, beauty, and truth.

There were other civilizations long before them and contemporary with them, far richer and grander; but only the Greeks *thought*, thought hard and constantly, and thought constantly in human terms. They saw themselves as surrounded on all sides by "barbarians"—which for them meant people who did not live reasonably . . . . Perhaps Nietzsche was right in saying that they felt a constant and terrible pressure of barbarism, not only from around them but from within; and that their civilization was not an effortless growth, but the product of courageous effort sustained by acute tension. They must often have felt like a few sane men living in a world of maniacs and constantly endangered by the infection of madness.[2]

Athenian high civilization was about as flawed as all civilizations have been—and still are. The society that celebrated rationality and high human values was also responsible for the execution of the philosopher Socrates. Its prosperity was built in large part on slavery, but so was that of every Mediterranean society in that faraway world. Nor was there equality of the sexes, again, like most ancient cultures and much of today's world. Male dominance in Athens was at the expense of the women, who were accorded no place at all in the democracy. The women were, however, freeborn and some did assert themselves, as vigorously emphasized by Lysistrata in the comedy bearing her name (see p. 79). Alone among ancient cultures this society openly pondered its flaws and criticized its achievements.[3]

The Greeks were certainly not the only thinkers, for no one can dispute the importance of the humanistic thought of the Buddha in India, Confucius in China, or countless others in world cultures. Rather, the Greeks thought *systematically* about the cosmos and their relationship to it, which led not only to the invention of philosophy but also to the concurrent invention of pure science, the essence of which is the pursuit of objective knowledge about the world in which we live. This is the significance of the quotation given above from Gilbert Highet; "a few sane men" transformed human society for all time to come.

1. Trefil, James, *The Dark Side of the Universe; A Scientist Explores the Cosmos* (New York: Macmillan, 1988), p. 10.
2. Highet, Gilbert, *Man's Unconquerable Mind* (New York: Columbia University Press, 1954), p. 14.
3. American philosopher Charles Taylor contends that the progression from ancient Greek aristocratic conceptions of politics to a universal respect for human dignity is a progress in understanding that was generated by tensions within the ancient conceptions themselves, with their unarticulated acknowledgment of the humanness of women and slaves. In other words, some Greek intellectuals were aware of the paradoxical nature of Athenian democracy in which one gender participated and the other did not. See Charles Taylor, *Sources of the Self: The Making of the Modern Identity* (Cambridge: Harvard University Press, 1990), p. 106.

A MATTER OF HONOR

Shortly after the battle of Thermopylai

There came now a few deserters from Arcadia to join the Persians—poor men who had nothing to live on and were in want of employment. The Persians brought them into the king's presence, and there inquired of them, by a man who acted as their spokesman, what the Greeks were doing. The Arcadians answered, "They are holding the Olympic games, seeing the athletic sports and the chariot races." "And what," said the man, "is the prize for which they contend?" "An olive-wreath," returned the others, "which is given to the man who wins." Hearing the men say that the prize was not money but a wreath of olive, . . . Tritantaechmes could not forbear from exclaiming before them all, "Good heavens, [General] Mardonius, what manner of men are these against whom you have brought us to fight—men who contend with one another, not for money, but for honor!"

Herodotos, *The Persian Wars*, VIII:26

The Ionian Philosophers

The first philosopher-scientists lived in the Ionian city of Miletus (my-LEET-us) where Thales (THAY-leez; ca. 636–546 BC) was their leading thinker. The questions they asked are more important than the answers they found, for the questions are those that constantly return to challenge people's minds. The answers change as our knowledge of the universe expands.

One problem consistently bothered the philosophers of the Ionian (or Milesian) School. They were intrigued by the constant change of everything around them. Soil changed to plant life; plant life changed to animal; wherever they turned they observed movement from one form of existence to another. They postulated that there must be one basic substance accounting for all forms of being, so that the process of change is simply the transformation of the basic element. The first question Thales asked, then, was, What is the single element, the basic stuff of which the universe is composed?

Thales answered that this basic element is water, for all things need water for their existence, and water itself changes to a gas (steam) when heated, or to a solid (ice) when chilled. As these things are true and observable by our relatively coarse sensory equipment, it appeared that all sorts of other changes and transformations that are not sense-apparent could take place in water. Other philosophers, following the line of thought first explored by Thales, argued for earth or air as the basic world-stuff. That his theory was incorrect is not important; it was the question that was critical. In today's world we assume that most

people are naturally curious about the universe and everything in it. It is still startling to realize that the Greeks actually invented scientific and philosophical speculation.

The key point is that the Greeks, beginning with Thales, were the first to make informed guesses that were completely **naturalistic** (without reference to supernatural powers). One of the Babylonian creation myths, for example, stated that the world was once all water and that the god Marduk then made a rush mat and piled dirt beside it to construct the dry lands.

What Thales did was leave Marduk out. He, too, said that everything was once water. But he thought that the earth and everything else had been formed out of water by a natural process, like the silting up of the Delta of the Nile. It is an admirable beginning, the whole point of which is that it gathers into a coherent picture some observed facts *without letting Marduk in.*[4]

A follower of Hippocrates (hy-POK-ra-teas; 460–377 BC), the Greek physician, wrote of the mysterious ailment known as epilepsy (then termed the divine malady):

It seems to me that the disease is no more divine than any other. It has a natural cause, just as other diseases have. Men think it divine merely because they do not understand it. But if they called everything divine which they do not understand, why, there would be no end of divine things.[5]

Another Ionian, Anaximander (a-NAKS-uh-man-der; ca. 611–547 BC), a student of Thales, posed the second important question: How do specific things emerge from the basic element? His answer, though seemingly unsatisfactory and vague, is probably more scientifically accurate than those of many of his contemporaries or successors. He rejected physical substances such as water, earth, or air, and simply labeled his basic stuff "the Boundless." This, he suggested, was a form of being we cannot perceive with our senses; that is, it permeates everything and surrounds everything. In specific answer to the question he raised, he asserted that all forms that we can see—trees, living animals, all specific things—are formed by "separating out" of this boundless element. Thus all forms that our senses can know, all physical things, simply congeal out of the non-sense-apparent "boundless" and eventually lose their form and disappear back into it.

Herakleitos (Hair-uh-KLY-toss; ca. 535–475 BC), a later philosopher-scientist from Ephesos on the Ionian coast, extended the speculation of Thales and Anaximander by asking a third major question: What guides the process of change? He granted a basic element from which all particular forms emerged, but he felt there must be some sort of controlling force to keep the process of universal change

---

4. Benjamin Farrington, *Greek Science* (Baltimore: Penguin, 1961), p. 37.
5. Farrington, p. 81.

orderly so that, for example, an elm tree always produces elm trees rather than crocodiles.

Herakleitos denied the possibility of *being*, for he felt that the universe was not static but in a process of flow. His basic belief was that nothing *is*; everything is *becoming*. Thus his famous statement that one cannot step into the same river twice. The appearance of the river may be "the same," whatever that may mean, but by the time one has pulled a foot out of the river and immediately plunged it back in, the water has changed, the bank has changed—nothing is exactly the same. The universe, said Herakleitos, was not created in time but existing from all eternity and is ever in flux. Between *now* and *now* it has flowed, changed, varied; it is no longer what it was even though it may seem the same.

Perhaps to illustrate this contention, he chose fire as his basic element. One may watch a blaze in a fireplace for half an hour and say to a companion, "I have been watching that same flame for thirty minutes." Though the flame may seem constant, the burning gas that is the flame is never the same, even for a microsecond. This is the universe envisioned by Herakleitos.

But such a universe needs a guiding force, for the mind finds it perplexing to live with an image of an ever-changing world without some order and direction. So Herakleitos proposed a great **logos** as the guiding force. *Logos* in Greek sometimes means "word."[6] Thus in the Bible the Gospel according to John, originally written in Greek, starts with the sentence, "In the beginning was the Word"—*logos* in Greek. But for John (see p. 170), as for Herakleitos, it obviously had a greater significance than our "word." For Herakleitos it meant, in part, a great Intelligence that permeated the world and somehow guided the constant change of the flame-like element of which all things were composed. This sense of all things "knowing" what shapes they should take, what forms they should assume, is one of the great mysteries of the universe. (How does each maple leaf differ from every other maple leaf in the world, yet take a characteristic shape that can be identified at a glance? How does it "know" the form it must take?)

Herakleitos' theory of a universe ruled by *logos* also concerns the human ordering of the continuously changing world as people think and talk about it. In this sense *logos* can be translated as "reason" or "rational discourse." Nature and *logos* are often deemed one and the same, but Herakleitos' *logos* represents nature's overall rational structure and not the whole of the natural order. For not all natural creatures have reason (*logos*) within them. That cows cannot chat rationally about the universe is only one of many possible examples.

Ionian thought seems reasonable enough in its attempts to explain the element that is One and yet so many, which seems to be always the same and yet so varied. However, the fundamental postulate is one of constant change and, furthermore, all the conclusions reached are based on the testimony of the five senses. We see, hear, taste, feel, or smell the phenomena of the world and the changing nature of all things. The search for a basic element from which it is all made is essentially a quest for "That Which Is Real."

But we can take an entirely different tack in this quest. We can declare, for example, that whatever is real cannot always be changing. The mind can equate permanence with reality and reason that only permanent, unchanging things are real. Furthermore, one can easily prove that our senses cannot be trusted. We know they give us varying reports about the "same" thing. For example, water at a specific temperature as measured by a thermometer will be either "hot" or "cold" depending on the temperature of our hands when touching the water. Perhaps only the "thought process," independent of the senses, can be trusted as a guide to truth. Here is the difference between scientists—people who trust their senses as they can be refined through such instruments as they can make—and pure philosophers, those who depend solely on their minds to lead them to truth. This distinction appeared early in Greek thought.

Pythagoras

Pythagoras (ca. 582–507 BC) was one of the most original and engaging Greek philosophers. An Ionian Greek from the island of Samos, he was most influential in Magna Graecia (southern Italy), where he established a religious brotherhood in Crotona. Pythagoras taught that "number" was the essence of all things, in the same sense that other philosophers saw ultimate reality as water, the boundless, or fire. He believed that number was more than symbolic, that all matter was essentially numerical, and that all relationships in the universe could be expressed through number. The first Greek philosopher to reject the geocentric theory that the sun revolved around the earth, Pythagoras relegated the earth to the status of a planet that revolved around the fixed point of a central fire.

In his search for "that which is most real," Pythagoras kept returning to the universality of mathematical relationships. Most famous now is the formula in plane geometry called the Pythagorean theorem: in right-angle triangles the square of the hypotenuse is equal to the sum of the square of the other two sides. Although the triangles can be dissimilar in appearance, one fact about them is true: $AB^2 + AC^2 = BC^2$. In Euclidean geometry this relationship was true before it was ever discovered, and it will remain true with no one left to be aware of it. Here is an "idea" that has no substance, that exists entirely apart from

---

6. *Logos* comes from the root of the Greek verb *lego*, "to say." Its earliest meaning was "connected discourse," but its other (later) meanings included: "argument," "proportion," "reason," "portion," and "rational discourse."

people's minds. In this numerical relationship we have the pattern for a physical thing. Pythagoras is therefore credited with three major accomplishments: the discovery of pure mathematics, the development of mathematical proofs, and the awareness that form and structure give objects individual identities. These achievements provide the framework for the Eleatic philosophers, especially Plato (see pp. 84–91), upon whom Pythagoras was the single most important influence.

The first to demonstrate a correlation between mathematics and the harmonies of music, Pythagoras discovered that vibrating strings had certain fixed relationships depending on their relative lengths. Building on these musical connections, Pythagoras developed his theory of the relationships among the planets. He pictured the heavenly bodies as revolving from east to west in orderly circular orbits around a central fire. There was, he said, an agreement between nature (the planets) and number (the musical intervals). The predictability of nature, like the musical intervals on a vibrating string, was therefore musical and the wheeling arcs of the celestial globes formed the "*harmonia* of the cosmos": the music (or harmony) of the spheres.

Pythagoras was both a speculative and a practical philosopher, applying his ideas to the religious community that he founded at Crotona. Philosophy was central to a religious way of life that was also intellectual, political, and ethical. Small communities functioned within the larger community, each a social and religious unit as well as a scientific study group. Property was held in common, music and mathematics were integral parts of social life, and there was no discrimination according to gender. Pythagoras may have derived his view of sexual equality from the earlier earth goddess religions in Old Europe and from Minoan culture.

If the sexes were deemed equal, who was in charge? Aesara of Lucania (ee-SAHR-uh; fl. 400 BC), a late Pythagorean philosopher, explained the situation in her *Book on Human Nature*. She said that women bore the responsibility for creating *harmonia* (order and justice; "music" is an alternate translation) in the home and men had the same responsibility in the city.

> Just, harmonious cities require their component parts, households, also to be just and harmonious. Therefore, social justice depends on women raising just, harmonious individuals in those households. In the Pythagorean view, women are not peripheral to social justice; they make it possible.[7]

To be sure, not many people today would see this as true sexual equality, but it was a substantial improvement upon views in other Greek city-states.

Perhaps the best-known Pythagorean creed is the doctrine of the transmigration of souls. Pythagoreans believed that souls were reincarnated in a series of lives as they struggled to ascend to an ideal existence in a life of divine bliss. One could approach the ideal only through purification, emphasis upon intellectual activity, and renunciation of fleshly pleasures. Salvation was attained only after a final escape from the cycle of intermediate births.

Affirming a brotherhood of all living things, the Pythagoreans believed in spiritual purification through music and science and physical purification through medicine and gymnastics. They advocated a humane society in which people would live always in harmony and friendship. Eventually they were either killed or forced to flee their communes by hostile neighboring tribes who considered them a threat to established religious practices.

Literary Selections

When the two-volume *Humanities in Western Culture* is compressed into this Brief Edition something has to go, but only those parts that will not compromise the basic book. The organization has been retained but bibliographies, study questions, and figures have been reduced, and the long literary selections have been deleted. These works are referred to, however, with the expectation that some of them may be studied, whenever feasible, from other sources. Of prime importance for this chapter are the *Iliad* and the *Odyssey*, preferably in the Fitzgerald translations. Book XI (*Odyssey*) is particularly recommended; this provides the proper background for the similar descent into the underworld in the *Aeneid* and, later, portions of Dante's *Inferno*.

STUDY QUESTIONS

1. For a culture as rich as that of Greece, a time line is both useful and instructive. Create one by assigning each of the following topics a date (sometimes approximate) or bracket of dates. Then arrange them in chronological order. This will provide an outline of Greek history up to the beginning of the Classical Period (480 BC). Finally, explain the significance of each topic as it contributed to the development of Greek civilization.

   a. Reforms of Cleisthenes
   b. Dorian invasions
   c. Persian wars
   d. Mycenaean culture
   e. Traditional date of the Trojan War

---

7. Mary Ellen Waithe, *A History of Women Philosophers; Vol. 1: Ancient Women Philosophers, 600 BC–AD 500* (Boston: Martinus Nijhoff Publishers, 1987), p. 11.

f. Peak of Minoan culture
g. Homer and Hesiod active
h. Volcanic eruption on Thera
i. Solon's reforms
j. Linear B script
k. Early Cycladic culture in the Aegean
l. First Olympic Games
m. Introduction of coinage

2. Greek religion functioned at about four levels of belief/disbelief:

a. Olympians believed in literally at face value.
b. Gods/goddesses seen as representing aspects of the forces of nature.
c. Gods/goddesses understood as symbolizing abstract ideas such as power, love, intellectuality, civilized living, and fine craftsmanship.
d. Gods/goddesses believed to have been invented by people, usually in their own image.

Explain each level and what each might imply about religious beliefs in general. Then consider other religions and whether or not some or all of these levels are relevant to them. You can include, but need not be limited to, Christianity, Islam, Judaism, Hinduism, and Buddhism.

SUMMARY

Introduced in this background chapter were threads that were later woven into the glorious tapestry known as the Athenian Golden Age. The basic strand was the mainland geography that had so much to do with the development of Greek character and the expansion of commerce.

Individualistic to the extreme, the Greeks had no organized religion and, consequently, no hierarchy of priests. Their pantheon of Olympian gods can be viewed as highly imaginative explanations of natural phenomena, as symbols of power, love, intellect, and as the Greeks themselves, writ large.

Our knowledge of early Greece has been obtained in large part from Hesiod and Homer. A commentator on the archaic period, Hesiod spoke as a farmer caught in a losing battle with the aristocracy. Homer sang of the Mycenaeans and the Heroic Age, but he spoke to Greeks of all periods. The Homeric view on women, however, did not appear to carry over to later Greeks. "Altho women suffered disabilities under the patriarchal code, they were not considered inferior or incompetent in the Homeric epic. When Agamemnon and Odysseus sailed to Troy, they had no qualms about leaving their wives to manage their kingdoms in their absence."[8]

The Greeks were highly competitive and this drive seems partially to explain the upward mobility of the land-poor farmer who migrated to a colony to improve his opportunities to get ahead. The rise of trade, a natural consequence of home cities and overseas colonies, was very competitive in the quality of goods and the expansion of markets. A key factor in the vertical ascent of the lower classes was the surplus of goods created by Greek artisans. A society that labors from dawn to dusk just to make ends meet cannot expand its economy or have much time for leisure. By producing far more goods than they needed the Greeks enlarged their economy and gained leisure time for other pursuits.

Athens achieved dominance in large part because of a series of political reforms inaugurated, in turn, by Draco, Solon, Pisistratus, and Cleisthenes. The movement from tyranny to oligarchy to democracy was not smooth by any means but it was headed in the right direction. Actually, the evolution of Athenian democracy was a natural consequence of the individual drive and initiative of a growing middle class of artisans, traders, and businessmen. A good income and some discretionary time made the middle class avid for more of each. To accomplish this they had to get involved in politics, to become part of the government that enacted and administered laws on coinage, trade, and taxes. Of course the four tribes did not meekly submit to political reforms but, given the clout of the new moneyed class, they had no alternative.

With the reforms of Cleisthenes, democratic government was well established, and Athens had convincingly demonstrated her capabilities as a political and economic power. Her military power, however, was put to the test by the Persians.

When the Athenians confronted the Persian army at Marathon in 490 BC, they felt they could do little more than slow the Persian juggernaut. No one, it seems, believed the Persians could be defeated. But the small Greek force outwitted the Persian invaders and drove them back to their ships in a humiliating retreat.

The Greek victory profoundly shocked and enraged the Persians. Consequently, the second invasion of Greece—some ten years later—was supposed to redeem the loss of face at Marathon. The army and navy would sweep the land and the sea and the arrogant Greeks would be humiliated. By this time the Greeks were, if anything, even prouder and their military power was considerably greater. The battle at Thermopylai was lost against overwhelming odds but, from then on, the Greeks outfoxed and outfought the enemy and profoundly changed the course of history.

In one form or another the questions posed by the

8. Sarah B. Pomeroy, *Goddesses, Whores, Wives, and Slaves: Women in Classical Antiquity* (New York: Schocken Books, 1975), p. 28.

Ionian philosophers are still being asked today. If the Greeks had made only one contribution to Western civilization, the search for *what is* and the introduction of speculative philosophy would have been more than sufficient to earn the gratitude of all humankind. Moreover, their invention of scientific speculation eventually made possible the improvement of the quality of life.

THE MILKMAID AND HER PAIL

A farmer's daughter had been out to milk the cows, and was returning to the dairy carrying her pail of milk on her head. As she walked along, she fell to musing after this fashion: "The milk in this pail will provide me with cream, which I will make into butter and sell in the market. With the money I will buy some eggs and these, when hatched, will produce chickens, and by and by I shall have a large poultry yard. Then I shall sell some of my fowls and with the money I will buy myself a new gown, which I shall wear to the fair, and all the young men will admire, and want to make love to me. But I shall toss my head and have nothing to say to them." Forgetting all about the pail, and suiting the action to the word, the milk was spilled, and all her fine castles in the air vanished in a moment!

> Do not count your chickens
> before they are hatched.

> Aesop, *Fable*, sixth century BC

Samuel Croxall translated the *Fables* in 1722, adding the moral at that time. Aesop's fables have been used to teach ethics, wit, and common sense in schools and other places for 2,500 years.

CULTURE AND HUMAN VALUES

The Dorian migrations of ca. 1100–800 BC caused a major step backward into the Greek dark ages. In every sense of the term it was a period of chaos. Then, sometime after 850 BC or so, a long period of adjustment led to a maturing society, but where the adjustment matured into the balance of the Golden Age is difficult to say. From 490 to 480 was very likely the final decade of adjustment, from the victory at Marathon to the triumph at Salamis. Defeating the Persians seemed to provide the inspiration necessary to take a confident stride into classical Greek civilization.

Their military victories gave the Greeks assurance, but it was the development of their values during the archaic period that propelled them into the achievements of the Golden Age. No one can say just why these people were so intensely individualistic and competitive or why they felt compelled to achieve excellence in whatever they did. Nor can we explain how they developed their aesthetic sense as they pursued the ideal of beauty or why they were so passionate about justice. Every one of these values is manifested in some degree in nearly everything they did, said, wrote, or made. The value system in any society is a chicken and egg puzzle. Did justice, for example, come into being because it was a noble theory, or was a particular court decision so objective and so just that it set a precedent? Either is possible and perhaps both; the Greeks were noted for both their idealism and their pragmatism. Perhaps it was a combination of the two that fed the fires of creativity that sparked the achievements of the archaic, classical, and Hellenistic periods.

(NOTE: See summary of Greek culture and values on pp. 123–4.)

CHAPTER 5

Hellenic Athens:
The Fulfillment of the Good Life

ATHENS: THE GOLDEN AGE

> Numberless are the world's wonders but none more
> wonderful than man.
>
> Sophocles

The city of Athens in 461 BC must have been an exciting
place in which to live. It was prosperous and strong and,
though no one knew it at the time, about to enter its Golden
Age, that astonishing era (ca. 460–430 BC) during which the
resident artists, writers, statesmen, and philosophers would
enrich a society based on the value of the individual and on
a commitment to truth, beauty, and justice. It was not a
perfect society—far from it—but it did aspire to perfection.
For a fleeting moment life was enveloped in the lusty embrace
of a city-state that dared to compete with the gods.

Athenian Greeks may have been the most verbal
people in the ancient world. Blessed with a sophisticated
language that was "one of the most exquisite instruments
ever devised by human beings" (Gilbert Highet), they talked,
discussed, argued, and debated everything under the sun:
politics, society, love, and especially philosophy, because
the intellectuals among them were fascinated by the world
of ideas. The Herakleitean belief in constant change had
its supporters, while others contended that reality could
be expressed through numerical relationships, as
Pythagoras had stated. Into this debate now came new ideas
from Elea, a prosperous Greek colony in southern Italy.
Led by Parmenides (par-MEN-uh-deez; born ca. 514 BC),
the Eleatic School refused to accept the Herakleitean idea
that nothing *is* and that the universe is in a constant state
of *becoming*. They based their deliberations on the idea
that whatever is real must be permanent and unchanging.
Turning that statement around may seem more logical:
anything that constantly changes its state of being cannot

be real. Further, they attacked the method of the Ionian
philosophers, who depended entirely upon their five senses for the discovery of truth. The Eleatics were quick to
emphasize that one cannot trust the senses; but if the senses are not reliable as a guide to truth, what is? The Eleatic
philosophers asserted that the mind is the only sure guide.
They pointed to truths established by such geometers as
Pythagoras to support their theory that the mind can arrive
at truth without the aid (or handicap) of the senses. These
thinkers were much like the Pythagoreans, and form a sort
of bridge between Pythagoras and Plato (see pp. 64 and 84).

The development of material philosophy reached its
high point with the Athenian Leucippus and his student,
Democritos (Di-MOK-ruh-toss; ca. 460–370 BC). Democritos
synthesized the attempts of the Ionians to understand the
physical world and developed a theory of this world that
could not be verified until the twentieth century. Using only
the power of his mind he postulated Greek atomic theory,
stating that all matter consists of minute particles called
atoma (Gk. *atomas*: indivisible). These atoms exist in space,
combine and separate because of "necessity," and represent a strict conservation of matter and energy, that is, the
same number of atoms always exists; only the combinations differ. Contemporary nuclear physics confirms a strict
conservation of matter and energy when taken together but
probability replaces necessity when linking cause and effect.
Atoms do exist, of course, and some of them can be split
or fused.

Athenian intellectuals were fascinated with the world
of ideas but average citizens were far more interested in
the tangible world and their place within it. They lived in
a city whose dominant mood, following the Persian wars,
was enthusiastically optimistic, where unlimited opportunities challenged free people in a democratic society. The
Persians had burned the entire city, giving the Athenians
an unprecedented opportunity to rebuild Athens to match
their visions of its greatness. Possibilities for growth and
progress lay everywhere but someone had to point the way.
For development of the human spirit in a free society,
Athenians looked primarily to that unique Greek institution: the theatre.

Opposite   Stone carving of theatrical mask from Ephesos,
Turkey. Ca. 400 BC. Limestone, height ca. 36" (91.4 cm).
Photo: Sonia Halliday, Weston Turville, U.K.
The Graeco-Roman theatre here seated 25,000 spectators.

THE THEATRE:
A GREEK INVENTION

The Greeks created **tragedy**, **comedy**, melodrama, mime, ballet, the art and craft of acting, costume and set design, stage machinery, and the theatrical structure itself. All this began with the first formal staging of tragedy during the Athenian Greater Dionysia festival in about 534 BC. Thespis was the name of the actor who led that theatrical troupe and "thespians" is what we sometimes call actors today. The Greater Dionysia was the more important of the two religious festivals held each year in honor of Dionysos, god of fertility and wine and patron of Athenian drama. (Curiously, secular drama evolved out of religious rites twice: in Greece and later in medieval Christian churches.)

Strictly speaking, drama is but one branch of literature, but Greek drama is far more than this. Encompassing poetry, music, dance, and such wide-ranging themes as the nature of truth, beauty, freedom, and justice, Greek theatre represented virtually the whole of that remarkable civilization. Theatres functioned as centers of education, enlightenment, and entertainment, probably in reverse order. No self-respecting Greek would tolerate a boring play, no matter how educational and enlightening. Simply stated, Greek drama can be defined as an alliance of moral passion and entertainment.

The state took full responsibility for every aspect of the festivals from selecting judges to funding and supervising casting and production. A small admission fee partially offset expenses; those too poor to afford even this received the price of a ticket from a "seeing fund." The prime government responsibility, though, was the location, design, construction, and maintenance of the theatre itself.

Theatres and Performances

The climate enabled the Greeks to spend much of their lives out-of-doors, so naturally the theatres were in the open air, with spectators' seats ascending an inward curving hillside. No theatre was ever "built"; it was carved into the side of a hill so that it became part of its environment. Chorus performed in the circular space (**orchestra**) that filled the flat area at the base of the hill. (Chorus was usually thought of as a single actor and was thus a singular noun.) Behind the orchestra and facing the audience was a long, low building (**skene**; SKAY-nuh) with a room at

---

5.1 Polykleitos the Younger, Theatre at Epidauros, Greece. Ca. 350 BC.
This view shows the great size (13,000 capacity) typical of Greek theatres.

either end (dressing and storage) and a platform (stage) between the rooms.

Because they were important centers for the entire populace of a city-state, theatres were suitably large; seating was for 13,000 at Epidauros (fig. 5.1), 18,000 at Athens, 25,000 at Ephesos (in Turkey). The **acoustics** of these semicircular stadiums were so fine that actors could be understood fifty rows above the stage. All-male casts wore large masks of easily identifiable character types (which also aided gender distinction; see chapter opener on p. 68). Violence took place off stage as described (usually) by a messenger though there were some exceptions in the comedies of Aristophanes. Each play had a chorus of up to a dozen members that reacted to the action in a variety of ways. Each play used one stage set, while the main stage machinery was the *mekhane* (me-KAY-nee), a crane that transported actors who played gods. This was the celebrated **deus ex machina**, the "god in a machine."

Greek drama was to a considerable degree a musical experience, a unique amalgam for which there is no modern equivalent. Neither opera nor musical play, Greek dramas (both tragedies and comedies) moved on their own plane somewhere in between. Chorus was central as it chanted, sang, and danced to the pungent, plaintive sounds of the **aulos** (OW-los; a double reed-pipe, somewhat like the modern oboe). The instrument of Dionysos, god of the theatre, the aulos was intimately involved in the pace and mood of the drama, commenting, underscoring, highlighting. (Modern stage directions referring to "flute" or "flute-girl" always mean aulos and aulos-player.)[1]

A single set, all-male cast, masks, chorus, music, dance, and off-stage violence were conventions that challenged spectators to use their imaginations to the fullest. What about the imaginations of the playwrights? Did state sponsorship limit what could be said or done? The Greek response to these issues is the key to the eminence and influence of the theatre.

Athens did have some restrictions concerning religion but the stage was the totally uncensored forum of the democracy. The freedom for dramatists to write anything whatever was protected by a society that delighted in the free expression of ideas and the airing of controversial topics. Playwrights, especially the comic dramatists, assaulted politicians, philosophers, civic leaders, and even other dramatists. As might be expected, corruption, hypocrisy, greed, politics, and war were favorite targets.

Compared with our ready access to theatre, the Greeks had limited opportunities to experience the artistry, wit,

and wisdom of their playwrights. Athens had only two festivals a year—the Greater Dionysia and the Linaea. Consequently, the festivals were eagerly anticipated and heavily attended. What better way to hear what some of the foremost men of their time had to say? In terms of general interest one can roughly compare the two festivals with the World Series and the Superbowl but with significant differences in impact. The plays generated a year or more of passionate discussions/arguments about the issues, ideas, and controversies presented on stage. Whatever message a writer had to impart to the entire population of the city, drama was the nearly perfect vehicle.

Aeschylus, 525–456 BC

Though many of their plays have been lost, enough has survived to demonstrate that three of the greatest tragedians in Western history were Greeks, all of whom lived in Athens at about the same time. The first dramatist was Aeschylus (ES-ka-luss), whose life and works were of profound importance in the development of Greek culture, especially the culture of Athens. Though a prize-winning playwright, his tombstone memorializes (at his request) his soldiering at the battle of Marathon. An aristocrat by birth, he synthesized some traditional ideas with those of the most enthusiastic liberals. Critics sometimes accuse Aeschylus of being more of a preacher than a dramatist; all his plays do carry clear messages designed to raise the ethical level of Athenian life. Greek scholar Edith Hamilton points out, however, that he was so instinctive a dramatist that when a suitable dramatic form did not exist, he invented it. Before his time the cast consisted of chorus and one speaking actor. Aeschylus added a second speaking actor, thus introducing true dialogue, real conflict, and the resolution of competing ideas.

Aeschylus wrote about ninety plays of which just seven survive. Of these only the trilogy called the *Oresteia* (o-res-TYE-ya), the story of Orestes, is discussed here. *Agamemnon*, the *Libation Bearers*, and the *Eumenides* (you-MEN-i-deez) make up the trilogy. All three are discussed as if they were three acts of a single drama. They relate the story of a system of justice based on tradition, fear, and revenge as it evolved into justice as administered by the law courts of a free society.

Agamemnon: Clytemnestra's Revenge

Agamemnon is a drama of murder, adultery, and revenge. The Greeks have won the Trojan War and Agamemnon is returning to Mycenae in triumph. Awaiting him is Queen Clytemnestra (kly-tem-NES-tra), who is bent on avenging the death of her daughter Iphigeneia (IF-i-je-NY-ya), whom Agamemnon had sacrificed ten years earlier to appease the goddess Diana. Accompanied by a captive Trojan prophetess, Cassandra, in his war chariot, Agamemnon arrives at

---

1. Greek plays are no longer performed in their original version because all of the accompanying music has been lost. Over a long period of time those who copied and recopied the manuscripts began omitting the musical notation because they were no longer able to decipher it. The words were transmitted to future generations but the music is gone forever.

TWO WINNERS

Greeks in general and Athenians in particular were the most critical and competitive people in the ancient world. *Arete* (ARE-uh-tay; diligence in the pursuit of excellence) was a creed that applied to everything from pots to temples, music to athletics. The laurel wreath was awarded at the Pythian Games in Delphi for track and field, poetry and music, and sculptures carved to commemorate the victors. In this fiercely competitive society what could be more natural than playwrights vying for the Athenian ivy wreath?

Dramatists competed at two levels; anyone could submit plays but only three finalists were chosen for the three-day festivals. A tragic **trilogy** (three plays on a related theme) was performed each morning followed by a single comedy in the afternoon. The eagerly awaited finale saw the twelve judges issue lists ranking the tragic playwrights and actors, comic playwrights and actors, and the choruses. The victors were crowned with ivy wreaths, and the two top dramatists received the added distinction of a guaranteed appearance at the next festival. Finally, as was the Greek custom, the winners had their names inscribed in stone.

his citadel, where Clytemnestra and her lover Aigisthos (i-JIS-thos) greet him. The queen encourages her arrogant husband to stride through the Lion Gate on a royal carpet so expensive it was reserved for the gods. The play ends shortly after she murders her husband and the Trojan captive and haughtily dismisses her horrified subjects (box 5.1).

What does all this mean? The most prevalent image is that of a net or web. The purple carpet is called a web, and Agamemnon has a net thrown over him in his bath so that he cannot escape the murderous blows. Perhaps Aeschylus felt that this net was the old traditionalism, the belief in fate, and the idea of justice as revenge. Chorus is bound up in this web with many speeches against pride, or wealth that breeds pride, or any sort of innovation. Chorus is constrained by ancestral traditions but if they had broken down the palace door they might have also shattered the barrier between themselves and freedom. Curiously, Cassandra tries to inspire them to act, but she, too, is imprisoned by the net. As she enters the palace to meet her known fate, Chorus admonishes her that even slightly delaying her death is a small victory; she can only reply that her time has arrived.

Of all the characters in the play, Clytemnestra alone seems free to act as a human being. True, she blames the curse on the House of Atreus but this only briefly placates Chorus. Her action, however, is destructive, a type of freedom that civilized society cannot tolerate. So, at the end

of *Agamemnon* we have two conditions of human existence: Chorus which consults tradition for guidance in life, and Clytemnestra, whose devastating freedom would destroy society. In the remaining two plays the playwright must free one segment and control the other.

Libation Bearers

The second play, the *Libation Bearers*, is primarily a transition play that brings the problems of vengeance and justice to a head. Apollo has ordered Orestes to avenge his father's murder by killing his mother and her lover. This, interestingly enough, is a directive from the new generation of progressive gods. On the other hand, tribal tradition decrees that anyone spilling kindred blood is hounded to death by the Furies. Caught between contradictory commands, Orestes is damned if he does and damned if he doesn't. But he does commit matricide, is attacked by the Furies and, as the play ends, driven from the stage.

Eumenides

The *Eumenides* may be translated as the "Gracious Ones," and the change of the Furies (the Erinyes; i-RIN-e-eez) to the Eumenides is part of the resolution of the concluding

BOX 5.1   THE HOUSE OF ATREUS

Like most old Greek families the roots go back to Zeus, in this case through Tantalus, a mortal who was permitted nectar and ambrosia at the table of the gods. To trick the gods and show them as fallible Tantalus hosted a banquet and served them a stew made of his son Pelops. The furious immortals dispatched Tantalus to Hades to suffer eternal hunger and thirst for he was guilty of **hubris** (overbearing pride), the worst of all sins. The family curse continued with the sons of Pelops. Thyestes (thigh-ES-teez) seduced Aerope, his brother's wife; Atreus, in revenge, killed three of Thyestes' four sons (Aigisthos survived) and served them to their father as a meat course. In his *Oresteia* trilogy Aeschylus dramatizes the working out of the curse.

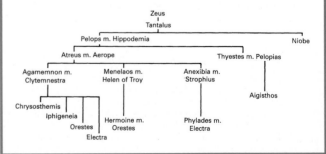

Only let them not tamper with the laws,
But keep the fountain pure and sweet to drink.
I warn you not to banish from your lives
All terror but to seek the mean between
Autocracy and anarchy; and in this way
You shall possess in ages yet unborn
An impregnable fortress of liberty
Such as no people has throughout the world.

The jury then returns a tied vote, with Athena casting her ballot for acquittal. Orestes immediately leaves the scene though one-third of the play still remains. Its hero is not Orestes, however, but rather the idea of *justice*. During the rest of the play the Furies are transformed into the Eumenides through the strenuous efforts of Athena, goddess of wisdom and persuasion, who convinces them that their new role as defenders of the city will accord them worship and honor.

The universal significance of the trilogy may be described as follows: the people, as represented by Chorus in the *Agamemnon*, are set free simply because their eyes are turned forward rather than backward. No longer will they function under the shadow of tradition and superstition, because each case will be tried using its own evidence and decided according to just laws enacted by human beings.

The *Eumenides* presents the thesis that people must establish the parameters of their own actions, with limits determined by the degree of freedom each can have without compromising the freedom of others. This applies also to the Clytemnestras of the world. Their acts will be brought before the same tribunal and judged by the identical standard. Humanity—at least in Athens of the Golden Age—was encouraged to do so in ways that would serve both the individual and the state.

play. The trilogy had begun in darkness in rural Argos and concludes in the sunlit city of Athens where, according to Apollo, Orestes will receive justice.

Chorus (the Furies at this point) laments that they, the older gods, have been shamed and dishonored. If Orestes goes free they predict that children will murder their parents at will, forcing the Furies to blight the land. Athena takes charge by declaring the matter too grave to be decided by ordinary people or by a god. She impanels a jury of citizens to hear the case and render a verdict, a shrewd and civilized solution. A trial by jury transcends the judgment of mortals because juries will, over time, build a body of law that provides a basis for rational, objective judgments.

As defense attorney, Apollo presents the evidence, after which Athena establishes the court, the Areopagus (are-ee-OP-uh-gus; "at the foot of the Acropolis"), and charges it with its duties as the highest court of justice. Her speech cannot be quoted often enough, for never in the ancient or medieval world and seldom in today's world has there been a clearer statement of how to achieve liberty and justice for all:

Here reverence
For law and inbred fear among my people
Shall hold their hands from evil night and day,

One further point. The Furies prospered on rule by fear, and it is tempting to discard that aspect of the new order advocated by Aeschylus. However, he has Athena insisting that a certain element of fear is still necessary. Though optimistic about human nature and behavior in a free society, he knew as well as anyone that people act in their own self-interest and that venality and greed cannot be legislated out of existence. To curb these tendencies an inbred fear of punishment must remain, a dread more deeply felt than a purely intellectual respect for law. Some critics have seen the Furies' conversion to the Gracious Ones as a sort of birth of conscience—this should be an ethical conscience that incorporates some degree of fear into a concern for the safety and welfare of society. Perhaps more than any other culture, the ancient Greeks saw men and women both as they were and as they should be.

Athenians revered Aeschylus for the lofty idealism of his dramas and his deep concern for the well-being of his city and its inhabitants. His brief and touching epitaph was written by his younger colleague, the comic playwright Aristophanes (air-i-STOF-uh-neez; his work is discussed on pp. 78–9):

> Gentle he was in this life,
> Gentle in life beyond.

THE AGE OF PERICLES, CA. 495–429 BC

The other two major tragic playwrights, Sophocles and Euripides (you-RIP-uh-deez), lived and worked in Athens during its Golden Age, which coincided with the rule of Pericles (PAIR-i-kleez). It is best, therefore, to consider the Age of Pericles before discussing the playwrights themselves.

Athenian democracy was most fully realized with the inspired leadership of Pericles, truly the best man at the right time. He was first elected general-in-chief in 461 BC and, except for two years when he was voted out of office, he directed Athenian affairs until he succumbed to the plague shortly after the beginning of the Peloponnesian War (431–404 BC) that ended the Golden Age.

The population of Attica (Athens and the surrounding territory it governed) at this time has been estimated at about 230,000 people. Of these, 40,000 were free male citizens, the actual voting population that participated in the democracy; 40,000 were women who, at best, were second-class citizens; 50,000 were foreign-born; and 100,000 were slaves. One must remember that Athenian democracy involved only the 40,000 free men. The rest of the free people (the Athenian women) participated on the periphery, and slaves not at all.

It is nevertheless a miracle of history that such a small group of citizens could, in a single century, have produced one great comedy writer, three of the finest writers of trag-

ic drama in the history of literature, and two philosophers whose ideas have helped shape Western civilization for 2,500 years. The continuing influence of their architecture and sculpture, pottery and poetry, cannot be overestimated. Their music and painting are apparently irretrievably lost and, considering that they themselves regarded music as their best developed art and their sculpture as inferior to their painting, this is a terrible loss.

Most significantly, the people of this glorious century achieved a way of life that in its freedom for the individual, coupled with a concern for the welfare of the state as a whole, has been envied (and sometimes emulated) by the Western world ever since. This was the quality of life toward which the dramas of Aeschylus pointed. The Greek ideal is succinctly stated by C. M. Bowra (*The Greek Experience*): "A man served his state best by being himself in the full range of his nobility, and not by sacrificing it to some abstract notion of political power or expediency."

Abstract notions and generalizations about political power and expediency were anathema to a culture that spent much time and effort trying to define itself. The Greeks are known, quite correctly, as idealists who envisioned the world as it should be. They were, however, clear-eyed and literal-minded, seeing themselves and their culture as they really were. Certainly they asked philosophical questions about the nature of justice, freedom, beauty, and love. These are, of course, abstractions but they sought the answers in the concrete reality of the world of here and now. Justice, for example, was literally to be found in the law courts. If justice was not present then injustice had replaced it. If a higher, purer form of justice could be idealized then that was what should be present in the courts. Injustice did not come into being because justice—in the all-too-familiar phrase—"failed to live up to its potential"; justice was either present in the courts or it was not.

This kind of idealistic pragmatism (Gk., *pragmatikos*, "to do business, a thing done") can also be applied to the idea of beauty. After reaching some sort of agreement about ideal beauty (beauty-in-and-of-itself), the proper thing to do is to find beauty in a particular pot, painting, poem, building, song, statue, or whatever. As much as a certain object possesses the attributes of beauty, then it is to that degree that beauty literally resides in the object. The Greeks knew that perfect beauty was not a realistic goal in an imperfect world, but this did not deter them from striving for perfection. As stated before, diligence in the pursuit of excellence (*arete*) was a Greek passion.

Little political change occurred during the Age of Pericles because a reasonably fair and just democratic system was already in place. The quest, then, was for a higher quality of life for the individual and for society. Pericles and some of his compatriots had a vision of Athens as the leading city in the world, in which resided freedom, justice, and beauty. Among other things, he encouraged the free exchange of ideas by reconstructing the marketplace of commerce and ideas (the agora) and literally beautified the city by commissioning the new temples on the Acropolis. Even in their current ruined condition these ancient temples symbolize the Golden Age, some of whose beauty still lingers on atop the Athenian Acropolis.

During the Periclean age the precarious balance between individual aims and the welfare of the state shifted toward greater individualism; there was less concern for Athens and still less for the well-being of other city-states. This was first noticeable in the city's international relations; it converted the Delian League (organized to fight Persia) into what was really an Athenian empire and shifted the treasury from the island of Delos to Athens. It was this treasury that paid for the temples on the Acropolis, leading, predictably, to vigorous protests from League members. The haughty response was that Athens had shouldered the burden of protecting the League and Athens would therefore decide how the League's money was spent.

As a self-anointed international power Athens became increasingly autocratic. The older values of reverence for the state and the gods that had triumphed at Marathon and that Aeschylus had propounded in his plays, faded in the shift toward self-centered individualism. This metamorphosis probably began (or was confirmed) with the teaching of atomists such as Democritos, who argued for total materialism—including the gods, thus removing their spiritual quality—and ascribed all change to pure chance. In this random atomic world with an unpredictable future and gods offering neither guidance nor inspiration the only dependable reality was material pleasure.

Probably taking their cue from the atomists, the sophists (SOF-ists) became the leading teachers of Athens. Their leader was Protagoras (pro-TAG-uh-rus; ca. 481–411 BC), a high-minded thinker whose chief dictum was that "man is the measure of all things." By itself, this is simply a slogan-like restatement of the centrality of human values long espoused by Athenian intellectuals. But there were problems. All is well if humankind is the measure; if an individual is the yardstick then whatever he or she does is proper, with as many yardsticks as there are individuals. The later sophists did indeed move toward this position, teaching that the laws, for instance, were merely a set of opinions; those with different opinions could act on those beliefs. This could lead, of course, to anarchy, one of the extremes cited by Athena in the *Eumenides*. As for religion, Protagoras said, "about the gods I have no knowledge either that they are or that they are not or what is their nature."

Much can be said for sophist philosophy for it introduced a healthy questioning of old traditions and uncritical veneration of the gods. Conversely, complete relativism could undermine the cohesion of society and make all thought and action a matter of expediency. The delicate balance between the welfare of the state and that of the individual was indeed shifting in the direction of the individual. It was against this philosophical backdrop that Sophocles and Euripides produced their plays.

Sophocles, ca. 496–406 BC

A contemporary of Pericles, Sophocles was a general, a priest, and the most popular dramatist in Athenian history. He is reputed to have written 123 plays and to have won first prize more than twenty times; he was never placed lower than second. Of the seven plays that survived, only *Oedipus the King* (ED-uh-pus, or EED-uh-pus) is discussed here.

Oedipus the King is a tale of patricide, murder, incest, suicide, and self-mutilation. This is perhaps the best-known of all Greek tragedies, partly because it became the model tragedy in Aristotle's *Poetics* (see p. 91). All the classic elements of tragedy are here: a man of exalted stature is brought low because of a fatal flaw in his personality; the unities of time (a single day) and of place (the exterior of the royal palace at Thebes); the calling forth of the emotions of fear and pity in the spectator; and the final purging or catharsis. One can define catharsis as feeling that the action has worked itself out to its one unavoidable conclusion. In doing so the emotions of pity and fear are purged in the spectator, who is left in peace. The ending, though tragic, is right; there is no more to be said or done.

As the play opens the city of Thebes is gripped by a terrible plague that can be lifted, according to the Delphic Oracle, only when the murderer of Laios (LYE-os), the former king, is discovered and punished. Oedipus, the present king, who has married, according to custom, the widowed queen Jocasta (yoe-KOS-ta), swears he will save the city by finding the murderer. He makes this vow in the face of two prophecies, one of which was known to Jocasta and Laios. It was foretold that their son would kill his father and marry his mother (box 5.2). Accordingly, after their son was born, Laios (without Jocasta's consent) had the baby exposed and left to die on the slopes of Mount Cithaeron (KEE-the-ron). The second prophecy, known to Oedipus when he grew up in Corinth as the son of the king and queen there, was that he would kill his father and marry his mother. To avert this he had fled Corinth. During his flight he had an altercation with an old man and his bodyguards at a place where three roads came together. In a fit of rage Oedipus killed the entire group, except a servant who escaped. He then proceeded to Thebes where he freed the city from the plague of the evil Sphinx by solving the riddle: "What walks on four legs in the morning, two legs at noon, and three legs at night?" Oedipus' correct answer was "humankind." Chosen king by a grateful populace, he married Jocasta and fathered four children.

The play is riddled with irony; the audience knows that Oedipus is the murderer he is seeking and that the curse he pronounced on the killer will fulfill itself on him. This expected event comes to pass: Jocasta commits suicide, and Oedipus pierces his eyeballs and exiles himself from the city.

The tragedy ends with the oracles upheld and the gods inflicting a just punishment on the errant king. Taken as a whole, the drama can be interpreted as a clear admonition: the gods are all-powerful and should receive

ASPASIA AND THE EDUCATION OF WOMEN

Aspasia of Miletus (d. 401 BC) exerted considerable influence on Pericles and on intellectual life in general in Athens. An educated and highly intelligent foreigner, Aspasia was a former hetaera (Gk., *hetaira*, female companion). The hetaerae of ancient Greece were companions—physically, intellectually, and emotionally—to influential men in Athenian society. Well-educated and adept in music, dancing, conversation, and other social graces, they fulfilled a role generally denied to Greek wives who, though undisputed mistresses of their households, were not allowed to partake fully in life outside the home. (Most Greek wives were encouraged to learn the domestic arts of spinning, sewing, weaving, and cooking, but little else.)

Though criticized by some because of her former profession and her political influence, Aspasia established, in Pericles' home, what might be called the first salon. Here she entertained notable artists, philosophers, and political leaders, including the more liberated women of Athens. Some men broke with tradition and brought their wives to Aspasia's dinner parties to participate in discussions about the need for better educated wives to be intellectual companions for their husbands. Credited by Socrates with teaching Pericles the art of rhetoric, it is likely that the brilliant Aspasia assisted Pericles in composing some of his speeches which, according to Plato (*Menexenus*, 236b), included the *Memorial Oration*.

reverence and honor. But was Oedipus only a pawn in a cosmic drama or the agent of his own destruction? Was the king himself a warning to the Athenians?

A common Greek tragic situation is one in which whatever the hero does is wrong. Agamemnon must either kill his daughter or betray his command; Orestes must disobey Apollo or kill his mother; Oedipus must discover the truth or watch his city die.

Whether the hero has erred unknowingly or must err against his will, there could be still another error that justified divine retribution. Consider Agamemnon as he walked upon the purple carpet, colored with a dye so expensive it was reserved for the gods. This was an act of overweening pride guaranteed to incur the wrath of the gods. This was hubris.

Pride was a virtue in ancient Greece. Diligence in the pursuit of excellence (*arete*) could result in impressive achievement and, for the creator, a justifiable feeling of self-esteem. Pride in achievement was expected; the accomplishment somehow enlarged everyone. Pride in onself as the achiever was another matter because that kind of vanity, that hubris, tended to elevate the one person and demean the many. Far more than vanity, hubris was an overweening pride that was harmful to others.

A careful study of *Oedipus the King* reveals many instances of Oedipus' placing himself above all others as the sole seeker of truth. Though justifiably proud of solving the riddle and saving the city, from the time the play begins he has become the all-knowing savior of Thebes. Hubris—his fatal flaw—led Oedipus to gratuitously attack Teiresias and Creon and to pronounce himself judge and jury in deciding the future of Thebes.

If the fatally-flawed king was indeed self-destructive, was his tragic end a warning to the people of Athens? *Oedipus the King* was produced around the beginning of the Peloponnesian War but it was the *cause* of the war—the Athenian empire itself—that distressed many Athenians. For several decades the empire had been expanding, acquiring riches and power largely at the expense of its commercial and political rivals. That power corrupts and that it is perhaps the ultimate aphrodisiac, are truisms that apply to the majority populist party of middle-class Athenians who lusted after the might of empire. Warnings by Sophocles and others went unheeded by an arrogant populace convinced of Athenian superiority in everything. The ruling populist party fought much of the war with a guns-and-butter philosophy, maintaining a luxurious lifestyle while contending with the "inferior" Spartans.

The size and strength of an empire that many thoughtful citizens had never wanted virtually invited the Spartans

BOX 5.2   HOUSE OF CADMOS, FOUNDER OF THEBES

The King of Sidon had a daughter, Europa, who was abducted by Zeus in the form of a bull and carried quite willingly to Crete, where she became the mother of Minos and Rhadamanthys. The King of Sidon sent his sons to search for her. One of them, Cadmos, consulted the oracle at Delphi; she told him to found his own city and forget Europa. He was instructed to follow a heifer and to build his city of Thebes on the heifer's first resting place. First, however, he had to kill a dragon, whose teeth Athena ordered him to sow; armed warriors sprang up, killing each other until just five survived. With the five Cadmos built Thebes and had five daughters and a son. Though Cadmos was a good man misfortune tormented his descendants—none more than Oedipus and Antigone.

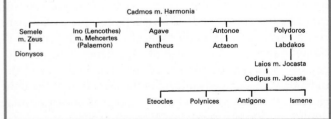

A SPARTAN LIFE

The word Spartan is still used to describe something austere, rigorous, disciplined. What was life like in the original Sparta?

The dominant warrior class in this collectivist society was supported by freemen engaged in commerce and crafts and by a large number of slaves (helots) who were owned by the state. The Spartan process began with babies inspected at birth and the weak ones left to die on a mountainside. Military training started at age seven with no clothing permitted until age twelve. Spartans became hoplites (soldiers) at age twenty, lived in military barracks until age thirty and moved into clubs until age sixty, after which those still alive retired from military life. Marriage and robust children were encouraged; a man could spend an evening with his wife but never a whole night. Spartan women received the physical training deemed necessary for producing sturdy babies. The men practiced war, the women raised future soldiers and mothers of soldiers, and the helots did most of the work.

to "put out all their strength and overthrow the Athenian power by force of arms" (Greek historian Thucydides). Hubris helped cause the war and hubris was certainly a factor in the final defeat of the haughty city.

Euripides, 484–406 BC

The third tragedian directed his tragic vision toward psychological drama with plots revolving around the plight of the underdog; the inferior status of women; the rejected wife; the exploited wife; the abuse of peasants; those who lose wars. Aristotle declared that Aeschylus composed properly without knowing it and that Sophocles had said: "I portray men as they ought to be, but Euripides portrays them as they are." Euripides mercilessly exposed the realities of suffering and experienced the customary fate of artists who deal with unpopular truths. He wrote ninety-two plays but won only four first prizes, the last one posthumously. However, nineteen plays have survived, more than the combined extant dramas of Aeschylus and Sophocles, an ironic twist that Euripides probably would have relished.

Their different versions of *Electra* provide an excellent example of the contrasting styles of the three dramatists. In his *Electra* Aeschylus portrays Orestes and his sister Electra as vehicles for developing an idea of justice; Sophocles writes a classic study of an Electra possessed and driven almost mad by the indignities heaped upon her;

Euripides presents Electra and Orestes as cold-blooded butchers bent solely on revenge.

During the last two years of his life Euripides exiled himself from civilized Athens, choosing to live in primitive Macedonia, where he died. There he wrote *The Bacchae* (BOCK-ee), in which he repudiated the rationalistic civilization he had known, a civilization that had rejected him and that he, in turn, had spurned. Though Euripides did not live to see his play produced, Sophocles used his own immense prestige to see that the tragedy received the production it merited in the city that deserved it. *The Bacchae* won first prize, suggesting that there was some magnanimity remaining in the Athenian spirit.

Thucydides spoke for future generations when he wrote Euripides' epitaph:

All Greece is his monument, though his grave
Lies in Macedon, refuge of his last days.
Hellas of Hellas, Athens his land, who gave
So much joy by his art, whom so many praise.

War and Peace

Throughout the careers of the three tragedians the growing might of the Athenian empire posed an ever-greater threat to the welfare of Sparta and its allies. Sparta finally attacked Athens in 431 BC, launching the Peloponnesian War that was to drag on for an entire generation. Athens was too strong to allow a quick Spartan victory but much too casual about besting an inferior culture. Pericles did foresee a long war of attrition and abandoned the land surrounding Athens to the powerful Spartan army. Gathering the people inside the city wall, he depended on the navy to bring in supplies and to attack the Spartan confederation. The strategy was successful until plague broke out in Athens and damaged the war effort. The remainder of the conflict provided some classic examples of the horrors of warfare, particularly the tactics of the hubristic Athenians. Several times Athens could have ended hostilities without serious damage to its precious honor, but the ruling hawks demanded nothing less than total victory.

Several Athenian actions illustrate the temper of the war. In 416 BC the Athenians attacked the tiny neutral island of Melos on the general principle that if you are not with us, you must be against us. Athens won the mismatch in a single day, killing all the men and selling the women and children into slavery. It was this atrocity that probably spurred Euripides to write his impassioned anti-war play, *The Trojan Women*.

In the following year Athens mounted a massive attack on the city of Syracuse in Sicily; by 413 this foolhardy Sicilian expedition had failed completely. Generals Nikias and Demosthenes were dead, the navy lost, and most of the army either dead or pressed into slavery. Though the war was to grind on until 404, the Sicilian disaster marked the moment of decline for the once glorious culture. It prompted Aristophanes, the leading writer of Greek comedy, to compose *Lysistrata* (li-SIS-tra-ta) in which he introduced a novel way to end the war, or any war for that matter. (The play is discussed below.)

The third leader of the Sicilian expedition, Alcibiades (al-ki-BY-uh-deez), was also the only surviving general, which was far from coincidental. Alcibiades the survivor represented the new egocentric individualism that was becoming so prevalent in Athens. His self-serving actions and ethical relativism could be construed by his sophist contemporaries as proper, that is, successful, behavior. It was Alcibiades who talked the ruling hawks into the Sicilian campaign, and it was probably Alcibiades and his followers who defaced some Athenian shrines during several drunken farewell parties. Even before reaching Sicily Alcibiades had defected to Sparta. After a subsequent desertion to Persia he finally returned home a national hero (!) and was reelected to a generalship. Perhaps this was an extreme case, but that such conduct was not only tolerated but rewarded reveals much about the decline in formerly cherished values in late fifth-century Athens.

The History of the Peloponnesian War was written by Thucydides (ca. 460–ca. 400 BC), considered the greatest ancient Greek historian. He deemed the war pivotal, believing that his account would have permanent value because such conflicts would inevitably occur in later eras "so long as human nature remained the same." The war cost Athens its empire but total victory eluded the Spartans. Their rule proved too harsh for rebellious former Athenian satellites and they lacked the skills and manpower—depleted by the war—to administer and defend an empire. A resilient Athens regained its commercial leadership and reinstated a government that vacillated between an autocratic faction and the still powerful democrats. Surprisingly, Athenian culture thrived despite widespread ethical relativity. This was, after all, the age of Socrates, Plato, Aristotle, and Aristophanes.

THE CRITICS OF ATHENS: SOCRATES AND ARISTOPHANES

Unquestionably the most persistent questioner of Athenian values was the philosopher Socrates (469–399 BC), of whom we know little since he spoke and debated in public but never wrote; the only reports we have are from his pupils, principally Plato and Xenophon (ZEN-o-fon). An outspoken advocate of the acquisition of knowledge, Socrates saw that the end of the good life was happiness, which is not only the avoidance of the bitter fruits of ignorance, but the virtue that comes from knowledge. To know rightly, to make right choices, is virtue, he said, for it alone can satisfy reason.

Socrates spent much of his life posing embarrassing questions and demanding that Athenians examine their presumed virtue and their reasons for living as they did.

He was exceptionally popular with the young intellectuals who shared his views about the decay of the old values but less than cherished by self-serving citizens, especially the politicians. The latter finally had him arrested on trumped-up charges of impiety and corrupting the youth. In 399 BC a jury of his peers found him guilty on both counts and sentenced him to death. At his trial he described himself as the gadfly of Athens who insisted that the well-examined life was the only one worth living. Socrates tried to help others by asking them what they meant by the words they used—what do you mean by "justice"?—and then by a series of ever sharper questions finally proving that people did not know what they were talking about. His method was always the same: ask a question and arrive at a seemingly fruitful answer, paring away the portions that prove to be false, until the original answer is refined to truth by the process of logical, rational thought. This was the **dialectic**, the Socratic method, and it worked very well indeed—so well that frightened politicians used judicial murder to silence the "gadfly of Athens."

Another powerful critic of Athenian life and values was Aristophanes (ca. 448–380 BC), the foremost writer of Old Comedy (so called to differentiate it from later comedies based on situations rather than ideas). Socrates was vulnerable because he used the agora (marketplace) for his Socratic method but Aristophanes had the stage, where he could present his plays with impunity. A conservative aristocrat and opponent of the populist majority, Aristophanes used irony, satire, and caricature to ridicule the foibles of humankind, especially those humans who resided in Athens.

Comedy, like tragedy, originated in religious festivals honoring Dionysos. Added to the Greater Dionysia program in 486 BC, comedy became an essential part of the contest for best tragedy and best comedy. Comedy used the conventions of tragedy (masks, chorus) but actors also continually displayed the phallic symbol and chorus occasionally stopped the action to speak directly to the audience. The phallus was used, of course, in the Dionysian fertility rites but the origin of the stop-action choral interludes is unknown. Unlike the tragedians who preferred subtle implications, comic playwrights had every intention of impressing their views on the audience through dialogue and, especially, through barbed and biting choral commentary.

Aristophanes used the stage to attack living persons (such as Socrates and Euripides), but also to fight hypocrisy, corruption, stupidity, greed, and war. In the *Clouds* he depicted Socrates as a sophist who, for a fee, taught either right logic or wrong logic, which did not help matters at the trial, as Socrates pointed out during his *Apology*. The *Wasps* poked fun at lawyers, who could be found, he said, by lifting any rock, while the *Frogs* was a literary satire about Aeschylus and, especially, Euripides, of whom he was sharply critical. In the *Knights* he specified the characteristics of popular politicians: a horrible voice, bad breeding, and a vulgar manner.

Of his eleven extant plays *Lysistrata* best illustrates the theme that concerns us here: the futility of war, particularly the Peloponnesian War that ended Athens' most glorious days. An Athenian woman, Lysistrata, enlists the cooperation of all Greek women (including Spartans) in a simple but wonderfully effective scheme to stop warfare: no sex until the fighting stops. Given a choice between making love and making war, the warriors, with much breast-beating followed by some pitiful pleading, choose the blessings of peace and love.

The satirical comedies of Aristophanes dealt primarily, and brilliantly, with universal themes—stupidity, for example, never goes out of style—which accounts for their immense popularity throughout antiquity and the many performances in today's world. Some four centuries after the Golden Age the poet Antipater (an-TIP-a-ter) wrote the following epitaph:

> These are Aristophanes' marvelous plays,
> so often crowned with ivy from his deme.
> What Dionysian pages, and how clear
> That ringing voice of comedy edged with charm—
> Heroic dramatist fit to take on Greece,
> Hating the bad and making fun of it.
>
> Alistair Elliot, translator

STUDY QUESTIONS

1. The chorus of *Agamemnon* cautions against the evils of wealth. We, too, have a proverb about money as the root of evil. How have the Greeks developed since Aeschylus wrote of the earlier populace? How might Pericles have argued with our own proverb?
2. What similarities in terms of purpose and ideals do you see between this oration and Lincoln's "Gettysburg Address" (delivered when our own nation was undergoing the ordeal of a Civil War)? Are the ideals of either any less relevant today?

SUMMARY

The fifth century BC in Athens was truly astonishing. Brief but brilliant, the Golden Age began with the pride of victory over the Persians, with the triumph of democracy, and with the promise of the good life as revealed in the noble plays of Aeschylus. During the early years of Pericles' leadership Athenian citizens realized that good life about as much as it can ever be. It ended in a time of military defeat; a time when the dominant mood was self-serving individualism; a time when Athenians listened no longer to the voice of its most astute philosopher/critic while also ignoring the

serious issues in the comedies of Aristophanes.

The loftiest assertion of the human spirit in these exhausted times came at the very end with the trial of Socrates and a glimpse of the philosopher as hero. In the *Apology* he spoke to the jury as an urbane, civilized man, disdaining high-flown rhetoric on the one hand, and sentiment on the other. Instead, he speaks almost in a conversational tone about his own life and his devotion to his highest ideals for human conduct. The most poignant statement about integrity and justice comes after the vote that condemned him to death:

> And there are many other ways of avoiding death in every danger if a man is willing to say and to do anything. But, my friends, I think that it is a much harder thing to escape from wickedness than from death, for wickedness is swifter than death. And now I, who am old and slow, have been overtaken by the slower pursuer: and my accusers, who are clever and swift, have been overtaken by the swifter pursuer—wickedness. And now I shall go away, sentenced by you to death; and they will go away, sentenced by truth to wickedness and injustice. I abide by my penalty, they by theirs.

LITERARY SELECTION 2

Memorial Oration

Pericles (ca. 495–429 BC)

As you read this eloquent address, you should remind yourself of the questions about human aspirations raised in the plays of Aeschylus. In the *Agamemnon* Chorus railed against great wealth, insisting that the humble life was the best. In the *Eumenides* the question was whether justice should be dispensed by reason or by stern revenge within the family. The playwright examined the conflict between people and an absolute god who ruled through fear. Further questions in the Greek mind (and our own) could be: must the state protect itself with a standing army?; does a life of cultural pursuits weaken the state? Perhaps the most significant question for their time (and ours) is whether a democracy can function efficiently and effectively. The argument on the other hand is that an absolute government can operate quickly and efficiently, while in a democracy people talk so much that they rarely get anything done. Aristotle later put his finger squarely on the basic problem: "Democracy arises out of the notion that those who are equal in any respect are equal in all respects; because men are equally free, they claim to be absolutely equal" (from *Politics*).

This portion of Pericles' famous oration is taken from *The History of the Peloponnesian War* by Thucydides. Pericles made this address at the public funeral of some Athenian young men who had been killed in the war. Pericles surveyed the waiting throng and said:

Before I praise the dead, I should like to point out by what principles of action we rose to power, and under what institutions and through what manner of life our empire became great. For I conceive that such thoughts are not unsuited to the occasion, and that this numerous assembly of citizens and strangers may profitably listen to them.

Our form of government does not enter into rivalry with the institutions of others. We do not copy our neighbors, but are an example to them. It is true that we are called a democracy; for the administration is in the hands of the many and not of the few. But while the law secures equal justice to all alike in their private disputes, the claim of excellence is also recognized; and when a citizen is in any way distinguished, he is preferred to the public service, not as a matter of privilege, but as the reward of merit. Neither is poverty a bar, but a man may benefit his country whatever be the obscurity of his condition. There is no exclusiveness in our public life, and in our private intercourse we are not suspicious of one another, nor angry with our neighbor if he does what he likes; we do not put on sour looks at him, which though harmless are not pleasant. While we are thus unconstrained in our private intercourse, a spirit of reverence pervades our public acts: we are prevented from doing wrong by respect for authority and for the laws; having an especial regard to those which are ordained for the protection of the injured, as well as to these unwritten laws which bring upon the transgressor of them the reprobation of the general sentiment.

And we have not forgotten to provide for our weary spirits many relaxations from toil; we have regular games and sacrifices throughout the year; at home the style of our life is refined; and the delight which we daily feel in all these things helps to banish melancholy. Because of the greatness of our city the fruits of the whole earth flow in upon us; so that we enjoy the goods of other countries as freely as of our own.

Then again, our military training is in many respects superior to that of our adversaries. Our city is thrown open to the world; and we never expel a foreigner, or prevent him from seeing or learning anything of which the secret, if revealed to an enemy, might profit him. We rely not upon management of trickery, but upon our own hearts and hands. And in the matter of education whereas they from early youth are always undergoing laborious exercises which are to make them brave, we live at ease, and yet are equally ready to face the perils which they face . . . .

If, then, we prefer to meet danger with a light heart but without laborious training, and with a courage which is gained by habit and not enforced by law, are we not greatly the gainers? Since we do not anticipate the pain, although, when the hour comes, we can be as brave as those who never allow themselves to rest; and thus too our city is equally admirable in peace and in war. For we are lovers of the beautiful, yet simple in our tastes, and we cultivate the mind without loss of manliness. Wealth we employ, not for talk and ostentation, but when there is a real use for it. To avow poverty with us is no

disgrace; the true disgrace is in doing nothing to avoid it. An Athenian citizen does not neglect the State because he takes care of his own household; and even those of us who are engaged in business have a very fair idea of politics. We alone regard a man who takes no interest in public affairs, not as a harmless but as a useless character; and if few of us are originators, we are all sound judges, of a policy. The great impediment to action is, in our opinion, not discussion, but the want of that knowledge which is gained by discussion preparatory to action. For we have a peculiar power of thinking before we act, and of acting too; whereas other men are courageous from ignorance but hesitate upon reflection. And they are surely to be esteemed the bravest spirits, who, having the clearest sense both of the pains and the pleasures of life, do not on that account shrink from danger. In doing good, again we are unlike others; we make our friends by conferring, not by receiving favors. Now he who confers a favor is the firmer friend, because he would fain by kindness keep alive the memory of an obligation; but the recipient is colder in his feelings, because he knows that in requiting another's generosity he will not be winning gratitude, but only paying a debt. We alone do good to our neighbors not upon a calculation of interest, but in the confidence of freedom and in a frank and fearless spirit.

To sum up: I say that Athens is the school of Hellas, and that the individual Athenian in his own person seems to have the power of adapting himself to the most varied forms of action with the utmost versatility and grace. This is no passing and idle word, but truth and fact; and the assertion is verified by the position to which these qualities have raised the State. For in the hour of trial, Athens alone among her contemporaries is superior to the report of her. No enemy who comes against her is indignant at the reverses which he sustains at the hands of such a city; no subject complains that his masters are unworthy of him. And we shall assuredly not be without witnesses: there are mighty monuments of our power, which will make us the wonder of this and of succeeding ages; we shall not need the praises of Homer or of any other panegyrist, whose poetry may please for the moment although his representation of the facts will not bear the light of day. For we have compelled every land and every sea to open a path for our valor, and have everywhere planted eternal memorials of our friendship and of our enmity. Such is the city for whose sake these men nobly fought and died: they could not bear the thought that she might be taken from them; and every one of us who survive should gladly toil on her behalf.

Other Literary Selections

The plays discussed at some length are strongly recommended: *Agamemnon* and the *Eumenides* by Aeschylus, *Oedipus the King* by Sophocles, and *Lysistrata* by Aristophanes.

SUMMARY

The achievements of the individuals discussed in this chapter demonstrate what can happen when people have the freedom to excel in a society that values and rewards excellence. First and foremost, the Greeks towered over all other societies in that they thought and thought hard, thereby inventing both philosophy and theoretical science. The Eleatics, particularly Parmenides, saw that whatever was real must be permanent and unchanging, a position that challenged the idea of the individual as the ultimate reality. Democritos, on the other hand, postulated an atomic theory that confirmed the materialistic view of reality and the individual.

The passion for excellence spurred achievements that enriched both the artist and society. With his *Oresteia* Aeschylus won the ivy wreath while challenging his fellow citizens with a model of how true justice should work in a court of law. But when Sophocles wrote *Oedipus the King* it was time to alert the populace to what hubris could call down on a man such as Oedipus or a city such as Athens. *The Trojan Women* won a first prize for Euripides while mercilessly exposing the ethical degeneration of the once heroic Greeks. The decline had begun after the death of Pericles and accelerated as the Peloponnesian War dragged on and on.

The Post-Periclean decline was identified and satirized by Aristophanes, whose plays after *Lysistrata* gradually subsided into amusing and popular comedies designed only to entertain a city no longer avid for enlightenment. One can only speculate as to what might have been had the Athenians and the Spartans listened to Lysistrata and ended the war with singing and dancing. The trial and death of Socrates in 399 BC signified the end of the postscript to the Golden Age and the beginning of a world that was to become less and less interested in freedom, truth, and justice.

But we should not overreact. The use of terms such as "degeneration" and "decline" are undeniably appropriate when describing Greece after the Golden Age. However, this was still an exceptional culture that, for centuries to come, was superior to all others. Late classicism and the Hellenistic age are notable for the achievements of Plato, Aristotle, Euclid, Archimedes, and Alexander the Great, to mention only a few celebrated names.

CULTURE AND HUMAN VALUES

In terms of the culture-epoch theory (as discussed in the Prologue), the Periclean Age was the golden moment of a period of balance that extended from the Greek classical period to the beginning of the long decline of the Roman Empire (ca. 480 BC–AD 180). Whatever its flaws, and they were abundant, this Graeco-Roman epoch was distinguished, on the whole, by a rational approach to civilized living in the secular world of the here and now. This achievement is even more remarkable when one considers what followed classical civilization, namely the decline and fall of Rome and the ensuing chaotic times of the early Middle Ages.

A balance was struck during the Periclean age between the rights of the individual and the welfare of the group. An idealistic society that firmly believed in what people *should* be, the Athenians advocated freedom, beauty, truth, and justice as the necessary foundations for the art of civilized living. From that time to ours Athenian achievements in the arts, government, and philosophy testify to the high goals these remarkable people set for themselves.

(NOTE: See summary of Greek culture and values on pp. 123–4.)

CHAPTER 6

Greece: From Hellenic to Hellenistic World

Had Greek civilization never existed . . . we would never have become fully conscious, which is to say that we would never have become, for better or worse, fully human.

W. H. Auden

"The name Greek is no longer a mark of race, but of outlook, and is accorded to those who share our culture rather than our blood," said the Athenian orator Isocrates in 380 BC. By then the Greek city-states no longer dominated the eastern Mediterranean but Greek culture continued its expansion throughout the Mediterranean and even into the vast Persian Empire. What caused the decline of the Greek city-states? Their fervor and pride had enabled them to rout the far larger forces of the Persian Empire because they were, for the first and last time, united against a common foe. Afterwards their pride and belligerent independence caused endless squabbles, culminating in the disastrous war between Athens and Sparta plus assorted allies on both sides. The Persian wars (490–479 BC) inspired confidence but the internecine Peloponnesian War (431–404 BC) left despair and decay in its wake. Not one city-state was strong enough to take control, making a federation impossible. Sparta dominated for a time, followed by Thebes, Athens[1] and Corinth, but always with the tireless Persians in the background manipulating events through bribery and coercion.

In the middle of the fourth century BC, in a backwater of Greek civilization, King Philip of Macedonia began his move toward an empire that was to unite all of Greece. Military strategy achieved some of his objectives but most were realized through a series of wily political and diplomatic moves, accomplished despite repeated warnings by the Athenian orator Demosthenes (De-MOSS-th-neez). Upon Philip's assassination in 336 BC, his brilliant young son, Alexander (see chapter opener opposite), a student of Aristotle's, became king. In one extended and remarkable

campaign Alexander brought Greece, Egypt, all of the Persian Empire (including the territory of modern Turkey), and lands as far east as India, into one vast empire. In doing so, he disseminated Greek culture throughout that immense territory.

Alexander apparently intended to establish what amounted to a Greek "league of nations." The conquered peoples would retain a certain amount of autonomy and all of their customs. Greek language and culture would be added throughout the empire so that the entire known world could benefit from Greek accomplishments. Alexander died at the age of thirty-three bemoaning the lack of new worlds to conquer, but he may have been referring to cultural, as well as geographical, conquest

To further his dream of a universal Greek culture Alexander had established many new cities—such as Antioch in Syria and about a dozen Alexandrias stretching as far east as Bactria (present-day Afghanistan)—in which he built libraries, museums, and other centers of civilization. The Alexandria constructed in Egypt supplanted Athens as the cultural center and largest city of antiquity. Established by Ptolemy I (TAHL-uh-me), the first Greek ruler of Egypt, the famous Library at Alexandria was the wonder of the ancient world with over 700,000 manuscripts by Julius Caesar's time (first century BC). Remnants of Alexander's empire survived until 146 BC, when Rome finally conquered the last Achaean League, but Hellenistic art and philosophy were influential throughout most of the Roman period, a span of some seven centuries.

"Hellenism" is the name of the civilization disseminated throughout the Mediterranean and the Near East in the wake of Alexander's conquests. This was the first great international culture of the West. The language was Greek and the milieu was the city, particularly all those cities named Alexandria. The politics were aristocratic but there was always a measure of participatory democracy. A person's ethnic origins were virtually incidental because the culture was remarkably universal. To become Greek was to be

---

Opposite Leochares(?), Portrait bust of Alexander the Great. Ca. 330–325 BC. Marble. Acropolis Museum, Athens. Photo: Scala, Florence.

Alexander, history's greatest military genius, conquered and Hellenized the then known world in just twelve years.

1. After ineffectual Spartan rule, Athens underwent a reign of terror under Critias and the Thirty Tyrants, followed by a brief civil war. Democracy was restored in 401 BC. It was the insecure government of a reestablished Athens that tried and condemned Socrates in 399 BC.

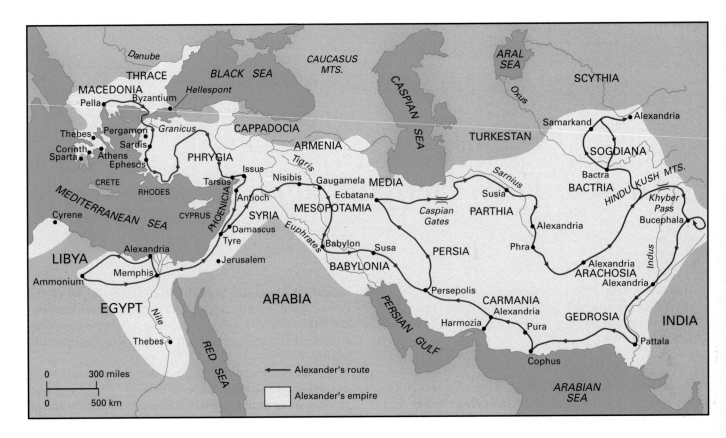

Map 6.1 Alexander's Empire, 323 BC.

truly educated, the real key to participation in the era's international civilization. Models for educated people throughout the culture were the scholars and scientist-mathematicians of Alexandria and the philosophers Plato and Aristotle, who epitomized the Greek characteristic of thinking and thinking hard.

PLATO, 427–347 BC

Born two years after the death of Pericles, Plato was a young man when Athens lost the Peloponnesian War. He was an ardent student of Socrates. No one can distinguish between the thought of Plato and that of Socrates in Plato's early writings, for most are dialogues with Socrates the principal speaker. Plato probably included much of his own thought in these dialogues, or perhaps he reported the Socratic ideas with which he agreed. Only in the latter part of his life did he speak entirely for himself, as in the *Laws*.

· Plato's thought about that-which-is-real is perhaps his most significant contribution to world philosophy. He began with the work of Pythagoras and the Eleatic philosophers by accepting permanence and unchangeability as the basic criteria for reality, and the mind as the only way to a knowledge of the real. Thus he denied the reality of all the sense-apparent objects around us: trees, animals, humans, or even abstract concepts such as love or justice. He regarded all sense-apparent things as shadows of the Real, made imperfect by an alliance with material stuff, which is illustrated in "The **Allegory** of the Cave" (p. 89).

Reality

Reality, for Plato, consisted of Ideas (or Forms) of all basic things, Forms that exist beyond the grasp of the senses or even the mind. These Ideas have no physical attributes or material substance; they are the "pure form" of all things we see and know in our earthly existence. These Forms are not, however, ideas-in-the-minds-of-people. Trying to imagine the perfect tree or chair has nothing to do with Plato's Forms. His Ideas[2] exist, are unchanging, and are the source of all things: the eternal Forms of everything in the universe. But the individual thing—what we perceive—is always a distorted or impure shadow of its Form. Because it is involved with matter it is at least one step removed from its Idea.

We can illustrate this by assuming that we have commissioned an architect to design a building. After prolonged wrestling with design problems, the architect suddenly has a flash, a mental image of a perfectly completed structure. "Eureka!" she cries. "This is *it*!" She rushes to the drawing board. But changes have to be made that affect the original concept: practical problems involving heating, cooling, lights, and service areas. The final blueprints reveal a building already substantially different from the original idea. Construction begins. A strike forces the substitution of one material for another. Costs go over budget, necessitating space cutbacks and less expensive finishing materials.

2. "Ideas" and "Forms" are used interchangeably because it takes both words to approximate Plato's conception.

Finally the building is complete, existing in its material form for people to use.

When was the structure most real? One can argue that it was most real when it was pure idea and that it became less authentic with every compromise in structure or materials. Certainly the architect sees the final product as a mere shadow of her original vision. For the moment, let us accept this as true: the physical building is but a clumsy manifestation of the "real" idea.

Now, assume that the architect is an eternal creator and the building the universe. The ideas for all things existed in this entity's conception and these Forms exist forever. But they are altered and distorted as they are mixed with material substance: animal, vegetable, mineral. Now, perhaps, we have Plato's belief about true reality, but we must take one more step and subtract the creator. Though Plato spoke of the gods—and sometimes of God—he did not believe that a creator had originated the Forms; they had existed eternally.

This Platonic version of reality had philosophical repercussions, of which the most significant is the separation of the soul from the body. That is, the belief that a soul that relates to the realm of the essences is imprisoned by a base, material body. This has been a major issue in Christian belief. Augustine, for example, borrowed heavily from Platonism in formulating the first unified Christian theology. Specifically, Plato believed that there was a hierarchy in the realm of ideas that started at the bottom with the essences of plants and animals and ended at the top with the idea of the Good. This is reflected in the image of light or fire encountered in "The Allegory of the Cave." Early Christian theology converted this Good into a concept of God as the highest and best ideal and the goal toward which all Christians should strive.

Arts and Ethics

His concern for the soul led Plato to ponder the role of poetry, music, and the other arts—especially music—in Athenian life. He believed, as did others, that music influenced the will in three ways. It could (1) provoke action; (2) help strengthen character (or conversely, it could undermine it); and (3) suspend normal will power and thus make people unaware of their actions. The emphasis upon ethical imperatives led to the Greek doctrine of **ethos,** with Plato as its most eloquent advocate.

The doctrine of ethos (EE-thos; Gk., *ethos*, "character") is concerned with the ethical, ideal, or universal element in an art work, as distinguished from its emotional appeal. (The Greek word for the latter is *pathos*, which means "suffering.") The doctrine of ethos brought external order into music's domain, for Plato saw an analogy between movements of the soul and musical progressions. He therefore felt that music must transcend mere amusement and set a goal of harmonic education and perfection of the soul.

ALEXANDRIAN SCIENCE

Euclid (fl. 300 BC): The acclaimed geometer whose *Elements* (of geometry) was not challenged until a non-Euclidian geometry was devised in the 19th century. Probably instructed by a student of Plato's, he founded and taught at a school of mathematics in Alexandria, Egypt, during the reign of Ptolemy I Soter (323–283 BC).

Aristarchus of Samos (ar-i-STAHR-kus; ca. 310–230 BC): Originated a sun-centered world system that Copernicus would rely on 1,900 years later to develop his own heliocentric system.

Archimedes (ar-kuh-MEE-dez; ca. 298–212 BC): Working in Egypt and his native city of Syracuse, he was antiquity's greatest mathematician. He developed fundamental theorems on the gravity centers of plane and solid figures and the weight of a body immersed in a liquid (Archimedes' Principle). He improved the catapult, and invented the compound pulley—a water raising device known as Archimedes' Screw—and a burning mirror to defend Syracuse against the Romans. "Give me a lever long enough," he once boasted, "and a place to stand and I can move the earth."

Eratosthenes of Cyrene (air-uh-TAHS-thuh-neez; ca. 276–195 BC): Best known for his amazingly close calculation of the earth's circumference, he served as chief librarian of the museum in Alexandria, Egypt.

Music's primary role was therefore a pedagogical one that helped build character and promote ethical behavior. The practice of music was necessarily public rather than private, an affair of state rather than of the home. Every melody, rhythm, and musical instrument had its unique effect on the ethical nature of humankind, and therefore upon the ethics of the state. Good music promoted the welfare of the state whereas bad music was harmful to the individual and to society.

All Athenian citizens received musical training until they were thirty and all, regardless of age, sang in a chorus on proper social, political, and religious occasions. Music education was mandatory and universal but prohibited for slaves because it was a mark of nobility and of education reserved for free Athenians.

In the *Republic,* Plato recognized that there should be a balance between music and gymnastics in education but felt that music should precede and dominate gymnastics. Music first ennobles the soul, after which the soul should then build up the body. He included dance (as well as wrestling) in gymnastics and combined poetry with music, because performers usually recited or sang poetry with musical accompaniment. Plato insisted that the latter two should be subject to state control, that is, censorship. By advocating censorship of music and poetry he implicitly acknowledged the power of these arts. Like all Athenians, he had attended performances of tragedies by Aeschylus, Sophocles, and Euripides. One can imagine the waves of powerful emotions that swept over the 18,000 spectators, emotions so intense as to be almost palpable. No wonder Plato was concerned that music and poetry should educate the young to take pleasure in the right things.

Plato and Aristotle considered the Dorian and Phrygian modes (two of the various Greek musical pitch organizations) ethically superior to the other modes (Lydian and Mixolydian), but, given their preference for rigor and austerity, the Dorian might be considered preeminent because it was strong and dignified. Phrygian was ecstatic and religious and exerted a positive influence on the soul. Lydian was considered piercing and suitable only for lamentations; Mixolydian was intimate and lascivious.[3]

These ethical doctrines also applied to the two national instruments. Restrained and elegant, the lyre was seen as proper for the performance of Dorian melodies. The aulos (see p. 71) was strong and powerful and thus particularly suitable for the emotional intensity of Phrygian melodies. This intensity made the aulos the chosen instrument of Greek comedies and, especially, tragedies.

In sum, the doctrine of ethos was a manifestation of the cult of Apollo and was designed to control the Dionysian power of the aulos and music, poetry, dance and, by extension, tragedy. Tragedy was, of course, an ingenious combination of all these elements. As noted earlier, it was probably the dramatic performances themselves that convinced Plato of the need for imposing rational control over them. But it was in the *Republic* that Plato expanded the idea of rational control to society itself.

The *Republic*

Because the Athenian democracy had executed Socrates, Plato sought a definition of true justice, one that would rise above his ironic description of a democracy, which is "a charming form of government, full of variety and disorder and dispensing a sort of equality to equals and unequals alike."

Plato was deeply committed to the idea that all citizens had an obligation to participate in government: "The punishment which the wise suffer who refuse to take part in the government, is to live under the government of worse men." The dialogue called the *Republic* provides a comprehensive view of the Socratic-Platonic ideas of human personality and the nature of government. The *Republic* is

not Plato's formation of an ideal state (or Utopia, as Sir Thomas More later called it); it is, instead, an extended dialogue between Socrates and his students about the nature of justice. Not a problem when someone lives alone on an island, justice becomes a critical issue in a populous city-state composed of rich and poor, saints and scoundrels, masters and slaves. So in the *Republic*, discussants formulate a picture of a luxurious city-state (that goes beyond minimal human needs) as they seek the elusive quality—justice—that exists to a greater or lesser degree in the interrelationships of human beings.

Plato believed that men and women were dominated by one of three qualities: appetite, spirit, or intellect. So he divided people into three classes of metal: iron, silver, and gold. Those driven primarily by appetite, iron, were to be the workers, including all who followed commercial pursuits. The silver, people of spirit, formed the auxiliaries or soldier class, who had no property or money to distract them from their duty: protection from foreign enemies and maintenance of order at home. The men and women of intellect, the guardian class of gold, were educated to become the stewards of the state, the rulers, the philosopher-kings.

Education was the key to the formation of this state. The lowest class would receive whatever education they could pick up on their own. The soldier or auxiliary group would train in gymnastics (to give them strong bodies, fit for their duties) and music and poetry (to make them sensitive and considerate). Socrates used the example of the good watchdog to illustrate his point, for such an animal is gentle toward the master and known friends but fierce toward enemies. The soldier class should have such a nature, with their spirits tempered by the study of music. The guardian class would have all of the education of the soldiers as well as studies in reasoning—emphasizing mathematics—and philosophy. After many years of formal education, they were to be subjected to a series of trials and temptations testing their strength of character and ability to make decisions that contributed to the greater good of the state. Selected from the best specimens of both sexes, these educated executives were to be highly original scientific thinkers and persons of impeccable integrity. Finally, at about age fifty, the guardians would be called upon to govern the city as philosopher-kings.

Socrates (as leader of the *Republic* dialogue) advocates strict control of the arts, particularly stories, poetry, and music, so that girls and boys would be educated in a beautiful environment. The highest good would enter into their souls because they were exposed to only the best and most morally uplifting of the arts. This is, once again, the doctrine of ethos. (The idea that the state should control—censor—the arts to maintain high moral standards has provoked arguments on both sides that continue, without resolution, to this day.)

Material possessions would neither encumber nor influence the soldiers or the guardians. Wealth was

---

3. A rough approximation of the Dorian mode can be made by playing the white keys of the piano from *e* to the next *e* above or below. Phrygian is *d* to *d*, Lydian *c* to *c*, and Mixolydian *b* to *b*.

banished as was poverty. Socrates was convinced that wealth would spoil a person's character and that vested interests affected judgment. On the other hand, poverty could break the human spirit and render men and women unfit to be public servants as soldiers or guardians.

By far the largest class, the men and women of iron included workers, farmers, sailors, artisans, merchants, professionals, and entrepreneurs. Their possessions were expressly their own; property held in common was explicitly forbidden. Plato's *Republic* was not communistic. The two small classes of guardians and soldiers—servants of the state—were denied property ownership for economic reasons: to eliminate conflicts between self-interest and public duty by putting a chasm between political power and financial influence. Everyone who did not serve the state (the bulk of the population) worked as individuals of varying degrees of wealth, from a farmer or worker to the owner of a merchant fleet.

At first glance the iron-silver-gold classes of the *Republic* seem as structured as the caste system still prevalent in today's India. But "caste" means something people are born into, above which they can never rise. Most societies have class structures in which the ease or difficulty of vertical movement depends on the rigidity of the society or nation in question. The opportunity for moving across class lines—up or down—was considerably greater in the *Republic* than it is in, say, Britain.

Socrates believed that heredity was a powerful force in shaping a person's character and abilities, and was therefore convinced that most people would find their rightful place in their parents' class. Some would be unfit for this, while others had the ability and ambition to rise above their origins, even from iron to gold. The authorities could identify any girl or boy as worthy of preparation for the highest responsibilities because class mobility was necessary in a state dependent upon an elite of philosopher-kings.

And where does justice come in? Each citizen, of whatever class, has theoretically found a proper niche in society with little inclination or opportunity to interfere with the rights of others. Potters make pots and merchants make profits, police keep the peace, soldiers guard the state, the rulers govern fairly and justly. Citizens are guaranteed equality of educational opportunities irrespective of class or gender. The people of iron may indulge their appetite for money and possessions, those of silver may gratify their spirit with honor and glory, and the men and women of gold may exercise their intellect to the fullest in the responsible governance of the state. Based on the principle of specialization of function according to vocation, justice has been established on a grand scale.

Did Plato believe that his theoretical city-state could really work? Think back to the hypothetical case of the architect and her building. Plato's *Republic* and the completed blueprints for the structure are roughly analogous, but both are already one step removed from the original conceptions of perfect justice and a perfect building. If constructing the building requires compromises in materials and design, what might the problems be if we tried to construct a complex human society? Plato had no illusions. At one point in the *Republic* he introduces the story of a young shepherd boy, "The Ring of Gyges." After Gyges discovers a ring that makes him invisible (and thus not accountable for his actions), he embarks on a successful career of robbery and murder that leads him to the richest and most powerful position in his native land.

Though the "Ring of Gyges" may or may not be an extreme example, Plato believed that no normal human being could maintain an intact virtue when guaranteed immunity from detection. If no one knew what we were doing, would we lower our standards? Do we ever act out of self-interest rather than out of duty? Plato saw that narrow self-interest, greed, envy, and other human failings would be potentially fatal problems in any republic, no matter how perfectly constructed.

As for the nature of justice, Plato and Socrates take the middle ground, the Golden Mean, ever a Greek ideal. Intellect should be in control, so that appetite would be curbed to the point of temperance, spirit limited to the point of courage, and intellect finally become wisdom. Justice would emerge when these conditions were met, meaning that behavior would be ethical and scrupulous and therefore just. These qualities—temperance, courage, wisdom, and justice—were the great Platonic virtues. Christians later added faith, hope, and love to establish the seven cardinal virtues. The difference between the Platonic intellectual virtues and the Christian emotional and spiritual virtues illustrates a fundamental distinction between the aspirations of the two cultures.

ARISTOTLE, 384–322 BC

Aristotle's background differed considerably from that of Plato. Though he studied with Plato at the Academy, his answers to the important questions are quite different, perhaps because of the dissimilarities in youthful experience. Aristotle's father was a physician who was called, early in Aristotle's life, to serve the court of King Philip II at Pella. Perhaps Aristotle's inquiring mind about sense-apparent things, his interest in experimentation, his concern with change rather than permanence, and his refusal to accept the mind alone as a guide to truth came from his father's interest in similar things. In fact, exactly as Plato's thought had its source in Pythagoras and the Eleatics, Aristotle's mature conclusions are rooted in the Ionians.

Aristotle's was one of the most extraordinary minds of all time. The keenness of his intellect, the range of his interests and studies, and the staggering amount of information and speculation in his enormous collection of writings rouse the admiration and awe of all who read his work. Not the least of his distinctions is that he tutored the youthful Prince Alexander of Macedonia (see p. 83) and must have greatly influenced that monarch's brilliant career. After this period of tutoring, Aristotle moved to Athens and founded his own school, the Lyceum. Along with Plato, he was to shape the course of Western thought.

As we have seen, Plato's quest for the permanent, the Idea or Form, rather than the actuality of experience, led him into a dualism that separates form from substance, soul from body. By contrast, Aristotle, who was profoundly interested in the changing life about him, tried to reconcile the two. The difference can be expressed as follows. When Plato considered the state he wrote the *Republic* and the *Laws*, which were theoretical constructions of an imaginary state. When Aristotle pondered the state, he and his students collected and studied the constitutions of 158 Greek city-states as a prelude to writing the work known as *Politics*.

The extent of Aristotle's writings is astonishing. His speculations range from logic and the proper process of thought through biology, physics, metaphysics, ethics, law and politics, and literary criticism. Only two of his ideas concern us here: one is his view of the nature of reality; the other is how life should be lived because of that view.

For Aristotle, the abstract Idea or Form of Plato's teaching could not be separated from the matter or substance by which it was known; the two somehow had to come together as different aspects of the same thing. Thus Plato's "ideal" chair did not exist for Aristotle apart from the actual wood and metal that composed it. A brick is a brick only when the "idea" brick and the clay composing it come together; then the brick is "real." The brick may then become the matter or substance of another "idea," and become house; and the house, in turn, may be substance to the idea of town or city. At every stage, the union of substance and form, of matter and idea, is necessary to constitute "reality"; and there is a progression, upward or downward. The substance that Plato is not concerned with becomes for Aristotle the basis for higher, more complex realities when it is informed by idea or form. Such is the direction of the difference between the two men; Plato's static view becomes more dynamic in Aristotle's teaching.

Aristotle accounts for the process of change (which Plato never satisfactorily explains) in his theory of enteleche (en-TEL-uh-key), which consists of the prefix *en* ("within") and the *telos* ("purpose") and *echaia* ("having"). Thus it is in the nature of things that they have an inner goal, a destiny, to fulfill: the seed becomes plant, for that is its enteleche; the clay becomes brick for its enteleche, but clay can become pot for a different enteleche. The upward movement through increasing complexity is the enteleche of the universe. The cause of the process, drawing all things toward their own perfection, is God, the First Cause, who moved all things without being moved—in Aristotle's phrase, the "Unmoved Mover."

The motive power of Aristotle's God is apparently not love, as Christianity might contend, nor will, as Judaism might argue. Rather there seems to be a cosmic yearning toward perfection, and that perfection is, by definition, God. Aristotle's customary view of the necessity for the union of both form and matter to constitute reality here breaks down (or more kindly, transcends itself?), for such a God must be pure form, with none of the inherent weakness or imperfection of the material world.[4] God is the only instance of pure form separated from matter.

And what about the good life? Aristotle was no ascetic, and he matter-of-factly assumed that everyone had enough material resources to enable them to choose among reasonable alternatives. Given adequate wealth, what does one do? The enteleche of which Aristotle speaks implies that there is a goal, or end, reached when a person or thing is functioning properly—that is, in accord with its inner purposes. When conditions permit, one can attain a highest good—what later philosophers would call a *summum bonum* (Lat. "greatest good"). Thus the enteleche of humans leads them to their own *summum bonum*, the worthy and proper fulfillment of their humanity. Because the human being is, for Aristotle, the "rational animal," that fulfillment is the life of reason. When people are living harmoniously, using their minds, functioning in family and state (for Aristotle also calls us political, that is, social animals), they have achieved their greatest good. Such a life has many implications, two of which concern us here.

One is that such a life will be one of virtue, or excellence. But virtues may fail by being deficient, or by being carried to excess. What one should desire is the middle ground between extremes. Courage, for instance, is a virtue; but deficiency may pervert it into cowardice, or a no less perverted excess becomes foolhardiness or rashness. Generosity is also a virtue but excessive generosity becomes prodigality and wastefulness, while its deficiency becomes stinginess. To mediate between extremes, to discover the "Golden Mean"—which is relative and not an absolute matter—is to achieve virtue.

The other implication, then, is that the finest use of reason is in a life of contemplation. People must have time to read, to talk, to think about the whole idea of excellence, that they may achieve the high-mindedness that is their *summum bonum* (the word that Aristotle uses is "magnanimity"). Such a quality is not to be won in the heat and dust of the marketplace. For although good people can perform their duties as members of society, the life of action cannot compare with the life of contemplation.

---

4. "Such then is the principle upon which depend the heavens and the world of nature. And its life (i.e., the principle, or God) is like the best that we enjoy, and enjoy but for a short time; for it is ever in this state, which we cannot be. And if then God is always in that good state in which we sometimes are, this compels our wonder; and if in a better state, then this compels it yet more. And God is in a better state. We say therefore, that God is a living being, eternal, most good; so that life and a continual eternal existence belong to God; for this is God." (Aristotle, *Metaphysics*, XII, 7.)

THE GREEK PHILOSOPHICAL LEGACY

Plato and Aristotle are generally considered the most influential philosophers in the history of Western culture. Plato's search for knowledge had an astonishing range and depth, embracing physics, metaphysics, mathematics, ethics, politics, religion, literature, music, and art. His influence on Aristotle is incalculable; surely this is the most remarkable teacher-student combination in human history.

Their answers might vary, sometimes considerably, but Plato and Aristotle asked many of the same questions: What are the moral, ethical, and legal bases of life? How, in a democracy, can we define the public good? Where is the line between protecting the individual and guarding the community? What is the good life and how may one achieve it?

Aristotle's influence has perhaps been greatest in the field of logic, particularly his invention of the **syllogism** as a tool for deductive reasoning. That the syllogism was a less than perfect tool for logical deduction was not Aristotle's fault. As Plato's greatest student, he stood alone at the end of the golden age of Greek philosophy. Aristotle followed Plato but not for 2,000 years did anyone follow Aristotle. For centuries he was the unquestioned authority—the philosopher—of medieval scholars, especially the Scholastic philosophers of the High Middle Ages.

Plato's influence was particularly strong during the formation of the early Christian church's theology. There have been revivals of Platonism during the Italian Renaissance, throughout the Age of Reason, and into our own century. That he was also among the finest literary artists of Western civilization is a whole other topic. Perhaps Alfred North Whitehead (1861–1947), the British philosopher and mathematician, best summarized Plato's contributions with his oft-quoted remark: "The safest general characterization of the European philosophical tradition is that it consists of a series of footnotes to Plato."

Plato's *Apology*

Socrates was tried in 399 BC before a generally hostile jury of 501 citizens on vague charges of impropriety toward the gods and corruption of the young. Long regarded as a suspicious character because of his relentless questioning of fellow Athenians, Socrates, due to a general amnesty, could not be charged for any offenses prior to the defeat of Athens in 404 BC. The unspoken charges were: (1) being the teacher of Alcibiades the traitor (interpreted as a corrupter of youth); (2) associating with the Thirty Tyrants (viewed as possible collaboration); (3) accepting money for teaching argumentation (mistakenly taking him for a sophist); (4) causing political and intellectual unrest. In Plato's account of the trial, Socrates cheerfully admits to

causing unrest, contending that the gods had commanded him to search into himself and other men to find the truth. This trial is his apology (or "defense") for his philosophical life. The recommended translation is by F. J. Church and R. D. Cummings.

STUDY QUESTIONS

1. Explain the doctrine of ethos and how it worked in Greek education, society, and the arts. Are there any modern parallels? Some claim, for example, that certain kinds of popular music are "satanic" or that it "corrupts the young." In the 1920s and 1930s the accusations were that jazz (swing, dance music) was sinful and corrupted the listeners and dancers. Similar charges have been aimed at rock. Are any of these charges based on objective facts? Is the music to blame or something else? Who makes these charges and what impels them to do so?
2. Plato's concept of reality is based on a static universe while Aristotle's thinking involves an ever-changing universe, which is essentially the difference between the ideas of the Eleatics and the Ionians.
   a. Explain the differences between the ideas of the two philosophers concerning the nature of reality.
   b. How much did Plato and Aristotle believe one could know of reality?
   c. What, for Aristotle, guides the process of change?

LITERARY SELECTION 3

Republic
Plato

The *Republic* is discussed on pages 86–7. The following excerpt is from the translation by F. M. Cornford.

Book VII

The Allegory of the Cave

Next, said I, here is a parable to illustrate the degrees in which our nature may be enlightened or unenlightened. Imagine the condition of men living in a sort of cavernous chamber underground, with an entrance open to the light and a long passage all down the cave.[5] Here they have been from childhood, chained by the leg and also by the neck, so that they cannot move and can see only what is in front of them, because the chains will not let them turn their heads. At some distance higher up is the light of a fire burning behind them; and between the   10

5. The length of the "way in" (*eisodos*) to the chamber where the prisoners sit is an essential feature, explaining why no daylight reaches them.

prisoners and the fire is a track[6] with a parapet built along it, like the screen at a puppet-show, which hides the performers while they show their puppets over the top.

I see, said he.

Now behind this parapet imagine persons carrying along various artificial objects, including figures of men and animals in wood or stone or other materials, which project above the parapet. Naturally, some of these persons will be talking, others silent.[7]

It is a strange picture, he said, and a strange sort of prisoners.   20

Like ourselves, I replied; for in the first place prisoners so confined would have seen nothing of themselves or of one another, except the shadows thrown by the fire-light on the wall of the Cave facing them, would they?

Not if all their lives they had been prevented from moving their heads.

And they would have seen as little of the objects carried past.   30

Of course.

Now, if they could talk to one another, would they not suppose that their words referred only to those passing shadows which they saw?[8]

Necessarily.

And suppose their prison had an echo from the wall facing them? When one of the people crossing behind them spoke, they could only suppose that the sound came from the shadow passing before their eyes.

No doubt.   40

In every way, then, such prisoners would recognize as reality nothing but the shadows of those artificial objects.

Inevitably.

Now consider what would happen if their release from the chains and the healing of their unwisdom should come about in this way. Suppose one of them set free and forced suddenly to stand up, turn his head, and walk with eyes lifted to the light; all these movements would be painful, and he would be too dazzled to make out the objects whose shadows he had   50
been used to see. What do you think he would say, if someone told him that what he had formerly seen was meaningless illusion, but now, being somewhat nearer to reality and turned towards more real objects, he was getting a truer view? Suppose further that he were

shown the various objects being carried by and were made to say, in reply to questions, what each of them was. Would he not be perplexed and believe the objects now shown him to be not so real as what he formerly saw?   60

Yes, not nearly so real.

And if he were forced to look at the fire-light itself, would not his eyes ache, so that he would try to escape and turn back to the things which he could see distinctly, convinced that they really were clearer than these other objects now being shown to him?

Yes.

And suppose someone were to drag him away forcibly up the steep and rugged ascent and not let him go until he had hauled him out into the sunlight, would   70
he not suffer pain and vexation at such treatment, and, when he had come out into the light, find his eyes so full of its radiance that he could not see a single one of the things that he was now told were real?

Certainly he would not see them all at once.

He would need, then, to grow accustomed before he could see things in that upper world. At first it would be easiest to make out shadows, and then the images of men and things reflected in water, and later on the things themselves. After that, it would be easier to   80
watch the heavenly bodies and the sky itself by night, looking at the light of the moon and stars rather than the Sun and the Sun's light in the day-time.

Yes, surely.

Last of all, he would be able to look at the Sun and contemplate its nature, not as it appears when reflected in water or any alien medium, but as it is in itself in its own domain.

No doubt.

And now he would begin to draw the conclusion that   90
it is the Sun that produces the seasons and the course of the year and controls everything in the visible world, and moreover is in a way the cause of all that he and his companions used to see.

Clearly he would come at last to that conclusion.

Then if he called to mind his fellow prisoners and what passed for wisdom in his former dwelling-place, he would surely think himself happy in the change and be sorry for them. They may have had a practice of honoring and commending one another, with prizes for   100
the man who had the keenest eye for the passing shadows and the best memory for the order in which they followed or accompanied one another, so that he could make a good guess as to which was going to come next. Would our released prisoner be likely to covet those prizes or to envy the men exalted to honor and power in the Cave? Would he not feel like Homer's Achilles, that he would far sooner "be on earth as a hired servant in the house of a landless man" or endure anything rather than go back to his old beliefs and live in   110
the old way?

Yes, he would prefer any fate to such a life.

Now imagine what would happen if he went down again to take his former seat in the Cave. Coming suddenly out of the sunlight, his eyes would be filled with darkness. He might be required once more to

---

6. The track crosses the passage into the cave at right angles, and is above the parapet built along it.

7. A modern Plato would compare his Cave to a movie theatre where the audience watched the play of shadows thrown by the film passing before a light at their backs. The film itself is only an image of "real" things and events in the world outside the cinema. Instead of film, Plato has to employ the clumsier apparatus of a procession of artificial objects carried on their heads by persons who are merely part of the machinery, providing for the movement of the objects and the sounds whose echo the prisoners hear. The parapet prevents these persons' shadows from being cast on the wall of the Cave.

8. Adam's text and interpretation. The prisoners, having seen nothing but shadows, cannot think their words refer to the objects carried past behind their backs. For them shadows (images) are the only realities.

deliver his opinion on those shadows, in competition with the prisoners who had never been released, while his eyesight was still dim and unsteady; and it might take some time to become used to the darkness. They would laugh at him and say that he had gone up only to come back with his sight ruined; it was worth no one's while even to attempt the ascent. If they could lay hands on the man who was trying to set them free and lead them up, they would kill him.[9]
120

Yes, they would.

Aristotle's *Poetics*

Aristotle's *Poetics* is a critical examination of the nature of art and what constitutes good art. Specifically, the treatise is directed to the problems of poetry in the writing of tragedy, which Aristotle feels is the highest form of art. With no word for fine art, the Greek term for art is *techne*, which also translates as "craft" or "skill." Art is therefore the "making" of a thing, which in its highest form is crafted with exceptional skill. The *Poetics* is the first clear statement in the history of **aesthetics** correlating the experience of a work of art with the skill of making the work itself.

For Aristotle, all art is an imitation of nature, and tragedy is

the imitation of an action that is serious and also, as having magnitude, complete in itself; in language with pleasurable accessories, each kind brought in separately in the parts of the work; in a dramatic, not a narrative form; with incidents arousing pity and fear, wherewith to accomplish a catharsis of such emotions.

The theoretical perfect plot of a tragedy must have a single issue, which should be resolved within a twenty-four-hour day. Further, a good man will be reduced from happiness to misery because of some great error on his part, his so-called "fatal flaw."

The six elements of a tragedy are:

Plot (Fable). The action—what happens.
Character. Moral qualities of the agents.
Diction. Metrical structure of the poetry as revealed in speech, recitation, chant, or song.
Thought. Implied themes and theses (universal truths) as exposed by all the elements together.
Spectacle. The stage appearance of set, costumes, movement, dance.
Melody. Aristotle takes this for granted, saying that it is "too completely understood to require explanation."
Melody refers to tunes played on the aulos (see p. 71) and the musical reciting, chanting, and singing of the actors and Chorus. With the statement that

"melody is the greatest of the pleasurable accessories of tragedy," Aristotle acknowledges the sensual elements of drama.

The *Poetics* ends with the discussion of tragedy, although Aristotle had earlier said that he would also deal with comedy and other kinds of poetry. Even as an incomplete work, this has been among the most influential of Aristotle's treatises.

SUMMARY

Greek civilization began within the shadow of superstition and tradition in ancient times. Slowly those bondages had been pared away until, early in the reign of Pericles, a precarious balance was achieved between the freedom of each individual and the welfare of society. The philosophers, the writers, and the artists of the time took an active interest in politics, and conducted their affairs in the bright sunlight of the Agora.

But change is inevitable. In Athens the knife-edge between individuality and the welfare of the group was apparently too thin, the balance too delicate, for a society to maintain an equilibrium for very long. The skeptical sophists taught that complete individuality was the goal—violating Aeschylus' doctrine of the mean between autocracy and anarchy. The original strength of the city was sapped, but enough vitality remained to give rise to a new and different kind of strength in the broadened horizons of Hellenistic culture. Both Plato and Aristotle (except for their brief efforts to educate a king: Plato as tutor for the Syracusan Dionysius, Aristotle as Alexander's tutor) stood apart from politics and the vigorous life of the time; they deserted the active marketplace. They were contemplatives, aware that something had gone wrong, that the dream had somehow failed, and each in his own way examined himself and his culture to discover what had caused their civilization to falter. Probably nothing had really gone "wrong." Change had simply taken place that led to different patterns of life, new types of exploration into human existence, altered ideas of freedom.

What could have gone "right" was Alexander's dream of turning the ancient world into a kind of United Nations with Greek culture as its unifying and elevating core. This was a monumental task but, had he succeeded, there would have been a functioning world federation over 2,200 years prior to two similar attempts in our own century. However, a critical part of Alexander's vision did survive. Hellenism became the first international culture, flourishing for over seven centuries throughout the Mediterranean and the Near East.

(NOTE: See summary of Greek culture and values on pp. 123–4.)

9. An allusion to the fate of Socrates.

CHAPTER 7

The Greek Arts

Life is short, and Art long.
                    Hippocrates

According to Greek mythology, Daidalos (DED-uh-los) was the first and greatest of artists, a legendary Minoan artificer who created amazing figures in wood, bronze, and stone, and even invented the Minoan maze that housed the fabled Minotaur. The myth celebrates Greek commitment to creative activity: to invent, design, sculpt, and build. Daidalean Greeks studied nature and used their discoveries to create dynamic new images and structures radiating the illusion of vitality and life. This urge to create is the hallmark of Greek genius.

The Daidalos story has a tragic ending but it does point to a primary artistic consideration of Greek artists. According to the legend, Icaros, Diadalos' undisciplined son, prevailed upon his father to invent wings made of wax and feathers that enabled the lad to soar birdlike in the air. Disregarding his father's warning not to fly too near the sun, the reckless aviator soared high enough to melt his wings, plummeting him to his death in a sea that now bears his name. A cautionary fabrication that reveals a higher truth, this myth symbolizes Greek respect for the laws of nature. Thus, through Daidalos and his hubristic son we see reflected the Greek search for artistic freedom through the study of nature, invention, and allegiance to reason.

CHRONOLOGICAL OVERVIEW

900–700 BC	Geometric period
700–480 BC	Archaic period
480–323 BC	Classical period
	Early 480–450
	High 450–400
	Late 400–323
323–30 BC	Hellenistic Period

Opposite Sosias painter, *Achilles Bandaging Patroclos' Wound,* detail of cup, from Vulci. Ca. 500 BC. Red-figure pottery, diameter of cup 12½" (32 cm). Antikenmuseum, Staatliche Museen Preussischer Kulturbesitz, Berlin. Photo: B.P.K., Berlin (Ingrid Geske-Heiden).

GREEK CIVILIZATION, CA. 900–30 BC

The principal visual arts of ancient Greece were sculpture, pottery, painting, jewelry, and architecture and the main performing arts were music, poetry, and dance All of the Greek arts continually evolved as artists pursued the ideal of excellence in invention, design, and execution; that does not mean, however, that the nine centuries of Greek civilization reached ever higher levels of quality. The apex in all the arts came during the high classical period, especially the Age of Pericles, and was followed by a very gradual decline throughout the Hellenistic period.

GEOMETRIC PERIOD, CA. 900–700 BC

The invasions of Greek-speaking Dorians (ca. 1100–800 BC) ended Mycenaean dominance, disrupted the lives of all the Hellenes, and greatly affected the once flourishing arts of sculpture and architecture. Military invasions always disturb the arts; political and economic turmoil is not conducive to the commissioning of major works such as temples and life-sized statues. While impoverishing many artists and interfering with technological progress, the waves of Dorian invaders had little impact upon the utilitarian arts of furniture, textiles, glassware, and, above all, pottery. Because most of the pottery produced during these chaotic times emphasized geometric decoration, this is called the Geometric period.

Pottery

Practiced since the Stone Age, the craft of making pots made a great leap forward with the invention (probably in Sumer—Iran—ca. 3250 BC) of the potter's wheel. Introduced into Crete around 2000 BC the wheel enabled Minoan potters to lead the Aegean world in transforming the craft of making utilitarian vessels into an art form that reached its apex with the classic Greek vase.

As early as the ninth century BC, geometric conven-

7.1 *Amphora of the Dipylon*. Ca. 750 BC. Terra-cotta, height 5'1" (1.55 m) with base. National Archaeological Museum, Athens. Photo: Hirmer, Munich.

tions of pottery decoration had evolved into a vocabulary of **meanders**, concentric circles, horizontal bands, wheel patterns, shaded triangles, swastikas, and zigzags. Artisans used abstract animal and figure patterns in two-dimensional form in either full front or profile views. Sophisticated, aesthetically appealing, and utilitarian, the *Amphora of the Dipylon* (fig. 7.1) is a masterwork of the potter's art. Once cremation had been abandoned, these monumental vases served as grave markers and as receptacles for liquid offerings, which filtered down to the honored dead through openings in the base. The representational scene is a *prothesis* (PROTH-uh-sis), or lying-in-state of the deceased, flanked by triangulated geometric figures of mourners with their arms raised in grief. Alternating bands separate different versions of the meander motif with a band of grazing antelope highlighting the neck. Created several decades after the inauguration of the Olympic Games in 776 BC, this heroic vase can symbolically mark the beginning of the Homeric Age of ca. 750–700 BC.

Statuettes

Among the most popular products of the Greek artisans, statuettes were produced in quantity throughout ancient Greek history. Though not as impressive as life-sized statuary, diminutive figures can be held and examined closely—a very personal relationship. The statuette shown in the unit opener on p.41 is a votive offering, bearing on its

thighs the inscription "Mantiklos dedicated me to the Far Darter of the silver bow, as part of his tithe. Do thou, Phoibos, grant him gracious recompense." The geometric elements are obvious but the unknown artist also shows a concern for volume, modeling, and some anatomical details—design elements that place this work on the borderline between the geometric and archaic periods.

ARCHAIC PERIOD, 700–480 BC

"Archaic" is a term derived from a Greek word meaning "ancient" and is not to be confused with such current definitions as "antiquated, outdated, or old-fashioned." Greek genius blossomed in the sixth century BC with the creation of brilliant works of art. This was one of the most fruitful and imaginative periods in the history of art, a vigorous era that also produced the world's first democracy.

Pursuit of the Ideal

Throughout Greek art, beginning with the archaic period, Greek sculptors evolved new representational modes that differed from all previous artistic conceptions. Fascination with the human body and its complex mechanics led to the creation of fully three-dimensional sculpture, increasingly faithful to the natural world. In a culture that studied the real world and that, above all, valued the individual, the movement toward naturalism seems, in retrospect, to have been inevitable. It was the ideal, the quest for excellence, that impelled Greek artists, just as the philosophers and statesmen sought excellence in a free society. Writing around the time of the Battle of Marathon (490 BC), a Greek poet succinctly described the ideal Greek: "In hand and foot and mind built foursquare without a flaw." And in the twentieth century:

> Greece is in a special category. From the point of
> view of the present day, the Greeks constitute a
> fundamental advance on the great peoples of the
> Orient, a new stage in the development of society.
> They established an entirely new set of principles for
> communal life. However highly we may value the
> artistic, religious, and political achievements of earlier
> nations, the history of what we can truly call
> civilization—the deliberate pursuit of an ideal—does
> not begin until Greece.[1]

1. Gilbert Highet, *Man's Unconquerable Mind* (New York: Columbia University Press, 1954), p. 15.

Sculpture

Two main subjects preoccupied sculptors throughout the sixth century BC: the standing nude male and the standing fully clothed female. Apparently serving as votive or commemorative statues, these figures were not personalized portraits but rather idealized representations placed somewhere between humankind and the gods. No one really knows why the men were always nude and the women fully clothed and, moreover, we can apply only vague and unsatisfactory names to these freestanding figures: **kouros** (KOO-rose; "youth") and **kore** (KORE-ay; "maiden"). Probably adapted from Egypt and Mesopotamia, these two subjects were repeated again and again, never exactly duplicated

---

7.2 *Kore of Auxerre*, from France. Ca. 630–600 BC. Limestone with traces of paint, height 29½" (75 cm). Louvre, Paris. Photo: R.M.N., Paris.

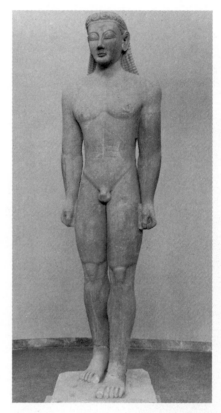

7.3 *Kouros of Sounion*. Ca. 600 BC. Marble, height 10' (3.05 m). National Archaeological Museum, Athens. Photo: Alison Frantz, Princeton.

---

but rather with the competitive drive that leads to constant innovation. The intensity of this ceaseless striving for something different, something better, sets the Greeks apart from all other cultures.

An early work, the *Kore of Auxerre* (fig. 7.2) stands as stiffly as an Egyptian statue, but when compared with Egyptian conventions, it reveals significant differences (see fig. 2.4). Unlike his Egyptian predecessor, the sculptor has cut away some needless stone to outline the figure rather than encasing it. The hair is braided in the geometric manner but the way the wide belt cinches the waist conveys a very human touch. From the light shoulder covering to the swelling hips, there is a skillful contrast between curved and straight lines.

Compare the colossal statue of the *Kouros of Sounion* (fig. 7.3) with the pharaoh (fig. 2.4). The Egyptian figure is "imprisoned" in stone in the manner of a very high relief, whereas the kouros has been liberated from unnecessary stone, except for the hands. The pharaoh stands in repose with his weight on the back foot. The equal distribution of weight of the kouros gives the illusion that he is striding forward, an effect heightened by the taut thigh muscles. Vestiges of geometric ornamentation remain in the rosette hair with meticulous braids and, especially, in the scrolls (**volutes**) that serve as ears. We see the most critical dif-

7.4 *Moschophoros* (*Calf-Bearer*), detail. Ca. 575–550 BC. Marble, height 5'6" (1.68 m). Acropolis Museum, Athens. Photo: Hirmer, Munich.

ference between the Egyptian and Greek sculptures in the eyes and facial expression. Displaying the typical relaxed serenity of Egyptian portraiture, the pharaoh gazes dreamily into an undefined distance. Conversely, the *Kouros of Sounion* manifests the characteristic dynamism of Greek art, with tension present in every line of the face. Egyptian figures seem never to have known stress, whereas tension and striving are hallmarks of the restless Greeks. Such were the contrasting views of the cultures in terms of reality and of human values: the pharaoh-gods constituted reality and their subjects lived for eternity; Greek reality was the individual and the time was now. Greek civilization, as Nietzsche said, "was not an effortless growth, but the product of courageous effort sustained by acute tension."

The *Calf-Bearer* (fig. 7.4) was something new in Greek art, a composition of two figures so unified that neither subject is conceivable without the other. A bearded man with a cloak draped over his upper body is gently balancing a bull calf on his shoulders as he strides confidently forward. With the corners of his mouth lifted in the "archaic smile," he stares ahead with hollow eyes that once contained realistic inlays. Characteristic of the archaic style, his braided hair and close-cropped beard are stylized, contrasting with the naturalistic depiction of the calf.

Architecture

By the sixth century BC, Greek city-states had established colonies in North Africa and from Byzantium (Istanbul) westward to Sicily, Italy, France, and Spain. Magna Graecia (southern Italy) was particularly important; Pythagoras founded his religious brotherhood here (see p. 64) and Parmenides and Empedocles established the Eleatic School of philosophy (see p. 69). One of the better-preserved of the surviving archaic temples is that of Hera I at Paestum (fig. 7.5), the site of two of the religious centers of Magna Graecia. Though employing an unusual nine-column front, this structure has all the elements of the basic Greek temple: rectangular floor plan, columns on four sides, three steps rising from the foundation to the top level on which the columns rest, and an enclosed inner shrine. Apparently the odd number of columns was never tried again. Regularity was an important quality for the Greeks, as exemplified in the six- or eight-column fronts of classical temples (see figs. 7.26 and 7.33). Other archaic features are the heavy, bulging columns that taper sharply as they near the oversize, pillowlike capitals. The whole effect is ponderous, creating a sense of physical strain, unlike the Parthenon (fig. 7.26), which appears light and free of stress.

Black-Figure Pottery

Painting was, for the Greeks, one of the supreme art forms, yet very little survives, mainly because pigments are perishable when applied to stone and especially so when painted on wood. Many more vases than paintings survived because pottery fired in a kiln is virtually indestructible; experts can restore badly fragmented vases to something approaching their original condition (fig. 7.6).

7.5   Temple of Hera I, Paestum, Italy. Ca. 550 BC. Photo: Dagli Orti, Paris.

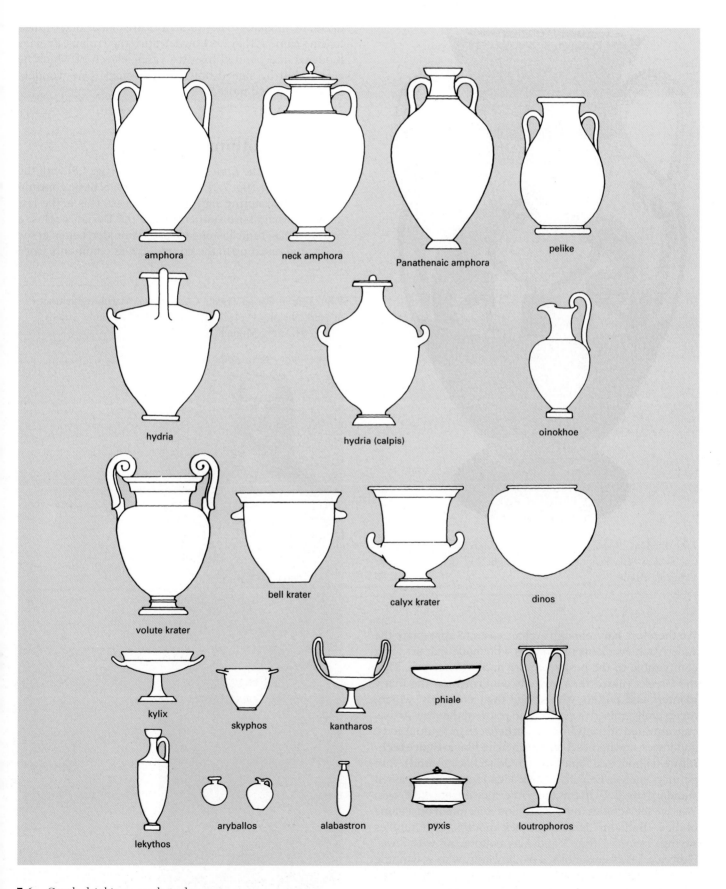

7.6   Greek drinking vessels and vases.

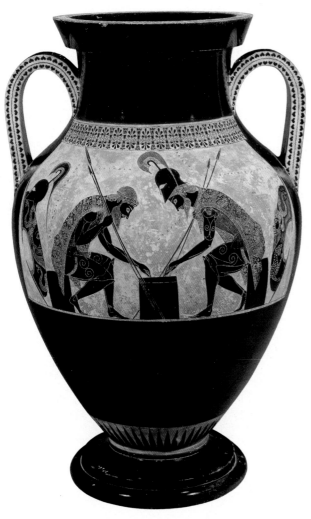

7.7 Exekias, *Amphora with Achilles and Ajax Playing Dice*. Ca. 530 BC. Black-figure pottery, height 24" (61 cm). Musei Vaticani, Rome.

We therefore have enough archaic vases to appreciate the superb achievements of painters who made that art form comparable to the best sculpture and architecture. That the Greeks valued their vases is confirmed by the many painters and potters who signed their creations, which, incidentally, raised the value (and price) of the vase. Artists concentrated on lively interaction between individual gods, goddesses, and heroes. Using an incisive **black-figure technique** (silhouetted figures on a reddish background), vase painters such as Exekias (e-ZEE-ki-as) set an unsurpassed standard (fig. 7.7). In this quiet interlude during the Trojan War we see Achilles (on the left) and Ajax intent on a game of dice. "Balloons" issue from their mouths, with Achilles saying *"tesara"* ("four") and Ajax countering with *"tria"* ("three"). (This does not tell us, however, who is winning the game.) The composition is sparse but elegant, with a sure line sustained by finely incised details in clothing and hair. The scene is quiet and dignified but permeated with

dramatic intensity. These warriors are just as determined to win a game as they were on defeating the Trojans. Exekias modeled and painted his own vases, eleven of which he signed, but he signed only two paintings. One wonders which he valued more.

Art and Clothing

By comparing the *Kore in Dorian Peplos* (fig. 7.8) with the *Kore of Auxerre* (fig. 7.2), one can observe a basic continuity while also noting significant changes. This is the last known archaic kore statue to wear the Dorian peplos, a heavy woolen tunic fastened at each shoulder, belted at the waist, and reaching to the ground. It was commonly worn

7.8 *Kore in Dorian Peplos*. Ca. 530 BC. Marble with traces of paint, height 4' (1.22 m). Acropolis Museum, Athens. Photo: Hirmer, Munich.

pleasure-loving orientation of an Ionian society as compared with the sober peplos and stolid, group-oriented residents of the Dorian city of Sparta. All Greek (and Mesopotamian, Egyptian, and Roman) women were responsible for the production of textiles and clothing. Ionian women were particularly well-known for their elegant, exquisitely decorated fabrics. Some of the sculpted fabrics and vases depicting clothing have survived but very little actual cloth remains from any ancient culture.

Naturalism

The *Anavyssos Kouros* (fig. 7.10), which was placed over the grave of a warrior named Kroisos, signals a major advance toward naturalism, i.e., fidelity to the actual

7.10 *Anavyssos Kouros*. Ca. 525 BC. Marble with traces of paint, height 6'4" (1.93 m). National Archaeological Museum, Athens. Photo: Alison Frantz, Princeton.

7.9 *Kore from Khios*. Ca. 520 BC. Marble with traces of paint, height 22" (56 cm) (lower part missing). Acropolis Museum, Athens. Photo: Hirmer, Munich.

over a light, sleeved tunic called a khiton. There is still a rectangular frontality about this figure but there is no doubt about the presence of a young, nubile body beneath the peplos. With its lovely smile and arched eyebrows, the softly rounded face radiates a serene happiness. The remaining paint on the graceful braids suggests that the young woman was a redhead, a valued hue in ancient Athens.

The Ionian himation worn by the *Kore from Khios* (fig. 7.9) contrasts sharply with the severe Dorian peplos. Made of much lighter material than the peplos, this elegant mantle could be draped over the body in a variety of graceful arrangements. Artists obviously enjoyed sculpting the sinuous lines of the garment, given the many surviving works. Moreover, Athenian women enthusiastically adopted the stylish himation symbolizing the individualistic, appearance of the natural world. The revolutionary changes already apparent in the *Kouros of Sounion* (see fig. 7.3) are more fully realized in this portrait of the finely tuned body of a youthful wrestler who died on some unknown battlefield. Though the knees and calves are emphasized, following earlier conventions, the muscles of the powerful thighs and taut arms swell with lifelike vitality. Based on an increasing concern with skeletal structure and anatomical details, the sculptor has concentrated on portraying the body as anyone might perceive it. From their very first efforts at monumental sculpture, Greek artists were never interested in portrait busts; their concern was the whole person. This does not imply that the head was secondary—far from it—but rather that Greek artists worked in a culture in which reality was the individual, one who possessed, ideally, a sound mind in a healthy body.

Whatever the reason for portraying men nude and women clothed, it had nothing to do with modesty. Nudity in the context of athletics or gymnastics was commonplace in the Greek world. Near Eastern prejudice against nudity was, for the Greeks, a sure sign of barbarism. Further, the male and female poses were consistently different. The women always stand with feet together, one arm at the side and the other raised (see figs. 7.2, 7.8, and 7.9). The men are always striding forward with the left foot, their hands at their sides (see figs. 7.3 and 7.10). To summarize, we know little of the purpose of these figures and nothing at all about conventional poses or clothing or the lack of it. We know only that their existence enriches our world.

Red-Figure Pottery

Around 530 BC vase painters began working with a color scheme of red figures against a black background, the reverse of black-figure technique. The luminous new **red-figure style** allowed secondary markings such as hair, muscles, details of dress, and even discreet shading. The two styles coexisted for thirty or forty years, but the red-figure technique, with its greater opportunities for delicacy and subtlety, became the dominant style of the classical period. In the red-figure cup by the Sosias painter (see chapter opener on p. 92), we see the first known example of eyes painted as they appear in profile. This was a significant advance beyond the Egyptian convention of always depicting the frontal view of eyes. In the painting, Achilles is tending his friend's wound while, in a very human reaction, Patroclos has turned his head away as if he were not a party to this painful event—or wishes he weren't. Differences between red-figure and black-figure technique are readily apparent when one compares this painting with that of Exekias (fig. 7.7). We cannot say that one work is better than the other, only that different techniques lead to diverse styles. Black-figure painting is characteristic of the vigorous archaic period, while red-figure vases typify the serenely confident classical style.

CLASSICAL PERIOD, 480–323 BC

Early Classical, 480–450 BC

The year 480 BC marked a critical turning point in Athenian history. Invaded and humiliated by Xerxes' Persian forces, their city ravaged and in ruins, the Athenians and their allies struck back by destroying the Persian fleet at Salamis and defeating the army the following year. A resurgent Athens moved confidently toward power, prosperity, and a legendary Golden Age.

Severe Style

The *Kritios Boy* (fig. 7.11), a prime example of the Severe style of early classicism, was created about the time that Aeschylus was gaining fame as a playwright. Somewhat like the innovations of Aeschylus, this statue represents a new principle in art. Wearing an expression of composed, classical solemnity (compare this with the archaic smile), this is truly a standing figure. Archaic sculptures were generally limited to a striding pose with an equal distribution of weight. Here is a formal composition with a fine balance of tense and relaxed muscles, the head turned slightly, one hip a bit elevated, the weight on one leg with the other at rest. This is how any of us might stand in repose.

Also representing the Severe style is the *Delphi Charioteer* (fig. 7.12), which was once part of a large

7.11   *Kritios Boy*. 481 BC. Marble, height 34" (86.4 cm). Acropolis Museum, Athens. Photo: Hirmer, Munich.

composition including a chariot and four horses. Chariot races were entered by the owners of racing teams and driven by skilled charioteers, much as professional jockeys ride today's thoroughbred horses. Overlooking the disheveled, dusty condition of a charioteer after a grueling race, the artist idealizes a proud champion, his khiton falling in fluted folds resembling a Doric column (see fig. 7.24).

One of the finest original Greek bronzes, *Poseidon* (*Zeus* according to some; fig. 7.13) stands majestically, prepared to hurl his trident (thunderbolt?). The figure is stridently asymmetrical: arms, legs, even the head, turn in different angles from the torso, which in turn shows the competing muscular strains and tensions. More so than even the most naturalistic archaic statues, this body has muscles rippling beneath taut skin. The concavities and convexities of the bronze surface reflect a shimmering light that further animates the figure. It matters little that if Poseidon's arms were lowered his hands would dangle at the knees; that the eyes are hollow sockets (once filled with colored stones); or that the hair, beard, and eyebrows are stylized; the work exudes a kinetic energy never achieved in earlier sculptures.

The idealism of Greek art—depicting people not as they were but as they should be—applied also to the gods (fig. 7.14). Whether Poseidon the earthshaker or Zeus of

7.12 *Above   Delphi Charioteer.* Ca. 478 or 474 BC. Bronze, height 5'11" (1.81 m). Archaeological Museum, Delphi. Photo: Sonia Halliday, Weston Turville, U.K.

7.13   *Poseidon (Zeus?).* Ca. 460 BC. Bronze, height 6'10" (2.08m). National Archaeological Museum, Athens. Photo: Dagli Orti, Paris.

7.15   Myron, *Discus Thrower (Discobolus)*. Reconstructed Roman copy of a bronze original of ca. 450 BC. Marble, height 5' (1.52 m). Museo Nazionale Romano, Rome. Photo: Hirmer, Munich.

7.16   *Riace Bronze* (Statue A). Ca. 460–450 BC. Bronze, height 6'6" (1.98 m). Museo Nazionale di Reggio Calabria, Italy. Photo: Alinari, Florence.

7.14   *Poseidon (Zeus?)*, detail of fig. 7.13. Photo: Dagli Orti, Paris.

the thunderbolt, this is how a god ought to look. Compare this regal demeanor with the idealized faces of figures 7.15, 7.16, and 7.17 and gauge the difference.

High Classical, 450–400 BC

More than any other style, the high classical boldly displayed the values of the Athenians of the Golden Age: optimism, freedom, individuality, competitiveness, the pursuit of excellence, and pride of achievement. This was the age of Pericles, Sophocles, Euripides, Socrates, and some of the most extraordinary sculptors, vase painters, metalworkers, and architects in the history of Western civilization.

Sculpture and Vase Painting

Myron's *Discobolus* (*Discus Thrower*; fig. 7.15) is intended to be viewed from the left of the figure, so one becomes totally involved in the moment before explosive action. Though a celebrated classical statue, the figure follows some Egyptian conventions. It is designed on a frontal plane, with head and legs in profile and the upper torso turned toward the front. Balanced by the arc of the arms and the angle of the head and left leg, this is a formal composition with the harmonious proportions characteristic of the classical style. With simplified anatomical details and a stylized pose, all is in readiness for the athlete to wheel about and hurl the discus. Excellence of form counted for half the score with the distance counting for the other half, a procedure comparable to scoring today's competitive diving or gymnastics. An athlete could win the olive wreath with a second-place throw, provided he displayed form comparable to the *Discobolus*. (See also the Olympic Games on pp. 138–9.)

The *Riace Bronze* (ree-AH-chee; fig. 7.16) is one of two original Greek bronzes discovered together in 1972 in the sea off Italy's southern coast and named after Riace township in Calabria. Statue A originally had a shield and a small sword; the eyes are now without pupils; and a tuft of hair is missing. Otherwise, this is a stunning representation of a youthful warrior in the prime of his vigorous life. Bronze is the primary material, but the teeth are silver, the corneas of the eyes ivory and limestone, and the lips, nipples, and eyelashes made of copper. The pose is fascinating; the right turn of the head and the steady far-off gaze express strength and resolution. Thrown-back shoulders strikingly fix the warrior in space.

The creator of this splendid addition to the tiny treasure of original Greek art is unknown. Some scholars say the bronze is worthy of the great Pheidias of Athens (and it is) while others attribute it to the sculptor in Magna Graecia called Pythagoras. It could have been imported from Athens or made in Italy. Stylistically, the warrior

7.18 *Victory Untying Her Sandal*, from the parapet of the Temple of Athena Nike, Acropolis, Athens. Ca. 410 BC. Pentelic marble, height 3'6" (1.07 m). Acropolis Museum, Athens. Photo: Dagli Orti, Paris.

stands somewhere between the *Poseidon* (fig. 7.13) and the canon developed by Polykleitos (polly-KLY-toss) of Argos, who is known today only through Roman copies of his work.

This copy of Polykleitos' *Doryphoros* (dory-FOR-os; fig. 7.17) is of sufficiently high quality to demonstrate how it exemplified a "canon" (system of proportions), which became a model for several generations of artists. Displaying the powerful body of a finely conditioned athlete, the young man rests his full weight on the right leg, with the left bent at the knee and his toes lightly touching the ground. With the head barely turned to the right and the right shoulder dropped slightly, we can trace a long S curve from the feet to the head. At rest as no sculpted figure had ever been before, the composition is a dynamic equilibrium of tension and relaxation throughout the body. Harmoniously proportioned and with a classic balance of artistic and natural form, this is the confident style of the Golden Age.

The relief *Victory Untying Her Sandal* (fig. 7.18) illustrates Greek sculpture's wet drapery effect. Sculptors apparently dipped a filmy material in a starchlike substance, draped the nude female model, and arranged the folds for

7.17 Polykleitos, *Spear Bearer (Doryphoros)*, Roman copy of a bronze original of ca. 450–440 BC. Marble, height 6'6" (1.98 m). Museo Nazionale, Naples. Photo: Scala, Florence.

7.19 *Stele of Hegesco*, grave relief. Ca. 400–390 BC. Marble, height 4'10½" (1.49 m). National Archaeological Museum, Athens. Photo: Hirmer, Munich.

best artistic effect. Portrayed here is a rather awkward human action, but one accomplished so gracefully that the work is a marvel of softly flowing lines in a perfectly balanced design.

A sculptured gravestone known as the *Stele of Hegesco* (fig. 7.19) shows a serving maid offering her seated mistress, the commemorated deceased, a casket of jewels. Common to sculpture of the classical period is the serenity of the facial expressions, whether the subjects are participating in a procession, a battle, or a meeting of the gods. Note, also, that the heads of the standing servant and seated mistress are close to the same level. This **isocephalic** (i-so-se-FALL-ik) convention, the tradition of keeping all heads on approximately the same level, gives exceptional clarity to Greek relief art. It is so subtly executed that one's sense of rightness remains undisturbed.

Vase painters of this period were just as skilled as the architects and sculptors, and their best work compares favorably with paintings by Renaissance artists such as Raphael or Leonardo da Vinci. Though most artists preferred red-figure paintings, some used a variety of colors on a white background in what is called the white-ground

technique. Before being fired in the kiln, a white clay was added in the area to be decorated and the painting done after firing. Though subject to fading because the color was not baked into the vase as in the red-figure technique, white-ground paintings are similar to easel paintings, but with the additional complication of working on curved surfaces. Some artists chose the permanency of red-figure painting, while others, like the Achilles Painter (fig. 7.20), favored the color range of white-ground decorations. Though he did not sign his work, his distinctive style appears on more than 200 vases. Here, sitting quietly on the sacred mountain of the muses, Polyhymnia, the muse of solemn hymn and religious dance, reverently plucks her seven-string kithara. (See The Greek Muses in box 4.1, p. 57.) Lightly decorated at top and bottom, there is nothing to draw our attention from the solitary figure with a lone bird at her feet. Graceful line and harmonious composition make this a superb example of the classical style.

7.20   Achilles Painter, *Muse on Mount Helicon*, detail of lekythos (funerary vase). Ca. 440–430 BC. White-ground pottery, height 14½" (35.5 cm). Glypothek, Munich. Photo: Studio Kopperman, Munich.

Were the common people of Athens appreciative of these and other great art works? According to Aristotle, there are only two criteria for art: 1) it should entertain and instruct; 2) it should disclose not secrets to the few but treasures to the many. We have ample evidence proving that all the Greek arts served up treasures to a large and appreciative public.

Architecture

Greek temples had evolved into their canonical form during the early archaic period (ca. 600 BC). Fundamental to the temple canon is the architectural system of post and lintel (fig. 7.21). After planting a post at all four corners of the space to be enclosed, the builder placed a **lintel** on top of and across the posts. Roof beams (joists) were placed at regular intervals to link the opposite lintels and then covered with a roof. Spaces between the posts were filled, as needed, with walls, windows, and doors. First employed in wood, then in brick, and eventually in stone construction, the post and lintel system was used for all major buildings. Though aware of the greater strength of arches and the arched vault (see Roman Architecture and Engineering, pp. 152–3), architects used this technology for minor projects such as tunnels and sewers.

A typical temple floor plan (fig. 7.22) shows a **cella**, a central room housing the statue of the deity. This basic core was provided with a columned porch at the front and, usually, one at the back, with the latter sometimes enclosed to house a treasury. Large and important temples had exterior columns on all four sides forming a colonnade or **peristyle**.

The plan appears to be simple, but a diagram of a **facade** (fig. 7.23) reveals a progression beyond the basic post and lintel system. Because the Mediterranean area is subject to heavy winter rains, a sloping or saddle-back roof was developed to facilitate drainage. It was covered with terra-cotta or marble tiles, equipped with gutters and rain spouts, and adorned with sculpture. The triangular space at each end, the **pediment**, was usually decorated with large-scale high reliefs or freestanding sculpture.

The architects constructed steps (usually three) on a stone foundation called a stereobate with the top level, the stylobate, forming the floor of the temple. From the stylobate rose columns (shafts with capitals) that supported the lintel, also called an architrave. The ends of the roof joists are called triglyphs, a term derived from the three vertical grooves that had become a decorative stone adaptation of the natural grain of wood joist ends. The spaces between the triglyphs were filled by plain, painted, or relief rectangles called metopes.

The Acropolis

Most ancient Greek cities developed around a fortified hilltop (*akra*; "high place"). As cities grew more prosperous and powerful, this "people's high place" (acropolis) became the center of religious and civic activity, suitably adorned with

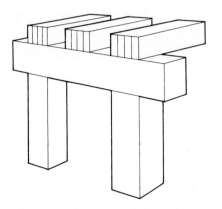

7.21 Post and lintel system.

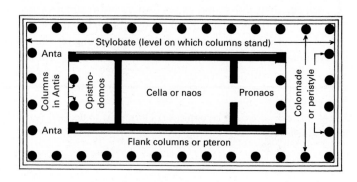

7.22 Typical Greek temple floor plan.

7.23 Typical Greek temple facade.

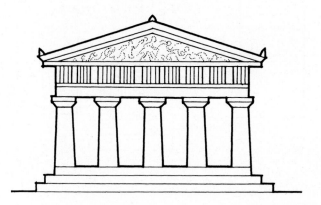

THE GREEK ORDERS

Determining the general mode of the basic temple plan was a problem that was resolved with the inspired conception of the classic Greek orders: **Doric, Ionic,** and **Corinthian** (fig. 7.24). Placed directly on the **stylobate,** the Doric column was about seven times as tall as its diameter, a ratio probably derived from the height of a man in relation to foot size. Fluted to provide visual depth and swelling in subtle convex curves (**entasis;** EN-ta-sis), it rose to a capital (**echinus;** eh-KY-nus), under an **abacus** (AB-a-kus), the square block that joined the **architrave.** Surmounting the columns was a Doric **frieze** of alternating **triglyphs** (TRY-glifs) and **metopes** (MET-o-pays). (See figs. 7.26, 7.32, and 7.33.)

The contrasting Ionic order is lighter than the Doric and more graceful, with a slender shaft about eleven times its diameter (approximately a woman's height in proportion to the size of her foot). Its components are a tiered base, a delicate shaft with softer, spaced fluting, and a capital formed of paired scrolls (volutes) capped by a highly decorated abacus. Usually subdivided into three projecting bands, the Ionic architrave normally consists of a continuous sculptural frieze. (See figs. 7.30 and 7.31.)

A variant of the Ionic, the Corinthian order, adored by the Romans, is considerably more decorative, even opulent. Taller and more slender than the Ionic, its column culminates in an inverted bell shape encrusted with stylized **acanthus** leaves, an ingenious transition from a circular shaft to a rectangular architrave. (See fig. 7.43 for the only Corinthian temple in Greece.)

Like multiple layers of a cake, the columns consisted of stone **drums** that were roughed out in the quarry. After delivery to the site, the drums were fitted with metal pegs coated with lead to resist corrosion and stacked into columns. The assembled columns were then finished under the supervision of the architect, who personally controlled the entire project.

With only one form and three modes of expression, Greek architecture might seem a limited achievement. Not so. The secret is in the limitations. For perfection of proportion and clarity of outline, subtlety of refinement, and visual appearance of solids and spaces in equilibrium, the Greek temple has never been surpassed.

7.24   Greek orders of columns: (a) Doric, (b) Ionic, and (c) Corinthian.

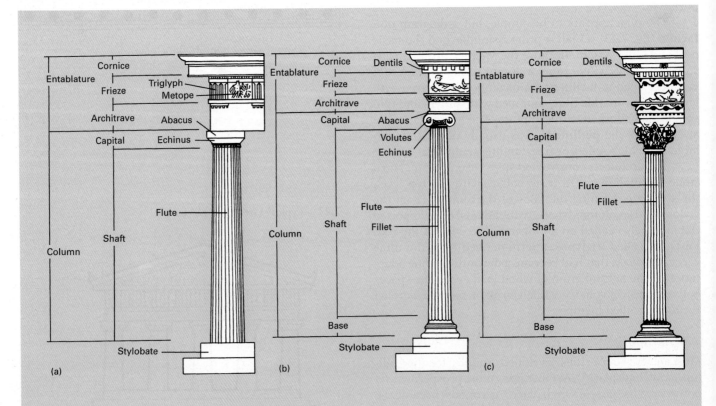

governmental buildings, libraries, and temples dedicated to the gods. According to legend, the Acropolis of Athens (fig. 7.25) was both the burial place of the fabled King Erechtheus and the site where Poseidon and Athena contended for authority over the city.

Under the leadership of Pericles, the Athenians completed a building and art program on the Acropolis surpassing in splendor and artistic quality anything the world had ever seen. It signified the beginning of the Golden Age, in about 460 BC, when Pericles appointed Pheidias overseer of all works on the Acropolis. By 405 the Parthenon, Erechtheion, Propylaia, and Temple of Athena Nike had been built, and the brief period of glory was at an end.

Parthenon Built under the direction of architects Ictinus (ik-TIE-nus) and Callicrates (ka-LIK-kra-teez), the temple of Athena Parthenos or the Parthenon (fig. 7.26) was created as the crowning glory of the Acropolis, complete with sculptural reliefs and a massive gold and ivory statue of

Athena created by Pheidias. Although it is the largest Doric temple ever built on the Greek mainland, with refinements so subtle that the building symbolized the Periclean ideal of "beauty in simplicity," its basic plan was still that of the sixth-century archaic temple. Though they invented nothing new, its architects clearly saw just how refined the temple form could be. Despite the great size (228 × 101' [69.54 × 30.8 m] with 34' [10.37 m] columns), this was still a rectangular box surrounded by columns and surmounted by a triangular prism. A temple in which the Doric order achieved perfection, the Parthenon is so unified and harmonious that its immense size belies its lightly poised serenity.

That the building has virtually no straight lines or true right angles is at first surprising. By using slight deviations from mathematical regularity, presumably to correct optical distortions, the architects created the appearance of mathematical precision. This bothered Plato, who could not reconcile the discrepancy between perfection and the illusion of perfection. Thus, the cella walls lean slightly inwards; the stylobate rises 4¼ inches (10.9 cm) at the center of the 228-foot (69.5 m) sides and 2¾ inches (7 cm) at the center of the other two sides.

7.25 Acropolis (view from the west) Athens. Photo: Sonia Halliday, Weston Turville, U.K.

7.26 Ictinus and Callicrates, Parthenon (view from the northwest), Acropolis, Athens. Ca. 447–432 BC. 228 × 101' (69.5 × 39.8 m). Photo: Spectrum, London.

All columns lean inward about 2½ inches (6 cm), except the corner columns, which lean diagonally inward, so much so that, if extended, all four would meet at a point about a mile (1.6 km) above the temple. Echoing the stylobate, the cornice, frieze, and architrave are all slightly higher in the center.

Further adjustments are found in the greater diameter of the corner columns, each of which is about 24 inches (60 cm) closer to its neighbors than the other columns. Corner columns are seen most directly against the sky, thus the deviations were probably intended to make them seem more supportive. Most Doric buildings show some signs of "correction," for the Doric column always had a slight outward curve called the entasis. In early temples the entasis is a bulge about a third of the way up the column; but the deviation from a straight line is only ¹¹/₁₆ inch (1.7 cm) within the 34-foot (10.4-m) Parthenon column. A longstanding convention, the fluting of Doric columns was not

only visually attractive but also made an optical correction; smooth-surfaced columns seem, from a distance, flat, lacking enough substance to perform support functions.

Adorned with some of antiquity's greatest marble carvings, the Parthenon was a visual encyclopedia of activities of the gods and of the Athenians themselves. A reconstruction of the east pediment (fig. 7.27) illustrates the story of the miraculous birth of Athena, who has just emerged from the brow of Zeus. The gods and goddesses are freestanding, larger than life-size, and carved in broad, clear planes and sharply delineated lines that made for better viewing at ground level.

A Parthenon metope depicting the *Combat between a Lapith and a Centaur* (fig. 7.28) is a skillfully executed high relief symbolizing the ascendancy of human ideals over human nature's bestial side. Studies of the ninety-two other metopes reveal consistent improvement in quality from the early, rather crude carvings to the exceptional work of such later pieces as the metope of figure 7.28. The stonemasons obviously benefited from some kind of on-the-job training under Pheidias.

The inner frieze, about 3 feet 9 inches (1.1 m) in height and over 500 feet (153 m) in length, ran along the outer walls of the cella. A marble **bas-relief** depicting the Athenians

7.27 *Above* Reconstruction of central section of east pediment of Parthenon. Original height at center ca. 11' (3.35 m). Acropolis Museum, Athens.

7.28 *Left   Combat between a Lapith and a Centaur*, south metope XXVII from Parthenon. Ca. 447–443 BC. Pentelic marble, height 4'5" (1.35 m). British Museum, London. Photo: Hirmer, Munich.

7.29 *Below   Horsemen*, from north frieze of Parthenon. Ca. 440 BC. Pentelic marble, height ca. 3'6" (1.07 m). British Museum, London. Photo: Hirmer, Munich.

7.30 Mnesikles, Erechtheion (view from the east), Acropolis, Athens. Ca. 421–405 BC. Height of porch figures ca. 8' (2.44 m). Photo: Hirmer, Munich.

and their gods in the Greater Panathenaea celebration, it portrayed a procession carrying a peplos to the statue of Athena in the Parthenon. Apparently at the very moment that the procession is getting underway, the horsemen (fig. 7.29) ready their mounts to escort the singing maidens to the temple. With about 600 persons and numerous horses, this scene depicts but one moment of activity; this is simultaneous narration, a sculptural version of the classic unities of Greek drama. The frieze is remarkable for its depiction of hundreds of Athenians on a temple frieze, something unthinkable in other ancient cultures. One has only to think of the dark and forbidden recesses of the Temple at Luxor (fig. 2.10) to understand some fundamental differences between Egyptian and Greek civilizations.

Erechtheion The complex design of the Erechtheion (AIR-ek-thee-on; fig. 7.30) probably results from both the uneven site and the legendary contest between Athena and

Poseidon. As both competed for the guardianship of the city, Poseidon struck a rock with his trident and sea water, symbol of Athenian sea power, gushed forth. Athena then struck the ground with her spear and a full-grown olive tree appeared. Judging olives more important because they were so useful, the other Olympians awarded the city to Athena. The canny Athenians, however, dedicated shrines to both within the same temple, and covered all bets by naming the building after the mythical King Erechtheus who had supposedly lived on the site.

The higher (eastern) level of this graceful Ionic temple was dedicated to Athena, while the lower level (right background) was Poseidon's sanctuary. Three **porticos**, each of different design and dimensions, project from three sides. Best known is the south porch with its six **caryatids** (karry-AT-ids; female figures used as columns). Measuring only 10 feet (3 m) deep by 15 feet (4.6 m) wide, the porch has an architrave supported by statues of young women whose drapery suggests the fluting of columns. Grouped as if in a procession toward the Parthenon, three figures on one side bend their right legs while those on the other side bend their left legs to give the illusion of animation. All columns suggest physical strain; despite the individual beauty of these figures, substituting a human form for a supporting column tends to place an undue burden on our imagination. One might characterize these caryatids as an excellent solution for a less than satisfactory idea. The caryatid to the right of the figure on the left corner is a copy of the figure Lord Elgin carried off to England in 1806 (along with considerable booty from the Parthenon and other buildings) as part of a questionable attempt to "save" Greek art.[2] Compounding the irony, all of the figures were moved to a protected environment and replaced with fiberglass copies, including a copy of the copy. Air pollution, rather than the Turks or an English lord, is the latest and most deadly threat to the Athenian Acropolis.

Temple of Athena Nike   A classic example of architectural unity, the exquisite Temple of Athena Nike (fig. 7.31) is a tiny building (17' 9" × 26' 10" [5.4 × 8.2 m]) of pentelic marble. Though architecture is usually defined as the art of enclosing space, Greek temples embody more than this. Each temple was designed as a series of receding planes from steps to columns to cella wall, with temple reliefs in comparable planes from surface to deepest recesses. Both a strongly defined form and a four-sided sculptural relief, the Greek temple is architectural but it is also a massive sculptural composition. Rather than just enclosing space the temple also fills space, and none any better than the elegant Temple of Nike, goddess of victory. The temple originally housed a statue of the victory goddess with her wings clipped so that she could never leave Athens. Twenty years after the completion of the building Athens fell to Sparta, never to regain her political and military supremacy. Demolished by the Turks in the eighteenth century to build a fort, the Temple of Athena Nike was later reconstructed by retrieving the stones from the wrecked fort. That the temple dedicated to the victory goddess could be restored to its original form symbolizes the enduring quality of a culture that survived invasions by Persians, Spartans, Romans, Venetians, Turks, Italians, and Germans.

Doric Temples—Sicily

Two of the most sophisticated Doric temples of the Periclean age are found not in Greece but in Sicily, the southernmost portion of Magna Graecia. Both the Temple of Concord at Agrigento and the Temple of Segesta are in relatively good condition, but for quite different reasons.

The prosperous Greek city of Akragas (ah-kra-GOSS; "high ground"; modern Agrigento) was built on a plateau overlooking the Mediterranean to the south. Because there

2. See Theodore Vrettos, *A Shadow of Magnitude: The Acquisition of the Elgin Marbles* (1974), about which the British novelist and poet Lawrence Durrell wrote, "So thoroughly researched and energetically executed, this is the first portrait in depth of that ignoble monomaniac Lord Elgin, who lives in history as the man who despoiled the Parthenon." The Greek government has repeatedly pressed Britain for the return of the Elgin Marbles removed from the Parthenon.

7.31   Callicrates, Temple of Athena Nike, Acropolis, Athens. Ca. 427–424 BC. Pentelic marble, 17' 9" × 26' 10" (5.4 × 8.2 m). Photo: Alison Frantz, Princeton.

was no acropolis, the citizens of Akragas built five Doric temples on the southern slope between the city and the sea. Lined up in a widely spaced "avenue of temples," the buildings provided a cohesive link between the city, the land, and the sea. Seen first when arriving by sea, the temples identified Akragas as a Greek city in a foreign land. One can say that the Greek gods were at home in Greece but they had to be imported into the very different environment of Italy and Sicily.

Temple of Concord   Placed on a high spot midway between the city and the coastal plain, Concord is a hexastyle (six-column front) Doric temple. It has 23-foot (7-m) columns arranged in a thirty-four-column peristyle, with six and eleven on alternate sides (fig. 7.32). Like the Parthenon, it has rising stylobates and entablatures on both sides but the six-column front is set in a straight line. The overall effect is a static front with longitudinal columns moving lightly down each side. When compared with the Parthenon the most significant difference is the hexastyle facade. For most people six columns can be taken in at a glance as a unit. However, one cannot see the eight-column front (octastyle facade) of the Parthenon (see fig. 7.26) as a unit; for most observers the Parthenon insists upon a second or third look. Compare the facade of Concord with that of the Parthenon. The latter appears to be restless and challenging; Concord reflects its name in its serenity, grace, and charm.

7.32 *Above* Temple of Concord, Agrigento, Sicily (ancient Akragas, Magna Graecia). Ca. 425 BC. Limestone, ca. 55 × 129' (16.8 × 39.3 m). Photo: Scala, Florence.

7.33 Temple of Segesta, Sicily. Ca. 420s BC. Limestone, ca. 76 × 191' (23 × 58 m). Photo: Scala, Florence.

The Temple of Concord was, like all Greek temples, a sacred site, probably a sanctuary for Demeter, goddess of fertility, agriculture, and peace. Despite its sacred character, the temple escaped destruction only because it was converted into a Christian church in AD 597. Greek religious architecture used by Christians was always substantially altered but the alternative was the destruction meted out to all other sanctuaries.

Temple of Segesta   Akragas was a very large Greek city (with a population of about 250,000) but Segesta was neither populous nor Greek. Why, then, did it have a large Greek theatre and one of the most interesting of all Doric temples? Located in the mountainous northwest of Sicily, Segesta was within the orbit of Carthaginian influence. Its vulnerable location led it to look to Greece, adopting the language and some of the customs, and eventually reaching an agreement with Athens.

The Temple of Segesta (fig. 7.33) is a hexastyle Doric structure considerably larger than Concord. The columns rise 32 feet (9.8 m) and are arranged in a thirty-six-column peristyle (6 x 12). The temple is sometimes referred to as "anonymous"; no one knows which god it served, only that the god was not Greek. The architect was probably Athenian (maybe even Ictinus) and certainly a knowledgeable and skillful master of the classical style. The architectural historian, Vincent Scully, calls him an "architectural Euripides."

Left in an unfinished condition for unknown reasons, the temple has no roof and no indication that an inner cella was ever planned. The columns are in place awaiting the fluting that never took place.

As in Concord and the Parthenon, the longitudinal stylobate and entablature of Segesta arch upward but much more sharply than in the other two temples. The straight, six-column front combined with the swift and tensile longitudinal arc give the building a strange and impressive energy. The architect may have chosen not to flute the columns after he saw their solid mass contributing to the extraordinary power of the structure; maybe the temple was deliberately left unfinished. That it was not destroyed by invading armies or zealous Christians was due to its isolation in the mountain wilderness of northwestern Sicily.

A comparison of the Temples of Concord and Segesta clearly reveals the range available to an imaginative architect. Both structures are readily classified as Doric by the elements identified in figure 7.24 (except for Segesta's lack of fluting). The aesthetic impact, however, is remarkably different. Concord is serene; Segesta is restless. Concord is graceful; Segesta is massive and muscular. Concord was probably dedicated to Demeter, the Greek goddess of peace. Segesta was intended for an unknown, non-Greek (meaning uncivilized) god. Concord could be transported to an appropriate site in Greece. Segesta is completely at home in the rugged mountains of Sicily. What Concord and Segesta had in common with the Parthenon and all other Greek temples was cogently expressed by an American writer:

Not magnitude, not lavishness,
But form—the site;
Not innovating willfulness,
But reverence for the archetype.

Herman Melville, 1891

The Golden Age ended with the Spartan defeat of Athens in 404 BC. That Sophocles, Euripides, and Socrates died within a few years of this date further marked the end of an era. Throughout the following century, until the death of Alexander in 323 BC, the classical tradition was maintained, though in a somewhat more theatrical manner. Greek artists prided themselves on adhering to the high standards of the preceding century. Athens no longer ruled the seas but it was still the cultural center of the ancient world.

Late Classical, 400–323 BC

The more pleasing and personal qualities of late classical sculpture and the superbly executed naturalism are largely due to Praxiteles of Athens (prax-SIT-uh-leez), the most celebrated of all Greek sculptors. In his *Hermes with the Infant Dionysos* (fig. 7.34) we see, perhaps, an example of the artist's exceptional skill in working marble. Praxiteles

7.34   Praxiteles, *Hermes with the Infant Dionysos*. Copy of probable bronze original of ca. 340 BC. Marble, height 6'1" (1.86 m). Archaeological Museum, Olympia. Photo: Alinari, Florence.

7.36   *Boy from the Bay of Marathon*. Ca. 340–300 BC. Bronze, height 4' 3" (1.3 m). National Archaeological Museum, Athens. Photo: Hirmer, Munich.

7.35   Praxiteles, *Aphrodite of Knidos*. Roman copy of marble original of ca. 350 BC. Marble, height 6'8" (2.03 m). Musei Vaticani, Rome.

was apparently among the first to exploit the shimmering, translucent quality of marble. There are no sharp angles; everything is smooth, rounded, polished. Compare, for example, the striking clarity of the *Doryphoros* (fig. 7.17) with the softly sensuous treatment of the *Hermes*. Slimmer and more relaxed, the *Hermes* looks positively decadent compared with the earnest *Spear Bearer*. Long regarded as the only surviving original by Praxiteles, this lovely sculpture is in the current expert consensus very likely a

Hellenistic copy of what was probably a bronze original. The infant's head is proportionately too small and the rumpled drapery inconsistent with the late classical style. The most telling discrepancy is the marble bar bracing the hip. Greek sculptors usually designed their works to be self-supporting, but a marble copy of an inherently strong bronze original would need bracing.

Definitely a copy, and a good one, the *Aphrodite of Knidos* (fig. 7.35) is a revolutionary work. The single most popular statue in all antiquity, the *Aphrodite* was lavishly praised by the Roman historian Pliny (XXXVI, 20) as the finest statue in the world, so marvelous that it was placed in a shrine to be universally admired. (Pliny was equally enthusiastic about the *Laocoön*—fig. 7.44—and named *it* the world's finest sculpture.) Abandoning the traditional concept of a figure occupying a rectangular space, Praxiteles designed a slender goddess with sinuous lines rising from her feet to the quizzical tilt of her head. The slight outward lean of the right leg increases the sensuous curve of the right hip. Echoing the swelling curve of the hip, the left leg is flexed so that the thighs are pressed gently together with the knees nearly touching. From the knees—the narrowest part of the composition—the figure ascends in an hourglass configuration to the startled reaction of a woman surprised in the act of bathing. In line, pose, proportion, and structure Praxiteles has created an incomparable idealization of femininity, the essence of womanhood. Though nude males were portrayed in a variety of activities, Greek artists invariably depicted women in normal situations that warranted nudity: bathing, making love, functioning as flute girls, or as hetairai.

Looking somewhat like a male version of the *Aphrodite* (fig. 7.35), the original bronze found in the Bay of Marathon (fig. 7.36) was probably derived from the work of Praxiteles. The innate strength of bronze enabled the anonymous artist to dispense with visually irritating supports like the marble bar previously discussed (*Hermes;* fig. 7.34). The lightly poised figure, difficult to achieve in bronze but virtually impossible to reproduce in marble, is similar to the *Hermes*,

especially in the modeling of the surfaces and the melting gaze of the eyes.

Lysippos, sculptor to the court of Alexander the Great, was probably the most revolutionary artist of the late classical period. His *Apoxyomenos* (a-pox-e-o-MAY-nos; fig. 7.37) was as pivotal in the fourth century as the *Doryphoros* of Polykleitos (fig. 7.17) was a century earlier; both works established new sculptural canons. Departing from the earlier canon, Lysippos introduced new proportions: smaller head, taller and more slender body, and long, lithe limbs. Using an S-shaped tool called a strigil, the athlete is scraping oil, dust, and sweat from his body, a standard procedure following athletic contests. Utilizing the space in front of the body, the extended arms break through the invisible barrier of the frontal plane, violating a convention dating back to Egypt's Old Kingdom art of ca. 2500 BC. There is a new sense of movement with trunk, head, and limbs turned in different directions. This is sculpture conceived, executed, and meant to be viewed in the round—all 360 degrees. As epitomized in the *Apoxyomenos,* these revolutionary ideas were not fully understood until the Italian Renaissance 1,700 years later.

Jewelry
Jewelry was popular in Greece from Homeric times onward as adornment and as a sign of affluence. Much fine jewelry was made during the early archaic period, especially in Magna Graecia, but comparatively little remains from about 580 to 480 BC, perhaps because of a shortage of gold

7.37 Lysippos, *Scraper (Apoxyomenos)*. Roman copy of bronze original of ca. 330 BC. Marble, height 6'9" (2.06 m). Musei Vaticani, Rome. Photo: Alison Frantz, Princeton. (The museum added the fig leaf.)

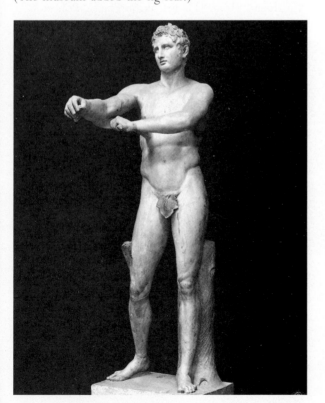

7.38 Necklace, from Taranto (Tarentum), Italy. 350–330 BC. Gold, length 11" (27.9 cm). British Museum, London.

during that time. Production increased after the Persian wars as Athens moved into its most prosperous era. The Greek general Xenophon noted that men spent their wealth on armor, horses, and houses; women collected expensive clothes and gold jewelry. A well dressed woman would select from her diadems, earrings, necklaces, pendants, brooches, bracelets, and rings. Unlike people of other cultures, Athenians generally preferred elegant gold jewelry without precious or semiprecious stones. This preference is characteristic of a culture that valued moderation and simplicity while also esteeming loveliness. Gemstones did not become popular until the Hellenistic era.

The gold necklace from Tarentum in southern Magna Graecia (fig. 7.38) is a choice example of the skillful gold-smithing of Greek artisans. Generously decorated with delicate filigree, the basic necklace is composed of interlocking rosettes. The pendants consist of flower buds and miniature female heads in two different sizes. The custom of burying favorite jewelry with its owner saved many pieces of fine jewelry, including this necklace.

HELLENISTIC PERIOD, 323–30 BC

Symbolized by the death of Alexander, the end of the long and enormously productive classical age had arrived. Artists were no longer concerned with idealized portraits and classical harmony, but instead became increasingly interested in actual appearances and in the infinite variety of human nature and experience. In the midst of the rapid disintegration of the Alexandrian empire, the emphasis was upon survival in a world beset by constant sectional strife.

However, Alexander had left in his wake Hellenism, the first international culture in which Greek was the common language and which venerated scholarship, education, and the arts.

Sometimes described as decadent, Hellenistic art did indeed include banalities, trivialities, pathos, and empty virtuosity. Greek genius was not yet exhausted, however, for the age also saw the production of exceptional art works that were no less admirable than those of the classical era but which were certainly different.

Sculpture and Architecture

A Celtic tribe that ravaged Asia Minor until subdued by Attalos I of Pergamon, the Gauls were immortalized in the remarkable figure of *The Dying Gaul* (fig. 7.39). Also known as the *Dying Trumpeter* because of the discarded battle trumpet in the right foreground, the hair, facial features, and ornamental neck collar realistically portray a Gallic tribesman. The figure is, however, in the heroic Greek tradition of the nude warrior; the treatment of the vanquished barbarian is sympathetic, portraying a poignant nobility as the dying man braces his right arm against the ground in a futile effort to ward off an ignoble death.

The *Nike of Samothrace* (fig. 7.40) is not only one of the most dramatic and compelling works ever created but

7.39 *The Dying Gaul.* Roman copy of bronze original from Pergamon, Turkey. Ca. 230–220 BC. Marble, life-size. Museo Capitolino, Rome. Photo: Alison Frantz, Princeton.

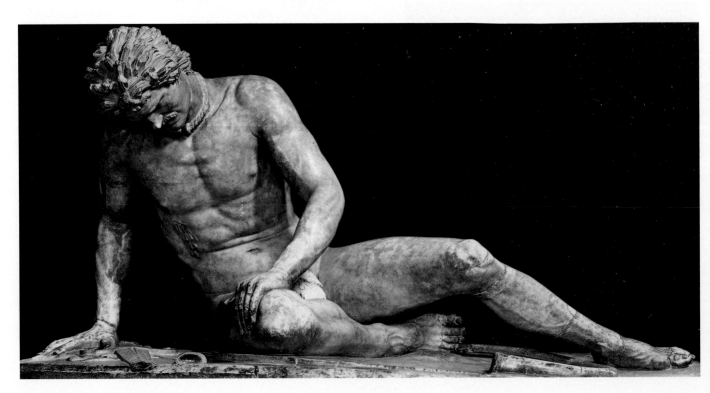

a prime example of the continuing power of the classical theme of Nike, the goddess of victory. Attributed to Pythokritos (py-THOCK-ri-toss) and erected in a sanctuary on the island of Rhodes in honor of a naval victory over King Antiochus III of Syria, Victory is portrayed alighting on the symbolic prow of a ship. With her great wings still extended, she is moving into a wind that becomes a tangible presence as it shapes the flowing draperies into deep diagonal folds, carrying our eyes restlessly over the entire surface. Aptly characterized as poetry in motion, Victory communicates both the immediacy of the moment and a feeling for ongoing action in a pervasive atmosphere of wind and sea.

One of the wonders of the ancient world, the great Altar of Zeus (fig. 7.41), was built by the son and successor of Attalos I to commemorate his father's military victories. Though designed as an Ionic structure for an Ionian site, the altar has none of the delicacy of the classic Ionic style. With a base 100 feet (30.5 m) square, this monumental altar is intended to impress rather than inspire. The immense frieze around the base is over 400 feet (122 m) long and 7 feet 8 inches (2.34 m) high (fig. 7.42). Using the traditional Greek device of portraying actual historical

7.40 *Above*   Pythokritos of Rhodes, *Nike of Samothrace.* Ca. 190 BC. Marble, height 8' (2.44 m). Louvre, Paris. Photo: Giraudon, Paris.

7.41   Altar of Zeus, west front (restored), from Pergamon, Turkey. Ca. 180 BC. Base 100' (30.5 m) square. Staatliche Museen, Berlin. Photo: Marburg.

7.42 *Above   The Battle of the Gods and Giants,* relief segment
from the Altar of Zeus, Pergamon. Ca. 180 BC.
Height 7'8" (2.34 m). Staatliche Museen, Berlin.

events in mythological terms, this is an emotional and dramatic work. Here is a world of giants, an exaggeration of
physical and emotional force that, in its own way, accomplishes its goals fully as well as the Parthenon frieze (see
fig. 7.29). Comparing the friezes defines the significant differences between the classical and Hellenistic styles, thus
reflecting the contrast between confident optimism and a
constant struggle for survival.

As dramatic as the Altar of Zeus and of equally monumental proportions, Hellenistic public buildings stressed
sheer size over classic restraint and harmonious proportions. Even in the scanty remains of the Temple of the
Olympian Zeus (fig. 7.43 and p. 54) one can detect some
of the grandeur of a temple that originally had 104 columns
over 56 feet (17 m) in height. Built in the Corinthian order
and entirely of pentelic marble, the temple measured 130
by 340 feet (40 × 104 m), as compared to the 101 by 228
feet (31 × 70 m) of the Parthenon. Though the photograph
shows only a few remaining columns, it also reveals the
full stylobate of the temple, clearly indicating its enormous
size. Affirming the Roman preference for the ornate

7.43   Cossutius, Temple of the Olympian Zeus, Athens.
Ca. 174 BC–AD 131. Pentelic marble, 130 × 340' (40 × 104 m).
Photo: © 1989 Loyola University of Chicago (R.V. Schoder,
S.J.).

Corinthian, the architect was Italic and the grandiose project completed by the Roman emperor Hadrian.

The *Laocoön and His Sons* (lay-OK-o-on; fig. 7.44) is
an extravagantly dramatic version of the fate of the Trojan
priest. Supposedly punished by Poseidon's sea serpents
because he warned his people of the Trojan horse scheme,

7.44 Hagesandros, Polydoros, and Athenodoros of Rhodes, *Laocoön and His Sons*. 1st century AD. Marble, height 8' (2.44 m). Musei Vaticani, Rome. Photo: Hirmer, Munich.

the three Trojans writhe and struggle, their faces distorted with terror. Despite his bulging muscles the priest is at the mercy of the god. When discovered in 1506 this work's striking virtuosity made an enormous impression on Michelangelo and other Renaissance artists. The Romans probably imported the *Laocoön* because it represented a vital episode in pre-Roman history. Forewarned of Troy's fall by the priest's punishment, Aeneas escaped from the doomed city to fulfill his destiny as the legendary founder of Rome.

MUSIC

Music was a requisite for the good life in ancient Greece. The education of the young men of Athens was not complete without extensive instruction in the ethical qualities of music with approximately equal time devoted to music performance. Further, there must be instruction in gymnastics roughly equal to the time and effort expended on music. Music and gymnastics had to be evenly balanced to reach the goal of a sound mind in a healthy body. According to Plato, too much time in the gymnasium makes men "more brutal than they should be," while too much music making causes performers to be "softer than is good for them."

The concept of the balanced regimen apparently

originated with Pythagoras, who drew an analogy between a vibrating, finely tuned string and the human mind and body. When stretched to the proper tension and plucked or bowed, the string will produce the exact musical tone that the performer requires. If stretched too tight, the string will break; if the tension is insufficient, the string will be dull and unresponsive. In other words, the mind (musical tone) and the body (tensed string) function best when they are completely in harmony with each other.

The Greek word for music (*mousike*; MOO-si-kay) means "of the Muses": the nine goddesses who presided over the arts, literature, and science (see box 4.1, p. 57). "Music" was therefore an umbrella term, but music as we understand the word was prominent in everyday life in four distinct ways:

1. The arts of singing and of playing a musical instrument. The relationship of poetry and music was symbiotic; rarely did one art form appear without the other.
2. Music in the educational process, that is, performing and listening to music as a vital part of the ethical training that inculcates virtue and "sobriety in the soul" (Plato). This is the doctrine of ethos that figured so prominently in Greek philosophy.
3. The study of the scientific basis of music, emphasizing acoustics (the science of sound) and mathematics.
4. Music and mathematics as a key to understanding the harmony of the universe, the Pythagorean "music of the spheres."

All Athenian citizens were involved in performance, listening, and music education. Plato, Aristotle, and other philosophers dealt with other aspects of music, from the Muses to mathematics to metaphysics.

Musical Instruments

The principal instruments were the lyre, a larger version of the lyre called the kithara, and the aulos. According to mythology the infant Hermes, son of Zeus, killed a turtle and strung gut strings across the hollow shell. That the strings were made from intestines of oxen stolen from his brother Apollo complicated the situation. Hermes craftily avoided further trouble by allowing Apollo to play his lyre. Thus the beginning of the legendary lyre and with it the lyre-playing tradition of the cult of Apollo (fig. 7.45).

The seat of the Apollonian cult was the island of Delos and subsequently Delphi. The myths extol the virtues of the early musical life of a Greek mainland untouched by alien influences. Marvelous were the deeds of heroes and of divinely endowed musicians such as Orpheus, Amphion, and others, all with names connected with ancient tribes in the northern part of the mainland. As the tribes migrated they carried their music with them. The Dorians moved to Sparta and as far south as Crete, the Aeolians settled in the eastern Aegean, and the Ionians moved from the west

7.45 *Lyre Player of "The Boston Throne."* Ca. 470–450 BC. Three-sided marble relief, height at center 38" (96.5 cm). Museum of Fine Arts, Boston (H. L. Pierce Fund). The lyre was usually played from a sitting position.

7.46 *Aulos Player of the Ludovisi Throne.* Ca. 460 BC. Marble, height 4' (1.2 m). Museo Nazionale Romano, Rome. Photo: Hirmer, Munich.
One of the few known female nudes from the classical period, this lovely work is also notable for the relaxed and casual pose. The aulos could be played standing or sitting.

to the east central mainland and to Asia Minor.

The Ionians brought with them their music and their national instrument, the lyre. The influence of Oriental elements synthesized the two cultures which, in turn, led to the founding of Greek classical music, poetry, and dance. Characteristically, mythology depicts the Ionian migration by relating how Orpheus accidentally dropped his lyre, which drifted eastward across the Aegean to the island of Lesbos, the home of Sappho, the famous poet-musician.

The Near East produced the other national instrument, the reed pipe, or aulos (fig. 7.46). The inventors of this pungent-toned instrument (which sounded somewhat like a modern oboe) came from Phrygia in Asia Minor. The aulos was associated with the Phrygian mode and the cult of Dionysos, as contrasted with the lyre, the instrument of the Dorian mode and the cult of Apollo. There was a notable conflict between the two cults. The East did not fully accept the lyre, possibly because its tone quality was too delicate compared to the reedy, nasal quality of the aulos. Legend recounts a musical competition between Olen the Lycian on the lyre and Olympos the Phrygian on the aulos. The results of the contest were inconclusive, indicating that the competing instruments attained a state of parity. The whole of Greek musical culture reflected this kind of balance of power between the Apollonian lyre and the Dionysian aulos, between the intellect and the passions.

The Musicians

The earliest musicians were apparently the blind singers who performed the Homeric epics. Greek legends abound with accounts of singers so full of hubris they challenged the gods. Thamyris was blinded by the Muses because of his boasting. The blind singer Teiresias (as in Sophocles' *Oedipus*) suffered the same penalty for revealing things men should not know.[3] Misenis lost a musical contest to the sea gods and was drowned in the Aegean. The satyr Marsyas was a spectacular loser. First, he picked up the aulos that Athena had discarded because she felt she looked undignified while playing it. She had Marsyas beaten for his impudence. Failing to take the celestial hint, he then challenged Apollo to a playing contest, for which

3. Because Teiresias had been both a woman and a man, Zeus asked him which enjoyed sex more. When Teiresias replied that women did, Hera was so angry to have the secret revealed that she struck the poet-musician blind. As partial compensation, Zeus awarded him the gift of prophecy.

audacity he was flayed alive.

The most famous singer-poet was Orpheus, reputedly the son of Apollo and Calliope. The powers attributed to Orpheus were staggering. In order to rescue Eurydice (you-RID-uh-sea), he enchanted the underworld with his lyre. He cast spells on all aspects of nature, and he was credited with inventing poetic meter and even the alphabet. The last attribute may refer to the musical notation that was based on the Greek alphabet.

The earliest historical figure to emerge from the legendary past personified by the mythical Olympos is the kithara-player, Terpander of Lesbos (ca. 675 BC). His musical powers were so renowned that the Delphic Oracle ordered him to Sparta to help quell dissension within the state. As the first known musician, Terpander is regarded as the founder of Greek classical music.

WORDS AND MUSIC

Most Greek musicians were, like Orpheus, singer-poets (or poet-musicians) who played the accompaniment as they sang their poetry. The first of these **lyric** poets—that is, those who sang with the lyre—was Archilochos (are-ki-LOW-kos; fl. 660 BC) of Paros, a major musical innovator. Before his time each note of music was closely linked to the words. He added "dissenting" notes that were not in unison with the melody, and added embellishments that were improvised on between stanzas. In brief, he made the lyre a solo instrument and a more interesting partner in song. Archilochos was a part-time poet-musician, by occupation a mercenary soldier who died on an unknown battlefield. Later, many poet-musicians, such as Sappho and Simonides, could devote themselves fully to their art.

The illustrious poet-musician Sappho was born on the Aegean island of Lesbos and lived most of her long life there. At a time when Solon was legislating in Athens and Jeremiah was prophesying in Palestine, she was at the height of her fame—and fully aware of her reputation:

> The Muses have made me happy
> And worthy of the world's envy,
> So that even beyond death
> I shall be remembered.

Celebrated in both the Greek and Roman worlds, her poems were preserved until the third century AD by Alexandrian editors but were later almost totally destroyed by zealous Christians along with other so-called pagan literature. The three surviving poems and many fragments remain to testify to the beauty of her lyric poetry, sung to the delicate sounds of the lyre. "Lead off, my lyre,/And we shall sing together."

Sappho's poems focus on her erotic passions and jealousies, but there are also references to two brothers and to her daughter, Kleïs. Though knowledge of her personal life is fragmentary, Sappho certainly enjoyed the social and domestic freedom of a society in which highly educated women mixed freely with men as their equals. Not confined to a subordinate existence like Ionian women or subject to a military discipline like the Dorians of Sparta, Aeolian women were devoted to the arts of beauty—especially poetry, music, and dance.

LITERARY SELECTION 4

God's Stunning Daughter
Sappho (fl. 6th century BC)

In the following complete poem, Sappho appeals to Aphrodite to help her win the affections of a reluctant girl. Aphrodite's response is good-natured but a bit impatient; Sappho has made this kind of request before and she will certainly make it again. Moreover, as Aphrodite points out, the girl refuses your gifts today but you will refuse hers tomorrow.

God's stunning daughter deathless Aphrodite,
A whittled perplexity your bright abstruse chair,
Don't blunt my stubborn eye with breathlessness, lady,
To tame my heart.

But come down to me, as you came before,
For if ever I cried, and you heard and came,
Come now, of all times, leaving
Your father's golden house

In that chariot pulled by sparrows reined and bitted,
Swift in their flying, a quick blur aquiver,   10
Beautiful, high. They drew you across steep air
Down to the black earth;

Fast they came, and you behind them, O
Hilarious heart, your face all laughter,
Asking, What troubles you this time, why again
Do you call me down?

Asking, in your wild heart, who now
Must you have? Who is she that persuasion
Fetch her, enlist her, and put her into bounden love?
Sappho, who does you wrong?   20

If she balks, I promise, soon she'll chase,
If she's turned from gifts, now she'll give them.
And if she does not love you, she will love,
Helpless, she will love.

Come, then, loose me from cruelties.
Give my tethered heart its full desire.
Fulfill, and, come, lock your shield with mine
Throughout the siege.

The next poem is also complete except for the last four words added by the translator. The theme is jealousy, a recital of physical torments brought about by the loved one's interest in conversing with a man. The emotions are strong but recollected in tranquility in carefully chosen words. Translated into Latin by Catullus, it was praised by Plutarch as "a masterpiece among poems of passionate love."

He Seems to Be a God

Sappho

He seems to be a god, that man
Facing you, who leans to be close,
Smiles, and, alert and glad, listens
To your mellow voice

And quickens in love at your laughter.
That stings my breasts, jolts my heart
If I dare the shock of a glance.
I cannot speak,

My tongue sticks to my dry mouth,
Thin fire spreads beneath my skin,
My eyes cannot see and my aching ears
Roar in their labyrinths.

Chill sweat slides down my body,
I shake, I turn greener than grass.
I am neither living nor dead and cry
From the narrow between.

But endure, even [this grief of love].

As a young man Plato liked to write poetry, including this tribute to another poet:

Some say there are nine Muses; but they're wrong.
Look at Sappho of Lesbos; she makes ten.

THE ART OF DANCE

Human beings seem to have always enjoyed dance, and few people have relished dance more than the ancient Greeks. Greek dance probably began as a form of worship, ritual, witchcraft, enchantment, and sexual symbolism in association with fertility rites. Plato believed that dance was a natural expression of emotions and that it might have grown out of the use of gestures to imitate words and phrases.

All of our knowledge of steps and movements is based on the figures on vases, on architectural friezes, and, to some extent, on various writings referring to dance. The dancing figures in Greek art display a variety of design and gesture, but over many centuries certain positions occur repeatedly. Arm movements were built either upon a straight line of the arm from shoulder to fingertip or upon the angularity of bending the arm at the elbow to form a right angle. The two basic positions could be somewhat curved by increasing the angle at the elbow, by bending at the wrist, or both at the same time. The intrinsic designs, however, were maintained. The straight lines and curves were normally associated with light and delicate Appollonian dances, while the angular positions were used in dramatic Dionysian

dances. These were invariably emotional and frequently frenzied. Dancers sometimes wore the animal skins of the Dionysian cult: bull, fawn, goat, fox, and panther. For the wild mountain dances they carried snakes. The revelers were called maenads, thyiades, bacchantes, and satyrs. The two Dionysian festivals held every year included dancing, sacrificial processions, banquets, choruses conducted by the poets, and the tragedies and comedies that were the eagerly awaited highlights of each festival.

Unfortunately no actual music has come down to us from the Periclean age. In fact, only a few scattered works and some fragments have survived even from Hellenistic times. However, the *Seikolos Song*,[4] which was found engraved on a tombstone in Asia Minor, provides something akin to the sound of ancient Greek music. The epitaph is still timely: "As long as you live, be cheerful; let nothing grieve you, for life is short and time claims its tribute."

Listening Example 1
GREEK MUSIC

Anonymous, *Seikolos Song*
Ca. AD 50

Time: 0:25
Cassette 3, track 1[5]

Seikolos Song (Phrygian mode)   **Anonymous (ca. AD 50)**

As long as you live, be cheerful; let nothing grieve you. For life is short, and time claims its tribute.

STUDY QUESTIONS

1. Compare vases of the four basic styles: geometric, black-figure, red-figure, white-ground.
   Which style do you find most appealing? Why?
2. Select a piece of sculpture from each of the four major periods of Greek art. Describe how they differ, each from the other, and then relate them to what was going on in Greek society at each particular time. Which style is most appealing for you? Why?

---

4. T. Reinach, *La Musique Grecque* 1926, p. 193.
5. Many of the musical examples for this text are selected from the four CDs entitled *Listener's Guide to Musical Understanding*. This is CD 1, track 1.

3. Prepare a project on "Greek Architectural Influence in _____," specifying your own community or college town. Which buildings are essentially Doric, Ionic, or Corinthian? Which have elements of two or more orders? Are there any structures patterned after the Greek temple plan, with or without modifications? Are there Greek facades stuck on other architectural styles?

The key to the project is the identification of Greek elements followed by an analysis of how they are used with other styles. Your project can culminate in a slide show, photo album, video tape, or perhaps a collection of drawings.

4. Consider the two basic forms of Greek dance—Apollonian and Dionysian. Are there any modern dances (popular, jazz, ballroom) that are Dionysian? Apollonian? A bit of both? Identify the dances and describe the movements.

SUMMARY

The Greeks yearned for reassurance that they lived in a rational and orderly universe in which there were certain eternal truths and, most important, an appropriate place for humanity. Their passion for beauty and order was manifested as early as the geometric period (900–700 BC) in which even the simplest utilitarian vase was meticulously decorated. During the archaic period (750–480 BC) there was a slow but constant evolution from the rigid sculpture early in the period toward a naturalism that characterized later works such as the *Kore from Khios* and the *Anavyssos Kouros*. The movement from formalism to realism also characterized vase painting as the stark and dramatic black-figure technique was superseded by the red-figure style.

The classical period (480–323 BC) was the crowning glory of every aspect of Greek culture from the visual arts to music, poetry, drama, dance, vase painting, and the philosophy of Socrates, Plato, and Aristotle. Masterpieces of the Periclean age included the *Poseidon*, *Discobolus*, *Doryphoros*, the Riace bronze, the Parthenon pediments, metopes, and frieze, and the perfected temples: Parthenon, Erechtheion, Athena Nike, and Concord. Their achievements in red-figure and white-ground painting were not even approached until the Renaissance.

The Greeks themselves considered music the most important of all the arts. A proper balance of instruction in the visual arts, literature, music, and gymnastics formed the educational foundation of every citizen, with music education (in poetry and music) providing a rigorous ethical training according to the doctrine of ethos. Through the acoustics of music the Greeks

determined the mathematical relationship of sounding bodies and constructed a theory of unity and perfection symbolized by a vibrating string. This eventually led to a metaphysical concept of a universe that the human mind could comprehend.

Poetry, dance, and music were allied arts in the Greek theatre, notably in the plays of Aeschylus, Sophocles, Euripides, and Aristophanes. Lyric poetry was all poetry accompanied by the lyre, the instrument of Apollo. Dramatic poetry was declaimed, chanted, and sung on stage to the accompaniment of the aulos, the instrument of Dionysos. Whatever the art form, the ideal was to combine the rationality of Apollo, god of reason and invention, with the emotional drive of Dionysos, god of fertility and wine, but always with the rational mind in control.

Although there was a gradual diminution in quality during the Hellenistic period (323–30 BC), Greek culture still gave the world such dynamic sculptures as *The Dying Gaul*, *Nike of Samothrace*, and the *Laocoön* (see figs. 7.39, 7.40 and 7.44), and such monumental buildings as the Temple of the Olympian Zeus (see p. 54 and fig. 7.43). It was the latter that symbolized the passing of the cultural torch from Greece to Rome. Begun in the middle of the Hellenistic period, the massive structure was completed by an Italic architect during the reign of Emperor Hadrian.

CULTURE AND HUMAN VALUES

The Athenian Golden Age lasted only one generation (ca. 460–430 BC) and yet its achievements, some of which are summarized above, are still among the most significant in human history. Why was this brief period so spectacular? The answer seems to lie in certain values directed to human ends that Athenians held in common. Athenians of this unique age valued optimism, a belief that anything and everything could be achieved or at least tried. Freedom was cherished by all, as were the rights of the individual to compete in a society in which vigorous competition was the norm. Excellence was the goal of every endeavor and the pride engendered by notable achievements was confirmed as an appropriate consequence. Let us examine each of these values.

Optimism
Within a ten-year period the upstart Greeks, led by the Athenians, had twice defeated the mighty Persian Empire. For a loose confederation of highly individualistic city-states this was an incredible accomplishment, after which just about anything seemed possible. The truism that nothing succeeds like success carried a certain weight in Athens. Pericles commissioned a noble temple honoring the city's patron

and the magnificent Parthenon rose on the Acropolis. Plans for a temple honoring Athena and Poseidon resulted in the remarkable Erechtheion. A tiny structure to house Victory became a perfect Ionic temple that charmed all who saw it. It was this kind of continuous reinforcement that inspired the Athenians and amazed their rivals.

Freedom

The progressive political reforms of Solon, Pisistratos, and Cleisthenes were carried out at the highest effective level by the astute leadership of Pericles. Political freedom provided the necessary framework for the pursuit of truth, beauty, and justice. Citizens optimistically assumed that a free society best served the interests of all the people, which became a self-fulfilling prophecy. The most critical freedom was the unrestrained pursuit of knowledge in a society that valued learning for its own sake. With neither an organized religion nor a priestly caste with vested interests in the status quo, individuals were free to seek answers wherever they might be found. Ignorance and superstition were, as always, conspicuous but not threatening, because they were not institutionalized by creeds or dogmas.

Individuality and Competition

That we know so many Greeks by name is not surprising for a society in which reality was the individual. The individual was paramount in Greece because personal achievements were the measure of all things.

Emphasizing individuality characterized the city-states while it also prevented any long-term federation. Athens was an Ionian city in which life was sophisticated and elegant. Sparta was Dorian and life was lean and "Spartan." Athens was a cosmopolitan seaport; Sparta was landlocked and provincial. Athenians loved to joke about Sparta. Spartans, they said, fought to the death on the battlefield so they wouldn't have to go back to Sparta. Spartans didn't make jokes; life was a serious business. Athens and Sparta were not only vastly different but, as might be expected, very competitive. Each thought its society superior to the other leading, perhaps inevitably, to the war that drained all combatants.

The Olympic, Delphic, and other athletic, poetic, and musical contests provided special arenas for head-to-head competition. Winning was all-important with one winner for each event and everyone else an also-ran. Drama contests were just as competitive with the eagerly sought prize awarded to the best intellectual creation. These contests were considered so vital that second-place dramatists were granted a return engagement.

The Pursuit of Excellence

As discussed earlier, the Greek word for skill is *arete*

(ARE-uh-tay), best translated as "diligence in the pursuit of excellence." Whether an artist, poet, politician, or athlete, each Greek assumed that he could be the best at whatever he chose to do and that, moreover, his accomplishment could be the best in its field. Greek artists, for example, competed against each other for pride of place, but they also competed against an unspoken standard of excellence known only to each artist.

Pride

A justifiable pride in superior accomplishments was the hallmark of the Greek passion for excellence. Contrary to Judeo-Christian doctrine, pride was not a vice but a virtue. The virtue of pride should not be confused, however, with the vice of hubris, which identified an excessive pride that could harm another human being (such as Oedipus). The proper balance was struck by observing the Greek motto "Nothing in excess." For Pythagoras the standard was the "Middle way" and, for Aristotle, the "Golden Mean." However stated, it was the sensible Greek approach to moderation in all things.

The Legacy of Greece

The Greeks of antiquity established a superb foundation for the development of most of Western civilization. They constructed a rational, viable, and humanistic culture in which the emphasis was upon the individual and each person's pursuit of excellence. Their achievements were by no means limited to the arts and philosophy discussed in this text, for they also excelled in commerce, seafaring, medicine, coinage, engraved gems, decorative metalwork, painting and mosaics, glassware, furniture, and textiles. Adding up all of these contributions reveals a marvelously rounded culture that achieved, during the Golden Age, a quality of life never to be seen again. They established standards that serve as thesis or antithesis for contemporary judgments and achievements throughout our cultural life.

It is important that the great age of Greece came before Christ. The stimulating, even subversive place of Greece comes from belonging within a Western world fundamentally based on Christianity.[6]

Skeptical, resilient, frequently cantankerous, the Greeks celebrated excellence and despised mediocrity. Constantly seeking an understanding of the world and everything in it, they asked not only "Why?" but also "Why not?" And they expected sane and sensible answers. There has never been anyone quite like them.

---

6. Oliver Taplin, *Greek Fire: The Influence of Ancient Greece on the Modern World* (New York: Atheneum, 1990), p.33.

Rome:
The
International
Culture

Rome

753 BC–AD 476

	Key Dates	People and Events	Literature	Art and Architecture	Religion, Science, Philosophy
600 BC	**753** Founding of Rome (trad.)	**606–509** Etruscan period with Tarquin kings			
500	**509–27** Roman Republic	**509** Tarquins overthrown			
400	**450** Romans colonize Italy			**ca. 500** *She-Wolf of the Capital* (Etruscan)	
300	**343–290** Samnite wars: Rome dominant in Italy	**390** Gauls sack Rome	**Theocritus** 310?–250 poet		**Epicurus** 341–270 **Zeno the Stoic** 335?–263?
200	**264–241** First Punic War with Carthage; Rome acquires Sicily, Corsica, Sardinia **218–201** Second Punic War; Rome rules western Mediterranean **214–146** Macedonian wars: Rome rules Greece **200–133** Conquest of Near East	**287** *Lex Hortensia* ends patrician-plebeian conflict **216** Hannibal invades Italy; defeats Romans at Cannae **202** Scipio Africanus invades Africa	**Plautus** 254?–184 dramatist **Polybius** 205–133 historian		
100	**149–146** Third Punic War; Carthage destroyed	**146** Corinth destroyed	**Terence** 190?–159 dramatist **Cicero** 106–43 **Caesar** 102–44 *Commentaries*		
0	**88–82 BC** Civil War: Sulla/Marius **80–43** Age of Cicero **60** First Triumvirate: Pompey, Crassus, Caesar **49** Caesar crosses Rubicon **44** Caesar assassinated by Brutus, Cassius, and others **43** Second Triumvirate: Mark Antony, Lepidus, Octavian (Augustus) **42 BC–AD 17** Augustan golden age **31** Naval battle of Actium	**82–79 BC** Sulla: dictator **73–71** Slave revolt; Spartacus **63** Cicero as consul **59** Caesar as consul **58–51** Caesar conquers Gaul **48–45** Caesar campaigns in Asia Minor, Egypt (Cleopatra), Spain **27 BC–AD 14** Reign of Caesar Augustus **4 BC?** Birth of Christ	**Sallust** 86–34 BC historian **Catullus** 84–54 poet **Virgil** 70–19 *Aeneid* **Horace** 65–8 *Odes* **Livy** 59 BC–AD 17 *History of Rome* **Ovid** 43 BC–AD 17 *Art of Love; Metamorphoses* **Seneca the Younger** 3 BC–AD 65 dramatist	**Vitruvius** ca. 50–ca. AD 10 *De architectura* **ca. 50–** Villa of the Mysteries, Pompeii **27–** Roman Forum, *Ara Pacis*, Baths of Agrippa, Theatre of Marcellus, Rome **20** *Augustus of Primaporta* **20–10** Pont du Gard, Nîmes **19** Maison Carrée, Nîmes	**Lucretius** ca. 96–55 *On the Nature of Things* (Epicureanism)
AD 100	**27 BC–AD 476** Roman Empire **27 BC–AD 180** *Pax Romana* **AD 17–130** Silver Age **70** Titus destroys Jerusalem and the Temple of Solomon **79** Mount Vesuvius destroys Pompeii and Herculaneum **96–180** The "Good Emperors"	**14–37** Reign of Tiberius **37–41** Caligula **41–54** Claudius **54–68** Nero **69** Galba, Otho, Vitellius, Flavian Caesars **69–79** Vespasian **71–81** Titus **81–96** Domitian, Antonine Caesars **96–98** Nerva **98–117** Trajan	**Petronius** d. 66 *Satyricon* **Pliny the Elder** 23–79 naturalist **Quintilian** 35–ca. 100 *Institutes of Oratory* **Lucan** 39–65 poet **Martial** 40–104 *Epigrams* **Plutarch** 46–120 historian **Tacitus** 55–120 historian **Juvenal** 60–140 *Satires* **Pliny the Younger** 62–114 writer **Suetonius** ca. 70–160 *Lives of the Caesars*	**54** Roman baths in England **70** *Herakles Discovering the Infant Telephos in Arcadia* **72–80** Colosseum, Rome **81** Arch of Titus, Rome	**d. 29?** Jesus Christ **d. 64?** Apostle Peter **d. 67?** Apostle Paul **Epictetus** ca. 60–110 Stoic philosopher: *Discourses*
200	**180–476** Decline and fall	**117–138** Hadrian **138–161** Antoninus Pius **161–180** Marcus Aurelius **180–192** Commodus **193–211** Septimius Severus	**Lucian** ca. 117–180 Greek satirist **Apuleius** fl. 160 *Golden Ass*	**106–113** Column, Baths, and Forum of Trajan, Rome **118–125** Pantheon, Rome **135–139** Hadrian's tomb and villa, Tivoli **161–180** Equestrian Statue of Marcus Aurelius, Rome	**Marcus Aurelius** 121–180 *Meditations* **Ptolemy** fl. 126–151 astronomer **Galen** ca. 130–200 physician
300		**211–217** Caracalla **222–235** Alexander Severus **235–284** "Barracks Emperors" (25 out of 26 murdered) **284–305** Diocletian		**ca. 212** Baths of Caracalla, Rome **298–306** Baths of Diocletian, Rome	**Plotinus** 205–270 founder of Neoplatonism
400	**313** Edict of Milan; freedom of worship **330** Constantine establishes Eastern capital in Constantinople **395** Theodosius proclaims Christianity sole permitted state religion	**307–337** Constantine I **337–361** Constantius **361–363** Julian **363–364** Jovian **364–378** Valens **379–395** Theodosius I **395–403** Honorius		**312–315** Arch of Constantine, Rome **330** *Constantine the Great*	**St. Jerome** 340–420 **St. Ambrose** 340–397 **St. Augustine** 354–430

The Roman Empire "fell" in 410 with the sack of Rome by the Visigoths or in 476 when the last Roman emperor was deposed.

CHAPTER 8

A Thousand Years of Rome

ROMAN LEGENDS AND VIRTUES

"So great a labor," wrote Virgil, "was it to found the Roman race." And it all began, according to legend, with Romulus and Remus, twin sons of Mars, god of war, and of Rhea Silvia, daughter of King Numitor. It seems that Amulius, Numitor's wicked brother, usurped the throne, forced his niece into service as a Vestal Virgin,[1] and, to secure his rule against future claimants, ordered the infants placed in a flimsy basket and set adrift on the Tiber River. Rescued and suckled by a she-wolf, the ancient symbol of Rome, they were discovered by a shepherd couple and raised to vigorous manhood.

Upon learning their identity they demonstrated their straightforward Roman nature by immediately killing Amulius and restoring Numitor to the throne. Ignoring an omen pointing to Romulus as Rome's founder, they resolutely set off to fulfill their destiny: establish a mighty city on the seven hills by the Tiber. The inevitable quarrel between Romulus, the serious twin, and the lighthearted Remus leads to the latter's death, apparently because Remus made fun of a wall constructed by Romulus and fell a victim to his brother's self-righteous wrath. Romulus subsequently raised an army, supplied the soldiers with Sabine wives (the Rape of the Sabines), and, to make a long story short, founded Rome right on schedule in 753 BC. And much as Moses received the tablets of law on the mountain, he accepted the first constitution from the gods and completed his imperative by becoming the first king of the Romans.

Establishing the Roman Republic was the first step; the Roman Empire had its own legendary beginning as related by Virgil (see pp. 140–1) in his epic poem, the *Aeneid*. "It is the nature," boasted Ovid, "of a Roman to do and suffer bravely," and Aeneas (uh-NEE-us) was the prototype of the stoic Roman hero. As Troy fell to the Greeks under Agamemnon, Aeneas and a loyal band of Trojan warriors escaped the debacle and sailed west to confront their destiny. Dumped on a North African shore by a mighty storm,

they made their way to nearby Carthage where Queen Dido (DIE-doe) received them with full honors while promptly falling in love with Aeneas. As much as stern duty would allow, Aeneas responded in kind, knowing that he must abandon her to fulfill his sacred mission of founding Rome. A despairing Dido chose suicide and, while she lay on her funeral pyre, still hopeful of a last-ditch rescue, Aeneas sailed resolutely to Sicily and finally to the banks of the Tiber. There he fought and defeated Turnus, married Lavinia the beautiful daughter of King Latinus, and dutifully established the "first among cities, the home of gods, golden Rome" (Ausonius).

Rome was fated to be a city of warriors, grandeur and glory, and its legends of Romulus and Remus and of Aeneas were actually self-fulfilling prophecies. Romulus was descended from the god of war and Aeneas was the progenitor of the stalwart city that would restore Trojan honor by conquering the wily Greeks of the wooden horse. Rome was nourished by the forces of nature, symbolized by the she-wolf, and raised to maturity by good people of the soil, the peasant couple who reared the twins. Rome pursued its imperative by seizing the Sabine lands and women, and established its legitimacy with a god-given constitution.

The Romans saw themselves as destined for world leadership; as Cicero said, "We were born to unite with our fellowmen, and to join in community with the human race." They would triumph because they were a no-nonsense, practical people with the exemplary virtues of thrift, honesty, loyalty, and dedication to hard work. Little interested in abstractions or theory, they had two questions: "Does it work?" and "How can we get the job done?" As Remus discovered, building an illustrious city was no laughing matter; obligations to the city took precedence over everything else, even passion, a lesson lost on the ill-fated Queen of Carthage. Duty to golden Rome was the noblest virtue of all.

Etruscan Influence

The Aeneas legend may have been based on the Etruscans, the mysterious people who emerged in northern Italy during the ninth century BC. Herodotos said they were an advanced culture from the Kingdom of Lydia in western

---

[1]. Selected daughters of the best families served the goddess Vesta in chastity and obedience. Amulius undoubtedly forced Rhea Silvia into the arms of the goddess so that she would not bear a legitimate heir to the throne.

Asia Minor (near Troy), a view today's historians cannot contradict. The Etruscans used letters derived from an archaic Greek alphabet but their language resembles no other tongue, in Lydia or anywhere else. Leaving an immense quantity of art, partially decoded inscriptions, and some undeciphered literature, their origins may never be known.

The Etruscans conquered most of central and northern Italy and ruled Rome itself during the sixth century BC. The decisive battle at Lake Vadimon in 308 BC broke Etruscan political and military power, but the cultural inheritance was exceptionally strong. From Etruscan civilization Rome derived street plans for cities, the idea of the triumphal procession, gladiatorial combat, and the masonry arch, the critical technological contribution. Etruria was densely populated and enjoyed a high standard of living, with large cities surrounded by market towns, villages, and exceptionally productive agricultural areas. Etruscans supported their affluent life-style with the most sophisticated sanitary and civil engineering in the Mediterranean world. Rome's spectacular achievements in engineering and construction were based on the expertise of their conquered enemies.

But Rome did not accept all things Etruscan. Such concerns as life after death, elaborate tombs, and most especially, luxurious living, did not suit sober Roman sensibilities. The pursuit of pleasure shocked the austere and dutiful Romans. Moreover, Etruscan women and men enjoyed about the same rights and liberties, whereas Roman women had scarcely any freedom at all. Etruscan tomb paintings portrayed women drinking wine with men but Roman women couldn't even socialize with men, much less drink with them. The status of Etruscan women so enraged the Romans that they accused them of gross promiscuity, even temple prostitution, judgments that tell us more about self-righteous Romans than it does about Etruscan morality. Nor were the chauvinistic Greeks any less critical of Etruscan society.

Greek Influence

Rome came under Greek influence very early, in the eighth century BC, when Greek immigrants founded colonies in southern Italy and Sicily in what the Romans called Magna Graecia. Syracuse, Naples, Paestum, Elea, the Pythagoreans of Crotona, the pleasure-loving Greeks of Sybaris—all flourished under the stern gaze of Romans who were always ambivalent about the Greeks. Awed by an obviously superior civilization, they were also hostile, for Greek culture amounted to a reversal of Roman values: urbane, artistic, intellectual, sophisticated, always seeking the good life. Roman enmity was not unexpected from an austere, rigid, and self-righteous society that stressed manly virtues, physical prowess, and duty to the state. From this point of view the Greeks were obviously dissolute and debauched.

THE REPUBLIC, 509–27 BC

Rome was not built in one day.
John Heywood, *Proverbs*, 1546

According to still another Roman tradition, the Republic began in 509 BC with the expulsion of the Etruscan king Tarquin the Proud. Never interested in abstractions or political theory, they pragmatically accepted their kingless state and made adjustments as necessary. We can call it the let's-try-it-this-way-and-see-if-it-stops-hurting philosophy of government. Tarquin's hurried departure left behind an oligarchy (government by the few), which became the basis of the new state. (Plato defined an oligarchy as "A government resting on the valuation of property, in which the rich have power and the poor man is deprived of it.") The oligarchs, the land-owning aristocrats, established a republic with full citizenship reserved for themselves, the patricians (Lat., *pater*, "father"). The other 90 percent or so of the population, the plebeians (pluh-BEE-uns; Lat., *plebs*, "the multitude"), could neither hold office nor marry into the patrician class. They could make money, however, making political adjustments inevitable.

Patricians and Plebeians

The patrician class supplied the executive heads of state, the two consuls who governed with full power for one year (except that each had veto power over the other). Already senators themselves, the consuls appointed patricians to life terms in the 300-member Senate. The other legislative body, the Centuriate Assembly, had less power than the Senate but it did elect the consuls and passed on laws submitted to it by the consuls or Senate. From among the exconsuls the Assembly elected two censors who determined eligibility for military service and ruled on the moral qualifications of Senate nominees.

Consuls were commanders of the army but, in time of war, their mutual veto power could jeopardize the state. Rome invented another adjustment, of course, a dictator, a supreme military commander who received his authority constitutionally and relinquished it at the end of his six-month term. When Julius Caesar had himself elected dictator for life his enemies had their worst fears confirmed.

The Roman oligarchy kept the plebeians in an intolerable situation but their growing financial power did force the Senate to create the new office of tribune, protector of the people. Later in the century (fifth century BC) ever more powerful plebeian forces accused the judges of abusing their office because there were no written laws. The reaction was most uncharacteristic; the Senate sent a commission to Athens to observe Solon's reformed legal system. The commission returned to compose the Twelve Tables of Law, at which point Roman conservatism reasserted itself. The new laws were as harsh as Draco's fierce legal code of nearly two centuries earlier (see p. 60), the very system that Solon's humane reforms had replaced.

Economics and the Military

Roman pragmatists never solved the problem of ownership of the land, a failure that had much to do with the Empire's demise. From the beginning of the Republic absentee landlords controlled a large part of the agricultural market, leaving the working farmer, with his small acreage, struggling to make ends meet. Competition from estate holders plus drought and pestilence forced him into debt and finally into a slavery decreed by the severe Twelve Tables. Large estates grew larger, operating with lower overheads because they used war-booty slaves. The inexorable price for noncompetitive farms was bankruptcy. (There were strikingly similar dilemmas in the American South before the Civil War.) Even after reforms barring debt-slavery and attempts to redistribute land, many farmers ended up as urban poor: landless and unemployed. Unable to work the land their ancestors had farmed for centuries and unfit for employment in a city that relied on slave labor, they became part of the permanent welfare program. By the first century BC about 80 percent of Rome's population was either slave laborers or subsisting on "bread and circuses." The welfare program was a failure because, as Plutarch observed, "The man who first ruined the Roman people was he who first gave them treats and gratuities."

Roman talent for organization was most spectacularly evidenced by their awesome military power. Reducing the ponderous 8,000-man phalanx to 3,600 men armed with javelin and short Roman sword, they created a mobile striking force that could march 24 miles (39 km) in five hours, each man carrying a 60-pound (27-kg) pack. Steely discipline honed a war machine that gave no quarter and asked none.

Some apologists claim that Rome backed into empire, much as England did in the nineteenth century, but this is simply not so. Roman conquest clearly became an end in itself during Republican days. The point at which Rome set out to deliberately conquer the world was probably 146 BC, the final year of the Punic Wars with Carthage (264–146 BC). The First Punic War began when Carthage, the powerful Phoenician colony in North Africa, attempted to expand its trading empire in eastern Sicily. Responding to the appeals of their Greek allies, Roman armies found themselves opposing the Carthaginian navy. Hurriedly building their first fighting fleet, the Romans somehow managed to defeat Carthage while losing more ships through ineptness than to enemy action.

Spain, which had resisted Roman domination for two centuries, became the Carthaginian base for the Second Punic War (218–201 BC). Stating that "we will either find a way or make one," the remarkable general Hannibal crossed the Alps with his elephants and attacked Rome

from the rear. Unable to compete with his brilliant tactics, a desperate Rome attacked his vulnerable homeland thus ending Carthage's dominance of the western Mediterranean. The Third Punic War, however, was a different kind of conflict.

Marcus Porcius Cato (Cato the Elder, the Censor; 234–149 BC) was a senator, consul, censor, and writer, and a prime instigator of the final attack on Carthage. Renowned for his devotion to Roman ideals of simplicity, honesty, courage, ability to endure hardship, rigorous sexual morality, and loyalty to Rome and the family, Cato opposed luxury, cultivation of the arts, and extravagance in any form. He hated the Greeks. Believing that fathers should educate their sons in the home, he boasted of teaching his son reading, Roman law and history, and training him in the "arts" of the javelin, riding, armed combat, boxing, and swimming.

Long since recovered from the Second Punic War but not a military threat to Rome, Carthage was a ripe target for Cato and other land-hungry Romans who lusted after her fertile soil and abundant harvests. After returning from a fact-finding mission to Carthage, Cato delivered an impassioned speech in the Senate about a resurgent foe that concluded, as did all his subsequent speeches and writings, with a call to arms: "Delenda est Carthago!" ("Carthage must be destroyed!"). In 149 BC Rome launched an unprovoked attack upon an astonished and unprepared Carthage.

Rome described the conflict with Carthage as preventive warfare, but armed robbery would be a more

---

CICERO ON LAW, HISTORY, AND PHILOSOPHY

The people's good is the highest law.
He used to raise a storm in a teapot.
Let the punishment match the offense.

De Legibus, III, 3, 16, 20

History is the witness that testifies to the passing of time; it illumines reality, vitalizes memory, provides guidance in daily life, and brings us tidings of antiquity.

De Oratore, II, 36

There is nothing so ridiculous but some philosopher has said it.

De Divinatione, III, 119

I would rather be wrong with Plato than right with such men as these [Pythagoreans].

Socrates was the first to call philosophy down from the heavens and to place it in cities, and even to introduce it into homes and compel it to inquire about life and standards and goods and evils.

Tusculanae Disputationes, I, 17 and V, 4

appropriate term.[2] Carthage was not only captured but demolished and the area sown with salt. The Romans killed the men and sold the women and children into slavery, which prompted Tacitus to write, "they make a desert and call it peace." This was in 146 BC, the fateful year in which another rapacious Roman army administered the same treatment to Corinth, the richest city in Greece. "To the victors belong the spoils" was Ovid's comment, but Seneca wrote: "We are mad, not only individually, but nationally. We check manslaughter and isolated murders; but what of war and the much vaunted crime of slaughtering whole peoples?"

Heading for Civil War

A new and very rich class of war-profiteering contractors, merchants, estate owners, province governors, and generals arose; known as *equites* ("knights"), they could afford to buy equipment for the cavalry, the most expensive branch of the military. The city bulged with plunder, slaves, and increasing numbers of landless, jobless Romans. Reform was long overdue and, during the 130s and 120s, the patrician brothers Tiberius and Gaius Gracchus attempted to speak for the dispossessed. Although no one knew it then, it was the last opportunity the Senate would have to salvage the integrity of the state. The Senatorial response was to murder Tiberius and force Gaius into suicide, thus unwittingly setting the stage for one-man rule.

The first of the generals to seize power, Marius won victories against North African and Celtic tribes, but his reorganization of the army was the critical change. He began converting the army from amateurs, who bought their own equipment and farmed between campaigns, to full-time professionals with battle gear provided by the state. With the beginning of Rome's war against King Mithridates in 88 BC, Marius emerged from retirement to claim command. The Senate chose Sulla instead, causing a bloody civil war that ended in 84 BC with Sulla's conquest of Mithridates in Asia Minor. A veteran of Sulla's campaign, the arrogant and ruthless Pompey next rose to power, eventually forming a ruling triumvirate with Crassus and Julius Caesar.

The First Caesar

Gaius Julius Caesar (ca. 102–44 BC)[3] saw himself as the best man to rescue the foundering Republic. Not everyone agreed with him, then or now, and Caesar remains one of history's most controversial figures. A man of enormous energy and even greater ambition, his mastery of power politics made his career a textbook example of how to take over a state. He enjoyed spectacular success in war, politics, oratory, and statesmanship. Caesar's *Commentaries* on the Gallic campaigns were masterpieces of concise and lucid Latin and his social graces were remarkable. Cicero, who hated him, remarked that he would rather spend an evening conversing with Caesar than in any other way.

Family background was important in tradition-minded Rome, and Caesar had impressive credentials; the Julian *gens* ("clan", "family") was among Rome's oldest and most powerful. The patrician Caesar astutely saw the need to side with the foes of an entrenched and unpopular aristocracy and cast his lot with the popular (democratic) party. He passed rapidly through the usual offices, made dazzling orations, and, with a daring speech defending the legal rights of a treasonous conspirator, secured in one bold stroke the enmity of the Senate and the adulation of the people. Caesar added gloss to his growing reputation with a public office in Spain while reducing his staggering debts resulting, it was said, from paying huge bribes to the right people. He married his daughter to Pompey, the most successful general of the time, and completed an unbeatable combination by forming an alliance with Crassus, the richest man in Rome. The next step was by now inevitable: Caesar, Pompey, and Crassus became a ruling coalition called the First Triumvirate, a short-lived association, however, because, as Lucan pointed out, "It is a law of nature that every great man inevitably resents a partner in greatness."

Caesar's self-improvement program was not yet complete because military power was the necessary base for political strength. Appointed governor of the conquered portion of Gaul, his seemingly invincible army overpowered the rest of Gaul and established his reputation as one of history's most successful generals. What Tacitus called "the terror of the Roman name" was confirmed by Caesar: "It is the right of war for conquerors to treat those whom they have conquered according to their pleasure." Though the Gauls thoroughly understood his military prowess Caesar needed strong support back in Rome. His inspired solution was the carefully composed *Commentaries on the Gallic Wars* (what would Latin classes do without Caesar?), which was widely distributed in Rome, becoming a veritable bestseller.

The Die Is Cast

By 49 BC Gaul was secured according to Caesar's pleasure, Crassus was dead in Parthia, Pompey had gone over to the Senate, and Caesar and his loyal army were poised on the banks of the Rubicon in northern Italy. An apprehensive Senate reminded him of the standing order that all field commanders must return to Rome without their troops. Never known for indecisiveness, Caesar observed that "the die is cast," and invaded and conquered all of Italy in several weeks. (With his keen sense of history, Caesar stated his decision in Greek rather than Latin.) Following his

---

2. "From the Punic Wars on, [Rome's] internal history is that of a successful gang of cutthroats quarreling over the division of the swag." Basil Davenport, *The Portable Roman Reader* (Baltimore, Penguin, 1977), p. 7.

3. All Romans had three names: first name, family name, last name.

triumphant return to a wildly enthusiastic Rome (except the Senate and aristocracy, obviously), he won a war in Spain and defeated his rival, Pompey, in Greece. He further solidified his power and filled his purse by campaigning in Egypt where he stabilized the reign of Cleopatra, Queen of Egypt, fathered a child by her, and guaranteed almost the entire tax revenues of Egypt for himself. In four brilliant years after crossing the Rubicon, Julius Caesar had triumphed in Italy, Spain, Greece, Syria, Egypt, and North Africa, strengthening and consolidating the Empire as he went. When he returned to Rome in 45 BC he was undisputed master of the Roman world and a legend in his, and our, time. Less than a year later, on the Ides of March, he died of twenty-three stab wounds on the Senate floor at the base of Pompey's statue. There were about sixty assassins.

The motives for murder ranged from patriotic concerns over constitutional violations to plain jealousy. Moreover, some of Caesar's reforms interfered with corrupt practices of the bloated aristocracy, providing additional incentive for murder. On the other hand, the people, who supported Caesar throughout his meteoric career, considered him a martyr to the ravenous greed of the aristocracy. Saying "the Ides of March have come" when he was attacked, Caesar was obviously aware of the conspiracy but did nothing to protect himself.

Caesar's will left three-quarters of an enormous fortune to his adopted grandnephew, Octavian, but Octavian's true legacy was the opportunity to acquire Rome itself. Though only eighteen when Caesar died (and unaware of the will), Octavian reacted like a veteran politician. He formed a Second Triumvirate with Mark Antony and Lepidus, brutally suppressed all dissent and used terror and the threat of death to raise some fighting money. To his everlasting discredit he failed to stop Mark Antony from having Cicero murdered. He avenged Caesar in Macedonia by defeating and driving to suicide two of his assassins, Brutus and Cassius. (Shakespeare has Brutus say, "Not that I loved Caesar less, but that I loved Rome more.") After he dropped Lepidus from the triumvirate, Antony and Cleopatra tried to use Ptolemy XV (Caesar's son) in their own bid for the empire. After the machinations and intrigue the final showdown was anticlimactic. Octavian won a naval battle off the northwest coast of Greece, near Actium, and the losers returned to Egypt, where Antony committed suicide. Unable to ignite a relationship with Octavian, Cleopatra followed Antony in suicide a year later.

THE EMPIRE, 27 BC–AD 476

Octavian (Caesar Augustus)

Though Octavian is considered Rome's first emperor, he was actually the second, with most Romans never realizing that constitutional government had ended with Caesar. While prudently maintaining the appearance of restoring the Republic, Octavian orchestrated his power by redesigning the creaky governmental machinery to better control the business of empire. Careful to avoid the appellation of emperor, he did accept the Senate titles of *Augustus* ("revered one") and *princeps* ("first citizen"). Though ruling indirectly he had as much control as any titled emperor.

Among many significant innovations, Augustus created a civil service based on merit, endowed a veteran's pension fund from his own capital (secured by the taxes of Egypt), added a sales tax, rebuilt Rome ("I found Rome brick and left it marble"), created the first police and fire departments, overhauled the armed forces, and sponsored army construction of public works projects throughout the Empire. He adjusted the bureaucratic machinery of imperial Rome so it could continue to function under good, mediocre, or incompetent leadership, and even the tenures of such murderous tyrants as Caligula, Nero, Commodus, and Caracalla.

Pax Romana

The **Pax Romana** ("Roman peace") began with Caesar Augustus in 27 BC and ended with the death of Marcus Aurelius in AD 180 (map 8.1). With no major wars in over two centuries, the Roman world was relatively peaceful and the whole Western world stable and orderly for the first time in history. People felt quite safe in their homes and even when traveling over the roads and sea routes of the prosperous Empire. Roman coins replaced the "owls of Athena" as the monetary standard of the ancient world. All was not rosy, however, because, as Juvenal observed, "We are suffering the evils of a long peace. Luxury, more deadly than war, broods over the city, and avenges a conquered world."

Decline and Fall

No one becomes depraved in a moment.
Juvenal, *Satires*, II, 1.83

After Marcus Aurelius the professional army usually decided the position of emperor, with the legions supporting any general who offered the greatest benefits to the military. The problems all emperors faced were much the same: an increasing national debt because of military expense, a declining population in Italy, a growing disinclination to take public office in the cities outside Rome (the officers were held responsible for paying the cities' taxes to the central government, and with increasing rural poverty no one wanted to bankrupt himself by holding office), and growing rebellion on the borders of the Empire. A vast population movement from the north and east pushed Germanic, Gothic, and Vandal peoples west and south until they overran Italy and Spain.

The century of decline from Commodus to Diocletian

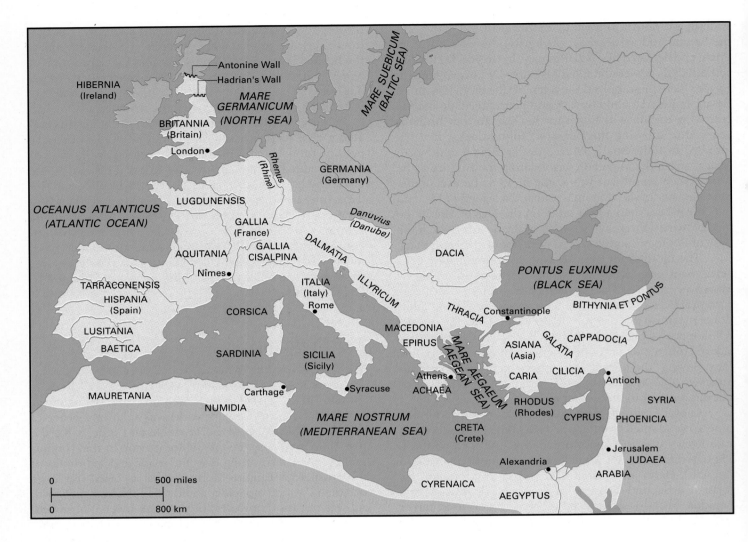

Map 8.1 The Roman Empire, AD 180.

(180–284) marked the beginning of the end though Diocletian's reforms temporarily halted the deterioration. The growth of Christianity posed an additional challenge to which Constantine responded with the Edict of Milan (313), granting freedom of worship throughout the Empire. Constantine also divided the Empire into west and east and located the capital of the Eastern Empire in the new city of Constantinople, built on the site of the old Greek colony of Byzantium. Theodosius made Christianity the official religion of the Empire, marking the beginning of vigorous Christian persecution of other religions. As the barbarian invasions intensified, the western emperor Honorius (395–403) moved to Ravenna, leaving the Pope to defend Rome as best he could. Rome was sacked in 410 and again in 455; in 476 the first non-Roman occupied the throne of Caesar and the Roman Empire passed into history. The painfully protracted decline led Emerson to remark that "the barbarians who broke up the Roman Empire did not arrive a day too soon."

ROMAN RELIGIONS AND PHILOSOPHY

Paganism

During the Republic's early years Roman religion encompassed household gods and earthly spirits appropriate to a farmer's simple life. This traditional religion remained viable for those who clung to the land; the word "pagan" (literally, "country dweller") described those who followed the old Roman religion. Agrarian beliefs became inadequate, however, for urban life in an expanding empire, and Rome again looked to Greece for suitable models. The Greek pantheon was adopted and given Roman names, albeit with different characteristics (see box 4.1, pp. 56–7). For example, playfully amorous Aphrodite, who represented beauty and the pleasures of love, became Venus, the mother of Aeneas, bringer of good fortune and victory and protector of female chastity; Athena, the goddess of wisdom and patroness of the arts, was transformed into Minerva, the goddess of learning and handicrafts; Poseidon, the powerful earthshaker and god of the sea, became Neptune, the god of water.

Jupiter, tho' called the best and the greatest, he was never, like Zeus, the supreme arbiter of the universe and the governor of the world. Zeus reigned from the heights of Mt. Olympus, Jupiter from a low and easily accessible hill. Zeus belonged to the shining space of the air, while Jupiter, as represented by the Romans, belonged to the earth as much as to the sky. Zeus was free. Jupiter was rigid. When we compare the two gods, we find we are comparing the imagination of the Greeks to the imagination of the Romans; they had almost nothing in common.[4]

The practical mind-set of the Romans also manifested itself in their religious practices. The pragmatic Ovid commented that "it is expedient that there should be gods, and as it is expedient, let us believe that they exist." In the interest of efficiency and the glory of the state, the Pantheon (Gk. "of all gods") housed in one sumptuous structure the seven planetary gods (see fig. 9.18). Rome promoted patriotism by elevating the emperors, usually during their lifetime, to godly status. After Caesar Augustus, the Senate deified most emperors and emperor worship became the official religion of the Empire, confirming Seneca's observation: "Religion is regarded by the common people as true, by the wise as false, and by the rulers as useful."

The official religion served the state but did little for the spiritual needs of the common people. The diverse cultures within the Empire led, therefore, to a variety of religions imported to satisfy those needs.

WHILE ROME BURNED

The fire that destroyed a large part of old Rome in AD 64 burned for six days and seven nights. Historians of the time agree that it was started on orders of Emperor Nero, who vacationed at a seaside resort until Rome was burning lustily. There is no agreement about motive but it was most likely boredom and the desire for a bigger and better royal residence. Returning to his flaming palace, Nero watched the fire from a tower in his garden, reportedly exclaiming about "the beauty of the flames." He then put on a tragedian's costume and sang verses from *The Fall of Troy* while accompanying himself on the lyre. Forbidding anyone to search the rubble for loot because he wanted it all, Nero built a colossal palace with a statue of himself 120 feet (37 m) tall in the entrance hall and a pillared arcade about a mile (1.6 km) long. While moving into the palace he remarked, "Good, now I can at last begin to live like a human being." Four years later he committed suicide, lamenting, while dying, "What an artist the world is losing in me!"

Isis and Cybele

Egypt contributed Isis, the mother of Horus and wife of Osiris, the dynamic goddess who raised her husband from the dead. Much more than Diana or Minerva, she appealed to Roman women because she was a giver of health, beauty, wisdom, and love and, moreover, she needed both priests and priestesses.

Cybele, the Great Mother goddess of Phrygia (in Asia Minor), appeared in Rome during the Second Punic War with Hannibal. According to the legend, she loved the glorious youth Attis, who, like Osiris, was raised from the dead (a standard motif for fertility cults). Her frantic grief over his death and abandoned delirium at his rebirth were followed by his unfaithfulness, at which point she castrated him. All of this dramatic spectacle was echoed in the ecstatic and bloody (including self-castration) rites of Cybele's followers. Aghast at the orgies and blood baths, Rome made periodic attempts to regulate the mayhem.

Mystery Religions and Mithraism

The Eleusinian mysteries and Dionysian rites, both Greek mystery religions, had their Roman adherents, but the vows of silence of both sects have been frustratingly effective; we know so little. Dionysian ritual celebrated the non-rational but the particulars are obscure. The Eleusinian mysteries are particularly intriguing because it appears that the worshipers could overcome their fear of death. Eventually the ceremonies at Eleusis (near Athens) were halted by Christianity; any religion that could conquer humanity's deepest fear had to be suppressed.

Imported from Persia was the resolutely virtuous worship of Mithras, the unconquered intermediary between Ahura-Mazda, lord of life and light, and Ahriman, lord of death and darkness. Mithras was the protector of humanity whose believers had to be courageous and morally pure. Soldiers were strongly attracted to this male-oriented religion which was, in the third century AD, Christianity's greatest rival.

Christianity

Emperor worship as the state religion separated monotheistic Christianity (and Judaism) from all other religions. Viewed as a threat to the state, Christians were traitors who refused to place the emperor above their God. Aristocratic Romans sneered at early Christians as common rabble while the people feared them as radical trouble makers. The Roman historian Tacitus called them criminals which, by law, they were.

4. Robert Payne et al., *Horizon Book of Ancient Rome* (New York: American Heritage Publishing Company, 1966), p. 68.

As early as AD 64 Christianity was prominent enough for Nero to blame Christian fanatics for the burning of Rome but not until 249 under Decius did systematic persecutions begin. What Christians called persecution the authorities justified as defending the state, except Nero, who needed a convenient scapegoat. Though very sporadic, the attacks created many Christian martyrs and put the church on the defensive. Literally driven underground into the **catacombs** outside Rome, Christianity formed a true community of believers. Rome's efforts to defend the state helped solidify the church while the long periods of tolerance (or indifference) allowed proselytizing throughout Roman society. (Christianity is discussed in detail on pp. 169–73.)

Astrology and Magic

Millions of believers looked to the stars as powerful deities on a par with Jupiter, Isis, and Cybele; astrology was the champion superstition of an age in which countless numbers preferred to believe the movements of heavenly bodies controlled their lives. Originating in Babylonia, astrology was known to Plato (he found it amusing) but it was not until Alexander's conquest of the Middle East that this persistent nonsense penetrated the Greek world and, ultimately, the entire Roman spectrum. The Eastern religions attracted different sectors of the populace but astrology fascinated everyone from slaves to emperors. Greek skeptics asked how it was that people fated to die at different times all went down in the same shipwreck, or how one-twelfth of humankind could share the basic characteristics of a Capricorn, but these rational queries simply bored true believers. (In fact, the earth has rotated on its axis—called precession by astronomers—to a point where the hopelessly outdated astrological signs are now about three weeks too early.) Augustus and Tiberius, never ones to take chances, banned astrologers from Rome, not to curtail larceny, but fearing rivals with horoscopes predicting an enticing throne. Practitioners of magic also did a thriving business. With fraud flourishing on its usual grand scale, spells, charms, incantations, amulets, fetishes, curses, and hexes were sold to an endless procession of fervently gullible Romans.

Epicureanism

Epicureanism and Stoicism, two eminent Athenian schools of philosophy of the third century BC, developed ethical systems that could help individuals feel more secure in an unstable and hostile world. Materialistic and practical, both philosophies suited thoughtful, educated Romans who chose to confront the problems of living an ethical life in a society plagued by dissension, vice, and corruption.

Based on the **materialism** of Democritos (see p. 69), the philosophy of Epicurus (341–270 BC) aimed primarily to secure tranquility. He considered pleasure the ultimate

good and adhered, with remarkable consistency, to the consequences of this view. "Pleasure," he said, "is the beginning and the end of the blessed life." And further, "I know not how I can conceive the good if I withdraw the pleasures of love and those of hearing and sight. The beginning and the root of all good is the pleasure of the stomach; even wisdom and culture must be referred to this." The mind's pleasure is contemplating the pleasures of the body. Socrates and Plato would disagree of course, but they did not face the uncertainties of a violent age. For Epicurus one acquired virtue by "prudence in the pursuit of pleasure." Justice was not even a virtue but a defense mechanism against pain, a practical matter of behaving without causing fear and resentment in other people.

Epicureanism, like all materialistic philosophies, contained elements of a hedonistic pursuit of physical pleasures, but Epicurus advocated intellectual pleasures as superior to sensual delights and always preferred quiet pleasures to violent joys. Eat moderately for fear of indigestion and drink sparingly for fear of the morning after; avoid politics, love, and other turmoil; do not present hostages to fortune by marrying and having children; above all, avoid fear. Holding public office raised the fear level because envious enemies multiplied as a man achieved power. "The wise man will try to live unnoticed so that he will have no enemies."

Epicurus identified the two greatest sources of fear as religion and dread of death. He believed that the gods, if they even existed, never intervened in human affairs and that the soul perished with the body. Not a consolation but a threat, religion was supernatural interference with nature and a source of terror because immortality denied release from pain. Death was both extinction and liberation.

In his poem, *De Rerum Natura* ("On the Nature of Things"), the Latin poet and philosopher Lucretius (loo-KREE-shus; ca. 96–55 BC) explained the workings of the universe as seen by the Epicurean: a rational, materialistic interpretation of how all things came to be. The poet Horace (65–8 BC) exemplified an Epicurean life and recorded in his poetry the ethical results of the philosophy. He advocated moderation in all things though he did warn against the inconvenience of poverty; above all, he said, avoid lofty positions because lightning strikes the tallest trees and highest mountains. A sophisticated man with a lively sense of humor, he recognized the foibles of his time, laughed at most of them, and unashamedly participated in a goodly number. As the creed of a cultivated minority, Epicureanism survived about 600 years, though with diminishing vigor.

Stoicism

Stoicism was taught by Zeno the Stoic (335?–263? BC), a Phoenician who lived and taught in Athens. He believed totally in common sense which, in Greece, meant materialism. He trusted his senses and had no patience with metaphysical subtleties. When the skeptic asked Zeno what he meant by the real world the reply was, "I mean solid and material, like this table." "And God," asked the skeptic, "and the soul?" "Perfectly solid," answered Zeno, "more solid than the table." In response to further questioning Zeno added virtue and justice to his list of solid matter. Later Stoics like the Emperor Marcus Aurelius (AD 121–180) abandoned materialism but retained the ethical doctrines in virtually the same form. Stoicism was less Greek than any other doctrine because it was emotionally limited and somewhat fanatical. Moreover, its sober austerity contained religious elements the Greeks seemed unable to supply or endorse. In short, it had qualities that appealed to the Romans.

The main doctrines of Stoicism involve cosmic **determinism** and human freedom. "There is no such thing as chance," said Zeno, "and the course of nature is determined by natural law." The natural world was originated by a Lawgiver, a supreme power called, variously, God or Zeus or Jupiter, who is the soul of the world. Each person has within a part of the Divine Fire. All things are part of a single system called Nature and the individual life is good when in harmony with nature. In one sense, people are in agreement with nature because they cannot violate natural laws, but in the Stoic sense virtue is achieved when the individual will is directed to ends that coincide with nature. The wicked obey God's laws involuntarily, like horses driven by a charioteer.

Virtue is the sole good in an individual's life; health, happiness, possessions are of no account. Because virtue resides in will power, everything good or bad in a person's life depends entirely on that person. A person may be poor but virtuous, or sentenced to death, like Socrates, regarded by Stoics as a patron saint. Other people may have power over externals but virtue, the only true good, is internal. Everyone can have perfect freedom by freeing themselves from all mundane desires. The doctrine has a non-Greek coldness that condemns not only bad passions but all passions. The Stoic sage does not feel bereft when his wife and children die because his virtue is undisturbed. Friendship is all very well but don't let your friend's misfortunes interfere with your detached calm. Participation in politics is tolerated but helping other people does nothing for virtue.

Stoic doctrine has at least two logical difficulties. If virtue is the only good then the divine lawgiver must promote virtue; why, then, are there more sinners than saints? Also, how can injustice be wrong if, as Stoics liked to suggest, it provided Stoics with more opportunities to endure and thus become ever more virtuous?

The Romans were acquainted with Stoicism mainly through the writings of Cicero, but the three most influential Roman Stoics were Seneca, Epictetus, and Marcus Aurelius: a minister, a slave, and an emperor, in that order. Seneca (ca. 3 BC–AD 65) was Nero's teacher and a multimillionaire, which casts some doubt on both his teaching and his Stoicism. Falsely accused of plotting Nero's assassination, he was ordered to commit suicide. His final words

to his grieving family were, "Never mind, I leave you what is far more valuable than earthly riches, the example of a virtuous life."

Epictetus (ep-ik-TEE-tus; ca. AD 60–110) was a Greek and a slave who finally won his freedom. The slave and the emperor, Marcus Aurelius, lived totally different lives but were in nearly complete agreement about the elements of Stoicism. Marcus Aurelius was devoted to Stoic virtue, of which he had great need, for his reign (AD 161–180) saw an endless procession of pestilence, insurrections, wars, and earthquakes. A conscientious ruler, he was mainly unsuccessful and certainly frustrated. Because Christian rejection of the state religion threatened the already besieged empire, he tried, in vain, to stamp out the sect. Epictetus lived a relatively short and uneventful life but his teaching profoundly affected early Christianity. Consider, for example, the implications of the following:

On earth we are prisoners in an earthly body.
God is the Father of all men and we are all brothers.
Slaves are the equal of other men because all are alike in the eyes of God.
We must submit to God as a good citizen submits to the law.
The soldier swears to respect no man above Caesar but we are to respect ourselves first of all.
We must love our enemies.

Late Stoicism, in the philosophy of Epictetus and Marcus Aurelius, emphasized the brotherhood of all humankind. Since the great intelligence (divine spark) is within each person, and each is a necessary part of the rational scheme of things, then all are brothers in the changing universe. Roman law interpreted this as all being equal before the law.

Neoplatonism

Becoming more of a religion than Stoicism, Neoplatonism was the third Greek philosophy to invade Rome. Its vision of an afterlife offered consolation to those who enjoyed little satisfaction or self-fulfillment in their earthly existence. Based on Platonic doctrines, Neoplatonism came to Rome from the **Academy** founded by Plato, the still-flourishing school (until AD 529) in Athens. The Neoplatonists began with the Platonic concept of Ideas as the true reality. But, said the Neoplatonists, ideas in their pure form are unknowable. We can appreciate beauty, for example, as manifested in a beautiful person, or beautiful landscape or picture, but we cannot imagine pure beauty apart from any of these things. Further, we cannot picture pure mind but we can approach a knowledge of the mind as we see people acting according to the dictates of their minds, that is, evidence of the mind at work but not the reality. Similarly, the true reality of Good is something people cannot envision in this life. The goal is to approach as near as possible to an understanding of reality while on earth so that, upon death, one is fit to enter the City of Good and contemplate the True Reality. Neoplatonism initiated the idea of salvation and eternal life for those who lived their earthly lives in contemplation and with a desire for true wisdom. These ideas strongly influenced Christianity, for it was St. Augustine (354–430), a Neoplatonist in his youth, who laid the foundation for the doctrine of the early Christian church in his monumental *The City of God*.

ROME'S ACHIEVEMENTS

Law and Government

Rome's major and most enduring contribution to Western civilization was her legal system: the art and science of law. Administration of justice was an art, while science (jurisprudence) defined justice and injustice. There is no clearer evidence of Roman preference for facts as opposed to abstractions than in a body of law founded, as Cicero stated, "not on theory but on nature." Justice was a process rather than a concept, a way of dealing with everyday problems. "Law is nothing but a correct principle drawn from the inspiration of the gods, commanding what is honest and forbidding the contrary" (Cicero). Venality and rapacity were human characteristics the state had to control so that "the stronger might not in all things have their way" (Ovid). Bertrand Russell wryly said that in his ideal society everyone would be honest and he would be the only thief. Roman law stood guard against the thief in all of us. Rome used its experience of empire to build a body of international law based on a rational appraisal of consistent human behavior in a variable environment.

The legal system worked but that need not imply a government of comparable efficiency. Modern research has shown that the Romans were not masters of the arts of governance. Until the time of Caesar Augustus government was a chaotic mess of corruption and inefficiency caused not by a republic trying to administer an empire but by time-honored inequities and improbabilities. Augustus did make some reforms, but he followed the Roman habit of shuffling parts around when what he needed was a new chariot. Diocletian (reigned 284–305) did design an efficient new system, but by this time it was like harnessing a team of lively horses to a broken-down chariot.

Province management was a permanent problem because there was little governing; the governors were responsible primarily for sending money to Rome. Charging whatever taxes the traffic would bear and rendering "unto Caesar that which is Caesar's," they pocketed the rest. Moreover, Rome's vaunted toleration of provincial cultures was more pragmatic than magnanimous: do nothing that will jeopardize the tax potential of conquered territories. Except for Greece,[5] Rome treated all foreign cultures with equal indifference.

Science

Roman science dealt entirely with empirical data; theoretical science was something left to the Greeks. For example, an Alexandrian Greek named Eratosthenes (air-uh-TOSS-thuh-neez) used reason, empirical data, and math to prove the earth round and measure its circumference within a few miles. Pliny the Elder (see pp. 114–15) observed that the masts of ships approaching shore were visible before he saw the hulls, leading to the deduction that the world had a curved surface. Roman medical science benefited when they combined their organizational talent with their passion for war to produce the field hospital, a predecessor of the general hospital.

Public Projects

A 50,000-mile (80,000-km) network of paved roads linked Rome to all parts of the Empire. All roads did lead to Rome. Originally designed as military highways, they carried the efficient postal service plus peripatetic Romans. Guide-books, highway patrols, a stable every 10 miles (16 km), and an inn every 30 miles (48 km) made traveling easier and safer than at any other time before the late nineteenth century.

> Of all societies in western Asia and Europe from antiquity until the nineteenth century, only the Romans set out to build a carefully planned road system, with properly installed and drained surfaces.[6]

Skillful engineering also produced the aqueducts that supplied the huge amounts of water needed for the luxurious public baths and for the many affluent households that used water for sanitary facilities. Only a few aqueducts remain, such as the one still serving Segovia in Spain, and some of the plumbing—in the Pantheon, at Pompeii, and at Bath—still works. Almost everything else has vanished, including the vast irrigation system that watered productive farms in the northern Sahara and the 300 miles (483 km) of aqueducts that served Rome.

As urbanization gradually supplanted Rome's early agrarian society, city building became a new specialty. Many residential units were five- and six-story apartment houses with such built-in services as nurseries, convenience markets, and neighborhood snack bars. Rome and other large cities always had extensive **forums** that served as civic centers (suitable backdrops for Roman pomp and ceremony) and open-air markets comparable to today's shopping malls. Rome was not, however, a neat and orderly city.

---

5. The love-hate relationship with Greece was largely involuntary. As Horace wrote, "Greece, taken captive, captured her savage conqueror, and carried her arts into clownish Latium."

6. Donald Hill, *A History of Engineering in Classical and Medieval Times* (La Salle, Ill.: Open Court Publishing Company, 1984), p. 76

Except for several thoroughfares there were no names for the 54 miles (86.4 km) of streets nor any house numbers. (Sample conversation: "See Marius in the leather shop behind the Pantheon; he knows where your friend, Sepulvius, lives.") There was pollution ("cease to admire the smoke, wealth and noise of prosperous Rome."—Horace) and, as Sallust observed, corruption: "A city for sale and doomed to speedy destruction, if it finds a purchaser."

City facilities always included public baths, the most popular of all Roman institutions. Cicero once remarked that the gong that each day announced the opening of public baths was "a sweeter sound than the voices of the philosophers in their schools." Emperors who needed to improve their public image, which included most of those who stayed alive long enough, built elaborate facilities larger than several Grand Central Stations.[7] All the baths included mixed bathing until Hadrian decreed separate times for the sexes. These hedonistic temples contained indoor and outdoor swimming pools, gymnasiums, libraries, lounges, restaurants, bars, and gardens, with brothels sometimes included as added attractions. Early in the Republic the baths facilitated cleanliness but they evolved into what Cicero's gong symbolized: public palaces that made life as pleasant as possible.

The baths soothed and entertained individuals in a variety of ways while mass entertainment was a spectacular Roman specialty. A large amphitheatre, such as the Colosseum, occupied the center of each city, where the favorite spectacle was gladiatorial combat. Other entertainments included wild animal hunts, naval battles, and an occasional gladiator, in a bid for freedom, singlehandedly killing an elephant.

Rome's bequest to the Western world was a curious compound of justice under law, military conquest, the Latin language, and Greek culture. Implicit in the laws that recognized the constitutional rights of citizens was the germinal idea that laws required the consent of the governed. The military conquests were a devastating legacy, but perhaps so was Horace's pious statement, *"dolce et decorum est pro patria mori"* ("it is sweet and glorious to die for one's country").

Rome's finest contributions to Western civilization were law and Greek culture. The Greek temple style was adopted, though mainly the ornate Corinthian order; Greek sculpture was copied so often that most of what we know of Greek work exists in Roman copies. The work of Greek artists, serving Roman tastes, appeared in the frescoes, murals, and mosaics of their houses and public buildings. Greek slaves tutored Roman children in the Greek language and the classics: Homer, Hesiod, and the plays of Aeschylus, Sophocles, and Menander. Roman tourists made the obligatory pilgrimage to Greece to view the centuries-old wonders on the Acropolis and to consult the oracle at Delphi. Rome contributed the language, organization, and law upon which the Church of Rome and medieval civilization were built; at the same time, Rome preserved and transmitted the Greek humanism that sparked the Renaissance and illuminated the Age of Reason.

> The worlds of classical Greece and Rome deserve our most careful study for two reasons. First, theirs is an extraordinary story, infinitely rich and of worth. And, second, they are the forerunners of the political, social, cultural, economic, and religious traditions of the West, and unless we know something about them, we are adrift in our own world—and at a loss how to manage the future.[8]

CONTRASTING VALUES IN GREECE AND ROME

When Greece and Rome are considered together the reference is to a Graeco-Roman civilization that was literate, rational, and secular, whose high (classical) period dates from ca. 480 BC to ca. AD 180. Taken separately, we can effectively compare the two very different cultures by discussing education and sports.

Education

Roman parents were responsible for their children's education either as teachers or by hiring tutors. As discussed earlier, the elder Cato boasted of teaching his son reading,

---

GREECE, ROME, EUROPE, AND THE UNITED STATES

Rome, with little high culture of its own, absorbed the intellectual and artistic heritage it had conquered, and was in turn conquered by it, as the poet Horace observed. Rome and the Latin language left their mark on everything they touched; but Rome's high culture was derivatively Greek. There is some analogy with the United States in relation to Europe. In Rome, as in America, this produced a tension, since in almost every sphere except culture the Romans were fundamentally dissimilar to the Greeks.

To complete the analogy, the United States inherited European culture but, in general, Americans are just as different from Europeans as the Romans were from the Greeks.

---

7. The New York landmark was modeled after Rome's Baths of Caracalla.
8. Michael Grant, *Readings in the Classical Historians* (New York: Charles Scribner's and Sons, 1992), p. 1.

Roman law and history plus the "arts" of the javelin, riding, swimming, and armed combat. When writing, simple arithmetic, and some Greek and Roman literature are added we have the standard Roman curriculum. This is pragmatic instruction designed to produce Romans useful to the state as citizens and soldiers. The Romans valued education and scorned the uneducated, whether Roman or foreigner. Ignorance, wrote Cicero, condemned these impoverished souls to "the tyranny of the present." While still a slave, Epictetus asserted that "only the educated are free."

Greek parents were also responsible for their children's education. All citizens studied reading and writing, arithmetic, art, poetry recitation, music, dance, and gymnastics. Talented students advanced to instruction in mathematics, rhetoric (oratory), and philosophy. Everyone received ethical education according to the doctrine of ethos. Greek education emphasized imagination, creativity, and, especially, thinking. It was an open-ended process that encouraged excellence in its highly individualistic citizens. Moreover, when teachers followed Plato's advice any talent would be recognized and nourished— "Let early education be a sort of amusement; you will then be better able to find out the natural bent."

Law and history were the two mandatory "academic" subjects in the Roman curriculum, neither of which required much imagination or original thinking. Education reinforced those qualities most highly valued by each culture. Where reality was the State, duty, conformity, discipline, and courage were prime values in a pragmatic society. Individuality, verbal skills, creativity, originality, and imaginative thinking were highly prized in a culture that encouraged diligence in the pursuit of excellence. In neither culture, however, did women have equal educational opportunities; educated Roman and Greek women were a distinct minority. Aristotle summed up the Greek view of education: "Educated men are as much superior to uneducated men as the living are to the dead."

Sports

Let us now consider athletic contests in the ancient world as another way of highlighting the differences. The Olympic Games and gladiatorial combat were both athletic contests, though we might refer to the Olympics as "games" and call battling gladiators something quite different. First we shall describe the games the Greeks played and then look at the Roman versions. By comparing the radically different approaches to athletics (sports), the reader can draw further conclusions about the two cultures.

Olympic Games

Greek festivals featured contests in drama, music, poetry, and athletics, especially athletics. It seems that the cities of Sparta, Elis, and Pisa were always squabbling and, rather than settling their difficulties by fighting, they decided upon a truce built around a footrace to decide superiority. This worked so well that by 776 BC almost the entire Hellenic world was involved in footracing and other contests at the sacred site of Olympia. 776 was considered so significant that the Greeks recorded their subsequent history based on that date. The contests were held every four years (the Olympiad); 776 was the first Olympiad, 772 the second Olympiad, and so on through the 320th Olympiad in AD 392: 1,168 years of Greek history.

From the beginning the critical factor was a truce unique to the Olympic Games. The conditions were simple: no one was to bear arms in Elis (the province of the games); all athletes and spectators were guaranteed safe access to Elis from anywhere in the Greek world; all fighting would cease throughout that world for a period of ten months plus travel time to and from the games. True to style, the Greeks pledged on their honor to abide by these rules. When the Spartans violated the truce the entire Greek-speaking world was called upon to witness their shame; there were no further violations.

Athletic contests were staged throughout Greece with the greatest at Olympia, not just because of the caliber of competition but because Olympia symbolized peace. Sportsmanship and brotherhood were also basic components of the games. Cheating was not tolerated but the Greeks were realistic enough to require an oath of fair play from each athlete. The games recognized the kinship of all Greeks with competition open to all of Greek descent regardless of rank, class, or native city. Brotherhood was national rather than universal, however, because barbarians (foreigners) were barred. The dominating spirit of the games was precisely the same as for all Greek culture: *kalos k'agathos* ("the beautiful and the good").

Selected by competition, the best athletes in each city started training exactly ten months before the festival; no one contestant had an unfair advantage. Because training was forbidden at the sacred site, they held final warm-ups at Elis, after which everyone moved to Olympia for five days of competition dedicated to Zeus and Hera. Because the Olympiad was Greece's top event it was scheduled for both good weather and maximum attendance. Consequently, competition began on the third full moon of summer (in July or August), which placed the festivities after the grain and olive harvests and before fall planting.

The basic events of the games were footraces, primarily because all Greeks took great pride in their speed and stamina as runners.[9] They based the unit of distance (stade) on the length of the stadium at Olympia, which was about 600 feet (183 m). There were sprints of one-stade, two-stade, and so on up to distances of about 3 miles (4.8 km). The Olympics had no second or third place finishes;

9. Cross-country running was, surprisingly, not one of the Olympic events. The marathon, based on the Marathon-to-Athens run of Phidippides to announce the wondrous victory over the Persians, was introduced at the modern Olympics which began at Athens in 1896.

there was one winner with everyone else an also-ran. The prize, a simple olive wreath,[10] was the most sought after in Greece; though the leaves soon withered and fell, the winner's name was recorded in the roll of the Olympics and, ever after, his descendants would recall his name.

The winner of a footrace in modern track and field is, of course, the first to break the tape, unless disqualified by a foul. The Greeks were more sophisticated; the position of finish counted only 50 percent. The other half was evaluated independently by judges searching for something special: grace, poise, rhythm, what we might call, in a word, style.[11] The Greek word for it is *arete*, which translates as skill, or stylish grace or, more precisely, diligence in the pursuit of excellence.[12] Besides the quality of *arete*, the games differed from the modern version in one other significant respect. Though the Greeks honored tradition they were not bound by the past, preferring instead to live enthusiastically in the present. They kept meticulous records of each Olympiad but they never recorded winning distances or times; athletes competed with each other, not with the past.

Except for chariot racing the ancient Olympic events are still a basic part of the modern Olympics: footracing, broad jump, discus, javelin, and boxing and wrestling. The composite event, the pentathlon,[13] featured the kind of individual the Greeks especially admired, a well-rounded person with skills in several areas. The Romans prized specialists but the Greeks preferred generalists.

The high point of the 1,168 years of the Olympic Games was reached, not unexpectedly, during the Age of Pericles. A slight decline in quality and integrity after that time accelerated rapidly beginning in 146 BC, the year in which Carthage and Corinth were razed and the Romans took over Olympia. Typical of the Roman way was Nero's behavior, who had himself declared winner of any event he entered. The games ended in AD 392, after the 320th Olympiad, when, in the name of Christianity, Emperor Theodosios issued an edict forbidding the games because they "promoted the worship of heathen and false gods." No mention was made of the ancient truce when the emperor completed his work by ordering the destruction of the

statues and temples. *Arete, kalos k'agathos* ("skill, beauty, and goodness") vanished from the sacred groves of the peaceful river valley at Olympia.

Roman Spectacles

Roman games were originally conceived and produced to honor the gods but, by the time of the Empire, private citizens were sponsoring extravagant spectacles honoring themselves more than the gods. While the Romans had frequent athletic contests the public was far more entranced by the giant spectacles staged in the Colosseum and Circus Maximus (see figs. 9.13 and 9.14). These were the *ludi* ("games," from which we get the word "ludicrous"), which referred to five types of extravaganzas produced for immense arenas: chariot races, gladiatorial combats, wild animal hunts, naval battles, and mythological pantomimes. Not concerned with style or beauty, these *ludi* were intended to amuse vast crowds and thus Rome invented mass entertainment.

Romans particularly enjoyed chariot races but gladiatorial combat was on a higher plane. Unique to Roman civilization, it characterized Roman values. There has been a tendency, probably dating from Napoleon, to ascribe the Roman virtues of nobility, courage, and honesty to the austere days of the Republic, and thus blame the Empire for much of the brutality and decadence for which Rome is justly infamous. It was the Republic, however, that bred gladiatorial combat, beginning in 264 BC, the same Republic that brutally destroyed Carthage and Corinth in 146 BC.

The ritual of mortal combat always began with the ceremonial march of the gladiators into the arena and the famous words to the royal box: *"Ave, Caesar, morituri te salutamus"* ("Hail, Caesar, we who are about to die salute you"). Following the drawing of lots and inspection of arms, a typical match-up would be a Thracian type gladiator versus the *hoplomachi* fighting style. The Thracian wore a heavy helmet and leather and metal armor, and carried a small shield and curved sword. The nearly naked *hoplomachus* wore a heavy helmet and carried a large, oblong shield and a Roman sword. A variety of clothing and armament protected each combatant from disabling minor wounds. The crowd enjoyed a skillful, courageous, and even fight; given this kind of battle, public sentiment tended toward a thumbs-up verdict so the loser could fight another day. The decision, however, lay with the editor, the sponsor of the day's games, and the verdict could just as well be thumbs-down. Of course the crowd expected the loser to display his superb training by presenting his naked throat to his conqueror's sword. Anguish and gore enough it seems, but the Romans further embellished the bloody scene with an actor dressed as a god and brandishing a white-hot staff, which he jabbed into the fallen man to make certain he was dead. The tattered body was then hooked behind a horse and dragged away and the entire arena sprayed with perfume, after which the crowd settled contentedly back for the next contest.

Next were the great crowd pleasers, a *retiarius* and a *secutor*. Possessing neither helmet nor shield, the *retiarius*

10. The other games of the sacred circuit awarded the laurel at Delphi (Pythian), pine at Corinth (Isthmian), and wild celery at Nemea (Nemean). The olive branch of the Olympic Games remains as a nearly universal symbol of peace.
11. Athletes competed in the nude so that judges could better evaluate their performance. It should also be noted that women were forbidden to attend the games under penalty of death, a prohibition based on religious reasons rather than the fact of nudity, which was not a problem for the Greeks, who looked upon their readiness to strip in public as one of the traits that separated them from barbarians.
12. Style is a factor in judging such modern Olympic events as diving, gymnastics, and ice skating.
13. Five events: sprint, broad jump, wrestling and boxing, discus, and javelin. The decathlon (ten events) of the modern Olympics dropped the wrestling and boxing and added shot put, pole vault, high jump, 110-meter hurdles, and 100-, 400-, and 1,500-meter races.

had a dagger in his belt, while one hand gripped a net and the other a trident. His *secutor* opponent wore a helmet and carried a long rectangular shield and a sword, plus the standard dagger. In a contest pitting a runner against a human tank the *retiarius* had to be very mobile.

The two pairs described above appeared at most spectacles. Other combats included fighting from chariots, dwarf gladiators, female combatants, and whatever else amused the common people in the upper tiers. Staging these extravaganzas was so expensive that the government had to assume responsibility for special schools, which in Rome alone trained and housed some 2,000 gladiators. Amphitheatre combat was probably scheduled only several times a year; this kept expenses down, helped maintain a full complement of gladiators (about 600 pairs fought in each production) and most importantly, heightened expectations for the next spectacular event.

Other spectacles involved elaborately staged hunts, which featured an African jungle, for example, in the Colosseum with hunters and assorted lions and tigers stalking each other, though it is doubtful the frightened creatures wanted anything more than a place to hide from their tormentors. Thousands of wild animals were slaughtered in this manner, so many that whole species were annihilated. Fought in pools built for the occasion, naval battles were reenactments of famous engagements, bloody reminders of the power of Roman arms at sea. Finally, there were dramatic pantomimes based on familiar mythological plots and starring condemned criminals in their first and last performance. Treated to mythology in action, audiences witnessed Heracles consumed by flames, Dirce lashed to the horns of a maddened bull, Icaros of the failing wings falling among wild beasts, and other edifying splendors. Roman efficiency prevailed; the mob was entertained; justice was served.

The Roman games were so appallingly brutal that some apologists have tried to rationalize the whole bloody business into justifiable entertainment for potentially dangerous mobs. Others have sought evidence that educated Romans disapproved of the institution; they have looked in vain, however, since Romans of every class and station attended and enjoyed the games, which continued in the Colosseum until they were banned by Honorius in 404. With the possible exception of Seneca and Pliny the Younger, we know of not one Roman who ever voiced any concerns, humane or otherwise, about the events staged in the Colosseum. Death, in this ancient time, was not a significant consideration for those in power, particularly when the powerless were doing the dying.

> Our critical assumption that the spectators must have been inhuman brutes never occurred to any Roman, philosopher or not. The gladiators brought Rome a strong dose of sadistic pleasure of which people fully approved: pleasure at the sight of bodies and at the sight of men dying."[14]

TO HELEN

Helen, thy beauty is to me
  Like those Nicean barks of yore,
That gently, o'er a perfumed sea,
  The weary, wayworn wanderer bore
To his own native shore.

On desperate seas long wont to roam,
  Thy hyacinth hair, thy classic face,
Thy Naiad airs have brought me home
  To the glory that was Greece
And the grandeur that was Rome.

Edgar Allan Poe (1831)

Ironically, the one event that was vigorously denounced was the *sparsio*, the bonus episode that usually followed the final gladiatorial contest. While the upper class beat a hasty retreat, a machine with a rotating arm that hurled clay or wooden tablets in the general direction of the upper tiers was wheeled into the arena. Whatever the tally depicted was redeemable in kind: a water buffalo, ten pounds of ostrich feathers, an elephant, two lower tier tickets for the next attraction, and so on. Horace spoke for the upper class when he wrote: "I hate the vulgar herd and hold it far."

THE BEST OF THE ROMAN IDEAL

Artistically and creatively, Rome reached its peak during the "golden age" of Caesar Augustus. Augustus had, at long last, won the civil war, bringing peace to an embattled Republic that emerged from the chaos as the mighty Roman Empire. While rebuilding Rome he turned his attention to a literary project perhaps more important than rebuilding a city in gleaming marble—the fabulous history of the city destined to rule the world, Virgil's *Aeneid*.

The *Aeneid*

Augustus selected Virgil (70–19 BC) as his poet of Roman greatness and commissioned him to write an epic poem celebrating the Augustan victory at Actium in 31 BC, depicting the emperor as the noble conqueror of the forces of darkness led by Mark Antony and Cleopatra. What

14. Philippe Aries and Georges Duby, gen. eds., *A History of Private Life I—from Pagan Rome to Byzantium* (Cambridge, Mass.: The Belknap Press of Harvard University Press, 1987), p. 20.

happened to the sponsored project was something not only unexpected but infinitely better. Virgil wrote the *Aeneid*.

Virgil saw that much of the greatness of Athens result-ed from the tradition provided by Homer's *Iliad* and *Odyssey*. Well versed in Homer's epics, Virgil deliberately patterned his poem upon them to give Rome the same kind of gold-en past that the Greeks had enjoyed, and to provide inspi-ration for the creation of great and noble works.

Books I–VI of the *Aeneid*, concerned with the wan-derings of Aeneas after his escape from Troy, are based on the *Odyssey*. Books VII–XII are based on the *Iliad* and tell of war and death in Italy as Aeneas follows his destiny. Virgil's major innovation was not writing an adventure story but tackling a noble subject: founding an empire. Reality, for the Romans, was the state; therefore the prin-cipal aim of all literature was to stir patriotism. The *Aeneid* is literature and it is also propaganda for a great nation. But what's the matter with propaganda for a noble cause?

Virgil created Aeneas as both Homeric and Roman, ancient and modern, a contemporary of Achilles and Odysseus but also a true Augustan Roman. Clearly we can see Virgil thinking to himself: "Tomorrow we are going to start the old tradition of Roman greatness." Somehow the overthoughtful, rather pompous figure of Aeneas falls short of the glory-bound Achilles and Hector, not to mention the clever Odysseus. In Aeneas, the Homeric hero is redefined as a man who can launch a whole civilization, who can write past, present, and future in himself and whose hero-ism consists in the fact that he can do this and others can-not. In no other person—real or fictional—are the superior qualities of the noble Roman better exemplified.

The hero is middle-aged and has gained the wisdom that sometimes comes with maturity. Aeneas sees clearly that a kind of sadness underlies all heroic acts and that many of people's actions are dictated by external forces. Compared with Homer, Virgil lacks dash; what he offers instead is a sorrowful and chastened wisdom.

Like Stoic philosophy, the *Aeneid* views adherence to duty as the loftiest of all human values. Virgil wonder-fully gives Rome its highest creed—its duty to the world—when Anchises tells his son Aeneas:

Others will cast more tenderly in bronze
Their breathing figures, I can well believe,
And bring more lifelike portraits out of marble;
Argue more eloquently, use the pointer
To trace the paths of heaven accurately
And accurately foretell the rising stars.
Roman, remember by your strength to rule
Earth's peoples—for your arts are to be these:
To pacify, to impose the rule of law,
To spare the conquered, battle down the proud.

This was the highest of Roman ideals. While it sacrificed much in the realm of human value, while it denigrated such qualities as imagination and joy, it provided a noble code of conduct so long as the Romans adhered to it.

LITERARY SELECTION 5

Poetry
Gaius Valerius Catullus (ca. 84–54 BC)

Catullus, the leading Latin lyric poet, composed his love poetry for the enchanting Clodia (Lesbia in the poems), wife of Quintus Metellus. She became the most notoriously faithless beauty in Rome, while Catullus struggled with a virulent passion for her that slowly shriveled to despair before subsiding into bitter maledictions. Poems 5, 51, 58, 72, and 75 testify to the stages of his infatuation. The first three stanzas of poem 51 are a partial translation by Catullus of a poem by Sappho, the sixth-century Greek poet of Lesbos. Poem 1 is concerned with poets and poetry, while 42 reveals a frustrated poet suffering from writer's block.

1

Who do I give this neat little book to
all new and polished up and ready to go?
You, Cornelius, because you always thought
there was something to this stuff of mine,
and were the one man in Italy with guts enough
to lay out all history in a couple of pages,
a learned job, by god, and it took work.
So here's the book, for whatever it's worth
I want you to have it. And please, goddess,
see that it lasts for more than a lifetime.

5

Let's you and me live it up, my Lesbia,
and make some love, and let old cranks
go cheap talk their damn fool heads off.
Maybe suns can set and come back up again,
but once the brief light goes out on us
the night's one long sleep forever.
First give me a kiss, a thousand kisses,
then a hundred, and then a thousand more,
then another hundred, and another thousand,
and keep kissing and kissing me so many times
we get all mixed up and can't count anymore,
that way nobody can give us the evil eye
trying to figure how many kisses we've got.

42

Calling all syllables! Calling all syllables!
Let's go! I need all the help I can get!
Some filthy whore's playing games with me
and won't give me back my manuscripts with
your pals inside! Are you going to let her?
Who is she, you ask? Well go take a look,
she's over there shaking her ass all around
and flashing smiles like a Pomeranian bitch.
Ready? Okay, line up and let her have it!
"O foul adulteress, O lascivious witch,
give me back my notebooks, you dirty bitch!"

10

What? Up yours, you say? You slut, tramp,
you've sunk so low you look up to see down!
Still, we can't let her get away like this,
if all else fails, at least let's see whether
we can force a blush from the hard-faced beast.
Try again, fellas, good and loud this time!
"O FOUL ADULTERESS, O LASCIVIOUS WITCH,
GIVE ME BACK MY NOTEBOOKS, YOU DIRTY BITCH!"
No use. It won't work. Nothing moves her.   20
We've got to switch to different tactics,
almost anything will work better than this.
"O maiden so modest, O virgin so pure . . . ."

51

To me, that man seems to be one of the gods,
or to tell the truth, even more than a god,
sitting there face to face with you, forever
looking, listening

to you laughing sweetly, while poor me, I take
one look at you and I'm all torn up inside,
Lesbia, there's nothing left of me. I can't
make a sound, my tongue's

stuck solid, hot little fire flashes go
flickering through my body, my ears begin
ringing around in my head, my eyes black out,
shrouded in darkness . . .

This soft life is no good for you. Catullus,
you wallow in it, you don't know when to stop.
A soft life's already been the ruin of both
great kings and cities.

58

Caelius, our Lesbia, that Lesbia,
the Lesbia Catullus once loved
more than himself and all he owns,
now works streets and back alleys
groping big-hearted sons of Remus.

72

Time was you said only Catullus could touch you,
that God in heaven couldn't have you before me.
I loved you then, not just as a guy does a girl,
but the way a father loves his sons and grandsons.
Now I know you, Lesbia, and if my passion grows,
you're also much cheaper to me and insignificant.
How's that? Because, hurt a man in love and he
lusts for you more, but the less he really cares.

75

My mind's sunk so low, Lesbia, because of you,
wrecked itself on your account so bad already,
I couldn't like you if you were the best of women,
or stop loving you, no matter what you do.

STUDY QUESTIONS

In poems 5, 51, 58, 72, and 75 Catullus seems to have mixed emotions about his Lesbia. What does he love about her? Hate about her? What is romantic love? Can it last?

LITERARY SELECTION 6

Odes

Horace (Quintus Horatius Flaccus; 65–8 BC)

Horace specialized in writing **odes**, such as the two below in modern translations by M. A. Crane. The first is a wry commentary about Pyrrha, his former mistress, while the second is an expression of Horace's Epicurean philosophy.

1

On the bulletin board there's a picture of me
Luckily saved from disaster at sea
Donating my gear to the God of the Ocean.
Tonight, some boy smelling of after-shave lotion
Is making a play for you, Pyrrha, my fair,
Trying that innocent look with your hair.
His turn will come soon to complain of foul weather
If he thinks that after you're going together
You'll stay bland and easy as on this first date.
Until you up anchor, all dinghies look great!

2

The peace that the sailor seeks in the storm
And the rest that's the warrior's aim
Can't be purchased with wealth in any form
Nor, Grosphus, with power or fame.
The pauper who wants only what he can afford
Sleeps soundly. But he who would fly
To new fortunes, although he hastens aboard
Speedy vessels, sees his troubles stand by.
Fools nourish dreams of perfect joy;
I'll take less, having witnessed a hero
Die young and watched rotting old age destroy
Tithonus, reduced to a jibbering zero.
It may be *I* have just those things that *you* need
Amidst your horses, fine clothing, and cattle—
Subsistence, and joy from the poems I read,
And no jealous mob doing me battle.

STUDY QUESTIONS

1. A "conceit" is an extended poetic comparison (**metaphor**) between two unlike things, applying the qualities of one to the other. In Ode 1 what conceit does Horace develop, and to whom or what is it applied?
2. According to the Epicurean philosophy expressed in Ode 2, what is necessary for happiness? Where do material possessions rate on the happiness scale? Why?

LITERARY SELECTION 7

Epigrams

Martial (Marcus Valerius Martialis; ca. 40–104)

Martial wrote hundreds of epigrams, which are brief poems, often satiric, ending in a surprise twist or climax. His style can be described as terse, sardonic, sparse, acerbic, sarcastic, witty, and, withal, strikingly and delightfully modern.

I, i
Here he is—the one you read,
the one you ask for—Martial,
recognized the world over
for his witty books of epigrams.
Learned reader, you've given him
(while he's still alive to enjoy it)
the glory poets rarely get
after they've turned to ashes.

I, xxxv
You take me to task for writing
poems that aren't as prissy
and prim as they might be, Cornelius.
Not the kind a schoolmaster
would read aloud in the classroom.
But my little books wouldn't satisfy
(any more than husbands can
their wives) without a little sex.
Would you want me to write a wedding-song
without using the words that wedding-songs   10
always use? Would you cover up
Flora's nymphs with a lot of clothing
or let prostitutes hide their shamefulness
under ladies' robes? There's a rule
that merry songs can't be merry
unless they're a bit indecent.

So forget your prudishness, please,
and spare my jokes and my naughtiness,
and don't try to castrate my poems.
Nothing's worse than Priapus posing   20
as a eunuch of Cybele.

II, xxxvi
I don't say you should curl your hair,
but you could comb it.
I don't say your body should be oiled,
but you could take a bath.
You needn't have a eunuch's beard
or a jailbird's. I don't insist
upon too much manliness,
Pannychus, or too little.
As it is, your legs are hairy
and your chest is shaggy with bristles,
but your mind, Pannychus, is bald.

III, xxxviii
Tell me, what brings you to Rome
so self-confidently, Sextus?
What are you after, and what
do you expect to find there?
"First of all, I'll plead cases
more eloquently than Cicero
himself. There won't be anyone
in the three forums to touch me."
Atestinus and Civis
(you know them both) pled cases,   10
but neither one of them took in
enough to pay the rent.
"Well, if nothing comes of that,
I'll write poems. When you hear them,
you'll say they're Virgil's work."
You're crazy. Wherever you look
you'll see Ovids and Virgils—all of them
shivering in their thin cloaks.
"Then I'll cultivate rich men."
That sort of thing has supported   20
maybe three or four. The rest
of the crowd are pale with hunger.
"What *will* I do? Advise me.
I'm determined to live in Rome."
Well, Sextus, if you're honest,
you'll be lucky to stay alive.

V, xiii
I'll admit I'm poor, Callistratus,
and always have been. And yet
two Emperors gave me a knighthood
and I'm not altogether unknown,
and my reputation isn't bad.
I've got a great many readers
everywhere in the world who will say
"That's Martial," and recognition
such as few receive after they're dead
has come to me while I'm alive.   10
On the other hand, your house-roof
is supported by a hundred columns,
and your money-boxes contain
a freedman's wealth, and wide fields
near Syene on the River Nile
call you master, and Parma in Gaul
shears its countless flocks for you.
That's what we are, you and I.

But you can never be what I am,
while anyone at all can be like you.   20

VI, xiv

You keep insisting, Labierus,
that you know how to write fine poems.
Then why is it you're unwilling
to try? Knowing how to write
fine poems and never doing it!
What will power, Labierus!

XI, lxvi

You're a spy and a blackmailer,
a forger, a pimp, a pervert,
and a trainer of gladiators,
Vacerra. I can't understand
why you aren't rich.

STUDY QUESTIONS

1. Try to identify the timeless qualities in Martial's art.
   For example, substitute the name of some well-
   known public figures of today in several epigrams;
   make sure the shoe fits!
2. Try rewriting several epigrams, altering as necessary,
   e.g., XI, lxvi:
   You're a fink and a toady,
   a cheat, a liar, a thief,
   and a politician,
   (add appropriate name). I can't understand
   why you aren't rich.

LITERARY SELECTION 8

Discourses of Epictetus

Arrian (b. AD 108)

This lecture of Epictetus (ca. 60–138), as recorded by his student Arrian, together with the meditations of Marcus Aurelius, which follows, presents the Stoic point of view. This philosophy assumes that the great *logos* ("intelligence") pervades the entire world and directs all that happens. Therefore, as will be seen in the selections, it is essentially a stern philosophy of acceptance, duty, and brotherhood of all men.

Book I, Chapter 1: On Things in Our Power and Things Not in Our Power

Of our faculties in general you will find that none can take cognizance of itself; none therefore has the power to approve or disapprove its own action. Our grammatical faculty for instance: how far can that take cognizance? Only so far as to distinguish expression.

Our musical faculty? Only so far as to distinguish tune. Does any one of these then take cognizance of itself? By no means. If you are writing to your friend, when you want to know what words to write grammar will tell you; but whether you should write to your friend or should not write grammar will not tell you. And in the same way music will tell you about tunes, but whether at this precise moment you should sing and play the lyre or should not sing nor play the lyre it will not tell you. What will tell you then? That faculty which takes cognizance of itself and of all things else. What is this? The reasoning faculty: for this alone of the faculties we have received is created to comprehend even its own nature; that is to say, what it is and what it can do, and with what precious qualities it has come to us, and to comprehend all other faculties as well. For what else is it that tells us that gold is a goodly thing? For the gold does not tell us. Clearly it is the faculty which can deal with our impressions. What else is it which distinguishes the faculties of music, grammar, and the rest, testing their uses and pointing out the due seasons for their use? It is reason and nothing else.   10   20

The gods then, as was but right, put in our hands the one blessing that is best of all and master of all, that and nothing else, the power to deal rightly with our impressions, but everything else they did not put in our hands. Was it that they would not? For my part I think that if they could have entrusted us with those other powers as well they would have done so, but they were quite unable. Prisoners on the earth and in an earthly body and among earthly companions, how was it possible that we should not be hindered from the attainment of these powers by these external fetters?   30

But what says Zeus? "Epictetus, if it were possible I would have made your body and your possessions (those trifles that you prize) free and untrammelled. But as things are—never forget this—this body is not yours, it is but a clever mixture of clay. But since I could not make it free, I gave you a portion in our divinity, this faculty of impulse to act and not to act, of will to get and will to avoid, in a word the faculty which can turn impressions to right use. If you pay heed to this, and put your affairs in its keeping, you will never suffer let nor hindrance, you will not groan, you will blame no man, you will flatter none. What then? Does all this seem but little to you?"   40   50

Heaven forbid!

"Are you content then?"

So surely as I hope for the gods' favor.

But, as things are, though we have it in our power to pay heed to one thing and to devote ourselves to one, yet instead of this we prefer to pay heed to many things and to be bound fast to many—our body, our property, brother and friend, child and slave. Inasmuch then as we are bound fast to many things, we are burdened by them and dragged down. That is why, if the weather is bad for sailing, we sit distracted and keep looking continually and ask, "What wind is blowing?" "The north wind." What have we to do with that? "When will the west wind blow?" When it so chooses, good sir, or when Aeolus chooses. For God made Aeolus the master   60 of the winds, not you. What follows? We must make the best of those things that are in our power, and take the rest as nature gives it. What do you mean by "nature"? I mean, God's will. 70

"What? Am I to be beheaded now, and I alone?"

Why? Would you have had all beheaded, to give you consolation? Will you not stretch out your neck as Lateranus did in Rome when Nero ordered his beheading? For he stretched out his neck and took the blow, and when the blow dealt him was too weak he shrank up a little and then stretched it out again. Nay more, on a previous occasion, when Nero's freedman Epaphroditus came to him and asked him the cause of his offense, he answered, "If I want to say anything, I will say it to your master." 80

What then must a man have ready to help him in such emergencies? Surely this: he must ask himself, "What is mine, and what is not mine? What may I do, what may I not do?"

I must die. But must I die groaning? I must be imprisoned. But must I whine as well? I must suffer exile. Can any one then hinder me from going with a smile, and a good courage, and at peace?

"Tell the secret!" 90

I refuse to tell, for this is in my power.

"But I will chain you."

What say you, fellow? Chain me? My leg you will chain —yes, but my will—no, not even Zeus can conquer that.

"I will imprison you."

My bit of a body, you mean.

"I will behead you."

Why? When did I ever tell you that I was the only man in the world that could not be beheaded?

These are the thoughts that those who pursue philosophy should ponder, these are the lessons they should write down day by day, in these they should exercise themselves. 100

Thrasea used to say "I had rather be killed today than exiled tomorrow." What then did Rufus say to him? "If you choose it as the harder, what is the meaning of your foolish choice? If as the easier, who has given you the easier? Will you not study to be content with what is given you?"

It was in this spirit that Agrippinus used to say—do you know what? "I will not stand in my own way!" News was brought him, "Your trial is on in the Senate!" "Good luck to it, but the fifth hour is come"—this was the hour when he used to take his exercise and have a cold bath—"let us go and take exercise." When he had taken his exercise they came and told him, "You are condemned." "Exile or death?" he asked. "Exile." "And my property?" "It is not confiscated." "Well then, let us go to Aricia and dine." 110

Here you see the result of training as training should be, of the will to get and will to avoid, so disciplined that nothing can hinder or frustrate them. I must die, must I? If at once, then I am dying: if soon, I dine now, as it is time for dinner, and afterwards when the time comes I will die. And die how? As befits one who gives back what is not his own. 120

STUDY QUESTION

What is the proper Stoic attitude toward those things we cannot control?

LITERARY SELECTION 9

Meditations

Book II

Marcus Aurelius (121–180)

Begin the morning by saying to thyself, I shall meet with the busybody, the ungrateful, arrogant, deceitful, envious, unsocial. All these things happen to them by reason of their ignorance of what is good and evil. But I who have seen the nature of the good that it is beautiful, and of the bad that it is ugly, and the nature of him who does wrong, that it is akin to me, not only of the same blood or seed, but that it participates in the same intelligence and the same portion of the divinity, I can neither be injured by any of them, for no one can fix on me what is ugly, nor can I be angry with my kinsman, nor hate him. For we are made for cooperation, like feet, like hands, like eyelids, like the rows of the upper and lower teeth. To act against one another then is contrary to nature; and it is acting against one another to be vexed and to turn away. 10

2. Whatever this is that I am, it is a little flesh and breath, and the ruling part. Throw away thy books; no longer distract thyself: it is not allowed; but as if thou wast now dying, despise the flesh; it is blood and bones and a network, a contexture of nerves, veins, and arteries. See the breath also, what kind of a thing it is, air, and not always the same, but every moment sent out and again sucked in. The third then is the ruling part: consider thus: Thou art an old man; no longer let this be a slave, no longer be pulled by the strings like a puppet to unsocial movements, no longer be either dissatisfied with thy present lot, or shrink from the future. 20

5. Every moment think steadily as a Roman and a man to do what thou hast in hand with perfect and simple dignity, and feeling of affection, and freedom, and justice; and to give thyself relief from all other thoughts. And thou wilt give thyself relief, if thou doest every act of thy life as it were the last, laying aside all carelessness and passionate aversion from the commands of reason, and all hypocrisy, and self-love, and discontent with the portion which has been given to thee. Thou seest how few the things are, that which if a man lays hold of, he is able to live a life which flows in quiet, and is like the existence of the gods; for the gods on their part will require nothing more from him who observes these things. 30 40

9. This thou must always bear in mind, what is the nature of the whole, and what is my nature, and how this is related to that, and what kind of a part it is of what kind of a whole; and that there is no one who hinders thee from always doing and saying the things which are according to the nature of which thou art a part.

11. Since it is possible that thou mayest depart from life this very moment, regulate every act and thought accordingly. But to go away from among men, if there are gods, is not a thing to be afraid of, for the gods will not involve thee in evil; but if indeed they do not exist, or if they have no concern about human affairs, what is it to me to live in a universe devoid of gods or devoid of Providence? But in truth they do exist, and they do care for human things, and they have put all the means in man's power to enable him not to fall into real evils. And as to the rest, if there was anything evil, they would have provided for this also, that it should be altogether in a man's power not to fall into it. Now that which does not make a man worse, how can it make a man's life worse? But neither through ignorance, nor having the knowledge, but not the power to guard against or correct these things, is it possible that the nature of the universe has overlooked them; nor is it possible that it has made so great a mistake, either through want of power or want of skill, that good and evil should happen indiscriminately to the good and the bad. But death certainly, and life, honor and dishonor, pain and pleasure, all these things equally happen to good men and bad, being things which make us neither better nor worse. Therefore they are neither good nor evil.

16. The soul of man does violence to itself, first of all, when it becomes an abscess and, as it were, a tumor on the universe, so far as it can. For to be vexed at anything which happens is a separation of ourselves from nature, in some part of which the natures of all other things are contained. In the next place, the soul does violence to itself when it turns away from any man, or even moves towards him with the intention of injuring, such as are the souls of those who are angry. In the third place, the soul does violence to itself when it is overpowered by pleasure or by pain. Fourthly, when it plays a part, and does or says anything insincerely and untruly. Fifthly, when it allows any act of its own and any movement to be without an aim, and does anything thoughtlessly and without considering what it is, it being right that even the smallest things be done with reference to an end; and the end of rational animals is to follow the reason and the law of the most ancient city and polity.

17. Of human life the time is a point, and the substance is in a flux, and the perception dull, and the composition of the whole body subject to putrefaction, and the soul a whirl, and fortune hard to divine, and fame a thing devoid of judgement. And, to say all in a word, everything which belongs to the body is a stream, and what belongs to the soul is a dream and vapor, and life is a warfare and a stranger's sojourn, and after-fame is oblivion. What then is that which is able to conduct a man? One thing and only one, philosophy. But this consists in keeping the daemon within a man free from

violence and unharmed, superior to pains and pleasures, doing nothing without a purpose, nor yet falsely and with hypocrisy, not feeling the need of another man's doing or not doing anything; and besides, accepting all that happens, and all that is allotted, as coming from thence, wherever it is, from whence he himself came; and, finally, waiting for death with a cheerful mind, as being nothing else than a dissolution of the elements of which every living being is compounded. But if there is no harm to the elements themselves in each continually changing into another, why should a man have any apprehension about the change and dissolution of all the elements? For it is according to nature, and nothing is evil which is according to nature.

STUDY QUESTIONS

Consider the "ruling part" of human nature; according to Marcus Aurelius, should it be reason, passion, conscience, tradition, authority, or revelation? Why?

SUMMARY

The pragmatic Romans cherished their flawed institutions and their proclivity for war, plunder, and profits, but they did have the saving grace of being able to laugh at themselves. Enthusiastically adapting satire to Roman tastes, they lambasted all they held dear: politics, material possessions, manners, and morals. The Romans were, in the final analysis, rational and (apart from their blood-sports) civilized people, and there is no clearer evidence of this than in their literature. No more given to profundities than their society in general, Roman writers were, collectively, sophisticated, worldly-wise, and often jaded. They sought to entertain and to inform rather than to enlighten, and they accomplished this with great style and a lusty elegance. The literature is consistently entertaining, frequently irreverent, often lewd; it makes lovely reading.

CULTURE AND HUMAN VALUES

The Greeks and the Romans were realists living in a world about which they had few illusions. However, the Greeks were also idealists who believed that people should (and could) be better than they were, that they could achieve freedom, beauty, truth, and justice.

Though not denying the desirability of these ideals, the Romans were total pragmatists. They rejected theory and precedent in favor of practical approaches and expediency. The value of a course of action lay in its observable consequences, the sum of which was its meaning. Serving the Roman state, for example, as a member of a Roman legion brought security, status, discipline, and a reasonable income. The sum of these benefits meant that soldiering was a good life and one that benefited first the state and then the individual. The state rather than the soldier was the true reality, a direct reversal of Greek values that placed the individual above the state. Duty, honor, and patriotism were Roman virtues as opposed to the Greek ideals of freedom, truth, and beauty.

Justice was a deep concern for both cultures, but in very different ways. The Greeks pursued the theory of perfect justice in an ordered society. Roman justice was pragmatic, a process that dealt with practical problems in everyday life. Such human failings as venality and greed were controlled by the state in order to prevent the strong from triumphing over the weak. Roman law implied the consent of the governed, and every citizen, regardless of class, had the right to "appeal to Caesar." Moreover, Roman law was international and based on a pragmatic appraisal of consistent human behavior regardless of the environment. Though we may admire the Greek ideal of justice, it is Roman law that has provided the basic framework of today's body of laws.

The state of balance of the culture-epoch theory was essentially maintained from the beginning of the classical period in Greece to the death of Marcus Aurelius, the sixth and last of the so-called good emperors (480 BC–AD 180). Though ending some eighteen centuries ago, the brilliant Graeco-Roman era set a standard of civilization rarely approached in the ten centuries or so that followed. Most of the so-called progress since that distant age has been technological with little positive effect on the quality of life or the viability of human institutions.

> Those who are most easily depressed about the precarious future of Western civilization are usually people who do not know the full history of its past. They also very generally misunderstand our relation to the Greeks and the Romans. They imagine them as remote peoples whose lives and achievements interest antiquarians alone, and whose languages and thoughts are "dead." Certainly they always conceive the Greeks and Romans as being less than ourselves, instead of being in many ways more mature and more advanced in knowledge and experience.[15]

15. Gilbert Highet, *Man's Unconquerable Mind* (New York: Columbia University Press, 1954), p. 15.

CHAPTER 9

Roman Art and Architecture: The Arts of Megalopolis

ETRUSCAN CIVILIZATION

The Etruscans controlled northern Italy for about 400 years and even ruled Rome for nearly a century. Their influence on Roman civilization was considerable but there was almost no mutual exchange. Rome did not impress the Etruscans but Greece did, especially her sculpture, painting, and vases, particularly vases, for much Greek pottery has been recovered from Etruscan tombs.

Despite the strong Greek influence the Etruscans did develop a distinctive kind of art. Provincial, sometimes homespun, with an occasional masterpiece, their work had an earthy vigor that impressed their Roman conquerors. In fact, we know more of Etruscan art than of their culture in general. With an undeciphered literature and little more than some massive stone walls remaining of their fortified hilltop cities, our scanty knowledge of Etruscan culture is based almost entirely on the contents of thousands of tombs found throughout central Italy (map 9.1). Etruscan skill in making terra-cotta objects is exemplified by the funerary sculpture (fig. 9.1) found in the *necropolis* (Gk., "city of the dead") outside Cerveteri,

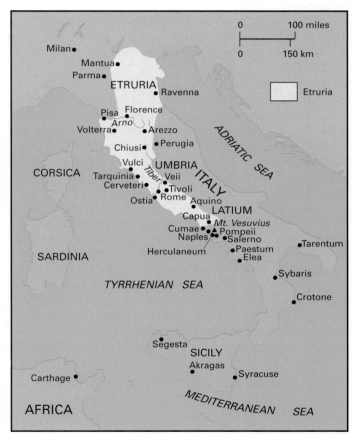

Map 9.1 Etruscan and Roman Italy.

Opposite *Apollo Slaying the Python*, House of the Vettii, Pompeii, detail. Ca. AD 65. Mural painting. Photo: Alinari, Florence.

9.1 *Left* Etruscan sarcophagus, from Cerveteri, Italy. Ca. 510 BC. Painted terra-cotta, length ca. 6'7"(2 m). Museo Nazionale di Villa Giulia, Rome. Photo: Hirmer, Munich.

9.2 *Chimera of Arezzo*, from Italy. Etruscan. Ca. 380–360 BC. Bronze, height 31½" (80 cm). Museo Archeologico, Florence. Photo: Viollet, Paris.

ART FORGERIES

Art forgers make objects designed to deceive a potential purchaser, a practice probably as old as collecting art objects. However, the earliest records of fraudulent art date only from ancient Rome. The influx of Greek art after the conquest of the Greek mainland created a demand for Greek paintings and sculpture. Collecting Greek art was a sure sign of taste, breeding, and social position (and money), and enterprising crooks found a ready market for counterfeit Greek art, especially sculpture. Many were the forgeries sold bearing the famous names of Myron, Polykleitos, Pheidias, Praxiteles, and Lysippos, among others. These ancient transactions haunt today's experts who are still puzzling over the authenticity of some Greek sculptures.

northwest of Rome. A deceased couple is shown resting their left elbows on a couch as if attending a celestial banquet. The smooth bodies, braided hair, and archaic smiles in the Greek manner are typical of the Etruscan style, as is the display of mutual affection and the couple's individualized features. The exact meaning of festive banquet scenes like this and many others is unknown, but continuation of the good life after death is likely.

The remarkable *Chimera* (fig. 9.2) is a masterful monster that radiates the vigor so characteristic of Etruscan art. In Greek mythology a chimera was usually a fire-breathing monster with the head of a lion, body of a goat, and a serpent for a tail. Here the head and tail fit the pattern, but the body is more "lion" than "goat" and the pattern down the backbone seems to be dragonlike. Compounding the four-footed hybrid is the head of a goat protruding from the back with the left horn caught in the fangs of the snake. (A mistake in reconstruction placed the snake's head too low; it

should be raised so that its fangs can intimidate observers.) There is no Greek influence here. The Greeks polished off the rough edges of their demons but the Etruscans created a whole company of monsters that specialized in tormenting the dead in the underworld. This seems to reflect the Asiatic origins of the Etruscans, about which Herodotos was so positive. This creature has precedents that go back to Egyptian sphinxes (see fig. 2.2) and the winged, man-faced bulls of Assyria (see fig. 1.11).

The Etruscans were highly skilled workers in precious metals as confirmed by their gold and silver jewelry and bronze sculptures such as the *Chimera*.

That the Etruscans were exceptional goldsmiths is shown by the gold disks in figure 9.3. The granulation is extremely fine and the filigree and gold wire work exceptionally delicate. For best effect this figure should be studied with a magnifying glass.

9.3 Etruscan gold disks. Late 6th century BC. Diameter 1¾" (4.4 cm). Antikenmuseum, Staatliche Museen Preussischer Kulturbesitz, Berlin. Photo: B.P.K., Munich (Ingrid Geske-Heiden).

THE ROMAN ARTS, CA. 753 BC–AD 476

Art for the stern Romans was a dissolute influence that could undermine the moral fiber of the people, especially the Republic's citizen-soldiers. As late as the third century BC Rome was, according to Plutarch, a metropolis devoid of refinement and beauty, a dreary city full of hostages, battle trophies, barbarous weapons, and ostentatious triumphal arches. The penetration of Greek culture, especially Greek art, was a slow process that gathered momentum with Roman triumphs over Greek territories. During the conquest of the luxurious cities of Magna Graecia (southern Italy) in 212 BC, for example, one general returned bearing Greek statues and paintings while another general displayed such "proper" booty as gold and jewels. After the 146 BC conquest of the Greek mainland, a huge volume of confiscated art works flooded the city, overwhelming old guard hostility and establishing Rome as the prime custodian of the Hellenic artistic tradition.

Though much of what we call Roman art is derived from Greek models and often created by Greek artists, the Romans did make some significant contributions with their realistic portrait busts, landscape painting, and, especially, their architecture. Justly famous for the monumental architecture of the imperial period, the Romans must also be credited with developing the "art" of civilized living. During the early days of the Republic more attention was paid to the efficient design of military camps than to the urban planning of Rome and other growing cities of the rapidly expanding Republic. With the shift from a simple rural to an affluent urbanized society, the Romans had to tackle city planning. Taking their cue from Etruscan hill towns, they learned how to design and build the basic requirements for urban life: fortifications; streets; bridges; aqueducts; sewers; town houses; apartment houses; and recreational, shopping, and civic centers.

9.4   Two sections, west colonnade of the forum, Pompeii, Italy. Whole forum 125 × 466' (38.13 × 142.13 m). Photo: Viollet, Paris.

Pompeii

With no art and very little architecture remaining from the early centuries of the Republic, we begin our study of the arts of Rome with Pompeii, the only surviving city of the Roman Republic. The eruption of Mount Vesuvius in AD 79 buried Pompeii under cinders and ashes that, in effect, preserved the city as a museum of Roman civilization. Probably founded in the sixth century BC, Pompeii was inhabited by Italic Oscans and Samnites, plus some Greeks, until its conquest by Rome in about 80 BC.

City Plan
Containing the earliest extant amphitheatre and public baths, Pompeii was built in a modified Greek grid plan around the most important early forum outside Rome (fig. 9.4). Reflecting Greek influence, the Doric colonnade with superimposed Ionic columns was a device later extended to four levels in the Colosseum. There are, in fact, so many different elements of Etruscan, Greek, and Italic contributions to Pompeiian decoration that it is impossible to decide who did what. Measuring 125 by 466 feet (38.2 × 142.2 m), the civic center, or forum, was bordered on the west and east by matching two-story colonnades, ending at arches that flanked the primary city Temple of Jupiter, Juno, and Minerva. One arch and part of the temple base are visible in the right background of figure 9.4. (Also visible in the right background is the looming bulk of Mount Vesuvius.) Combining religious, commercial, and civil functions, forums were the hub of every Roman city, reflecting Roman concerns for centralized authority and control.

Domestic Architecture
Because the city-center forum was always closed to vehicular traffic, the network of streets began at the perimeter

POMPEII

It was already hot on the morning of 24 August 79. Pliny the Elder and his nephew Pliny the Younger, seeking cooler air, moved to the balcony of their villa overlooking the Bay of Naples. Suddenly they saw a burgeoning cloud across the bay over Vesuvius. The younger Pliny later wrote to Tacitus: "like an immense tree-trunk it was projected into the air, and opened out with branches, sometimes white, sometimes dark and mottled." Seconds later they heard an enormous explosion and felt earth tremors so violent that the nephew and his mother fled their villa and joined a panic-stricken crowd struggling to get out of the debris-filled air. Above the volcano there now "loomed a horrible black cloud ripped by sudden bursts of fire, writhing snakelike and revealing sudden flashes larger than lightning." Ash was falling so thickly that they had to keep moving to avoid being buried in it. The tremors and falling pumice and ash seemed to last several terrifying hours. As darkness gradually lightened to let a dim sun shine through, they could see that the whole top of Vesuvius had been blown away. Where there had once been farms, vineyards, Pompeii, Herculaneum, and Stabiae was now a deadly silent gray carpet of ash. Though the elder Pliny was a writer and lawyer, it was his dedication as a naturalist that compelled him, despite the pleading of his sister and nephew, to investigate this incredible natural wonder. He had set off in a galley for a closer look when he was trapped and died amid clouds of sulfurous fumes.

9.5 Atrium, House of the Silver Wedding, Pompeii. 1st century AD. Photo: Canali, Brescia.

and expanded outward to the suburbs. Much as old Italian towns are today, the streets nearer the forum were lined by shops, which were flanked by houses of shopkeepers and other citizens. The domus, single-family residence, was entered through a front doorway set in a windowless wall that guaranteed privacy and shut out city noise and dirt. An entrance hall led to the atrium (fig. 9.5), a typical Italic-Roman design for larger houses and for the still more elaborate villas in the surrounding countryside. A rectangular, windowless court that kept out heat while admitting light and air, the atrium had an inwardly sloping roof that drained rainwater into the pool below, from which it was piped to a cistern. Surrounding the central atrium were the kitchen, and parlors for everyday living. Beyond the atrium were the bedrooms, whose porches fronted on an open courtyard surrounded by a peristyle of, in this case, Doric columns. As was customary with Roman houses, the many blank walls were either brightly painted or decorated with murals. The combination of Roman atrium and Hellenistic Greek peristyle court, which was adopted in the second century BC, makes the Roman house or villa an ideal design for hot Mediterranean summers.

A vivid mythological scene decorates a wall of the gar-den room of the House of the Vettii (see chapter opener on p. 148). Apollo strums his kithara as the vanquished python trails down from an altar where Diana stands at the left with the sacrificial bull. Above the panel is a fantastic architectonic construction under which a goddess plays her cymbals; this may be Euterpe, muse of lyric poetry and music. Left and right of the muse are statues of herms (for Hermes, god of fertility). This is the latest and most elaborate of the four Pompeiian styles.

Architecture and Engineering

The Roman Temple
Though no intact Augustan temples remain in Rome, the remarkably well preserved temple nicknamed the Maison Carrée (marble house; fig. 9.6) embodies the qualities advocated by the emperor. Unlike their Greek counterparts, Roman temples stand on high podiums and are entered from the front by a single flight of steps. The open form of the Greek temple, with a walkway and three steps on all four sides, has been converted to the closed form of buildings designed to enclose space. This temple uses the rich Corinthian order (fig. 9.7) favored by most Roman architects and engaged columns attached to the cella walls in a decorative device from Republican days. A small building measuring 59 by 117 feet (18 × 35.7 m) with 30-foot (9.2 m) columns, the Maison Carrée became a prototype of temples honoring notable emperors, much as the Jefferson Memorial in Washington memorializes an illustrious president. This building, in fact, inspired Thomas Jefferson to

9.6 Maison Carrée, Nîmes, France. 1st century BC. 59 × 117' (18 × 35.7 m). Photo: Helga Schmidt-Glassner, Stuttgart.

9.7 *Above*   Corinthian capital.

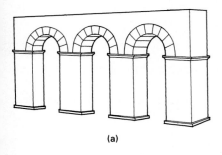

(a)

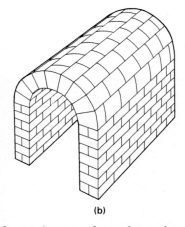

(b)

9.8   (a) Semicircular arch arcade, and (b) barrel or tunnel vault.

utilize the classic style of Rome in his neoclassic designs of the Virginia State Capitol, the University of Virginia, and his own home of Monticello.

The Roman Arch

Rome made a lasting contribution to the development of the rounded arch and vault as structural architectural principles. Used for centuries in Asia Minor and Greece for lesser works like gates, storage areas, corridors, and sewers, the arch was exploited by Roman engineers on a massive scale. Concerned with spanning and enclosing space, they

used arches to build bridges, aqueducts, baths, and basilicas, the secular structures necessary for the efficient operation of Roman cities. A semicircle of stone blocks, or bricks and mortar (fig. 9.8), spanning spaces between **piers** or walls, the arch was better suited to the utilitarian needs of Roman engineering than the post and lintel system. Not intended to bridge large spaces, the lintel is the weaker portion of the system because it can support a limited amount of weight. To bear greater loads it must be enlarged, the columns moved closer together, or both. In the arch, the wedge-shaped blocks called **voussoirs** (voo-SWAHR) curve up to the **keystone** at the apex of the arch, providing strength and stability because of the mutually supporting pressures from pier to keystone. From the keystone the thrust is transmitted through the voussoirs down through the pier, or wall, to the ground. When the arches are side by side they form an **arcade**, as in the Pont du Gard (see unit opener on p. 125). When extended longitudinally along its axis, the arch is called a **barrel** or tunnel **vault**, as in the Arch of Titus (fig. 9.15).

Aqueducts

Representing Roman engineering and power, aqueducts were a highly visible portion of the network of waterways and roadways that interconnected the Empire. Built by Agrippa, a lieutenant under Augustus, the Pont du Gard (see p. 125) is 180 feet (54.9 m) high and in its present condition about 900 feet (275 m) long. It carried water some 25 miles (40 km) from the mountains, across the gorge of the Gard River, and into Nîmes. Spanning over 80 feet (24 m), each massive arch supports an arch of similar dimensions but with much less masonry, which in turn undergirds the watercourse itself. Supported by three small arches for each large one, the water flowed steadily down an approximate 1 percent grade. Using stones weighing up to 6 tons (6,000 kg) each and assembled without mortar, the bridge of the bottom arcade has been in continuous use for 2,000 years.

Sculpture, Painting, and Minor Arts

Maintaining a strong sense of identity was a major concern for Roman families; they preserved collections of wax portrait masks of their ancestors. Recognizable portrayals were therefore required, accounting for the long tradition of starkly realistic marble portrait busts as represented, for example, by the bust of Julius Caesar (fig. 9.9). As the man responsible for the final demise of the embattled Republic, Caesar is depicted as history has revealed him to be: imperious, ruthless, a charismatic leader of men. With their no-nonsense approach to reality, the Romans insisted upon an exactitude that included every wart, pimple, line, and blemish. This bust may have been done from life; if so, Caesar probably relished the portrait, particularly the confident tilt of the head.

9.9 *Above* Bust of Julius Caesar. 1st century BC. Marble, height 38" (96.5 cm). Museo Archeologico Nazionale, Naples. Photo: Mansell Collection, London.

Caesar Augustus, 63 BC–AD 14

There are no blemishes on the commanding statue of Caesar Augustus from the Imperial Villa at Primaporta (fig. 9.10). Idealized in the Greek manner, this is Augustus the noble ruler. Based on the *Doryphoros* (see fig. 7.17), with the imperious gesture probably derived from Near Eastern art, this is an official portrait. With his likeness on Roman coins and with thousands of busts distributed throughout the Empire, Augustus created the imperial image of mighty Rome. Augustus' divine origins are revealed in the cupid and the dolphin, symbols of Venus, mother of Aeneas, who was, according to Virgil, the emperor's ancestor. The relief sculpture on the armor details the emperor's road to power. The only realistic elements are the tactile illusions of leather, metal, and cloth that give the feeling of actuality prized by Romans but considered trite by Greeks. Becoming a stock device for depicting kings, emperors, and dictators, this is a superb example of didactic art.

Painting

In figure 9.11 we see an example of the continuing interest in classical themes, which formed one of the bridges between Greek and Roman cultures. The powerful Herakles

9.11 *Herakles Discovering the Infant Telephos in Arcadia*, from Herculaneum, Italy. Roman copy of ca. AD 70 of a Hellenistic original of the 2nd century BC. Mural painting, ca. 7 × 6' (2.1 × 1.9 m). Museo Nazionale, Naples. Photo: Scala, Florence.

9.10 *Augustus of Primaporta.* Ca. 20 BC. Marble, height 6'9" (2.06 m). Musei Vaticani, Rome. Photo: Scala, Florence.

9.12   Roman jewelry: earrings, brooch in the form of a dog, hair ornament, pendant, and necklace. 1st–4th century AD. Gold with garnets, sapphires, emeralds, and pearls. British Museum, London.

Greek Theory and Roman Practice

A comparison of the assemblage of visual images of the *Herakles* (fig. 9.11) with the figure of the *Doryphoros* (see fig. 7.17) illustrates some fundamental differences between Greek and Roman cultures. More concerned with practice than theory, the Romans itemized rather than conceptualized. The *Herakles* is a kind of visual catalog of a specific event: Herakles finding his son in Arcadia. The *Doryphoros* is not a specific person but a realization of the ideal athlete, the embodiment of a concept against which individual athletes measured themselves. The Romans portrayed people as they were and the Greeks depicted them as they should be. The Romans were practical, the Greeks theoretical. It is no wonder that the Romans viewed the Greeks with awe, contempt, envy, and suspicion. The Romans accepted the imperfect world as it was; the Greeks wanted something better. The quarreling Greek city-states were forcibly united by Alexander; Rome conquered the world.

The Romans acknowledged Greek culture as generally superior and made Greek literature, art, and architecture basic strands in the fabric of Roman civilization. The Empire was, in fact, administered in two languages—the Latin of the ruling Romans and the Greek of the conquered Hellenes. (Try to imagine Napoleon administering the French Empire in both French and German.) Where the two cultures differed significantly was in sheer size. The population of Athens of the Golden Age was about 100,000; Imperial Rome had a much larger population and greater wealth, but it also endured the endless problems that plague large cities in any culture.

stands before a classically conceived woman representing the mythical Arcadia, where everyone lived at peace with nature and one another. The lion is painted in a vaguely impressionistic manner, while the doe in the left foreground is light and graceful. The disparate figures appear to have been placed in a preexisting space with little concern for their interrelatedness or to the painting's unity. Like much Roman painting, the work does display, however, great technical skill in the manipulation of light, lines, and shapes, and in the illusion of three-dimensional space.

Minor Arts
The citizens of the Republic were as disdainful of such luxury items as jewelry as they were of the visual arts, making surviving examples very rare. However, by the beginning of the Empire in 27 BC, the old austerity had quickly become passé. **Mosaic** work decorated the floors of Roman houses, temples, baths, and other buildings. Rome's annexation of the lands of the Hellenistic world included, inevitably, the opulent culture. Essentially a continuation of the Hellenistic style, Roman jewelry was an equally skillful combination of gemstones and precious metals. In the necklace (second century AD) in figure 9.12 gold links alternate with emeralds. The hair ornament from Tunis (third century AD) is inlaid with emeralds with a pearl border. The pendant is a sapphire flanked by two pearls. These two pieces in particular symbolize the elegance of the Empire at its height.

9.13   I Gismondi, Reconstruction of 4th-century Rome, detail. Museo Nazionale Romano, Rome.

The Imperial City

Shown in figure 9.13 is part of the center section of a city with over 50 miles (80 km) of streets, almost none with names, and a population in the second century AD of about 1,200,000. Much of this area was constructed by the Flavian emperors (reigned 69–96); the monumental civic structures were completed by Nerva, Trajan, and Hadrian (76–138).

In the far upper left of the model are the Baths of Trajan; with a central complex of thermal, exercise, and dressing rooms surrounded by landscaped grounds, this became the prototype for all subsequent imperial baths. Near the bottom of the figure is the Circus Maximus, the primary stadium for chariot racing and the common meeting ground for all levels of Roman society. Achieving its final form in about AD 329, the stadium enclosed a race course measuring 660 by 1,950 feet (201.3 × 594.8 m). Seating about 150,000 spectators and operating a full racing program on 240 days of the year, the Circus Maximus could total about 8,000,000 admissions a year. This was mass entertainment, Roman style. Directly above the Circus

Maximus are the Imperial Forums and the Claudius Aqueduct leading to the Palatine, highest of the seven hills of Rome and urban abode of the aristocracy. At the upper right is the Colosseum, the single most representative building of the Roman Empire, then and now.

The Colosseum

Designed for the staging of battles between various combinations of animals and gladiators, the Colosseum seated about 50,000 spectators around an arena measuring 156 by 258 feet (47.6 × 78.7 m). With underground corridors for gladiators, animals, and technicians, and elaborate stage equipment for crowd-pleasing effects, the Colosseum was a complete entertainment center. Built on four levels, the exterior is unified by four superimposed orders of columns. Beginning with a simplification of the Doric column called Tuscan, the columns mount upwards through the Ionic and Corinthian orders to flat Corinthian piers called **pilasters**. Topping the wall are sockets for pennants and for a removable canvas covering that protected against sun and rain. A key design unit in the exterior wall is the characteristic combination of a Roman arch flanked by a Greek order. Called the Roman arch order, the basic elements are a Roman arch set in a Greek post and lintel frame. Used in triumphal arches and other structures, this device was revived in the Italian

9.14   Colosseum, aerial view. Photo: Fototeca Unione, Rome.

GAMES IN A RING

Chariot races (*ludi circenses*; "games in a ring") were staged at six racetracks in and about Rome. Racing was a frenzied and dangerous sport, if one can call driving four-horse chariots on a tight oval track that had only one rule—to the victor go the spoils—a sport. The stakes were high enough; winning drivers made a great deal of money and enjoyed a status comparable to the combined charisma of a pro football star and a Grand Prix champion. There is no contemporary equivalent for a day at the races in Rome's Circus Maximus, which was a combination sports, social, and gambling center. Try to imagine an oval track 2,000 feet (610 m) in circumference, four tense and tough racing teams (blues, greens, whites, reds) and 150,000 fanatical spectators who had millions riding on every race. And some were even betting on who got killed.

Renaissance and can be seen today in neoclassic building facades in Europe and the Americas.

The Colosseum is an amphitheatre (Gk., *amphi*, "both"; *theatron*, "theatre"), a structure invented by the Romans as a derivation of Greek theatre design. As the name indicates, this structure is actually two theatres facing each other to form an oval-shaped bowl (fig. 9.14). Brilliantly designed and executed, the Colosseum exemplifies the qualities the Roman architect Vitruvius (first century BC) considered basic for superior design: firmness, commodity, and delight. Structurally sound (firmness), the Colosseum was a spacious arena with eighty portals for easy ingress and egress, comfortable seating, and unobstructed sightlines (commodity). Though not a prime Roman concern, it does have a quality of "delight," an aesthetic appeal that makes a work of art exalted and memorable.

Erected by the Flavian emperors, the Colosseum, also known as the Flavian Amphitheatre, was largely built by prisoners of the Jewish Wars, which had ended in AD 70 with the conquest of Jerusalem and the Temple of Solomon's destruction. Dedicated by Titus in AD 80, the Colosseum opened with inaugural ceremonies that lasted 100 days and that were, according to contemporary accounts, very successful, costing the lives of some 9,000 wild animals and 2,000 gladiators.

Immediately recognized as an extraordinary achievement, the Colosseum was elevated by Martial to one of the Seven Wonders of the World:

On the Dedication of the Colosseum in Rome

Barbaric Egypt, boast no more
    The wonders of your pyramids!
Babylon, vaunt no longer now

The gardens of Semiramis!
Let not the soft Ionians swell
    With pride for their great Artemis
Whose temple splendor long has been
    The claim and fame of Ephesus.
Let Delos hide its head in shame
    And say no more Apollo
Himself did rear the altar there
    (A claim both weak and hollow).
Let not the Carians wildly praise
    The wondrous, sculptured tomb
The queen at Halicarnassus raised
    When Mausolus met his doom.
Let every wonder of the past
    Yield now to this great wonder.
Fame shall cling to this at last,
    Her applause as loud as thunder.

The Triumphal Arch

Julius Caesar contended that the only truly effective way of controlling conquered people was to execute the entire population. The practical alternative to extermination was the conversion of prisoners of war into a tractable slave labor force. One of the most effective propaganda devices for impressing their bondage on the slaves was the triumphal arch, a symbolic representation of the yoke of oxen. In a ritualistic dramatization of Roman might, victorious generals marched their prisoners through hastily erected temporary arches to the accompaniment of battle trumpets and drums. What the Romans called the Triumph was meant to be awesome for the spectators and humiliating for the vanquished—and it undoubtedly was.

SPARTACUS

Despite steely Roman policies controlling their war-booty slaves, there were three major slave revolts. The Romans frantically covered up details of two rebellions they thought could never happen. Nothing at all could suppress news of the 73 BC slave insurrection led by a gladiator of Thracian origin named Spartacus. Proving himself a brilliant general, Spartacus and a slave army of 90,000 men ravaged southern Italy and scored seven dazzling victories over the humiliated Roman armies. Not until Spartacus was killed in 71 BC while battling Crassus, Pompey and two Roman legions was the rebellion finally crushed. To make certain this would never happen again the Romans crucified selected rebel slaves, lining the 120 miles (193 km) of road from Capua north to Rome with 6,000 crosses. The victorious Romans found 3,000 unharmed Roman prisoners in Spartacus' camp.

9.15 Arch of Titus, Rome. AD 81. Marble, height ca. 50' (15 m), width ca. 40' (12 m). Photo: Alinari, Florence.

To commemorate his brother Titus' destruction of Jerusalem in AD 70, Domitian had a permanent version of the triumphal arch erected where the Via Sacra enters the Roman Forum (fig. 9.15). (By the end of the Empire there would be over sixty triumphal arches in Rome and many more throughout the Empire.) Constructed of concrete with a marble facing, the Arch of Titus utilized a Roman arch order similar to that of the Colosseum. Massive piers with dual-engaged columns provided a post and lintel frame for a deep Roman arch vault (see fig. 9.8). With a superstructure called the attic bearing the commemorative inscription, the walls of the vault were decorated with high reliefs depicting Titus' successful campaign against the Jews.

Trajan's Column

The assassination of Domitian in AD 96 ended the Flavian dynasty and ushered in the era of the so-called good emperors (reigned 96–180): Nerva, Trajan, Hadrian, Antoninus Pius, and Marcus Aurelius. The first non-Italian to occupy the throne, the brilliant Spanish general, Trajan, led Rome to the maximum expansion of its empire. Among the monuments commemorating his phenomenal successes is the Column of Trajan (fig. 9.16), an unprecedented conception. Carved in low relief in 150 scenes, the 658-foot (200 m) frieze winds twenty-three times around the column as it narrates the highlights of Trajan's two campaigns into Dacia (modern Romania and Hungary). To "read" the story, one

walks round and round the column, but it soon becomes impossible to read it without binoculars. How and if this story was read in its entirety has never been satisfactorily explained.

Though the inspiration for this unusual monument is unknown, it is perhaps significant that it was placed between the Latin and Greek libraries of Trajan; the column is quite similar to library books of the time—*rotuli* ("scrolls"), which were wound on two spindles. The basic inspiration, however, is the "continuous narration" technique, which is so typically Roman, as opposed to Greek "simultaneous narration." The Greek unities of time, place, and action as observed in the Parthenon frieze (see fig. 7.29) were apparently not suitable for the day-to-day world of empire building. Reflected in the Column of Trajan is Roman interest in biography and history; the basic unity is the focus on the leadership of Trajan while history is served by the unfolding scenes of campaigns. Executed under the direction of a single artist, the frieze is a masterpiece of didactic art in the tradition of the *Augustus of Primaporta* (see fig. 9.10). The column was originally topped by a statue of Trajan, which was destroyed during the Middle Ages and since replaced by a sixteenth-century statue of St. Peter. Symbolizing the church's triumph over Rome, the first pope stands above a visual record of two bloody Roman campaigns.

Hadrian, 76–138

Probably the best educated of all Roman emperors and certainly the most cosmopolitan, Hadrian (reigned 117–138) was more interested in improving the cultural life of the

9.16 Column of Trajan, Rome. Ca. AD 106–113. Marble, height (with base) 125' (38.13 m). Photo: Alinari, Florence.

9.17 The Pantheon, Rome. Ca. 118–125. Marble, brick, and concrete, portico height 59' (18 m). Photo: Calmann & King, London (Lieberman).

works. The Pantheon is the best preserved of all Roman buildings because it became a Christian church early in the history of the Church of Rome.

The eight-column front of Corinthian capitals topping polished granite columns is, in effect, a Greek portico opening into a massive drum derived from the circular Greek tholos. The impressiveness of the interior—one of the most astounding spatial accomplishments in architecture—is communicated better by the Panini painting (fig. 9.18) than by any contemporary photograph. Originally painted blue, the hemisphere of concrete was highlighted with rosettes of gilded bronze set into each coffer. Softly colored columns alternate with marble panels, pilasters, and niches, forming a harmonious blend within a single, self-sufficient, uninterrupted space. Dedicated to the worship of the seven planetary gods, the Pantheon is a stunning human version of the sky itself, the Dome of Heaven.

Empire than in extending political frontiers. Indicating his style of life, Hadrian lived and worked in Britain, southern France, Spain, Morocco, Asia Minor, Greece (twice), Tunisia, Syria, Palestine, and Egypt. After ten years abroad he finally returned to build Hadrian's Villa at Tivoli near Rome. A student of all things Greek, Hadrian was more concerned with supporting Greek intellectual life than with whatever took place in Rome's mercantile environment. He did, however, strongly support the most advanced concepts of Roman architects in their interior space designs.

The Pantheon

One of the most revolutionary and authoritative structures ever built, the Pantheon (fig. 9.17) has influenced the architecture of every age from ancient Rome to the present day. The inscription on the frieze, "M. AGRIPPA L.F. COS TERTIUM FECIT" ("Marcus Agrippa, son of Lucius, consul for the third time, built this"), does not refer to this building but to previous structures erected in 27–25 BC by Agrippa, son-in-law of Augustus. Because the original buildings included baths and a temple called Pantheon, Hadrian, displaying his fine sense of Roman history, had the original inscription repeated on the new temple. With a portico 59 feet (18m) high and measuring 142 feet (43.2 m) in the interior (diameter and height), the Pantheon is topped by one of the largest **domes** ever constructed. (St. Peter's dome is 139 feet [42.5 m] in diameter.) Twenty feet (6.1 m) thick at the outside edge, the poured concrete dome decreases to less than 5 feet (1.5 m) at the center. Resting on eight enormous piers and providing interior lighting with a circular opening (oculus) 28 feet (8.5 m) in diameter, the dome is coffered (indented panels) to decrease the weight without sacrificing structural strength. Rainwater can be drained away in minutes by a plumbing system that still

9.18 Giovanni Paolo Panini, *The Interior of the Pantheon*, after restoration. Oil on canvas, height 50" (127 cm), width 39" (99 cm). National Gallery of Art, Washington, D.C. (Samuel H. Kress Collection).

9.19 *Equestrian Statue of Marcus Aurelius*, Rome. Ca. AD 161–180. Gilded bronze, height 11'6" (3.5 m). Piazza del Campidoglio, Rome. Photo: Scala, Florence/Art Resource, New York.

Marcus Aurelius, 121–180

The last of the illustrious Antonine emperors,[1] Marcus Aurelius (reigned 161–180) was an unusual combination of distinguished general and Stoic philosopher. Most un-Roman in his detestation of war, he confined his military activities to defending the borders against barbarian incursions, particularly in the Balkans. It was on that distant frontier that the philosopher-king died in the performance of his Stoic duty. As depicted in the only equestrian statue surviving from

1. The very last Antonine was Commodus (reigned 180–192), the son of Marcus Aurelius. Anything but illustrious, he was corrupt, demented, and, ultimately, the victim of a household conspiracy.
2. Constantine himself personified Roman decadence. "Twice married, he murdered Crispus, his son by his first wife, in 326. He had his second wife drowned in the bath; killed his eleven-year-old nephew, then his brother-in-law, after giving his assurance of safe conduct under oath. He murdered his co-regent, Licinius, to become the sole emperor of the West and East." Peter De Rosa, *Vicars of Christ: The Dark Side of the Papacy* (New York: Macmillan, 1988), p. 18.

the ancient world (fig. 9.19), the emperor wore a beard in the Greek style first adopted by Hadrian. With his right arm extended in the characteristic gesture of a general about to address his troops, the emperor is both commanding and resigned to fulfilling his responsibilities. Vigorous and impatient, the high-spirited warhorse displays the artist's exceptional knowledge of equine anatomy. Mistaken identity assured the survival of the imperial bronze; Christians thought it depicted the Emperor Constantine.

Rome in Decline

The Empire was in almost continual disruption after the death of Marcus Aurelius in 180. Between 235 and 284 there were no less than twenty-six "barracks emperors" sponsored by various army factions. The accession of Diocletian in 284 replaced anarchy with a rigid despotism under which the Roman Senate lost the last vestige of its by then ephemeral powers. A time of agony and despair, the chaotic third century saw the flourishing of many mystery cults as people sought spiritual salvation in the midst of nihilism. It was the worst of times.

Constantine, 272–337

Seizing power from his co-regent, Constantine (reigned 312–337) represented the last effective authority in an empire doomed to destruction from external assaults and from internal corruption and decadence.[2] Built to celebrate his assumption of sole imperial power, the Arch of Constantine (fig. 9.20) was wholly dependent on its

9.20 Arch of Constantine, Rome. AD 312–315. Photo: Scala, Florence.

9.21 Head of colossal statue of Constantine, from the Basilica of Constantine, Rome. Ca. AD 330. Marble, height of head as shown 8'6" (2.6 m) (dimensions of entire statue are not known). Palazzo dei Conservatori, Rome. Photo: Alinari, Florence.

eyes of a mere man; this is an exalted being, unique in authority and vision, with godlike eyes fixed upon infinity. Symbolizing sanctity and sometimes saintliness, oversized eyes become a convention in early Christian and Byzantine art.

Boethius, ca. 475–524

Though a miniature in fact and truly minuscule when compared with the head of Constantine, the *Diptych of Consul Boethius* (bow-E-thi-us; fig. 9.22) is similar to the bust in that the artist has denied the physical reality of Boethius and emphasized instead his authority and spirit. Costume, body, and space are reduced to patterned lines that are more emotional than representational. One of the last Roman consuls and the author of *Consolation of Philosophy* (524), the other-worldliness of Boethius can be compared to the physical reality of the *Augustus of Primaporta*. Both share the commanding arm gesture—a symbol of authority—but all else has changed. In the *Augustus* we see a man with supreme authority and in the *Boethius* there is depicted supreme authority that happens to be a man.

predecessors for its impressive appearance. In an attempt to recapture the glorious past, the three-arch design was copied from the Arch of Septimus Severus (ca. 203) in the Roman Forum, while the eight Corinthian columns are literally from Domitian's time (reigned 81–96). The free-standing statues, with heads recarved to resemble Constantine, were lifted from monuments to Trajan, Hadrian, and Marcus Aurelius. Despite the borrowed design and transferred columns and statues, there is little trace of the Hellenic tradition. The inferior craftsmanship of the carved reliefs can be explained by a shortage of skilled artists; there had been no official relief sculpture in nearly a century. Despite the technical inadequacies, the shift from classical to a new Constantinian style appears, however, to have been deliberate. Compare, for example, the classical style of the *Augustus of Primaporta* (see fig. 9.10) with the head of Constantine the Great (fig. 9.21). In addition to the notable stylistic differences, it is clear that the latter is intended as a much more obvious symbol of both imperial majesty and spiritual superiority. Part of a colossal statue enthroned in his basilica, the masterful modeling of the head demonstrates a total awareness of the Hellenistic tradition with the significant exception of the extraordinary eyes. Carved even with a marble fleck representing light reflecting from the cornea, these are not the

9.22 *Diptych of Consul Boethius.* Ca. 487. Ivory miniature. Museo Romano, Brescia, Italy. Photo: Scala, Florence.

STUDY QUESTIONS

1. The Romans obviously admired Greek art as indicated by so many copies and yet they were frequently uncomfortable with it. Why? Are there any parallels in American attitudes toward twentieth-century art?
2. The poem given in a feature box on page 140 by Edgar Allan Poe extols "the glory that was Greece, and the grandeur that was Rome." Explain how this statement applies to the visual arts of the two civilizations.
3. How is the influence of Roman architecture evident in the history and culture of the United States? Consider, for example, government buildings and athletic facilities. What are some prime examples?

SUMMARY

Roman achievements in architecture were notable and still act upon the modern world. The first to achieve mastery of enclosing space, Roman prototypes are visible today in grandiose train stations, monumental public buildings, and the ubiquitous football and soccer stadiums patterned after the Colosseum. With their superbly designed roads, bridges, and aqueducts, Roman engineers made essential contributions to civilizing and humanizing people that were fully as important as their monuments, buildings, and stadiums. Indeed, roads, bridges, and sewers may be as essential for civilized living as art, music, and literature.

Sculpture was as common in the Roman world as billboards are in the United States, but considerably more attractive. Streets, buildings, and homes were filled with portrait busts and freestanding statues or reliefs of the gods of all major and minor religions. Included were masterpieces confiscated from Greece and Egypt and mass-produced copies of Greek works of all periods. Greeks characteristically created while the Romans were often content to copy; Roman artists excelled in portraiture and historical narrative precisely because they copied the world as they saw it.

The little that is left of Roman painting was found mainly in the ruins of Pompeii and Herculaneum (see chapter opener on p. 148), which were buried by the eruption of Vesuvius in AD 79. Excavations that began in the eighteenth century have revealed at least four major styles of painting. Whether this work was accomplished by Greek, Hellenistic, or Roman artists cannot be determined. Furthermore, later development of painting during the enlightened regimes of the Antonines may

never be known. Deeply indebted to Greek developments in painting techniques, Roman painters, it is safe to assume, produced works comparable to the Pantheon and the *Augustus of Primaporta*.

CULTURE AND HUMAN VALUES

The Romans were as pragmatic about their art and architecture as with most everything else in their lives. Does it do what it is supposed to do? was a more pertinent question than Is it beautiful? Portrait busts, for example, exactly recalled emperors, statesmen, and ancestors. Their function was to graphically represent a specific person, warts and all, with absolutely no doubt about the subject. The aesthetic quality was of no concern and, indeed, rarely apropos.

Triumphal arches pose a similar problem. Designed to awe and intimidate Rome's conquered foes, they apparently fulfilled their function very well or the Romans wouldn't have built so many. Historically interesting, they are not as artistically inspiring as other structures such as, for example, the amphitheatres.

In fact, roads, bridges, aqueducts, and amphitheatres are consistently more interesting than busts or arches. Why is this so? The answer, in a word, is engineering. An engineer is a problem solver and the Romans produced superb problem solvers. How do I cross the river? Build a bridge. How do I obtain fresh water daily? Construct an aqueduct and plumb the houses and public baths. How do I get from here to there? Design a road.

Roman amphitheatres were designed to solve many problems: large capacity, easy ingress and quick exit, good sightlines, unobtrusive stage equipment, and so forth. The Colosseum is an outstanding example of Roman engineering at its best. All 50,000 spectators could easily see the arena and the sun/rain cover could be cranked into position in a few minutes and retracted just as quickly. After each contest perfume was sprayed throughout the amphitheatre through built-in ducts and the structure could be cleared in five minutes after the last performance. Good architecture, according to the Roman architect Vitruvius, must have firmness, commodity, and delight. The Colosseum is remarkably successful on all counts thanks largely to its sophisticated engineering.

The main point about Roman pragmatism is that it usually worked, which means that, by definition, the Roman virtues of duty, honor, and love of country were true. When combined with Roman practicality and efficiency, the Roman virtues helped build the mightiest empire that the world had yet seen. Theories, concepts, ideas, and ideals may occupy a higher ground but Roman pragmatism made its civilization the dominant way of life in much of Europe, North Africa, and the Middle East.

UNIT 4

Judaism and Christianity

	Key Dates	People and Events	Religion	Philosophy and Theology	Art and Literature
1900 BC	**After 1900** Abraham and Israelites migrate from Ur to the Land of Canaan				
1600	**ca. 1600** Israelites follow Joseph into Egypt				
1300	**1300/1200** Moses leads Children of Israel out of Egypt	**ca. 1230** Joshua takes Jericho			
1100	**ca. 1165–1050** Israelite armies battle with Canaanites				
1000		**1020–1000** King Saul defeats Philistines			
900	**933–722** Kingdom of Israel **933–586** Kingdom of Judah	**1000–960** King David **960–933** King Solomon			
800			Prophet: Elijah		
700	**722** Assyria conquers Kingdom of Israel	**722–** "Lost tribes of Israel"	Prophets: Amos, Hosea, Isaiah I, Micah		
600			Prophet: Jeremiah		
500	**586** Nebuchadnezzar II conquers Kingdom of Judah **538–332** Palestine vassal state of Persian Empire	**586–538** Babylonian Captivity	Prophets: Ezekiel, Isaiah II		**ca. 550** Sacred writings in form somewhat like Old Testament
300	**332–63** Palestine vassal state of Alexander and of Egypt				
100					**ca. 100** Old Testament arranged in present form
0	**63 BC** Palestine conquered by Rome; becomes protectorate **ca. 4 BC–AD 29** Jesus Christ	**37–4 BC** Herod, king of Judea **27 BC–AD 14** Reign of Caesar Augustus		**Philo Judaeus** ca. 30 BC–AD 50 Hellenistic Jewish philosopher	**Virgil** 70–19 BC *Aeneid*
AD 100	**50–300** Rise of papacy	**64** Persecution of Christians under Nero **70** Romans destroy Jerusalem and Temple; disperse Jews **93** Persecution of Christians under Domitian	Writing of New Testament (dates approx.): **55** Paul's epistles to Corinthians **60** Acts of Apostles **70** Mark **80–85** Matthew; Luke **93** Revelation **100–120** John	**Epictetus** ca. 60–110 Stoic philosopher, *Discourses*	
200	**180–476** Decline and fall of Rome	**111** Trajan classifies Christians as traitors	**d. 165?** Justin Martyr, *First Apology*	**Tertullian** 160?–240? Latin Father of Church **Origen** 185?–254? Father of Christian theology	
300		**250** Persecution of Christians under Decius	**ca. 200** New Testament becomes canonical Christian text	**Plotinus** 205–270 Founder of Neoplatonism	**ca. 250** Earliest known Christian church, Dura-Europos, Syria; *The Good Shepherd*, Catacombs of St. Callistus, Rome
400	**300–** Growth of monasticism **313** Constantine's Edict of Milan legalizes Christianity throughout Roman Empire **325** First Council of Nicaea condemns Arian heresy **330** Constantine establishes new capital at Constantinople **375–500** Invasions of empire by barbarian tribes **395** Theodosius proclaims Christianity official and only religion of Rome	**302** Persecution of Christians under Diocletian **306–335** Reign of Constantine **314–335** Pope Sylvester I **379–395** Reign of Theodosius I; empire splits into West and East; persecution of non-Christians begins	**ca. 330–379** St. Basil; rules established for Greek church and monasticism **374–397** St. Ambrose as Bishop of Milan	**St. Augustine** 354–430	**ca. 313–** St. John Lateran Basilica, Rome **ca. 330–** Old St. Peter's, Rome **ca. 359** Sarcophagus of Junius Bassus **386–** Basilica of St. Paul's Outside-the-Walls, Rome **397** Augustine, *Confessions*
500	**402** Ravenna new capital of Western Roman Empire **410; 455** Rome sacked by Visigoths and by Vandals **451** Attila the Hun defeated at Battle of Chalons **476** Last Roman emperor deposed **ca. 493–527** Theodoric and Ostrogothic Kingdom; capital at Ravenna	**400–600** Invasions of England by Angles and Saxons **440–461** Pope Leo I the Great; saves Rome from Attila the Hun **St. Benedict** 480–543	**ca. 400** St. Jerome: *Vulgate* (Latin Bible) **413–425** Augustine: *City of God*	**Boethius** ca. 480–524? *The Consolation of Philosophy*	**425–450** Mausoleum of Galla Placidia, Ravenna **430** *Crucifixion*, Church of Santa Sabina, Rome **440–** Basilica of Santa Maria Maggiore, Rome

Hebrew lettering, meaning "Hear O Israel."

CHAPTER 10

The Star and the Cross

Life in the later years of the Roman Empire was marked by increasing pessimism and disillusionment. Epicureanism is grounded on pessimism; Stoicism was at best a resignation to the evils of the world; cults and mystery religions provided little abiding fulfillment. The general malaise was shared by aristocrats, intellectuals and, most especially, the common people. A frequently used Roman epitaph proclaims the melancholy mood of the age:

I was not
I was
I am not
I do not care

One could scarcely go further in apathetic world-weariness.

Of the two conflicting preferences during this period, one was the general disbelief in religion, especially the old Olympian beliefs. The other, paradoxically, was the appeal, however transitory, of mystical religious cults, usually of oriental origin: Mithraism, the worship of Isis, and the cult of Cybele. Whatever the scoffing or indifferent disregard at society's upper level, the poor and uneducated were eager for the emotional appeal of any religiosity that softened their uncertainties and insecurities.

Graeco-Roman culture advocated living according to reason, an intellectual rather than a spiritual existence. For an Aristotle or a Cicero, such a life could be worthwhile and satisfying, but not many men or women in any generation are of such caliber, and even those few are often seen as wanting in human warmth. At best, the God in whom Aristotle found perfection was distant and detached from human affairs, a noble but serenely dispassionate concept.

As important as reason is, it has never been the only human attribute. Call it spirit, emotion, belief, faith—there is something not in the same category. No one can give six good reasons why he or she loves the beloved, for love is not "reasonable," though it is not necessarily contrary to reason; it simply moves in another dimension. The "something" beyond reason may be the compulsion of an ethical ideal or a yearning for spiritual satisfaction. More pronounced in some people than in others, it is rarely totally absent. It is precisely such a range of human experience that the intellectualized traditions of Greece and Rome failed to satisfy.

While the Greek and Roman cultures were developing—cultures devoted to rationalism—an entirely different kind of society had arisen in Palestine. A vast amount of pure intellectual power has gone into the development of Jewish doctrine, but the core of Judaism is faith, as faith is different from but not opposed to reason. The Jewish religion itself, as it has had wider influence through Christianity, wove another strand into the majestic amalgam we call Western civilization.

THE CHOSEN PEOPLE

The Jews would have been just another set of Near Eastern tribes, small in number and lacking talent for art and invention, had it not been for their remarkable religion. Other civilizations have come and gone; Jews have maintained their culture essentially intact for 4,000 years.

The Jews were first called Hebrews (from *Habiru* or *Ibri*; "alien, outcast, nomad"), a descriptive term used mostly by their enemies and still employed today to designate the biblical Jews. Long before the Bible was written, however, these desert nomads had named themselves after the grandson of Abraham, a man originally called Jacob and subsequently named Israel. These, then, were the Israelites, the Children of Israel.

Early Jewish History

Sometime after 1900 BC the Israelites followed Abraham from the Sumerian city of Ur "of the Chaldees," according to the Bible, into the lands northwest of the Euphrates river valley. Several generations later, nomads no longer, they moved west into the Land of Canaan—subsequently called Palestine after the Philistine inhabitants. Sometime after 1600 BC and probably prompted by famine, many Israelites followed Joseph into Egypt, where they prospered along with Joseph, who achieved a position of considerable importance. Time passed until there was a new Pharaoh "who did not know Joseph," according to the Bible. The Children of Israel were reduced to slavery but were finally delivered out of bondage by an Israelite with the Egyptian name of

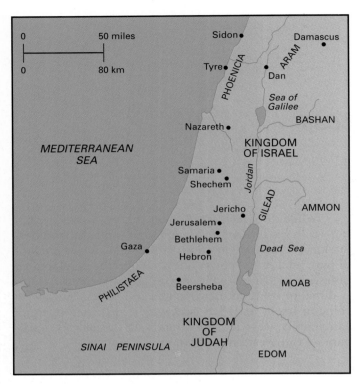

Map 10.1   Palestine, ca. 900 BC.

Moses. Leading his people out of Egypt and into Sinai (ca. 1300 BC), Moses gave them the concept of a single tribal god, Yahweh (later mistranslated as Jehovah), and a **covenant** with Yahweh based on their acceptance of the commandments that, according to the Book of Exodus, Moses had carried down the mountain.

Following the death of Moses, after about forty years "in the wilderness," the Promised Land "flowing with milk and honey" was taken by conquest, with the key city of Jericho falling to Joshua around 1230 BC. By 1020 the twelve tribes had been unified and a monarchy forged with Saul as the first king. It was under Saul's leadership that the tenacious Philistines were finally subdued.

The height of Israelite political power was reached with the Twelve Tribes of Israel under King David (1000–960 BC) and his son Solomon (960–933 BC). After Solomon's death the accumulated resentment against his policies of forced labor and high taxes led to the secession of the ten northern tribes to form a separate Kingdom of Israel. The two southern tribes of Judah and Benjamin, though holding to the capital of Jerusalem, were left with the apparently weaker Kingdom of Judah[1] (map 10.1).

Israel did not survive long as a divided kingdom, falling to the Assyrians in 722 BC. Following the standard Assyrian procedure, the kingdom was brutally ravaged and the Ten Tribes dispersed forever, to be known thereafter as the Lost Tribes of Israel. Judah managed to survive until 586 BC, when it was conquered by Nebuchadnezzar II and most

of its citizens sent into an exile known to history as the Babylonian Captivity (586–538 BC). The subsequent Persian conquest of Babylon freed the Jews, some of whom returned to Jerusalem where they eventually rebuilt the Temple of Solomon. No longer a commonwealth, they were politically subservient to three successive empires: the Persian (538–332 BC); Alexander and the Ptolemies of Egypt (332–63 BC); and the might of Rome, which proved fatal.

The Romans never knew what to do with the Jews because nothing worked. After their conquest of Palestine in 63 BC, the Romans gave the country a special status as a protectorate. Among other privileges, the Jews were excused from military service and permitted freedom of religion. This was not enough. In AD 66 the Jews launched what turned out to be their most disastrous rebellion against Rome. By AD 70 Jerusalem was totally destroyed and much of the population dead or driven from the land, a Diaspora (dea-AS-po-ra; "scattering") that lasted until the establishment of the State of Israel in 1948.

Four Unique Aspects of Judaism

The Jews' will to resist and to survive was based on their religion, Judaism,[2] four aspects of which were different from all other Near Eastern religions.

1. **Monotheism:** there was only one God and he came to be viewed as universal.
2. **Covenant:** God chose Israel to be his people and they accepted him as their God.
3. **Graven images:** images of God or of any living thing were prohibited.
4. **The name of God** (Yahweh, meaning "he causes to be" or "the creator") was not to be taken "in vain," i.e., was not to be spoken.

Let us examine each of these concepts. Beginning with the Mosaic period in the Sinai, Yahweh was the primary God among many: "You shall have no other gods before me" (Exodus 20:3). This concept gradually evolved into a monotheism in which there was one Israelite God and, later, one universal God. The first people to insist upon monotheism, the Jews, throughout their history, found this to be their greatest source of strength.

The covenant was a bond with Yahweh that the Hebrews made of their own free will. Moses climbed the mountain and returned with knowledge of God's will— "commandments" inscribed on tablets of stone and subsequently amplified in the **Torah**. In a narrow sense the Torah

---

1. The inhabitants of Judah (later called Judea) were thereafter known as Jews.
2. A term coined by Greek-speaking Jews to distinguish their religious way of life from that of the Hellenes. Though the term is late, the religion to which it refers goes back to the beginnings of Jewish spiritual life.

consists of the first five books of the Bible, the so-called **Pentateuch**, or Books of Moses. The word "torah" means "law" but it also means "teaching" or "direction." In the broad modern sense, Torah refers to the total content of God's unending revelation to and through Israel.

The prohibition of graven images separated Judaism from all other religions, which represented their gods in a variety of ways. This stricture, a defense against idolatry, effectively nullified any significant artistic development. The injunction against using the Lord's name in vain emphasized a reverence unknown to other ancient religions. In sum, Judaism was a People in covenant with God, a Book (the Hebrew Scriptures), a Way of Life, and a Hope grounded in Faith.

Prophecy

The Jewish prophets of the eighth to fifth centuries BC emerged from a tradition of augurs and seers who sought to ascertain the divine will and to forecast the future through dreams, divinations, and induced ecstasy. Eventually these professionals were denounced as "false prophets" and replaced by a succession of preachers, mystics, moralists, and poets who felt they were speaking for Yahweh. Stressing righteousness and justice, prophets such as Amos and Isaiah functioned as restorers and conservators of Israel's inspiring spiritual heritage. Not always accepted by various classes of society, they preached an uncompromising and lofty doctrine: Yahweh was the only god and he demanded the highest ethical standards.

Amos

The first and perhaps most important of the notable eighth-century prophets, Amos preached against luxury, corruption, and selfishness, pointing the way to altruism and a higher form of religion.

> [11]Therefore because you trample upon the poor
> and take from him exactions of wheat,
> you have built houses of hewn stone,
> but you shall not dwell in them;
> you have planted pleasant vineyards,
> but you shall not drink their wine.
> [12]For I know how many are your transgressions,
> and how great are your sins—
> you who afflict the righteous, who take a bribe,
> and turn aside the needy in the gate.
> [13]Therefore he who is prudent will keep silent in such a time;
> for it is an evil time.
> [14]Seek good, and not evil,
> that you may live;
> and so the LORD, the God of hosts, will be with you,
> as you have said.
> [15]Hate evil, and love good,
> and establish justice in the gate;
> it may be that the LORD, the God of hosts,
> will be gracious to the remnant of Joseph.
>
> Amos 5:11–15

Isaiah

Active around 740–700 BC, Isaiah[3] was the prophet of faith, preaching an abiding trust in the providence of God. A prophet of doom like the other preachers, Isaiah saw that a purging was necessary in the interest of spiritual betterment in a kindlier and more loving world. He was among the first to picture a warless world under the benign rule of a Prince of Peace, a Messiah ("anointed one") descended from the House of David.

> [1]There shall come forth a shoot from the stump of Jesse,
> and a branch shall grow out of his roots.
> [2]And the Spirit of the LORD shall rest upon him,
> the spirit of wisdom and understanding,
> the spirit of counsel and might,
> the spirit of knowledge and the fear of the LORD.
> [3]And his delight shall be in the fear of the LORD.
> He shall not judge by what his eyes see,
> or decide by what his ears hear;
> [4]but with righteousness he shall judge the poor,
> and decide with equity for the meek of the earth;
> and he shall smite the earth with the rod of his mouth,
> and with the breath of his lips he shall slay the wicked.
> [5]Righteousness shall be the girdle of his waist,
> and faithfulness the girdle of his loins.
> [6]The wolf shall dwell with the lamb,
> and the leopard shall lie down with the kid,
> and the calf and the lion and the fatling together,
> and a little child shall lead them.
> [7]The cow and the bear shall feed;
> their young shall lie down together;
> and the lion shall eat straw like the ox.
> [8]The sucking child shall play over the hole of the asp,
> and the weaned child shall put his hand on the adder's den.
> [9]They shall not hurt or destroy
> in all my holy mountain;
> for the earth shall be full of the knowledge of the LORD
> as the waters cover the sea.
>
> Isaiah 11:1–9

For unto us a child is born,
to us a son is given;

---

3. The Book of Isaiah contains prophecies attributed to Isaiah or his disciples (chapters 1–35) and those by an unknown prophet of the sixth century called Second Isaiah (Deutero-Isaiah; chapters 40–55). Chapters 56–66 were written still later by a Third Isaiah (Trito-Isaiah). Chapters 36–39 were taken directly from 2 Kings. Two manuscripts of the book were found among the Dead Sea Scrolls.

THE DEAD SEA SCROLLS

First found in caves near the Dead Sea in Jordan in 1947, these were one of the great historical and scholarly discoveries of the century. Written in Hebrew, Aramaic, and Greek, they date from the first century BC to about AD 50 and were left there by the Qumran community, which some scholars identify with the Essenes, a strict ascetic Jewish communal sect. The scrolls were mostly bits and pieces but, when painstakingly assembled, they included many parts of the Old Testament (including two manuscripts of the Book of Isaiah; fig. 10.1), some New Testament, and much non-Biblical Jewish literature. The Old Testament material is much older than any existing manuscripts. Some parallels between the Qumran scrolls and the New Testament led to the much-disputed suggestion that Jesus and John the Baptist were Essenes. The concern that some of this material might contradict or invalidate any part of the Bible has proven, so far, to be unjustified.

10.1 The Great Isaiah Scroll, columns, XLVIII–LI (Chapters 58:6–65:4), from Qumran Cave, Israel. Ca. 100 BC. Parchment, length 24' (7.34 m). Israel Museum, Jerusalem.

and the government will be upon his shoulder,
and his name will be called
"Wonderful Counselor, Mighty God,
Everlasting Father, Prince of Peace."

Isaiah 9:6

Ezekiel

During the Babylonian Captivity, when his people were far from home, their city and temple destroyed, Ezekiel preached the universality of the faith and of the personal relationship between the individual Jew and his God. God existed wherever the people were; the city and the temple were not indispensable. Each person had the option of selecting good over evil and turning from evil ways to a righteous life.

25"Yet you say, 'The way of the Lord is not just.' Hear now, O house of Israel: Is my way not just? Is it not your ways that are not just? 26When a righteous man turns away from his righteousness and commits iniquity, he shall die for it; for the iniquity which he has committed he shall die. 27Again, when a wicked man turns away from the wickedness he has committed and does what is lawful and right, he shall save his life. 28Because he considered and turned away from all the transgressions which he had committed, he shall surely live, he shall not die. 29Yet the house of Israel says, 'The way of the Lord is not just.' O house of Israel, are my ways not just? Is it not your ways that are not just?

30"Therefore I will judge you, O house of Israel, every one according to his ways, says the Lord GOD. Repent and turn from all your transgressions, lest iniquity be your ruin. 31Cast away from you all the transgressions which you have committed against me, and get yourselves a new heart and a new spirit! Why will you die, O house of Israel? 32For I have no pleasure in the death of any one, says the Lord GOD; so turn, and live."

Ezekiel 18:25–32

Isaiah

The celebrated unknown prophet of the exile, generally known as Second Isaiah, was the great architect of Jewish ethical monotheism. Climaxing the prophetic movement, his ethical and religious insight set the sufferings of the Jews against a background of God's eventual redemption of the entire world. He saw the Jews as a people chosen to exemplify in their characters and lives the spiritual presence of the Lord. "A light to the nations" (Isaiah 42:1), their suffering had not been in vain. The world would say of Israel:

3He was despised and rejected by men;
    a man of sorrows, and acquainted with grief,
and as one from whom men hide their faces
    he was despised, and we esteemed him not.
4Surely he has borne our griefs
    and carried our sorrows,
yet we esteemed him stricken,
    smitten by God, and afflicted.
5But he was wounded for our transgressions,
    he was bruised for our iniquities;
upon him was the chastisement that made us whole,
    and with his stripes we are healed.
6All we like sheep have gone astray;
    we have turned every one to his own way;
and the LORD has laid on him
    the iniquity of us all.

Isaiah 53:3–6

They were to return to the New Jerusalem where the

work of redemption would be a model for all the world.

¹Comfort, comfort my people,
  says your God.
²Speak tenderly to Jerusalem,
  and cry to her
that her warfare is ended,
  that her iniquity is pardoned,
that she has received from the LORD'S hand
  double for all her sins.
³A voice cries:
  "In the wilderness prepare the way of the LORD,
  make straight in the desert a highway for our God.
⁴Every valley shall be lifted up,
  and every mountain and hill be made low;
the uneven ground shall become level,
  and the rough places a plain.
⁵And the glory of the LORD shall be revealed,
  and all flesh shall see it together,
  for the mouth of the LORD has spoken."
⁶A voice says, "Cry!"
  And I said, "What shall I cry?"
All flesh is grass,
  and all its beauty is like the flower of the field.
⁷The grass withers, the flower fades,
  when the breath of the LORD blows upon it;
  surely the people is grass.
⁸The grass withers, the flower fades;
  but the word of our God will stand for ever.
⁹Get you up to a high mountain,
  O Zion, herald of good tidings,
lift up your voice with strength,
  O Jerusalem, herald of good tidings,
  lift it up, fear not;
say to the cities of Judah,
  "Behold your God!"

                                        Isaiah 40:1–9

The profound insights of Second Isaiah strongly influenced later Judaism but were even more significant for early Christianity. His writings were studied and pondered by those who awaited the coming of the Messiah. In particular the story of the sufferings of Israel (see Isaiah 53:3–6 above) was so specific and individualized that later generations came to believe that he was speaking of a particular person, a Messiah who would redeem the world through his suffering. In Jesus of Nazareth the early Christians found that Messiah.

CHRISTIANITY
Some of the Teachings of Jesus

Jesus was born in the year we now call 4 BC, or possibly 6 BC,[4] a time that was ripe for his message of hope and love. He preached for possibly three years, but in the 2,000 years

since that time—whether people have believed his teachings or not, whether they have acted upon them or not—men and women throughout what was once called "Christendom" have been hearing the teachings of Jesus. What are the cardinal points of his teaching? These: that one God (a Personal Spirit, not an abstract idea nor a principle) is not only the Creator but also the loving Father of all humankind; that all people are consequently the children of God, and that as a result all men and women are brothers and sisters; that as children of God, human beings are capable of better lives than they lead; that their human inadequacies, imperfections, and shortcomings can be forgiven if they are repentant; that life is eternal, and death is not extinction; that "all the Law and the Prophets" hangs upon the joint commandment to "Love thy God, and thy neighbor as thyself"; and that the intention—the act of the personality—is of greater importance than the deed—the act of the person.

Not the least of the appeals of Christianity is the joy and hope that it carries with it because of its doctrine of Christ as Redeemer. Theologically, one of several explanations may be stated in this way: because of the sin of Adam, humankind as a whole carried with it the taint of original sin, a sort of moral disease. But God, loving all people, sought to redeem them. This was accomplished through the mystery of **Incarnation** in which God became man, taking to himself all of humankind's inherent guilt. Then, in Christ's death as a mortal, the guilt is atoned, and human beings are set free. The possibility of salvation and eternal life with God, from that moment on, lies before each person. In the world-weary and guilt-ridden time of the late Roman Empire such a possibility could bring hope and joy to the believer.

All of these teachings affect the world of here and now, for Christianity is a "social" religion; its effects are seen in the daily acts of people in society. It is not necessarily a religion in which the believers isolate themselves and seek individual salvation through private contemplation, although some have followed this path. For most Christians their faith entails involvement and commitment. Love must prompt the worshiper to perform acts of love, mercy, and compassion as evidence of an inward change. The three words that Jesus addressed to Peter can summarize his teaching: "Feed my sheep."

Early Christianity

Jesus left no written record of his work nor are there any surviving accounts contemporary with his ministry. A collection of his sayings, written in Aramaic, disappeared

4. The idea of denominating the years of the Christian era was introduced in AD 525 by Dionysius Exiguus; the BC sequence extending backwards from the birth of Christ was not added until the seventeenth century.

WOMEN AND EARLY CHRISTIANITY

The role of women in the early development of the Christian religion has only recently been studied. After the death of Christ women served as missionaries, deaconesses, and ministers. The book of Acts (16:14–15) mentions Lydia, the first Christian convert of Paul's ministry in Macedonia, and the early evangelist Prisca (or Priscilla; 18:18). Numerous letters of the Apostle Paul cite the work of women. Phoebe is identified as a deaconess and Mary and Junia are called "co-workers" by Paul in Romans 16. He also says in Philippians 4:2–3 that Eodia and Syntyche "labored side by side with me in the gospel."

Epiphanius (d. ca. 403), an early Christian writer, argued against women baptizing and performing priestly functions, a sure sign that women were doing these things. As the church grew more formal in its theology, dogma, and rituals, the role of women became ever more constricted. Between the third and fifth centuries they were gradually eliminated from any meaningful participation in official church rites. Tertullian (ca. 160–230) and John Chrysostom (d. ca. 407) were adamant in their hostility to women in the church and their writings reinforced the position adopted by the Church of Rome for the past fifteen centuries.

before AD 60, and scholars are still debating some of the references to Jesus in the Dead Sea Scrolls. His life, character, and message inspired hope and joy but without any documentation this was not sufficient basis for a new religion. Christianity is concerned above all with God's relation to human beings. It remained for the followers of Jesus to construct a systematic theology as a solid foundation for the propagation of the new faith.

Written accounts in Greek began to appear several decades after Christ's death: St. Paul's Epistles to the Corinthians (ca. AD 55); the Acts of the Apostles (ca. AD 60); the four Gospels telling the story of Jesus: Mark (ca. AD 70); Matthew and Luke (ca. AD 80–85); and John (ca. AD 100–120). By about AD 200 the texts were revised in Alexandria into a canonical Christian text.

Paul

An upper-class Jew of Orthodox parentage, St. Paul (Saul of Tarsus) was first a persecutor of Christians and later one of the most ardent missionaries of the faith. A Hellenized Jew, Paul took the position that "there is neither Jew nor Greek" (Galatians 3:28). St. Peter at first disagreed, contending that the Christian message was intended only for Jews and converted Gentiles. Paul argued (and Peter later agreed) that the Law was no longer valid, even for Jews; it could only bring people to an understanding of their dependence on Christ in a new covenant with Christ the Savior. Sweeping aside Jewish rituals and practices, Paul, the "apostle to the Gentiles," carried the message of salvation through faith in Christ throughout the eastern Mediterranean and into Rome itself.

An enthusiastic teacher, organizer, and administrator, Paul was neither a theologian nor a logician. Confirmed by his conversion experience on the road to Damascus, Paul believed that faith was a gift of God. Christians had only to accept the discipline of the church and to lead quiet, faithful, and firmly Christian lives.

Logos and John

A synthesis of Judaic, Greek, and Christian ideas, Christian theology developed separately from the work of the Apostle Paul. In his Prologue, which introduces the fourth Gospel, John states that

> [1]In the beginning was the Word, and the Word was with God, and the Word was God. [2]He was in the beginning with God; [3]all things were made through him, and without him was not anything made that was made. [4]In him was life, and the life was the light of men. [5]The light shines in the darkness, and the darkness has not overcome it.
>
> John 1:1–5

In the Greek of the New Testament, "word" is a translation of *logos*, a word as old as the Greek language. Introduced by Herakleitos in the fifth century BC, *logos* was a principle of cosmic interpretation. Constantly changing, the cosmos was a total process becoming controlled by an agency called *logos*. To avoid chaos, change had to conform to fixed patterns; *logos* was thus an intelligent and eternal agent that imposed an orderly process upon change.

Though the concept of *logos* is vague and unspecified in Plato and Aristotle, the Stoics took it from them but used *logos* to designate a divine element present in all men. It remained for Philo Judaeus of Alexandria (ca. 30 BC–AD 50) to go beyond the Stoics and consciously construct a synthesis of Hebraic and Hellenic philosophy. Philo saw *logos* as a mediator between God and man and as a translation of the Hebrew word for "wisdom." As a personal agent of God in the creation of the world, *logos* was not identical with God but distinctly separate from him.

The Prologue of John is thus a creation story; Jesus is a divine being whose existence antedates the world itself. God's relation to this imperfect world was through the intervention of the *logos*; in Christ "the Word became flesh and dwelt among us, full of grace and truth" (John 1:14). It can be said that Herakleitos and Second Isaiah meet in John, representing two contrasting civilizations which are synthesized into a Christian philosophy of history.[5]

---

5. See chapter 12 for subsequent developments in Christian theology.

THE IMPACT OF CHRISTIANITY

Objective study of the historical Jesus and of the facts about his life and death leaves some basic questions unanswered. Was he the Messiah, "Son of God," "son of man," a religious reformer, prophet, humanitarian, inspired teacher? Or was he, as his Jewish critics claim, a blasphemer and an impostor? Currently available sources have failed to settle the issue, and the multiplicity of Christian beliefs (Roman Catholic, Orthodox, varieties of Protestantism) testifies to the different interpretations of the evidence.

Nevertheless, the Christian emphasis on the importance of the human personality carries a religious sanction weightier than the speculations of the philosophers. The worth and dignity of the individual soul, and its responsibility to itself, has been a shaping influence in Western thought.

As discussed earlier, reality, for the Greeks, was the individual and for the Romans it was the state. What the two cultures had in common was their secular view of the world. Neither the Greeks nor the Romans rejected religion or religious beliefs. There were, in fact, several religions and many believers but religion did not play a central role in the classical world. The rise of Christianity caused a massive shift from a secular to a religious worldview with God as the ultimate reality. The new view of reality caused major changes in values and value systems, which we shall examine in later chapters.

Christianity's expansion was almost in direct proportion to the decline of the Roman Empire, spreading inexorably from an obscure, remote Roman province practically throughout the known world.[6] Its message of hope, joy, salvation, and a merciful and loving God in a world that knew only the sterner aspects of justice in a declining empire made its welcome assured (map 10.2). Encompassing the whole of life, and able to take to itself the good things of any civilization, Christianity could appropriate the best of Greek thought, as well as Rome's most notable products of organization and law. With the passage of time it produced such diverse offshoots as the elegance and beauty of Chartres Cathedral, the terror of witchcraft trials, and the horrors of the Inquisition. Its impact upon the Western world is fundamental.

---

6. Christianity was not exclusively a Western development, having been well established in Ethiopia as early as the third century.

Map 10.2   The early Christian world.

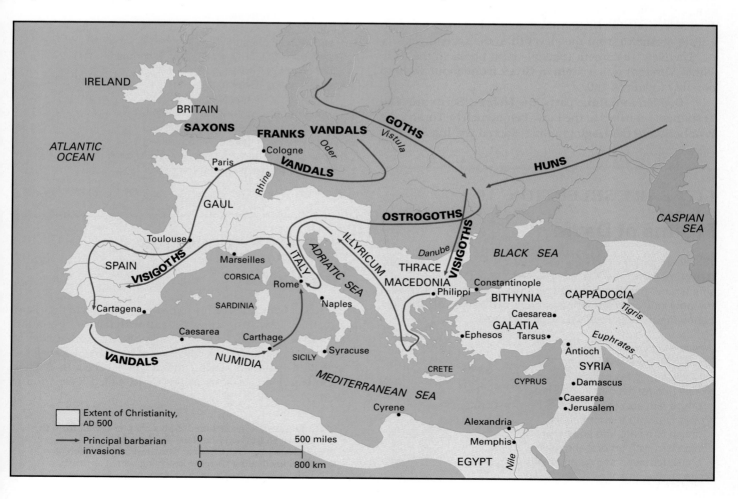

STUDY QUESTIONS

1. What were the significant events that occurred on approximately the following dates? BC: 1900, 1300, 1230, 1000, 933, 586–539, 332–63, 63, 4; AD: 64, 200, 313. What was going on in Egypt and Mesopotamia on or about these dates (through 63 BC)?
2. Four aspects of Judaism differentiated it from all other Near Eastern religions. What were these?
3. What were the basic teachings of Jesus and how did these differ from the Judaism of his time?

THE BIBLE

The Bible (Gk., *Ta Biblia,* "The Books") has exercised a more profound influence upon Western civilization than any other literary work. Its style alone has burnished the tongues of poets and writers from Chaucer to Shakespeare to Lincoln, and its ethical tenets have become basic to the codes and customs of Western culture. Of its two main divisions, the Old Testament (thirty-nine books in the King James Version) was written almost entirely in Hebrew (with a little Aramaic) from the eleventh to the second century BC. The New Testament (twenty-seven books in the King James Version) was written in Greek from about AD 40 to possibly as late as 150.

Divided into three parts, the Hebrew Scripture (Old Testament) consists of the Law (Pentateuch or Torah), the Prophets, and the Hagiographa ("Sacred writings").

LITERARY SELECTION 10

Psalms of David

The Hagiographa includes the **Psalms,** a hymnal (**Psalter**) reflecting the whole history of Jewish worship. The Psalmists sing Israel's praise of God the creator, intone their sorrow for national guilt and tribulations, and carol the songs of salvation. Following is a Psalm of salvation and glory.[7]

¹Praise the LORD!
Praise God in his sanctuary;
    praise him in his mighty firmament!
²Praise him for his mighty deeds;
    praise him according to his exceeding greatness!
³Praise him with trumpet sound;
    praise him with lute and harp!
⁴Praise him with timbrel and dance;
    praise him with strings and pipe!
⁵Praise him with sounding cymbals;

praise him with loud clashing cymbals!
⁶Let everything that breathes praise the LORD!
Praise the LORD!

                                            Psalm 150

Apparently composed during the Babylonian Captivity (586–538 BC), Psalm 137 is a Lamentation. Though the condition of the Jews in Babylon was relatively favorable, they mourned the destruction of Jerusalem and their separation from the homeland.

This magnificent poem was frequently used in the worship services of American slaves in remembrance of their African homeland.

¹By the waters of Babylon,
there we sat down and wept,
    when we remembered Zion.
²On the willows there
    we hung up our lyres.
³For there our captors
    required of us songs,
and our tormentors, mirth, saying,
    "Sing us one of the songs of Zion!"
⁴How shall we sing the LORD'S song
    in a foreign land?
⁵If I forget you, O Jerusalem,
    let my right hand wither!
⁶Let my tongue cleave to the roof of my mouth,
    if I do not remember you,
if I do not set Jerusalem
    above my highest joy!
⁷Remember, O LORD, against the E'domites
    the day of Jerusalem,
how they said, "Rase it, rase it!
    Down to its foundations!"
⁸O daughter of Babylon, you devastator!
    Happy shall he be who requites you
    with what you have done to us!
⁹Happy shall he be who takes your little ones
    and dashes them against the rock!

                                            Psalm 137

LITERARY SELECTION 11

Revelation

For several centuries before and after Christ, there flourished a distinctive writing known as **apocalypse** or revelation. Apocalyptic thought was based on the Jewish eschatological[8] view of history. A portion of the Book of Daniel is an apocalypse, and Paul included several apocalyptic verses in 2 Thessalonians. The last book of the Bible, called Revelation or

---

7. The translations included in this chapter are all from the American Revised Standard Version (RSV).
8. Eschatology (Gk., *eschatos,* "furthest") is a branch of theology dealing with the last things, such as death, judgment, resurrection, and immortality.

Apocalypse of John, is the only full apocalypse in the New Testament. Writing to seven besieged churches around AD 93 during Domitian's savage persecution of Christians, John of Patmos declares, in visionary terms, the ultimate triumph over the Roman Empire and his perception of a new heaven, a new earth, and a new Jerusalem after all souls have been raised from the dead for the Last Judgment. In the early church there was a widespread belief that the Second Coming of Christ was imminent.

In the following selection, Christ opens four of the seven seals, releasing the Four Horsemen of the Apocalypse: Conquest, War, Famine, and Death.

¹Now I saw when the Lamb opened one of the seven seals, and I heard one of the four living creatures say, as with a voice of thunder, "Come!" ²And I saw, and behold, a white horse, and its rider had a bow; and a crown was given to him, and he went out conquering and to conquer.

³When he opened the second seal, I heard the second living creature say, "Come!" ⁴And out came another horse, bright red; its rider was permitted to take peace from the earth, so that men should slay one another; and he was given a great sword.

⁵When he opened the third seal, I heard the third living creature say, "Come!" And I saw, and behold, a black horse, and its rider had a balance in his hand; ⁶and I heard what seemed to be a voice in the midst of the four living creatures saying, "A quart of wheat for a denarius, and three quarts of barley for a denarius, but do not harm oil and wine!"

⁷When he opened the fourth seal, I heard the voice of the fourth living creature say, "Come!" ⁸And I saw, and behold, a pale horse, and its rider's name was Death, and Hades followed him; and they were given power over a fourth of the earth, to kill with sword and with famine and with pestilence and by wild beasts of the earth.

Revelation 6:1–8

Following the Last Judgment, John presents a golden vision of the world to come:

¹Then I saw a new heaven and a new earth; for the first heaven and the first earth had passed away, and the sea was no more. ²And I saw the holy city, new Jerusalem, coming down out of heaven from God, prepared as a bride adorned for her husband; ³and I heard a great voice from the throne saying, "Behold, the dwelling of God is with men. He will dwell with them, and they shall be his people, and God himself will be with them; ⁴he will wipe away every tear from their eyes, and death shall be no more, neither shall there be mourning nor crying nor pain any more, for the former things have passed away."

Revelation 21:1–4

SUMMARY

The secular Graeco-Roman world was gradually superseded by two strains of religion, first by Judaism and later by Christianity. The basic strength of the Jews was their religion, the first monotheistic religion of the Western world. Judaism was, briefly stated, the religion of a people who had a covenant with God, a book (the Hebrew Scriptures), a way of life, and a hope based on faith. This sustained them through conquests by Assyrians, Babylonians, Persians, Alexander, and the Romans. They were without a homeland from the Diaspora (scattering) in AD 70 until the reestablishment of the state of Israel in 1948.

The strongest impact upon Rome was that of Christianity, a new faith derived partly from Judaism and based on the teachings of Jesus, recognized by Christians as the Messiah. With its doctrine of Christ as the Redeemer, Christianity was a religion of joy and hope in the jaded days of the late Roman Empire.

CULTURE AND HUMAN VALUES

The rise of Rome caused a shift from the Greek view of the individual as the ultimate reality to one in which reality was the state. With the decline of the Empire and the growth of Christianity the view of reality shifted once again. God became the ultimate reality and the goal of all Christians was to join Him in the Heavenly Kingdom.

The advent of Christianity also caused a major change in values. Prudence, temperance, fortitude, and justice were accepted as the four cardinal virtues (as earlier identified by Plato and the Stoics) to which were added the Christian (theological) virtues of faith, hope, and love. Justice was administered as best they could by courts of justice in the City of Man but only God the Father could dispense infallible justice in the City of God.

CHAPTER 11

The Beginnings of Christian Art

The first two centuries of Christianity had little need for art in any form. Meeting in small groups in private homes, early Christians conducted simple services centered on the **Eucharist**: the consecrated bread and wine commemorating Christ's sacrifice on the cross. Dating from about 250, the earliest known church building is a Greek peristyle house in Dura-Europos, Syria. Suitable for a congregation of no more than sixty, this was a private home converted to liturgical use though it was devoid of decorations or architectural distinction. No Christian art survived from the first two centuries and very little from the third century, and that almost entirely from the catacombs of Rome.

ROMAN CATACOMBS

Initially and during most of the first two centuries, Christians were buried in regular (surface) Roman cemeteries. Rejecting customary cremation because of their belief in resurrection of the body, Christians continued using surface cemeteries, except in the outskirts of Rome, Naples, and Syracuse, where porous stone (tufa) was easily excavated for subterranean tombs. During the late second century Christian communities became increasingly interested in separate areas where they could perform private rites for the dead and safeguard the tombs against vandals. Because Roman law forbade burials within city limits, Christians bought land alongside the major highways leading into Rome, sites that already contained the funerary monuments of wealthy Roman families. Using surface chapels and subterranean passages, these cemeteries suited Christian concerns for seclusion and security as guaranteed by Roman law.[1]

The Roman catacombs had up to five subterranean levels with superimposed niches for sarcophagi eight to ten deep on each level. Each cemetery included small chapels for burial and commemorative services. In the chapels and sometimes over the burial niches are found the earliest examples of Christian figurative art. Executed by artisans working by lamplight in a dark, dank, and undoubtedly malodorous environment, the representations were generally simple, often hastily executed, and aesthetically indifferent. Christians wanted to convey a message or a prayer understood by the Christian community and, above all, by God.

The *Orans*

The most common representation in the catacombs was the *orans* (OR-an; from the Latin word for "praying"; see chapter opener opposite), a figure presented frontally, standing with arms raised in prayer or supplication. The *orans* can symbolize the soul of the deceased praying for salvation or reflect the Hellenistic view: a personification in human form of such abstract ideas as resurrection or salvation.

The Good Shepherd

The figure of Jesus as *The Good Shepherd* (fig. 11.1), a commonly used representation throughout the centuries, appears frequently in catacomb frescoes. Not unexpectedly, the "good shepherd" motif itself, as distinguished from Christ, is found in most cultures in which herding sheep is an important occupation. There is, for example, the *Calf-Bearer* (see fig. 7.4) of archaic Greek sculpture and, in the Hebraic tradition, David the shepherd boy, giant-killer, psalmist, and king. Christ as the Good Shepherd symbolized his guardianship of the faithful; further, Jesus was descended from the David who tended sheep in Palestine.

CHRISTIAN SYMBOLS

Artistic representation of the concepts inherent in the new religion caused difficulties never dreamed of by Egyptian, Greek, and Roman artists. The Greeks, for example, had

1. Not used after the sixth century, the catacombs were completely forgotten until rediscovered in the sixteenth century.

11.1 *The Good Shepherd*, Catacombs of St. Callistus, Rome. Ca. 250. Ceiling fresco. Photo: Scala, Florence.

created the gods in their own image, thus making the divinities instantly available for artistic representation: Zeus with a thunderbolt symbolizing the power principle, Poseidon with his trident, Aphrodite as the goddess of love, and so forth. How, then, was the Christian artist to depict such abstractions as the Trinity (God the Father, God the Son, God the Holy Spirit), the Eucharist, salvation, redemption, immortality?

In time, artists worked out a variety of solutions using biblical stories, parables, and symbols. Immortality, for example, could be represented through biblical scenes of

Ιησους
Χριστος
Θεου
Ὑιος
Σωτηρ

11.2 Acronym derived from Greek for "Jesus Christ, the Son of God, Savior."

CROSSES

The cross is a very old and virtually universal symbol. In preliterate societies the vertical and horizontal arms represented a series of opposing qualities: spiritual and worldly, celestial and terrestrial, positive and negative, active and passive. The four points also symbolized earth, air, fire, and water and the spatial dimensions of height, length, width, and depth. The swastika (1), whose Sanskrit name meant "good luck," was a major symbol of ancient Asian, European, and pre-Columbian American civilizations. For pre-Columbian Americans it represents the wheel of life but Hindus perceive it as a sign of a resigned spirit. Buddhists believe it is emblematic of the Buddha's mind. This ancient left-directed cross is not to be confused with the right-directed swastika that Germany's Nazis mistakenly took for an Aryan symbol.

Christianity has been responsible for over fifty different cross designs, with some of the more important ones illustrated here. The **Latin cross** (2) is the primary symbol of Western Christianity while the **Greek cross** (3) is the principal symbol for Orthodox Christianity. The ankh (4) is an ancient Egyptian symbol of life that later became a Christian symbol. The Tau cross (5) has the shape of the Greek letter *Tau*. According to legend, the Israelites on Passover eve in Egypt marked their doors with blood-drawn Tau crosses to identify themselves as followers of Yahweh. The Maltese cross (6) is associated with the Crusader Knights of Malta and also used as the German military decoration called the Iron Cross. The Celtic or Iona cross (7) developed in medieval Ireland and Scotland while St. Andrew's cross (8) is so named because Andrew, the patron saint of Scotland, was supposedly crucified on a cross of this shape. The cross of Lorraine (9) is usually associated with archbishops and patriarchs but during World War II it was the symbol of the Free French forces led by Charles de Gaulle.

salvation: Moses leading his people out of Egypt, Jonah released from the whale, Daniel escaping from the lion's den, Lazarus rising from his tomb. The anchor came to represent hope, the dove was peace or the Holy Spirit, and the palm victory through martyrdom. Symbolizing Christ was the Chi-Rho (KYE-ro) monogram, which superimposes the first two letters of Christ's name (Christos) in Greek: ☧ . The first and last letters of the Greek alphabet, Alpha (A) and Omega (Ω), symbolize infinity as in Christ's statement, "I am Alpha and Omega, the Beginning and the End." Multiple meanings are symbolized by the fish: (1) the Last Supper; (2) Christian evangelism, as represented in Christ's exhortation to his fishermen disciples to be "fishers of men"; and (3) an acronym upon a Greek phrase, the initial letters of which form the Greek word *ichthus* ("fish"; fig. 11.2).

The one event not represented in catacomb paintings was the Crucifixion. As the most ignoble and horrible method of Roman execution, crucifixion was reserved for criminals judged guilty of foul and heinous acts. The Romans executed Christ as an "enemy of the state," treason being the worst of all crimes. For early Christians, the simple geometric form of the cross was sufficient to symbolize Christ's sacrifice. Perhaps the earliest extant crucifixion scene produced for a public place is a small, wooden, low-relief panel on a door of the Church of Santa Sabina (fig. 11.3). Set amid a door rich with elaborately carved panels this, the simplest panel, may be a deliberate attempt to tone down the horror of the crucifixion.

CHRISTIAN SCULPTURE

Early Christians refrained from producing sculpture in the round, especially life-size figures. Religious conservatives interpreted God's commandment literally: "Thou shall not make unto thee any graven images." However, early church fathers did recognize and approve the educational value of painting, an attitude summed up by Pope Gregory the Great (reigned 590–604): "Pictures are used in the church in order that those who are ignorant of letters may, merely by looking at the walls, read there what they were unable to read in books." Supplementing this realistic position was the theological argument that since Jesus was "made flesh and dwelt among us," he had a human likeness and nature that could be represented in art. Conservatives still associated freestanding statues with gods of other religions. This is the primary reason why there was very little monumental sculpture in Europe between the fall of Rome and the tenth century, when new attitudes toward religious art began to emerge.

Despite the rarity of Christian sculptures in fourth-century Rome, two pieces do survive. Classical in pose and reminiscent of the catacomb painting in figure 11.1, the *Good Shepherd* (fig. 11.4) is as carefully detailed as the finest Hellenistic sculpture. Stylistically it still relates to the *Calf-Bearer* (see fig. 7.4) that was created about 1,000 years earlier.

11.4 *Good Shepherd*. Ca. 350. Marble, height 39" (99 cm). Musei Vaticani, Rome. Photo: Islay Lyons, Siena.

11.3 *Crucifixion*, west door, Church of Sta. Sabina, Rome. Ca. 430. Wooden relief, 11 × 15¾" (28 × 40 cm). Photo: Hirmer, Munich.

11.5 *Christ Enthroned.* Ca. 350–360. Marble, smaller than life-size. Museo Nazionale, Rome. Photo: Hirmer, Munich.

The statue of *Christ Enthroned* (fig. 11.5) depicts Jesus in the guise, perhaps, of a young, clean-shaven philosopher. Features, clothing, and gestures are classical, as is the smooth, idealized face. Though the universal image today, the concept of a bearded Christ was not accepted until later. Because this was art of the spirit rather than the flesh, literal depiction was not the goal; this is Christ the symbol, the Son of God.

Relief sculpture appeared relatively early in the Christian era as a means of decorating sarcophagi. By the middle of the third century important church leaders were being entombed in these stone sarcophagi, but the practice was not widely accepted until Christianity was legalized in the fourth century. At first the subject matter was drawn from the Old Testament but, by the middle of the fourth century, sarcophagi began to emphasize New Testament scenes as shown in the Sarcophagus of Junius Bassus (fig. 11.6). The front panel, illustrated here, is divided into ten reliefs on two levels. The top level includes: (1) the Sacrifice of Isaac, (2) the Arrest of St. Peter, (3) Christ Enthroned between St. Peter and St. Paul, and (4–5) Christ before Pilate. The bottom level shows: (1) the Misery of Job, (2) Adam and Eve after the Fall, (3) Christ's Entry into Jerusalem, (4) Daniel in the Lion's Den, and (5) St. Paul Led to His Martyrdom. Many interpretations are possible for a series this complex: the sacrifice of Isaac is in response to God's command, as is the testing of Job; Daniel, Abraham, and Job represent salvation; the fall of Adam and Eve

11.6 *Below* Sarcophagus of Junius Bassus, St Peter's, Rome. Ca. 359. Marble, 3'10½" × 8' (1.17 × 2.44 m). Photo: Alinari, Florence.

11.7 *The Abbot Mena, Protected by Christ*, from Egypt. Coptic. 5th century. Painted icon. Louvre, Paris. Photo: R.M.N., Paris.

---

represents humanity's condition that is redeemed by Christ's sacrifice; the triumphal entry into Jerusalem signals the eternal triumph of the resurrected Christ directly above. To modern eyes the choice of scenes may seem rather odd, but early Christians emphasized the divinity of Christ rather than his earthly existence. His suffering and death are merely suggested in the appearance before Pilate and in the low-keyed martyrdom of St. Paul. All the panels have a detached but controlled air about them; the old classical style was in decline but obviously still influential. The Old and New Testament figures look like Romans of the time and, in fact, the Roman sky god, Caelus, is holding up the firmament on which Christ rests his feet.

COPTIC ART

The native Egyptian church was a result of the rivalry between Alexandria and Constantinople: Egyptian nationalism versus Byzantine imperialism. Though created during Roman domination, most Coptic[2] art reveals the opposite pulls of the Greek classical tradition and the spirituality of the Christian faith. The icon in figure 11.7 is one of the best examples of Coptic painting, for it is a skillful synthesis of Greek realism and Christian sanctity. The realistic facial expressions of the two figures leave no doubt about who is protecting whom. There are very real bodies under the artfully draped robes, but the deliberate disproportions of large heads on shortened bodies reflects the more intellectual orientation of the Hellenistic (Alexandrian) tradition. The large eyes of both men and

2. The word "Copt" is derived from *Kubt*, the Arab version of the Greek word *Aigyptios*.

11.8   Giambattista Piranesi, *Interior, St. Paul's Outside the Walls*. 1749. Etching.

the greater size of the figure of Christ characterize the Byzantine style of Constantinople. The gold **nimbus** of light and glory surrounding the heads of Christ and Abbot Mena first appeared in Christian art in the fifth century but was known earlier in India and Egypt.

THE AGE OF CONSTANTINE

Christianity made its great leap forward after Constantine proclaimed freedom of religion in the Edict of Milan:

> When we, Constantine Augustus and Licinius Augustus, met so happily at Milan, and considered together all that concerned the interest and security of the State, we decided . . . to grant to Christians and to everybody the free power to follow the religion of their choice, in order that all that is divine in the heavens may be favorable and propitious towards us and towards all who are placed under our authority.
>
> From a rescript issued at Nicomedia by Licinius, 13 June, 313.[3]

Though it came soon after the two most severe and methodical persecutions of Christians, by Decius in 249–251 and Diocletian in 303–305, this declaration of religious freedom found organized Christianity ready to build churches and otherwise assume a prominent role in the Empire.

Basilicas

For centuries the Romans had constructed **basilicas** that served as meeting halls, mercantile centers, and halls of justice. The basilica was a prototype of the large, dignified structure Christians needed for worship services.

None of the great basilica-type churches built in Constantine's Rome have survived as such. Old St. Peter's was replaced by the present church, and hardly anything original remains of St. John Lateran after many restorations. St. Paul's Outside the Walls was destroyed by fire in 1823 and faithfully reconstructed in 1854, insofar as that was possible. Piranesi drew the original church (fig. 11.8), clearly illustrating a basic Western church design used throughout the medieval period. People entered the secular basilica from its longitudinal sides but Christians

---

3.   Laotantius, *De Mortibus Persecutorum*, xlviii. Constantine did not assume sole leadership of the Empire until 324, when he had Licinius, his co-regent, executed.

shifted the entrances to a shorter side, usually the western end, thus orienting the building along a longitudinal axis. The interior space was divided into a large area called the **nave**, because it seemed to symbolize a ship (Lat. *navis*, the "ship" of souls), flanked by two aisles on each side. The nave joins a secondary space, the **transept**, which is placed at right angles to the nave proper and forms an interior Latin cross. Later churches would lengthen the transept so that even the exterior walls assumed a cruciform shape, the most characteristic church design in Western Christendom. Behind the transept is a semicircular space called an **apse** in which the altar is placed on a raised platform. The nave was covered with an A-shaped **truss roof**; at a level well below the nave, lean-to truss roofs topped the aisles so that the **clerestory** (or clearstory) windows could be set in the upper nave wall to illuminate the interior. Corinthian columns connected a nave arcade above which was the triforium, usually painted or covered with mosaics; above that was the clerestory area with alabaster windows. Aesthetically, the basilica interior is complex and stimulating, for there is no single point from which one can comprehend the space. The strong rhythm of the nave arcade seems to march inexorably toward the eastern end and the triumphal arch that frames the ultimate focus of the design: the high altar where the sacraments are celebrated.

An obvious choice for Christian use, the basilica had imperial associations that suited the triumph of Christianity and a spacious interior that could hold thousands of worshipers; Old St. Peter's was said to have a capacity of 40,000. Besides the interior space, large churches like St. Paul's and Old St. Peter's were fronted by an atrium (open courtyard), which was surrounded on three sides by a covered arcade called an ambulatory (walkway). On the fourth side of the atrium was a **narthex** (porch) that led to the front doors of the church. Adapted from Roman house plans, the atrium was later moved to the south side of monastic churches to become the medieval **cloister**.

RAVENNA AND THE BYZANTINE WORLD

Serving briefly as an imperial city for the Romans, Ostrogoths, and the Byzantine Empire, provincial Ravenna was a most unlikely capital. Located south of Venice in the midst of extensive swamps, the port of Ravenna did provide the Western emperors with an easily defensible site and, perhaps more importantly, a low profile compared with once-mighty Rome, now the target of every barbarian invader. Becoming the capital of the Western Empire under Honorius in 404, Ravenna fell to Odoacer in 476 but emerged as the capital of Theodoric's Ostrogothic kingdom (489–526), and concluded its royal career as the Western capital of Justinian's Byzantine Empire (527–565) (map 11.1). Modern Ravenna contains notable art works from all three imperial periods.

Map 11.1   The Byzantine world under Justinian, AD 565.

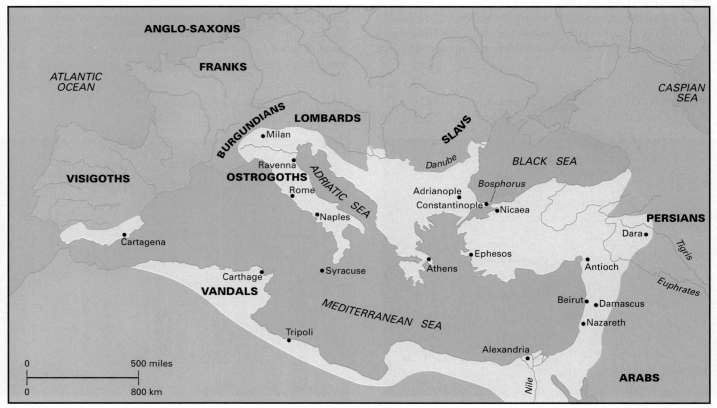

11.9   *The Good Shepherd*, Mausoleum of Galla Placidia, Ravenna, Italy. Ca. 425–450. Mosaic. Photo: Giraudon, Paris.

The mausoleum that Empress Galla Placidia, half sister of Honorius, built for members of her family contains some of the best-preserved and most splendid mosaics of the fifth century. Set in a **lunette** (lew-net), a semicircular wall of a vaulted room, the mosaic of *The Good Shepherd* (fig. 11.9) depicts a majestic Christ watching over six attentive sheep, who balance him in pyramid formations of three on each side, thus symbolizing the Trinitarian doctrine. The regal pose spirals upward from the right hand, feeding a sheep, to the left hand, which grasps a knob-ended cross signifying the earthly death of the King of Kings. In the Hellenic tradition of classical painting, the forms give the illusion of three-dimensional bulk and appear in a real

space. Particularly notable is the rocky landscape, which though increasingly stylized remained in the repertoire of landscape painting throughout the Byzantine tradition and into the late medieval style of such painters as Giotto.

Marking the true beginning of the Byzantine style, the reign of Justinian (reigned 527–565) was notable for artistic production and for the Justinian legal code, plus the dubious distinction of closing, after 1,000 years, Plato's Academy in Athens. Operating from his capitals of Constantinople in the East and Ravenna in the West, Justinian was both an emperor in the Roman tradition and an Oriental potentate in what later became the Byzantine Empire. Except for some architecture in Constantinople, most Byzantine art created before 1204 can be found in Ravenna. The rape of Constantinople by the Fourth Crusade (1204) destroyed most of the art and much of the city, which was not retaken from the Latins until 1261.

San Vitale

The most "Byzantine" of the many religious buildings in Ravenna is the octagonal, domed church of San Vitale (fig. 11.10), a prototype of the central-plan churches that were to dominate the world of Orthodox Christianity just as the basilica plan prevailed throughout Western Christendom. The brick exterior is a complex and subtle interplay of angular patterns around a central core, marred only by an added Renaissance doorway. The interior is a veritable jewel box (fig. 11.11), with polychromed marble walls, pierced marble screens, hundreds of decorative and pictorial mosaics, marble floor mosaics, and carved alabaster columns. San Vitale is an octagonal structure surmounted by an octagonal drum on which the circular dome rests. The transition from the octagonal drum to the round dome was

11.10   Church of San Vitale, Ravenna. Ca. 526–547. Photo: Canali, Brescia.

11.11   San Vitale, Ravenna, interior. Photo: Canali, Brescia.

accomplished by using **squinches**: stone lintels placed diagonally across corners formed by the octagonal walls (fig. 11.12). Topping the aisle surrounding the nave is a vaulted triforium gallery reserved for women, as was customary for Orthodox Christianity. Compact and intimate, San Vitale functioned for the imperial court somewhat like a diminutive, luxurious theatre. The vertical emphasis of the central plan can be seen as a spatial metaphor for the more hierarchal rigidity of the Eastern church while the design also divides the congregation by official rank and gender.

Facing the altar from opposite sides are the two justly celebrated mosaics of Emperor Justinian (fig. 11.13) and Empress Theodora (fig. 11.14). Though extensively restored, these ceremonial works are still the best extant examples of early Byzantine mosaics. Illustrating the new ideal of the Byzantine style, all the figures are tall and slim with small feet, solemn faces, and large oval eyes. Frozen in time without a hint of movement, the solemn participants are depicted in full frontality, highly stylized, but still revealing individual differences while clearly showing the distinctions in official rank. Flanked by twelve male companions suggesting the twelve Apostles, Justinian stands in the exact center holding the offering of bread for the **Mass**. He is crowned with both the imperial diadem and a halo, representative of the unity of the spiritual force

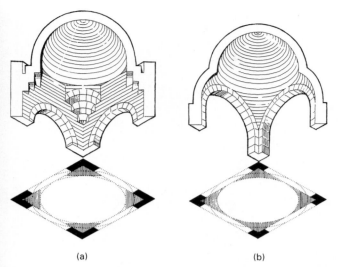

11.12 Supporting a dome with (a) squinches, and (b) **pendentives**.

11.13 *Emperor Justinian and His Courtiers*, San Vitale, Ravenna. Ca. 547. Mosaic. Photo: Gian Carlo Costa, Milan.

11.14 *Empress Theodora and Retinue*, San Vitale, Ravenna. Ca. 547. Mosaic. Photo: Gian Carlo Costa, Milan.

of the church and of the temporal power of the state. At Justinian's left is Bishop Maximianus, who was responsible for the completion of San Vitale and whose importance is signified by the label over his head. The composition of the work delineates the threefold structure of the Empire: the six soldiers represent the army, the three staff members the state, and the three clergymen the church. One of the soldiers holds a shield with the Chi-Rho insignia that not only symbolizes the name of Christ but allegorically becomes a combination of the cross and shepherd's crook, suggesting Christ's death and his pastoral mission.

Unlike the emperor, Theodora is depicted in a more specific setting, probably the narthex of San Vitale, thus indicating both her high rank and her inferior position as a woman. About to pass through a doorway to which she is beckoned by one of her female attendants, she is carrying the offering of wine in a gold chalice encrusted with precious stones. With her huge diadem, ropes of pearls, and luxurious ceremonial gown in royal purple, Theodora is portrayed as the strong-willed, intelligent, and beautiful

empress history has revealed her to be, and considerably removed from her reputed early career as circus performer and courtesan. Pictured on her gown are the Magi bringing their offerings to the infant Jesus, suggesting a parallel with her gift-bearing activity. Both mosaics achieve some of their clarity by conforming to the Greek isocephalic convention of placing all heads on about the same level. They also underscore the separation of the sexes mandated by Orthodox Christianity.

THE CITY OF CONSTANTINE

Dedicated by Constantine in 330 as "New Rome," Constantinople, as the city quickly became known, was the sumptuous center of Byzantine civilization for over 1,000 years. The Orthodox faith was totally dominant in this city, but it was still under the aegis of the emperor who built the churches and appointed the patriarch of Constantinople.

Justinian's building program for Constantinople began as a matter of necessity. In 532 the Blues and Greens, rival chariot-racing factions, joined forces in a powerful revolt against the autocratic rule of Justinian and Theodora. Before the imperial troops put down the revolution by slaughtering about 30,000 people, most of the public buildings had been destroyed, including the Basilica of Hagia Sophia (HA-jeh SO-fee-ah; Church of Holy Wisdom). Only the determined resistance of Empress Theodora kept Justinian from fleeing the city. Justinian's reign depended, in fact, on Theodora, whose influence on public policy and the fate of ministers was usually decisive.

Hagia Sophia

Disdaining the usual procedure of selecting an architect, Justinian appointed the noted mathematician, Anthemius of Tralles, to design the new Hagia Sophia. Assisted by Isidorus of Miletus and possibly Justinian himself, Anthemius invented a revolutionary new design unlike anything in either the Roman or Byzantine world (fig. 11.15). Combining the longitudinal axis of the basilica plan with the domed structure of a central plan, abutted on east and west by half domes, the new Hagia Sophia was a beautiful and inspiring building, truly a majestic architectural achievement. No wonder Justinian supposedly exclaimed as he rode up to the church for its consecration, "O Solomon, I have excelled thee!"

The interior of Hagia Sophia is breathtaking (fig. 11.16) with the dome seemingly floating on light as it rests upon a tightly spaced ring of forty windows. The entire interior is flooded with light from hundreds of windows in the thin, shell-like walls. Adding to the magical effect of all this light were thousands of tesserae that were set into the walls, but later covered with plaster and paint when the Turks converted the building into a **mosque**. With an interior measuring 233 by 252 feet (71 × 77 m), crowned by a dome 112 feet (34 m) in diameter and extending to 184 feet (55 m) above the pavement, this is one of the largest space enclosures achieved prior to this century. At the corners of a 100-foot (30.5-m) square area under the dome are 70-foot (21.35-m) piers that support massive arches. They in turn are connected by pendentives (pen-DEN-tivs), which effect the transition from the basic square to the circular rim of the dome. Best described as concave spherical triangles, two of the four pendentives can be seen at the top of figure 11.16 (see also fig. 11.12). A more graceful transition from a square base to a round dome than squinches, pendentives also facilitate the covering of more floor space. Their origin remains unknown and their use on the monumental scale of Hagia Sophia is unprecedented. Subsequently used in most Byzantine architecture,

11.15 Anthemius of Tralles and Isidorus of Miletus, Hagia Sophia, Constantinople (Istanbul). 532–537. (The minarets were added later.) Photo: Sonia Halliday, Weston Turville, U.K.

11.16   Hagia Sophia, interior. Photo: Explorer, Paris.

pendentives became standard structural devices from the Renaissance to the present day.

As sometimes happens with highly original buildings, there were some technical problems, the most serious being the collapse of the dome twenty-one years after its completion. The present higher-arched dome solved that problem. Byzantium never produced another structure to equal Hagia Sophia. Though it inspired similar designs seen all over Istanbul, it remains unique—the first and best of its kind. First a church and then a mosque, Hagia Sophia is now a museum.

The Iconoclastic Controversy

Brutally terminating the first Byzantine golden age, the Iconoclastic controversy lasted off and on, mostly on, from 726 to 843. Issuing an imperial decree forbidding idolatry, Leo III ordered the destruction of all images of Christ, saints, and prophets. Representations of all sorts, including mosaics in Hagia Sophia, were destroyed along with the entire legacy of pictorial art of Justinian's age, except in Byzantine Italy and on Mount Sinai. Iconoclasts (image-destroyers) mutilated, blinded, tortured, and sometimes executed those trying to protect sacred images. Ostensibly a religious issue based on the commandment forbidding graven images, the controversy was essentially a conflict between church and state. The monastic movement had achieved great wealth and power and won considerable respect from the faithful, much to the consternation of the emperors; furthermore, monasteries were diverting revenue from the state and paying little or no taxes. As principal repositories for sacred images, monasteries were attacked, sometimes confiscated, and their resident monks executed, without, however, stamping out the image-worshiping monks in the West. A later Empress Theodora

allowed images again in 843, but the Western and Eastern branches of Christianity were already launched on a parting of the ways, which led, in 1054, to a schism that has yet to be healed. Though the extent of the loss of priceless art works can never be known, the disaster was not total. The controversy did help to spark a renewed interest in secular art and late classical motifs, setting the stage for the second Byzantine golden age of ca. 900–1100.

THE SECOND GOLDEN AGE

The largest and most profusely decorated church of the second golden age, St. Mark's of Venice, is also the most ambitious structure outside the Empire. St. Mark's differs from Hagia Sophia in that the Greek cross form is clearly visible from within and that, in addition to the central dome, each arm of the cross is capped by a full dome. From the exterior and especially from the air (fig. 11.17), St. Mark's, with each of its five domes encased in wood covered by gilt copper sheathing and topped by ornate lanterns, is the splendid showcase the republic of Venice intended it to be. As required by law, every ship's captain had to return to Venice with something of value for construction or decoration of the cathedral. Because of the law, many treasures from the 1204 sack of Constantinople found their way to Venice. Despite Romanesque and Gothic elements, the Greek cross plan, multiple domes, strong interior lighting, and glittering mosaics make St. Mark's a Byzantine masterpiece.

One of the many treasures in St. Mark's is the sumptuous plaque of the archangel St. Michael (see unit opener on p. 163). On the border polished but uncut gems alternate with **cloisonné** medallions. Other parts are of

11.17   St. Mark's, Venice, aerial view. Begun 1063. Photo: Alinari, Florence.

11.18 Byzantine Miniature Painter of the Macedonian Period, *David Between the Personifications of Wisdom and Prophecy*, from the *Vatican Psalter*. 10th century. Tempera on parchment, 13 × 9½" (33 × 24.1 cm). Musei Vaticani, Rome. Photo: Canali, Brescia.

STUDY QUESTIONS

1. Explain what is meant by "squinch" and "pendentive" and what purpose they served.
2. Many animals, birds, flowers, and objects function as symbols in Christian art. What is symbolized by the dove, rose, fish, anchor, lion, peacock, ox, eagle, lily, cup, lamb? What are some of the symbols for salvation, communion, immortality, and peace? Are any of these symbols of pre-Christian or non-Christian origin?
3. Compare the Parthenon, Pantheon, and Hagia Sophia in terms of purpose, size, and style.

SUMMARY

The simple services of the early Christian congregations had no need for art. There were, moreover, two negative factors: (1) the Judaic prohibition of graven images and (2) a basic dislike—even fear—of classical art. However, the explosive growth of the church in the fourth century called for more and more churches, resulting in a need to instruct masses of new converts in the tenets of the faith. The Bible was basic, but artists significantly broadened religious instruction by developing symbols for Christian themes that they used in murals, mosaics, and relief sculptures. By the time of Pope Gregory the Great (reigned 590–604) the church was actively supporting the production of Christian art with special attention to its didactic function.

As the classical age receded further into the past, there was less and less concern with representational art. For the new faith, physical reality was not so important as authority and spirit. Except for the basilica architectural plan, the early Christians rejected virtually the whole of classical culture from styles to ideals. In its place they introduced different sources of inspiration, thereby changing the entire nature of art.

The Byzantine Empire was an outgrowth of the Roman Empire, beginning with Constantine's transfer of his capital to Constantinople in 330. The stream of culture was unbroken from the Hellenistic Age through the ascendancy of Rome to Byzantium itself. The main ingredient of that culture was Greek but the Christian synthesis included Oriental elements. Also Eastern was the absolutism of the emperor, who claimed that his power came directly from God. Eastern features of Byzantium's highly developed art included its abstract nature, its deliberate two-dimensionality, brilliant colors, and elaborate ornamentation.

The Hagia Sophia was one of the great triumphs of Byzantine art, a magnificent conception that influenced

beaten and painted copper but with a preponderance of gold. The medallion of Christ at the top is flanked by two patriarchs. This colorful masterpiece is so typical of Byzantium that it can be used to define the Byzantine style.

Byzantine art was exceptionally splendid under the Macedonian dynasty of the tenth and eleventh centuries. The renewal of classical ideals that emerged in the post-iconoclastic era is particularly notable in the miniature paintings of the period (fig. 11.18). This page from the *Vatican Psalter* reveals a style that harks back to the Hellenistic roots of Byzantine civilization. The classical influence can be clearly seen when this painting is compared with the mosaics in San Vitale (figs. 11.13 and 11.14). The Byzantine character of this work is apparent in the elegant, if mannered, fold of the drapery, the courtly pose of the figures, and the mixture of gold and bright colors.

The Byzantine style in painting, architecture, and the decorative arts spread throughout the Balkans, into Russia, and as far west as Sicily. It strongly influenced some of the Western art of the Middle Ages, while continuing to flourish in Eastern Europe for centuries beyond the demise of the Byzantine Empire itself, which fell to the Turks in 1453.

Christian and Islamic architecture, especially the latter. A more direct influence on Western art were the mosaics and churches of Ravenna during its glory days as capital of the Western empire. Many of the sacred buildings were built in the Eastern style and most of the pictorial art was created by artisans from Constantinople.

The two basic styles of church architecture were developed during these early centuries. From Rome came the basilica form with a long central hall or nave, and one or two side aisles, usually ending with a semicircular apse at the far end. Byzantium contributed the central-plan building, usually in the shape of a Greek cross, with a central dome over the intersection of the arms of the cross.

The ancient prohibition of graven images returned with a vengeance during the Iconoclastic controversy (726–843) that ended Byzantium's first golden age. The next major shock was the **Great Schism** of 1054 that led to the continuing separation of the Eastern Orthodox churches from the Church of Rome. Inspired by the second golden age (ca. 900–1100), St. Mark's of Venice was constructed as the most elaborate church outside the Byzantine Empire. Byzantine art flourished for centuries after the demise of the Eastern empire in 1453 and is still a force today.

CULTURE AND HUMAN VALUES

During its long decline Rome presided over a world growing increasingly chaotic; the barbarian invasions that contributed to its death throes only added to the confusion. The waning of a strong central authority left a power vacuum gradually filled by the Christian church. The final step in the organization of the church was the establishment of a firm leadership that could assure unity of practice and purpose, and resolve any issue that divided the bishops. For a variety of reasons the Bishop of Rome assumed a place of primary importance in the Christian world. By the fifth century the bishop was calling himself the pope (Lat., *papa*, "father"), Christ's vicar on earth. For members of the Western church he possessed the "keys of the kingdom." Though acknowledged as the Father of the Church in the West, the pope was not regarded as supreme in the East, leading eventually to a schism in 1054 that split the Latin and Greek churches.

The administrative authority of the church hierarchy was paralleled by the development of biblical authority. The bishops, in fact, used their authority to decide what the Scriptures would and would not include. These determinations were completed near the end of the fourth century, when the pope declared Jerome's Latin translation as the standard text—which it still is today for the Church of Rome.

Although Christian art was concerned with the spiritual world-view of the young church, the dominant concept was authority in any form, from church doctrine to the Bible, the bishops, the pope, Jesus, and God the Father. Representational art of the classical world was rejected; instead, people were depicted in terms of their authority—what they represented rather than how they might look.

Artists also depicted other values, particularly the seven virtues of faith, hope, love, justice, fortitude, temperance, and prudence. The seven deadly sins of pride, envy, anger, avarice, dejection, gluttony, and lust were, supposedly, unfit subjects for art; nevertheless, these attitudes or activities were occasionally graphically depicted as examples of how not to behave.

Christian values dominated Western culture for the next 1,000 years or so. In varying degrees, they retain their importance today for those who adhere to one of various Christian beliefs.

The Age
of Faith

The Middle Ages

500–1453

Key Dates	People and Events	Art, Architecture, Music, Literature	Religion	Philosophy, Science, Education
500 527–565 First Byzantine golden age	527–565 Reign of Emperor Justinian 529 Justinian closes Plato's Academy 533 Legal Code of Justinian 590–604 Pope Gregory the Great; establishes political power, codifies liturgy and chant 597 St. Augustine's mission to England	ca. 500 Early materials of *Ring of the Nibelung* ca. 526–547 San Vitale, Ravenna ca. 530–539 Church of Sant' Apollinare in Classe, Ravenna 532–537 Hagia Sophia, Constantinople (Istanbul)	ca. 529 Benedictine Order founded by St. Benedict at Monte Cassino **Muhammad** 570–632	ca. 500 Origin of Seven Liberal Arts
600 600–800 Irish golden age	622–732 Islamic conquest of Middle East, western Asia, north Africa, Portugal, and Spain	ca. 698–721 *Lindisfarne Gospels*	622 Muhammad's flight from Mecca (the Hegira) 630 Muhammad captures Mecca	
700 750–900 Carolingian Period	732 Battle of Poitiers; Muslim expansion checked by Charles Martel 751– Pepin, King of the Franks 768–814 Reign of Charlemagne (Carolingian Empire)	ca. 740 *Beowulf* ca. 760–820 *Book of Kells* 785–990 Mosque of Córdoba 792–805 Palatine Chapel of Charlemagne, Aachen		781 Charlemagne's Palace School established. Beginning of Carolingian Renaissance
800 800–1100 Development of Feudalism	800 Charlemagne crowned Holy Roman Emperor by Pope Leo III ca. 820 Beginning of Viking raids on England and France, later on Italy and Sicily	806 Germigny des Pres		
900 900–1100 Second Byzantine golden age	955 Invading Magyars stopped by German King Otto 987 Foundation of French monarchy by Hugh Capet		ca. 900 Conversion of Kievan Russia to Orthodox Christianity	
1000 1000–1200 Romanesque Period	ca. 1000 Viking Leif Eriksson reached North America (?) 1042–66 Edward the Confessor, Anglo-Saxon king 1061–91 Norman conquest of Sicily 1066 Norman conquest of England by William the Conqueror	ca. 1000 *Song of Roland* written down 1004–1218 St.-Benoit-sur-Loire 1017– Mont-St.-Michel 1037–67 Abbey of Jumièges 1056– Westminster Abbey, London 1063–1272 Pisa Cathedral 1064 St. Etienne, Caen ca. 1070–80 Bayeux Tapestry 1080– Tower of London 1080–1120 St.-Sernin, Toulouse	1054 Separation of Eastern and Western churches 1095 First Crusade preached by Pope Urban II 1096–1291 Period of major crusades	ca. 1000–1100 Battle of Universals (Realist-Nominalist controversy) **Abelard** 1079–1142 philosopher and theologian
1100 1140–1200 Early Gothic Period	**Eleanor of Aquitaine** 1122–1204 (m. Louis VII of France and Henry II of England) 1152–90 Reign of Frederick Barbarosa, Emperor of Holy Roman Empire 1154–89 Reign of Henry II, first Angevin king of England 1189–99 Reign of Richard the Lion-Heart	ca. 1104–32 Ste.-Madeleine, Vézelay 1140–4 Gothic choir, St.-Denis, near Paris ca. 1160 *Tristan et Iseult* written down 1163–1250 Notre Dame, Paris 1174– Canterbury Cathedral fl. 1183 Pérotin, composer at Notre Dame, Paris 1194–1260 Chartres Cathedral	1147–9 Second Crusade **St. Francis of Assisi** 1182–1226 *Little Flowers of St. Francis* 1198–1216 Pope Innocent III; apex of church political and ecclesiastical power	ca. 1150 Complete works of Aristotle become available from Islam; founding of University of Paris ca. 1163 Founding of Oxford University
1200 1200–1300 High Gothic Period	1215 King John signs Magna Carta 1220–50 Reign of Frederick II, Holy Roman Emperor; royal vs. papal power 1226–70 Reign of Louis IX of France (St. Louis) 1295 Model Parliament of Edward I (Angevin), England	ca. 1200 *Ring of the Nibelung* written down ca. 1220–88 Notre Dame, Amiens ca. 1225– Beauvais Cathedral **Cimabue** 1240–1302 painter 1245–8 Ste.-Chapelle, Paris **Duccio** ca. 1255–1319 painter **Dante Alighieri** 1265–1321 **Giotto** ca. 1266–1337 painter **Philippe de Vitry** 1291–1361 Ars Nova in music	1210 St. Francis founds Franciscan order	**Roger Bacon** ca. 1214–94 scientist **Thomas Aquinas** ca. 1225–74 scholastic philosopher **William of Occam** ca. 1270–1347 Nominalist philosopher
1300 1300–1500s Late Gothic Period: International Style	1322–8 Charles IV, last of Capetian kings of France 1328–50 Philip VI, first Valois king of France 1337–1453 Hundred Years' War: England vs. France 1347–9 Black Death sweeps through Europe 1377–99 Richard II, last Angevin king of England 1399–1413 Henry IV, House of Lancaster, England	*Petrarch 1304–74 *Boccaccio 1313–75 *Decameron* *Chaucer 1340–1400 *Canterbury Tales* 1354–1427 Alhambra, Granada *Christine de Pisan ca. 1365–ca. 1431 writer *Gentile da Fabriano 1370–1427 painter *Brunelleschi 1377–1446 architect *Fra Angelico 1387–1455 painter	1305–76 Papacy at Avignon ("Babylonian Captivity") 1378–1417 Great Schism of the Church of Rome	
1400 1453 Constantinople falls to Ottoman Turks; end of Eastern Roman Empire		ca. 1485 *Everyman*		ca. 1400 Arabs transmit compass and astrolabe to Europe

*These artists and writers represent the Early Renaissance, clearly indicating that a new movement arises as the previous era fades away

CHAPTER 12

Building Medieval Walls

Whether we accept 410 or 476 as the date of the "fall" of Rome makes little difference; the decline of Roman power began in the third century and accelerated throughout the fifth century. Roman civilization, however, never died; many physical remains suffered from vandalism but some were sufficiently intact for Renaissance studies 1,000 years later. Moreover, Roman law, language, organization, and its practical approach to power were incorporated into the fabric of the Church of Rome as it expanded to fill the power vacuum. Formerly (and mistakenly) called the Dark Ages, the Early Middle Ages (ca. 500–ca. 800) saw the steady rise of what is now the oldest major institution in Western civilization.

THE EARLY CHURCH

Christianity originated in the teachings of Christ, but became an institutionalized church largely through the efforts of Paul, Peter, and Augustine. Peter wanted to limit the new faith to Jews, but Paul prevailed with his belief that Christianity had a message for the whole world. Paul preached to the Gentiles but it was Peter, credited with being the first Bishop of Rome and thus the first pope, who placed the leadership of the new church in the best possible setting to inherit what remained of the Roman Empire. Paul, Peter, and a succession of popes worked diligently but the church needed a clear, unified doctrine to become a widely accepted institution for the preservation and propagation of the faith. This task was accomplished in large measure by Augustine.

Augustine the Searcher, 354–430

A North African from Thagaste, Augustine received a fine education followed by further study in Carthage. Always a searcher for a firm belief, the young man considered and rejected the Christian faith of his mother, Monica. He first became a Manichean, an austere religion founded by a third-century Persian named Mani. The religion's core was a dualistic belief (derived in part from Zoroastrianism) in powers of good and evil conflicting in the world and in

people. In this ascetic faith the "elect" or "perfect" led a Spartan life and practiced strict celibacy to ensure immediate happiness after death. Augustine could not accept all of this doctrine—particularly celibacy—and later, in Rome, became a skeptic, a believer in nothing, not even his own existence.

Augustine then considered the Neoplatonists, later crediting this period as the crucial stepping stone to Christianity, for his doctrine incorporated much of Neoplatonism while omitting Greek rationalism. This was in Milan, where he was serving as a municipally appointed teacher and where Bishop Ambrose's preaching had a powerful effect on him. Influenced by Ambrose and by his Christian mother, who had joined his household, he experienced his famous mystical conversion as described in his *Confessions*. Baptized by Ambrose in 387, he led a contemplative life until his appointment as Bishop of Hippo, where he became a powerful advocate of the church against the heresies of the Manicheans and the Arians.

Strengthening the Institution

The Arian and Donatist heresies were serious problems for a young institution that would not tolerate dissent. Roman persecution induced some priests to collaborate with authorities by handing over sacred texts. After Constantine's edicts of toleration in 311 and 313, these "handers-over" (*traditores*) resumed their priestly roles only to be challenged by Donatus, Bishop of Carthage. Donatus would punish collaborating priests by declaring their administration of the sacraments invalid, a politically dangerous position because it gave believers a chance to judge priests. Because the controversy was political, Constantine wielded his imperial prerogative by ruling that once the church ordains a priest, his administration of the sacraments remains valid even though his actions may become reprehensible.

The Arian heresy, after Arius, an Alexandrian priest, maintained that God the Son could not be of precisely the same essence as God the Father because the begetter must be superior to and earlier in time than the begotten. This view threatened to diminish the divinity of Christ and demolish the Holy Trinity, as emphasized by Arius' bitter opponent, Athanasius, Bishop of Alexandria. Disdaining logic and espousing mystery, Athanasius and his followers exhorted Christians to accept on faith the Trinity of Father, Son, and Holy Ghost as equal and contemporary. Unable to settle the quarrel, Constantine called, in 325, an ecumenical council (Gk., *oikoumene*, "the inhabited world"), the first meeting involving the whole church. Meeting at Nicaea, across the straits from Constantinople, the assembled bishops backed Athanasius, resulting in the famous Nicene Creed ("I believe in one God"), which Constantine issued with all the force of an imperial decree. It took several centuries, however, to completely suppress the Arian movement.

In his administrative role as Bishop of Hippo Augustine constantly faced the problem of the sacraments (only through which one gained salvation) when performed by heretical or corrupt priests. He decided that the efficacy of the sacraments lay in the priestly office for, if the benefit of the sacraments depended on the quality of the priest, people would be judging God's grace. The resulting doctrine that the priestly office was infallible helped establish the idea of the church as infallible since its power was in its offices. This power, it was argued, descended directly from the apostles, the original bishops of the church. From them it passed to other bishops and on to the priests through the "laying on of hands." This act, which could not be revoked, conferred the power to administer the sacraments.

Theology

Our discussion of Augustine is limited to an overview of his ideas about the nature of God, creation, free will; his philosophy of history; and the infallibility of the church. These beliefs form the backbone for European civilization through the Late Middle Ages.

A New Reality

With the demise of the Roman Empire the time was ripe for a new idea of reality. According to Augustine, God was the only reality, who created the world out of nothingness. This God was a mystic being, not a Neoplatonist intellectual principle; knowledge of God and life in him was available to all human beings, whether or not they were philosophers. Although Augustine regarded his own philosophic speculations as stepping-stones to belief, he felt that his conversion came about not through human efforts but by the grace of God that is available to all people. For Augustine and all believers throughout the Middle Ages, union with God was the only true goal and the only genuine happiness for people, all of which happened in the hereafter.

According to Augustine, the process of creation-from-nothingness took place because of two aspects of the mind of God, roughly corresponding to the Platonic essences, but with significant differences. One such aspect corresponds to the eternal truths, such as the fact that the sum of the angles of a triangle always equals 180 degrees. Such truths, existing before creation and after the destruction of the world, constitute the basic patterns and harmonies of the universe. Another aspect of God's mind consists of the "seminal [seed] reasons" for created things. These are the patterns that acquire physical substance and form the visible entities: human bodies, trees, earth, and the other myriad things that are apparent to our senses. Such sense-apparent things exist in time; they rise, disintegrate, and pass away, and because of their transitory nature are the least important of God's creations.

Time and Eternity

Implicit in the last statement is Augustine's dualistic concept of time. He believed in a direct flow of time in which humanity's activities moved upward toward eventual perfection, toward the godlike. The flow of time and all the changes that occur within it are characteristic of the temporal world. God, however, with all the attributes of his mind, dwells in eternity, which is really a timeless instant. In this realm past and future have no meaning; all is present.

Augustine reconciled the problem of God's foreknowledge of all events and humanity's free will by asserting that people had free will, even though God knew every event that would take place. How does one avoid fatalism and the idea of predestination if a person's actions are known in advance? The answer is that God's seeing all things as present-time allows for foreknowledge in what we call time, yet the "seeing" of things does not influence them. All events are simultaneous for God, and thus he can know them without influencing them.

The Material World

Augustine was ambivalent in his attitude toward the body and the material world. If this world is God's creation then it must be good. On the other hand, being overly concerned with the acquisition of worldly goods can turn a person away from God, and that is sinful. The matter of bodily pleasures was especially disturbing. Before his conversion, Augustine had lived a lusty life of fleshly pleasures; his proclivities were dramatized in his famous prayer: "O Lord, make me chaste, but not yet." He shifted to the other extreme after his conversion and condemned sexual pleasure. He included music in this censure because, like the sex act, it kept the mind from contemplating God.

Platonic doctrine strongly influenced Augustine's view of the material world. He believed that the physical things of the world are all passing away and changing. In *The City of God* (426), for example, he notes that many people lost their worldly goods when barbarians sacked Rome in 410, yet Christians remained happy because their "possessions" were spiritual and could not be taken away. Augustine's position here is not completely dualistic, in that it does not actually despise the flesh and worldly things, yet it tends in that direction. Later on, some Christian thinkers were to turn completely against the world and the flesh, asserting even more strongly than Plato and Augustine that these things were traps for the mind and spirit of humanity. Much of the puritanical thought in the history of Western civilization comes from this reasoning.

Philosophy of History

In the first complete formulation of a Christian philosophy of history, Augustine viewed the story of humanity as a conflict between two cities. (He used the word "city" as we might use the word "community," e.g., "business community.") One was the City of God, the other the City of Man. In the beginning, when time was created, he stated, everything belonged to the good city, yet with the revolt of the angels and Satan's expulsion from heaven, the other city came into being. From that time until the birth of Christ, almost all of humanity belonged to the earthly city. Only a few Hebrews who had faith in the coming of a Savior belonged to the City of God. With Christ's coming for the redemption of mortals, and with the formation of the church, the membership in the two cities was more sharply divided, since all members of the City of God were also members of the church. This, he was careful to assert, did not work conversely; not all members of the church were necessarily members of God's City. The end of history will come with the Last Judgment and the final and complete separation of the two cities. The saved will be reclothed in their perfect bodies and take their place with God; the damned will undergo eternal torture with Satan. Because, according to Augustine, those destined for the good city are already known to God, this can be the basis for the doctrine of predestination, a tenet enunciated by Calvin during the Reformation.

Augustine's philosophy of history has at least one other important consequence. If the original members of the City of God are to be found only among the Hebrews, they alone know truth. Thus all other learning—that of the Greeks, for example—is false and must not be studied. This condemnation of the Graeco-Roman heritage plagued the development of Western civilization for many centuries.

The Church in Rome

Sometime after the death of Augustine the bishops of Rome asserted their supremacy over the other bishops by placing the final authority of the church in Rome. The argument was both pragmatic and biblical. Peter had founded the church in Rome and he was, moreover, Christ's spiritual successor. Biblical authority rested on Christ's words concerning Peter, "Upon this rock [*petras*] will I build my church." Leo, Bishop of Rome (reigned 440–461), first made this claim to ecclesiastical authority, and later, Pope Gregory the Great (reigned 590–604), a skillful diplomat, guaranteed universal acceptance (in the West) of the primacy of the pope. These moves reinforced the stability of an institution that maintained its authority throughout the troubled years of the Early Middle Ages as the only source of order throughout Europe.

FEUDALISM

The Church of Rome replaced imperial Rome as the unifying power of Western civilization but there was no comparable secular authority capable of organizing and governing large territories. Instead, medieval Europe became a patchwork quilt of small fiefdoms. The governmental system, **feudalism**, did not develop fully until the tenth century, but it is discussed here as the slowly evolving political system of the Middle Ages.

Feudalism was, essentially, the division of the former Empire into units small enough for a single man to rule. It also engendered a fighting society, because the lords constantly raided adjoining territories, and all were subject to the forays of the northern tribes from Germany and Scandinavia.

In the wake of Roman civilization many kings lacked enough wealth or power to hold their kingdoms together. To survive, they split their kingdoms among the nobility, starting with the high-ranking barons. In return for land the barons swore allegiance to the monarch and agreed to furnish some fighting men whenever anyone attacked the kingdom. A baron thus became the king's vassal (meaning "servant"). But the barons also lacked sufficient power to administer their lands, leading to the creation of their own vassals and further subdivision of the land. This successive land division continued down to the knight, who owned one demesne (di-MAN): a village and the surrounding farmlands. Each nobleman was thus absolute ruler over the land he controlled, administering justice as he saw fit, and subject only to the oaths of fealty sworn to the lord immediately over him.[1]

MANORIALISM

Coexisting with feudalism on the lowest level of land division was the manorial system. **Manorialism**, as it is also called, regulated the life of rural communities during the Middle Ages. It had its beginnings during late Roman times, when the peasants were forced to stay on the land and became serfs. It reached its zenith during the tenth and eleventh centuries and then began a long decline that did not end until the modern era.

The manorial system was the totality of the life

---

1. Feudalism was far from universal in Europe being largely confined to northern France, western Germany, England, the Norman kingdom of Sicily, and northern Spain. Other parts of Europe experienced some feudalism but many areas were never feudalized.

SERFDOM

The serf and the lord were obligated to each other by a complex web of interrelationships. The serf pledged labor, loyalty, and some material goods to the lord in return for protection and the use of some land for subsistence farming. Bound to the land, the serf and his descendants were inherited by the lord and his descendants. Though they were not slaves and had certain established rights, serfs were not free to leave the manor. They could buy their freedom, but few managed to save enough money. Another alternative was to flee the manor; those determined ones who could survive in a city for a year and a day were finally rid of all manorial obligations. With increasing prosperity throughout Europe beginning in the eleventh century, more and more serfs could rise above their lowly station to become peasants with only voluntary ties to the land. Although manorialism generally ended in the sixteenth century there were lingering remains. Serfs were not freed in the Austrian Empire until 1781 and it took the 1789 revolution to sweep away remaining pockets of serfdom in France. The czar finally freed Russian serfs in 1861 but, not surprisingly, elements of medieval manorialism survived until the 1917 revolutions.

12.1 Aigues-Mortes, France, aerial view. Photo: Lesley and Roy Adkins Picture Library, Langport, U.K.
Located on the Mediterranean coast, this perfectly preserved medieval town was founded as a staging area and supply base for the Crusades. Walls were a common denominator throughout medieval Europe.

within one of these villages. Here the lord resided in his manor unless he was away at war. A priest took care of the community's spiritual needs with the church and parish house at the center of the village. Other buildings usually included a community bake-oven, a winepress, and a mill for grinding grain. The farming land (averaging about 1,000 acres [405 hectares]) was divided into three main sections, two of which were planted each year (summer and winter crops) and the third left fallow. The lord retained about half of the land (his demesne, the best part) as his personal property (though serfs farmed it), the priest received a small parcel ("God's acre"), a section was preserved as common woodland, and another as a common meadow. Each serf was given certain strips of land in each of the three fields—each strip was usually an eighth of a mile (0.2 km) in length and about 17 feet (5 m) wide.[2] The serf and his family were "attached" to the land; they could not leave, but neither could they be turned away. The serf gave part of his produce to the lord and was obligated to work a set number of days on the lord's land. The lord, in turn, protected his villagers and provided justice, though he was the only judge in legal disputes and his word was final.

The manorial system ensured a fairly secure but poverty-stricken and almost totally isolated existence. The manor provided the bare necessities and the serf scarcely ever traveled beyond it. There was no news of the outside world except when the lord returned from a war, or when an occasional itinerant peddler happened through. Formal education was unknown, and illiteracy the norm for the serfs and even for many lords. Life on the manor was an endless round of hard work, birth, marriage, and death, with time off only for religious holidays. Existence was maintained at a minimal level behind medieval walls (fig. 12.1), which shut out hostile forces but which also, figuratively speaking, kept out ideas that might disturb the rigid order enforced by the church and the barons. No wonder people regarded the world as a vale of tears as they hopefully anticipated a glorious afterlife in heaven.

THE RISE OF ISLAM

Western Christianity, Byzantium, and Islam had the common heritage of Graeco-Roman civilization but the three cultures generally preferred emphasizing their differences.

2. Replacing the scratch plow, a new kind of plow was invented (late seventh century) that was equipped with a vertical knife to cut the furrow, a horizontal plowshare to slice under the sod, and a moldboard to turn it over. Pulled by eight oxen (communally owned), it attacked the land with such violence that cross-plowing was unnecessary and fields tended to be shaped in long strips. Found nowhere else in the world (for centuries to come), this plow marked the beginning of a technological revolution that would transform the European from nature's partner to an exploiter of natural resources, leading, in part, to today's ecological problems.

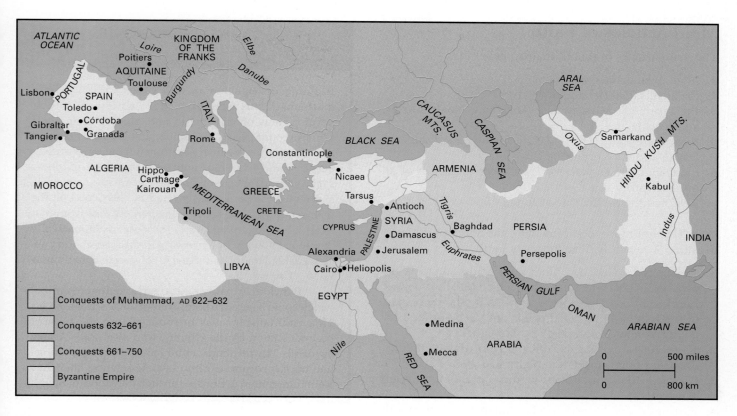

Map 12.1   Expansion of Islam, 622 to ca. 750.

During the Early Middle Ages the West, the most primitive and backward civilization, accused the Muslims of being "infidels" and saw Byzantium as "decadent" and "treacherous." In fact, Eastern and Western Christianity and Islam were monotheistic faiths with their roots deep in Judaism. However reluctant, medieval Europe had much to learn from Islam and Byzantium and, in time, it was strongly influenced by its neighbors as it evolved a unique synthesis of classical, Christian, and Germanic traditions.

For over twelve centuries the relations between Islam and Christianity have ranged from distrust and fear to open warfare; the Muslim conquest of Spain and invasion of France, the Crusades, and the Christian reconquest of Spain are only a few of the major conflicts. Politics and economics, however, cause more alienation and hostility between the two cultures than does ideology. Centuries ago the problems involved Muslim control of Palestine and trade routes to the Far East. Today those problems include Palestine, trade, oil, and Israel.

Islam was the last of the great monotheistic religions, but it made up for lost time with the breathtaking speed of its expansion. Beginning in the Arabian Peninsula in 622, the militant faith, in little more than a century, spread east to the borders of China and west to North Africa and the Iberian Peninsula, an area greater than the Roman

Empire at its height (map 12.1).

Pre-Islamic Arabia was a hot, dry, barren, and backward land inhabited mainly by nomadic Bedouin tribes who worshiped trees, stones, and pieces of wood supposedly inhabited by supernatural powers. Human virtues, by their standards, were courage, manliness, loyalty, and generosity. The chief Arabian city was prosperous Mecca, the hub of the lucrative caravan trade and site of the Kaaba, Arabia's holiest shrine. Chief deity of the city was Allah, creator of the universe but still only one of some 300 gods.

Muhammad

Muhammad (or Mohammed or Mahomet) was born in this bustling city in about 570. After supporting himself by tending sheep and then as a merchant, he became an agent for a rich widow in her commercial enterprise and later married her. It was undoubtedly on his business trips for her that he encountered Judaism and Christianity. At about age forty he began his practice of retiring to a mountain cave to meditate where he received spiritual insights that he later compared with "the breaking of dawn." He had visions of an angel and then of a giant Archangel Gabriel. After a second revelation ordering him to "rise and warn" the people, Muhammad began preaching in Mecca in 613. His ministry angered the wealthy and powerful Meccans, and he fled for his life (the Hegira [hi-GYE-rah]) to the city of Yathrib (later called Medina, "City of the Prophet"). This was in 622, which became the first year of the new faith.

Main Articles of Faith

The main articles of that faith are a belief in:

1. Allah, who is the only God;
2. the angels (Gabriel and others);
3. the Prophets (Muhammad, Abraham, Noah, Moses, and Jesus);
4. the sacred books (Old and New Testaments, Psalms of David, and the Koran);
5. the Qadar (God's plan for the collective benefit of all humankind);
6. Resurrection on the Day of Judgment.

The minimum requirement for the religious duties of Muslims is called the Five Pillars of Faith:

1. "There is no God but Allah, and Muhammad is his prophet." This is the Shahadah, which Muslims believe implies all six articles given above. A fundamental part of the religion, this creed needs only to be uttered for any person to be accepted as a Muslim.
2. The obligation of the five daily prayers (dawn, midday, midafternoon, sunset, and nightfall).
3. Giving to the poor (once voluntary, this is now an assessment).
4. Fasting during the month of Ramadan, the ninth month of the Muslim lunar calendar. According to Islamic belief this marks the month in which Allah gave the Koran to Gabriel for revelation to Muhammad.
5. Pilgrimage to Mecca. Though many cannot do this, millions have done so for the experience of mingling as an equal with other believers and for the sense of Islamic unity.

In the early stages of Islam, a sixth duty was required for all able-bodied men: to fight in the **jihad** (holy war). Each caliph ("successor" to Muhammad) felt obligated to reduce the infidel "territory of war" by armed conquest in the name of Allah. With the exception of Spain and Portugal, all territories converted by the sword remain Muslim to this day.

The Koran

Islam is based on the Shahadah, the Koran, which embodies all of Muhammad's teachings, and the Hadith (traditions), a collection of the Prophet's sayings and decisions (some of which are apocryphal). The believer has only to submit to the will of Allah. The Arabic word for submission is *"Islam,"* the faith; he who submits is a *"Muslim,"* a believer. Submitting unreservedly to an all-powerful God, believers make up a religious community that follows the Koran's detailed rules for every aspect of daily life. Compiled from the writings of the Prophet some twenty years after his death in 632, the Koran is the only authority, the last word in theology, law, and all social institutions. By far the

HINDU MATHEMATICS

Building on Babylonian and Greek efforts, Hindu mathematicians were even more advanced in their development of arithmetic and algebra than their Chinese counterparts. In addition to the whole numbers and fractions of ordinary arithmetic, algebra involves negative and irrational numbers. Irrational numbers such as *pi* and the square root of 2 that are not expressible as fractions were first discovered by the Greeks in the fifth century BC and used by mathematicians from that time on. Negative numbers were systematically developed in India by Aryabhata in the sixth century AD. This enabled mathematicians to solve such equations as $x + 4 = 2$ in which x is −2.

Babylonian mathematics had lacked a zero symbol which could be used to hold an empty place in a number. This vital concept was introduced into the present base-10 system by the Hindus, who also used "Arabic numerals." By the tenth century all of these innovations had been incorporated into Islamic science; later they were transmitted to Europe through the Moors of Spain.

most important textbook in Muslim universities, the Koran should be read by the faithful in its original language, Arabic, the one language of the faith.

Islamic civilization reached its high point during the tenth century as a kind of Middle Eastern renaissance. The culturally backward Arabs contributed little more than the language, but that was a decisive factor. The language of the Koran is the great unifier of the faith, just as Latin was once the common language of the Church of Rome. The Arabic form of writing was also important, leading, in Islamic art, to the development of an infinite variety of abstract ornament and a remarkable system of linear abstraction that is uniquely Islamic.

Islamic Culture

Islamic culture was a synthesis of Greek, Syrian, Persian, and Indian (Hindu) traditions. But Islam digested as well as borrowed, enriching virtually every field of human endeavor, most significantly in medicine, astronomy, navigation, and mathematics. Omar Khayyam, the Persian astronomer and poet of the *Rubaiyat*, devised a remarkably accurate calendar. Philosophers studied Plato and Aristotle, translating them from Syriac (Syrian scholars had earlier translated the Greek) into Arabic. Trade routes were opened through India and on to China so that material goods and immaterial ideas flowed freely throughout the Islamic world. Learning flourished in the great universities at Cairo and

Toledo. The art of gracious living was finely developed, particularly in the luxurious cities of Baghdad and Córdoba. While Western Europe was slogging along in the mud a high culture flourished in the lands of the mosques, the riches of which would not be known until after the Crusades began in the last years of the eleventh century.

Art and architecture were distinctive features of this high culture. National styles of the pre-Islamic era made important contributions but Muslim artistic achievements were not of a particular people or country. Unified and shaped by religion, Islamic art and architecture were among the glories of an entire civilization.

Islamic Architecture

The Mosque

Islam provided direct access to God through prayer; there was no liturgy, sacraments, or priestly class and thus no need for a special kind of architecture. Praying could be done literally anywhere and Muhammad did teach and pray everywhere including his own home. Paradoxically, a religion that had no architectural requirements developed a mosque design that remained essentially the same throughout the vast Muslim world.

The open-court mosque was derived from encampment mosques of the conquering Muslim armies. The "army mosque" was an open field with a ditch and a rustic prayer shelter on the **kibla** side—the wall facing Mecca. Permanent mosques used the basic idea of a large open court enclosed

12.2 Muhammad Ago ibn Ahd al-Muin, Mosque of Sultan Ahmet I, Istanbul, Turkey. 1609–16. Photo: Sonia Halliday, Weston Turville, U.K.

12.3 Mosque of Sultan Ahmet I, interior. Photo: Spectrum, London.

on three sides by covered arcades with a roofed prayer hall on the kibla side. (The arcades provided areas shaded from the torrid desert sun.) Inside the hall a central niche, the **mihrab**, was added to the kibla wall. To the right of the mihrab was the **minibar**, or pulpit, for readings from the Koran and the Friday sermon. A characteristic feature from the earliest days, the **sahn**, a pool for ritual ablutions, was located in the courtyard. Though *muezzins* (mu-EZ-ins; criers) could call the faithful to prayer from any high place, **minarets** or tall, slender towers quickly became standard features of the total mosque design.

The Mosque of Sultan Ahmet I (fig. 12.2, also known as the Blue Mosque) was apparently designed by a student of Koca Sinan, Turkey's greatest architect. Here the original prayer hall of early Islamic architecture has been enlarged into the domed mosque, the finest architectural achievement of the Ottoman Turks. Minarets are placed at the four corners of the mosque and at the two corners of the arcade. There was no mandatory number of minarets; the sole stipulation was that no mosque may have seven minarets like the Great Mosque in Mecca.

To the left of figure 12.2 is Hagia Sophia, the astonishing sixth-century church (now a museum) constructed by Justinian (see figs. 11.15 and 11.16). A comparison of the mosque with the former church reveals the inspiration for Ottoman Turk central-domed mosques. The higher dome and lack of interior decoration give the interior of Hagia Sophia a much different feeling from that of the Blue Mosque. They do represent two very different religious views. Also to the left of figure 12.2 is the site of the Roman Hippodrome, where the chariot races were staged, with a column called the Obelisk of Theodosius that the emperor had moved to Constantinople from the Temple of Karnak. Istanbul has been, in turn, a Greek, Roman, Byzantine, Christian, and Muslim city.

The interior of a mosque (fig. 12.3) illustrates the "dissolution of matter" that was so fundamental to the Islamic style. In the mosque everyone must have a feeling of being equal before Allah. Further, there must be a concern about eternity coupled with a disregard for earthly existence. Highly ornamented surfaces help to disguise and "dissolve" matter. Solid walls are, in effect, camouflaged with tiles and plaster decorated with arabesques and endlessly repetitive designs called "infinite patterns." This feature of Islamic design is very different from ancient Greek architecture, which emphasized the function of architectural members, e.g., the entasis (slight swelling) of columns to suggest their load-bearing function.

The Great Mosque

Begun by Caliph Abd ar-Rahman in the tenth century, the mosque of the caliphs of Córdoba (fig. 12.4) is so large that a sixteenth-century Christian church was built in its midst. With no axis and thus no focus, the forest of columns—

12.4 Great Mosque (arcades of Abd ar-Rahman I), Córdoba, Spain, interior. Height of columns 9'9" (2.9 m). Photo: Sonia Halliday, Weston Turville, U.K.

856 in all—symbolizes the worshipers, who are as individual as the columns but who are all united in common prayer as part of the great community of believers. The striped arches are a Muslim invention, but the columns themselves were recycled, having been taken from Roman and Christian buildings. In common with mosques throughout the Muslim world, the Great Mosque has no sculpture and no figurative decoration. Although there is no prohibition of figurative art—or even any mention of it—in the Koran, idolatry was expressly prohibited, and to avoid any possibility of this, mosques never contain any representations of living forms.

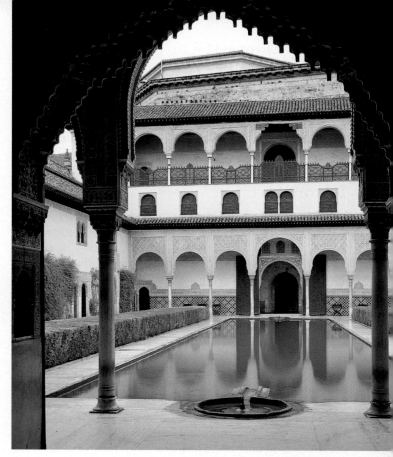

AN ORIENTAL PALACE

To the traveler imbued with feeling for the historical and poetical, so inseparably intertwined in the annals of romantic Spain, the Alhambra is as much an object of devotion as is the Caaba to all true Muslims. How many legends and traditions, true and fabulous; how many songs and ballads, Arabian and Spanish, of love and war and chivalry, are associated with this Oriental pile!

1832, Washington Irving (1783–1859), American author

12.5 Court of Myrtles, the Alhambra, Granada, Spain. 1354–91. Photo: Dagli Orti, Paris.

12.6 Court of Lions, the Alhambra. Photo: Dagli Orti, Paris.

The Alhambra

The ponderous exterior of the palace of the caliphs of Granada, the Alhambra, shields an inner architectural fairyland resonating to the liquid murmur of running water. Because of its desert origins, Islam pictures Hell and Paradise as extensions of the natural environment; Hell is an arid and flaming inferno while Paradise is like an oasis: cool, wet, and luxuriant. Drawing unlimited water from the snows of the Sierra Nevada, the caliphs built an earthly paradise: delicate, intimate, cooled and soothed by playful fountains and the channels of water coursing throughout the palace, the embodiment of an Arabian Nights setting. The main units of the palace are patios framed by architecture. The Court of Myrtles (fig. 12.5) is essentially a reflecting pool with the illusion of floating columns and arches. Multi-colored tiles and plaster casements are decorated with elegant infinite patterns.

The famous Court of Lions (fig. 12.6) is a kind of reverse image of the Court of Myrtles. Here the water runs through the court in slender ribbons, tying the unit together in an intimate arrangement. Fittingly, this is the area reserved exclusively for the ruler, his harem, his family, and the servants. Guarded by sculptures of stylized lions, the fountain adds its bubbling sounds to the flowing waters of a fantastic courtyard of delicate columns and arches decorated with tiles and stucco. Lacy arabesques and airy stuccoed ceilings contribute to what is actually a lucid, rhythmic design. Not one column is perfectly tapered and precisely vertical, thus symbolizing the imperfections of earthly

existence. Even this manufactured Eden is but a defective version of the heavenly paradise to come. The last notable structure built in Moorish Spain, the Alhambra fell to Ferdinand and Isabella in the eventful year of 1492.

Islamic Art

From the thirteenth to the sixteenth centuries in Syria and Egypt workers in the decorative arts developed superlative skills. Master craftsmen abounded: potters, ivory and wood carvers, and workers in plaster and metal. This marvelous Syrian bottle (fig. 12.7) has a wealth of ornamentation but all so delicately done that the effect is exquisite. Mongol influence is seen in the warriors of the bottom border and in the Phoenix on the neck band but all else is Muslim from the blue arabesques to the geometric and naturalistic motifs.

Figure 12.8 illustrates an especially beautiful example of Islamic manuscript painting. With the poetic text condensed into the tiny area at the top, the artist has concentrated on nature, from the garden's trees and flowering plants to the star-studded sky. The skillful use of curving lines makes the picture seem to undulate. The use of such colors as pale blue and gold, the soft reds and greens, the deep blue and light rose provide a magical lyrical effect. It was this kind of elegant painting that attracted Henri Matisse (1869–1954) to Persian miniatures.

12.7 Bottle, decorated with three arabesques above a wide band of mounted warriors, from Syria. Late 13th century. Free-blown and tooled glass, enameled and gilded, pontil on base, height 17⅛" (43.5 cm). Metropolitan Museum of Art, New York (Rogers Fund, 1941.41.150).

12.8 Junaid, *Bihzad in the Garden*, from the poems of Khwahju Kirmani. Persian. 1396. Illumination. British Museum, London.

MUSLIM INDIA

When British India was subdivided into Pakistan and India in 1947 there were over a million casualties in the ensuing warfare between Hindus and Muslims. Moreover, Muslim Pakistan and secular—but largely Hindu—India have fought two wars since that time. One can hardly believe that India was a Muslim empire from the thirteenth to the nineteenth century, when the British arrived. Things began badly in 1206 when Asian converts to Islam, mainly Turks, Persians, Afghans, and Mongols installed a Delhi Sultanate that persisted through thirty-four sultans despite an unceasing record of tyranny, corruption, and bloodshed. The opposite extreme was reached when the dissolute sultanate was overthrown in 1526 by Babur, a remarkable warrior from Persia and descendant of Mongol conquerors Genghis Khan and Tamerlane. A series of able emperors subsequently added to the glory of the new Mogul dynasty. They developed the administrative machinery that is still basic today and did much to combine Hindu and Muslim motifs in art, architecture, literature, and music. Mogul art and, especially, architecture, which culminated in the Taj Mahal (1630–1648?), have had a lasting impact on Indian culture.

CHARLEMAGNE AND THE CAROLINGIAN RENAISSANCE

Islam's expansion into France was halted by Charles Martel (688?–741), "mayor of the palace" of the Frankish kingdom of the House of Pepin. Chief official of the kingdom, Martel ("the Hammer") was the first of the Carolingian line (after *Carolus*, Latin for Charles). Facing the **Moors** (also called Saracens) at Poitiers in western France, he used his tightly knit cavalry to drive the enemy back to Spain. Because this was the northernmost Muslim penetration of Europe, the Battle of Poitiers of 732 became a landmark in European history.

Pepin the Short (ruled 751–768), son of Charles Martel, declared himself king of the Franks and vigorously consolidated a kingdom that was subsequently inherited by his son Charlemagne (Charles the Great; ruled 768–814). The most important political and humanistic period of the Early Middle Ages, Charlemagne's reign lit the first bright spark in European culture since the demise of Rome. His Carolingian Renaissance proved that the light of civilization had not been extinguished.

First, Charlemagne expanded and solidified the kingdom of the Franks, fighting the Muslims in Spain, the Norsemen up to the Danish border, and the Germanic Lombards in Italy. The Battle of Roncevaux in 778 in which the Saracens ambushed and killed Charles' knight, Count Roland, furnished the kernel for the great cycle of songs and stories relating to the exploits of Charles. In return for this warring activity against the pagans, and as a shrewd political move, the pope crowned Charles "Emperor of the Romans" on Christmas Day in the year 800.

A Learning Revival

Politics aside, the significant factor is that Charles had a great respect for learning and brought scholars from all over Europe to his court at Aix-la-Chapelle (today's Aachen). The architecture of this court itself is a landmark in Western culture, for Charles had visited Ravenna where he had marveled at the magnificent architecture and gleaming mosaics. The chapel at Aachen (fig. 12.9) is modeled after the Church of San Vitale in Ravenna (figs. 11.10 and 11.11), and it was responsible for introducing Roman stone construction and Eastern ideas of beauty to the Western world.

Charles established the Palace (or Palatine) School

Map 12.2 The Empire of Charlemagne, AD 814.

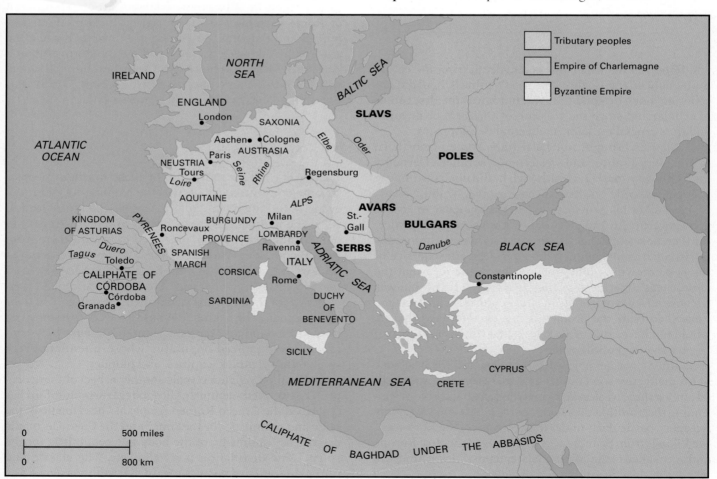

12.9 Odo of Metz, Interior of the Palantine Chapel, Aachen, Germany. 792–805. Photo: Roebild, Frankfurt.

and imported the English scholar Alcuin from the cathedral school at York to direct it. The Palatine School did not generate much original thought, but it was the first center of scholarship since the collapse of Classical civilization and thus crucial for later intellectual development.

Charles brought northern Italy, some of northern Spain, all of France, and western and southern Germany under his rule (map 12.2). Although he did not try to impose a single law code on these diverse people, he did, however, have all of his provinces inspected regularly to ensure good government and the proper administration of justice. Further, he strengthened the power of the church by forcibly Christianizing all conquered people. One consequence of the pope crowning him emperor lay in the idea that the church was superior to secular authority, a belief that was to cause all sorts of trouble in later centuries. Charlemagne himself foresaw the problem when he remarked that he would not have gone to St. Peter's that Christmas Day had he guessed the pontiff's plan.

After Charlemagne's death in 814, and the brief rule of his ineffective son Louis the Pious, his empire was divided among three weak grandsons who were incapable of continuing the tradition they had inherited. The empire rapidly fell apart, particularly under the invasions of the Norsemen, the Vikings from Scandinavia who ravaged much of Europe and even sailed to the continent later named North America, where they briefly established colonies.

THE ASSIMILATION OF CULTURES

"Middle Ages" is a less than satisfactory term that Renaissance humanists applied to the thousand-year period between the end of Graeco-Roman civilization and the self-conscious "rebirth" of the classical world. For the humanists this middle era was an uninteresting, if extended, interlude between the glories of antiquity and the revival of Graeco-Roman culture. But the humanists failed to see that a new culture had evolved out of the fusion of the Graeco-Romans of the south with the Celto-Germanic peoples of the north.

We have already examined the sophisticated, balanced, and intellectual culture of the Graeco-Roman era, whose horizontal-linear architecture and canons of art and architecture testify to a rational civilization. From the third to the sixth centuries many northern people had come into the empire by invitation, infiltration, and military conquest. These were people of a very different character. Primitive and coarse when compared with the cultivated southerners, their architectural line was energetic, vertical, and angular, their decorations intricate, twisted, and unpredictable. Canons of art or architecture were unthinkable.

From around 500 to about 1000 the clashing cultures made this transitional period one full of fear, doubt, confusion, and strife. All was not darkness however. The Church of Rome grew ever stronger, agricultural methods improved and the vital horsecollar was invented, while the sea-worthy Viking ships that could sail the stormy Atlantic became the design of choice. Who were these intrepid sailors who dared to cross the Atlantic to a New World that Columbus "discovered" many centuries later?

The Norsemen

The basic social organization of these northern peoples was the **comitatus**, which was the banding together of a group of fighting men under a warrior chieftain's leadership. The men pledged their loyalty and their strength to the chief and he, in turn, promised to reward them from captured plunder. Thus in the early Anglo-Saxon poem of *Beowulf*, which is based on a Scandinavian legend, both the hero and another leader, Hrothgar, are called "ring-givers" from their roles as leaders distributing gold to their fighting men. The Viking dragonships were fearsome visitors in England and on the Continent because they contained an organized comitatus whose intentions were singleminded: attack, capture, and plunder.

But their religion reveals another aspect of these people. The twentieth-century philosopher Lewis Mumford has described the Graeco-Roman people as "pessimistic of the body and optimistic for the soul," and the Celto-Germanic peoples as "optimistic of the body but pessimistic for the spirit." The distinction is a valid one. The classic and Christian southern peoples regarded earthly existence as a brief period of pain and sorrow followed, they believed, by a joyous afterlife in heaven. The Celto-Germanics ate greatly, drank deeply, killed and raped widely, but were ultimately pessimistic about the afterlife. Theirs was perhaps the only religion that envisions the ultimate defeat of the "good" gods by the forces of evil and darkness.

The Norsemen worshiped a group of anthropomorphic gods who inhabited a celestial residence called Valhalla. Wotan was the king of the gods but the most active was Thor, the god of thunder. Baldur represented the idea of beauty, springtime, and warmth while Loki was the trickster. Even in the heavenly abode the pessimistic nature of these gods emerges for, through a trick of Loki's, Baldur is slain. Norse warriors were promised an afterlife among the gods, but far different from any heaven conceived of by Christians or Muslims, for example. When a warrior died in battle, semidivine maidens (the Valkyrie) swooped over the battlefield to take him to Valhalla, where the hero continued his fighting, eating, and drinking.

An awful fate was predicted, however, for the gods and heroes, for Valhalla was surrounded by the land of the giant Jotuns, who probably represented the cold and darkness of the northern climate. The gods and the Jotuns were engaged in constant petty warfare and trickery. Ultimately, it was believed, a great battle between the two forces would result in victory for the Jotuns and the death of the gods. Thus the ultimate and total pessimism of the spirit of the Celto-Germanic people.

Boethius, ca. 475–524

We have already noted the difference between the Graeco-Roman and Celto-Germanic cultures in their art and architecture. A comparison of their literature is even more revealing. There is no better example of late Graeco-Roman literature than the *Consolation of Philosophy* by Boethius, who served as a Roman consul almost fifty years after the "official" collapse of the Empire. The book is a thoroughly rational dialogue between the author as a man deeply troubled by his unhappy fate, and a vision of philosophy as a stately woman. The discussion includes such subjects as fortune and chance, happiness, the existence of evil, and free will. The entire exchange reads like a Socratic dialogue, and indeed Boethius was heavily indebted to Platonic thought. Although the ideas in the following excerpt are not new, the reader is constantly aware of a classic coolness and dignified withdrawal from the passions of life.

> "But it has been conceded that the highest Good is happiness?"
>
> "Yes," I said.
>
> "Therefore," she said, "it must be confessed that God is Happiness itself."
>
> "I cannot gainsay what you premised before," said I,

"and I perceive that this follows necessarily from those premises."

"Look, then," she said, "whether the same proposition is not proved more strongly by the following argument: there cannot be two different highest Goods. For it is clear that where there are two different goods the one cannot be the other; wherefore neither one can be the perfect Good while each is wanting to the other. And that which is not perfect is manifestly not the highest; therefore, if two things are the highest Good, they can by no means be different. Further, we have concluded that both God and happiness are the highest Good; therefore the highest Deity must be identical with the highest happiness."

"No conclusion," said I, "could be truer in fact or stronger in theory or worthier of God."

"Over and above this," she said, "let me give you a corollary such as geometricians are wont to do when they wish to derive a deduction from the propositions they have demonstrated. Since men become happy by attaining happiness, and happiness is identical with divinity, it is plain that they become happy by attaining divinity. And as men become just by attaining justice and wise by attaining wisdom, so by the same reasoning they become God-like by attaining divinity. Every happy man, then, is God-like; but, while there is nothing to prevent as many men as possible from being God-like, only one is God by nature: men are God-like by participation.[3]

NORTHERN HEROIC EPICS

An urbane, civilized discussion such as the selection above would have utterly bewildered the action-oriented northern people. We can get some idea of their very different Celto-Germanic world by considering the hero epics about Beowulf and Roland.

Beowulf

Although it was written down around the year 1000, *Beowulf* probably dates back to ca. 680, according to evidence that emerged in 1939 in a spectacular archaeological discovery at Sutton Hoo in Suffolk, northeast of London. This was a ship-tomb of an East Anglian king dating from the seventh century and containing a harp, ornaments, jewels, and armor like those described in the poem (fig. 12.10). The intricate, skillfully crafted purse cover vividly suggests a dynamic, vigorous culture. The poem even includes a description of a ship-funeral—that of Beowulf himself.

3. Boethius, *The Consolation of Philosophy*, ed. James J. Buchanan (New York: Frederick Ungar Publishing Co., 1957), pp. 31–2.

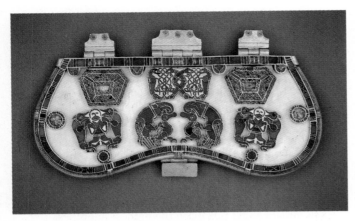

12.10   Purse cover, from the Sutton Hoo ship burial, England. Ca. 655. Gold and enamel, length 7½" (19 cm). British Museum, London.

Beowulf is a warrior from southern Sweden who sails to his uncle's court in Denmark where he slays the monster Grendel. As a trophy Beowulf carries home the monster's arm and shoulder that he has wrenched from the giant's torso. Of course there is a great victory feast followed by drunken slumber on the banquet hall floor. After all are asleep Grendel's mother creeps in, kills some of the sleeping men, and carries the bloody "trophy" back to her home beneath the waters of a dismal swamp.

The next morning Beowulf tracks Grendel's mother to the swamp. Fearlessly he dons his armor and plunges down to the opening of her cave. After a mighty battle with the hag-monster, he kills her with a weapon forged by the giants of old. Following is the closing section of "Beowulf's Fight with Grendel's Dam." The modern translation in alliterative verse is by Charles W. Kennedy.

But fixed of purpose and firm of mood
Hygelac's earl was mindful of honor;
In wrath, undaunted, he dashed to earth
The jewelled sword with its scrolled design,
1503–1533

The blade of steel; staked all on strength,
On the might of his hand, as a man must do
Who thinks to win in the welter of battle
Enduring glory; he fears not death.
The Geat-prince joyed in the straining struggle,
Stalwart-hearted and stirred to wrath,
Gripped the shoulder of Grendel's dam
And headlong hurled the hag to the ground.
But she quickly clutched him and drew him close,
Countered the onset with savage claw.
The warrior staggered, for all his strength,
Dismayed and shaken and borne to earth.
She knelt upon him and drew her dagger,
With broad bright blade, to avenge her son,
Her only issue. But the corselet's steel

Shielded his breast and sheltered his life
Withstanding entrance of point and edge.
    Then the prince of the Geats would have gone his
        journey,
The son of Ecgtheow, under the ground;
But his sturdy breast-net, his battle-corselet,
Gave him succor, and holy God,
The Lord all-wise, awarded the mastery;
Heaven's Ruler gave right decree.
    Swift the hero sprang to his feet;
Saw mid the war-gear a stately sword,
An ancient war-brand of biting edge,
Choicest of weapons worthy and strong,
The work of giants, a warrior's joy,
So heavy no hand but his own could hold it,
Bear to battle or wield in war.
1534–1563

Then the Scylding warrior, savage and grim,
Seized the ring-hilt and swung the sword,
Struck with fury, despairing of life,
Thrust at the throat, broke through the bone-rings;
The stout blade stabbed through her fated flesh.
She sank in death; the sword was bloody;
The hero joyed in the work of his hand.
The gleaming radiance shimmered and shone
As the candle of heaven shines clear from the sky.
Wrathful and resolute Hygelac's thane
Surveyed the span of the spacious hall;
Grimly gripping the hilted sword
With upraised weapon he turned to the wall.
The blade had failed not the battle-prince;
A full requital he firmly planned
For all the injury Grendel had done
In numberless raids on the Danish race,
When he slew the hearth-companions of Hrothgar,
Devoured fifteen of the Danish folk
Clasped in slumber, and carried away
As many more spearmen, a hideous spoil.
All this the stout-heart had stern requited;
And there before him bereft of life
He saw the broken body of Grendel
Stilled in battle, and stretched in death,
As the struggle in Heorot smote him down.
The corpse sprang wide as he struck the blow,
The hard sword-stroke that severed the head.
    Then the tried retainers, who there with Hrothgar
Watched the face of the foaming pool,
Saw that the churning reaches were reddened,
1564–1594

The eddying surges stained with blood.
And the gray, old spearmen spoke of the hero,
Having no hope he would ever return
Crowned with triumph and cheered with spoil.
Many were sure that the savage sea-wolf
Had slain their leader. At last came noon.
The stalwart Scyldings forsook the headland;

Their proud gold-giver departed home.
But the Geats sat grieving and sick in spirit,
Stared at the water with longing eyes,
Having no hope they would ever behold
Their gracious leader and lord again.
    Then the great sword, eaten with blood of battle,
Began to soften and waste away
In iron icicles, wonder of wonders,
Melting away most like to ice
When the Father looses the fetters of frost,
Slackens the bondage that binds the wave,
Strong in power of times and seasons;
He is true God! Of the goodly treasures
From the sea-cave Beowulf took but two,
The monster's head and the precious hilt
Blazing with gems; but the blade had melted,
The sword dissolved, in the deadly heat,
The venomous blood of the fallen fiend.
                        1595–1619

    The poem's last episode recounts Beowulf's final days when, as chief of his tribe, a dragon threatened his own land. Once more Beowulf sallied forth to slay the dragon but this time he was mortally wounded. The poem ends with his funeral pyre as a Viking chieftain and the construction of his ship-tomb as a landmark for Viking ships at sea.

    Beowulf was never tender, never kind, never sympathetic. When his friends die in battle or in the great hall of Heorot, he does not weep for them or extol their virtues. Instead, he swears vengeance and strides forth with sword raised high. He is the mighty warrior, the stalwart adventurer, an authentic Germanic hero.

    This was the warrior's world, full of adventure and courage, revenge and death. By the tenth century this ethos had begun slowly to change as the two cultures merged. Many northerners had moved to the south, become Christianized, and given up some of their savage ways. The Angles and Saxons, from Germany, settled in England. Norsemen put down roots in a part of northern France later named for them: Normandy. Throughout Europe the once-restless Germanic people settled on the land. The northern chieftain moved into the evolving feudal system, becoming a baron or a count, a duke or a knight, holding land from his overlord, or suzerain, and granting fiefs to those under him. It was still a warlike society, but a somewhat more settled one, in which the former chieftain gave up his wooden hall for a castle built of stone. The highest virtue continued to be a mutual loyalty between the lord and his vassals.

Song of Roland

The *Song of Roland* is a good example of this new civilization. This minor epic was written in French at about the time of the First Crusade (the 1090s), but the written version simply records a hero-story sung and recited concerning the events that happened, legendarily, three centuries before in the days of Charlemagne. The persons of the story are Franks, the Germanic conquerors who gave their name to France; the central figure is Roland, the emperor's nephew. The poem's chief event is the Saracen ambush of the rear guard of Charlemagne's army in a Pyrenees pass at Roncevaux. (Medieval Christians called all Muslims Saracens regardless of nationality. These Saracens were Moors from Spain.) Prompted by envy and revenge, Roland's treacherous kinsman Ganelon arranged the ambush. Roland, his companion Oliver, and the militant Archbishop Turpin are the last survivors of the Frankish host. Facing overwhelming odds, they too are killed. One of the best-known episodes is Roland's stubborn refusal, despite Oliver's urging, to blow his ivory horn (oliphant) to recall Charlemagne's host before the battle begins. When he realizes that he and his fellow Franks are doomed, he at last blows three mighty blasts that Charlemagne hears, 30 leagues (possibly 100 miles or 160 km) away; the emperor returns to rout the Saracens and avenge the death of Roland and his companions. The epic concludes with the trial and punishment of Ganelon.

    This is a truly feudal poem, full of the vigorous, active, restless spirit of the northern soldier. Roland is the warrior, a splendid barbarian, courageous in the face of overwhelming odds, loyal to his friends, utterly devoted to God, his spiritual overlord, and to Charlemagne, his temporal one. He is blood brother to his earlier northern kinsman, Beowulf; both heroes represent the all-out, do-or-die, go-for-broke spirit of the heroic age. Following is the 176th stanza, or "laisse," of the poem:

And now Count Roland,   lying beneath a pine,
Has turned his face   to look toward pagan Spain;
And he begins   remembering these things:
The many lands   his valor won the king,
Sweet France, his home,   the men of his own line,
And Charlemagne   who raised him in his house—   2380
The memories   make him shed tears and sigh.
But not forgetting   how close he is to death,
He prays that God   forgive him all his sins:
"O my true Father,   O Thou who never lied,
Thou who delivered   Lazarus from the grave,
Who rescued Daniel   out of the lions' den,
Keep now my soul   from every peril safe,
Forgive the sins   that I have done in life."
Roland, in homage,   offers his glove to God.
Saint Gabriel comes   and takes it from his hand.   2390
His head sinks down   to rest upon his arm;
Hands clasped in prayer,   the count has met his end.
God sends from heaven   the angel Cherubin,
Holy Saint Michael   who saves us from the sea,
And with these two   the Angel Gabriel flies.
Count Roland's soul   they bring to Paradise.

    The similarities and differences between this story

and that of *Beowulf* are immediately apparent. *Roland*, with its heavy Christian overlay, is more "civilized" than the early epic, but it is still a savagely militaristic poem, extolling the glories of war, bravery, and loyalty. The final act of Roland reveals much of the spirit of the time, for offering his glove to God means pledging loyalty to a feudal lord. Roland, Charlemagne's vassal, has now accepted a new suzerain in God, and Gabriel takes the glove to signify God's approval of Roland as a vassal in the celestial feudal system.

STUDY QUESTIONS

1. Explain how each heresy—Arian and Donatist—differed from the official doctrine of the Church of Rome. Why didn't the church permit several versions of doctrine? What did the church do to eliminate these heresies? Can violence against those labeled as heretics be justified? Why or why not?

2. Review, in your own words, the basic articles and duties of Islam and explain what they mean. Compare these with Roman Catholicism and with some specific Protestant church. What are the critical differences between the three religions? How does Islam compare with Judaism?

3. Explain how and why Islam expanded so rapidly. Can violence in the name of religion be justified? Have Christians ever waged "holy" wars?

SUMMARY

People of the early Middle Ages built walls around their villages—wooden palisades in the early days; later, the walls were stone and the lord's house and the whole village a fortified enclave. Life paralleled those confining fortifications because people had battlements around their minds, barriers that were reinforced by the church.

Their universe was based on the teachings of the church of Rome, which, in the Middle Ages, allowed no questioning of its tenets or its actions. Further, the church took a dim view of worldly pleasure and repressed any consideration of the physical world. Science as we know it did not exist; the natural world was a closed book, to be interpreted only as a vague shadow of the intention and mind of God. Earthly life was viewed as a brief and transitory journey through a dismal land, with real life and genuine happiness reserved for the next world. Furthermore, as is explicit in the morality play of *Everyman*, the only way to achieve the blissful afterlife lay in the unquestioning acceptance of the doctrines and sacraments of the church.

The economic system of manorialism bound most people to the 1,000 or so acres of the manor itself. There

was little chance of escape; the few who left the enclave needed special permission. In fact, the average serf never strayed even a kilometer from the demesne. Food, clothing, and meager physical comforts were limited to what the manor could produce. Not even the mind could escape the narrow confines; reading was almost unknown because most people were illiterate, including many clergymen. Illiteracy and minimal travel meant also that news of the outside world almost never penetrated the closed miniworld of the manor.

The political system of feudalism was equally narrowing. Justice lay entirely in the hands of the feudal lord or, more often, his deputy. Except for the specific obligations of serf to lord and vassal to suzerain, which were generally known and accepted, the law was made up on the spot, and the individual never knew what to expect.

About the only contact feudal society had with the outside world were the bloody incursions of barbarian Norsemen or Magyars, or as victims of Muslim holy wars. Not until the middle of the Middle Ages (ca. 1000) would the Norsemen and Magyars be absorbed by Christian societies and the advanced culture of Islam acknowledged, studied, and drawn into the evolving Western synthesis. Western civilization would not be what it is today without the vital infusion of Islamic culture.

The narrow confines of church, manorialism, and feudalism provided the walls that closed in upon the human spirit. Creativity and freedom of thought were almost unknown. But, with the withdrawal of Roman protection and with all the dangers from bands of marauders, these walls provided protection for the individual. If ordinary serfs could not live well, they could at least live safely.

But the human spirit is never content with mere security. Particularly with the gaining of a little freedom, as happened in the tenth and eleventh centuries, it clamors more and more for expansion. The seeds that were to germinate and eventually break down medieval walls were already planted. Some of the directions for that growth may be indicated.

First, the human spirit has never long been content *not* to examine the world around it. The varied forms of the world, its beauties, and reason for being demand attention. Both art and science express this quest for an exploration of the sensory world.

Second, the two personality types of Europe, the rational Graeco-Roman and the emotional and energetic Germanic lived side by side but not in unison by the year 1000. Some form of synthesis between these two personality types, almost exactly opposite each other, needed to be found.

Third, a problem limited largely to politics: the question of supremacy of church or state demanded settlement. At a time when the secular power was so weak as to be almost nonexistent, the church could and did assert its authority over kings and lords. But with the growth of the powers of the world a struggle was inevitable, a bitter conflict of church and state that has been waged all over the Western world and which is still not fully resolved.

Fourth, and perhaps most important, people need joy in their lives but this was sternly denied by the church. A desire for immediate physical and intellectual pleasure in life now would necessarily conflict with the doctrine that life here was nothing, the afterlife everything. The pull of life as opposed to the church-dictated pull of death was bound to cleave the human personality until some synthesis could be effected.

These are the latent problems one sees at the end of the Early Middle Ages. Their solutions will be considered in subsequent chapters.

CULTURE AND HUMAN VALUES

The centuries from about 500 to around 1000 were a tumultuous period of transition. The former realities of the Individual and then of the State had been superseded by the vision of God as the true reality and the Church of Rome as the sole possessor of the Keys of the Kingdom. For most people the church was the most easily comprehensible reality. For the faithful it promised salvation and a glorious existence in the afterlife. A sparse and meager existence in this harsh world would be more than made up for by eternal life in the paradise to come. Strict adherence to the church's teaching of the Scriptures and to church doctrine—plus avoidance of sin—virtually assured admission to eternal bliss.

The virtues and vices as specified by the church can be considered from another point of view. The church was the only absolute authority and intended to remain so. Some scholars have suggested that the church-defined virtues and vices also served to reinforce the power and authority of Rome. The first and foremost value was obedience to authority. After this, the seven virtues of faith, hope, love, temperance, prudence, fortitude, and justice would reinforce the dominance of Rome. Condemnation of the sins of pride, lust, envy, anger, avarice, dejection, and gluttony would help guard against any temptation to tinker with the status quo. One should be reminded that justice was the foremost value in ancient Greece, pride was a virtue, and Aphrodite was adored by all. Whatever the interpretation, life during these perilous times was bleak and dismal for most of the population and was to remain so for centuries. There was hope but precious little joy. It must be emphasized that the Early Middle Ages was a difficult transitional period from the chaos of the post-Roman era to the period of balance of the High Middle Ages when a synthesis emerged that emphasized spirituality without sacrificing earthly pleasures.

CHAPTER 13

The Late Middle Ages: Expansion and Synthesis

A NEW CENTURY

There was no single reason for the liberation of a whole social structure, but looking back over the centuries we know it began in eleventh-century Europe. Release from a dreaded Doomsday was one of the many causes of the transformation. Some claimed that the world would end at the dawn of the year 1000, a prophecy believed by some of the peasantry. One must imagine the wonder when people woke up on New Year's morning to discover that they were not only alive but hungry, not for spiritual food, but for a very physical breakfast. Such a reprieve was certainly one of the symbols of the general awakening of Europe. This was still the Middle Ages with God the accepted Reality, but what a difference was soon to be discovered in the lives and thoughts of men and women!

Many were the instruments of change. The shift from feudalism's fierce warrior code to the more cultured ideals of chivalry was a major civilizing influence. The existing church doctrine was widely viewed as austere and remote, which led to the more personal cult of the Virgin, the most popular religious force in the High Middle Ages. Even the Crusades led, however inadvertently, to increasing knowledge of the luxurious Islamic civilization and its priceless hoard of ancient Greek culture. New cities were created while older ones expanded. Universities, destined to influence all of Europe, were founded, supporting a revival of humanistic studies which sparked an intellectual life that had lain dormant for centuries. Perhaps a metaphor for the entire transformation was the philosophic ferment about the nature of reality itself, which culminated in the "Battle of Universals."

Opposite "Christine de Pisan Presenting her Poems to Isabel of Bavaria," fol. 3, Harley Ms 4431, detail. Manuscript illumination. British Library, London.

The Rise of Cities

New cities and the expansion of existing cities was central to the transformation of Europe. Cities are essential for the development of any civilization; agriculture is the business of rural areas while culture is the business of cities. Of the many reasons for the rise of medieval cities, one lay in the increase of land available for agriculture because of the drainage of swamps, for cities require a guaranteed food supply. Another impetus to the gathering of people was the nobles' need for central military forces for quicker mobilization to fight ever bigger wars. But increasing trade and commerce were probably the most important forces driving urban development.

The itinerant peddler, who traveled from manor to manor, had been a standard fixture of the Early Middle Ages. Sometime during the eleventh century some peddlers-become-merchants set up stalls under the protection of the churches or abbeys. This caused a change comparable to reinventing the wheel: the reintroduction of money in place of bartering as the medium of exchange. For centuries the nobles had received their manorial dues in goods and produce, but money offered far greater freedom in fuelling their ambitions. In return for tax money they granted charters to cities while awarding varying degrees of freedom from feudal responsibilities. Thus they encouraged the growth of urban centers that keyed a general stirring of the human spirit.

Throughout Europe the word went around, "City air is free air." Living in a city for a year and a day made a serf a free man. Here tradesmen organized guilds to regulate the quality and price of their goods and to provide insurance and some social life for the members and their families. As these guilds—first only craft guilds, later also merchant guilds—prospered, grand guildhalls were built flanking the cathedral to form a quadrangle about the open marketplace, a central grouping characteristic of medieval towns and cities.

The Crusades

For a variety of reasons the Crusades were a major force for change. Preached by Pope Urban II in 1095, the First Crusade captured Jerusalem in 1099—the only successful venture in a series of failed Crusades lasting into the Renaissance—and that success was only temporary (map 13.1). The stated intent of the Crusades was to rescue the Holy Land from its Muslim inhabitants so that Christian shrines might become more accessible for Western pilgrims. The hidden agenda included a lust for Middle Eastern lands and riches plus papal attempts to deflect to a foreign foe the increasing criticism of the Holy See. The West justified the Crusades as holy wars freeing biblical lands from infidels but Muslims saw only unprovoked aggression by barbarous heathens. The repercussions have yet to end.

The long-lasting effects of Middle Eastern invasions did, however, include significant benefits. Although Europeans had already encountered Islamic culture in Sicily and Spain, the Crusaders entered the heart of this rich civilization, and what they found there caused substantial changes in virtually every aspect of European life. The luxurious booty carted home by the soldiers, following the ancient custom of all warriors, stoked rising expectations for a better life. First imported as luxuries, such foods as sugar, saffron, rice, citrus, and melon and such manufactured goods as silk, damask, muslin, and cotton soon became necessities. More important than food and textiles, however, was the rich reservoir of Islamic science and the carefully tended heritage of ancient Greece. The way was still long and tortuous but semibarbaric Europe began, finally, to develop the arts of civilized living.

Feudalism and Chivalry

One of the key transformations was the movement from feudalism's warrior ethic to chivalry's more civilized code of behavior. During the later Middle Ages, especially in France, aristocratic women began to assume a more prominent role in shaping the world in which they lived while their husbands were off fighting. They efficiently managed their estates, introduced poetry and music to the courts, and elevated the standards of behavior, dress, and manners.

Epitomizing this metamorphosis was the remarkable Eleanor of Aquitaine (1122–1204), Queen of France and then of England. Insisting on accompanying her first husband, King Louis VII of France, on the Second Crusade in 1147, Eleanor was fascinated by the sophistication of Constantinople and quick to add elements of Byzantine and Muslim culture to her already extensive education. Along with her daughter, Marie of Champagne, and granddaughter, Blanche of Castile, Eleanor established Courts of Love that were to write legal-sounding codes of etiquette. Lyrical love songs composed and performed by aristocratic **troubadours** replaced epic tales of stalwart heroes fighting bloody battles. This shift in emphasis can be seen clearly in the contrast between Roland's lament over the fallen Franks at Roncevaux, representative of feudal ideals, and the lament over the dead Lancelot, an exemplary knight of the age of chivalry. Surveying the field of death where his comrades in arms lie, Roland says:

> Lords and barons, now may God have mercy upon you, and grant Paradise to all your souls that you may rest among the blessed flowers. Man never saw better men of arms than ye were. Long and well, year in and year out, have you served me, and many wide lands have ye won for the glory of Charles. Was it to such an end that he nourished you? O France, fair land, today art thou made desolate by rude slaughter. Ye Frankish barons, I see you die through me, yet I can do naught to save and defend you. May God, who knows no lie, aid you!

When Lancelot, the legendary knight of chivalry, lies dead, we hear the following lament from Guinevere:

> Thou wert the courtliest knight that ever bare shield, and thou wert the truest friend to thy lover that ever bestrode horse, and thou wert the truest lover among sinful men that ever loved woman, and thou wert the kindest man that ever struck with sword, and thou wert the goodliest person that ever came among the crowd of knights, and thou wert the meekest man and the gentlest that ever are in hall among ladies, and thou wert the sternest knight to thy mortal foe that ever put spear in breast.

Here is a transformation from a fighting code to a humane and courtly standard. Both codes are present in the lament over Lancelot but kindness, love, and humility—never even considered by feudal warriors—are, once again, virtues. Given the vagaries of human nature, the elaborate codes of chivalry were undoubtedly violated about as often as they were observed. They assisted nevertheless in the laborious process of recivilizing Europe.

Powerful women such as Eleanor of Aquitaine were in a position to contribute to the civilizing process, but what of those medieval women who were neither powerful nor royal? With the exception of the Etruscans, Minoans, and the Aegean culture of Lesbos, the role of women in Western civilization was always secondary and subservient. However, determined women could help change the role of their gender in medieval society. Though it was considerably more difficult for women outside a court setting to influence society, Christine de Pisan (ca. 1364–ca. 1431), considered France's first professional writer, was one of the most significant writer/thinkers to do so. An early feminist who was always firm but cheerfully well-mannered within a male-dominated society, she had a voice of reason and restraint—and courage.

Born in Venice, Christine de Pisan spent most of her life in the shadow of the court of Charles V in Paris, where her father was court physician. After ten years of a happy marriage she was suddenly widowed at twenty-five and faced with making her way in a man's world. Utilizing her excellent education, she became so successful as a professional writer that she supported her three children, her mother, and assorted relatives (see chapter opener on p. 208). Many of her forty-one works were concerned with the advancement of women, particularly the *Book of the City of Ladies* and *A Medieval Woman's Mirror of Honor: The Treasury of the City of Ladies* (see pp. 222–4).

The Church of Our Lady

Closely allied to chivalry's evolution was the development of beauty and warmth within the church. Church doctrine was an intellectual monument centered on the **Trinity**—Father, Son, and Holy Ghost—a Three who were always One, and administering the uncompromising justice described by Augustine. For guilt-ridden men and women justice was the last thing to be desired. They sought mercy, not justice, turning to the Virgin, the highest of the saints, the Queen of Heaven. She was the essence of purity, an idealized version of love, warmth, and beauty. A manifestation of the polarized medieval view of women, the cult of the Virgin venerated one woman, pure in body and soul, possessor of all the womanly virtues. Her diametric opposite was Eve, Adam's temptress, the "fallen" woman beguiled by Satan, a misogynous concept with disastrous consequences, then and now.

The Virgin was the loving Mother who could mercifully intercede for the faithful, and it was to her that many of the majestic cathedrals were dedicated. Indeed, in France one asks not the way to the cathedral, but how to get to Notre Dame, the church of "Our Lady." The two are almost synonymous. As the nineteenth-century American historian Henry Adams noted in *Mont-St.-Michel and Chartres*:

> The measure of this devotion [to the Virgin], which proves to any religious American mind, beyond possible cavil, its serious and practical reality, is the money it cost. According to statistics, in the single century between 1170 and 1270, the French built 80 cathedrals and nearly five hundred churches of the cathedral class, which would have cost, according to an estimate made in 1840, more than five thousand millions to replace. Five thousand million francs is a thousand million dollars,[1] and this covered only the great churches of a single century . . . . The share of this capital which was—if one may use a commercial figure—invested in the Virgin cannot be fixed . . . but in a spiritual and artistic sense, it was almost the whole . . . .
>
> Expenditure like this rests invariably on an economic idea . . . . In the thirteenth [century] they trusted their money to the Queen of Heaven—because

of their belief in her power to repay it with interest in the life to come.

Therein lay the power of the Virgin in bringing human understanding and sympathy into the remote structure of church doctrine. While theologians wrangled about materialism and spiritualism, the common people were consoled by the presence, in their church, of a beautiful statue representing a person with human sympathy and warmth. Such faith reveals itself in the many stories of the mysteries of the Virgin, including "Our Lady's Juggler" (see pp. 219–21).

Scholasticism

The medieval church insisted upon absolute authority. Despite his early philosophic speculations, St. Augustine finally said, "I believe in order that I may know." Thus faith in the Scriptures and the biblical commentaries of the early church fathers and total submission to these sources was the mandatory first step for the Christian life. Knowledge was secondary; whenever doctrine was inexplicable or contrary to reason, doctrine was believed and intellect denied.

Scholars built the elaborate structure of Christian Scholasticism on this steadfast base. Although Scholasticism was complex the reasoning procedure was simple. A scholar answered any question by studying the Bible and writings of the church fathers to find all passages pertaining to his subject. This was his only source for basic data; exploration of other writings or of the sensory world was forbidden. Secondly, he used Aristotelian logic to work on his source. Such logic is built upon the three-part syllogism: a major premise, *all men are mortal*; a minor premise, *Socrates is a man*; a conclusion, *therefore Socrates is mortal*. The conclusion can then be used as a major or minor premise in further syllogisms until the final, refined answer is found.[2]

Faith and Reason

As early as the ninth century the philosopher Johannes Scotus Erigena had recognized some differences between faith and reason, but he insisted that both reason and the Scriptures had come from God, making conflict "impossible." But the church held to its stand on faith alone, which Anselm of Canterbury reaffirmed in the eleventh century.

---

1. This is the money values of 1840. If we multiplied the figure by a hundred, it might still be low for the late twentieth century.
2. Today's students might scoff at this type of reasoning until they are reminded that every culture sets similar limits to its thought processes. In the twentieth century, for example, the searcher for truth investigates the physical world and then uses the scientific method to refine the raw data and gain knowledge about the world in which we live.

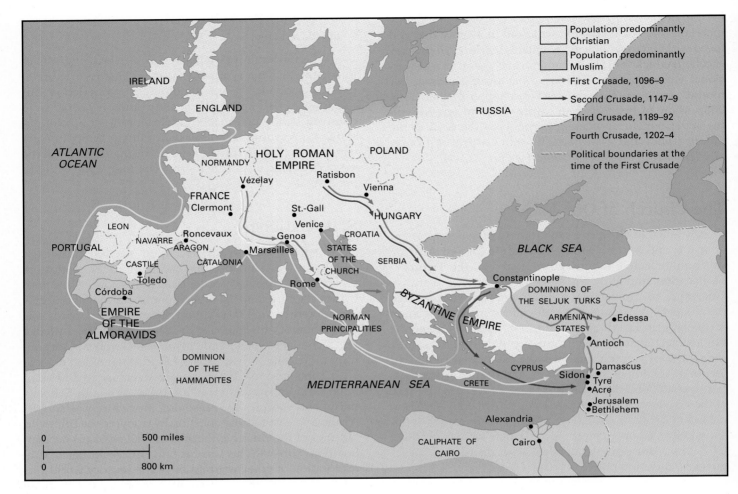

Map 13.1   The major Crusades.

Late in that century, however, this reaffirmation was challenged by a philosophic dispute that became known as the Battle of Universals. The "battle" was a controversy (greatly simplified here) about the nature of reality. Today's student may consider this an esoteric dispute between ivory-tower philosophers, but the issue was critical. Because a commonly held concept of reality determines the nature of a civilization, any change in the concept will necessarily alter the way people live and think. These philosophers were leading scholars in the central institution of the age, as important in their time as Einstein and Stephen Hawking have been in our century. Any change in the church's position affected everyone from kings to serfs.

The Realist Position
Church doctrine was based on an adaptation of Plato's belief in Forms/Ideas as constituting an ultimate reality that is permanent, unchanging, without material substance, and, according to the church, existing in the mind of God. Thus physical things, which are subject to change, are only illusory shadows, as described in Plato's "Allegory of the Cave." The human body is to be disregarded and a study of the physical world is wasted time better spent seeking eternal truths. This Neoplatonic/Augustinian doctrine was the Realist position and the position held by the church.

The Nominalist Position
The French philosopher Johannes Roscellinus (ca. 1050–after 1120) first challenged this doctrine with a nominalist position that is close to what many people believe today. Claiming that physical things were the only reality, he stated that, for example, each sense-apparent tree is real and that no higher "treeness" exists. How can we know the idea of tree? We can speak of trees, or people, or elephants, or justice when no specific example is present to our senses. Roscellinus said that these "ideas" were only names (hence the word "nominalist") and that we form the idea as a generalization only after experience with a number of individual things. We experience, he said, specific examples of elms, oaks, pines, and so forth. We then generalize and form the "idea" tree so that we can discuss the species—and understand each other—in the middle of the ocean with no tree within 1,000 miles.

The two positions in the battle were thus established, as opposite as opposites can be. William of Champeaux

(1070–1121) and others stoutly defended the realist position, the standard doctrine of the church. If the defenders should fail, the church itself would be in danger, they said, and indeed it was.

The Conceptualist Position

A middle position was suggested by the brilliant thinker Peter Abelard (1079–1142), probably the most popular teacher in the early University of Paris. Having studied with both Roscellinus and William of Champeaux, Abelard was in a perfect position to propose a compromise. Abelard's conceptualist position anticipated Aristotle's view of the problem even before that whole body of knowledge was known to Europe. The conceptualist view can be stated briefly, for it will become better developed by Thomas Aquinas. Abelard contended that idea is real but that it does not exist either before or after a particular physical thing. That is, reality as idea exists only in the sense-apparent object. Abelard's intellectual daring was condemned by the church but, nevertheless, the battle of the three positions continued until, a century later, Thomas Aquinas formed a synthesis that would become the official dogma of the church.

But the imaginative Abelard was not finished. He tossed a bombshell into religious thought when he published *Sic et non* ("Yes and No"). One remembers that the only valid sources of knowledge then were the Bible and the commentaries of the church fathers. In *Sic et non* Abelard raised a number of important religious questions; then, in opposite columns, he quoted the answers of each father, thus exposing all sorts of contradictions and sending a shudder throughout the church. If this source of knowledge was contradictory then how wrong were the conclusions based on these writings? The sources were faulty and the challenge of authority was inevitable.

Aristotle Rediscovered

Still another blaze broke out in the structure of the church with the late twelfth-century rediscovery of all of Aristotle's works. His logic, his only known work, had been universally used as the only method of reasoning, which made Aristotle the most venerated philosopher of the Early Middle Ages and the Philosopher to one and all.

Everyone appreciated Aristotle, which helps explain the preservation of his work for sixteen centuries and its circuitous route back to Europe. Aristotle had written in Greek, of course, which Syrian scholars translated into Syriac. Translated later into Arabic, his works were brought into Muslim Spain where they were discovered, rendered into Latin, and made available to all of Europe. The discovery of this treasure trove of knowledge revealed, among other things, that the philosopher developed his knowledge by investigating and classifying physical things, not by relying entirely on reason. The church was opposed to such

knowledge, yet this man, more revered than some of the saints, had broadened his experience by studying the things of this world. The impact was about as great as if we learned that Einstein made his discoveries by consulting a witch doctor. What was the church to do?

The predictable first reaction was to ban something already too well known for a ban to work, so authorities retreated to "authorized" versions that deleted everything contradicting church doctrine. But the scholars who idolized Aristotle the logician could not be denied and everything became available and avidly studied. Incredibly, the most revered thinker of the Middle Ages had, among many other things, studied anatomy by dissecting animals and classified plants according to their structure. Thus another problem confronted the church, demanding a reasonable solution if the institution was to maintain its authority.

THE UNIVERSITIES

The civilizations of Greece, Rome, Byzantium, and Islam all had centers of learning that predated European universities. The rise of the universities, however, was especially significant in the development of Western civilization. Their origin is obscure, for we have little knowledge of them

PSEUDOSCIENCE

Suppose that you could turn common metals into gold. Suppose, also, that you discovered a panacea, a single cure for all diseases and a way to prolong life indefinitely. The name for these vain pursuits is alchemy. Emerging in both China and Egypt in the third century BC, alchemy sought the secret substance called a "philosopher's stone" that converted base metals into gold and produced a magic elixir that preserved and prolonged life. This pseudoscience merged in Mesopotamia with astrology which fused metals with planetary bodies; the sun was gold, the moon silver, Venus copper, Mars iron and so on. Descending inevitably into further superstition and chicanery, alchemism was revived in the eighth century in Alexandria by the Arabs and transmitted to Europe during the Middle Ages, where it initially received a hearty welcome. Alchemists contributed mystical theories and such practical recipes as how to distill wine, make gunpowder, and construct a telescope. Pragmatic alchemist Paracelsus (1493–1531) turned from pursuing gold to preparing medicinals. Some unfortunates who failed to manufacture gold for sponsoring sovereigns were executed in a variety of unpleasant ways. The mostly incidental chemical facts that accrued over the centuries eventually became the basis for modern chemistry.

until their formal charters were issued. In Christian Europe (as distinguished from Muslim Spain) the University of Salerno, specializing in medicine, dated from the eleventh century, but, being situated in southern Italy, it had little influence on the general dawn of culture. The University of Bologna, with its eminent law school, received a formal grant of rights in 1158. The University of Paris was granted a royal charter in 1200 but began much earlier. Its papal license of 1231 reopened a university that had been closed for two years because of a riot between students and city authorities. (Few things are new under the sun!) Oxford had been formed in the twelfth century when some teachers and students seceded from Paris, and Cambridge was founded by a dissident group from Oxford. Growth was so rapid that, by the end of the Middle Ages, some eighty universities were scattered throughout Europe.

Universitas

Universitas is Latin for a corporation such as a trade guild. A university came into being when teachers and students joined together as a legal body. Protected by a charter granted, usually, by the pope or a king, universities were generally freed from local jurisdiction, though they could not avoid "town and gown" conflicts that seem endemic to university communities. Their operation paralleled that of craft guilds, with guild masters (professors) awarding qualifying certificates (degrees) to apprentices (students), who were working to become masters in the teaching corporation (university). Graduation of the apprentices marked their "commencement" as certified teachers.

Flourishing in the largest medieval city (population 300,000), and offering instruction in all recognized fields of knowledge, the University of Paris was the leading institution of the time, with faculties of medicine, law, theology, and liberal arts. As a prerequisite for professional courses, the liberal arts curriculum followed the seven liberal arts pattern of monastic schools: the **trivium** (grammar, rhetoric, logic) and the **quadrivium** (arithmetic, geometry, astronomy, and music, plus the works of Aristotle). In today's terms, trivium subjects were humanistic and those of the quadrivium mathematical.

Studies began with the trivium (including philosophy, literature, and history) but without prescribed hours or units of credit. Comprehensive oral examinations measured achievement with successful candidates awarded the bachelor of arts (B.A.) degree, the prerequisite for studying the quadrivium. Passing the second set of examinations certified the graduate to teach the liberal arts as a master of arts (M.A.). Doctors of law, medicine, or theology were teaching degrees, with the doctor of philosophy (Ph.D.) added later for advanced study in the liberal arts. Usually based on four years of study beyond the M.A., doctorates were awarded to candidates who passed more rigorous examinations and successfully defended a "thesis"

(proposition) before a faculty board. The comparative few who survived this ordeal were granted both a doctorate in the appropriate profession and the opportunity to host a banquet for the examiners.

Although Plato's Academy had admitted women and some noted Hellenistic scholars were women, medieval universities were operated by and for men. The assumption that women needed no formal education continued the subordination of women as practiced in the Graeco-Roman world. Woman's inferior position in Christian Europe was, if anything, even more pronounced. The Old Testament expressed the Hebraic view that a wife was a lesser being who was her husband's property. The New Testament offered little improvement and the church fathers were unanimous in their contempt for women, most notably Paul, Jerome, Tertullian, and Augustine. The myth of Eve having originated in Adam's rib was universally believed in an age that accepted biblical stories and myths as facts. The rediscovery of Aristotle's works gave additional ammunition to the church's repression of women, for the still-revered philosopher had called women simply a necessary reproductive adjunct to the superior sex. For medieval universities the end result was the incalculable loss of the brain power of half the human race.

Nonexistent in the Early Middle Ages, scholars were a new class, notable for their enthusiasm in the pursuit of all sorts of knowledge and experience. Their motto may well have been Abelard's famous teaching "for by doubting we come to inquiry, by inquiry we discover the truth." Some of these zealous scholars were increasingly restless in a culture dominated by an authority that allowed no questioning of itself. Here, as in most areas of life in the High Middle Ages, we find a surge of energy, a quickening of the spirit.

SUMMARY

We have seen that medieval men and women sheltered themselves within the narrow walls of the authoritarian church, the rigid structure of feudalism, and manorialism's closed society. Literal and figurative walls provided a measure of physical and psychological safety but left little room for growth. Urban development and the increasing intellectual ferment in the universities helped breach the barriers in the first explorations for knowledge since the end of Graeco-Roman civilization. Virtually overnight the rediscovery of Aristotle raised the intellectual level of Western culture. Most importantly, contacts with more advanced Muslim and Byzantine cultures and the civilizing effects of chivalry and Courts of Love indicated that life on earth could be made immeasurably better.

THE MEDIEVAL SYNTHESIS

The conflicts in the late Middle Ages were between new secular ways of thinking and living and the older religious ways. Where was the art that could bring these together in a new synthesis? Where were the people who could define new relationships between human beings and the universe, human beings and God, the individual and society as a whole? Where were the artists who could suggest new purposes for life now that the old were so sorely challenged?

The new synthesis can be seen in the work of three men, one of them unknown. Thomas Aquinas constructed a new philosophic system that accommodated the divergent positions of the Battle of Universals. The nameless master-builder of Chartres cathedral designed a structure in which form merged with function. In literature, the new balance was represented by Dante Alighieri in *The Divine Comedy*. Let us examine each of these remarkable achievements.

Philosophy: Thomas Aquinas, 1225–74

From the philosophy of Thomas Aquinas (henceforth called Thomism), we focus on his reconciliation of some medieval contradictions. In discussing Thomism one cannot resist borrowing his equilateral triangle as a representation of an individual, a nation, or an empire (fig. 13.1). Aquinas chose this shape deliberately, of course, because it symbolizes the Holy Trinity. For us it suggests both firmness and upward motion—a synthesis of Celto-Germanic energy and Graeco-Roman stability.

Form and Matter
Thomism reconciled Aristotelian thought with that of the church by accepting the central Aristotelian doctrine that matter and form (or idea) cannot exist separately. Matter has only potentiality—the possibility of being itself—until it is entered into by the idea of the thing; it then becomes that thing. Clay, for example, is not brick, nor is there brick without clay; but when clay, which has only potentiality, is joined with the form or idea of brick, then the brick exists.

Thomism goes on to state that lower forms of existence are merely to be used to create higher forms. Everything is moving, growing, turning into something else. All this movement is toward perfection, which is God. God the First Mover does not move things from behind but is the goal toward which all things are moving. Since things must desire that toward which they move, the motive force is love of God. The First Mover, also called the Unmoved Mover, represents the most important of the five Thomistic proofs of the existence of God. If there is movement then a first attracting power must exist and that power is God. (These proofs could not withstand later analysis but they were accepted in their time.)

In the Thomistic version of reality both form and matter are necessary, thus reconciling the conflict in the Battle

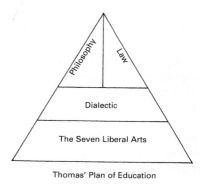

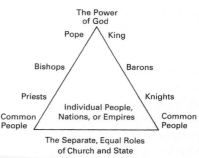

13.1   Thomistic triangles of education and of the separate, equal roles of church and state.

of Universals. The question is whether form (idea) has existence *before* or only *in* a specific thing, and whether it exists *after* the specific has vanished. All three says Thomism. The idea exists (as potentiality) before the thing; it exists in the thing; because of its continuing upward progress it exists after the particular thing. Thus, borrowing heavily from the conceptualist view, the three positions are joined in a harmonious whole.

Knowledge and Doctrine
The doctrine of lower and higher forms in motion toward perfection also helped resolve the conflict between worldly knowledge and the church's position that knowledge was useless, a study of nothingness. As illustrated in the Thomistic triangle of education (fig. 13.1), philosophy and law are the highest human studies. Philosophy is a study of the humanly knowable laws for the discipline of the spirit; law is a study of the rules for the governing of our physical nature. According to the Aristotelian-Thomistic concept of reality, both are necessary and equal. To begin a study of these subjects one must first study all forms and all matter. People attain their highest human perfection through knowledge. Or, as Socrates had said eighteen centuries earlier, virtue is knowledge.

Theology, which has its source in God, is, according to Thomism, another realm of knowledge that is complementary to philosophy. However, it can be understood only by revelation, never by learning. The two, however, are not opposed to each other. A knowledge of philosophy leads to the possibility of revelation, and revelation presupposes a knowledge of philosophy. True knowledge, the union with the divine science, comes only after death. It is the duty of everyone to acquire as much natural knowledge as possible so that each is ready to receive the final revelation of God in the afterlife.

Body and Soul

The pull of life and death, perhaps the greatest question of all, was solved, similarly, by the premise that form and matter exist only when together and in each other. Because natural knowledge, gained through the five senses, was necessary for human perfection, it followed that body and soul exist together and equally. Thus Thomism banished the dualism that had existed since Augustine and the cities of God and Man. Henceforward, both body (matter) and soul (form) were considered necessary for earthly perfection.

Just as cities were swelling beyond their encircling walls, so this great intellectual synthesis opened the way for people to begin to develop themselves. Science—true science—was expanding, too, with scientific research conducted both within and without the universities. Thomism was an effective synthesis for the increasing numbers of intellectuals but what about the common people?

A PEASANT GIRL

We know the names of medieval royalty and can identify some of the lords and clergy but the peasants are invariably anonymous—with one exception. This peasant girl was only nineteen when she died for her country but the short life of Joan of Arc (ca. 1412–1431) has been extensively documented and remains endlessly fascinating. She was illiterate, which was normal for her station, but she was well versed in the teachings of the church as she amply demonstrated in a church trial she could not win. Always poised and self-possessed, she convinced the Dauphin of France (later Charles VII) that hers was a divine mission to rid her nation of the British. A remarkably quick learner of military strategy and fighting techniques, she also displayed a solid knowledge of political and military issues as she led French troops to victory over the English at Orléans. Captured by the Burgundians and sold to the English, who turned her over to the church, she was condemned on trumped up charges of heresy and witchcraft and burned at the stake. Within a generation, however, her martyrdom helped inspire the French under Charles VII to expel the English and end the Hundred Years' War. Joan of Arc represents the peasants of France, who would never again be underestimated.

The Cathedral: "Bible in Stone"

Literally and symbolically the cathedral was central in people's everyday lives. Standing tall at the center of the city, it represented the best of the sacred and secular worlds. Cathedral and civic center, church of Our Lady and theatre, school, court, concert hall, and general meeting place, the Gothic cathedral was a three-dimensional synthesis of church and state and of aspirations both spiritual and worldly.

A Gothic cathedral always thrust strongly upward (see fig. 14.20). Impelled by the dynamic pointed arches, the beholder's gaze moved up its great towers until the spire was reached with its sharp finger pointing toward heaven. Partly because of its architectural sculpture, the cathedral has been called a "Bible in stone." Much of its art is indeed didactic, but a Gothic cathedral is more than the sum of its parts. It is power and glory and spirituality personified. The richly colored light filtered through the stained glass windows, the gliding sound of Gregorian chant, the musky aroma of incense, the pageantry of the celebration of the Mass—all these added beauty, majesty, and joy to people's lives. Building one of these great structures provided a creative outlet for many people for this was a communal effort shared by nobility, burghers, and the common people. In a very real sense the cathedral belonged equally to all who built it and all who used it.

Dante's *Divine Comedy*: An Intellectual Vision

The most significant aspect of the *Divine Comedy* or *Commedia* was the removal of age-old restrictions. The final goal was still the heavenly kingdom but, according to Thomism and Dante, everyone was now relatively free to achieve the blissful afterlife in his or her own way. Morality plays such as *Everyman* no longer applied because God was not an accountant; rather, in Dante's vision, he was perfect wisdom and love. The purpose and goal of humankind, like Aristotle's enteleche, were union with God. For Dante the heavenly state was the ultimate home of humankind which must be ever earned anew because of Adam's fall from grace. While they are alive people cannot fully know the love of God but salvation can be achieved through God's grace. Faith and good works alone will not suffice.

Although people cannot achieve union with God solely by their own efforts, they may prepare for it by gaining the maturity that accompanies the earthly wisdom stressed by Thomism. Paradoxically, Dante calls this mature condition innocence: the happy state of Adam and Eve before the Fall. Thus Dante places the Garden of Eden at the top of the mountain of Purgatory, from which God elevates men and women to Paradise.

Hell

What were the choices? The way of God is discipline and order, that of Satan is chaos. God himself is perfect freedom, and the route toward him is marked by an increase in freedom. Sin is the opposite, the loss of free will, which can be illustrated with the simple example of an addiction such as smoking.

At first, with cigarettes, the individual is ignorant, with no firsthand knowledge of the pleasures or problems of smoking. Even after a person smokes a cigarette the act itself is not sinful, nor are subsequent smoking experiences. There comes a time, however, when the smoker has lost the power to say no. One aspect of the freedom of choice has been sacrificed and this, for Dante, is sin. Free will is the ability to say yes, no, or anything in between. Sin is loss of that ability; in Dante's Hell the degree of sin is gauged by the deviation from free will. Those who can no longer choose freely are destined for Hell. Over the mouth of Hell Dante envisions the words "Abandon hope all ye who enter," which express the irreversible state of the condemned. The punishments inflicted on the souls in Hell symbolize what they have made themselves to be. Step by descending step we traverse the cone of Hell, in each lower level viewing the souls ever deeper in sin. Step by descending step we see these souls increasingly enslaved until, at the bottom of the pit, we find Satan immobilized by his sins, forever frozen in ice.

Purgatory

Emerging with Dante at the base of the mountain of Purgatory, we find a very different scene. These souls have strayed from the path of wisdom but they still have hope. Expiating their sins is laborious but they are joyful as they anticipate wisdom, maturity, and the heavenly Paradise. Each soul determines when it is sufficiently purged of sin to ascend to a higher cornice on the mountain. This is explicitly stated when Dante and his guide Virgil encounter the Latin poet Statius, who has just moved up a niche. The mountain is shaken by the momentous occasion while all the souls shout "Gloria in excelsis."

Paradise

Finally in Paradise, and guided by Beatrice, Dante receives instruction in theology, the science of God. Here he views the perfect order of the universe, both of humans and of angels. He sees the church and its officers as the guardians of the human spirit and observes the kings' importance to God, for they maintain temporal order on earth. Here, too, he finds freedom, as opposed to the ever-increasing levels of bondage he witnessed in Hell. Though the souls in Paradise are symbolically assigned to different spheres as a result of their different capacities for joy and love, they can pass through all the spheres and approach the throne of God. In the final cantos of the *Paradise* Dante comes as close as any human being can to expressing, as living experience, the mystic union of the soul with God.

Dante Today

What is Dante saying to twentieth-century readers, who may be Catholics, Protestants, Muslims, Buddhists, or **atheists**, or whatever? Like all great literature, the *Commedia* has a universal appeal that speaks to every age. Dante says that we all have free will and that we can choose order and discipline over disorder and chaos. He envisions a life at once balanced and aspiring—one that seeks broad worldly knowledge including a thorough understanding of science. The *Commedia* unites body and soul in a life that men and women must choose for themselves in their contemporary world. In the *Commedia* and its architectural counterpart, the Gothic cathedral, we see the artist proposing answers to the pressing questions of humankind.

Freedom

In the period of balance of the thirteenth and fourteenth centuries what were the extent and nature of freedom? As with all balanced periods this was a typically brief era in which the generally accepted view of reality was mirrored by the values of the High Middle Ages. During these two centuries we see a kind of freedom that might prompt many world-weary people of our time to look back with longing.

The fundamental characteristic of the period was the sense of unity that set rules for human behavior but that provided room for individual values. Rather than a paradox or a contradiction, individual endeavor within a communal solidarity is a special kind of freedom. Consider, for example, the Gothic cathedral, whose basic design was very formalized. It had to be oriented with its altar toward the East so that worshipers could move toward Jerusalem. Its shape had to be cruciform, and its representations included the saints, Jesus, Mary, and Joseph, the Nativity, the Resurrection, and Day of Judgment. Yet consider the freedom of the individual in helping to build a Gothic church, of which no two are even remotely alike. If the stonecutter wanted to carve fat little angels or lively animals he had seen or imagined, that was his decision. One sees this kind of work high on capitals or on the underside of seats in the choir stalls. Here a woodcarver thought it would be fun to carve a pig playing a fiddle. No sooner said than done! Or a carver felt compelled to caricature a local burgher and proceeded to do so. Gothic churches are replete with a variety of images and fantasies.

This kind of freedom within limits existed in all spheres of activity. The craftsman, for example, necessarily belonged to his guild, an association that regulated the quality of his work and the price he could charge. Beyond that, the guild served as an insurance and burial society, a social group, and a dramatic society that participated in the mystery and miracle plays that educated, inspired, and amused the local townsfolk. The guildhall was not only a business center but a social hall where wedding festivities, banquets, and balls were enjoyed by all.

The guild regulated membership and supervised the levels of apprentice, journeyman, and master craftsman, but within these standards the cobbler, say, was absolutely free. When business was slow he could take his family, apprentices, and journeymen for an outing in the country. Every pair of shoes he made was an individual creation in which he took justifiable pride. Whether or not his apprentices did the preliminary work, the master craftsman was totally responsible for the finished product, on which he staked his reputation. In the late twentieth century it is difficult to imagine the satisfaction of someone who exercised total control from inception to production of the finished product.

The story of "Our Lady's Juggler" (see pp. 219–21) exemplifies a similar sort of freedom within an authoritarian religion. The creed was strict and the rules absolute but, given human ingenuity, there was still room for creativity. Dante's concept of freedom as participation in the wisdom, order, and love of God was paramount in the value system of the era. However mistaken some choices might be, the Christian scheme of things viewed any straying from grace as only human. Errors must be purged, of course, but only a deliberate desire to do evil led to eternal damnation.

The idea of freedom in this period of balance was reinforced by the stability, however brief, of the culture. Freedom, individuality, and creativity were available to all who respected the rules of the society. But the balance, like all others we have seen, was too delicate to last. The secular forces that boiled up during the Middle Ages were to triumph, breaking down the still recent designs made by Dante, Thomas Aquinas, and the master builders of the mighty cathedrals. The cathedrals remained, of course, but the fundamental beliefs of medieval culture were to change drastically in a new period of ferment called the Renaissance.

The Church in Turmoil

The supreme irony of the High Middle Ages was the agony of the inner structure of the Church of Rome. Even while cathedrals were rising and Thomism was becoming accepted, the all-powerful and supposedly infallible institution proved, during a century of internal strife and corruption, to be all too fallible. The power struggle between Rome and royalty peaked in the bitter quarrel between Philip IV of France (reigned 1285–1314) and Pope Boniface VIII (reigned 1294–1303), whom Dante had called the "black beast." The corrupt Boniface prevailed but, after his death, a vengeful Philip engineered the election of a subservient pope (Clement V; reigned 1305–14) and transferred the papacy to Avignon in the south of France. Thus began the "Babylonian Captivity" of 1305–78 when French kings controlled the Church of Rome. Newly located in a strange land, the papal court rapidly became notorious for its corruption and decadence. Writing anonymously because he "did not want to be burned," court poet Petrarch described the papacy at a low ebb:

> The shame of mankind, a sink of vice, a sewer where is gathered all the filth of the world. There God is held in contempt, money alone is worshiped and the laws of God and man are trampled underfoot. Everything there breathes a lie: the air, the earth, the houses and above all the bedrooms.

The Babylonian Captivity ended in 1378 with a bad situation made worse by the election, in Rome, of Urban VII. After the new pope managed to alienate just about everyone, the cardinals chose Robert of Geneva (Anti-pope Clement VII), who fled from Urban VII to establish a thoroughly dissolute court in Avignon. This was the Great Schism of 1378–1417 with rival popes in Rome, Avignon, and even Pisa. It was the Pisan anti-pope John XXIII about whom the eighteenth-century English historian Edward Gibbon wrote: "The most scandalous charges were suppressed: The Vicar of Christ was only accused of piracy, murder, rape, sodomy, and incest."[3]

Caused, in part, by the French captivity and multiple popes, the view of what constituted the real world began to shift from God as the ultimate reality to the belief that human earthly existence had its own validity. This did not mean that there was any widespread unrest or denial of Christianity; rather, growing resentment over corruption in the church hierarchy led people to question whether this powerful bureaucracy provided the best way to the Kingdom of Heaven. The Great Schism certainly forced many to wonder which of the two or three popes was the true keeper of the keys of the kingdom.

STUDY QUESTIONS

1. Imagine growing up on a medieval manor and then moving to the city. What opportunities might come your way? What new temptations? What new problems? Which aspects of rural life might you miss?
2. Given the European point of view, what were the positive aspects of the Crusades? Negative aspects? Now try answering these two questions from the Muslim point of view.

---

3. It was not until 1958 that a pope again chose, quite deliberately, the name of John. Pope John XXIII became one of the greatest popes in the history of the Church of Rome.

LITERARY SELECTION 12

Songs of the Wandering Scholars

The pull of life was strong when new ideas were assaulting medieval walls. And students (even the many who were to become learned clergymen) were much the same then as they are now.

Gaudeamus Igitur

Let us live, then, and be glad
    While young life's before us!
After youthful pastime had,
After old age, hard and sad,
    Earth will slumber o'er us.

Where are they who in this world
    Ere we kept, were keeping?
Go ye to the gods above;
Go to hell; inquire thereof;
    They are not; they are sleeping.   10

Brief is life, and brevity
    Briefly shall be ended;
Death comes like a whirlwind strong,
Bears us with his blast along;
    None shall be defended.

Live this university,
    Men that learning nourish;
Live each member of the same,
Long live all that bear its name,
    Let them ever flourish!   20

Live the commonwealth also,
    And the men that guide it!
Live our town in strength and health,
Founders, patrons, by whose wealth
    We are here provided!

Live all gods! A health to you,
    Melting maids and beauteous;
Live the wives and women too,
Gentle, loving, tender, true,
    Good, industrious, duteous!   30

Perish cares that pule and pine!
    Perish envious blamers!
Die the Devil, thine and mine!
Die the starch-neck Philistine!
    Scoffers and defamers!

Lauriger Horatius

Horace with your laurel crowned,
Truly have you spoken:
Time, a-rush with leap and bound,
Devours and leaves us broken.

Where are now the flagons, full
Of sweet wine, honey-clear?
Where the smiles and shoves and frowns
Of blushing maiden dear?

Swift the young grape grows and swells;
So do comely lasses!
Lo, on the poet's head, the snows
Of the Time that passes!

What's the good of lasting fame,
If people think it sinful
Here and now to kiss a dame
And drink a jolly skinful!

STUDY QUESTIONS

1. Prominent in these songs is the theme of *carpe diem* ("seize the day,"—eat, drink, and be merry for tomorrow we may die). Is this theme present in any of today's songs?
2. These students were certainly aware of the church's teaching about virtue and sin. How, then, do you account for their attitudes about sex, drinking, gambling, stealing, and other forbidden activities?

LITERARY SELECTION 13

Our Lady's Juggler

This delightful story reveals some of the attraction and charm of the cult of the Virgin, especially for the common people for whom chivalry and philosophy were meaningless.

In the days of King Louis there lived a poor juggler by the name of Barnabas, a native of Compiègne, who wandered from city to city performing tricks of skill and prowess.

On fair days he would lay down in the public square a worn and aged carpet, and after having attracted a group of children and idlers by certain amusing remarks which he had learned from an old juggler, and which he invariably repeated in the same fashion without altering a word, he would assume the strangest postures and balance a pewter plate on the tip of his nose. At first the crowd regarded him with indifference, but when, with his hands and head on the ground he threw into the air and caught with his feet six copper balls that glittered in the sunlight, or when, throwing himself back until his neck touched his heels, he assumed the form of a perfect wheel and in that position juggled with twelve knives, he elicited a murmur of admiration from his audience, and small coins rained on his carpet.   10

Still, Barnabas of Compiègne, like most of those who exist by their accomplishments, had a hard time making a living. Earning his bread by the sweat of his brow, he bore rather more than his share of those miseries we are all heir to through the fault of our Father Adam.   20

He had never thought much about the origin of

wealth nor about the inequality of human conditions. He firmly believed that if this world was evil the next could not but be good, and this faith upheld him. He was not like the clever fellows who sell their souls to the devil; he never took the name of God in vain; he lived the life of an honest man, and though he had no wife of his own, he did not covet his neighbor's, for woman is the enemy of strong men, as we learn by the story of Samson which is written in the Scriptures.

Verily, his mind was not turned in the direction of carnal desire, and it caused him far greater pain to renounce drinking than to forgo the pleasure of women. For, though he was not a drunkard, he enjoyed drinking when the weather was warm. He was a good man, fearing God, and devout in his adoration of the Holy Virgin. When he went into a church he never failed to kneel before the image of the Mother of God and to address her with his prayer:

"My Lady, watch over my life until it shall please God that I die, and when I am dead, see that I have the joys of Paradise."

One evening, after a day of rain, as he walked sad and bent with his juggling balls under his arm and his knives wrapped up in his old carpet seeking some barn where he might go supperless to bed, he saw a monk going in his direction, and respectfully saluted him. As they were both walking at the same pace, they fell into conversation.

"Friend," said the monk, "how does it happen that you are dressed all in green? Are you perchance going to play the part of the fool in some mystery?"[4]

"No, indeed, father," said Barnabas. "My name is Barnabas, and my business is that of juggler. It would be the finest calling in the world if I could eat every day."

"Friend Barnabas," answered the monk, "be careful what you say. There is no finer calling than the monastic. The priest celebrates the praise of God, the Virgin, and the saints; the life of a monk is a perpetual hymn to the Lord."

And Barnabas replied: "Father, I confess I spoke like an ignorant man. My estate cannot be compared to yours, and though there may be some merit in dancing and balancing a stick with a denier[5] on top of it on the end of your nose, it is in no wise comparable to your merit. Father, I wish I might, like you, sing the Office every day, especially the Office of the Very Holy Virgin, to whom I am specially and piously devoted. I would willingly give up the art by which I am known from Soissons to Beauvais, in more than six hundred cities and villages, in order to enter the monastic life."

The monk was touched by the simplicity of the juggler, and as he was not lacking in discernment, he recognized in Barnabas one of those well-disposed men of whom Our Lord has said, "Let peace be with them on earth." And he made answer therefore:

"Friend Barnabas, come with me and I will see that you enter the monastery of which I am the Prior. He who led Mary through the Egyptian desert put me across your path in order that I might lead you to salvation."

Thus did Barnabas become a monk. In the monastery which he entered, the monks celebrated most

magnificently the Cult of the Holy Virgin, each of them bringing to her service all the knowledge and skill which God had given him.

Perceiving so great a competition in praise and so fine a harvest of good works, Barnabas fell to lamenting his ignorance and simplicity.

"Alas!" he sighed as he walked by himself one day in the little garden shaded by the monastery wall, "I am so unhappy because I cannot, like my brothers, give worthy praise to the Holy Mother of God to whom I have consecrated all the love in my heart. Alas, I am a stupid fellow, without art, and for your service, Madame, I have no edifying sermons, no fine treatises nicely prepared according to the rules, no beautiful paintings, no cunningly carved statues, and no verses counted off by feet and marching in measure! Alas, I have nothing."

Thus did he lament and abandon himself to his misery.

One evening when the monks were talking together by way of diversion, he heard one of them tell of a monk who could not recite anything but the *Ave Maria*. He was scorned for his ignorance, but after he died there sprang from his mouth five roses, in honor of the five letters in the name Maria. Thus was his holiness made manifest.

In listening to this story, Barnabas was conscious once more of the Virgin's beneficence, but he was not consoled by the example of the happy miracle, for his heart was full of zeal and he wanted to celebrate the glory of his Lady in Heaven.

He sought for a way in which to do this, but in vain, and each day brought him greater sorrow, until one morning he sprang joyously from his cot and ran to the chapel, where he remained alone for more than an hour. He returned thither again after dinner, and from that day onward he would go into the chapel every day the moment it was deserted, passing the greater part of the time which the other monks dedicated to the pursuit of the liberal arts and the sciences. He was no longer sad and he sighed no more. But such singular conduct aroused the curiosity of the other monks, and they asked themselves why Brother Barnabas retired alone so often, and the Prior, whose business it was to know everything that his monks were doing, determined to observe Barnabas. One day, therefore, when Barnabas was alone in the chapel, the Prior entered in company with two of the oldest brothers, in order to watch, through the bars of the door, what was going on within.

They saw Barnabas before the image of the Holy Virgin, his head on the floor and his feet in the air, juggling with six copper balls and twelve knives. In honor of the Holy Virgin he was performing the tricks which had in former days brought him the greatest fame. Not understanding that he was thus putting his best talents at the service of the Holy Virgin, the aged brothers cried out against such sacrilege. The Prior knew that Barnabas had a simple soul, but he believed that the man had lost his wits. All three set about to remove Barnabas from

---

4. Mystery—one of the religious dramas of the time.
5. Denier—a small coin.

the chapel, when they saw the Virgin slowly descend from the altar and, with a fold of her blue mantle, wipe the sweat that streamed over the juggler's forehead.

Then the Prior, bowing his head down to the marble floor, repeated these words:

"Blessed are the pure in heart, for they shall see God."   150

"Amen," echoed the brothers, bowing down to the floor.

LITERARY SELECTION 14

The Art of Courtly Love

Andreas Cappelanus (fl. 1174–1186)

Countess Marie of Champagne established a Court of Love at Troyes, where Andreas was probably chaplain to the court, or so he claimed. Andreas was an accomplished writer whose treatise on love provides us with a vivid and probably accurate picture of courtly life. Specifically, Andreas intended his manual as a portrayal of the Poitiers court of Marie's mother, Queen Eleanor of Aquitaine, as it was between 1170 and 1174.

Undoubtedly commissioned by Countess Marie, the manual is a codification of the etiquette of love. Andreas combines quotations from classic Latin writers (mainly Ovid) and the spirit of lyric love poetry by troubadours such as Bernart de Ventadorn (see p. 252) with his own observation of actual practices, producing a unique work known throughout Europe in a variety of translations.

Book I: Introduction to the Treatise on Love

We must first consider what love is, whence it gets its name, what the effect of love is, between what persons love may exist, how it may be acquired, retained, increased, decreased, and ended, what are the signs that one's love is returned, and what one of the lovers ought to do if the other is unfaithful.

Chapter 1. What Love Is

Love is a certain inborn suffering derived from the sight of and excessive meditation upon the beauty of the opposite sex, which causes each one to wish above all things the embraces of the other and by common desire to carry out all of love's precepts in the other's embrace.

That love is suffering is easy to see, for before the love becomes equally balanced on both sides there is no torment greater, since the lover is always in fear that his love may not gain its desire and that he is wasting his efforts. He fears, too, that rumors of it may get abroad, and he fears everything that might harm it in any way, for before things are perfected a slight disturbance often spoils them. If he is a poor man, he also fears that the woman may scorn his poverty; if he is ugly, he fears that she may despise his lack of beauty or may give her love to a more handsome man; if he is rich, he fears that his parsimony in the past may stand in his way. To tell the truth, no one can number the fears of one single lover.[6] This kind of love, then, is a suffering which is felt by only   10

one of the persons and may be called "single love." But even after both are in love the fears that arise are just as great, for each of the lovers fears that what he has acquired with so much effort may be lost through the effort of someone else, which is certainly much worse for a man than if, having no hope, he sees that his efforts are accomplishing nothing, for it is worse to lose the things you are seeking than to be deprived of a gain you merely hope for. The lover fears, too, that he may offend his loved one in some way; indeed he fears so many things that it would be difficult to tell them.   20

That this suffering is inborn I shall show you clearly, because if you look at the truth and distinguish carefully you will see that it does not arise out of any action; only from the reflection of the mind upon what it sees does this suffering come. For when a man sees some woman fit for love and shaped according to his taste, he begins at once to lust after her in his heart; then the more he thinks about her the more he burns with love, until he comes to a fuller meditation. Presently he begins to think about the fashioning of the woman and to differentiate her limbs, to think about what she does, and to pry into the secrets of her body, and he desires to put each part of it to the fullest use.[7] Then after he has come to this complete meditation, love cannot hold the reins; but he proceeds at once to action; straightway he strives to get a helper and to find an intermediary. He begins to plan how he may find favor with her, and he begins to seek a place and a time opportune for talking; he looks upon a brief hour as a very long year, because he cannot do anything fast enough to suit his eager mind. It is well known that many things happen to him in this manner. This inborn suffering comes, therefore, from seeing and meditating. Not every kind of meditation can be the cause of love, an excessive one is required; for a restrained thought does not, as a rule, return to the mind, and so love cannot arise from it.   30   40   50

Book II: Chapter 8

In Chapter 8 (Book II), Andreas presents the Rules of Love as the climax of a properly romantic mission. It seems that a knight of Britain cannot win the love of "a certain British lady" until he has brought her the hawk sitting on a golden perch in King Arthur's court. And, he is told,

you can't get this hawk that you are seeking unless you prove, by a combat in Arthur's palace, that you enjoy the love of a more beautiful lady than any man at Arthur's court has; you can't even enter the palace until you show the guards the hawk's gauntlet, and you can't get this gauntlet except by overcoming two mighty knights in a double combat.

After defeating the pugnacious keeper of a golden bridge, the Briton then vanquishes a giant and rides on to Camelot where he manfully accomplishes the assigned tasks. While seizing the hawk he discovers a written parchment and is told

---

6. Ovid, *Art of Love*, II, 517 ff.
7. Compare Ovid, *Metamorphoses*, VI, 490–93.

that "this is the parchment on which are written the rules of love which the King of Love . . . pronounced for lovers. You should take it with you and make these rules known to lovers."

These are the rules.

  I.   Marriage is no real excuse for not loving.
  II.   He who is not jealous cannot love.
  III. No one can be bound by a double love.
  IV.   It is well known that love is always increasing or decreasing.
  V.   That which a lover takes against the will of his beloved has no relish.
  VI.   Boys do not love until they arrive at the age of maturity.
  VII. When one lover dies, a widowhood of two years is required of the survivor.
  VIII. No one should be deprived of love without the very best of reasons.
  IX.   No one can love unless he is impelled by the persuasion of love.
  X.   Love is always a stranger in the home of avarice.
  XI.   It is not proper to love any woman whom one would be ashamed to seek to marry.
  XII. A true lover does not desire to embrace in love anyone except his beloved.
  XIII. When made public love rarely endures.
  XIV. The easy attainment of love makes it of little value; difficulty of attainment makes it prized.
  XV.   Every lover regularly turns pale in the presence of his beloved.
  XVI. When a lover suddenly catches sight of his beloved his heart palpitates.
  XVII. A new love puts to flight an old one.[8]
  XVIII. Good character alone makes any man worthy of love.
  XIX. If love diminishes, it quickly fails and rarely revives.
  XX.   A man in love is always apprehensive.
  XXI. Real jealousy always increases the feeling of love.
  XXII. Jealousy, and therefore love, are increased when one suspects his beloved.
  XXIII. He whom the thought of love vexes eats and sleeps very little.
  XXIV. Every act of a lover ends in the thought of his beloved.
  XXV. A true lover considers nothing good except what he thinks will please his beloved.
  XXVI. Love can deny nothing to love.
  XXVII. A lover can never have enough of the solaces of his beloved.
  XXVIII. A slight presumption causes a lover to suspect his beloved.
  XXIX. A man who is vexed by too much passion usually does not love.
  XXX. A true lover is constantly and without intermission possessed by the thought of his beloved.
  XXXI. Nothing forbids one woman being loved by two men or one man by two women.

8. Compare Cicero, *Tusculan Disputations*, IV.

These rules, as I have said, the Briton brought back with him on behalf of the King of Love to the lady for whose sake he endured so many perils when he brought her back the hawk. When she was convinced of the complete faithfulness of this knight and understood better how boldly he had striven, she rewarded him with her love. Then she called together a court of a great many ladies and knights and laid before them these rules of Love, and bade every lover keep them faithfully under threat of punishment by the King of Love. These laws the whole court received in their entirety and promised forever to obey in order to avoid punishment by Love. Every person who had been summoned and had come to the court took home a written copy of the rules and gave them out to all lovers in all parts of the world.

STUDY QUESTION

As the selection indicates, many characteristics of romantic love were first articulated during the Middle Ages. Considering the definition and rules in the text, which concepts are still basic to romantic love?

LITERARY SELECTION 15

A Medieval Woman's Mirror of Honor: The Treasury of the City of Ladies

Christine de Pisan (ca. 1364–ca. 1431)

Written specifically for women, this book was intended to help women gain a sense of self-worth, to prepare them to make their own way in the world, whatever problems they might encounter. As with other medieval writers, de Pisan composes an allegory using the three virtues of Reason, Rectitude, and Justice to guide her. As compared with the sacred virtues of Faith, Hope, and Charity, these are secular qualities that were more appropriate for her world.

Christine de Pisan was not only a successful writer but a famous one. William Caxton, the first English printer, translated and published one of her works, noting that she was "the mistress of intelligence." A contemporary male writer claimed that she was the equal of Cicero for eloquence and Cato for wisdom. De Pisan herself remarked, perhaps ironically, that "women are enhanced by knowledge so it is indeed surprising that some men should oppose it." Certainly her efforts on behalf of women were long overdue, for numerous men had written tracts intended to prepare women for religious or domestic duties or as guides to a suitable marriage, that is, to condition them for a secondary role in a world controlled by men. Nothing had ever been written to help single, married, or widowed women deal with adult situations and problems encompassing every aspect of the everyday world.

Books I and II are addressed mainly to court women and those in religious orders. Book III is directed to all women regardless of class. Her choice of problems to discuss was obviously personal, for the author had to undergo the very experiences she so dispassionately describes. The translation is by Charity Cannon Willard.

Book III.4 Which speaks of widows young and old [ca. 1405]

In order for this work to be more completely profitable to women of all classes, we will speak now to *widows* among the more common people, having already discussed the case of widowed princesses.

Dear friends, we pity each of you in the state of widowhood because death has deprived you of your husbands, whoever they may have been. Moreover, much anguish and many trying problems afflict you, affecting the rich in one manner and those not rich in another. The rich are troubled because unscrupulous people commonly try to despoil them of their inheritance. The poor, or at least, those not at all rich, are distressed because they find no pity from anyone for their problems. Along with the grief of having lost your mate, which is quite enough, you must also suffer three trials in particular, which assault you whether rich or poor.

First is that, undoubtedly, you will find harshness and lack of consideration or sympathy everywhere. Those who honored you during the lifetime of your husbands, who may well have been officials or men of importance, now will pay little attention to you and barely even bother to be friendly. The second distress facing you is the variety of lawsuits and demands of certain people regarding debts, claims on your property, and income. Third is the evil talk of people who are all too willing to attack you, so that you hardly know what you can do that will not be criticized. In order to arm you with the sensible advice to protect yourself against these, as well as other overpowering plagues, we wish to suggest some things you may find useful.

Against the coldness you undoubtedly will find in everyone—the first of the three tribulations of widowhood—there are three possible remedies. Turn toward God, who was willing to suffer so much for human creatures. Reflecting on this will teach you patience, a quality you will need greatly. It will bring you to the point where you will place little value on the rewards and honors of this world. First of all, you will learn how undependable all earthly things are.

The second remedy is to turn your heart to gentleness and kindness in word and courtesy to everyone. You will overcome the hardhearted and bend them to your will by gentle prayers and humble requests.

Third, in spite of what we have just said about quiet humility in words, apparel, and countenance, nevertheless you must learn the judgment and behavior necessary to protect yourself against those all too willing to get the better of you. You must avoid their company, having nothing to do with them if you can help it. Rather, stay quietly in your own house, not involving yourself in an argument with a neighbor, not even with a servingman or maid. By always speaking quietly while protecting your own interests, as well as by mingling little with miscellaneous people if you don't need to, you will avoid anyone taking advantage of you or ruining you.

Concerning the lawsuits that may stalk you, learn well how to avoid all sorts. They damage a widow in many ways. First of all, if she is not informed, but on the contrary is ignorant in legal affairs, then it will be necessary for her to place herself in the power of someone else to solicit on behalf of her needs. Those others generally lack diligence in the affairs of women, willingly deceiving them and charging them eight crown for six. Another problem is that women cannot always *come and go at all hours*, as a man would do, and therefore, if it is not too damaging for her, it may be better to let go some part of what is her due rather than involve herself in contention. She should consider circumspectly any reasonable demands made against her; or if she finds herself obliged to be the plaintiff, she should pursue her rights courteously and should attempt alternatives for achieving her ends. If assailed by debts, she must inform herself of what rights her creditors have and make an appropriate plan of action. Even presupposing there is no official "owing" letter or witness, if her conscience tells her that something is owing, she must not keep anything that really belongs to another. That would burden her husband's soul as well as her own, and God indeed might send her so many additional, expensive misfortunes that her original losses would be doubled.

But if she protects herself wisely from deceitful people who make demands without cause, she is behaving as she should. If, in spite of all this, she is obliged to go to court, she should understand three things necessary for all to take action. One is to act on the advice of wise specialists in customary law and clerks who are well versed in legal sciences and the law. Next is to prepare the case for trial with great care and diligence. Third is to have enough money to afford all this. Certainly if one of these things is lacking, no matter how worthy the cause, there is every danger the case will be lost.

Therefore, a widow in such a situation necessarily must look for older specialists in customary law, those most experienced in various sorts of cases, rather than depending on younger men. She should explain her case to them, showing them her letters and her titles, listening carefully to what they say without concealing anything which pertains to the case, whether in her favor or against her. Counsel can utilize in her behalf only what she tells him. According to his advice, either she must plead steadfastly or accede to her adversaries. If ever she goes to court, she must plead diligently and pay well. Her case will so benefit.

If it is necessary for her to do these things, and if she wishes to avoid further trouble and bring her case to a successful conclusion, she must take on the heart of a *man*. She must be constant, strong, and wise in pursuing her advantage, not crouching in tears, defenseless, like some simple woman or like a poor dog who retreats into a corner while all the other dogs jump on him. If you do that, dear woman, you will find most people so lacking in pity that they would take the bread from your hand because they consider you either ignorant or simple-minded, nor would you find additional pity elsewhere because they took it. So, do not work on your own or depend on your own judgment, but hire always the best advice, particularly on important matters you do not understand.   120

Thus, your affairs should be well managed among those of you widows who have reached a certain age and do not intend to remarry. Young widows must be guided by their relatives or friends until they have married again, conducting themselves particularly gently and simply so as not to acquire a doubtful reputation that might cause them to lose their prospects and their advantage.   130

The remedy against the third of the three misfortunes pursuing any widow—being at mercy of evil tongues—is that she must be careful in every way possible not to give anyone reason to talk against her because of appearance, bearing, or clothing. All these should be simple and seemly, and the woman's manners quiet and discreet regarding her body, thus giving no cause for gossip. Nor should the widow be too friendly or seemingly intimate with any man who may be observed frequenting her house, unless he is a relative.   140 Even then discretion should be observed, including the presence of a father-in-law, brother, or priest, who should be permitted few visits or none at all. For no matter how devout a woman herself may be, the world is inclined to speak evil. She should also maintain a household where there is no suspicion of great intimacy or familiarity, however fine she knows her staff to be and despite the innocence of her own thoughts. Nor should her household expenses give people opportunity for slandering her. Moreover, to protect her property better,   150 she should make no ostentatious displays of servants, clothing, or foods, for it better suits a widow to be inconspicuous and without any extravagance whatsoever.

Because widowhood truly provides so many hardships for women, some people might think it best for all widows to remarry. This argument can be answered by saying that if it were true that the married state consisted entirely of peace and repose, this indeed would be so. That one almost always sees the contrary in marriages should be a warning to all widows.   160 However, it might be necessary or desirable for the young ones to remarry. But for all those who have passed their youth and who are sufficiently comfortable financially so that poverty does not oblige them, remarriage is complete folly. Though some who want to remarry say there is nothing in life for a woman alone, they have so little confidence in their own good sense that they will claim that they don't know how to manage their own lives. But the height of folly and the greatest of all absurdities is the old woman who takes a   170 young husband: There a joyful song rarely is heard for long. Although many pay dearly for their foolishness, nobody will sympathize with them—for good reason.

Displaying a thoroughly unmedieval concern for renown and influence, de Pisan wrote near the end of the book:

> I thought I would multiply this work throughout the world in various copies, whatever the cost might be, and present it in particular places to queens, princesses and noble ladies. Through their efforts, it will be the more honored and praised, as is fitting, and better circulated among other women.

Nineteen manuscripts still exist in addition to three printed editions in French plus a Portuguese translation.

STUDY QUESTIONS

1. De Pisan comments that some men charge women "eight crown for six." Does this problem still exist? Think, for example, about what some men may charge women for automotive repairs.
2. What is de Pisan's opinion of women who tearfully throw up their hands and give up? Is she justified?

SUMMARY

The eleventh century marked the beginning of a new era we call the High Middle Ages. Cities began to grow and develop. The walls behind which men and women had sheltered themselves—the authoritarian church, the rigid structures of feudalism and manorialism—began to crumble. International trade began not long after the first Crusader entered Jerusalem in 1099. Even more importantly, contact with the civilized Middle East tapped the reservoir of Islamic science, medicine, and mathematics plus the culture of ancient Greece that Islamic scholars had carefully preserved.

Partly because of the increasing influence of important women, feudalism began to give way to the more civilized code of chivalry. Running parallel to this was the cult of the Virgin, in whose honor hundreds of magnificent churches were erected.

The tenets of Scholasticism, the dominant mode of Christian thought, were challenged by the Battle of Universals that marked the beginning of a conflict between faith and reason. The rediscovery of the complete works of Aristotle also challenged the theologians. Further, the proliferation of medieval universities led inevitably to intellectual challenges of the monolithic church.

In philosophy, the synthesis of the High Middle Ages was made by Thomas Aquinas, who merged Christian and Aristotelian thought. Dante's *Divine*

Comedy delineated the options available to humankind. The goal was still heaven but people were free to pursue it under their own power and through the discipline of their own will. In Gothic religious architecture—notably in the great cathedrals—the world of the senses and the world of the spirit were triumphantly united.

CULTURE AND HUMAN VALUES

The period of balance of the High Middle Ages was glorious, an era of magnificent achievements in art, architecture, literature, music, and philosophy. Although Christian doctrine remained central, there was a discernible shift in attitudes and values in the ever-growing educated class. Church teachings that had been accepted for centuries were increasingly questioned. The issue was not just the faith but the hierarchy. This is not to say that there was widespread unrest, but the Avignon papacy (Babylonian Captivity) and Great Schism had exposed an all too fallible power structure. The church preached obedience to authority, but what if that authority were corrupt?

In looking back on the volatile fourteenth century, one can perceive the beginning of the restless stirring that would eventually lead to the Renaissance, the Reformation, and the modern world. Call it 20–20 hindsight, but the ingredients were there: the rise of science; the proliferating universities; the rediscovery of Aristotle, followed by ancient Greek culture as preserved in the Islamic world.

A new value emerged during the age, a marvelous rediscovery called knowledge. Monasteries had preserved and endlessly copied what the church deemed important from the classical past, but there had been no real search for knowledge since the expiration of Graeco-Roman civilization. Thomism had responded to the new movement by justifying the acquisition of knowledge as a prerequisite for philosophy, law, and divine understanding. Whether the thirst for knowledge prompted the founding of universities or whether the universities sparked the search cannot be known. Whatever the case, there arose a need for knowledge for its own sake—a burning desire to know everything about the physical world. This ceaseless drive accounts for the rise of science, for "whatever scientists do, the most significant thing they do is to try to find out things that are not known."[9] Science investigates the material world; and so began a slow but inexorable shift from the spirituality of the Middle Ages to the materialism of the modern world.

9. Dennis Flanagan, *Flanagan's Version: A Spectator's Guide to Science on the Eve of the 21st Century* (New York: Alfred A. Knopf, 1988), p. 13.

CHAPTER 14

The Medieval Synthesis in Art

The giants of medieval art are comparable to Dante and Chaucer but few names have come down to us. For one thing, the creation rather than the creator was much more important in the God-centered world of the Middle Ages; the cathedral dedicated to Our Lady and built for the greater glory of God far transcended the identity of the master builder who supervised its construction. Moreover, individual personalities were generally submerged in the groups of artists who labored on such cooperative projects as illuminated manuscripts, tapestries, stained glass windows, architectural sculpture, and, especially, the majestic Romanesque and Gothic churches and cathedrals that rose all over Europe.

The complexity of that art and architecture and the sheer length of the era we are examining—from the seventh through the fifteenth centuries—make it necessary (and prudent) to divide this chapter into the following periods or styles (all dates approximate):

CHRONOLOGICAL OVERVIEW

600–800	Hiberno-Saxon Style
750–900	Carolingian Art
1000–1150/1200	Romanesque Style
1140–1200	Early Gothic Style
1200–1300	High Gothic Style in France
	Gothic Style Elsewhere in Europe
1300–1500s	Late Gothic Style

Opposite Bishop Eadfrith (?), "X–P Page," fol. 29, *Lindisfarne Gospels*. Ca. 698. Illuminated manuscript, 13½ × 9¾" (34.3 × 24.8 cm). British Library, London.

HIBERNO-SAXON PERIOD, CA. 600–800

Though never part of the Roman Empire, Ireland was known to the Romans, who called it *Hibernia*. This later became *Ivernin* in Old Celtic and then *Erin* in Old Irish. Occupied by Celts and Christianized by St. Patrick of Gaul, Ireland was cut off from the continent by the Anglo-Saxon conquest of England. This isolation led to the development of a unique form of Christian monasticism patterned after the solitary hermits of Egypt rather than the urbanized Roman version of Christianity. Founding monasteries in the countryside, Irish monks cultivated a strict ascetic discipline and, unlike the desert saints, a deep devotion to scholarship. Preempting the power of the bishops, Irish monasteries sponsored a remarkable missionary program in England and western Europe resulting in a spiritual and cultural ascendancy fittingly called the Irish Golden Age (ca. 600–ca. 800).

Manuscripts were produced in abundance to supplement these missionary activities, especially numerous copies of the Bible, all elaborately decorated to signify the supreme importance of the sacred texts. Displaying little interest in the figurative art of Roman Christianity, monks synthesized Celtic and Germanic elements to produce a richly decorated art based on geometric designs and organic abstractions derived from plant and animal forms. Created at a monastery on the island of Lindisfarne off the east coast of England, the *Lindisfarne Gospels* is a superb example of Hiberno-Saxon decorative art. As meticulous as printed electronic circuitry, the "X–P (khi-rho) Page" (see chapter opener opposite) is lovely testimony to the masterful use of color to enhance but not compete with either the linear composition or importance of the gospel text. Inside the letters is a miniature maze of writhing shapes and mirror-image effects. With details so fine they are best studied with a magnifying glass, one wonders how this work was accomplished.

The last of the remarkable Hiberno-Saxon illuminated manuscripts, the *Book of Kells* is also the most elaborately decorated. On one page the Greek letters XPI (khri), an abbreviation of the name of Christ, dominate a design

14.1 *Above* "XPI Page," fol. 34, *Book of Kells*. Ca. 760–820. Illuminated manuscript, 13 × 10" (33 × 25 cm). Library of Trinity College, Dublin.

swirling with animal and abstract interlaces and geometric decoration (fig. 14.1). Whorls within circles within larger circles dazzle the eye, but closer study reveals two human faces and, on the left vertical of the X, three human figures depicted from the waist up. Near the bottom and to the right of the same vertical is a playful **genre** scene featuring two cats and four mice.

Hiberno-Saxon manuscripts typify the early period of intricate and painstaking northern craftsmanship, which included metalworking, woodworking, jewelry, ivory carving, stone carving, and by the eleventh century stained glass, a tradition that led to spectacular achievements in the Gothic age and, eventually, to machine design and the industrial revolution. An important factor in the development of northern crafts may have been climate, for these are mainly indoor activities that could be carried on despite inclement weather and long, bleak winters.

CAROLINGIAN ART, CA. 750–900

Ruling from 768 to 814 as a Frankish king, Charlemagne saw himself as a successor to the Caesars of Rome, a notion reinforced in 800 when the pope crowned him Emperor of the Holy Roman Empire. To his capital at Aachen (formerly Aix-la-Chapelle), in present-day Germany, Charlemagne brought scholars, artists, and craftsmen to help revive the civilization of classical antiquity. Short-lived, but vital for later developments, the Carolingian Renaissance drew upon Celto-Germanic and Mediterranean traditions to produce a Carolingian art that combined classic forms with Christian symbols and subject matter.

Societies tend to develop an architecture based on the availability of building materials, and at that time the vast forests of northern Europe provided an endless supply of wood for the timber-frame construction of private and public buildings. Charlemagne, however, preferred impressive palaces and churches built in the Roman manner. He imported southern techniques of building in stone and southern masons to work the stone and instruct northern craftsmen. This educational process was to culminate in the expert stonework of the great medieval cathedrals.

One of the few buildings to survive intact from the age of Charlemagne, the chapel of his palace at Aachen (see fig. 12.9) is an impressive example of northern European stone construction. As might be expected during this early period, the columns and most of the capitals were simply taken from existing Roman buildings. One suspects that Charlemagne fancied using columns of the Caesars for his personal chapel.

14.2 "St. Mark," fol. 18v, *Gospel Book of Archibishop Ebbo of Reims*. 816–35. Illuminated manuscript, ca. 10 × 8" (25.4 × 20.3 cm). Bibliothèque Municipal, Epernay, France. Photo: Giraudon, Paris.

14.3 "Crucifixion Cover," *Lindau Gospels.* Ca. 870. 13¾ × 10½" (34.9 × 26.7 cm). Pierpont Morgan Library, New York.

Painted shortly after Charlemagne's death, the "St. Mark" (fig. 14.2) derives from a classic model. The Hiberno-Saxon influence is discernible in the draperies swirling about the torso in lines as dynamic as those in an Irish manuscript. Rather than a scholar writing a book, Mark is a man inspired by divine guidance, a transmitter of the sacred text. This follows the ancient view that poets—Homer for example—are divinely inspired and possess superhuman powers.

Influenced possibly by Byzantine decorative arts, Carolingian book covers were made of precious metals and richly ornamented with jewels. Created during the waning influence of the Carolingian dynasty, the "Crucifixion Cover" of the *Lindau Gospels* is made of gold, with the figures of Christ and angels delineated in graceful, sinuous lines (fig. 14.3). The artist outlined the golden Greek cross with gold beads and precious and semiprecious stones, then echoed the cross motif with jeweled crosses in the four panels and all around the border. Major stones are set above the gold surface so that reflected light can add to their brilliance. No one could doubt the importance of the text within such a cover.

After the remarkable reign of Charlemagne the Holy Roman Empire declined in power and influence. Nevertheless, the revival of Greek and Roman learning sparked a synthesis of classical civilization and Celto-Germanic culture, elements of which are still discernible in modern Europe and America.

ROMANESQUE STYLE, CA. 1000–1150/1200

By about AD 1000 virtually all of Europe had been Christianized, and, after centuries of ferocious attacks, the barbaric Vikings and Magyars had finally been assimilated by their erstwhile victims. Major building programs began all over Europe to replace damaged structures and to construct new churches and monasteries. With at least one new church in every hamlet, village, town, and city, architecture and architectural sculpture became the dominant art forms of this vigorous new age.

Vaulted Churches

Christians had been making pilgrimages to scenes of Christ's life since the third century and, since Charlemagne's time, in ever-increasing numbers. By the tenth century it was commonly believed that viewing sacred relics of Christ and the saints secured God's pardon for sins, a belief

14.4 St.-Benoit-sur-Loire, France, nave, looking east. End of 11th century. Photo: B.P.K., Berlin.

encouraged by the churches containing such relics. One of these was the Abbey of Fleury (now St.-Benoit-sur-Loire). Claiming to contain the bones of St. Benedict, the abbey became one of the prime destinations for organized parties of pilgrims. Rebuilt in the eleventh and twelfth centuries after brutal Viking raids in the ninth century, St.-Benoit-sur-Loire is another fine example of the Cluniac style. Its nave has a barrel vault with ornamental ribs (fig. 14.4). The

14.7   Abbey of Jumièges, near Rouen, France, west facade. 1037–67. Photo: James Austin, Cambridge, U.K.

14.5 *Above*   Basilica of St.-Sernin, Toulouse, France, nave. Ca. 1080–1120. Length of nave 377' 4" (115 m). Photo: Dagli Orti, Paris.

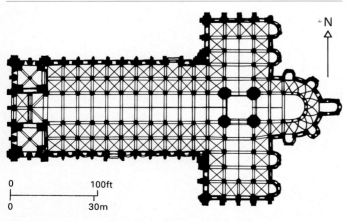

14.6   St.-Sernin, plan after Kenneth John Conant.

clerestory windows, which admit considerable light for a Romanesque church, are set above a blind arcade that decorates the upper wall. Adorned only with architectural details, the masonry walls are supported by majestic columns connected by Roman (semicircular) arches. The interiors of French Romanesque churches are always restrained, depending for their effect on a unity of basic design and discreet architectural embellishment without recourse to wall mosaics, murals, frescoes, or similar pictorial decorations. The result is a rational design of awesome power.

Many pilgrimage churches were monastic. An important stop on the pilgrimage road from Italy and Provence to Spain's Santiago de Compostela, the Basilica of St.-Sernin in Toulouse is a superb example of the Romanesque style and of the influence of pilgrimages on church architecture. The barrel vault is punctuated by nonstructural transverse arches evenly distributed down the nave (fig. 14.5), which is flanked by double aisles to accommodate the many pilgrims. Constructed on the module of the **crossing** square under the tower, the size of each compartment between the columns, called a **bay**, is exactly half the area of the crossing square under the central tower. (fig. 14.6). In the side aisles each square is one-quarter of the module (the crossing). The piers with their attached compound columns are two stories high with arches supporting a gallery that runs above the side aisles and that was probably used by some of the pilgrim throngs. Minus the triumphal arch of early Christian churches, the evenly spaced columns and identically sized bays lead inexorably down the nave to the focal point of the altar. St.-Sernin is a classic example of French Romanesque design, unified and lucid.

Now one of the most imposing ruins in France, the Abbey of Jumièges, in Normandy, was built in the eleventh century on the site of a seventh-century building which had been destroyed by Vikings in the ninth. It was reconsecrated in 1067 in the presence of William the Conqueror, himself a descendant of Viking marauders (fig. 14.7). With its 141-foot (43-m) twin towers and projecting porch, Jumièges represents the impressive Norman style of Romanesque that was established in England (where it is called, simply, Norman) by the conquerors. The present state of Jumièges typifies the fate of French monasteries during the French Revolution. After the monks were dispersed, the abbey was auctioned off in 1793 to a timber merchant who quarried and sold many of the stones. The ruins now belong to the nation.

The Bayeux Tapestry

Probably designed by a woman and embroidered on linen by Saxon women, the Bayeux Tapestry is the most precise medieval document that has survived intact, providing daily life scenes and details of clothes, customs, and weapons. The rivalry between King Harold of England and Duke William of Normandy for the English throne is depicted in fifty-eight scenes, culminating in the Battle of Hastings (fig. 14.8). In the episode shown, the English, identified by their mustaches, are beginning to succumb to the superior numbers and better equipment of the Normans. At the far left in the battle scene a rider protects himself with a large shield while brandishing his lance. Unlike the British, the Norman cavalry had stirrups in which they stood as they

COMMUNITIES OF WOMEN

Most women in the medieval world could look forward to marriage, raising a family, and requisite domestic chores with little opportunity for anything else—with one exception. They could join an abbey (monastery, later called a convent) where they could acquire an education and learn a variety of skills as they dedicated their life to God. Because abbeys were usually independent institutions run by an abbess, they had to be self-supporting, with nuns trained in the tasks that kept the order functioning.

The nuns had to import a priest to say Mass and hear confessions, but they performed all other duties, including the preservation of knowledge through manuscript copying and research. Some abbeys became prominent centers of learning staffed with notable intellectuals. Hrotsvit, abbess of Gandersheim (ca. 930–90), wrote histories and plays. Hildegard of Bingen (1098–1179) was a composer, scientist, and theologian. Herrad of Landsberg, abbess at Hohenberg (1165–95), assisted by her nuns, wrote the *Hortus Deliciarum* (*Garden of Delights*), an encyclopedia of knowledge and world history (see chapter opener on p. 246). Beginning in the thirteenth century, universities began replacing abbeys as educational institutions while women's education became virtually nonexistent for the next five or six centuries.

14.8 "The Battle Rages," detail of the Bayeux Tapestry. Ca. 1070–80. Wool embroidery on linen, height ca. 20" (51 cm), entire length 231' (70.5 m). Musée de l'Evêche, Bayeux. Photo: Scala, Florence.

14.9 *Above*   Basilica of Ste.-Madeleine, Vézelay, Burgundy, France, nave. Ca. 1104–32. Photo: Lonchampt-Delehaye, C.N.M.H.S./© DACS 1995.

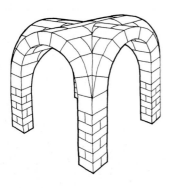

14.10 *Left*   Schematic drawing of a cross vault.

relentlessly mowed down the enemy with their deadly lances. The tripartite design features an ornamental band above the violent battle scene and a lower band depicting the casualties. Despite the stylized design, the details are brutally realistic; warriors and horses have died in agony.

Ste.-Madeleine, Vézelay

The Abbey Church of Ste.-Madeleine in the village of Vézelay is intimately associated with another kind of warfare: holy war. Originally scheduled for Vézelay, the First Crusade was preached by Pope Urban II from Clermont in 1095, calling on all Christians to free the Holy Land from the Saracens. In 1146 Vézelay was the site for St. Bernard's Second Crusade and, in 1190, King Richard the Lion-Hearted of England and King Phillip Augustus of France departed from Vézelay on the Third Crusade, a disastrous failure, as was every Crusade from the Second to the Eighth.

One of the most distinctive of all Romanesque interiors, the nave of Ste.-Madeleine (fig. 14.9) is high—about 90 feet (27 m)—with unusual transverse arches of white and pinkish brown stone, probably inspired by such Islamic buildings as the Great Mosque in Córdoba (see fig. 12.4). The tunnel, or barrel, vault was no longer used because of its inherent drawback: an unbroken series of arches pressed back to back can be lighted or opened only on the opposite ends. Any and every opening in the supporting wall weakens the entire structure. One of the earliest French churches to abandon the barrel vault, Ste.-Madeleine's uses a vault that is intersected at right angles by another vault to form a **groin** or cross vault (fig. 14.10).

Note that at this high level the groin vaults of Vézelay permit considerable illumination from the clerestory windows. Close study of the interior also reveals that the architect used groin vaults that were too heavy for the exterior wall, vaults so massive that the upper walls are pushed outward. External flying **buttresses** (see an example of the principle in fig. 14.18) had to be added to balance the **thrust** of the vaults, thus stabilizing this lovely nave.

A striking architectural sculpture at another Burgundian church portrays the most powerful subject in Christendom. *The Last Judgment* **tympanum** at Autun (fig. 14.11) exemplifies the revived relationship of architecture and sculpture in the Romanesque style. Set between the arch and lintel, the tympanum is a compendium of sermons warning the faithful about the terrors of Hell. Staring straight forward, the imposing figure of the final Judge holds his hands out as in a set of scales. Along the lower edge the dead are rising from their graves. On the left the saved are passing into Heaven, and on the right the damned are being

14.11 *Left*   Gislebertus, *The Last Judgment*, tympanum of the central portal, Cathedral of St.-Lazare, Autun, France. Ca. 1130. Photo: Viollet, Paris.

14.12 Buscheto, Pisa cathedral and campanile. 1063–1272. Photo: Alinari, Florence.

thrust into Hell by hideous devils and demons. Heated by a fervent faith, the Romanesque imagination knew no bounds in graphic warnings to transgressors.

Tuscan Romanesque

The basic Romanesque style of Roman (round) arches and vaults, heavy walls, and alternating square piers and columns spread throughout western Europe, always displaying, however, certain variations depending on regional conventions and traditions. In Tuscany and other parts of northern Italy, the style adhered closely to the basilica plan of early Christian churches, and also evidenced an increased interest in classical art, a heritage that had never been totally forgotten. The most distinguished complex in the Tuscan Romanesque style is the cathedral group at Pisa (fig. 14.12). Constructed of readily available white marble, the cathedral resembles an early Christian basilica, but with Romanesque characteristics: the dome over the crossing; the superimposed arcades on the west front; the blind arches encircling the entire building. The extended transepts with an apse at each end add to the poise and serenity of the design, which makes the famous Leaning Tower, the **campanile**, all the more striking. Begun in 1174 by Bonanno Pisano on an unstable foundation, the tower began to tilt well before its completion in 1350. The three upper sections were adjusted slightly to the north in an attempt to compensate for the southward incline. Now 16 feet 6 inches (5 m) off the perpendicular, the tower—whose bells haven't rung in decades—is apparently no longer moving. In May 1992 two steel bands were wrapped around it and covered with stucco to match the rest of the tower. Also added was a counterweight of 800 pounds (363 kg) of lead.

Eventually, engineers will add a total of eighteen bands as they check to see if the tower is stabilized.

Mont-St.-Michel

In all its manifestations, Romanesque art finds its unity in architecture; the church is the Fortress of God where the apocalyptic vision is ever called to mind. No more vivid representation of this idea exists than the Abbey of Mont-St.-Michel in the Sea of Peril (fig. 14.13), which rises in awesome majesty off the coast of Normandy. The abbey was begun about 1020 by Abbot Hildebert and Richard II, Duke of Normandy, grandfather of William the Conqueror. Its building spanned five centuries, as abbot succeeded abbot and style succeeded style. Mont-St.-Michel summarizes medieval architecture, a glorious mixture of Norman, Norman Romanesque, and Early, High, and Late Gothic styles.

EARLY GOTHIC STYLE, CA. 1140–1200

> Mankind was never so happily inspired as when it made a cathedral.
>
> Robert Louis Stevenson (1850–94)

Erected usually in the countryside as part of monastic communities, Romanesque churches were built by and for "regular" clergy, those who lived under the rule (*regula*) of a religious order. The rise of the great cities on the Continent

14.13 Mont-St.-Michel. Ca. 1017–1144; 1211–1521. Photo: Robert C. Lamm, Scottsdale.
This view also illustrates the stormy weather so typical of this portion of the northern coast of France.

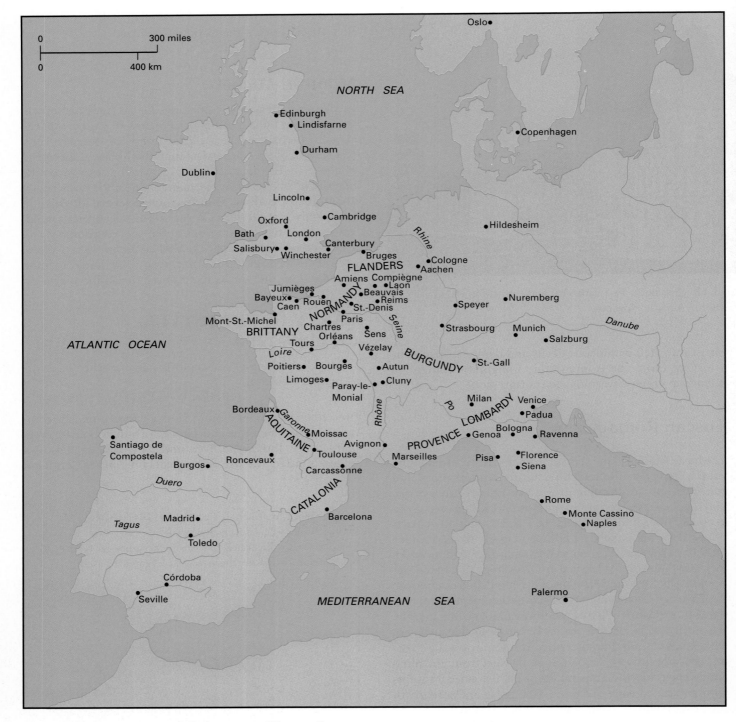

Map 14.1   Romanesque and Gothic sites in Western Europe.

was paralleled by the development of the new Gothic style (map 14.1).[1] Staffed by the "secular" clergy, priests who lived "in the world" (*in saecula*), Gothic churches were urban establishments designed to serve city parishes. Each city's glory and chief community center, the Gothic cathedral was not only the seat (*cathedra*) of the bishop but a theatre, class-room, concert hall, court, and general meeting place.

Gothic Vaulting

Though the basic structural elements of Gothic architec-ture were developed and used during the Romanesque peri-od, it remained for an unknown architectural genius to put it all together at St.-Denis, just north of Paris. It was car-ried out under Abbot Suger, who left a detailed account of

---

1. Known initially as the "French style," it did not acquire the name "Gothic" until the sixteenth century.

The most striking difference at St.-Denis is the marked increase in light. Stained glass windows function as light converters, transforming the interior into a hazy luminosity of shifting colors. The windows are subdivided first by **mullions** (carved stone posts), then by stone **tracery** to form still smaller glass panels, and finally by thin lead strips to hold in place the individual pieces of colored glass. The light penetrating the stained glass creates a polychromatic effect, making the glass translucent, while the stone and metal dividers become opaque black lines separating and highlighting the colors. The mystical coloration of Gothic interiors represents the philosophical idea of light as a Neoplatonic form of ultimate beauty, an earthly manifestation of the divine light of the heavenly kingdom (see figs. 14.24 and 14.25).

On 11 June 1144 Abbot Suger proudly presided at the dedication of the choir of St.-Denis in the company of hundreds of priests and laymen, five archbishops, and Louis VII of France and his Queen, Eleanor of Aquitaine. This was a truly momentous occasion, sparking a veritable frenzy of Gothic construction in the Ile de France, the region surrounding Paris. The cathedral at Chartres was begun in 1142, even before the formal dedication at St.-Denis, Laon in 1160, Notre Dame of Paris in 1163, Bourges in 1185, and Chartres again in 1194 after a catastrophic fire. These cathedrals, all major enterprises, were followed by hundreds of other churches in a vast building program that, in a single century, included every major city in northern Europe.

14.14 Cathedral of St.-Denis, near Paris, interior. 1140–4. Photo: C.N.M.H.S./© DACS 1995.

his administration (1122–51), and his goals. Suger wished to give the church a new choir and ambulatory, one that would be full of light—symbolic of the presence of God (fig. 14.14). The cramped, dark ambulatory of the existing church, with its thick walls between chapels, was to be replaced with walls of colored glass. To achieve this, the architect supported the weight of the vaults with pointed arches, which are more stable than semi-circular ones. The arch principle is one of mutual support; the two halves lean against each other so that the force (gravity) that would cause either to fall actually holds them in place. However, the flatter the arch the greater the lateral thrust at the springline, that is, the outward push where the arch begins (fig. 14.15). This thrust is significantly reduced when the pointed arch is used because the springline is angled more nearly downward. Hence, the more pointed the arch, the less the tendency to push its supporting pier outward, thus reducing the need for massive supports.

The round arch has a fixed radius because it is always half of a circle. Since it has no unalterable diameter, the pointed arch can rise to almost any height and span virtually any space (fig. 14.16). In the illustration the first rounded arch spans the short side, the second the long side, and the third the diagonal, necessitating piers of different heights. With their identical height, pointed arches simplify the engineering and improve the aesthetic effect with slender columns topped by capitals at a uniform height.

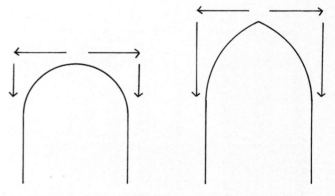

14.15 *Above* Schematic drawings of Romanesque and Gothic arch thrusts.

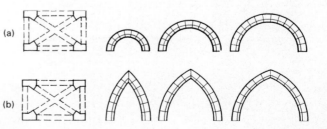

14.16 (a) Cross vault of semicircular arches over an oblong bay, (b) cross vault of pointed arches over an oblong bay.

Notre Dame of Paris

The imposing facade of Notre Dame of Paris (fig. 14.17) has been justly admired for over seven centuries as a supreme example of rational design. Solidly buttressed at the corners, the facade rises effortlessly in three levels on which sculptural embellishment is subordinate to the architecture. Unlike the projecting porches of later Gothic cathedrals, the three portals are recessed from the frontal plane and topped by a row of carved saints. The rose window centerpiece is flanked by smaller roses over double windows, above which there is a line of lacy pointed arches. With their subtly embellished cornices and elongated windows, the square towers complete the design with restraint and dignity. This majestic west front is a fitting symbol for the ascendancy of Paris as the cultural center of Europe.

The view of the east end of Notre Dame (fig. 14.18) displays in no uncertain terms that critical component of Gothic design, the flying buttress. Springing from massive piers around the ambulatory, two sets of arches curve upward to support the piers of the upper stories, providing the counterbalancing force needed to stabilize the structure. It is the flying buttress principle that enabled architects to utilize the curtain walls of stone pierced by numerous

14.18   Notre Dame, Paris, apse with flying buttresses. Photo: James Austin, Cambridge, U.K.

14.17   Notre Dame, Paris, west facade. Plan 1163–1250; facade ca. 1200–50. Photo: Marburg.

stained glass windows. Also visible in figure 14.18 is the late Gothic flèche ("arrow"), the slender spire that rises above the crossing. Flying buttresses represent an exposed engineering that provides both the needed physical support and the psychological assurance that the building is totally solid and safe, as indeed it is.

The floor plan of Notre Dame is a long rectangle with a rounded eastern end, but most Romanesque and Gothic churches were designed in the shape of a Latin cross—that is, a cruciform plan. Figure 14.19 is a simplified plan illustrating the basic outline. The terminology for the various parts of the church is standard and applies to all cruciform designs. The orientation of the plan is also standard; worshipers enter through a west door and walk toward Jerusalem in the East (Orient). (Some churches do not follow this geographical rule, although they use the same terminology.) In this plan there are six bays in the nave and three in each transept.

HIGH GOTHIC STYLE, CA. 1200–1300

After a disastrous fire in the village of Chartres in 1194, which left intact only the Early Gothic facade of the still unfinished cathedral, the rebuilding of Chartres Cathedral commenced immediately and moved rapidly, with the basic structure completed by 1220. The idea that Gothic cathedrals took decades or even centuries to build is erroneous

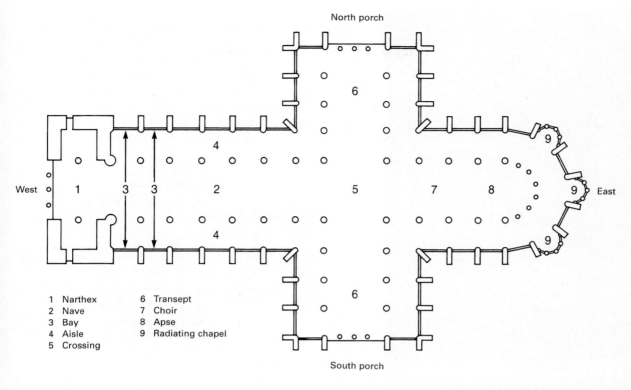

North porch

West   East

6

4

1   3   3   2   5   7   8   9

4

6

South porch

1 Narthex   6 Transept
2 Nave   7 Choir
3 Bay   8 Apse
4 Aisle   9 Radiating chapel
5 Crossing

14.19 *Above*   Cruciform floor plan of a hypothetical church.

and probably based on the fact that these buildings were never fully completed; there was always something to be added or elaborated.

Chartres Cathedral

The first masterpiece of the mature period, Chartres Cathedral has been called the "Queen of cathedrals," the epitome of Gothic architecture (fig. 14.20). Typically High Gothic but unique to Chartres, the south (right) tower begins with a square base that evolves smoothly into the octagonal shape of the fourth level. From here the graceful spire soars to a height of 344 feet (105 m), the characteristic "finger pointing to God" of the Gothic age. The elaborate north tower, which was not completed until well into the Northern Renaissance, lacks the effortless verticality of the south tower. Verticality was a hallmark of Gothic; cities competed in unspoken contests to erect cathedrals with the highest vaults and the tallest towers. An inspiring House of God was also a symbol of civic achievement. With a facade 157 feet (48 m) wide and measuring 427 feet (130 m) in length, Chartres cathedral is as prominent a landmark today as when it was built, thanks in part to modern zoning ordinances that control building heights throughout the village.

Incorporated into the facade when the cathedral was rebuilt, the Royal Portal (western doorways) of the earlier church emphasizes the Last Judgment theme of

14.20   Notre Dame, Chartres, France, west facade. Ca. 1142–1507. Photo: Kersting, London.

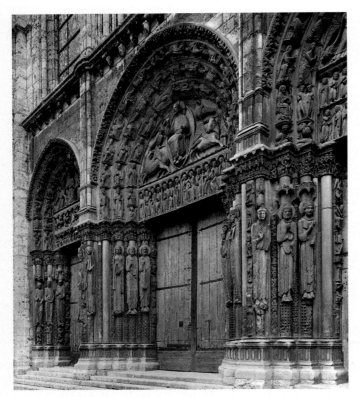

14.21 Notre Dame, Chartres, central doorway of Royal Portal. Ca. 1140–50. Photo: Kersting, London.

With the development of cathedral schools such as those at Paris and Chartres, Mary was viewed much like Athena, as patroness of arts and science. The right doorway of the Chartres Royal Portal includes portraits of Aristotle, Cicero, Euclid, Ptolemy, Pythagoras, and symbols of the **seven liberal arts**. In fact the school associated with Chartres cathedral was a renowned center of classical learning, and this portal, like the Gothic cathedral itself, represents the medieval synthesis of spiritual and secular life at its best.

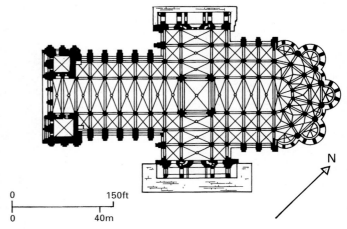

14.22 *Above*   Notre Dame, Chartres, floor plan after Dehio.

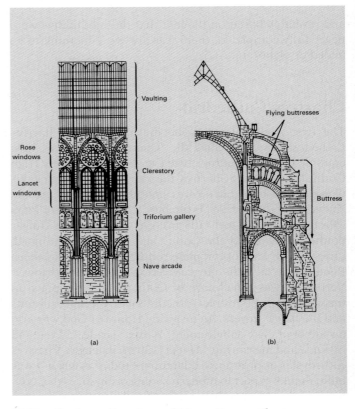

14.23 Goubert, Drawings of Notre Dame, Chartres. (a) Section of nave wall, (b) diagram of vaulting.

Romanesque portals but with significant differences (fig. 14.21). Rather than the harsh Damnation of the Last Judgment, the theme is now the Second Coming with its promise of salvation. No longer is there the inventive freedom of the Romanesque; all is unified and controlled. The outer frame is provided by the twenty-four elders of the Apocalypse on the **archivolts** and the lower row of twelve Apostles. Surrounded by symbols of the four Evangelists, the now benign figure of Christ raises an arm in benediction in the manner of Caesar Augustus (see fig. 9.10). Beneath the tympanum are the **jamb figures**, a wholly new idea in architectural sculpture. Conceived and carved in the round, the figures were very likely fashioned after live models rather than copied from manuscripts, a further indication of the emerging this-worldly spirit of the age.

The most significant manifestation of the new age was the dedication of the cathedrals themselves. Named after apostles and saints in previous eras, the new churches were almost invariably dedicated to Our Lady (Notre Dame). Mary was Queen of Heaven, interceding for her faithful who, sinners all, wanted mercy, not justice. This was the Cult of the Virgin Mary, the popular spiritual movement of the Gothic age. The Romanesque was the style of the age of feudalism and conflict; the more cultivated Gothic represented the Age of Chivalry, as derived from Courts of Love sponsored by powerful women like Eleanor of Aquitaine.

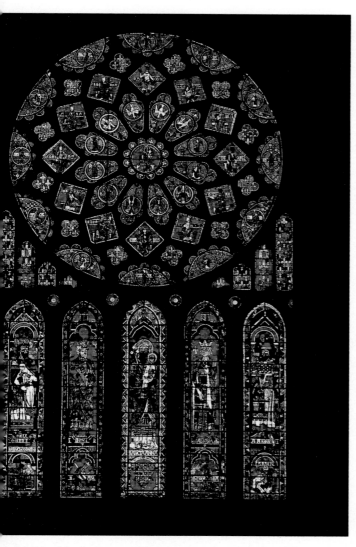

14.24 Notre Dame, Chartres, northern rose and lancets. Early 13th century. Diameter of rose window ca. 42' (12.8 m). Photo: Sonia Halliday, Weston Turville, U.K.

is a treasure house of the art, with clerestory windows 44 feet (13.4 m) high, all in all some 20,000 square feet (1,858 m²) of medieval glass. Located at the north end of the transepts, the northern rose is like a gigantic multicolored jewel set above the five figurative **lancet windows** (fig. 14.24). As a northern exposure window the color leans toward the cool part of the spectrum with a preponderance of blue. Its counterpart, the southern rose (not illustrated), transmits the warmer colors: red, orange, and yellow. Contrary to what one might expect, direct sunlight on any of the windows upsets their chromatic balance for they were designed to function best under the even, cool light characteristic of northern France.

Other French Cathedrals

Reims Cathedral is the traditional site for the consecration of French kings for it was here, in 496, that Bishop Remi baptized Clovis, leader of the conquering Franks. The inspiring interior is both beautiful and delightful. The gorgeous rose window within the pointed arch is crowned by an even more dazzling rose at the top of the 125-foot (38-m) vaulting (fig. 14.25). The most remarkable aspect of Reims is its homogeneous design. The four master builders who followed the original design of Jean d'Orbais (master until 1231) left the nation a priceless legacy: the majestic Coronation Church of France.

14.25 Notre Dame, Reims, France, interior looking west. Begun 1210. Photo: Bulloz, Paris.

The nave of Notre Dame of Chartres is 53 feet (16 m) wide, the most spacious of all Gothic naves. The total length is 130 feet (40 m) and the height 122 feet (37 m)—the loftiest vault of its day. Around the apse are the tall pointed arches of the arcade and above them, the **triforium**, an arcaded passageway. Five huge windows, dedicated to the Virgin, flood the choir with colored light.

Chartres has six bays in the nave and two in each transept, a single aisle in the nave, and a double aisle in the choir and apse (fig. 14.22). Figure 14.23a depicts a full bay (center) and the three levels of the nave wall. The diagram of the vaulting (fig. 14.23b) gives some idea of the complexity of the exterior support system.

One of the chief glories of Gothic interiors is the kaleidoscopic color cascading from the mighty stained glass windows. Retaining most of its original windows, Chartres

Completed in less than thirty-three months for Louis IX of France, later St. Louis, Sainte Chapelle is today a small chapel set in the midst of the Palais de Justice. With virtually no stone walls, the structure is a set of piers supporting stained glass curtains. Topped by a spire reaching 246 feet (75 m) into the sky, the upper chapel, with its 49-foot (15-m) windows, rests on a lower level intended for the use of servants. With almost 6,700 square feet (622 m^2) of glass containing 1,134 scenes, the upper chapel is a triumph of the **rayonnant** *("radiant")* style: a jewelbox of color dominated by brilliant reds and luminous blues (fig. 14.26). Because there are no side aisles, there are no flying buttresses to impede the penetration of light into a building whose walls are about 75 percent glass. Rivaling Chartres in the extent and quality of its original glass, Sainte Chapelle

14.27   Cathedral of St.-Pierre, Beauvais, France, aerial view of choir. Begun ca. 1225. Photo: Bernard, Paris.

14.26   Sainte Chapelle, Paris, upper level of interior. 1245–8. Photo: Jean Feuillie, C.N.M.H.S./© DACS 1995.

managed to survive the Revolution; damaged and neglected, it became a storage area for old government files. Restored in the nineteenth century to an approximation of its original condition, the remarkable fact is that its basic structure is so flawless, so perfectly engineered that it survived intact for seven centuries.

With the building of the cathedral at Beauvais, the competition to build the highest vault came crashing to an end (fig. 14.27). The vault, which reached the amazing height of 157 feet (48.9 m), was a wonderment to all until its collapse in 1284; only the apse was left standing. Rebuilt over a period of forty years, the choir remains today as a testament both to Gothic vertical aspirations and to the waning of enthusiasm for building enormously expensive churches. The money ran out along with the spirit. Previously it was thought that stone simply could not support such a lofty vault as that of Beauvais, but modern engineering research[2] points to a design flaw in an exterior pier, the deterioration of which was not detected. The nature of the 1284 disaster ironically confirmed the nature of Gothic engineering, in which the stability of the vaulting depends on the proper functioning of all components. When the single pier failed due to undetected weathering, it was only the choir vaults that came tumbling down; the structurally independent apse remained standing. Interestingly enough, the design flaw in the defective pier was corrected during the rebuilding program, meaning that the entire cathedral could then have been completed as originally planned. Today, looking at the magnificent choir, one wonders what might have been at Beauvais.

2.   Robert Mark, *Experiments in Gothic Structure* (Cambridge, Mass.: MIT Press, 1982), pp. 58–77.

Gothic Style Elsewhere in Europe

By the second half of the thirteenth century the Gothic style had been accepted throughout most of Europe, though Italy was less than enthusiastic. Regional variations gave each area its own brand of Gothic. Taking to Gothic as if they had invented it, the English built in the style with enthusiasm, but showed a clear intention to give it their own stamp. Whereas French cathedrals are marked by verticality, their English counterparts are noted for their length, often including double sets of transepts. The choir end is usually squared off rather than curved, and includes a Lady chapel, devoted to the Virgin. The clean lines of French verticality were abandoned at the outset in favor of a profusion of patterns—reflected in the name applied to mature English Gothic of the late thirteenth and fourteenth centuries: Decorated. Veritable forests of ribs adorn the vaults of many English cathedrals, as we can see in that of Winchester (fig. 14.28). It is the vault, rather than the arcading, that is of primary interest here. Another difference is that many English cathedrals were built over a longer time span than French ones and incorporated more diversity of styles including, often, some Norman (Romanesque) features. Although the total effect lacks the serene harmony of French Gothic, it offers much visual and historic interest. Unfortunately, little remains of English medieval stained glass, most of which was destroyed by iconoclastic Protestants during the sixteenth and seventeenth centuries. The English see French interiors as cold and

14.29 Giovanni Pisano, Siena Cathedral, facade. Begun ca. 1285. Photo: Spectrum, London.

impersonal while viewing their version of Gothic as warmly intimate and hospitable. Different styles suit different folks.

Italy took up the Gothic style slowly and with reservations; Italians were, after all, the people who had, in the sixteenth century, labeled the "French style" as a barbaric creation of northern Goths. Distinctly unclassical, a Gothic cathedral is restless, unsettled, always unfinished, whereas a classical temple is serenely complete. Nevertheless, the Gothic spirit was on the move in Italy, becoming part of the classical and Romanesque traditions.

For all its Gothic elements, the west front of the cathedral of Siena (fig. 14.29) has square doorways, triangular pediments, and a balanced design reminiscent of the classical past. Gothic features include a rose window, but without stained glass, the unobtrusive Gothic towers, lacy blind arcading, and the three portals. Most of the statuary has been liberated from its architectural bondage and the tympanums display colorful mosaics. Faced with multicolored marble, the facade is a lively ensemble of Gothic and Tuscan Romanesque elements, all in all a notable example of Italian reaction to the Gothic spirit.

Whatever its regional variations, the Gothic cathedral epitomizes the explosive creativity and intellectual boldness of the High Middle Ages. Never completely finished, a process rather than an end product, it stood at the center of the storm of changes that would sweep away the medieval synthesis. It represents both the triumphant climax of the Age of Faith and the end of the Middle Ages. The German author Heinrich Heine (1797–1856)

14.28 Winchester Cathedral, England, nave. Begun 1079. Photo: E.T. Archive, London.

14.30 *Abraham and the Three Angels*, from the *Psalter of St. Louis*. 1253–70. Illuminated manuscript, 8½ × 5½" (21 × 14.5 cm). Bibliothèque Nationale, Paris.

14.31 *Below, left Beatus* page, fol. 14r from the *Peterborough Psalter*. 1300. Illuminated manuscript. Bibliothèque Royale, Brussels.

succinctly characterized the Middle Ages: "People in those old times had convictions; we moderns only have opinions. And it needs more than a mere opinion to erect a Gothic cathedral."

Decorative Arts

Although architecture was the dominant art of the High Middle Ages, the so-called minor, or decorative, arts were notable for both quality and quantity. The page from the *Psalter of St. Louis* is a stunning example of Gothic **illumination** (fig. 14.30). It shows three angels appearing to Abraham and, on the right, Abraham and Sarah serving supper to the angels. Vibrating with color, the two scenes are separated by a marvelously decorative oak tree. Notice the architectural setting; Gothic features such as vaults, arcading, and tracery are incorporated into many medieval works of art, reflecting the primacy of architecture in this period. Reliquaries, in particular, often resemble Gothic churches or chapels. (Conversely, the Sainte Chapelle is, in effect, a large reliquary.)

Medieval manuscripts, being mainly of a religious nature, were customarily illuminated with a variety of sacred scenes and events. However, the *Beatus* page from the *Peterborough Psalter* (fig. 14.31) illustrates how important the secular world had become. This is the beginning of Psalm I, but one would be hard pressed to discover a single figure or object related to the text. Instead, we see a broad selection of scenes from everyday life, all done in a realistic and sometimes whimsical style.

LATE GOTHIC STYLE, CA. 1300–1500s

The extraordinary richness and sensuosity of the *Beatus* page, painted in 1300, brings us to the period when medieval art was in full flower: confident, exuberant, and, in many cases, unashamedly pretty. It was also a period in which large-scale painting (as contrasted with manuscript illumination) began, slowly, to be revived.

Created in the Late Gothic age, the Reliquary of the Holy Thorn (fig. 14.32) is splendidly luxurious at a time when this kind of opulence was expected in a sacred vessel. The gold armature and base are abundantly embellished with large pearls and pink rubies. Bearing a golden crown of thorns, the exquisitely sculpted angel has an enameled robe and wings. The interior of the vase holds a tiny

14.32 *Left* Reliquary of the Holy Thorn, Notre Dame, Reims, France. 11th-century vase with 15th-century setting. Rock crystal, gold, pearl, ruby, enamel, 10 × 37 × 31½" (25.5 × 94 × 80 cm). Photo: Giraudon, Paris.

golden angel gripping a thorn supposedly taken from Christ's crown of thorns. The overall effect is both secular and sacred, a vase fit for royalty surmounted by the most elegant of angels.

An integral part of Gothic architecture, stained glass windows and relief sculpture served the pictorial purposes once provided by mosaics, murals, and frescoes. Virtually nonexistent in the Gothic north, large-scale paintings were still done in Italy, which had maintained its contact with Byzantium. It was Italian painters who synthesized Byzantine and Gothic styles to create new procedures crucial to the future development of Western painting.

Cimabue

Renowned for his skill as a fresco and **tempera** painter,[3] the Florentine Cimabue (chee-ma-BOO-uh; 1240?–1302) introduced features that were incorporated into the developing Italian style. His *Madonna Enthroned* (fig. 14.33) illustrates the new characteristics of strong, forceful figures in a serene setting. The human scale of the lower figures emphasizes the towering dignity of the Madonna

14.34   Giotto, *Madonna Enthroned*. Ca. 1310. Tempera on wood, 10' 8" × 6' 8" (3.25 × 2.03 m). Galleria degli Uffizi, Florence. Photo: Dagli Orti, Paris.

holding the mature-looking child. Distinguished from Byzantine icons by its much greater size, the gable shape and solid throne are also Gothic in origin as is the general verticality. The rigid, angular draperies and rather flat body of the Madonna are from the Byzantine tradition, but the softer lines of the angels' faces and their lightly hung draperies were inspired by works from contemporary Constantinople.

Giotto

Cimabue's naturalistic, monumentally scaled work had a profound influence on his purported pupil Giotto (JOT-toe; ca. 1267–1337), the acknowledged "father of Western painting." Giotto was a one-man revolution in art. He established the illusionary qualities of space, bulk, movement, and human expression—all features of most pictorial art for the next six centuries. His indebtedness to Cimabue is obvious in his *Madonna Enthroned* (fig. 14.34), but there

14.33   Cimabue, *Madonna Enthroned*. Ca. 1280–90. Tempera on wood, 12' 7½" × 7' 4" (3.85 × 2.24 m). Galleria degli Uffizi, Florence. Photo: Scala, Florence.

3. Fresco paintings are made on fresh wet plaster with pigments suspended in water; tempera uses pigments mixed with egg yolk and applied, usually, to a panel. Because the drying time for both techniques is very fast, corrections are virtually impossible without redoing entire areas. Therefore, artists had to work rapidly and with precision.

14.35 Duccio, *The Calling of the Apostles Peter and Andrew*. 1308–11. Tempera on panel, 17⅛ × 18⅛" (43.5 × 46 cm). National Gallery of Art, Washington, D.C. (Samuel H. Kress Collection).

are significant changes that make it not necessarily better but certainly different. Giotto abandoned the Byzantine tradition and patterned his work after Western models, undoubtedly French cathedral statues. His solid human forms occupy a three-dimensional space surrounded by an architectural framework. His *Madonna Enthroned* is highlighted by the protruding knee of the Madonna, indicating a tangible body underneath the robe, a figure of monumental substance. When compared with Cimabue's angels, we see that Giotto's angels, especially the kneeling ones, are placed firmly at the same level on which the base of the Gothic throne rests. The ethereal quality of Byzantine painting has been supplanted by the illusion of tangible space occupied by three-dimensional figures.

Two Artists from Siena

Two Sienese artists, whose work was unlike that of either Cimabue or Giotto, established the International Style, the first international movement in Western art. Duccio (DOOT-cho; ca. 1255–1319) painted Byzantine-type faces except for the eyes, but in a style comparable to northern Gothic manuscripts and ivories. The most elegant painter of his time, his *Rucellai Madonna* (see unit opener on p. 189) is highly decorative, with sinuous folds of background drapery and a remarkable delicacy of line for so large a work. Contrasting with the Byzantine-style flatness of the

Madonna, the kneeling angels are portrayed much more in the round, combining the Hellenistic-Roman naturalistic tradition with that of Gothic architectural sculpture. This one work is a virtual encyclopedia of the International Style synthesis of Mediterranean and northern cultures.

In his *Calling of the Apostles Peter and Andrew* (fig. 14.35), Duccio depicts a world of golden sky and translucent greenish sea where the commanding yet elegant figure of Christ beckons gently to the slightly puzzled fishermen. It is a lovely creation, the world of Duccio, and this is the style the popes at Avignon and the northern kings and queens admired and encouraged their artists to emulate.

Serving the pope's court in Avignon, Duccio's pupil Simone Martini (1284–1344) combined the grace of the Sienese school with the exquisite refinement of Late Gothic architecture. His *Annunciation* (fig. 14.36) epitomizes the courtly style. Completely Gothic, the frame is replete with **crockets**, or ornamental leaves and flowers, and finials, or carved spires; signifying eternity, the gold-leaf background is Byzantine. Delineated in graceful curved-lines, the Angel Gabriel kneels before the Virgin to proclaim "Hail Mary, full of grace . . . ." As the words travel literally from his lips, she draws back in apprehension, her body arranged in an elaborate S-curve and covered by a rich blue robe. Between the two figures is an elegant vase containing white lilies symbolic of Mary's purity. As delicately executed as fine jewelry, the artistic conception is aristocratic and courtly, comparable to the polished **sonnets** of Petrarch, who also served the papal court at Avignon.

With its combined classical, Byzantine, and Gothic attributes, the International Style was promulgated

14.36 Simone Martini, *Annunciation*. 1333. Tempera on wood, 8' 8" × 10' (2.64 × 3.05 m). (Saints in side panels by Lippo Memmi.) Galleria degli Uffizi, Florence. Photo: Scala, Florence.

throughout the religious and secular courts of Europe. It found an enthusiastic response wherever wealthy clients prized grace, delicacy, and refinement in art, music, dress, and manners. Aesthetic pleasure was the goal, not spiritual enlightenment.

STUDY QUESTIONS

1. Medieval churches were very expensive, but many hundreds of them were built, indicating that they were highly valued by society. Which of the following are most valued by our society?

   Museums   Sports facilities

   Airports   Scientific facilities

   Office buildings   Nuclear power plants

   Educational buildings   Other

   Military bases

   What does this tell us about modern American values?

2. Architectural historians still argue about which building is better (greater, more beautiful, more inspired): the Parthenon or Chartres Cathedral. Pick one and defend your choice.

SUMMARY

A curious backwater during Roman times, Christianized Ireland launched missionary activities that led to a golden age highlighted by the production of exquisite manuscripts in the Hiberno-Saxon style. Establishing a tradition of meticulous northern craftsmanship, the *Lindisfarne Gospels* and the *Book of Kells* were among the first and best of a long history of illuminated manuscripts.

Charlemagne seized the opportune moment to create the Holy Roman Empire and launch the Carolingian Renaissance. Importing technology and stonemasons from the Mediterranean area, he set in motion the forces that would produce the Romanesque style and climax in the Gothic Age.

The year AD 1000 marked the Christianization of virtually all of Europe and the launching of a vast building program of monasteries and churches. Inspired by Roman models, builders constructed stone-vaulted churches such as the pilgrimage churches of St.-Benoit-sur-Loire, St.-Sernin, Toulouse, and Ste.-Madeleine, Vézelay. Notable among the numerous monasteries built during the period were Jumièges and Mont-St.-Michel.

Inspired by the revolutionary design of the choir of St.-Denis, which launched the Gothic style, French master builders erected some of the most sublime buildings ever conceived by humankind, most notably the cathedrals of Chartres, Amiens, and Reims. The style spread to other European countries, where it acquired various regional variations. It also influenced decorative arts, such as jewelry and manuscript illumination.

Though relatively immune to Gothic architecture, Italian artists synthesized classical, Byzantine, and Gothic elements to create the first International Style in art. A medieval man like Dante and his friend and fellow Florentine Giotto carried medieval art to its final consummation. Indeed, Dante's work marks the end of the Middle Ages and sets the stage for the Renaissance.

CULTURE AND HUMAN VALUES

Of the many significant artistic achievements of the Middle Ages, the Gothic cathedral would have to rank as the crowning glory. These amazing structures represented, simultaneously, inspired engineering, breathtaking architecture, appropriate settings for Christian worship, and notable symbols of civic pride. The church ranked pride among the seven deadly sins but pride—a sense of one's own dignity and value—was a vital factor in artistic achievement, as well as stimulating the competitive drive in commerce. The striving for excellence was matched by the vying for position, profit, or prizes.

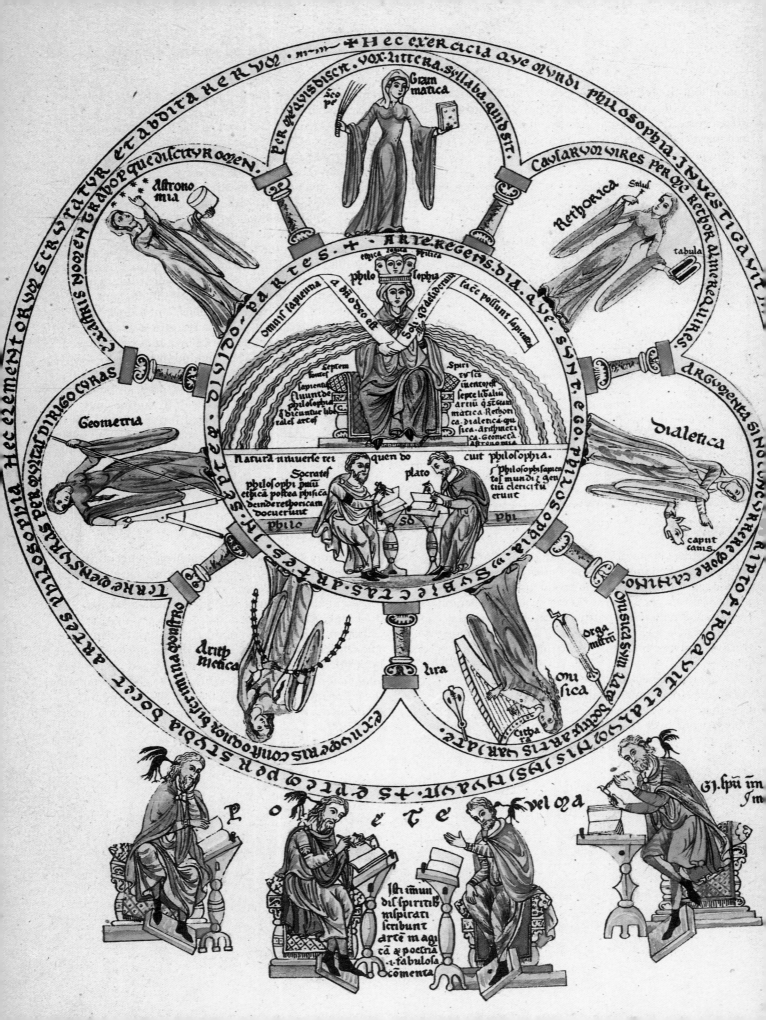

CHAPTER 15

Medieval Music and Dance: Sacred and Secular

The line today between secular music and music used for religious purposes is often very fuzzy, with some of the same music turning up on both sides of the line. Inherently, music is neither sacred nor secular, but it is used for sacred and secular purposes, which is the only way to tell the difference. We can't even say, for example, that "dance music" doesn't belong in church because people do dance in some churches and, conversely, anyone can pray in a nightclub or at a football game. What this adds up to, of course, is that we live in a secular society, and have ever since this country was founded.

Medieval Europe was not a secular society. To be sure, what took place out of sight of the authorities was probably no different than everyday life today. Nevertheless, the society was structured and it was rigid, with everyone knowing his or her place from the village cobbler through the millers, squires, yeomen, knights, earls, barons, kings, monks, priests, bishops, and on and on. Music also knew its place. Only in certain strictly defined ways could it appear in church. It was sacred music and it had to serve God. The service was dictated, of course, by the church, for it made the rules.

SACRED MUSIC

Throughout the world, the oldest type of music is **monophonic**, a single melodic line with no other parts or accompaniment. This kind of unadorned melody line became the liturgical (officially authorized) music of the Church of Rome. The music is monophonic in a style called **Gregorian chant**, or **plainsong**.

Opposite Abbess Herrad von Landsberg, "The Seven Liberal Arts," fol. 32 from the *Hortus Deliciarum* (modern reconstruction; see fig. 15.3). Original ca. 1170. Manuscript. Photo: A.K.G., London.

Gregorian Chant

According to legend, Pope Gregory the Great (reigned 590–604; fig. 15.1) ordered a body of liturgical music organized, priests trained in singing the music, and a common liturgy disseminated throughout the Western church. He did reorganize the church, but the chant that bears his name reached its final form during and shortly after the reign of Charlemagne (reigned 768–814). Consisting today of nearly 3,000 melodies, Gregorian chant is a priceless collection of subtle and sophisticated melodies.

Gregorian chant is monophonic, **a cappella** (unaccompanied), and sung by male or female voices (solo and chorus) in Latin. The authorized texts determine the note values and musical accents, that is, the rhythm of the music

15.1 "King David as Organist *[left]* and Pope Gregory the Great," fol. 5v, Codex Lat. 17403, Bayerische Staatsbibliothek, Munich. 1241. Illuminated manuscript. The Psalms, many of which are attributed to David, formed a large part of the Gregorian repertoire. Inspired by the dove of the Holy Spirit and holding a **monochord** (an instrument for measuring the mathematical relations between musical tones), Gregory is depicted in his legendary role as codifier of liturgical chant.

15.2 "Guido d'Arezzo," fol. 35v, Codex 51, Vienna Staatsbibliothek. 12th century. Illuminated manuscript. Seated at the left, Guido is demonstrating on a monochord the two-octave scale (A–B–C–D–E–F–G, etc.) which was converted to neumes and placed on the staff.

matches the rhythm of the words. There is no steady pulsation or beat, no division into regular accents as there is in a march or waltz. The undulating melodies flow smoothly, resonating through the cavernous stone churches, weaving a web of sound, and evoking in the worshipers feelings of awe and reverence.

Like secular music, Gregorian chant existed for centuries as a purely oral tradition. The precise musical notation of the ancient Greeks had been lost, and it was not until the eighth century that a new notational system began to evolve. Symbols for musical pitches, called **neumes**, were at first vague about the precise pitch, leading the monk Guido of Arezzo (ca. 990–1050) to remark that, "In our times, of all men, singers are the most foolish." He blames the lack of precise musical notation for

1. Simple musical notation is used on a modest scale throughout this text; once you understand how to read this, it will make your listening more meaningful and enjoyable. See the Appendix, "Music Listening and Notation," for the basic principles of reading music.
2. CD1, track 3.

"losing time enough in singing to have learned thoroughly both sacred and secular letters." To solve this problem Guido invented a four-line musical **staff** on which neumes could symbolize precise pitches (fig. 15.2).

Many Gregorian melodies were adapted from Jewish synagogue chant, especially the **Alleluias** (Hebrew, *Hallelujah*, "praise ye the Lord"). The seventh item of the Christian Mass (see table 15.1), Alleluias are characteristically **melismatic**, with many notes sung to one syllable. Following is an Alleluia from the Mass for Epiphany (the visit of the Magi).

Listening Example 2
GREGORIAN CHANT

Anonymous, "Alleluia Vidimus stellam"
Codified 590–604[1]
"Alleluia. We have seen his star in the East, and have come with gifts to worship the Lord. Alleluia."

Time: 1:04
Cassette 3, track 2[2]

Alleluia, Vidimus stellam   **Anonymous (codified 590–604)**

The Mass

The two basic types of Catholic services are the Mass and the Daily Hours of Divine Services, usually called **Office hours**. The latter are celebrated eight times a day in religious communities such as monasteries and convents. The Mass, also celebrated daily, is the principal act of Catholic worship. In form this **sacrament** is an elaborate reenactment of the Lord's Supper and its climax is the consecration of the bread and the wine and the partaking of these elements by the congregation. Everything else in the service is either preparation for Communion (the Eucharist, Gk., "thanksgiving") or a postscript to this commemorative act.

In a "low Mass," the words are enunciated by the priest in a low (speaking) voice in front of a silent congregation. In a "high Mass," the service is recited and sung in a high (singing) voice using either Gregorian chant or a combination of chant and other music.

The Mass consists of the proper, in which the texts vary according to the **liturgical** calendar, and the ordinary, which uses the same texts throughout the church year. Both proper and ordinary have texts that are recited or chanted by the celebrants (clergy) or sung by the choir.

The complete Mass is outlined in table 15.1 (italics indicate the sung portions of the text). Although modernization of the Mass permits the use of indigenous modern language, increased lay participation, and congregational singing, the essential structure remains unchanged.

TABLE 15.1   THE MASS

Ordinary (same text)	Proper (changing texts)
	1. *Introit*
2. *Kyrie*	
3. *Gloria*	
	4. Oratio (prayers, collect)
	5. Epistle
	6. Gradual
	7. *Alleluia* (or *Tract* during Lent)
	8. Gospel
9. *Credo*	
	10. *Offertory*
	11. Secret
	12. Preface
13. *Sanctus*	
14. Canon	
15. *Agnus Dei*	
	16. *Communion*
	17. Postcommunion
18. *Ite missa est* (or *Benedicamus Domino*)	

Tropes

A **trope** (Lat., *tropus*, "figure of speech") is a textual addition to an authorized text, an interpolation in the chant. Sentences or even whole poems were inserted between words of the original text. Sometimes, added words were fitted to preexisting notes; at other times both words and music were injected together into the established text. For example, the chant *Kyrie eleison* ("Lord have mercy upon us"), with an interpolated trope, might read: Lord, *omnipotent Father, God, Creator of all*, have mercy upon us.

The practice of troping could have resulted from boredom, a desire for creativity, an inability to remember the notes, or varying combinations of all three. The authorized texts had not only remained the same for centuries but many of them—particularly the texts of the ordinary—were sung countless times. More positively, troping permitted exercises in creativity that could enliven the unvarying liturgical music without unduly disturbing the authorities.

Sequences

The oldest form of trope was that inserted into the last syllable, the "ia" (ja) of the Alleluia (see the example of an Alleluia given above). Many Alleluias, because of their Eastern origin, ended with an exotic and elaborate melisma on the final syllable. New poetry was added to this melisma and then, in time, the last section was detached from the Alleluia to become a separate composition called a **sequence**—that which follows. After this separation had occurred, composers felt free to alter the melodic line—a chance, finally, to move beyond the church-imposed formulas for sacred music.

The sequence marked the beginnings of musical composition for its own sake, a new development that would lead eventually to the works of such composers as Palestrina, Beethoven, and Stravinsky. Composing sequences was a first step away from the rigidity of a prescribed musical repertoire. Composers began to explore ever more musical innovations and thus to breach and, ultimately, to break down medieval walls.

The proliferation of sequences threatened for a time to dominate traditional Gregorian chant—a development that alarmed some churchmen. The Council of Trent (1545–63), formed to oppose the Reformation, abolished sequences, which caused such a furor that four sequences were returned to the repertoire. Following is the oldest of the surviving sequences, the so-called Easter Sequence by Wipo of Burgundy (WEE-po; ca. 1024–50), chaplain to the Holy Roman Emperor Henry III. This melody also served later as the basis for a Lutheran Easter **chorale**, "Christ Lay in the Bonds of Death," with text by Martin Luther.

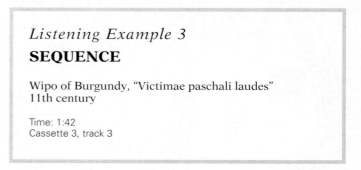

Listening Example 3
SEQUENCE

Wipo of Burgundy, "Victimae paschali laudes"
11th century

Time: 1:42
Cassette 3, track 3

Victimae paschali laudes   **Wipo of Burgundy (11th century)**

Vic - ti - mae pas - cha - li lau - des   im - mo - lent Chri - sti - a - ni.
(Let Christians dedicate their praises to the Easter victim.)

Liturgical Drama

Religious ceremonies, such as the Mass, extend themselves into the realm of the theatre. The dramatic reenactment of the Last Supper in the Mass led, in time, to the development of medieval drama. The impulse was somewhat similar to that which saw classical Greek drama evolve from the cult of Dionysos. There were notable differences, however. Greek tragedy dealt with ethical choices made under stress; illiterate medieval peasants were concerned with representations of the Nativity, the Shepherds, the Three Wise Men, and other specific events connected with their religion. Apparently the earliest surviving complete liturgical drama (words and music) was written by Hildegard (1098–1179), abbess of Bingen, who told the story of a contest between the devil and a human soul (*anima*).

At first the actors were priests and the plays episodes from the life of Christ, particularly the Christmas and Easter stories. During the liturgy, priests interpolated paraphrased dialogues from the Gospels, frequently using tropes. But these miniature dramas were too brief and too abstract for the unlettered congregation. Gradually the actors (clergy) gave priority to the Scriptures by using Latin for the formal sections and the vernacular for the dialogues. Eventually whole plays were performed in the native language, which in the early plays was French. Dramas were originally enacted in front of the altar; as vernacular elements were added performances were moved to the church portal and acting parts taken by laypeople who, in time, formed their own confraternities or societies of actors.

Liturgical dramas were mainly musical, relying for their effects on singing and on a rich variety of accompanying instruments. Of the dozens of instruments available, favorites included the **organ**, **harp**, lyre, **horn**, **trumpet**, **recorder**, rebec (precursor of **viols** and then violins), **drums**, and other **percussion** instruments (fig. 15.3).

The following opening dialogue (sung in Latin) is from *The Play of the Three Kings*, which dates from the late eleventh century. Some of the melodies were borrowed from plainsong, but much of the music was undoubtedly composed for the occasion. This recorded performance is *a cappella*, but instruments could have been added to underscore the Oriental origins of the Magi.

Listening Example 4

LISTENING EXAMPLE 4
LITURGICAL DRAMA

Anonymous, "Infantem vidimus"
11th–12th century; excerpt
Shepherds
Infantem vidimus
(We have seen the Infant.)
Boys
Qui sunt hi, quos stella ducit nos adeuntes, inaudita ferentes?
(Who are those whom the star leads, approaching us and bearing strange things?)
Magi
Nos sumus quos cernitis reges Tharsis et Arabum et Saba, dona offerentes Christo Reginato Domino.
(We are those whom you see—the kings of Tharsis, Arabia, and Sheba, offering gifts to Christ the King, the new-born Lord.)

Time: 1:08
Cassette 3, track 4

15.3 Abbess Herrad von Landsberg, fol. 32 from the *Hortus Deliciarum*. Ca. 1170. Manuscript fragment. Photo: Marburg. Formerly in the town library of Strasbourg, the manuscript was destroyed in the 1870 Franco-Prussian War. Hanging at the right is a rebec—a bowed string instrument of Arab origin. The female performer holds a harp, and at the left there hangs a wheel-lyre (organistrum). This instrument has three strings set in motion by a revolving wheel operated by a hand crank and is an ancestor of the hurdy-gurdy.

Conductus

The conductus was a processional used to "conduct" important characters on and off the stage. One of the most familiar of these was the "Song of the Ass,"[3] which was often used to describe Mary's flight into Egypt riding on a donkey. This song is shown as it was used in the twelfth-century *Play of Daniel*. Accompanying the Virgin as she rides into the church on a donkey, the conductus, as befits its function as processional music, is metrical. It has four beats to each **measure** in the manner of a solemn march. Only one of the seven verses is given here.

---

3. G. M. Dreves, *Analecta hymnica* xx, 217, 257; H. C. Greene, *Speculum* vi.

Play of Daniel: "Song of the Ass," Verse 1   **Anonymous (12th century)**

A
O - ri - en - tis par - ti - bus Ad - ven - ta - vit a - si - nus
(Out from lands of O - ri - ent Was the ass di - vine - ly sent.

B
Pul - cher et for - tis - si - mus Sar - ci - nis ap - tis - si - mus,
Strong and ve - ry fair was he, Bear - ing bur - dens gal - lant - ly.

Coda
Hez, Sir As - ne, hez.
Heigh, Sir Ass, oh heigh!)

Beginning in the fourteenth century, liturgical drama developed into mystery plays (Lat., *ministerium*, "service") performed entirely in the vernacular under secular sponsorship. Using music only for processions, fanfares, and dances, these dramatic portrayals of biblical stories (the Creation, the life of Jesus, and so forth) were the forerunners of modern European drama.

SECULAR MUSIC

Goliards

The **goliards** of the tenth through thirteenth centuries were a motley collection of rebellious vagabonds: disenchanted students, defrocked priests, minstrels, rascals, artists, and dreamers. Generally dissatisfied with established values and entrenched institutions, they took their name from a "Bishop Golias," whom they claimed as a patron—a very tolerant patron.

The goliards' songs treat many subjects: love, drinking, springtime, and more love, and include material both moral and immoral. Generally light-hearted and frequently obscene, their songs reflect, according to contemporary accounts, the licentious conduct of the goliards themselves.

Though little of their music is extant, many of their poems have survived, including those quoted on page 219 and a thirteenth-century manuscript published as *Carmina Burana*. Selections from this collection have been set to music by the modern German composer Carl Orff (1895–1982). A sampling of the opening lines from this poetry indicates some basic themes.

"Were the world all mine from the sea to the Rhine, I would gladly forsake it all if the Queen of England were in my arms."
"In rage and bitterness I talk to myself."
"I am the Abbot of Cluny, and I spend my time with drinkers."
"When we are in the tavern we don't care who has died."
"The God of Love flies everywhere."
"Sweetest boy I give myself completely to you."

The debauched conduct of the goliards and their assault upon established values led inevitably to conflicts with the church. However, the movement died out, not because of clerical opposition, but due to the rise of universities, which replaced wandering students with resident ones. However, conflict between the church and the universities, between authority and knowledge, became ever more strident.

Jongleurs

The **jongleurs** of France (and the *Gauklers*, their German counterparts) were generally not as educated as the goliards. Appearing first during the ninth century, these wandering men and women were seldom composers but always entertainers. They played music and sang songs that others had written, did tricks with trained animals, and generally helped to brighten weddings and other special events. Though some of them were sufficiently talented to be socially acceptable, many were considered disreputable as far as a despairing clergy was concerned.

The jongleurs' repertoire included **chansons de geste**, epic chronicles of the valorous deeds of heroes such as Charlemagne and Roland. Because the melodies consisted of easily remembered tunes, there was no real need to write down the music and thus very little of it has survived. In a twelfth-century manuscript of the *Chanson de Roland* there are musical fragments that were apparently used to sing of the exploits of Roland and his horn. The chant-fable, part prose and part verse, was similar to the chanson de geste but with a slightly different form. The best-known chant-fable is *Aucassin and Nicolette*.

Troubadours and Trouvères

A manifestation of the age of chivalry, the troubadours of Provence and their later followers in northern France, the **trouvères**, produced the finest repertoire of lyric song of the Middle Ages. These educated aristocrats, both men and women, composed love poetry in the tradition of Ovid, whose love poems and *Art of Love* were known to the cultured nobles of the south of France. The repertoire is large (2,600 troubadour poems, about 300 melodies; 4,000 trouvère poems, 1,400 melodies) and covers many subjects: the Crusades, travel, adventure, and, above all, romantic love. Despite the relative paucity of surviving melodies, all of the poems were meant to be sung. According to the troubadour Folquet of Marseilles (ca. 1155–1231), "A verse without music is a mill without water."

The earliest known troubadour, Duke William IX of Aquitaine (1071–1126), was a Crusader, poet, and performer, whose lusty life and romantic pursuits are reflected in his poetry, of which eleven poems and one melody have survived. The boldly masculine attitude in the following poem is comparable to Ovid's most aggressive style.

LITERARY SELECTION 16

Troubadour Songs

Duke William IX of Aquitaine

1. Friends, I'll write a poem that will do:
   But it'll be full of fun
   And not much sense.
   A grab-bag all about love
   And joy and youth.

2. A man's a fool if he doesn't get it
   Or deep down inside won't try
   To learn.
   It's very hard to escape from love
   Once you find you like it.   10

3. I've got two pretty good fillies in my corral:
   They're ready for any combat—
   They're tough.
   But I can't keep 'em both together:
   Don't get along.

4. If I could tame 'em the way I want,
   I wouldn't have to change
   This set-up,
   For I'd be the best-mounted man
   In all this world.   20

5. One's the fastest filly up in the hills,
   And she's been fierce and wild
   A long, long time.
   In fact, she's been so fierce and wild,
   Can't stick her in my pen.

6. The other was born here—Confolens way—
   And I never saw a better mare,
   I swear
   But she won't change her wild, wild ways
   For silver or gold.   30

7. I gave to her master a feeding colt;
   But I kept myself a share
   In the bargain too:
   If he'll keep her one whole year,
   I will a hundred or more.

8. Knights, your advice in this affair!
   I was never so troubled by
   Any business before.
   Which of these nags should I keep:
   Miss Agnes? Miss Arsen?   40

9. I've got the castle at Gimel under thumb,
   And over at Nieul I strut
   For all the folks to see.
   Both castles are sworn and pledged by oath:
   They belong to me!

Considerably more subtle, the next poem is designed to create a romantic, seductive atmosphere.

1. I'm going to write a brand-new song
   Before the wind and rain start blowing.
   My lady tries and tests me
   To see the way I love her.
   Yet despite the trials that beset me,
   I'd never break loose from her chain.

2. No, I put myself in her bondage,
   Let her write me into her charter.
   And don't think that I'm a drunkard   10
   If I love my good lady thus,
   For without her I couldn't live.
   I'm so hungry for her love.

3. O, she's whiter than any ivory statue.
   How could I worship any other?
   But if I don't get reinforcements soon
   To help me win my lady's love,
   By the head of St. George, I'll die!—
   Unless we kiss in bower or bed.

4. Pretty lady, what good does it do you
   To cloister up your love?   20
   Do you want to end up a nun?
   Listen: I love you so much
   I'm afraid that grief will jab me
   If your wrongs don't become the rights I beg.

5. What good will it do if I'm a monk
   And don't come begging round your door?
   Lady, the whole world's joy could be ours,
   If we'd just love each other.
   Over there at my friend Daurostre's
   I'm sending this song to be welcomed and sung. 30

6. Because of her I shake and tremble,
   Since I love her with the finest love.
   I don't think there's been a woman like her
   In the whole grand line of Lord Adam.

William's son governed the duchy for a few years, followed by his granddaughter, the celebrated Eleanor of Aquitaine (1122–1204), who established a court of love in Poitiers in 1170. Eleanor sponsored several troubadours and trouvères, the most notable of whom was Bernart de Ventadorn (d. 1195). Dante conferred the title of master singer on Arnaut Daniel and consigned another troubadour, Bertran de Born, to Hell but modern critics have ceded the palm to the poet-musician from Ventadorn as the finest lyric poet of the age.

Forty poems, eighteen with music, by Bernart de Ventadorn are known today. Lively, witty, and eminently singable, the subject is immutable: love rewarded, unrequited, noble, sacred, or profane, but always love. In the following canso (love song; **chanson** in northern France) the first of six verses is given in both Provençal, the language of the troubadours, and in English.

Listening Example 5
TROUBADOUR CANSO

Bernart de Ventadorn, "Be m'an perdut"
12th century; excerpt
Be m'an perdut lai enves Ventadorn tuih meo amic,
(I am indeed lost from the region of Ventadorn / To all my friends,)
pois ma domna no m'ama; et es be dreihz que jamais lai no torn
(for my lady loves me not; With reason I turn not back again,)
c'a des estai vas me salvatj' egrama.
(For she is bitter and ill-disposed toward me.)
Veus per quem fai semblan irat emorn;
(See why she turns a dark and angry countenance to me;)
car en s'amor me deleih e'm sojorn!
(Because I take joy and pleasure in loving her!)
ni de ren als no's rancura ni's clama.
(Nor has she ought else with which to charge me.)

Time: 0:52
Cassette 3, track 5[4]

"Be m'an perdut"   Ventadorn (d. 1195)

After her divorce from the king of France, Eleanor married, in 1152, Henry II, Duke of Normandy and, later, King of England. The next poem implies that Bernart has followed her to England and that the haughty highborn lady is either Eleanor herself or a member of her court.

LITERARY SELECTION 17

Lancan vei per mei la landa

Bernart de Ventadorn

1. Whenever I see amid the plain
    The leaves are drifting down from trees
    Before the cold's expansion,
    And the gentle time's in hiding,
    It's good for my song to be heard,
    For I've held back more than two years
    And it's right to make amends.

2. It's hard for me to serve that woman
    Who shows me only her haughty side,
    For if my heart dares make a plea,   10
    She won't reply with a single word.
    Truly this fool desire is killing me:

I follow the lovely form of Love,
    Not seeing Love won't attend me.

3. She's mastered cheating, trickery,
    So that always I think she loves me.
    Ah, sweetly she deceives me,
    As her pretty face confounds me!
    Lady, you're gaining absolutely nothing:
    In fact, I'm sure it's toward your loss   20
    That you treat your man so badly.

4. God, Who nurtures all the world,
    Put it in her heart to take me,
    For I don't want to eat any food
    And of nothing good I have plenty.
    Toward the beautiful one, I'm humble,
    And I render her rightful homage:
    She can keep me, she can sell me.

5. Evil she is if she doesn't call me
    To come where she undresses alone   30
    So that I can wait at her bidding
    Beside the bed, along the edge,
    Where I can pull off her close-fitting shoes
    Down on my knees, my head bent down:
    If only she'll offer me her foot.

6. This verse has been filled to the brim
    Without a single word that will tumble,
    Beyond the land of the Normans,
    Here across the wild, deep sea.
    [Apparently England.]
    And though I'm kept far from Milordess,   40
    She draws me toward her like a magnet:
    God, keep that beauty ever safe!

7. If the English king and the Norman duke
    Will it, I'll see her soon
    Before the winter overtakes us.

8. For the king I remain an English-Norman,
    And if there were no Lady Magnet,
    I'd stay here till after Christmas.

A number of female troubadours have been identified, including Azalais of Porcairagues, Maria of Ventadorn, Lombarda, and the Countess Garsenda of Provence. The most notable poet-musician, whose work is comparable to that of any male troubadour, was the Countess of Dia (present-day Die), who lived in the Drôme valley in southern France during the twelfth century and was known as Beatritz. Her voice is as distinctive as that of Sappho (see pp. 121–2). In the following dialogue song the lady sweeps aside male rationalizations and exacts a pledge of loyalty, devotion, and a love to be shared equally.

4. C. Appel, *Bernart von Ventadorn* (Halle, 1915), Plate ix (citing Milan manuscript *Chansonnier G*, folio 14). The form is AAB (see pp. 553–4).

LITERARY SELECTION 18

Troubadour Songs

Beatritz, Countess of Dia

1. Friend, I stand in great distress
   Because of you, and in great pain;
   And I think you don't care one bit
   About the ills that I'm enduring;
   And so, why set yourself as my lover
   Since to me you bequeath all the woe?
   Why can't we share it equally?

2. Lady, love goes about his job
   As he chains two friends together
   So the ills they have and the lightness too   10
   Are felt by each—in his fashion.
   And I think—and I'm no gabber—
   That all this deep-down, heartstruck woe
   I have in full on my side too.

3. Friend, if you had just one fourth
   Of this aching that afflicts me now,
   I'm sure you'd see my burden of pain;
   But little you care about my grief,
   Since you know I can't break free;
   But to you it's all the same   20
   Whether good or bad possess me.

4. Lady, because these glozing spies,
   Who have robbed me of my sense and breath,
   Are our most vicious warriors,
   I'm stopping: not because desire dwindles.
   No, I can't be near, for their vicious brays
   Have hedged us in for a deadly game.
   And we can't sport through frolicsome days.

5. Friend, I offer you no thanks
   Because my damnation is not the bit   30
   That checks those visits I yearn for so.
   And if you set yourself as watchman
   Against my slander without my request,
   Then I'll have to think you're more "true-blue"
   Than those loyal Knights of the Hospital.

6. Lady, my fear is most extreme
   (I'll lose your gold, and you mere sand)
   If through the talk of these scandalmongers
   Our love will turn itself to naught.
   And so I've got to stay on guard   40
   More than you—by St. Martial I swear!—
   For you're the thing that matters most.

7. Friend, I know you're changeable
   In the way you handle your love,
   And I think that as a chevalier
   You're one of that shifting kind;
   And I'm justified in blaming you,
   For I'm sure other things are on your mind,
   Since I'm no longer the thought that's there.

8. Lady, I'll never carry again   50
   My falcon, never hunt with a hawk,
   If, now that you've given me joy entire,
   I started chasing another girl.
   No, I'm not that kind of shyster:
   It's envy makes those two-faced talk.
   They make up tales and paint me vile.

9. Friend, should I accept your word
   So that I can hold you forever true?

10. Lady, from now on you'll have me true,
    For I'll never think of another.   60

More direct than much of the poetry of her male counterparts, the following song leaves no doubt about the lady's fiery passion. The slighting reference to the husband may have amused the Count, for this is, after all, a fictional account of a woman who has much in common with the Wife of Bath in Chaucer's *Canterbury Tales*.

1. I've suffered great distress
   From a knight whom I once owned.
   Now, for all time, be it known:
   I loved him—yes, to excess.
      His jilting I've regretted,
   Yet his love I never really returned.
   Now for my sin I can only burn:
      Dressed, or in my bed.

2. O, if I had that knight to caress
   Naked all night in my arms,   10
   He'd be ravished by the charm
   Of using, for cushion, my breast.
      His love I more deeply prize
   Than Floris did Blancheflor's.
   Take that love, my core,
      My sense, my life, my eyes!

3. Lovely lover, gracious, kind,
   When will I overcome your fight?
   O, if I could lie with you one night!
   Feel those loving lips on mine!   20
      Listen, one thing sets me afire:
   Here in my husband's place I want *you*,
   If you'll just keep your promise true:
      Give me everything I desire.

By the middle of the twelfth century, troubadour influences had spread to northern France, where notable trouvères included Blondel de Nesles (b. ca. 1155), minstrel to Richard the Lionhearted (reigned 1189–99 and himself a trouvère). Like troubadour cansos, trouvère chansons were monophonic with accompaniment an option depending on available instruments. The following **virelai** is a trouvère form that begins with a refrain that repeats after each verse. Composed by an unknown trouvère, this is a superb example of the sophisticated style of northern France.

"Or la truix"   **Anonymous (12th–13th century)**

In 1208 Pope Innocent III preached a crusade against the Albigensian heresy (latter-day Manicheans; see p. 191), stating that the church must "use against heretics the spiritual sword of excommunication, and if this does not prove effective, use the material sword." His army killed 12,000 Christians in a single day. Exploiting the Albigensian Crusade as an excuse to plunder the south of France, nobles, the French crown, and the papacy destroyed the high culture that had fostered the troubadour tradition, chivalry, and the Courts of Love.

POLYPHONIC MUSIC

The high point of medieval music was the development of **polyphony**. Polyphony (Gk., *poly-phonos*, "many sounds") is a style of music in which two or more melodies are played and/or sung together. "Row, Row, Row Your Boat," when sung as a **round**, is an example of one kind of polyphonic music in which the same melody is sung at different times. "Jesu, Joy of Man's Desiring," by J. S. Bach, combines three different melodies.

5. Bodleian Oxford, Douce 308, folios 226 and 237. The form is
    ABAA.

Related to polyphonic music is a style that evolved in the late seventeenth and early eighteenth centuries, and is called **homophonic** (Gk., *homo-phonos*, "like sounds"). Homophonic music consists of a single melody plus accompaniment or, to put it another way, melody and **harmony**. For example, "The Star Spangled Banner" and "The Battle Hymn of the Republic" are homophonic.

Polyphonic and homophonic styles of music are closely related with neither style usually existing in a pure form. Music that emphasizes two or more melodies of roughly equal importance is termed polyphonic. Homophonic music, on the other hand, emphasizes a predominant melody accompanied by harmony that enriches the melodic line. The two styles may be illustrated as follows:

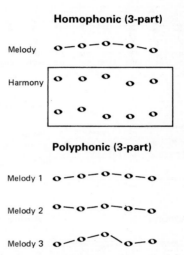

Non-Western music (from the Middle and Far East and Africa) has not developed polyphonic or homophonic styles of music. Although polyphony may occur in the music of these cultures, it is spontaneous rather than planned, the result of accidental conjunctions of melodies rather than a premeditated polyphonic composition, as we find in Western music.

It is this multi-voiced quality (both polyphonic and homophonic) that makes Western music unique. The development of polyphony during the Middle Ages was thus a crucial step leading to the enormous proliferation of musical styles: those of Bach, Beethoven, Bob Dylan, and Bruce Springsteen; the blues, ragtime, jazz, country-western, rock, and all the others.

The earliest medieval polyphony drew on the rich treasury of monophonic chants. Early attempts at multiple melodies, beginning in the tenth century, were quite literal: another voice was added at a fixed interval from the original chant (parallel **organum**). Later, in free organum, the two voices generally moved in contrary motion. That is, when one voice went up the other would go down. Still later, in melismatic organum, one voice moved slowly on prolonged notes (the original chant) while the other traced elaborate melismas.

Listening Example 7

EARLY POLYPHONY: ORGANUM

Parallel: "Rex caeli, Domine"[6]
Free: Trope, "Agnus Dei"[7]
Melismatic: "Benedicamo Domino"[8]

Time: 2:29
Cassette 3, track 7[9]

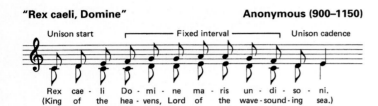

"Rex caeli, Domine"   Anonymous (900–1150)

"Agnus Dei"   Anonymous (900–1150)

"Benedicamo Domino"   Anonymous (900–1150)

Cantus Firmus

Eventually the chant melody was consistently placed in the lowest voice and referred to as the **cantus firmus** ("fixed song"). The chant was identified by quoting the initial phrase of the Latin text. The cantus firmus was also called the **tenor** (Lat. *tenere*, "to hold") because it held (retained) the original chant.

All polyphonic compositions of the medieval period were based on a cantus firmus, usually assigned to the tenor voice. The practice of using authorized liturgical music (plainsong) as a foundation for composing original music is comparable to basing a sermon on a scriptural quotation. Both procedures quoted an approved source as the prerequisite for what was essentially an exercise in creativity.

Polyphonic writing developed rapidly during the twelfth century due, in part, to the invention of rhythmic notation by composers of the school of music associated with the Cathedral of Notre Dame in Paris. The Paris composers wanted the larger sound of more voices for the cavernous nave of Notre Dame. They began writing three- and four-part compositions after they discovered how to synchronize the different voices, how to keep the singers moving together to the right notes at the right time. This Notre Dame notation (now called rhythmic modes) was based on the poetic meters such as iambic, dactylic, trochaic, and so forth. These were patterns of long and short sounds that were transformed into musical notation. The remarkable thing about rhythmic notation was that "it represented the first symbolic manipulation of measured time—time independent of motion and detached from the environment."[10] The Notre Dame composers were the first to discover how to measure time.

Following is a three-part organum by Pérotin, the foremost composer of the **Notre Dame school**. The beginning measures are given in musical notation so that the two voice parts plus instrumental line can be seen as well as heard. The music is now "measured" with a **time signature** and bar lines separating the measures. Any of the melodies can be sung, whistled, or played on an instrument. The complexity of polyphony results from the simultaneity of, in this case, uncomplicated melody lines.

Listening Example 8

THREE-PART ORGANUM

Pérotin, "Alleluya" (Nativitas)
12th century; excerpt

Time: 1:35
Cassette 3, track 8[11]

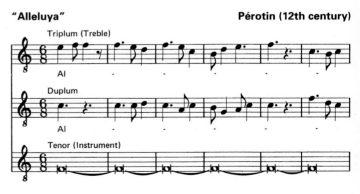

"Alleluya"   Pérotin (12th century)

---

6. M. Gerbert, *Scriptores* (St. Blaise, France, 1784) Vol. I, p. 167.
7. Besseler, *Die Musik des Mittelalters* (Potsdam, 1931), p. 95.
8. F. Ludwig, *Handbuch der Musikgeschichte* (Frankfurt am Main, 1924), p. 148.
9. CD 1, track 4.

10. Szamosi, Geza, "The Origin of Time: How Medieval Musicians Invented the Fourth Dimension." *The Sciences* 26 (September/October 1986): 33–7.
11. Y. Rokseth, *Polyphonies du XIIIe siècle* (Paris, 1935).

The **motet**, one of the most important forms of sacred music, was developed in the thirteenth century. This polyphonic form was based originally on a passage of plainsong, which was used as the cantus firmus. Above this, the composer wrote one, two, or more melodic lines, each with its own set of words. The first of these was called the motetus (Fr., *mot*, "word"). A third voice added to the cantus firmus and the motetus was called the triplum; a fourth voice, the quadruplum.

The motet offered enormous scope for variation. Not only could the different voices sing different words, but they might be in different languages: the cantus firmus being in Latin, for example, and the upper voices being in the vernacular. It was not long before secular poetry was being used for the upper voices, at which point the sacred Latin text of the cantus firmus was often dropped and this line performed instrumentally. This type of secular motet is illustrated by the following example, in which the upper voices sing variations on a French love song. Its title contains, as was customary, the first few words of each line, those of the tenor line serving only to identify the original chant. Here again, the opening measures of notation illustrate the uncomplicated nature of the individual melodies.

Listening Example 9
MOTET

Anonymous, "En non Diu! Quant voi; Eius in Oriente"
13th century; excerpt

Time: 1:07
Cassette 3, track 9[12]

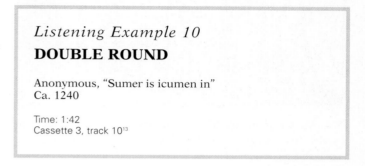

"En non Diu! Quant voi; Eius in Oriente"   **School of Notre Dame (13th century)**

Triplum
En non Diu! que que—nus   di - e, Quant voi l'her-be__   vert__et
(Now in truth! what-e'er they   tell__ us,When the grass is__   green and)

Motetus
Quant voi la__ rose es - pa - ni - e, L'her-be   vert__ et__ le - tans
(When I see__ the ro - ses bud-ding, Grass-es   green__ and__ wea-ther)

Tenor EIUS IN ORIENTE

The earliest extant piece of music in six parts is the "Reading Rota," a double round found at Reading Abbey and set to a Middle English text: "Sumer is icumen in." The top melody is sung by four voices as a four-part round. One voice begins alone, the second voice begins when the first has gotten to the asterisk, and so on. At the same time the lower two voices sing a two-part round to the words "sing cuccu."

Listening Example 10
DOUBLE ROUND

Anonymous, "Sumer is icumen in"
Ca. 1240

Time: 1:42
Cassette 3, track 10[13]

"Sumer is icumen in"   **Anonymous (ca. 1240)**

Sum - er is i - cum - en in,____ Lhu - de sing cuc - cu
Sing   cuc - cu   nu,____ Sing   cuc - cu

Sing   cuc - cu,   Sing   cuc - cu

Polyphonic Mass

Musical styles developed very rapidly during the High Middle Ages, and some composers acquired international reputations (in contrast to the great master builders of Gothic cathedrals, most of whom remain anonymous). Guillaume de Machaut (ca. 1300–77), equally proficient as poet and as a composer of both sacred and secular music, was the most acclaimed of the gifted artists of the Late Middle Ages (fig. 15.4). He was the first to write a polyphonic setting of all five movements of the ordinary of the Mass, a practice that was subsequently followed by every major composer through the sixteenth century and by many composers up to the present day.

The following "Agnus Dei" is sung by the upper three voices and accompanied by an instrument on the *contratenor* part, as indicated by the absence of text. The tenor, now the next lowest voice, still sings the cantus firmus. The polyphonic Mass, as distinguished from a motet, uses the Latin text of the monophonic chant. The beginning of the movement is notated here in an open score (one staff for each part) so that the more complex movement of the melodies can be compared with the examples previously given of an organum and a motet.

---

12. Y. Rokseth, *Polyphonies du XIIIe siècle* (Paris, 1935).
13. CD 1, track 5.

15.4 Master of Bocqueteaux, "Machaut Receiving Honors of Royalty and Clergy." Miniature. Bibliothèque Nationale, Paris.

This first known portrait of a Western composer is indicative both of Machaut's reputation and of the status of a creative artist in late medieval France.

Listening Example 11
POLYPHONIC MASS

Machaut, "Agnus Dei," Mass of Notre Dame
1364; excerpt

Time: 1:30
Cassette 3, track 11[14]

Mass of Notre Dame, "Agnus Dei" **Machaut (ca. 1300–77)**

14. CD 1, track 7. H. Besseler, *Die Musik des Mittelalters und der Renaissance* (Bucken, *Handbuch der Musikwissenschaft*) (Potsdam, 1931), p. 149.

MEDIEVAL DANCE
Sacred Dance

Although the Church of Rome officially disapproved of dance in worship because of its non-Christian associations, dancing as a glorification of God was widely accepted in some Christian communities up until the High Middle Ages, when it was universally banned. Especially popular was the "Hymn of Jesus," a round dance (or ring dance) with twelve dancers representing the twelve disciples and the twelve signs of the zodiac. The idea of zodiac dancing to restore order to the cosmos can be traced as far back as the ancient Egyptians. However, a direct influence was probably the Pythagorean concept of the music of the spheres. This ring dance was also called the Ring Dance of Angels or simply Angel Dance.

The tripudium dated from early Christianity and was one of the few dance steps to survive into the medieval period. A tripudium was a three-step dance with two steps forward and one step backward. The dance symbolized both the Holy Trinity and, possibly, the concept of two (spiritual) steps forward and one step (of human frailty) backward.

"The Way to Jerusalem" was a stately dance that symbolized a pilgrimage to the Holy City. The dance was executed on the design of a labyrinth inlaid in the nave floor of some cathedrals. A chosen leader determined the pace and the steps that matched the pattern of the floor tiles. This was a slow, spiraling dance that coordinated the dance steps with an accompanying chant. To make it all the way to Jerusalem, the leader had to arrive at the center of the labyrinth at the precise moment that the final syllable of the chant was sung. The dance was usually performed on a labyrinth modeled after the Cretan version in the Knossos Labyrinth. The labyrinth in the cathedral of Chartres dates from the twelfth century and is 40 feet (12.2 m) in diameter.

Choreomania, a kind of dance mania, probably first appeared in England in the twelfth century. It was characterized by group psychosis and frenzied, even demented dancing. The Dance of Death (*Danse Macabre*) was a phenomenon that appeared during the Black Death. Enacting the superstition that the dead danced on their graves to lure the living, some plague victims did their Dance of Death in the cemetery.

Secular Dance

Little is known of dancing in the Early Middle Ages, but by the eighth or ninth centuries social dancing was a universal activity enjoyed by people at every level of society. The frequent fairs and festivals, with the attendant vigorous dancing, enabled the peasantry to forget temporarily their generally bleak and meager existence.

THE BLACK DEATH

No pestilence to date has been more devastating than the Black Death of the Middle Ages. Active in Central Asia in 1338, the plague infiltrated every European country with a port city and killed about a third of the population—75 million people. Spread by fleas who had fed on the blood of infected rodents, the disease traveled aboard rat-infested ships. Symptoms included vomiting, delirium, muscular pain, and swollen lymph nodes called buboes, thus "bubonic plague," with death certain 60 to 90 percent of the time. Inhaling droplets from a victim whose disease had spread to the respiratory system caused pneumonic plague, when death was literally in the air, swift and virtually inevitable. What caused the sickness was unknown but Christians blamed non-Christians and sinners, who were supposedly reaping God's punishment. Scapegoats were everywhere: cripples, lepers, Arabs, and Jews—especially Jews, who were massacred in Germany, southern France, the Low Countries, and parts of Spain. The Jews in Basel, Switzerland, were locked in wooden buildings and burned alive. Ironically, a non-Christian civilization had already found the answer in the fifth century AD, when the Indian physician Susrata noted the relationship of malaria to mosquitoes and of plague to rats. Plague is still a menace and still kills if antibiotics are not started within hours of the first symptoms. The disease is apparently not as virulent as the earlier strain but the emergence of AIDS signals a plague that could surpass the medieval killer.

The earliest form of European social dancing was performed by a group of people arranged either in a ring or in a chain. One of the most popular early dances was the **branle**, which was danced in an arc or in a closed circle, moving in a clockwise direction, interrupted by occasional steps to the right, producing a swaying effect. Like many other dances, the branle was taken up by the nobility, who used its basic steps to devise more refined and complex dances. Some of these new aristocratic dances were performed by couples—a development that may have first taken place in twelfth-century Provence. The earliest known couple dance, called the **estampie** (Provençal, *estamper*, "to stamp"), remained the most popular dance through the High Middle Ages. The music for the estampie was in triple meter and consisted of short, rotating phrases that were repeated many times during the course of the dance. To begin the dance, couples stood side by side in a semicircle. The first part of the dance began with both starting on the same foot with a step, close, step, close to first

15. Wooldridge, *Early English Harmony* (London, 1897), p. 19.

position with heels together. The dancers moved first to the right, then backward, then forward, then backward once more, and then began the pattern all over again.

Following is a two-part estampie with the parts labeled simply as cantus superior and cantus inferior. They were to be played by any available instruments. To get a sense of what it was like to dance in a medieval court, try executing the steps of the estampie to an accompaniment of the cassette or any two or more different percussion instruments like the drum, tambourine, bells, or triangle.

Listening Example 12
ESTAMPIE

Anonymous, "Instrumental Dance"
13th century; excerpt

Time: 1:26
Cassette 3, track 12[15]

"Instrumental Dance"   Anonymous (13th century)

STUDY QUESTIONS

1. Hearing an authentic performance of music that has been sung for 1,000 years or more is a moving and exhilarating experience. Find a vocal group in your area that sings Gregorian chant, possibly in a Catholic church or monastery or a college music department.

2. How does a Protestant service (Presbyterian, Methodist, Baptist, and so on) differ from the Catholic Mass? (NOTE: The several denominations also differ considerably from each other.) What do the Mass and various forms of Protestant services have in common?

3. What, if anything, do rock lyrics have in common with troubadour songs? You might want to look up additional troubadour songs for better comparisons.

SUMMARY

The first medieval music to be written down was composed for the church. This was monophonic music of a form known as Gregorian chant or plainsong, performed by monks or nuns without accompaniment as part of the Mass or the Divine Office. In time, these chants were elaborated by the introduction of tropes and sequences—extra words and notes that varied the pattern in interesting ways. These embellishments led, in turn, to the development of liturgical drama as part of the Mass, and then to spoken drama in the form of mystery plays.

Medieval secular music consisted at first of songs, performed by various groups of musicians, from the vagabond goliards and jongleurs to the aristocratic troubadours and trouvères of Provence and northern France, respectively, who composed their own songs, mainly about love.

Beginning in the tenth century, composers began to experiment with polyphony ("many sounds"), adding one or more melodic lines to an existing chant. In time, such experiments were to lead to a rich variety of musical textures, using several melodies together and, in other cases, a single melody supported by harmony—called homophonic music. The High Middle Ages produced some wonderfully complex polyphonic music, including the first polyphonic Mass, by Guillaume de Machaut.

Early medieval dance included some forms intended for worship, but this practice came to an end in the High Middle Ages. Peasant dances, originally performed in a ring or a chain, were refined and elaborated by the aristocracy into couple dances such as the estampie.

CULTURE AND HUMAN VALUES

The history of medieval music is much more than the study of the musical practices of a cultural period. Music of any era, in the playing and the singing, reflects and expresses the hopes, aspirations, frustrations, and fears of people of all classes and stations in life. Music is still the nearest equivalent to an international language that humans have yet devised.

Medieval music, when properly performed, is an aural time machine. It can bring alive the vast panorama of medieval musical life, from Gregorian chant to liturgical drama, from troubadour love songs to peasant dances. Because its sound is so different from that of music we normally hear, it seems to conjure up the whole world that produced it.

The sound of the music has a correlation with the architectural styles of the period. Gregorian chant, for example, was intended for participating worshipers—monks or nuns—rather than for an audience. It is therefore most effective and persuasive heard in a church or, better still, a monastery or convent, with its narrow windows, heavy walls, and pervasive quietude.

The development of more complex forms in music during the Middle Ages was paralleled by the increasing complexity of architecture. The spare line of monophonic chant is complemented by the equally austere forms of early Romanesque churches. Each has a simplicity and purity capable of refreshing the spirit. Similarly, the development of polyphony reflects—and is reflected by—the flowering of the Gothic style of architecture, with its intricate structures of rib vaults and flying buttresses, its delicate tracery and glittering stained glass windows. Both the music and the architecture of the High Middle Ages display a love of elaboration and a delight in scaling the heights of creativity.

The High Middle Ages achieved the first period of balance since Graeco-Roman civilization, a long and torturous trek up the mountain of culture. The Church of Rome reached its pinnacle of power at the same time, only to see its formidable structure begin to crack with the "Babylonian Captivity" in Avignon and the Great Schism, while the Renaissance and Reformation waited impatiently in the wings. Even as the medieval synthesis settled into place, the forces that were to hurl Europe into the chaos of the Renaissance were already undermining the foundations of society: science, universities, Aristotle, humanism, burgeoning commerce and trade, and rising nationalistic expectations. There was, however, an enormous difference between the fall of Rome and the waning of the Middle Ages. Rome's extended demise left a vacuum that was largely filled by the barbarians within and those at the gates. The vibrant Gothic age was gradually supplanted by another version of reality that bred new values and goals. Rather than taking a step backward, European civilization was poised at its medieval apex as its leaders, artists, and intellectuals sought new directions in a rapidly changing world.

The Renaissance, 1350–1600

The Renaissance

1350–1600

People and Events	Art and Architecture	Literature and Music	Philosophy, Science, Discovery
1350			
1305–76 Papacy at Avignon **1348–50** Black Death **1382** Wiclif's Bible	**Limbourg Brothers** fl. 1385–1416 *Très Riches Heures du Duc de Berry*	**Petrarch** 1304–74 sonnets **Boccaccio** 1313–75 *The Decameron*	
1400			
1415 Jan Hus burned at stake; Henry V of England defeats French at Agincourt **1378–1417** Great Schism of church **1428** Joan of Arc defeats English **1436** Dedication of Florence Cathedral **1419–67** Philip the Good of Burgundy **1453** Hundred Years' War ends; Constantinople falls to Turks **1449–92** Lorenzo de' Medici **1456** Gutenberg Bible printed **1469–1504** Reign of Ferdinand and Isabella of Spain **1492–1503** Alexander VI (Borgia pope) **1494** Beginning of French and Spanish invasions of Italy **1498** Savonarola burned at stake; Petrucci obtains printing monopoly in Venice	**Brunelleschi** 1377–1446 Florence Cathedral dome; Pazzi Chapel **Donatello** 1386–1466 *David* **van Eyck** 1390–1441 *Ghent Altarpiece* **Uccello** 1397–1475 *Battle of San Romano* **van der Weyden** 1400–64 *Portrait of a Lady* **Masaccio** 1401–28? *Tribute Money* **Alberti** 1404–72 Santa Maria Novella **Verrocchio** 1435–88 *David* **Memling** 1440–94 *The Presentation in the Temple* **Bramante** 1444–1514 Tempietto **Botticelli** 1445–1510 *Birth of Venus* **Bosch** 1450–1516 *Garden of Delights* **da Vinci** 1452–1519 *The Last Supper*	**Dunstable** 1390–1453 English composer **Dufay** 1400–74 Burgundian composer **Lorenzo Valla** ca. 1407–57 proved *Donation of Constantine* a forgery **Issac** 1450–1517 German composer at Medici court **Josquin** 1450–1521 Franco-Flemish composer **Mirandola** 1463–94 *Oration on the Dignity of Man* **Erasmus** 1466–1536 *The Praise of Folly* **Machiavelli** 1469–1527 *The Prince* **Sir Thomas More** 1478–1535 *Utopia* **Castiglione** 1478–1529 *The Book of the Courtier* **1498** *The Witches' Hammer,* a manual for finding witches	**Prince Henry the Navigator** 1394–1460 improves compass and navigation charts **Ficino** 1433–99 translates Plato for Platonic Academy **1462** Cosimo de' Medici founds Platonic Academy **Copernicus** 1473–1543 heliocentric theory **1486** Diaz sails down African coast **1492** Columbus discovers America **1497** John Cabot lands in America; North America claimed by England **1497–99** Vasco da Gama sails around Africa to India
1500			
1503–13 Julius II (Warrior pope) **1517** Luther posts 95 Theses **1521** Diet of Worms: Luther's formal break with Rome **1509–47** Henry VIII of England **1515–47** Francis I of France **1519** Cortés conquers Aztecs in Mexico **1527** Rome sacked by Charles V **1531–33** Pizarro conquers Incas in Peru **1534** Church of England founded by Henry VIII **1540** Society of Jesus officially sanctioned **1545–64** Council of Trent; Inquisition renewed **1547** Calvin's Bible **1588** English defeat Spanish Armada	**Grünewald** 1483?–1528 *The Small Crucifixion* **Dürer** 1471–1528 *Erasmus of Rotterdam* **Giorgione** 1475–1510 *Adoration of the Shepherds* **Michelangelo** 1475–1564 *David, Pietà,* Sistine Chapel **Raphael** 1483–1520 *School of Athens* **Titian** 1488–1576 *Venus with a Mirror* **Holbein** 1497–1543 *Sir Thomas More* **Parmigianino** 1503–40 *Madonna with the Long Neck* **Tintoretto** 1518–94 *The Last Supper* **Palladio** 1518–80 Villa Rotunda **Bruegel the Elder** 1525–69 *Winter (Return of the Hunters)* **Veronese** 1528–88 *Christ in the House of Levi*	**Rabelais** 1490–1553 *Gargantua and Pantagruel* **Vasari** 1511–74 *Lives of Architects, Painters, Sculptors* **Palestrina** 1524/5–94 Roman composer **Lassus** 1532–94 Flemish composer **Montaigne** 1533–92 *Essays* **Cervantes** 1547–1616 *Don Quixote* **Gabrieli** 1557–1612 Venetian composer **Shakespeare** 1564–1616 *The Tempest* **Farnaby** 1565–1640 English composer **Bennet** 1575–1625 English madrigal composer	**1513** Balboa discovers Pacific **1519–22** Magellan sails around world **Tycho Brahe** 1546–1601 astronomer **Francis Bacon** 1561–1626 empirical science Illustration from Kepler's *Prodromus Dissertationum Cosmographicarum.* Photo: A.K.G., London.
1600			
1558–1603 Elizabeth I of England	**El Greco** 1541–1614 *The Resurrection of Christ*		

CHAPTER 16

A New Way of Looking at the World

A remarkable period of intellectual energy and artistic creativity, the Renaissance (ca. 1350–1600) ushered out the Middle Ages and set the stage for the emergence of the modern world. It was also a turbulent time of social unrest, political turmoil, religious conflict, and, particularly in Italy, constant warfare. Seen by its contemporaries as a "rebirth" of classical civilization, the era was also a period of chaos that followed upon the breakdown of the balanced culture of the High Middle Ages. Graeco-Roman civilization had neither died nor been "lost." Rather, it had been both replaced and partly absorbed by 1,000 years of what humanists designated the "Middle Age" between the fall of Rome and the revival of Graeco-Roman culture.

The emphasis in medieval Christendom on eternal salvation in another world as the sole purpose of human existence gradually gave way to the idea that life on earth had its own worth and that the life of each individual man and woman was unique and valuable. Everyone had worth and dignity and a free will that enabled them to use their God-given capacities to transform the world. They could and should develop their minds by study and reflection, activities advocated by Cicero as worthy of the "dignity of the human race" (*On Duties*, I, 30). Renaissance men and women were often as sanctimonious, superstitious, and naive as their medieval ancestors, but they were also more individualistic, materialistic, and skeptical than almost anyone in that vanished world. The enthusiastic revival of their ancient heritage reinforced their pride in being singular individuals who would create a brave new world.

Glorification of the distant past originated in Italy and spread to France, England, and the Low Countries, none of which even possessed a classical heritage, though all contained Roman ruins. What Italy and the northern countries had in common was vigorous trade, the growth of capitalism, expanding craft guilds, burgeoning industries, growing cities, and a widespread spirit of creative endeavor.

THE RISE OF HUMANISM

On 8 April 1341 the Latin scholar with the Latinized name of Petrarch (Francesco Petrarca; 1304–74) was crowned with a laurel wreath as the first poet laureate of modern times. Symbolizing an intellectual movement called **humanism** that had begun in Verona and Padua a century earlier, the ceremony took place, fittingly, in Rome. Humanists believed in the worth and dignity of the individual and that belief led, in turn, to the rediscovery of the culture of classical antiquity: literature, history, rhetoric, ethics, and politics. Describing his abandoned law studies at Bologna as "the art of selling justice," Petrarch devoted his life to acquiring what he called the "golden wisdom" of the ancients: proper conduct of one's private life; rational governance of the state; the enjoyment of beauty; and the quest for truth. Humanism was a union of love and reason that stressed earthly fulfillment rather than medieval preparations for paradise. The humanists had rediscovered their ancestors, seeing them as real people able to lend assistance in the restatement of human values. Petrarch wrote letters to Cicero, whom he called his father, and to Virgil, who was, he said, his brother.

There had been earlier stirrings of classical revivals in the ninth century at Aachen, where Charlemagne established his famous school, and in the twelfth century at the Cathedral School of Chartres and the Court of Eleanor of Aquitaine; but not until the middle of the fourteenth century did the rediscovery of antiquity become a true cultural movement. Petrarch's friend, the writer Giovanni Boccaccio (bo-KOTCH-yo; 1313–75), was one of the first Westerners to study Greek, but by 1400 nearly all the Greek authors had been recovered and translated into Latin and Italian: Homer, Herodotos, Thucydides, Aeschylus, Sophocles, Euripides, Aristophanes, and all of Plato's dialogues. Human history was divided into three ages, said the humanists: ancient, middle, and their own modern era. The middle was the Middle Ages, deemed a benighted phase between the fall of Rome in 476 and the rebirth of classical cultures. The men and women of the Renaissance were, in effect, discovering themselves as they recovered the past. They were aware that their time was significantly different from the Middle Ages, that they were the spiritual heirs of a distant past that was being reborn through their own efforts. There was no Latin word for rebirth, but Giorgio Vasari (1511–74) invented the word *rinàscita* ("renaissance") in his *Lives of the Most Excellent Italian Architects, Painters, and Sculptors from Cimabue to our own Times* (Florence, 1550).

Vasari's term was applied to the fine arts that had developed out of early humanism, but the label now describes an era that consciously freed itself from the bondage of medievalism.

Lorenzo Valla (ca. 1407–57), one of the few Renaissance scholars not associated with Florence, confined his activities mainly to Rome and Naples, where he translated Herodotos and Thucydides into Latin. A dedicated scholar of immense learning, he dared to challenge any authority. He criticized Cicero's supposedly flawless Latin, wrote a philological critique of the New Testament and, most notably, exposed the *Donation of Constantine* as a forgery. This was the document that willed Constantine's entire empire to the Church of Rome and on which Rome based its claims to temporal power.[1]

Valla would be called a bookworm today. He was one of the many scholars who devoted their careers to conserving antiquity by copying and translating ancient documents. Other humanists, such as Boccaccio and Rabelais, preferred writing in the vernacular, whereas still others tried to synthesize the classical past with the Christian present. Marsilio Ficino (fi-CHEE-no; 1433–99) and Pico della Mirandola (PEA-ko del-la mere-AN-do-luh; 1463–94) were two of the most important of the synthesizers, particularly for the Platonists of Florence.

Platonic Academy

A celebrated center of humanistic studies, the Platonic Academy was founded at Florence in 1462 by the banker Cosimo de' Medici (1389–1464), the sire of a family that was to dominate Florence throughout most of the Renaissance. The guiding force of the academy, Marsilio Ficino, promoted the study of Platonism through his translations into Latin of Plato, Plotinus, and other philosophers. In his major work, the *Theologia Platonica* (1482), Ficino described a universe presided over by a gracious and loving God who sought to bring humankind to him through beauty, one of his attributes. The contemplation of the beauty of nature, of beautiful things, of glorious art became a sort of worship of this God. When beauty was arranged in words or paintings (as in fig. 17.14), these works of art, too, became part of the circle of love by which people reached beyond themselves to a loving God. Ficino's theory of "Platonic love," a spiritual bond between lovers of beauty, had strong repercussions in later English, French, and Italian literature.

Pico della Mirandola was a colleague of Ficino and a major influence on the Florentine humanists. His broadly based classical education in Greek and Latin was enriched

by studies in Hebrew and Arabic that brought him into contact with Jewish and Arabic philosophy. Pico's attack on astrology impressed even the astronomer Johannes Kepler. More importantly, his conception of the dignity of the human race and the ideal of the unity of truth were significant contributions to Renaissance thought. His *Oration on the Dignity of Man* has been called "The Manifesto of Humanism." The following excerpts from Pico's ringing affirmation of the nobility of humankind epitomize Renaissance optimism.

LITERARY SELECTION 19

Oration on the Dignity of Man, 1486

Pico della Mirandola

I have read in the records of the Arabians, reverend Fathers, that Abdala the Saracen, when questioned as to what on this stage of the world, as it were, could be seen most worthy of wonder, replied: "There is nothing to be seen more wonderful than man." In agreement with this opinion is the saying of Hermes Trismegistus: "A great miracle, Asclepius, is man." But when I weighed the reason for these maxims, the many grounds for the excellence of human nature reported by many men failed to satisfy me—that man is the   10
intermediary between creatures, the intimate of the gods, the king of the lower beings, by the acuteness of his senses, by the discernment of his reason, and by the light of his intelligence the interpreter of nature, the interval between fixed eternity and fleeting time, and (as the Persians say) the bond, nay, rather, the marriage song of the world, on David's testimony but little lower than the angels. Admittedly great though these reasons be, they are not the principal grounds, that is, those which may rightfully claim for themselves the privilege   20
of the highest admiration. For why should we not admire more the angels themselves and the blessed choirs of heaven? At last it seems to me I have come to understand why man is the most fortunate of creatures and consequently worthy of all admiration and what precisely is that rank which is his lot in the universal chain of Being—a rank to be envied not only by brutes but even by the stars and by minds beyond this world. It is a matter past faith and a wondrous one. Why should it not be? For it is on this very account that man is rightly   30
called and judged a great miracle and a wonderful creature indeed.

But hear, Fathers, exactly what this rank is and, as friendly auditors, conformably to your kindness, do me this favor. God the Father, the supreme Architect, had already built this cosmic home we behold, the most sacred temple of His godhead, by the laws of His mysterious wisdom. The region above the heavens He had adorned with Intelligences, the heavenly spheres He

---

1. C. B. Coleman (ed.), *The Treatise of Lorenzo Valla on the Donation of Constantine* (New Haven: Yale University Press, 1922).

had quickened with eternal souls, and the excrementary and filthy parts of the lower world He had filled with a multitude of animals of every kind. But, when the work was finished, the Craftsman kept wishing that there were someone to ponder the plan of so great a work, to love its beauty, and to wonder at its vastness. Therefore, when everything was done (as Moses and Timaeus bear witness), He finally took thought concerning the creation of man. But there was not among His archetypes that from which He could fashion a new offspring, nor was there in His treasurehouses anything which He might bestow on His new son as an inheritance, nor was there in the seats of all the world a place where the latter might sit to contemplate the universe. All was now complete; all things had been assigned to the highest, the middle, and the lowest orders. But in its final creation it was not the part of the Father's power to fail as though exhausted. It was not the part of His wisdom to waver in a needful matter through poverty of counsel. It was not the part of His kindly love that he who was to praise God's divine generosity in regard to others should be compelled to condemn it in regard to himself.

At last the best of artisans ordained that that creature to whom He had been able to give nothing proper to himself should have joint possession of whatever had been peculiar to each of the different kinds of being. He therefore took man as a creature of indeterminate nature and, assigning him a place in the middle of the world, addressed him thus: "Neither a fixed abode nor a form that is thine alone nor any function peculiar to thyself have we given thee, Adam, to the end that according to thy longing and according to thy judgment thou mayest have and possess what abode, what form, and what functions thou thyself shalt desire. The nature of all other beings is limited and constrained within the bounds of laws prescribed by Us. Thou, constrained by no limits, in accordance with thine own free will, in whose hand We have placed thee, shalt ordain for thyself the limits of thy nature. We have set thee at the world's center that thou mayest from thence more easily observe whatever is in the world. We have made thee neither of heaven nor of earth, neither mortal nor immortal, so that with freedom of choice and with honor, as though the maker and molder of thyself, thou mayest fashion thyself in whatever shape thou shalt prefer. Thou shalt have the power to degenerate into the lower forms of life, which are brutish. Thou shalt have the power, out of thy soul's judgment, to be reborn into the higher forms, which are divine."

O supreme generosity of God the Father, O highest and most marvelous felicity of man! To him it is granted to have whatever he chooses, to be whatever he wills. Beasts as soon as they are born (so says Lucilius) bring with them from their mother's womb all they will ever possess. Spiritual beings, either from the beginning or soon thereafter, become what they are to be for ever and ever. On man when he came into life the Father conferred the seeds of all kinds and the germs of every way of life. Whatever seeds each man cultivates will grow to maturity and bear in him their own fruit. If they be vegetative, he will be like a plant. If sensitive, he will

become brutish. If rational, he will grow into a heavenly being. If intellectual, he will be an angel and the son of God. And if, happy in the lot of no created thing, he withdraws into the center of his own unity, his spirit, made one with God, in the solitary darkness of God, who is set above all things, shall surpass them all. Who would not admire this our chameleon? Or who could more greatly admire aught else whatever? It is man who Asclepius of Athens, arguing from his mutability of character and from his self-transforming nature, on just grounds says was symbolized by Proteus in the mysteries. Hence those metamorphoses renowned among the Hebrews and the Pythagoreans.

For the occult theology of the Hebrews sometimes transforms the holy Enoch into an angel of divinity whom they call "Mal'akh Adonay Shebaoth," and sometimes transforms others into other divinities. The Pythagoreans degrade impious men into brutes and, if one is to believe Empedocles, even into plants. Muhammad, in imitation, often had this saying on his tongue: "They who have deviated from divine law become beasts." And surely he spoke justly, for it is not the bark that makes the plant but its senseless and insentient nature; neither is it the hide that makes the beast of burden but its irrational, sensitive soul; neither is it the orbed form that makes the heavens but its undeviating order; nor is it the sundering from body but his spiritual intelligence that makes the angel. For if you see one abandoned to his appetites crawling on the ground, it is a plant and not a man you see; if you see one blinded by the vain illusions of imagery, as it were of Calypso, and softened by their gnawing allurement, delivered over to his senses, it is a beast and not a man you see. If you see a philosopher determining all things by means of right reason, him you shall reverence: he is a heavenly being and not of this earth. If you see a pure contemplator, one unaware of the body and confined to the inner reaches of the mind, he is neither an earthly nor a heavenly being; he is a more reverend divinity vested with human flesh .

Are there any who would not admire man, who is, in the sacred writings of Moses and the Christians, not without reason described sometimes by the name of "all flesh," sometimes by that of "every creature," inasmuch as he himself molds, fashions, and changes himself into the form of all flesh and into the character of every creature? For this reason the Persian Euanthes, in describing the Chaldaean theology, writes that man has no semblance that is inborn and his very own but many that are external and foreign to him. But why do we emphasize this? To the end that after we have been born to this condition—that we can become what we will— we should understand that we ought to have especial care to this, that it should never be said against us that, although born to a privileged position, we failed to recognize it and became like unto wild animals and senseless beasts of burden, but that rather the saying of Asaph the prophet should apply: "Ye are all angels and sons of the Most High," and that we may not, by abusing the most indulgent generosity of the Father, make for ourselves the freedom of choice He has given into something harmful rather than salutary. Let a certain holy ambition invade our souls, so that, not content with the mediocre, we shall pant after the highest and (since we may if we wish) toil with all our strength to obtain it.

Let us disdain earthly things, despise heavenly things, and, finally, esteeming less whatever is of the world, hasten to that court which is beyond the world and nearest to the Godhead. There, as the sacred mysteries relate, Seraphim, Cherubim, and Thrones hold the first places; let us, incapable of yielding to them, and intolerant of a lower place, emulate their dignity and their glory. If we have willed it, we shall be second to them in nothing.

170

RENAISSANCE SCIENCE AND TECHNOLOGY

The Copernican Revolution

The medieval idea of the universe was based on Ptolemy's geocentric theory, which identified the earth as the center of the universe, with the moon, planets, and stars revolving around it in more or less fixed spheres, or orbits. Around the whole lay the crystalline sphere, beyond which was the realm of God. However, many medieval scientists—particularly the Arabic astronomers—had observed movements of stars and planets that did not fit into this scheme but required additional spheres. Working within the confines of Ptolemaic assumptions, these scientists postulated backward loops of heavenly bodies to account for variations in their rotation periods. By the Renaissance, astronomers had compiled a complicated system of more than seventy spheres surrounding the earth, with each of the heavenly bodies performing an epicycle (little backward rotation of its own) around a central point on its orbit.

The Ptolemaic system was first questioned by the Polish astronomer and mathematician Nicholas Copernicus (1473–1543). Copernicus never advanced the theory that the earth was not the center of the universe; he believed that mathematical calculations would be less complicated if one accepted the sun as a stationary point and based one's computations on a heliocentric system. Though he failed to design a simpler system or to eliminate mistaken assumptions about orbits, his contribution was monumental. Copernicus opened the door to modern astronomy.

Today we honor Copernicus not because he produced the modern view of the solar system (he didn't) or because his system was simpler than Ptolemy's (it wasn't), but because he was the first person in "modern times" who had the courage and perseverance to carry his idea beyond the realm of philosophical speculation. It was he who pointed out

2. James Trefil, *The Dark Side of the Universe; A Scientist Explores the Cosmos* (New York: Macmillan, 1988), p.18.

that the emperor's new clothes might be missing. After him everyone came to see geocentrism as just an assumption, one that could be challenged like any other.[2]

Paradoxically, other advances in Renaissance science were made by translating the ancient writings of Galen, Archimedes, Hippocrates, and other Greek scientists into Latin. Additionally, there were improvements in anatomical and geological studies but, on the whole, Renaissance scientific studies were mainly preparation for the scientific revolution of the seventeenth century.

Technology

Printing was invented in China in 756, gunpowder around 1100, and the magnetic compass a decade or two later. Like many Chinese innovations, these were so rigidly controlled by the imperial government that they had no value for the common people. With no equivalent central authority in Europe the impact of just these three inventions was dramatic. Movable type was invented in the 1440s in the Rhine valley of Germany, possibly in Mainz by Johannes Gutenberg (1398?–1468). Once the privilege of the few who could afford hand-copied books, learning became available to all. The invention of printing made possible the most rapid expansion of knowledge that we have known prior to the proliferation of computers in our own time. By 1500 there were over 1,000 printshops and millions of volumes in print. The printing press was the key to the success of the Protestant Reformation—Martin Luther's tracts attacking the Church of Rome were rushed into print and spread like wildfire throughout Europe.

The technique of making gunpowder was imported from China and first used during the latter part of the Hundred Years' War (1337–1453) between England and France. Subsequent improvements in firearms and artillery made gunpowder, in effect, a great leveler. One man with a gun was more than a match for a knight on horseback, and even primitive cannons could bombard medieval castles into submission. The feudal age ended abruptly and, one might say, explosively.

EXPLORATION AND DISCOVERY

Trade between European cities and the Near and Middle East was an important factor in the evolution of the Renaissance. A few intrepid travelers, the most famous of whom was the Venetian Marco Polo (1254?–1324?), made their way along the great land routes to India and China (map 16.1). Marco Polo returned to Venice after spending many years in China (1271–95), but no one believed any of the wonders that he related. The conquests of the Ottoman Turks, especially the capture of Constantinople in 1453, had cut off the traditional Mediterranean routes.

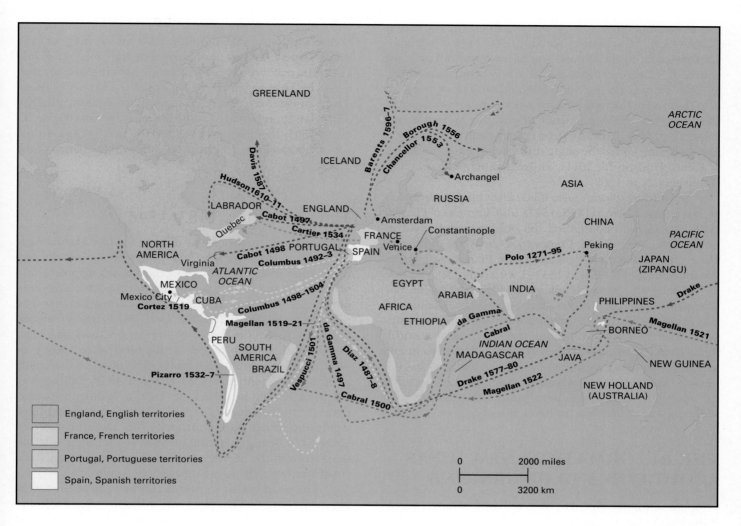

GREENLAND

ARCTIC OCEAN

Barents 1596-7
Borough 1556
Chancellor 1553

ICELAND

•Archangel

ASIA

RUSSIA

Davis 1587

Hudson 1610-11

LABRADOR

ENGLAND

CHINA

PACIFIC OCEAN

Quebec

Cabot 1497

•Amsterdam

Cartier 1534

FRANCE
•Constantinople

Peking

Cabot 1498 PORTUGAL
SPAIN
Venice•

Polo 1271-95

JAPAN (ZIPANGU)

NORTH AMERICA

Columbus 1492-3

Virginia

ATLANTIC OCEAN

EGYPT

INDIA

Drake

MEXICO

ARABIA

PHILIPPINES

Mexico City•

CUBA

Columbus 1498-1504

AFRICA

da Gamma

Magellan 1521

Cortez 1519

ETHIOPIA

BORNEO

Magellan 1519-21

Cabral

PERU

SOUTH AMERICA

da Gamma 1497

INDIAN OCEAN
MADAGASCAR

JAVA

NEW GUINEA

Vespucci 1501

Diaz 1487-8

Drake 1577-80

Magellan 1522

Pizarro 1532-7

BRAZIL

Cabral 1500

NEW HOLLAND (AUSTRALIA)

0   2000 miles
0   3200 km

☐ England, English territories

☐ France, French territories

☐ Portugal, Portuguese territories

☐ Spain, Spanish territories

Map 16.1 World exploration 1271–95; 1486–1611.

Limited navigational aids forced sailing vessels to remain within sight of Mediterranean shores, which became unsatisfactory when other routes to the East had to be found. Not until the fifteenth century did European sailors have the capability to circumnavigate Africa to reach China, and the driving force behind this exploration was Prince Henry the Navigator (1394–1460), son of King John I of Portugal. Apparently without referring to Chinese work, a crude magnetic compass had been invented in the twelfth century. Henry improved this crucial device, had accurate maps and tables drawn, improved the design of ships, and reintroduced the **astrolabe**, an Arab invention. A ship's latitude could be calculated to within about 30 miles (48 km) by using the astrolabe to determine the angle of the sun above the horizon at noon. This figure was then compared with Henry's tables of the sun's declination at known latitudes for each day of the year.

Navigation could not be made more precise until the marine chronometer was invented in 1760 to determine

longitude. Nevertheless, navigational aids were adequate for voyages of exploration. In 1497, for example, Vasco da Gama (ca. 1469–1524) sailed southwest and then south from Portugal for ninety-seven days before turning east and sailing directly to the known latitude of his African destination, the Cape of Good Hope. He continued around Africa and on to India, returning to Lisbon in 1499.

Before da Gama's successful voyage, India had been the destination of Christopher Columbus (ca. 1451–1506), who sailed west rather than south and discovered instead a New World—new to Europeans, that is, with the exception of earlier Viking voyages. Columbus claimed the land for Spain, and the claim was confirmed in 1493, when Pope Alexander VI drew a vertical line in the Atlantic and awarded the Americas to Spain and Africa to Portugal. No one knew that the line ran through Brazil until it was accidentally discovered a year later by a Portuguese captain, leading to a treaty confirming Portugal's ownership. It apparently occurred to no one that the Americas and Africa were already inhabited by people who were never consulted by their new "owners." European colonialism had begun.

Spain and Portugal intended to divide the entire overseas world between them but England and France had other ideas. An Italian mariner whom the English called John Cabot (1450–98) was dispatched in 1497 to find a "northwest passage" to the Indies. The passage did not exist, of course, but Cabot's landings somewhere around Labrador and Newfoundland provided England with an opportunity to claim all of North America. The explorations of Jacques Cartier (1494–1553), plus later discoveries by Samuel de Champlain (1567?–1635), gave France competing claims, and the Dutch joined the competition with the explorations of Henry Hudson (d. 1611), an Englishman who entered Dutch service in 1609.

Maritime explorers were followed by adventurers such as Hernando Cortés (1485–1547) and Francisco Pizarro (1471–1541), who conquered the only two high civilizations of the New World. Cortés took the Aztec empire of Mexico in 1519 with 600 soldiers, and Pizarro conquered the Inca empire of Peru in 1531–3 with only 180 soldiers.

There was treasure aplenty in the New World, but Europeans found another in their own minds. Accounts of the voyages of explorers inspired Renaissance imaginations much as space exploration fascinates today's world. Renaissance Europe had opened up new frontiers in art, literature, philosophy, and science, and now there was the lure and challenge of new lands as well. America became, for many Europeans, the literal utopia that Sir Thomas More used as the setting for his fictional *Utopia*.

THE REFORMATION: NEW IDEAS ABOUT GOD AND HUMANKIND

Concepts about the world and the universe changed rapidly during the Renaissance, but it was the Reformation that transformed the face of Europe. It not only divided a once monolithic institution but kindled social, political, economic, and intellectual revolutions. There had been earlier challenges to the authority of the Church of Rome, but the Reformation inaugurated by Martin Luther was the first to succeed on a large scale.

Centuries earlier, in 1170, a French merchant named Peter Waldo (d. 1217) founded a puritan sect known as the Waldenses. Preaching apostolic poverty, they rejected Rome and its papal claims. Though excommunicated in 1184 and persecuted for centuries, the sect survives today as the Vaudois in the Alps of Italy and France.

In England, John Wiclif (or Wycliffe; ca. 1320–84), an Oxford scholar, revived interest in St. Augustine and openly questioned the need for a priestly hierarchy. Contending that God and the Scriptures were the sole sources of spiritual authority, he translated the Bible from the Vulgate into English and urged everyone to read it for themselves. He was silenced by the church, but the Wiclif Bible was undisputed after 1534, when Henry VIII broke away from the Church of Rome with the Act of Supremacy and confiscated all church property.

Jan Hus (or Huss; 1369–1415) was a Wiclif follower and a priest/professor at Charles University in Prague. His opposition to the sale of indulgences led to charges of the Wiclif heresy, and he was burned at the stake on 6 July 1415. His martyrdom caused bloody riots in Bohemia, followed by an evangelical movement of the Unitas Fratrum (Unity of Brethren). By 1500 the Brethren (later called the Moravian church) had over 200,000 members in 400 parishes. In 1501, the church published the first hymnal in the vernacular and placed it, and the Bible, in the hands of the people.

Martin Luther, 1483–1546

The term "reformation" was used in the late Middle Ages by individuals and groups who protested against the secularization of Christianity and the abuses of power and privilege by the church hierarchy, from parish priests to popes. An unbroken succession of corrupt Renaissance popes, from Sixtus IV (reigned 1471–84) to Leo X (reigned 1513–21), fueled the flames of a revolt that was ignited by Martin Luther when he posted his ninety-five Theses, or statements for public debate, on the door of the castle church at Wittenberg on 31 October 1517. Luther was incensed at what he called the "sale" of indulgences, particularly the fund-raising activities of a monk named Tetzel. Operating under papal authority, the Dominican John Tetzel was dealing in indulgences—soliciting contributions to swell the depleted papal treasury and finance the construction of the new St. Peter's in Rome.

Luther intended, at first, a clarification of the teachings of the church. The origins of the Reformation are found primarily in Luther's religion. An **Augustinian** friar and professor of theology at the University of Wittenberg, Luther had experienced a spiritual crisis. Convinced that he was a lost soul and destined for Hell, Luther took the advice of a confessor and plunged with characteristic fervor into intensive study of the Bible. He rediscovered, in the epistles of Paul, a faith in salvation by grace. The central doctrines of the Church Fathers, especially Augustine, confirmed his belief in the authority of the Word of God; faith alone was sufficient for salvation. Church doctrine stipulated that good works and the intercession of priests were also necessary, but Luther was convinced that he expressed the true faith of the church. Faith and the Bible were enough for Luther, making the break with Rome inevitable.

Why was Luther so concerned about indulgences? Indulgences were remissions by the church of temporal punishment on earth or in **purgatory**. The sacrament of penance of the Church of Rome consists of contrition, confession, absolution, and satisfaction on the part of the penitent. The penitent must feel contrition for his or her sins, confess to the priest, and be absolved of guilt. The sinner satisfies God's justice by working out the penalties assigned by the priest. Indulgences could be granted for the guilt or

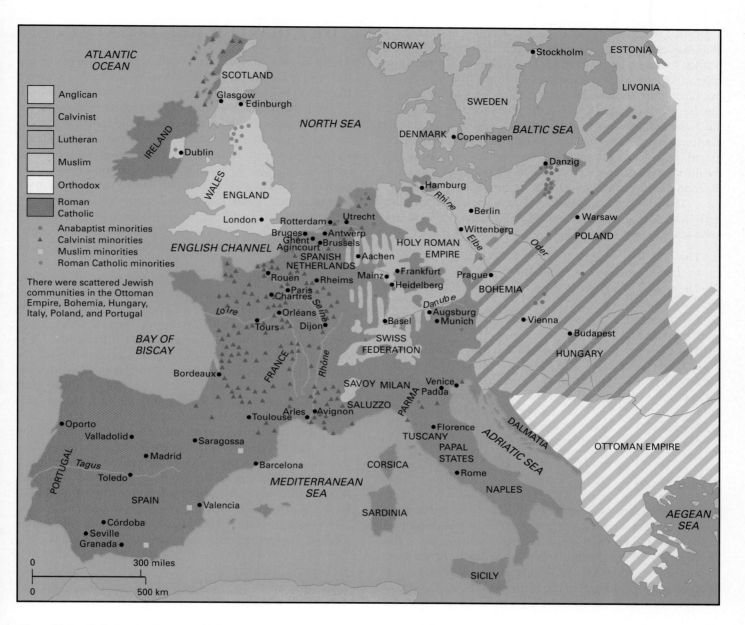

Map 16.2 Religion in Europe, 1565.

punishment in purgatory, according to the church, but the sin remained after confession. According to the doctrine of Thesaurus Meritorum, the church had a treasury of spiritual merits accumulated from the crucifixion of Christ for the sins of the world and the martyrdom of the Saints. Indulgences transferred spiritual merit from this treasury to the penitent. Tetzel, among others, misled the people when he chanted his favorite **refrain**: "As soon as the coin in the coffer rings/A soul from Purgatory springs." The doctrine behind indulgences was too complex for lay persons to understand, many of whom believed that even sins could be absolved if they could buy enough indulgences, which misunderstanding, as Luther observed, "put a grievous instrument in the hands of avarice."

"Therefore those preachers of indulgences err who say that a papal pardon frees a man from all penalty and assures his salvation" was one of Luther's theses. Arguing some of his theses with the theologian John Eck, Luther publicly admitted that his statements attacked an institution that could have him burned alive. When shown that his position was similar to that of Jan Hus, Luther dared to assert that the church was in error in burning Hus. Jan Hus was a condemned heretic, and Luther put his life on the line by openly challenging the authority of the pope and the councils of the church.

In 1521, Emperor Charles V convened the estates of the **Holy Roman Empire** in the town of Worms to compel Luther, already excommunicated by the pope, to retract his writings. "I neither can nor will make any retraction, since it is neither safe nor honorable to act against conscience" was his response. Insisting that "the Church universal is the number of the elect," Luther concluded his defense, according to tradition, with the words, "Here I stand. I cannot do otherwise. God help me. Amen." The Diet of Worms declared Luther an outlaw, but the verdict was academic because Luther had many supporters among the German princes. Church corruption and forming a new faith helped promote Luther's church, but a rising tide of nationalism and the desire to end the flow of money to the papal treasury were perhaps even more significant in the rapid spread of the Reformation throughout the Holy Roman Empire and Scandinavia (map 16.2).

The principles of Lutheranism were later formulated by a Lutheran scholar, Philip Melanchthon (1497–1560), who stated them as follows:

1. The only final authority either for conduct or belief is in the Scriptures (*Sola Scriptura*).
2. The one condition of salvation is faith or trust in Divine Love (*Sola Fide*).
3. Faith itself is a gift of God, not a human achievement (*Sola Gratia*).
4. The community of the faithful is the true church whose only head is Christ. The growth of this church is fostered by preaching the gospel and the observance of two sacraments, Baptism and the Lord's Supper. In sum, Lutheran belief stresses individuality; salvation and a knowledge of God are direct processes, needing no church or priestly intercessor.

Calvinism

The Reformation in Germany was closely followed by a notable movement in Switzerland, first led by Ulrich Zwingli (1484–1531), who even more than Luther believed in the individuality of worship and the authority of the Scriptures. Later, this group was led by John Calvin (1509–64), a French Protestant originally educated for the law as well as theology. Persecuted in France, he fled to Geneva, where he established a theocratic republic, that is, a government ruled by elders of the church.

Calvin stated the philosophy of his faith in *The Institutes of the Christian Religion* (final form in 1559). This rests on the unconditional sovereignty of God; whatever transpires is because God wills it so. The assistance of a Saviour is necessary because Calvin believed in humanity's abject helplessness and total depravity. Predestination is rigorous and universal: a few of the elect will be saved through faith in God but many will be forever damned. Finally, he stated that the group of the elect constitutes the church, the preservation of which is the duty of both religious and civil authorities. An infraction of divine law therefore requires civil punishment by officials subject to church authorities. This, as one can see, was a very stern belief; Calvin forbade many of the ordinary pleasures of life in Geneva and vigorously persecuted all who did not follow his faith.

THE COUNTER-REFORMATION

The Catholic Reformation, also called the Counter-Reformation, was the papal response to Luther's revolt. Convened by Pope Paul III (reigned 1534–49), the Council of Trent met from 1545 to 1563 and reaffirmed every element of Roman doctrine attacked by the reformers: original sin, grace, redemption, the sacraments, the sacrifice of the Mass, and purgatory. Every violation of discipline was denounced, reforms were enacted, and observance was demanded under pain of censure. The music of the church was reformed, and there was a strong thrust of Counter-Reformation art and architecture (see p. 349). The Counter-Reformation was given a mighty assist by the Jesuits (Society of Jesus), founded by Ignatius Loyola in 1534 and later approved by Pope Paul III. The Jesuits led the disciplined drive of the movement, but the popes also revived the Inquisition, an old and seasoned mechanism for stamping out heresy. Sitting as medieval courts and employing medieval methods of torture, the papal and Spanish inquisitions sentenced convicted heretics to "purification." The operative term was *auto-da-fé* (Portuguese, "act of the faith"), meaning that secular authorities purified the victims by burning them at the stake (fig. 16.1). Judicial murders failed to stem the Protestant tide but the Spanish Inquisition was not abolished until 1834.

How can we sum up the influence of the Reformation on the lives of people? First, it encouraged national identity, the strongest single force of this period. Second, it had a marked influence on education, in many cases divorcing it from ecclesiastical domination. On the other hand, because of Calvinist influence, education was limited largely to subjects of immediate utilitarian value. The Reformation encouraged religious independence; if the Bible is

---

16.1   Bernard Picart, *Execution and burning of heretics in Spain*, from *Cérémonies et coutumes religieuses*, vol. 1, *Cérémonies en usage chez les Catholiques* (Amsterdam: J. F. Bernard). 1723. Copperplate engraving. Photo: A.K.G., London.

the sole basis for religious beliefs, there are any number of possible interpretations. As a result, Protestantism generated a host of sects in which one could find virtually any type of religious belief. Finally, Protestantism influenced the growth of capitalism, for the ideal Calvinist, Methodist, or Lutheran took the beginning of the first psalm to heart:

> ¹Blessed is the man that walketh not in the counsel of the ungodly, nor standeth in the way of sinners, nor sitteth in the seat of the scornful. ²But his delight is in the law of the Lord; and in his law doth he meditate day and night. ³And he shall be like a tree planted by the rivers of water, that bringeth forth his fruit in his season; his leaf also shall not wither; and whatsoever he doeth shall prosper.

Clearly this psalm tells us that good people shall prosper. In a time when making, saving, and spending money became more and more the surest signs of success, men and women concluded that prosperous people were good people. Furthermore, the sober, steady, shoulder-to-the-wheel and nose-to-the-grindstone way of life advocated by most of the new sects was exactly the sort of life that would promote industrious work and prudent spending. And so began the Protestant work ethic, which produces the ideal person for a capitalist system.

THE RELATION OF THE INDIVIDUAL TO THE GROUP

Capitalism

The growth of capitalism is but one more example of the trend toward individualism that characterized a transitional period in a European society that was busily rebuilding itself to match the new view of reality. There was considerable mercantile activity in the Middle Ages, especially in the twelfth and thirteenth centuries, but the economic system called mercantile capitalism did not come into full flower until the Renaissance. Before this time economic affairs had been dominated by political or religious concerns, granted that merchants always keep an eye on the bottom line. Just as knowledge of the real world developed into science, so evolved an economic system free of religious or political considerations.

Medieval **guilds** produced solely for human needs, and manufacturing and selling were interrelated processes. A cobbler, for instance, made shoes only to order; with no orders he could close his shop and go on a picnic. His guild regulated the quality of materials and workmanship and set the prices. There was no competition and the business died with the cobbler, unless he had a son yearning to follow in his footsteps.

The rising fortunes of the Fugger family in what is now Germany illustrate the development of Renaissance capitalism. Anton Fugger became a weaver in Augsburg in 1380 and soon began collecting and selling other weavers' products. His son, Jacob Fugger I, continued a business later vastly enlarged under Jacob Fugger II, the leading capitalist of the era. Jacob expanded into metals within the Hapsburg Empire, dealing in silver and copper in Austria and silver and mercury in Spain. Lending huge sums (at high interest) to the Hapsburg emperors, he received, in return, monopolies on the ores he mined. Inevitably, he bought the mines to control all his products from raw materials to market. Fugger set prices at whatever the traffic would bear and no one supervised product quality. Finally, he formed a company that piled up profits far exceeding the needs of the Fuggers or any other family. From this example we can explore the essential attributes of capitalism.

Characteristics of Capitalism

Capitalism creates "companies" that exist separately from the people who form them. The company can conduct business, make contracts, assume debts, distribute and/or reinvest profits, and be subject to litigation. The purpose of the company is to make money with no limit whatever on the amount of money (and power) that can be amassed (fig. 16.2). Capitalism assumes that making money is the goal of economic activity because, after all, no sensible person goes into business to lose money.

A company is a rational organization that must plan and control every step of its operation from raw materials to the marketplace. It must have an accounting system that

16.2 Quentin Matsys, *The Money Lender and His Wife*. 1514. Oil on wood, 28 × 26¾" (71.1 × 67.9 cm). Louvre, Paris. Photo: R.M.N., Paris.
Distracted from reading her Bible, the wife is as fascinated as her husband as he lovingly examines his money.

CROWN VERSUS POPE

England's break with the Church of Rome had little to do with the theology or politics of the Reformation. Henry VIII wanted a male heir to further the Tudor line and his first wife, Catherine of Aragon, was unable to cooperate. When Rome also failed to cooperate by granting an annulment, Henry's chief minister suggested that England break with the papacy so that the Archbishop of Canterbury could grant a divorce. Parliament passed the legislation in 1533, leaving Henry VIII free to marry Anne Boleyn. Now the head of the Church of England, Henry proceeded to confiscate every Roman monastery, nunnery, and church in the land. Later, he executed Anne Boleyn for infidelity and failing to bear a son. Ironically, it was Boleyn's daughter who became the exalted Queen Elizabeth.

keeps track of materials, money, and human energies. Capitalism shapes ends to means and the end is making a profit. This is a rational goal with no room for feeling or emotion. The system is pragmatic; whatever works is good and what doesn't is eliminated. An irrational aspect of early capitalism was the lack of safety standards, whether installed by industry itself or imposed by government. Competition between companies could and did exploit the consumer. Moreover, workers were paid as little as possible and worked as long as possible.

Effects of Capitalism

The flourishing of capitalism dramatically increased the possibilities of individualism. Those who made it to the top of the economic heap acquired the power to do whatever they wished. The only limits on individuals lay in their own imagination, creativity, and ability to spot and exploit opportunities. A second effect was the marked increase in available goods. Guilds made goods when people wanted them, but capitalists made more of everything and sold the surplus to ever-expanding markets. The rapid rise of the standard of living in sixteenth-century Europe was due almost entirely to the expanded economic system. In material terms capitalism was a whopping success.

Capitalism transformed cities. Medieval stores, such as they were, had been booths at fairs or traveling wagons with itinerant peddlers. In the guild system the factory was the workshop and living quarters for the craftsman, his apprentices, and his family. But capitalists had to get their merchandise before the public, and this required buildings in which goods were "stored." The impact on Renaissance cities of the expanding industry of retail sales was, of course, remarkable. To appreciate this, try to imagine a city without a single retail store.

The Development of Sovereign Power

Perhaps the most striking Renaissance development was the increase of royal power. The beginning of this movement had emerged during the latter part of the Middle Ages, when the inadequacies of feudalism had become obvious. There was no common currency, feudal tariff barriers hindered trade, justice was inconsistent at best, and competent civil servants didn't exist. Kings drove to new power with their might increasingly keyed to the extravagant stream of treasure from the newly discovered lands across the sea. The Spanish monarch, for example, claimed a fifth of all riches brought to Spain by the *conquistadores*. With seemingly unlimited funds, kings created brilliant courts that attracted the nobles from their muddy country estates and inevitably made them totally dependent on the monarch. Most nobles were willing to exchange their rural independence for the privilege of participating in the rituals, grand balls, and resplendent festivals of the royal courts in England, France, and Spain.

Not only did the nobles pledge their allegiance to the sovereign, but the common people looked to the throne as the single source of order in a world changing so rapidly they could scarcely keep up. Order had been the rule in the Middle Ages but "future shock" was present in the Renaissance as it is today. Protestantism shattered the monolithic authority of Rome, science demolished the unity of the universe, and capitalism dismembered the old economic order controlled by the guilds. The king was the single stabilizing influence in all this chaos. Wherever we turn, we find references to the centrality of the sovereign. In Shakespeare's play *Hamlet*, Rosencrantz speaks of the monarch's importance:

> The cease of majesty
> Dies not alone, but, like a gulf doth draw
> What's near it with it; it is a massy wheel,
> Fix'd on the summit of the highest mount,
> To whose huge spokes ten thousand lesser things
> Are mortis'd and adjoin'd; which, when it falls,
> Each small annexment, petty consequence,
> Attends the boisterous ruin. Never alone
> Did the king sigh, but with a general groan.

Historically, the Renaissance saw the brilliant reigns of the Tudor rulers in England, especially Henry VIII (reigned 1509–47) and Elizabeth I (reigned 1558–1603). These two monarchs understood the rising importance of trade and commerce and the vital role the middle class played in England's growing prosperity. It was under Elizabeth, also, that the English navy defeated the mighty Spanish Armada in 1588, making England mistress of the seas until well into the twentieth century.

In France, Francis I (reigned 1515–47) set a pattern for later kings, such as Louis XIV (reigned 1643–1715), by bringing the best artists to a sumptuously furnished court that became a model for all of Europe. Francis I cemented

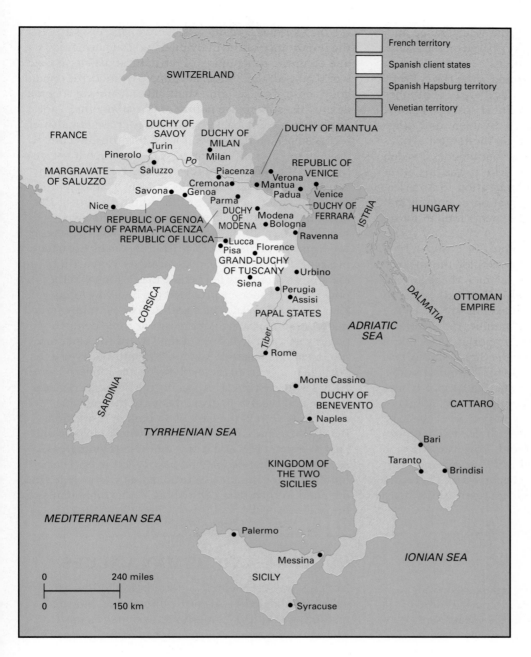

Map 16.3 Renaissance Italy.

national feeling by a series of wars fought largely by mercenary soldiers in a helpless and divided Italy. France was later bitterly embroiled in a struggle between the Protestant Huguenots, led by the house of Bourbon, and the Catholics, led by the house of Guise. This struggle came to a head in 1589, when Henry of Navarre took the throne as Henry IV, the first Bourbon king (reigned 1589–1610). Henry professed himself a Catholic, but by the Edict of Nantes (1598) guaranteed certain rights to the Huguenots in selected cities—rights that Louis XIV cancelled in 1685, at which time thousands of Huguenots left the country.

Spain reached its single high point of brilliance at this time, at first under the rule of Ferdinand and Isabella (1469–1504). They and later rulers enjoyed tremendous profits from the Spanish conquests in Central and South America. In fact, the decline of Spain can be attributed to their disinterest in permanent colonies; they preferred instead to plunder their holdings. Later, Spain became one of the countries ruled over by the Hapsburgs, for Charles I of Spain (reigned 1519–56) also held the title of Archduke of Austria.

In 1566 the Netherlands revolted against the Hapsburg kings, a revolt provoked in large part by the importation of the ruthless Inquisition. After a series of bloody wars Holland became an independent nation in 1648, but the area known today as Belgium did not free itself until 1713. Portugal also achieved full independence during the Renaissance and, like Spain, achieved a short-lived glory based on the wealth plundered from its hapless possessions.

Germany became the battleground of the Thirty Years' War (1618–48), which began as a conflict between Catholics and Protestants and ended as a political struggle against the Hapsburgs by Holland, France, Sweden, and other nations. Germany was devastated as the largest armies since Roman days surged over the countryside. Sweden alone had over 200,000 men in the field. It was this bitter and disastrous war that spurred emigration to America, where there would be a clear separation of church and state and no more religious disagreements fought out on a battlefield.

Italy's fate deserves a special note, for it was in Italy that humanism first appeared, not to mention the inspired creations of artists such as Leonardo da Vinci, Michelangelo, and Raphael. Early mercantile capitalism was made to order for enterprising individuals to exploit in flourishing city-states. As a result, a few powerful families rose to prominence, each controlling one of the important cities. The Visconti family ruled in Milan, and the Sforza family was a power in Lombardy and later in Milan. The most notable of the ruling families was the Medici clan in Florence, whose leading member was the famous Lorenzo the Magnificent (1449–92)—banker, ruler, artist, and patron of the arts. A council of rich merchants took over the Venetian republic. Like the Greek city-states of old, however, the rich and powerful Italian cities could never unite, and went into decline after 1500, when Italy became a battleground for internal squabbles and rampaging foreign armies (map 16.3).

STUDY QUESTIONS

1. Give a definition of Renaissance humanism in your own words. What is a humanist in today's world? How does a humanist differ from a humanitarian?
2. The invention of movable type and gunpowder changed history. Which, in your opinion, has had the greater impact? Why?
3. Have nuclear weapons changed history as much as gunpowder?

SUMMARY

There has scarcely been a time, except perhaps our own, when people busied themselves so industriously exploring the dark room of their universe. Wherever they went they turned up new facts that upset old balances and archaic institutions. Humanism, as one of the manifestations of the secular spirit, stripped the allegory from all manifestations of nature and helped people to

see the world as it really was. Humanism also stressed the importance of the individual and the harmonious and complete functioning of the natural person in a rich world guided, the humanists hoped, by moderation and good sense. To a certain extent, humanism was a revolt against the submissive nature of Christian ethics, not only in its turning back to classical sources, but also in its insistence on the reason for leading the good life: it was not the hope of eternal bliss in heaven, but because the good life was its own reward. The view of what constituted the real world was shifting from the medieval idea that God was the ultimate reality to the belief that human existence on earth had its own validity. This shift did not necessarily mean that there was widespread denial of Christianity or the Christian message. Rather, growing resentment over corruption in the church hierarchy led people to question whether this powerful bureaucracy provided the best way to the Kingdom of Heaven. The Great Schism certainly forced many to wonder which of the two or three competing popes was the true keeper of the keys of the kingdom. Amidst all the negative factors, humanism served as a positive bridge from the medieval to the modern world.

The new science, especially the heliocentric solar system and the mechanistic theory of the universe, completely shifted the base of all human institutions. Before that time God had been the whole purpose and goal of human life, and it was on these **teleological** assumptions that people had based their lives. That foundation for human aspirations was swept aside, and men and women regarded themselves as inhabitants of a brave new world.

CULTURE AND HUMAN VALUES

Not only was the theoretical foundation for human values invalidated by scientific discoveries, but the institution that had formerly controlled life's most important functions was questioned and rejected. The keystone of the revolt against the Church of Rome was the dazzling realization that people could live in a direct relation to God with no necessity for an intermediary. Those who needed religious authority to direct their lives could turn to the Scriptures and interpret for themselves. And those who did not need or want religious authority could live their lives without fear. The new churches, however, did institute their own authorities with restrictions sometimes comparable to those of the old Church of Rome. Ultimately, the movement from a monolithic church to a multiplicity of faiths meant that people had a choice.

Vast areas for human endeavor opened at the same time. The idea, as much as the reality, of the New World swept aside musty medieval walls and liberated the European mind. One tangible reality did come from the

New World, and that was money. Wealth poured into the countries who sent their buccaneers forth, and the new riches bought ease and luxury. Capitalism offered another marvelously stimulating outlet for individual enterprise. The sky was the limit for creative, ambitious, and resourceful individuals.

Renaissance Men and Women: Real and Ideal

> What a piece of work is a man! How noble in reason! how infinite in faculty! in form, in moving, how express and admirable! in action how like an angel! in apprehension how like a god! the beauty of the world! the paragon of animals! And yet, to me, what is this quintessence of dust? man delights not me . . . .
> William Shakespeare, *Hamlet*, II, ii

When contemplating the Renaissance, one can call to mind the glories of exploration and discovery and names such as Michelangelo, Luther, Copernicus, Shakespeare, Cervantes, and Elizabeth I. We picture the era as a time of radiant optimism and expansion of the human spirit. The possible zones of human action were widened, it seems, in every respect: geographically, with the new discoveries; spiritually, with the Reformation; economically, with the growth of capitalism. This, of course, is true but it is only part of the total picture. Hamlet says, "man delights not me."

This hints at another aspect of the Renaissance as important as the first exuberant picture. A troubling melancholy strain ran throughout the whole period, a deep-seated pessimism concerning human nature. What is Hamlet saying? Primarily, that in appearances, actions, and potentialities, people are great. Yet somehow in reality they fall short of greatness. Such pessimism usually indicates a failure to reach some ideal.

The Renaissance Problem

What was the problem that confronted the thinkers of the time? On the one hand they had opportunity unlimited with beckoning horizons extending in all directions. Human beings, with their awesome achievements, could at last become godlike creatures.

Yet at the same moment, the very forces that opened these new possibilities undermined the concept of human beings as special among all of God's creations. Matters of the soul and divinity were relegated to an inferior position below material things. Even further, the more the hopes held out for humankind, the more it seemed people's animal nature won out. All too often venality and greed triumphed as people seized opportunities savagely and selfishly. Not only did those of low station show themselves unworthy, but even the best and the wisest, the noblest among men and women stared deeply into their own personalities and found there the same base instincts.

Here, then, is the problem. How can people's animal nature be controlled so they may become the noble creatures they were apparently destined to be? How can the rough, crude, and selfish aspects of human nature be disciplined so that all men and women may achieve fulfillment in the expanding world in which they live? Philosophers, theologians, artists, psychologists, men and women in all walks of life have wrestled with the problem, but the question remains.

CHAPTER 17

Renaissance Art: A New Golden Age

THE EARLY RENAISSANCE IN FIFTEENTH-CENTURY ITALY

Florence (from *flora*), the city of flowers, dates back to the Bronze Age (3000 BC). Influenced by the Greeks as early as the eighth century BC, it flourished under Roman rule and even prospered during the difficult centuries following the demise of the empire. As early as 1199 it was a city of bankers and wealthy craft guilds, destined to become a leading financial power and the city most closely identified with the Renaissance (fig. 17.1). Intended to symbolize Florentine influence and wealth, the great cathedral Santa Maria del Fiore (St. Mary of the Flower) was begun by Arnolfo di Cambio in 1296. Work slowed down after Arnolfo's death in 1302 and stopped altogether during the terrible days of the Black Death in 1348 and several subsequent years. Like many cities in Europe, Florence was devastated by the plague, its population falling in just a few summer months from about 130,000 to around 65,000. Recovery was relatively swift, however, and in 1368 the cathedral design was finalized and building resumed, though no one had the faintest idea of how to construct the dome.

Filippo Brunelleschi, ca. 1377–1446

In 1417 a special commission announced a competition for the design of the dome, optimistically trusting in Italian ingenuity to solve the problem. The expected genius materialized in the person of Brunelleschi (broo-nuh-LES-key), one of the three founders of the Florentine Renaissance

Opposite Lorenzo Ghiberti, *Story of Adam and Eve*, detail of fig. 17.4. Gilt on bronze, 31¼ × 31¼" (79.4 × 79.4 cm). Photo: A.K.G., London.

17.1 View of Florence across the Arno River. From left to right: the Gothic tower of the Palazzo Vecchio, the square white tower of Giotto's campanile and the Cathedral of Sta. Maria del Fiore with its mighty dome. Photo: Scala, Florence.

(with Donatello and Masaccio) and the greatest architect of the Renaissance. His design was selected in 1420 and triumphantly completed sixteen years later.

On 25 March 1436 all of Florence was bursting with anticipation. Pope Eugene IV was to preside over the long-awaited consecration of the cathedral. On the day of the Feast of the Annunciation, the pope, accompanied by thirty-seven bishops, seven cardinals, the ruling Signoria, and envoys of foreign powers, began the solemn procession from the doors of the monastery. Moving along the specially constructed passageway (sumptuously carpeted and decorated with tapestries, damask, silk, and fresh flowers), the notables turned into the Via de' Banchi where the major banking houses were located. Passing through the eleventh-century **baptistery**, the dignitaries entered the spacious cathedral nave, where a five-hour service celebrated the completion of what was then the largest church in Christendom. The most famous composer of the time, Dufay (doo-FYE; see p. 314), was present to hear the choir sing his motet *Nuper Rosarum Flores (Flower of Rose)*, commissioned for the occasion by the Florentine Republic.

Brunelleschi began his artistic career as a sculptor, but after losing the 1401 competition for the north doors of the baptistery to Ghiberti, he turned to architecture. He subsequently made several trips to Rome in the company of the young sculptor Donatello to study and measure the existing buildings of ancient Rome. His design for the largest dome since the Pantheon consisted of eight massive ribs arching upward from an octagonal drum and held in place by a classically inspired **lantern**. Within the dome a complex web of smaller ribs and horizontal buttresses tied the main ribs firmly together, all done without expensive scaffolding. Brunelleschi's hoisting device was so practical and simple that city authorities had to issue injunctions forbidding children from riding it to the dome. Averaging 140 feet (42 m) in diameter, the dome was 367 feet (136 m) high—the dominant feature of the Florentine skyline from that day to this.

It was in the Pazzi Chapel (fig. 17.2) that Brunelleschi applied his knowledge of classical designs. A diminutive building measuring only 59 feet 9 inches by 35 feet 8 inches (18.2 × 10.9 m), its Renaissance design is clearly apparent, perhaps because the architect was not preoccupied with complex structural problems. In this beautifully proportioned building the break with the Gothic tradition is total. Gothic arches are replaced with Corinthian columns and pilasters in even, harmonious spacing. The walls are treated as solid, flat surfaces and, overall, there is a subtle and graceful balance of horizontal and vertical elements.

Rather than dominating the building, the central dome rests effortlessly on its supporting rim. From within (fig. 17.3), it seems to float on the light of the twelve *oculi*, somewhat in the manner of Hagia Sophia. The white stucco is articulated by the *pietra serena* (It., "clear stone") pilasters and moldings of clear gray Tuscan limestone and highlighted by the deep blue backgrounds of the terra-cotta reliefs and the Pazzi coat of arms on the pendentives. The harmonious proportions of the facade are confirmed by an interior space that is also shaped into clear geometric units. The Pazzi Chapel is a prototype of the new Renaissance style, which revived the concept of harmonious proportions on a human scale—a point of view even more germane to the work of Renaissance sculptors and metalworkers.

17.2 *Left* Filippo Brunelleschi, Pazzi Chapel, Cloister of Church of Santa Croce, Florence. Ca. 1441–60. Photo: Angelo Hornak, London.

17.3 *Opposite* Pazzi Chapel, interior, looking up into the dome. Photo: Scala, Florence.

Lorenzo Ghiberti, 1378–1455

Though initially trained in the International Gothic style, Ghiberti (gee-BEAR-tee) later mastered perspective and classical motifs to excel as a metalworker of the Early Renaissance. Winner over Brunelleschi of a competition to design the north doors of the Baptistery in 1401, Ghiberti went on to design the east doors that were quickly pronounced (by Michelangelo) as worthy of the Gates of Paradise. Illustrating ten scenes from the Old Testament, the bronze, gilded doors are a classically inspired landmark of the Early Renaissance style (fig. 17.4). Contrary to the International Style, the figures and their settings are perfectly proportioned, creating the illusion that these events are taking place on stage right before our eyes. The *Story of Adam and Eve* (top of the left door; see p. 276) is designed in three receding planes using high, middle, and low **relief**. In the left center foreground is the creation of Adam and Eve. The Garden of Eden appears in the middle ground, with the background representing God and his angels as part of a remote past. Bordering the panels are figures and portrait busts representing Hebrew prophets and sibyls of antiquity who had supposedly foretold the coming of Christ.

Donatello (Donato de Niccolò Bardi), 1386?–1466

When Donatello (don-a-TEL-o) completed his statue of a biblical prophet (fig. 17.5), he is said to have commanded it, "Speak, speak or the plague take you." The story may be apocryphal, but Renaissance artists did view themselves as creators, not as mere makers of things. With an assurance that the ancient Greeks would have admired, these artists hacked, hewed, painted, and composed as though they partook of the Divine Spirit. Though still regarded by society as craftsmen engaged in manual labor, they repeatedly proclaimed their preeminence as artists—an elevated status finally accorded Leonardo, Raphael, and Michelangelo in the sixteenth century. Created for a niche in Giotto's campanile, Donatello's biblical prophet displays the rude power of a zealot, a man of God fiercely denouncing wickedness and vice. Known in Donatello's time as Zuccone ("pumpkin head," i.e., baldy), the figure is not a category but a specific individual. Wearing a cloak thrown hurriedly over his body, the prophet is intent on his mission: calling down the wrath of God on the faithless.

After a prolonged stay in Rome studying Roman art,

17.5 Donatello, *Prophet ("Zuccone")*. Ca. 1423–5. Marble, height 6'5" (1.96 m). Originally on the campanile, Florence; now in the Museo dell'Opera del Duomo, Florence. Photo: Alinari, Florence.

17.4 *Opposite* Lorenzo Ghiberti, "Gates of Paradise," east doors of Baptistery of S. Giovanni, Florence Cathedral. Commissioned 1425, executed 1429–52. Gilt on bronze, height 18'6" (5.64 m). Photo: Scala, Florence.

Donatello returned to Florence in the early 1430s, where he created his *David* (fig. 17.6), a favorite image of Republican Florence, which saw itself as a latter-day David, champion of liberty. Representing a second stage in the development of Renaissance art, *David* is more classical than the biblical prophet, standing in a pose reminiscent of Praxiteles' *Hermes*. Though the gracefully flowing lines and the balance of tension and relaxation are classical, this is the body of an adolescent boy, not a Greek warrior. The Tuscan shepherd's cap and warrior boots emphasize what is possibly the first life-size freestanding nude since antiquity. The agony evident in the face of the slain Goliath contrasts sharply with the curiously impassive expression of the shepherd boy. The Middle Ages interpreted David's triumph as symbolic of Christ's victory over death, but Donatello's intentions remain a tantalizing mystery.

17.6   Donatello, *David*. Ca. 1430–2, but possibly later. Bronze, height 5'2" (1.57 m). Museo Nazionale del Bargello, Florence. Photo: Alinari, Florence.

Donatello's colossal equestrian statue of the Venetian soldier of fortune (condottiere) Gattamelata (fig. 17.7) was commissioned by the general's family, which led to a ten-year sojourn in Padua. This, in effect, exported the Florentine Renaissance to northern Italy, spawning a whole school of painting and sculpture influenced by Donatello's powerful personality. The statue itself was possibly inspired by the vigor of the equestrian statue of Marcus Aurelius in Rome, then thought to portray Constantine. Donatello's work, however, exceeded the representation of the Roman

emperor in the concentrated power of his figure's commanding presence. Apparently guiding his charger by sheer willpower (note the slack reins and spurs), the general is an idealized image of majestic power. Outfitted with a combination of Roman and Venetian armor, the horse and rider have a composition unified by the vigorous diagonals of the general's baton and long sword. Donatello not only solved the technical problems of large-scale bronze casting, but created a masterpiece[1] in the process.

Though no one knows exactly what Donatello meant by his *David*, the intentions of Early Renaissance painters are quite clear—they were concerned with representing the natural world regardless of metaphysical symbols. Artists studied anatomy to determine how the human body was constructed and how it functioned. Using scientific procedures they developed linear and aerial perspectives to create the illusion of actual space. They studied optics, light, and color to add the final touches to the illusion of light and personality. Through keen observation they confidently developed new forms for the new age.

17.7   Donatello, *Equestrian Monument of Gattamelata*, Piazza del Santo, Padua. 1443–53. Bronze, height 12'2" (3.71 m). Photo: Alinari, Florence.

---

1. Some nowadays consider "masterwork," "masterpiece," etc. politically incorrect. However, one cannot change the past. Historically speaking, a masterpiece is a work presented to a guild by a craftsman for admission to the rank of master. The term is probably a translation of the Dutch *meesterstuk* or German *Meisterstück*. It has been used for centuries to describe anything superlative.

Masaccio (Tommaso di Ser Giovanni di Mone), 1401–28?

Renaissance painting appeared in the 1420s in fully developed form in the work of a single artist, whose nickname of Masaccio ("Slovenly Tom") indicated so much preoccupation with art that personal appearance was neglected. Though only in his mid-twenties, Masaccio (ma-SOT-cho) created a fresh repertory of illusionist techniques avidly studied by later Renaissance painters, especially Leonardo and Michelangelo. Working with his colleague Masolino, Masaccio painted a series of frescoes in the Brancacci Chapel, of which his *Tribute Money* (fig. 17.8) is the acknowledged masterpiece. The subject is based on Matthew 17:24–27, in which the Roman tax collector, wearing the short tunic, demands his tribute of Peter. Christ instructs Peter to cast a hook and take the first fish caught. In the fish's mouth Peter will find a shekel that he will give to the tax collector "for me and for yourself." Told in continuous narration in the Roman manner (as on Trajan's Column), Peter appears first in the center, fishing at the left, and finally handing the coin to the tax collector at the right. Masaccio convinces us that we are looking into deep space by using four illusionist devices: linear perspective, visual perspective, atmospheric perspective, and **chiaroscuro** (key-AR-o-SCOOR-o).

Paolo Uccello, 1397–1475

For an age already using crossbows, gunpowder, and cannons, Renaissance warfare was paradoxical, a cultivated legacy from the Age of Chivalry. The system followed the tradition of medieval lists: armored knights in formal combat, complete with code of honor and the pageantry of

17.8   Masaccio, *Tribute Money*, Brancacci Chapel, Sta. Maria del Carmine, Florence. Ca. 1425. Fresco, 8'4" × 19'8" (2.54 × 6 m). Photo: Scala, Florence.

A MATTER OF PERSPECTIVE

Literally meaning "clear-seeing," perspective comprises the techniques giving the illusion of three-dimensional spatial relationships on a two-dimensional surface. Apparently first developed by Brunelleschi, linear perspective is based on the principle of all lines converging on a single **vanishing point** located, in figure 17.8, at the head of Christ. Visual perspective suggests depth of space by overlapping shapes and by the smaller size of distant objects. Perhaps invented in Italy by Masaccio, atmospheric perspective is based on the optical fact that colors become dimmer and outlines hazier as they recede into the distance. Flooding *Tribute Money* from outside the pictorial space, light strikes the figures at an angle, outlining the bodies in a tangible space. With light sculpting the bodies in gradations of light and shadow, called chiaroscuro (literally "clear-dark"), the illusion communicates weight, substance, and bulk. Masaccio's contemporary in northern Europe, Jan van Eyck, also used these perspectives in varying degrees, indicating that naturalistic painting had become, virtually simultaneously, the goal of a number of widely separated artists.

wheeling and charging with trumpets blowing and banners flying. For the Florentines, the relatively minor fray at San Romano epitomized fifteenth-century concepts of honor and, most especially, *virtù*. Immortalized by Uccello (oo-CHELL-o) in three magnificent panels, the *Battle of San Romano* originally hung in the bedchamber of Lorenzo the Magnificent. The central panel (fig. 17.9) portrays the climax of the battle. Uccello was obsessed with the problems of scientific linear perspective, and thus more concerned with the patterns of lances, armor, trumpets, and crossbows than with the ferocity of warfare. The result is a stylized composition of a bloodless battle, with horses looking like transplants from a merry-go-round. The work is both a study in perspective and a memorial to military honor, Renaissance-style.

17.9   Paolo Uccello, *The Rout of San Romano*. Ca. 1455. Tempera on wood, 6' × 10'6" (1.83 × 3.2 m). National Gallery, London. Photo: A.K.G., London.

17.10   Leonbattista Alberti (designer) and Bernardo Rossellino (architect), Palazzo Rucellai, Florence, facade. Begun 1461. Photo: Alinari, Florence.

Leonbattista Alberti, 1404–72

During the first half of the fifteenth century such classical elements of the Roman past as columns, capitals, and arches were examined by Brunelleschi, Donatello, and others. By mid-century the whole of antiquity was scrutinized, under the leadership of the remarkable humanist Alberti, who adopted the glorious past as a way of life. The first to study in detail the works of the Roman architect Vitruvius (first century BC), Alberti wrote enormously influential scientific treatises on painting, architecture, and sculpture. His design for the facade of a wealthy merchant's townhouse was inspired by Roman architecture but, there being no precedents for such a building in an ancient society in which the rich lived in country villas, Alberti invented for the Palazzo Rucellai (fig. 17.10) a new architecture based on his classically derived system of ideal proportions. Divided into three clearly articulated stories separated by friezes

17.11   Leonbattista Alberti, Sta. Maria Novella, Florence, facade. 1470. Photo: Scala, Florence.

harmonious whole of the facade was the result of a rigorous set of proportions. Width and height are identical with a ratio of 1:1. The upper structure can be encased in a square one-fourth the size of the basic square, or a ratio of 1:4. The lower portion is a rectangle of double squares forming a ratio of 1:2. Throughout the facade the proportions can be expressed in whole-number relationships: 1:1, 1:2, 1:3, and so on. Along with Brunelleschi, Alberti was convinced that beauty was inherent in these ratios.

Andrea del Verrocchio, 1435–88

An overriding characteristic of Renaissance artists was their individuality, their compulsion to be uniquely, unmistakably themselves. In Verrocchio (veh-ROE-key-o) we see distinct manifestations of this drive for individuality when treating the same subject. Verrocchio's *David* (fig. 17.12) is totally different from Donatello's conception. Donatello's figure is essentially a composition of sinuous and graceful lines; in his young warrior, Verrocchio emphasizes texture by a delicate rendering in gleaming bronze of skin, underlying veins, muscle, and bone. These are qualities that, unfortunately, can be best appreciated only when walking around the actual work. The tactile qualities are enhanced by clothing the figure in a skintight short skirt designed to look like leather. That Verrocchio used his pupil, Leonardo da Vinci, as a model may or may not be true, but the age and looks are about right.

Donatello's *Equestrian Monument of Gattamelata* (see

and **architraves**, the structure is faced with rusticated blocks of identical patterns in each bay, changing to related patterns in the upper two stories. Alberti adapted the articulation of superimposed pilasters from the Colosseum, but without the deep spaces. He used the **Tuscan order** for the ground floor and the Corinthian for the top floor. In between he invented his own composite order—a layer of acanthus leaves around a palmette—maintaining that a thorough knowledge of classical designs enabled architects to extend the vocabulary, and then proving his point.

Alberti was responsible for two Florentine buildings, the Palazzo Rucellai and the facade of the Church of Santa Maria Novella, neither of which had any noticeable effect on contemporary Florentine artists. Outside of Florence, however, Alberti's classical designs influenced all Renaissance architects, especially Bramante, Michelangelo, and Palladio. His design for the facade of Santa Maria Novella (fig. 17.11) had to cope with the existing Gothic arches on the ground level, a challenge which he met brilliantly by topping them with blind arches and matching their green and white marble with the corner pilasters and the four pilasters on the second story. His masterstroke was the addition of **volutes** on both sides of the narrow upper temple, which solved two problems: (1) it supplied needed buttressing for the nave walls, and (2) it beautifully filled the space above the side aisles of a basilica-plan church. The

17.12   Andrea del Verrocchio, *David*. Ca. 1465. Bronze, height 4'1⅝" (1.26 m). Museo Nazionale del Bargello, Florence. Photo: Alinari, Florence.

17.13 Andrea del Verrocchio (completed by Leopardi), *Equestrian Monument of Bartolommeo Colleoni*. Ca. 1481–96. Bronze, height 13' (3.96 m). Campo SS Giovanni e Paolo, Venice. Photo: Alinari, Florence.

fig. 17.7) is idealized, but Verrocchio's portrayal of Bartolommeo Colleoni (fig. 17.13) is strikingly realistic, with the fiercely scowling general readying his mace as he rides boldly into battle. Twisting in his saddle, the powerful figure seems almost too massive for the sprightly horse to carry. The tensions of horse and rider are portrayed at a dynamic moment in time, an instant before the battle.

Sandro Botticelli, 1445–1510

Three of the leading painters of the last quarter of the century—Botticelli, Ghirlandaio, and Perugino—were all vastly different in temperament and style. Botticelli (bot-tee-CHEL-lee), in fact, stands alone as one of the great masters in the use of line. In his celebrated *Birth of Venus* (*Venus Landing on the Shore*; fig. 17.14), Botticelli subordinates perspective and "correct" anatomical proportions and details to the elegant and sensual lines that make his style so delightfully unique. Like many of his generation, especially the elite circle of Lorenzo de' Medici and the Platonic Academy, Botticelli was fascinated with themes from classical mythology. According to an ancient myth, Venus was born from the sea, a legend interpreted by Ficino as an allegory of the birth of beauty. What the Florentine **Neoplatonists** actually did believe is still debated. Much of Plato's work had become available, but there was also a large body of Neoplatonist writings with Christian elements superimposed on Platonic theories.

Whether Botticelli's *Venus* symbolizes non-Christian or Christian ideas, or both, she is certainly lovely. Possibly inspired by a poem by Poliziano, Botticelli has painted her poised lightly on a conch shell, being blown gently to shore by two Zephyrs as one of the Hours hastens to drape her body with a flowered mantle. This is poetry in motion. The sea is flat, marked by upward-thrusting, V-shaped lines and bound by a stylized shoreline to form a serene setting for the sinuous lines of the moving figures. Probably inspired by classical statues in the Medici collection, the body of the goddess of spiritual and intellectual beauty is elongated and exquisitely curved, proportionately larger than the scale of the landscape. The gold-line shading on the trees is a further indication that Botticelli intended no realistic representation of the landscape. It was this sort of stylized treatment of the background that led to his friend Leonardo's wry comment that Botticelli created landscapes by throwing a sponge at the canvas.

Domenico del Ghirlandaio, 1449–94

Botticelli was favored by the intellectual elite of Florence, but the style of Ghirlandaio (gear-lan-DAH-yo) was preferred by the merchants and bankers of the city. Not interested in mythological fantasies, Ghirlandaio was a conservative painter for a commercial clientele and, as might be expected, a very successful artist. His *Old Man with a Child* (fig. 17.15), one of his most endearing works, is a compassionate portrayal of an elderly man holding an adoring child who could be his grandson, though the subjects have never been identified. Perhaps influenced by the naturalism of Flemish painting, which was well known in Italy by this time, the objective treatment of thinning hair and a deformed nose adds to the tender scene of familial love. As was customary in Renaissance portraiture, the human subjects totally dominate a composition that is reinforced by the lovely and distant landscape.

17.14 *Above* Sandro Botticelli, *Birth of Venus (Venus Landing on the Shore)*. After 1482. Tempera on canvas, 5'8" × 9'1" (1.73 × 2.77 m). Galleria degli Uffizi, Florence. Photo: Scala, Florence.

Perugino (Pietro Vanucci), ca. 1445–1523

Until about the middle of the fifteenth century, the Early Renaissance was essentially Florentine; the second half of the century saw the dissemination of Renaissance techniques throughout Italy, notably by artists such as Perugino and Bellini. Though his early training is a mystery, Pietro Vanucci was in Florence by 1472, where he acquired his knowledge of drawing and perspective, probably from Verrocchio. It was in the Umbrian city of Perugia that he established his reputation and acquired the name by which he is known today: Perugino (pay-roo-GEE-no), the "Perugian." In his *Crucifixion with the Virgin, Saint John, Saint Jerome, and Saint Mary Magdalene* (fig. 17.16), Perugino created a wonderful pictorial space that is much

17.15 Domenico del Ghirlandaio, *Old Man with a Child*. Ca. 1480. Panel, 24⅜ × 18" (61.9 × 45.7 cm). Louvre, Paris. Photo: R.M.N., Paris.

17.16   Perugino, *The Crucifixion with the Virgin, Saint John, Saint Jerome, and Saint Mary Magdalene.* Ca. 1485. Oil on panel, transferred to canvas: center 39⅞ × 22¼" (101.3 × 56.5 cm); wings each 37½ × 12" (95.2 × 30.5 cm). National Gallery of Art, Washington, D.C. (Andrew W. Mellon Collection).

more open than Florentine landscapes, with a sky stretching to infinity. As polished and cool as the work of the Flemish painter Hans Memling (see fig. 17.22), and probably influenced by his work, the **altarpiece** shows none of the usual emotions of Florentine crucifixions. Christ is not racked by pain nor do Mary at the left nor John at the right display any grief. In the wings St. Jerome and Mary Magdalene stand serenely in counterbalancing poses. In the vast expanse of the natural setting all is quietude. Whether the absence of emotion reflects Vasari's statement that Perugino was an atheist is a moot point. Though religious convictions were important for many people at that time, Renaissance artists were valued chiefly for their skills, not their spirits.

THE EARLY RENAISSANCE IN THE NORTH

Limbourg Brothers, ca. 1385–1416

A focus of significant new developments in art and in music was the sumptuous court of the dukes of Burgundy, from which the dukes governed the most prosperous lands in Europe (see map 18.1, p. 314). Philip the Bold and his brother, the Duke of Berry, sponsored leading artists such as the Limbourg brothers: Paul, Herman, and Jean. Their work in manuscript illumination marked the high point of the International Style (late Gothic), while also moving beyond to a new naturalism. Commissioned by the Duke of Berry, they created for him a personal prayer book, a Book of Hours containing passages of Scripture, prayers, and Office hours, all lavishly decorated and illustrated with paintings. Of particular interest are the twelve illuminated calendar pages; ten include peasants and aristocrats and two are devoted solely to peasant genre scenes. "February" (fig. 17.17 and p. 322) has, at the top, a zodiac representing the route of the chariot of the sun and including, in this case, the zodiacal signs of Aquarius and Pisces. The scene is an intensely cold, snowy landscape—the first convincing snow scene in Western art. On the upper level a peasant cuts firewood as another herds a donkey laden with faggots toward a distant village. In the tiny farmyard snow caps the beehives and covers the roof of the sheep pen except for the unrepaired hole in the roof. At the right a woman blows on her icy hands and stamps her feet to try to restore circulation. With the front wall removed for our benefit, we see a man and a woman seated before the fire with skirts raised high to gather in the welcome warmth. At the doorway, the lady of the house rather more decorously lifts her skirt; the cat is, of course, cozily warm and comfortable. The perspective that gives the illusion of depth is empirical rather than mathematically precise, the way the artists actually perceived the scene. Marking the beginning of the northern tradition of naturalistic art, the overriding concern is with the visible world, with loving care devoted to minute details in all their complexity.

The decisive victory of the English king, Henry V, at Agincourt in 1415 effectively ended, for some forty years,

17.17 Limbourg Brothers, "February" from the *Très Riches Heures du Duc de Berry*. 1413–16. Illuminated manuscript. Musée Condé, Chantilly, France. Photo: Giraudon, Paris.

the dominance of the French court and thus royal sponsorship of the courtly International Style. The center for art shifted to the Low Countries, where Philip the Good (reigned 1419–67) maintained his Burgundian court and negotiated hardheaded trade alliances with England. Artists found in the flourishing cities of Flanders—Bruges, Ghent, Louvain, Brussels—new patrons in the bankers and merchants who were the true arbiters of the wealthiest society in Europe. The society was **bourgeois**, but cosmopolitan rather than provincial, with powerful banking and trade connections throughout Europe. This solid middle class wanted art that pictured the real world and, by a strange coincidence, there were several artists of genius available to help fulfill the passion for naturalism.

Jan van Eyck, ca. 1390–1441

The leading painter of the early Flemish school, indeed of any age, van Eyck (van IKE) first served the court of John of Bavaria and later at the Burgundian court of Philip the Good. Credited by Vasari with inventing oil painting, van Eyck probably perfected an existing procedure. Using a technique still not fully understood, he probably put a **gesso** coating, or ground, on his panel; then, by applying

alternate layers of opaque and translucent color, he enhanced the brilliance of his colors. He made infinitely subtle and smooth gradations between color tones, obtaining a jewel-like radiance comparable to medieval stained glass. He undoubtedly learned some of his techniques from manuscript painters such as the Limbourg brothers, but it also seems likely that van Eyck was influenced, possibly inspired, by Gothic stained glass.

Ghent Altarpiece

The greatest work of early Flemish painting and a monumental accomplishment in any age, the *Ghent Altarpiece* (fig. 17.18) is a polyptych, a central painting with two hinged wings. The twenty different panels of the work range from the Annunciation on the outer panels to the Adoration of the Mystic Lamb within. In the lunettes of figure 17.18, the prophet Zechariah (left) with the Erytraean Sibyl, Cumean Sibyl, and prophet Micah symbolize the coming of Christ. The Annunciation figures are placed in a contemporary room containing Romanesque and Gothic elements that probably symbolize the Old and New Testaments. In the center panels below, the simulated sculptural figures of St. John the Baptist and St. John the Evangelist are flanked by the donors Jodoc Vyt and his wife.

In the open altarpiece (fig. 17.19), the lower central panel shows the community of saints, come from the four corners of the world to worship at the altar of the Mystic Lamb, from whose heart blood cascades into a chalice. In

OIL REPLACES EGG YOLK

Until early in the fifteenth century tempera (TEM-pur-uh; Lat., "to mingle or temper") painting was the standard medium. Artists mixed powdered pigments in egg yolk and painted, usually, on a wood panel. They had to paint rapidly and precisely because the paint dried so fast. Capable of details and bright colors, the medium had a narrow range between light and dark; colors too dark became dead while very light ones became chalklike.

Northern artists mixed their pigments in linseed oil and painted on canvas, which held paint better than wood. The surface was prepared as in tempera with gesso (plaster of Paris mixed with glue), and paint then applied in layers. Colors ranged from the lightest to the darkest with no loss of intensity, attaining, in the Flemish school, the rich glow that characterizes their work. With oil, artists could paint minute still-life details and vast landscape vistas; it dried slowly, giving them time to correct, revise, enrich. One wonders which came first: northern artists' obsession with painting everything they saw (leading to the invention of oil painting) or the discovery of a medium that enabled them to paint what they saw.

the foreground the Fountain of Life pours from spigots into an octagonal basin, running toward the observer as the "river of life" (Revelation 22:1). In the left-hand panel, judges and knights ride to the altar; on the right, hermits, pilgrims, and the giant St. Christopher walk to an altar scene backed by the heavenly Jerusalem in the distance. Forming a continuous view of Paradise, the five lower panels are designed with a rising perspective, another of the artist's innovations. On the upper level, the Lord has Mary as the Queen of Heaven on his right hand and St. John the Baptist on his left. To either side are choirs of angels with St. Cecilia seated at the portative (portable) organ, flanked by Adam and Eve on the outer panels.

The first large nudes in northern panel painting, the figures of Adam and Eve reveal a keen appreciation of the human body and innovative painting techniques in perspective and lighting. Once bowed by shame, the figures

17.18 *Right*   Jan van Eyck, *Ghent Altarpiece* (closed). Ca. 1425–32. 11'3" × 7'2" (3.43 × 2.18 m). St. Bavo, Ghent, Belgium. Photo: Paul M.R. Maeyaert, Zelzate, Belgium.

17.19 *Below*   Jan van Eyck, *Ghent Altarpiece* (open). 11'3" × 14'5" (3.43 × 4.39 m). Photo: Scala, Florence.

17.20 Jan van Eyck, *The Arnolfini Wedding Portrait*. 1434. Oil on canvas, 32¼ × 23½ " (81.9 × 59.7 cm). National Gallery, London.

stand erect as the First Man and First Woman. The placement of the altarpiece puts the feet of the two nudes at eye level, which accounts for the view of the sole of Adam's foot. This bit of naturalism is typical of a visual reality so precise that botanists can identify dozens of plants in this awesome work.

The *Ghent Altarpiece* was created early in the supremacy of the Duchy of Burgundy but, even as van Eyck worked on it, Joan of Arc (ca. 1412–31) was leading Charles VII and the French army to victory (in 1428) over the English invaders. By 1453 Charles had triumphantly ended the Hundred Years' War with England (1337–1453) and absorbed Burgundy, Picardy, and Flanders.

The Arnolfini Wedding

The meticulous details in a van Eyck painting are fascinating, but the whole of a picture—its unity—is greater than the sum of its parts. In a work commissioned by Giovanni Arnolfini, an Italian merchant, he and his bride, Jeanne Cenami, apparently pose for a portrait as a form of wedding certificate, duly witnessed by the artist (seen in the convex mirror) and notarized on the back wall: "Jan van Eyck was here" (fig. 17.20). The light, space, volume, and the two distinct personalities are all unified, both visually and psychologically. Patron and artist must have been more than acquaintances; two individuals make up this couple, joined in a tender moment without the slightest hint of sentimentality. The texture of cloth, glass, metal, wood, and even the furry little dog are exquisitely detailed.

Though unobtrusive, symbols abound. The single lighted candle is, according to custom, the last to be extinguished on the wedding night, but it may also symbolize Christ as the light of the world. Carved on the post of a bedside chair is the image of St. Margaret, the patron saint of childbirth. (The lady is not pregnant but holding up her full-skirted dress in the contemporary fashion.) The dog represents fidelity (Lat. *fides*; hence "Fido"), and the abandoned slippers are a reminder that the couple is standing on holy ground. By uniting the classical concern for naturalism and spatial depth with the Christian idea that every material object has transcendent importance, Flemish painters developed a radically new style of painting. Craftsmanship at this level verges on the superhuman; indeed, nothing like this had ever been done before.

Rogier van der Weyden, ca. 1400–64

Because his paintings were perfect in their own marvelous way, van Eyck had many admirers in northern Europe, Spain, and Italy, but no emulators. There were imitators,

17.21 Rogier van der Weyden, *Portrait of a Lady*. Ca. 1460. Oil on panel, painted surface 13⅜ × 10⅙" (34 × 25.5 cm). National Gallery of Art, Washington, D.C. (Andrew W. Mellon Collection). Photo: Richard Carafelli.

17.22 Hans Memling, *The Presentation in the Temple*. Ca. 1463. Oil on panel, 23½ × 19" (59.7 × 48.3 cm). Photo: Bridgeman, London.

of course, but no disciples who could even approach his rare gifts. Adopting a more expressive and emotional style than that of van Eyck, van der Weyden (van dur VYE-den) was the leading Flemish painter of the next generation, becoming City Painter for Brussels in 1435. When he traveled to Italy for the Holy Year of 1450, he influenced Italian art and was, in turn, impressed by what he saw there. As technically accomplished as van Eyck, he painted portraits with a psychological depth then unknown in Flemish painting.

Portrait of a Lady (fig. 17.21) is a study of a young woman tentatively identified as Marie de Valengin, the daughter of Philip the Good, Duke of Burgundy. Her forehead and eyebrows are shaved, a fashionable indication of intellectual acumen. Also high fashion, the high-waisted dress and triangular coif focus attention on the exquisite modeling of the face. The portrait is both beautiful and baffling. The impression of an almost ascetic contemplation is contradicted by the sensuality of the full mouth with its ripe underlip. The overall impression is that of an assertive personality—an intelligent, self-confident, and strong-willed young woman. She certainly looks like a princess.

Contrasting curiously with the broad facial planes, the thin fingers are almost Gothic in style. Bewitching and beguiling, this is a great psychological study by one of the first of a long line of Low Country painters leading directly to Hals and Rembrandt.

Hans Memling, ca. 1440–94

Memling served his apprenticeship in his native Germany, but then moved to Flanders (at that time a French province) where he apparently studied with van der Weyden. A contemporary of Ghirlandaio in Italy, his style is similarly genial and rather naive. It appealed to a large clientele of merchants and led ultimately to a considerable fortune. Using extensive studies of earlier Flemish masters, particularly van Eyck, he developed a somewhat melancholy art of extreme refinement. In *The Presentation in the Temple* (fig. 17.22) the figures are immobile, frozen in time, or even outside time. The light falls on people grouped in harmony with their imaginary setting; the overall feeling is unworldly and slightly sad.

Memling's work was in tune with a general feeling of pessimism, an erosion of confidence in the moral authority of the church, an almost prophetic feeling of the impending Reformation. In Italy the pessimism was fully warranted, for it was in 1494—the year of Memling's death—that the Medicis were expelled from Florence, coinciding with the invasion of the French armies of Charles VIII, which launched a tumultuous era in Italy called the Italian Wars.

17.23 Hieronymus Bosch, *Garden of Delights*. Ca. 1505–10. Oil on panel, sides 86 × 36" (218.4 × 91.4 cm); center 86 × 76" (218.4 × 193 cm). Museo del Prado, Madrid.

Hieronymus Bosch, ca. 1450–1516

This pessimistic age found its supreme artist in the person of Bosch (bahs), one of history's most enthralling and enigmatic painters. He lived and worked in present-day southern Holland, but little else is known about either his life or his artistic intentions. Art historians have wondered about his bizarre iconography, and so have psychiatrists. This was an age obsessed with death and with an almost pathological fear of the devil and his demons. His work makes it plain that Bosch had a pessimistic view of human nature—though some would call his vision realistic—and he certainly raged against sinfulness.

One of his major and most enigmatic works is the huge triptych entitled *Garden of Delights* (fig. 17.23). The side panels of this incredible work depict an idyllic Garden of Eden and a spectacularly disastrous Hell, both rendered in an unconventional but fairly consistent manner. The central panel is quite another matter. Complex, bizarre, and bewildering, the sparse landscape teems with hundreds of naked men and women and various animals, both real and imaginary—and in all sizes. There are several lakes, a pond, giant strawberries, mussel shells, eggs, and assorted mysterious and grotesque objects. Frail of body and seeming all the same age—about twenty-one—men and women frolic and tease and gambol about the strange arena.

Despite the universal nudity and much pairing off, there is no explicit sexual activity. The general ambiance is certainly erotic, but no one displays any sexual desire except, perhaps, by stroking a giant strawberry. Most are busy with silly activities. One cuddling couple wears an owl for a headdress and someone rides a lion while clutching a giant fish. The foolishness is virtually endless, but apparently harmless. The faces are generally calm and composed; the entire scene appears to resemble a genteel nudist camp.

What does all this mean? In the absence of a universally accepted interpretation, there are several

possibilities. Perhaps there are messages hidden behind symbolic acts and objects—a vocabulary taken from non-Christian traditions, Flemish folklore, and medieval bestiaries. Pursuing this line leads one into a quagmire of ambiguities that apparently have no resolution. Too much of the old symbolic vocabularies has been lost over the intervening centuries.

Others take the view that this is a message in code directed to people practicing a secret religion. This kind of activity amounts to heresy and a possible death sentence— hence the code. But can we accept these vapid people as high practitioners of a secret sect? Their actions seem too ridiculous for that. Nothing in this picture has any religious connotation whatsoever, and this at a time when religion pervaded every nook and cranny of life.

We can never know exactly how Bosch's contemporaries viewed this painting but, in our own time, there are startling flashes of recognition. All too familiar is the aimless pursuit of pleasure, the lack of ambition, direction, or purpose, the games people play. Did Bosch anticipate the twentieth century, or has he perhaps indicted all humankind for persistent foolishness and failure?

When considering Bosch's total output, there is no denying his pessimism; his was perhaps the darkest vision in an age of deep pessimism. This painting seems to be, therefore, a despairing depiction of the human condition in which there is no Christ, no Redemption, no Salvation. Humanity is doomed, not because it is vicious or depraved, but because it is vain, vapid, and silly. The Incarnation is useless because folly was present in the Garden of Eden and remains as the dominant characteristic of the human race.[2] This interpretation leaves us no alternative but to see Bosch as the ultimate pessimist: humankind will move endlessly from folly to damnation with no hope of heaven.

Enormously popular in the sixteenth century, Bosch's paintings typify an age that groveled in a sickening undercurrent of fear of the devil, leading to fierce, misdirected religious zeal. In 1484 Pope Innocent VIII declared witchcraft (activities of women possessed by the devil) a prime heresy. During the next two centuries a tidal wave of sadism and misogyny led to the torture, hanging, and burning of some 100,000 to 200,000 women, plus many men (and children) who were enveloped in the madness. Two unscrupulous Dominican monks wrote a handbook for self-appointed witch-hunters, *The Witches' Hammer*,[3] a bestseller that ran to thirty editions, a melancholy testimony to the dissemination of printed books.

The career of Hieronymus Bosch marked the end of the Early Northern Renaissance and the beginning of a tormented period of warfare in Italy, of corrupt and dissolute

---

2. See also Erasmus, *The Praise of Folly*, discussed on p. 324.
3. Heinrich Kramer and James Sprenger, *Malleus Maleficarum*, trans. Montague Summers (London: Pushkin Press, 1928). Approved by the pope, the handbook was originally published in 1490.

popes, and of spiritually bankrupt religious orders. One year after Bosch's death, Martin Luther published his ninety-five Theses to set in motion the Reformation.

THE HIGH RENAISSANCE IN ITALY, CA. 1495–1520

The relatively peaceful and prosperous existence of Florence ended in two rough jolts in the fateful years of 1492 and 1494. Lorenzo the Magnificent—a strong, moderating force in the fortunes of Florence—died in 1492, the same year in which Ferdinand and Isabella captured Córdoba, the last Moorish stronghold in Spain. Columbus, using a map drawn in Florence, discovered the New World. In Rome, Rodrigo Borgia was crowned as Pope Alexander VI, the embodiment of a decadent and corrupt Renaissance pontiff and a merciless enemy of the Florentine Republic.

In 1494, concerned about the military support of Lorenzo's dim and feckless son Piero, Ludovico Sforza of Milan encouraged Charles VIII of France to invade Italy. Charles, who was spoiling for a fight, willingly did so. For the next thirty-five years French and Spanish armies, the latter freed by the removal of the Moors, fought the Italian Wars against the city-states and, for good measure, each other. Always assuming that each invasion was the last, the Italian city-states never banded together to expel their foreign tormentors. Paradoxically, High Renaissance art flourished against this backdrop of continuous warfare. Exploiting and refining Early Renaissance discoveries in Italy and the North, Leonardo da Vinci, Michelangelo, Raphael, and Bramante created masterworks that crowned the Italian Renaissance.

Leonardo da Vinci, 1452–1519

The illegitimate son of a peasant girl known only as Caterina, and Piero da Vinci, a notary, Leonardo da Vinci (lay-o-NAR-do da VIN-chee) was the acknowledged universal man of the Renaissance, the most astounding genius in an age of giants. Inventor, civil and military engineer, architect, musician, geologist, botanist, physicist, anatomist, sculptor, and painter, Leonardo left untouched only classical scholarship, poetry, and philosophy. Theology was of no interest to him, for he was a lifelong skeptic who recognized no authority higher than the eye, which he called the "window of the soul."

As was customary with bastardy during the Renaissance, Leonardo was acknowledged by his father and, at about age fifteen, apprenticed to Verrocchio in Florence. Though little else is known about the first thirty years of his life, records indicate that Leonardo, like Masaccio and Botticelli before him, was admitted to the guild as a craftsman in painting. Unlike Early Renaissance masters, however, Leonardo, along with Michelangelo, launched a successful campaign to raise the status of artists from mere artisans to members of the highest level of society.

In 1481 Pope Sixtus IV summoned the "best" Tuscan artists to work in the Vatican, including Botticelli, Ghirlandaio, and Perugino, but not Leonardo. Furious at the slight, Leonardo decided to leave Florence, but not before he had completed a commission for the de' Benci family of wealthy bankers. His portrait of *Ginevra de' Benci* (fig. 17.24), the only Leonardo painting in the United States, is an enchanting study of a lovely but strangely tense and wary young woman. She was known to be a very devout person, ill at ease in the fun-loving exuberance of Florence, and sternly disapproving of Lorenzo de' Medici's long-term affair with her aunt. Framing her golden curls in juniper branches (Ginevra means "juniper"), Leonardo has created a melancholy work; the pallid face is set against a thinly misted background, with details deliberately softened and blurred. Though not invented by Leonardo, this **sfumato** (foo-MAH-toh, literally "smoky") technique was one of his significant contributions to the art of painting. The twilight atmosphere is another innovation, contrasting sharply with the sunlit scenes of other painters. The painting is minus some 6 inches (15.2 cm) at the bottom, which may explain why the lady's hands are not shown.

Seeking a more appreciative patron than the Medici or the pope, Leonardo wrote to Ludovico Sforza, duke of Milan, touting his expertise as a military engineer but mentioning, in just two sentences, that he was also a sculptor and a painter. During his stay in Milan (1482–99) Leonardo produced *The Last Supper* (fig. 17.25), a treatment of the familiar theme unlike anything before or since. The High Renaissance begins with this magnificent composition.

17.24 Leonardo da Vinci, *Ginevra de' Benci*. Ca. 1474. Oil on panel, 15¼ × 14½" (38.8 × 36.7 cm). National Gallery of Art, Washington, D.C. (Ailsa Mellon Bruce Fund). Photo: Jose A. Naranjo.

17.25 Leonardo da Vinci, *The Last Supper*. Ca. 1495–8. Mural, oil and tempera on plaster, 14'5" × 28' (4.39 × 8.53 m). Refectory of Sta. Maria delle Grazie, Milan. Photo: Scala, Florence.

After suffering the indignities of Leonardo's experimentation with fresco painting, damp walls, Napoleon's troops, and World War II bombing, the painting has been restored, but only to an approximation of its original condition.

The moment of the painting is not the traditional one of the Eucharist, but Christ's electrifying statement: "One of you shall betray me." Except for Christ, Leonardo used life models for the disciples and had difficulty only in finding a suitable Judas. According to Vasari, when the prior of Santa Maria complained to Sforza that Leonardo was "lazy" in his execution of the painting, Leonardo remarked that locating a Judas was difficult but that the prior would serve nicely. Leonardo's contemporaries would have looked for Judas where other artists had placed him—across the table from Jesus. Instead, we see the villain as part of the first group of three Apostles to the left of Christ, composed in a tight, dark triangle with his face in darkness. Clutching a bag of money, he is in the group but not a part of it. His dark bulk is in sharp contrast to the lighted profile of Peter and the luminous radiance of John. Each Apostle is an individual psychological study, reacting to Christ's startling statement in a manner consistent with his personality.

The design of *The Last Supper* has a mathematical unity, with divisions of groups of threes and fours that add up to seven and multiply into twelve. The three windows place Christ's head in the center window as the second person of the Trinity. The shocked Apostles are grouped into four units of three each, divided in the middle by the isolated triangular design of Christ. Echoing the four groups are the wall panels on either side, and on the ceiling there are seven beams running from both front to back and side to side. Leonardo may have had Christian number symbolism in mind (Holy Trinity, Four Gospels, Seven Cardinal Virtues, Twelve Gates of the New Jerusalem) but three, four, and seven also stand for the *trivium* and *quadrivium* of the seven liberal arts. Moreover, Pythagorean number symbolism included the concept of one as unity, three as the most logical number (beginning, middle, end), and four as symbolizing Justice. Given Leonardo's skepticism and explicit anticlerical feelings, something other than Christian symbolism would be an appropriate interpretation.

There is no question, however, about the picture as a whole. Despite the mathematical precision of the perspective, there is no place from which a spectator can view the perspective "correctly"; it exists as a work apart, on an ideal level beyond everyday experience. This is the elevated style of formal design and noble theme that characterizes the Italian High Renaissance.

Leonardo insisted that painters were noble creatures and that painting should be a part of the seven liberal arts. For him, sculptors were craftsmen standing in dust and debris chiseling away at stubborn marble. Michelangelo, on the other hand, claimed that sculpture was as superior to painting as the sun was to the moon.

Michelangelo Buonarroti, 1475–1564

Perhaps the greatest artistic genius who ever lived, Michelangelo (me-kell-AHN-djay-lo) excelled in sculpture, architecture, painting, and poetry. A towering figure even in his own time, he was the "Divine Michelangelo." Words and more words have been written trying to account for such a man, but there is no accounting for him. Born of a vain and mean-spirited father and a dimly pathetic mother to whom he never referred, he appeared with prodigious gifts at a time and place seemingly destined to make him immortal. He learned painting techniques in Ghirlandaio's studio and sculpting both from a pupil of Donatello and from ancient works in the Medici collection.

His first masterpiece, the *Pietà* (fig. 17.26), is more characteristic of the fifteenth century than the sixteenth in style, with elegant lines reminiscent of Botticelli. The triangular composition is fashioned of contradictions. Though Christ is dead, the blood pumps through his veins as if he were asleep. The Virgin is portrayed as younger than her son, her lovely face composed rather than distorted by grief; only her left hand indicates her sorrow. The figure of Christ is life-size but that of the Virgin is elongated. Her head is the same size as Christ's, but in proportion she would be about 7 feet (2.1 m) tall if she were standing. The overall visual effect of these distortions is a super-authenticity beyond earthbound reality.

17.26 Michelangelo, *Pietà*. 1498–1499/1500. Marble, height 5'8½" (1.74 m). St. Peter's, Rome. Photo: Anderson-Giraudon, Florence.

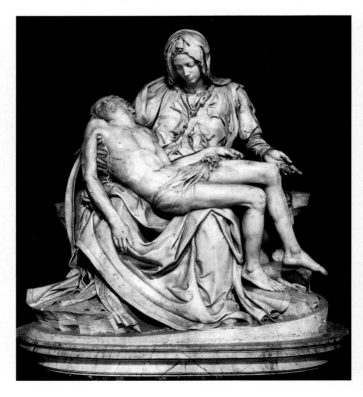

17.27 Michelangelo, *David*. 1501–4. Marble, height 13'5"
(4.09 m). Galleria dell'Accademia, Florence. Photo: Alinari,
Florence.

The *Pietà* was a youthful work but the *David* (fig.
17.27), initiated only a year or so later, was the first monumental statue of the High Renaissance, a product of
Michelangelo's already mature genius. Though the Palazzo
della Signoria proudly possessed three Davids, two by
Donatello (fig. 17.6) and one by Verrocchio (fig. 17.12), one
more hero was not too many for a city battling to maintain its power and independence. A Florentine Republic
was established after the Medici were expelled in 1494 but
it did not last long. While Michelangelo was working on

his *David*, the dangerous Alexander VI died, in 1503, and
shortly thereafter the incompetent Piero de' Medici, known
as Piero the Unfortunate, drowned while fighting with the
French in an attempt to gain reentry into the city. By 1504
Florence was finally at peace and the prime civic concern
was where to place Michelangelo's mighty *David*. The commission to select the site included Leonardo, Botticelli, and
Perugino, attesting to the status the nearly completed work
had already acquired. Originally scheduled to be placed
high on Florence Cathedral, *David* was triumphantly set in
front of the center of government, the Palazzo Vecchio,
where it became the symbol of a republic ready to do battle against all enemies. During the nineteenth century the
statue was moved indoors to protect it from the weather
and replaced by a copy.

The Davids of Donatello and Verrocchio were adolescent boys; this is a strapping young man standing alert,
every muscle vibrant with power. The head might be that
of Apollo and the body that of Herakles, yet this is the
portrait of a Platonic ideal as well as David the King. His
father was both Hebrew and, collectively, Lorenzo, Ficino,
and the Florentine Platonic Academy.

The fame of the *David* was instant, and Michelangelo
had more commissions than he could handle, including
one to construct a vast tomb for Pope Julius II. The tomb
project was never finished as originally planned; instead,
Michelangelo somehow found himself in 1508 lying atop
the scaffolding in the Sistine Chapel. How all this came
about has never been satisfactorily explained, but one
plausible theory involves the alleged machinations of
Bramante, the recently appointed architect of the new St.
Peter's. He was known to be concerned about funds for his
project and was also intensely jealous of Michelangelo.
Julius had lavished enormous sums on his tomb project—
money that Bramante needed for his mighty basilica. If
the pope could be encouraged to put Michelangelo to work

BONFIRE OF THE VANITIES

A Dominican monk, Girolamo Savonarola (1452–98),
established a theocracy in Florence after the Medici were
expelled and even declared Christ king of the city. A virtual dictator, he imposed rigid reforms while warning
of approaching doom. Railing against materialism, he
condemned ownership of anything beautiful or valuable
as sinful and urged people to burn their "vanities," which
many dutifully did. Friends of Botticelli barely managed
to keep him from burning his paintings. Inevitably
Savonarola came into conflict with the corrupt Alexander
VI. When the monk ignored the pope's excommunication, he was arrested, tortured, tried, hanged (and then
burned) for heresy and schism.

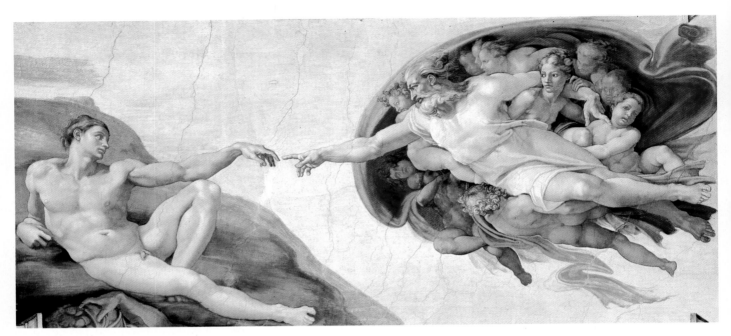

17.28   Michelangelo, *Creation of Adam*, Sistine Chapel ceiling, detail. 1511. Fresco. Vatican, Rome. Photo: Nippon Television, Tokyo. This photograph was taken after the ceiling was cleaned in the 1980s.

painting the Sistine Chapel ceiling, a monumental undertaking Bramante felt not even Michelangelo could bring off, then he would have no further financial or artistic competition. Whatever transpired behind the scenes, Michelangelo was, in fact, the only artist who was capable of tackling the project.

With a ceiling proportionately too high (68'; 20.7 m) for its length and width (132 × 44'; 40.2 × 13.4 m), the private chapel of the popes was neither intimate nor monumental. Michelangelo's frescoes made it monumental. In only four years, 1508–12, he filled the entire 700 square yards (630 m²) of barrel-vaulted ceiling with over 300 powerful figures. Relating the Genesis story from the Creation to the Flood, Michelangelo fused Judeo-Christian theology with ancient mythology and Neoplatonic philosophy to create one of the truly awesome works of Western art. In just one detail, the *Creation of Adam* (fig. 17.28), one can perceive some of the majesty of the total work. Embracing an awestruck Eve and with his left hand resting on the shoulder of the Christ child, God the Father extends his

finger and the spark of life to an inert Adam. Against a background of generations waiting to be born, the twisting, dynamic figure is lovingly paternal, imparting to Adam the soul that will actuate his potential nobility.

After protesting for four years that he was a sculptor, not a painter, Michelangelo proved that he was both; all the figures are sculptural forms, conceived in the mind's eye of a sculptor and executed in paint on wet plaster.[4] A recent cleaning of the entire ceiling has brilliantly revealed the original rich, even dazzling, colors employed. Totally overwhelming the work of many notable artists on the walls, the ceiling frescoes express the optimism of a supreme artist at the peak of his powers.

The following sonnet[5] embodies Michelangelo's personal and agonizingly physical reaction to four years of lying on his back and painting over his head:

Sonnet V

To Giovanni da Pistoia
"On the Painting of the Sistine Chapel"
(I' ho gia fatto un gozzo)

I've grown a goitre by dwelling in this den—
As cats from stagnant streams in Lombardy,
Or in what other land they hap to be—
Which drives the belly close beneath the chin:
My beard turns up to heaven; my nape falls in,
Fixed on my spine: my breast-bone visibly
Grows like a harp: a rich embroidery
Bedews my face from brush-drops thick and thin.
My loins into my paunch like levers grind:
My buttock like a crupper bears my weight;
My feet unguided wander to and fro;
In front my skin grows loose and long; behind,
By bending it becomes more taut and strait;

4. On his first paycheck he pointedly wrote, "I, Michelangelo Buonarroti, sculptor, have received 500 ducats on account . . . for painting the vault of the Sistine chapel." From Peter De Rosa, *Vicars of Christ: The Dark Side of the Papacy* (New York: Macmillan, 1988).
5. John Addington Symonds (trans.), *The Sonnets of Michelangelo Buonarroti and Tommaso Campanella* (London: Smith, Elder & Co., 1878), p.35. See pp.329–30 for another poem by Michelangelo.

Crosswise I strain me like a Syrian bow:
Whence false and quaint, I know,
Must be the fruit of squinting brain and eye;
For ill can aim the gun that bends awry.
Come then, Giovanni, try
To succour my dead pictures and my fame;
Since foul I fare and painting is my shame.

Donato Bramante, 1444–1514

The dominant political figure and artistic patron of the High Renaissance was Pope Julius II (reigned 1503–13), known as the Warrior Pope. Determined to obliterate the appalling memories of Alexander VI and the Borgia crimes, he refused even to live in the apartment of his decadent predecessor. Julius II restored order to the city of Rome, ruthlessly reconquered papal provinces with the sword, and proceeded energetically to rebuild his beloved Rome. A fortuitous quirk of history put a dynamic pope in power at precisely the time when he could utilize the mature talents of Michelangelo, Raphael, and Bramante. Bramante of Urbino, the foremost architect of the High Renaissance and a close friend of the pope, was entrusted with many building projects, with the new St. Peter's leading the list. Julius II decided, in 1505, that the 1,100-year-old Basilica of St. Peter's was to be replaced by a Renaissance structure worthy of the imperial splendor of the new Rome—a project not completely finished until 1626, some fourteen architects, twenty popes, and one Reformation later.

Though much of Bramante's design can still be seen in St. Peter's, his architectural genius is better illustrated by

17.29 Donato Bramante, Tempietto, S. Pietro in Montorio, Rome. 1502. Height 46' (14 m); external diameter 29' (8.8 m). Photo: Kersting, London.

a circular structure of only modest size but of immense influence in architectural history. Constructed on the spot where St. Peter was supposedly crucified, the Tempietto ("little temple"; fig. 17.29) became the prototype of classical domed architecture in Europe and the United States. The exquisitely proportioned building was placed on a three-step base like a Greek temple and conceived as an articulated work of sculpture in the manner of classical Greek architecture. Influenced by Leonardo's radial designs, the building is distinguished by the severely Doric colonnade, above which are classical triglyphs and metopes topped by a lightly rhythmical **balustrade**. The overall effect of majestic serenity in a small building may have been the decisive factor in Bramante's selection as the papal architect.

Raphael (Raffaello Sanzio), 1483–1520

The third artist working in the Vatican, in addition to Bramante and Michelangelo, was Raphael (RAHF-ee-el), one of the greatest painters in Western art. Born in Urbino like Bramante, Raphael studied first with Perugino and then, as many artists had done before him, moved to Florence, where he studied the works of Leonardo and Michelangelo and painted many famous Madonnas.

Raphael is the most reproduced painter of the Renaissance and his works, especially the Madonnas, are perhaps too familiar. He was an intellectual painter whose works should be studied for both form and content; but viewers tend to see his Madonnas as pretty and sweet, partly because they were intended as sympathetic portrayals of Mother and Child and partly because there have been countless sentimental imitations.

The *Alba Madonna* (fig. 17.30) is a tightly controlled triangular composition derived from Leonardo's style, but designed as a *tondo* (circular painting). Unlike Leonardo and other Madonna painters, Raphael used life models, usually in the nude, sketching the basic figure until he had all elements just right. In this work he was concerned with subtly contrasting the humanity of John the Baptist with the divinity of the Christ child, who is the focal point of the painting. The counterbalancing diagonals of the left arm of the Madonna and the back of the kneeling John form the top of the pyramid. The left leg of Christ echoes the reverse diagonal that extends from the Madonna's left forearm and down her leg. Enclosed within the space between the blue-draped leg and the fur-covered back of John, the figure of the Christ child is essentially vertical. The one horizontal element in the composition is the right arm of Christ, leading our eye to the slender cross so lightly held. Like so many of Raphael's paintings, this work suffers perhaps from too much loving care; it has been so vigorously cleaned that the colors are not as vibrant as they undoubtedly once were.

Raphael was an active member of a philosophical circle dedicated to reconciling the views of Plato and Aristotle,

17.30 *Above* Raphael, *Alba Madonna*. Ca. 1510. Oil on panel, transferred to canvas, diameter 37¼" (94.5 cm). National Gallery of Art, Washington, D.C. (Andrew W. Mellon Collection). Photo: Jose A. Naranjo.

and when he was commissioned to decorate the papal apartments, he was eager to put his ideas into visual form. The result was four giant wall murals depicting the four branches of human knowledge and wisdom: theology, law, poetry, and philosophy. The last painting, the so-called *School of Athens* (fig. 17.31), is itself a summary of Renaissance humanism. Grouped on the left side of the painting are the Greek philosophers who were mainly concerned with ultimate mysteries, from Plato at the top to Pythagoras writing on a slate at the lower left. Holding the *Timaeus*, Plato (a likeness of Leonardo) points to the heavens as the source of his ideas/forms. Herakleitos sits in the foreground with his elbow on a block, but his face is probably that of Michelangelo. At the upper left we see Socrates in a typical dialogue with some of his students. Aristotle holds his *Ethics* as he indicates the earth as the rightful object of all observations. Diogenes sprawls on the steps, and at the lower right, Euclid bends over a slate, but his face is that of Bramante. Continuing the portraiture, Raphael depicts

17.31 Raphael, *School of Athens*. 1501–11. Fresco, 26 × 18' (7.92 × 5.49 m). Stanza della Segnatura, Vatican, Rome. Photo: Scala, Florence.

himself at the extreme right looking at the viewer. The statue of Apollo, patron of poetry, presides at the upper left, whereas Athena, goddess of wisdom, watches over the empirical philosophers and scientists. Though Plato used poetic images and Aristotle utilized rational analysis, Raphael and his circle were convinced that the philosophers agreed in substance even though they disagreed in words. Raphael has here harmonized not only the schools of philosophy but the ancient and Christian worlds as well.

The premature death of the frail Raphael signaled the end of the High Renaissance in Rome.[6] By this time the innovations of Leonardo, Michelangelo, Bramante, and Raphael were being studied and applied throughout Italy, especially in Venice, and northward into Germany, France, and the Netherlands (today's Holland and Belgium).

HIGH AND LATE RENAISSANCE AND MANNERISM IN SIXTEENTH-CENTURY ITALY

Giorgione da Castelfranco, ca. 1475/7–1510

The High Renaissance style emerged very clearly in the work of a shadowy figure known first as Giorgio and later as the famous Giorgione ("big George"; giorge-o-nay). Very little is known about the man or even his work. He was, according to Vasari, a humanist, musician, and lover of conversation, parties, nature, and women—probably in reverse order.

Though another hand has added some distant figures in the left landscape, Giorgione's *Adoration of the Shepherds* (fig. 17.32) is a superb example of the new pastoral poetic style that he introduced to painting in general and to the Venetian school in particular. One of the most innovative and influential Renaissance painters, Giorgione used his mastery of light and color to paint magical landscapes in which human figures become part of the Arcadian mood. The natural setting is, in fact, so prominent that we can call this a landscape with nativity scene. The setting is depicted not in ideal naturalistic terms, as in the works of van Eyck or Leonardo, but as nature in the raw viewed through the eye of the poet. The figures are not drawn but rather formed of contrasting light and shadow, with the body of the child and the heads of the parents radiating a heavenly light against the gloomy recesses of the cave. The high moral tone and noble values of the Florentine and Roman High Renaissance are utterly foreign to this romantic evocation of mood and feeling.

6. Historical periods in any field (art, music, society, government, whatever) are identified after the fact, usually long after, by historians who look for significant defining events.

17.32 Giorgione, *The Adoration of the Shepherds*. 1505–10. Oil on panel, 35¾ × 43½" (90.8 × 110.5 cm). National Gallery of Art, Washington, D.C. (Samuel H. Kress Collection). Photo: Richard Carafelli.

Giorgione died of the plague at an early age, leaving a number of works unfinished. Though it is known that Titian completed some of the paintings, what may never be known is which paintings were involved and what "completed by Titian" really means. To confuse matters further, Giorgione probably contributed to some of Titian's paintings, but again we have no sure knowledge of which specific paintings were involved.

Michelangelo and Mannerism

The art of the remainder of the century can be considered as two basic stylistic streams: Mannerism and Late Renaissance. The High Renaissance, with the beauty, harmony, and proportions of its paintings, sculpture, and architecture, was seen at this time as a golden age, an era in which Leonardo, Michelangelo, and Raphael had convincingly demonstrated that there was nothing an artist could not do.

What was left for subsequent artists? Vasari used the term *maniera* ("style") of working "in the manner of" supreme artists such as Raphael and Michelangelo. Later artists could either adopt the techniques of the masters or use these techniques as a point of departure, to replace the serenity of the High Renaissance with a Mannerist virtuosity that delighted in twisting, confusing, and distorting human figures. Raphael and Michelangelo studied nature; the Mannerists studied Raphael and Michelangelo, especially Michelangelo.

The so-called Mannerist crisis may also have been a reaction to the momentous events of the 1520s, both local

17.33 Michelangelo, *The Last Judgment*, after restoration.
1536–41. Fresco, 48 × 44' (14.63 × 13.41 m). Altar wall
of the Sistine Chapel, Vatican, Rome. Photo: Nippon
Television, Tokyo.

and international, that affected the viewpoints and lives of just about everyone. Florence's power came to an end, as the proud city became a pawn in the hands of the Medici popes, Leo X (reigned 1513–21) and Clement VII (reigned 1523–34). Luther's defiance of Pope Leo X led to the dissolution of unified Christianity, followed by over a century of sectarian warfare. In 1527 the political machinations of Clement VII led to the sack of Rome by the rampaging armies of the Holy Roman Emperor, Charles V of Germany. In 1529 Clement VII refused to annul the marriage of Henry VIII of England and Catherine of Aragon, leading to England's break with Rome. It was a decade of disasters. In the New World, rapidly becoming a significant factor in European culture, the decade was prefaced by Cortés' conquest of the Aztecs in Mexico (1519) and followed by Pizarro's conquest of the Incas in Peru (1533).

Michelangelo's Later Works

During a visit to Rome, Michelangelo discussed the Sistine Chapel with Clement VII. The east, or altar, wall contained the *Assumption of the Virgin* by Perugino, but Clement wanted this replaced with a Resurrection. By the time the new pope, Paul III (reigned 1534–49), had commissioned the artist to paint the entire wall, the subject had become the Last Judgment, though how this came about is not clear. Paul III was a Counter-Reformation pope whose most significant act was the convening of the Council of Trent (1545–64) to reform the church and to counter the challenge of Protestantism. However, nepotism was rampant during Paul's reign and he, along with his illegitimate sons and daughters, lived the lavish life of a Renaissance pontiff. Michelangelo, on the other hand, was deeply religious and was, moreover, sixty-one years old when he accepted the commission.

Preoccupied with the fate of humanity and that of his own soul, Michelangelo apparently began *The Last Judgment* (fig. 17.33) with the conviction that the world had gone mad. (He began his project in the same year that Henry VIII defied Rome and established the Church of England.) The ideal beauty and optimism of the chapel ceiling had been superseded by a mood of terror and doom, with the gigantic figure of Christ, based on Matthew 24:30–31, come to judge the quick and the dead. Everyone "will see the Son of Man coming on clouds of Heaven with power and great glory," his body twisted and his arm raised in a gesture of damnation. In an energetic clockwise motion, the figures at the bottom rise toward Christ and are either gathered in by waiting angels or pulled by demons down into Hell. The resurrected women (always clothed) and men (generally nude) float into the helping arms of angels, who are unencumbered by wings or halos. The scale of the figures is from small in the region of the Damned, close to eye level, to monumental at the distant top section in the region of the Blessed. The nervous energy and the twisting, writhing, elongated figures are techniques adopted by the Mannerists.

17.34 Michelangelo, *Rondanini Pietà*. Ca. 1554–64. Marble, height 5'4" (1.63 m). Castello Sforza, Milan. Photo: Alinari, Florence.

In this powerful fresco, however, they are manifestations of the unique artistic vision of a master, a natural evolution, given the subject matter, of his mature style.

Only a few days before his death, Michelangelo was reworking his *Rondanini Pietà* (fig. 17.34), cutting the head back into the Virgin's shoulder and making the composition a slender, unified work of infinite pathos. Far removed from the High Renaissance style, the elongated figures are reminiscent of the jamb statues of the Royal Portal of Chartres, seeming to symbolize the artist's direct appeal to God. His death in his eighty-eighth year, probably of pneumonia, left this sculpture unfinished and his major project, the dome of St. Peter's, still under construction.

Michelangelo's apse and dome of St. Peter's (fig. 17.35) were not a commission but, in his words, done "solely for the love of God." Whether or not Michelangelo's late style

17.35 Michelangelo, Dome of St. Peter's, Rome, from the west. 1546–64, completed by della Porta in 1590. Height 452' (138 m). Photo: Alinari, Florence.

can be described as Mannerist—still a moot point—his late architectural style is powerful and confident. The great dome is a huge sculptured shape rising above an apse, distinguished by enormous pilasters. This is Michelangelo's "colossal order"—pilasters that are both decorative and structural. Their upward thrust is repeated and reinforced by the double columns of the drum and carried ever upward by the arching ribs to a climax in the lantern. The vertical stress of classic forms, a new Renaissance procedure, is visible proof that classicism can be as emotional and as transcendental as the High Gothic style of Chartres Cathedral. Though the nave was extended far beyond Michelangelo's Greek cross plan, the dome is still the major landmark of Rome, a fitting symbol for the art and life of Michelangelo.

Parmigianino (Francesco Mazzola), 1503–40

Unquestionably a Mannerist, Parmigianino (par-me-dja-ah-NEE-no) painted in an elaborate, tense, elegant, and artificial style in sharp and deliberate contrast to the harmonious naturalism of the High Renaissance. His *Madonna with the Long Neck* (fig. 17.36) is a marvel of decorative beauty. With a swanlike neck, exceptionally long fingers, and cold, ivory-smooth flesh, the Madonna smiles tenderly on a seemingly lifeless Christ child. The background figure of the biblical prophet is dramatically small, and the rising, uncompleted columns add to the artificiality and strange mood of unreality. Parmigianino planned a complete temple in the background but left it incomplete, further illustrating, perhaps, the perverseness of an artist notorious for flaunting social and artistic conventions.

LATE RENAISSANCE AND MANNERISM IN ITALY AND SPAIN
Titian (Tiziano Vecelli), ca. 1488–1576

With an artistic career spanning sixty-eight years, Titian (TISH-un) was a giant of the High and Late Renaissance, excelling in every aspect of the painter's craft. After Raphael, he was the finest portrait artist of the century, courted by the nobles and royalty of Europe. Titian achieved the social status advocated by Leonardo, acquiring a towering reputation that led to many honors, the title of count, and a princely life. He repeatedly celebrated the goddess of love, and his late painting, *Venus with a Mirror* (fig. 17.37), is permeated by a tangible sensuality that is, however, not erotic, but instead expresses the natural loveliness of woman. The famous color tones are exceptionally rich rather than just brilliant, mellowed by layer on layer of glazes. Titian produced several variations on the Venus-and-mirror theme; this painting he kept for himself and willed to his son. Perhaps more than any other Renaissance artist, Titian understood the spirit of classical art. Drawing on the Greeks, he incorporated High Renaissance techniques and some Mannerist devices in what is best described, in this work, as Late Renaissance style.

17.36 Parmigianino, *Madonna with the Long Neck*. 1534–40. Oil on panel, 7'1" × 4'4" (2.16 × 1.32 m). Galleria degli Uffizi, Florence. Photo: Scala, Florence.

17.37 *Above*   Titian, *Venus with a Mirror*. Ca. 1555. Oil on canvas, 4'1" × 3'5½" (1.24 × 1.05 m). National Gallery of Art, Washington, D.C. (Andrew W. Mellon Collection).

Tintoretto (Jacopo Robusti), 1518–94

Titian's Venetian contemporary, Tintoretto (tin-toe-RET-toe), developed a more fervent style that blended Mannerist devices with the drawing technique of Michelangelo. A comparison of Tintoretto's *The Last Supper* (fig. 17.38) with that by Leonardo (see fig. 17.25) dramatically illustrates the differences between the High Renaissance style and the Mannerist style of the Late Renaissance. In Tintoretto's version the table is sharply angled and placed at the left. The size of the disciples diminishes from foreground to background, with Christ highlighted only by the brilliant glow of his halo. Almost lost in the agitation, Judas, dressed as a servant, sits on the opposite side of the table, a pathetic, isolated figure. This is the moment of the Eucharist, what Roman Catholics regard as the transubstantiation of consecrated bread and wine into the flesh and blood of Christ. The agitated clutter of servants, hovering angels, flaming lamp, and radiant halo combine to proclaim the emotional spirit of the Counter-Reformation.

17.38   Tintoretto, *The Last Supper*. 1592–4. Oil on canvas, 12' × 18'8" (3.66 × 5.69 m). S. Giorgio Maggiore, Venice. Photo: Scala, Florence.

17.39 Palladio, Villa Rotonda, Vicenza. Begun 1550 and finished by Vincenzo Scamozzi. Photo: Alinari, Florence.

Palladio (Andrea di Pietro), 1518–80

The intense dramatic style of Tintoretto heralds the coming age of the Baroque, but the architectural designs of Andrea Palladio (pah-LAH-djo) are clearly, lucidly classical. The only north Italian architect comparable to Brunelleschi, Alberti, Bramante, and Michelangelo, Palladio was born Andrea di Pietro but is known to posterity by a name derived from Pallas Athena, goddess of wisdom. An avid student of classical and Renaissance architecture, Palladio designed churches, public buildings, and private homes. His Villa Rotonda (fig. 17.39), one of nineteen Palladian villas still in existence, was built in the countryside near Venice, much in the manner and style of Roman villas. From a central square identical porticoes thrust out from each side, each with a different view and a slightly variable climate at different hours of the day. Palladian designs became popular for English stately homes, and this particular design became a model for southern plantation homes in the American South, where outdoor living was customary for much of the year. In the Villa Rotonda the proportions of length and breadth, height and width, of and between the rooms were based on the Pythagorean ratios of the Greek musical scale.

Paolo Veronese, 1528–88

Paradoxically, only the country villas of Palladio were placed in the natural settings that the Venetian painters Giorgione, Titian, Tintoretto, and Veronese celebrated in their richly colored paintings. Venice itself, except for private gardens, was a congested city of marble, brick, stone, and waterways with few plants, flowers, or trees. The fourth of the great Venetian masters, Veronese (vair-oh-NAY-se), like

17.40 Paolo Veronese, *Christ in the House of Levi* (originally *The Last Supper*). 1573. Oil on canvas, 42' × 18'3" (12.8 × 5.56 m). Accademia, Venice. Photo: Scala, Florence.

his contemporaries glorified nature in his work, but unlike other artists he concentrated on the sumptuous material world. Pleasure-loving Venetians preferred luxurious paintings that dazzled the eye and soothed the conscience. In *Christ in the House of Levi* (fig. 17.40) Veronese demonstrated his skill in *di sotto in sù* (It., "looking up from below") perspective. A superb example of Veronese's theatrical style, the elaborate perspective opens to the sky like a stage set. Although Christ and his disciples occupy the center, the rest of the painting is crowded with exotic characters totally unrelated to the biblical text. Veronese was called before the Inquisition because the unorthodox details lacked the mandatory seriousness and piety for a Last Supper and was given three months in which to modify the composition. Rather than wreck his grand design, he simply gave the painting a less exalted title. That this painting caught the attention of the Inquisition is a kind of backhanded testimony to the power of this work.

El Greco (Domenikos Theotokopoulos), 1541–1614

Veronese's style is lavishly and opulently Late Renaissance and basically secular, but that of El Greco is mystical, a fervent expression of the Counter-Reformation spirit. The last and possibly the most gifted of the Mannerists, Domenikos Theotokopoulos, known as El Greco ("the Greek"), was born in Crete, then a Venetian possession, and trained in late Byzantine art and Venetian Mannerism before moving to Spain in 1576. Even before the defeat of the Spanish Armada in 1588 Spain was a fading power, artistically provincial and obsessed with the Counter-Reformation. Yet it was the proper environment for an artist of El Greco's religious convictions. Combining the Byzantine tradition with his thorough knowledge of the Venetian masters, El Greco created a passionately religious art that was the embodiment of Spanish mysticism. In his *Resurrection of Christ* (fig. 17.41) the illusion is of Christ floating upward as the Roman soldiers are afflicted with various contortions indicating their awe and terror. This very shallow space is enlivened by shimmering splashes of light that add to the mystical quality of the work.

A nation supercharged with religious zeal, Spain formed the spearhead of the Counter-Reformation as the birthplace of the Society of Jesus (Jesuits) and the stronghold of the merciless Inquisition. El Greco was its peerless master of religious subjects, an artist who, more than any other, made visible the spiritual content of the Catholic faith. Widely admired in his time, El Greco had a reputation that declined rapidly as most of western Europe (though not Spain) plunged enthusiastically into the scientific and intellectual discoveries of the Enlightenment. It was not until the twentieth century that El Greco's unique and intensely personal art received proper recognition.

17.41 El Greco, *The Resurrection of Christ*. Ca. 1597–1604. Oil on canvas, 9'4¼" × 4'2" (2.85 × 1.27 m). Prado, Madrid.

HIGH AND LATE RENAISSANCE IN THE NORTH, CA. 1500–1600

For most of the fifteenth century, northern artists and some Italians were influenced by the dazzling naturalism of the Flemish masters. Not until the end of the century did Italian influences begin to beguile northern patrons with their scientific rules and especially a literary tradition that included a vocabulary of art criticism. Noble patrons were delighted with classical examples of "good" and "bad" art. Increasingly, this meant that art based on models from antiquity was good, but the rest, including the entire Flemish tradition, was "wrong" or at best "primitive." With remarkable suddenness, Italian artists were busily engaged with important projects for patrons such as Henry VII of England and the French royal family, whereas northern artists were traveling to Italy to study the masters of the Early and High Renaissance.

During the sixteenth century it became fashionable to view northern culture as backward and its artists as inferior, especially those who had not been blessed with Italian instruction in the rules of perspective and proportion. Speaking, in essence, for the Italian Renaissance, Michelangelo remarked to the Portuguese painter Francesco da Hollanda that Flemish landscape paintings were fit only for "young women, nuns, and certain noble persons with no sense of true harmony." "Furthermore," he observed, "their painting is of stuffs, bricks, mortar, the grass of the fields, the shadows of trees and little figures here and there. And all this," said he, "though it may appear good in some eyes, is in truth done without symmetry or proportion." Consigned to the attic of northern art, the matchless paintings of the Flemish masters were, for over three centuries, derided as primitive or naive. It was not until 1902 that the first international show of fifteenth-century Flemish art opened in Bruges, and only considerably later in this century that the derogatory labels were finally dropped.

Albrecht Dürer, 1471–1528

For reasons still unknown, Italian art caught on first in Germany, where Dürer (DOO-rer) became the founder of the brief but brilliant German High Renaissance. His two trips to Italy (1494–5 and 1505–7) exposed him to all the Italian techniques, but he was never attuned to Italian form, preferring instead the strong lines of the northern tradition. Though Dürer became a master painter, his most significant achievements were in the graphic arts of engraving and woodcuts, which were printed in quantity and sold throughout Germany, making the artist a wealthy man.

Northern art retained a Gothic strain—a fascination with the bizarre, the grotesque, and the supernatural—as embodied, for example, in *Knight, Death, and the Devil* (fig. 17.42). The subject was apparently derived from the

17.42 Albrecht Dürer, *Knight, Death, and the Devil*. 1513. Engraving, 9¾ × 7⅝" (24.8 × 19.4 cm). Metropolitan Museum of Art, New York (Harris Brisbane Dick Fund).

Manual of the Christian Soldier by Erasmus of Rotterdam (1466–1536). With death mounted on a decrepit horse in the background and a hideous devil behind him, the Christian knight rides confidently along the path of faith. Mounted on a superb horse and accompanied by his faithful dog, he fixes his unwavering gaze on his ultimate goal of the Heavenly Kingdom. The drama, control, and incredible detail of this powerful work are highly representative of the vigorous Northern Renaissance, created by an artist who had chosen to follow the faith of Martin Luther.

Dürer was deeply involved in the religious and political movements in Germany and in the Italian humanism that flourished briefly on German soil until the winds of the Reformation swept away what was essentially a Catholic point of view. The leading humanist of sixteenth-century Europe, Erasmus influenced many intellectuals of the period, including artists such as Dürer and Hans Holbein the Younger. In the *Erasmus* portrait by Dürer (see fig. 19.1) the scholar sits in his study surrounded by books, some presumably his own publications, as he drafts a new work. Behind him in Latin is the elaborate title of the print and the name of the artist. At the bottom is Dürer's monogram, above which is the date and above that a Greek inscription

that translates as, "His writings portray him even better," meaning that his books were a more accurate measure of the man than Dürer's reverential portrait. The northern passion for detail is, to say the least, clearly evident in this print.

Matthias Grünewald (Mathis Gothardt Neithardt), 1483?–1528

Dürer was internationally famous, but his worthy contemporary Grünewald, though widely known in his own time, was neglected until this century. A highly original artist, Grünewald was familiar with the work of Dürer and possibly that of Bosch, but there is no evidence of Italian classical influence, as one glance at his *Small Crucifixion* (fig. 17.43) immediately reveals.

17.43 *Left* Matthias Grünewald, *The Small Crucifixion.* Ca. 1511–20. Oil on panel, 24⅛ × 18⅛" (61.3 × 46 cm). National Gallery of Art, Washington, D.C. (Samuel H. Kress Collection).

17.44 *Below* Pieter Bruegel the Elder, *Winter (Return of the Hunters).* 1565. Oil on panel. 3'10" × 5'3¾" (1.2 × 1.6 m). Kunsthistorisches Museum, Vienna. Photo: A.K.G., London (Eric Lessing).

This is the brutal reality of nailing a man to a cross and leaving him there to die. His body a mass of cuts and suppurating sores, his limbs twisted, his skin gray and speckled with dried blood, Christ is depicted in relentless detail as having died for the sins of all humankind. The grief of John, Mary, and Mary Magdalene is vibrant with intense pain and sorrow. Grünewald has elevated the horror of the Passion to the level of universal tragedy, producing a composition as convincing as anything in Western art.

Hans Holbein, 1497–1543

Fully conversant with all that the Italians had to teach, Holbein (HOL-bine) the Younger was the last of the superb painters of the German High Renaissance and one of the finest portrait painters in the history of art. He traveled widely in France, Switzerland, and Italy, then finally settled down in London, where he became the favorite painter of Henry VIII, who furnished a special suite in St. James's Palace for "master Hans." Holbein gained access to the English court through Erasmus, who provided him with a letter of recommendation to Sir Thomas More. His portrait of More (see fig. 19.2) is a noble portrayal of the humanist statesman. Depicted realistically, including a stubble of beard, More wears the luxurious clothes of his rank and the heavy chain of his office as Lord Chancellor of England. With meticulous attention to detail in the manner of van Eyck, Holbein depicts the dignity and determination of a man who was later to be executed for opposing Henry's establishment of the Church of England.

Pieter Bruegel the Elder, 1525?–69

Most of the Renaissance art of France was courtly but, as mentioned previously, there was a growing number of middle-class art patrons in the Netherlands, which in the latter sixteenth century became a battleground of religious and political strife. Militantly Protestant, particularly in the north (today's Holland), the Netherlands fought to overthrow a rigid Spanish rule that became even more brutal under the fanatical Philip II and the imported Spanish Inquisition. Nevertheless, the Netherlandish school of painting flourished and produced Bruegel (BRU-gul), the only northern genius to appear between Dürer and Rubens. A highly educated humanist and philosopher, Bruegel studied in Italy from 1551 to 1555, returning home with a love of Italian landscapes and a profound knowledge of Italian control of form and space.

In *Winter (Return of the Hunters)* (fig. 17.44) Bruegel demonstrates his mastery of perspective as he details what first appears to be a simple genre scene. Two moods are conveyed: the bleak coldness of nature and the warmth and activity of human beings. Our attention is drawn to the hunters and their dogs as, cold and exhausted, they return to their frosty hamlet. Before them are all sorts of activities from work to play and the promise of a warm fire in a cozy house. Bruegel has presented us with a microcosm, an image of his time and place as he saw it. But there is also the universality that great works have in common. This is not just 1565 in a northern clime but a sensitive portrayal of human activities in a hostile environment: working, playing, coping, surviving.

STUDY QUESTIONS

1. Compare and contrast the *David* sculptures of Donatello, Verrocchio, and Michelangelo. Consider first every detail then the overall effect.
2. Compare and contrast the Pazzi Chapel with Sainte-Chapelle in Paris. Then, using the two chapels as representative of their ages, compare and contrast the Gothic era with the Renaissance.

SUMMARY

Symbolized by Brunelleschi's dome and the dedication of Florence Cathedral in 1436, a new age came into being in fifteenth-century Florence. This was a city of bankers and craftsmen whose self-image was personified by the Davids of Donatello, Verrocchio, and Michelangelo. To create the new style, a fresh repertory of illusionist devices was developed by Masaccio and later used by all painters.

By the second half of the century, classical designs had been fully assimilated, leading to the classically based architecture of Alberti and the mythological painting of Botticelli. Florentine innovations spread throughout Italy, promoted by Perugino and by Bellini, the founder of the Venetian school.

The Renaissance in the North took another course. Influenced by the International Style and a long tradition of brilliant craftsmanship in manuscript illumination and stained glass, van Eyck perfected the new technique of oil painting and created matchless works of meticulous naturalism. Rogier van der Weyden and Hans Memling continued in the naturalistic style but, coinciding with the rising pessimism and fear of death and the devil, the bizarre art of Hieronymus Bosch epitomized the religious torment of a society on the brink of the Lutheran Reformation.

The High Renaissance in Italy was a time of constant warfare, but was illuminated by the incredible achievements of Leonardo in scientific investigation, invention, and painting. Excelling in the arts of sculpture, architecture, painting, and poetry, the "divine Michelangelo" created, among other works, the *Pietà*, *David*, and the frescoes of the Sistine Chapel ceiling. Raphael achieved a classic balance of form and content that became the hallmark of the High Renaissance, and Bramante, in his Tempietto, designed the prototype of classical domed structures.

In sixteenth-century Venice, Giorgione was the first of the Venetian colorists, followed by the assured painting of Titian and the luxuriant style of Veronese. Michelangelo influenced such Mannerist painters as Parmigianino, Tintoretto, and the Spanish painter from Crete called El Greco. During the latter stages of his career Michelangelo painted the awesome *Last Judgment* and designed the apse and dome of St. Peter's. Marking the end of the Renaissance in Italy, Palladio's villas became models for eighteenth- and nineteenth-century domestic architecture in England and the United States.

In sixteenth-century Germany Albrecht Dürer, Matthias Grünewald, and Hans Holbein the Younger were the leading painters of the High Renaissance. In France, Italian styles influenced French courtly art and contributed to the designs of elegant châteaux in the Loire valley. Renaissance art in the strife-torn Netherlands culminated in the work of Pieter Bruegel the Elder.

By the end of the sixteenth century the ideals and aspirations of the Renaissance had perished in the wreckage of cultures beset by religious wars—with the worst yet to come. Marking the end of an era, the Renaissance set the stage for the emergence of the modern world.

CULTURE AND HUMAN VALUES

The importance and influence of creative artists changed considerably during the Renaissance. During the Early Renaissance their role was basically defined by a continuation of the medieval guild system that trained artisans, not artists. The painters' guild to which Leonardo belonged, for example, was established primarily for people who painted walls and ceilings.

All that had changed by the time of the High Renaissance. More than anything else, the newly acquired importance of the individual helped elevate the artist to a position comparable to his or her artistic achievements. The individual was not, however, the ultimate reality, as had been the case in ancient Greece. The analogy, rather, is with ancient Rome, in which the individual was free to act in accordance with the needs of the state. Reality in the Renaissance was the division of power between the monolithic Church of Rome and the secular authority of the many ducal states that dotted western and southern Europe. For the artists, reality was the protective power of such patrons as the papacy, a dukedom, or an emerging national state.

If one had to list a single virtue in the chaos and violence marking the transition from the medieval to the modern world, that ideal quality would be survival. Artists often had to work under trying, even dangerous circumstances. Yet they survived, and some of them, like Raphael, Michelangelo, and Titian, attained enduring fame and influence. Given all the rigors of the age, one can only marvel at the artists who survived and created, and wonder even more at the quality and quantity of the art and architecture that survived the Renaissance.

CHAPTER 18

Renaissance Music: Court and Church

NORTHERN ORIGINS OF THE MUSICAL RENAISSANCE

Renaissance music dates from about 1420 to 1600, music that can be characterized, in large part, as optimistic, lively, and worldly. The once-rigid distinctions between sacred and secular music no longer applied. Sacred music was not always synonymous with devotional, noble, and edifying sounds any more than secular music was necessarily shallow, common, or folksy. The subject matter rather than the style now determined whether the work was sacred or secular. Just as a painter's model could become a madonna, or nymph, or Venus, so composers used melodies where they worked best, with popular songs sometimes serving as a basis for liturgical motets or Masses.

As previously discussed, the Renaissance began around 1350 in Italy and eventually moved north to encompass most of Europe. For reasons still not clearly understood, the musical Renaissance began in the North—in England, the Low Countries, and northern France. The most notable of the English composers, John Dunstable (1380?–1453), was a contemporary of the early Renaissance composers on the continent and probably influenced them with what his admirers called his "sweet style." On the continent some court and church composers of northern France and the Low Countries (Flanders) formed a group known today as the Franco-Flemish school. True Renaissance artists, they were individualistic, materialistic, and boldly experimental. They had mastered the craft and art of a new style of music, and they delighted in demonstrating their compositional skills with intricate **canons** and musical puzzles for educated amateurs.

In their quest for new materials and fresh ideas they traveled to Italy, where the simple folk melodies and dance tunes provided further opportunities for polyphonic devices and techniques. Considering the travel hardships then, the mobility of Franco-Flemish composers in the fifteenth century was astounding. The composer Dufay, for example, was discovered at the age of nine in Cambrai in France by talent scouts seeking out precocious young musicians. Before he was twenty-six, Dufay had traveled to Italy, studied in Paris, held a post in northern France, served the court in Bologna, and sung in the papal choir in Rome.

Franco-Flemish composers such as Dufay and others dominated Italian musical life in the courts and in the churches for over a century. St. Mark's in Venice, one of the most important musical centers in Europe, employed only Flemish composers until the latter part of the sixteenth century. When Florence dedicated its magnificent cathedral in 1436, Dufay was commissioned to write special music for the occasion.

Music was an integral part of the complex fabric of Renaissance society. A retinue of musicians became a fixture of court life, with the dukes of Burgundy setting the style. Castiglione (see p. 326), the chief social arbiter of the Renaissance, viewed his ideal courtier as proficient in both vocal and instrumental music.

> I regard as beautiful music, to sing well by note, with ease and beautiful style; but as even far more beautiful, to sing to the accompaniment of the viol, because nearly all the sweetness lies in the solo part, and we note and observe the fine manner and the melody with much greater attention when our ears are not occupied with more than a single voice, and moreover every little fault is more clearly discerned,—which is not the case when several sing together, because each singer helps his neighbor. But above all, singing to the viol by way of recitative seems to me most delightful, which adds to the words a charm and grace that are very admirable.
>
> All keyed instruments also are pleasing to the ear, because they produce very perfect consonances, and upon them one can play many things that fill the mind with musical delight. And not less charming is the music of the stringed quartet, which is most sweet and

---

Opposite St Mark's, Venice, interior, arch showing the Passion of Christ and domes depicting the coming of the Holy Spirit at Pentecost and the Ascension of Christ. 12th century and ca. 1200. Mosaic. Photo: A.K.G., London.

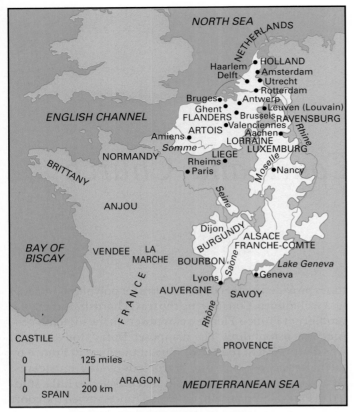

Map 18.1 Lands of the Dukes of Burgundy, 1477.

exquisite. The human voice lends much ornament and grace to all these instruments, with which I would have our Courtier at least to some degree acquainted, albeit the more he excels with them, the better.[1]

The Courts of Burgundy

At different times a kingdom, a county, and a duchy, Burgundy became the most powerful and influential political entity in Europe in the first half of the fifteenth century. From Philip the Bold in 1336 through John the Fearless and Philip the Good to Charles the Bold (reigned 1467–77), the rulers of Burgundy made the court in the capital city of Dijon one of the most magnificent in Europe (map 18.1).

The Flemish painter Jan van Eyck served the "court of plume and panoply" of Philip the Good at the time of its greatest splendor. The court was ostentatious and even flamboyant, but nevertheless, according to contemporary accounts, it resembled a sort of fairyland. Women wore hennins, cone-shaped headdresses with long sheer veils hanging from the pointed tops. Their gowns were opulent, frequently decorated with fur and set off by gold throat bands and necklaces. Elaborate furniture and interior designs provided a tasteful setting for the elegance of the court.

The ducal court set the styles in dress, manners, dancing, music, and the other arts. The principal court dance was the *basse danse*, which was performed with gliding

steps, possibly accounting for the designation *basse* (Fr. "low"). The *basse danse* belonged to a family of related dances: the *basse danse* proper and the *pas de Brabant* (It. *saltarello*). It was the custom to follow the dignified *basse danse*, referred to as the "imperial measure," by the quicker *pas de Brabant*, thus producing a contrasting pair of slow and fast dance movements, a typical procedure for Renaissance dances. Both used the same basic music; only the rhythms were changed.

Tapestries and miniatures of the period show various instrumental ensembles playing for the dancers. The standard group of instruments consisted of two shawms (early **oboes**) and a slide-trumpet, with the harp, **lute**, and **flute** forming the other group. The former group consisted of *haut* (Fr. "high, loud") instruments, the latter of *bas* (Fr. "low, soft") instruments. The *haut* instruments were used for festive occasions and were usually played from a balcony or *loggia*. The *bas* instruments were used for more intimate dancing and were placed near the dancers.

Court life at Dijon was lively and elegant. It was, in many respects, an updated version of the medieval Court of Love with music, both lively and sedate, for dancing and for songs, true French chansons extolling love, joy, and beauty. Secular music was in great demand for everything from the intimate rites of courtship to elaborate ceremonial music for the court. There was a remarkable development of sophisticated secular music, but not at the expense of sacred music, which incorporated the techniques and some of the melodies of secular music into a highly refined style.

The Burgundian School

Guillaume Dufay, ca. 1400–74

Dufay (doo-FYE) was the most famous composer of the Burgundian school of the Franco-Flemish tradition and one of the greatest of French composers. Following is the beginning of a Dufay Mass movement that illustrates the smooth, rich sounds of Renaissance music. Dufay broke down the "Kyrie eleison" into three separate movements: "Kyrie eleison," "Christe eleison," and "Kyrie eleison." The texture is characteristic of early Renaissance music with mixed vocal and instrumental sounds and with instruments playing the wordless portions of the Mass.

1. Baldassare Castiglione, *The Book of the Courtier* (trans. Leonard Eckstein Opdycke) (New York: Horace Liveright, 1929).
2. Smijers, *Algemeene Muziek Geschiedenis* (Utrecht, 1938), p.101.
3. Musical notation is used on a modest scale throughout this book to give brief quotations from works to be studied. These are guides to listening just as literary quotations are guides to reading. Using musical quotes is a necessary, basic procedure that is in no way "technical." Performing music is technical; but reading music is a simple procedure easily learned by anyone. Please consult the Appendix: Music Listening and Notation.
4. Josquin des Près, *Werke* (Amsterdam, 1935), vol.1, p.1.

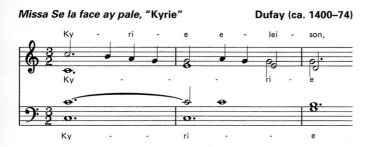

Listening Example 13
MASS MOVEMENT

Dufay, *Missa Se la face ay pale*, "Kyrie 1"[2]
15th century

Time: 1:45
Cassette 3, track 13[3]

THE FRANCO-FLEMISH TRADITION

During the latter part of the fifteenth century the center of musical activity gradually shifted from Burgundy to northern France and the Low Countries of Flanders and the Netherlands. The fusion of French elegance, Flemish polyphonic techniques, and Italian vigor led to the cosmopolitan style of the Late Renaissance. Whatever followed from this—even the music of such giants as Palestrina and Lassus—was a continuation of northern genius suffused with Italian taste and supported by Italian patronage.

No one person was responsible for the development of the new music. It simply happened that many gifted northern composers were active at about the same time and that most, at varying times, were involved in Italian musical life. There were important composers from the Netherlands and northern France but Josquin of Flanders outshone them all.

Josquin des Près, ca. 1450–1521

Martin Luther reportedly said that "Others follow the notes; Josquin makes them do as he wishes." Josquin (JOSS-can) was known in his own time as the "prince of music." He and his Franco-Flemish contemporaries developed all the basic features of the Late Renaissance musical style and, in so doing, established it as an international style in western European culture. Josquin was to music what Leonardo, Michelangelo, and Raphael were to the visual arts. A master of compositional techniques, he sometimes invented and consistently refined the methods and materials of Renaissance polyphonic music.

The motet "Ave Maria" by Josquin is an example of the serene lucidity and beauty of the music of the High Renaissance. The smoothly flowing lines are woven into an elegant tapestry of luminous sound, a sound somehow comparable to the undulating arches of a Renaissance arcade. Motets are still sacred music, similar to polyphonic Masses, but the text is non-scriptural. Instruments are no longer combined or alternated with the voices as in Early Renaissance music; the singing is now consistently unaccompanied (*a cappella*). The vocal texture is continuous, with new phrases overlapping preceding phrases to produce an unbroken stream of simultaneous melodies. This ceaseless flow of intricately intertwined melodies is a hallmark of High and Late Renaissance vocal music.

The voices enter one at a time in imitation; that is, each of the four voices has essentially the same melodic line when it makes its entrance. Josquin used the text of the "Ave Maria" (Lat., "Hail Mary, full of grace . . .") and selected his basic theme from a portion of an "Ave Maria" chant:

Ave Maria chant theme

Listening Example 14
MOTET

Josquin des Près, "Ave Maria"
Ca. 1480; excerpt

Time: 2:06
Cassette 3, track 14[4]

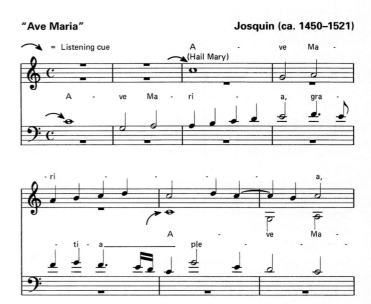

Orlando de Lassus, 1532–94

The Flemish composer Lassus was one of the finest composers of a celebrated era, the golden age of polyphony of the sixteenth century. His 1,250 compositions were literally international: Latin masses and motets; secular vocal music in French, German, and Italian; and instrumental music in different national styles. Representative of his secular music, the following Italian **madrigal** is a playful love song spiced with cheery nonsense syllables: "don don don diri diri don don don don."

Listening Example 15
ITALIAN MADRIGAL

Lassus, "Matona mia cara"
1550; excerpt

Time: 2:10
Cassette 3, track 15[5]

"Matona mia cara"   Lassus (1532–94)

Ma - to - na   mi - a   ca - ra.   Mi fol - lere can - zon.
(Ma - to - na, my be - lov - èd,   be be-witched by   my   song.)

Matona, my beloved, be bewitched by my song. I sing beneath the window to win you for my good wife. I pray to you, listen to my pretty singing; it will make you love me more, like the obstinate Greek [Odysseus]. Command me to go hunting, to hunt with the falcon, and I will bring you a woodcock as fat as kidneys. If I were not able to speak to you with so many good reasons, Petrarch himself would not be able to, nor the Springs of Helicon [home of the Muses].

DEVELOPMENTS IN ITALY

During the latter part of the sixteenth century, Italian genius finally surfaced in the compositions of native Italians. Italian music had been invigorated by the presence of resident Flemish composers and by the dynamic Counter-Reformation response to Luther's revolt. Flemish composers had fled Spanish tyranny in the Low Countries to pursue their profession in a less hostile setting. There was, moreover, a real need to develop a new style of sacred music because things had gotten out of hand, as Erasmus of Rotterdam cogently pointed out:

We have introduced an artificial and theatrical music into the church, a bawling and agitation of various voices, such as I believe had never been heard in the theatres of the Greeks and Romans. Horns, trumpets, pipes vie and sound along constantly with the voices. Amorous and lascivious melodies are heard such as elsewhere accompany only the dances of courtesans and clowns.[6]

The Council of Trent (1545–64) was convened to deal with the abuses pointed out by Luther and other reformers. The problem of music was only incidental to overall concerns, but musical difficulties occupied most of the attention of the Council for over a year. Final recommendations were negative rather than positive. Certain practices were forbidden and particular results were prescribed without, however, specifying the means. The canon finally adopted by the Council in 1562 banned all seductive or impure melodies, whether vocal or instrumental, all vain and worldly texts, and all outcries and uproars, so that "the House of God may in truth be called a House of prayer."

After passing the canon against decadent musical practices, the Council considered banning all polyphonic music, especially polyphonic Masses. This ultraconservative movement was countered by Lassus and Palestrina, who, among others, submitted polyphonic music to a special Commission in a successful attempt to preserve their reformed style of polyphonic music. Perhaps the Commission simply recognized its inability to appraise the quality of liturgical music, a judgment best made by the musicians themselves.

Giovanni Pierluigi da Palestrina, 1524/5–94

Palestrina was one of the supreme exponents of Roman Catholic polyphonic music of the Renaissance. Romanticized in the nineteenth century as a lonely and poverty-stricken artist who was wedded to the church, Palestrina was actually a successful professional musician. He briefly considered the priesthood after the death of his first wife, but chose instead to marry a wealthy widow. He was paid well for the music that he wrote for the church and even refused several more lucrative positions rather than leave Rome.

Present-day music students study Palestrina's music for classes in "strict **counterpoint**," that is, writing polyphonic music in the manner of the sixteenth century with Palestrina as the model composer. Though his compositions serve as a guide to correct contrapuntal writing, Palestrina's music is anything but dogmatic. A model it is, but one of clarity, conciseness, and consistency. Using existing plainsong melodies as a point of departure, he wrote

---

5. CD 1, track 9.
6. Erasmus, *Opera Omnia*, VI, 1705, col.731.

in a beautifully balanced style of what can be described as simultaneous plainsong.

The following plainsong, "Veni sponsa Christi," forms the basis for a Palestrina Mass:

"Veni sponsa Christi"   **Anonymous**

Palestrina began with this simple melody, transforming it into a serenely flowing melodic theme:

Missa Veni sponsa Christi, **"Agnus Dei I"**   **Palestrina**
                                              (1524/5–94)

"Veni sponsa Christi" (named after the plainsong) is a short composition based on this characteristic Palestrina melody. Notice how the smoothly flowing text is fitted to graceful melodic lines.

Listening Example 16
MASS MOVEMENT

Palestrina, *Missa Veni sponsa Christi,* "Agnus Dei I"
Before 1554

Time: 2:21
Cassette 3, track 16[7]

Missa Veni sponsa Christi, **"Agnus Dei I"**   **Palestrina**

7. Ioannis Petrealoysii Praenestini, *Opera Omnia* (Leipzig, 1886), vol.18, p.35.

Italian Vocal-Instrumental Music

During the Late Renaissance, instrumental music began to rival the preeminence of vocal music, assisted particularly by the musical directors of the Cathedral of St. Mark's in Venice. St. Mark's Byzantine splendor was typical of the grandiose palaces, churches, ceremonies, and even paintings of that ornate city (see fig. 11.17 and p. 312).

As a trading center and crossroads of the world, Venice deliberately and successfully used pomp and pageantry to impress visitors with its magnificence. Grand productions inside the cathedral were necessary for the desired effect, but the arrangement of the church did not lend itself to large musical groups.

St. Mark's floor plan formed a Greek cross (fig. 18.1). Following the conventions of the Eastern church, the main floor was reserved for men and the smaller balcony level for women. This design was exploited by creating a new polychoral style of antiphonal singing—a procedure whereby the ensemble (chorus with or without orchestra) was divided into several different groups singing and/or playing in alternation. Musical productions would include the use of the two organs in their fixed positions plus choirs and brass choirs stationed on several balconies throughout the church. The listener would be overwhelmed by vocal and instrumental music alternating between left and right, front and rear. Arrangements of choirs and brass choirs could be selected from some of the possibilities indicated in figure 18.1 (see also fig. 18.2).

18.1 St. Mark's, Venice, simplified floor plan.

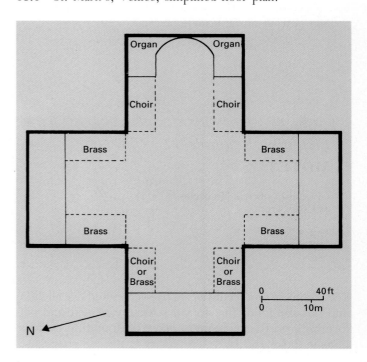

18.2   St. Mark's, Venice, interior. Photo: Marburg.
This view is from the west, where one organ is located in
the balcony, looking east to the small chancel with the other
organ and space for a small choir. Brass choirs were placed
on the balcony under massive arches at one or more of the
four upper corners. The conductor stood on the high
podium in front of the main-floor choir.

Verse 1	In ecclesiis benedicite Domino, (Praise the Lord in the congregation)	Sopranos (Chorus I) Organ
	Alleluia	Sopranos (Chorus I) Chorus II Organ
Verse 2	In omnia loco . . . , (In every place of worship praise him)	Tenors (Chorus I) Organ
	Alleluia	Tenors (Chorus I) Chorus II Organ
Sinfonia (orchestral interlude)		
Verse 3	In Deo, salutari meo . . . , (In God, who is my salvation and glory, is my help, and my hope is in God)	Altos (Chorus I) Tenors (Chorus I) Orchestra
	Alleluia	Altos (Chorus I) Tenors (Chorus I) Chorus II Orchestra

---

Listening Example 17
MOTET

Giovanni Gabrieli, "In ecclesiis"
1615; excerpt

Time: 4:20
Cassette 3, track 17

The complete motet consists of five verses and five alleluias
and has the following overall structure of text and performing groups (which sing or play from four different loca-
tions in the church):

Music Printing

Prosperous Venice was also the setting for the development of printed music. Over 9,000,000 books had been
printed by the year 1500, but no one had thought of printing music on that scale. A 1457 *Psalterium* that included
music had been printed at Mainz and a Roman *Missale*
was printed in 1476 in Milan using, for the first time, movable type.

Ottaviano de' Petrucci (peh-TROO-tchee; 1466–1539)
used movable type in his printing shop. He was an enterprising businessman and in 1498 he petitioned the Signoria of Venice for a twenty-year license (amounting to a
monopoly) to print music to meet a growing demand for
domestic music. In 1501 he produced the *Harmonice
Musices Odhecaton A (One Hundred Songs of Harmonic
Music)*, the earliest printed collection of part-music. Rich
in Franco-Flemish chansons, this anthology was followed
by fifty-eight more volumes of secular and sacred music
produced for music-hungry amateurs and an increasing
number of professional musicians. An expanding market
led, of course, to lower prices and even wider dissemination of music. By the end of the sixteenth century, music
publishers were in business throughout Europe.

INSTRUMENTAL MUSIC

Renaissance instrumental music continued to be primarily functional; that is, it was associated with dances, plays, masquerades, and extravaganzas of noble courts, rather than as a performance art with its own special audience (fig. 18.3).

Dance and music have always been associated and rarely more effectively than in the sixteenth century, which has been called "the century of the dance." The church had long suppressed dancing as both heathen and lascivious, but Renaissance society ignored such medieval strictures and invented social dancing. Accompanied by wind and stringed instruments, men and women of the Italian and French courts joined hands for the first time for folklike round dances and courtly pair dances such as the *danse royale*.

Because of its portability and mellow tone the lute was the preferred instrument of the age. Its chief rival was the **harpsichord**—also called cembalo, clavecin, **virginal**, spinet—the principal keyboard instrument of the sixteenth through the eighteenth centuries. Harpsichords have various shapes, which are generally similar in external appearance to grand, upright, and spinet pianos. The tone is produced by quills plucking the strings and is bright and sharp. Unlike the piano, harpsichords cannot vary their **dynamics** (degrees of loudness or softness) except by using two keyboards, muted strings, or different types of quills. Whole sections are played at one dynamic level; variation is achieved by changing to a louder or softer tone quality in the next section.

In England, the harpsichord was called a virginal, supposedly in honor of the "maiden Queen Elizabeth." English music had flourished under Henry VIII, Edward VI, and Mary, and reached, under Elizabeth, a level rarely approached thereafter. English power and wealth, the importation of foreign talent, and increased travel all combined to assist the assimilation of the Italian style and make the sixteenth century one of the outstanding periods in English musical history. Tudor sacred music was superb, but the secular forms of English music—the madrigals, lute music, virginal music, and fancies for **viols**—had special importance in the richness of the Elizabethan age.

ENGLISH SECULAR VOCAL MUSIC

The English madrigal school was inspired by Italian models, but its growth and development have made the English madrigal virtually synonymous with Elizabethan England. A madrigal, whether English or Italian, is a secular, unaccompanied part-song, usually in four voices. English madrigals tend toward a balanced texture of polyphonic and homophonic writing, and can be either merry or melancholy. The outstanding characteristic, however, is the sheer delight in the sounds, rhythms, and meanings of the English language.

The madrigalists are fond of natural word rhythms.

18.3 *Lady playing a Dulcimer*, from the early 16th-century manuscript of the 14th-century poem, "Les Echecs amoreux," fol. 143v, Bibliothèque Nationale, Paris. A few of the many Renaissance instruments are depicted here. The elegantly gowned lady is playing her dulcimer (an instrument still in use) with small hammers. A harp leans against the wall at the left and a portable organ rests on the floor at the right. In the background are singers and players. Reading from left to right, the instruments are: recorder (still used today: ancestor of the flute), shawm (ancestor of the oboe), and bagpipes (probably of Asian origin; introduced to Europe by the Romans during the first century AD).

They also like to play with **onomatopoeia**, alliteration, metaphor, and **simile** and take exceptional pleasure in exploiting double meanings. Wordplay with triple meanings is even better. Word painting is another notable method by which composers manipulate the sounds of the music so that they can imitate, imply, or describe the sounds of nature and/or the meanings and sounds of words.

In the following pastoral madrigal, the composer quietly poses the question "Thyrsis? Sleepest thou?" and then continues to press the question until Thyrsis is awakened with some vigorous "hollas." The cuckoo song is imitated, the music "sighs" as the shepherd "sighed as one all undone" and requests to be "let alone alas." The repetitious text of "drive him back to London" pushes the madrigal to an animated conclusion.

Listening Example 18
MADRIGAL

Bennet, "Thyrsis? Sleepest thou?"
Before 1625

Time: 1:50
Cassette 3, track 18[8]

"Thyrsis? Sleepest thou?"   John Bennet (ca. 1575–1625)

Opera

Opera was invented during the Renaissance in, of course, Florence. A group of humanists known as the Florentine Camerata met on a regular basis to reconstruct what ancient Greek music must have been like. They began by trying to imagine what the music of Greek drama sounded like and came up with a declamatory solo vocal line with instrumental accompaniment. This became the operatic recitative followed by the lyrical **aria**. Like the madrigal, opera migrated to England, where Henry Purcell was the greatest operatic composer. Following is a recitative and aria from Act III of Purcell's *Dido and Aeneas*.

Listening Example 19
OPERA

Purcell, *Dido and Aeneas*, Act III, "Dido's Lament"
1689

Time: 4:12[9]

Recitative
Thy hand, Belinda! darkness shades me,
On thy bosom let me rest,
More I would, but death invades me.
Death is now a welcome guest.

Aria
When I am laid in earth,
May my wrongs create no trouble in thy breast.
Remember me, but ah! forget my fate.

After the introductory recitative a descending **chromatic** bass line is heard a total of eleven times, accompanying an independent vocal melody. This is called a "ground" because it is the unvarying foundation for the vocal line.

Dido and Aeneas, "Dido's Lament"   **Purcell (1659–95)**

SUMMARY

The environment of music experienced notable changes during the Renaissance, with the inevitable result that the forms of music changed accordingly. The forces of secularization, which were set in motion during the Gothic period, began to moderate the power of the church. The expansion of the universities, the development of city centers of trade and commerce, and the rise of a mercantile middle class led to a development of secular music.

Outdoor concerts using orchestras composed of violins, shawms, trombones, and drums, and indoor concerts of recorders, viols, and harpsichord became common. Some of the outdoor performances provided music for dancing, which had changed from improvised music for one or two instruments to composed music for groups of instruments (consorts).

The demand for musical instruments for domestic use spurred the development and production of lutes, viols, and especially the instrument that could play both homophonic and polyphonic music, the harpsichord. An even more common household instrument was the clavichord.[10]

The newly awakened interest in classical culture, in humanism, and in the creative individual was reflected in the active participation in the arts by educated amateurs. Large and small social gatherings featured performances of solo songs accompanied by lute or harpsichord (or clavichord), a variety of **chamber music** and, particularly in England, the singing of part-songs such as madrigals and catches.

The proliferation of secular music did not provoke a decline in sacred music; rather there was a merging of techniques, instruments, and styles. Burgundian composers such as Dufay combined voices with instruments for their church music.

---

8. John Bennet, *Madrigals to Four Voices* (London, 1599), no.8.
9. CD 1, track 12.
10. The tone of the clavichord is produced by depressing the keys so that metal tangents on the other end of the keys strike the strings. The instrument is portable and the tone light and flexible.

Josquin des Près wrote Masses and motets, Italian secular music, and French chansons. Lassus wrote 1,250 compositions in Latin, French, German, and Italian. Palestrina, serving the church in Rome, wrote much sacred music and a variety of Italian madrigals. In Venice, Gabrieli wrote antiphonal, vocal-instrumental music and considerable instrumental music. The Florentine Camerata invented opera.

The growth of music during the Renaissance was astounding. Within a single century, music changed from an esoteric, church-dominated art form to an international language heard in every court and noble residence, and in many middle-class homes throughout Europe.

CULTURE AND HUMAN VALUES

Musicians achieved the superior status accorded High Renaissance artists if they were composers or if they were amateur performers who had no need to make music for a living. Professional musicians, no matter how adept they were in the skillful manipulation of musical instruments, were ranked with cobblers, tailors, and other artisans. This situation reflected the medieval world's class division into the elite (aristocracy and clergy) and the rest of humankind.

Throughout the Renaissance the class structure gradually changed with the rise of a middle class. The new merchant class experienced its strongest growth in northern Europe, particularly in Burgundy and Flanders. And that was precisely where the musical Renaissance began and flourished. One can logically conclude that there is a connection between music and a middle class, but what is the connection?

In the first place, music is an art form that can entertain an audience of one (the performer) up to an audience of thousands. It is a social art whose appeal transcends all social barriers. Whether used in conjunction with dance, theatrical productions, or as a performing/listening art in its own right, music is generally perceived as the most universal of all art forms. Thus this most accessible and widespread art form found a new patron in the flourishing merchant class. Merchants and traders enthusiastically embraced music in all its forms, much as their seventeenth-century descendants commissioned portraits by Rembrandt, Hals, and other Dutch artists.

Did businessmen patronize music solely for its intrinsic value? Hardly. Heretofore, only the elite were patrons of the arts, literature, and theatre. What better way to announce your newly acquired wealth than to "buy in" to a higher social class by sponsoring music and, later, portraiture? This is not to say that every burgher was a calculating social climber. Some could credit sponsorship of the arts as good business, but others could truly enjoy participating in some of the "finer things of life."

For growing numbers of people the grim rounds of bleak survival in a feudal society had become a distant memory. Peasants still tilled the soil in overwhelming numbers but capitalism, trade, merchandising, and education began to change all that. For centuries people had been able only to hope for a glorious afterlife that supposedly compensated for the miseries of earthly existence. Now there was hope for a better life on this earth and, increasingly, the belief that individuals could better their lives through their own efforts took hold. Perhaps the most positive aspect of the Renaissance was the change in attitude, from mute acceptance of the old *status quo* to one of rising expectations. Envisioning something better can move mountains.

STUDY QUESTIONS

What was the long-range significance of the bourgeois aspects of fifteenth-century music? How, for example, would you categorize, in social and economic terms, today's popular music? Where does rock fit in? Jazz? Symphonic music?

ADDITIONAL LISTENING

1. Palestrina, Pope Marcellus Mass, Kyrie. This is one of the best known of the composer's liturgical compositions (CD 1, track 10).
2. Morley, "My bonny lass she smileth." This cheerful composition has five voices (CD 1, track 11).

CHAPTER 19

Shadow and Substance: Literary Insights into the Renaissance

The linguistic dualism of the Renaissance had a very positive effect on the development of literature, philosophy, and science. Church-preserved Latin was the common language of all intellectuals and, moreover, a direct link to the classical past. No wonder Petrarch and other humanists viewed Cicero and Virgil as contemporaries; all wrote in the same language. Developing during the Middle Ages as the spoken languages of the people, the vernaculars became the accepted languages of popular culture. Latin remained the proper scholarly language, but the vernaculars evolved into recognized national languages that became acceptable vehicles for literary expression. Latin provided a kind of intellectual unity, whereas English, French, Italian, and Spanish each reinforced a sense of national cohesion and purpose. Each nation developed its own modern literary tradition, but languages were not isolated by the rise of nationalism. Translations of every language, including Latin, flowed back and forth over national borders, making Renaissance literature as international, in its own way, as art and music.

RENAISSANCE AUTHORS

In a survey such as this only literary peaks can be discussed, for almost everyone of any consequence was an author of sorts, as well as an amateur painter and musician. Most of the authors possessed the quality of *virtù*, the highest ideal of a Renaissance man; they were, in some measure, universal men, active leaders in their turbulent times. Erasmus was known as the most brilliant intellect of his time, friend and adviser to popes and kings. Both Thomas More and Francis Bacon served as Lord Chancellors of England

(roughly equivalent to the chief justice of the United States Supreme Court). Petrarch was among the foremost of the humanists, and both Castiglione and Machiavelli were prominent diplomats. The achievements of Michelangelo and Shakespeare were exceptional even in an age of awesome talents. Cervantes fought in the last Crusade and, a unique distinction, was captured and held prisoner by pirates. We know little about Rabelais beyond the fact that he was once a monk and priest and later a physician. He did take rakish delight in his voluntary separation from the church. The single exception among these activists was Montaigne, who retired to his study to compose his penetrating essays on Renaissance life and mores.

Miguel de Cervantes Saavedra, 1547–1616

Although he came late, in spirit it was Cervantes (sir-VAHN-teez) who tolled the knell of medievalism. Cervantes was in a better position than most of his contemporaries to utter the words that closed the Middle Ages and opened up the Renaissance; he had been a part of the final burst of chivalry, having accompanied the fleet of Don John of Austria on the last Crusade. He fought at the Battle of Lepanto (1571) and had seen, at first hand, the last knight of Christendom. Perhaps Lord Byron expressed it best in his *Don Juan*: "Cervantes smiled Spain's chivalry away."

Don Quixote is Cervantes' reaction to the medieval noble gesture. This lank, hungry, and apparently demented man rides the Spanish roads as he battles injustice. The Don's problem was his medieval point of view. His encounter with a common barber reveals a hostile knight, barmaids become noble damsels in distress, and windmills turn into giants. For Don Quixote and the medieval mind as a whole, things were never what they appeared to be. We, who are practical-minded like the people of the Renaissance, recognize that barbers are barbers and windmills are windmills, and we laugh, as did Renaissance readers, at the knight of the woeful countenance riding his flea-bitten nag. Yet the only trouble with Quixote was that he was born 100 years too late. A century earlier, he would have been the hero of a tale of chivalry, and his windmills *would* have been giants. After Cervantes, the tale of chivalry—the most popular form of medieval literature—could no longer be taken seriously. It became as outdated as the melodrama of the beautiful daughter, the mortgage coming due, the villain fingering his waxed mustache, and the hero arriving in the nick of time.

Have we lost something in giving up these fond delusions and embracing stark naturalism? Chesterton raises this question in his poem "Lepanto," in which he compares Don John, a true hero, with the paltry figures of other Renaissance rulers. Cervantes, too, must have wondered the same thing, for in the second part of his book the reader smiles at his hero, but the smile, like the author's, is sympathetic. Cervantes was apparently disillusioned with the pragmatism of the age and longed for vanished glories. This comparison of past and present, as seen in the two parts of *Don Quixote,* brings to a focus the central problem of the Renaissance, as first discussed in chapter 16. With all the new freedoms, wealth, economic order, and a science that relegated the human soul to a secondary position below sense-apparent objects—with all these, what is man? "What a piece of work is man! ... And yet to me what is this quintessence of dust?" Shakespeare confronts this problem in *The Tempest* and suggests a solution.

Petrarch (Francesco Petrarca), 1304–74

Petrarch was recognized in his own time as the preeminent poet and humanist of a new age. In 1341 the Roman Senate awarded him the laurel wreath as the first poet laureate since the ancient world. Though he cherished his elaborate Latin poems, he is best known today as the inventor of the Italian sonnet and creator of elegant Italian love poetry. As the court poet of the papal palace at Avignon, he was appalled at the decadence of the French popes of the Babylonian Captivity.

Erasmus of Rotterdam, 1466–1536

Italian humanism had a distinctly pagan flavor, but across the Alps the movement was entirely Christian, with Erasmus (fig. 19.1), the "Prince of Humanists," in the forefront. A true cosmopolitan, he made all Europe his home, from England to Italy. Although at first well-disposed toward Luther's reforms, he could not accept Luther's denial of free will. "I laid a hen's egg," wrote Erasmus; "Luther hatched a bird of quite another species."

A strong supporter of overdue reforms, Erasmus wrote that "Luther was guilty of two great crimes—he struck the Pope in his crown, and the monks in their belly." In

19.1   Albrecht Dürer, *Erasmus of Rotterdam.* 1526. Engraving, 9¾ × 7½" (24.8 × 19 cm). Metropolitan Museum of Art, New York (Fletcher Fund, 1919). The Latin inscription states that this was a drawing from life.

another vein he sternly admonished the church: "By identifying the new learning with heresy you make orthodoxy synonymous with ignorance." Erasmus preferred a purified church to a divided one.

During a journey from Italy to England Erasmus conceived the idea of a satire on just about every aspect of contemporary society. Written partly during his stay with the English humanist Sir Thomas More, and dedicated to him, the book was called *Moria* (Gk., "folly") in a punning reference to his English friend's name. Appearing in thirty-six editions in his own lifetime, the *Praise of Folly* was, after the Bible, the most widely read book of the century. Erasmus had brilliantly reinvented the classical paradoxical encomium in which everyone and everything unworthy of praise are ironically celebrated.

Niccolò Machiavelli, 1469–1527

If man is the measure of all things, as the humanists joyously avowed, what then is man? Machiavelli (mak-ee-uh-VEL-li) attacked the problem with a clinical eye in *The*

Prince, the most famous and influential of his many publications. Having observed the confusion following the fall of Cesare Borgia's autocratic government in Urbino, Machiavelli claimed that a ruler should be pragmatic rather than virtuous. The book examines the techniques of exercising power. As such, it is rather closely allied to both the art and the science of the Renaissance. Machiavelli uses the *scientific* method of his time to dissect the successes and failures of many rulers to see what made them tick, to come to an understanding of the *art* of governing successfully. Machiavelli delineated this art with such skill and frankness that the nineteenth-century historian Jacob Burkhardt observed that a Renaissance prince manipulated the state much as an artist manipulates his art.

Machiavelli's first premise is that anything is good for a state that allows it to survive and prosper; his second premise is that any means that will work in achieving that goal is good. (Machiavelli did not write that "the end justifies the means." Rather, he used the phrase *si guarda al fine*, meaning "one considers the end.") With these two premises he sweeps aside ideals and sentiment. The state, he assumes, does not exist for the happiness or well-being of people; the people exist only for the good of the state. The resulting thinking is detached, practical, and painfully accurate, though it is based on the lowest possible estimate of the worthiness of people. Its analytic method sweeps aside all mystery and disregards previous conceptions about justice and the ruling power. A typical, but depressing example of the cold, clear vision of the age, Machiavelli gave the Renaissance its first candid picture of human nature with the idealism of medievalism and humanism stripped away. He said simply:

> For of men it may generally be affirmed that they are thankless, fickle, false, studious to avoid danger, greedy of gain, devoted to you while you are able to

confer benefits upon them, and ready, as I have said before, while danger is distant, to shed their blood, and sacrifice their property, their lives and their children for you; but in the hour of need they turn against you . . . . Love is held by the tie of obligation, which, because men are a sorry breed, is broken on every whisper of private interest.

Machiavelli's verdict was not the opinion of a misanthrope, soured on the world, but that of a social scientist investigating human affairs with the detachment of a Kepler charting planetary orbits. After considering the fate of governments from Athens to his own time, he concluded that people were beasts, at best, and the successful ruler was one who treated them accordingly.

Disengagement: Michel de Montaigne, 1533–92

Nor was Machiavelli alone in this conclusion. Montaigne (mon-TEN-je) wrote:

> The frailest and most vulnerable of all creatures is man, and at the same time the most arrogant. He sees and feels himself lodged here in the mud and filth of the world, nailed and riveted to the worst, the deadest and most stagnant part of the universe, at the lowest story of the house and the most remote from the vault of heaven, with the animals of the worst condition of the three; and he goes and sets himself in imagination above the circle of the moon, and brings heaven under his feet.

Though not included in this text because of limited space, "On Cannibals" is one of the most candid and entertaining of the author's essays. The cannibals described by Montaigne also live in the New World, in Brazil. More used his Utopians to criticize his own society, but Montaigne is more direct. His cannibals are compared with Europeans and, cannibalism notwithstanding, judged superior:

> We may, then, well call these people barbarians in respect to the rules of reason, but not in respect to ourselves, who, in all sorts of barbarity, exceed them.

We find two disparate attitudes emerging from the new freedom of the Renaissance. The first, resulting from such opinions as those quoted above, displayed extreme pessimism and despair. Allied with that was the fear and uncertainty caused by losing the security of the old faith. But the second attitude is most commonly associated with the Renaissance. With all ties cut, with wealth abounding and frontiers stretching across the seas to unknown lands, people could be free. To secure freedom a person must obtain some kind of power, and the possibilities were apparently unlimited.

A RENAISSANCE PRINCE

Soldier, politician, and ecclesiastic, Cesare Borgia (CHAYS-uh-ray BORE-ja; 1476?–1507) was, like many of his contemporaries, corrupt, treacherous, and cruel. One of the four illegitimate children of Pope Alexander VI, he was made a cardinal at the age of eighteen. His father later named him Duke of Romagna, which enabled him to extend his military conquests. When rebels attempted to reclaim the Duchy of Urbino, Cesare lured them into one of his castles, where he had all of them executed. After his father's death his many enemies deprived him of his extensive lands and had him imprisoned. He later escaped to Navarre but was killed in action in an expedition against Castile. It is generally assumed that he is the prototype of Machiavelli's prince.

19.2 Hans Holbein the Younger, *Sir Thomas More*. Ca. 1530. Frick Collection, New York. Holbein's superb portrait reveals a visionary and a man of conscience, who died at the hands of Henry VIII rather than compromise his religious conviction.

François Rabelais, ca. 1490–1553

One reaction to a freewheeling society lusting after power was to withdraw from the rat race, a response that our own century has witnessed in many different forms. Symbolically this desire to retreat is revealed in the number of utopias that were written during the Renaissance. In his *Gargantua and Pantagruel*, Rabelais (rab-uh-leh) included a brief section on "The Abbey of Theleme" as his version of utopia. Actually, the "abbey" was a country club version of a monastery that has been turned upside down. Instead of "Poverty, Chastity, and Obedience" the sole injunction is to "Do What Thou Wilt." The Abbey of Theleme was a quiet retreat where the "rougher element" (and at no time in Western history has that element been so rough as during the Renaissance) was excluded, and where everyone behaved with perfect manners.

Baldassare Castiglione, 1478–1529

An elegant aristocrat and skilled diplomat, Castiglione represented a viewpoint advocated by Rabelais but opposed to both Montaigne and Machiavelli. Little concerned with humankind's capacity for evil and very much a man in and of the world, Castiglione advocated urbane lives of mannered civility. His code for Renaissance patricians, *The Book of the Courtier*, was a best-seller for the next two centuries.

Thomas More, 1478–1535

Sir Thomas More (fig. 19.2) quite rightly ranks as one of the heroes of the humanist movement. For his greatest work, *Utopia*, More seized on everyone's curiosity about the New World. As a framework for his story, he relates a conversation with a sailor, Raphael Hythlodaeus, who had sailed with Amerigo Vespucci to locate a new land named Utopia. More uses this Utopia (Gk., "no place") to criticize severely his own country and to describe a perfect government, which is a curious mixture of Plato's ideas and some of the most progressive concepts of More's time—or ours. Rather than the combination of private property and communism described by Plato, practically everything in Utopia is held in common. Most of the political officers are elected by the people in free elections, though More also provides for a monarch and a slave class. He believes that everybody—men and women and members of all the professions, including the clergy—should do real work, especially manual labor. With everyone working, all chores can be accomplished in a six-hour day, leaving ample time for creative leisure. His Utopians work as farmers and then move to the city to perform urban tasks. These population shifts are staggered so that the population in both country (on collective farms) and city remains constant.

More's *Utopia* has always been taken seriously, yet its conception of the state is naive. Actually, More seeks to return to medievalism while incorporating the advances of his own age. In the first place, More opposes the new capitalism, complaining of the evils that result from a society in which "money beareth all the swing." He proposes that all property should be held in common, that all houses should be the same (except for the gardens, where he allows individual initiative), and that people should trade houses at regular intervals. Gold would be used for chamber pots and jewels serve as children's toys so that citizens would not covet such things. Yet the state is to use gold and jewels to buy goods from neighboring countries.

Like Rabelais, More insists on equality and proposes representative local and federal governments similar to those of Switzerland. His equality means that every person should work at a trade except the few selected to be priests and scholars. Even with this ingenious planning, More cannot escape the dirty work done in any civilization, and he, like Plato, has slaves for labor unworthy of the Utopians. So much for equality.

More was appalled by the ceaseless strife and warfare of his time, and he insisted that his Utopians would have none of it—or little, at least. He proposes that all wars be conducted on neighboring lands and that the Utopians hire mercenary soldiers to do the fighting. Most fortunately, a neighboring nation is inhabited by a fierce and warlike people who are eager to wage war—at a price—for the Utopians.

The limitation of More's thinking is paradoxical, for he can extend his ideal state only to the borders of the nation. He degrades the people of other countries so that his Utopians may live well. And how like Shakespeare's Caliban the warrior group is! The good life, it would seem, must float on a vast sea of all that we regard as evil. When we consider the Utopians and this crude race of warriors, when we consider Prospero and Caliban, we recognize that they are as unlike as day and night, yet both seem necessary for human life. More was able to place his exploitable savages just outside the borders of his nation and our consideration; yet in everyday life, they are here and now and with us always.

Particularly abhorrent for More was the religious dissension that split nations, and that would eventually cause his own death. So in *Utopia* we find complete religious freedom. Most of the people adhere to one faith, but those of other faiths or no faith are neither chastised nor penalized. Only bigots are punished, for they provoke dissension by insisting that their faith is better than any other.

More did not write a guidebook to the perfect civilization. Practically, it won't work, and he knew this as well as Plato before him. He is to be taken seriously for the ideas that lay behind the practical operation of a utopia for civilized people. Most importantly, the necessity for human equality, religious tolerance, and his conviction that life should be lived for the pleasure of each individual are grand Renaissance ideas that foreshadow the thoughts of Rousseau, Jefferson, Madison, and others of later epochs. Indeed, they are our own best ideals, and we are still at a loss for ways of making them work, even as was More.

William Shakespeare, 1564–1616

Shakespeare knew all the intricacies of the Renaissance problem, not as theory, but as one who experienced within himself the perplexities of the age. In each of his plays one finds his reactions to the nature of Renaissance people, and, as Shakespeare matured and developed, the scope of his concerns became ever more comprehensive.

By the time of his last complete play, *The Tempest*, Shakespeare, viewing this resolution ever more clearly, renders up his account and gives us a summation of the totality of his experience. The best of the previous plays had been tragic, but is this final play a tragedy? No, for the author has gone beyond tragedy. He places *The Tempest* in a world of imagination sufficiently removed from the workaday world to bring together all the disparate elements of the Renaissance and resolve the conflicts. Shakespeare achieves the truth-beyond-appearances on Prospero's island.

What forces are represented here? Primarily there are the dark human failings that we try to deny, but which are with us always. Among the mortals, this old evil is represented by Stephano and Trinculo, Sebastian and Antonio; among the spirits, it is symbolized by Caliban. This is the force represented by the barbaric warrior race in More's *Utopia*, the force found in the myths of every culture. It is Grendel and his mother in *Beowulf*, the mindless drives in Freudian psychology, the dark creature that the Earth-Spirit and the Walpurgis-Night Scene represent in *Faust*. Sometimes we think of this force as lust, yet that is too limited. The Caliban thrust is all the drives that make human beings distorted and destructive, the force that Dante observed in Hell.

Represented by Prospero and symbolized by Ariel, the opposing thrust is the power of the intellect, which stands at the heart of the various utopias. Prospero is the humanist who has gone stale, as humanism did in the late Renaissance, and who belatedly realizes his responsibility to humanity. He describes himself as being "for the liberal arts without a parallel: those being all my study." The Ariel force, then, represents the highest nature of humankind, the intellect, which in the Renaissance view made men and women akin to the angels.

We explore the nature of evil with Caliban, who clearly recognizes his opposition to intellect when he speaks of his only profit from language as knowing how to curse, and when he tells Trinculo and Stephano to "burn his Book" if they want power over Prospero. Caliban's nature is confirmed when he celebrates his new "freedom" at the very moment when he is most in bondage, for he is drunk and has taken Stephano as a cruel master. Yet Caliban is more perceptive than his mortal counterparts, for when they advance with their evil purpose of overpowering Prospero, he knows the difference between the show of power (the spangled garments hung on the line) and real power, which involves pressing on about their business. His more foolish mortal masters are tricked by the flashy garb and routed by Prospero and Ariel. It is only after all these experiences that Caliban can say, "How fine my master is! . . . What a thrice-double ass was I, to take this drunkard for a god, And worship this dull fool!"

But the other side of the coin is that Prospero and Miranda cannot exist without Caliban. Although he is revolting in appearance and nature, so much so that Miranda says, " 'Tis a villain, sir, I do not love to look on," Prospero wisely answers,

> But as 'tis
> We cannot miss him: he does make our fire,
> Fetch in our wood; and serves in offices
> That profit us.

The Caliban nature, then, wisely used and ruled by the human will, serves a useful function in life.

But it was the state that was Shakespeare's main concern. Because the church could no longer control society, another type of order was necessary. This was the secular state, ruled by a king. Throughout the play, the political world is out of joint, for the right duke is not on the throne, and evil governs in place of good. Quite early, Shakespeare has Gonzalo propose a utopia—one not much different from that of More or of Rabelais. But the idea is ridiculous. Gonzalo starts his speech, "Had I plantation of this isle . . . and were the king on't," but he ends the speech, saying that there would be no sovereign. In a stroke

Shakespeare dismisses the utopian dream.

But we need more than this if the state is to survive while providing a sound framework for its inhabitants. Enter Ferdinand and Miranda, who are carefully schooled throughout the play in right living. Their marriage unites the man of action with the woman of spirit. One is reminded of Plato's philosopher-king, but the philosophy here is more sprightly and lighthearted. With the consummation of this marriage, and the return to Italy, we can predict an order, neither Machiavellian (as was Alonso's) nor too idealistic (as was Prospero's). This is the proper nature of the state.

What is Shakespeare's conclusion? In the first place he recognizes the folly of most of the things people do. He realizes that ninety years hence it will make little difference what anyone has done or failed to do.

> We are such stuff
> As dreams are made on, and our little life
> Is rounded with a sleep.

Perhaps our present activities will not affect the future but they are important here and now. Shakespeare's final choice is with humankind, men and women of good and evil mixed most wondrously. How else are we to interpret that little passage between Miranda and her father as she views all these mortals for the first time, people whom we have seen in all sorts of wicked conspiracies and evildoing? She looks on them and says:

> O Wonder!
> How many goodly creatures are there here!
> How beauteous mankind is! O brave new world,
> That has such people in 't!

And Prospero wisely answers: " 'Tis new to thee."

Francis Bacon and the Decline of the Renaissance

All balances must fail, which we have seen in every period that we have studied. One so delicate as that suggested in *The Tempest* cannot last for long. Sir Francis Bacon (1561–1626) proposed how the scales were to fall. He was skilled in many fields, but his greatest work lay in his scientific writing, in which he consistently revealed the clear-sighted realism that was the hallmark of the Renaissance.

Bacon wrote a utopia called *The New Atlantis*, which, not surprisingly, is inhabited by scientists. These are men who follow the lead of Descartes in ruling by reason alone, reason divorced from the spirit. It can weigh the actions of a man such as Ferdinand, judging by the results whether they are good or bad, but reason cannot measure the loveliness of a Miranda. So Bacon and those that followed him in the next period, the Age of Reason, downplayed such qualities as imagination and sentiment. They gained greatly in sureness; their way had the hard brilliance of a diamond. But is clarity worth the price of loveliness?

This, then, was the Renaissance. Its early discoverers brought to it more new big ideas than any civilization had ever faced before. At its outset the change was overwhelming, for all the basic ideas of the Middle Ages had to be adjusted in the face of a mass of new knowledge about the world. Out of this chaos of change emerged two basic attitudes. One orientation led to the glories of the Renaissance: daring explorers, superb artists, powerful capitalists, great monarchs. Some were as fine as Leonardo or Raphael, others as corrupt as Renaissance popes or princes, or as ruthless as English sea dogs or Spanish *conquistadores*. The opposing trend of thought was one of deep pessimism. Montaigne and others who felt this assumed that somehow people were not fine enough in their basic nature properly to use their new freedom. In their dreams of the good life, these people retreated to their utopias. Near the end of his career Shakespeare saw that the balance lay in the powerful king in whose person imagination and action were joined by love. This is the pattern that enlightened despots tried to achieve, but the delicate balance was easily disturbed. In its decline it moved toward the emerging modern world in which science and technology would become ever more central to the culture.

STUDY QUESTION

Describe Machiavelli's view of human nature and explain why this might contribute to the pessimism of the time. Does Machiavelli's view apply to rulers today? Consider, for example, the various governments in the Western world, the Middle East, and selected African nations.

LITERARY SELECTION 20

Poetry
Petrarch (Francesco Petrarca), 1304–74

Though Petrarch intended his epic poem *Africa* to be his major work, his Italian sonnets have been far more influential. His love poetry was inspired by Laura, whom he first saw in the Church of St. Clara of Avignon on 6 April 1327. The following sonnet commemorates that momentous meeting while also alluding to the day on which Christ supposedly died: 6 April.

Sonnet III
(Era il giorno ch'al sol si scolarara)

'Twas on the morn when heaven its blessed ray
    In pity to its suffering master veil'd,
    First did I, lady, to your beauty yield,

Of your victorious eyes th' unguarded prey.
Ah, little reck'd I that, on such a day,
   Needed against Love's arrows any shield;
   And trod, securely trod, the fatal field:
Whence, with the world's, began my heart's dismay.
On every side Love found his victim bare,
   And through mine eyes transfix'd my throbbing heart;
   Those eyes which now with constant sorrows flow:
But poor the triumph of his boasted art,
   Who thus could pierce a naked youth, nor dare
   To you in armor mail'd even to display his bow!

Like Dante's Beatrice, Laura was an ideal, the object throughout Petrarch's life of an unrequited poetic passion. Unlike Beatrice, whom Dante idealized from afar, Laura accepted the poet as a friend—but no more than that. She was married and destined to be the mother of ten children. A sonnet is, by definition, a fourteen-line lyric poem that expresses a single idea or thought, in this case the poet's reaction to Laura's physical beauty.

Sonnet LXIX
(Erano i capei d'oro all' aura sparsi)

Her golden tresses were spread loose to air,
   And by the wind in thousand tangles blown,
   And a sweet light beyond all brightness shone
   From those grand eyes, though now of brilliance bare;
And did that face a flush of feeling wear?
   I now thought yes, then no, the truth unknown.
   My heart was then for love like tinder grown,
   What wonder if it flamed with sudden flare?
Not like the walk of mortals was her walk,
   But as when angels glide; and seemed her talk
   With other than mere human voice, to flow.
A spirit heavenly, a living sun
   I saw, and if she be no longer so,
   A wound heals not, because the bow's undone.

Petrarch was tormented by his passion, but he was also inspired as a poet because the one-way love affair appealed to his vanity. He was a Renaissance artist, a self-conscious man of letters seeking earthly fame, as the following sonnet clearly reveals.

Sonnet XLVII
(Benedetto sia l' giorno e l' mese e l' anno)

Blest be the day, and blest the month, the year,
   The spring, the hour, the very moment blest,
   The lovely scene, the spot, where first oppress'd
   I sunk, of two bright eyes the prisoner:
And blest the first soft pang, to me most dear,
   Which thrill'd my heart, when Love became its guest;
   And blest the bow, the shafts which pierced my breast.
   And even the wounds, which bosom'd thence I bear.
Blest too the strains which, pour'd through glade and grove,

Have made the woodlands echo with her name;
   The sighs, the tears, the languishment, the love:
And blest those sonnets, sources of my fame;
   And blest that thought—Oh! never to remove!—
   Which turns to her alone, from her alone which came.

   Laura died on 6 April 1348 of the Black Death, as did millions of Europeans during that ghastly summer. Petrarch was devastated, as well as transfixed by the date.

Sonnet CCXCII
(Gli occhi di ch' io parlai si caldamente)

Those eyes, 'neath which my passionate rapture rose,
   The arms, hands, feet, the beauty that erewhile
   Could my own soul from its own self beguile,
   And in a separate world of dreams enclose,
The hair's bright tresses, full of golden glows,
   And the soft lightning of the angelic smile
   That changed this earth to some celestial isle—
   Are now but dust, poor dust, that nothing knows.
And yet I live! Myself I grieve and scorn,
   Left dark without the light I loved in vain,
   Adrift in tempest on a bark forlorn;
Dead is the source of all my amorous strain,
   Dry is the channel of my thoughts outworn,
   And my sad harp can sound but notes of pain.

STUDY QUESTIONS

1. In line 11 of Sonnet III, the image of the eyes as a gateway to the heart was a poetic commonplace. Is that image still used today in poetry and songs? Give a few examples.
2. What is the meaning of the image of the "bow" in the last line of Sonnets III and LXIX?

LITERARY SELECTION 21

Poetry
Michelangelo Buonarroti, 1475–1564

The musicality of sonnets by Petrarch and his followers was the accepted style of the Italian Renaissance, but Michelangelo followed his own course in his poetry just as he did in sculpting, painting, and architecture. His sonnets were, as he himself said, "unprofessional, rude, and rough." Michelangelo did not consider himself a poet in Petrarchian terms, but he was praised at the time as a poet in his own right. His sonnets, like the personality of their creator, are powerful and unique, and constitute, at their best, the finest lyric Italian poetry of the Renaissance. No knowledge of Michelangelo the sculptor and painter can be complete without knowing the artist as poet. The following poem was written for Michelangelo's close friend Tommaso de' Cavalieri.

Sonnet XXXII
(S'un casto amor)

If love be chaste, if virtue conquer ill,
    If fortune bind both lovers in one bond,
    If either at the other's grief despond,
    If both be governed by one life, one will;
If in two bodies one soul triumph still,
    Raising the twain from earth to heaven beyond,
    If Love with one blow and one golden wand
    Have power both smitten breasts to pierce and thrill;
If each the other love, himself foregoing,
    With such delight, such savor, and so well,
    That both to one sole end their wills combine;
If thousands of these thoughts, all thought outgoing,
    Fail the least part of their firm love to tell:
    Say, can mere angry spite this knot untwine?

Michelangelo met Vittoria Colonna, the Marquise of Pescara, while he was working on the *Last Judgment* (1536–1541; see fig. 17.33) in the Sistine Chapel. Probably the only woman he ever loved, Vittoria was an astute judge of his work, but valued the man even above his creations. Michelangelo viewed her as "God inside a woman." Her death in 1547 was a painful loss for a seventy-two-year-old artist who was already obsessed with the fear of death and hell. In much of the poetry written for Vittoria, Michelangelo used sculpture as a theme; God had created Adam and that made him a sculptor.

SUMMARY

The dynamic Renaissance was notable for its artistic creativity, intellectual energy, widespread violence, and almost constant warfare. Almost everything was writ large because European civilization experienced drastic changes over a relatively short period of time. The Middle Ages died hard, partly because of the intransigent stance of the church. Determined to relinquish none of its vast power, the Church of Rome ultimately lost some of its authority in southern Europe and all control in northern Europe.

Critical elements of the Italian Renaissance were the rise of humanism and the retrieval of the Graeco-Roman heritage. Other factors included the expansion of capitalism and a steady increase in trade, industry, and banking. Northern Europe had no classical heritage, but its livelier economy, coupled with creative enterprise, produced considerable prosperity and a growing middle class.

Science made notable advances with the Copernican theory replacing the old Ptolemaic system and with Galileo's development of his laws of motion. Using his improved telescope, Galileo also helped confirm the Copernican thesis.

This was the age of exploration, with the magnetic compass, astrolabe, and tables of Henry the Navigator assisting the voyages of discovery of Columbus, Cabral, Cabot, and Magellan. The New World was explored by Cartier, Champlain, and Hudson; Cortés conquered the Aztec empire in Mexico, and Pizarro captured the Inca empire in Peru.

Assisted mightily by the invention of movable type, the Reformation broke the universal power of the Church of Rome. Led by Martin Luther, John Calvin, and others, the Protestant reformers established a variety of denominations throughout northern Europe. Politically, the Renaissance saw the rise of nation-states that in many ways supplanted the controlling power of the Roman church. The new nations of England, France, and Spain became the most powerful in Europe.

All of these forces contributed significantly to human freedom, but they raised the question of whether human beings were equipped to use their freedom wisely. Could selfish, greedy people rise above their animal natures to become what the Renaissance called the "noblest creatures of God" and use their God-given capacities to transform the world? That remained, for the Renaissance, an open question.

CULTURE AND HUMAN VALUES

If one were to ask what final answers were arrived at for the Renaissance problems stated here and in previous chapters, one would have to look not so much to ideas as to the lives of individuals. These were people who fulfilled the concept of "universal." This kind of person was completely free to live as he or she pleased, gaining freedom along with the ability to master knowledge and power.

Symbolic of this Renaissance person is Michelangelo's *Creation of Adam* (see fig. 17.28). One sees in the eyes of the reclining figure infinite longing, the type of yearning that will carry this man far. In the strongly muscled body one sees the strength that will help him fulfill that longing. Representing both of the sexes, this person is free, with the creative vigor to conquer new worlds, to unlock the secrets of the universe, to dare and to do in a world welcoming ambition and achievement.

UNIT 7

The
Early
Modern
World,
1600–1789

	People and Events	Art and Architecture	Literature and Music	Philosophy and Science
1600	**1600** English East India Company founded **1602** Dutch East India Company founded **1609** Truce in Dutch revolt against Spain **1603–25** James I of England **1618–48** Thirty Years' War **1621–65** Philip IV of Spain **1625–49** Charles I of England **1632** Galileo condemned by Inquisition **1635** French Academy of Language and Literature established **1642–6** English Civil War **1643–1715** Louis XIV of France **1648** French Academy of Painting and Sculpture established **1649** Charles I of England executed **1649–60** Cromwell's Commonwealth **1660–85** Restoration: Charles II of England **1666** Great Fire of London **1669** Paris Opera established **1682–1725** Peter the Great of Russia **1685** Louis XIV revokes Edict of Nantes **1685–8** James II of England **1688** England's Glorious Revolution **1688–1702/1694** William and Mary of England	**Vignola** 1507–73 *Il Gesù* **Jones** 1573–1652 *Queen's House* **Caravaggio** 1573–1610 *The Conversion of St. Paul* **Rubens** 1577–1640 *The Assumption of the Virgin* **Hals** ca. 1580–1666 *The Laughing Cavalier* **Gentileschi** 1593–1652 *Judith Slaying Holofernes* **Poussin** 1594–1665 *Holy Family on the Steps* **Bernini** 1598–1680 *St. Peter's Piazza and Colonnade* **Borromini** 1599–1644 *S. Carlo alle Quattro Fontane* **Velasquez** 1599–1660 *Maids of Honor* **van Dyck** 1599–1641 *Charles I of England* **Rembrandt** 1606–69 *The Descent from the Cross* **Leyster** 1609–60 *Self-Portrait* **Ruisdael** 1628–82 *View of Haarlem from the Dunes at Overveen* **Vermeer** 1632–75 *The Girl with the Red Hat* **Wren** 1632–1723 *St. Paul's* **Pozzo** 1642–1709 *Apotheosis of Saint Ignatius* **Mansart** 1646–1708 *Palace of Versailles*	**Donne** 1573–1631 *Holy Sonnets* **Milton** 1608–74 *Paradise Lost On His Blindness* **Molière** 1622–73 *Tartuffe* The 1456 appearance of Halley's comet, from Conrad Lycosthenes, *Prodigiorum ac ostentorum chronicon*. 1557. Woodcut. Photo: Ann Ronan Picture Library, Taunton, U.K. 	**Bacon** 1561–1626 *Novum Organum* **Galileo** 1564–1642 *Dialogues Concerning the Two Chief World Systems* **Kepler** 1571–1630 elliptical planetary orbits **Hobbes** 1588–1679 *Leviathan* **Descartes** 1596–1650 *Discourse on Method* **Spinoza** 1632–77 *God in nature* **Locke** 1632–1704 *Two Treatises of Government*
1700	**1701–13** Frederick I of Prussia **1702–14** Anne of England **1713–40** Frederick William I of Prussia **1714–27** George I of England **1715–74** Louis XV of France **1727–60** George II of England **1740–86** Frederick the Great of Prussia **1748** Excavations begin at Pompeii **1755** Lisbon earthquake **1760–1820** George III of England **1762–91** Catherine the Great of Russia **1774–93** Louis XVI of France **1775** Watt's improved steam engine **1775–83** American Revolution **1780–90** Joseph II Emperor of Austria	**Watteau** 1684–1721 *A Pilgrimage to Cythera* **Hogarth** 1697–1764 *Marriage à La Mode* **Chardin** 1699–1779 *The Kitchen Maid* **Boucher** 1703–70 *Venus Consoling Love* **Gainsborough** 1727–88 *Mrs. Richard Brinsley Sheridan* **Fragonard** 1732–1806 *The Swing* **Kauffmann** 1741–1807 *Pliny the Younger and His Mother at Misenum* **Houdon** 1741–1828 *Voltaire* **David** 1748–1825 *Death of Socrates*	**Swift** 1667–1745 *Gulliver's Travels; A Modest Proposal* **Couperin** 1688–1733 *Le Croc-en-jambe* **Bach** 1685–1750 *French Suite No. 4* **Vivaldi** 1685–1743 *The Four Seasons* **Handel** 1685–1759 *Messiah* **Pope** 1688–1744 *Essay on Man* **Montesquieu** 1669–1755 *Spirit of the Laws* **Voltaire** 1694–1778 *Candide* **Rousseau** 1712–78 *Confessions* **Diderot** 1713–84 *Encyclopedia* **Haydn** 1732–1809 *String Quartet in C Major* **Mozart** 1756–91 *Symphony No. 35*	**Newton** 1642–1727 *Principia Mathematica* **Bayle** 1647–1706 *Historical and Critical Dictionary* **Halley** 1656–1742 *Halley's comet* **Hume** 1711–76 *A Treatise of Human Nature* **Smith** 1723–90 *Wealth of Nations* **Kant** 1724–1804 *Critique of Pure Reason*
1800	**1789–1815** French Revolution	**Stuart** 1755–1828 *Mrs. Richard Yates* **Canova** 1757–1822 *Pauline Borghese as Venus* **Johnson** 1765–1830 *The Westwood Children* **Charpentier** 1767–1849 *Mlle. Charlotte du Val d'Ognes*	**Jefferson** 1743–1826 *Declaration of Independence* **Beethoven** 1770–1827 *Symphony No. 5*	**Laplace** 1749–1827 French astronomer

CHAPTER 20

Science, Reason, and Absolutism

THE SEVENTEENTH CENTURY

Europe emerged from medievalism into what is generally called the Modern World[1] during the tumultuous Renaissance, but not until 1648 did the passions unleashed by the Reformation and Counter-Reformation begin to subside. Initially a conflict between Catholics and Protestants, the Thirty Years' War (1618–48) evolved into an international conflict between modern nation-states. The Peace of Westphalia of 1648 that ended the slaughter was a landmark in European history, finally laying to rest the last vestiges of medievalism. Once viable values and institutions completely disappeared. As viewed from the early modern world, the medieval idea of a unified Christian commonwealth was a relic of the distant past as were papal claims to political power. Adopting the strategies of diplomacy and alliances initiated by Italian city-states, sovereign nations staked out boundaries and competed with each other in the struggle for a new balance of power. The strongest competing powers were France, England, the Hapsburg empires of Austria and Spain, and the Ottoman empire (map 20.1).

Rapid advances in science and technology revealed vast new horizons, and international trade opened up the whole world to European dominance and, inevitably, European exploitation. The English East Indies Company was founded in 1600; its Dutch counterpart was chartered two years later, followed by the French. The prevailing mood in northern Europe, with its growing power and wealth, was as positive as the joyful optimism voiced by Miranda in Shakespeare's *The Tempest*.

---

1. Our modern world began in around 1600 but the difference between "modern" in that sense and "modern" meaning our own century can sometimes be confusing. The modern period is frequently divided into three parts: the Early Modern World: 1600–1789; the Middle Modern World: 1789–1914; the Twentieth Century. The French Revolution of 1789 marked a major change from one era to another as did the onset of World War I in 1914. The Baroque, the Age of Reason, the Enlightenment, and so forth are, of course, subheads within the modern period.

Science and Philosophy

Francis Bacon, 1561–1626

The career of Francis Bacon spanned the late Renaissance and the emerging modern world, which is why he is discussed here and in the preceding chapter. Along with Galileo and Descartes, he ranks as one of the founders of modern science and philosophy. He formulated no new scientific hypotheses nor did he make any dramatic discoveries, but he did inquire into the function and ethics of science and scientific research in relation to human life. For Bacon, knowledge was not recognition of any given reality but a search for truth, a journey rather than a destination. Bacon knew that the old culture was being replaced by a dramatically new epoch. Inventions such as gunpowder, the printing press, the compound microscope (ca. 1590), and the telescope (ca. 1608) changed the material world, spawning new beliefs, institutions, and values. Scientific knowledge and invention, Bacon believed, should be public property to be shared democratically and to be used for the benefit of all people. In his *Novum Organum* (1620) Bacon stated the logic of scientific inquiry and the principles of the inductive method. Factual information would be collected through experiment and observation, leading to general statements based solely on observable data. For Bacon the principal task of scientific investigation was to remedy the poverty of factual data, to embark on an exhilarating voyage of scientific discovery that had been delayed about 2,000 years. There was an explosion of knowledge as seventeenth-century scientists explored a world that had been virtually unknown since the groundbreaking efforts of the Hellenistic scientists of the ancient world (map 20.2).

Galileo Galilei, 1564–1642

Professor of mechanics and astronomy at the University of Padua, Galileo Galilei contributed mightily to the accumulation of factual information. His was a threefold scientific method based on a Pythagorean faith in a mathematical order of nature, the practice of abstracting and intuiting mathematical laws, and, most importantly, experimentation under rigidly controlled conditions. With his improved telescope he empirically proved the heliocentric theory, discovered sun spots, and viewed the moons

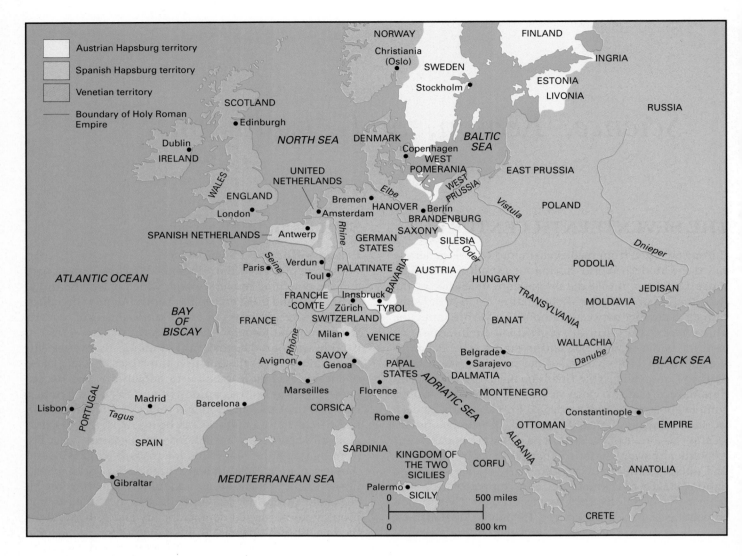

Map 20.1   Europe in the 17th century.

of Jupiter. He devised two laws of motion, invented the thermometer, improved the compound microscope, investigated the principles of the lever and the pulley, measured air pressure, and studied the properties of magnetism and sound vibrations. Even more importantly, he invented the modern method of forming a theory, testing it experimentally, and adjusting the theory to conform to observable results.

It can be said that modern science began on 24 August 1609, the date of Galileo's letter to the Doge of Venice in which he described his telescopic observations. But Galileo's was the only voice promoting examination of the heavens with his improved telescope. His fellow scientists unanimously rejected this marvelous new scientific instrument. Why was this so?

The magnifying power of a convex mirror was known to Euclid in 300 BC, but for the next 1,900 years no one was interested in concave mirrors nor were they concerned

with the three-power spyglass that Dutch artisans had copied from a 1590 Italian model. Philosophers and scientists had learned not to trust the senses, especially visual phenomena. The problem was compounded because lenses and concave mirrors made one see figures that were contradicted by the sense of touch. Galileo's thirty-power telescope was therefore rejected as dispensing false information. The Catholic cardinals who refused to view moon craters through it had a long tradition behind them.

The startling contents of the famous letter to the Doge became common knowledge, leading to ever-growing controversy. After Galileo published his *Dialogues Concerning the Two Chief World Systems* (1632), the Inquisition charged him with heresy. The Holy Office (Inquisition) claimed that Galileo had agreed, in a signed statement, not to promulgate his heliocentric views. The statement was a forgery, and Galileo was not allowed to appear before the court in his own defense. He was judged, nevertheless, a heretic, forced to recant, and sentenced to lifetime house arrest. First condemned to public burning, the book was later merely prohibited.

Galileo managed to get his book published in Switzerland and followed that with the publication (in Holland) of *The New Sciences* (1638), the first great work on modern physics. Galileo had successfully defied Rome but his life was a shambles and Italian science was set back for generations. (In October 1992 the Church of Rome officially declared that Galileo had been treated unfairly.)

René Descartes, 1596–1650

The Reformation raised the question of the reliability of religious knowledge, of whether Catholic beliefs were more or less true than Protestant or any other creeds. The rise of

Map 20.2   The spread of the intellectual revolution in 17th- and 18th-century Europe.

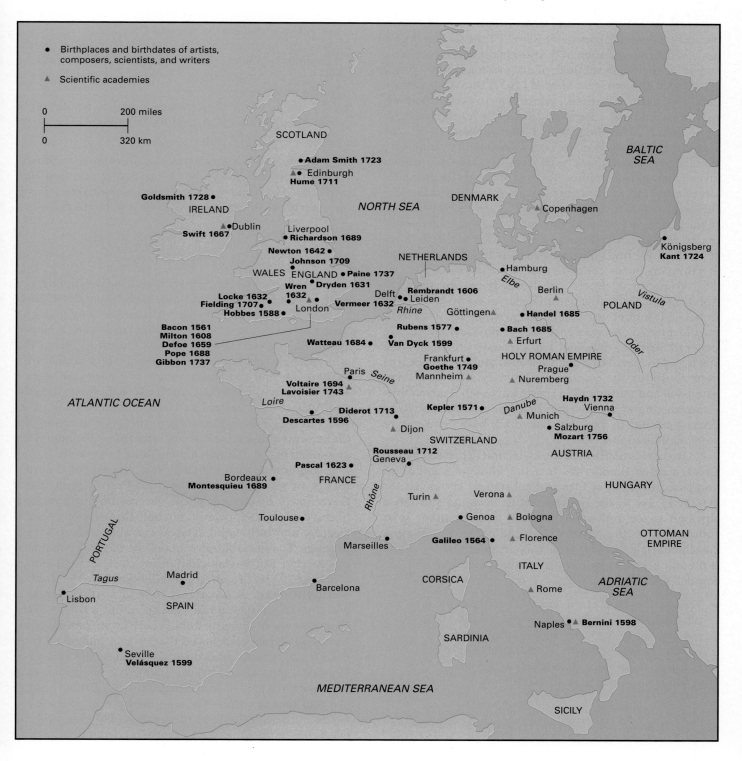

science extended the question to the reliability of all knowledge. Skeptics maintained that doubt was always present, with no certain knowledge possible, but Bacon argued that the inductive method, augmented by mechanical aids such as the compound microscope, provided certain knowledge about the world. Like many philosophers and scientists, René Descartes distrusted sensory evidence. Indeed, he went even further, following the arguments of skeptics such as Montaigne and Mersenne to their logical conclusion and rejecting everything as "true" or knowable except his own mental existence: *Cogito, ergo sum* ("I think, therefore I am"). On this foundation of "Cartesian doubt," he was able to erect a system, or method, of discovering truth.

In his *Discourse on Method* (1637) Descartes formulated his "natural method," which was to accept nothing as true except what "clearly and distinctly" presented itself to his mind. It was not until his *Meditations* (1641) that Descartes responded to attacks on all knowledge. Admitting that the senses could not be trusted, Descartes postulated an evil demon who confused people about the truth or falsity of anything, even whether a square had four sides. The Cartesian solution was to exorcise the demon by believing in the goodness of the all-powerful God. Descartes doesn't doubt that God exists, but how does he know that he himself exists? He finds his answer in the realization that he is a thinking person: *"Cogito ergo sum."*

Whatever is clearly and distinctly perceived by the mind is true. From this point Descartes constructed a rational philosophy that established the reliability of the senses and proved the existence of the physical world. He believed, further, that God had created two substances, spirit and matter. The mind was spirit and its essence was consciousness; the essence of the body, or matter, was extension and movement in space. Cartesian dualism thus established a gulf between mind and body that later philosophers removed by proving that mind, body, and nature were all interconnected.

Descartes reaffirmed the ideas first expressed by the Greek atomist Democritos that the whole of matter was composed of items of identical substance. All reality, for Descartes, lay in the motion of this absolute substance through space and time. For him and the many who followed him, the perfect God had created a flawless (mathematical) world; God was an engineer who had built and set in motion a very complicated machine. As Randall summarizes:

> To Descartes thenceforth space or extension became the fundamental reality in the world, motion the source of all change, and mathematics the only relation between its parts. . . . He made of nature a machine and nothing but a machine; purposes and spiritual influences alike vanished.[2]

2. J. H. Randall, Jr., *The Making of the Modern Mind* (New York: Columbia University Press, 1976), pp. 241–2.

Mathematics was "queen of the sciences" for Descartes and all anyone needed to explain a mechanical universe. Applied mathematics enabled scientists to study and understand an orderly cosmos that operated according to natural laws, a position with which Galileo was in complete agreement. Copernicus had proposed the heliocentric theory; Kepler had confirmed it by observation and, with mathematics, determined the three laws of planetary motion:

1. The planets move around the sun in ellipses with the sun at one focus of the ellipse.
2. We can imagine a line joining the sun and a planet. Though the planet's speed varies in its orbit around the sun, yet this imaginary line "sweeps out" equal areas in equal times.
3. The square of the time for one complete revolution of each planet is proportional to the cube of its average distance from the sun.

Bacon, Galileo, Descartes, and the early astronomers built a firm foundation for the scientific eruption that inspired Newton and that subsequently made Western culture unrivaled among the civilizations of the world.

Absolutism

At the beginning of the century both England and France were governed by absolute monarchs who based their claims on Divine Right. The thrones of England and Scotland were united by the accession of James I (reigned 1603–25), the son of Mary Stuart, Queen of Scots. His attempt to govern absolutely brought him into conflict with Parliament, and the absolute rule of Charles I (reigned 1625–49) finally led to Civil War (1642–6) between the king and Parliament. Charles I was tried and executed for treason and the Interregnum began, the Puritan era of the Commonwealth and the Protectorate (1649–59) under what amounted to the dictatorship of Oliver Cromwell.

Beginning with the Civil War, the Social Contract theory of government became ever more prominent. Government by consent of the governed did not imply a liberal democracy, however, but only that the power of the wealthy and influential classes was able to curb kingly excesses. The Social Contract concept was a strong political current but it was challenged by Thomas Hobbes (1588–1679) in *Leviathan*, published in 1651. Hobbes revived the idea of a contract based on subjection to a monarch's sovereign power, but ruled out a Divine Right king. Convinced that peace and security were prerequisites for society, Hobbes believed that certain individual freedoms had to be sacrificed for the good of the state. For Hobbes a state of nature was anarchy; there had to be a superior force to restore and maintain the stability of society, and that would be the unlimited power of the king. Given the Social Contract theory, the Civil War, and the execution of the king, the Hobbesian position became, of course, anathema to Cromwell and Parliament.

On the death of Cromwell in 1659, power passed to his son, Richard, but within a year Charles II (reigned 1660–85), son of Charles I, was invited to restore the Stuart line. Charles managed to go his own way without openly confronting Parliament, but James II (reigned 1685–8) was not so clever and was forced to abdicate, leaving in his wake the conviction that a Catholic king was dangerous to English liberties. Mary, the daughter of James II, was Protestant and married to William of Orange, a Dutch Protestant. Providing they accepted the new Bill of Rights, William and Mary were invited to ascend the English throne. This was the bloodless Glorious Revolution of 1688 that established a constitutional monarchy. Absolutism was virtually finished in England.

Absolutism in France had a far longer and more violent history. Succeeding to the throne after the assassination of Henry IV, Louis XIII reigned from 1610 to 1643, but royal power was gradually taken over by his chief minister, Cardinal Richelieu, who operated as a virtual dictator from 1624 to 1642. It was Richelieu who established the royal absolutism to which Louis XIV succeeded in 1643 at the age of five under the regency of his mother. During the longest reign of any French monarch, Louis XIV (1643–1715; fig. 20.1) promoted the arts, built the magnificent palace at Versailles (see fig. 21.15), and made France the most powerful monarchy in Europe. The nation was crippled, however, by an archaic economic system with local customs barriers, tax farming, and a nobility that paid no taxes at all. Raising revenues simply increased the misery of the people. Further, the king's revocation of the Edict of Nantes (1685), that protected the Huguenots (French Protestants) from persecution, was a disaster. Over 250,000 mostly middle-class craftsmen and their families fled the country, marking the beginning of the end of Louis' greatness and, ultimately, of the French monarchy itself.

THE EIGHTEENTH CENTURY
The Enlightenment, ca. 1687–1789

"Enlightenment" and "Age of Reason" are the two terms that describe the intellectual characteristics of the eighteenth century. The Enlightenment is usually dated from 1687, the year in which Newton's epochal *Principia Mathematica (Mathematical Principles of Natural Philosophy)* appeared, to the beginning of the French Revolution in 1789. An alternative beginning date would be 1688, the year of the Glorious Revolution in England. No matter; the *Principia* and the Glorious Revolution were major milestones marking the advance of science, rationalism, and freedom.

The Enlightenment was a self-conscious and extremely articulate movement that was to transform all Western societies. Europe had experienced some rude shocks, what

20.1 French school after Gianlorenzo Bernini, *Bust of Louis XIV*. Ca. 1700. Bronze, 33⅛ × 39⅜ × 17" (84.2 × 100 × 43.2 cm). National Gallery of Art, Washington, D.C. (Samuel H. Kress Collection).
Versailles was decorated and furnished in the Baroque style represented by this bust, but the exterior is essentially Neoclassic, the preferred architectural style of Louis XIV.

some writers called the "three humiliations": the earth was not at the center of the universe; people were creatures of nature like other animals; and their reason was subject to passions and instincts. These new truths represented intellectual advances that enabled people to redefine their responsibilities: discover truth through science; achieve personal happiness in a viable society; explore the full meaning, and limitations, of liberty. Newton's discoveries provided convincing evidence that the world was orderly and knowable and that, by the same token, human societies could be made orderly and rational through the exercise of enlightened reason.

Montesquieu (1689–1755) was apparently among the first to expand Cartesian ideas about natural law, contending that both physical and political phenomena were subject to general laws. The Marquis de Condorcet (1743–94) went still further. He assumed that one could discover universally valid truths in ethics, economics, and government that were as certain as the facts of mathematics and science. The accumulation of new knowledge would guide decisions and actions and help to free men and women from prejudices, superstitions, and undesirable restraints of society and government. This was the doctrine of progress that so fascinated the intellectuals of the Enlightenment. Just as the sciences progressed ever upward by discovering new facts, so would society move to an ever fuller realization of human potential. These optimistic beliefs had the force of self-fulfilling prophecies, leading to major improvements in many areas before the realization dawned that ethics, economics, society, and government had far more variables than anyone had ever dreamed.

Science and Philosophy: Newton and Locke

Isaac Newton, 1642–1727

Newton was the scientific hero of the Enlightenment. He electrified Western culture with his discovery of the universal law of gravitation, made important investigations into optics, and invented the branch of mathematics known as calculus (also invented independently by Baron von Leibniz; 1646–1716). As important as these specific discoveries were, Newton was revered by his peers more for his methodology. Some of Newton's discoveries have been modified by later scientists, but his scientific method stands to this day as a model for every scientist. Willing to give credit where it was due, Newton supposedly remarked, "If I have seen a little farther than others, it is because I have stood on the shoulders of giants." There were many giants, including Copernicus, Brahe, Bruno, Kepler, and Galileo, but Newton effected the grand synthesis that explained the

operation of the cosmos. First, he refined Galileo's laws of motion:

1. A body remains in a state of rest or of uniform motion in a straight line unless compelled by an external force to change that state. In other words, a body's inertia keeps it in a state of rest or its inertia keeps it moving in a straight line. External force has to be applied to move it from either its state of rest or its straight-line motion.
2. A change in momentum is proportional to the force causing the change and takes place in the direction in which the force is acting. In other words, the increase or decrease in velocity is proportional to the force.
3. To every action there is an equal and opposite reaction. We see this law in action every time a rocket roars into space.

Celestial Calculations

Galileo had demonstrated the principles of movement of bodies on earth, but not the motion of heavenly bodies. Why were their orbits curved? Newton hypothesized that all celestial bodies were mutually attracted to each other. He concentrated his studies on the moon's inertial movement in space, and then determined that its orbit was curved because it was continuously falling toward the earth (fig. 20.2). Its inertia causes it to fly out in a straight line, as shown by the dotted arrows, but the gravitational pull of the earth overcomes the straight-line tendency. Action and reaction are equal and the moon remains in orbit at a standard distance from the earth, just as today's manufactured satellites remain in orbit. Newton calculated the mass of the moon and its distance from the earth and determined that the gravitational pull was inversely proportional to the square of its distance from the earth. Newton also calculated the mass of the sun, the planets, and their moons and discovered that each planet would travel according to Kepler's laws by using the same formula: the gravitational pull of the sun was inversely proportional to the square of a planet's distance from the sun. The mathematical formula was the same whether the object was an apple falling from a tree or the moon, a law that worked here on earth and far out in space. This was the universal law of gravitation.

Universal Principles

Newton (and Edmund Halley) demonstrated that comets obey the same universal principle. Newton measured the flattening of the earth at its poles due to its rotation and proved that the size of a planet determined the length of its day. He showed the effect of latitude on the weight of an object and explained that the tides resulted from the combined attraction of the sun and the moon. All these examples of gravitation illustrate some of the different phenomena that can be explained with one law. No wonder Alexander Pope wrote:

20.2   Forces acting on the moon to determine its motion.

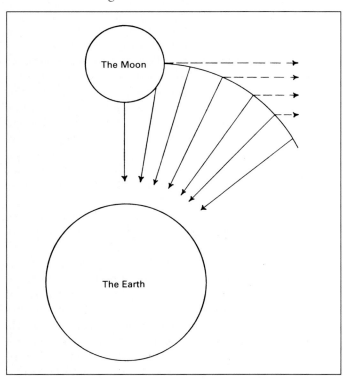

Nature and Nature's laws lay hid in night:
God said, *Let Newton be!* and all was light.

The philosophic implications of this unification of scientific principles were astounding. Picture the universe as Newton saw it, a vast and intricate system of whirling bodies in space, a configuration both orderly and predictable. Each planet, each moon, each solar system was balanced in the cosmic plan, a balance determined by mechanical forces pulling against each other. Absolute and unvarying, these forces would keep the machine in working order. What, then, was God's place? For all practical purposes God was ruled out, but Newton assigned two functions to the Divinity. Scientists noticed slight irregularities in the motions of the heavenly bodies in terms of Newtonian physics. Therefore one function of God was to make certain periodic readjustments, with a second function the maintenance of an even flow of time and space. Thus God became a sort of celestial engineer, turning a wheel here, opening a valve there, keeping an eye on the dials. Even before the close of the eighteenth century, however, a French astronomer, the Marquis de Laplace, extended the mechanism of gravitation and proved that the irregularities were periodical and subject to a law that kept them within bounds. This led to the belief held by certain deists that God existed as the master designer of a perfect world-machine needing no further tending.

Given these developments, we see clearly and distinctly the reliance on intellect that characterized the Enlightenment. Human beings using the marvelous mechanisms of their minds could, in time, unlock the most hidden secrets of the universe. And what of human institutions? The cosmos was orderly, rational, and knowable; why couldn't people use their reason to design an orderly, rational society? It was precisely this optimism that inspired the American Founding Fathers to construct a democracy that would be a model and a beacon of hope for the entire world.

John Locke, 1632–1704

The founders of the American republic had derived some political ideas from Montesquieu's *Spirit of the Laws* (1748), but they drew mainly from John Locke. Returning from exile after the Glorious Revolution, Locke wrote his *Two Treatises of Government* (1690) to justify constitutional monarchy. In the fifteenth essay from his *Second Treatise on Civil Government* Locke takes this position:

> Now this power, which every man has in the state of Nature, and which he parts with to the society in all such cases where the society can secure him, is to use such means for the preserving of his own property as he thinks good and Nature allows him; and to punish the breach of the law of Nature in others; so as (according to the best of his reason) may most conduce to the preservation of himself and the rest of mankind. So that the end and measure of this power, when in every other man's hands, in the state of Nature, being the preservation of all his society, that is, all mankind in general; it can have no other end or measure, when in the hands of the magistrate, but to preserve the members of that society in their lives, liberties, and possessions.

Locke assumed a natural law that operated in the affairs of human beings much as Newton's world-machine functioned according to natural law, a position also reflected in the opening paragraph of the Declaration of Independence as composed by Thomas Jefferson:

> When, in the course of human events, it becomes necessary for one people to dissolve the political bands which have connected them with another, and to assume, among the powers of the earth, the separate and equal station to which the laws of nature and of nature's God entitle them, a decent respect to the opinions of mankind requires that they should declare the causes which impel them to the separation.

According to Locke, this natural law gave people certain rights that were unalienable, and these were life, liberty, and property. Jefferson substituted for "property" a much more striking and challenging phrase:

> We hold these truths to be self-evident, that all men are created equal, that they are endowed by their Creator with certain unalienable Rights, that among these are Life, Liberty, and the pursuit of Happiness. That to secure these rights, Governments are instituted among Men, deriving their just powers from the consent of the governed.

Jefferson later explained how he regarded the Declaration:

> Neither aiming at originality of principles or sentiments, nor yet copied from any particular or previous writing, it was intended to be an expression of the American mind.

Locke wrote that government existed and had authority only because the people brought it into existence and gave it its authority. If the government violated its trust, the people had a natural right to set up a new government. They had a right to revolt.

The Wealth of Nations: Adam Smith, 1723–90

Exactly as Locke and Jefferson sought natural law as a guide to political affairs and Newton found such a law to be the binding force of the universe, so did Adam Smith seek a unifying principle for economic affairs. His work, interestingly enough, followed the scientific method that Bacon had established in the previous epoch; his investigations of the facts of economic life were conducted in a pin factory, leading to generalizations based on his factual findings.

Smith presented his principles of capitalism in 1776 in a book that quickly became a classic: *An Inquiry into the Nature and Causes of the Wealth of Nations*. In Smith's day capitalism had taken the form called mercantilism, a strictly regulated trade system controlled by each nation's government and based on the assumption that wealth depended on how much gold and silver that nation possessed. Increasing the supply of precious metals required a favorable balance of trade, i.e., more exports than imports. With every nation seeking a favorable trade balance the system will inevitably collapse—with one way out. A colonial nation can exploit its colonies as a source of cheap raw materials and a dumping ground for more expensive manufactured goods—so England treated its American colonies. Eventually, colonies will either develop their own manufacturing or be bled dry by the mother country. The system fails again.

Some French economists, called physiocrats, were the first to revolt against mercantilism. They claimed that a nation's wealth depended on its raw materials rather than the supply of money. They also believed that government regulation of trade and commerce was detrimental to economic well-being and progress. Adam Smith studied with this group while fleshing out his own theories.

Smith sought a reasonable balance in economic affairs that would insure an adequate supply of goods to meet the needs of human beings. He wanted these produced and sold at a fair price so that most people could buy the goods while the laborer earned a decent wage and the manufacturer reaped a reasonable profit. To solve this intricate problem he proposed a return to nature in economic affairs: the removal of all restrictions on wages and the manufacture and sale of goods. This is the unfettered competition called *laissez-faire* that can be demonstrated by the following example.

Smith's first premise is that people are acquisitive by nature with an endless craving for wealth. So an enterpriser with investment capital sees that people need shoes. He builds a shoe factory and charges whatever the traffic will bear. Other capitalists eye the large profits and rush into the shoe business. As the number of shoes increases, the price necessarily drops if, according to *laissez-faire* doctrine, everyone has equal access to raw materials and to markets with no regulation whatever. Eventually there are more shoes than buyers and prices are slashed to stimulate sales, driving the least efficient manufacturers out of business. As demand overtakes supply the price begins to regulate itself. Finally, production is adequate for people's needs, the price is stable, and the most efficient producers can make a fair profit. Labor, however, is still missing from this formula.

Labor, says Smith, is a commodity for sale just like shoes. Wages will be high in a new field and laborers will flock to this work, but wages will decline as workers become plentiful. Finally, the labor market in shoe production will become glutted, and wages will fall to less than a living wage, forcing the least competent workers into other employment. Eventually the price of labor, like that of shoes, will stabilize, with the most efficient workers employed at a fair wage. Those laid off will find other work at which they are more efficient, and, presumably, better able to make a living.

From these examples we can abstract the principles of Smith's *laissez-faire* economy. First, labor is the source of a nation's wealth. Second, all people are acquisitive. Third, there must be unregulated access to raw materials, labor, and markets. Fourth, each person has a natural endowment of skills that should determine the kind of work to be done; a free choice of employment should lead the worker into the most congenial job. Fifth, if all the conditions above exist, the law of supply and demand will solve the problem of sufficient goods, satisfactory price, adequate profit, and fair wages. Furthermore, each person will be doing what he or she can do best, and thus the most enjoyable kind of occupation. Q.E.D.

Or almost Q.E.D. One problem remained, which Smith recognized, without producing an adequate solution. He realized that monopolies might limit or eliminate competition and proposed that governments protect free competition by controlling monopolies; he could not, however, suggest any procedures that did not also regulate industry. Modern capitalist nations have solved the problem with regulations and controls that still permit the operation of Smith's laws of supply and demand in a relatively free marketplace. Constant vigilance against monopolies is, of course, essential.

Smith's economic system was similar to Locke's political philosophy and to the universal law of gravitation. The first step is a return to nature; human differences and limitations are the natural parameters. Nature will then provide a self-regulating economic mechanism. The natural forces of supply and demand, like the mutual gravitational pulls of planets and suns, like the pulls of executive and legislative branches of government, will shape the economy into a smoothly operating machine. Adam Smith contributed a principle on which an economy could be organized and operated, leading, in the fullness of time, to productive and affluent societies. Today's capitalistic economies do not function as well as everyone would like, but there is no doubt that modern capitalism, like modern democracy, functions better than anything else yet devised. The catastrophic failure of socialism's central-planning economies that had neither private property nor free enterprise vividly highlights the basic validity of Smith's theories.

Philosophy and *Les Philosophes*

Locke and Educational Theory

John Locke made yet another contribution that greatly influenced education and other human institutions. He said that the mind, at birth, was a complete blank, a *tabula rasa* (Lat., "blank slate"). This contradicted royalists, clergymen, and others, who insisted that the natural inclination, at birth, was submission to authority. Not so, said Locke. The mind was a spotless tablet on which would be written all the experiences the individual had throughout life. Shaping men and women into good citizens who were honest and responsible members of society required, therefore, positive, reinforcing experiences beginning early in life. Beyond the family, a formal education, according to Locke, was the best way of providing the good experiences that help form healthy and independent personalities.

The process is rational. One starts with the human mind as raw material and molds it, so to speak, with a solid education. The finished product is, at least theoretically, a good person. The process can, of course, work in the opposite direction, for bad experiences could produce a bad person. Most of our current ideas of universal education in a constructive environment are based on Locke's educational philosophy. Along with Socrates, men and women of the Enlightenment believed that virtue was knowledge and ignorance vice, and that an educated mind was its own reward. It still is.

David Hume, 1711–76

Locke's theories of mind and understanding revealed some inconsistencies that were later filled in by the Scottish philosopher David Hume, a lucid and urbane man who epitomized the enlightened thinker. Beginning with Locke's empiricist theory of knowledge, Hume proved that human reason has its limits. Anticipating a great public outcry, he published, in three volumes, *A Treatise of Human Nature, being an Attempt to Introduce the Experimental Method of Reasoning into Moral Subjects* (1739–40). Instead, no one noticed the book at the time; as Hume sadly noted, "it fell dead-born from the press." It could not, however, be ignored for long. In the first volume Hume granted certain knowledge only to arithmetic and algebra, and to geometry providing the axioms are true. Beyond that, he said, there was only probable knowledge, thus anticipating modern scientific thought.

Hume's principal concern was with cause and effect, or causality. If we observe that a certain event A is always followed by B, then we assume that A causes B. If, for example, we hold a match to a piece of paper and see the paper burn, we connect the two events and say that the flaming match caused the paper to burn. Not so, says Hume. That paper always burns when a match is held to it is a *belief* developed through *custom*, that is, experience. Because we have seen this happen so often we assume that it must happen every time. Therein lies the rub. Because A (the match) does not cause B (paper) to burn, we cannot assume that the paper is certain to burn; it is a probability but not a certainty. The paper, for example, could have been soaked in a chemical that no amount of flame would set afire. Further, we cannot bite into an apple with the certainty that it will taste like an apple; it could taste like roast pork.

We assume that the sun will rise tomorrow, but it is impossible to establish that it must necessarily rise. Newton's law of universal gravitation is therefore probable and not necessarily universal. As space vehicles have probed ever deeper into the cosmos, scientists have watched with extreme curiosity to see if Newton's law remains valid. There have been no inconsistencies to date, but no scientist would be willing to predict what the situation might be somewhere way out there. As Hume says, human reason has its limits. He accepted a world based on probability rather than certainty. Through observation and reasoning we can determine, short of certainty, how nature operates, but not why.

Hume's skepticism also applied to religion and religious beliefs and followed a long history of serious doubts about the truths of Judaism and Christianity. In the sixteenth century Uriel da Costa, a Portuguese Jewish refugee in Holland, started out questioning the truths of orthodox Judaism and ended up maintaining that all religions were made by human beings. The French skeptic Isaac la Peyrère wrote *Man Before Adam* (1656) in which he claimed that there were people all over the world before Adam; therefore, the Bible could not be an accurate account of human history. La Peyrère's work led two biblical scholars, Baruch de Spinoza (1632–77) and Father Richard Simon (1638–1712), to reexamine religious knowledge. Spinoza concluded that the Bible was not divine revelation but merely a history of Jewish activities and superstitions. He proposed instead a religious pantheism in which all existence was embraced in one substance (God or Nature), a position that would appeal to the coming Romantic movement. Father Simon, the greatest biblical scholar of his age, declared that scholars could never find an accurate text of

---

THE SALONS OF PARIS

Invented in Paris in the early seventeenth century, the European Salon rose to great popularity during the eighteenth century in Rome, Vienna, Berlin, London, and, especially, in Paris. Salons were usually formed by women, *salonières*, who opened their homes to the intellectual, artistic, and social elite of the time. The most fashionable salons were hosted by witty, well-informed, and intelligent *salonières* who provided a gracious atmosphere, fine foods, and a large number of very interesting guests. Attended mostly by men, including Voltaire, Hume, and many of the Encyclopedists, salons were increasingly criticized later in the century because they were controlled by women. David Hume chided France for allowing itself to be governed by women. John Locke omitted women from his idea of natural freedom and Rousseau contended that women should stick to their domestic activities and leave intellectual and artistic pursuits to men. The demise of the salon was not far behind.

NATURAL DISASTER AND THE ENLIGHTENMENT

On 1 November 1755 Lisbon, in Portugal, was a wealthy trading city widely known for great piety. The three tremendous earthquakes that shook and burned and flooded the city on that day destroyed most of the wealth, 17,000 out of 20,000 homes, and the lives of over 60,000 people. Why Lisbon? Stern priests daily preached hundreds of sermons telling the stunned survivors that God was punishing them for their sins and would do so again if they did not repent. But, knowing how many children had perished on that dreadful day, people began to question God's mercy and compassion. Further, they asked the priests why God destroyed so many churches while sparing a whole street of brothels. No one had an answer. Among those writing pamphlets on the controversy were scientists who blamed the quake not on human sins but on movements of the earth. The relentless priests were eventually jailed to shut them up. The Lisbon earthquake marked a critical turning point in human attitudes toward natural disasters.

the Bible nor discover what it really meant. Unlike Spinoza, Simon was convinced that there was a biblical message and tried, in vain, to determine what the message was.

The most famous of the French skeptics, Pierre Bayle (1647–1706), wrote a *Historical and Critical Dictionary* (1697–1702), in which he undermined the metaphysical theories of Descartes, Spinoza, Locke, and Leibniz, attacked all existing theologies, ridiculed the heroes of the Old Testament, and challenged all rational knowledge. He advocated abandoning reason in favor of blind faith, for all things, all understandings, were doubtful — except, perhaps, historical descriptions. Voltaire called Bayle's *Dictionary* the "Arsenal of the Enlightenment."

An avid reader of Bayle, Hume saw, as apparently no other Enlightenment thinker did, the plight of human beings if Bayle's skepticism could not be countered. Hume never doubted that people could be certain about the evils of murder, stealing, and the like, nor need they be unsure about Newton's laws. Uncertainty belonged in the philosopher's study. Hume anticipated modern science by stating that there were no absolute truths and, further, that one should not, must not, believe anything absolutely. He was particularly concerned about religious conflicts. "Errors in religion," he wrote, "are dangerous; those in philosophy only ridiculous." He believed, in the final analysis, that people could lead their lives as he did his, exercising their natural passions and common sense as they cheerfully enjoyed the uncertainties of everyday life.

Immanuel Kant, 1724–1804

The leading thinker of the German Enlightenment, Kant responded to Hume's skepticism with the famous remark that he had been "awakened from his dogmatic slumbers." In his three *Critiques* (*Pure Reason*, 1781; *Practical Reason*, 1788; *Judgement*, 1793) Kant presented a complete philosophical system. He showed that knowledge *a priori* was possible because people could perceive the world of space, forms, and causality and, because of the intrinsic nature of the human mind, understand phenomena. As he said, we can know only such appearances as colors, shapes, and sounds, but never the thing-in-itself; true knowledge cannot transcend experience. But we can have reliable knowledge because all minds function in the same way.

In ethics Kant stated that good actions must be performed from a sense of duty and that moral law was derived from his categorical imperative: "Act only according to the maxim which you at the same time will to be a universal law." People, he said, were independent moral agents with the freedom to choose right actions. As a practical necessity Kant postulated the existence of God for those who desired (or required) a belief in divinity, so that virtue could be crowned with happiness and immortality, and the pursuit of moral perfection continue in the afterlife.

With ethical and moral theories that appealed to the heart as opposed to Hume's dispassionate rationalism, Kant was the founder of the German philosophical movement known as Idealism. Subsequently, his philosophy had enormous appeal for the German Romantic movement. Kant was, however, an enlightened rather than a proto-Romantic thinker. His principle that every person had to be considered as an end in herself or himself is a form of the Enlightenment doctrine of the Rights of Man. Kant coined, moreover, the prevailing motto for the Enlightenment: "Dare to Know!"

Les Philosophes

Called *les philosophes* ("the philosophers") or *Encyclopédistes* because most of them wrote articles for Diderot's monumental *Encyclopedia*, the *philosophes* included writers, poets, artists, dramatists, mathematicians, and scientists. What they had in common was the French language, which had become the international language of the Enlightenment, leading to the comment that everyone had two homelands: his own and France. One of the leading *philosophes*, Denis Diderot (dee-duh-ro; 1713–84), was editor-in-chief of the *Encyclopedia* (1747–72), which he conceived of after he had translated the groundbreaking *Cyclopedia* of the Scotsman Ephraim Chambers. With characteristic wit he remarked that "there is no need to understand a language to translate it, since one translates it only for people who understand it not." For Diderot translation became creation, leading to his own *Encyclopedia*. For Diderot and the other *philosophes*, it was time for a secular, more democratic, world to replace a hierarchical, religious one. Published in twenty-eight volumes but suppressed in 1759 by the government and thereafter print-ed clandestinely, the work was a summary of all human knowledge, a brilliant response to Kant's "Dare to Know!" Its prevailing spirit was scorn for the past and for all orga-nized religions, and glorification of reason, the arts, the experimental sciences, and industry. The *Encyclopedia* assumed that religious toleration and freedom of thought would win out and implied throughout that the condition of the common people should be the main concern of the government. A call to arms in twenty-eight volumes, the *Encyclopedia* was probably, for the intellectuals, the key influence that led to the French Revolution.

In his *Persian Letters* (published anonymously in 1721) Montesquieu (mon-tes-kyu; 1689–1755) satirized European, especially French, society, leaving no phase of human activ-ity untouched by his devastating wit and irony. His most influential book, *The Spirit of the Laws* (1748), was a sci-entific study of comparative government whose theories of checks and balances found their way into the United States Constitution.

Diderot, Voltaire, and Rousseau were the most influ-ential of the French *philosophes*. A kind of reverse image of Voltaire the rationalist, Rousseau was a powerful influ-ence on the Romantic movement (see p. 396).

Absolutism and the Enlightenment

Louis XIV was a despot but, with some justification, he could also be called an enlightened monarch. The same cannot be said for the next two kings. Louis XV, great grand-son of Louis XIV, ruled ineptly but luxuriously from 1715 to 1774, and his weak and vacillating grandson, Louis XVI (reigned 1774–93), went to the guillotine.

A rival state, the kingdom of Brandenburg-Prussia, rose to power during the decline of French authority. Frederick I was crowned the first king of Prussia in 1701, followed by Frederick William I (reigned 1713–40), who began Prussian expansion. Frederick the Great (reigned 1740–86) excelled at waging war and made Prussia the dominant military power in Europe. Known as a "benev-olent despot," he promoted social and legal reforms and established a glittering court with musical performances by Johann Sebastian Bach and by Frederick himself. But the king did remark that "my people say what they please and I do as I please." Enlightenment had a way to go.

The founder of the modern Russian state, Peter the Great (reigned 1682–1725), mercilessly "westernized" his country and savagely destroyed his enemies. He was admit-tedly a genius and undoubtedly more than a bit mad. To this day he has been admired as an enlightened leader and viewed with horror as a sadistic monster. Catherine the Great (reigned 1762–91) was of German birth, but she became thoroughly Russianized. Influenced by the Enlightenment, she planned vast reforms, but a peasant revolt in 1773–5 and the French Revolution caused her to reverse course. She issued, among other authoritarian decrees, one to enslave the peasants. Absolutism during the Enlightenment was anything but enlightened.

Only in Great Britain was there any real political free-dom. Under the Hanoverian kings George I (reigned 1714–27) and George II (reigned 1727–60), Robert Walpole became, in fact if not in name, the prime minister (in office 1721–42). William Pitt (in office 1757–61) was a strong prime minister, but resigned when the next king, George III (reigned 1760–1820), decided he wanted to direct poli-cy. Lord North was an acquiescent prime minister and between king and prime minister they inadvertently brought a new democratic republic into being.

LITERATURE, 1600–1789

John Donne, 1573–1631

Although the seventeenth century is often referred to as the Baroque era, the term is more appropriate for art and music (see chapters 21 and 22) than it is for literature. Donne's poetry does display some of the opulence and splendor asso-ciated with the Baroque, but Donne has, instead, been char-acterized as the leader of the Metaphysical school, referring, in general, to the powerful intellectual content of his work, his concentrated images, and his remarkable ability to range between the intensely personal and the cosmic. Poets such as Andrew Marvell were influenced by Donne, but they formed no organized school nor would they have endorsed the Metaphysical label that John Dryden and Samuel Johnson affixed to the poetry of Donne and Marvell.

Poet, prose stylist, and preacher, John Donne was an experienced man of the world who spoke with great intel-lectual vigor in his love poems and in his Holy Sonnets. Neglected for three centuries after his death, he is now rec-ognized as one of the finest poets in the English language.

In the following song (given here in modernized spelling) Donne uses six vivid images to express the impos-sibility, as he saw it, of woman's constancy.

LITERARY SELECTION 22

Song

John Donne

Go and catch a falling star,
    Get with child a mandrake root,
Tell me, where all past years are,
    Or who cleft the devil's foot,
Teach me to hear mermaids singing,
Or to keep off envy's stinging,
    And find

What wind
Serves to advance an honest mind.

If thou be'st born to strange sights,   10
    Things invisible to see,
Ride ten thousand days and nights,
    Till age snow white hairs on thee;
Thou, when thou return'st, wilt tell me
All strange wonders that befell thee,
        And swear
        Nowhere
Lives a woman true and fair.

If thou find'st one, let me know,
    Such a pilgrimage were sweet;   20
Yet do not, I would not go,
    Though at next door we might meet,
Though she were true when you met her,
And last, till you write your letter,
        Yet she
        Will be
False, ere I come, to two, or three.

The following poem employs unique images that reflect Donne's secret marriage to his patron's niece, a happy union but one that clouded the rest of the poet's life. Only John Donne could effectively express life, love, and loving in terms of a flea.

The Flea

John Donne

Mark but this flea, and mark in this,
How little that which thou deniest me is;
It sucked me first, and now sucks thee,
And in this flea, our two bloods mingled be;
Thou know'st that this cannot be said
A sin, nor shame, nor loss of maidenhead,
    Yet this enjoys before it woo,
    And pampered swells with one blood made of two,
    And this, alas! is more than we would do.

Oh stay, three lives in one flea spare,   10
Where we almost, yea more than married are.
This flea is you and I, and this
Our marriage-bed, and marriage-temple is;
Though parents grudge, and you, we're met
And cloistered in these living walls of jet.
    Though use make you apt to kill me,
    Let not, to that, self-murder added be,
    And sacrilege, three sins in killing three.
Cruel and sudden, hast thou since
Purpled thy nail, in blood of innocence?   20
In what could this flea guilty be,
Except in that drop which it sucked from thee?
Yet thou triumph'st, and say'st that thou
Find'st not thyself, nor me the weaker now;
    'Tis true, then learn how false, fears be;
    Just so much honor, when thou yield'st to me,
    Will waste, as this flea's death took life from thee.

Of Donne's large volume of religious poetry some, near the end of his career, reflected his obsession with the thought of death. In the following Holy Sonnet he uses intense language and vivid images to put death in perspective.

Holy Sonnet X

John Donne

Death, be not proud, though some have called thee
Mighty and dreadful, for thou art not so;
For those whom thou think'st thou dost overthrow
Die not, poor Death, nor yet canst thou kill me.
From rest and sleep, which but thy pictures be,
Much pleasure, then from thee much more must flow;
And soonest our best men with thee do go,
Rest of their bones, and soul's delivery.
Thou art slave to Fate, chance, kings, and desperate men,
And dost with poison, war, and sickness dwell,
And poppy or charms can make us sleep as well
And better than thy stroke; why swell'st thou then?
One short sleep past, we wake eternally
And Death shall be no more; Death, thou shalt die.

STUDY QUESTION

Donne's poetry has been aptly called "strong-lined" because of his powerful images and sharp changes in rhythm. Try reading his "Song" aloud, listening for the abrupt change in rhythm of "And find/What wind" plus similar changes in the second and third stanzas. How much do these contribute to "strong-lined" poetry?

Andrew Marvell, 1621–78

Late in his career Marvell wrote stinging political satires, but he is best known today for his classically inspired lyric poetry about love and nature. "To His Coy Mistress" is a seduction poem in the tradition of Catullus and other classical writers. The theme is the fleeting moment and the tone is urgent. We must seize the moment and make love now. Though the theme is serious, the style is both graceful and playful.

LITERARY SELECTION 23

To His Coy Mistress

Andrew Marvell

Had we but World enough, and Time,
This coyness Lady were no crime.

We would sit down, and think which way
To walk, and pass our long Loves Day.
Thou by the *Indian Ganges* side
Should'st Rubies find: I by the Tide
Of *Humber* would complain. I would
Love you ten years before the Flood:
And you should if you please refuse
Till the Conversion of the *Jews*.   10
My vegetable Love should grow
Vaster than Empires, and more slow.
An hundred years should go to praise
Thine Eyes, and on thy Forehead Gaze.
Two hundred to adore each Breast:
But thirty thousand to the rest.
An Age at least to every part,
And the last Age should show your Heart.
For Lady you deserve this State;
Nor would I love at lower rate.   20
   But at my back I alwaies hear
Times winged Charriot hurrying near:
And yonder all before us lye
Deserts of vast Eternity.
Thy Beauty shall no more be found,
Nor, in thy marble Vault, shall sound
My echoing Song: then Worms shall try
That long preserv'd Virginity:
And your quaint Honour turn to dust;
And into ashes all my Lust.   30
The Grave's a fine and private place,
But none I think do there embrace.
   Now therefore, while the youthful hew
Sits on thy skin like morning dew,
And while thy willing Soul transpires
At every pore with instant Fires,
Now let us sport us while we may;
And now, like am'rous birds of prey,
Rather at once our Time devour,
Than languish in his slow-chapt pow'r.   40
Let us roll all our Strength, and all
Our sweetness, up into one Ball:
And tear our Pleasures with rough strife,
Thorough the Iron gates of Life.
Thus, though we cannot make our Sun
Stand still, yet we will make him run.

STUDY QUESTION

Did the Coy Mistress acquiesce? Look again at the first
and last lines, at the progression from not having
enough time to the illusion of time flying by.

John Milton, 1608–74

An ardent supporter of the Puritan cause, Milton became
Latin secretary in Cromwell's government and, in several
important tracts, one of its principal defenders. On the
restoration of the Stuart monarchy with Charles II (1660),
Milton was fined and forced to retire, after which he dic-
tated his epic poems, *Paradise Lost* (1667) and *Paradise
Regained* (1671). One of the world's great epic poems,
Paradise Lost relates the story of Satan's rebellion against
God and the Fall of Man. Milton's intention was, as he said,
to "justify the ways of God to man."

    The epic poems were among the first to use blank verse
(unrhymed iambic pentameter), but Milton also wrote some
notable sonnets. Considered to be among his finest work in
small form, the two sonnets given below are in the standard
form of fourteen lines in rhymed iambic pentameter.

    On Easter Sunday in 1655, in the Piedmont region of
northwestern Italy, the Duke of Savoy slaughtered about
1,700 members of the Protestant Waldensian sect that dated
back to 1170. The pope celebrated the occasion with a special Mass but Protestant Europe was horrified; Milton's
response was a sonnet tense with low-keyed fury. The "martyred blood" refers to Tertullian's statement that "the blood
of the martyrs is the seed of the Church." The "triple Tyrant"
is the pope, whose tiara has three crowns, and "Babylonian
woe" is a reference to Revelation 18 in which the oblitera-
tion of the city of luxury and vice is described. Along with
many Protestants, especially Puritans, Milton saw the
destruction of Babylon as an allegory of the ultimate fate of
the Church of Rome.

LITERARY SELECTION 24

On the Late Massacre in Piedmont (1655)

John Milton

Avenge, O Lord, thy slaughtered Saints, whose bones
   Lie scattered on the Alpine mountains cold;
   Even them who kept thy truth so pure of old,
When all our fathers worshipped stocks and stones,
Forget not: in thy book record their groans
   Who were thy sheep, and in their ancient fold
   Slain by the bloody Piedmontese, that rolled
Mother with infant down the rocks. Their moans
The vales redoubled to the hills, and they
   To heaven. Their martyred blood and ashes sow
O'er all the Italian fields, where still doth sway
   The triple Tyrant; that from these may grow
A hundredfold, who, having learnt thy way,
   Early may fly the Babylonian woe.

Milton's eyesight, owing to overwork, had become impaired as early as 1644, and by 1652 he was totally blind. The first of two sonnets about his blindness, the following poem signals the poet's submission to fate though he had not yet found his way to using, in darkness, "that one talent which is death to hide."

On His Blindness (1655)

John Milton

When I consider how my light is spent
    Ere half my days in this dark world and wide,
    And that one Talent which is death to hide
Lodged with me useless, though my soul more bent
To serve therewith my Maker, and present
    My true account, lest He returning chide,
    "Doth God exact day-labour, light denied?"
I fondly ask. But Patience, to prevent
That murmur, soon replies, "God doth not need
    Either man's work or his own gifts. Who best
    Bear his mild yoke, they serve him best. His state
Is kingly: thousands at his bidding speed,
    And post o'er land and ocean without rest;
    They also serve who only stand and wait."

STUDY QUESTION

Milton seethes with indignation over the fate of the slaughtered saints in Italy, but not over the loss of his sight. What are some of the words that convey this mood of resignation? Consider, for example, such words as "spent," "bent" "mild," and "murmur."

Thomas Jefferson, 1743–1826

The American Revolution (1775–1783) was hailed as the first significant triumph of rationalism. The causes of the uprising were certainly as much economic as ideological, yet liberal rational beliefs prevailed over the imposition of absolute authority. One of the clearest voices of the new nation was that of Thomas Jefferson, author of the Declaration of Independence, third president of the United States, and founder of the University of Virginia, the last being, for Jefferson, his most significant achievement. Jefferson's address on first assuming the presidency (First Inaugural Address) is a masterful speech that summarizes the ideals of the Enlightenment.

SUMMARY

It was not until the 1648 Peace of Westphalia that Europe was fully launched on a new age freed from medievalism. The physical world had been transformed by inventions such as gunpowder and the printing press, and the work of Bacon, Descartes, and Galileo began to change ways of thinking about the world.

At the beginning of the seventeenth century England and France had absolute monarchs, but the Glorious Revolution of 1688 saw William and Mary on the English throne as rulers of a constitutional monarchy. In France, however, Louis XIV was a divine-right king throughout the longest reign (1643–1715) of any monarch.

The publication of Newton's *Principia* in 1687 marked the dawn of the Enlightenment, an optimistic new age that relied on the intellect to design a rational society in a knowable universe. Newton had discovered the law of universal gravitation, John Locke relied on natural law as a guide to political affairs, and Adam Smith developed a similar unifying principle for economic affairs. Locke's theories of knowledge were later refined by David Hume, who granted certain knowledge only to mathematics, with all other knowledge as only probable. Immanuel Kant reacted to Hume's skepticism with an idealistic philosophy that highlighted the German Enlightenment. In France, the *philosophes* Diderot, Montesquieu, Voltaire, and others wrote articles for the *Encyclopedia*, a monumental summary of all human knowledge.

Paradoxically, the Enlightenment had little influence on the absolute rulers in France, Prussia, and Russia. Only in England was there any political freedom; the most democratic nation in Europe set the forces in motion that led to the triumph of the Enlightenment in the New World.

CULTURE AND HUMAN VALUES

The Enlightenment was victorious in the United States from 1776 but failed in France only thirteen years later. How could the Enlightenment fail in its country of origin—the land of Voltaire, Diderot, and Montesquieu?

Both revolutions intended to replace an autocratic regime with a republican form of government, but there the similarity ends. A prime ingredient in the American success story was the extended and invaluable experience in the art of self-government. The British crown had long pursued a policy of benign neglect; acts of the colonial assemblies were rarely questioned, let alone vetoed by a royally appointed governor or the king himself. There was no titled nobility and, most importantly, no state church. Colonial society had a backbone of a solid middle class of farmers and merchants, particularly in the northern colonies. Further, the Founding Fathers, firmly grounded in Enlightenment ideals, were convinced that human beings had the ability to govern themselves in a sane and rational manner. They not only assumed that people could realize their potential, but designed a government and a constitution that enabled its citizens to do so.

The French revolted against a royal power unchallenged for centuries, a creaking monarchy that had piled up a mountain of abuses. It was not the only problem, however. France was more advanced than other continental nations, but its social organization was inherited from the Middle Ages. By the eighteenth century the class structure had evolved into a First Estate (clergy), a Second Estate (nobility), with 97 percent of the population lumped into a Third Estate (commoners). The Third Estate and some of the clergy and nobility favored reforms, but the commoners had been abused by everyone and longed for an end to the throne, the nobility, and the church. But, with no experience in government, there was no workable alternative to the Old Regime.

Hatred of the Old Regime and its abuses was such a dominant factor there was no room left for restraint and reason. Liberty was quickly achieved, but equality was an impossible dream. Within just a few years any feelings of fraternity had vanished during the unleashed passions that led to the Reign of Terror and, finally, to the dictatorship of Napoleon and the Napoleonic Wars. The French Revolution had, at the time, failed just as completely as the American Revolution had succeeded. But it was the establishment of a New World democracy that provided hope and inspiration for a weary Old World.

In terms of the culture-epoch theory the period from 1600 to 1789, the Early Modern World, can be seen, in retrospect, as one of relative balance, preceded by the tumultuous Renaissance and followed by the French Revolution and the Napoleonic Wars. Certainly both the seventeenth and eighteenth centuries were glorious years of superb artistic achievement.

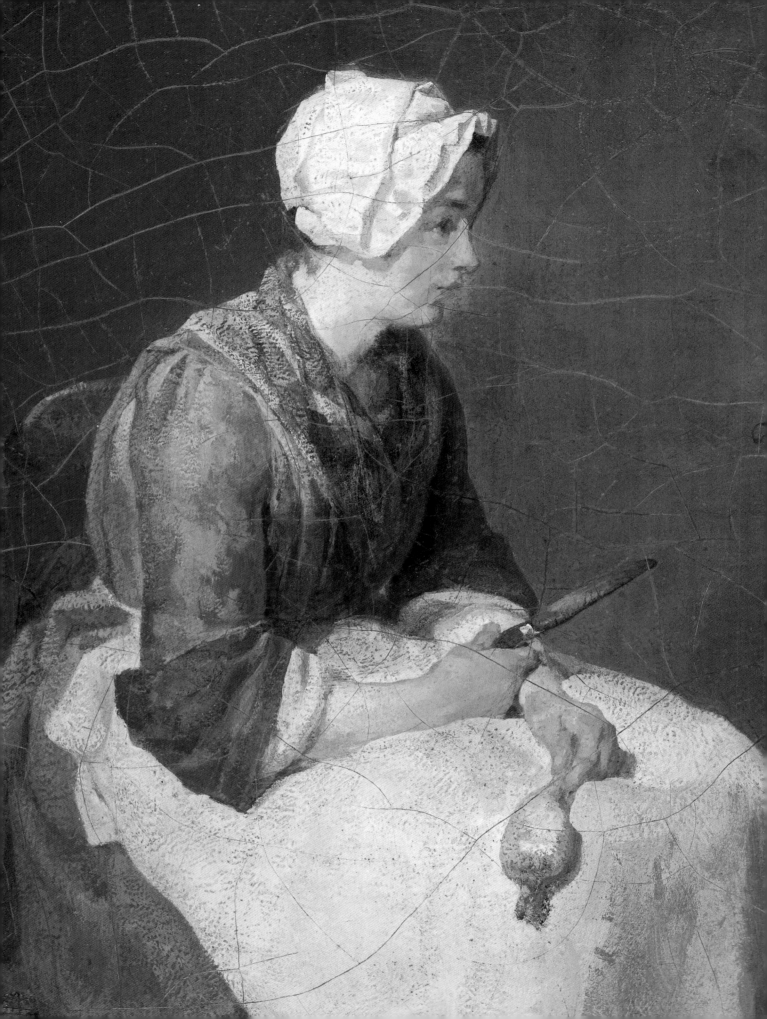

CHAPTER 21

Art: Baroque, Rococo, and Neoclassic

THE BAROQUE AGE, CA. 1580–1700

An age of expansion following the Renaissance era of discovery, the Baroque was a period of conflicts and contradictions that encompassed extremes: Louis XIV and Rembrandt; Bernini and Descartes; Milton and Bach. In architecture and the visual arts the Baroque began in the last quarter of the sixteenth century; and it extended into the eighteenth, culminating in the music of Bach and Handel (see pp. 376–8).

The characteristics of Baroque art are movement, intensity, tension, and energy, traits that are more often associated with music than with the more static arts of painting, sculpture, and architecture. Nevertheless, revolutionary innovations in all the arts generated a Baroque style that could be extravagant, excessive, or even grotesque. At its best, Baroque art is vigorous, dazzling, opulent, colorful, and frequently theatrical, all in marked contrast to the High Renaissance canon of balance, restraint, and control. Most especially, the new style proclaimed the vigorous beginning of the contentious Early Modern World.

The sometimes contradictory variations of the Baroque style can be examined under three broad categories of patrons: the Counter-Reformation Church of Rome; the aristocratic courts of Louis XIV of France and the Stuarts of England; and the bourgeois merchants of Holland. Though drive, intensity, and contrast are common characteristics of all Baroque art, the style will be considered here as a set of reactions to the needs of these patrons and labeled Counter-Reformation, aristocratic, and bourgeois Baroque art.

21.1 *Right* G. B. Vignola (plan) and G. C. della Porta (facade), Il Gesù, Rome, 1568–84. Photo: Scala, Florence.

Opposite Jean-Baptiste-Siméon Chardin, *The Kitchen Maid*, detail. 1738. Oil on canvas, full painting 18⅛ × 14¾" (46.2 × 37.5 cm). National Gallery of Art, Washington, D.C. (Samuel H. Kress Collection).

Counter-Reformation Baroque

Founded in 1534 by Ignatius of Loyola, the Society of Jesus (Jesuits) formed the spearhead of the Counter-Reformation. The mother church of the order, Il Gesù ("Church of Jesus"), was the first building in the new style. It became a model for church design throughout the Roman Catholic world, especially in Latin America (fig. 21.1). The four pairs of pilasters on each level visually stabilize the facade and add a rhythmic punctuation that the evenly spaced columns of the classical style do not have (see fig. 17.2). Baroque architecture, from its very beginning, is characterized by the strong accents of paired columns or pilasters. The dramatic effect of paired pilaster and column framing a central portal under a double **cornice** exemplifies the theatricality of the Baroque style, making the entrance seem like an invitation to hurry into the church. The proportions of the two stories and the framing volutes are derived from Alberti's Santa Maria Novella (see fig. 17.11), whereas the classical pediment is reminiscent of Palladio (see fig. 17.39). Il Gesù

21.2 Il Gesù, Interior. Photo: Scala, Florence.

21.3 Caravaggio, *The Conversion of St. Paul*. Ca. 1601. Oil on canvas, 7′ 6″ × 5′ 9″ (2.29 × 1.75 m). Sta. Maria del Popolo, Rome.

is not a wholly new design but rather a skillful synthesis of existing elements in a new and dramatic style.

In the interior (fig. 21.2), chapels recessed in the walls replace side aisles, making the richly decorated central space a theatre for the enactment of the Lord's Supper. Light pours through the dome windows and on the high altar in this architectural embodiment of the militant and mystical Society of Jesus.

Michelangelo Merisi da Caravaggio, 1573–1610

The Baroque style of painting appeared abruptly in the person of the northern Italian artist called Caravaggio (ca-ra-VOD-jo), perhaps the first artist to deliberately shock not only the public but also his fellow artists. The most important Italian painter of the seventeenth century, Caravaggio was militantly opposed to such classical concepts as balance and restraint, claiming that nature would be his only teacher. Using chiaroscuro and nonrealistic dramatic lighting, his paintings had an intense psychological impact that profoundly influenced most Baroque artists, including Rembrandt and Velasquez. *The Conversion of St. Paul* (fig. 21.3) must have shocked everyone who saw it, for this is no reverent depiction of a biblical scene. This is the moment after Saul of Tarsus, while riding on the road to Damascus, experiences his vision of Christ, who asks why Saul persecutes him. In that instant Paul becomes a missionary for the new religion. The lighting is harsh and dramatic and the effect highly theatrical. The vivid contrast between light and dark (chiaroscuro) was a major innovation, one that first shocked and then enthralled contemporary artists. In a composition further dramatized by slashing diagonals, the realistically depicted horse towers over the recumbent Paul. Caravaggio was vividly explicit about his rejection of tradition, especially Renaissance idealism, which would hardly surprise anyone viewing this painting.

Caravaggio's life was as dramatic as his art. A man of violent passions, he killed another man in a fight and, badly wounded, fled Rome for Naples. Later thrown into prison, he violated his oath of obedience and escaped to Sicily, but subsequently returned to Naples where he was nearly fatally wounded in another fight. Destitute and ill with malaria, he died during a violent rage over a misunderstanding on the very day that his papal pardon was announced.

Artemisia Gentileschi, 1593–1652/3

A student of her father, who was a follower of Caravaggio, Gentileschi (jen-ti-LES-ki) was also strongly influenced by that artist's use of chiaroscuro and his frequently violent subject matter. Her preferred subjects were heroic women,

21.5 Gianlorenzo Bernini, *David*. 1623. Marble, life-size. Galleria Borghese, Rome. Photo: Alinari, Florence.

21.4 Artemisia Gentileschi, *Judith Slaying Holofernes*. 1620. Oil on canvas, 6' 6" × 5' 4" (1.98 × 1.63 m). Galleria degli Uffizi, Florence. Photo: Scala, Florence.

particularly Judith, whom she portrayed many times. In *Judith Slaying Holofernes* (fig. 21.4) she selected the exact moment in which Judith beheaded the enemy general, having tricked him to gain access to his tent. The Hebrew heroine works with the cold efficiency of an executioner as she also avoids the rush of blood. The extreme chiaroscuro emphasizes the drama and horror of the scene. Criticism from some of her contemporaries that her violent images were not "feminine" deterred her not at all. Unlike most women of her day, she had received a good education in painting solely because her father was a highly skilled artist, and she took full advantage of that training.

Gianlorenzo Bernini, 1598–1680

In his life and in his art Caravaggio was at odds with his time, but Bernini (bear-NEE-nee) was the Counter-Reformation personified. A superbly gifted sculptor and architect, with a virtuosity comparable to that of Michelangelo, Bernini was regarded in his own century as not only its best artist but also its greatest man. He himself saw that his renown would decline with the waning of Counter-Reformation energy, but his emotional art has now regained some of its luster. His *David* (fig. 21.5) is a young warrior tensely poised over his discarded armor and harp; every muscle strains to hurl the fatal stone at an unseen Goliath, who seems to be approaching from behind and above the level of the viewer. Compared with Michelangelo's *David* (see fig. 17.27), Bernini's sculpture has the intense energy of the Baroque, so much so that there is an impulse to leap out of the way of the stone missile. The bit lip is Bernini's own expression as copied from a mirror, and realism is further heightened by the grip of David's foot on the actual base of the statue. Completed just nine years before the Inquisition condemned Galileo (in 1632), *David* epitomizes Counter-Reformation fervor.

21.6   St. Peter's, Rome. Apse and dome by Michelangelo (1547–64); nave and facade by Carlo Maderno (1607–26); colonnade and piazza by Gianlorenzo Bernini (1617–67). Photo: Spectrum, London.

Rome was Bernini's city and he left his stamp on it literally everywhere, but nowhere else so effectively as in his enhancement of St. Peter's (fig. 21.6). The oval piazza, together with the embracing arms of the colossal colonnade, form a spectacular entrance to the largest church in Christendom. The 284 massive Doric columns are 39 feet (11.7 m) in height and are topped with 15-foot (4.5-m) statues of 96 saints, demarcating a piazza that can accommodate about 250,000 people. Bernini used the pavement design, the Egyptian obelisk, and the two fountains to unify the piazza and give it human scale. This fifty-year project was the crowning architectural achievement of the Counter-Reformation. Ironically, it was completed one year after the Great Fire of London had reduced much of that Protestant stronghold to rubble.

Once in the awesome nave of the church, the visitor is surrounded by other manifestations of Bernini's genius: monumental sculptures, the Throne of St. Peter, elegant

21.7   Gianlorenzo Bernini, Baldacchino. 1624–33. St Peter's, Rome. Photo: Scala, Florence.

21.8   Gianlorenzo Bernini, *Ecstasy of St. Theresa*. 1645–52. Marble and gilt, life-size. Cornaro Chapel, Sta. Maria della Vittoria, Rome. Photo: Scala, Florence.

relief carvings, even the patterned marble floor. Under Michelangelo's soaring dome stands the Baldacchino (ball-da-KEY-no; fig. 21.7), a canopy 85 feet (25.5 m) in height over the tomb of St. Peter. The title is derived from the Italian: *baldacco* is a silk cloth draped as a canopy over important people or places. In this case, the drapery is bronze as is the entire canopy, including the intricate designs covering the four columns. The Baldacchino was commissioned by the Barberini Pope Urban VIII, who ordered the bronze plates to be removed from the dome of the Pantheon and melted down, prompting the pope's physician to remark that "what the barbarians didn't do the Barberini did." Bernini patterned the serpentine column design after the twisted marble columns saved from Old St. Peter's, which were thought by Constantine to have survived from Solomon's Temple. Some critics refer to the Baldacchino as architecture and others as sculpture; in either case, it is an artistic triumph under difficult circumstances. It had to be large enough to be significant under Michelangelo's enormous dome, but not disproportionate to the size of the nave. Bernini himself called the solution one that "came out well by luck."

The appeal of Bernini's *Ecstasy of St. Theresa* (fig. 21.8) is emotional, mystical, spiritual, and, withal, palpably sensual. It is based on the writings of St. Theresa, the Spanish mystic, who is depicted in the throes of rapture as the angel is about to pierce her with the golden arrow of Divine Love. Epitomizing the Roman High Baroque, the altarpiece has become a stage for a theatrical work of intense religiosity, a visual counterpart of the *Spiritual Exercises* of Ignatius of Loyola that Bernini himself practiced every day.

Francesco Borromini, 1599–1644

Bernini was Pope Urban VIII's favorite, but by no means the only artist supported by the lavish building program that drained the Vatican treasury. One of Bernini's severest critics was rival architect Borromini (bor-o-ME-nee), a brooding and introspective genius who resented Bernini's favored status and grand reputation. Rejecting Bernini's predilection for rich marbles and lavishly painted stucco, Borromini concentrated on the interplay of elaborate curves and lines. In the small monastic Church of S. Carlo alle Quattro Fontane (fig. 21.9), Borromini used a series of

21.9 Francesco Borromini, *S. Carlo alle Quattro Fontane,* Rome. Begun 1638. Photo: Alinari, Florence.

21.10 Diego Velasquez, *Maids of Honor (Las Meninas).* 1656. Oil on canvas, 10' 5" × 9' (3.18 × 2.74 m). Museo del Prado, Madrid. Photo: Oronoz, Madrid.

intersecting ellipses in an undulating facade richly embellished with columns, sculpture, plaques, and scrolls, all in stone and relying for their effect on design rather than on opulent materials. The impression of restless, mystical passion must have had great appeal, for this small church was emulated throughout southern Europe.

Diego Velasquez, 1599–1660
Unlike his Spanish contemporaries, Velasquez (ve-LASS-kis) was not interested in religious subjects. Allegorical figures, swirling clouds, and rhapsodic faces were never part of a unique style that was concerned with nature and the optical effects of light. During his studies in Italy he became fascinated with the paintings of Titian and Tintoretto, but he cared not at all for the style of Raphael, nor was he influenced by Rubens even though they were friends. A court painter to King Philip IV for thirty years, Velasquez worked with the effects of light on objects and colors, producing candid portraits that never descended to the level of common courtly pictures. His *Maids of Honor* (fig. 21.10) is his acknowledged triumph and one of the most celebrated works of the century. The painting is a symphony of deep pictorial space, light, and images of reality, including what we actually see in the room and also the implied presence of the king and queen, whose images are reflected in the mirror. The artist apparently adapted the mirror idea from van Eyck's *Arnolfini Wedding Portrait* (see fig. 17.20), which was then in the Spanish Royal Collection.

The painter himself looks back at us as he works on a painting that is probably the one at which we are looking. At the front of the picture plane light falls on the dog with the child's foot placed on its back, on the court dwarf, and, in the near foreground, on the Infanta Margarita and her two attendants. Standing behind a lady-in-waiting and wearing the cross of the Order of Santiago, the artist pauses with paintbrush poised; slightly deeper in the middle ground we see a couple engaged in conversation. The mirror on the back wall marks the next step in receding space and, behind the courtier in the open doorway, space recedes to infinity. What at first looks like a genre scene in the artist's studio is actually a stunning spatial composition of five or six receding planes. As it is usually displayed in the Prado Museum, the painting faces a mirror on the opposite wall in which the spectator sees an electrifying image of receding space, an illusion that further confuses reality because the mirror includes the viewer as part of the painting. Space was a major preoccupation of the Baroque, from the large interiors of Baroque churches to the great piazza fronting St. Peter's, and the fascinating illusion of deep space in the *Maids of Honor.* Like most of the paintings of the period, the title was added in the nineteenth century when it was viewed by people other than the royal couple for whom it was originally painted. *Maids of Honor* so fascinated Pablo Picasso that he painted, in 1957, no less than forty-five different studies of all or part of this monumental creation.

Aristocratic Baroque

Peter Paul Rubens, 1577–1640

Rubens lived during an age marked by extremes. Galileo, Kepler, and Descartes were helping shape a new vision of the world, but there was also the dark and bloody side of misogynistic witchcraft trials, the Inquisition, and the savage Thirty Years' War. Throughout his entire lifetime Rubens' own country, the Netherlands, was struggling to free itself from ruthless Spanish power with its pitiless Spanish Inquisition, and yet Rubens painted works that jubilantly praised the human spirit and celebrated the beauty of the natural world. He was not indifferent to human suffering—far from it—but his temperament was wholly sunny and positive. He possessed a rare combination of robust health, good looks, common sense, a talent for business, phenomenal artistic ability, and a remarkable intellect. He was fluent in six modern languages and classical Latin and was reputed to be capable of listening to a learned lecture while painting, conversing, and dictating letters.

21.11   Peter Paul Rubens, *The Assumption of the Virgin*. Ca. 1626. Oil on panel, 49⅜ × 37⅛" (125.4 × 94.2 cm). National Gallery of Art, Washington, D.C. (Samuel H. Kress Collection).

One of the most gifted and accomplished painters who ever lived, Rubens amassed a fortune and enjoyed it all.

In only eight years of study in Italy Rubens mastered the classical style of ancient Rome plus the styles of the High and Late Renaissance. On completing a series of paintings for Marie de' Medici, the Dowager Queen of France, he established his reputation as the preeminent painter for kings, nobles, and princes of the church. *The Assumption of the Virgin* (fig. 21.11), though considerably smaller than his many giant paintings, is charged with the boundless energy that characterizes all his work. In diametric opposition to Caravaggio's stark realism, his figures are richly and colorfully garbed, with pink and chubby cherubs and solicitous angels effortlessly wafting the Virgin into heaven. The rich sensual quality of Rubens' work was prized by aristocratic patrons and by the church; glamor, grandeur, and glory provided favorable answers to any doubts of the faithful, assuring them that heaven and earth alike were equally splendid.

Anthony van Dyck, 1599–1641

No one knows how many assistants Rubens employed in his huge studio in Antwerp. As a court painter he paid no guild tax and therefore kept no records of the people who copied popular works or roughed out canvases that the master would complete and sell at a price based on the square footage and the extent of his involvement. Of the few assistants who were successful in their own right, van Dyke is by far the most notable. Unable to develop his talents in the overpowering presence of his teacher, van Dyck left to seek his fortune, which he found in abundance at the court of Charles I of England. With his aristocratic and refined style, van Dyck became the century's foremost portrait painter for court and church, producing elegant portrayals that always improved on the appearance of the model. Van Dyck portrays Charles I in a quiet moment in a beautiful English landscape (fig. 21.12). He conveys a feeling of both dignity and certitude, for this is no tentative monarch. This is a model of the art of portraiture in the grand manner.

Nicolas Poussin, 1594–1665

Throughout his mature career Poussin (poo-sã) painted in the grand manner, but in a style entirely different from that of van Dyck and especially Rubens. Emphasizing line, lucidity, and control, Poussin chose only lofty subject matter drawn from ancient history, mythology, and biblical stories. He was an elitist, an aristocrat of paint and canvas, a French classicist in an age of Baroque exuberance. Religious subjects were treated, he thought, in a base and vulgar manner in most of the works by Caravaggio and his followers. Poussin's Baroque classical style attracted followers just as did the quite different Baroque style of Rubens, touching off a controversy between "Rubenists" and "Poussinists" that may never be resolved. The basic disagreement was between color and line. Line and drawing were absolute values in representing things according to the Poussinists, and color

21.12 Anthony van Dyck, *Charles I of England*. 1635. Oil on canvas, 8' 8¾" × 6' 9¼" (2.66 × 2.07 m). Louvre, Paris. Photo: R.M.N., Paris.

was merely incidental because it depended on light. But Rubens and his followers were addicted to color. Rubenists painted the multicolored world as they perceived it, whereas the Poussinists constructed idealized forms of the world as it should be. Actually, the conflict was not just Rubenists versus Poussinists but the eternally opposing views of artists who were, in general, inclined toward romanticism as opposed to artists who were classically oriented. Romanticism in the nineteenth century is a stylistic period and is not to be confused with romantic or classical tendencies of artists in any period. When considered in very broad terms, the Renaissance was classically oriented, where-

as the Baroque was inclined toward romanticism except, of course, for Poussin. Classicists emphasize objectivity, rationality, balance, and control; romanticists stress subjectivity, nonrationality, and the restless expression of emotion. Leonardo, Raphael, Poussin, Haydn, and Mozart are classicists; Tintoretto, the later Michelangelo, El Greco, Rubens, Verdi, Tchaikovsky, and Delacroix are romanticists.

In *Holy Family on the Steps* (fig. 21.13) Poussin has designed an upward-angled perspective that is enforced by the steps across the bottom of the painting. Reminiscent of Raphael's style that Poussin studied assiduously, the triangular composition is slightly off-center, putting the head of Christ almost precisely in the mathematical center of the painting. From vases to temples the setting is Roman and the mode is derived, according to Poussin, from the ethos of the Greek musical scales which, in this case, may be the sweetly lyrical quality of the Ionic scale. Appearing

21.13 Nicolas Poussin, *Holy Family on the Steps*. 1648. Oil on canvas, 27 × 38½" (68.6 × 97.8 cm). National Gallery of Art, Washington, D.C. (Samuel H. Kress Collection).

at first to be starkly geometric, the composition has a drama and a classical beauty that are apparent in the balance of solids and voids, cylinders and cubes, and in the balanced contrast of hard stone and soft foliage, drapery and coolly supple flesh. To compare this work with the Rubens painting (fig. 21.11) is to understand the difference between classicism and romanticism in the broad sense in which these terms are used here.

Louis XIV and Versailles

French tastes were attuned to a rationalized version of the Baroque as represented in the work of Poussin and, on a grand scale, in the enormous royal palace at Versailles. Soon after Louis XIV assumed full control of the government in 1661, French classicism was deliberately used to create a "royal style" that reinforced and enhanced the absolute rule of the king of the most powerful nation in Europe. Classical architecture has, since that time, been used by banks to indicate their financial stability and by rulers and dictators from Napoleon to Hitler and Stalin to symbolize authority and power.

Originally a hunting lodge for Louis XIII, the Palace of Versailles was rebuilt and vastly enlarged for Louis XIV, the self-styled "Sun King" whose power was so immense that he supposedly declared that *"L'état, c'est moi"* ("I am the state"). He certainly said, "It is legal because I wish it." The royal portrait (fig. 21.14) illustrates the judgment of the English statesman Viscount Bolingbroke: "If he was not the greatest king, he was the best actor of majesty that ever filled a throne." Designed initially by Louis le Vau (VO; 1612–70) and completed by Jules Hardouin Mansart (mä-sar; 1646–1708), the Palace was oriented along an east-west axis with the western front facing the extensive gardens (fig. 21.15 and p. 331). Far too large to photograph at ground level in its entirety, the view shown is part of the garden

21.14 Hyacinthe Rigaud, *Portrait of Louis XIV*. 1701. Oil on canvas, 9' 1½ " × 6' 2⅝" (2.78 × 1.9 m). Louvre, Paris. Photo: R.M.N., Paris.

21.15 Louis le Vau and Jules Hardouin Mansart, Palace of Versailles, central section of garden facade. 1669–85. Photo: Robert Harding, London.

21.16 Frans Hals, *The Laughing Cavalier*. 1624. Oil on canvas, 33¾ × 27" (85.7 × 68.6 cm). Wallace Collection, London.

facade. The three-floor design is basically classical, with windows equally spaced and lined up above each other from ground-level French doors to the square top windows. The paired Ionic columns on the projecting fronts are Baroque and intended to enliven an exterior that would otherwise be bland and boring.

Bourgeois Baroque

Dutch art flourished in an environment utterly unlike the regal splendor of France or the flamboyant Baroque of the southern Catholic countries. Freed at last from the Spanish yoke, Holland became a prosperous trading nation: Protestant, hard-working, and predominantly middle class. Calvinism opposed images in churches, and there was no royal court or hereditary nobility, meaning that there were no traditional patrons of the arts. The new patrons were private collectors and there were many. Just about everyone in the nation of nearly 2,000,000 inhabitants wanted paintings for their living rooms, and schools of painting at Amsterdam, Haarlem, Delft, and Utrecht labored to supply a demand somewhat comparable to the Golden Age of Greece or fifteenth-century Florence.

Frans Hals, ca. 1580–1666

The first of the great Dutch masters, Hals was one of history's most brilliant portraitists. There is no precedent for the liveliness of his canvases or the spontaneous brilliance of his brushwork. In *The Laughing Cavalier* (fig. 21.16), a portly gentleman with hand on hip, his head jauntily tilted, stares at the viewer. Large surfaces are treated casually but the lacework and brocade are incredibly precise. Not a deep character study, this is a portrait of a passing acquaintance captured in a brief moment, but rendered as a momentary but uncompromising truth.

Judith Leyster, 1609–60

Leyster (LIE-ster) specialized in genre paintings, especially of musicians, and was one of the few artists prior to this century who could suggest musical performance through form, line, and color. In *Self-Portrait* (fig. 21.17) Leyster portrays herself in formal dress but in a relaxed and casual pose that echoes, in a lower key, the laughing violinist

21.18   Rembrandt van Rijn, *The Descent from the Cross*. 1650–5. Oil on canvas, 4' 8¼" × 3' 7¾" (1.43 × 1.11 m). National Gallery of Art, Washington, D.C. (Widener Collection). Photo: Richard Carafelli.

21.17   Judith Leyster, *Self-Portrait*. Ca. 1630. Oil on canvas, 29⅜ × 25⅞" (74.6 × 65.7 cm). National Gallery of Art, Washington, D.C. (Gift of Mr. and Mrs. Robert Woods Bliss). Photo: Lorene Emerson.

on her canvas, who is actually playing the instrument rather than just holding it. Although influenced by the Utrecht school of Caravaggio disciples and her teacher, Frans Hals, her style is clearly her own. However, it was not until this century that "Leyster" replaced "Hals" on several paintings that she had completed during her late teens or early twenties. She was, in fact, a well-known artist at the age of eighteen and the only woman among the thirty or more master painters in the Haarlem guild in the 1630s. However, she did not receive her first retrospective until 1993 when "A Dutch Master and Her World" opened at the Worcester Art Museum in Massachusetts.

Rembrandt van Rijn, 1606–69

Some Dutch artists such as Hals specialized in portraits, Leyster painted genre scenes, and others concentrated on history or landscapes. Rembrandt, however, worked with consummate ease in all areas. Sometimes called the Shakespeare of seventeenth-century painters, he is one of a handful of supreme masters of the entire European tradition. Calvinism frowned on religious images, which may explain why sculpture was not popular, but, on the other hand, the Reformed Church rejected all authority except individual conscience. This meant, in effect, that artists could study the Bible and create sacred images as they personally envisioned them, which is precisely what Rembrandt did. He could not accept the stern God of the Calvinists and he never painted a Last Judgment. He was concerned instead with the human drama of the Old Testament, the loving and forgiving God of the New Testament, and the life and passion of Christ. In *The Descent from the Cross* (fig. 21.18) the two main focal points of the drama are the body of Christ and the face of his fainting mother. Eliminating all superfluous details with his characteristic dark background, the artist conveys the tenderness with which the broken body is being lowered from the cross. The composition is extremely tight, concentrating our attention on the key figures and, through the skillful use of chiaroscuro, flooding the canvas with the most profound grief.

Jan Vermeer, 1632–75

Vermeer (ver-MEER) did not paint monumental subjects with the passion of Rembrandt, but he did possess a special magic that transmuted everyday reality into eternal

21.19   Jan Vermeer, *The Girl with the Red Hat*, after restoration. Ca. 1665. Oil on panel, 9⅛ × 7⅛" (23.2 × 18.1 cm). National Gallery of Art, Washington, D.C. (Andrew W. Mellon Collection). Photo: Richard Carafelli.

symbols. Fewer than forty of his paintings survive, and all but three are of sparsely furnished interiors of modest size. Vermeer, in fact, did for ordinary rooms what High Renaissance artists did for ordinary human bodies: elevated them to the level of universals. With an eye for detail comparable to van Dyck's, Vermeer specialized in light—natural light streaming into the interior, usually from the left, and filling a space punctuated by objects. His figures are seemingly suspended in light. In *Woman Holding a Balance* (see frontispiece on p.ii) Vermeer has created an apparently simple scene of a woman, probably his wife, Catharina, in one of her eleven pregnancies, holding an empty balance. With jewelry on the table and a painting of the Last Judgment on the wall, one might assume that this is a moral analogy, a weighing of worldly possessions against a background of divine judgment. Dutch Calvinists would not have had a Last Judgment anywhere in the house, but this may be Catharina's room and she, unlike her husband, was Catholic. Nevertheless, the mood is introspective and her expression serene. Catharina was married to a painter who never sold a painting, a man of extravagant tastes with a host of creditors, and in this painting she may simply be contentedly contemplating jewelry received from her loving husband. The highest level of art may not be to encourage laughter, passion, or tears but to invoke dreams, and dreams are perhaps best left unexplained.

After Vermeer's premature death, his paintings were used to satisfy creditors who undoubtedly had no more appreciation of his worth than the rest of a society that had ignored him. Not rediscovered until the 1860s, his paintings, with their use of color and light, were a revelation to the Impressionists, who thought themselves the first to discover that shadows were not black but also had color. In *The Girl with the Red Hat* (fig. 21.19), there is a technical mastery that, in combination with Vermeer's scientific study of light, makes this one of the finest works of the artist's brief mature period. Remarkable in its own right, the painting is also a tribute to the rapidly developing science of optics, for it is virtually certain that Jan Vermeer actually sought to simulate the camera obscura's effects. The principle of the camera obscura was described by Leonardo da Vinci and developed by Johannes Kepler: light passing through a small hole in the side wall of a dark room projects an image of outside objects onto an interior wall. Filling the hole with one of the new improved lenses would make the inside image as vivid as a color photograph. The artist did not copy the camera image; rather, he suggested the luminosity of such an image. Here, as if they were visualized molecules, we see floating globules of colored light. Light glints from an eye, an earring, and the lips of a young woman unexpectedly caught in a soft-focus candid "photograph."

Jacob van Ruisdael, 1628–82

Vermeer exploited color and light, but Ruisdael (ROISdale) specialized in space. The finest Dutch landscape

21.20 Jacob van Ruisdael, *View of Haarlem from the Dunes at Overveen*. Ca. 1670. Oil on canvas, 25 × 22" (63.5 × 55.9 cm). Mauritshuis, The Hague.

painter and one of the greatest in Western art, Ruisdael painted the immensity of space from memory and imagination. In his *View of Haarlem* (fig. 21.20) a spacious sky dominates the composition, taking up over two-thirds of the canvas. Ruisdael's landscapes are frequently devoid of people and when they are present, as here, they are inconsequential figures compared with the magnificence of nature. The atmospheric perspective encourages the illusion that we are looking into space so deep it verges on infinity.

Rachel Ruysch, 1664–1750

Emerging late in the Dutch Baroque style, Ruysch (roys) became one of the leading still-life painters of the era. Court painter to the Elector Palatine at Düsseldorf, she successfully combined her profession with marriage and children. Though she has the characteristic Dutch dark background for her flower arrangement (fig. 21.21), she uses vivid colour to enliven and dramatize her composition.

ROCOCO ART, CA. 1715–89

With the death of Louis XIV in 1715 the academic classical art of the Baroque lost its chief patron. It was with immense relief that the French court abandoned the palace of Versailles and the Baroque, moving back to Paris and

21.21 Rachel Ruysch, *Flowers in a Vase*. 1698. Oil on canvas, 23 × 17½" (58.5 × 44.5 cm). Städelsches Institut, Frankfurt am Main.

to a new way of life in elegant townhouses, where manners and charm were far more interesting than grandeur and geometric order. This was the Age of Enlightenment and of the Rococo style of art, contradictory but not mutually exclusive. In fact, the Enlightenment and the American and French revolutions cannot be fully understood without knowing what the Rococo was all about. That Rococo is merely Baroque made small or Baroque made light are bromides that do have a certain element of truth, but Rococo is also a style in its own right. Rococo art illustrates with astonishing accuracy the superficial values of an aristocracy whose languid days were numbered. Imposing Baroque forms were reduced to depictions of the pursuit of pleasure and escape from boredom. Rococo art was not decadent but the society it portrayed most certainly was.

21.22 *Below* Jean Antoine Watteau, *Embarkation for Cythera*. 1717. Oil on canvas 4' 3" × 6' 2½" (1.3 × 1.89 m). Louvre, Paris. Photo: R.M.N., Paris.

France

Jean Antoine Watteau, 1684–1721

Watteau (vah-toe), the first and greatest French Rococo artist, was born of Flemish parents in Valenciennes, a city that had been French for only six years. Yet he transformed French art from the classicism of Poussin into a new style of gaiety and tenderness, casual but elegant, that even today is recognized as Parisian in the sophisticated tradition later reinforced by artists such as Renoir and Degas. Watteau's *Embarkation for Cythera* (fig. 21.22), an early Rococo work completed only two years after the death of Louis XIV, is also the most important. Cythera was the legendary island of Venus, whose statue at the right presides over the amorous festivities. Grouped couple by couple, the elegantly garbed party is preparing to board a fanciful boat attended by cherubs, anticipating the pleasures to be enjoyed on the isle of love. Characteristic of Rococo design is the reverse *C* that can be traced from the heads at the lower left, curving past the couple on the hillock, and then turning back to the left along the delicate tips of the tree branches. Though it is a large painting, the scene is remarkably intimate. Each couple is totally preoccupied with itself and forms a distinct unit as they talk, smile, whisper, or touch. Beneath the frivolity and charm is a warm feeling of agreeable people and pleasant times. Watteau has transformed the amorous dalliances of an idle and privileged class into lyric poetry.

François Boucher, 1703–70

Venus was queen of the Rococo at its height in the 1750s, and Boucher (boo-shay) was her most talented interpreter. The protégé of Madame de Pompadour, mistress of Louis XV and arbiter of Rococo style, Boucher was a master of the sensual and frequently erotic art of the period. With astounding energy and prodigious virtuosity he produced paintings, designed tapestries, decorated porcelain, and created opera and ballet settings. With his many students and widely circulated engravings, he became the most influential artist in Europe. His *Venus Consoling Love* (fig. 21.23) depicts a slim and delicate beauty who would be more comfortable at the French court than on Mount Olympos. She was, in fact, at the French court, for this is one of Boucher's many portraits of Mme. de Pompadour, to whom the painting belonged. Here are the characteristic ivory, pink, blue, silver, and gold colors of the Rococo, all elegantly detailed by one of the virtuosos of the painter's brush. The painting is frankly pretty, and meant to be, but its subtle design is a carefully controlled interplay of sinuous curves; nowhere is there a straight line. A study of the apparent diagonals of the goddess' body discloses a series of curves, flattering curls of supple and creamy flesh. This is an idealized version of Pompadour, totally different from other Boucher paintings that reveal her intellectual brilliance. Her physician, Dr. Quesway, quoted her foreboding remark, *"Après moi le déluge!"* ("After me the flood!", that is,

21.23 François Boucher, *Venus Consoling Love*. 1751. Oil on canvas, 42⅛ × 33⅜" (107 × 84.8 cm). National Gallery of Art, Washington, D.C. (Chester Dale Collection).

disaster), and Voltaire wrote, on the occasion of her death in 1764, that he would miss her because "she was one of us; she protected Letters to the best of her power."

Jean-Honoré Fragonard, 1732–1806

The most eminent pupil of Boucher and Chardin and the last of the exceptional Rococo artists, Fragonard (frah-go-nar) lived to see the revolution destroy the Rococo age and all it represented. A master of the elegantly erotic paintings that delighted his patrons, Fragonard also had a technical skill and an eye for composition that enabled him to make powerful artistic statements. *The Swing* (fig. 21.24) is an apparently lightweight erotic diversion with a statue of Cupid at the left and the lolling figure of a young man below, actually Baron de Saint-Julien, who commissioned the work. As directed by the baron, Fragonard has shown his lady friend whimsically kicking her pump off to give him a better view up her skirt. Almost unnoticed is the key to the composition, the swing-pulling servant in the right background. Fragonard has portrayed a decadent class that neither works nor pays taxes, a frivolous aristocracy totally supported by the labors (and taxes) of 97 percent of a population symbolized by the shadowy figure of the servant. This was painted when the publication of Diderot's

21.24 Jean-Honoré Fragonard, *The Swing*. 1766. Oil on canvas, 32 × 25½" (81.3 × 64.8 cm). Wallace Collection, London.

Encyclopedia was nearing completion and the revolution itself was waiting impatiently in the wings.

Jean-Baptiste-Siméon Chardin, 1699–1779

But there was another current, one that celebrated the sober virtues of the middle class. Chardin (shar-dā) sought the underlying nobility that could be found in scenes of daily life. Nothing was so humble that his brush could not reveal its charm. *The Kitchen Maid* (see p. 348) has a natural dignity in sharp contrast to the artificiality of the courtly Rococo style. Chardin painted what he saw, which was,

essentially, light falling on pleasing shapes: face, apron, basin, turnips. The result is a quietly beautiful composition by the finest **still life** painter of the eighteenth century.

England

Thomas Gainsborough, 1727–88

The artificial elegance of the French Rococo had no place in an English society that was less frivolous than the French and certainly less decadent. In both subject matter and style Gainsborough's portrait of *Mrs. Richard Brinsley Sheridan* (fig. 21.25) symbolizes the dashing, worldly taste of English high society. This is the beautiful singer who married Sheridan, the wit, brilliant member of Parliament, and writer of such plays as *School for Scandal* and *The*

21.25 Thomas Gainsborough, *Mrs. Richard Brinsley Sheridan.* Ca. 1783. Oil on canvas, 7' 2½" × 5' ½" (2.2 × 1.5 m). National Gallery of Art, Washington, D.C. (Andrew W. Mellon Collection).

21.26 William Hogarth, *Marriage à la Mode II.* 1745. Engraving by B. Baron after an oil painting of 1743. British Museum, London.

21.27 Dominikus Zimmermann, Wieskirche, Upper Bavaria, Germany. 1745–54. Photo: Angelo Hornak, London.

Rivals. Here nature is synthetic, arranged as a proper background to highlight the natural beauty and unpretentious air of the sitter. In contrast to the sprightly sophistication of Boucher's women, Mrs. Sheridan is the very picture of the tasteful elegance so admired by British society.

William Hogarth, 1697–1764

Painter, engraver, and above all a master satirist, Hogarth delighted in attacking foolishness, frivolity, hypocrisy, and other vulnerable aspects of English society. He can, in fact, be considered a visual Jonathan Swift. Perhaps his finest work is the series of six paintings entitled *Marriage à la Mode* in which he satirized everything that could go wrong in marriage for money. When the engravings were published in 1745 there were very many indignant people all over London. In the second engraving (fig. 21.26) the husband is sprawled on a chair, obviously exhausted from a night out with a woman friend, whose hat the dog is drawing from his pocket. The black mark on the husband's neck indicates the presence of syphilis. The wife leans back in a suggestive pose, probably indicating some interrupted activity on her part, perhaps with a hastily departed music teacher. Her father protests to heaven about the accumulating bills but he must know there is no end in sight. The design of the two rooms is clearly Palladian and made even more classical by the huge number of Rococo decorations and furnishings.

Rococo Architecture

Rococo architecture is charming and beguiling in small structures and, when tastefully done, even in larger buildings. The pilgrimage church of Wieskirche (VEEZ-keer-ka; Church in the Meadow) was built in a remote rural area where the faithful believed a miracle had transpired. Pilgrims from near and far would travel to a pilgrimage church in the expectation of a miraculous cure or deliverance from some sort of evil. The interior of the church (fig. 21.27) is a celestial arrangement of white **stucco**, gold gilt, and profuse decoration set off to best advantage by the north-south orientation of the building and the large clear-glass windows. Most of the elegantly textured decorations are carved wood, and the "marble" columns are wood painted to look like marble. The spritely terra-cotta angels pose gracefully on stucco clouds, above which the painted vaulting soars effortlessly. Despite the multiplicity of details the rich ensemble is completely harmonious; the overwhelming impression is a mystical, deeply emotional experience.

NEOCLASSIC ART
English Architecture

The visual arts of the Renaissance and the Baroque made little impact on English culture. Apparently preoccupied with their justly celebrated achievements in dramatic literature, poetry, and music, the English continued to build in the Gothic and Tudor styles and to import painters such as Holbein, Rubens, and van Dyck. After a visit to Italy, Inigo Jones (1573–1652), the king's surveyor (architect), inaugurated a revolution in English architecture. Jones' middle-class sensibilities were offended by the extravagance of Michelangelo's style, but he was profoundly impressed with Palladio's architectural designs. Jones did not copy Palladian buildings, but instead selected classical characteristics as a basis for his own architectural style. His Queen's House (fig. 21.28) is the first English building designed in the Neoclassic style that was to become so prominent in England and North America. Chaste and clean with the poise of pure Roman classicism, the house has slight rustication on the ground floor derived from an early Renaissance style long since abandoned by the Italians (see

21.28   Inigo Jones, Queen's House, Greenwich, England, north facade, 1610–18. Photo: Topham, Edenbridge, U.K. (William Gordon Davis).

fig. 17.10). With simple window openings and matching lower and upper balustrades, the curving double stairway adds a discreet touch of dignity and grace.

English architecture was influenced by Palladian and Baroque characteristics more rapidly than anyone might have anticipated. In 1666 King Charles II commissioned Christopher Wren (1632–1723) to design a new dome for the Gothic Cathedral of St. Paul's, a design that Wren planned in the "Roman manner." A professor of astronomy at Oxford and an amateur architect, Wren soon had more than he bargained for; the Great Fire of 1666 destroyed most of London, necessitating a major rebuilding program with Wren as the chief architect. Of the more than fifty churches that Wren designed, the most important was the new St. Paul's, an eclectic design influenced by Jones, Palladio, and the French and Italian Baroque, and masterfully synthesized by Wren (fig. 21.29). St. Paul's is one of a limited number of English buildings with Baroque characteristics, but overall the design is dominated by the classical dome that is reminiscent, on a massive scale, of Bramante's Tempietto (see fig. 17.29). Punctuated by paired Corinthian columns in the Baroque manner, the facade is basically classical, but the ornate twin towers are similar to Borromini's curvilinear style (see fig. 21.9). None of Wren's London churches is quite like any other, though most are classical; some have towers, others steeples, and a few are crowned with domes.

French Neoclassicism

In France the Rococo style was deemed too frivolous for public buildings and the Baroque too elaborate, leaving the way open for a French version of Neoclassicism. Ange-Jacques Gabriel (1698–1782), court architect for Louis XV, made his reputation with his design for the Petit Trianon on the royal grounds at Versailles (fig. 21.30). Restrained, symmetrical, and exquisitely proportioned, the diminutive

21.29 *Above* Christopher Wren, St. Paul's Cathedral, London, west facade. 1675–1710. Photo: Angelo Hornak, London.

21.30 Ange-Jacques Gabriel, Petit Trianon, Versailles, south facade. 1762–8. Photo: Giraudon, Paris.

palace was constructed for Mme. de Pompadour who was, in effect, the ruler of France in place of the inept Louis XV. Clearly reflecting her classical architectural tastes, the Petit Trianon is in the austere Augustan style of republican Rome, a style that became dominant in Paris and other French cities during the second half of the eighteenth century.

Jacques-Louis David, 1748–1825

Both a gifted and a visionary artist, David (da-veed) developed his Neoclassic style during his studies in Rome (1775–81). Refusing to merely copy Roman statues and paintings, to become an antiquarian, he chose instead to be a propagandist, to place his talent at the service of revolutionary ideals. David used the forms of ancient art to extol the virtues of patriotism and democracy. Painted shortly before the French Revolution, *The Death of Socrates* (fig. 21.31) became one of the most popular paintings of the century and set the tone for didactic art of the highest quality. The Greek philosopher is depicted here as the apostle of reason, the patron saint of such Roman Stoics as Epictetus and Marcus Aurelius. With the body of a young athlete and the face of a benign sage, Socrates dominates a sharply focused composition that recalls Caravaggio's dramatic use of chiaroscuro. The figures of the twelve disciples—no coincidence—are rendered as precisely as marble statues, meticulous detail being a David trademark.

21.31   Jacques-Louis David, *The Death of Socrates*. 1787. Oil on canvas, 4' 3" × 6' 5¼" (1.3 × 1.96 m). Metropolitan Museum of Art, New York (Wolfe Fund, 1931. Catharine Lorillard Wolfe Collection 31.45).

David's message is unmistakable: men of principle should be willing to die in defense of their ideals. Nobles and tradesmen, philosophers and priests, seemingly everyone bought an **engraving** of the painting, including the doomed Louis XVI, who admired its noble sentiments.

David's works, with their detailed, painstaking realism and appeal to reason, were conceived and executed as cries for revolution. During the revolution itself David was a member of the Convention that sentenced Louis XVI and Marie Antoinette to death. For twenty-five years he was a virtual dictator of the arts in France. Following his dicta, Rococo salons were stripped of their sensuous paintings and curvaceous furnishings, remodeled in Neoclassic style, and equipped with furniture patterned after Greek vase paintings and Pompeiian murals. Fashionable men and women adopted Roman names such as Portia and Brutus, styled their hair in the antique manner, and even costumed themselves in classical togas.

Constance Marie Charpentier, 1767–1849

David was a highly successful artist with many students and, of course, numerous imitators. As with any well-known artist, paintings were sometimes attributed to him so they could command a higher price, which is what happened with the portrait of *Mlle. Charlotte du Val d'Ognes* (see p.2). Purchased in 1917 as a David for $200,000, the painting has since been attributed to Charpentier (shar-pā-ty-ay), a Parisian artist who studied with David and several other noted painters. Winner of a gold medal and an exhibitor in ten salons, her work appears to be hidden away—either in private collections or behind the names of more famous artists. That the painting could ever have been attributed to David is very

21.32 Angelica Kauffmann, *Pliny the Younger and his Mother at Misenum*, AD 79. 1785. Oil on canvas, 3' 4½" × 4' 2½" (1.03 × 1.28 m). Art Museum, Princeton University (Museum Purchase, Gift of Franklin H. Kissner).

odd. Though the style is Neoclassic, the brushwork firm and lucid, and the garb elegantly classical, the mood is totally alien to David's style. Strangely haunting, the work has a brooding and unreal quality that prompted critics to call it a "mysterious masterpiece." André Malraux described it as "a merciless portrait of an intelligent, homely woman against the light and bathed in shadow and mystery. The colors have the subtlety and singularity of those of Vermeer. A perfect picture, unforgettable." Made while the painting bore David's name, these comments are just as appropriate for a masterpiece by Constance Marie Charpentier.

Angelica Kauffmann, 1741–1807

Daughter and pupil of the artist J. J. Kauffmann, the Swiss painter became, at age twenty-four, a member of the Accademia di San Luca in Italy but was not allowed in the nude drawing classes because she was a woman. She nevertheless had a successful career as a history painter. One of the founding members of the British Royal Academy of Art, she produced hundreds of portraits and also designed the interiors of houses —mainly homes conceived by classicist Robert Adam. Upon marrying Antonio Zucchi and returning to Rome, she became the unofficial head of the Roman school of painting. Bristling with contained emotion, her painting shows Pliny the Younger and his mother, sister to Pliny the Elder, fearfully awaiting the news that the ever-so-curious Elder had lost his life as he investigated the eruption of Vesuvius at Pompeii (fig. 21.32).

21.33 Elisabeth Vigée-Le Brun, *Self-Portrait*. 1791. Oil on canvas, 39 × 31¾" (99.1 × 80.6 cm). Ickworth, Suffolk, U.K. Photo: National Trust Photographic Library, London (Angelo Hornak).

Elisabeth Vigée-Le Brun, 1755–1842

A student of her father, a portrait artist, Le Brun was already supporting her family at the age of fifteen. She married Le Brun, an art dealer and inveterate gambler, but chose to pursue a career as an internationally recognized portrait painter with over 900 paintings to her credit, a virtual *Who's Who* of late-eighteenth- and early-nineteenth-century European aristocrats. She served as painter to Queen Marie Antoinette but escaped, after the French Revolution, with her daughter to Italy, and continued to receive commissions throughout Europe. Her *Self-Portrait* (fig. 21.33) shows the artist painting a portrait of her daughter, whose face is captured in almost ghostlike fashion. Meticulously detailed from sash to lacework to hat, this is classical portraiture at its best. Particularly notable is the strong light on the hat and collar that creates a virtual miniature portrait of the head and shoulders.

Jean-Antoine Houdon, 1741–1828

Portrait sculpture, as might be expected, was a natural for the Neoclassic style, but there were no sculptors comparable to David. Houdon (ooh-dō), the finest French sculptor of the age, was admired by the *philosophes*, many of whom he portrayed with great accuracy. His reputation led to a commission in the United States for a statue of George Washington. His portrait bust of Voltaire (fig. 21.34) is a realistic depiction of the aging writer, clearly communicating his personality with twinkling eyes and wry and cynical smile.

Antonio Canova, 1757–1822

Houdon was acquainted with other revolutionaries, including George Washington and Benjamin Franklin, and created a portrait of Franklin and two statues of Washington. Despite his revolutionary background and realistic portraits, Houdon won only reluctant acceptance from Napoleon, who much preferred the Neoclassic style of Italian sculptor Canova (ka-NO-va), whose art, like that of David, became a propaganda tool for the Empire. Canova's lovely study of *Pauline Borghese as Venus* (fig. 21.35) is an idealized version of feminine charm, a very sensual portrait of Napoleon's sister and, though classical, an evocation of imperial luxury rather than the noble dignity of Republican Rome.

Neoclassicism in the United States

Gilbert Stuart, 1755–1828

The Neoclassic style found a congenial home in the young republic of the New World. The leading American painter was Stuart, who painted many Founding Fathers, particularly George Washington, whose portrait on the dollar bill is from a Stuart work. In his portraits Stuart displayed a mastery of flesh tones, having determined, like the much later Impressionists, that flesh coloration was a combination of colors. His portrait of *Mrs. Richard Yates* (fig. 21.36) is typical of the Neoclassic style in a new democracy in which neither dress nor background gives a clue to the social status of the sitter. European portraiture customarily added a proper setting and adornment indicating a regal or noble subject. In this portrait of the wife of a New York importer we see a coolly poised and confident woman. Her strongly featured face with the raised eyebrows and slightly drooping eyelids is faintly skeptical, the face of a shrewd and capable Yankee.

Joshua Johnson, 1765–1830

Johnson was one of the most celebrated of a long line of limners who traveled through New England and New York painting family portraits. The name was derived from "illuminator," a decorator of illuminated manuscripts. Though the National Gallery has a number of Johnson's portraits, many are still retained by descendants of the original families. *The Westwood Children* (fig. 21.37) has a charming modern appeal with its artful asymmetrical arrangement of the children, the dog, and the tree outside. The children are dressed in identical outfits but each is distinguished by hair style, placement of the feet, and the held objects. It was customary for limners to have the clothing already painted with faces and other personal factors added later.

21.34   Jean-Antoine Houdon, *Voltaire*. 1778. Marble, 20¾ × 17⅞ × 13⅛" (52.7 × 45.5 × 33.3 cm). National Gallery of Art, Washington, D.C. (Widener Collection).

21.35 *Above* Antonio Canova, *Pauline Borghese as Venus*. 1805. Marble, life-size. Galleria Borghese, Rome. Photo: Scala, Florence.

21.36 *Below, left* Gilbert Stuart, *Mrs. Richard Yates*, 1793. Oil on canvas, 30¼ × 25" (76.8 × 63.5 cm). National Gallery of Art, Washington, D.C. (Andrew W. Mellon Collection).

21.37 *Below* Joshua Johnson, *The Westwood Children*. Ca. 1807. Oil on canvas, 3' 5⅛" × 3' 10" (1.04 × 1.17 m). National Gallery of Art, Washington, D.C. (Gift of Edgar William and Bernice Chrysler Garbisch).

21.38   Thomas Jefferson, State Capitol, Richmond, Virginia, from roof of Sovran Bank. 1785–9. Photo: Library of Virginia (Mark Ranier).

Thomas Jefferson, 1743–1826

As United States Minister to France, Jefferson had an opportunity to study French Neoclassic architecture and especially Roman architecture in France and Italy. In particular, he was fascinated by the Maison Carrée in southern France. The first time he visited the building he studied it for seven hours, remarking afterward that he was as transfixed as a man admiring his beautiful mistress. His love affair with this temple compelled him to introduce Roman architecture into the United States. Jefferson's design of the State Capitol of Virginia (fig. 21.38) was patterned after the Maison Carrée, but with Ionic capitals, and constructed of wood painted gleaming white. Larger than the Roman temple, the Virginia Capitol has an aura of noble dignity precisely as intended by its designer.

Neoclassicism is popular because it is easily comprehended. Political themes and purposes aside, the classical impulse is toward physical and intellectual perfection as embodied in buildings that express the essence of poised, serene beauty. The Greeks not only invented the style but perfected it, and for twenty-five centuries the Western world has copied it.

STUDY QUESTION

Compare and contrast the Davids by Donatello, Verrocchio, Michelangelo, and Bernini. Which, in your opinion, best exemplifies the shepherd boy of the Old Testament? How does the Bernini statue symbolize the Baroque, particularly when compared with Michelangelo's *David*?

SUMMARY

The seventeenth and eighteenth centuries witnessed diversity and conflict in virtually every field of human endeavor. In the arts, the term Baroque embraced contradictory styles and trends, all of which had a common denominator of restless and powerful energy. The emergence of the Modern World in the seventeenth century was reflected in the development of four predominant styles in response to three categories of patronage:

1. The Counter-Reformation Baroque, a dynamic, colorful, and frequently flamboyant style favored by the Counter-Reformation Church of Rome. Leading artists included Caravaggio, Bernini, and Borromini.
2. The aristocratic Baroque, a splendidly regal style as embodied in the work of Rubens and van Dyck, and largely supported by the court nobles of France and England.
3. The Baroque classical style of Nicolas Poussin, a typically rationalistic French counterpart of the aristocratic style. Poussin emphasized line as opposed to the use of color by Rubens, setting up a confrontation between Poussinists and Rubenists, between painters who objectively controlled the lines and those who expressed themselves through color.
4. The bourgeois Baroque as exemplified in the painting of Hals, Rembrandt, Leyster, Ruisdael, and Vermeer, and patronized by the bourgeois merchants of Holland. As an artistic style by and for the Protestant middle class, this contradicted the aristocratic style and, most emphatically, the Counter-Reformation Baroque of the Church of Rome.

In retrospect, we can see the first two styles as the beginning of the end of the old world, whereas the bourgeois Baroque signified the coming age of world trade, free enterprise, industrial development, and democratic societies.

These multiple aspects of the Baroque had in common a presentation of monumental form; an exuberance of action, expression, and idealism; and an audience that was international. To this audience Baroque artists, with their outstanding accomplishments, brought Western men and women to a realization of their potential as enterprising and creative human beings. This was probably the greatest achievement of the Baroque.

With the death of the "Sun King", Louis XIV, in 1715, the academic classical art of the Baroque lost its chief secular patron. The French court and the aristocracy moved from Versailles, that most monumental of Baroque palaces, and began a new way of life in the elegant, intimate salons of their Parisian townhouses, where manners and charm were emphasized over splendor in the grand manner. Although the eighteenth century was the Age of the Enlightenment, and science was thought to be the key to most aspects of life, in art the refinement of men, women, and nature was the overriding concept. The artists of the Rococo celebrated the cult of pleasure and sentimentality, of genteel seduction and love in an enchanted land. Watteau was elegant and refined; Boucher was the flashy style-setter; Fragonard was unabashedly sensual.

By mid-century the antagonism between the aristocracy and the bourgeoisie had become blatantly apparent. The *philosophes* celebrated middle-class morality and the simple life as embodied in the art of Chardin but found their ultimate artistic exemplar in Jacques-Louis David, who turned to classical antiquity for literary and stylistic inspiration. David placed his talent at the service of revolutionary ideals and painted to inspire honor, duty, and patriotism.

By the end of the eighteenth century all Europe was ablaze with revolutionary fervor and Neoclassicism reigned supreme. The Neoclassic style gave historical sanction to both liberalism and conservatism because it was so readily comprehensible. Any power structure could manipulate the style to defend and justify its existence.

CULTURE AND HUMAN VALUES

There was a critical change in art patronage during the Early Modern Age that foretold the growth of capitalism and the rise of a middle class. Churches and courts were still the main supporters of working artists, but the bourgeois Baroque style was a clear sign of something new and different; nor was the middle-class sponsorship of art the only indication of a significant change in European society. The founding of the Dutch and English East India societies formed the leading edge of the coming European domination of international trade that gradually evolved into imperialism. Increased trade meant greater prosperity for a growing number of capitalists. No longer was a title or a bishop's mitre the only way to power and recognition in this world; money and power were there for the taking by a growing class of bourgeois capitalists.

The view of reality had changed again, from the Renaissance idea of individuals as the most beloved of God's creations to a materialistic view as described by Newton: a world that operated like a machine. Further, the world machine was inhabited by societies that, according to the Enlightenment, functioned rationally—a view confirmed by the American Revolution, but denied by the French Revolution that ended the Enlightenment in Europe.

CHAPTER 22

Music: Baroque, Rococo, and Classical

BAROQUE MUSIC, 1600–1750

Modern music, music as we know it, began sometime around the year 1600 as the Renaissance waned and the new Age of Reason began to take shape. The unbroken line of development leading from early organum to the smoothly flowing symmetry of the *a cappella* vocal music of the golden age of polyphony came to an end. The old world of private music for the church, the courts, and a cultural elite steadily declined in influence and importance. The modern world in which music became a public art was taking shape amid the intellectual, political, and social ferment of the seventeenth century.

Given the continuing rivalry between the Reformation and Counter-Reformation, churches could no longer take the faith of their congregations for granted. They built edifices with a maximum of floor space that resembled theatres more than they did Gothic or Renaissance churches. In a setting bursting with agitated forms and twisting, curving shapes with elaborate decorative details, these audiences were preached to, firmly and fervently.

This new Baroque style was applied to all public buildings whether they were churches, concert halls, or opera houses. Even the Baroque palaces (such as Versailles) of ruling heads of state assumed a quasi-public character in their dual roles as royal residences and showcases of national prestige and power.

There was a consistent dualism in the Baroque era, a sometimes precarious balance of opposing forces: church and state, aristocracy and affluent middle class. Baroque architecture reflected this dualism, achieving a sculptured effect by balancing the massiveness of its basic structure with elaborate decoration and exploitation of three-dimensional effects. Even the cylindrical columns of the facades were grouped in pairs. Baroque music displayed its dualism with balanced vocal-instrumental groups, consistent use of two-part (binary) forms, and the reduction of the

Opposite Anonymous, *Queen Elizabeth I Dancing the Volta with Robert Dudley, Earl of Leicester*, detail. Late 16th century. Oil on canvas. Private collection, England. Photo: A.K.G., London.

eight church modes to the two modes of either major or minor.

The emergence of instrumental music to a position of equal importance with vocal music virtually eliminated the *a cappella* style. All Baroque vocal music had an instrumental accompaniment, whether it was a mass, motet, **oratorio**, passion, **cantata**, or opera. Purely instrumental music established new forms such as the balanced participation of small and large groups in the **concerto grosso** and the pieces for two solo instruments with keyboard accompaniment called trio sonatas. Even the dynamics were dualistic, with consistent use of alternating loud and soft passages.

KEYBOARD MUSIC

Harpsichord

Dance Suite

Dancing has been a fundamental activity since the dim dawn of the human race—dances to appease the gods, to exorcise evil spirits, to invoke fertility, and for the sheer exhilaration of physical and emotional release. Dancing attained a new prestige during the seventeenth century, with magnificent balls in the great royal courts. Lords and ladies refined lusty and sometimes crude peasant dances into a social art of grace and charm (see chapter opener opposite).

During the early Baroque period, short instrumental pieces were composed in the manner and style of various popular dances. The exotic and erotic sarabande, for example, was transformed into a stylized and sophisticated art form that sometimes subtly implied what the original boldly proclaimed. Later on, in the nineteenth century, a similar process changed the waltz from an "indecent" dance into a popular social dance, leading finally to an art form, for example, "The Blue Danube" by Johann Strauss, Jr. Late twentieth-century composers are likely to accord similar treatment to dances of the 1980s and 1990s. During the seventeenth century these stylized dances were combined in collections of chamber music called suites, which were played by harpsichords, other solo instruments, and various instrumental ensembles. There are usually five or six dances (or movements) in a suite, each a different type of dance with a standard sequence: allemande, courante, sarabande, gigue. The suite was truly international in character; the original folk dances were, respectively, German, French, Spanish, and English (jig). Each dance suite had, however, a basic unity: each dance was in the same key.

For the first time in history, music acquired a firm and rational foundation: a key. Centuries before, the many modes of the Greeks had been reduced to the eight church modes that formed the musical material of everything from plainsong to Renaissance polyphonic music. The Baroque saw the emergence of two new concepts:

1. all music came to be written in a consistent pitch relationship called a key, with a choice of either major or minor mode, and
2. a temporary disenchantment with the complexities of polyphonic music led to compositions based on blocks of sound called **chords** or harmony.

By exploiting homophonic (one-sound) music (that is, one block of harmony following another) and a fixed pitch relationship, composers were merely reflecting the new view of reality. The "old music" was gradually replaced by less complicated music that was considered to be lucid and rational, though of course always expressive. This is not to say that this was a conscious decision by anyone or that there was instant recognition of the drastic changes that had taken place. Rather, musicians, like all artists, reacted to the new view of reality with a combination of old and new techniques that gave a fresh sound to a new age.

This new sound, as in the music of Johann Sebastian Bach, can be considered the beginning of modern music. Compositions by twentieth-century composers such as Stravinsky, Prokofiev, and Bartók are more closely related to the music of Bach than Bach's is, in turn, to the Renaissance. Palestrina, Lassus, and other Renaissance musicians were writing for the Church of Rome and for an educated aristocracy. Bach, though sometimes serving as a court composer, wrote, played, and conducted music for the largely middle-class Lutheran church.

The music of Bach is admired for its artistry and its superb craftsmanship. In his own day, however, Bach composed much of his music in response to specific demands. Many of his organ works were written and performed for church services and special programs. His sacred cantatas, written for particular Sundays of the liturgical year, were normally performed only once. Having served their purpose, they were consigned to storage where, many years later, a young Mozart could discover them and exclaim, "Now here is a man from whom I can learn," or words to that effect.

Much of Bach's output was intended for performance by amateur musicians and, more importantly, to be listened to by audiences composed essentially of middle-class German burghers. This middle class, of increasing affluence and influence, was becoming the primary audience not only of that period, but of all subsequent periods. Today's mass audience is a logical development of the processes that began during the eighteenth century.

The following dance suite for harpsichord is typical of solo keyboard music of the Baroque. The performance could be as simple as an amateur playing in the parlor of a middle-class home or as elaborate as a professional playing at a royal court on a highly decorated harpsichord. The suite is in six movements.

Listening Example 20
DANCE SUITE

J. S. Bach, French Suite No. 4 in E-Flat Major, 6th movement, Gigue
1720–4

Time: 2:34
Cassette 3, track 19[1]

French Suite No. 4   **J.S. Bach (1685–1750)**

Organ

The prime keyboard instrument for the performance of preludes, **fugues** and chorale preludes was the pipe organ. Baroque organs were solo instruments capable of filling Baroque churches and concert halls with a variety and volume of sound unequaled by any other instrument. The clarity and grandeur of these magnificent instruments have never been surpassed. The proof of this statement can still be heard throughout Europe; many of the original instruments have never ceased pouring forth the unique color and brilliance of the Baroque.

Chorale Prelude

An organ composition consisting of variations on a chorale melody is called a chorale prelude. The variations are to be played before the congregation sings the chorale (what Lutherans call a **hymn**)—hence the term "prelude." The intention of the organist is to set the general mood of the chorale so that the congregation can sing it with more understanding.

The following chorale prelude is based on the Lutheran chorale "Wachet auf" ("Sleepers, Awake"). The

---

1. CD 1, track 13.

opening section has a sprightly melody over a smoothly striding bass. The first part of the chorale melody becomes a third voice about halfway through the opening section, after which the entire section is repeated. In the second (concluding) section the chorale melody is interspersed throughout.

Listening Example 21
CHORALE PRELUDE

J. S. Bach, Schubler Chorale Prelude No. 1, BWV 645, "Wachet auf"
1746

Time: 4:40
Cassette 3, track 21[2]

Schubler Chorale Prelude No. 1, BWV 645, "Wachet auf"   J.S. Bach

INSTRUMENTAL MUSIC

Trio Sonata

Baroque music was particularly notable for the widespread development of private music-making by performers who played or sang for the sheer joy of making their own music. Not all of them were as skilled as professionals, but self-expression was more important than technical proficiency. These multitudes of musicians, whose personal pleasure was more than sufficient payment for performance, were amateurs: true lovers of music in the best sense of the term.

Musical instruments became necessary functional furniture for a burgeoning middle class growing ever more affluent. Baroque music was, however, in many respects difficult for amateur performances. Composers did not indicate the exact speed or tempo of their compositions, nor did they do more than provide occasional directions regarding dynamics (relative loudness or softness). These procedures gave amateurs considerable margin for error. Moreover, specific directions as to which instruments were to be used were frequently omitted, leaving it to the discretion, and resources, of the performers.

The ubiquitous trio sonata provided ideal material for amateurs because it was written in the conventional form of two melodic lines plus generalized directions for keyboard accompaniment. The two melodies could be

performed by any two available instruments and the accompaniment by any keyboard instrument (clavichord, harpsichord, or pipe organ). The pivotal figures in trio sonatas (and large compositions) were the keyboard performers; it was assumed that they were the most competent musicians, which was usually the case. They provided the foundation for the continuation of the piece, which led to the adoption of the Italian word *continuo* to describe the function of the keyboard musicians. It was up to them to fill in the harmony and to cover up the blank spots whenever the less expert performers played wrong notes, lost their place, or otherwise strayed from grace.

Baroque chamber music was highly improvisational (as were arias in operas and oratorios) because performers were expected to add their personal touches to a given melodic line. Compositions were "personalized" through available instruments, the expertise and imagination of performers and, most importantly, the musical challenge presented by the composer. Not until jazz appeared on the scene during the latter part of the nineteenth century did performers again have so much individual freedom as that accorded amateur and professional musicians of the Baroque period.

Concerto

The classic Baroque **concerto** was the *concerto grosso* in which a small group of soloists (*concertino*) performed in conjunction with a full orchestra (*tutti* or *concerto grosso*). Bach, Handel, and Vivaldi did write solo concertos for single instruments, but Baroque composers generally preferred the sonority of the concertino as it blended and contrasted with the full orchestra.

The Italian composer Antonio Vivaldi wrote more than 450 concertos, the most famous of which are *The Four Seasons* for solo violin and orchestra. Each season—spring, summer, autumn, winter—has three movements that together evoke different aspects of the season. The four concertos are remarkable early examples of **program music**, that is, music describing or communicating extra-musical ideas. As might be expected, the first concerto is bright and cheerful, full of allusions to nature's annual rebirth.

Listening Example 22
VIOLIN CONCERTO

Vivaldi, *The Four Seasons*, "Spring," 1st movement
Before 1725; excerpt

Time: 2:25
Cassette 3, track 20

---

2. CD 1, track 16.

The Four Seasons, "Spring"   Vivaldi (ca. 1675–1741)

VOCAL-INSTRUMENTAL MUSIC

Chorale

Martin Luther translated the Bible into German because he believed that every Christian should have direct access to the text. He was also concerned about congregational participation in the service of worship because it tended to bind the congregation and the clergy together in a common endeavor. Moreover, music had, in Luther's opinion, a spiritual, transcendental quality that enriched and elevated worship. Unlike John Calvin, Luther, once a priest of the Church of Rome, culled the rich musical heritage of the church, selecting and adapting plainsong to the needs and capabilities of Protestant congregations. For the first time in many centuries, common people once again took an active part in worship as they raised their voices in song. They sang what we would call hymns, though hymn tunes of the Lutheran church are called "chorales."

The typical Lutheran service of the eighteenth century began at 7:00 A.M. and concluded at noon. In the larger churches professional musicians (such as Bach) were expected to teach school during the week, maintain the organ, train a volunteer choir, compose special instrumental and vocal music for each Sunday of the year, and play the organ and direct the choir during the Sunday service. Each Sunday occupied a specific place in the liturgical year, with special emphasis on Advent, Epiphany, Easter, and Pentecost. The music for each Sunday had to correspond with the special meaning of that Sunday—from the opening chorale prelude through the hymns, the cantata, and the concluding postlude.

Oratorio

An oratorio is a sacred or epic text set to music and performed in a church or concert hall by soloists, chorus, and orchestra; it can also be described, somewhat loosely, as a concert version of a sacred opera. In the latter part of his career George Frederick Handel, the foremost composer in eighteenth-century London, turned from composing operas for an indifferent nobility to writing oratorios for the middle class. Of his twenty-one oratorios, the most celebrated is *Messiah.* This extended composition was written in feverish haste—completed in only three weeks—leading Handel to believe it was divinely inspired. Based mainly on the New Testament, it is divided into three sections. Concluding the second section, the brilliant Hallelujah Chorus so impressed George II that he sponta-

neously rose to his feet, thus setting the tradition of a standing audience for this stirring chorus. The text consists primarily of "hallelujah," a Hebrew word of jubilation that has been called the college cheer of Christendom.

Listening Example 23
ORATORIO

Handel, *Messiah,* 44th movement, Hallelujah Chorus
1742

Time: 3:59
Cassette 3, track 22

Messiah, Hallelujah Chorus   Handel (1685–1759)

Hal - le - lu - jah!   Hal - le - lu - jah!   Hal-le - lu-jah!

Opera

Opera (It., from Lat. *opera,* "works") is generally considered to be the most "Baroque" of all the artistic media of the age. As discussed earlier, opera began as a "reform" movement, an attempt to return to the proper combination of words and music in ancient Greek tragedies. Text was all-important, vocal lines were sparse, and accompaniment minimal. However, within a remarkably short period opera developed into full-blown music drama with elaborate sets, costumes, and choruses. Despite various regional differences in style between Florence, Rome, Venice, Vienna, Paris, and London, opera became the most popular and spectacular art form of the period. Elaborate opera houses were built all over Europe for an art form which, in a manner of speaking, put the vitality of an era on stage for all to see and hear.

Italian operas became the favorite artistic import for most of the nations of western Europe. French nationalism, however, strongly resisted the dominance of Italian music. Critics lambasted Italian operas as being too long, monotonous, too arty, archaic in language, and with flamboyant singing that obscured the sound and the sense of the words, thus leaving no appeal to the logical French mind. Additionally, the male sopranos and altos—the *castrati*—were said to horrify the women and to cause the men to snicker. But the French resisted Italian opera because they valued dance over drama. Dance—French ballet—was central to the French musical stage but only minimal in Italian opera.

The struggle between French and Italian music became an actual confrontation when the Italian opera composer, Pietro Francesco Cavalli (1602–76), was commissioned to write a festive opera for the wedding of Louis XIV. The director of the king's music, Jean-Baptiste Lully

(1632–87)—born Gianbattista Lulli in Florence—turned the occasion to his advantage. The opera was indeed performed in 1662 for the king's wedding and it was monumental, lasting some six hours. However, each act concluded with one of Lully's large-scale ballets. The French reaction to this spectacle was interesting: the production was seen, not as a music drama with interpolated dances, but as a gigantic ballet with operatic interludes. Cavalli returned to Italy, vowing never to write another opera while Lully continued his intrigues becoming, in time, as absolute a sovereign in music as Louis XIV was in affairs of state. Cavalli's career was finished but Lully went on to accumulate one of the greatest fortunes ever amassed by a musician.

ROCOCO, 1725–75

In art and architecture the last stage of the Baroque period is characterized by an even more elaborate style called Rococo (from the Fr., *rocaille*, "rock," and *coquilles*, "shells"). The grandeur of the Baroque was scaled down to an emphasis on interior design and decorative scroll and shell work, resulting in a sort of domesticated, sometimes decadent, Baroque.

In music, Rococo is the "gallant style," a highly refined art of elegant pleasantness suitable for intimate social gatherings in fashionable salons. Among the chief exponents were François Couperin and Domenico Scarlatti with styles comparable to the paintings of Watteau, Boucher, and Fragonard.

François Couperin (1668–1733)

The foremost Rococo composer was Couperin, usually referred to as "le Grand." His music crystallizes the miniature world of the Rococo. French to the core, it is scintillating, elegant, refined, and witty. He wrote twenty-seven *ordres* or sets of dances for harpsichord, all with evocative titles. The name of the following composition is typically whimsical. It translates literally as "hook in leg" and means tripping someone. In this case it is the music that goes tripping along, lighthearted and saucy.

Listening Example 24
DANCE MOVEMENT FOR HARPSICHORD

Couperin, Ordre No. 22, *Le Croc-en-jambe*
1730

Time: 2:14
Cassette 3, track 23

Ordre No. 22, *Le Croc-en-jambe*   Couperin (1668–1733)

CLASSICISM IN MUSIC, 1760–1827

The Classical period in music dates from about 1760, the beginning of Haydn's mature style, to about 1827, the year of Beethoven's death. Haydn, Mozart, and Beethoven were musical giants in what has been called the golden age of music, an era of extraordinary musical achievements. Other eras have perhaps been as musically productive, but none has become so mutually identifiable as the Classical period, the golden age, and the musical output of Haydn, Mozart, and Beethoven. The basic homophonic style of Classicism has many antecedents in several earlier periods of music. It is therefore appropriate to briefly review these earlier periods.

Renaissance music was primarily polyphonic and written in the old liturgical modes. On the other hand, some Renaissance music, English madrigals in particular, was quite homophonic and was, moreover, tonal; that is, it was written in either a major or a minor key rather than in a liturgical mode. The music of Gabrieli in Venice was also strongly homophonic with a preference for sonorous harmonies rather than the multiple melody lines used by Renaissance composers such as Josquin, Lassus, and Palestrina.

At the beginning of the seventeenth century there was a relatively brief period of strongly homophonic music as composers attempted to re-create what they thought was the text-oriented musical style of the ancient Greeks. These experiments in words and music led to the development of the new style of music called opera. Opera, the epitome of the new Baroque style, quickly became elaborate and ornate and combined homophonic and polyphonic music. The vocal-instrumental music of the age developed a new and complex style of polyphony, culminating in the music of Handel and Bach.

Rococo music used Baroque **ornamentation**, but the style was much more homophonic, less profound, and more stylishly elegant. Some characteristics of the Rococo, notably the less complex homophonic techniques, were incorporated into a new style called Classicism, Neoclassicism, or Viennese Classicism. Classicism is the preferred term for music of the period, whereas Neoclassicism is generally applied to the sister arts.

At no time are the stylistic periods of the arts precisely synchronized. Careful study of the comparative outline given (table 22.1) will indicate that the prevailing world-views of the periods since the Renaissance are reflected in the arts at different times. Any number of inferences can be drawn regarding the influence of an era on the arts and the arts on each other. However, the artistic

TABLE 22.1   COMPARISON OF STYLISTIC PERIODS OF THE ARTS

	Approx. Dates	Important Individuals
Period: The Age of Reason	1600–1700	Descartes, Galileo, Kepler, Bacon, Spinoza
Artistic Style: Baroque		
Architecture	1575–1740	Bernini, Wren, Mansart, Perrault, Le Vau
Music	1600–1750	Corelli, Lully, Vivaldi, Handel, Bach, Purcell
Painting	1600–1720	Rubens, Rembrandt, Steen, Hals, Vermeer, van Dyck, Velasquez
Sculpture	1600–1720	Bernini
Period: The Enlightenment	1687–1789	Newton, Voltaire, Diderot, Locke, Hume, Kant, Rousseau, Frederick II, Jefferson, Franklin
Artistic Style: Rococo		
Architecture	1715–60	Erlach, Hildebrandt, Asam, Cuvilliés, Fischer
Music	1725–75	Couperin, some of Haydn and Mozart
Painting	1720–89	Watteau, Chardin, Boucher, Fragonard
Sculpture	1770–1825	Clodion, Falconet
Artistic Style: Neoclassic		
Architecture	1750–1830	Chalgrin, Vignon, Fontaine
Music (Classicism)	1760–1827	Haydn, Mozart, Beethoven, Gluck
Painting	1780–1850	David, Ingres
Sculpture	1800–40	Canova, Thorwalden, Houdon

production of specific individuals is of paramount concern. The uniqueness of a work of art reflects the uniqueness of the individual artist who created it.

The Classical period of music might also be called the "Advanced Age of the Amateur Musician." Baroque music, with its figured bass accompaniments and demands for improvisation, was partially the province of the professional but with real possibilities for gifted amateurs. On the other hand, the latter part of the eighteenth century featured modern notation, with every note written down plus indications for interpretation (tempo, dynamics, etc.), thus providing an even better opportunity for music-making by amateurs. Baroque musicians could improvise and stray from the musical score but, in the Age of Reason, you acceded to the composer's intentions by playing the music exactly as written.

The vastly increased demand for music for all occasions resulted in a flood of mostly instrumental compositions. There were serenades for outdoor parties, chamber music for indoor gatherings, **symphonies** for the newly established symphony orchestras, and operas for the increasing number of private and public opera houses. The newly invented piano (ca. 1710 by Cristofori), with its ability to play soft and loud (It. *pianoforte*) on a single keyboard, rapidly replaced the harpsichord and the clavichord as the standard home instrument for amateur performance.

Amateur chamber music societies were organized for the presentation of programs ranging from **sonatas** to duets and trios for the various instruments, including the quartets for a homogeneous group of string instruments called, naturally enough, string quartets.

All of this musical activity was of little benefit to those who tried to earn a living from their music. Eighteenth-century musicians were, on the whole, accorded a lowly position on the social scale. Typically, composers such as Franz Joseph Haydn worked for a noble family like the Esterhazy, wore servant's livery, and sat at the dinner table "below the salt." Not until the latter part of his life did Haydn achieve any financial independence, and he had to go to the London concert scene to do it. Ironically, the descendants of the once powerful Esterhazy family are notable today only to the extent that some of Haydn's unpublished music may still be in their possession.

Franz Joseph Haydn, 1732–1809

Haydn's professional life was typical of the vicissitudes of a musical career, yet he fared better than many of his contemporaries. In a short sketch that he contributed to a 1776 yearbook, Haydn wrote that he sang at court in Vienna and in St. Stephen's Cathedral until his voice changed and he was summarily dismissed.

When my voice finally changed I barely managed to stay alive by giving music lessons to children for about eight years. In this way many talented people are ruined: they have to earn a miserable living and have no time to study.

There were numerous musical opportunities for a musician in Vienna, but most of them paid very little. Musicians were forced to hold down a number of positions in order to survive. Haydn had as many as three jobs on a Sunday morning: playing the violin at one church, the organ at another, and singing in the choir at a third. When he finally achieved full employment with the Esterhazy family, he was quite willing, at that time, to relinquish a certain amount of personal freedom.

Classical composers had tired of the late Baroque proclivity for ever more elaborate and sometimes ponderous polyphony. A simpler homophonic style emerged and began gradually to replace the polyphonic manipulation of a single musical theme. By abandoning the polyphonic vocal-instrumental style, composers were faced with a dilemma: how to develop a coherent style of purely instrumental music. A certain unity was inherent in vocal music because of the text. Without a text, composers were faced with the possibility of a chaotic mass of instrumental sounds. One of the solutions was to give shape to instrumental music by using the form of theme and variations: a long subject or theme was followed by a series of variations that, usually, grew gradually more distant from the theme, before concluding with the original theme.

Haydn, as the first of the composers in the Classical style, led the way in establishing such basic instrumental ensembles as the symphony orchestra and the string quartet. Large enough to produce a rich, full tone but small enough to be intimate and to leave room for personal expression, the string quartet was the preferred Classical musical group. Consisting of first and second violin, viola, and cello, corresponding to the SATB division of voices in choral music, the three members of the violin family can achieve a fine balance of unified tone. The second movement of his String Quartet in C has the Theme and Variations form. Further, the theme was Haydn's gift to the Austrian people, the Austrian national anthem, best known as the Austrian National Hymn.

Listening Example 25
SLOW MOVEMENT OF STRING QUARTET

Haydn, String Quartet in C, Op. 76 No. 3, "Emperor," 2nd movement
1798

Time: 7:33[3]

Wolfgang Amadeus Mozart, 1756–91

Musical genius has been a subject of considerable interest to twentieth-century psychologists, but the exact nature of the qualities that can be labeled "genius" remains tantalizingly elusive. Thus the accomplishments of Mozart, possibly the greatest musical genius who ever lived, are both awesome and inexplicable.

Mozart devoted virtually his entire life to the composition and performance of music. Like Haydn, he endured the slights of a society as yet unready and unwilling to recognize, let alone support, his incredible gifts. Unlike Haydn, he never found a noble patron. His brief, poverty-stricken life and eventual burial in an unmarked grave testify eloquently to the status of a musician in Vienna during the golden age of music.

There are many accounts of Mozart's precocity but none more typical of his manner of composition—and lifestyle—than the premiere of his opera *Don Giovanni*. The opera was complete except for the overture that was, according to the composer, "finished." On the day of the premiere, Mozart was busily engaged in shooting billiards, one of his favorite occupations. In reply to urgent questioning, he reiterated that he had completed the overture. When pressed to produce a musical score, he finally admitted that the piece was indeed completed—in his head—but not yet written down. Many cups of coffee later, the complete parts, still dripping with wet ink, were rushed to the opera house where the orchestra had to sightread the music. Characteristically, the thousands of musical notes that Mozart had mentally arranged added up to a gem in operatic literature. Some critics feel, in fact, that *Don Giovanni* is the greatest opera ever written but others single out *The Marriage of Figaro* or *The Magic Flute*, also by Mozart.

Mozart wrote over fifty symphonies, with most of the movements using sonata form,[4] which neither he nor Haydn is credited with inventing. The inventor is, in fact, unknown. Sonata form was the prime eighteenth-century solution to the problem of finding a rational design for instrumental music. In a very real sense, sonata form reflected Enlightenment ideals: it was lucid, logical, and symmetrical.

The technical term "sonata form" is a label for a procedure that uses a dual subject rather than the single subject of the Baroque style. The first of these two subjects is usually vigorous and dynamic, while the second is generally quieter and more lyrical. The two subjects should be, musically speaking, logical parts of the whole; the second subject should somehow complement and balance the first.

The dual subjects of sonata form are theme A and theme B. These two contrasting subjects (or themes) are

---

3. CD 2, track 1.
4. Sonata form was not limited to sonatas, which are compositions for piano or a solo instrument with accompaniment. The form was also used for trios, quartets, concertos, and symphonies.

connected by a bridge, a transitional passage, which leads smoothly from theme A to theme B. Following theme B there is a closing section called a codetta ("little ending"). The complete unit of two themes with connecting transition and closing section contains all the thematic material which has been presented or to which the ear has been exposed. This unit is therefore called an exposition and can be outlined as indicated below. During the Classical period expositions were normally repeated, as indicated by the sets of double dots.

```
                Exposition
        ‖: theme A    bridge    theme B    codetta :‖
```

After the basic material has been presented in the exposition, the composer proceeds to manipulate and exploit selected thematic material in the development section. Any and all material may be subjected to a variety of treatment.

Near the end of the development section, the composer usually introduces the return, a transitional section that prepares the way for a recapitulation of the material from the exposition. The recapitulation repeats, more or less, the material from the exposition, but there are subtle variations that help avoid monotony.

After the codetta of the recapitulation, the composer may add a final coda if he or she believes that something more is needed to bring the movement to a satisfactory conclusion. A complete sonata form can be outlined as follows:

```
Exposition              Development      Recapitulation
‖: A bridge B codetta :‖:                return A bridge B codetta (coda) :‖
```

Mozart's Symphony No. 35 was written for a festive occasion in the house of Siegmund Haffner, the mayor of Salzburg. Originally a six-movement serenade, it was completed in the amazing time of only two weeks. Six months after finishing it he wrote to his father that "the new Haffner symphony has quite astonished me, for I do not remember a note of it. It must be very effective." Mozart's evaluation of his new symphony is modest, for this is a joyful work of great brilliance. The first, second, and fourth movements use sonata form while the third movement follows the ternary form of ABA.

Symphony No. 35, "Haffner," Fourth movement   Mozart (1756–91)

The Magic Flute is a comic opera commissioned by a theatrical impresario who wanted a popular and profitable opera, which it was. Its combination of fantasy, frolic, and solemn rites has made it popular on the operatic stage, as a movie, as several different television productions, and even as a production of the Salzburg Marionettes for the annual Mozart Festival in Salzburg. In the following solemn aria Sarastro, the high priest, comforts a despairing Pamina by assuring her that Prince Tamino will soon be free to marry her.

Listening Example 27
OPERATIC ARIA

Mozart, *The Magic Flute,* Act II, "Within these hallowed portals"
1791

Time: 4:15[6]

Within these hallowed portals,
Revenge and discord die;
Here when a brother falleth,
A brother's help is nigh.

Led by a kind and friendly hand,   } 3 times
He seeks, rejoiced, the better land.

Here on our peaceful mountain,
In holy love we live;
And here no hatred lurketh,
But all their wrongs forgive.

He who by love is not made free,   } 3 times
Doth not deserve a man to be.

English translation by Samuel Langford

Listening Example 26
SYMPHONY

Mozart, Symphony No. 35 in D, K.385, "Haffner"
1782

Time: 7:59, 4:25, 3:05. 3:34
Cassette 3, track 24 (4th movement)[5]

---

5. CD 1, track 19 (1st movement); CD 1 track 20 (2nd movement); CD 1, track 21 (3rd movement).
6. CD 1, track 18.

Ludwig van Beethoven, 1770–1827

Unlike Haydn and Mozart, Beethoven forged a place for himself as an economically independent musician. He was not above selling the same composition to different publishers and did so quite often. He reasoned that the publishers had cheated composers long enough; he was merely collecting retribution for a long chain of abuses.

Beethoven's finances were generally sound though somewhat chaotic. His health was another matter. He noticed a hearing loss at an early age that gradually evolved into total deafness. This silence became, at times, almost more than a musician could bear. That some of Beethoven's greatest music was composed while he was completely deaf is a testament to his genius and to his unconquerable spirit. He himself conducted the premiere of his Ninth Symphony, that powerful and imposing work dedicated to the exalted ideal of world brotherhood. At the conclusion of the symphony he remained facing the orchestra, solitary in his silence, and thinking that the work had failed. Finally, someone turned him about to face the thunderous applause of an audience that was both inspired and deeply moved.

Beethoven's Third Symphony, the "Eroica," was originally dedicated to Napoleon, whom Beethoven regarded as a true Faustian man who labored to improve the lives of all the people. There were many victims of Napoleon's march to power—"while man's desires and aspirations stir, he cannot choose but err"—but it appeared that he was using his energy to make the world a better place in which people could work out their freedom. However, Napoleon declared himself emperor, and Beethoven furiously erased his name from the dedicatory page of the "Eroica," leaving the work implicitly dedicated to the heroic impulses of a Faustian man or, simply, to an unknown hero.

Beethoven poured the very essence of Classical symphonic music into his Fifth Symphony, a work that has often been cited as the perfect symphony. Though sometimes threatening to break the bounds of Classical form, Beethoven channeled all his titanic energy into the driving rhythms of this mighty work. The Fifth Symphony is a summary of many aspects of Beethoven's genius: the terse, surging energy of the first movement, the moving and mellow lyricism of the second movement, the exuberant vitality of the **scherzo**, and the sheer drive of the finale.

The orchestra as Beethoven knew it was simply not large and expressive enough for this symphony. He enlarged his tonal palette by adding instruments at both ends of the spectrum and trombones in the middle to obtain the full and rich sound that he had to have. The instrumentation for the enlarged orchestra needed to perform his Fifth Symphony is: piccolo, two flutes, two oboes, two clarinets, two bassoons, contra-bassoon, two French horns, two trumpets, three trombones, two timpani, sixteen violin I, fourteen violin II, ten violas, eight cellos, six basses. (The number of strings can vary; these are approximations.)

The Fifth Symphony achieves a maximum effect with the utmost economy of musical materials. Essentially, the entire symphony is built out of one musical interval and one rhythmic pattern:

Interval of 3rd plus pattern of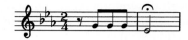

This motive is so brief that it is referred to as a germ motive from which the entire symphony is germinated. This first movement is in sonata form.

The Fifth Symphony is a prime example of the Classical style: logical, direct and to the point, objective, controlled, achieving maximum effect with a minimum of means.

Listening Example 28
SYMPHONIC MOVEMENT

Beethoven, Symphony No. 5 in C Minor, Op. 67,
3rd movement
1808

Time: 4:30
Cassette 3, track 26

Symphony No. 5, Third movement   **Beethoven (1770–1827)**

Beethoven is considered by some to be a pivotal figure in musical styles, standing midway between Classicism and the dawning age of Romanticism. However, his heroic style and even his introspective later works all testify to his fundamental Classical outlook, namely, his rational control of his material. Beethoven's music served *him;* he was the master who, with disciplined creativity, molded (and sometimes hammered) his musical materials into the structured sounds of the Classical style.

SUMMARY

From about 1600 to 1750 the Baroque style built a new kind of music on the Classical foundations of the Renaissance. The flexible modal system of the past was narrowed down to a single tonal center, or key, with the modal possibilities reduced to two: major or minor. Compensating for the limiting of tonal materials to a single major or minor key were the new possibilities for composing by contrasting keys and modulating from one key to another.

The ubiquitous trio sonata was perhaps most representative of Baroque music-making because of the emphasis on instrumental music with improvised accompaniment in the *continuo* part. Concertos were more formal because of the larger number of instrumentalists involved, but the continuo still played an important accompanying part for orchestra and soloist(s).

Following the Reformation, the German sacred songs called chorales assumed an important place in congregational singing and in organ literature in the form of chorale preludes. Cantatas, oratorios, and operas were the most important vocal forms of the Baroque, although there was still a tradition of composing Masses and motets.

The surface elements of the ornate Baroque style assumed a primary emphasis in the style called Rococo. The Rococo, or "gallant style" of music (1725–75), with its light, airy texture and elegant ornamentation, served as a bridge between the sumptuous Baroque and the gracefully refined style of the Classical period.

During the Classical period (1760–1827), instrumental musicians, whether professional or amateur, came into their own. The improvement in musical instruments and the great interest in amateur performance encouraged the composition of chamber music (sonatas, string quartets, etc.) and orchestral music ranging from serenades for soirées to symphonies for the growing number of concert halls. Monothematic polyphony was replaced by a dual-subject structure called sonata form in which composers could combine two contrasting themes into an expressive and balanced whole.

The Classical period, coinciding with the height of the Enlightenment, created chamber music and the symphony orchestra virtually as they are known today. Even more important, music progressed from a more or less private concern of the aristocracy or the church to a public art available to all.

CULTURE AND HUMAN VALUES

All of us are so accustomed to the ready availability of all kinds of music that we tend to forget that mass audiences for music are a relatively recent phenomenon. As late as the seventeenth century, the musical patrons were still the courts and, to a lesser extent, the Church of Rome. After the Reformation, Protestant churches, particularly Lutheran, became active in commissioning music and hiring organists and choirmasters. The common element in the Lutheran churches and in Holland was the growing middle class.

By the eighteenth century music had become much more of a public art. Virtually anyone with money could rent a hall and hire musicians, but few could make a living as a composer. Handel did fairly well in London, particularly with his oratorios, but Bach's reputation was largely based on his remarkable skills as a performer. Mozart attempted to survive in Vienna as a composer without a patron but only eked out a bare living. At the end of the century, however, Beethoven proved that music had finally become a profession in which one could make a living composing and performing. It was at this point that one can say musical art had gone public.

STUDY QUESTIONS

1. Explain the forces that helped convert music from a private to a public art.
2. What are the pressures when music depends on an admission-paying public?

ADDITIONAL LISTENING

1. Bach, *The Well-Tempered Clavier*, vol. I, Fugue in G minor. This is a good example of the monothematic (one-subject) Baroque style (CD 1, track 14).
2. J. S. Bach, *Partita No. 3 in E* for violin, Gavotte en Rondeau. This is in the rondo form of ABACAD (CD 1, track 15).
3. Beethoven, Piano Sonata No. 2 in A, Op. 2, No. 2. The fourth movement is also in rondo form (CD 2, track 2).
4. Beethoven, Piano Sonata No. 8 in C minor, Op. 13. The first movement, after the dramatic introduction, is in sonata form (CD 2, track 3).
5. Beethoven, Violin Sonata No. 5 in F, Op. 24, "Spring." The scherzo is in three-part form (ABA) (CD 2, track 4).

The
Middle
Modern
World,
1789–1914

The Middle Modern World

1789–1914

	People and Events	Art and Architecture	Literature and Music	Philosophy, Science, Invention
1800	**1760–1820** George III of England **1774–93** Louis XVI of France **1789–1815** French Revolution **1801–25** Alexander I of Russia **1804–12** Napoleon Emperor of France **1814–24** Louis XVIII of France **1815** Napoleon defeated at Waterloo **1820–30** George IV of England **1821–30** Greek revolt from Turks **1824–30** Charles X of France **1825–55** Nicholas I of Russia **1830** July Revolution in France **1830–48** Louis Philippe of France, constitutional monarch **1830–7** William IV of England **1837–1901** Victoria of England **1848** *Communist Manifesto* by Marx and Engels **1851** Crystal Palace, "Great Exhibition of the Works of All Nations" **1852–70** Napoleon III of France **1853–6** Crimean War **1855–81** Alexander II of Russia **1859** *Origin of Species* by Darwin **1861–78** Victor Emmanuel II of Italy **1870–1** Franco-Prussian War **1871–1940** Third Republic in France **1871** *Descent of Man* by Darwin **1871–88** Wilhelm I, Emperor of Germany **1878–1900** Humbert I of Italy **1881–94** Alexander III of Russia **1888–1918** Wilhelm II, Emperor of Germany **1889** Paris Exhibition; Eiffel Tower **1894–1918** Nicholas II of Russia **1899–1902** Boer War	**Goya** 1746–1828 *Gran hazaña! Con muertos!* **Turner** 1775–1851 *Keelman Heaving Coals by Moonlight* **Constable** 1776–1837 *Wivenhoe Park, Essex* **Ingres** 1780–1867 *Grande Odalisque* **Géricault** 1791–1824 *The Raft of the Medusa* **Corot** 1796–1875 *Forest of Fontainebleau* **Delacroix** 1799–1863 *Arabs Skirmishing in the Mountains* **Cole** 1801–48 *Oxbow* **Paxton** 1801–65 The Crystal Palace **Daumier** 1808–79 *Third-Class Carriage* **Bingham** 1811–79 *Fur Traders Descending the Missouri* **Millet** 1814–75 *The Gleaners* **Courbet** 1819–77 *Burial at Ornans* **Manet** 1832–83 *Olympia* **Degas** 1834–1917 *Four Dancers* **Whistler** 1834–1903 *The White Girl: Symphony in White, No. 1* **Homer** 1836–1910 *Breezing Up* **Cézanne** 1839–1906 *Mont Sainte-Victoire* **Rodin** 1840–1917 *The Thinker* **Monet** 1840–1926 *Rouen Cathedral* **Renoir** 1841–1919 *Le Moulin de la Galette* **Morisot** 1841–95 *In the Dining Room* **Eakins** 1844–1916 *The Gross Clinic* **Cassatt** 1844–1926 *The Bath* **Rousseau** 1844–1910 *The Dream* **Gauguin** 1848–1903 *Where Do We Come From?* **van Gogh** 1853–90 *The Starry Night* **Seurat** 1859–91 *Sunday Afternoon on the Island of La Grande Jatte* **Toulouse-Lautrec** 1864–1901 *Quadrille at the Moulin Rouge*	**Rousseau** 1712–78 *Emile* **Goethe** 1749–1832 *Faust* **Schiller** 1759–1805 "Ode to Joy" **Blake** 1757–1827 "The Tyger" **Wordsworth** 1770–1850 "The World Is Too Much With Us" **Coleridge** 1772–1834 "Kubla Khan" **Byron** 1788–1824 "Prometheus" **Shelley** 1792–1822 "To a Skylark" **Mary Shelley** 1797–1851 *Frankenstein* **Keats** 1795–1821 "La Belle Dame Sans Merci" **Schubert** 1797–1828 *Gretchen am Spinnrade* **Berlioz** 1803–69 *Symphonie fantastique* **Emerson** 1803–82 "The Rhodora" **de Tocqueville** 1805–59 *Democracy in America* **Mendelssohn** 1809–47 Italian Symphony **Poe** 1809–49 "Annabel Lee" **Tennyson** 1809–92 "Ulysses" **Chopin** 1810–49 *Ballade in G minor* **Liszt** 1811–86 *Les Preludes* **Whitman** 1819–92 "I Hear America Singing" **Melville** 1819–91 *Moby Dick* **Dostoevsky** 1821–81 "The Grand Inquisitor" **Arnold** 1822–88 "Dover Beach" **Dickinson** 1830–86 "A Service of Song" **Brahms** 1833–97 Symphony No. 3 **Twain** 1835–1910 "The Notorious Jumping Frog of Calaveras County" **Hardy** 1840–1928 "Neutral Tones" **Tchaikovsky** 1840–93 "The Nutcracker" **Crane** 1871–1900 "War Is Kind"	**Bentham** 1748–1832 *Utilitarianism* **Hegel** 1770–1831 *Philosophy of History* **Schopenhauer** 1788–1860 *The World as Will and Idea* **Daguerre** 1799–1851 photography **Faraday** 1791–1867 electromagnetic induction **Morse** 1791–1872 painting, telegraph, and Morse Code **Mill** 1806–73 *On Liberty* **Kierkegaard** 1813–55 *Fear and Trembling* **Marx** 1818–83 *Das Kapital* **Pasteur** 1822–95 begins bacteriology **Mendel** 1822–84 genetics **Thomson** 1824–1907 transatlantic cable (1858) **Lister** 1827–1912 antiseptic surgery (1860) **James** 1842–1910 pragmatism **Nietzsche** 1844–1900 *Thus Spake Zarathustra* **Röntgen** 1845–1913 X-rays (1895) **Edison** 1847–1931 inventor **Bell** 1849–1922 telephone (1870s) **Friese-Greene** 1855–1921 movies (1880s) **Freud** 1856–1939 psychoanalysis **Hertz** 1857–1894 wireless that led to Marconi's radio in 1895 **Diesel** 1858–1913 diesel engine (1897)
1900	**1900–46** Victor Emmanuel III of Italy **1901–10** Edward VII of England	**Munch** 1864–1944 *The Scream*	**Puccini** 1858–1924 *La Bohème* **Debussy** 1862–1918 *La Mer* **Strauss** 1864–1949 *Till Eulenspiegel's Merry Pranks* **Dunbar** 1872–1906 "Sympathy"	**Planck** 1858–1947 quantum theory (1900) **Wright brothers** 1867–1912; 1871–1948 heavier-than-air flight (1903) **Curie** 1867–1934; radium (1910) **Einstein** 1879–1955 relativity (1905)

CHAPTER 23

Revolution, Romanticism, Realism

REVOLUTION TO WATERLOO

On 14 July 1789 a Parisian mob stormed the hated prison called the Bastille only to find a handful of bewildered prisoners. When Louis XVI asked the next day if this were a riot, the response was: "No sire, a revolution." The revolt erupted only eight years after French money and troops had materially helped the American colonies win their independence from Great Britain. Due partly to the American effort, the national debt was enormous and getting worse because of huge defense expenditures. Failed harvests and mismanaged financial crises led to widespread shortages and skyrocketing food prices. Whatever was wrong was blamed on the government. Hunger and anger finally touched off a revolution long in the making. The American example had inspired, of course, much revolutionary fervor, but the enemy was not a distant colonial power but the French establishment itself. Nothing less than the total destruction of the *ancien régime* would suffice. In a nation at war with its own institutions, fury and brutality energized the revolution from the storming of the Bastille to the busy guillotine and the Reign of Terror. St. Just stated the ultimate goal quite simply: "The Republic consists in the extermination of everything that opposes it." Like many revolutions (with the notable exception of the American), the political outcome was a tyranny and the economic consequences catastrophic. As Barzini observed in *The Europeans*, "the French Revolution did not correct the fundamental defects of French life. It magnified and perfected them." In retrospect we can see that this ferocious bloodbath marked the beginning of what we have called the Middle Modern World of 1789 to 1914, the period between the beginning of our modern world in about 1600 and the twentieth century.

Royalty, aristocracy, and all their properties were targeted for destruction and indeed many nobles were summarily executed while howling mobs ravaged rich estates. The revolution feasted on ferocity so pervasive that 250,000 people (one-third of the population) died in just one area of the country (the Vendée). Any who opposed, hindered, or even failed to strongly support the revolution could be consumed in the firestorm of savagery and death, and many thousands were.

The revolutionary battle cry of "Liberty, Equality, Fraternity" was a thrilling slogan that had nothing to do with reality. How can you have both total individual liberty and a strong, efficient government? How can you abolish privilege and place everyone on the same social, brotherly level in a country with few teachers, lawyers, and doctors and millions of illiterate peasants? It certainly wasn't the first time that ideals clashed with the real world.

The revolution had been incredibly destructive but there were some positive results, particularly the noble "Declaration of the Rights of Man and the Citizen." Feudalism, titles, and privileges had been abolished, the monastic orders suppressed, and church properties confiscated, but the enemies of France were assaulting the borders and internal disorder was increasing. The execution of Robespierre in 1794 ended the Terror, but it took the establishment of the Directory in 1795 to temporarily stabilize the state. Composed of men of conspicuous wealth, the Directory ruled from 1795 to 1799 with the assistance of the military, most notably the Corsican general Napoleon Buonaparte (1769–1821). Under the guise of saving the revolution Napoleon seized power in a coup d'état in 1799 and declared himself First Consul. Proclaiming himself emperor in 1804, he launched a course of conquest that engulfed much of Europe and part of Africa. Waterloo (18 June 1815) was an anticlimax to the fall of a conqueror who lost his entire Grand Army of 500,000 men on the scorched steppes of Russia.

Napoleon saw himself as the enlightened, benevolent despot who had rescued the revolution (fig. 23.1), but he maintained order and control only with the army and, especially, his secret police. He did establish the Code Napoleon, a model of modern civil laws that buried the inequities of the *ancien régime* and set the stage for the rise of the middle class. The Napoleonic legend of the military and political genius who fostered liberalism and nationalism contains, therefore, minor elements of truth. The ideals of the French Revolution did, in time, inspire the spread of democracy throughout the Western world. The other side of the coin was dark and bloody; two decades of Napoleonic wars destroyed lives and property on a staggering scale (map 23.1).

Napoleon's conquerors were deep in deliberations at

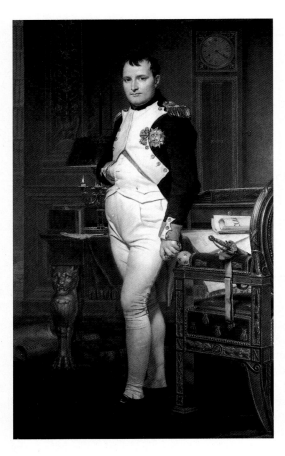

the Congress of Vienna when he escaped from Elba and rallied his still loyal armies for a Hundred Days' campaign that ended, once and for all, on the field of Waterloo. Final banishment to the remote island of St. Helena and a heavy guard assured the allies of a peace on their terms.

Called the "peace concert of Europe," the Congress of Vienna (1814–15) involved Austria, Prussia, Russia, and England, but its guiding spirit was Prince Clemens von Metternich (MEH-ter-nikh; 1773–1859), the chief minister of Austria. A reactionary and arch defender of the old order, Metternich secured a balance of power that favored Austria and reinforced established monarchies at the expense of all

---

23.1 Jacques-Louis David, *Napoleon in His Study*. 1812. Oil on canvas, 6' 8¼"× 4' 1¼" (2.04 × 1.25 m). National Gallery of Art, Washington, D.C. (Samuel H. Kress Collection).
Wearing the Legion of Honour, Napoleon is pictured by his court painter as a conscientious ruler who has stayed up until 4:12 A.M. working for his subjects.

Map 23.1 Napoleon's empire at its greatest extent, 1812.

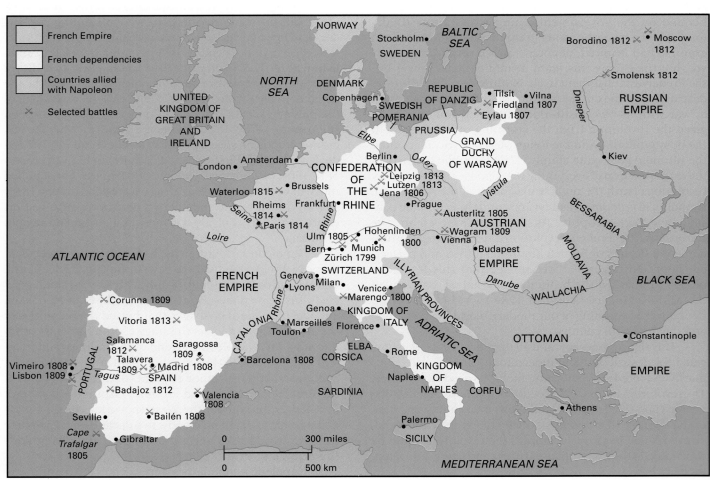

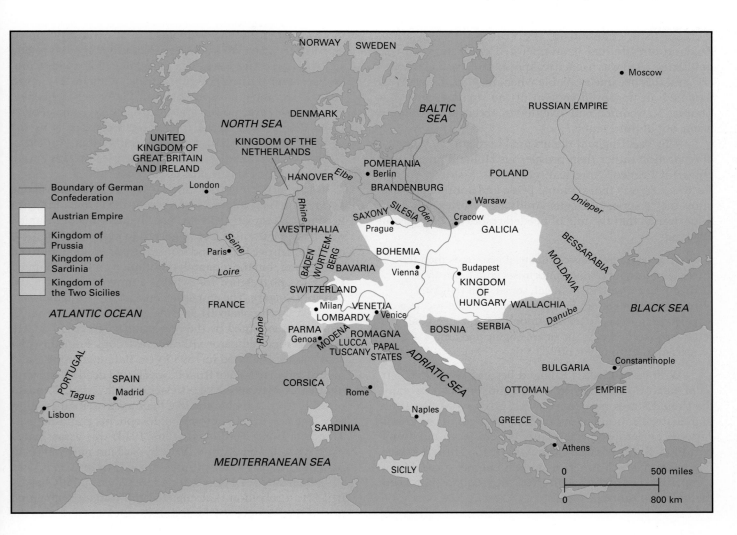

Map 23.2   Europe, 1815.

liberal movements, marking the period of 1815–48 as the Age of Metternich (map 23.2).

Napoleon's foreign minister, Prince Charles Maurice de Talleyrand (1754–1838), betrayed Napoleon, won easier peace terms for his country, and effected the restoration of the Bourbon kings with Louis XVIII (reigned 1814–24), the brother of Louis XVI.

THE REVOLUTIONS OF 1830 AND 1848

The heavy-handed, reactionary rule of Charles X (1824–30), who succeeded Louis XVIII, led to the July Revolution of 1830 in which the workers of Paris challenged the government. When the troops and police refused to fire on the rioters, the king quickly abdicated, delighting the liberals, who saw a possibility of relieving the misery of workers oppressed by the monarchy and the factory-owners. On the invitation

of the Chamber of Deputies, Louis Philippe (reigned 1830–48) assumed rule of a "bourgeois monarchy," which catered to the wealthy middle class and ignored the industrial workers. The brief July Revolution sparked violence in Germany, Italy, Spain, Portugal, Poland, and Belgium, all of which was overcome by force except in Belgium which, in 1831, won its independence from Holland.

A wave of revolutions swept Europe in 1848, the year in which Marx and Engels published *The Communist Manifesto*. The suppressed forces of liberalism erupted in France, Prussia, Austria, Hungary, Bohemia, Croatia, and the Italian possessions of the Hapsburgs. Repression was even more severe than in 1830 but, as Marx and Engels wrote, "The specter of Communism" was haunting Europe.

THE INDUSTRIAL REVOLUTION

Between 1750 and 1850 England's economic structure changed drastically as the nation shifted from an agrarian society to modern industrialism. The transformation was astonishingly rapid because so many important factors already existed: capitalism, international trade, mercantilism, colonialism, the Protestant work ethic. England already had hand-operated domestic (cottage) industries; what was needed was power to drive the machinery, and this became available when, in 1769, James Watt patented an improved version of the steam engine that Thomas Newcomen had invented in about 1700 to pump water out of mine shafts.[1]

Why was England the original home of the industrial revolution rather than prosperous Holland or rich and powerful France? American economic historian W. W. Rostow suggests that national pride and confidence were buoyed by a series of English military victories but, more importantly, that the mix of needed resources was best in England:

> Britain, with more basic industrial resources than the Netherlands; more nonconformists, and more ships than France; with its political, social, and religious revolution fought out by 1688—Britain alone was in a position to weave together cotton manufacture, coal and iron technology, the steam engine and ample foreign trade to pull it off.[2]

With its head start England became the textile center of the world but, after 1850, Belgium, France, Germany, the United States, and Canada were also involved not only in industrialization but in dramatic changes in communications, agricultural chemistry, machinery, and transportation. Railroads and steamships helped turn northern Europe and North America into an energetic and highly competitive complex that, in effect, functioned like an economic community.

DEVELOPMENT OF THE WESTERN NATIONS

Only in France did the 1848 revolution succeed and then just briefly. The Second Republic lasted from 1848 to 1852, followed by the Second Empire of Napoleon III (1852–70). Deliberately provoked by Bismarck, the Franco-Prussian War (1870–1) toppled the inept emperor and humiliated the nation. The Third Republic of 1871 finally exorcised the monarchy in France, but the Dreyfus Affair (1894–1906) nearly ripped the nation asunder. Falsely accused of treason, Captain Alfred Dreyfus (dray-fus; 1859–1935) was cashiered from the army and sentenced to life imprisonment on notorious Devil's Island. Generally speaking, anti-Semites, royalists, militarists, and Catholics backed the army whereas republicans, socialists, intellectuals, and anticlericals supported Dreyfus. Emile Zola, for example, was jailed for his inflammatory newspaper article, *"J'accuse"* (1898). It took a civil court to exonerate Dreyfus and reinstate him in the army as a major. Monarchists and Catholics were discredited, paving the way for the separation of church and state.

Otto Fürst von Bismarck (1815–98), the first minister of Prussia (1862–71), personally created the German Empire in 1871, when he had Wilhelm I of Prussia proclaimed emperor (reigned 1871–88). Consolidating his gains after a series of aggressive wars, the "iron chancellor" made a unified Germany the new power in Europe. Wilhelm II (reigned 1888–1918), the grandson of Queen Victoria, had his own ideas about royal power and dismissed his chancellor in 1890. Bismarck criticized the Kaiser unceasingly as the emperor armed his nation for the conflict that erupted in 1914. Wilhelm II abdicated in 1918 after leading his nation to defeat in the catastrophic Great War.

During the reign of Francis II (1792–1835) Austria was defeated on four different occasions by the French. Emperor Ferdinand (reigned 1835–48) had frequent fits of insanity, which left Metternich free to govern in his name. The 1848 revolution drove Ferdinand from the throne and Metternich from power, but the monarchy continued under the ill-fated Franz Joseph (reigned 1848–1916), Emperor of Austria and King of Hungary. The emperor's brother, Maximilian I, was installed by Napoleon III as Emperor of Mexico (1864–7), but he was executed by the revolutionary forces of Juarez after the French emperor withdrew his troops. Franz Joseph's wife was assassinated in 1898 by an Italian anarchist, and his only son, Archduke Rudolf, was found dead (along with his mistress Baroness Maria Vetsera) at Mayerling. Thought possibly to be a double suicide, the tragedy remains a mystery. The heir-apparent to Franz Joseph, his grand-nephew Archduke Franz Ferdinand (1863–1914) was assassinated (with his wife) on 28 June 1914 by Serbian nationalists at Sarajevo, leading to the ultimate tragedy of the Great War.

Ruled by the Turks since 1456, Greece finally began, in 1821, a rebellion that engaged the romantic imagination of the Western world. Extolling ancient Greece as the birthplace of democracy and of Western culture, Philhellenic (pro-Greek) committees in Europe and North America sent supplies and money while demanding that civilized nations intervene directly. Eventually, England, France, and Russia did. The war was ferocious, with Greek peasants slaughtering every Turk in sight and the Turks retaliating, for example, by killing or selling into slavery all 30,000 residents of the island of Chios, which inspired Delacroix's painting, *The Massacre at Chios* (fig. 23.2). Lord Byron could not resist the siren call of Greek independence and died there of fever in 1824. By 1832 independence had been achieved, but Greek nationalism was not fully victorious until after World War II.

Early in the nineteenth century Italy was temporarily unified under Napoleon, but the Congress of Vienna

1. Reinvented would be a more appropriate word. The ancient Greeks were apparently the first to invent the steam engine. Judging by the drawings of Heron (or Hero) of Alexandria (ca. second century AD), steam power was used in toy gadgets that caused birds to sing and Tritons to blow their horns. See Robert S. Brumbaugh, *Ancient Greek Gadgets and Machines* (Westport, Conn.: Greenwood Press, 1975).
2. W. W. Rostow, *The Stages of Economic Growth* (New York: Cambridge University Press, 1960), p. 33.

23.2 Eugène Delacroix, *The Massacre at Chios*. 1822–4. Oil on canvas, 13' 10" × 11' 7" (4.22 × 3.53 m). Louvre, Paris. Photo: Marburg/Art Resource, New York.

again reduced it to petty states. Following several abortive revolts, Giuseppe Garibaldi (1807–82) spearheaded the *Risorgimento* (rie-sor-jie-MEN-toe; "resurgence") which, by 1861, established Italy, under King Victor Emmanuel II (reigned 1861–78), as a unified political entity for the first time since the demise of the Roman Empire. By 1870 the Papal States had been incorporated into the kingdom, but not until 1929 was Vatican City established by Benito Mussolini as a separate sovereign state of 108 acres.

Plagued by Czarist repression and widespread corruption, poverty, and ignorance, Russia was the most backward country in Europe. Czar Alexander I (reigned 1801–25) attempted some reforms but, under the influence of Metternich, he became a reactionary; his successor, Nicholas I (reigned 1825–55), was even more rigid. The campaign of Nicholas to dominate southeast Europe led to the Crimean War (1853–6) in which the allied powers of Turkey, England, France, and Sardinia stopped, for a time, Russian expansionism. The main battle was the successful siege of the Russian naval base at Sevastopol, but the war itself was notorious for the outrageous neglect of wounded soldiers and general incompetence of command. Nothing could save the troops from tragic blunders— epitomized by the futile gallantry of the Light Brigade.

ANGEL OF MERCY

Trained as a nurse in France and Germany at a time when most nurses were untrained menials, Florence Nightingale (1820–1910) offered to leave her job as a hospital superintendent in London to nurse soldiers in the Crimea. The minister of war immediately (surprisingly) accepted her proposal and helped her lead thirty-eight nurses to the pitifully inadequate hospitals behind the battlefields. Having saved untold lives, she returned to London after the war to open the Nightingale School, the first to train nurses as medical professionals. She was the very first woman to be awarded, belatedly in 1907, the British Order of Merit.

Tennyson's poem, "The Charge of the Light Brigade," typifies the romantic fantasies about national honor and glory that helped plunge Europe into the Great War of 1914–18.

European Monarchs

The reign of Alexander II (1855–81) was about as authoritarian as that of Nicholas I, but he did belatedly liberate about 40,000,000 serfs with his 1861 Emancipation Act. The assassination of Alexander II led to the brutally oppressive regime of Alexander III (reigned 1881–94) and the inept but equally oppressive reign of Nicholas II (reigned 1894–1918), the last of the czars.

The long reign of England's George III (1760–1820) actually ended in 1811 when the king became totally insane. Functioning as Prince Regent (1811–20) and then king, George IV (reigned 1820–30) led a wildly profligate life that earned him the contempt of his subjects. William IV (reigned 1830–7) agreed to the Reform Bill of 1832 that extended suffrage to people who owned property but not to the large majority who did not. His niece, Victoria (reigned 1837–1901), reestablished the prestige of the crown while presiding over the enormous expansion of the British Empire, symbolized by her crowning as Empress of India in 1876. Though the English monarchy was largely decorative, Victoria determinedly took her role seriously, presiding over the conversion of the country into a political democracy with humanitarian reforms and a measure of social and economic democracy. Paradoxically, the British developed a liberal democracy at home while pursuing aggressive imperialism abroad.

Several decades before Victoria's death Victorian earnestness and sobriety had become, for many writers and artists, increasingly boring. They were as ready for a new era as Edward VII (reigned 1901–10) was eager to rule, having been Prince of Wales for sixty years. The Edwardian Age, as flashy and flamboyant as the king himself, was a great age for those who could afford to frolic in the grand manner. The accession of George V (reigned 1910–36) restored some measure of decorum but all that ended in 1914 with the guns of August.

America's Civil War

Inspired in part by the doctrine of **Manifest Destiny**, the United States tripled its size during the nineteenth century and increased its population twentyfold. Even more remarkable was the fact that the nation could expand so enormously and still maintain its union. The Civil War (1861–5) was a cruel test sufficient to destroy perhaps any other nation. Slavery was the basic issue but the conflict also stemmed from widely divergent ways of life and different economic structures. The mainly industrial North was vigorous and aggressive in the spirit of Calvinism, whereas the South was primarily agricultural, with a relaxed and cavalier life-style. Lee surrendered to Grant at Appomattox, the war was over, and that fact was accepted, despite

23.3 Mathew Brady, *Portrait of Lincoln*. Photograph. Photo: Hulton Deutsch, London.

UNCLE TOM'S CABIN

The scenes of this story, as its title indicates, lie among a race hitherto ignored by the associations of polite and refined society; an exotic race, whose ancestors, born beneath a tropic sun, brought with them, and perpetuated to their descendants, a character so essentially unlike the hard and dominant Anglo-Saxon race, as for many years to have won from it only misunderstanding and contempt . . . .

But another and better day is dawning . . . . Unhappy Africa at last is remembered; Africa, who began the race of civilization and human progress in the dim, gray dawn of early time, but who, for centuries, has lain bound and bleeding at the foot of civilized and Christianized humanity, imploring compassion in vain . . . .

The object of these sketches is to awaken sympathy and feeling for the African race, as they exist among us; to show their wrongs and sorrows, under a system so necessarily cruel and unjust as to defeat and do away the good effects of all that can be attempted for them, by their best friends, under it.

From Harriet Beecher Stowe (1811–96),
Preface, *Uncle Tom's Cabin*, 1852

the four years of ferocious combat, by most Southerners as the final end of a rebellion that would never again be seriously considered. Reconstruction would surely have proceeded less radically had Lincoln not been assassinated but, nevertheless, his views seemed to eventually temper vengeful northern radicals and encourage the moderates. In his memorable Second Inaugural Address, given just five weeks before the end of the war, Lincoln (fig. 23.3) set the tone of what would ultimately prove to be the sanest and wisest attitude in the aftermath of the nation's internal agony, as summarized in the final paragraph:

With malice toward none; with charity for all; with firmness in the right, as God gives us to see the right, let us strive on to finish the work we are in; to bind up the nation's wounds; to care for him who shall have borne the battle, and for his widow, and his orphan—to do all which may achieve and cherish a just and lasting peace among ourselves, and with all nations.

THE END OF AN ERA

The industrial revolution was a major factor in the complex chain of events leading to the Great War. Germany, England, France, and Russia were competing in the quality and price of industrial products while also searching for new colonial

markets that would absorb some of their booming production. In Europe, after the unification of Germany and Italy, there was very little territory "available" for annexation. There were, in other words, more predatory nations than suitable victims, with the latter located mainly in Africa (maps 23.3 and 23.4). To protect what they had and hoped to acquire, nations enlarged their armies and navies and equipped them with the latest weaponry.

National identity was another crucial factor. As late as the 1860s citizens of Florence, for example, saw themselves as Florentines or Tuscans; residents of Normandy were Norman rather than French; the population of Munich was Bavarian first and German second, and so on. The physical unification of Germany and Italy stimulated a sense of national identity symbolized by the powerful image of Great Britain as a sovereign nation, with national pride fueled by feelings of national superiority.

The Romantic idea of the sovereign individual was enlarged to include each citizen as a critical component in the noble and heroic image of the sovereign state. There was for the Romantic no true identity separate from the homeland, as Sir Walter Scott emphasized, when he wrote: "Breathes there the man, with soul so dead,/Who never to himself hath said,/ This is my own, my native land!"

Map 23.3   European colonies in Africa, 1878.

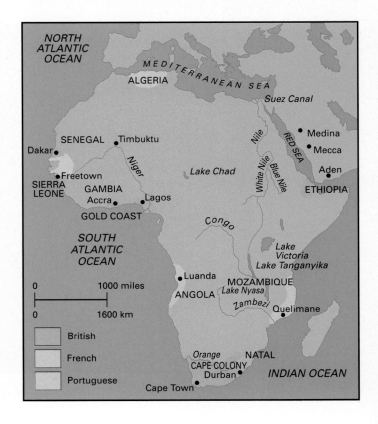

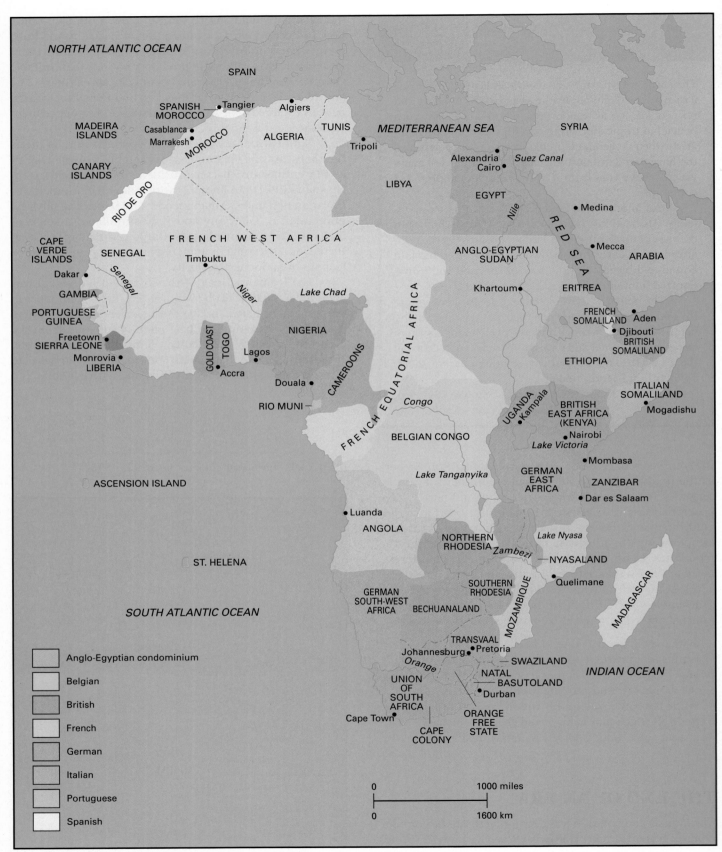

Map 23.4   European rule in Africa, 1914.

The Balkan Tinderbox

Nations forged alliances that were supposed to maintain a balance of power and thus avoid open warfare. Bismarck effected a Triple Alliance in 1882 of Germany, Austria-Hungary, and Italy to offset French power. France and Russia countered in 1894 with a Dual Alliance that made Germany uneasy about a two-front war and, in 1907, Great Britain joined the two nations in what was called a "close understanding" (Triple Entente). The tinderbox was the Balkans, where nationalist ambitions were continually clashing. Russia wanted to make the Black Sea a Slavic lake, but Great Britain saw a Russian thrust as a threat to the empire. By this time Turkey, the "sick man of Europe," was virtually powerless, newly independent Serbia was a threat to the Austro-Hungarian Empire, and Germany had her eye on Balkan conquests. The high level of international tension was extremely dangerous because all nations were armed to the teeth.

Nationalist activities touched a spark to the Balkan tinder and nationalist stubbornness, duty, and honor provoked a war that many diplomats and statesmen believed was preferable to seeing their nation humiliated by loss of face. On 28 June 1914, a Serbian nationalist assassinated the Austrian Archduke Franz Ferdinand and his wife. After obtaining Germany's backing for whatever it should choose to do in response—a true "blank check"—Austria delivered an ultimatum to Serbia that was promptly rejected. Claiming that compromise was inconsistent with "national honor," Austria rebuffed a British offer to mediate and declared war on Serbia on 28 July 1914. Fearful of German might, the panic-stricken Russian government ordered full mobilization, prompting a German ultimatum, ignored by the Kremlin, to cease or face a fight. On 1 August 1914 Germany began mobilizing while simultaneously declaring war, which says something about German readiness. Two days later the confident Germans declared war on the frantically mobilizing French. Great Britain dithered and delayed until Germany announced her intention to violate Belgium's neutrality as established in 1839. Great Britain's subsequent declaration of war prompted the German chancellor to sneer that the English had gone to war over a "scrap of paper" (map 23.5).

Map 23.5   Europe, 1914.

World War I

The war was fought, generally speaking, with twentieth-century weapons (machine guns, tanks, poison gas, artillery) and nineteenth-century tactics (mass frontal assaults, artillery duels, use of cavalry). There were many theatres of action but the 300-mile (483-km) Western Front was the main meat-grinder with mass charges launched between trenches into pointblank machine-gun fire. In four years sixteen nations had casualties (killed, died, wounded, missing) of about 50,000,000. One example indicates the extent of the slaughter. In the center of the small French village of Sully-sur-Loire stands a war memorial designed as a tall obelisk. On one side are listed, in categories, the villagers who died in World War II. The categories themselves communicate much about the conflict with Nazi Germany: "Killed in Action," "Murdered by the Gestapo," "Died in Concentration Camp," and "Missing." Eight names are engraved on the World War II side. On the opposite World War I side, the single category is "Killed in Action." There are ninety-six names. Throughout Western history no event has ended an era with such finality as did the Great War.

ROMANTICISM

More an attitude to be explored than a term to be defined, Romanticism began around 1780 as a reaction against the Enlightenment. The Romantic movement itself lasted from about 1780 to about 1830, but Romantic ideas and issues were present in a variety of forms right up to 1914.

In its initial stages Romanticism was mainly a German movement but it drew its inspiration from Jean-Jacques Rousseau (1712–78). Rousseau began his *Social Contract* (1762) with a ringing proclamation: "Man is born free and everywhere he is in chains." The source of the trouble, according to Rousseau, was too much education, and of the wrong kind at that. Self-forged chains could not be thrown off with more "progress"; instead, people must emulate the Noble Savage by returning to a state of innocence in nature. Civilization had corrupted us, claimed Rousseau, and a return to nature was the proper antidote. More a call to action than a coherent program, just what Rousseau meant by "back to nature" has been debated for centuries. Some idea of his attitude can be obtained from his analysis of the "wrong kind of education" in the *Discourse on the Arts and Sciences* (1749):

Astronomy was born of superstition, eloquence of ambition, hatred, falsehood, and flattery; geometry of avarice; physics of an idle curiosity; and even moral philosophy of human pride. Thus the arts and sciences owe their birth to our vices; and we should be less doubtful of their advantages, if they had sprung from our virtues.

Their evil origin is, indeed, but too plainly reproduced in their objects. What would become of the arts were they not cherished by luxury? If men were not unjust, of what use were jurisprudence? What would become of history if there were no tyrants, wars, or conspiracies? In a word, who would pass his life in barren speculations if everybody, attentive only to the obligations of humanity and the necessities of nature, spent his whole life in serving his country, obliging his friends, and relieving the unhappy?

THE ROMANTIC MOVEMENT
Germany

Johann Gottfried von Herder (1744–1803) was the leader of the precursor of Romanticism, the *Sturm und Drang* (SHTOORM oont DRAHNG) movement in German literature, a term derived from Klinger's novel, *Der Wirrwarr; oder Sturm und Drang* ("Chaos; or Storm and Stress"). A passionate opponent of French rationalism and the Enlightenment, Herder emphasized the *Volksgeist* ("spirit of the people") in Germany, claiming that each *Volk* found its *Geist* in its language, literature, and religion. This was, in effect, a cultural particularism that became the basis of later German nationalism.

In his early writings Johann Wolfgang von Goethe (GUHR-tuh; 1749–1832) was one of the leading exponents of the movement. Written after an unhappy love affair, *The Sorrows of Young Werther* (1774) was a morbidly sensitive tale full of sentiment and gloomy feelings that culminated in the suicide of the tragic Werther. Though Goethe was later to regret the storm and stress of his little book, it made him an instant celebrity.

The philosopher Friedrich Wilhelm Joseph von Schelling (1775–1854) contributed the theory that nature and mind were inseparable and differed only in degree rather than in kind. For Schelling the creative artist was the "ideal Romantic man," a genius who presented his work as instinctively created apart from any conscious effort. From this idea Nietzsche developed his notion of the creative genius as a "superman" who was "beyond good and evil."

Second only to Goethe in German literature, Friedrich von Schiller (1759–1805) was influenced by Kant and, in turn, became a major inspiration for modern German literature. An idealist who hated tyranny, Schiller envisioned the universal fellowship of all humankind. It was his poem *"An die Freude"* ("To Joy") that Beethoven used in the final movement of his mighty Ninth Symphony.

Contributing his pessimistic theories to the movement, Arthur Schopenhauer (1788–1860) claimed that reality was a blind driving force manifested in individuals as Will. Individual wills inevitably clashed, causing strife and pain, from which there was no escape except by a negation of the will. Temporary escape was possible, however, through creative acts in art and science. According to

Schopenhauer and other Romantics, creativity emerges from the unconscious, but there are also instinctual drives that conflict with the creative impulses. The unconscious cuts both ways and the Romantics were vividly aware of the "night-side" that could release demonic destruction, as Schopenhauer noted in *The World of Will and Idea* (1818). Blind human will achieves only unhappiness or, as Goya said, "The sleep of reason produces monsters." Schopenhauer concluded that reason must permit the release of creativity while simultaneously controlling the passions, but he was not optimistic about the outcome.

England

Romanticism was effectively expressed in nineteenth-century art and music, in historical novels, Gothic tales, and romantic stories of love and adventure. For an English-speaking audience the Romantic mood is never better expressed than in the work of the English poets.

William Blake, 1757–1827

A self-proclaimed mystic with minimal formal schooling, Blake was a fundamentalist Protestant who believed that the Bible was the sole source of religious knowledge. A militant individualist, he detested institutionalized religion, claiming that the human imagination was the sole means of expressing the Eternal. Blake referred to people as the Divine Image, the possessors of the humane virtues of mercy, pity, peace, and love. Equally gifted as an artist, Blake illustrated all but one of his volumes of poetry plus the Book of Job, Dante, and the poems of Thomas Gray.

The collection of poems called the *Songs of Innocence* (1789) coincides with the beginning of the French Revolution that, for Blake, held so much promise of a better life for all people. The following poem from that collection celebrates the joys of a Christian life and a simple pastoral existence.

LITERARY SELECTION 25

The Lamb (1789)

William Blake

Little Lamb, who made thee?
Dost thou know who made thee?
Gave thee life, and bid thee feed,
By the stream and o'er the mead;
Gave thee clothing of delight,
Softest clothing, woolly, bright;
Gave thee such a tender voice,
Making all the vales rejoice?
Little Lamb, who made thee?
Dost thou know who made thee?   10

Little Lamb, I'll tell thee,
Little Lamb, I'll tell thee:
He is callèd by thy name,
For He calls Himself a Lamb.
He is meek, and He is mild;
He became a little child.
I a child, and thou a lamb,
We are callèd by His name.
Little Lamb, God bless thee!
Little Lamb, God bless thee!   20

The *Songs of Experience* address a sick and corrupt world in which good and evil coexist. In "The Tyger" Blake asks the age-old question: did the good God create evil?

The Tyger (1794)

William Blake

Tyger! Tyger! burning bright
In the forests of the night,
What immortal hand or eye
Could frame thy fearful symmetry?

In what distant deeps or skies
Burnt the fire of thine eyes?
On what wings dare he aspire?
What the hand dare seize the fire?

And what shoulder, and what art,
Could twist the sinews of thy heart?   10
And when thy heart began to beat,
What dread hand? and what dread feet?

What the hammer? what the chain?
In what furnace was thy brain?
What the anvil? what dread grasp
Dare its deadly terrors clasp?

When the stars threw down their spears,
And water'd heaven with their tears,
Did he smile his work to see?
Did he who made the Lamb make thee?   20

Tyger! Tyger! burning bright
In the forests of the night,
What immortal hand or eye,
Dare frame thy fearful symmetry?

STUDY QUESTIONS

In *The Marriage of Heaven and Hell* Blake wrote that "Attraction and Repulsion, Reason and Energy, Love and Hate are necessary to Human Existence." Is this attitude reflected in the poems about the lamb and the tiger? Is the tiger, in other words, evil or a symbol of necessary vigor and energy?

William Wordsworth, 1770–1850

The greatest of the English nature poets, Wordsworth was influenced by Rousseau and the spirit of the French Revolution. Strongly opposed to the flowery artificiality of Neoclassic poetry, Wordsworth and Samuel Taylor Coleridge published *Lyrical Ballads* (2nd edition, 1800), which contained a new poetic manifesto. Wordsworth referred to his poetry as "emotion recollected in tranquillity" but, as he stated in the manifesto, he deliberately chose to write in "the language of conversation in the middle and lower classes of society."

The following sonnet mourns a world so overwhelmed with materialism that it may lose its spiritual qualities. Proteus and Triton are from Greek mythology and symbolize the poet's conviction that the wonders of nature that delighted the ancients cannot, in the long run, be destroyed by the Industrial Age. Wordsworth was a Romantic optimist.

LITERARY SELECTION 26

The World is Too Much With Us (1802)

William Wordsworth

The world is too much with us; late and soon,
Getting and spending, we lay waste our powers:
Little we see in Nature that is ours;
We have given our hearts away, a sordid boon!
This Sea that bares her bosom to the moon;
The winds that will be howling at all hours,
And are up-gathered now like sleeping flowers;
For this, for everything, we are out of tune;
It moves us not.—Great God! I'd rather be
A Pagan suckled in a creed outworn;
So might I, standing on this pleasant lea,
Have glimpses that would make me less forlorn;
Have sight of Proteus rising from the sea;
Or hear old Triton blow his wreathèd horn.

STUDY QUESTIONS

If Wordsworth were to write "The World is Too Much With Us" today, would he be as optimistic about the survival of nature's wonders? Why or why not?

Samuel Taylor Coleridge, 1772–1834

Though he did not consider himself a Romantic poet, Coleridge did make a classic Romantic statement: "Each man is meant to represent humanity in his own way, combining its elements uniquely." Coleridge set great store on imagination over fancy, claiming that fancy was only the ability to copy or elaborate on previous examples; imagination was the ability to create new worlds. "Kubla Khan" is a notable example of an inspired vision whether or not, as Coleridge claimed, the poem was composed during an opium reverie and later written down. Coleridge and many other Romantics were fascinated with the exotic Orient. The grandson of Mongol conqueror Genghis Khan, Kubla Khan (1215?–94) founded the Yuan dynasty of China and sponsored Marco Polo as his agent to the West.

LITERARY SELECTION 27

Kubla Khan (1797)

Samuel Taylor Coleridge

In Xanadu did Kubla Khan
A stately pleasure-dome decree:
Where Alph, the sacred river, ran
Through caverns measureless to man
Down to a sunless sea.
So twice five miles of fertile ground
With walls and towers were girdled round:
And, there were gardens bright with sinuous rills,
Where blossomed many an incense-bearing tree
And here were forests ancient as the hills,   10
Enfolding sunny spots of greenery.
But oh! that deep romantic chasm which slanted
Down the green hill athwart a cedarn cover!
A savage place! as holy and enchanted
As e'er beneath a waning moon was haunted
By woman wailing for her demon-lover!
And from this chasm, with ceaseless turmoil seething,
As if this earth in fast thick pants were breathing,
A mighty fountain momently was forced,
Amid whose swift half-intermitted burst   20
Huge fragments vaulted like rebounding hail,
Or chaffy grain beneath the thresher's flail:
And 'mid these dancing rocks at once and ever
It flung up momently the sacred river.
Five miles meandering with a mazy motion
Through wood and dale the sacred river ran,
Then reached the caverns measureless to man,
And sank in tumult to a lifeless ocean:
And 'mid this tumult Kubla heard from far
Ancestral voices prophesying war!   30
    The shadow of the dome of pleasure
    Floated midway on the waves;
    Where was heard the mingled measure
    From the fountain and the caves.
It was a miracle of rare device,

A sunny pleasure-dome with caves of ice!
   A damsel with a dulcimer
In a vision once I saw:
   It was an Abyssinian maid,
   And on her dulcimer she played,   40
Singing of Mount Abora.
   Could I revive within me
   Her symphony and song,
   To such a deep delight 'twould win me,
That with music loud and long,
I would build that dome in air,
That sunny dome! those caves of ice!
And all who heard should see them there,
And all should cry, Beware! Beware!
His flashing eyes, his floating hair!   50
Weave a circle round him thrice,
And close your eyes with holy dread,
For he on honey-dew hath fed,
And drunk the milk of Paradise.

STUDY QUESTIONS

Coleridge claimed that "Kubla Khan" appeared to him in a dream and that what he later wrote down was "a fragment." Is the poem incomplete? Could the first thirty-six lines be an exercise in creative imagination and the remainder a lament over the loss of poetic power? In these terms is the poem complete or incomplete?

George Noel Gordon, Lord Byron, 1788–1824

The most flamboyant and controversial personality of the age, Lord Byron epitomizes the Romantic hero. With his egotism and superhuman vigor he gloried in physical and mental license, learning relatively late, and only in part, the virtue of moderation. He wrote his words, he said, "as a tiger leaps" and aimed many of them at conventional social behavior, cant, and hypocrisy. Much of his poetry was prosaic when compared with the iridescent style of Shelley and Keats but, as he said, his genius was eloquent rather than poetical. His reputation was early and firmly established with *Childe Harold's Pilgrimage*, a poetic travelogue, but his greatest work is *Don Juan*, a long poem full of irony and pathos. Byron wrote in the Dedication:

I want a hero: an uncommon want, . . .
But can't find any in the present age
Fit for my poem (that is, for my new one):
So, as I said, I'll take my friend Don Juan.

Almost to the day of his premature death Byron was torn between the heroic defiance of Prometheus and the worldly, cynical insolence of Don Juan. In the end, he tried to choose the Promethean way but died of fever during the Greek struggle for independence.

Percy Bysshe Shelley, 1792–1822

Shelley and Keats established Romantic verse as the prime poetic tradition of the period; to this day "Shelley and Keats" and "Romantic poetry" are virtually synonymous. A life-long heretic who was expelled from Oxford because of his pamphlet, *The Necessity of Atheism*, Shelley saw all humankind as the Divine Image to whom poets spoke as the "unacknowledged legislators of the world" (*A Defence of Poetry*). His finest achievement is *Prometheus Unbound*, a lyrical drama in four acts in which he gave full expression to his "passion for reforming the world." Also written at Leghorn, Italy, and published with *Prometheus Unbound* was "To a Skylark," the composition of which was described by Mary Wollstonecraft Shelley:

It was on a beautiful summer evening while wandering among the lanes, whose myrtle hedges were the bowers of the fireflies, that we heard the caroling of the skylark, which inspired one of the most beautiful of his poems.

LITERARY SELECTION 28

To a Skylark (1820)
Percy Bysshe Shelley

Hail to thee, blithe spirit!
   Bird thou never wert,
That from heaven, or near it,
   Pourest thy full heart
In profuse strains of unpremeditated art.
   Higher still and higher
      From the earth thou springest
Like a cloud of fire;
      The blue deep thou wingest,
And singing still dost soar, and soaring ever singest.   10
   In the golden lightning
      Of the sunken sun,
O'er which clouds are brightning,
      Thou dost float and run;
Like an unbodied joy whose race is just begun.
   The pale purple even
      Melts around thy flight;
Like a star of heaven,
      In the broad day-light
Thou art unseen, but yet I hear thy shrill delight,   20
   Keen as are the arrows
      Of that silver sphere,
Whose intense lamp narrows
      In the white dawn clear,
Until we hardly see, we feel that it is there.
   All the earth and air
      With thy voice is loud,
As, when night is bare,
      From one lonely cloud
The moon rains out her beams, and heaven is overflowed.   30

What thou art we know not;
    What is most like thee?
From rainbow clouds there flow not
    Drops so bright to see,
As from thy presence showers a rain of melody.
    Like a poet hidden
        In the light of thought,
    Singing hymns unbidden,
        Till the world is wrought
To sympathy with hopes and fears it heeded not: 40
    Like a high-born maiden
        In a palace tower,
    Soothing her love-laden
        Soul in secret hour
With music sweet as love, which overflows her bower:
    Like a glow-worm golden
        In a dell of dew,
    Scattering unbeholden
        Its aërial hue
Among the flowers and grass, which screen it from the
    view: 50
    Like a rose embowered
        In its own green leaves,
    By warm winds deflowered,
        Till the scent it gives
Makes faint with too much sweet these heavy-winged
    thieves:
    Sound of vernal showers
        On the twinkling grass,
    Rain-awakened flowers,
        All that ever was
Joyous, and clear, and fresh, thy music doth surpass: 60
    Teach us, sprite or bird,
        What sweet thoughts are thine:
    I have never heard
        Praise of love or wine
That panted forth a flood of rapture so divine.
    Chorus Hymenaeal,
        Or triumphal chaunt,
    Matched with thine would be all
        But an empty vaunt,
A thing wherein we feel there is some hidden want.   70
    What objects are the fountains
        Of thy happy strain?
    What fields, or waves, or mountains?
        What shapes of sky or plain?
What love of thine own kind? what ignorance of pain?
    With thy clear keen joyance
        Languor cannot be:
    Shadow of annoyance
        Never came near thee:
Thou lovest; but ne'er knew love's sad satiety.   80
    Waking or asleep,
        Thou of death must deem
    Things more true and deep
        Than we mortals dream,
Or how could thy notes flow in such a crystal stream?
    We look before and after,
        And pine for what is not:
    Our sincerest laughter
        With some pain is fraught;

Our sweetest songs are those that tell of saddest thought.   90
    Yet if we could scorn
        Hate, and pride, and fear;
    If we were things born
        Not to shed a tear,
I know not how thy joy we ever should come near.
    Better than all measures
        Of delightful sound,
    Better than all treasures
        That in books are found,
Thy skill to poet were, thou scorner of the ground!   100
    Teach me half the gladness
        That thy brain must know,
    Such harmonious madness
        From my lips would flow,
The world should listen then, as I am listening now.

STUDY QUESTION

How does Shelley achieve the seemingly effortless buoyancy of "To a Skylark"? Consider the rhythm and the use of words such as "blithe," "springest," "soar," "float," and many others.

Mary Wollstonecraft Godwin Shelley, 1797–1851

Mary Shelley deserves special mention here. She was the daughter of noted feminist Mary Wollstonecraft (1759–97), author of *Vindication of the Rights of Woman* (1792), and the equally notable social reformer William Godwin (1756–1836), a disciple of Jeremy Bentham and a man who strongly influenced Shelley's reforming zeal. Shelley had left Harriet, his wife, for Mary and moved to the continent where he later married her. While reading ghost stories one evening, Lord Byron suggested that each should write a tale of the supernatural. Mary Shelley's contribution was *Frankenstein; or, The Modern Prometheus* (1818). Using the central themes of Faustian ambition and Promethean creativity, Mary told the story of the scientist Frankenstein who dared to create life itself. Frankenstein's creation needed love and sympathy, but was greeted instead, even by his creator, with disgust and revulsion. Symbolizing Romantic ideas of isolation and alienation, Frankenstein's creation turned from a search for love to hatred of all humankind and murderous destruction. Mary Shelley's story is even more influential today as a modern myth about the horrifying potential of human creativity such as, for example, nuclear weapons.

John Keats, 1795–1821

The poems of both Keats and Shelley have a musicality that sets them apart from all other Romantic poetry. Trained as an apothecary with no thought of becoming a poet, Keats

THE RIGHTS OF WOMAN

Dedication: To M. Talleyrand-Perigord, Late Bishop of Autun

Sir, Having read with great pleasure a pamphlet which you have lately published, I dedicate this volume to you; to induce you to reconsider the subject and maturely weigh what I have advanced respecting the rights of woman and national education: and I call with the firm tone of humanity; for my arguments, Sir, are dictated by a disinterested spirit—I plead for my sex—not for myself. Independence I have long considered as the grand blessing of life, the basis of every virtue and independence I will ever secure by contracting my wants, though I were to live on a barren heath.

It is thus an affection for the whole human race that makes my pen dart rapidly along to support what I believe to be the cause of virtue: and the same motive leads me earnestly to wish to see woman placed in a station in which she would advance, instead of retarding, the progress of those glorious principles that give a substance to morality. My opinion, indeed, respecting the rights and duties of woman, seems to flow so naturally from these simple principles, that I think it scarcely possible, but that some of the enlarged minds who formed your admirable constitution, will coincide with me.

From Mary Wollstonecraft (1759–97),
A Vindication of the Rights of Woman, 1792

LITERARY SELECTION 29

La Belle Dame Sans Merci (1819)

John Keats

O what can ail thee, knight-at-arms,
    Alone and palely loitering?
The sedge has withered from the lake,
    And no birds sing.

O what can ail thee, knight-at-arms,
    So haggard and so woe-begone?
The squirrel's granary is full,
    And the harvest's done.

I see a lily on thy brow,
    With anguish moist and fever dew;   10
And on thy cheek a fading rose
    Fast withereth too.

I met a lady in the meads,
    Full beautiful—a faery's child;
Her hair was long, her foot was light,
    And her eyes were wild.

I set her on my pacing steed,
    And nothing else saw all day long;
For sidelong would she bend, and sing
    A faery's song.   20

I made a garland for her head,
    And bracelets too, and fragrant zone;
She looked at me as she did love,
    And made sweet moan.

She found me roots of relish sweet,
    And honey wild, and manna-dew;
And sure in language strange she said,
    "I love thee true."

She took me to her elfin grot,
    And there she wept and sighed full sore: 30
And there I shut her wild, wild eyes
    With kisses four.

And there she lullèd me asleep,
    And there I dreamed—Ah! woe betide!
The latest dream I ever dreamed,
    On the cold hill-side.

I saw pale kings and princes too,
    Pale warriors—death-pale were they all;
Who cried, "La Belle Dame Sans Merci
    Hath thee in thrall!"   40

I saw their starved lips in the gloam,
    With horrid warning gapèd wide;
And I awoke, and found me here
    On the cold hill's side.

And this is why I sojourn here,
    Alone and palely loitering;
Though the sedge is withered from the lake,
    And no birds sing.

began writing when he was eighteen with a sense of urgency, having noted the symptoms of the tuberculosis that had already carried off his mother and his brother. Keats was the first to admit that his initial volume of poetry had many flaws, but not that it was "alternately florid and arid," as one critic bitingly observed. Keats' own reaction to a barrage of criticism was quite relaxed: "About a twelvemonth since, I published a little book of verses; it was read by some dozen of my friends, who lik'd it; and some dozen whom I was unacquainted with, who did not."

Most Romantics adored what they imagined the Middle Ages to have been; none would have tolerated for a moment the reality of the medieval world. "La Belle Dame sans Merci" ("The Lovely Lady without Pity") is perhaps the finest example of Romantic medievalism. Though the title is taken from a medieval poem by Alain Chartier, the ballad is the poet's own magical version of the ageless myth of the hapless mortal who succumbs to the irresistible charms of a supernatural and pitiless seductress. The first three stanzas are addressed to the distraught knight by an unknown questioner; the balance forms his anguished reply.

STUDY QUESTION

How does Keats maintain the medieval mood in "La Belle Dame Sans Merci"? Look, for example, at obvious words such as "thee," "knight-at-arms," and "dancing steed" and subtle words such as "meads," "garland," and "elfin."

SUMMARY

The Romantic movement is perplexing if we consider only what these individual writers and philosophers advocated. What most Romantics were opposed to provides a clearer picture, and the Enlightenment was their main target. Empiricism, geometric thinking, Neoclassicism, all were areas subject to reason and, said the Romantics, all were mechanized and dehumanized. Even the great Newton had become only a materialist and a narrow materialist at that.

Romantics emphasized individuality, the non-rational component of the personality, a sense of the infinite, and a quest for religious reality beyond sensible experience to find God in nature and within the human heart. Far from a return to orthodoxy, the impulse to re-create wonder in the world by finding God in nature was common to many Romantics, except for those such as Byron and Shelley, who sought no God at all. The closest

23.4 Kaspar David Friedrich, *Cloister Graveyard Under Snow*. 1819. Oil on canvas, 3' 11" × 5' 10" (1.19 × 1.77 m). Formerly Nationalgalerie, Staatliche Museen, Berlin (destroyed in 1945 during the Battle of Berlin). Photo: B.P.K., Berlin.

approach to a Romantic consensus was the emphasis on the primacy of human concerns, the celebration of the emotional nature of human beings, and the necessity for creative activity through the exercise of an unfettered imagination.

Perhaps more than any other period, the Romantic era was expressed as well in literature as in music and the visual arts. "Art," wrote Oscar Wilde, "is the most intense mode of individualism that the world has known." In no era was the creative role of the individual more consciously and effectively fulfilled than in the Romantic age. Art was, moreover, highly social, because it was the "result of a relationship between the artist and his time" (James Adams). This was an era of extreme sensitivity to social issues. The Romantics, whether writers, artists, or composers, were generally attuned to certain themes that were endlessly fascinating. Figure 23.4 depicts in a single work five of the most powerful of these themes: nature, the Middle Ages, mysticism, religion, and death. The fate of this painting represents a final Romantic irony.

PHILOSOPHY, SCIENCE, AND SOCIAL THOUGHT
Hegel and Marx

The most important German philosopher after Kant, Georg Wilhelm Hegel (HAY-gul; 1770–1831) influenced European and American philosophers, historians, theologians, and political theorists. Described by Bertrand Russell as "the hardest to understand of all the great philosophers," Hegel and those doctrines of his that influenced Karl Marx will be our focus here. Hegel believed in an all-encompassing Absolute, a world Spirit that expressed itself in the historical process. Basing his logic on the "triadic dialectic," Hegel stated that for every concept or force (thesis) there was its opposite idea (antithesis). Out of the dynamic interaction between the two extremes would emerge a synthesis that, in turn, would become a new and presumably higher thesis. Absolute Being, for example, is a thesis whereas Absolute Unbeing is its antithesis. The synthesis is Absolute Becoming, meaning that the universe is eternally recreating itself.

The notable cultures of the past were, according to Hegel, stages in the evolutionary development of the world Spirit toward perfection and freedom. Human beings and their institutions must inevitably clash because all are subject to error; nevertheless, they must act and, through striving, find the "path of righteousness." Essentially Faustian in the conviction that perfectibility was attainable only through continuous activity and unavoidable conflict, Hegel's philosophy of history was evolutionary. Not only all humankind but the world itself was progressing ever upward, away from imperfection and toward the Absolute.

By mid-century, few could see progress of any kind, particularly for the oppressed lower class. The horrible working conditions and dismal lives of factory workers concerned social reformers throughout Europe. Many spoke out against the exploitation of the working class, but none so dramatically as the Communists in the following extracts from their *Manifesto*.

LITERARY SELECTION 30

Manifesto of the Communist Party (1848)

Karl Marx and Friedrich Engels

A spectre is haunting Europe—the spectre of Communism. All the Powers of old Europe have entered into a holy alliance to exorcize this spectre: Pope and Czar, Metternich and Guizot, French Radicals and German police spies.

Where is the party in opposition that has not been decried as Communistic by its opponents in power? Where the Opposition that has not hurled back the branding reproach of Communism against the more advanced opposition parties, as well as against its reactionary adversaries?   10

Two things result from this fact:

  I. Communism is already acknowledged by all European powers to be itself a power.
  II. It is high time that Communists should openly, in the face of the whole world, publish their views, their aims, their tendencies, and meet this nursery tale of the Spectre of Communism with a Manifesto of the party itself.

To this end, Communists of various nationalities have   20 assembled in London, and sketched the following Manifesto, to be published in the English, French, German, Italian, Flemish, and Danish languages.

I Bourgeois and Proletarians

The history of all hitherto existing society is the history of class struggles.

Freeman and slave, patrician and plebeian, lord and serf, guild-master and journeyman, in a word, oppressor and oppressed, stood in constant opposition to one another, carried on an uninterrupted, now hidden, now open fight, a fight that each time ended, either in a   30 revolutionary reconstitution of society at large, or in the common ruin of the contending classes.

In the earlier epochs of history, we find almost everywhere a complicated arrangement of society into various orders, a manifold gradation of social rank. In ancient Rome we have patricians, knights, plebeians, slaves; in the Middle Ages, feudal lords, vassals, guild-masters, journeymen, apprentices, serfs; in almost all of these classes, again, subordinate gradations.

The modern bourgeois society that has sprouted from   40 the ruins of feudal society, has not done away with class antagonisms. It has but established new classes, new conditions of oppression, new forms of struggle in place of the old ones.

Our epoch, the epoch of the bourgeoisie, possesses, however, this distinctive feature: it has simplified the class antagonisms. Society as a whole is more and more splitting up into two great classes directly facing each other: Bourgeoisie and Proletariat . . . .

Each step in the development of the bourgeoisie was   50 accompanied by a corresponding political advance of that class. An oppressed class under the sway of the feudal nobility, it became an armed and self-governing association in the medieval commune: here independent urban republic (as in Italy and Germany); there, taxable "third estate" of the monarchy (as in France); afterwards, in the period of manufacture, serving either the semi-feudal or the absolute monarchy as a counterpoise against the nobility, and, in fact, cornerstone of the great monarchies in general. The   60 bourgeoisie has, at last, since the establishment of Modern Industry and of the world market, conquered for itself, in the modern representative State, exclusive political sway. The executive of the modern State is but a committee for managing the common affairs of the whole bourgeoisie . . . .

IV Position of the Communists in Relation to the Various Existing Opposition Parties

. . . The Communists turn their attention chiefly to Germany because that country is on the eve of a bourgeois revolution that is bound to be carried out under more advanced conditions of European civilization   70 and with a much more developed proletariat than that of England in the seventeenth and of France in the eighteenth century, and because the bourgeois revolution in Germany will be but the prelude to an immediately following proletarian revolution.

In short, the Communists everywhere support every revolutionary movement against the existing social and political order of things . . . .

Finally, they labour everywhere for the union and agreement of the democratic parties of all countries.   80

The Communists disdain to conceal their views and aims. They openly declare that their ends can be attained only by the forcible overthrow of all existing social conditions. Let the ruling classes tremble at a Communist revolution. The proletarians have nothing to lose but their chains. They have a world to win.

WORKINGMEN OF ALL COUNTRIES, UNITE!

Translation by Samuel Moore, 1888

Because he believed in the basic goodness of human beings, Karl Marx (1818–83), along with his collaborator Friedrich Engels (1820–95), formulated a doctrine of inevitable progress that would lead to the perfect classless society in which private property and the profit motive would be relics of the imperfect past. From Hegel he took the dialectic, not as world Spirit, but as material forces, a concept espoused by the German philosopher Ludwig Feuerbach (1804–72). In effect, Marx turned Hegel's dialectic upside down, contending that it was not consciousness that determined human existence but the social existence of people that defined their consciousness.

For Marx, the way people made a living, their "means of production," determined their beliefs and institutions. To demonstrate the working of dialectical materialism Marx concentrated on medieval feudal society. The *thesis* was the ruling class of the nobility and clergy. With the development of trade an increasingly affluent middle class, the bourgeoisie, rose as the *antithesis* in the class struggle. Following the American and French revolutions the bourgeois class merged with the vanquished nobility as the *synthesis*. Traders, bankers, and factory-owners made up the ruling class of capitalists, the new thesis, whereas the oppressed workers, the proletariat, were the antithesis. The final class struggle between capitalists and workers would, according to Marx, inevitably result in victory for the proletariat, who would take over the means of production. Under the "dictatorship of the proletariat" the entire capitalist apparatus would be collectivized. With only one class remaining, the class struggle would cease. According to Marx, the state, with its laws, courts, and police served only to oppress the proletariat and would no longer be necessary; it would therefore "wither away."

It was not until late in the twentieth century that Marx was finally and decisively proven wrong, along with those who used their versions of his theories. The failure of Communism is discussed in the concluding unit of this text.

STUDY QUESTIONS

1. Marx claimed that Communism would first overcome the most advanced societies. Why didn't this happen?
2. Communism succeeded in Russia, the most backward nation in Europe. How did this happen? Why?

Charles Darwin, 1809–82

Anaximander of Miletus (610–ca. 547 BC) postulated an elementary theory of evolution, but it was not until the nineteenth century that the theories of Erasmus Darwin, Jean-Baptiste de Lamarck, Thomas Malthus, and the detailed naturalistic observations of Charles Darwin finally led to Darwin's publication of *On the Origin of Species by Means of Natural Selection* (1859). After serving as naturalist on the surveying ship *Beagle* (1831–6) Darwin read, in Thomas Malthus's *Essay on the Principle of Population* (1798), the thesis that population increased by a geometric ratio (1:2:4:16 etc.), whereas the food supply increased arithmetically (1:3:5:7:9 etc.). The limited food supply, Malthus observed, placed a natural check on population increase. Darwin wrote:

> It at once struck me that under the circumstances favourable variations would tend to be preserved and unfavourable ones destroyed. The result of this would be the formation of a new species. Here then I had a theory by which to work. This is the doctrine of natural selection, the result of chance enabling, in Herbert Spencer's phrase, the survival of the fittest.

Modern evolution theory confirms Darwin's facts and deductions, but adds some significant variations in terms of modifications, mutations, and recombinations. Modification is a variation due to external or internal factors and is not the result of inheritance. Take, for example, identical twins, one leading an active and healthy life and the other immersed in alcoholism. Barring an accident one twin will almost certainly survive the other.

The copying of genes in the process of reproduction is not always precise. A copy that differs slightly from the original is a mutation, and the mutated gene will continue to reproduce itself unless the mutation results in an unfavorable variation that increases the chances against survival. Mutations tend, on the whole, to result in unfavorable variations.

Darwin was not aware of the full implications of Gregor Mendel's (1822–84) experiments in genetics, specifically the fact that sexual reproduction results in a recombination of existing genetic units that may produce or modify inheritable combinations. Take, for example, twelve children born of the same parents. Though there is generally a familial resemblance, each child will be distinctly different because of the different recombination of genes.

Darwin was reluctant to publish his theories until he learned that Alfred Russel Wallace (1823–1913) had independently developed a theory of evolution. Both men submitted a paper to the Linnaean Society on the theory of natural selection; both papers were read on 1 July 1858, and later published. Even when Darwin published his *Origin of Species* the following year he considered his work a brief abstract of twenty-five years of detailed studies.

Darwin's work provoked a great controversy, of course, because it denied supernatural intervention in the functioning of the universe. He rode out the theological storm, but not the attacks of naturalists who claimed a special place for *Homo sapiens* separate from other species. In the introduction to *The Descent of Man* (1871) Darwin noted that he had many notes on the origin or descent of man, but that he had been determined "not to publish, as I thought that I should thus only add to the prejudices against my views." Indeed, *Origin of Species* implied "that man must be included with other organic beings in any general conclusion respecting his manner of appearance on this earth."

What is the status of Darwinism today? As Dennis Flanagan states it, evolution by natural selection is simply "the testing of variations in the laboratory of the environment." With the theory of evolution

> the trouble lies with the word "theory." The everyday meaning of "theory" is speculation but the scientific meaning of the word is a substantial body of reasoning. It is like that with the Darwinian theory of evolution. *Evolution itself is not a theory; it is an inescapable fact.* Charles Darwin did much to call attention to that fact. Modern Darwinian theory, however, is an effort to explain how life evolves.[3]

The difference, in science, between "law" and "theory" can be further illustrated by citing the *law* of gravity, which states that objects in space are attracted to each other. The *theory* of gravity, on the other hand, is the inquiry into how and why objects attract each other. As with evolution, that inquiry continues to challenge scientists.

Social Darwinism

English philosopher Herbert Spencer (1820–1903) argued that evolution occurred not only in nature but in human institutions as well. Spencer's phrase, "survival of the fittest," meant, according to the Social Darwinists, that the rich were better adapted to the rigors of competitive life because they were better able to survive than the poor. Opposed to government interference in economic affairs, to trade unions, and to socialist ideas such as welfare, powerful capitalists (John D. Rockefeller, Andrew Carnegie, and others) claimed that unrestrained competition had a scientific basis comparable to evolution in nature. This position was, of course, an attempt to justify *laissez-faire* capitalism.

On a larger scale, Social Darwinism reinforced the idea that some nations were more competent than others; defeating an adversary in warfare would thus demonstrate that superiority. Indeed, it became almost a moral duty, in Social Darwinian terms, to conquer "inferior" people and populate their lands with fitter human beings. Late nineteenth-century imperialism thus had an ideal social philosophy to justify the ruthless growth of empire. British imperialist Cecil Rhodes went even further by claiming that a world of Anglo-Saxons was the best of all possible worlds, thus adding racism to the social evolution theory. In 1845 a journalist and diplomat named John Louis O'Sullivan coined the term "manifest destiny"—a phrase that, when reinforced by Social Darwinism, provided the justification of American imperialism.

Darwinian views spread into every corner of the intellectual domain: anthropology, sociology, history, literature, art, music, legal and political institutions. Just about everything was investigated in terms of origin, development, and survival or disappearance.

There is no denying the enormous influence of evolutionary theory in all these areas, but great care has to be taken when applying a scientific theory to non-scientific areas. "Natural selection," for scientists, means the way things work in nature and no more than that. Social Darwinists manipulated evolutionary theory to justify individuality and unfettered competition as if the marketplace were a scientific laboratory. Scientific terminology was selected to undergird the way things were supposed to be. "Survival of the fittest" supposedly proved that the wealthy and powerful were fit and no one else. In fact, the most competent creatures in Darwin's natural world were those who, over a period of time, left the most dependents who could survive natural selection. Not necessarily the smartest, largest, or strongest; just survivors.

Furthermore, many of those who claimed that a capitalist economy was a struggle for existence with only the fittest surviving refused to compete in a free market. They wanted high tariffs to protect them from foreign competition and would tolerate no competition for improved wages and working conditions on the part of organized labor. Rockefeller and Carnegie, for example, argued for competition, but they effectively eliminated it and made billions from their virtual monopolies in oil and steel. Social Darwinism is a twisted play on the good name of Charles Darwin. The true social philosophy of America's "robber barons" at the height of *laissez-faire* capitalism can best be summed up in the callous statement attributed to William Vanderbilt: "The public be damned!"

Liberalism

Jeremy Bentham (1748–1832) was the founder of the rationalist philosophy of utilitarianism, a doctrine whose central idea is that, in themselves, actions are not right or wrong; they can be judged only by their consequences. Utilitarianism is based on the assumption that all human beings pursue happiness by seeking pleasure and avoiding pain. The criterion of the value of deeds is their utility, that is, whether they lead to the greatest happiness of the greatest number. Bentham's ethics are, in effect, an inversion of those of Kant. Kant calls for action as a duty and on principle; Bentham's values are based on the consequences of actions.

3. Dennis Flanagan, *Flanagan's Version: A Spectator's Guide to Science on the Eve of the 21st Century* (New York: Alfred A. Knopf, 1988), p. 26.

Bentham believed, along with classical (*laissez-faire*) economists, that government governs best when it governs least and that it should be relatively passive in social affairs. He was, however, an ardent reformer and his detailed studies of English institutions convinced him that the pleasure derived by some in the pursuit of self-interest caused pain for others, sometimes many, many others. He and his followers, the Philosophic Radicals, finally concluded that the state should intervene to help provide the greatest happiness for the greatest number. Their influence led to considerable administrative, legal, and economic reforms that broadened, in the twentieth century, into the concept of the welfare state that aimed to care for all its citizens "from the cradle to the grave."

John Stuart Mill, 1806–73

James Mill was a disciple of Bentham and the director of a rigorous "educational experiment" for his son, John Stuart Mill. By the age of three, young Mill had learned Greek and, at seven, he was reading Plato's dialogues. During the following year he taught Latin to his sister. By the time John Stuart Mill started college, he had what he called a twenty-five-year head start on his classmates. There were drawbacks, however. "I grew up," Mill wrote in his celebrated *Autobiography* (1873), "in the absence of love and in the presence of fear." Referring to himself as a "reasoning machine," Mill had a breakdown at twenty from which he recovered by turning to music and the Romantic poets, especially Coleridge and Wordsworth. It was also during this period of crisis that Mill met Harriet Taylor, the wife of a London merchant. A woman of remarkable intellect comparable to that of Mill, Harriet was his intense Platonic love and intellectual companion until 1851, when her husband died and they were married. The belated education in music and art plus the association with Harriet, whom Mill credited with much assistance in his writing, helped make Mill the foremost humanitarian liberal of the century.

Mill adopted utilitarianism at an early age, but he distinguished pleasures by qualities rather than by mere quantities as Bentham had done. For Mill the greatest pleasures were intellectual, ranking far above sensual pleasures. As he said, he would "rather be Socrates dissatisfied than a fool satisfied." Mill's position was comparable to that of the Epicureans: he said that "human beings have faculties more elevated than the animal appetites, and when once conscious of them, do not regard anything as happiness which does not include their gratification." Among the greatest pleasures for Mill were freedom of thought, speech, and action, but only up to the point where this freedom might impinge on that of another. His famous political essay, *On Liberty* (1859), explores the "nature and limits of power which can be legitimately exercised over the individual." His arguments defending free speech in a democratic society are just as convincing today, and his repeated warning against the "tyranny of the majority" is equally apropos.

To help secure the greatest good for the greatest number, Mill was an extremely active reformer, pressing for extended suffrage, measures to protect children, and actions to improve the lot of the poor. Virtually alone among thinkers of his time, Mill was convinced that women were the intellectual equals of men. Vigorously opposed to the inferior status of women, he wrote the *Subjection of Women* (1869), a strongly worded book that was responsible for some altered laws and a number of modifications in opinions. Though he did not reject classical economics, Mill did see that adjustments were necessary and long overdue. In the midst of self-righteous materialistic Victorians, Mill's sane and sophisticated voice was hailed, by his supporters, as a generous breath of fresh air.

Victorian Poets

By the later Victorian period England was a bustling and prosperous country. Mechanized, industrialized, and urbanized, it was also a tiny island on whose flag the sun never set, the most powerful and far-flung empire the world had ever known. Early Romantics had envisioned a new society flourishing in a golden age, but later Victorians witnessed endless colonial wars, smoke blanketing the countryside from hundreds of belching smokestacks, and miles of dreary row houses inhabited by overworked and underpaid factory workers. The industrial revolution had defiled nature but, after Darwin, there was no solace in nature, which Tennyson described as "red in tooth and claw." What, then, was the role of the poet?

Alfred, Lord Tennyson, 1809–92

The most representative poet of the mid-Victorian era, Tennyson reflected the mood of the period in poetry that was sad, quiet, contemplative, melancholy, sometimes wistful, and often pessimistic. The old optimism of the early Romantics had vanished.

Tennyson wrote often about contemporary events such as "The Charge of the Light Brigade," but his best poetry is about the past, particularly the classical past. In "Ulysses" the Greek hero has returned, after twenty years, to Penelope, his "aged wife," and Telemachus, a dutiful son who is content to stay at home and "make mild a rugged people." Ulysses is always the man of action, the embodiment of the Faustian man, whose mission in life is succinctly stated in the last line of the poem.

LITERARY SELECTION 31

Ulysses (1842)

Alfred, Lord Tennyson

It little profits that an idle king,
By this still hearth, among these barren crags,

Matched with an aged wife, I mete and dole
Unequal laws unto a savage race,
That hoard, and sleep, and feed, and know not me.
I cannot rest from travel: I will drink
Life to the lees: all times I have enjoyed
Greatly, have suffered greatly, both with those
That loved me, and alone; on shore, and when
Through scudding drifts the rainy Hyades   10
Vext the dim sea. I am become a name;
For always roaming with a hungry heart
Much have I seen and known: cities of men
And manners, climates, councils, governments,
Myself not least, but honoured of them all,—
And drunk delight of battle with my peers,
Far on the ringing plains of windy Troy.
I am a part of all that I have met;
Yet all experience is an arch wherethrough
Gleams that untravelled world, whose margin fades   20
For ever and for ever when I move.
How dull it is to pause, to make an end,
To rust unburnished, not to shine in use!
As though to breathe were life! Life piled on life
Were all too little, and of one to me
Little remains: but every hour is saved
From that eternal silence, something more,
A bringer of new things; and vile it were
For some three suns to store and hoard myself,
And this grey spirit yearning in desire   30
To follow knowledge, like a sinking star,
Beyond the utmost bound of human thought.

This is my son, mine own Telemachus,
To whom I leave the sceptre and the isle—
Well-loved of me, discerning to fulfil
This labour, by slow prudence to make mild
A rugged people, and through soft degrees
Subdue them to the useful and the good.
Most blameless is he, centred in the sphere
Of common duties, decent not to fail   40
In offices of tenderness, and pay
Meet adoration to my household gods,
When I am gone. He works his work, I mine.

There lies the port: the vessel puffs her sail:
There gloom the dark broad seas. My mariners,
Souls that have toiled, and wrought, and thought with
    me—
That ever with a frolic welcome took
The thunder and the sunshine, and opposed
Free hearts, free foreheads—you and I are old;
Old age hath yet his honour and his toil;   50
Death closes all: but something ere the end,
Some work of noble note, may yet be done,
Not unbecoming men that strove with Gods.
The lights begin to twinkle from the rocks:
The long day wanes: the slow moon climbs: the deep
Moans round with many voices. Come, my friends,
'Tis not too late to seek a newer world.
Push off, and sitting well in order smite
The sounding furrows; for my purpose holds
To sail beyond the sunset, and the baths   60
Of all the western stars, until I die.

It may be that the gulfs will wash us down:
It may be we shall touch the Happy Isles,
And see the great Achilles, whom we knew.
Though much is taken, much abides; and though
We are not now that strength which in old days
Moved earth and heaven, that which we are, we are,—
One equal temper of heroic hearts,
Made weak by time and fate, but strong in will
To strive, to seek, to find, and not to yield.   70

STUDY QUESTIONS

In Tennyson's version is Ulysses a noble hero who refuses to submit meekly to old age and death or is he an arrogant, self-centered old man with little concern for his family? Why shouldn't he be "matched with an aged wife"? Penelope is younger than Ulysses and she did wait twenty faithful years for her husband to return from his Odyssey. Whatever your opinion, is he believable as a human being?

Matthew Arnold, 1822–88
As a poet and literary critic Arnold was as pessimistic as his colleagues about human beings and their institutions, but through sheer force of will he created a cheerful demeanor and purposeful character for himself. Possibly the most anti-Victorian figure in Victorian England, Arnold was an apostle of high culture and a lifelong enemy of Puritanism, the "Barbarians" (aristocracy), and the "Philistines" (middle class). His despairing view of human alienation in a hostile universe is memorably expressed in "Dover Beach." When the poet says to his female companion, "Ah love, let us be true to one another!" the objective is not love but survival. Arnold was a realist, not a romantic.

LITERARY SELECTION 32

Dover Beach (1867)

Matthew Arnold

The sea is calm to-night.
The tide is full, the moon lies fair
Upon the straits; on the French coast the light
Gleams and is gone; the cliffs of England stand,
Glimmering and vast, out in the tranquil bay.
Come to the window, sweet is the night air!
Only, from the long line of spray

Where the sea meets the moon-blanch'd land,
Listen! you hear the grating roar
Of pebbles which the waves draw back, and fling,   10
At their return, up the high strand,
Begin, and cease, and then again begin,
With tremulous cadence slow, and bring
The eternal note of sadness in.

Sophocles long ago
Heard it on the Aegaean, and it brought
Into his mind the turbid ebb and flow
Of human misery; we
Find also in the sound a thought,
Hearing it by this distant northern sea.   20

The Sea of Faith
Was once, too, at the full, and round earth's shore
Lay like the folds of a bright girdle furled.
But now I only hear
Its melancholy, long, withdrawing roar,
Retreating, to the breath
Of the night-wind, down the vast edges drear
And naked shingles of the world.

Ah, love, let us be true
To one another! for the world, which seems   30
To lie before us like a land of dreams,
So various, so beautiful, so new,
Hath really neither joy, nor love, nor light,
Nor certitude, nor peace, nor help for pain;
And we are here as on a darkling plain
Swept with confused alarms of struggles and flight,
Where ignorant armies clash by night.

STUDY QUESTIONS

1. What happened to the "sea of faith"? Why?
2. What are the many implications inherent in the last line? Consider the levels of meaning in each of the key words—"ignorant," "armies," "clash," "night"—and then reflect on the entire line. How far have we come from the opening lines?

Thomas Hardy, 1840–1928
Though he denied being a pessimist, the novels, short stories, and poems of Thomas Hardy reveal a pessimism every bit as profound as that of Matthew Arnold and Feodor Dostoevsky. Hardy claimed that human effort could make the world a better place, but his prose and poetry overflow with sadness over the waste and frustration of life. Though he outlived the Victorian era, Hardy's output typifies the late Victorian mood of ironic melancholy as, for example, in "Neutral Tones" in which the imagery is consistent and convincing.

LITERARY SELECTION 33
Neutral Tones (1898)
Thomas Hardy

We stood by a pond that winter day,
And the sun was white, as though chidden of God,
And a few leaves lay on the starving sod;
—They had fallen from an ash, and were grey.
Your eyes on me were as eyes that rove
Over tedious riddles of years ago;
And some words played between us to and fro
On which lost the more by our love.
The smile on your mouth was the deadest thing
Alive enough to have strength to die;
And a grin of bitterness swept thereby
Like an ominous bird a-wing . . .
Since then, keen lessons that love deceives,
And wrings with wrong, have shaped to me
Your face, and the God-cursed sun, and a tree,
And a pond edged with greyish leaves.

Written on the last day of the nineteenth century, "The Darkling Thrush" morosely defines a century that ends, for Hardy, with a whimper, and anticipates a new hundred years that seem to offer little hope of anything better.

The Darkling Thrush (1900)
Thomas Hardy

I leant upon a coppice gate
    When Frost was spectre-grey,
And Winter's dregs made desolate
    The weakening eye of day.
The tangled bine-stems scored the sky
    Like strings of broken lyres,
And all mankind that haunted nigh
    Had sought their household fires.
The land's sharp features seemed to be
    The Century's corpse outleant,   10
His crypt the cloudy canopy,
    The wind his death-lament.
The ancient pulse of germ and birth
    Was shrunken hard and dry,
And every spirit upon earth
    Seemed fervourless as I.
At once a voice arose among
    The bleak twigs overhead
In a full-hearted evensong
    Of joy illimited;   20
An aged thrush, frail, gaunt, and small,
    In blast-beruffled plume,
Had chosen thus to fling his soul
    Upon the growing gloom.
So little cause for carolings
    Of such ecstatic sound

Was written on terrestrial things
    Afar or nigh around,
That I could think there trembled through
    His happy good-night air   30
Some blessed Hope, whereof he knew
    And I was unaware.

ROMANTICISM AND REALISM IN AMERICA

For the United States the nineteenth century was the great age of expansion, from thirteen states to forty-five, plus three territories, Alaska, Hawaii, the Philippines, Puerto Rico, Guam, and American Samoa (map 23.6). Part of this growth was at the expense of the many American Indian tribes whose lands were dotted all across the country. The Indian Wars had begun in 1540 when Coronado's conquistadores first clashed with the Zuni in what is now New Mexico. Three and a half centuries later the wars ended with the 7th U.S. Cavalry massacre of Big Foot's band of Oglala Sioux at Wounded Knee, South Dakota, in 1890.

I am tired of fighting.
Our chiefs are killed.
Looking Glass is dead.
Toohulhulsote is dead.
The old men are all dead.
It is the young men who say no and yes.
He who led the young men is dead.
It is cold and we have no blankets.
The little children are freezing to death.
My people, some of them,   10
Have run away to the hills
And have no blankets, no food.
No one knows where they are—

Map 23.6   Growth of the United States.

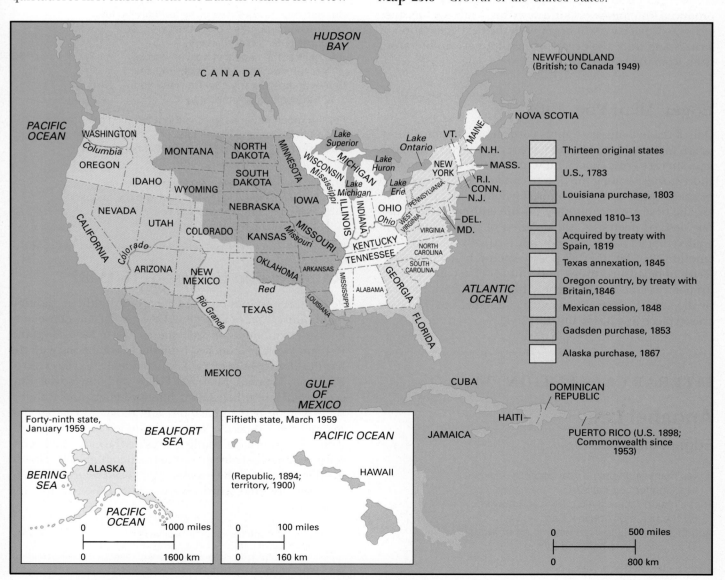

Perhaps they are freezing to death.
I want to have time to look for my children
And see how many of them I can find.
Maybe I shall find them among the dead.
Hear me, my chiefs, I am tired.
My heart is sad and sick.
From where the sun now stands   20
I will fight no more forever.
                    Surrender speech of Nez Perce[4] Chief Joseph
                                        (ca. 1840–1904)

America's vast physical growth and economic development were not paralleled, however, by significant developments in the fine and literary arts—not for some time. Early in the century writers were still intimidated by British letters though seeking ways to declare their literary independence. The emergence of Romanticism in England struck a responsive spark in America, and writers such as Washington Irving (1783–1859), William Cullen Bryant (1794–1878), and James Fenimore Cooper (1789–1851) produced Romantic works in a new American style. Because of limited space we will begin with the next generation of writers and trace the development of American literature from Romanticism to Realism.

Edgar Allan Poe, 1809–49

One of the few literary figures with an international reputation that the United States has produced, Poe was a brilliant literary critic, poet, and writer of highly imaginative short stories. Among the first to condemn crass American materialism, Poe devoted himself wholly to his art, becoming the first American to live his life entirely as an artist. Poe defined poetry as "the creation of beauty" and contended that all poetry should appeal equally to reason and emotion. Poe felt that all poetry should be composed in terms of beauty, restraint, and unity of effect and, indeed, his poetry is the embodiment of his theory of art. Inspired by the loss of a beautiful woman, "Annabel Lee" is a lyric masterpiece in a lilting musical style.

LITERARY SELECTION 34

Annabel Lee

Edgar Allan Poe

It was many and many a year ago,
    In a kingdom by the sea,
That a maiden there lived whom you may know
    By the name of Annabel Lee;
And this maiden she lived with no other thought
    Than to love and be loved by me.

I was a child and she was a child,
    In this kingdom by the sea,
But we loved with a love that was more than love,
    I and my Annabel Lee;   10
With a love that the wingèd seraphs of heaven
    Coveted her and me.

And this was the reason that, long ago,
    In this kingdom by the sea,
A wind blew out of a cloud, chilling
    My beautiful Annabel Lee;

So that her highborn kinsmen came
    And bore her away from me,
To shut her up in a sepulchre
    In this kingdom by the sea.   20

The angels, not half so happy in heaven,
    Went envying her and me;
Yes! that was the reason (as all men know,
    In this kingdom by the sea)
That the wind came out of the cloud by night,
    Chilling and killing my Annabel Lee.

But our love it was stronger by far than the love
    Of those who were older than we,
    Of many far wiser than we;
And neither the angels in heaven above,   30
    Nor the demons down under the sea,
Can ever dissever my soul from the soul
    Of the beautiful Annabel Lee:

For the moon never beams, without bringing me dreams
    Of the beautiful Annabel Lee;
And the stars never rise, but I feel the bright eyes
    Of the beautiful Annabel Lee;

And so, all the night-tide, I lie down by the side
Of my darling—my darling—my life and my bride,
    In her sepulchre there by the sea,   40
    In her tomb by the sounding sea.

Ralph Waldo Emerson, 1803–82

Poe was a conscious representative of a Southern tradition in literature, that of a Virginia Cavalier. Just as consciously, Emerson and his colleagues were New England Romantics who reconciled romantic abstractions with the hardheaded realities of Yankee individualism. The creed of Emerson, Thoreau, Margaret Fuller, and others was transcendentalism, a belief that human beings and the universe were in perfect harmony and moving in a Hegelian manner toward perfection. High-minded and highly individualistic, transcendentalists stressed the individual's conscience as the sole judge in spiritual matters, total self-reliance in all matters, and the necessity for social reforms.

Beauty and truth were critical issues for the

---

4. Chief Joseph was one of the Nez Perce chiefs responsible for the skillful eluding of the enemy during a 1,000-mile (1,610-km) flight from Oregon to Montana, where the tribe finally surrendered to the U.S. Army.

transcendentalists. For Poe poetry was beauty. Emerson viewed it as a necessary function for the individual who was seeking truth. Emerson wrote his essays but, in a sense, he thought that his poems wrote him. Many of Emerson's poems are the result of the poet's attempts to perceive the deeper meaning of nature. One such was "The Rhodora," which was emblematic of the beauty bestowed by spirit on the world and implanted in human beings.

LITERARY SELECTION 35

The Rhodora

On Being Asked, Whence is the Flower?

Ralph Waldo Emerson

In May, when sea-winds pierce our solitudes,
I found the fresh Rhodora in the woods,
Spreading its leafless blooms in a damp nook,
To please the desert and the sluggish brook.
The purple petals, fallen in the pool,
Made the black water with their beauty gay;
Here might the red-bird come his plumes to cool,
And court the flower that cheapens his array.
Rhodora! if the sages ask thee why
This charm is wasted on the earth and sky,
Tell them, dear, that if eyes were made for seeing,
Then Beauty is its own excuse for being:
Why thou wert there, O rival of the rose!
I never thought to ask, I never knew:
But, in my simple ignorance, suppose
The self-same Power that brought me there brought you.

Walt Whitman, 1819–92

In his essay, "The Poet," Emerson wrote that the poet has a special mission because "the experience of each new age requires a new confession, and the world seems always waiting for its poet." It was the age of affirmation of American aspirations, and the exuberant voice of American democracy was that of Walt Whitman, which Emerson himself immediately recognized. On receiving the first edition of *Leaves of Grass* (1855), Emerson wrote Whitman that this was "the most extraordinary piece of wit and wisdom that America has yet contributed" and greeted the poet "at the beginning of a great career." Few writers, not to mention an indifferent general public, were as perceptive as Emerson, and even he later advised Whitman to go easy on the erotic poetry, advice which Whitman consistently ignored. *Leaves of Grass* was to be the poet's only book. Through nine editions (1855–92) it grew with his life and, in effect, became his life. "This is no book," wrote Whitman; "who touches this touches a man."

A poet of many voices, Whitman rejected the genteel tradition and what he called "book-words," selecting instead the language of the common people, a unique blend of journalistic jargon, everyday speech, and a great variety of foreign words and phrases. A pantheist, mystic, and ardent patriot, Whitman advocated humanity, brotherhood, and freedom, not only in the United States, but throughout the world.

The following chantlike poem is in Whitman's "catalog style" and illustrates his lusty mode as the "bard of democracy."

LITERARY SELECTION 36

I Hear America Singing

Walt Whitman

I hear America singing, the varied carols I hear,
Those of mechanics, each one singing his as it should be blithe and strong,
The carpenter singing his as he measures his plank or beam,
The mason singing his as he makes ready for work, or leaves off work,
The boatman singing what belongs to him in his boat, the deck-hand singing on the steamboat deck,
The shoemaker singing as he sits on his bench, the hatter singing as he stands,
The wood-cutter's song, the ploughboy's on his way in the morning, or at noon intermission or at sundown,
The delicious singing of the mother, or of the young wife at work, or of the girl sewing or washing,
Each singing what belongs to him or her and to none else,
The day what belongs to the day—at night the party of young fellows, robust, friendly,
Singing with open mouths their strong melodious songs.

Always an ardent supporter of the Union, Whitman was tormented by the "peculiar institution" of slavery and became an active Abolitionist. His involvement in the Civil War turned personal when he began caring for his wounded brother, George, in an Army hospital and stayed on to nurse others stricken by the war. The following poem is from *Drum-Taps*, which was added to *Leaves of Grass* in 1865.

By the Bivouac's Fitful Flame

Walt Whitman

By the bivouac's fitful flame,
A procession winding around me, solemn and sweet and slow—but first I note,
The tents of the sleeping army, the fields' and woods' dim outline,
The darkness lit by spots of kindled fire, the silence,

Like a phantom far or near an occasional figure moving,
The shrubs and trees, (as I lift my eyes they seem to be
   stealthily watching me,)
While wind in procession thoughts, O tender and
   wondrous thoughts,
Of life and death, of home and the past and loved, and
   of those that are far away;
A solemn and slow procession there as I sit on the
   ground,
By the bivouac's fitful flame.

Herman Melville, 1819–91

Born in the same year as Whitman and also influenced by
Emerson, Melville had not one but two literary careers.
Like Whitman, Melville was fascinated by the sea and
images of the sea, but Whitman's vision was essentially
positive whereas Melville's was ironic and tragic, the viewpoint of a realist as opposed to Whitman the romantic.
Several years after publishing his greatest novel, *Moby Dick*
(1851), Melville turned, for reasons still unknown, to an
exclusive preoccupation with poetry. (He did leave at his
death the manuscript of *Billy Budd*, but with no clues as
to when it was written.) Melville's ten-year career as a prose
writer and thirty-year sequel as a poet were as unnoticed
by the general public of the time as was the poetry of
Whitman.

Deeply disturbed by the prospect of civil war, Melville
followed the self-appointed mission of the Abolitionist John
Brown who, in his zeal to free the slaves, had secured support from Emerson, Thoreau, and many others. Brown's
capture of the U.S. Arsenal at Harper's Ferry was a major
step in his campaign, but the government recaptured the
Arsenal and hanged John Brown. Melville's brooding poem
uses the image of the dead Abolitionist as a prologue to
war.

LITERARY SELECTION 37

The Portent (1859)

Herman Melville

Hanging from the beam,
   Slowly swaying (such the law),
Gaunt the shadow on your green,
   Shenandoah!
The cut is on the crown
(Lo, John Brown),
And the stabs shall heal no more.
Hidden in the cap
   Is the anguish none can draw;
So your future veils its face,
   Shenandoah!
But the streaming beard is shown

(Weird John Brown),
The meteor of the war.

One of the bloodiest conflicts of the Civil War, the Battle
of Shiloh (6–7 April 1862) cost the lives of thousands of soldiers and forecast both the terrible battles to come and the
inevitable defeat of the Confederacy. No one, not even
Whitman, wrote more eloquently and sadly about the war than
did Herman Melville.

Shiloh

A Requiem (April 1862)

Herman Melville

Skimming lightly, wheeling still,
   The swallows fly low
Over the field in clouded days,
   The forest-field of Shiloh—
Over the field where April rain
Solaced the parched ones stretched in pain
Through the pause of night
That followed the Sunday fight
   Around the church of Shiloh—
The church so lone, the log-built one,
That echoed to many a parting groan
And natural prayer
   Of dying foemen mingled there—
Foemen at morn, but friends at eve—
   Fame or country least their care:
(What like a bullet can undeceive!)
   But now they lie low,
While over them the swallows skim,
   And all is hushed at Shiloh.

Emily Dickinson, 1830–86

The poetry of the "recluse of Amherst" is also realistic.
Twain's universe was the exterior world; Dickinson's was
the inner world of her own psyche. Published years after
her death, her 1,775 poems were written as if they were
entries in a diary, the private thoughts of a solitary person
who took just a little from society and shut out all the rest.
Her gemlike, frequently cryptic, verses are unique, unlike
poetry of any writer of any age.

LITERARY SELECTION 38

Poetry

Emily Dickinson

VI

Some keep the Sabbath going to church;
I keep it staying at home,
With a bobolink for a chorister,
And an orchard for a dome.

Some keep the Sabbath in surplice;
I just wear my wings,
And instead of tolling the bell for church,
Our little sexton sings.

God preaches,—a noted clergyman,—
And the sermon is never long;
So instead of getting to heaven at last,
I'm going all along!

XI

Much madness is divinest sense
To a discerning eye;
Much sense the starkest madness.
'Tis the majority
In this, as all, prevails.
Assent, and you are sane;
Demur,—you're straightway dangerous,
And handled with a chain.

XVII

I never saw a moor,
I never saw the sea;
Yet know I how the heather looks.
And what a wave must be.

I never spoke with God,
Nor visited in heaven;
Yet certain am I of the spot
As if the chart were given.

XXVII

Because I could not stop for Death,
He kindly stopped for me;
The carriage held but just ourselves
And Immortality.

We slowly drove, he knew no haste,
And I had put away
My labor, and my leisure too,
For his civility.

We passed the school where children played,
Their lessons scarcely done;
We passed the fields of gazing grain,
We passed the setting sun.

We paused before a house that seemed
A swelling of the ground;
The roof was scarcely visible,
The cornice but a mound.

Since then 'tis centuries; but each
Feels shorter than the day
I first surmised the horses' heads
Were toward eternity.

Paul Laurence Dunbar, 1872–1906

Emancipation released the slaves from bondage only to suspend African Americans somewhere between African cultures to which they could not return and an American culture that refused to admit them. The first black poet to reach a national audience, Dunbar wrote a poignant poem still quoted today.

LITERARY SELECTION 39

Sympathy

Paul Laurence Dunbar

I know what the caged bird feels, alas!
    When the sun is bright on the upland slopes;
When the wind stirs soft through the springing grass,
And the river flows like a stream of glass;
    When the first bird sings and the first bud opes,
And the faint perfume from its chalice steals—
I know what the caged bird feels!

I know why the caged bird beats his wing
    Till its blood is red on the cruel bars;
For he must fly back to his perch and cling   10
When he fain would be on the bough a-swing;
    And a pain still throbs in the old, old scars
And they pulse again with a keener sting—
I know why he beats his wing!

I know why the caged bird sings, ah me,
    When his wing is bruised and his bosom sore,—
When he beats his bars and he would be free;
It is not a carol of joy or glee,
    But a prayer that he sends from his heart's deep core,
But a plea, that upward to Heaven he flings—   20
I know why the caged bird sings!

Stephen Crane, 1871–1900

Though sometimes identified as a writer in the realistic style called naturalism, Crane was actually influenced by Monet, Renoir, and other Impressionists. A journalist by profession and a war correspondent, Crane used word-painting in a manner comparable to the Impressionists' use of color. *The Red Badge of Courage* (1895) is perhaps the finest short novel in the English language, and "The Open Boat" and "The Blue Hotel" rank at the top of American short stories. Of Crane's poems, the following two seem most appropriate to conclude this survey of nineteenth-century life and literature.

LITERARY SELECTION 40

Two Poems (Untitled)

Stephen Crane

Do not weep, maiden, for war is kind.
Because your lover threw wild hands toward the sky
And the affrighted steed ran on alone,
Do not weep.
War is kind.
    Hoarse, booming drums of the regiment,
    Little souls who thirst for fight
    These men were born to drill and die.
    The unexplained glory flies above them,
    Great is the battle-god, great, and his kingdom—   10
    A field where a thousand corpses lie.
Do not weep, babe, for war is kind.
Because your father tumbled in the yellow trenches,
Raged at his breast, gulped and died,
Do not weep.
War is kind.
    Swift blazing flag of the regiment,
    Eagle with crest of red and gold,
    These men were born to drill and die.
    Point for them the virtue of slaughter,   20
    Make plain to them the excellence of killing
    And a field where a thousand corpses lie.
Mother whose heart hung humble as a button

On the bright splendid shroud of your son,
Do not weep.
War is kind.

. . . . .

A man said to the universe:
"Sir, I exist!"
"However," replied the universe,
"The fact has not created in me
A sense of obligation."

SUMMARY

The revolutionary surge that began in France in 1789 was sidetracked by the imperial conquests of Napoleon and, even more effectively, by the 1815 Congress of Vienna. From 1815 to 1848, the arch-conservatism of the age of Metternich helped to maintain the *status quo* of absolutism, disturbed only by the waves of revolution that rolled over Europe in 1830 and 1848. By mid-century the industrial revolution had helped turn western Europe and North America into a powerful economic community, but political divisions became ever sharper with the rise of militant nationalism.

Revolution, civil war, and aggressive imperial wars became the hallmark of the last half of the so-called Romantic century. The Greek struggle for independence did spark the Romantic imagination, but the Crimean and Franco-Prussian wars were bloody preludes to the Great War of 1914–18.

Italy finally became an independent nation in 1861 and, after the Civil War ended in 1865, the United States began to assume its place as a world power. In 1871 France became, once again, a republic; Bismarck proclaimed the German Empire; and the rival British Empire girdled the globe. Nationalism, imperialism, and militarism led, perhaps inevitably, to the conflict that ended what has been called the Age of Progress.

CULTURE AND HUMAN VALUES

The nineteenth century was noted for the prosperity stimulated by the industrial revolution, the growing middle class, and the enormous increase in manufactured products. The prevailing view of reality was more materialistic than ever; the world was a well-oiled machine bursting with machines turning out a flood of products. When these factors are combined with steady advances in science, transportation, communications, and other technologies, one can see why this has been grandly labeled as the Age of Progress.

This designation was, however, self-anointed and

self-serving for the industrially advanced nations of western Europe and North America. And not even in these industrialized countries was "progress" even remotely uniform. A large (growing ever larger) class of underpaid industrial workers, child labor, inadequate health and safety standards, and woefully substandard sanitation and housing were just some of the basic problems plaguing the working class. The poor were without power or influence in the factory, at home, and at the voting booth, whereas the rich got richer and more powerful.

What of the rest of the world—those non-industrial nations of Central and South America, Africa, and Asia? Many of them became involuntary outposts of Western civilization. The monumental problem of the nineteenth century—that spilled over into the twentieth—was colonialism, and its negative after-effects haunt us still.

In the colonies of England, Germany, France, Belgium, Italy, Spain, and Portugal, the locals (natives) had to accept whatever culture and values the foreign overlords brought with them. As arbitrary extensions or pawns of the mother country, colonies were fair game for commerce, the military, politicians, and as many industrial products as the market would bear.

When considering the culture-epoch theory the period is full of paradoxes. On the one hand, there was the notable increase in prosperity in the industrial nations but a *status quo* at best in the colonized nations. The industrial, imperialist powers enforced a certain stability as they competed to maintain a balance of power, and certainly Europe imposed its values on much of the world. But the Age of Progress was headed for a fall signaled by the onset of the Great War, the so-called "war to end all wars."

CHAPTER 24

Romanticism in Music

The ever-changing sequence of artistic styles can be seen in broad perspective as a constant back-and-forth movement between two extremes. In painting, these outer boundaries were represented by the Rubenists, who emphasized color, and the Poussinists, who advocated line and drawing. Delacroix was a Rubenist; Ingres and David were Poussinists. These extremes are referred to, in music, as romanticism and classicism. As in painting, romantic music emphasizes color whereas the classical style stresses line and design. The two extremes can be outlined as follows:

Classicism	Romanticism
intellectual	emotional
objective	subjective
rational	non-rational
tranquil	restless
simple	ornate
Apollonian	Dionysian

No artistic style can be classified as wholly classic or wholly romantic. An inclination in favor of either extreme results in a classification of the style *as* that extreme, a process that can be compared to a seesaw touching ground at one end because of a slight shift of balance. Though it is absurd to consider all of Mozart's music, for example, as intellectual but not emotional, tranquil and simple rather than ornate and restless, the fact remains that Mozart's music is essentially classic in its meticulous detail, restraint, and clarity of design.

The Romantic style in music is either miniaturized or grandiose with comparatively little in between. There are intimate art songs for solo voice and piano and single-movement piano pieces at one extreme, and grandiose symphonic works at the other. The emphasis is on tone color (or sound), that fourth element of music (melody, harmony, rhythm, tone color). Symphonies have a wider range of instrumental tone color and a greater volume of sound than at any time since the invention of the symphony

orchestra. The international aspects of seventeenth- and eighteenth-century music are superseded by highly individualistic styles of writing and strong nationalistic expression. The "Austrian" quality of the classical music of Haydn and Mozart is not relevant to their work. During the Romantic period, however, the "German" characteristics of Wagner, Schubert, and Schumann and the "Italian" qualities of Verdi, Rossini, and Donizetti are essential components of the stylistic picture. Along with literature and art, Romantic music mirrors the rise of nationalism.

Typical of the Romantic mode is the brooding, melancholy painting by Arnold Böcklin (BOEK-lin; 1827–1901), which the artist called "a picture for dreaming about" (fig. 24.1). The strange and mysterious scene was enormously popular; it simply exists in its own bizarre world with no explanation necessary or even desirable.

GERMAN *LIEDER*

The Romantic movement generated a new style, the setting of preexisting poetry—almost always Romantic—to music in an adroit matching of mood and meaning. Nationalism was again a salient characteristic, for the new

24.1 Arnold Böcklin, *Island of the Dead*. 1880. Oil on wood, 29 × 48" (73.7 × 121.9 cm). Metropolitan Museum of Art, New York (Reisinger Fund, 1926).

Opposite Eugène Delacroix, *Arabs Skirmishing in the Mountains*, detail. 1863. Oil on linen, 36⅜ × 29⅜" (92.5 × 74.6 cm). National Gallery of Art, Washington D.C. (Chester Dale Fund).

style was a synthesis of words and music, and the language was German.

Viennese composer Franz Schubert (1797–1828) created the new artistic medium when, in 1814, he wrote music for "Gretchen am Spinnrade" from Goethe's *Faust*. Schubert invented the art song movement; the generic term *Lieder* applies to the German Romantic songs of Schubert, Schumann, Brahms, and others, though *Lied* is the German word for any song.

Composers have always set poetry to music, from Sappho to the troubadours to Bach and beyond. *Lieder* are not just songs, however, for German composers displayed a remarkable unity of purpose—the re-creation of a poem in musical terms. Art songs (*Lieder*) were significant miniatures in an era that indulged itself with the grandiose or doted on the diminutive. There was little middle ground, for the Romantics sought the heights and plumbed the depths with scant patience for the ordinary. Complexity was preferred and simplicity abhorred. If one art form was good then two art forms were even better. Art songs embodied the essence of Romanticism for they synthesized poetry and music in a new and rarefied style.

From the poem comes the song, which attempts to capture the feelings, the mood, indeed the essence of what the poet is saying. The rhythm, inflection, sound, and meaning of the language are corroborated and heightened by the composer's own personal language of melody, harmony, rhythm, and tone color.

Following is the Schubert *Lied* that inaugurated the German *Lieder* movement. German art songs are always sung in German because a translation spoils the unity of words and music. The German text with English translation is provided so that the listener can follow one and understand the other. There are ten verses, as indicated by the numbers in the text.

Listening Example 29
GERMAN ART SONG (*LIED*)

Schubert, "Gretchen am Spinnrade" ("Gretchen at the Spinning Wheel")
1814

Time: 3:48
Cassette 3, track 26

Synopsis: Margaret sits in her room at the spinning wheel and sings of her love for Faust, knowing that this love will prove fatal. The scene occurs near the end of Part I of *Faust*.

1. Mei-ne Ruh' ist hin, mein Herz ist schwer;
   ich finde, ich finde sie nimmer und nimmer mehr.
   (My peace is gone, my heart is sore:
   I shall find it never and never more.)

2. Wo ich ihn nicht hab', ist mir das Grab,
   die ganze Welt ist mir vergällt.
   (He has left my room an empty tomb
   He has gone and all my world is gall.)

3. Mein armer Kopf ist mir verrückt,
   mein armer Sinn ist mir zerstückt.
   (My poor head is all astray,
   My poor mind fallen away.)

4. Meine Ruh' ist hin, mein Herz ist schwer;
   ich finde, ich finde sie nimmer und nimmer mehr.
   (My peace is gone, my heart is sore;
   I shall find it never and never more.)

5. Nach ihm nur schau' ich zum Fenster hinaus,
   nach ihm nur geh' ich aus dem Haus.
   ('Tis he that I look through the window to see
   He that I open the door for—he!)

6. Sein hoher Gang, sein' edle Gestalt,
   seines Mundes Lächeln, seiner Augen Gewalt,
   (His gait, his figure, so grand, so high,
   The smile of his mouth, the power of his eye,)

7. Und seiner Rede Zauberfluss,
   sein Händedruck und ach, sein Kuss! (Piano)
   (And the magic stream of his words—what bliss
   The clasp of his hand and, ah, his kiss!)

8. Meine Ruh' ist hin, mein Herz ist schwer;
   ich finde, ich finde sie nimmer und nimmer mehr.
   (My peace is gone, my heart is sore:
   I shall find it never and never more.)

9. Mein Busen drängt sich nach ihm hin.
   Ach, dürft' ich fassen und halten ihn!
   (My heart's desire is so strong, so vast;
   Ah, could I seize him and hold him fast.)

10. Und küssen ihn, so wie ich wollt'
    an seinen Küssen vergehen sollt',
    O könnt' ich ihn küssen, so wie ich wollt',
    an seinen Küssen vergehen sollt',
    an seinen Küssen vergehen sollt'!
    (And kiss him forever night and day,
    And on his kisses pass away!)
    Meine Ruh' ist hin, mein Herz ist schwer. (Piano)
    (My peace is gone, my heart is sore.)

PIANO MUSIC

The Romantic emphasis on the uniqueness of the individual was symbolized by the dominance of the piano as the most popular musical instrument—as typical of the Romantic era as the guitar is of contemporary life. The piano was ubiquitous because it could accompany *Lieder*, blend into a chamber music ensemble or, in a piano concerto, dominate a symphony orchestra. Its prime attraction, however, was its independence, for it is a superb solo instrument.

Eighteenth-century pianos were relatively small with a clear and delicate tone. Nineteenth-century pianos were larger, more sonorous than clear, and loud enough to fill the largest concert hall. The range of tone was representative of the Romantic propensity for extremes. Whether playing the tender "Lullaby" by Brahms or the thunderous "Revolutionary Etude" by Chopin, the pianist was a commanding figure throughout the Romantic period. Pianists also dominate today's concert world because of the enduring popularity of the Romantic repertoire.

Frédéric Chopin, 1810–49

Frédéric Chopin (shaw-pã) was a superb concert pianist, but he did not confuse virtuoso performance with the circus showmanship of Paganini and Liszt. Though he was successful in the concert hall he gave fewer than seventy-five public concerts in his entire career. In temperament and style he was much more at home in the fashionable

24.2 Eugène Delacroix, *Frédéric Chopin*. 1838. Oil on canvas, 18 × 15" (45.7 × 38.1 cm). Louvre, Paris, Photo: R.M.N., Paris.
Delacroix seldom painted portraits on commission; instead, he depicted some of his personal friends, the victims, like himself, of what he and other artists called the "Romantic agony."

salons of Paris. He was the "poet of the keyboard," whose personal style epitomizes the Romantic spirit (fig. 24.2).

His musical poetry is not unlike the blending of words and music in German art songs. The formal designs of his music—sonata form, binary, and ternary forms—are traditional, but the content is unique. Some of the range of Chopin's piano style can be appreciated by considering just three compositions: two preludes and an étude.

Chopin wrote twenty-four preludes in Opus 28, each in a different key. As befits a prelude, which for Chopin is a short piano piece in one movement, there is only one subject. Prelude No. 4 is a short and melancholy meditation in the minor mode. Prelude No. 7 is a very brief and beautiful composition in the major mode.

Listening Example 30
PIANO PRELUDES

Chopin, Preludes, Op. 28 No. 4 in E Minor and No. 7 in A Major
1839

Times: 1:53, 0:43[1]

Chopin wrote a number of studies (études) that concentrated on various technical problems in playing the piano. Brief and brilliant, the G-Flat Major ("Black Key") Etude is a delightful exercise for playing on the black keys of the piano. The problem is performing at breakneck speed on narrow keys less than half the width of the white keys—³⁄₈" to ⁷⁄₈" (0.95–2.2cm).

Listening Example 31
PIANO ETUDE

Chopin, Etude in G-Flat Major, Op. 10 No. 5
1830

Time: 1:46
Cassette 3, track 27

Etude in G-Flat Major, Op. 10, No. 5   **Chopin (1810–49)**

1. CD 2, track 9 (Prelude No. 4); CD 2, track 10 (Prelude No. 7).

SHOWMANSHIP

The nineteenth century was a fabulous age of virtuosos, which is what spectacular performers were called. Virtuosity and showmanship were so widely admired that some performers added extramusical tricks. Violin virtuoso Niccolò Paganini, for example, would conclude a concert with a razor blade hidden in his right hand. Near the end of an already sensational performance he would deftly cut the violin strings, one by one, until he could triumphantly conclude on the last remaining string.

Virtuoso pianist Franz Liszt was fond of planting a female admirer in the front row of the concert hall. At the most dramatic moment the young lady, obviously enthralled by Liszt's performance, would be drawn to her feet and then ecstatically faint away. The maestro would carry her onstage and, holding her artistically draped body over one arm, triumphantly conclude his performance with one hand.

THE SYMPHONY

The greatly augmented symphony orchestra with its strong brass and percussion sections and enlarged body of woodwinds provided a particularly effective medium for Romantic music. The classical orchestra had a nucleus of strings plus a small woodwind section and just a few brass and percussion instruments. Romantic composers added full sections of woodwinds and brass that could play as independent sections as well as filling in the ensemble.

24.3   Typical seating plan of a modern symphony orchestra.

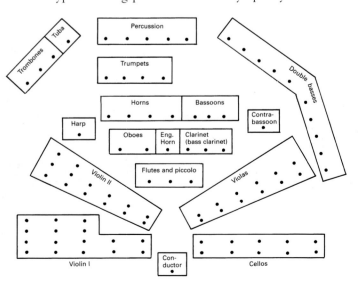

Figure 24.3 is a seating plan observed in principle by most modern orchestras. Because of their limited volume the strings are seated in front and the woodwinds in the center; brass, bass instruments, and percussion bring up the rear.

As might be expected, composers were highly individualistic in their approach to the symphonic tradition. The remarkable variety of orchestral music will be surveyed by considering one work by each of three different composers: Hector Berlioz, Johannes Brahms, and Peter Tchaikovsky.

Hector Berlioz, 1803–69

Hector Berlioz (bear-lee-os; fig. 24.4) was a red-headed Romantic from the south of France, a revolutionary artist whose only personal instrument was the guitar, but whose preferred instrument was the entire symphony orchestra. Despite his flamboyance—his lifetime dream was to hear

24.4   Hector Berlioz.

10,000 trumpets from a mountain top—he was a solid musician and an orchestral innovator who strongly influenced Liszt, Wagner, Tchaikovsky, and Strauss.

One of his most successful and controversial works, the *Symphonie fantastique*, was completed in 1830, only three years after Beethoven's death. Berlioz had been influenced by the popular *Confessions of an English Opium Eater* (1821) by Thomas de Quincey and he thought of combining an opium dream with music. He also fell madly in love with a Shakespearean actress named Harriet Smithson. It is now impossible to tell what the components were of this frenzied, desperate love affair that led to a short-lived and disastrous marriage.

Entranced by what he saw as the Romantic elements in Shakespeare's plays, Berlioz was as stage-struck by the Shakespearean women played by Miss Smithson as he was infatuated with the actress herself. In the midst of their stormy marriage Berlioz blended his conception of Shakespeare's women, his passion for Harriet, and his interest in opium into the fanciful story-line (program) that created the *Symphonie fantastique*.

Berlioz viewed classical forms as empty shells. He created, instead, an *idée fixe* (Fr. "fixed idea"), a single theme that was the common thread for each of the five movements of his daring new symphony. The *idée fixe* was a kind of *Leitmotif*—a procedure that Wagner was to exploit—that represented both the ideal of perfect love and the artist's idealized version of Harriet Smithson.

Following are the titles of the five movements of the *Symphonie fantastique* plus a brief explanation of what the composer apparently had in mind when he wrote the music.

I. *Reveries—Passions* ("Daydreams—Passions"). The artist, despairing of ever possessing his beloved, attempts to poison himself with opium. What follows in this and in the other movements is a series of opium-induced dreams, fantasies, and nightmares. This first movement is a frequently euphoric reverie about the artist's passion for his beloved.

II. *Un bal* ("A ball"). There is a fancy ball at which the beloved appears, slipping in and out of the dancers. The *idée fixe*, representing the beloved, is heard as she appears among the dancers.

III. *Scène aux champs* ("Scene in the country"). An idyllic scene of calm serenity in the bucolic countryside.

IV. *Marche au supplice* ("March to the scaffold"). In his delirium, the artist imagines that he has killed his beloved and that he is being taken on a tumbrel to the guillotine.

V. *Songe d'une nuit de Sabbat* ("Dream of a Witches' Sabbath"). Following his execution the artist dreams that he is present at a gruesome Witches' Sabbath, complete with a parody of the Dies irae (Lat., "Day of Judgment") as a part of a Black Mass. The *idée fixe* is also parodied as his beloved appears as a debased prostitute.

Listening Example 32
PROGRAM SYMPHONY

Berlioz, *Symphonie fantastique*, 4th movement, March to the Scaffold
1830

Time: 4:56
Cassette 3, track 28

Symphonie fantastique, Fourth movement, "March to the Scaffold"
Berlioz (1803–69)

Johannes Brahms, 1833–97

More than any other composer of the last half of the nineteenth century, Brahms was responsible for the reviving of "absolute music," that is, compositions that were strictly interplays of sound and totally independent of any kind of extramusical program. In this respect he was seen as a successor to Beethoven—so much so that his First Symphony was also nicknamed "Beethoven's Tenth." Brahms followed the Viennese classical tradition that emphasized form over novelties and innovations. While all of Europe was mesmerized by the special effects and innovations of Richard Wagner's operas, Brahms stubbornly stuck to the traditions of Mozart and Beethoven and thereby forged a unique place for himself as the foremost composer of the German Romantic movement. The third movement of his Second Symphony is a charming and lighthearted example of his symphonic style. The form is a five-part rondo: ABACA.

Listening Example 33
SYMPHONY

Brahms, Symphony No. 2 in D Major, Op. 73, 3rd movement
1877

Time: 5:33[2]

2. CD 2, track 19.

Peter Ilich Tchaikovsky, 1840–93

Tchaikovsky (chy-KOF-skee) seldom succeeded in mastering musical forms, but he was remarkably skillful in his handling of the symphony orchestra. The lush sounds of Tchaikovsky's orchestra have become a kind of hallmark for the dramatic intensity and emotional extremes of the Romantic movement.

Tchaikovsky's orchestral music ranges from ponderous melodrama to vapid sentimentality and yet, at his best, he has created enormously popular works for ballet—"Swan Lake," "The Nutcracker," "Sleeping Beauty"—and three successful symphonies, the Fourth, Fifth, and Sixth.

"The Nutcracker"

The subject for his ballet "The Nutcracker" was drawn from stories by Alexandre Dumas and E. T. A. Hoffmann. It begins with a Christmas tree party hosted by Marie for children and mechanical dolls. She is fascinated by a German nutcracker fashioned in the figure of an old man with massive jaws. Some rough boys break the nutcracker, and that night Marie lies sleepless in pity for it. Getting out of bed to look after her broken darling, she watches the Christmas tree grow and the toys come to life, including the cakes, tidbits, and nutcracker. Mice attack the toys and the nutcracker challenges the king of mice to single combat, a battle being won by the mouse until Marie kills it with a well-aimed shoe. The nutcracker is immediately transformed into a handsome young prince who thanks Marie for his life as he escorts her to his enchanted kingdom.

The scene in the second act is a jam mountain in the realm of the Sugarplum Fairy. There follows a series of eight dances which comprise the suite that Tchaikovsky made from the ballet score. The Russian Dance (*Trepak*) is extremely lively and is based almost entirely on the rhythmical figure in the opening measure.

Listening Example 34
BALLET MUSIC

Tchaikovsky, Suite from the ballet "The Nutcracker,"
Op. 71a, 4th movement, Russian Dance (*Trepak*)
1892

Time: 1:09
Cassette 3, track 29[3]

Nutcracker Suite, Fourth movement, "Russian Dance (Trepak)"

OPERA

Opera underwent drastic changes in style and intent during the nineteenth century. Early in the century, Beethoven's *Fidelio* (1805) represented what might be called international opera. With the emergence of Romanticism there was a corresponding rise in national schools of opera with Italy dominating the European (and American) scene.

Italian opera, as typified by Verdi's *Rigoletto* (1851), was a mélange of melodramatic plots, popular-type melodies, and "effective" solos and ensembles. There was more emphasis on *bel canto* (It., "beautiful singing") than on the development of plot and character. Later operas, Verdi's *Aïda* (1871) for example, evidenced an ever-increasing concern with dramatic values, culminating in the complex "music dramas" of Richard Wagner. Wagner conceived of opera, his *Tristan und Isolde* (1859) for example, as a super art form, a viewpoint roughly comparable to Byron's conception of himself as a superhero and Nietzsche's theory of a superman.

Wagner's insistence on the musical-literary totality of his myth-based music dramas provoked strong reactions in favor of so-called realism in subject matter and a new simplicity in musical treatment. A similar reaction against academic painting led to the emergence of such Romantic realists as Millet and Corot of the Barbizon School and, especially, the realists Daumier and Courbet. A comparable movement in literature, called naturalism, was led by Emile Zola.

Giuseppe Verdi, 1813–1901

Probably the greatest of all Italian opera composers, Verdi (VAIR-dee) had an exceptionally long and productive career. His last two operas, *Otello* (1887) and *Falstaff* (1893), based on Shakespeare and undoubtedly his best works, were composed long after most composers would have considered their careers over and done with. His operas are noted for their emotional intensity, tuneful, singable melodies, and highly dramatic characterizations. The following example is a tenor aria that deals playfully with women's frivolity: "How fickle women are, Fleeting as falling star, Changing forever; Constant, ah! never."

Listening Example 35
ITALIAN OPERA

Verdi, *Rigoletto*, Act IV, "La donna è mobile"
1851

Time: 2:11[4]

---

3. CD 3, track 2.
4. CD 2, track 17.

Georges Bizet, 1838–75

Bizet (Bee-zay) wrote only one successful opera, but that was quite enough to make him one of the century's great operatic composers. Oddly enough, *Carmen* was poorly received when first performed, a great disappointment for the composer, who died shortly after the thirty-first performance. Bizet based his opera on the novella *Carmen* by the French author Prosper Mérimée. Numerous French Romantic writers and composers had great success in using Spanish themes and placing their work in Spain. In the following selection Carmen compares love with a bird that cannot be tamed and with a wild and lawless gypsy child, warning anyone who loves her to be forever on guard. The arrogance of the beautiful Spanish gypsy is unmistakable.

Listening Example 37
OPERA

Bizet, *Carmen*, Act I, Habanera
1875

Time: 5:38[6]

IMPRESSIONISM IN MUSIC

By the end of the nineteenth century the main stream of Romanticism had about run its course. The decline was marked by the appearance of what was thought to be the new style of Impressionism. Just as the Renaissance had faded into Mannerism and the Baroque into Rococo, the refined essence of Romanticism was distilled into a final stage named after the painting style of Monet, Degas, Renoir, and others.

The so-called "impressionistic" music of Debussy and Ravel—Debussy detested the term "impressionism"—spearheaded a French revolt against the domination of German Romanticism and particularly the overwhelming exuberance of Wagner. The competition of German and French nationalism was a major factor in the Impressionist movement. Debussy cultivated an art that was subtle, delicate, and discreet, an art that was a sensuous rather than an emotional experience. For Debussy, German Romanticism was ponderous and tedious whereas French music possessed the Gallic spirit of elegance and refinement.

Many similarities exist between the painting of the Impressionists and the sophisticated music of Debussy and Ravel. The Impressionists tried to capture the play of color and light; favorite images included dappled sunlight through

24.5   Giacomo Puccini. Photo: Viollet, Paris.

Giacomo Puccini, 1858–1924

Giacomo Puccini (poo-CHEE-nee; fig. 24.5) was the leading Romantic Realist in operatic literature. His tragic operas *La Bohème*, *Madame Butterfly*, and *Tosca* are among the most popular works in the standard repertoire of leading opera companies. Though not the musical or dramatic innovator that Verdi was, Puccini had an inherent feeling for the stage which, together with the instrumental colors of his orchestral writing, assured him of international success. Along with Verdi's, his work continues to define Italian opera around the world. In the following example Tosca, an opera star, sings of her lover's imminent execution: "Love and music, these I have lived for, nor ever have harmed a human being . . . why, Heavenly Father, why hast Thou forsaken me?"

Listening Example 36
ITALIAN OPERA

Puccini, *Tosca*, Act II, "Vissi d'arte"
1900

Time: 3:08[5]

---

5. CD 3, track 4.
6. CD 2, track 18.

leaves and the play of light on water, fields, flowers, and buildings. The musicians dealt with an art of movement that attempted to translate this interplay of color and light into shimmering sounds.

Closely related to Impressionism in painting and music was the symbolism of the French poets, Mallarmé, Verlaine, and Baudelaire. They achieved an indefiniteness with words that had been the privilege of music alone. They likened their poetry to music and sought tone color in word sounds and symbolic meanings of words rather than any definite meaning. Wordplay, as with the tonal play of impressionistic music, was, according to Verlaine, "the gray song where the indefinite meets the precise."

The effects that musical impressionism achieved were the result of a number of innovations and extensions of musical resources.

Stylistic Characteristics

Modes

The old church modes came into favor again during late Romanticism and were exploited further by the impressionists. The effects they sought were counter to the clear tonality of the major-minor system. The modes, among other scales, provided a wider range of colors and a vagueness of tonality.

Other Scales

A strong Asian influence was reflected in the use of the pentatonic scale (five-tone scale) that is the basis for the folk music of Bali, China, and other Asian cultures.

Pentatonic scale

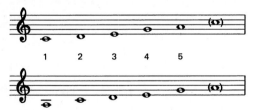

Particularly appropriate for the vague tonalities and drifting harmonies of impressionism was the whole-tone scale. This was a six-tone scale with a whole step between each pitch. With all tones equidistant, there was no clear tonal center. In fact, there were only two whole-tone scales possible: one starting on a white note and ending on a black note, and the other starting on a black note and ending on a white note.

Whole-tone scale

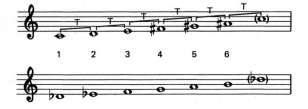

Form

Classical forms were generally abandoned in favor of the vague outlines, drifting quality, and dreamlike effects so basic to the style. This is not to say that the music is formless—there is a beginning, middle, and end—but rather that the forms are subtle and dictated by the impressions sought by the composer.

Orchestration

The massed woodwind and/or brass sounds of the orchestras of Brahms and Wagner were anathema to the impressionists. They replaced the dark and ponderous sound of the Germanic orchestras with a much lighter, shimmering effect and much more individualistic use of instruments. They delighted in the exotic sounds of the English horn and the flutes and clarinets in the low register. Violins frequently played in extremely high registers and were often muted. Trumpets and horns, too, were frequently muted. The characteristic sounds of the orchestra were supplemented by the harp, triangle, lightly brushed cymbals, and the bell tones of the small keyboard instrument called the celeste. The treatment of the pure sounds of the individual instruments was very much like the use of tiny brushstrokes of pure colors by the painters.

The piano remained a favorite instrument for the impressionists, but the sounds had little in common with the style, for example, of Chopin. The emphasis was on coloration, sensation, subtle harmonic effects, delicacy of tone. Everything was programmatic, whether a tonal description of a specific event or the evocation of a general idea, image, or sensation.

Claude Debussy, 1862–1918

Claude Debussy (deh-buh-see) used shifting harmonies and tone colors to suggest the shimmering effects of light and shade in the paintings of the Impressionists. His music has a luminous quality that compares with, for example, Renoir's sun-dappled nudes. Below is a piano composition that is titled "Voiles" (Fr., "Sails"). Using the whole-tone scale and a bit of pentatonic, Debussy weaves drifting patterns of melody and harmony that encourage the listener to make any association appropriate to the music and the ambiguous one-word title.

Listening Example 38
PIANO SOLO

Debussy, Preludes for Piano, Book I, 2nd movement, "Voiles"
1913

Time: 2:42
Cassette 3, track 30

Preludes for Piano, Book 1, Second movement, "Voiles (Sails)"

Debussy (1862–1918)

SUMMARY

Some of the elements of nineteenth-century Romanticism were present in the later works of Beethoven, but the lyric strains of full-blown Romanticism were paramount in the vocal and instrumental works of Franz Schubert. The characteristic style of German art songs (*Lieder*) which he created was developed by the German composers Schumann, Brahms, and Wolf. Frédéric Chopin made the piano his personal instrument with his unique style, and the very nature of Romanticism reinforced this individuality of personal expression. The music of Tchaikovsky, Brahms, Verdi, Bizet, and Puccini reflected this intensely subjective approach to artistic experience. They, like Rousseau, if not better than other men, were "at least different."

The decline of absolute music in favor of a full range of miniature to grandiose program music was probably the most significant musical characteristic of the century. The abstract titles of the eighteenth century (sonata, serenade, symphony) were, to a considerable extent, abandoned for descriptive or poetic titles. Dreamy nocturnes, cute capriccios, and dashing rhapsodies were distinguished more by sound and fury than by strong intrinsic design. Filled with emotion for its own sake and thus unabashedly sentimental, and lacking also the disciplined energy of the pre-Napoleonic era, Romantic music provided the sounding-board of the age.

The latter part of the century saw a gradual leveling off in the growth of the symphony orchestra. The tone poems of Strauss and the huge vocal-instrumental works of Mahler and Bruckner represented a point of no return, a stage reached after a reaction against the grandiloquence had already set in. Brahms responded to the extravagant use of musical materials and orchestral sounds by deliberately returning to the more disciplined practices of an earlier age. Debussy, Ravel, and other impressionists sharply reduced the orchestra in order to concentrate on the pure tone colors of individual instruments. However, they did continue in the Romantic tradition of program music, carrying it to its ultimate conclusion with techniques similar to those used in the Symbolist poetry of Mallarmé and Verlaine. The transition from nineteenth-century Romanticism to the so-called "new music" of the twentieth century was accomplished in large part by the impressionists, who inaugurated many of the materials of modern music while writing the final chapter of Romantic music.

CULTURE AND HUMAN VALUES

Though we live in an era not particularly notable for romantic sentiment, nineteenth-century music still forms a large part of today's musical repertoire. Why is the Romantic style still so popular?

Some of this appeal would have to be attributed to its familiarity: American audiences are notorious for their attachment to the tried and true compositions of the past. There is, however, an additional appeal that seems to have an enduring value—the fervent individualism of Romantic composers. The music of Chopin, for example, is totally unique, as is the music of Brahms, Verdi, and others. Each Romantic composer was fiercely independent and self-consciously "different."

Many of us are painfully aware of the anonymity of modern life in which people feel that they are little more than facts and figures imprisoned in the memory bank of a computer. Romantic composers, by contrast, loom large as heroic individuals from a recent past.

Romantic music is also unabashedly emotional, dramatically revealing the strains and stresses of life in all its complexity. Restraint is not a characteristic of the Romantic style. Nor can we say that our own era is particularly noted for restraint; in fact, energy, emotion, and dramatic intensity are notable components of much of modern music, with particular reference to several styles of rock.

There is, perhaps, more than a trace of nostalgia in our fondness for the Romantic style. Here is daring and derring-do. Laced with sentiment and surging emotions, Romanticism appeals to a large and faithful cross-section of today's audiences.

ADDITIONAL LISTENING

1. Chopin, Mazurka No. 24 in C, Op. 33 No. 3 (1838). The form of this piano solo is ABA (CD 2, track 11).
2. Wagner, *Lohengrin*, Prelude to Act III. This is a good illustration of the dynamic Wagnerian style at its best (CD 2, track 16).
3. Franck, Violin Sonata in A, last movement. This features a canon between the violin and piano (CD 3, track 1).
4. Sousa, *Hands Across the Sea*. The "March King" was an outstanding Romantic composer. The form is standard march form: an introduction followed by AABBCDC (CD 3, track 3).

CHAPTER 25

Nineteenth-Century Art: Conflict and Diversity

THE ROMANTIC MOVEMENT AND THE NEOCLASSIC STYLE

The Romantic movement first manifested itself in literature and music in the poetry of Wordsworth and Coleridge and the *Lieder* of Schubert. The visual arts were, however, in thrall to David, Napoleon's court painter, and to Napoleon's determination to confirm the legitimacy of his empire with the classical architecture of Imperial Rome. In 1806 Napoleon commissioned Jean François Chalgrin (shal-grã; 1739–1811) to construct a mighty arch to honor the victories of the French fighting forces (fig. 25.1). Placed in the center of twelve radiating avenues, the arch is 164 feet (49 m) in height and 148 feet (44.5 m) wide, larger than the triumphal arch of any Caesar. It stands today at the climax of the Avenue des Champs Elysées over the tomb of the Unknown Soldier, commemorating French imperial glory and the military triumphs of an emperor who did not live to see its completion.

The Church of St. Mary Magdalen, known as The Madeleine (fig. 25.2), was originally begun in 1764 and later razed to be replaced by a building modeled after the Pantheon in Rome. Napoleon required a new temple, a massive building dedicated to the glory of his Grand Army. The Madeleine has fifty-two majestic Corinthian columns running completely round the building, each 66 feet (20 m) tall. The eight-column front and complete peristyle are reminiscent of the Parthenon, but the podium, 23 feet (7 m) in height, is of Roman origin and similar to the Maison Carrée. Napoleon's Temple of Glory (also completed after his death) is a skillful synthesis of Graeco-Roman elements in a unified and imposing design.

Opposite Claude Monet, *Rouen Cathedral, West Facade Sunlight*, detail. 1894. Oil on canvas, full painting 39½ × 26" (100.3 × 66 cm). National Gallery of Art, Washington, D.C. (Chester Dale Collection).

25.2 *Right* Pierre Vignon, The Madeleine, Paris. 1806–42. Photo: Viollet, Paris.

25.1 *Above* Jean François Chalgrin (and others), Arch of Triumph, Place Charles de Gaulle, Paris, eastern facade. 1806–36. Photo: Giraudon, Paris.

Jean-Auguste-Dominique Ingres, 1780–1867

Only nine years old when the revolution began, Ingres (āgre) was never an enthusiastic supporter of Napoleon's self-proclaimed revolutionary ideals. He was, however, David's most talented pupil and an advocate of a Neoclassic style that had evolved from revolutionary art into state-endorsed dogma. Contending that David's style was too heavily incised, Ingres developed a fluid drawing technique influenced by Pompeiian frescoes and patterned after the elegant linear figures of Greek vase paintings. His *Grande Odalisque* (fig. 25.3) is not a classical version of feminine beauty; it is, however, a superb example of the artist's unique mix of Neoclassic and Romantic ideas. The reclining-nude pose can be traced to Titian and the smoothly flowing contours of the sculpturesque body are coolly classical; but the subject is an odalisque, a harem slave girl who represents an exotic concept dear to the Romantics. The small head, elongated limbs, and languid pose are very mannered in the decorative style of Parmigianino (see fig. 17.36).

25.3 Jean-Auguste-Dominique Ingres, *Grande Odalisque*. 1814. Oil on canvas, 35¼ × 63¾" (89.5 × 161.9 cm). Louvre, Paris.

Francisco de Goya, 1746–1828

The first of the illustrious painters of the Romantic era, Goya (GO-ya) was unique even in a time of remarkably individualistic artists. A contemporary of David, with whom he had nothing in common, Goya was influenced by Velasquez and Rembrandt, but not at all by antiquity or the Renaissance. Excelling in both portraiture and vigorous action canvases, Goya was appointed painter to the court of Spain in 1799. In his many acutely candid studies of the incompetent royal family of Charles IV that presided over a corrupt and decadent administration he was both a Romantic and a realist.

Goya extended his critical appraisal of the royal family to a general view of human folly, vice, and stupidity as depicted in a series of eighty etchings called "The Caprices." He had sold only twenty-seven copies when the Inquisition shut down the enterprise. Then, in 1808, Napoleon's invasion and conquest of Spain provided the artist with a powerful new subject: the bestiality and utter futility of war. Goya and many of his countrymen had hoped for French reforms of the debased Spanish court; instead, the merciless brutality of French soldiers provoked an equally savage resistance. Among the tragic results were a series of executions of Spanish patriots. Commissioned in 1814 by a liberal government after the expulsion of the French, Goya selected the executions of the Third of May (fig. 25.4) to vividly portray the underside of Napoleonic conquest. The firing squad is a faceless monster with many legs. Firing at point-blank range—the usual procedure for these

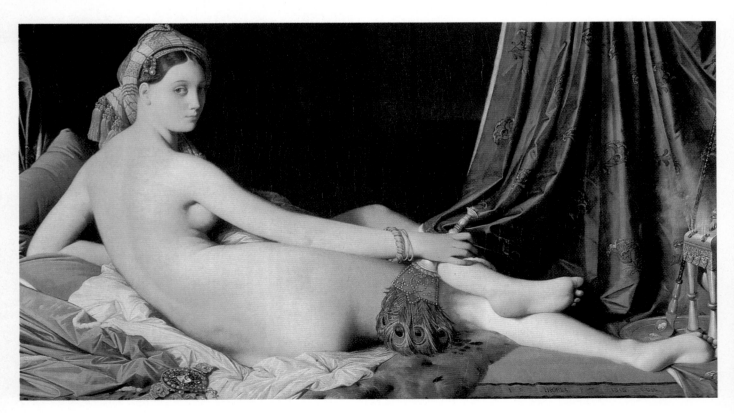

25.4 Francisco de Goya, *The Third of May, 1808, at Madrid: The Shootings on Príncipe Pío Mountain*. 1814. Oil on canvas, 8' 8¾ × 11' 3⅞" (2.66 × 3.45 m). Museo del Prado, Madrid. Photo: Bridgeman, London.

executions—the soldiers operate in a symbolic blackness of night illuminated only by a single lamp. This is probably the first of its kind, a work of art that protests against the barbarism of military conquest. Later in the century, so-called social-protest works of art became ever more common as artists attacked a variety of social evils. Careful study of Goya's painting, of the dead and those about to die, reveals a powerful universal statement about the lot of common people at the mercy of invading armies.

Goya's art was intensely personal and impossible to classify. He was a true Romantic, however, in his refusal to place much faith in reason, that goddess of the Enlightenment—the era that ended in bloody revolution, the Reign of Terror, and Napoleon. Goya left Spain in 1824 during a period of repression and died in self-imposed exile in France. His art was not known outside Spain until late in the Romantic era.

Théodore Géricault, 1791–1824

The most talented French painter of early Romanticism, Géricault (zhay-ree-ko) won artistic immortality with his painting of *The Raft of the "Medusa"* (fig. 25.5). Like other Romantic artists, Géricault seized on a contemporary event, a tragedy that caused a national scandal, as his subject matter. Jammed with colonists bound for French West Africa in 1816, the *Medusa* ran aground off the African coast because of the incompetence of the ship's captain, who then filled the *Medusa*'s six life-boats with his own party and sailed safely to shore, leaving about 150 men and one woman to shift for themselves.[1] In the painting, the few remaining survivors on their makeshift raft have just sighted a rescue ship on the horizon and are frantically signaling for help. This was the *Argus*, which did not sight the raft until the following day. Géricault researched the tragedy like an investigative reporter, interviewing survivors, studying corpses in the morgue, even building a raft to scale in his studio. The result is not just a realistic reporting of the event but a drama of heroic proportions of men against the sea. The

---

1. For details of the century's worst French scandal prior to the Dreyfus Case, see Alexander McKee's *Death Raft: The Human Drama of the Medusa Shipwreck* (New York: Warner Books, Inc., 1977).

25.5 Théodore Géricault, *The Raft of the "Medusa."*
1818–19. Oil on canvas, 16' × 23' 6" (4.8 × 7.05 m).
Louvre, Paris.

slashing diagonals and vivid chiaroscuro lead our eye to the triangle formed by the extended arms, with the waving figure at the apex; all movement is projected forward toward the distant sail. There is no movement in the left foreground, however, where an older man broods over the youthful corpse sprawled across his lap. The dejected man seems to be mourning the inhuman price all of them had to pay, for this composition is taken from an earlier sketch depicting the cannibalism that kept the survivors alive. But, if these men had been adrift for fourteen days with almost no provisions, why do the figures look so muscular, so healthy? Simply stated, emaciated figures with shriveled flesh and horrible wounds would be pitiful, tugging too directly on our emotions. But these sturdy figures transmit such power that we are lifted past the particular to the universal. This is how you turn a catastrophe into art.

Géricault's graphic realism was characteristic of the Romantic intent to shock the sensibilities of the viewer and evoke an emotional response. Government attempts to cover up the errors of a French naval officer stirred the public to a frenzy and focused attention on the painting as a political statement, much to the artist's dismay. (Géricault had at first hoped to avoid this reaction by calling the paint-

ing *Scene of Shipwreck.*) However, the *Medusa* affair has receded into history, leaving behind this vivid example of social-protest art whose timeless appeal transcends the tragedy that inspired it.

Eugène Delacroix, 1799–1863

Following Géricault's early death as a result of a riding accident, Delacroix (de-la-krwah), a peerless colorist, became the leading Romantic artist. The expansion of the French colonial empire into north Africa (beginning with Algeria in 1830) opened new vistas to French writers and artists. The first major French artist to visit Islamic countries, Delacroix was fascinated with the colorful vitality of Muslim cultures. In *Arabs Skirmishing in the Mountains* (see p. 416) he demonstrates a vibrant range of intense hues and strong contrasts of light and dark. As the artist wrote in one of his journals, "the more the contrast the greater the force." His ability to capture the illusion of movement makes the dramatic impact of the pitched battle all the more convincing. Continuing the squabble between color and line (one aspect of Romanticism versus Classicism), Delacroix was the Rubenist and his rival, Ingres, the Poussinist of the early nineteenth century. For a colorist such as Delacroix the perfect style, as he said, was a combination of Michelangelo and the recently discovered Goya.

Romantic painters were enamored of the sister arts:

25.6 John Constable, *Wivenhoe Park, Essex*. 1816. Oil on canvas, 22⅛ × 39⅞" (56.2 × 101.3 cm). National Gallery of Art, Washington, D.C. (Widener Collection).

the plays of Shakespeare, medieval romances, English romantic poetry, and especially music. Delacroix preferred, surprisingly, the classical style of Mozart to the flamboyant romanticism of his French contemporary Hector Berlioz but he was a friend of Chopin, whose poetic piano music had a special appeal, not only for Delacroix, but also for many writers and artists of the time. His portrait of Chopin (see fig. 24.2) epitomizes the melancholy suffering of the Romantic genius.

John Constable, 1776–1837

English artists responded more readily to Rousseau's back-to-nature movement than to the ideological drive of the French Revolution and subsequent Napoleonic wars. English Romantic poets—Wordsworth, Coleridge, Shelley, Keats—described the beauties of nature in highly personal terms. Landscape was prominent in their poetry but not as description for its own sake; rather, poets responded to aspects of the natural scene that stimulated their thinking, leading to meditations on nature that, as Wordsworth observed, involved the "Mind of Man." On the other hand, nature was frequently the subject matter for Romantic painters. Constable, one of the finest of all English painters, studied landscapes with a scientific objectivity. Rather than simply recording actual objects he sought the intangible qualities of atmosphere, light, and sky. The justly famed "Constable sky" is the dominating element in his poetic response to the peaceful scene at *Wivenhoe Park, Essex* (fig. 25.6). Sunlight shining on the wind-driven clouds and the effect of sunshine on fields and water have a luminosity rivaling even the Dutch masters, and the entire canvas has a freshness never before achieved in painting. The lustrous sky is the crowning glory of the picture, triumphantly confirming the artist's claim that this area was the "principal instrument for expressing sentiment." After his first exposure to Constable's work, Delacroix repainted the sky of an already completed work; the Impressionists were no less dazzled by the skies of Constable.

Joseph M. W. Turner, 1775–1851

The Impressionists, especially Monet, were just as enthralled by the heightened, liberated colors of Turner, Constable's eminent contemporary. A Londoner by birth

25.7 Joseph M. W. Turner, *Keelmen Heaving Coals by Moonlight*. Probably 1835. Oil on canvas, 36¼ × 48¼" (92.1 × 122.5 cm). National Gallery of Art, Washington, D.C. (Widener Collection).

and preference, Turner had none of Constable's attachment to peaceful nature. He was fascinated by light, the bright southern light of Italian cities, especially Venice. His sensitivity to light enabled him to develop a subtle, colorful art of freedom and refinement. His concentration on light and extreme effects of storms, sunsets, and fires put him ahead of his time and his indifference to finished details made his art unique. His *Keelmen Heaving Coals by Moonlight* (fig. 25.7) includes many of Turner's prized effects: moonlight, fires, and the use of color for atmospheric effects. The details are typically unclear with an overall effect that reveals Turner at his Romantic best.

Thomas Cole, 1801–48

American Romanticism had all the characteristics of the European variety but with some distinct variations that reflected a youthful nation in the New World. George Catlin, for example, spent many years studying and painting various Indian tribes, and John James Audubon devoted twelve years to the publication of his monumental *Birds of America*. But it was the American landscape that enthralled Thomas Cole and many other artists.

Cole emigrated from England to Philadelphia at the age of seventeen and later became an influential member of a group of artists now known as the Hudson River School. Cole and his colleagues viewed their landscape paintings as a high moral imperative in which they celebrated the beauty and purity of the American wilderness. In his *Essay on American Scenery* Cole pointed out that "the most distinctive, and perhaps the most impressive characteristic of American scenery is its wildness." He contrasted this with civilized Europe in which "the primitive features of scenery have long since been destroyed or modified." With its

---

25.8   Thomas Cole, *The Oxbow: View from Mount Holyoke. Northampton, Massachusetts, After a Thunderstorm.* 1836. Oil on canvas, 4' 3½" × 6' 4" (1.31 × 1.93 m). Metropolitan Museum of Art, New York (Gift of Mrs. Russel Sage, 1908. 08.228).

25.9 George Caleb Bingham, *Fur Traders Descending the Missouri*. Ca. 1845. Oil on canvas, 29 × 36½" (73.7 × 92.7 cm). Metropolitan Museum of Art, New York (Morris K. Jesup Fund, 1933.33.61).

relatively untouched forests and mountains and newly established republic, the United States was viewed as the new Eden, the light and hope of an exhausted Old World. Cole's view of *The Oxbow* (fig. 25.8) is an elaborate celebration of nature, a realistic depiction of an actual location with Romantic overtones of an idealized storm that, along with the twisted tree, helps frame the river. As with most of Cole's paintings, the human figure (right foreground) is dwarfed by the majesty of nature. Currently there is a considerable revival of interest in the work of the Hudson River School occasioned, in part, by environmental concerns. Depictions of the new Eden are, after all, only about a century and a half in a past that can never be recaptured.

George Caleb Bingham, 1811–79

Bingham pursued still another aspect of American Romanticism. Though he was born in Virginia he moved to Missouri when he was eight, there to paint the fur traders, boatmen, and politicians in what was then raw frontier country. This was also Mark Twain country, and one can find many images in the artist's work that illustrate life on the Missouri and Mississippi rivers as described in Twain's novels. *Fur Traders Descending the Missouri* (fig. 25.9) communicates some of the mystery and mystique of life on the leading edge of a developing nation. Bingham saw these figures as exotic explorers of the American wilderness— the first title for the painting was "French Trader and Half-Breed Son." His use of primary colors (red, yellow, blue) for the figures is echoed in the landscape by paler hues throughout the composition. The two figures stare out at us as though they are momentarily frozen in time. Though the water is like a mirror we still have the impression of watery motion from right to left. This is clearly a Romantic work but there are classical overtones in the balanced design, luminous light, and meticulous purity of details.

Robert Scott Duncanson, 1817–72

Influenced by the Hudson River School, Duncanson was recognized in his own time as an exceptional landscape painter. His *Blue Hole* (fig. 25.10), like much of Thomas Cole's work, has a double scale: the fishermen have been made very small so that the enlarged landscape can dominate the composition. Like other artists in the Hudson River tradition, Duncanson regarded America, with its magnificent landscapes towering over insignificant human beings, as the new Garden of Eden.

25.10   Robert Scott Duncanson, *Blue Hole, Flood Waters, Little Miami River.* 1851. Oil on canvas, 42¼ × 29¼" (107.3 × 74.3 cm). Cincinnati Art Museum (Gift of Norbert Heerman and Arthur Helbig).

Architectural Inspiration from the Past

The largest and most successful architectural recollection of the past was the Houses of Parliament in London, designed by Sir Charles Barry (1795–1860) with the assistance of Gothic scholar Augustus Welby Pugin (1812–52; fig. 25.11). More than the French or Germans, the English felt that the Gothic style was an exemplary expression of the national past, a heritage both noble and Christian. Consequently, a parliamentary commission decreed that the design for the new seat of government be either Gothic or Elizabethan and nothing else. Barry favored the Neoclassic style, but Pugin convinced him that the English Late Gothic style was the proper glorification of the British spirit and a celebration of medieval craftsmanship in the face of mass-produced items of the industrial age. Actually, the body of the building is symmetrical in the Palladian manner surmounted by a Gothic fantasy of turrets, towers, and battlements.

REALISM
Millet, Corot, and the Barbizon School

Countering the Romantic fantasies of their literary and artistic contemporaries, the realists concentrated on the real world as they perceived it, with an objective matter-of-factness that alienated the followers of Géricault and Delacroix. Settling near the village of Barbizon in the Forest

25.11   Barry and Pugin, The Houses of Parliament, London. 1836–60. Photo: John Bethell, St. Albans, U.K.

25.12 Jean-François Millet, *The Gleaners*. 1857. Oil on canvas, 33 × 44" (83.8 × 111.8 cm). Louvre, Paris. Photo: R.M.N., Paris.

of Fontainebleau south of Paris, painters of the Barbizon School imitated Rousseau's back-to-nature movement while simultaneously escaping the disorder and confusion of the 1848 Revolution. Rousseau's "noble savage" was interpreted by Barbizon painter, François Millet (me-yay; 1814–75), as a heroic peasant who exemplified the dignity of working the land. In *The Gleaners* (fig. 25.12) Millet's peasants have the monumentality of Michelangelo and an earthy quality comparable to the bourgeois Dutch tradition. Himself the son of peasants, Millet chose to live the life of a peasant and he sympathetically depicted his figures as actors in a kind of divine drama in a style antithetical to the French academic tradition.[2]

Though he did not consider himself a member of the Barbizon School, Jean-Baptiste-Camille Corot (ko-row; 1796–1875) lived in the area and shared their strong commitment to direct visual experience. In the *Ville d'Avray*

(fig. 25.13) Corot painted the full range of light and dark values, depicting visual reality at a single moment in time, as in a photograph. Working very quickly, Corot sought the underlying rhythm of nature, composing his landscapes so that the magic moment of truth would be revealed to all. One of the finest Western landscape painters, Corot became, according to the poet Baudelaire, "the master of an entire younger generation."

Honoré Daumier, 1808–79

Corot, Millet, and the Barbizon School can be described as Romantic realists for there is an element of escapism in their work. In Paris, however, the realities of political and social unrest before and after the 1848 Revolution were of far greater concern to a hard-bitten realist such as Daumier (doe-me-ay). Known to his contemporaries as a

2. Disdained since about 1860 as artistically inferior, French academic art has, since about 1965, experienced a rebirth. See, for example, *The Encyclopedia of World Art*, vol. XVI (New York: McGraw-Hill, 1983), pp. 230–1.

25.13   Jean-Baptiste-Camille Corot, *Ville d'Avray*. 1870. Oil on canvas, 21⅝ × 31½" (54.9 × 80 cm). Metropolitan Museum of Art, New York (Bequest of Catherine Lorillard Wolfe, 1887). Photo: Tintometer Ltd., Salisbury, U.K.

caricaturist, Daumier created over 4,000 **lithographs**³ satirizing the major and minor foibles of the day.

Daumier was just as forceful a contemporary social critic in oils as he was in his lithographs, claiming that scenes of contemporary everyday life had to be painted because "one must be of one's own time." In *Third-Class Carriage* (fig. 25.14) he used a strong chiaroscuro in the manner of Rembrandt, whom he greatly admired, to depict the isolation of each figure in the railway car; each person is utterly alone with his or her own thoughts. This painting is both Romantic and realistic. Daumier accurately caught a stark moment in the anonymity of urban life but the painting is suffused with the emotion of an artist who has sympathetically identified with a car full of lonely strangers.

3. One of the graphic arts, lithography is a printmaking process that was widely used in the nineteenth century for newspaper and magazine illustrations. In lithography (Gk., "writing on stone") the design is drawn on stone or a metal plate with a greasy printing ink and then reproduced by the standard printing process.

25.14   Honoré Daumier, *Third-Class Carriage*. Ca 1862. Oil on canvas, 25¼ × 35½" (65.4 × 90.2 cm). Metropolitan Museum of Art, New York (Bequest of Mrs. H.O. Havemeyer, 1929; H.O. Havemeyer Collection. 29.100.129). Photo: Schecter Lee.

Gustave Courbet, 1819–77

Realism in art was given a name and a leader in the person of Courbet (koor-bay), who issued a "Manifesto of Realism." At the Andler Keller, one of the first Parisian beer halls, the swaggering, flamboyant Courbet held forth as the champion of the physical world of visible objects. "Show me an angel," he once remarked, "and I will paint you an angel." Courbet found his natural subjects in the common people of his home village of Ornans in eastern France. As he said, "to paint a bit of country, one must know it. I know my country." *Burial at Ornans* (fig. 25.15) depicts a rural scene on a monumental scale normally reserved for epic historical events. Much to the consternation of the critics, Courbet turned the somber reality of this simple country funeral into a noble occasion that he called "true history." Combining religious symbolism with realism, Courbet included the dog as it was depicted in the Office of the Dead in medieval manuscripts; the people were all painted from life in innumerable sittings demanded by the artist. Composed on a horizontal S-curve, the figures of clergy, pall-bearers, friends, and relatives stand in poses ranging from indifference to composed grief. The staff with the crucifix is positioned to give the illusion of Christ's death on Golgotha. This and other paintings were rejected by the Universal Exposition, leading to the construction of a shed, called by Courbet "The Pavilion of Realism," for the exhibition of his uncompromising works.

25.15   Gustave Courbet, *Burial at Ornans*. 1849–50. Oil on canvas, ca. 10' 6" × 13' (3.2 × 3.9 m). Musée d'Orsay, Paris. Photo: R.M.N., Paris.

Winslow Homer, 1836–1910

Realism spread throughout Europe as artists were attracted to the style, but it was especially popular in the United States, where pragmatism and realism were characteristics of the American way of life. Beginning his career as an illustrator for *Harper's Weekly*, Winslow Homer was influenced by Corot and Courbet, but not at the expense of his American point of view. Homer lived during the post-Civil War era that Mark Twain called the Gilded Age, a grossly materialistic era of pretentious opulence, but his style was firmly fixed in genre paintings in the mode of American realism. In *Breezing Up* (fig. 25.16) Homer celebrated his lifelong love-affair with the sea in a joyous composition of wind, salt air, and sparkling sea. Fatigued but happy with the day's catch, the fisherman and boys are returning home. With the catboat placed at eye-level and slanting away from the viewer, we are drawn into an illusion of movement and the feeling of a job well done. Exemplifying Homer's statement, "When I have selected a thing carefully, I paint it exactly as it appears," the details are finely drawn: wrinkled clothes, light sparkling from metal fittings, a lighthouse at the lower left, a wheeling gull at the upper right. Homer's ability to give the illusion of light emanating from his canvases paralleled the development of French Impressionism across the ocean.

Homer's career was remarkably divergent from that of his older contemporary, author Herman Melville. Both were New Englanders, fascinated by the sea, but Homer's vision was generally positive whereas Melville's was darkly ambiguous. Homer covered the Civil War as an illustrator for *Harper's Weekly*; Melville wrote two volumes of war poems that were totally unknown at the time. Homer was a highly successful and popular painter; Melville was

25.16 Winslow Homer, *Breezing Up (A Fair Wind)*. 1876. Oil on canvas, 24⅛ × 38⅛" (61.3 × 96.8 cm). National Gallery of Art, Washington, D.C. (Gift of the W. I. and May T. Mellon Foundation, 1943).

25.17 Thomas Eakins, *The Gross Clinic*. 1875. Oil on canvas, 8' × 6' 6" (2.4 × 1.95 m). Jefferson Medical College of Thomas Jefferson University, Philadelphia.

not recognized as one of America's greatest writers until many years after his unremarked death. Both were realists.

Thomas Eakins, 1844–1916

Eakins (ay-kins) called Homer the best living American artist, but Eakins himself ranks, with Homer, as one of the very best of American artists. His *The Gross Clinic* (fig. 25.17) is a monumental work. The scene is Philadelphia's Jefferson Medical Clinic, in which Dr. Gross and his surgical team are operating. Much in the manner of Rembrandt (see fig. 21.18) the focus is precisely on the chief surgeon and the incision in the leg of the anesthetized patient, whose mother on the left (present as a legal requirement) cannot bear to watch. As was customary at the time, the doctors wear street clothing (as did Eakins himself, on the far right). Not surprisingly, considering the era, the uncompromising realism of the painting raised a storm of objections. Though submitted for the Philadelphia Centennial of 1876, it was shunted aside and ended up in the obscurity of the U.S. Army Post Hospital exhibit. Eakins was never popular with the general public or with most critics of the time.

Architecture

Realism in painting can be compared, to some extent, with the development of late-nineteenth-century architecture. Abandoning copies of older styles, architects turned to modern building materials to design functional structures serving specific purposes. Epitomizing the new attitude toward utilitarian design, the Crystal Palace (fig. 25.18) was constructed of 5,000 prefabricated iron columns and girders and nearly 300,000 panes of glass. A gardener and greenhouse designer by profession, Sir Joseph Paxton (1801–65) oversaw the construction of an immense structure that covered eighteen acres in Hyde Park and contained almost a million square feet of floor space. Ironically, this first truly modern building was a response to an emergency brought about by the dithering of the Building Commission, which was unable to select a winning design from the more than 200 submitted. The Crystal Palace won by default because only Paxton's advanced technology could create a building in the little time remaining.

Assembled in only thirty-nine weeks, the Crystal Palace housed London's "Great Exhibition of the Works of All Nations of 1851," a triumphant display of the miracles wrought by the industrial revolution. The theme of the exhibition was "Progress," represented by the mechanized marvels within the glittering structure, itself a symbol of the "Age of Progress." The first of many similar buildings, the Crystal Palace was dismantled after the exhibition and reassembled south of London where, in 1936, it was destroyed by fire. Though cast-iron structures were vulnerable to fire, the Crystal Palace did establish the practicality of metal as a building material. With the invention of the Bessemer process of making steel in 1856, the technology became available for the construction of bridges and twentieth-century high-rise buildings.

The first high-rise structure in the world was designed by an engineer who had previously devised bridges and the metal framework for the Statue of Liberty. Gustave Eiffel

---

25.18 Joseph Paxton, Crystal Palace, London. 1850–1. Cast iron, wrought iron, and glass. Engraving (R. P. Cuff after W. B. Brounger). Royal Institute of British Architects, London (Drawings Collection).

25.19 Gustave Eiffel, Eiffel Tower, Paris. 1889. Original poster produced by Ch. Parvillers. Photo: Mansell Collection, London.

(I-fel; 1832–1923) designed the theme tower for the Paris Exhibition of 1889, another celebration of technological advances. Rising to an imposing height of 984 feet (295 m), the Eiffel Tower (fig. 25.19) symbolized the "Age of Progress" in France. Like a giant erector set, it was assembled on the site; 15,000 prefabricated and prepunched girders were bolted together in a masterful demonstration of precision design and production that was completed in two years, two months, and two days. The tower weighs almost 10,000 tons (10 million kg), but it is proportionately so light that a steel scale model 1 foot (30 cm) in height would weigh less than ¼ ounce (7g). Though denounced from the outset by purists who objected to the violation of the Parisian skyline, the tower stands today as the enduring symbol of the City of Light.

IMPRESSIONISM

In one respect Impressionism was an outgrowth of realism, but in another it was a revolutionary artistic movement almost as profound in its effect as the Early Renaissance in Italy. Impressionists saw themselves as the ultimate realists whose main concern was the perception of optical sensations of light and color. Whether the Impressionists were consciously aware of photographic techniques, scientific research in optics, or the physiology of the eye is not important; they painted as if the world were not matter in space but a source of sensations of light and color. Objects were perceived as agents for the absorption and reflection of light; there were no sharp edges, indeed no lines, in nature. In nature, form and space were implied by infinitely varied intensities of color and light, and shadows were not black but colored in relation to the objects casting the shadows. This is Impressionist theory in essence, but the individual artists developed styles, of course, that sometimes contradicted the theories.

There was one characteristic of Impressionism that differentiated the movement from all other styles; it was not limited to artists. There was a generally appealing quality that drew together not only painters and their models, but a number of writers, critics, and collectors. The general public was not part of the movement, of course, for this was a consciously **avant-garde** enterprise, a confident step into the modern world.

Edouard Manet, 1832–83

"From now on I will be of our times and work with what I see," Manet (ma-nay) said to friends after destroying most of his early paintings. A major innovator in Western painting, Manet was not a member of the Impressionist group, but his influence on the movement was critical. Realizing that modeled transitions did not exist in nature, he worked instead in planes. He was also one of the first artists to paint with pure colors, eliminating dark shadows that had been used for centuries. Manet was a pioneer in the use of light as his subject; light was the actual subject matter of the painting that he submitted in 1863 to the jury of the Paris **Salon**. An unconventional painting with a conventional title, *Déjeuner sur l'herbe* ("Luncheon on the Grass"; fig. 25.20) was refused by the jury but exhibited in a special Salon des Refusés, where it caused a storm of controversy. The contemporary dress of the men in combination with the unconcerned nakedness of the woman deeply shocked the public. Even Courbet criticized the work as flat and formless. Indeed, Manet had almost totally abandoned Renaissance perspective, accepting the canvas for what it really was: a two-dimensional surface. For example, the background figure is much too large: if corrected for perspective she would be 9 feet (2.7 m) tall. Also, the painting is lit from two different directions. The hue and cry over the work bewildered the artist; the subject, after all was light itself—as clustered around the nude, the background figure, and the still life in the left foreground. The grouping of the dark areas further emphasized the harsh light of day, giving the painting a powerful visual impact. For Manet and the Impressionists the objects and figures in their paintings were sometimes treated impersonally, as opportunities to depict light sensations. Frequently detached and non-judgmental, Manet and the Impressionists, except for Renoir, were often more entranced with optical sensations than with humanity.

The public, however, was not detached and it was very judgmental. The reaction to Manet's *Olympia* (fig. 25.21), which he exhibited at the 1865 Salon, caused one of the greatest scandals in art history. Critics called Manet "a buffoon" and the nude a "female gorilla" and "yellow-bellied odalisque." Boisterous crowds flocked to see a work that another critic advised pregnant women and proper young ladies to avoid at all costs. Manet had painted his model, Victorine Meurend (who also posed for the

25.20 Edouard Manet, *Déjeuner sur l'herbe*. 1863. Oil on canvas, 6' 9⅛" × 8' 10¼" (2.06 × 2.7 m). Musée d'Orsay, Paris. Photo: R.M.N., Paris.

25.21 *Below* Edouard Manet, *Olympia*. 1863. Oil on canvas, 4' 3¼" × 6' 2¾" (1.3 × 1.9 m). Musée d'Orsay, Paris. Photo: A.K.G., Berlin.

Déjeuner), as an elegant and world-weary lady of the evening. With an orchid in her hair and wearing only a black ribbon and a bracelet, she stares disdainfully at the viewer while ignoring the bouquet proffered by her maid. Critics were no more incensed by the flagrant nakedness than by the black-on-black coloration of the maid's face against the background, not to mention the black cat at the foot of the suggestively rumpled bed, also painted against a black background. The picture became a *cause célèbre*, pitting modernists against traditionalists. In his novel *Of Human Bondage* Somerset Maugham gleefully described the Latin Quarter in which reproductions of *Olympia* were prominent in virtually every student room, bistro, and café. Even today the picture is distinctly modern. Manet forces his viewers to look *at* his flat picture rather than *into* it. The traditional boxlike space behind the frontal picture plane has been eliminated, presenting a situation that leaves much to the imagination. Further, a comparison of *Olympia* and the *Odalisque* of Ingres (see fig. 25.3) reveals the difference, at that time, between acceptable nudity and the disagreeable reality of a naked prostitute.

Following the innovations of Manet, who went on to experiment in other directions, the Impressionists developed a definite system with its own aesthetic principles. For centuries artists had been painting what they knew. The Impressionists were interested in painting what they saw.

Claude Monet, 1840–1926

The spokesman and chief painter of the Impressionist style was Monet (mah-nay), who throughout his long and productive career relied wholly on his visual perceptions. For him, especially, there were no objects such as trees, houses, or figures. Rather, there was some green here, a patch of blue there, a bit of yellow over here, and so on. Monet was "only an eye," said Paul Cézanne, "but what an eye!"

The mechanics of vision were a major concern of

WELL-TIMED TECHNOLOGY

Until the late nineteenth century artists had to undergo the messy and time-consuming process of mixing their own paints and storing the results in jars or bladders. Advances in chemistry now produced new and brilliant pigments and the invention of collapsible tin tubes came at just the right time. With their bright colors in portable tubes artists were able to roam the countryside and paint *en plein air* ("in open air"). They were freed to paint what they saw and that was largely the glories of nature and the evanescent effects of sunlight and shade, clouds and water.

Monet and the other Impressionists. To achieve intensity of color, pigments were not combined on the palette but laid on the canvas in primary hues so that the eye could do the mixing. A dab of yellow, for example, placed next to one of blue is perceived, from a distance, as green, a brilliant green because the eye accomplishes the optical recomposition. Further, each color leaves behind a visual sensation that is its after-image or complementary color. The after-image of red is blue-green and that of green is the color red. The adjacent placement of red and green reinforces each color through its after-image, making both red and green more brilliant. Impressionists generally painted with pure pigments in the colors of the spectrum; conspicuously absent from the spectrum and thus from Impressionist canvases was black, a favorite of academic painters. Monet contended that black was not a color and he was scientifically correct; black is the absence of color. This, of course, did not keep Degas and Manet from using black with dramatic effect.

Portable paints in the open sunlight and color perception were two components of Impressionist technique. The third component was speed. Making natural light explode on canvas necessitated quick brushstrokes that captured a momentary impression of reflected light, a reflection that changed from minute to minute. Monet's procedure was to paint furiously for seven or eight minutes and then move quickly to another canvas to capture a different light. Should a painting require additional effort he would return to the same spot the following day at the same time, a procedure he followed in his forty paintings of Rouen Cathedral done at different times of day. Early in the morning the elaborate Gothic facade would appear to be quite solid, but later in the day, as in *Rouen Cathedral, West Facade Sunlight* (see p. 426), the stonework has dissolved into a luminous haze of warm colors. Monet was the first artist since the Renaissance to investigate the dimension of time.

"Impressionism" is a term used derisively by a critic who, on seeing Monet's 1872 painting entitled *Impression, Sunrise*, remarked that it was "only an impression." That the term is generally apropos is apparent in Monet's impression of sunlight on medieval stonework. An interesting and telling sidelight is the 1872 date of this important painting. This was only a year after France had been humiliated by Germany in the Franco-Prussian War of 1870–1. A study of French artistic output of the period points up the artists' total unconcern with politics and so-called national honor.

Auguste Renoir, 1841–1919

Monet was a magnificent "eye" whose achievements are far more appreciated today than in his own time. On the other hand, the work of his celebrated contemporary, Auguste Renoir (re-nwar), has always had great appeal, possibly because Renoir portrayed people rather than buildings, landscapes, or lily ponds. The finest painter of luscious nudes since Rubens, Renoir had a unique ability to create the illusion of soft and glowing human flesh. He painted females of all ages, once exclaiming that if "God had not created woman I don't know whether I would have become a painter!"

Much of the art of Millet and the realists depicts laborers at various tasks, but the Impressionists viewed a world without work. An astonishing number of Impressionist works portrayed people enjoying leisure activities: boating, bathing, picnicking, promenading, dancing, attending the theatre, opera, ballet, or music hall, going to the races. There is no finer representation of exuberant pleasure than Renoir's *Le Moulin de la Galette* (see p. 385), a dazzling display of painterly virtuosity. The scene is an outdoor café with a large and crowded dance floor. The radiant color and shimmering light emphasize the fresh and youthful vigor of the participants, especially the women; nowhere is there a trace of black for all shadows have some degree of color. Light, air, color, and the captured moment, this is what Impressionism is all about. Further, Impressionism also functioned as a social history of France in the latter part of the nineteenth century. People were shown enjoying leisure activities because so many more of them had the time and money to do so. The growth and rise of the middle class is right there in Renoir's painting for all to see.

25.23 Berthe Morisot, *In the Dining Room*. 1886. Oil on canvas, 24⅛ × 19¾" (61.3 × 50 cm). National Gallery of Art, Washington, D.C. (Chester Dale Collection).

Edgar Degas, 1834–1917

Degas (day-gah) also specialized in women, but women in their casual and graceful roles as ballet dancers. Delighting in studying forms in motion, he drew dancers and race horses with a remarkable vitality. *Four Dancers* (fig. 25.22)

25.22 Edgar Degas, *Four Dancers*. Ca. 1899. Oil on canvas, 4' 11½" × 5' 11" (1.51 × 1.8 m). National Gallery of Art, Washington, D.C. (Chester Dale Collection).

was one of his last large oil paintings, and it shows the influence of the pastel medium that he used in most of his later works. Of all the Impressionists, Degas was most interested in photography, both in taking pictures and in basing some of his works on photographs. This off-stage ballet scene has the appearance of a candid snapshot of dancers limbering up and checking their costumes before going onstage. Actually, Degas posed dancers in his studio to create the illusion of spontaneity. Degas' concern with composition—and his use of black—make his style less Impressionist than that of Monet or Renoir.

Berthe Morisot, 1841–95

The Impressionists were a cohesive group of *avant-garde* artists who revolved around the central personality of Manet. The regular meeting place of Manet's "school" was the Café Guerbois, where Manet, Monet, Renoir, Degas, Whistler, the photographer Nadar, Emile Zola, Baudelaire, and others congregated to argue passionately about the role of the modern artist. Morisot (more-ee-so) was a member of the group but, as a proper young woman, she was denied the opportunity to socialize at the café with her colleagues. A student of both Corot and Manet, she earned the unusual distinction of having her work accepted by both the Impressionists and the Salon. She was, in fact, one of

25.24   Mary Cassatt, *The Bath*. Ca. 1891–2. Oil on canvas, 39¼ × 26" (99.7 × 66 cm). Art Institute of Chicago (Robert A. Waller Fund). Photo: Arlette Mellaart.

the organizers of the first Impressionist exhibition at Nadar's Gallery in 1874. *In the Dining Room* (fig. 25.23) depicts her maid and a little white dog in a setting in which the forms are silhouetted as elements in a design literally flooded with shimmering color and light. Mallarmé, an enthusiastic admirer of her art, wrote in his catalog for an exhibition of her work: "To make poetry in the plastic arts demands that the artist portray on the surface the luminous secret of things, simply, directly, without extraneous detail."

Mary Cassatt, 1844–1926

Both of the American painters who exhibited with the Impressionists, Mary Cassatt and James Whistler, drew inspiration from Impressionist techniques, but each developed a different and very personal style. Cassatt was American by birth and training and, though she lived in

France for much of her life, is considered by the French to be the best artist America has yet produced. The influence of two-dimensional Japanese woodcuts (see fig. 25.29) is apparent in *The Bath* (fig. 25.24), but the extraordinary fluidity of the lines is uniquely her own. Both decorative and functional, they enclose what seems at first to be a simple domestic scene. But this is a highly stylized composition that we look down on, an intimate and tender moment presented in a closed form that shuts out the viewer and the

25.25   James McNeill Whistler, *The White Girl (Symphony in White No. 1)*, after restoration. 1862. Oil on canvas, 7' ½" × 3' 6½" (2.15 × 1.08 m). National Gallery of Art, Washington, D.C. (Harris Whittemore Collection). Photo: Richard Carafelli.

25.26 Auguste Rodin, *The Walking Man*. Probably ca. 1900. Bronze, 33¼ × 16¾ × 21⅞″ (84.5 × 42.6 × 55.5 cm). National Gallery of Art, Washington, D.C. (Gift of Mrs. John W. Simpson).

world. We experience the rich warmth of the scene but we are not a part of it. The frequently caustic and always chauvinistic Degas remarked, after examining her work in her studio, "These are real. Most women paint pictures as though they were trimming hats, not you." For Degas, this was high praise for a great artist.

James McNeill Whistler, 1834–1903

Whistler and Henry James considered American civilization an embarrassment. Like James, Whistler became an expatriate, even denying that he was born in Lowell, Massachusetts: "I shall be born when and where I want, and I do not choose to be born in Lowell." Whistler was highly critical, naturally, of American realists such as Winslow Homer (see fig. 25.16), advocating instead "art for art's sake." The Impressionists were sufficiently artistic for his tastes, and he adapted some of their modern techniques to his uniquely personal style. Subject matter, he felt, was of no importance. Of his *White Girl (Symphony in White, No. 1)* (fig. 25.25) Whistler remarked that no one could possibly be interested in the model, who happened to be the artist's mistress, Joanna Heffernan. Whistler added the subtitle several years after exhibiting the painting to emphasize the aesthetic appeal of his use of rhythm and

harmony in the manner of music. Some of his *avant-garde* colleagues recognized that art was its own subject matter, but not the art establishment. Rejected by both the Royal Academy in London and the Paris Salon, the painting became as notorious as Manet's *Déjeuner* (see fig. 25.20). Light was the subject of one painting and white the subject of the other.

Auguste Rodin, 1840–1917

During the eighteenth and nineteenth centuries sculpture failed to keep pace with painting and architecture. The work of Houdon (see fig. 21.34) was significant, but the sculptures of Daumier and Degas were scarcely known at the time. And then there was Rodin (ro-dā), the greatest sculptor since Bernini, a dynamo of a man who captured the spontaneity and immediacy of Impressionism in three-dimensional form. Like Renoir and Degas, Rodin was concerned with the human figure but, totally unlike any Impressionist, he depicted his figures in moments of stress or tension. *The Walking Man* (fig. 25.26), intended originally as a study for *St. John the Baptist Preaching*, is a study in motion—and motion is all that we sense. Headless and armless, the figure has neither expression nor gesture to distract our attention from the strongly striding torso moving its muscular legs in long steps. The surface shimmers

25.27 Auguste Rodin, *The Thinker*. 1880. Bronze, 28⅛ × 14⅜ × 23½″ (71.5 × 36.4 × 59.5 cm). National Gallery of Art, Washington, D.C. (Gift of Mrs. John W. Simpson).

with light, shaped by the artist to heighten the illusion of motion.

Rodin's commission for *The Gates of Hell* produced a number of figures extracted from a monumental work that was never finished. *The Thinker* (fig. 25.27), sitting atop the gates and brooding over Rodin's conception of Dante's *Inferno*, is a prodigious representation of tension in repose. Similar to Michelangelo's superhuman forms (which Rodin studied in detail), the figure is sunk deep in thought. What is he thinking of? Rodin said at one time that it was Dante contemplating his poem and at other times that it was a dreamer or a creator. Whether writer, dreamer, or creator, *The Thinker* remains a fascinating enigma.

25.28   Paul Cézanne, *Mont Sainte-Victoire seen from Les Lauves*. 1902–4. Oil on canvas, 27⅞ × 36⅛" (70.8 × 91.8 cm). Philadelphia Museum of Art (George W. Elkins Collection).

POSTIMPRESSIONISM
Paul Cézanne, 1839–1906

Postimpressionism is a catch-all term for some highly individual artists who reacted against the purely visual emphasis of Impressionism. The first and foremost of the Postimpressionists, Cézanne (say-zan) was, in fact, one of the giants of European painting. His art lay somewhere between representation and abstraction, an intellectualized approach to applying paint to canvas. For Cézanne the whole purpose of painting was to express the emotion that the forms and colors of the natural world evoked in the artist. His landscapes look like his native Provence but not literally; everything has been clarified and concentrated. Cézanne took liberties with ordinary visual experience that challenge our perceptions and force us to view the world in a new way, in Cézanne's way. In *Mont Sainte-Victoire seen from Les Lauves* (fig. 25.28) Cézanne gives us one of many versions of his favorite mountain. In common with his other

landscapes, it contains no living creatures and the forms of the trees and houses are synthesized with the artist's characteristically muted blue-green and orange hues. The Impressionists used color to dissolve form and space; Cézanne did precisely the opposite, using color to define form in a tangible space. Cézanne constructed his paintings slowly, methodically, with an intellectual control comparable to that of Poussin. *Mont Sainte-Victoire* has what he called a "durable museum quality" because Cézanne painted not just what he saw but what he knew.

Vincent van Gogh, 1853–90

Cézanne sold some of his paintings for as little as nine dollars but the Dutch artist van Gogh (van-go) sold only one painting during his ten-year career, depending entirely on his brother for support. Van Gogh began as an Impressionist but changed his style drastically after studying Japanese prints, which he found "extremely clear, never tedious, as simple as breathing" (fig. 25.29). Though van Gogh never attained this degree of facility, he did learn to treat the picture surface as an area to be decorated in masses of flat or slightly broken color. In *La Mousmé* (fig. 25.30) he painted a young girl from Provence, to which he had moved in 1888 to capture in the brilliant sunlight some of

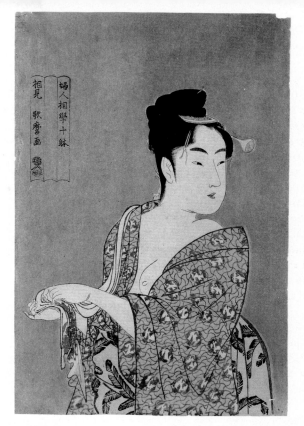

25.29 Kitagawa Utamaro, *Uwaki, Half-Length Portrait*, from the series *Fujin Sogaku Jittai: Studies in Physiognomy; Ten Kinds of Women*. Ca. 1794. Print; color and mica on paper, 14½ × 10" (36.8 × 25.4 cm). Cleveland Museum of Art (Bequest of Edward L. Whittemore).

25.30 Vincent van Gogh, *La Mousmé*. 1888. Oil on canvas, 28⅞ × 23¾" (73.3 × 60.3 cm). National Gallery of Art, Washington, D.C. (Chester Dale Collection). Photo: Bob Grove.

JAPANESE PRINTS

The Japanese *ukiyo-e* prints that inspired Mary Cassatt and Vincent van Gogh were popular during the eighteenth and nineteenth centuries (Edo period) in Japan. *Ukiyo-e* ("pictures of the floating world") was a tradition in Japanese painting and printmaking that tried to capture pleasurable scenes from everyday life: love or sexual scenes, festivals, theatrical performances, portraits of actors and dancers, and so forth.

Ukiyo-e prints were widely popular as independent, affordable works of art and book illustrations. Their commercial nature seems to have made the workshops less conservative than other art areas and open to large numbers of aspiring artists who signed on as apprentices in workshops run by master artists. A number of women artists also became apprentices in these workshops, leading some to credit the more liberal mercantile atmosphere for the unusual opportunity afforded women. Even more than European women, Japanese women were traditionally limited in their education and tied to domestic responsibilities. But further research identifies many of these women artists as producing art in a workshop run by a famous artist who was also their father. Not until well after World War II were Japanese women able to pursue careers in art or the professions.

the beauty that he imagined existed in Japan. The word *mousmé* was used in a contemporary romantic novel to characterize the innocent charm of youthful Japanese teahouse attendants. Poised motionless against a neutral background and holding some oleander flowers, the thirteen-year-old peasant girl seems totally removed from everyday experience. She represents the artist's aim "to paint men and women with that quality of the eternal which used to be suggested by the halo."

Twice confined to a hospital in Arles after an apparent mental breakdown in 1889, van Gogh resumed painting and continued to produce during his subsequent year-long confinement in an asylum at St.-Rémy. Painted in a field near the hospital, *The Starry Night* (fig. 25.31) is

an ecstatic vision of the power and glory of the universe. A tall cypress flames toward the whirling and exploding stars of a cosmic drama unknown to the inhabitants of the peaceful village below. This expressive work represents the artist's reverent celebration of the wonders of nature and is not, as some have contended, symptomatic of mental problems, although recent research has determined that the artist probably suffered from a debilitating illness called Ménière's disease. Symptoms include hallucinations and a ringing in the ears.

Moving northwest of Paris to the village of Auvers-sur-Oise after his release from the asylum, van Gogh completed about sixty paintings during the last two months of his tragic life. Why he chose to commit suicide at age thirty-seven with a bullet to the abdomen (that killed him several agonizing days later) has never been satisfactorily explained. At his funeral his friend and physician, Dr. Paul Gachet, said: "He was an honest man and a great artist. He had only two aims: humanity and art. It was the art that . . . will insure his survival."

25.31 Vincent van Gogh, *The Starry Night*. 1889. Oil on canvas 29 × 36¼" (73.7 × 92.1 cm). The Museum of Modern Art, New York (Acquired through the Lillie P. Bliss Bequest). Photo: © 1996 The Museum of Modern Art, New York.

Paul Gauguin, 1848–1903

Van Gogh's onetime friend, Gauguin (go-gā), has been a kind of folk hero for desk-bound romantics who dream of dropping out of the rat race to pursue their artistic muse. The reality of Gauguin's life and career is, however, not the stuff of dreams. An amateur painter for many years, Gauguin naively assumed that he would be as successful as a full-time painter as he had been as a stockbroker. Within three years of giving up his financial career in 1883 (because of a stock market crash), everything was gone: wife, family, money. He found himself living on borrowed funds at a rundown country inn in Brittany.

A rebel at odds with conventional behavior and society in general, Gauguin was seldom plagued with self-doubt. Writing to his absent wife (whom he had abandoned), he proclaimed that "I am a great artist and I know it." Forever restless, Gauguin was drawn to the warm weather of Provence where he roomed briefly, and quarreled, with van Gogh. He then drifted to tropical climates: Panama, Martinique, Tahiti, and the Marquesas, where he died. In Tahiti Gauguin found, he thought, an antidote to the sickness of European civilization, a "primitive life" that would nurture his style. Actually, the Society Islands were governed by the French and Gauguin had evolved his tropical style before settling down in Polynesia. Gauguin's dream of "solitude under the tropical sun" was compromised by illness, poverty, and harassment by French authorities, but his work did acquire a new vigor.

While critics of the time found Gauguin's colors bizarre and his drawing crude, the public accepted the content of his paintings as actual illustrations of Tahitian life and customs. Tahiti was, however, Westernized and middle-class, with a snobbish colonial bureaucracy and a pervasive overlay of Western missionary zeal. One looks in vain in a Gauguin painting for anything resembling the everyday details of colonial life: no officials, traders, sailors, ships, or any possessions of the Europeans who had been running this colonial outpost for sixty years. The Polynesia that we see in Gauguin's art was the creation of the artist.

Though Gauguin admitted that his Tahiti was a subjective interpretation of what was "vaguest and most universal in nature," we still have a romantic image of Tahiti in Gauguin's mode. In *Where Do We Come From? What Are We? Where Are We Going?* (fig. 25.32) Gauguin executed what he called his "spiritual testament," completed shortly before his abortive suicide attempt. Stating that "I will never do anything better or even like it," Gauguin painted this as a voyage of discovery, not as a statement of his rather confused ideas about birth, life, and death. The painting is a fusion of antitheses: sunlight and moonlight; night and day; the warmness of life and the coldness of death. The cycle of life can be read from childhood on the right to the old woman waiting for death at the left. Ultimately, this work attests, as Gauguin said, to "the futility of words" in any attempt to express the wonder and mystery of life. It may have been this painting that the Symbolist poet Mallarmé called a "musical poem that needs no libretto."

Georges Seurat, 1859–91

Causing nearly as much controversy as Manet and Whistler, Seurat (sue-rah) exhibited *Sunday Afternoon on the Island of La Grande Jatte* (fig. 25.33) at the eighth and final Impressionist show of 1886. Critics had a field day lambasting the dots of color, the "procession of pharaohs," and a "clearance sale of Nuremberg toys." Favorable critics, and there were some, labeled the new style "Neo-impressionism" or "Divisionism," though Paris wits chose

25.32 Paul Gauguin, *Where Do We Come From? What Are We? Where Are We Going?* 1897. Oil on canvas, 4' 6¾" × 12' 3½" (1.39 × 3.75 m). Museum of Fine Arts, Boston (Tompkins Collection).

the word "confettism." Seurat himself used the term "chromo-luminarium" to describe his method of painting with tiny dots using the colors of the spectrum. Aspiring to paint in a scientific manner based on the optical theories of Helmholtz and others, Seurat used his *petits points*, his dots, to construct a monumental composition of "museum quality," as advocated by Cézanne. The scene is a popular summer resort near Paris where middle-class city dwellers could bathe, picnic, and promenade. Though the dots of pure color were supposed to fuse in the eye this does not happen, save in the luminosity of the river. Instead, the spectator is conscious of the myriads of dots that, in a non-chromatic way, contribute as units of scale to the grandeur that Seurat achieved; his optical theories were, in practice, more artistic than scientific. In addition, he developed a control of line, proportions, and masses of light and shade that make this a classical composition in the manner of Poussin and David. In its psychological impact the work is curiously modern. People, animals, hats, and parasols are structural and decorative elements, as

25.33   Georges Seurat, *Sunday Afternoon on the Island of La Grande Jatte*. 1884–6. Oil on canvas, 10' 6" × 6' 9" (3.2 × 2.06 m). Art Institute of Chicago (Helen Birch Bartlett Memorial Collection).

isolated from each other as the passengers in *Third-Class Carriage* (see fig. 25.14). A typical Impressionist genre scene has become a melancholic comment on alienation and isolation in late Victorian society, symbolizing the underlying pessimism of the age.

Henri Rousseau, 1844–1910

The most influential of the Postimpressionists were Cézanne and an obscure toll collector named Rousseau. An isolated and enigmatic genius who began painting late in life, Rousseau taught himself to paint "alone," as he said, "and without any master but nature." His naive ideal was what he called the "truth" of the camera; he was actually convinced that his paintings were as "realistic" as photographs. His jungle landscapes were painted with a startling directness of vision that influenced Picasso and others, but these were tropics of the mind produced by the magical vision of a simple man who, apparently, never left France. Nothing in *The Dream* (fig. 25.34) is identifiable in botanical terms. What we see is a brooding and sinister jungle inhabited by a nude on a Victorian couch, some apparently tame animals, and a creature both animal and human who plays a musical instrument. Rousseau has combined the subjectivity of Romanticism with the so-called objectivity that was aspired

25.34 Henri Rousseau, *The Dream*. 1910. Oil on canvas, 6' 8½" × 9' 9½" (2.40 × 2.98 m). The Museum of Modern Art, New York (Gift of Nelson A. Rockefeller). Photo: © 1996 The Museum of Modern Art, New York.

to by the realists and Impressionists, giving us a vivid illustration of the never-never land between the two extremes.

Edvard Munch, 1864–1944

Van Gogh, Gauguin, Seurat, and Rousseau were critical of the disease of civilization, but their pervasive pessimism was not limited to French urban culture. The Norwegian painter Munch (moonk) manipulated themes of evil, terror, and death to depict the plight, as he saw it, of *fin de siècle* European civilization, themes similar to those of the poets Matthew Arnold and Thomas Hardy (see pp. 407–9). In *The Scream* (fig. 25.35) Munch portrayed a terror-stricken person whose sexual and facial identity has been obliterated by a piercing scream that is echoed in undulating lines of the landscape. Like his friend and associate, Henrik Ibsen, Munch dealt with the unbearable tensions

25.35 Edvard Munch, *The Scream*. 1893. Tempera and casein on cardboard, 36 × 29" (91.4 × 73.7 cm). National Museum, Oslo, Norway.

of the modern world that led to anxiety, alienation, and, as here, terror. Though his **iconography** was intensely personal, Munch's pessimistic vision strongly influenced the later German Expressionist movement (see p. 487).

A rather impromptu special event, the *banquet Rousseau*, symbolically marked the end of an era and the advent of the twentieth-century *avant-gard*e. Held in the studio of Picasso in 1908, three years after the revolutionary show of the Fauves (see p. 485), the guest of honor was Henri Rousseau, nearing the end of his career and still unrecognized by the public. Guests included artists Georges Braque and Marie Laurencin, writers Apollinaire, Max Jacob, and Gertrude Stein, and other luminaries of the new epoch. Picasso had ordered the food for the wrong day but there was ample wine and abundant good spirits, with violin entertainment provided by the guest of honor. The only real tribute the unassuming toll-collector-cum-painter ever received prompted him to whisper confidentially to Picasso that "after all, you and I are both great painters: I in the Modern style and you in the Egyptian." Though Picasso's "Egyptian" style was actually his African mask period, Henri Rousseau's remark was correct on both counts.

SUMMARY

Romanticism was a reaction in all the arts against the Enlightenment. For a time, however, the visual arts in France were in the service of Napoleon and David, his court painter. The Arch of Triumph and Church of the Madeleine made significant contributions to the neoclassic face of Paris, and the paintings of Ingres established an academic style against which later artists were to rebel.

Painting in a style uniquely his own, Goya was one of the most important painters of the century. The French Romantic style was established by the dramatic work of Géricault and continued by the peerless colorist Delacroix. John Constable was the leading Romantic landscape painter in England whereas Romantic architecture was revivalist, as manifested in the Gothic Revival Houses of Parliament. The art of Turner was a Romantic style in and of itself. The Romanticism of Cole, Duncanson, and Bingham had a distinctly American flavor.

By the second half of the century realists such as Millet, Corot, Daumier, and Courbet were dominating the Parisian art scene while, in America, Winslow Homer and Thomas Eakins were leading artists in the ongoing tradition of American realism. Imaginative uses of industrial technology saw the construction of prefabricated structures such as the Crystal Palace and the Eiffel Tower.

Led by the innovations of Manet, the Impressionist movement became the *avant-garde* of European art.

Considering themselves the ultimate realists, Monet, Renoir, Degas, Morisot, Cassatt, and others helped to establish Impressionism as one of the most influential of all artistic styles. Whistler did his own personal version of modern art and, in Paris, Rodin produced the most dramatic and expressive sculpture since the High Renaissance.

Reacting against the visual emphasis of Impressionism in very personal terms, the Post-impressionists included Cézanne, who distilled on canvas the forms and colors of the natural world, and Seurat, who used a similar approach but with dots of color. Van Gogh and Gauguin employed vivid colors to create very expressive works in very different styles. Rousseau created works from his private dream world that were a revelation to Picasso and others of the new *avant-garde*. Like many artists and writers of the late Victorian era, Munch reacted against modern urban society with themes of alienation and terror. A century that began with the Arch of Triumph ended with *The Scream*.

CULTURE AND HUMAN VALUES

The facts of science, a secular worldview, and materialism were the realities of the nineteenth century. Other factors included imperialism, the rising tide of nationalism, and the sporadic violence of an almost endless procession of revolutions and wars. The optimism of the Enlightenment seemed as remote as the Middle Ages. Though pessimism was not yet endemic, there were many, especially among writers and artists, who had strong feelings of foreboding. There is no more poignant expression of the doleful end of the century than Thomas Hardy's poem "The Darkling Thrush" (see p. 408). The entire age is brilliantly summed up by Stephen Crane's two untitled poems that end chapter 23.

STUDY QUESTIONS

1. Explain the basic differences between nineteenth-century Neoclassic and Romantic art by using two works from this chapter. Then repeat this exercise using two works not in this book.
2. What relationships can you find between the pessimistic Victorian poets in chapter 23 and some of the works discussed in this chapter? Relate all of these to some of the events of the period as outlined in the Time Chart for the Middle Modern World (see p. 386).

UNIT 9

The
Twentieth
Century

The Twentieth Century

People and Events

1905 Unsuccessful revolution in Russia; Fauves in Paris
1906 San Francisco earthquake
1907 Cubism in Paris
1909 Founding of NAACP
1910–36 George V of England
1913 Armory Show in New York; Stravinsky *Rite of Spring; Ballet Russe* in Paris
1914–18 World War I
1916 Beginning of Dada movement
1917 Lenin triumphs in Russia; U.S. enters WWI; beginning of International Style
1918 Worldwide flu epidemic kills 20 million
1919 Treaty of Versailles
1919–33 Weimar Republic
1919–39 League of Nations
1920 U.S. women win right to vote
1920–33 Volstead Act (prohibition)
1922 Mussolini triumphs in Italy
1924 Surrealist Manifesto in Paris
1927 Stalin dictator in Russia
1929 Great Depression begins
1931–45 Sino-Japanese War
1932–4 Geneva Disarmament Conference
1933–45 Hitler dictator of Germany
1933–45 Roosevelt U.S. president
1934–8 The Great Terror: Stalin's purges
1935 Congress passes Social Security Act
1935–6 Italy conquers Ethiopia
1935–40 WPA Art Project
1936 Edward VIII of England
1936–9 Spanish Civil War
1936–52 George VI of England
1938 Germany annexes Austria; Czechoslovakia dismembered
1939–45 World War II
1941 Pearl Harbor: U.S. enters war
1944 Beginning of modern jazz
1945 United Nations organized; atomic bombs on Japan
1945–90 The Cold War
1947 Beginning of Marshall Plan
1948 Israel becomes independent state
1950 U.S. advisors sent to Vietnam
1950–3 Korean War
1952 Elizabeth II of England
1954 School segregation disallowed
1955 Civil Rights movement begins
1961–89 Berlin Wall
1963 President Kennedy assassinated
1964–75 Vietnam War
1965 M. L. King leads Seima march; beginning of protests, hippies, flower children
1968 Assassination of M. L. King, R. F. Kennedy
1969 U.S. lunar landing; race riots in Watts, Detroit, New York
1970 National Guard kills 4 students at Kent State University
1974 Nixon resigns presidency
1979 American hostages seized in Iran
1980–8 The Reagan era
1989 Beginning worldwide collapse of Communism
1990 End of Cold War

Literature

Olive Schreiner 1855–1920 "Somewhere, Some Time, Some Place"
William Butler Yeats 1865–1939 "The Second Coming"
Sidonie Gabrielle Colette 1873–1954 "The Other Wife"
Virginia Woolf 1882–1941 "If Shakespeare Had a Sister"
Countee Cullen 1887–1946 "Yet Do I Marvel"
Robinson Jeffers 1887–1962 "Shine, Perishing Republic"
T. S. Eliot 1888–1965 "The Love Song of J. Alfred Prufrock"
Wilfred Owen 1893–1918 "Dulce et Decorum Est"
e e cummings 1894–1962 "anyone lived in a pretty how town"
Jorge Luis Borges 1899–1986 "The Disinterested Killer Bill Harrigan"
George Seferis 1900–71 "Helen"
Langston Hughes 1902–67 "Harlem"
Richard Eberhart 1904– "The Fury of Aerial Bombardment"
Jean-Paul Sartre 1905–80 "Existentialism"
Samuel Beckett 1906–89 *Waiting for Godot*
Naguib Mahfouz 1911– "The Happy Man"
Albert Camus 1913–66 "The Myth of Sisyphus"
Dylan Thomas 1914–53 "When All My Five and Country Senses See"
Ralph Ellison 1914–94 *Invisible Man*
Gwendolyn Brooks 1917– "We Real Cool"
James Dickey 1923– "Adultery"
Joseph Heller 1923– *Catch 22*
Yehuda Amichai 1924– "Jews in the Land of Israel"
Adrienne Rich 1929– "Two Songs"
Martin Luther King, Jr. 1929–68 "Letter from Birmingham Jail"
N. Scott Momaday 1934– *House Made of Dawn*
Kofi Awoonor 1935– "Night of My Blood"
Gail Godwin 1937– "A Sorrowful Woman"
Susan Griffin 1943– "I Like to Think of Harriet Tubman"

Art

Wassily Kandinsky 1866–1944 *Panel 3*
Käthe Kollwitz 1867–1945 *The Only Good Thing*
Henri Matisse 1869–1954 *The Blue Window*
Georges Rouault 1871–1958 *Christ Mocked by Soldiers*
John Sloan 1871–1952 *Roof Gossips*
Piet Mondrian 1872–1944 *Broadway Boogie Woogie*
Constantin Brancusi 1876–1956 *Bird in Space*
Paul Klee 1879–1940 *Twittering Machine*
Pablo Picasso 1881–1973 *Guernica*
Edward Hopper 1882–1967 *Nighthawks*
José Orozco 1883–1949 *Zapatistas*
Diego Rivera 1886–1957 *Liberation of the Peon*
Kurt Schwitters 1887–1948 *Sichtbar*
Marcel Duchamp 1887–1968 *The Bride Stripped Bare by Her Bachelors, Even*
Marc Chagall 1887–1985 *I and the Village*
Georgia O'Keeffe 1887–1986 *Jack-in-the-Pulpit*
Giorgio de Chirico 1888–1978 *The Nostalgia of the Infinite*
Josef Albers 1888–1976 *Homage to the Square*
Horace Pippin 1888–1946 *Victorian Interior*
George Grosz 1893–1959 *I Am Glad I Came Back*
Joan Miró 1893–1983 *Person Throwing a Stone at a Bird*
Stuart Davis 1894–1964 *Radio Tubes*
David Siqueiros 1896–1974 *Echo of a Scream*
Alexander Calder 1898–1976 *Many Pierced Discs*
Henry Moore 1898–1986 *Family Group*
René Magritte 1896–1967 *The False Mirror*
Jean Dubuffet 1901–85 *Portrait of Henri Michaux*
Mark Rothko 1903–70 *Number 10*
Willem de Kooning 1904– *Woman I*
Salvador Dali 1904–89 *The Persistence of Memory*
David Smith 1906–65 *Cubi XV*
Francis Bacon 1910– *Number VII from Eight Studies for a Portrait*
Jackson Pollock 1912–56 *Autumn Rhythm, No. 30, 1950*
Meret Oppenheim 1913– *Object*
Jacob Lawrence 1917– *Daybreak—A Time to Rest*
Roy Lichtenstein 1923– *Drowning Girl*
Robert Colescott 1925– *Les Demoiselles d'Alabama: Vestidas*
Robert Rauschenberg 1925– *Monogram*
Edward Kienholz 1927– *State Hospital*
Tony DeLap 1927– *Sentaro*
Helen Frankenthaler 1928– *Interior Landscape*
Marisol 1930– *Women and Dog*
Audrey Flack 1931– *World War II, April 1945*
Bridget Riley 1921– *Crest*
Christo and **Jeanne-Claude** 1935– *Running Fence*
Fritz Scholder 1937– *Waiting Indian No. 4*
Robert Smithson 1938–73 *Spiral Jetty*
Otto Duecker 1948– *Russell, Terry, J. T.*
Gerhard Richter 1932– *Vase*

Architecture, Music, Photography

Mathew Brady 1823–96 *Abraham Lincoln*
Antonio Gaudi 1852–1926 Church of the Holy Family
Alfred Stieglitz 1863–1946 *The Terminal*
Frank Lloyd Wright 1869–1959 "Falling Water"
W. C. Handy 1873–1958 "St. Louis Blues"
Charles Ives 1874–1954 *Three Places in New England*
Béla Bartók 1881–1945 *Concerto for Orchestra*
Igor Stravinsky 1882–1971 *The Rite of Spring*
Anton Webern 1883–1945 *Three Songs*
Walter Gropius 1883–1969 Bauhaus
Alban Berg 1885–1935 *Violin Concerto*
Ludwig Mies van der Rohe 1886–1969 Seagram Building
Le Corbusier 1887–1965 Notre Dame-du-Haut
Wallace Harrison 1895–1981 Secretariat Building of the United Nations
Paul Hindemith 1895–1963 *Mathis der Maler*
Dorothea Lange 1895–1965 *Migrant Mother*
Duke Ellington 1899–1974 "Old King Dooji"
Benny Goodman 1900–80 "Dizzy Spells"
Ansel Adams 1902–84 *Moonrise*
Margaret Bourke-White 1904–71 *Two Women, Lansdale, Arkansas*
Philip Johnson 1906– Chippendale Skyscraper
Eero Saarinen 1910–61 TWA Terminal
John Cage 1912–92 Aleatory music
Joern Utzon 1918– Sydney Opera House
W. Eugene Smith 1918–78 *Spanish Wake*
Michael Graves 1937– The Portland
Barton McLean 1938– *Etunytude*

Invention, Science, Philosophy

1900 Freud *The Interpretation of Dreams:* Planck's constant; quantum theory
1901 first transatlantic radio telegraphic transmission
1902 first phonograph recordings
1903 Wright brothers' first flight
1905 Einstein Special Theory of Relativity; first U.S. motion pictures
1908 Ford introduces Model T
1909 wireless radio
1912 discovery of insulin
1914 discovery of vitamins
1916 Einstein General Theory of Relativity
1922 radar invented
1926 first TV transmission; first liquid-fuel rocket
1927 Heisenberg Principle of Uncertainty
1928 first sound movie
1930 discovery of penicillin
1934 first use of antibiotics
1939 first commercial TV; first jet engine; automatic sequence computer
1940 first successful plutonium fission
1942 uranium fission, atomic reactor
1948 LP recordings marketed
1951 inauguration of transcontinental TV
1951 U.S. explodes hydrogen bomb
1956 first transatlantic telephone; inauguration of interstate highway system
1957 first earth satellite (U.S.S.R.)
1958 beginning of jet airline passenger service; laser beam invented
1961 first manned orbital flight (U.S.S.R.)
1962 Rachel Carson's *Silent Spring* launches environmentalist movement
1963 quasars discovered
1964 China detonates atom bomb
1965 foundation of National Organization for Women (NOW)
1967 first heart transplant
1972 UN Conference on the Human Environment
1973 first orbital laboratory (Skylab)
1974 first energy crisis
1976 genetic engineering developed
1978 first test-tube baby
1981 beginning of space shuttle flights
1990s expansion of high tech: computers, robotics, global communications

CHAPTER 26

Things Fall Apart: The Center Cannot Hold

HISTORICAL OVERVIEW, 1914–39

World War I can be viewed as Act I in a drama that began in 1871 with Bismarck's formation of the German Empire (the Prologue) and continued with World War II as Act 2 in a tragedy that engulfed most of the world. The period of 1918–39 can be seen, in retrospect, as an entr'acte that set the stage for what may or may not be the last act.

When the Allies and Germany agreed to an Armistice on 11 November 1918 the stated intent was to stop the fighting and arrange for a just peace. However, the Treaty of Versailles, signed on 28 June 1919, was harshly punitive. Germany and its allies were forced to sign the "war guilt" clause and to accept all responsibility for causing the war. War reparations were to be paid to all thirty-two allies; Germany lost virtually its entire armed services and overseas colonies plus large portions of its land area. Woodrow Wilson's attempts to curb the nationalistic zeal of Great Britain's Lloyd George and France's Clemenceau were essentially futile. Even Wilson's prize project, the League of Nations that was part of the Peace of Versailles, ended, finally, in failure—caused, in part, by the refusal of the United States to join this valiant, doomed attempt to civilize the conduct of nations. The League of Nations did settle a few disputes but it was powerless to prevent Japan's invasion of Manchuria in 1931, Germany's withdrawal from the League in 1933 in order to rearm, and Mussolini's invasion of Ethiopia in 1935.

The Allies had convinced the Germans that Kaiser Wilhelm II and his imperial government were primarily responsible for the war. But it was the new Weimar Republic that signed the dictated peace and it was the Republic that bore the onus of German humiliation at the conference table. Moreover, the Treaty of Versailles made no provision for the economic rehabilitation of Europe. Nor were there any assurances for the futures of new nations—Czechoslovakia and Yugoslavia—that had been carved out of the dismembered Austro-Hungarian empire. The Treaty of Versailles caused more discontent and unrest than even the 1815 Vienna Settlement after the Napoleonic wars.

The March 1917 revolution in Russia had disposed of the czar, but the new Provisional government, despite rising unrest, continued to pursue the war. V. I. Lenin (1870–1924) capitalized on new defeats at the front to seize the government and establish the All-Russian Congress of the Soviets. Concluding a separate disastrous peace with Germany, Lenin established a dictatorship of the Communist party that barely survived the ferocious Civil War of 1918–21. Under Leon Trotsky (1877–1940) a new Red Army destroyed the rebel White armies and then helped Lenin solidify his hold on the government. Lenin established himself as the unchallenged leader by having his secret police (Cheka) murder all his political opponents and potential opponents (some 60,000 or more), conforming to the dictator's rationale: "We are exterminating the bourgeoisie as a class. This is the essence of the Red Terror."[1] The Russian aristocracy had already been eliminated and the vast body of peasants posed no threat. Following Lenin's death in 1924, a power struggle between Trotsky and Joseph Stalin (1879–1953) saw Stalin emerge, in 1927, as the absolute dictator of the Soviet Union. (fig. 26.1)

26.1 Gustav Kluzi, "Lenin's Banner." 1933. Poster: photomontage with portrait of Stalin. Galerie Avantgarde N. Fedorowskij, Berlin. Photo: A.K.G., London.

1. Paul Johnson, *Modern Times: The World from the Twenties to the Eighties* (New York: Harper & Row, 1983), p. 71.

The democracies were beset by economic difficulties in the 1920s and assaulted by Communists on the left and hard-core nationalists on the right. Benito Mussolini (1883–1945) marched on Rome in 1922 and assumed full dictatorial powers by 1926. Designed to produce a corporate totalitarian state, the doctrines of Italian fascism stressed the dominance of the state and the subordination of the individual, the desirability of war, and the Social Darwinian "right" of Italy to expand at the expense of "inferior" nations.

The initial successes of Italian fascism impressed not only the older Western democracies but also many malcontents in Germany, who bitterly resented the war-guilt clause of the Treaty of Versailles. Compounding the discontent, the German military clique fostered the false belief that Germany had never been defeated on the field of battle; it had been betrayed at home, said the military, by pacifist liberals. Following the disastrous inflation of 1923 the

National Socialist German Workers Party (Nazis) launched a propaganda campaign that capitalized on the supposed sellout at Versailles. Coupled with the barrage was a virulent anti-Semitism that blamed the Jews for many of Germany's postwar problems while proclaiming the absolute supremacy of the Aryan master race. A spellbinding political orator, Nazi leader Adolf Hitler (1889–1945) mesmerized his audiences with what he called the Big Lie: "If you keep it simple, say it often, and make it burn the public will believe anything." The Nazis gained power when, in 1933, President von Hindenburg appointed Hitler as Chancellor of the Republic. Using the emergency powers of Article 48 of the constitution, Hitler eradicated all opposition with his bloody purge of 1934. He was now absolute ruler of a Third Reich that was to "last for a thousand years."

The direct road to World War II began, probably, with Japan's seizure of Manchuria in 1931; it was followed by her withdrawal from the League of Nations in 1933 and her invasion of China four years later. In order to arm secretly for war, Germany withdrew from the League in 1933, the year in which Hitler opened the first

Map 26.1   World War II in Europe.

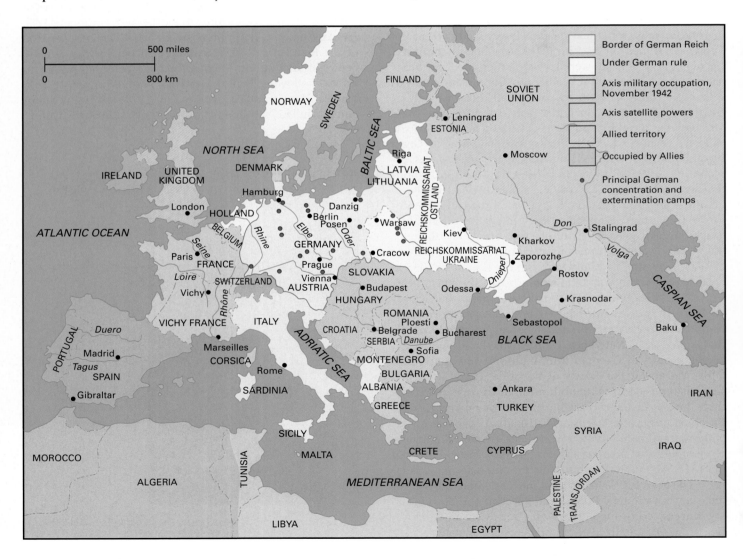

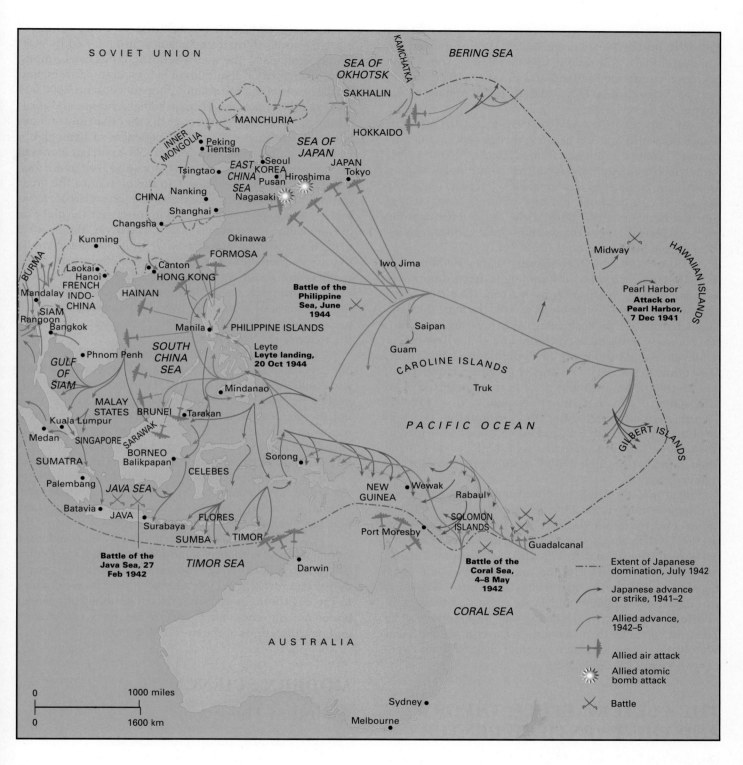

Map 26.2 World War II in the Pacific.

concentration camp at Dachau (DAH-kow; see pp. 472 and 520). Defying the Treaty of Versailles, Hitler occupied the Rhineland in 1936, a fateful step that is now seen as the last opportunity for England and France to avert war in Europe. From then on Hitler had the might to back up his threats.

The Spanish Civil War of 1936–9 had the effect of polarizing world opinion between the fascists and monarchists of "loyalist" Francisco Franco (1892–1975) and rebel factions led by anarchists, socialists, communists, and an assortment of liberals. Hitler backed Franco, using the opportunity to field-test his new war machines. It was German bombers that attacked the undefended Basque town of Guernica, an atrocity immortalized on canvas by Picasso (see fig. 28.7).

After signing the Rome-Berlin treaty with Mussolini in 1936, Hitler launched his campaign for a union (*Anschluss*) with German-speaking Austria, which he occupied in early 1938. The next target was the German-speaking Sudeten area of Czechoslovakia. After working up a full-scale crisis with his oratory, Hitler agreed to a four-power conference at Munich on 29 September 1938. Hitler, Mussolini, British Prime Minister Neville Chamberlain, and Premier Edouard Daladier of France conferred in an atmosphere of conciliation artfully orchestrated by Hitler. Chamberlain returned to England proclaiming "peace in our time" even though England and France had helped to dismember hapless Czechoslovakia. Hitler acquired the Sudetenland at Munich and all of Czechoslovakia by the following spring.

The final step was Poland. Germany and Russia signed a non-aggression pact on 23 August 1939 that relieved Hitler of his concerns about waging a two-front war. The secret portion of the pact carved up Poland and eastern Europe between Germany and Russia and "awarded" the Baltic republics of Lithuania, Estonia, and Latvia to Stalin. On 1 September 1939 the German armies rolled into Poland and, two days later, England and France honored their commitment to Poland by declaring war on Germany. The Treaty of Versailles that was supposed to confirm the Great War as the "war to end all wars" had lasted a scant twenty years (maps 26.1 and 26.2).

THE CULTURE-EPOCH THEORY AND THE TWENTIETH CENTURY

Our distance from past ages enables us to perceive the periods when a culture was balanced, when the balance tipped into chaos, when the adjustment began that led to a new period of balance, and so on (see pp. 3–5). Analyzing our own age is far more difficult, perhaps impossible, yet we try to understand where we are and where we might be going.

During the past several decades new attitudes have become increasingly important. We know through evolutionary studies, for example, that all living things are evolving—everything in the cosmos, in fact. Led by molecular biologists, the overwhelming consensus among today's scientists is that human beings, chimpanzees, and gorillas evolved from a common ancestor between 3,000,000 and 8,000,000 years ago. Human beings, chimps, and gorillas are more closely related to each other than any of them is to other primates. The DNA sequences of hemoglobin from human beings and chimps are 98.4 percent identical and the sequences from human beings and gorillas are 98.3 percent identical. Right down to the bottom of the great chain of being, all living creatures are interrelated. *Homo sapiens* has no proper claim to dominion over the globe or over so-called lower forms of life. Moreover, the balance of life in our world is precarious; we know, or should know, that we cannot alter our environment without worldwide repercussions and we cannot damage our environment without ultimately harming ourselves. It is a scientific fact that the flight of a butterfly over Tokyo can in some still unexplained way—the famous "butterfly effect"—influence the weather of New York City.

This holistic view of living things expands to include our concept of the cosmos as expressed by modern science and applies to the inner world of the human personality as probed by Freud and other psychologists. Contemporary holistic views of evolving personality, society, the environment, and the cosmos suggest a new age that may be called a planet in process, a world in which everything is in a continual stage of becoming. Goal-oriented cultures of the past may be replaced by change-oriented cultures of the future. Once people begin viewing their cultural identities as journeys rather than as destinations, the new age may have begun.

In this and the following chapters we will consider the status of modern science, the Information Age, the Global Village, the failure of Marxist-Leninism and the resurgence of free enterprise in democratic societies, massive damage to the environment, racism, nascent nationalism, gender issues, and the reactions of artists to the chaos, adjustment, and new directions of the twentieth century.

MODERN SCIENCE

Quantum Theory

The old social order was in disarray by about 1914, but the predictable world-machine described by Newtonian science was overthrown even earlier. In 1900 Max Planck (1858–1947) took a giant stride away from visible perceptions of the physical world to a theory that described the microcosmos by using mathematical abstractions. While studying the radiant energy given off by heated bodies, Planck discovered that energy was radiated, not in unbroken streams, but in discontinuous bits or portions that he called *quanta*. In terms of both the emission and the absorption of atomic and subatomic particles, Planck hypothesized that the energy transfer was discontinuous and involved a unit of energy (quantum) that could be calculated: "The uncertainty in the position of a particle times the uncertainty in its velocity times its mass can never be smaller than a certain quantity," which is known as Planck's constant.[2] Roughly a decimal point followed by 26 zeroes and ending in 6624, this minuscule number remains one of nature's most fundamental constants.

In conjunction with quantum theory, Werner Heisenberg (1901–76) developed, in 1927, his "Principle of Uncertainty," which states that, in effect, theory can accurately predict the behavior of statistically large numbers of particles, but not the behavior of individual particles. It is impossible simultaneously to determine the position and the velocity of, for example, an electron. If the position is observed, that act of observing will alter its velocity; conversely, the more accurate the determination of its velocity the more indefinite is the position of the electron. The fundamental equation of quantum mechanics is this: there is no such thing as an electron that possesses both a precise momentum and a precise position. The old science relied on a study of cause and effect (or causality and determinism), but the Principle of Uncertainty toppled these formerly sturdy pillars. Heisenberg won the Nobel Prize in 1932 for his work in quantum mechanics. His leadership of the German scientists who kept Hitler from developing the atomic bomb is also worthy of mention.[3] Even now the vision of Hitler with the bomb is just too dreadful to contemplate.

Quantum theory is strange and fascinating. Niels Bohr, Heisenberg's mentor and a leading physicist on the Manhattan Project that developed the bomb, cogently proclaimed that "anyone who is not shocked by quantum theory has not understood it." What is so astonishing?

In the first place, no one knows how the quantum world behaves the way it does; scientists simply do know that it behaves the way it does. "In the quantum world what you see is what you get, and nothing is real; the best you can hope for is a set of delusions that agree with one another."[4]

The double-hole experiment is perhaps the best way to view the eerie quantum world. Picture two walls separated by several feet with a small hole in each wall, either of which can be covered up. A single electron, or a single photon, on its way through one hole in the wall, obeys statistical laws which are appropriate only when it "knows" if the other hole is open.

This is the central mystery of the quantum world. The electrons not only know whether or not both holes are open, they know whether or not we are watching them, and they adjust their behavior accordingly.[5]

Scientists had shown in theory, in 1970, that an atom in one energy state cannot change its energy so long as it is being observed. By 1990 scientists at the National Institute of Standards and Technology had demonstrated that the act of looking at an atom prevented it from decaying. What

still remains to be proved is that continuous observation of unstable radioactive isotopes can prevent them from disintegrating radioactively. Theoretically, if a nuclear bomb were watched intently enough, it could not explode!

All of this bizarre behavior leads one to ask if there are any practical ways to convert quantum theory into quantum mechanics.

The physics is impossible, but the math is clean and simple, familiar equations to any physicist. As long as you avoid asking what it means there are no problems. Ask why the world should be like this, however, and the reply is: "we have no idea."[6]

Mathematical formulas based on quantum theory are basic to the development of television, VCRs, computers, and other high-tech marvels. Further, quantum theory has opened up a whole new area of philosophic speculation. Given a fantastic world that can be used but not explained, what, then, is reality?

Einstein and Relativity

Five years after Planck discovered quanta Albert Einstein (1879–1955; fig. 26.2) hammered another nail into the coffin of the Newtonian world-machine. He postulated that light photons were also quanta and developed his Special Theory of Relativity (1905). In essence, his Special Theory rests on the hypothesis that neither space nor time has an objective reality. Space is an arrangement of perceived objects and time has no independent existence apart from our measurements of a sequence of events. Our clocks are geared to our solar system. What we call an hour is actually a measurement of an arc of 15 degrees in space based on the apparent movement of the sun. A year is, therefore, the time it takes the earth to orbit the sun, which is 365¼ days. Mercury has an eighty-eight-day year and other planets have their own time-frame. As Einstein said, time is subjective and based on how people remember events as a sequence of "earlier" and "later" episodes.

Einstein's Special Theory stipulates, in particular, that the velocity of light is constant for all uniformly moving systems anywhere in the universe. There is neither absolute space nor absolute time, but the velocity of light is the absolute speed limit of the universe. There can be no fixed interval of time independent of the system to which

2. Stephen Hawking, *A Brief History of Time: From the Big Bang to Black Holes* (New York: Bantam Books, 1988), p. 55.
3. See Mark Walker, *German National Socialism and the Quest for Nuclear Power: 1939–1949* (Cambridge: Cambridge University Press, 1990).
4. John Gribbin, *In Search of Schrödinger's Cat: Quantum Physics and Reality* (New York: Bantam Books, 1984), p. 162.
5. *Ibid.*, p. 171.
6. *Ibid.*, p. 174.

26.2   Albert Einstein playing a violin at a chamber music rehearsal in Princeton, N.J. Photo: Bettmann Archive, New York.

it is referred nor can there be simultaneity independent of an established reference. Einsteinian physics assumes, for example, that there is an observer seated beside a railroad track who sees a bolt of lightning at the far left (bolt A) and another at the far right (bolt B). Assuming that the observer is positioned precisely between A and B, the bolts will be perceived as simultaneous because all events have the same frame of reference. Now, assume that a train is moving along the track from right to left at the brisk speed of light (186,284 miles or 300,000 km per second) and that another observer is riding on the top of the train. Assume, further, that observer 2 is exactly opposite observer 1 at the precise moment that bolts A and B strike. Observer 2 will perceive bolt A but not bolt B. The train is moving away from bolt B at the speed of light, meaning that the light waves of bolt B will never catch up with the train. Observer 2 is in a different frame of reference from the one occupied by observer 1.

Based on his Special Theory, Einstein determined that with an increase in velocity the mass of an object will also increase relative to an observer. Because motion is a form of kinetic energy, the increase in motion that leads to an increase in mass means that the mass has increased in energy. Einstein computed the value of the equivalent mass (m) in any unit of energy (e), leading to the equation that mass is equal to its energy over the square of the speed of light (c^2). The remaining algebraic step results in the equation $e = mc^2$, the most famous equation of our age. As Einstein demonstrated mathematically, mass and energy

were equivalent. What we normally call mass is concentrated energy that, with the proper trigger, can be released. The detonation of the first atomic device at Alamogordo, New Mexico, on 16 July 1945 demonstrated the transmutation of matter into energy in the forms of light, heat, sound, and motion.

Newton's laws still satisfactorily explain phenomena based on human experiences, but they cannot cope with modern physics. Einstein's laws of motion are based on the relativity of distance, time, and mass, what he called the "four-dimensional space-time continuum," that is, three dimensions of space and one of time. Relativity thus gives scientists the means to provide better descriptions of the workings of nature.

Einstein later expanded his system into the General Theory of Relativity, in which he examined what it is that guides all moving systems. His Special Theory had stated that the velocity of light was constant for all uniformly moving systems. His General Theory is broader and states that the laws of nature are the same for all systems regardless of their states of motion. The basic premise of his Special Theory—that all motion, uniform or non-uniform, had to be judged within some system of reference because absolute motion did not exist—held true. He could not, however, distinguish between the motion caused by inertial forces (acceleration, centrifugal forces, etc.) and motion caused by gravitation. This led to his Principle of the Equivalence of Gravitation and Inertia, a new theory of gravitation more accurate and complete than Newton's Law of Universal Gravitation. Newton had postulated gravitation as a force or attraction, but Einstein's Law of Gravitation simply describes the behavior of objects in a gravitational field by depicting the paths they follow.

Gravitation, for Einstein, was a form of inertia, leading him to conclude that light, like any material body, was subject to gravitation when passing through a very strong gravitational field. He then proved that light travels in a predictable curve given sufficient gravitational pull. Einstein's universe has no straight lines. Euclidean geometry defines a straight line as the shortest distance between two points but there are only vast circles delineating all of space that, though finite, is unbounded.

It took only a few years to verify Einstein's General Theory of Relativity:

> The modern world began on 29 May 1919 when
> photographs of a solar eclipse, taken on the island
> of Principe off the coast of West Africa and at Sobral
> in Brazil, confirmed the truth of a new theory of
> the universe.[7]

As Einstein observed, relativity defined the outer limits of our knowledge and quantum theory delineated the inner limits. What bothered him was that the two systems were unrelated to each other: "The idea that there are two

7. Johnson, *op. cit.*, p. 1.

structures of space independent of each other, the metric-gravitational and the electromagnetic is intolerable to the theoretical spirit." He went on to declare that "God does not play dice with the universe." A persistent believer in the fundamental uniformity and harmony of nature, Einstein devoted the latter part of his career to a futile search for a Unified Field Theory that would construct a bridge between relativity and quantum theory.

But Einstein was mistaken about the dice. In terms of quantum theory, physicist Stephen W. Hawking has declared that "God not only plays dice, he sometimes throws the dice where they cannot be seen." Physicist Joseph Ford approached the problem from another perspective, stating that "God plays dice with the universe, but they're loaded dice. And the main objective of physics now is to find out by what rules they were loaded and how we can use them for our own ends."[8]

The New Science of Chaos

Relativity eliminated the Newtonian illusion of absolute space and time; quantum theory abolished the Newtonian dream of a precise and controllable measurement process; chaos dispensed with the long-held belief that random events could not be subjected to scientific analysis.

That the remarkable scientific advances of this century have led to a brand new science should not be surprising. Since about 1976 physicists, biologists, astronomers, and economists have created a new way of understanding the evolution of complexity in nature. This new science of chaos is a way of seeing order and pattern where formerly only the erratic, the random, the unpredictable—the chaotic—had been observed. According to mathematician Douglas Hofstadter, "it turns out that an eerie type of chaos can lurk just behind a facade of order—and yet, deep inside the chaos lurks an eerier kind of order."

> Where chaos begins, classical science stops. For as long as the world has physicists inquiring into the laws of nature, it has suffered a special ignorance about disorder in the atmosphere, in the turbulent sea, in the fluctuations of wildlife populations, in the oscillations of the heart and the brain.[9]

Chaos has been used to study, among other things, weather patterns to determine how to make long-range predictions. Consider, for example, the "butterfly effect." Could the flight of a butterfly over Tokyo somehow affect the weather of New York City? The surprising answer is Yes!, though no one knows how this happens, there being so many variables (known and unknown). The variables are, in fact, so numerous that long-range predictions (more than five days) are impossible. Chaos mathematics has identified patterns that permit short-range weather forecasts, which become increasingly inaccurate after one, two, three, and four days. Chaos has also been used to study wave motion, water

turbulence, economic activity, wildlife populations, and other phenomena that were heretofore totally unpredictable, leading to the discovery that there are indeed underlying patterns that reveal "an eerier kind of order."

Chaos is a science in its infancy with no idea where its analyses of previously hidden patterns will lead. As with all science, the search is endlessly exciting because the explorers are moving ahead into what was not only unknown but, in this case, totally unexpected.

Another relatively new scientific area is complexity theory, which has been described as a first cousin to chaos theory. Complexity theory may, eventually, explain life on this planet. Scientists ask how it is that a chaotic universe organized itself into stars, galaxies, and planets and, against all known odds, produced a wild diversity of life on planet Earth. There may never be satisfactory answers but, this being what science is basically all about, the search is on.

How do relativity, quantum mechanics, complexity, and chaos affect us as human beings? In the first place, human mental processes cannot be explained by existing laws of physics. The answer may come, scientists believe, with the merger of general relativity, which concerns itself with gravity, and quantum theory, which governs the submicroscopic world, a bridge that Einstein called the Unified Field Theory. The two theories are mathematically incompatible but scientists, led by Stephen Hawking, are laboring to create a quantum version of gravity. One consequence would be to establish the boundaries of quantum mechanics, which says that particles can suddenly leap from one space to another without traversing the space between. What if these properties also apply to something as large as human brain cells in the process of creative thinking?

Indeed, quantum gravity could be behind consciousness itself. Consciousness has a peculiar quality that baffles physics: all humans perceive time as moving forward rather than backward. But virtually all the laws of physics are time-symmetric, working equally well either forward or backward. The speculative answer is that when quantum gravity is finally constructed it will begin with the Big Bang theory of creation and thus move only forward. Some scientists believe that human creativity and consciousness are the perceptible workings of the most basic laws of the universe, laws that are being explored using quantum, complexity, and chaos theories.

The uncertainty principle applies to virtually everything in our universe with only three fundamental constants remaining: gravity, Planck's constant, and the speed of light. Given so much uncertainty, philosophers have renewed their arguments for the existence of free will. Moreover, contemporary thinkers in many fields are exploring the nature of reality given the unexplained

8. Joseph Ford, as quoted in James Gleich, *Chaos: Making a New Science* (New York: Viking, 1987), p. 314.
9. *Ibid.*, p. 3.

mysteries of quantum theory and the incompatibility of the mathematics of general relativity and quantum mechanics. If physical events can be neither plotted nor explained, nor predicted with any certainty, then perhaps the still relatively unknown capabilities of the human intellect will be a decisive factor in the destiny of humankind.[10]

FREUD AND THE INNER WORLD

Though he wrote his celebrated *The Interpretation of Dreams* in 1900 and *The Psychopathology of Everyday Life* in 1904, the psychological theories of Sigmund Freud (1856–1939; fig. 26.3) did not become influential until after World War I. Freud evolved a theory of the tripartite personality consisting of the *id, ego,* and *superego*. There are no clear boundaries between these concepts but each can be described in isolation. Representing our biological endowment, the *id* (Lat., "it") resides in our unconscious as an amalgam of our drives and instincts. Hunger, thirst, elimination, and sex are some of the drives that compel us to avoid pain and to seek pleasure through gratification. Either through action or wish-fulfillment, pent-up energy is discharged and tension relieved. Freud considered life and love as positive life forces (*libido* or *Eros*) and aggressiveness, destruction, and the death-wish as negative forces.

The *ego*, according to Freud, is the reality-principle, the thinking, conscious self that interacts with objective reality. The well-developed *ego* controls the *id*, determining when and how instinctive drives are satisfied.

26.3   Sigmund Freud. Ca. 1921. Photo: Mary Evans, London (Max Halberstadt, courtesy of W. E. Freud).

Freud's *superego* is a combination of the moral code of the parents and the person, a kind of conscience that is a product of socialization and cultural traditions. Motivated by fear of punishment and desire for approval, the *superego* can perhaps be best described as a synthesis of the *ego*-ideal and conscience. The psychological rewards for the *superego* are feelings of pride and accomplishment; psychological punishment causes feelings of inferiority and guilt.

The well-balanced personality has a strong *ego* generally in control of the *id* and *superego*, restraining the *id* while recognizing the censorship of the *superego*. A neurotic person has lost some control, for whatever reason, over conscious actions, giving in to aggressive instincts from the *id*, or succumbing to feelings of guilt and inferiority exacted by the *superego*. Psychosis is a serious mental illness in which the patient has lost all touch with reality.

Freud invented what he called psychoanalysis, a systematic therapy for the treatment of neurosis. The task of the analyst was to help the patient uncover repressed matter, mainly through free association and the interpretation of dreams. Essentially, the analyst assisted the patient in understanding the reasons for abnormal behavior; once the patient uncovered the repressions that caused undesirable actions, the *ego* could consciously deal with the problem. Recognition of the basic problem(s) would theoretically help restore emotional balance.

Partly because he treated mostly neurotic patients, and partly because any new idea is likely to carry its originator to extremes, Freud rode his interpretations very hard in one direction. He believed that virtually all the mental disorders he treated were ultimately traceable to one basic frustration: the denial of the life-force, the *libido* or sex-drive. Freud's discovery that sexuality goes far back into childhood, even infancy, was a radical departure from the views of his day. It is, therefore, quite understandable that the sexual factor should loom so large in his investigations, for this human drive is hedged about with all sorts of taboos. Even in our own time, supposedly sexually liberated, there are a variety of sexual mores about how one should and should not act.

A number of scientists, including Adolf Grünbaum, Marshall Edelson, Frank J. Sulloway, and Peter Medawar now claim that none of Freud's concepts or hypotheses stand up to scientific scrutiny.[11] Most of his theories were not based on observation but derived from his premise that repression was the driving force of a neurosis. No one has been able to prove scientifically that this is indeed the case. Much of his work has, for this reason, been invalidated. As demonstrated by Marx's mistaken view of history, a correct doctrine cannot be erected on a false premise.

Why, then, was Freudian psychology so influential? Primarily, the time was ripe for his theories because they contributed to a new spirit of liberation. Freud's unchallenged achievement was to show that men and women were not always guided by their reason but driven to action by their impulses and passions. They did not, in other words, deliberately choose to act destructively. The liberating factor was that blame or censure need not focus on bad decisions; instead, one could consider the reasons why a person failed to control unconscious passions that produced negative results. The notion of "inner drives" was an idea whose time had come. Sigmund Freud was the first person to attempt a "scientific" exploration of the mysterious inner world of the human personality and for that alone he deserves a special place in the history of science. Moreover, as one critic (Michael Molnar, an editor of Freud's diaries) remarked, "Freud is in better shape than Marx."

Whatever illusions the nineteenth century may have preserved about the perfectibility of human behavior and human institutions perished during the four dreadful years of World War I. Much of the art and literature of the postwar period reflected a profound pessimism, a feeling that Western civilization carried the seeds of its own destruction. The following poems express some of the prevailing sentiments, some of the loneliness, alienation, and despair experienced by the postwar generation. And little did anyone know that within less than a generation the Great War was to receive a number.

LITERARY SELECTION 41

The Love Song of J. Alfred Prufrock
Thomas Stearns Eliot, 1888–1965

Written in England around the beginning of World War I, *Prufrock* is a dramatic monologue of a middle-aged and frustrated social misfit who is vainly trying to adjust to a petty and superficial society. The larger perspective is that of bankrupt idealism, a decaying of nations, societies, and religious institutions. With juxtaposed images enlarged by dramatic echoes of Hesiod, Dante, and Shakespeare, Eliot builds a mood of futility and despair.

S'io credesse che mia risposta fosse
a persona che mai tornasse al mondo,
questa fiamma staria senza più scosse.
Ma per ciò che giammai di questo fondo

---

10. Though this chapter is primarily concerned with the 1914–39 period, the discussion of twentieth-century science includes contemporary science because scientific knowledge and theory are continually evolving into ever more complex mosaics that encompass new discoveries and/or affirmations or denials of all past knowledge. A similar rationale also applies to the discussion of Freud and his contemporary critics.

11. According to Medawar, "psychoanalysis is akin to mesmerism and phrenology: it contains isolated nuggets of truth, but the general theory is false." Johnson, *op. cit.*, p. 6.

non torno vivo alcun, s'i'odo il vero,
senza tema d'infamia ti rispondo.[12]

Let us go then, you and I,
When the evening is spread out against the sky
Like a patient etherised upon a table;
Let us go, through certain half-deserted streets,   10
The muttering retreats
Of restless nights in one-night cheap hotels
And sawdust restaurants with oyster-shells:
Streets that follow like a tedious argument
Of insidious intent
To lead you to an overwhelming question . . .
Oh, do not ask, "What is it?"
Let us go and make our visit.

In the room the women come and go
Talking of Michelangelo.   20

The yellow fog that rubs its back upon the window-
     panes,
The yellow smoke that rubs its muzzle on the window-
     panes
Licked its tongue into the corners of the evening,
Lingered upon the pools that stand in drains,
Let fall upon its back the soot that falls from chimneys,
Slipped by the terrace, made a sudden leap,
And seeing that it was a soft October night,
Curled once about the house, and fell asleep.

And indeed there will be time
For the yellow smoke that slides along the street   30
Rubbing its back upon the window-panes;
There will be time, there will be time
To prepare a face to meet the faces that you meet;
There will be time to murder and create,
And time for all the works and days of hands[13]
That lift and drop a question on your plate;
Time for you and time for me,
And time yet for a hundred indecisions,
And for a hundred visions and revisions,
Before the taking of a toast and tea.   40

In the room the women come and go
Talking of Michelangelo.

And indeed there will be time
To wonder, "Do I dare?" and, "Do I dare?"
Time to turn back and descend the stair,
With a bald spot in the middle of my hair—
(They will say: "How his hair is growing thin!")
My morning coat, my collar mounting firmly to the chin,
My necktie rich and modest, but asserted by a simple pin—
(They will say: "But how his arms and legs are thin!")   50
Do I dare
Disturb the universe?
In a minute there is time
For decisions and revisions which a minute will reverse.

For I have known them all already, known them all—
Have known the evenings, mornings, afternoons,
I have measured out my life with coffee spoons;
I know the voices dying with a dying fall
Beneath the music from a farther room.

So how should I presume?   60

And I have known the eyes already, known them all—
The eyes that fix you in a formulated phrase,
And when I am formulated, sprawling on a pin,
When I am pinned and wriggling on the wall,
Then how should I begin
To spit out all the butt-ends of my days and ways?
     So how should I presume?

And I have known the eyes already, known them all—
Arms that are braceleted and white and bare
(But in the lamplight, downed with light brown hair!)   70
Is it perfume from a dress
That makes me so digress?
Arms that lie along a table, or wrap about a shawl.
     And should I then presume?
     And how should I begin?

                    .   .   .   .   .

Shall I say, I have gone at dusk through narrow streets
And watched the smoke that rises from the pipes
Of lonely men in shirt-sleeves, leaning out of windows? . . .
     I should have been a pair of ragged claws
Scuttling across the floors of silent seas.   80

                    .   .   .   .   .

And the afternoon, the evening, sleeps so peacefully!
Smoothed by long fingers,
Asleep . . . tired . . . or it malingers,
Stretched on the floor, here beside you and me.
Should I, after tea and cakes and ices,
Have the strength to force the moment to its crisis?
But though I have wept and fasted, wept and prayed,
Though I have seen my head (grown slightly bald)
     brought in upon a platter,
I am no prophet—and here's no great matter;[14]
I have seen the moment of my greatness flicker,   90
And I have seen the eternal Footman hold my coat, and
     snicker,
And in short, I was afraid.

And would it have been worth it, after all,
After the cups, the marmalade, the tea,
Among the porcelain, among some talk of you and me,

---

12. "If I thought I were making answer to one that might return
    to view the world, this flame should evermore cease shaking.
    But since from the abyss, if I hear true, none ever came
    alive, I have no fear of infamy, but give thee answer due."
    The speaker is Guido da Montefeltro, who was condemned
    to Hell as a Counsellor of Fraud (Dante, *Inferno*, XXVII,
    61–6). Dante has asked him why he is being punished and
    Guido, still fearful of what might be said about him, answers
    truthfully because he thinks Dante is also dead. Prufrock,
    like Guido, is fearful of society's judgment.
13. *Works and days* recalls Hesiod's poem entitled "Works and
    Days" (ca. 750 BC). Ironically contrasting with Prufrock's
    frivolous world, Hesiod's poem extols the virtues of hard
    labor on the land.
14. *I am no prophet*, that is, no John the Baptist, who was
    beheaded by Herod and his head brought in on a tray to
    please Salome, Herod's stepdaughter (Matthew 14:3–11).
    Prufrock views himself as a sacrificial victim, but he is
    neither saint nor martyr.

Would it have been worth while,
To have bitten off the matter with a smile,
To have squeezed the universe into a ball[15]
To roll it toward some overwhelming question,
To say: "I am Lazarus, come from the dead,[16]   100
Come back to tell you all, I shall tell you all"—
If one, settling a pillow by her head,
    Should say: "That is not what I meant at all,
    That is not it, at all."

    And would it have been worth it, after all,
Would it have been worth while,
After the sunsets and the dooryards and the sprinkled
    streets,
After the novels, after the teacups, after the skirts that
    trail along the floor—
And this, and so much more?—
It is impossible to say just what I mean!   110
But as if a magic lantern threw the nerves in patterns on
    a screen:
Would it have been worth while
If one, settling a pillow or throwing off a shawl,
And turning toward the window, should say:
    "That is not it at all,
    That is not what I meant, at all."

    . . . . . .

    No! I am not Prince Hamlet, nor was meant to be;
Am an attendant lord, one that will do
To swell a progress, start a scene or two,
Advise the prince; no doubt, an easy tool,[17]   120
Deferential, glad to be of use,
Politic, cautious, and meticulous;
Full of high sentence, but a bit obtuse;
At times, indeed, almost ridiculous—
Almost, at times, the Fool.

    I grow old . . . I grow old . . .
I shall wear the bottoms of my trousers rolled.[18]

    Shall I part my hair behind? Do I dare to eat a peach?
I shall wear white flannel trousers, and walk upon the
    beach.
I have heard the mermaids singing, each to each.   130

I do not think that they will sing to me.

I have seen them riding seaward on the waves
Combing the white hair of the waves blown back
When the wind blows the water white and black.

We have lingered in the chambers of the sea
By sea-girls wreathed with seaweed red and brown
Till human voices wake us, and we drown.

STUDY QUESTION

Describe, in your own words, Prufrock's physical appearance, personality, and social conduct.

LITERARY SELECTION 42

Dulce et Decorum Est
Wilfred Owen, 1893–1918

Perhaps the most promising English poet to die in the war, Wilfred Owen, unlike most of his contemporaries, saw no honor nor glory in a conflict that he referred to as "this deflowering of Europe." The closing quotation of this somber poem is from the poet Horace: "It is sweet and fitting to die for one's country." Owen apparently hoped that this "old Lie" would never again lead nations to war. He was killed in action on 4 November 1918, one week before the armistice that ended the fighting.

Bent double, like old beggars under sacks,
Knock-kneed, coughing like hags, we cursed through sludge,
Till on the haunting flares we turned our backs
And towards our distant rest began to trudge.

Men marched asleep. Many had lost their boots
But limped on, blood-shod. All went lame; all blind;
Drunk with fatigue; deaf even to the hoots
Of tired, outstripped Five-Nines that dropped behind.
Gas! Gas! Quick, boys!—An ecstasy of fumbling,
Fitting the clumsy helmets just in time,   10
But someone still was yelling out and stumbling
And flound'ring like a man in fire or lime . . .
Dim, through the misty panes and thick green light,
As under a green sea, I saw him drowning.

In all my dreams, before my helpless sight,
He plunges at me, guttering, choking, drowning.

If in some smothering dreams you too could pace
Behind the wagon that we flung him in,
And watch the white eyes writhing in his face,
His hanging face, like a devil's sick of sin;   20
If you could hear, at every jolt, the blood
Come gargling from the froth-corrupted lungs,
Obscene as cancer, bitter as the cud
Of vile, incurable sores on innocent tongues,—
My friend, you would not tell with such high zest
To children ardent for some desperate glory,
The old Lie: *Dulce et decorum est*
Pro patria mori.

---

15. *Universe into a ball* recalls "Let us roll all our Strength, and all our sweetness, up into one Ball" from the poem "To His Coy Mistress" by Andrew Marvell (see p. 345). Prufrock's attempt to raise the conversation to a cosmic level with an allusion to a love poem is doubly ironic; the imaginary lady casually brings the discussion back to trivialities (ll. 103–4).
16. *Lazarus* was raised from the grave by Christ (John 11:1–44). Can this society be brought back from the dead?
17. *Advise the prince* apparently refers to Polonius, the king's adviser in *Hamlet*. The cross-reference is to Guido da Montefeltro, also a false counsellor.
18. Cuffed (rolled) trousers were stylish at the time. Middle-aged and socially inept, Prufrock tries to appear young and fashionable.

LITERARY SELECTION 43

The Second Coming

William Butler Yeats, 1865–1939

Written by Yeats in 1920, the poem conveys a sense of the dissolution of civilization. His image of the cycle of history is a "gyre" (a rotating spiral). Imagine a falconer losing control of his falcon as the bird soars in widening circles and eventually breaks away. Lines 4–8 refer to the Russian Revolution of 1917, but they can also be taken as a portent of the rise of fascism in the twenties and thirties. *Spiritus Mundi* is the soul of the universe that connects all human souls in what Yeats calls the "Great Memory," or universal subconscious.

Turning and turning in the widening gyre
The falcon cannot hear the falconer;
Things fall apart: the centre cannot hold;
Mere anarchy is loosed upon the world,
The blood-dimmed tide is loosed, and everywhere
The ceremony of innocence is drowned;
The best lack all conviction, while the worst
Are full of passionate intensity.

Surely some revelation is at hand:
Surely the Second Coming is at hand.   10
The Second Coming! Hardly are those words out
When a vast image out of *Spiritus Mundi*
Troubles my sight: somewhere in the sands of the desert
A shape with lion body and the head of a man,
A gaze blank and pitiless as the sun,
Is moving its slow thighs, while all about it
Reel shadows of the indignant desert birds.
The darkness drops again; but now I know
That twenty centuries of stony sleep
Were vexed to nightmare by a rocking cradle,   20
And what rough beast, its hour come round at last,
Slouches towards Bethlehem to be born?

STUDY QUESTIONS

1. What is the implication of the "rocking cradle"?
2. Describe the feeling aroused by the last two lines of the poem.

LITERARY SELECTION 44

Shine, Perishing Republic

Robinson Jeffers, 1887–1962

Postwar America was a world power but Jeffers saw the darker side, a crass and materialistic nation mired "in the mold of its vulgarity." The reader can determine whether the poem, written in 1924, is still apropos.

While this America settles in the mold of its vulgarity, heavily thickening to empire,
And protest, only a bubble in the molten mass, pops and sighs out, and the mass hardens,
I sadly smiling remember that the flower fades to make fruit, the fruit rots to make earth.
Out of the mother; and through the spring exultances, ripeness and decadence; and home to the mother.

You making haste haste on decay: not blameworthy; life is good, be it stubbornly long or suddenly
A mortal splendor: meteors are not needed less than mountains: shine perishing republic.
But for my children, I would have them keep their distance from the thickening center: corruption
Never has been compulsory, when the cities lie at the monster's feet there are left the mountains.
And boys, be in nothing so moderate as in love of man, a clever servant, insufferable master.
There is the trap that catches noblest spirits, that caught—they say—God, when he walked on earth.

STUDY QUESTIONS

1. Identify the images that refer to the cycle of life and death.
2. What is implied by "meteors are not needed less than mountains"?

LITERARY SELECTION 45

Yet Do I Marvel (1924, 1925)

Countee Cullen, 1887–1946

One of the leaders of a 1920s literary movement called the Harlem Renaissance, Cullen can be seen, at first glance, as a voice of moderation compared with black protests since World War II. Cullen's references are from the Western literary tradition (Greek mythology, Dante) and the form is that of a sonnet. Line 12 is derived from the last two lines of "The Tyger" by William Blake (see p. 397). Blake asks how a good God can put evil in the world; Cullen ponders a similar question about the evil of racism. The tone is moderate but the sentiment is not.

I doubt not God is good, well-meaning, kind,
And did He stoop to quibble could tell why
The little buried mole continues blind,
Why flesh that mirrors Him must some day die,
Make plain the reason tortured Tantalus
Is baited by the fickle fruit, declare
If merely brute caprice dooms Sisyphus
To struggle up a never-ending stair.
Inscrutable His ways are, and immune
To catechism by a mind too strewn
With petty cares to slightly understand
What awful brain compels His awful hand.
Yet do I marvel at this curious thing:
To make a poet black, and bid him sing!

STUDY QUESTION

How many images are there of the way things are? Consider, for example, blind moles, Tantalus, and Sisyphus. (Tantalus was condemned by Zeus to stand up to his chin in water that receded everytime he tried to drink. Above his head hung fruit that the wind kept perpetually out of his reach. His name has given us the verb "tantalize.")

SUMMARY

The nineteenth-century Age of Progress had established a core of belief that held people together or provided a target against which they might revolt. World War I marked the point at which the balance was finally destroyed; after that time no such center existed and people found themselves cut loose from the comforting bonds of community and shared values, alone and alienated in a frightening new world. The Culture-Epoch theory highlights the chaotic nature of the period between the two World Wars. This, in turn, provides the framework for cultural changes later in the century.

Replacing the determinism of Newton's world-machine, the work of Planck, Heisenberg, and Einstein revolutionized scientific knowledge of the universe and

how it operates. Also revolutionary, the theories of Sigmund Freud, though fatally flawed, helped prepare the way to new insights into the human personality.

In "The Love Song of J. Alfred Prufrock" and "The Second Coming" Eliot and Yeats set the theme for the postwar reaction against the spiritual bankruptcy of the age. Wilfred Owen's poem "Dulce et Decorum Est" speaks for the generation of young men wasted in the trenches and, in "Shine, Perishing Republic," Jeffers depicts bankrupt idealism in a crass and vulgar nation. Harbinger of bad times to come, Cullen's "Yet Do I Marvel" highlights the destructive effects of racism in interwar America.

CULTURE AND HUMAN VALUES

Looking back from the distance of some three-quarters of a century, it is difficult to fully appreciate the devastating impact the Great War had on Western culture. Bad enough were the dreadful numbers killed, wounded, and maimed for life. But there was much more. Europeans considered their civilization as the world's most advanced, with the foremost science and technology, a superb educational system, and the world's highest standard of living. Science and technology, however, served the war-machines and contributed mightily to the general death and destruction. The best-educated nation in Europe—Germany—launched a long-planned war of conquest, with victims such as neutral Belgium sacrificed to imperial goals. Germany was by no means the sole transgressor; by the end of the war most nations had contributed their own barbarous acts. In the name of duty, honor, and love of country, politicians and generals violated virtually every precept of those vaunted ideals, not to mention justice and mercy.

Ideals and empires turned out to be equally vulnerable. By the end of the war the empires of Russia, Germany, and Austria-Hungary were finished and the British empire was on its last legs.

Actually, the old values had been disintegrating since the latter decades of the nineteenth century. The pressures of workers, unions, liberals, revolutionaries, socialists, and communists had forced changes on society, but not yet on the outmoded colonial empires. It remained for World War I to bring down the empires and start phasing out colonialism. We now see the war as the cataclysmic event that ended an era and set the stage for the search for new values: chaos followed by a period of adjustment.

CHAPTER 27

Ideas and Conflicts That Motivate the Twentieth Century

HISTORICAL OVERVIEW, 1939–90s

The Great Depression following the breakdown of economic systems was "cured" by the escalating production of weapons for war. England and France frantically, and belatedly, prepared for the resumption of hostilities with Germany in a war notably different from any other in humankind's interminable history of violence.

Soldiers fought in fields and pastures in the nineteenth century, in the trenches in 1914–18, but in 1939–45 the furious new battlefield described by American poet and playwright Richard Eberhart was the air itself. The bomber was the cost-efficient delivery system of World War II; targets included not only opposing armies but myriads of cities and their millions of inhabitants. Whether blasting Berlin and London, fire-bombing Dresden and Tokyo, or obliterating Hiroshima and Nagasaki, civilian casualties vastly outnumbered those of the military, and warfare was total.

LITERARY SELECTION 46

The Fury of Aerial Bombardment[1]

Richard Eberhart, b.1904

You would think the fury of aerial bombardment
Would rouse God to relent; the infinite spaces
Are still silent. He then looks on shock-pried faces.
History, even, does not know what is meant.
You would feel that after so many centuries
God would give man to repent; yet he can kill

Opposite Audrey Flack, *World War II (Vanitas)*, April 1945, detail. 1976–7. Oil over acrylic on canvas, full image 8 × 8′ (2.44 × 2.44 m). Incorporating a portion of Margaret Bourke-White's photograph "Buchenwald, April 1945." © Time, Inc. Photo: Louis K. Meisel Gallery, New York.

DEATH OF A CITY

On 13 February 1945 Dresden, Germany, held about 1,200,000 people, about twice its normal population. Refugees had gathered there because, with no important military targets, it was the safest city in Germany. The first wave of 244 English Lancaster bombers, dropping mostly incendiaries, set fires that the next wave of 529 Lancasters fed with about 650,000 fire-bombs. The third wave of 450 American Flying Fortresses finished the city off. Over 130,000 people (including Allied prisoners of war) were dead, mostly by fire, and the entire center of the city was gone. Why was a non-industrial city full of civilians destroyed? Allied air commanders justified the fire-bombing of German cities such as Berlin, Hamburg, Cologne, and others as part of the "progressive destruction and dislocation of the German economic and industrial system." Famous for its superb old buildings and splendid art collections, Dresden was known as the "Florence of the Elbe". The art had been stored elsewhere but the homes, churches, and palaces were gone forever.

As Cain could, but with multitudinous will,
No farther advanced than in his ancient furies.
Was man made stupid to see his own stupidity?
Is God by definition indifferent, beyond us all?
Is the eternal truth man's fighting soul
Wherein the Beast ravens in its own avidity?
Of Van Wettering I speak, and Averill,
Names on a list, whose faces I do not recall
But they are gone to early death, who late in school
Distinguished the belt feed lever from the belt holding pawl.

1. The Literary Selections in this chapter were picked for two reasons: literary merit and pertinent themes that could point up or flesh out a particular idea or conflict.

LITERARY SELECTION 47

Chorus of the Rescued

Nelly Sachs, 1891–1970

Sachs developed her poetry as a means of expression that would "make the unspeakable bearable." She escaped to Sweden in 1940 but returned to her native Germany after the war to confront the Holocaust, the basic theme of her poetry. She shared the 1966 Nobel Prize for literature with S. Y. Agnon.

We, the rescued
From whose hollow bones death had begun to whittle
    his flutes,
And on whose sinews he had already stroked his bow—
Our bodies continue to lament
With their mutilated music.
We, the rescued,
The nooses wound for our necks still dangle before us in
    the blue air—
Hourglasses still fill with our dripping blood.
We, the rescued,
The worms of fear still feed on us.   10
Our constellation is buried in dust.
We, the rescued.
Beg you:
Show us your sun, but gradually.
Lead us from star to star, step by step.
Be gentle when you teach us to live again.
Lest the song of a bird,
Or a pail being filled at the well,
Let our badly sealed pain burst forth again and carry us
    away—
We beg you: 20
Do not show us an angry dog, not yet—
It could be, it could be
That we will dissolve into dust—
Dissolve into dust before your eyes.
For what binds our fabric together?
We whose breath vacated us,
Whose soul fled to Him out of that midnight
Long before our bodies were rescued
Into the ark of the moment,
We, the rescued,   30
We press your hand
We look into your eye—
But all that binds us together now is leave-taking,
The leave-taking in the dust
Binds us together with you.

2. "If we assume the viewpoint of humanity and freedom, history does not know a despot as cynical as Stalin was. He was methodical, all-embracing, and total as a criminal. He was one of those rare terrible dogmatists capable of destroying nine-tenths of the human race to 'make happy' the one tenth." Milojan Djilas, *Conversations with Stalin* (New York: Harcourt, Brace & World, 1962), p. 190.

STUDY QUESTIONS

1. Which images best indicate what these survivors have endured?
2. Will these people ever fully recover?

THE COLD WAR, CA. 1945–90

World War II ended on 14 August 1945 with the Japanese surrender, and the whole world expected a new era of peace and stability. The United States, with its nuclear monopoly and enormous industrial capacity, emerged as an unrivaled superpower. Having learned some bitter lessons from the League of Nations, the United Nations began to function as the first real consortium of nations; with the assistance of the Marshall Plan, war-ravaged nations launched recovery programs that frequently verged on the miraculous. However, the anticipated era of peace and stability was delayed indefinitely with the Soviet Union's postwar expansionism and the detonation of its own atomic bomb in 1949. The sharply reduced power of the western European nations and the shambles of the old colonial order left a vacuum that was filled by the United States and the Soviet Union. Basically the confrontation was between the Western democracies led by the United States and the Eastern Bloc led by the Soviet Union under dictator Joseph Stalin (map 27.1).[2] Stalin moved quickly in 1945, creating "people's republics" in Poland, Romania, Hungary, Bulgaria, and later in Czechoslovakia and East Germany. Soviet attempts to take over Greece and Turkey were rebuffed by the Allies but, as it had for centuries before Lenin and Stalin, Russian imperialism continued to select targets of opportunity.

Communists tried and failed to win power in the Philippines, Indonesia, and Malaysia, but they did succeed in North Korea. Russian weapons (and the connivance of Stalin and Mao Zedong) encouraged the North Koreans to invade South Korea, thus launching the Korean War (1950–53) that eventually saw the People's Republic of China enter the war against United Nations troops comprised mainly of U.S. forces. The invasion ended in a stalemate near the original boundary between the two nations. Prolonged negotiations resulted in an armistice—not a peace treaty—in July 1953 that remains in effect.

The Viet Minh revolt that erupted in French Indochina after World War II ended in 1954 when the French stronghold at Dien Bien Phu surrendered to the insurgency led by Ho Chi Minh (1890–1969). A major power conference in Geneva subsequently recognized the independence of the former provinces of Cambodia and Laos. A Korean-style compromise divided the third province into Communist North Vietnam with its capital at Hanoi, and capitalist South Vietnam with Saigon as its capital.

By 1958 Communist-led guerillas, supported by Ho Chi Minh and known as the Viet Cong, had disrupted and terrorized much of South Vietnam. When the North Vietnamese army joined the Viet Cong in 1966, the American response was a rapid increase in troops, from several thousand in 1965 to 500,000 in 1967. The impact of the war on the United States was enormous, this being the first war to appear every evening on American television. The mounting casualties, the known atrocities, the corrupt South Vietnamese governments, the lack of a clear-cut rationale for an Asian war, and the inability of American arms to inflict a decisive defeat on a dedicated and relentless enemy led to massive anti-war protests in the United States.

Even now it is difficult to determine which came first: the anti-establishment free-speech revolt of the 1960s or the violent reaction to the slaughter in Vietnam that spun off a whole decade of activism, hippies, flower children, communes, campus sit-ins and riots, and the development of a drug culture. All were manifestations of a sea-change that affected every cranny of American society.

The war effectively ended the political career of President Lyndon B. Johnson and adversely affected the Nixon administration. A long-delayed cease-fire was finally arranged in January 1973, a pact that North Vietnam violated after most of the remaining American troops had left the country. Saigon fell to the North Vietnamese on 30 April 1975 as the remaining Americans frantically evacuated the American embassy on relays of helicopters. Though the war was widely believed to be an internal war of liberation, North Vietnamese leaders later admitted that they had used the Viet Cong as pawns in a well-planned war of conquest.

The war in Vietnam prompted violent reactions, but a large segment of the population tried to ignore American entanglement in an unpopular war. There was a desire not to become involved, not to think about distant, murderous jungles, especially when—as was often the case—no friends nor relatives were fighting in Asia. However, nearly 60,000 combatants died in Vietnam in the only war the United States ever lost.

Throughout the Cold War, mutual assured destruction (MAD), a balance of terror, kept nuclear weapons in their silos. So-called conventional (hot) wars, however, abounded. If a major war is defined as one in which there are more than 1,000 combatants, there have been over 100 wars since 1945. African and Asian nationalism, class conflicts in Central and South America, endless Middle East crises, including large-scale warfare—the trials and tribulations of our era never cease and yet the world looks hopefully toward better days with the freeing of captive nations and the widespread revival of democracies.

The major event—actually series of events—of the late 1980s was the widespread failure of Marxist-Leninism. The Soviet Union and its satellites had, by that time, demonstrated that Communism could not work, indeed had never achieved its goals. In *The Unperfect Society* (1969) Yugoslav author Milovan Djilas predicted the inevitable failure of Communism; he identified the source of the problem by tracing the ugly roots of Stalinism back through Lenin to Marx's utopianism, ideological rigidity, and scientific pretensions. He pointed out that Communist dictators assumed they had been named by a higher power—History—that awarded them the right to establish the Kingdom of Heaven (dictatorship of the proletariat) in this sinful capitalistic world. Why was History this higher power? Because Marx said so.

The flaw in Marxism was fundamental. Marx based his entire doctrine on the proclamation that began Section I of the *Communist Manifesto*: "The history of all hitherto existing society is the history of class struggles." If this statement were true then History was on the side of those who would eliminate class struggles by establishing a classless society. Hegel had claimed that past cultures were stages in the evolutionary development of the world Spirit toward perfection and freedom. Marx and Engels formulated a doctrine of inevitable progress leading to the perfect classless society by twisting Hegel's philosophy from the consciousness of his world Spirit to the consciousness of societies engaged in class struggle. In fact, however, some of the most important values and issues transcend class. Family, trust, loyalty, faith, fidelity, and the many varieties of love are just a few of the values that are cherished by peasants and poets, commoners and kings. The Marxian interpretation of history was, in plain words, wrong, thus making all subsequent Communist theory fatally flawed. This should not imply, however, that Marx's influence was wholly negative. He was genuinely interested in the welfare of the working class and his theories are, in part, responsible for the greatly improved status of the underprivileged of advanced societies.

In pragmatic terms, Communism failed because not one aspect of the system worked.[3] The classless society was never tried nor did the proletariat ever have any voice in the "dictatorship of the proletariat." Every Communist country suffered under a dictatorial party whose elite class controlled the masses by coercion, fear, censorship, rewriting history (of all subjects!), and the omnipresent secret police. One of the worst—and abiding—bequests of Communist inefficiency and mismanagement is the destruction of the environment. Throughout central Europe, forests, fields, streams, lakes, and the atmosphere were destroyed or severely contaminated in futile attempts to fulfill production quotas regardless of the consequences.

---

3. In 1983 Luigi Barzini wrote in *The Europeans*: "The Russian Revolution exaggerated the worst traits of Czarist authority: secret police, mass exiles to Siberia, forced labor camps, the concentration of all of the economy in the hands of the state. The Soviets dedicated the largest percentage of the national income to armaments and starved the peasantry, as has been done in Russia for centuries. In the end, the Communist regime turned out to be a caricature of what had existed before."

GENOCIDE

Not until Nazi Germany was finally defeated in 1945 did the world learn of the incredible extent of Nazi atrocities. As Allied troops liberated starving prisoners from Dachau (see p. 520), Auschwitz, Buchenwald (see pp. 468 and 509) and dozens more death camps, the horror grew ever greater. Of the estimated 12,000,000 victims who were gassed and cremated in the ovens, about 6,000,000 were Jews, whom Hitler's Holocaust had tried to erase from the face of the earth. The other 6,000,000 were Slavs, Gypsies, Masons, Communists, Socialists, homosexuals, prostitutes, and an unending supply of enemies of the state. Ironically, some of the troops whose relatives had been imprisoned in the United States, namely the Japanese-American 522nd Field Artillery Battalion, were among the Allied liberators.

The wonder of it all, as many have remarked, is not that Marxism-Leninism failed but that it took so long.

The most startling aspect of the demise of Communism was how abruptly it collapsed in so many countries. The sickly Soviet economy was a critical factor, of course, but one should also consider the pivotal role of the electronic devices of the Information Age. Television, camcorders, video tapes, and VCRs played a significant role in the public's knowledge of demonstrations, repression, and rebellion. It is no longer possible to keep a subject people in the dark about what transpires in the rest of the world, and this may be the most hopeful sign of what it means to live in a "Global Village."

The decisive conclusion of the Cold War followed closely on the jubilant destruction of the Berlin Wall in 1989. Stalin had reasoned that, American power notwithstanding, a divided Germany was the key to the USSR's unrivaled dominance in Europe. Germany was unified on 2 October 1990 and the Paris Charter was signed on 21 November 1990 by the United States, Canada, and every European nation except Albania. The Paris agreement guaranteed commitment to democracy and economic well-being for all signatories, thus ending the Cold War that had begun after World War II. 1990 is already viewed as one of the most important dates in the modern history of Western civilization, probably on a par with the end of the Thirty Years' War in 1648 and the termination of the Napoleonic wars in 1815.

We can now complete the dramatic allegory described on page 455 in which World War I was characterized as Act I. The entr'acte of 1918–39 connected the Great War to World War II (Act II), for the former did indeed lead to the latter. The third act was the Cold War that ended with the triumph of the Western democracies. The Western world and the European Community in particular now have a historic opportunity to secure a lasting peace. Serious problems in the Balkans, Middle East, the Far East, and Africa remain unresolved but the United Nations, with the strong backing of the United States and the EU, is in the best position in its history to bring some sort of stability to the entire world.

PHILOSOPHY

Probably every philosophical system ever invented has surfaced at one time or another during this troubled century. One of the most influential of these philosophies, existentialism, is more a mood or an attitude than a complete philosophical system. Formulated during World War II by French writer Jean-Paul Sartre during his years with the French Resistance, existentialism had an immediate appeal for a desperate world. Actually, the roots of the movement go back to several disparate personalities of the nineteenth century, particularly Kierkegaard, a Danish anticlerical theologian, and Nietzsche, a German atheist.

Søren Kierkegaard, 1813–55

A melancholy and lonely Dane, Kierkegaard (KEER-kuh-gard) was almost totally unnoticed in his own time. Kierkegaard's concern was with the individual, whom he saw as an actor on the stage of life. For each individual there was, according to Kierkegaard, the possibility of three ascending levels of existence along life's way: aesthetic, ethical, and religious. The aesthetic level was that of the pleasure-seeker, and the only goals were newer pleasant sensations. Eventually, the futile pursuit of pleasure ends in despair and life is absurd. The only way to rise above the aesthetic level is to recognize the reality of choice.

The second level is that of the ethical, which does not eliminate the aesthetic mode but rises above it. The ethical life is not, however, the same as advocating abstract ethical theories; one can know about ethical theories and still be an unethical slob. The ethical person, for Kierkegaard, is actively committed to long-range purposes, dedicated to the continuity of life, free to choose and be bound to a commitment. Choice is a necessity in the ethical life and, Kierkegaard says, the only absolutely ethical choice is between good and evil. But this is not enough. We are virtually helpless in facing the evils and injustices of everyday life; these evils can be overcome only by an outpouring of love and generosity beyond human justice and human powers. Such love and generosity is possible only if something transcending us breaks into history and works in our lives. Kierkegaard believed that the breakthrough of the eternal into history was the birth of Christ.

To recapitulate: after the vain pursuit of pleasure we feel despair; through choice we can raise ourselves to the ethical level and become committed to our responsibilities, but this eventually proves insufficient; each of us becomes a "knight of infinite resignation." At this point we

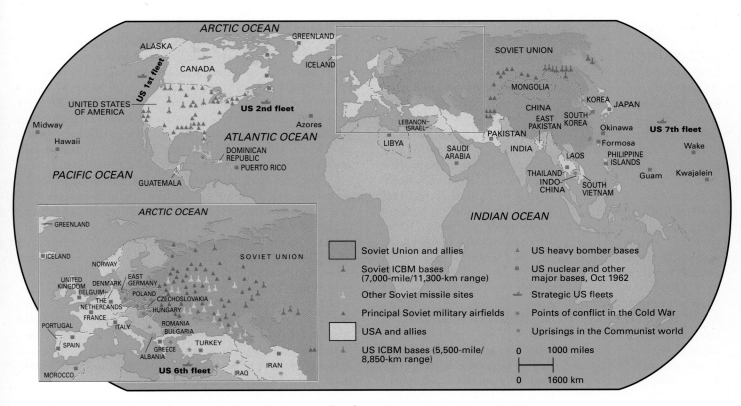

Map 27.1 The Cold War.

can choose to leap beyond reason to the religious mode of existence using the passion called faith ("where reason ends there begins faith").

Faith, for Kierkegaard, means total commitment to the inner personality of God. We cannot cleverly argue our way to God; we either accept God completely or reject him completely. The second and final leap of faith is into the arms of Jesus. However, Kierkegaard says, this leap to the God-man of Christian history is conceptually absurd. The intensity of the leap of faith to God is vastly increased by the second venture to the level of Christianity, which is unintelligible. As Kierkegaard wrote, "in an unpermissible and unlawful way people have become knowing about Christ, for the only permissible way is to be believing."

These absolute ventures are personal decisions taken in absolute loneliness with the utmost responsibility. The isolation of the individual in such a decision is absolute and this, says Kierkegaard, is what it means to be a human being. These leaps of faith make an existing individual. Speculative philosophy, according to Kierkegaard, plus the Christian establishment and the press had confused basic facts: "Christendom has done away with Christianity without being quite aware of it."

Values, for Kierkegaard, were not esoteric essences: "Good and evil are ways of existing and the human good is to exist authentically." Conversely, evil is an unauthentic, ungenuine existence. Authentic existence is a matter of choice and the existing person knows the risk and feels the dread of individual responsibility. But, as Kierkegaard observed, "dread is the possibility of freedom" and "man is condemned to freedom."

ECOLOGICAL SUICIDE

One of today's most serious concerns is the worldwide abuse of natural resources. This is not, however, a recent problem. The past is replete with chilling examples of cultures who, in effect, committed ecological suicide. A case in point are the Maya of Central America. This civilization can be traced back to around 2000 BC with a classic period (ca. AD 300–900) more advanced than European civilization in the same era, especially their mathematics and calendar. Equally notable were Maya achievements in astronomy, historical writing, architecture, and sculpture.

Numbering over 2,000,000 people at the height of their civilization, the Maya went into a long decline after 900 and, beginning around 1542, finally succumbed to Spanish conquest. Some archaeologists have theorized that this deterioration was caused by a combination of overpopulation and the devastation of natural resources through slash-and-burn agriculture. Widespread famine led to interminable civil wars over dwindling agricultural lands. The Maya left today still live in virtually the same geographical area, much of which is once again tropical jungle. Only haunting vestiges of their high culture remain.

Friedrich Nietzsche, 1844–1900

Nietzsche (NEE-chuh) stressed the absurdity of human existence and the inability of our reason to understand the world. A passionate individualist, he proclaimed the will to power as the only value in a meaningless world. Nietzsche rejected any ideas or system that would limit the freedom of the individual, particularly Christianity, which taught, he contended, a "slave morality" of sympathy, humility, and pity, qualities beneficial only to the weak and the helpless. His "noble" man was a superman, an incarnate will to power, who would rise above the herd (the "bungled and the botched") to establish a "master morality" of the "aristocratic" qualities of strength, nobility, pride, and power. "God is dead," Nietzsche proclaimed, meaning that all absolute systems from Plato onward had died with the God of the Judeo-Christian tradition.

A fervent admirer of the culture of ancient Greece, Nietzsche evolved an influential aesthetic theory of the Apollonian and Dionysian modes. The Apollonian mode is intellectual. It draws an aesthetic veil over reality, creating an ideal world of form and beauty. The Apollonian attitude found expression in Greek mythology, in Homer's epic poems, in sculpture, painting, architecture, and Greek vases.

The Dionysian mode, somewhat like Freud's *id*, is the dark, turgid, and formless torrent of instinct, impulse, and passion that tends to sweep aside everything in its path. Tragedy and music are typical Dionysian art forms: they transmute existence into aesthetic phenomena without, however, drawing a veil over authentic existence. The Dionysian represents existence in aesthetic form and affirms this, says Nietzsche, in the human condition. True culture, for Nietzsche, is a unity of life forces, the dark Dionysian element combined with the love of form and beauty that characterizes the Apollonian. The highest product of this balanced culture is the creative genius, the superman.

The basic theme of Nietzsche's life and thought was the antipolitical individual who sought self-perfection far from the modern world. His desire was "to live for one's education free from politics, nationality, and newspapers." For him, knowledge was power and the will to power was the use of education for the betterment of humankind. "Above all," he said, "become who you are!"

Kierkegaard and Nietzsche represent the two extremes of theistic and atheistic existentialism with Feodor Dostoevsky somewhere in between. In the Grand Inquisitor section of *The Brothers Karamazov* the latter denies all authority (symbolized by the Church of Rome) in favor of the individual search for faith, spirit, and redemption.

Jean-Paul Sartre, 1905–80

Sartre (sar-tru), an atheistic existentialist quite unlike Nietzsche, arrived at his conclusions using logic. Sartre contended that the idea of God was self-contradictory, that the man called Christ could not be both divine and human because the terms are mutually exclusive. In other words, said Sartre, divine means non-human and human means that which is not divine. You cannot draw a circular square or a square circle. And, if there is no God, there are no fixed values, no absolute right or wrong, no good or bad. In *The Brothers Karamazov* Dostoevsky has one of his characters say, "But you see, if there were no God, everything would be possible." And that is precisely Sartre's point, that human beings are the sole source of values and anything is possible.

Sartre's basic premise was that existence precedes essence. First, a person is; what he or she becomes is settled in the course of existence. For the existentialist things in the world just are; only human beings can create themselves. Liberty is unrestricted, our capacity for choice is absolute, and making choices is what makes us human. The only meaning that life has is in the significance of the values that we choose. Values are not waiting to be discovered; we invent values. To the question, "What meaning is there in life?", the existentialist replies, "only what you put into life." But, as Sartre warns, the exercise of freedom is inseparably linked with responsibility: "Man is condemned to be free; because once thrown into the world, man is responsible for everything he does."

You can never choose anything, wrote Sartre, without realizing that this is the choice you wish all humankind to make. If you choose truth then you want everyone to be truthful; if you choose to steal then you are willing that everyone should be a thief. In every choice you have chosen for all humankind, a crushing responsibility, a condition that Sartre calls "anguish."

What are the values for which the existentialist is willing to assume responsibility? The answer has a curiously old-fashioned ring: the values are those of individualism; value is in the individual; value is the individual. The supreme virtue is responsible choice, what we call integrity, and the ultimate vice is self-deception. "Know thyself," said the Greeks and the existentialist fervently agrees. What you choose determines what you will become but, Sartre emphasizes, you can change, you can redirect your steps. What gives meaning to life is not what happens to us but what we ourselves do. We are actors on the stage of life. As Sartre said: "Man is encompassed by his own existence and there is no exit." In 1947 Sartre wrote in *Existentialism*:

Existentialism is nothing less than an attempt to draw all the consequences of a coherent atheistic position. It isn't trying to plunge man into despair at all. But if one calls every attitude of unbelief despair, like the Christian, then the word is not being used in its original sense. Existentialism isn't so atheistic that it wears itself out showing that God doesn't exist. Rather, it declares that even if God did exist, that would change nothing. There you've got our point of view. Not that we believe that God exists, but we think the problem of his existence is not the issue. In this sense existentialism is optimistic, a doctrine of action, and it is plain dishonesty for Christians to make no distinction between their own despair and ours and then to call us despairing.

Existentialism owes its popularity in no small part to repeated failures in politics, economics, and social organizations that have scarred our century. Whatever shortcomings the movement may have, it is not just a body of philosophical speculations, but an attitude that still helps a great many people in this muddled world to pursue a personal freedom, a way of life that ranks quality over quantity.

RELIGIONS

The continuing influx of new citizens from Asia and the Middle East simply adds to the multiculturalism of the United States. Though there have always been religions in addition to Judaism and Christianity in this country, the numbers are now changing rather significantly. Throughout the country there are new mosques, Buddhist and Hindu temples, and one can study with a Zen master in any major city. Islam was discussed at length in chapter 12, but attention must be given to Hinduism, Buddhism, and Zen Buddhism.

Hinduism

The oldest of all world religions, Hinduism dates back to about 1500 BC. The word "Hindu" is derived from the Sanskrit word *sindhu*, meaning "river," specifically the Indus, where the earliest Indian civilization developed. Unlike any other religion, Hinduism's origins are unknown. It has no founder, it has more than one sacred book, and there is no single body of doctrine. Remarkably inclusive rather than exclusive, Hinduism is a blanket term for a wide diversity of beliefs and practices that do not, however, cause any conflicts or problems. Hindus worship many gods while also holding to the view that there is only one god, called Brahman, with all other divinities aspects of the unknowable Brahman.

A distinctive feature is the belief in the transmigration of souls and the idea that all living things are part of the same essence. An individual human soul may return many times in human, animal, or vegetable form. What a person does in a present life will affect the next life, which is the doctrine of *karma*, the law of cause and effect. The individual's goal is to escape the cycle of birth and death so that the soul, Atman, may become part of Brahman, the absolute soul.

India's caste system is a historic characteristic of Hinduism that originally divided all human beings into four classes: priests (or Brahmins), warriors, merchants, and servants. In today's India there are many castes, from the Brahmins at the top to the Untouchables (now outlawed as a caste) at the bottom. Adherents of Hinduism can be found around the globe but the caste system is confined to India.

Hindus regard many animals and plants as sacred, most notably the cow; beef is not eaten even among castes that are not vegetarian. Monkeys, tree squirrels, trees, and some snakes are also considered holy, as are some rivers, especially the Ganges. People are also sacred according to their position in life; thus parents are holy to their children, teachers to their students, and so on. It is estimated that there are more than 700,000,000 Hindus with 90 percent of them residing in India.

Buddhism

The religion of about one-eighth of all the people in the world, Buddhism is a complex set of beliefs built around the teaching of a single man. It was founded in northeast India in the fifth century BC by Siddhartha Gautama, known as the Buddha (the "Enlightened One"). Having lived a self-indulgent life and then one of bitter denial, Siddhartha sat for forty-nine days under a tree, where he was awakened to the truth about life. For many years he taught the Four Noble Truths and the Eightfold Path.

The first truth is that all life is suffering, pain, and misery. The second is that this suffering is caused by selfish craving and personal desire. But this selfishness can be overcome, which is the third truth. The fourth truth is that people can overcome this misery through the Eightfold Path. All Buddhists believe that people should not identify too strongly with their own personal existence in any one life. The cycle of reincarnation condemns the person to the suffering associated with being alive and striving. The goal, according to the Buddha, is to escape from being born as a suffering person—to attain Nirvana, the highest bliss. This is what he experienced under the tree.

The Buddha called his Eightfold Path the Middle Way between a luxurious life and one of unnecessary poverty. Not everyone can attain Nirvana, of course, but everyone can at least start down the road. But first they must take a basic step that precedes the Middle Way. Buddhists are supposed to follow Right Association, that is, to associate only with other seekers of truth in a spirit of love.

The Eightfold Path

1. Right Knowledge of life is revealed in the Four Noble Truths.
2. Right Aspiration means being committed on the Path toward Enlightenment.
3. Right Speech is speaking with clarity and always kindly.
4. Right Behavior means paying attention to one's behavior and to the five basic laws of behavior: not to kill, steal, lie, drink intoxicants, or commit sexual offenses.
5. Right Livelihood means choosing a career that promotes

life and good will rather than trying to make a lot of money.

6. Right Effort means learning to curb all selfish concerns.
7. Right Mindfulness is continual self-examination and awareness; as Socrates said, the unexamined life is not worth living.
8. Right Concentration is the final goal of being absorbed into a state of Nirvana.

The Eightfold Path, in reduced form, becomes the Threefold Learning: Discipline on Morality, Meditation, and Wisdom.

Schism

Two major traditions of Buddhism emerged early on and continue to this day. The older tradition, known as the Way of the Elders, is also called the Little Raft and also Theravada Buddhism. This is still the main tradition in Sri Lanka, Myanmar (Burma), Thailand, Laos, and Cambodia. The Greater Vehicle, Mahayana Buddhism, is the dominant form of Buddhism in Mongolia, Tibet, China, Taiwan, Japan, Korea, Vietnam, and Nepal. In all its forms Buddhism has three unchanging cornerstones, which are the Three Jewels: *Buddha*, the teacher; *Dharma*, the teachings or laws; and *Sangha*, the community of believers.

Zen (or Ch'an)

This is a Buddhist school that developed in China and later in Japan as a result of the fusion of Mahayana Buddhism with the Chinese philosophy of Taoism. Zen and Ch'an are the Japanese and Chinese ways of pronouncing the Sanskrit term *dhyana*, which connotes a state of mind roughly corresponding to contemplation or meditation. Zen is the peculiarly Chinese way of seeing the world just as it is, with a mind that neither grasps nor feels; it just contemplates. This is called "no-mind." Zen maintains that gradual practice cannot produce such freedom of the mind; it must come through insight. The world, according to Zen, is not many things; it is one reality. When reason analyzes the diversity of the world it obscures this oneness. But it can be apprehended by the non-rational part of the mind: intuition. Zen is fond of asking questions such as, "what is the sound of one hand clapping?", or, when asked about the Way of Zen, of replying "a cloud in the sky and water in the pail."

Zen has strongly influenced Eastern arts and crafts because it is concerned with acting rather than theorizing and because of its direct vision of nature rather than relying on interpretation. It has also appealed to many Western artists, philosophers, and psychologists. It has a special appeal for non-objective painters and sculptors. Philosophers have noted its similarities with the ideas of Ludwig Wittgenstein, the Austrian philosopher, and, to some extent, with existentialism as propounded by German philosopher Martin Heidegger.

CIVIL RIGHTS

Since World War II the United States has become more democratic, but it hasn't been easy. The so-called Second Reconstruction in American history began in the late 1940s with presidential decrees that banned discrimination in federal jobs and ordered desegregation of the armed forces. The target of the first stage of the civil rights movement, segregation in public education, was struck down by the landmark Supreme Court decision of 1954, Brown versus the Board of Education (Topeka). Despite sometimes violent opposition, the nation's schools were gradually integrated while, at the same time, other forms of discrimination were challenged with boycotts, sit-ins, and "freedom rides." Congress enacted, in 1957, the first civil rights legislation—to safeguard voting rights—since 1865, followed by voting legislation in 1960, and, in 1964, by a comprehensive Civil Rights Act that banned discrimination on the basis of race, sex, nationality, or religion in public places, employment, and unions.

The most powerful moving force behind the Civil Rights Movement was the Reverend Martin Luther King, Jr., the president of the Southern Christian Leadership Conference. He helped organize a coherent program of non-violent resistance to networks of segregation laws, a program best described in his famous "Letter from Birmingham Jail." Written on 16 April 1963 while he was confined for parading without a permit, the letter was addressed to certain Protestant ministers, Catholic priests, and a rabbi.

LITERARY SELECTION 48

Letter from Birmingham Jail
Martin Luther King, Jr., 1929–68

My dear Fellow Clergymen,

While confined here in the Birmingham City Jail, I came across your recent statement calling our present activities "unwise and untimely." Seldom, if ever, do I pause to answer criticism of my work and ideas. But since I feel that you are men of genuine goodwill and your criticisms are sincerely set forth, I would like to answer your statement in what I hope will be patient and reasonable terms.

I think I should give the reason for my being in   10
Birmingham, since you have been influenced by the argument of "outsiders coming in." Several months ago our local affiliate here in Birmingham invited us to be on call to engage in a nonviolent direct action program if such were deemed necessary. We readily consented and when the hour came we lived up to our promises. So I am here, along with several members of my staff, because we were invited here. Beyond this, I am in Birmingham because injustice is here.

Moreover, I am cognizant of the interrelatedness of all   20 communities and states. I cannot sit idly by in Atlanta and not be concerned about what happens in Birmingham. Injustice anywhere is a threat to justice everywhere. We are caught in an inescapable network of mutuality tied in a single garment of destiny. Never again can we afford to live with the narrow, provincial "outsider agitator" idea. Anyone who lives inside the United States can never be considered an outsider anywhere in this country.

You deplore the demonstrations that are presently taking place in Birmingham. But I am sorry that your statement did not express a similar concern for the conditions that brought the demonstrations into being. I would not hesitate to say that it is unfortunate that so-called demonstrations are taking place in Birmingham at this time, but I would say in more emphatic terms that it is even more unfortunate that the white power structure of this city left the Negro community with no other alternative.

In any nonviolent campaign there are four basic steps:

1. collection of the facts to determine whether injustices are alive;
2. negotiation;
3. self-purification; and
4. direct action.

You may well ask, "Why direct action? Why sit-ins, marches, etc.? Isn't negotiation a better path?" You are exactly right in your call for negotiation. Indeed, this is the purpose of direct action. Nonviolent direct action seeks to create such a crisis and establish such creative tension that a community that has constantly refused to negotiate is forced to confront the issue. So the purpose of the direct action is to create a situation so crisis-packed that it will inevitably open the door to negotiation.

My friends, I must say to you that we have not made a single gain in civil rights without determined legal and nonviolent pressure. History is the long and tragic story of the fact that privileged groups seldom give up their privileges voluntarily. Individuals may see the moral light and voluntarily give up their unjust posture; but as Reinhold Niebuhr has reminded us, groups are more immoral than individuals.

We know through painful experience that freedom is never voluntarily given by the oppressor; it must be demanded by the oppressed. For years now I have heard the word "Wait!" It rings in the ear of every Negro with a piercing familiarity. This "wait" has almost always meant "never." We must come to see with the distinguished jurist of yesterday that "justice too long delayed is justice denied." We have waited for more than three hundred and forty years for our constitutional and God-given rights.

You express a great deal of anxiety over our willingness to break laws. This is certainly a legitimate concern. Since we so diligently urge people to obey the Supreme Court's decision of 1954 outlawing segregation in the public schools, it is rather strange and paradoxical to find us consciously breaking laws. One may well ask, "How can you advocate breaking some laws and obeying others?" The answer is found in the fact that there are two types of laws. There are *just* laws and there are *unjust* laws. One has not only a legal but a moral responsibility to obey just laws. Conversely, one has a moral responsibility to disobey unjust laws.

Now what is the difference between the two? A just law is a man-made code that squares with the moral law or the law of God. An unjust law is a code that is out of harmony with the moral law. Any law that degrades human personality is unjust. All segregation statutes are unjust because segregation distorts the soul and damages the personality. It gives the segregator a false sense of superiority and the segregated a false sense of inferiority.

Let us turn to a more concrete example of just and unjust laws. An unjust law is a code that a majority inflicts on a minority that is not binding on itself. This is *difference* made legal. On the other hand a just law is a code that a majority compels a minority to follow that is willing to follow itself. This is *sameness* made legal. I hope you can see the distinction I am trying to point out. In no sense do I advocate evading or defying the law as the rabid segregationist would do. This would lead to anarchy. One who breaks an unjust law *openly, lovingly,* and with a willingness to accept the penalty by staying in jail to arouse the conscience of the community over its injustice, is in reality expressing the very highest respect for law.

Of course there is nothing new about this kind of civil disobedience. It was seen sublimely in the refusal of Shadrach, Meshach, and Abednego to obey the laws of Nebuchadnezzar because a higher moral law was involved. It was practiced superbly by the early Christians.

We can never forget that everything Hitler did in Germany was "legal" and everything the Hungarian freedom fighters did in Hungary was "illegal." It was "illegal" to aid and comfort a Jew in Hitler's Germany.

In your statement you asserted that our actions, even though peaceful, must be condemned because they precipitate violence. But can this assertion be logically made? Isn't this like condemning the robbed man because his possession of money precipitated the evil act of robbery? We must come to see, as federal courts have consistently affirmed, that it is immoral to urge an individual to withdraw his efforts to gain his basic constitutional rights because the quest precipitates violence. Society must protect the robbed and punish the robber.

Over the last few years I have consistently preached that nonviolence demands that the means we use must be as pure as the ends we seek. So I have tried to make it clear that it is wrong to use immoral means to gain moral ends. But now I must affirm that it is just as wrong, or even more so, to use moral means to preserve immoral ends. T. S. Eliot has said that there is no greater treason than to do the right deed for the wrong reason.

I wish you had commended the Negro sit-inners and demonstrators of Birmingham for their sublime courage,

their willingness to suffer, and their amazing discipline in the midst of the most inhuman provocation. One day the South will recognize its real heroes. They will include old, oppressed, battered Negro women, symbolized in a seventy-two-year-old woman of Montgomery, Alabama, who rose up with a sense of dignity and with her people decided not to ride the segregated buses, and responded to one who inquired about her tiredness with ungrammatical profundity: "My feets is tired, but my soul is rested." One day the South will know that when   150
these disinherited children of God sat down at the lunch counters they were in reality standing up for the best in the American dream and the most sacred values in our Judeo-Christian heritage, and thus carrying our whole nation back to great wells of democracy which were dug deep by the founding fathers in the formulation of the Constitution and the Declaration of Independence.

I hope this letter finds you strong in the faith. I also hope that circumstances will soon make it possible for me to meet each of you, not as an integrationist or a civil   160
rights leader, but as a fellow clergyman and a Christian brother. Let us hope that the dark clouds of racial prejudice will soon pass away and the deep fog of misunderstanding will be lifted from our fear-drenched communities and in some not too distant tomorrow the radiant stars of love and brotherhood will shine over our great nation with all of their scintillating beauty.

Yours for the cause of Peace and Brotherhood

Martin Luther King, Jr.

By 1965 the attack on segregation was essentially completed and stage two of the civil rights movement had begun. The rising demand was for equal opportunity, not only for jobs but in every area in American life. Mounting dissatisfaction with ghetto life, *de facto* segregation, and deteriorating urban environments fueled frustrations that writers such as Langston Hughes early saw as unbearable. Hughes, the leading writer of the Harlem Renaissance, summed up the smoldering situation in 1951 with a prophetic eleven-line poem.

LITERARY SELECTION 49

Harlem

Langston Hughes, 1902–67

What happens to a dream deferred?
Does it dry up
like a raisin in the sun?
Or fester like a sore—
And then run?
Does it stink like rotten meat?
Or crust and sugar over—
like a syrupy sweet?

Maybe it just sags
like a heavy load.

Or *does it explode?*

Harlem, Detroit, Watts, and other urban centers erupted in the 1960s and extreme violence did not subside until after 1969. Equal opportunity for many African Americans, Hispanics, Native Americans, and other minorities remains a "dream deferred."

LITERARY SELECTION 50

The Transport of Slaves From Maryland to Mississippi

Rita Dove, b. 1952

U. S. Poet Laureate Rita Dove uses much historical material in her poetry, including some powerful poetry about slavery, which is not that far in the past. Her Pulitzer Prize-winning *Thomas and Beulah* (1993) consists of linked poems that pay homage to her grandparents as they migrated north. Her verse play, *The Darker Face of the Earth* (1994), is based on the story of Oedipus but the setting is slaveholding antebellum South Carolina. The following poem is from her book of poetry entitled *The Yellow House on the Corner* (1993).

[On August 22, 1839, a wagonload of slaves broke their chains, killed two white men, and would have escaped, had not a slave woman helped the Negro driver mount his horse and ride for help.]

I don't know if I helped him up
because I thought he was our salvation
or not. Left for dead in the middle
of the road, dust hovering around the body
like a screen of mosquitoes
shimmering in the hushed light.
The skin across his cheekbones
burst open like baked yams—
deliberate, the eyelids came apart—
his eyes were my eyes in a yellower face.   10
Death and salvation—one accommodates the other.
I am no brute. I got feelings.
He might have been a son of mine.

"The Negro Gordon, barely escaping with his life, rode
into the plantation just as his pursuers came into sight.
The neighborhood was rallied and a search begun.
Some of the Negroes had taken to the woods but
were routed, ending this most shocking affray and murder."

Eight miles south of Portsmouth, the last handcuff
broke clean from the skin. The last thing   20
the driver saw were the trees, improbable as broccoli,
before he was clubbed from behind. Sixty slaves
poured off the wagon, smelly, half-numb, free.

Baggage man Petit rushed in with his whip.
Some nigger's laid on another one's leg, he thought
before he saw they were loose. Hold it! he yelled;
but not even the wenches stopped. To his right
Atkins dropped under a crown of clubs. They didn't
even flinch. Wait. You ain't supposed to act this way.

GENDER ISSUES

No man can make you feel inferior without your consent.

Eleanor Roosevelt, 1884–1962

A roll call of influential women in Western culture can be impressive—at first glance. Cleopatra, Eleanor of Aquitaine, Queen Elizabeth I, Queen Victoria, and Margaret Thatcher certainly made their mark. What of the rest of the feminine half of the human race? With the exception of women such as those cited above, human history has been, until recently, an uninterrupted saga of male domination of the subordinate "inferior sex." Perhaps the first feminist to protest against such treatment in print was Christine de Pisan in her *Book of the City of Ladies*,[4] published in 1405. Not surprisingly, there was no reaction from either sex. It was not until Mary Wollstonecraft (1759–97) published *Vindication of the Rights of Woman* (1792) that there began a feminist movement, though it was barely a ripple across the broad waters of male dominance. John Stuart Mill helped change that; drawing on ideas supplied by his wife, Harriet Taylor Mill, he wrote an essay, *The Subjection of Women* (1869), that had considerable impact, particularly on those in England who were pressing for democratic reforms. Reform moved faster in New Zealand, the first nation to give women the vote (in 1893), with the British following suit in 1918 (for some women) and 1928 (for all women).

As in other Western democracies, the initial target of the American feminist movement was suffrage. Reasoning that voting rights would lead to equal rights, Susan B. Anthony (1820–1906) spent most of her life campaigning for women's suffrage. Not until 1920 was that particular fight won with the passage and ratification of the Nineteenth Amendment.

The right to vote changed virtually nothing for American women. Males continued their domination in government, politics, the professions, business, and unions, thus provoking increasingly militant reactions. The latest, most powerful, and most effective feminist movement began in the 1960s in the general context of a push for equal rights for all Americans regardless of race, creed, sex, age, or national origin. A key work for the movement was *The Second Sex* (1949) by the French writer Simone de Beauvoir (1908–86). It was a brilliant exposition of misconceptions regarding women and their place in the world. But it was chiefly *The Feminine Mystique* (1963) by Betty Friedan (b. 1921) that sparked a wide popular reaction. Friedan analyzed the social and psychological pressures on women who were supposed to remain in the home and effectively attacked persistent stereotypes of feminine intellect and behavior.

By no means limited to women, the feminist movement includes many men who see the liberation of women as a necessary condition of freeing men from *their* traditional stereotypes. In fact, the proposed Equal Rights Amendment makes no reference to either sex.

LITERARY SELECTION 51

I Like to Think of Harriet Tubman
Susan Griffin, b. 1943

The women's movement toward equality in all areas of American life is far from over. Some say it has only begun. In this militant poem Susan Griffin cites Harriet Tubman as a heroic symbol of activism and freedom (fig. 27.1). Tubman (ca. 1820–1913) was an Abolitionist, an escaped slave who, before the Civil War, freed over 300 slaves through the Underground Railroad. During the Civil War she was a Union nurse, laundress, and spy.

I like to think of Harriet Tubman.
Harriet Tubman who carried a revolver,
who had a scar on her head from a rock thrown
by a slave-master (because she
talked back), and who
had a ransom on her head
of thousands of dollars and who
was never caught, and who
had no use for the law
when the law was wrong,   10
who defied the law. I like
to think of her.
I like to think of her especially
when I think of the problem of
feeding children.
The legal answer
to the problem of feeding children
is ten free lunches every month,
being equal, in the child's real life,
to eating lunch every other day.   20
Monday but not Tuesday.
I like to think of the President
eating lunch Monday, but not
Tuesday.
And when I think of the President
and the law, and the problem of
feeding children, I like to
think of Harriet Tubman
and her revolver.

---

4. Published in English in 1982 by Persea Books of New York.

27.1 Jacob Lawrence, *Harriet Tubman Series, No. 7.* 1939–40. Casein tempera on hardboard, 17⅛ × 12" (43.5 × 30.5 cm). Hampton University Museum, Hampton, Virginia.

And then sometimes   30
I think of the President
and other men,
men who practice the law,
who revere the law,
who make the law,
who enforce the law
who live behind
and operate through
and feed themselves
at the expense of   40
starving children
because of the law,
men who sit in paneled offices
and think about vacations
and tell women
whose care it is
to feed children

not to be hysterical
not to be hysterical as in the word
hysterikos, the Greek for   50
womb suffering,
not to suffer in their
wombs,
not to care,
not to bother the men
because they want to think
of other things
and do not want
to take the women seriously.
I want them   60
to take women seriously.
I want them to think about Harriet Tubman,
and remember,
remember she was beat by a white man
and she lived
and she lived to redress her grievances,
and she lived in swamps
and wore the clothes of a man
bringing hundreds of fugitives from
slavery, and was never caught,   70
and led an army,
and won a battle,
and defied the laws
because the laws were wrong, I want men
to take us seriously.
I am tired wanting them to think
about right and wrong.
I want them to fear.
I want them to feel fear now
as I have felt suffering in the womb, and   80
I want them
to know
that there is always a time
there is always a time to make right
what is wrong,
there is always a time
for retribution
and that time
is beginning.

STUDY QUESTIONS

1. You will note that the poem consists mostly of one- and two-syllable words with an occasional three-syllable word. There are only five different four-syllable words in the entire poem and two of these are related. What are the words? Is this a coincidence? What does the poet seem to have in mind?
2. What does Tubman's revolver signify?
3. What does Tubman herself symbolize?

RACISM

No one needs to be reminded that racism has always been a problem for the human race. There seems to be a fairly general human failing that compels one race or nation or society to feel and act superior to another. Whether this attitude is based on ignorance or arrogance, or both, there seems to be no limit to the amount of destruction inflicted on human potential and on human life itself. No nation or group of people is immune to the blight of bigotry and intolerance but that does not mean that the problem can ever be ignored.

The destructive effects of racism can be seen around the globe. In the United States there has been a shift from fighting for civil rights to combating racism as such. The Civil Rights Acts of 1964 and 1965 were positive steps that eliminated racial segregation in public places and established equal access to the voting booth. During the 1980s there was a shift from the quest for constitutional guarantees to a focus on changing attitudes; the effect of this thrust was to contend that the opinions, feelings, and prejudices of private individuals were legitimate targets for political action.

Many political leaders see this drive as not only inappropriate but dangerous. It is divisive because it divides humanity into "them" and "us." A member of "us" can see the self as victim; as a self-styled victim the person has endless opportunities for self-pity and self-righteous anger. This can lead to a society at war with itself because there is no constitutional right to be free from racism, anti-Semitism, or sexism. The legal principles of freedom and justice for all are established though certainly less than fully accomplished. The negative movement against racism can never accomplish its objective of eliminating prejudices held by individuals. What, then, is the solution to the abiding affliction of racism?

THE INFORMATION SOCIETY AND THE GLOBAL VILLAGE

During the several decades of civil rights and gender issues other fundamental changes were quietly transforming American life. Once a nation of farmers, the Industrial Revolution made laborers the dominant work force. By the mid-1950s, however, white-collar workers outnumbered blue-collar laborers; by the early 1990s the manufacturing work force had dwindled to about 13 percent and farmers to less than 3 percent of the working population. The United States and Canada had shifted from an industrial society to an information society based on high technology; computers, communication satellites, fax machines, modems, robots, and other electronic marvels herald what has been called, variously, the Age of Information, the Computer Age, or the Communications Age. By the early 1990s over 75 percent of all jobs were involved with high tech and the

products of high tech. Smokestack industries such as steel, textiles, and shipbuilding will probably continue to decline in the Western world as heavy industry expands in Third World countries that have large pools of cheap labor.

Not too many years ago children lived in a world not very different from that of their parents or grandparents. Information about the rest of the globe was confined to the printed word and technology was not even a word. The velocity of change was, metaphorically speaking, about ten miles an hour—the speed of a horse and buggy. In a society that was evolving almost imperceptibly, children tended to adopt the values, religion, and politics of their parents.

Today's world is so vastly different that comparisons boggle the mind. It has been estimated, for example, that human society has experienced more change during the past half-century than in all the preceding years of its history. The acceleration of change appears to be the single most important influence on our lives. We can choose a philosophical, religious, or humanistic point of view (probably very different from that of our parents), but we can neither avoid nor deny the reality of a future that so insistently crowds upon the present.

During the late 1960s Alvin Toffler wrote a book whose title, *Future Shock*, became a metaphor for the frustrations and anxieties thrust on us by the onslaught of rapid and relentless change. Toffler described the understandable reluctance of people to recognize and accept the existence of what he called the "accelerative thrust." The pace of change keeps quickening, keeps forcing people to cope with ever faster acceleration and still more future shock. Toffler's thesis was that the shock of change can be replaced by the recognition of change as the new reality of the late twentieth century. Change can be seen as proper and necessary in an age when process is reality. Children and young adults have made the transition with relative ease because rapid change is all that younger Americans have ever known. But many of those who once played 78 rpm records, placed phone calls through an operator, and are intimidated by computers have had their difficulties.

The magnitude of accelerating change can be comprehended by comparing the evolution of computers with the evolution of the automobile. If cars had progressed as rapidly as computers, a Rolls Royce today would:

1. cost $2.75
2. get 3 million miles per gallon
3. have enough power to propel the Queen Elizabeth II
4. fit six on the head of a pin.[5]

In a later book, *The Third Wave* (1980), Toffler predicted that individualized entertainment and information services would become readily available, and that there would be a whole new range of social, political, psychological, and religious adaptations throughout the Western

---

5. Paul Johnson, *Modern Times: The World from the Twenties to the Eighties* (New York: Harper & Row, 1983), pp. 128–9.

world and around the Pacific Basin: Japan, Korea, Hong Kong, Singapore, Taiwan, New Zealand, and Australia. No one is predicting any drastic changes (in the near future) for Third-World countries, especially those in sub-Saharan Africa, but some countries have managed to leapfrog over older technology—such as railroads—to land in the middle of the high-tech revolution.

Developing technology tends to follow the line of least resistance. The first book printed with movable type, the Gutenberg Bible, looked like a handwritten manuscript. The first automobiles were called "horseless carriages" because they were indeed motorized carriages. Early steamships were sailing ships outfitted with paddle wheels. Much computer usage has been concerned with improving older technology: faster computations, quicker information retrieval, and improved typewriting in the form of a word processor, and so on. No one can predict the different directions computers will take except to say that, inevitably, there will be startling new applications of computer technology.

Einstein gave us new conceptions of space, and the age of computers and telecommunications has forced us to recognize space as a concept connected by electronics and not just as a physical reality linked by interstate highways. International television with worldwide viewers, fax machines, modems, and other forms of rapidly evolving telecommunications have shrunk our earth to a Global Village. The late 1990s will see a fully operational commercial telephone network that will enable subscribers to phone absolutely anywhere in the world. All of Antarctica, New Guinea, and the backwaters of the Amazon will be as immediately accessible as our next-door neighbor. Moreover, the telephone connection will enable the caller to fax or transmit computerized material throughout the world. One important effect of electronic communications is to open all societies to the world outside despite the efforts of tyrants to control what their subjects can see and hear.

What will life be like in the Global Village? No one can predict what the globalization of culture will lead to, but the prognosis can be optimistic. The possibility of instantaneous close contact with people and their institutions can lead to closer human ties than at any time in human history.

SUMMARY

The long-awaited era of peace and prosperity that was supposed to follow World War II ended abruptly in 1949 when the Soviet Union joined the United States as a nuclear superpower. The next four decades saw a Cold War between the two powers highlighted by two very hot wars. Communist aggression was successfully resisted in South Korea, but not in Vietnam.

The widespread and surprisingly sudden collapse of Communist governments that began in 1989 was, of

course, the most important series of events in the late twentieth century. Though much has already been revealed, it may take years before the extent and degree of the damage to people, societies, and the environment will be fully known. The world has yet to recover fully from the Hitler years; the Lenin legacy will undoubtedly plague civilization for decades to come.

> The central tragedy of modern world history is that both the Russian and the German republics, in turn, found in Lenin and Hitler adversaries of quite exceptional calibre, who embodied the will to power to a degree unique in our time.[6]

Existentialism as developed by Kierkegaard, Nietzsche, and Jean-Paul Sartre is discussed as a significant postwar movement. Martin Luther King's "Letter from Birmingham Jail" outlines the strategy of non-violent resistance that helped make the Civil Rights movement effective in overcoming some barriers to equal opportunity. The poem "Harlem" by Langston Hughes predicted the racial violence that erupted in major American cities, violence that was precipitated by the realization that equal opportunity regardless of race still had a long way to go. Susan Griffin's poem "I Like to Think of Harriet Tubman" stresses the anger and frustration of women who deeply resent their position as the subordinate sex.

CULTURE AND HUMAN VALUES

The themes discussed and illustrated in this chapter were chosen to delineate some of the problems of our era. Though far from definitive, these are some of the important issues: civil rights, gender issues, violence, and racism. If there were a universal, overwhelming concern for human values and human rights, these problems would not exist—and we would be living in Utopia.

Violence seems to be a fact of human existence but there is no logical reason why a society cannot end overt discrimination and guarantee civil rights for everyone. This is no pipe dream but a goal that can be reached. Why, in the affluent world we are fortunate to inhabit, hasn't some kind of humane society come into being? Has there been enough time? Has there been enough effort?

There is another way to approach the problem. There have been three great technological revolutions in the history of humankind, all of which are still in progress:

1. Agricultural, 10,000 years ago;
2. Industrial, eighteenth and nineteenth centuries;

---

6. Christopher Evans, *The Micro Millennium* (New York: The Viking Press, 1980), p. 4.

3. Information, late nineteenth and twentieth centuries.

New discoveries are still being made in agriculture, robotics in home and industry is in its infancy, and who knows where the knowledge explosion will lead? If virtue is knowledge and ignorance is vice, as Aristotle, Socrates, and other Greeks contended, then perhaps the knowledge eruption can eventually lead the peoples of the world to form more rational and humane societies. Rapidly increasing scientific and technological knowledge can certainly improve our material existence; one must always consider the impact of technology on all of us.

> The universalizing imperative of technology is irresistible . . . it will continue to shape both modern culture and the consciousness of those who inhabit that culture.[7]

Moreover, knowledge tends to lead to greater tolerance of the differences between individuals and between the varieties of cultures, an acceptance of diversity that can help offset the bane of intolerance and its spin-offs of prejudice, bigotry, sexism, and racism. More than at any time in human history, we seem to be acquiring the means to make this a better world for all humankind.

Noted futurist Peter Drucker says that we are already deep in a new and vastly different century and living in what he calls a post-business society. The business values of enterprise and profit, according to Drucker, have receded before the growth of such values as knowledge and fuller development of human potential. That we are living in a knowledge society should be apparent to everyone. We already have the technology for self-teaching that will enable everyone to learn subjects while teachers are freed to teach people. Consequently, we can expect an acceleration in the rate of change in our educational system, particularly in light of the changes taking place in the rival trading nations in Europe and Asia.

Other authorities feel that we are living in what they call the post-modern world. In the modern movement in art, for example, artists sought originality and novelty and denied virtually the whole of the past. The postmodern movement in architecture (see p. 517) appears to reflect a general proclivity to depart from the *avant-garde* tendencies of most of this century, a desire to integrate much of the recent past with contemporary Western culture and, to some extent, non-Western cultures. There is a search for human values in the context of a global civilization. This movement seems to be, in part, a reaction to the speedily evolving Information Age and the growing realization that our world is becoming a Global Village. Another factor is the recognition that a mind-set that denies the past is severely hampered when trying to confront the complexities of contemporary life. Many feel that we have lost our way in this bewildering world and that we can improve our lives by incorporating elements from the Enlightenment, the Renaissance, the Middle Ages, even the Greek and Roman worlds. The previous values of novelty, originality, of being different have little appeal when we are constantly reminded that people of any age are no different from men and women of today. The world is changing rapidly but people haven't changed at all. Progress, success, invention, and innovation may be false gods that have nothing to do with such human values as truth, justice, love, family, fidelity, integrity, and honor. "Value education" is a buzz phrase in public education but one wonders how values are "taught." Values are learned from families, institutions, artists, philosophers, writers.

Finally, we should always keep in mind the profound question posed by philosopher William Barrett:

> What shall it profit a whole civilization, or culture, if it gains knowledge and power over the material world, but loses any adequate idea of the conscious mind, the human self, at the center of all that power?[8]

---

7. O. B. Hardison, Jr., *Disappearing through the Skylight: Culture and Technology in the Twentieth Century* (New York: Viking Penguin, 1989), p. 144.

8. William Barrett, *Death of the Soul: From Descartes to the Computer* (Garden City, N.Y.: Anchor Press/Doubleday, 1986), p. 56.

Art in the Twentieth Century: Shock Waves and Reactions

Art is either a plagiarist or a revolutionist.

Paul Gauguin

Would you realize what Revolution is, call it Progress; and would you realize what Progress is, call it Tomorrow.

Victor Hugo

PRELUDE

The beginnings of modern art can be traced back to the revolutionary innovations of Edouard Manet, especially as exemplified in his *Olympia* (see fig. 25.21). Manet insisted that the actual subject matter was "light," but the artist's response to the rapidly changing world about him was visible on the canvas. *Olympia* was a naked prostitute from Manet's contemporary world. She gazed unconcernedly at a shocked public that still expected art to be an academic enterprise, drawing its subject matter from myths and legends and instructing the viewer in the beauty of color and line. This was, however, the Age of Progress, the industrial era of cities, factories, slums, trains, Marx, Darwin, and Bismarck. The Renaissance tradition was no longer adequate or even appropriate. The Impressionists did paint from nature but even Monet painted many views of a Parisian train station crowded with powerful locomotives emitting clouds of steam. Gauguin fled to Polynesia to escape a civilization that he saw as corrupt and diseased. Cézanne's sources were nature, people, and objects of the world in which he lived, not stories and myths of the past. The contemporary world was the basis for the new reality of painting. The stage was set for the advent of modernism.

Opposite Marc Chagall, *I and the Village.* 1911. Oil on canvas, 6' 3⅜" × 4' 11⅝" (1.92 × 1.51 m). The Museum of Modern Art, New York (Mrs. Simon Guggenheim Fund). Photo: © 1996 The Museum of Modern Art, New York, © ADAGP, Paris and DACS, London 1995.

ARTISTIC STYLES TO 1945

Fauvism and Expressionism

Henri Matisse, 1869–1954

Modern art was in the air in 1905, especially in Collioure, a fishing port on the French Mediterranean coast a few miles from the Spanish border. Summering there with his family and a fellow artist, Matisse (ma-teess) saw some Tahitian paintings by Gauguin and was forcibly reminded of Gauguin's contention that color was whatever the artist perceived it to be. Still searching for a style, Matisse had become dissatisfied with copying nature as an Impressionist and he refused to even consider the dots-of-color technique of Seurat. At age thirty-six he found his style in Collioure. In the sparkling southern light he began painting in bold colors with broad and exuberant brushstrokes; he would delight in color for the rest of a long and marvelously productive career. When he displayed some of his Collioure pictures in Paris at the 1905 **Salon d'Automne**, critics were outraged, claiming that the "blotches of barbaric color" bore no relationship to real painting. There was, in fact, a whole room full of wildly colorful paintings by Matisse, his Collioure colleague, André Derain, and other French artists. Perhaps seeking to localize the repercussions, the judges assigned all their paintings to Room VII, leading the horrified public to believe that this was an organized school with Matisse, the eldest, as its leader. A critic's remark about a room full of *fauves* (Fr., "wild beasts")[1] gave the group a name, and critical and public hostility helped create a movement. For a public still unfamiliar with the works of van Gogh and Gauguin, Fauve paintings were shocking. Color was, after all, *true;* apples were red and trees were green. In *The Blue Window* (fig. 28.2) Matisse painted a landscape that is also a still life. The lampshade is green but the beautifully rounded trees in the background are blue. They are, nevertheless, still perceived as trees in an

---

1. Though commonly translated as "wild beasts," *fauves* actually means "deer"; the French call wild beasts *les grands fauves.*

28.2 Henri Matisse, *The Blue Window (Summer 1913)*. Oil on canvas, 51½ × 35⅜" (130.8 × 87.7 cm). The Museum of Modern Art, New York (Abby Aldrich Rockefeller Fund). Photo: © 1996 The Museum of Modern Art, New York, © Succession H. Matisse/DACS 1995.

elegantly cool and decorative composition of curving shapes within a series of carefully proportioned rectangles. Color has been freed to become whatever the artist wants it to be.

Marguerite Thompson Zorach, 1887–1968
American artist Thompson went to Paris in 1908 to study in the academic tradition at the Ecole des Beaux-Arts but her visit to the Salon d'Automne, where she saw the new art of Matisse and other Fauvists, changed everything. Entirely captivated by the new style, she became an active participant in the *avant-garde* intellectual life and a noted Fauvist in her own right. Her *Man Among the Redwoods* (fig. 28.1) is a richly decorated California landscape done with strong, pure colors and lavish brushwork. She later established her studio in New York, where she married the modern sculptor William Zorach.

28.1 *Opposite* Marguerite Thompson Zorach, *Man Among the Redwoods*. 1912. Oil on canvas, 25¾ × 20¼" (65.4 × 51.4 cm). Private collection, Hockessin, Delaware.

German Expressionism
Käthe Kollwitz, 1867–1945
German artists were more concerned with political and social conditions before and after World War I than were the French, and none more so than Kollwitz. Both a sculptor and a graphic artist, Kollwitz became, in 1918, the first woman to be elected to a professorship in the Prussian Academy of Arts and, later, the first woman to head a department there. A socialist and a feminist, she concentrated on themes of poverty and injustice, and the difficulty of being a woman and mother in militaristic Prussia. Her *Raped* from her "Peasants' War" series is an early depiction of the criminal violation from a woman's point of view. In *Unemployment* (fig. 28.3) the exhausted mother stares numbly at the viewer, her newborn baby on her chest, her other child nestled down in the bed. The baby is presumably a girl. When first published the print's caption read: "If they are not used as soldiers they at least deserve to be treated as children." Kollwitz's lifelong campaign against German militarism began well before her personal tragedies. Her son was killed in combat in World War I and her grandson met the same fate in World War II.

28.3 Käthe Kollwitz, *Unemployment*. 1909. Print, 7 × 5" (17.8 × 12.7 cm). Preussischer Kulturbesitz, Kupferstichkabinett, Staatliche Museen, Berlin. Photo: © DACS 1995.

Wassily Kandinsky, 1866–1944
The expressive qualities of strong color also impressed some Russian artists, especially Kandinsky. Russia had a long history of robust colors derived from its Byzantine tradition, which Kandinsky realized as he studied the intense colors of richly decorated peasant clothing, furniture, and houses. After moving to Munich he began painting in the German Expressionist style. It was not until about 1908 that he discovered, apparently accidentally, that color could operate independently of subjects. Red, for example, need

not be on an apple nor green on a tree; colors could function in expressive compositions without representing specific objects. Called the first Abstract Expressionist as early as 1919, Kandinsky developed theories about the spiritual qualities of colors and the interrelationship of music and art. As with many of his contemporaries, Kandinsky felt that the world was headed for disaster and that there was a real need for a spiritual rebirth in art and in life. He equated representational art with the materialism that appeared to be corrupting society, and thus removed all objective references from his paintings in an attempt to return to spiritual values. In *Painting Number 198* (also known as *Panel 3* or *Summer*; fig. 28.4) he created what can be described as "visual poetry" or "visual music," a celebration of the warmth and brightness of summer. That this work was completed in the year in which the Great War engulfed most of Europe may or may not be coincidental.

Cubism and Other Abstractions

Pablo Picasso, 1881–1973

The most famous and successful artist of this century, Picasso was a one-man art movement whose innovations throughout a long and enormously productive career make him impossible to classify or categorize. He is discussed under this heading because he, along with Georges Braque (brack; 1882–1963), invented Cubism.

Picasso's studies of ancient Iberian sculptures and African masks led him to produce a painting of five nude women that astonished and horrified art dealers, and even his friends. Unlike anything ever seen in art, *Les Demoiselles d'Avignon* (fig. 28.5) represented a breakthrough as epochal as Masaccio's *Tribute Money* (see fig. 17.8) at the beginning of the Italian Renaissance. Masaccio established Renaissance perspective; Picasso destroyed it with this painting. Just about all the rules were broken by his innovations: flat picture plane with no single point of perspective; angular and fragmented bodies; distorted faces with enormous eyes; two figures wearing grotesque African-like masks. With a remarkable economy of means Picasso created tense and massive figures whose heads and facial features are seen simultaneously in full-face and profile, marking a great step forward in the evolution of Cubism. A friend of the artist added the title later, a reference to a brothel on Avignon Street in Barcelona. About this painting Picasso remarked

28.4 *Above* Wassily Kandinsky, *Painting Number 198*. 1914. Oil on canvas, 64 × 36½" (162.5 × 92.1 cm). The Museum of Modern Art, New York (Mrs. Simon Guggenheim Fund). Photo: © 1996 The Museum of Modern Art, New York.

28.5 Pablo Picasso, *Les Demoiselles d'Avignon*. Paris, June to July 1907. Oil on canvas, 8' × 7' 8" (2.44 × 2.34 m). The Museum of Modern Art, New York (Acquired through the Lillie P. Bliss Bequest). Photo: © 1996 The Museum of Modern Art, New York, © DACS 1995.

28.6 Pablo Picasso, *Still Life*. 1918. Oil on canvas, 38¼ × 51¼" (97.2 × 130.2 cm). National Gallery of Art, Washington, D.C. (Chester Dale Collection). Photo: © DACS 1995.

28.7 Pablo Picasso, *Guernica*. 1937. Oil on canvas, 25' 5¾" × 11' 5½" (7.77 × 3.49 m). Museo del Prado, Madrid. Photo: © DACS 1995.

that "nature has to exist so that we may rape it!" Braque commented that it made him feel "that someone was drinking gasoline and spitting fire."

Picasso and Braque took Cubism through several phases, from a faceting of three-dimensional figures to flattened images and rearranged forms. In *Still Life* (fig. 28.6) Picasso uses forms from the "real" world to confuse reality and illusion. All is two-dimensional, and shadows cast by objects on the tilted tabletop further add to the confusion. What is reality here? Actually, colors and forms on canvas. Inspired in part by Cézanne's compressed forms (see fig. 25.28), Cubism was a refutation of the Mediterranean classical heritage as the sole model for creating and viewing art.

During the afternoon of 26 April 1937 the Spanish Civil War came home to the Spanish artist living in Paris. German bombers of the Condor Legion destroyed over 70 percent of the Basque town of Guernica and, twenty-five sketches and one month later, Picasso had completed his anguished protest against the brutal destruction of a defenseless town (fig. 28.7). The central figure is a wounded horse that, according to the artist, represents the people, whereas the bull symbolizes the pitiless brutality of fascism. Possibly representing the threatened Light of Reason, a light bulb is superimposed on the blazing sun. Painted on an enormous scale in a stark black, white, and gray, the work is a monumental protest against the impersonal cruelty of modern warfare. At the bottom center is one small symbol of life, a fragile flower above the broken sword. Picasso decreed that the work would remain on loan to the Museum of Modern Art in New York until democracy was restored in Spain. After difficult negotiations with heirs, politicians, and two art museums, the painting was officially inaugurated in Madrid on 24 October 1981.

American Modernists

Georgia O'Keeffe, 1887–1986

Undoubtedly reflecting her American training, O'Keeffe applied abstract concepts to American themes. She took special delight in painting organic forms found in the Southwest, to which she moved permanently after the death of her husband, the celebrated photographer Alfred Stieglitz. *Jack-in-the-Pulpit, No. 5* (fig. 28.8) is from the numerous series of floral images that she painted for over forty years, steering a middle path between nature and abstraction. Her imagery is a unique combination of graceful representation and elegant geometry.

28.8   Georgia O'Keeffe, *Jack-in-the-Pulpit, No. 5*. 1930. Oil on canvas, 48 × 30" (121.9 × 76.2 cm). National Gallery of Art, Washington, D.C. (Alfred Stieglitz Collection, Bequest of Georgia O'Keeffe). Photo: © ARS, New York and DACS, London 1995.

28.9   Alfred Stieglitz, *The Terminal*. Ca. 1890. Photograph. Art Institute of Chicago (Alfred Stieglitz Collection).

Alfred Stieglitz, 1864–1946

O'Keeffe and her husband operated the Little Gallery of the Photo-Secession that Stieglitz had earlier opened at 291 Fifth Avenue in New York. At "291," as the art world called it, the arts of photography and painting coexisted. Advocating "straight photography," Stieglitz used no gimmicks, relying instead on his eye, his camera, and his lens. Lonely in New York after nine years of study abroad, he came upon *The Terminal* (fig. 28.9), and captured a moment in a world of horse-drawn streetcars, quaint streetlamps, and men in bowler hats. In this photograph we share a personal instant in the life of the photographer.

Stieglitz was the strongest and most persuasive advocate of photography as an art form, but he was even more dedicated to the promotion of modern painting. His gallery showed, for the first time in America, works by Cézanne, Picasso, Toulouse-Lautrec, Rodin, Matisse, Brancusi, and Henri Rousseau.

The Armory Show

Early American abstract artists, like their European counterparts, had to combat the hostility of a public accustomed to representational art and the opposition of academicians and the Ash Can school (see p. 496). The modernists of "291" ended the internecine warfare by inducing academicians and Ash Can artists to form, in 1911, the Association of American Artists and Painters. An exhibition of contemporary American art was to be the first project, but the end result was the epochal New York Armory Show of 1913, still the most controversial exhibition ever staged in the United States. Convinced that the public was ready for new ideas, the organizers included European modernists in what was officially termed the International Exhibition of Modern Art. Works by Cézanne, Rousseau, Gauguin, van

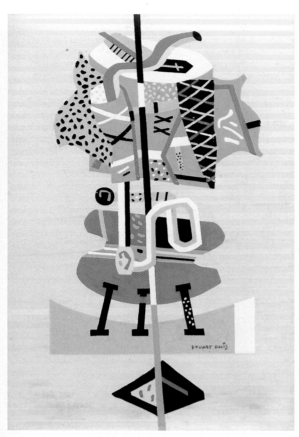

28.10 Stuart Davis, *Radio Tubes*. 1940. Gouache, 22 × 14" (55.9 × 35.6 cm). University Art Collections, Arizona State University (Gift of Oliver B. James). Photo: © Estate of Stuart Davis/DACS, London/VAGA, New York 1995.

28.11 Piet Mondrian, *Composition with Red, Blue, Yellow, Black, and Gray*. 1936. Oil on canvas, 16½ × 19" (41.9 × 48.3 cm). Toledo Museum of Art, Toledo, Ohio (Purchased with funds from the Libbey Endowment; Gift of Edward Drummond Libbey, 1978).

Gogh, Matisse, Duchamp, and Picasso astounded and infuriated artists, critics, and most of all the public. The shocked organizers dismissed the public reaction as militant ignorance, which it was, but American modernists were dismayed to see how far behind they themselves were. The Armory Show was "the greatest single influence that I have experienced," said Stuart Davis (1894–1964) as he altered his style and, like many other American artists, sailed to Paris. His Cubistic *Radio Tubes* (fig. 28.10) is a characteristically whimsical celebration of American technology at a time when advanced technology was naively thought to be uniquely American. Contending that the camera was the proper instrument for recording facts, Davis believed, as did most modernists, that his function was to make new statements. Though influenced by European Cubism, *Radio Tubes* is, in its own way, as American as the work of Georgia O'Keeffe.

Piet Mondrian, 1872–1944
Though he was attracted to the work of the French Cubists, the Dutch artist Mondrian felt that their art did not express what he called "pure reality." He sought "plastic expression" in a basic reality made up solely of colors and forms that had their own spiritual values. *Composition with Red, Blue, Yellow, Black, and Gray* (fig. 28.11) is a precisely balanced work in a style generally called Geometric Abstraction. No two of the rectangles are of the same size or shape nor are all the heavy black lines the same width. The poised serenity of Mondrian's "composition" is as classical as a Greek temple. His ideas influenced many artists but they have also been popularized, in simplified and sometimes distorted versions, in fashion, interior, and advertising design.

Constantin Brancusi, 1876–1957
The Romanian sculptor Brancusi (bran-KOOSH) was first influenced by Rodin when studying in Paris, but developed an abstract style that influenced many artists. His *Bird in Space* (fig. 28.12) conveys, in an elegantly swelling shape, the soaring spirit of flight. It is a magnificent work of transcendental beauty that epitomizes the sculptor's statement: "I bring you pure joy."

Fantasy

Marc Chagall, 1889–1985
Fantasy plays a large part in twentieth-century art, with the Russian artist Chagall (shah-GALL) a leading exponent. Chagall combines Fauve color and Cubist forms with a personal vision of his early life in a Russian village. In *I and the Village* (see chapter opener on p. 484) cow and peasant speak to each other; a peasant marches up the street after his wife, who floats upside down; and a magic tree grows out of a hand. Chagall's paintings are meant to be enjoyed as enchanting pictorial arrangements of images that fascinated the artist.

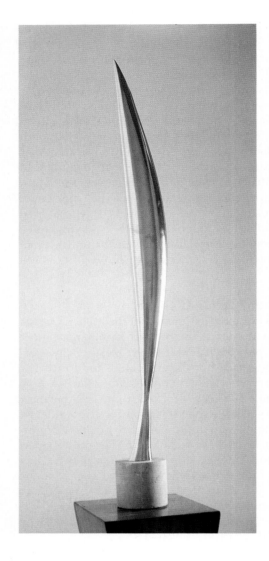

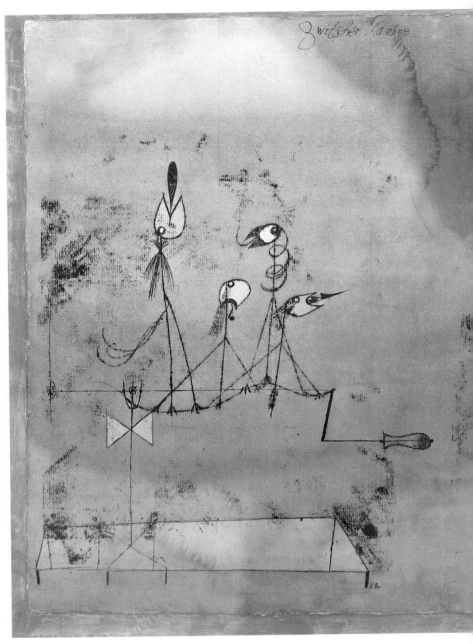

28.12 Constantin Brancusi, *Bird in Space*. Ca. 1928. Polished bronze, unique cast, 54 × 8½ × 6½" (137.2 × 21.6 × 16.5 cm). The Museum of Modern Art, New York (Given anonymously). Photo: © 1996 The Museum of Modern Art, New York, © ADAGP, Paris and DACS, London, 1995.

28.13 Paul Klee, *Twittering Machine*. 1922. Watercolor, pen, and ink on oil transfer drawing on paper, mounted on cardboard, 25¼ × 19" (64.1 × 48.3 cm). The Museum of Modern Art, New York (Purchase). Photo: © 1996 The Museum of Modern Art, New York.

Paul Klee, 1879–1940

The German-Swiss artist Klee (klay) was a master of fantasy. Through his teaching at the Bauhaus (see fig. 28.27) and his painting, Klee was one of the most influential artists of the century. Rejecting illusionistic art as obsolete, he turned to the art of children and primitives as inspiration for his paintings. *Twittering Machine* (fig. 28.13) is a whimsical fantasy of stick-figure birds twittering soundlessly in an unknown language. The "machine" is apparently an industrial concoction of no conceivable use.

28.14 Giorgio de Chirico, *The Nostalgia of the Infinite*. Ca. 1913–14 (?), dated 1911 on the painting. Oil on canvas, 53¼ × 25½" (135.3 × 64.8 cm). The Museum of Modern Art, New York (Purchase). Photo: © 1996 The Museum of Modern Art, New York, © DACS 1995.

Giorgio de Chirico, 1888–1979

The fantasies of de Chirico (day KEE-re-ko) were as subjective as those of Chagall but infused with pessimism and melancholy. Like Kandinsky and other intellectuals, de Chirico perceived a sick society defiled by materialism. Born in Greece of Italian parents, he studied in Athens and, like many other artists of the time, wound up in Paris, where he studied the Old Masters in the Louvre. Strongly influenced by the German philosopher Nietzsche (see p. 474), de Chirico looked on himself as a metaphysical painter who explored the mysteries of life. In *The Nostalgia of the Infinite* (fig. 28.14) he employed a distorted Renaissance perspective in a characteristic dreamlike cityscape in which everything is real, except that it isn't. Pennants are flying vigorously from a sinister and threatening tower in front

of which two minuscule figures cast disproportionately long shadows. Like most of his images, this building actually exists (in Turin), but the strange juxtaposition creates another reality that is not of the waking world.

Dada

Marcel Duchamp, 1887–1968

As early as 1914 it had become obvious to some artists that World War I marked the low point of a bankrupt Western culture. In February of 1916 some exiles from the war that was consuming Europe formed, in neutral Switzerland, the Cabaret Voltaire, a loose-knit and contentious group devoted to attacking everything that Western civilization held dear. These writers, artists, musicians, and poets chose the word *Dada* to identify their iconoclastic movement, a word intended as nonsense but immediately adopted by acclamation. Dada was an idea whose time had come, for it had happened even earlier in New York with the arrival, in 1915, of Marcel Duchamp (due-shā). Duchamp was the greatest exponent of the "anti-art" movement known as Dada, having already turned "found" objects into art by,

28.15 Marcel Duchamp, *The Large Glass; The Bride Stripped Bare by Her Bachelors, Even*. 1915–23. Oil, lead wire and foil, and dust and varnish on plate glass (in two parts), front 9' 1¼" × 5' 9⅛" (2.77 × 1.76 m). Philadelphia Museum of Art (Bequest of Katherine S. Dreier). Photo: © ADAGP, Paris and DACS, London 1995.

for example, hanging a snow shovel on a gallery wall and labelling it *In Advance of a Broken Arm*. He made the first mobile in 1913 by fastening an inverted bicycle wheel to the top of a stool and presenting it as a sculpture with moving parts. Typical of his assault on the citadel of art was a reproduction of the *Mona Lisa* to which he added a mustache and a goatee and the title of *L.H.O.O.Q.* that, when pronounced letter by letter in French, means "She's got a hot ass."

Duchamp found a congenial home in Stieglitz's "291" and began work on what turned out to be his greatest Dada work, the enigmatically titled *The Bride Stripped Bare by Her Bachelors, Even,* commonly referred to as *The Large Glass* (fig. 28.15). The following analysis is based on Duchamp's notes that, given the artist's proclivity for paradox and irony, may be accepted, modified, or rejected. According to Duchamp, this is the story of a bride, located in the upper section and symbolized by an internal combustion engine with a reservoir of love gasoline and a magneto of desire. She is lusted after by the nine bachelors in the left lower section: the reddish-brown molds resembling chessmen. Each bachelor is a stereotype of what were, at the time, masculine occupations: priest, delivery boy, policeman, warrior, gendarme, undertaker's assistant, busboy, stationmaster, and flunky. Capillary tubes carry gas from each bachelor mold to the center of the glass and to one of seven funnels, where the gas solidifies into large needles. These needles, in turn, break into spangles of frosty gas and then into liquid drops of semen that splash into the bride's domain. At the moment depicted in the glass the bride is stripped but she remains undefiled; bride and bachelors are caught between desire and possession/surrender. Duchamp intended the work to be humorous and sexual, satirizing machines, people, and social conventions.

Surrealism

The Dada movement was generally absorbed by the Surrealists, who coalesced around the Manifesto of Surrealism issued in 1924 by the writer André Breton, a disciple of Sigmund Freud. Surrealism in art is, briefly stated, the theory that dreams, and those waking moments when subconscious images overwhelm our intellect, furnish us with material far more relevant to our lives than traditional subject matter. The world of psychic experience, as explored by Freud and others, was to be combined with consciousness to create a super-reality called Surrealism.

Joan Miró, 1893–1983

Surrealism was an organized movement in revolt against conventional art and society, but there was no single style. Artists like Miró (ME-row) drew on their personal dreamworlds. In *Person Throwing a Stone at a Bird* (fig. 28.16) Miró does not abstract the human image but seems, instead, to humanize abstractions. In a witty and humorous style,

28.16   Joan Miró, *Person Throwing a Stone at a Bird*. 1926. Oil on canvas, 29 × 36¼" (73.7 × 92.1 cm). The Museum of Modern Art, New York (Purchase). Photo: © 1996 The Museum of Modern Art, New York, © ADAGP, Paris and DACS, London 1995.

sometimes called Biomorphic Abstraction, he creates an amoebic person with one huge foot, bulbous body, and orange and yellow eye. This being seems to fall back in wonder as an oblong stone falls toward an appealing bird with a crescent torso from which a longline neck projects to a lavender head topped by a flaming cock's comb. This is super-reality. "Everything in my pictures exists," stated Miró; "there is nothing abstract in my pictures."

Salvador Dali, 1904–89

The self-appointed spokesman of the Surrealist movement, Dali (DAH-lee) stressed paradox, disease, decay, and eroticism. *The Persistence of Memory* (fig. 28.17) is a tiny painting of a vast landscape in which watches hang limply and dejectedly. A strange chinless creature with protruding tongue (alive? dead?) lies in the foreground of a Renaissance perspective construction lit by an eerie glow. A dead tree grows out of a table (?) on which the only flat watch lies, a metal timepiece infested with sinister-looking bugs. Anything is possible in dreams.

Meret Oppenheim, 1913–85

Startling distortions or juxtapositions are basic to Surrealism, as Oppenheim's *Object* (fig. 28.18) demonstrates. The absurdity of a fur-lined teacup has become a symbol of Surrealism. Her now familiar but bizarre ensemble is typical of the push-pull effect of many Surrealist works. Our intellect is titillated, but our senses of touch and taste are outraged.

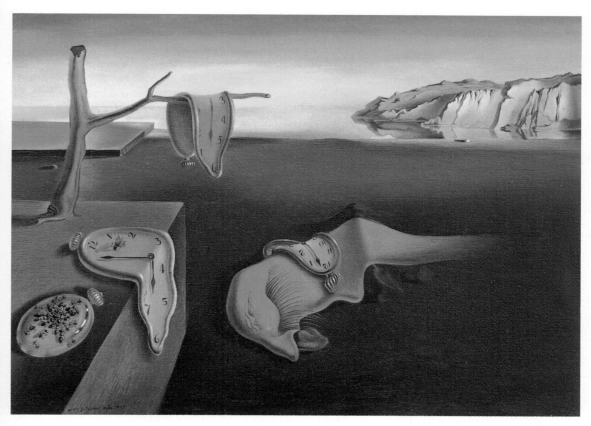

28.17 Salvador Dali, *The Persistence of Memory (Persistance de la mémoire).* 1931. Oil on canvas, 9½ × 13" (24.1 × 33 cm). The Museum of Modern Art, New York (Purchase). Photo: © 1996 The Museum of Modern Art, New York, © DEMART PRO ARTE BV/DACS 1995.

28.18 Meret Oppenheim, *Object.* 1936. Fur-covered cup, saucer, and spoon; diameter of cup 4¾" (12.1 cm); diameter of saucer 9⅜" (23.7 cm); length of spoon 8" (20.3 cm); overall height 2⅞" (7.3 cm). The Museum of Modern Art, New York (Purchase). Photo: © 1996 The Museum of Modern Art, New York, © DACS 1995.

René Magritte, 1898–1967

Belgian Surrealist Magritte was a witty, even mischievous, painter who consistently questioned the nature of reality by representing ordinary images in a strange and extraordinary manner. *The False Mirror* (fig. 28.19) portrays a huge but recognizable human eye with an iris of fluffy clouds in a blue sky. Are we looking into someone's eye while viewing the world from within that other organ? Or?

28.19 René Magritte, *The False mirror (Le Faux Miroir).* 1928. Oil on canvas, 21¼ × 31⅞" (54 × 81 cm). The Museum of Modern Art, New York (Purchase). Photo: © 1996 The Museum of Modern Art, New York, © ADAGP, Paris and DACS, London 1995.

28.20   Frida Kahlo, *The Two Fridas*. 1939. Oil on canvas, 5' 9" × 5' 9" (1.75 × 1.75 m). Museum of Modern Art, Mexico City.

Frida Kahlo, 1910–54

Mexican artist Kahlo is usually identified as a Surrealist because of the intensity of her paintings, her depiction of inner life and thought, and her unexpected, even strange arrangement of images. Kahlo, however, saw Surrealism as inherently misogynistic with women treated as objects of male fantasies. Further, she disavowed Surrealism because she claimed to be painting her own reality. *The Two Fridas*

(fig. 28.20) depicts the reality of her divorce from Mexican muralist Diego Rivera. Dressed in a traditional Mexican wedding dress, the Frida on the left is the woman Rivera loved. The other Frida is the modern and independent feminist whom he abandoned. The Fridas hold hands but the artery joining them has been ruptured. The divorced Frida uses forceps but cannot stop the flow of blood. In constant pain because she was injured for life by a streetcar accident, Kahlo painted her uncompromising works from a wheelchair.

Realism in America: The Ash Can School

From the early days of the Republic there has always been a strain of realism on the American scene, a tradition separate from European realists like Courbet and Millet. While European artists were experimenting with Impressionism, Americans such as Winslow Homer and Thomas Eakins (see figs. 25.16 and 25.17) continued to paint reality as they perceived it.

At the beginning of this century Robert Henri (hen-RYE; 1865–1929) founded a new school of realism called The Eight. Working almost entirely in New York, the followers of Henri painted city scenes of tenement life and everyday activities, mainly of the working class. A derogatory remark by a critic gave still another new style a label. After the caustic comment that they "even painted ash cans," The Eight proudly bore the label of Ash Can school.

John Sloan, 1871–1951

Sloan painted *Roof Gossips* (fig. 28.21) as if the three women on the tenement roof were the subject of a casual snapshot. Actually, the work is an artful composition of lines and forms. Reminiscent of the high viewpoint of Mary Cassatt's *The*

28.21   John Sloan, *Roof Gossips*. Ca. 1912. Oil on canvas, 24 × 20" (60 × 50.8 cm). University Art Collections, Arizona State University (Gift of Oliver B. James).

28.22   Edward Hopper, *Nighthawks*. 1942. Oil on canvas, 33 × 60" (83.8 × 152.4 cm). Art Institute of Chicago.

Bath (see fig. 25.24), we witness an intimate and relaxed scene but are not a part of it. Academicians were critical of the gritty realism of Sloan and the Ash Can school but they collaborated with them and the *avant-garde* of "291" to present the Armory Show the year after this work was painted.

Edward Hopper, 1882–1967
A student of Henri's in the early 1900s, Hopper was more concerned with formal design than were his Ash Can colleagues. He was fascinated with lonely people isolated in the urban landscape, with empty streets, with windows looking on vacant streets and the like. His *Nighthawks* (fig. 28.22) has a typical broad horizontal base and a scene starkly free of details, with a sharp contrast between the subdued buildings in the background and the garish lighting in the all-night café. Sitting speechless in isolated loneliness at the counter, the three figures convey both a melancholy mood and the aching anonymity so characteristic of urban life. The signs and advertising symbols present in many of Hopper's works may be a wry commentary on his other career as a commercial artist.

Horace Pippin, 1888–1946
A notable artist in the manner of colonial artisan-painters, Pippin was a self-taught painter whose style can be

28.23   Horace Pippin, *Victorian Interior*. 1946. Oil on canvas, 25¼ × 30" (64.1 × 76.2 cm). Metropolitan Museum of Art, New York (Arthur Hoppock Hearn Fund, 1958.58.26).

described as modernized abstractions of folk art traditions. Unlike the French primitive, Henri Rousseau, Pippin was acclaimed in his lifetime and his works were acquired by major American museums. One of his most elegant paintings is *Victorian Interior* (fig. 28.23). At first glance the painting appears closely related to simple folk art, but further study reveals a complex arrangement of strong color and selected areas of intricate linear designs. The end result

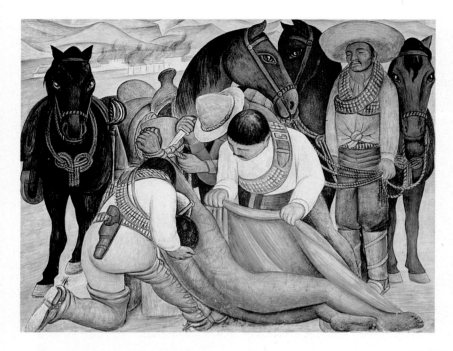

28.24   Diego Rivera, *The Liberation of the Peon*. 1931. Fresco, 6' 2" × 7' 11" (1.88 × 2.41 m). Philadelphia Museum of Art (Gift of Mr. and Mrs Herbert Cameron Morris).

is a happy medium between primitive folk art and modernism. Pippin was not a member of the Ash Can school, but his wry and unique style adds another dimension to realism.

Mexican Social Realists

Diego Rivera, 1886–1957
Though he lived and studied in Europe for many years, Rivera disavowed modernism in his zeal to create a distinctly Mexican style in the socialist spirit of the protracted Mexican revolution (1910–40). Rivera's statements were usually political and consistently on the side of the vast Mexican underclass. In *The Liberation of the Peon* (fig. 28.24) he shows revolutionary soldiers tenderly wrapping the body of a peon, or worker, who has been tortured and then murdered. The victim's bound hands are being "liberated," echoing the only freedom that a peasant could expect: death that freed him from a life of grinding poverty and ceaseless toil.

José Clemente Orozco, 1883–1949
Orozco was even more strongly influenced by Mexican Indian traditions than was Rivera, perhaps because he received much of his training in Mexico City. Like Rivera, his teacher and collaborator, he was deeply committed to the revolution. His *Zapatistas* (fig. 28.25) is a prime example of the painterly illusion of rhythm. Moving from right to left, the Zapatistas set up a kind of beat in a pattern of continuous movement that symbolizes the ongoing revolution. Along with Pancho Villa, Emiliano Zapata (ca. 1879–1919) was one of the leaders of the revolution; the representation here is of some of his loyal Indian followers.

28.25   José Orozco, *Zapatistas*. 1931. Oil on canvas, 3' 9" × 4' 7" (1.14 × 1.4 m). The Museum of Modern Art, New York (Given anonymously). Photo: © 1996 The Museum of Modern Art, New York.

David Alfaro Siqueiros, 1896–1974
Siqueiros (see-KEER-ohs) was a most politically active artist, who served a prison term for his leftist views. Though his early painting was heavy on Marxist ideology, his later work was directed more to humanistic concerns and universal problems. His *Echo of a Scream* (fig. 28.26) is a dramatic protest against the insanity of war. Set in the midst

28.26 David Alfaro Siqueiros, *Echo of a Scream*. 1937. Enamel on wood, 48 × 36" (121.9 × 91.4 cm). The Museum of Modern Art, New York (Gift of Edward M. M. Warburg). Photo: © 1996 The Museum of Modern Art, New York.

28.27 Walter Gropius, The Bauhaus, Dessau, Germany. 1925–6. Photo: Esto, New York (Wayne Andrews).

of a wasteland of debris, the enlarged head of the screaming child is the overwhelming center of attention. Forced to concentrate on the child's agonized face, we are confronted with the artist's passionate indictment of the madness called war. Edvard Munch's *The Scream* (see fig. 25.35) expressed the artist's reaction to critical tensions of the modern world: alienation, desperation, terror. In his painting Siqueiros has particularized the tensions into a single issue, an anti-war statement that appeared just two years before Hitler invaded Poland to launch World War II.

Architecture

The International Style

Walter Gropius, 1883–1969
The design school called the Bauhaus (BOUGH-house; fig. 28.27) was built expressly to exploit modern technology. As director of the Bauhaus, Gropius promoted instruction in painting, sculpture, architecture, and the crafts, with everything oriented toward the latest in technology and industrial design. As he wrote in 1919: "The separate arts must be brought back into intimate contact, under the wings of a great architecture." The workshop is a four-story box with an interior steel skeleton enclosed by window walls of glass, the latter a Gropius invention. The design established the principles of the International Style that was to dominate architectural design into the 1970s. Expensive to heat and to cool, not to mention washing the windows, many International Style buildings appear as anomalies in the energy-conscious 1990s. For half a century, however, they were the essence of modernity.

Le Corbusier (Charles-Edouard Jeanneret), 1887–1965
The International Style was brilliantly developed by the Swiss painter-architect Le Corbusier (luh core-boos-iay). For Le Corbusier, houses were "machines for living," as efficient as airplanes were for flying. Totally devoid of ornament, his Villa Savoye (fig. 28.28) is partially supported by slender columns but rests mostly on a recessed unit containing service functions, servants' quarters, entrance hall, and staircase to the living quarters on the second level. The living room is separated from an open interior terrace by floor-to-ceiling panes of glass, making the terrace a basic part of living arrangements.

Organic Architecture

Frank Lloyd Wright, 1867–1959
International Style buildings are, in effect, disdainful of their environment, thrusting away from the earth to create their own space. America's greatest architect disagreed totally with this concept. Wright's buildings are generally organic, seemingly a natural consequence of their environment. One of his most imaginative designs is the

28.28   Le Corbusier, Villa Savoye, Poissy-sur-Seine, France. 1929.

28.29   Frank Lloyd Wright, Kaufmann House ("Falling Water"), Bear Run, Pennsylvania. 1936. Photo: Ralph Lieberman, North Adams, Massachusetts/Calmann & King Ltd., London.

Kaufmann House (fig. 28.29). Built on a site that would challenge any architect and which obviously inspired Wright, the house is situated on a steep and rocky hillside over a waterfall. Combining native rock construction with daring cantilevers colored beige to blend with the environment, the structure cannot be imagined on any other site. The Villa Savoye and "Falling Water" (as the Kaufmann House is known) represent, between them, opposite theories of modern design. Subsequent developments tended to fall somewhere between the two extremes.

ARTISTIC STYLES SINCE 1945

Action Painting: Abstract Expressionism

Jackson Pollock, 1912–56

The new style of Abstract Expressionism developed in New York, which, after World War II, replaced Paris as the artistic capital of the Western world. Once a Social Realist in the manner of Rivera, Pollock became the acknowledged leader of the new movement. His personal style of Abstract Expressionism began to bloom when he quit easel painting and, instead, tacked a large, unstretched canvas to the floor. Walking all around the canvas he became completely absorbed as he dropped, dripped, poured, and spattered paint on the canvas. Though he had no preconceived ideas when he began a canvas he could, as he said, "control the flow of the paint," and he did complete works with brushstrokes as needed. His *Autumn Rhythm* (fig. 28.30) is an intricate and complex interplay of curvilinear lines and controlled spatters illustrating, as he remarked, "energy made visible." Pollock's energetic involvement in the act of painting led to the term "action painting" as a general description of the movement.

Willem de Kooning, b. 1904

The Dutch-American artist works in violent motions using a large brush heavy with paint. His favorite theme is that

28.31 Willem de Kooning, *Woman I.* 1950–2. Oil on canvas, 6' 3⅜" × 4' 10" (1.93 × 1.47 m). The Museum of Modern Art, New York (Purchase). Photo: © 1996 The Museum of Modern Art, New York, © Willem de Kooning/ARS, New York and DACS, London 1995.

28.30 Jackson Pollock, *Autumn Rhythm, No. 30, 1950.* 1950. Oil on canvas, 8' 9" × 17' 3" (2.67 × 5.26 m). Metropolitan Museum of Art, New York. Photo: © ARS, New York and DACS, London 1995.

of the eternal woman: earth mother and fertility goddess. *Woman I* (fig. 28.31) is a giant, earthy figure of a woman painted in slashing brushstrokes. An energetic portrayal of a goddess-cum-movie queen and sex symbol, this is one man's view of the other half of the human race.

Mark Rothko, 1903–70

In his mature style Rothko covered large canvases with luminous, softly bleeding rectangles of color. *Number 10* (fig. 28.32) is an extremely subtle combination of softly glowing colors separated by ragged, foggy edges. Compared with the dynamics of Pollock and de Kooning, this is Abstract Expressionism in a gentle and meditative mood—in a style frequently called "color field."

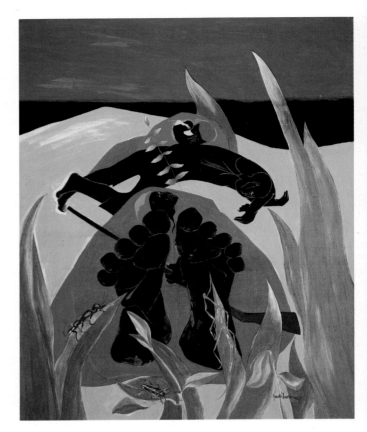

28.33 Jacob Lawrence, *Daybreak—A Time to Rest*. 1967. Tempera on hardboard, 30 × 24" (76.2 × 61 cm). National Gallery of Art, Washington, D.C. (Anonymous gift).

28.32 Mark Rothko, *Number 10*. 1950. Oil on canvas, 7' 6⅜" × 4' 9⅛" (2.29 × 1.45 m). The Museum of Modern Art, New York (Gift of Philip Johnson). Photo: © 1996 The Museum of Modern Art, New York, © ARS, New York and DACS, London 1995.

Jacob Lawrence, b. 1917

Lawrence uses vigorous silhouetted patterns and narrative subject matter in his unique abstract style. Deeply committed to African-American history in America, Lawrence is perhaps best known for the series *The Migration of the Negro* (1940–41) and his *Harlem* series of 1943. *Daybreak—A Time to Rest* (fig. 28.33) is related, like much of his work, to the life of an African-American hero, Harriet Tubman, a famed conductor of slaves to freedom on the Underground Railway. This is from a children's book entitled *Harriet and the Promised Land*, which he illustrated. The work is balanced between a dream-world and reality, an artful juxtaposition of identifiable images and abstractions. The huge feet are pointed north but, even when traveling the route to freedom, there must be a time to rest and to dream of the promised land.

Reaction Against Action: Pop Art

The emotional fervor of Abstract Expressionism burned itself out in about fifteen years, to be superseded by a Dada-type reaction. The self-confidence of America after World War II was jolted by the Korean conflict, the Cold War, and the military build-up in Vietnam. A new breed of artists was skeptical of American accomplishments and chose the banalities of American life to satirize the superficiality of

American culture. First called Neo-Dadaists, these artists used recognizable subject matter from American popular culture: soup cans, comic strips, road signs, and cult figures from rock music and commercial Hollywood movies.

Pop Art was the label applied to what seemed to be a uniquely American reaction to the numbing vulgarity of much of popular culture. Actually, the label and the movement had surfaced in England in the mid-1950s. English images tended, however, to be romantic and sentimental commentaries on popular idols, comic strips, and American movies; American reactions were much more aggressive, perhaps because the media hype in the United States was so blatant and all-pervasive.

Robert Rauschenberg, b. 1925

The movement burst on to the American scene in 1962, but Rauschenberg had been working his way from Abstract Expressionism to Pop Art since the mid-1950s. In his *Monogram* (fig. 28.34) he combined an old tire, a stuffed Angora goat, and pieces of stenciled signs into a wry and witty commentary on American life. The goat and tire are waste that has been recycled, so to speak. Paradoxically, they are still distasteful objects, retaining their identity and creating a tension between themselves and the total work.

28.34 Robert Rauschenberg, *Monogram*. 1959. Construction, 4 × 6 × 6' (1.2 × 1.83 × 1.83 m). Moderna Museet, Stockholm, Sweden. Photo: Per-Anders Allsten, © Robert Rauschenberg/DACS, London/VAGA, New York, 1995.

28.35 Roy Lichtenstein, *Drowning Girl*. 1963. Oil and synthetic polymer on canvas, 5' 7⅞" × 5' 6¾" (1.72 × 1.69 m). The Museum of Modern Art, New York (Philip Johnson Fund and gift of Mr. and Mrs. Bagley Wright). Photo: © 1996 The Museum of Modern Art, New York, © Roy Lichtenstein/DACS 1995.

They should not be there but they are, undeniably there, forever and ever. Rauschenberg has stated that painting is related to art and to life and that his function is to "act in the gap between the two."

Roy Lichtenstein, b. 1923

Rauschenberg generally retains the painterly quality of Abstract Expressionism but Lichtenstein adopted the mechanical techniques and imagery of comic strips, including the Benday dots used in newspaper reproductions of the comics. He also used the hard lines of comic strips but his paintings are monumental in scale. His cold and impersonal portrayal of a *Drowning Girl* (fig. 28.35) is an indictment of the casual and callous attitudes of many Americans toward violence in comic strips, in the streets, in Africa or the Middle East. The technique is that of the "low art" of the comics, but the result is a potent artistic statement. Lichtenstein, for obvious reasons, selected nothing from comic strips like *Peanuts* or *Doonesbury*.

Edward Kienholz, 1927–94

The sculptures of Kienholz have been called Pop but his work is also expressionistic and surreal. He combines painting, sculpture, collage, and the stage to depict some of the shabbiness, stupidity, and cruelty of modern urban life. In *The State Hospital* (fig. 28.36) he confronts us with an elderly patient—someone's father, someone's grandfather—who has been chained to a cot in a state facility. In the upper cot, encased in what appears to be a comic-strip balloon,

28.36 Edward Kienholz, *The State Hospital*. 1966. Mixed media, 8 × 12 × 10' (2.4 × 3.6 × 8.5 m). Moderna Museet, Stockholm, Sweden. © Edward Kienholz.

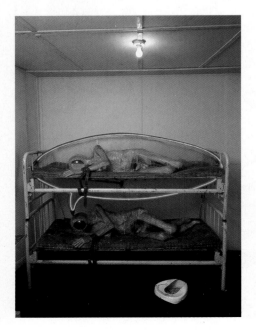

28.37 Marisol, *Women and Dog*. 1964. Wood, plaster, synthetic polymer, and miscellaneous items, 72¼ × 73 × 30¹⁵⁄₁₆" (183.5 × 185.4 × 78.6 cm). Whitney Museum of American Art (Purchase, with funds from the Friends of the Whitney Museum of American Art). Photo: Robert E. Mates, New Jersey, © Marisol/DACS, London/VAGA, New York 1995.

is the same figure, possibly representing the patient's vision of himself: chained, caged, and abandoned. Is this how life should end?

Marisol, b. 1930

Marisol's work is lighter in spirit than that of Kienholz but with oblique social commentaries that are sophisticated, witty, ironic, and often sardonic. A Venezuelan born in Paris and living in the United States, Marisol (Escobar is her unused surname) creates her own world with assemblages of wood, plaster, paint, and assorted objects. In *Women and Dog* (fig. 28.37) she uses painting, drawing, stencil, relief, collage, carving, and assemblage to present the somewhat Cubist and Surrealist tableau. As is her custom, all the faces are of Marisol herself, giving the scene an introspective dimension. She has created a world without men in which the feminine gender is the self-contained reality. (We may safely assume that the dog is female.) Rather than an anti-male work, this is an assemblage of self-reliant females.

Color, Geometry, and Optics

Josef Albers, 1888–1976

One of the first graduates of the Bauhaus, Albers emigrated from Nazi Germany in 1933 to the United States, where his work influenced the development of Abstract Geometric painting and Op Art. His *Homage to the Square* paintings were a serialization similar to Monet's paintings of haystacks and lily ponds, a process, not a solution. Working with three or four squares of different colors, Albers explored, in hundreds of paintings, the interaction of colors and straight lines. *Homage to the Square: Star Blue* (fig. 28.38) has an intensity based not on the squares themselves but on the relationship of the colors.

Helen Frankenthaler, b. 1928

Working against the currents of Abstract Expressionism and Geometric Abstraction, Frankenthaler stained the raw canvas to achieve a limpid freshness not seen in the work of any other artist. In *Interior Landscape* (fig. 28.39) the paint is applied in thin washes so integrated with the canvas that there is no illusion of either foreground or background. Like Pollock, she creates an open composition out of abstract shapes manipulated into patterns of color. In this sense she is an action painter. She begins with no preconceived idea; rather, the painting evolves as she

28.39 Helen Frankenthaler, *Interior Landscape*. 1964. Acrylic on canvas, 8' 8⅞" × 7' 8⅞" (2.66 × 2.35 m). San Francisco Museum of Modern Art (Gift of the Women's Board).

28.38 Josef Albers, *1. Homage to the Square: Star Blue*. 1957. Oil on board, 29⅞ × 29⅞" (75.9 × 75.9 cm). Cleveland Museum of Art, Cleveland, Ohio (Contemporary Collection, 65.1). Photo: © DACS 1995.

interacts with her washes and the canvas. In another sense she is a color-field artist, in that she creates abstract landscapes of color that can be interpreted in many different ways.

Louise Nevelson, 1900–88

Nevelson's assemblage of sculptures reflects the geometric forms of pre-Columbian sculpture, but her overriding interest in working with wood can be traced to her father's career as a cabinetmaker and her involvement with the wood in his shop. *Illumination—Dark* (fig. 28.40) is a large wooden wall on which the artist has arranged selected pieces of wood (culled from old houses) to form a three-dimensional geometric abstraction. With bronze-painted shapes against the flat black background of the wall, the piece resembles both a cupboard and a cityscape like the artist's native New York. As Nevelson has said, she "putters endlessly" with the design until she gets it right. The result here is a subtle blend of delicacy, mystery, and strength.

Bridget Riley, b. 1931

American painters like Albers were concerned with straight lines, but British artist Riley worked with the possibilities inherent in curved lines. *Crest* (fig. 28.41) is a large, complex composition that communicates directly with the eye and the optic nerve. Though she has been called an Op Artist (from "optical art"), Riley's style goes beyond merely confusing or tricking the eye. What we have here is a new way of perceiving and experiencing motion.

Fantasy and Expressionism

Jean Dubuffet, 1901–85

Dubuffet (due-boo-fay), the most notable French artist since World War II, found some of his inspiration in strangely different areas: art of the insane, children's art, and graffiti. Contending that there should be no essential division between the art of amateurs, children, psychotics, and artists, Dubuffet described his collection of non-professional art as *art brut*. Dubuffet's art could not be called *art brut* because he was neither untrained nor psychotic; he painted intuitively, somewhat like the Abstract

28.40 Louise Nevelson, *Illumination—Dark*. 1961. Bronze, dimensions variable: 10' 5" × 9' ½" (3.18 × 2.76 m). Whitney Museum of American Art, New York (Gift of the artist, dedicated to the Whitney Museum of American Art). Photo: Geoffrey Clements, New York.

28.42 Jean Dubuffet, *Portrait of Henri Michaux*, from *More Beautiful Than They Think: Portraits* series. 1947. Oil on canvas, 51½ × 38⅜" (130.7 × 97.3 cm). The Museum of Modern Art, New York (Sidney and Harriet Janis Collection). Photo: © 1996 The Museum of Modern Art, New York, © ADAGP, Paris and DACS, London 1995.

28.41 Bridget Riley, *Crest*. 1964. Emulsion on board, 5' 5½" × 5' 5½" (1.66 × 1.66 m). Private collection. Photo: Juda Rowan Gallery, London.

Expressionists, but his subjects were fantastic figures and landscapes. He combined pigments with different mixtures of plaster, sand, or twigs to make a thick **impasto** that he scratched and scored to make grotesque figures such as his *Portrait of Henri Michaux* (fig. 28.42). Like much of his work, this painting has a powerful primordial quality that both attracts and repels.

Francis Bacon, 1909–92

The Irish-born Bacon painted tormented visions distorted to the point of insanity. Preoccupied with deformity and disease, he selected works by Old Masters and restated them as anguished symbols of contemporary life. *Number VII from Eight Studies for a Portrait* (fig. 28.43) is based on the portrait of Pope Innocent X (reigned 1644–55) by Velasquez, who depicted the pope as a powerful, intelligent, and coolly confident pontiff. Bacon used Renaissance perspective but placed the pope in an isolation booth where his anguished screams tear his head asunder.

Fritz Scholder, b. 1937

The best-known Native-American artist, Scholder shows the influence of Expressionism and Pop Art, but his subject matter sets him apart from both styles. Scholder uses serialism to portray the paradoxical position of Native Americans in everyday life. With a poignant irony he has depicted stereotypes: a Super Chief eating an ice cream cone; a drunken Indian clutching a can of beer like a

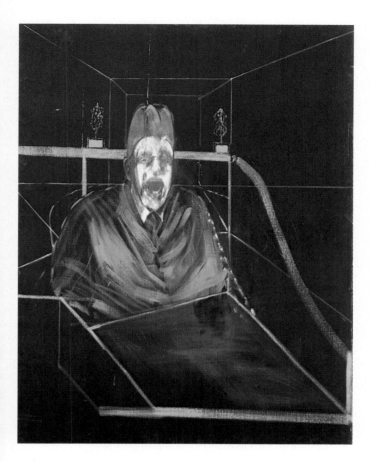

28.43 *Above* Francis Bacon, *Number VII from Eight Studies for a Portrait*. 1953. Oil on linen, 5' × 3' 10⅛" (1.52 × 1.17 m). The Museum of Modern Art, New York (Gift of Mr. and Mrs. William A. M. Burden). Photo: © 1996 The Museum of Modern Art, New York.

28.44 Fritz Scholder, *Waiting Indian No. 4*. 1970. Oil on canvas, 5' 10" × 5' 4" (1.78 × 1.63 m). University Art Collections, Arizona State University.

tomahawk; a Hollywood Indian and his captive "Anglo" maiden. Scholder's work is satirical and searching, depicting both the nobility and the degradation of his people. *Waiting Indian No. 4* (fig. 28.44) stands majestically in a barren landscape. In his awesome dignity he refuses to accept any part of a stereotype in the Anglo world.

Alexander Calder, 1898–1976

For centuries sculptors have labored to give their works the illusion of movement. Calder invented abstract works that actually moved. Influenced by Surrealism and Geometric Abstraction, Calder created the true mobile. *Many Pierced Discs* (fig. 28.45) is a fantasy of abstract shapes wired together and delicately balanced so that it can respond to the slightest breeze. An indoor mobile, this work rests on its pedestal in an art gallery where it can gently gyrate and bow to museum visitors.

Henry Moore, 1898–1986

Moore was the most important English artist of his time in any medium. Like Calder, he was influenced by Surrealism but went on to develop his unique abstract figural style. In *Family Group* (fig. 28.46) the figures are recognizable but abstracted into curving, rather primitive shapes that emphasize the unity and stability of a family.

28.46 *Below* Henry Moore, *Family Group.* 1948–9. Bronze (cast 1950), 59¼ × 46½ × 29⅞" (150.5 × 118 × 75.9 cm), including base. The Museum of Modern Art, New York (A. Conger Goodyear Fund). Photo: © 1996 The Museum of Modern Art, New York.

28.47 Tony DeLap, *Sentaro.* 1967. Aluminum, wood, plexiglass, and lacquer, 16 × 16 × 5" (40.6 × 40.6 × 12.7 cm). University Art Collections, Arizona State University (American Art Heritage Fund).

28.48 David Smith, *Cubi XV.* 1963–4. Stainless steel, 10' 5⅛" × 4' 10½" (3.23 × 1.49 m). San Diego Museum of Art, California (Gift of Mr. and Mrs. Norton W. Walbridge). Photo: © Estate of David Smith/DACS, London/VAGA, New York, 1995.

Minimal Art

Tony DeLap, b. 1927

Minimal Art began in the 1960s as a movement to reduce art to basics: one shape or one color or one idea. Also called primary structures or primary art, the style is easier to observe than to discuss. *Sentaro* (fig. 28.47) by DeLap is a sculpture/ painting reduced to a basic shape and a single color. This is a beautiful hunk of a bright red rectangular box that seemingly floats within its plastic case. DeLap used commercial staining and spraying techniques so that the saturated painting/sculpture is a solid color field with no trace of brushwork or other manipulation by the artist. The vitality and spontaneity of Abstract Expressionism has given way to a laid-back restraint comparable to Cool Jazz (see p. 533).

David Smith, 1906–65

American sculptor Smith applied his experience of working in an automotive plant and locomotive factory to sculpting with steel—something that, as he said, "had little art

history." His *Cubi XV* (fig. 28.48) is a gravity-defying combination of simple geometric components that set up a lively interplay of forms and space. The stainless steel is highly polished, with controlled light patterns that make the metal surface as sensual as works by Brancusi (see fig. 28.12) or Verrocchio (see fig. 17.12).

Varieties of Realism

Though never absent from the American scene, realism has again become a major factor in a variety of styles called New Realism, Magic Realism, or Photorealism. The sculptor Duane Hanson (b. 1925) makes casts of living people and paints the resulting figures to look completely lifelike, including real clothing and accessories. Richard Estes (b. 1936) projects a slide directly onto canvas and makes a precise copy with an airbrush. Hanson selects subjects like gaudily dressed tourists, junkies, and overweight shoppers, whereas Estes paints banal cityscapes totally devoid of people.

Audrey Flack, b. 1931

In their subject matter Hanson and Estes follow the orientation of Pop Art, but that Photorealism can pursue other paths has been illustrated by the work of Flack, the first Photorealist to have a painting purchased by the Museum of Modern Art in New York. Like others in the movement, she projects color slides onto a canvas and paints with an airbrush. Her subject matter, however, is a kind of collage, a still-life arrangement that conveys a specific idea or message. *World War II Vanitas, April 1945* (see p. 468) refers to the liberation of the Nazi concentration camp at Buchenwald. Flack's painting, based on Margaret Bourke-White's famous photograph, is a tribute to the survivors of the death camps and a memorial to the 12,000,000—including about 6,000,000 Jews—who perished there. The rose, burning candle, pear, watch, butterfly, and black border are all symbols of mortality or the commemoration of the dead. The printed statement is a rabbinical quotation affirming belief in God and concluding: "You can take everything from me—the pillow from under my head, my house—but you cannot take God from my heart." The various objects are so much larger than life-size that they appear not to be "real." The basic reality is, of course, the haunted faces of the survivors of Buchenwald.

Otto Duecker, b. 1948

Our society has apparently learned to accept many real/unreal mystifications of the everyday world such as, for example, twelve-foot cowboys on a giant movie screen or six-inch football players on TV. Indeed, when Duecker paints larger-than-life figures, cuts them out, and arranges them in galleries, homes, and warehouses, we are inclined to accept them as "real." In *Russell, Terry, J. T., and a Levi Jacket* (fig. 28.49) we see the artist posed in front of his four cutouts and appearing, in this photograph, somehow less real than his creations.

pinkish water. A dedicated environmentalist with a special interest in land-reclamation, Smithson was always intent on integrating his works with their natural setting. This was particularly successful with *Spiral Jetty* because the work and the environment have indeed become accepted as one. Tragically, this was one of the artist's last works; he was killed in a plane crash while scouting a new site.

28.49 Otto Duecker, *Russell, Terry, J. T., and a Levi Jacket.* 1979. Oil on masonite cutouts within a photograph. Elaine Horwitch Galleries, Scottsdale, Arizona. Photo: Don Wheeler, Tulsa, Oklahoma.

28.50 Robert Smithson, *Spiral Jetty*, Great Salt Lake, Utah. 1970. Rock, salt crystals, earth, algae; coil 1,500' (457 m). John Weber Gallery, New York. Photo: Gianfranco Gorgoni/Dawn Gallery, New York.

28.51 *Below* Christo and Jeanne-Claude (Christo and Jeanne-Claude Javacheff), *Running Fence, Sonoma and Marin Counties, California*. 1972–6. Fabric fence, height 18' (5.49 m), length 24½ miles (39.4 km). Photo: Jeanne-Claude. © Christo, 1976.

If each generation develops its own concepts of reality, then what is real now? For the present century—sometimes called the Age of Uncertainty—it might be accurate to say that several concepts of reality are acceptable, or tolerable, given the scientific environment of relativity, quantum, chaos, and complex theories.

Environmental Art

There are two basic kinds of Environmental Art: art that creates an artificial environment that one can enter and art that alters the natural or constructed environment. The latter type will be considered here in the work of three notable artists.

Robert Smithson, 1938–73

Smithson chose Rozel Point in the Great Salt Lake for his *Spiral Jetty* (fig. 28.50) because it was remote and because algae colored the water pink. The spiral design was suggested, he said, by the intense light radiating from the

28.52 Wallace K. Harrison and Associates, Secretariat Building of the United Nations, New York. 1947–50. Photo: United Nations, New York.

Christo and Jeanne-Claude (Christo and Jeanne-Claude Javacheff), both born 1935

These environmental artists have wrapped everything from a woman, a bicycle, and a machine, to a bridge in Paris. One of their largest projects was the arrangement of 1,000,000 square feet (92,900 m²) of fabric on an Australian coastline. One of their most successful and best-known works is probably the *Running Fence* (fig. 28.51). Laid across the rolling countryside north of San Francisco, the fence celebrated the landscape in a manner somehow comparable to the work of landscape painters. Running from a major highway down to the Pacific Ocean, the fence was in place for two weeks during September 1976. Though viewed by many, it caused thousands more to become aware of the beauty of the countryside through the two books and the movie about the project.

None of the Christos' projects remains in place for very long, which is a deliberate aesthetic decision on their part. Just as each stage of life is temporary—childhood, maturity, old age—they feel that each project is best appreciated knowing that it is momentary, possessing what Jeanne-Claude has described as the "lovely quality of impermanence."

Architecture: The International Style

Before World War II skyscraper designs were generally eclectic, clothing steel skeletons with older styles. The innovations of Louis Sullivan (1856–1924) and Frank Lloyd Wright were more influential in Europe than at home and the International Style had yet to make much of an impression outside Europe. Until the 1950s New York skyscrapers were circumscribed by the demands of clients and rigid zoning restrictions. Buildings were designed to occupy every square foot of expensive real estate but zoning ordinances required that some sunlight had to fall into

manmade canyons. The result was the so-called ziggurat, a setback design with upper floors terraced back from the street.

Beginning an international renaissance in architecture, the International Style appeared in New York with the design of the United Nations complex. Because modern buildings were so complicated, most were designed by a group of architects and engineers. Wallace K. Harrison (1895–1981) headed an international team that designed the Secretariat Building (fig. 28.52) in the shape of a giant slab, as suggested by Le Corbusier. Clothed on the sides in glass and on the ends in marble, the structure was the first American building to embody the Bauhaus tradition. Because it occupied only a portion of the riverfront site, it avoided the setback restrictions imposed on other high-rise structures.

Ludwig Mies van der Rohe, 1886–1969

The German architect Mies van der Rohe was initially influenced by Gropius but developed his own Minimalist version of the International Style. Illustrating his motto that "less is more," his Seagram Building (fig. 28.53) is a model of simplicity and elegance, a classic among glass skyscrapers.

28.53 Ludwig Mies van der Rohe, Seagram Building, New York. 1958. Photo: Ezra Stoller/Esto, New York. Courtesy Joseph E. Seagram & Sons, Inc.

28.54 Le Corbusier, Notre-Dame-du-Haut, Ronchamp, France. 1950–5. Photo: Ralph Lieberman, North Adams, Massachusetts.

Le Corbusier

Though he was an influential pioneer of the International Style, Le Corbusier later abandoned his boxes on stilts (see fig. 28.28) for a more sculptural style. His design for the pilgrimage chapel of Notre-Dame-du-Haut (fig. 28.54) was revolutionary, unlike any other building. The plan is irregular in every respect. Thick, curving white walls are topped by a heavy overhanging roof and flanked by a tall white tower on the left and a shorter tower on the right. The towers are decorative but they also transmit natural light to the two altars within. Window openings are cut through the massive walls to make tunnels of light. Randomly placed, the windows are of different sizes and cut through the walls in a variety of angles. Stained glass is used but each window has a different design and color scheme. The overall effect is intimate and magical.

Organic Architecture

Frank Lloyd Wright

Wright designed many buildings based on the circle but none as dramatic as the Solomon R. Guggenheim Museum in New York (fig. 28.55). The front circle is the administrative unit, with the gallery behind. The structure is essentially a cylinder rising in expanding circles. This is the antithesis, in every respect, of the International Style. Inside the building (fig. 28.56) a circular ramp rises to the top in six complete turns around a 90-foot (27-m) well that

climaxes in a skylight dome. Visitors are taken to the top in an elevator, permitting them to walk on a continuous downhill grade while inspecting art works placed on the outside wall. The design necessarily limits how art is displayed but the Guggenheim interior is one of Wright's boldest concepts.

Eero Saarinen, 1910–61

New York's JFK International Airport is an uninspired collection of architectural clichés with the sole exception of the TWA Terminal (fig. 28.57). Designed by Saarinen, the structure is a triumph, a curvilinear enclosure of space that actually looks like an air terminal. Built of reinforced

28.55 Frank Lloyd Wright, Solomon R. Guggenheim Museum, New York. 1943–59. Photo: Robert E. Mates.

28.56 Solomon R. Guggenheim Museum, interior. Photo: Robert E. Mates.

28.57 *Above* Eero Saarinen, TWA Terminal, JFK International Airport, New York. 1959–62. Photo: Ezra Stoller/Esto, New York.

28.58 Utzon, Hall, Todd, and Littleton, Sydney Opera House, Bennelong Point, Sydney, Australia. 1959–72. Photo: Associated Press/Topham, Edenbridge, U.K.

concrete, the continuously curving surfaces symbolize flight in a manner reminiscent of Brancusi's *Bird in Space* (see fig. 28.12).

Joern Utzon, b. 1918

The design competition for the new opera house in Sydney, Australia, was won by Danish architect Utzon in 1956, but it took thirteen years and several more architects to figure out how to build the unique concept (fig. 28.58). It is a cultural center that includes an opera house, exhibition hall, theatre, and other facilities, and the soaring gull-wing design—executed with a facing of brilliant white ceramic tiles—is a visual triumph, thanks in part to its location on one of the world's great harbors.

The Art of Photography

Anyone can take photographs, but there are few artists behind the camera. Mastering the technical aspects of photography is one thing, producing an artistic image quite another. Unlike painting or sculpture, there is no gradual build-up to a completed work, no chance to add, delete, modify, rework. The image can be altered after the fact, but the shot still begins with what the camera "sees" when the shutter is opened. What is a good photograph? For that matter, what is a good painting? Like all art, photography is communication, a personal statement that the artist is making. Moreover, the work of a good photographer has a recognizable style just as, for example, paintings by Monet are stylistically consistent.

Portrait photographers have a special talent, an ability to reveal the nature and character of their subjects. Few were as accomplished as Matthew Brady (1823–96). Brady took so many photographs of Abraham Lincoln that the latter is reputed to have said that his Cooper Union speech and Brady's photos put him in the White House. But it was quality, not quantity, that accounted for the fame of Brady's portraits of Lincoln. Even the calling-card photo (see fig. 23.3) clearly shows the strength, dignity, and nobility of the future president.[2]

Like many painters, photographers tend to concentrate on specializations such as portraiture, landscape, cityscape, sports, combat photography, and so forth. Landscape photographer Ansel Adams (1902–84) was one of the charter members of the photographic society named "Group f/64." This optical term was chosen because the group generally set their lenses to the smallest aperture to secure the greatest depth of field: maximum sharpness from foreground to background. For most of his career Adams produced very sharp photos of the landscape of the American West. His *Moonrise, Hernandez, New Mexico* (fig. 28.59) magically conveys the immensity of the landscape as it and the night sky tower over the isolation of the few inhabitants.

Photo-journalist W. Eugene Smith (1918–78), on assignment for *Life* magazine, did a memorable photo-essay on life in a Spanish village. His *Spanish Wake* (fig. 28.60) from that series has characteristics comparable to a fine oil painting. The dramatic chiaroscuro and powerful composition add to the impact of the range of grief.

2. Brady also produced a remarkable photographic record of the Civil War.

Also a photo-journalist for *Life*, Margaret Bourke-White (1904–71) photographed everything from industry and cities to natural disasters and World War II combat. It was her photograph of concentration camp survivors that inspired Photorealist painter Audrey Flack to create her memorial to the Holocaust (see pp. 468 and 509). Bourke-White's *Two Women, Lansdale, Arkansas* (fig. 28.61) is a serene study, taken during the Great Depression, of two companionable women who are totally at ease with themselves and with each other.

There is no more telling image of the Great Depression

28.60 W. Eugene Smith, *Spanish Wake*, from Spanish Village series. 1951. Photograph. © W. Eugene Smith Estate/Black. Photo: Center for Creative Photography, University of Arizona.

28.61 Margaret Bourke-White, *Two Women, Lansdale, Arkansas*. 1936. Gelatin-silver print. George Arents Research Library, Syracuse University, Syracuse, New York.

than the *Migrant Mother, Nipomo, California* (see p. 536) by Dorothea Lange (1895–1965). Lange's compassion and respect for the farmers who migrated from the Midwest Dust Bowl to California in search of a better life are clearly revealed. This single photograph sums up the unflinching determination of thousands of homeless, rootless farmers to survive. The subject matter is comparable to John Steinbeck's novel *The Grapes of Wrath,* in which the Joad family migrated from Oklahoma to California.

Photography's strong points include its immediacy and ease of replication. The earlier question about what makes a good photograph is answered by the examples printed in this volume (see figs. 23.3, 28.9, and 28.59–61). Each picture communicates more than the sum of its parts; each image is unique; and the personal communication from the artist is just as apparent in these works as in paintings by Rembrandt, Monet, or van Gogh.

Painting and Sculpture: Postmodernism

Art was self-consciously "modern" from around 1910 to about 1970. Artists viewed themselves as *avant-garde* creators who denied the past as they searched for new means of expression. Abstraction or a renunciation of representation, a taste for novelty that affirmed originality and denied tradition (no more imitations of the world or of earlier artists) were characteristics of Modernism. Beginning around 1970 or so, however, there was a general shift to a reweaving of the recent past and Western culture, a search for human values in the context of a world civilization. Representation and history were reintroduced, though without reverting to graphic realism. This was, of course, a reaction to the rapidly evolving Electronic/Information Age and the idea that the world was becoming a Global Village. For want of a better term this movement is called "postmodernism."

Postmodernism uses representation where appropriate and revives the connection with tradition by deliberately choosing between several traditions or by making explicit reference to tradition as such, which is anything but a traditional attitude. It recognizes the plurality of autonomous cultures within a world civilization.

Contemporary artistic styles are therefore wildly pluralistic. No one style predominates. A renewed interest in figurative painting called, for want of a better term, New Painting, seems to be significant, but some older styles persist and innovations abound. One of the newer innovations is Neo-Expressionism, which emerged in Germany in the 1980s, much as its ancestor surfaced some seven decades earlier. This is an authentic style practiced by a number of successful artists, notably Gerhard Richter (b. 1932). His *Vase* (fig. 28.62 and p. 453) is a vibrant abstraction achieved by superimposing many layers of pigment with a variety of brushes, including the wide brushes used by house painters. This is a very large work that exudes vigorous emotion.

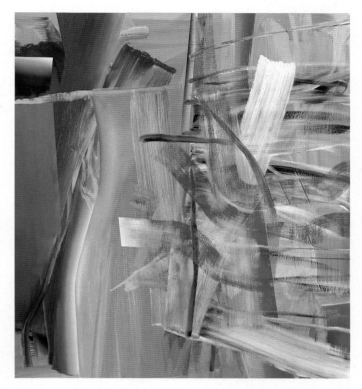

28.62   Gerhard Richter, *Vase*. 1984. Oil on canvas, 7' 4½" × 6' 6¾" (2.25 × 2 m). Museum of Fine Arts, Boston (Juliana Cheney Edwards Collection).

28.63   Sylvia Plimack Mangold, *Schunnemunk Mountain*. 1979. Oil on canvas, 5' ¼" × 6' 8⅛" (1.53 × 2.04 m). Dallas Museum of Art (General Acquisitions Fund and a gift of the 500, Inc. 1980.7).

28.64 *Left* Jennifer Bartlett, *Sad and Happy Tidal Wave*. 1978. Enamel, silkscreen on steel plate (62 plates); oil on canvas (2 panels), 10' 9½" × 14' 4" (3.29 × 4.37 m). Dallas Museum of Art (Foundation for the Arts Collection, gift of Susan and Robert K. Hoffman).

28.65 *Below* Robert Colescott, *Les Demoiselles d'Alabama: Vestidas*. 1985. Acrylic on canvas, 8' × 7' 8" (2.44 × 2.37 m). Phyllis Kind Gallery, New York, Chicago.

There are literally thousands of artists hard at work turning out untold numbers of art works. In the absence, at present, of any towering figures, we have selected three artists to represent the many who have yet to be recognized.

Sylvia Mangold, b. 1938

Mangold lives and works in upstate New York. Her *Schunnemunk Mountain* (fig. 28.63) is a night landscape framed by larger painted rectangles and strips of applied masking tape. The country scene viewed from her studio is representational but the added rectangles, stripe, and masking tape make the illusion ambiguous; perhaps the painting is not a landscape but a commentary on how art is constructed. This is thus a poetic image that is "presented" to the viewer.

Jennifer Bartlett, b. 1941

Contrasting sharply with the hushed image of the New York mountain, Bartlett's art is consistently cheerful and often exuberant, as in *Sad and Happy Tidal Wave* (fig. 28.64). This is a diptych with a left panel of Bartlett's distinctive painted steel tiles and the right panel a two-piece canvas. Both panels focus on the abstract figure of a swimmer, composed of oval shapes. Though color and design are similar the two panels are sharply different: gleaming brilliance on the left and a softer, almost pastel quality on the right. The artist is playing not only with color and shapes, but with the characteristics of different media as well.

Robert Colescott, b. 1925

Colescott has been among the leaders in a Postmodern movement that is reexamining the whole range of the Western pictorial tradition. His *Les Demoiselles d'Alabama: Vestidas* (fig. 28.65) is a delightful and wickedly witty "quotation" of Picasso's *Les Demoiselles d'Avignon* (see fig. 28.5), which was such a crucial step in modern art. Despite the many close similarities, this work is highly original, especially in the totally different mood the artist has given to his work as compared with the Picasso.

Outlook

Art in the 1990s is, in general, no longer a Bohemian activity and New York is no longer the primary center of artistic activity. Faced with a declining art market, some New York promoters seized on Neo-Expressionism as the new American style and then "discovered" artists who were working in the style, most of whom turned out to be Europeans. Happily discovered while working in Europe, Julian Schnabel is actually a Texan. He, along with Laurie Anderson and David Salle, is making a living out of Neo-Expressionism by promoting a "fast track" art market rivaling the hyped success of rock stars and soap-opera personalities. The marketing of art and "art stars" has become another American enterprise with the implication that "success" is more important than aesthetics. Where this will lead is anybody's guess,

but the prognosis does not favor artistic integrity. Art critic Robert Hughes has called the 1980s probably the worst decade in the history of American art, a nadir that will likely continue through the 1990s because the social conditions that fostered the era's cultural traits give no evidence of changing.

Following is a selective listing of styles, attitudes, and movements that indicate the wide range of contemporary artistic activity.

New Painting	Primitivism
Neo-Expressionism	Naives
French Nouveau Réalisme	Abstractionists
Italian Arte Povera	Nul/Zero
Pop and Post-Pop	Computer Art
Fluxus	Holograhic Art
Conceptual Art	Performance Art
Minimalism	Body Art
Earth Art	Vague Art
Noise or Sound Art	Light Art
Site Sculpture	Bad Painting
Postmodern Art	

Whether any one style will predominate in the manner of Impressionism or Cubism is unlikely, given the rapid interactions of our Global Village in the Communications Age. Artistic influences are international but artists are individuals. They will pursue their own goals, creating art works faster than critics can conjure up labels. This is as it should be. Works of art are always best judged on their own merits regardless of style, school, or movement.

Architecture: Postmodernism

The most important architectural movement since the Bauhaus, Postmodernism has developed—since about 1970—into a worldwide phenomenon. Strictly urban in orientation, the style has appeared in New York, Paris, Hong Kong, Tokyo, Portland, Los Angeles, and many cities in between. In fact, the rise of Postmodern design has co-incided with the increasing emphasis on city-based identities as opposed to traditional national boundaries. At the same time, these urban centers, with instant worldwide communications, are clearly part of the international community and the rapid evolution of the Global Village.

How can modernity be spoken of in the past tense? What is meant by *post*modern? During the middle segment of this century Modernism usually meant the *avant-garde*, unadorned geometry of the International Style. By the 1970s the stark boxes and towers that had long dominated cityscapes were increasingly viewed as cold and impersonal at best and, at worst, as profoundly anti-human. Not many buildings had the elegant proportions of the Seagram Building (see fig. 28.53).

Architectural critics and historians sometimes refer

28.66 Philip Johnson and John Burgee, with Simmons Architects, AT&T Building, New York. 1978. Photo: Peter Mauss/Esto, New York.

to the "coding" of a building. The Seagram Building, for example, is immediately recognizable as an office building; its code (design) reads "office building." But there is no other code or message, no reference to local or historical traditions. Postmodern design, on the other hand, is characterized by a double coding: the function of the structure coupled with architectural references to local and/or historical elements. The AT&T Building (fig. 28.66) by Philip Johnson (b. 1906) is a hotly debated example of Postmodernist dual coding. Basically a glass-and-steel skyscraper, it has an entrance that is reminiscent of Brunelleschi's Pazzi Chapel (see fig. 17.2) but the pediment resembles eighteenth-century furniture designed in England by Thomas Chippendale (1718–79). According to some detractors, this so-called Chippendale skyscraper looks very much like a grandfather clock. The design is both modern and traditional (Renaissance and Neoclassic) and the overall effect, according to some, is a welcome step away from the impersonal uniformity of the International Style.

The current architectural controversy is between latter-day Modernists and Postmodernists. The former,

unrepentant adherents of Modernism and the International Style, remain committed to advanced technology, efficiency, and austerity. The latter emphasize the city context of each building, the needs and values of the users, and the appropriate ornamentation for each structure. Postmodernism does not, however, take a backseat to Late-Modernism in the use of the latest technology.

The first significant competition for Postmodernism took place in Portland, Oregon, where Michael Graves (b. 1934) competed against a Late-Modernist firm. Graves won the competition (twice) and built a structure now known as The Portland (fig. 28.67). This, the first major monument of Postmodernism, has a clear three-part division: a broad green base, a buff-colored shaft, and a brown keystone resting atop brown pilasters that indicate interior elevator cores. Though still a rather heavy high-rise structure, it has been generally accepted by the citizens as an attractive public building that is comfortably at home in the city of Portland.

28.67 Michael Graves, Portland Public Services Building, Portland, Oregon, view from Fifth Avenue. 1980–2. Photo: Paschall/Taylor.

SUMMARY

The multiplicity of styles and the sheer number of artists of the present century cannot be adequately covered in a chapter or even in a set of books. The discussion of most major styles and some of the important artists should be considered as a preamble to continuing studies of what today's artists are creating. Twentieth-century art is as accessible in this country as Renaissance art is in Italy and can be viewed in any good-sized American city. Most of the illustrations for this chapter, for example, were drawn from the collections of American museums and galleries from New York to the West Coast.

Finally, consider art as what anyone elects to present to us as art, as evidence of human creativity. If we do not like an art work, perhaps it communicates something we already know but refuse to acknowledge. Paradoxically, a work of art that tells us something we know and understand can leave us dissatisfied. We do want the artist to challenge our emotions, our intellect, our knowledge. The more we study art the more likely we are to respond to it and to seek out challenges.

CULTURE AND HUMAN VALUES

Philosopher William Barrett wryly remarked that "modern art tells us most, if we have but eyes to see, about the nature of the modern age which we have traversed or which has almost finished us."[3] Certainly some artistic values changed—at least in emphasis—during the century, notably the long-held belief that art existed to communicate beauty and give pleasure. Beauty and pleasure have not been entirely abandoned, but art as the communication of unpleasant and even terrible truths has been prominent in many artistic movements. Consider, for example, Picasso's *Les Demoiselles d'Avignon* (see fig. 28.5) and its portrayal of the darker aspects of human nature. In *Guernica* (see fig.

28.7) the bombs are not only destroying a defenseless Basque village, but tearing at the very fabric of civilization itself. Kollwitz (see fig. 28.3) depicts common people at the mercy of a militaristic state.

On a smaller scale, most of the work of Pop Artists portrays the tacky, tawdry, and banal American materialism (see fig. 28.35). For a statement on the care and treatment of the elderly, Kienholz gives us *The State Hospital* (see fig. 28.36). The Mexican Social Realists have pictured the plight of peasants, not just in Mexico, but in all Third-World countries (see figs. 28.24–26).

Consider also the sickness and terror communicated by the works of Dubuffet (see fig. 28.42) and Bacon (see fig. 28.43), and the horror depicted by Flack (see p. 468). Whether institutionalized insanity or the madness of Nazi extermination camps, this is all part of the twentieth century.

Has modern art portrayed the twentieth century as thoroughly violent and hopeless beyond recall? Not at all. Some of the works of Brancusi (see fig. 28.12), Chagall (see chapter opener on p. 484), Le Corbusier (see fig. 28.28), Christo and Jeanne-Claude (see fig. 28.51), and Bartlett (see fig. 28.64) present a more positive image. In the final analysis, perhaps the best way to look at modern art is to recognize the truth, the beauty, the love, the faith, and the justice that artists have presented to all of us.

STUDY QUESTION

In the last section of this chapter, Culture and Human Values, the discussion centered on modern art as exemplifying the twentieth century in its ugliness, violence, and despair. From other sources select works that, in your opinion, communicate something of the dark side of the century, then balance this with six works that present a brighter side. Which examples were harder to find?

---

3. *Death of the Soul: From Descartes to the Computer* (Garden City, N.Y.: Anchor Press/Doubleday, 1986), p. 56.

CHAPTER 29

Modern Music

MODERNISM

Twentieth-century music has developed in what have been essentially two phases. Phase one has been a continuation and development of instruments, forms, and styles inherited from the rich tradition represented by Bach, Beethoven, and Brahms. Phase two began in the 1950s with the electronic age. Though the past is still fundamental, an exciting new world of music has burst upon the scene, providing a dazzling display of electronic sounds and instruments, synthesizers, and computer composition and performance, and the innovations continue to proliferate.

Igor Stravinsky, 1882–1971

Stravinsky is perhaps the modern composer whose career best summarizes the ceaseless experimentation and multiplicity of styles of this century. He exploited all the "neo" styles from neo-Gothic to Neoromantic, pausing along the way to try his hand at modern jazz. Thoroughly grounded in the music of the past—he admired the music of Bach above all—he was a superb musical craftsman as well as a bold and daring innovator. Always associated with the European *avant-garde*, he influenced Diaghilev, Cocteau, Picasso, and Matisse and was, in turn, influenced by all of them.

The first and perhaps strongest impetus came from Diaghilev, who commissioned several ballet scores for the Ballet Russe de Monte Carlo of which the first was *The Firebird*. Following the success of *The Firebird*, Stravinsky produced the popular *Petrouchka* ballet and then turned his attention to *The Rite of Spring*.

Success was not immediate for this daringly original work. The 1913 premiere in Paris set off a full-scale riot between Stravinsky's *avant-garde* partisans and his far more numerous detractors. The audience was restless even before the music began; the two camps of "liberal artist" and "conservative establishment" had, in effect, already taken sides. The liberals were as determined to relish the music and the ballet as the conservatives were bent on open hostility. Conservatives viewed the work as an assault on cherished

values of Western culture; liberals regarded it as a metaphor for the vulgar materialism and decadence of the age.

The high-**register** bassoon solo at the very beginning of the piece provoked sneers and audible laughs from the conservative camp and the evening went downhill from there. By the time the police arrived things had gotten totally out of hand and the premiere performance was history. On a television program aired many years later Stravinsky sat in that Parisian hall in the same seat that he had occupied in 1913. When asked what he did during the riot, Stravinsky replied, "I just stood up, told all of them to go to hell and walked out."

The Rite of Spring, subtitled *Pictures of Pagan Russia*, exploits a very large symphony orchestra and uses many unique instrumental effects to portray the primitive ceremonies. Built around the spring fertility rites of ancient Russia, the scenes include the coming of spring, various spring dances, games of the rival tribes, and the selection of the sacrificial virgin. The ballet concludes with the Sacrificial Dance: frenzied convolutions by the Chosen One until she collapses and dies, after which her body is solemnly placed on the sacred mound as an offering to the fertility gods.

Listening Example 39
BALLET MUSIC

Stravinsky, *The Rite of Spring*, Last scene, Sacrificial Dance
1913

Time: 4:37
Cassette 3, track 31[1]

Atonality

Atonality was a musical idea whose time had come. Strictly speaking, atonality was a twentieth-century technique that arbitrarily declared the twelve different notes in an octave to be created free and equal. No one tone would

---

Opposite Memorial Sculpture, Dachau, Germany, detail. Photo: Ullstein, Berlin (Rudolf Dietrich).

1. CD 3, track 6.

predominate; there would be no tonal center, no tonic, no tonality. Curiously symptomatic of the twentieth century, the new system was closely associated with mathematics.

Some modern composers developed what might be called mathematical music. Though atonal composers used no more than simple arithmetic, this was quite sufficient for their manipulations of notes, rhythm, and texture. Following is a brief description of the process of change from tonal to **atonal** music, a development that, in retrospect, was inevitable. Also included are some games that people can play with twelve-tone arithmetic.

The tonal music that had superseded the modes during the seventeenth century was based on the idea that the seven tones of a diatonic scale belonged to a key and that the other five tones were outside the key.[2] Composers relied increasingly on the five tones outside the key to give color and variety to their music. By the end of the nineteenth century musicians such as Wagner and Brahms were regularly using all of the tones as a twelve-tone system of tonality revolving around a central pitch called the tonic, or tonal center.

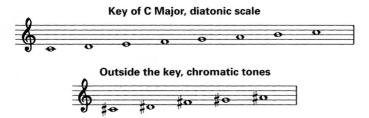

Arnold Schoenberg, 1874–1951

After World War I, Schoenberg (SHURN-burg) developed a system in which all twelve tones were considered exactly equal with no tonal center. There would be no dissonance or consonance as such because all the pitches could be used in any combination and without reference to the centrality of any single pitch. This system of twelve equal musical pitches is called atonality, or the dodecaphonic (twelve-tone) system.

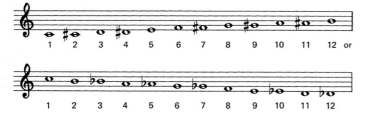

Without a tonic pitch to give the music some sort of unity, it was necessary to devise another kind of unifying system. This new device was called a tone row, or basic set. Composers invented melodic sequences of the twelve tones, using each tone only once and refraining from using any sequence of notes that would imply a key (tonality). Since it is neither necessary nor desirable to limit the twelve

different tones to one octave, a basic set (tone row) could look like this:

Basically, the twelve-tone system lends itself to polyphonic rather than homophonic writing, although almost anyone can devise and use a mixture of polyphonic and homophonic techniques. Because of the infinite possibilities of manipulating the row, the problem becomes one of selectivity, choosing those possibilities that make musical sense.

Twelve-tone composition is both a musical process and a mathematical or mechanical procedure. The finished composition might be very different and original in sound (and it might not). Whether it is good music or bad music still remains the province of the composer, who makes up one or more tone rows, manipulating, selecting, and modifying until he gets the musical results he wants. Neither a virtue nor a vice, twelve-tone technique is merely a means to an end. It may assist the composer to discover new melodic, rhythmic, and harmonic ideas and different combinations of these ideas, but it will not do a thing for the finished product; that's up to the creator.

Alban Berg, 1885–1935

Berg was one of the most musically creative of the twelve-tone composers. His style is also notable for clear, clean orchestral writing. For his Violin Concerto he used a small, versatile orchestra with a delicate contrapuntal texture.

Berg's tone row was not a mechanical contrivance but a point of departure for some lyrical music. He deliberately constructed a row with clear tonal implications, mixing G minor, A minor, and a portion of the whole-tone scale.

Listening Example 40
VIOLIN CONCERTO

Berg, Violin Concerto, 1st movement
1935; excerpt

Time: 2:12
Cassette 3, track 32

2. In the key of C major, for example, the white notes belong to the key and the black notes are outside the key.

NEOCLASSICISM, EXPRESSIONISM, AND NEOROMANTICISM

The styles of twentieth-century music are many and varied, as befits a dynamic art in a rapidly changing age. The vogue of neoprimitivism (*The Rite of Spring* and other similar compositions) had its day; Romanticism, whether called Neoromantic or Postromantic, continues to have some influence; nationalism is once again a characteristic of the works of some composers. One trend has been toward Classicism, as in the works of the twelve-tone school and, among many others, the music of the Hungarian composer Béla Bartók.

Béla Bartók, 1881–1945

Bartók was one of the outstanding composers of the century. Born in Hungary, he escaped the Nazi terror and settled in New York City where he made a meager living as a piano teacher and concert pianist. Only after his death was there any significant recognition of the consistently high quality of his music. The shy, soft-spoken Hungarian refugee wrote some powerful music characterized by great intensity and depth of feeling.

His style was an amalgam of Hungarian folk music, great rhythmic ingenuity, and a fundamental allegiance to Classical forms. He delighted in the folk music of southeastern Europe because it helped free him from the tyranny of the major-minor system and provided him with rhythmic conceptions. His preoccupation with formal unity and coherence led him to a unique style of continuous variations, a dynamic and thoroughly modern style of relentless tension and growth.

Bartók's Piano Concerto No. 3 has become a concert favorite. The third movement is in five-part rondo form: ABACA.

Listening Example 41
PIANO CONCERTO

Bartók, Piano Concerto No. 3, 3rd movement
1945

Time: 7:20[3]

Charles Ives, 1874–1954

The startling innovations of Charles Ives anticipated just about every important development of the first half-century: serial and aleatory music,[4] mixed meters and tempos, blocks of sound, free forms, the possibilities of accidental or chance acoustical experiences, assemblages, collages, and even early manifestations of Pop Art. However, despite an impressive array of *avant-garde* techniques, Ives was still

a traditional New Englander who wanted to maintain his philosophical relationship with the recent literary past. His important *Concord Sonata* for piano has four movements named after five Transcendentalists: Emerson, Hawthorne, the Alcotts, and Thoreau.

To understand what Ives is getting at in his music one must recognize the music that he quotes—the church hymns, dance music, and military band music. These quotes are comments on life in the small towns and rural areas of America. His nostalgic *Three Places in New England*, for orchestra, is replete with quotations from Americana and illustrates a concern for the American heritage as profound as that of Walt Whitman.

Listening Example 42
ORCHESTRAL MUSIC

Ives, *Three Places in New England*, 2nd movement, "Putnam's Camp, Redding, Connecticut"
1903–11; excerpt

Time: 3:05
Cassette 3, track 33[5]

Near Redding Center is a small park preserved as a Revolutionary Memorial; for here General Israel Putnam's soldiers had their winter quarters in 1778–9. Long rows of stone camp fireplaces still remain to stir a child's imagination. The scene is a "4th of July" picnic held under the auspices of the First Church and the Village Cornet Band. The child wanders into the woods and dreams of the old soldiers, of the hardships they endured, their desire to break camp and abandon their cause, and of how they returned when Putnam came over the hills to lead them. The little boy awakes, he hears the children's songs and runs down past the monument to "listen to the band" and join in the games and dances.

Charles Ives

Atonality: Postscript

The twelve-tone system of the Viennese School of Schoenberg, Berg, and Anton Webern (VAY-burn; 1883–1945) went into temporary decline in the 1930s and 1940s. Berg died in 1935 and many composers fled for their lives from totalitarian states that demanded simplistic music in a national style. Schoenberg emigrated to the

---

3. CD 3, track 12.
4. Aleatory (AY-lee-uh-tore-e) means "depending on chance, or luck: hence aleatory music allows for random choice in its composition.
5. CD 3, track 7.

United States. Webern, however, stayed on in Vienna, quietly creating rigorous twelve-tone music that was to captivate postwar composers. Ironically, Webern survived tyranny and the war only to be accidentally killed by an American soldier shortly after the end of the war.

The music of Webern is difficult to characterize apart from the sound: a kind of Cubist pointillism with meaningful breathing spaces. Webern wrote some of the most beautiful rests—the sounds of silence—in music. He used few notes in a short space of time, manipulating isolated, contrasted tone colors in a space-time continuum. All is rigorous, precise, twelve-tone mathematics, but Webern combined the isolation of single tones with the dissociation of sequential events to make up a total musical interrelationship. The contrasting tone colors in his *Three Songs* are soprano voice, clarinet, and guitar.

Listening Example 43

SONGS WITH INSTRUMENTAL ACCOMPANIMENT

Webern, *Three Songs*, Op. 18, 1. "Schatzerl klein" ("Sweetheart, Dear"); 2 "Erlösung" ("Redemption"); 3. "Ave, Regina" ("Hail, Queen") 1925

Times: 1:01, 1:05, 1:22
Cassette 3, track 34 ("Schatzerl klein")[6]

Serial Technique and Electronic Music

Partly because of the presence of Schoenberg, twelve-tone composition in the United States flourished during the war. After 1945 it was again prominent in western Europe. Eastern-Bloc countries, however, condemned its dissonant complexities as "bourgeois decadence." Some composers expanded twelve-tone writing from a method into an elaborate system called serial technique or serial composition. Although the old method was never a matter of simply arranging the twelve pitches into a row, the new procedure systematized other elements of music such as rhythm, harmony, tempo, dynamics, **timbre**, and so forth. For example, a serial composition could contain mathematical permutations of twelve pitches, a sixteen-unit rhythmic organization, a sequence of twenty-nine chords, and fourteen timbres (tone colors). When one considers that there are approximately half a billion ways of arranging just the twelve pitches, the mathematical possibilities of serial technique systems approach infinity. Whether these combined mathematical procedures produce music worth listening to is strictly up to the composer.

While the serialists pursue the manifold possibilities of their systems, other composers have concentrated on the exploitation of noise and timbre. Traditionally, tone color has been more ornamental than essential to Western music and the incorporation of "noise" was unthinkable. But musical sounds as such are only a minuscule part of the modern world of acoustical phenomena. We are surrounded and often engulfed by noise ranging from city traffic, electrical appliances, and factory din to the "noises" of nature: sounds of the animal world, thunder, rain, hail, seasounds, windsounds, and so forth.

The Electronic Revolution

Much of the experimentation with timbre and noise has been incorporated into the several varieties of electronic music. In fact, electronic music appears to be a natural stage in the evolution of Western music. In the early, predominantly vocal, era, the singer was his or her own instrument. During the Baroque period there was a general parity between vocal and instrumental music, after which instrumental music clearly dominated vocal music. Musicians began to use what amounted to mechanical extensions for music-making, with varying degrees of dissociation between performer and instrument. Wind players, for example, are in close contact with their instruments, string players have some direct control, but keyboard instruments, especially the pipe organ, are quite mechanical. The evolution from a personal instrument (the voice) to an instrument once-removed (for example, the trumpet) has now progressed to the introduction of instruments twice-removed, that is, wholly the product of technology and entirely removed from direct human contact.

This instrumental evolution seems to reflect the condition of contemporary culture, in which so many activities are carried on untouched by human hands. Computers are talking to computers whereas many people find it ever more difficult to communicate with each other. One might argue that the exclusion of human beings from the production of musical sounds spells the death of art and the triumph of technology. On the other hand, there is evidence that the electronic manipulations of sound can open up a whole new era of musical forms, while simultaneously stimulating new vitality in vocal and instrumental music. If this optimistic view proves to be the correct one, it will bear out the thesis emphasized throughout this book: that the ferment and rapid change in contemporary life are apparently a necessary prelude to a more humane society that may already be taking form. In any event, electronic music, along with all our highly developed technology, is here to stay.

The age of electronic music began in 1951 when Cologne Radio opened the first electronic studio. Other studios were subsequently opened in Paris, Milan, Tokyo,

---

6. CD 3, track 9 ("Schatzerl klein"); CD 3, track 10 ("Erlösung"); CD 3, track 11 ("Ave, Regina").

and at Columbia University and the Bell Laboratories in the United States—and many more are now in operation. Milton Babbitt began working in electronic music with the R.C.A. Electronic Sound Synthesizer. His *Ensembles for Synthesizer* uses a wide variety of tone colors and complex rhythms at tempos faster than human performers can hope to reproduce.

Listening Example 44

ELECTRONIC MUSIC

Babbitt, *Ensembles for Synthesizer*
1962–4; excerpt

Time: 1:05
Cassette 3, track 35

Barton McLean (b. 1938) composed the following composition at the Electronic Music Center of the University of Texas in Austin. He used a Fairlight Computer Musical Instrument (CMI). Computer-generated sounds are used exclusively. The title refers to the tunefulness of the composition and its étude-like character.

Listening Example 45

ELECTRONIC MUSIC

McLean, *Etunytude*
1982

Time: 5:28[7]

Chance Music

After the mid-1950s, the nature of *avant-garde* music began to change. Total serialism grew into new materials based on the many ways of transforming textures, colors, and sound densities. From the earlier "controlled chance" compositions, with some options controlled by the composer and others by the performer, the movement shifted to multiple forms of control and chance and to so-called "open forms" in which chance was the major factor. Aleatory music (Lat., *alea*; "dice") is a general term describing various kinds of music in which chance, unpredictability, ambiguity, and even sheer chaos are realized in performance. If strict serial music represents a kind of Newtonian, mathematical determinism, then aleatory music represents its exact opposite: a symbolic rolling of musical dice just to see what will happen.

This conflict between calculation and chance is a

musical equivalent to the current situation in science. The precision of the Newtonian world machine has been supplanted by a modern science that is forced to settle for contingent proofs, complementary truths, and/or mathematical concepts of uncertainty. Quantum theory recognizes the element of chance and its language has been carried over, however ineffectively, into aesthetic theories. Strict mathematical concepts (except for "pure" mathematics), whether in science or art, can lead only to dead ends: scientific "truths" that are jarred by further gains in knowledge and strict mathematics in music that lead to the sterility of nonart. Chance music is therefore a corollary of modern science, and a reflection of both the profundity and absurdity of contemporary life.

John Cage, 1912–92

John Cage (fig. 29.1) was one of the first American composers to experiment with chance music. In the late 1930s he worked with a "prepared piano" that was designed to produce percussive sounds and noises that were unrelated to its traditional sound. From the early 1950s on, he

---

29.1 John Cage "preparing" a piano. Photo: New York Times.

produced works of indeterminate length, of chance operations, of chance media (a concert of a group of radios tuned
to different stations), and similar techniques. One of his
most widely discussed compositions is a piano solo titled
4'33" during which the pianist merely sits quietly at the
piano for this period of time, after which he or she bows
and leaves the stage. Obviously the composition "sounds"
different at each performance because of the variance in
noise from the audience. This composition would have to
be considered the ultimate in Minimal art as well as an
achievement somewhat comparable to the "non-wheat" that
a farmer produces in exchange for government money. The
logical conclusion might be to have the government pay
artists for non-poetry, non-novels, and non-paintings. At
that point the ultimate absurdity would have been reached
and Dada would reign supreme.

And Dada is related to chance music, or vice versa, just
as are Cage's ideas of the Chinese chance technique of coin-
throwing from the *I Ching* and his fascination with Zen
Buddhism. Chance music may include instructions on manuscripts such as: "Start when you like and repeat as often as
necessary"; "Hold this note as long as you like and then go
on to the next one"; "Wait till the spirit moves you and then
make up your own piece." Performers may also be instructed to destroy their instruments, stare at the audience, propel vehicles about the stage, blow sirens, flash lights, and
perform other stimulating activities. The result might be
called Aimless Theatre rather than theatre of the absurd,
although there appear to be common elements.

Functional Music

Not all contemporary music is of the *avant-garde* variety.
Paul Hindemith (1895–1963) was a Neoclassicist in his
retention of tonal writing and his devotion to the style of
J. S. Bach. He also advocated *Gebrauchmusik* (Ger., "useful music," that is, functional) and wrote music for all ages
and degrees of musical skills and for numerous special
events that called for appropriate music. One of his best
works is the symphonic version of *Mathis der Maler*, a moving depiction in sound of the *Isenheim Altarpiece* by Matthias
Grünewald (1480–1528). The form of the second movement is ABA'Coda.

Listening Example 46
ORCHESTRAL MUSIC

Hindemith, *Mathis der Maler*, 2nd movement,
Grablegung (Entombment)
1934

Time: 4:08[8]

American Musical Theatre

After meeting the playwright Bertolt Brecht, Kurt Weill
(1900–50) deliberately rejected the complexities of modern music. In conjunction with Brecht he wrote *The
Threepenny Opera* and *The Fall of the House of Mahagony*.
Threepenny and *Mahagony* were partly responsible for the
blossoming of musical theatre in America, which began
with Rodgers and Hammerstein's *Oklahoma!* and continued through their *South Pacific, Carousel,* and *The Sound
of Music.* Bernstein's *West Side Story* and Lerner and Loewe's
My Fair Lady and *Camelot* are notable contributions to the
musical theatre. The finest talent in contemporary music
theatre is unquestionably Stephen Sondheim (b. 1930),
who writes both words and music. His musicals include
West Side Story (lyrics), *A Funny Thing Happened on the
Way to the Forum, A Little Night Music, Pacific Overtures,
Sweeney Todd, Passion*, and, based on Seurat's painting,
Sunday in the Park with George.

George Gershwin (1898–1937) may be one of
America's best composers. Criticized by musical snobs as
"popular" and thus, for some strange reason, beyond the
pale, his music has endured and much of it has become a
part of the standard repertory. *Rhapsody in Blue, An
American in Paris*, and the Concerto in F have all become
known throughout the world as truly representative of
American music. *Of Thee I Sing* is now recognized as musical theatre at its satirical best and *Porgy and Bess* is perhaps America's finest opera.

Minimalism

Philip Glass, b. 1937

Some critics claim that Glass is, after Gershwin, America's
best composer. Certainly one of the most provocative of
contemporary composers, Glass has developed his own
unique style of Minimalism. He combines Hindu rhythmic
cycles and other devices of non-Western music with some
Rock plus Western-style intervals and harmonies that have
been reduced to the barest essentials. The result—sometimes called "solid state music"—is not so austere as it
sounds, for Glass is not afraid to use elements from the
classical tradition. On the other hand, he is just as likely
to use the synthesis of Jazz and Rock styles called "New
Age" Fusion.

One of his first major successes was *Einstein on the
Beach* (1976), a 4½-hour multi-media production that has
been billed as an opera, but which is actually a series of
events. His first true opera was *Satyagraha* (1980), a complex work based on the *Bhagavad Gita* and sung entirely
in Sanskrit. This was followed by *Akhenaten* (1984), an
opera about the pharaoh who introduced monotheism to
ancient Egypt.

8. CD 3, track 13.

JAZZ IN AMERICA

Jazz is a uniquely different style of music, the result of a fusion—collision might be a better word—of certain elements of African and American musical cultures. Aside from Native American music, music in the United States and the rest of the New World was of European origin and influenced by European styles. Given the European heritage and the presence of African slaves and freedmen throughout the United States, the islands of the Caribbean, and Central and South America, the singular and significant fact remains that jazz originated solely in the United States. By the turn of the century, African-American spirituals, ragtime, blues, and jazz were established types or styles of music, none of which existed anywhere else in the Western Hemisphere.

The French, Spanish, Portuguese, Dutch, and even English cultures of the West Indies and Central and South America apparently provided a climate in which African arts, crafts, customs, and religious beliefs could coexist with their European counterparts. For whatever reasons, and there appear to be many, the dominant white culture of the American South was not as tolerant of African customs as were the transplanted European cultures south of the United States. There existed a strong conflict between white and black Americans in almost every area of life: religion, folklore, music, art, dance, and social and political customs.

In summary, jazz is a musical style that evolved out of three centuries of cultural and racial conflict, a clash between an inflexible dominant culture and a powerful and persistent subculture with its own age-old beliefs and customs. Jazz continues to evolve, of course, including even a change in name. A number of jazz musicians now refer to their music as African-American classical music.

The Elements of Jazz

The elements of jazz are those of any music: melody, harmony, rhythm, and tone color. The African-American mixture makes the difference. The development of any style of music normally follows an evolutionary process within a single culture. Outside influences, when they appear, tend to be transformed and absorbed into the stylistic development. The Viennese waltz, for example, is a modified, speeded-up version of an old Austrian folk dance called a *Ländler*. The *Ländler* was Austrian; the changes were compatible with Austrian concepts of melody, harmony, rhythm, and tone color. The finished product was in all respects the result of Austrian culture and the musical genius of one Johann Strauss, Jr. It would be ludicrous to remove a Strauss melody and insert a Russian boat song, an Irish jig, or a Hopi rain dance. Scale, harmony, rhythm, and tone color would be all wrong because an incompatible melody was introduced into a foreign context.

Jazz sounds the way it does because it *is* a compound of several different and even opposing concepts of melody, rhythm, and tone color. In very general terms, jazz is a musical style consisting of African-European melody, European harmony, African rhythm, and African-European tone color. A built-in conflict of musical styles lies at the root of jazz and probably accounts, at least in part, for the feelings of dislocation and sometimes anguish and even pain on the part of performers and listeners.

The fundamental conflict in the materials of jazz occurs in scale and tuning. Equal temperament, with its twelve equal semitones in each octave, is the tuning standard for Western music. On the other hand, African melody was and is based on the tones present in the overtone series. The distances between pitches range from whole steps and half steps, similar to those in the tempered scale, to other intervals between half steps, including quarter-tones. African harmony is quite rudimentary; melody, rhythm, and tone color are far more important.

African melodies, with their different-sized intervals, were, when transported to America, sung in a culture that did not use such a variety of intervals, that built musical instruments in equal temperament. In that culture African songs were often characterized as out of tune, primitive, or a poor imitation of "proper" singing.

Scale

The combining of African scales with the European diatonic scale produced a hybrid called the blues scale.[9] In terms of the equal-tempered piano the blues scale can be described as a diatonic scale plus three blue notes: flatted 3rd, 5th, and 7th.

Blues scale

Blue notes

Rhythm

Rhythm is the main ingredient in African music: highly developed, intricate, complex, as sophisticated in its own way as the harmonic system of Western culture. The African rhythms that have crossed over into jazz and into much of our modern music are but a relatively simple portion of a whole world of elaborate percussion music.

There are two interrelated fundamental characteristics of African rhythm: beat and syncopation. Emerging from the simultaneous rhythm patterns is a subjective beat, a rhythmic pulsation that is not necessarily played by any one drummer but which results from the combination of the whole. The beat is implicit. This beat (whether explicit or implicit) is so much a part of jazz that it can be called

---

9. The blues scale is not African in itself although its origins necessarily lie in African music. Rather it is an African-American scale, and it is the elemental component out of which jazz is made.

its heartbeat or pulse. Jazz can thus be defined as the "beauty of the beat."

Syncopation is a displacement or shifting of accents so that they disagree with natural metrical accents. It has the effect of tugging at the beat, a dynamic process that emphasizes the existence of the basic pulse by setting up a conflict with that pulse. The pull of syncopation against the ongoing beat gives a swing to the music, a buoyant resilience that is a fundamental characteristic of jazz.

Tone Color

The story is told of a World War II air base in Africa that stockpiled aviation gasoline in steel drums. The drums were unloaded and stacked by native laborers, one of whom accidentally dropped a drum and noticed a booming, reverberant tone as it hit the ground. His neighbor immediately dropped his drum to discover its tone color. Within a very few minutes, in their delight at discovering new tone colors, the entire crew was enthusiastically engaged in dropping, hitting, and scraping gasoline drums.

Beating on logs, sticks, bones, metal, or drums, scratching gourds, shaking rattles—all are activities designed to exploit tone colors within a rhythmic framework. An African drummer can obtain several dozen different timbres by using his thumbs, fingers, flat of the hand, or fist on various areas of a drumhead. All that is necessary for a percussion instrument is a distinctive sound and virtually no limit to the number and variety of possible tone colors.

Distinctive tone color in jazz is not confined to the drums. It extends to the colors obtained by using mutes, hats, plungers, handkerchiefs, or anything else that will give variety to the timbre of instruments such as trumpet and trombone. Instrumentalists also use growls, slurs, and slides to broaden their expressive range and impart a personal quality to their music. The colors may be cool or hot or anything in between; in any event, jazz musicians are concerned with their sound, the distinctive coloration of their performance.

Harmony

Harmony, one of the most highly developed elements of Western culture, is of only slight importance in African music. Consequently, the fusion of African and American music was essentially a combining of African melody, rhythm, and tone color with an established harmonic system. The result, as stated before, was a synthesis of conflicting stylistic elements and the beginning of a new style of music called jazz.

Pre-Jazz Styles (African-American Folk Music)

Some of the many types of folk music date back to the arrival of the first indentured workers and slaves in the seventeenth century; other music developed in response to—

or despite—the American environment. The African vocal tradition survived as it adjusted to the strange servile conditions and the new religion of Christianity. The instrumental tradition, especially drums, was rigorously suppressed by the slaveholders, who suspected, and rightly so, that African drums could communicate such terrifying possibilities as slave rebellions. The planters were thus inadvertently successful in their drive to break up tribal units and destroy their traditions. They did not know that tribal histories were entirely oral and perpetuated by the drummers and the language of the drum script.[10] The **banjo** (African, *banjar*) did manage to survive, but European instruments were gradually taken up by African-American musicians. Out of this mélange of African and American cultures emerged a remarkably rich tradition of folk music, much of which is still performed today.

Secular Music

The work song is closely related to an African tradition of rhythmic songs that have the effect of making hard work a bit easier. They are usually unaccompanied, but sometimes have a guitar or banjo accompaniment. They are associated with manual labor that has a rhythmic regularity: chopping wood, rowing a boat, driving railroad spikes.

Example: "Juliana Johnson"[11]

Hollers (field hollers) are sung during non-rhythmic fieldwork such as picking cotton or hoeing corn. Unaccompanied and with an irregular beat, they frequently use narration mixed with singsong chants.

Example: "Old Hannah"

The street cry is sung by street-sellers of fruit, vegetables, fish, and so forth. Unaccompanied, with constant repetition of the name of the product, the seller maintains interest with continuous changes in pitch and tone quality.

Examples: "Crab Man" and "Strawberry Woman" from Porgy and Bess *(George Gershwin)*

Narrative songs with numerous verses, **ballads** were originally African heroic songs of kings, warriors, and hunters. American versions are about folk heroes such as John Henry, the steel-driving man.

Example: "John Henry"

---

10. Some African languages, especially the varieties of Bantu, used different pitch-levels of vowel sounds for different word-meanings. Tribal historians were highly select drummers who were trained to play the talking drum by beating out the word rhythms while at the same time varying the pitch by means of a stretched membrane. The drum script was virtually a vocal sound that could be transmitted over considerable distances with the aid of relay drummers.

11. Titles and/or performers are sometimes given rather than specific recordings, which may or may not be available given the vagaries of the recording industry.

Blues

The blues are the most important single influence in the development of jazz. There are two basic kinds of blues: folk blues (rural blues) and urban blues (true jazz blues). They reflect African customs and musical traditions, but they are native to America. The blues are personal, subjective, introspective, a way of protesting misfortune and identifying trouble. Singing the blues is a survival technique for counteracting bad times, loneliness, and despair.

Blues lyrics usually consist of three lines of poetry. The first line is repeated (possibly with a slight variation) followed by a third line that completes the thought. Because blues are usually improvised, the repeating of the second line gives the singer more time to make up the last line. There may be only one verse or there may be many verses in a narrative blues. Favorite subjects are love, traveling, and trouble, but almost anything makes a fit subject, as shown by the following blues poems.

Love:
Love is like a faucet, you can turn it off or on, [twice]
But when you think you've got it, it's done turned off and gone.

Traveling:
I went to the deepot, an' looked upon de boa'd. [twice]
It say: dere's good times here, dey's better down de road.

Proverbs:
My momma tole me, my daddy tole me too: [twice]
Everybody grin in yo' face, ain't no friend to you.

Images:
Ef blues was whiskey, I'd stay drunk all de time. [twice]
Blues ain't nothin' but a po'man's heart disease.

Comedy:
Want to lay my head on de railroad line, [twice]
Let the train come along and pacify my mind.

Tragedy:
[one line images]
Got the blues but too damn mean to cry.
Standin' here lookin' one thousand miles away.
I hate to see the evenin' sun go down.
Been down so long, Lawd, down don't worry me.

Sacred Music

Most spirituals are derived from Protestant hymns, but with significant changes in text, melody, and rhythm (usually syncopated). Frequently improvised, especially during church services and prayer meetings, they use texts that are variations on existing hymns or paraphrases of biblical verses and stories. They are notable for vividness of imagery, the relating of biblical stories with direct and telling simplicity, and a strong concern for the sounds and rhythms of words.

Example: "Swing Low, Sweet Chariot"

The ring shout is similar to African circle dances in form and character. Usually performed outdoors after a church service, the worshipers form a ring while singing a spiritual to start the ring slowly revolving. Accompanied by hand claps and foot stomping, the spiritual is sung over and over until the accumulative effect is hypnotic.

Example: "Come and Go with Me"

A jubilee is a particular kind of spiritual that sings triumphantly of the Year of Jubilee "When the Saints Go Marching In."

Gospel songs differ from hymns and spirituals mostly in the texts, which are more personal and subjective. "I," "me," "my" are the key words in songs that tend to reduce religious experience to a personal viewpoint.

Example: "My God Is Real"

The song-sermon is delivered from the pulpit, usually beginning with a scriptural quotation. The vocal delivery of the minister moves gradually from the spoken word to a kind of intoned chant, culminating in ringing declamation and vocalized phrases on higher and higher pitches. The African custom of responding verbally to important personages, such as tribal chieftains, is reflected in the congregational response to the song-sermon. There are shouts of "amen," "yes sir," "hallelujah," and impromptu wordless crooning.

Example: "Dry Bones"

Voodoo (*vodun*) is the name given to the combination of African and Catholic religious rites and beliefs that was developed in Haiti by the Dahomeans of West Africa and that still exists in the West Indies and in portions of the United States, particularly Louisiana. Voodoo rites took place in Congo Square in New Orleans before being driven underground. Voodoo helped perpetuate African customs and music and made significant contributions to African-American folk music and to the development of jazz.

Example: "Drums of Haiti"

Entertainment

Dating from about the middle of the nineteenth century, minstrel shows were sentimentalized "scenes of plantation life" performed by an all-male, all-white cast. Characteristic African-American elements were present in some of the group dances, the use of rhythmic "bones," tambourine, and banjo, the soft-shoe dances and the cakewalk finale. Stephen Collins Foster's songs (many of them based on African-American folk music) were a popular staple. Minstrelsy dealt with stereotypes that no longer exist, if they ever did, but it can be credited with disseminating a portion of African-American musical culture throughout the United States and Europe and preparing the way for the more authentic music of a later period.

Ragtime

Ragtime is a written-down style of music originally composed for the piano and featuring syncopated rhythmic patterns over a regular left-hand accompaniment in **duple meter**. The essentials of ragtime probably were in existence prior to the Civil War, although Scott Joplin is formally credited as the first to write ragtime in the mid-1890s. Slaves in their quarters liked to imitate, even parody, the fancy balls in the plantation house by staging a cakewalking contest. The highest-stepping couple "took the cake." The basic cakewalk patterns consisted of duple meter plus two kinds of melodic syncopations:

Kinds of melodic syncopation

There is a considerable body of ragtime piano literature, but, since most of it is too difficult for the average pianist to play, there is also much watered-down semi-ragtime popular music from the period 1900–20. Almost any piece of music can be "ragged" by changing the meter to duple, if necessary, and converting the rhythms into ragtime patterns. In developed ragtime these syncopations would include the two patterns illustrated above plus the more difficult pattern of four-note groups in which every third note is accented:

Further ragtime pattern of syncopation

Examples: "The Entertainer" and "Maple Leaf Rag" by Scott Joplin

THE STYLES OF JAZZ

New Orleans Style

Jazz began at one or more places in the American South sometime between the end of the Civil War and the last decade of the nineteenth century. New Orleans may or may not be the birthplace of jazz, but it certainly figured prominently in the promulgation of the new music. Jazz, New Orleans style, began in the 1890s as brass-band performances of spirituals and gospel songs, and ragtime versions of standard band marches. This is the so-called traditional jazz that, in a more discreet version played by white musicians, became known as Dixieland jazz. The original New Orleans style, however, still exists and is normally referred to as such.

Brass bands secured many of their instruments from pawn shops, where they had been deposited after the Civil

War by returning military bandsmen. The instrumentation was typical of marching bands: trumpets, trombones, tuba, snare drum, bass drum, and usually one clarinet. The bands played and paraded for all special functions but especially for funeral processions. According to a long-standing tradition they played spirituals and dirges on the way to the cemetery and some of the same music in a jazz idiom on the way back.

New Orleans jazz is ensemble jazz; everyone plays all the time. In general, the first trumpet has the melody, the clarinet a moving **obbligato** above the trumpet, and the trombone a contrapuntal bass below the lead trumpet. The material is normally gospel songs, spirituals, and marches, and the meter invariably duple. ("In the churches they sang the spirituals. In the bright New Orleans sun, marching down the street, they played them.") Needless to say, all the music was played by ear and everyone was free to improvise a suitable part for himself. ("You play your part and I play mine. You don't tell me what you want and I don't tell you. We will all variate on the theme.") The texture was polyphonic, a crude but dynamic grouping of musical voices improvising simultaneously on the melodic and harmonic framework of preexisting music. One word that best describes New Orleans jazz is "exuberant."

In the following example New Orleans jazz has moved indoors and added vocal and instrumental solos—plus a piano.

Listening Example 47
NEW ORLEANS JAZZ

Hardin-Armstrong, *Hotter than That*
1927

Time: 3:02
Cassette 3, track 36[12]

Urban Blues

Urban blues are the heart of the true jazz idiom. The accompaniment has changed from the folk (or country) blues guitar to piano or jazz band. The subject matter revolves around the problems of urban (ghetto) life. The feeling is still bittersweet, and the form has crystallized into the classic twelve-bar blues accompanying the rhymed couplet in iambic pentameter. The blues may be sung or played by any instrument. Recorded in 1925, the following urban blues stars Bessie Smith as the blues singer with Louis Armstrong playing cornet.

12. CD 4, track 3.

Listening Example 48
BLUES

Handy, *St. Louis Blues*
1914

Time: 3:08[13]

Chicago Style

With the closing of Storyville, the legal red-light district of New Orleans (1897–1917), jazz musicians began moving north in increasing numbers. Prohibition and the rise of bootlegging in the Roaring Twenties helped make Chicago the home for unemployed musicians playing the new and exciting sounds of jazz. Briefly stated, Chicago jazz is New Orleans jazz moved indoors. The ensemble used on the march in the New Orleans sun now played in crowded speakeasies for such dances as the Fox Trot, Shimmy, Black Bottom, and Charleston.

Some of the simultaneous improvising remains, but bands are playing many popular songs in a more homophonic, though still lively and swinging, style. The meter is mostly duple, but the instrumentation has changed. The piano, a newcomer to jazz, furnishes the rhythmic harmonic background; drums, guitar or banjo, tuba, or string bass provide the rhythm. Varying combinations of trumpet, clarinet, trombone, and saxophone (another newcomer) play the melody and harmony. March tempos have been superseded by a range of tempos suitable for the various dances. The one word for Chicago style would be "frenetic."

Examples: Recordings made in the 1920s (and later): Jelly Roll Morton; Bix Beiderbecke

Swing

The Swing era began during the Depression years, the so-called Dancing Thirties. After the repeal of Prohibition in 1933 the speakeasies closed down, leaving many jazz musicians again out of work. The musical migration turned in the direction of New York City, with its radio stations, large ballrooms, and crowds of young dancers seeking cheap entertainment. (The usual cost of a dancing date was 25¢–30¢ admission plus two soft drinks.)

The six- or eight-piece bands of the Chicago era were large enough for the tiny speakeasies (with minuscule dance floors) but too small for the spacious ballrooms. More musicians had to be added and stylistic changes were made to accommodate them. The individuality of the New Orleans and Chicago styles was subordinated to ensemble playing mixed with improvised solo performances; Big Band jazz was born. Divided into three units of brass (two trumpets, two trombones), four saxophones, and a solid rhythm base (piano, drums, guitar, string bass), the swing band launched what is now recognized as the classic era of jazz. Swing was by far the dominant style of the Depression years through to the end of World War II.

Listening Example 49
BIG BAND SWING

Duke Ellington, *Old King Dooji*
1938

Time: 2:29[14]

Listening Example 50
JAZZ QUARTET

Benny Goodman, *Dizzy Spells*
1938

Time: 5:47[15]

After the Bop Revolution that followed World War II (see below) Big Band jazz surfaced again as Progressive jazz, a modern version of the basic swing style. By the 1970s the term was Mainstream jazz because the Big Band sound was once again in the mainstream of American jazz.

Examples: Recordings of the 1930s and 1940s (Swing) and 1970s, 1980s, and 1990s (Mainstream): Count Basie; Duke Ellington; Benny Goodman (fig. 29.2); Glenn Miller; Woody Herman; Stan Kenton; Don Ellis

New Orleans Revival

The revival of Swing was preceded by an even more basic revival, that of traditional New Orleans jazz. Some white San Francisco musicians took the first steps, in 1939, to save what was left of the original jazz style. First-generation jazz musicians were brought out of retirement and old records collected and studied. Some revivalists used the ragtime piano, banjo, tuba, clarinet, trumpet, trombone, and drums in the authentic two-beat New Orleans style. Others mixed New Orleans with the four-beat characteristics of Swing to create Dixieland. Typical Dixieland jazz uses the "front line" of obbligato clarinet, lead trumpet, and fluid trombone (tailgate trombone) backed by drums, bass, and piano.

13. CD 4, track 2.
14. CD 4, track 4.
15. CD 4, track 5.

29.2   Benny Goodman and His Orchestra. Photo: Range/Bettmann, London.

Other Examples: Preservation Hall Jazz Band; Pete Fountain; Al Hirt

The Bop Revolution

During the long musicians' recording and broadcast strike midway through World War II, an entirely new style of jazz was developing. On the resumption of recording and broadcasting the unsuspecting public heard, in the style known as Bop (or Rebop or Bebop), the startling sounds of the beginning of modern jazz. The increasingly regimented swing style had stifled most creative activity. Bop took musical control away from the arranger and returned it to the performing musician. The domination of Swing was not the only issue, for the emergence of Bop was much more of a revolution than most people realized at the time. The radical change in jazz was, it might be said, the first wave of the Civil Rights movement that began with full force in the mid-1950s. Led by African-American jazz musicians, the Bop movement was opposed to all aspects of the white establishment, especially the white swing bands that had a near-monopoly of the commercial market of records, radio, and television.

16. CD 4, track 6.

Bop groups were small combos of six or seven instruments who played jazz for listening rather than for dancing. With fast, often frenetic, tempos, highly elaborated melodic and rhythmic patterns, and modern dissonant harmonies, the Bop combo actually played chamber-music jazz. No longer confined to maintaining the beat, the piano and guitar were played much more melodically. The beat was lighter because it was laid down by the string bass rather than the Swing-style percussion of guitar, piano, and drums. The drummer was freed from the basic beat to become a more versatile percussionist.

Bop combos consistently improvised but they usually avoided the conventional pattern of paraphrasing an existing melody while "playing the changes" (improvising on the harmonies). They preferred to create new melodic lines out of existing harmonies. In this way, for example, Dizzy Gillespie and Charlie Parker converted a popular romantic ballad named "Whispering" into an uptempo Bop version called "Groovin' High."

Combining a new melody with the existing harmonies of a popular song had a critical extra-musical function: it enabled musicians to avoid what many truly detested—audience requests for specific titles. This was the primary reason for performing "Whispering" as "Groovin' High." Technically, the request of the bewildered customer/listener was granted, but only on terms that the performer could accept. The problem was not a basic antagonism between musicians and the public but different perceptions of jazz itself.

Modern Jazz

Shortly after Bop arrived on the scene (during the late 1940s) jazz passed almost imperceptibly from a form of entertainment (dancing and listening) to an art form in its own right. Assimilated Bop techniques made important contributions but the significant factor was the change in attitude: music-making that had no other purpose or function than aesthetic communication between performers and their listening audience. The performance of "requests" would henceforth have about as much validity as asking the Philadelphia Orchestra to play "When the Saints Go Marching In."

The leaders of modern jazz included Dizzy Gillespie, Charlie Parker, Bud Powell, Miles Davis, and the big bands

Listening Example 52
MODERN JAZZ

Kooper, *House in the Country*
1969

Time: 2:46[17]

of Count Basie, Duke Ellington, Woody Herman, and Stan Kenton. It was Kenton who used the term "progressive jazz" to describe what he and some others saw as consistent advances in contemporary jazz. It is only in retrospect that we can see "progress" in jazz as the shift from mere entertainment for a dancing public to the only totally new art form the United States has yet produced.

Third-Stream Jazz

Flowing between the parallel streams of classical music and jazz, Third-Stream jazz borrows techniques from both while attempting to remain in the jazz idiom. There had been earlier confrontations with classical music in the eras of ragtime ("ragging the classics") and swing ("swinging the classics"). Later jazz styles adopted instrumental, melodic, and harmonic techniques and musical forms from contemporary concert music. Third-Stream went a step further with combinations of jazz and string quartets, and jazz combos combined with symphony orchestras. In particular, the Dave Brubeck Quartet and the Modern Jazz Quartet have made interesting Third-Stream recordings.

The Listening Example is a modern cool version of a Gershwin song from *Girl Crazy* (1930), which was revived in 1993 as *Crazy for You*.

Listening Example 53
COOL JAZZ

Gershwin, *But Not for Me*
1965

Time: 3:46[18]

Liturgical Jazz

Liturgical jazz has met with considerably more success. Jazz has been a long-accepted practice in many African-American revivals and tent-meetings, but not until the 1960s did it begin to appear in the church services of major Protestant denominations. The prime moving force was the intent to update the liturgy by using more contemporary modes of thought and expression. (The basic thrust was, of course, the youth revolt against the Establishment and the war in Vietnam.) Though Liturgical jazz was generally accepted by liberal mainline churches there were those who opposed admitting a new art form to church. Some opponents confused jazz with popular music; others reasoned that music formerly associated with New Orleans bordellos, Chicago speakeasies, dance halls, and night clubs was obviously not good enough for church. The fact is, however, that much of the music presently used in

17. CD 4, track 8.
18. CD 4, track 7.

churches has similar humble origins. Moreover, there is no such thing as "sacred music"; there is only music used with sacred services. Duke Ellington's recordings of sacred concerts performed in church are interesting, valid modes of jazz used for religious purposes.

Crossover and Fusion

Current jazz styles range from traditional jazz in the New Orleans manner to ragtime, Dixieland, Chicago, Bop, and Mainstream. Added to this mélange are the eclectic styles called *Crossover* and *Fusion*. Crossover combines some jazz and rock with popular songs in a style that downplays the drive of both jazz and rock. Fusion is much closer to the jazz tradition; it is defined by *Downbeat* magazine as "an agreement between jazz, rock, and funk (soul)." Fusion generally uses mixtures of electronic instruments and acoustic instruments.

Examples: Recent recordings by Miles Davis and Chick Corea (fig. 29.3).

29.3   Chick Corea in a jazz parade at the Royal Festival Hall, London. 21 July 1987. Photo: Dat's Jazz Picture Library, Harrow, U.K. (Derick A. Thomas).

But the latest and more authentic jazz style, called acoustic jazz or straight-ahead jazz, is successfully promoted by exceptionally talented musicians such as Wynton Marsalis (b. 1961). Trumpeter Marsalis refers to himself as a neo-traditionalist who has studied such jazz immortals as Louis Armstrong, Duke Ellington, and Charlie Parker as he forges ahead in what has become a renaissance of African-American jazz. Marsalis, like many of his colleagues, is accomplished in both classical music and jazz, having won Grammies in both types of music, from Bach to the blues. The movement is little concerned with electronic instruments—hence the occasional label of acoustic jazz. The Listening Example is a modern cool jazz original in quintuple meter (five beats per bar) by alto saxophonist Paul Desmond.

> *Listening Example 54*
> **COOL JAZZ**
>
> Paul Desmond, *Take Five*
>
> Time: 2:05
> Cassette 3, track 38

SUMMARY

This chapter has dealt with only a few highlights selected from the bewildering complexities of modern music. Of course, twentieth-century music, like the music of any age, effectively mirrors the prevailing patterns of the age. The impending catastrophe of World War I was forecast in the primitive barbarity of Stravinsky's *The Rite of Spring*. Reflecting the rational, intellectual aspects of the Age of Analysis were the serial techniques of Alban Berg as he exploited the tone row to compose his Violin Concerto. Charles Ives anticipated many of the innovations of *avant-garde* twelve-tone composers such as Schoenberg, Berg, and Webern and, after World War II, the *avant-garde* developed the twelve-tone method into complete serial systems.

Electronic music in various forms exerted an ever-growing influence as reflected in much or all the work of McLean, Boulez, Stockhausen, and Cage. Aleatory music, with or without electronic assistance, is not dominating the musical scene but it is certainly making waves.

The essence of much of this century's music can be summarized in Yeats' phrase, "Things fall apart: the centre cannot hold." The old musical centers of clear-cut keys, major-minor tonality, and traditional musical instruments are no longer apropos. Composers have been trying to find new centers, new ways of relating to a rapidly changing world.

The search for new musical values has used mathematics (twelve-tone and serial techniques), technology (electronic media), the sounds of people, and the sounds of nature. Traditional music has been bent, borrowed, violated, and ignored. The search goes on and not until well into the the next century will people be able to see clearly where the search led and what twentieth-century music was all about.

The many faces of contemporary jazz and the infinite variety of the jazz-rock-pop scene seem to span the spectrum of twentieth-century life and thought.

New Orleans   basically the street band sounds of original jazz

Dixieland   a combination of New Orleans jazz and Swing for an exuberant, happy sound

Cool   romantic impressionism, always keeping its cool

Mainstream   a bit of Swing plus a bit more of Progressive and steering down the middle of the road

Hard Bop   uncompromising, blowing hard and hot

Soul   return to the roots, to unabashed emotion, to wholehearted involvement

Liturgical jazz   revitalization of the music of established churches

Crossover   some jazz with a little rock and much pop

Fusion   synthesis of jazz, rock, and funk

Straight-ahead jazz   a revival of traditional jazz combined with great technical virtuosity.

CULTURE AND HUMAN VALUES

It is generally agreed that music is the closest thing to an international language the world has. Some Western classical music has been performed around the world but classical music has not had nearly the international impact that jazz has had. As early as the 1920s, jazz was more popular in France than in its country of origin. After World War II, jazz became a worldwide phenomenon and continues to be widely popular around the globe.

The U.S. Department of State has consistently sent jazz groups as goodwill ambassadors to foreign countries. Considering the lingering after-effects of Western imperialism, and of international tensions in general, it appears that American jazz is a valuable American export and one that better exemplifies American values than, for example, the exportation of violent TV programs. Whether as a very personal and direct form of communication or as a universally admired art form, jazz sounds a positive note in a world that needs all the help it can get.

CHAPTER 30

Twentieth-Century Literature

The analogy of the broken center certainly applies to contemporary literature. Amid the wreckage of old values today's authors search for fresh meanings, new forms, and a revitalized sense of personal identity and community.

Almost any thesis about contemporary literature can be proposed and supported with a large body of writing, for ceaseless experimentation has produced many types, moods, and themes. Following are some generalizations about twentieth-century literature leading to comments on specific literary works. The reader is free to agree or disagree with any or all comments.

CONVENTIONS AND REVOLTS

Many writers of our century have violated most or all of the restrictions on form and idea that were characteristic of most nineteenth-century writing. There are at least two "literatures of the twentieth century," one before, the other after World War II. The two types are related because they are in revolt against both the literary tradition of the nineteenth century and the rigidity of Victorian mores. The literatures differ because early twentieth-century writers recognized a common core against which they might voice their protest; the writers since World War II are cast adrift, with little unifying force and few webs of connection, and with the urge, almost the necessity, to create anew the meanings and values of life.

The "conventional" revolt early in the century was predictable, as described by John Livingston Lowes: "The ceaseless swing of the artistic pendulum is from the convention of a former age to the revolt of a new day, which in its turn becomes a convention from which still newer artists will in their turn revolt."[1]

The poetic conventions of the nineteenth century generally favored the tight-knit structure of recognizable stanza form: blank verse or couplet, tercet or quatrain, or other nameable unit. There were exceptions of course, but in general a poem *looked* like a poem, because that was the way poems looked! The order and pattern and design appealed to an audience that liked design, approved of pattern, and believed in order.

But, in about 1914, the Imagist poets challenged the convention with *vers libre* (Fr., "free verse")—lines unrhymed and unmetrical. Not only is the form of T. S. Eliot's poem, "The Love Song of J. Alfred Prufrock" (see pp. 463–5), different from that of the past, but the meaning of the poem represents a revolt against the predominant nineteenth-century optimism (or even the pessimism). Yet, with all the innovations of form and meaning, Eliot works within a recognizable tradition. The poem is not only to be felt and experienced, it must be thought out as an intellectual poem within the rational tradition of European culture. Eliot expects his readers to share a common background of knowledge about Hesiod, Dante, and Shakespeare.

Because World War II involved the obvious choice between freedom or submission to inhuman systems ruled by power-mad dictators, the emotions and rituals of patriotism seemed appropriate, even noble. Yet, when the conflict ended, the world went back to its old ways, with the victors seeming to take more of a beating than the vanquished. An introspective United States focused on its shortcomings and the hollowness of much of its way of life. The old materialistic values, as opposed to standards involving the quality of life itself, seemed no longer appropriate. The wars in Korea, Vietnam, even in the Persian Gulf, challenged much of the enthusiasm for the "rightness" of our value system.

At the same time, the Western world was introduced to philosophies of existentialism that denied inherent intelligence and purpose in the universe, or intrinsic meaning in individual life. The effect on an ever-growing number of thoughtful individuals has been to destroy the old center of certainty: to force them to peer over the brink of life and discover nothing but senseless void beyond. Thus, for many, old values have been seriously questioned or destroyed completely.

Opposite Dorothea Lange, *Migrant Mother, Nipomo, California*, detail. 1936. Gelatin-silver print, full print 12½ × 9⅞" (31.8 × 25.1 cm).

1. John Livingston Lowes. *Convention and Revolt in Poetry*, New York, Gordon Press, n.d.

None of these literary developments is entirely new. Pessimism was not invented in the twentieth century; existentialism had its immediate source in Kierkegaard and Nietzsche in the nineteenth century and can be traced as far back as the ancient Greek philosopher Democritos; new forms for literature (black humor, science fiction) have antecedents. Whatever writers have done in the recent and distant past appears to have all flowed together to become a rich reservoir available for literary creation.

Taboos

Previous restrictions about ethics, language, and structure have been relaxed or even swept away, profoundly affecting present-day writing.

Ethics

Social taboos about ethics in general and sexual ethics in particular are much more lax. Not too long ago it was difficult to buy Henry Miller's novels or D. H. Lawrence's *Lady Chatterley's Lover* in the United States, since they supposedly shocked the general public's idea of "proper" literature. Social restrictions have now become so relaxed that these particular books are not even very exciting in terms of raw sex. There are still restrictions, of course, on so-called hard-core pornography, but any work that has artistic value is protected by the Constitution, thus guaranteeing society's right to know. The maturation of the public in terms of the freedom to explore the whole range of human experience has stimulated all who create and all who enjoy art works in any medium.

Language

"Polite" language, was the norm in most nineteenth-century literature, with the other words appearing in the underground erotic literature of the Victorian era. That taboo has vanished. Words found on the walls and stalls of restrooms appear regularly in our "better" magazines—in fiction, poetry, and non-fiction. This is freedom of expression as guaranteed by the Bill of Rights. By the time any boy or girl has reached junior high school, he or she is familiar with all the four-letter words; intrinsically, the word "excrement" is neither better nor worse than its four-letter synonym. Not surprisingly, many writers, especially screen-writers, jumped on the bandwagon and used so many expletives in one form or another that the intended shock values were dissipated in the murk of monotonous obscenities. People do use these words in everyday life but does art have to become a Xerox machine in the pursuit of the "real" world? Writers who feel compelled to use the short Anglo-Saxon words may find a true freedom by choosing, from the whole range of language, whatever words are best suited to the purpose of their art work. That is, in fact, precisely what many contemporary writers are doing.

The freedom to choose from all the words in the language has certainly helped recent translations of ancient, medieval, and modern foreign language literature. Generations of students have assumed that the classics of ancient Greece and Rome, for example, were written in the stilted, sanitary language adopted by earlier translators. Not so! Greek and Roman writers used the full range of their languages, including as many explicit words and phrases as found in languages throughout the world. All the works of Aristophanes, Ovid, Catullus, and Juvenal, to name a few, are now available in translations that do justice to their lustily explicit vocabulary. These writers selected their words from the entire realm of their richly expressive languages, which helps explain their lofty rank in the world's literature.

Structure

A third restriction was the apparent necessity for rational or chronological structure in prose, and for traditional "sense" in poetry. The expectation that a literary work have a beginning, a middle, and an end has vanished except for the requirements imposed by the printed page. Present-day writers need not string their words on a "plot." (Plot may be defined as the working out of a theme, usually clearly stated, which is developed in chronological order by the confrontation of two "sides" in opposition, with the ultimate victory of one side over the other.) Until the last generation or so, this has been (with notable exceptions) the standard structure for most fiction and drama. It is, of course, still used, but structure is not necessary, and many important writers have discarded the flow-of-time convention and the idea of opposing forces. Many playwrights have discarded logical development in an attempt to achieve immediate and direct feeling that does not fit Aristotelian concepts of either thought or dramatic art. With the old structures no longer required, writers are free to seek truth in many different ways. Experimentalism in form, sometimes successful, sometimes merely confusing, has become a commonplace in the writer's art.

POETRY

Experiments in Form, Subject, and Language

Form, subject, and language are three aspects of poetry that are so closely united as to be inseparable in total effect. However, poetry can be analyzed by arbitrarily considering each aspect separately.

The free verse in Eliot's "The Love Song of J. Alfred Prufrock" is an excellent example of formal innovation. Robinson Jeffers' "Shine, Perishing Republic," with its long, flowing lines, is another instance of free verse (see p. 466). The poem has rhythmic effects—with phrases often indicated by punctuation—but not conventional poetic meter.

A strikingly different experiment is the following poem

by e e cummings. The poet delights in typographical eccentricity—lack of capitals or punctuation, frequent parentheses—and the example below is mild in comparison with others among his poems. A notable characteristic is his use, avoidance, and distortion of rhyme: "town-down," "winter-did," "same-rain." Innovation in subject matter and form almost necessarily demands a difference in language. This does not simply mean that the modern poet talks about the artifacts of our culture—computers or space travel, for example—but that he or she uses a deliberately distorted grammar, syntax, and logic. Consider "anyone lived in a pretty how town." One must untangle the phrase, to find in it perhaps a sardonic amusement at a gushing cliché—"How pretty this little town is!" When the poet wishes to point out the passage of time, he does not say "time after time, as trees come out leaf by leaf"; he telescopes it to "when by now and tree by leaf," and the apparent nonsense suddenly becomes new sense.

LITERARY SELECTION 52

anyone lived in a pretty how town

e e cummings, 1894–1962

anyone lived in a pretty how town
(with up so floating many bells down)
spring summer autumn winter
he sang his didn't he danced his did.

Women and men (both little and small)
cared for anyone not at all
they sowed their isn't they reaped their same
sun moon stars rain

children guessed (but only a few
and down they forgot as up they grew   10
autumn winter spring summer)
that no one loved him more by more

when by now and tree by leaf
she laughed his joy she cried his grief
bird by snow and stir by still
anyone's any was all to her

someones married their everyones
laughed their cryings and did their dance
(sleep wake hope and then) they
said their nevers they slept their dream   20

stars rain sun moon
(and only the snow can begin to explain
how children are apt to forget to remember
with up so floating many bells down)

one day anyone died i guess
(and noone stooped to kiss his face)
busy folk buried them side by side
little by little and was by was

all by all and deep by deep
and more by more they dream their sleep   30
noone and anyone earth by april
wish by spirit and if by yes.

Women and men (both dong and ding)
summer autumn winter spring
reaped their sowing and went their came
sun moon stars rain

STUDY QUESTIONS

1. Much of the poetry of cummings is very rhythmic with considerable use of what is called the "variable foot." In stanza 1, for example, the variation occurs in the third line. Try reading the poem aloud to hear how the variations set off the nimble words in the other lines.
2. Many of the phrases are dissociated from expected relationships. Try rephrasing some of these to see what happens to the rhythm. Do the conventional versions become commonplace?

LITERARY SELECTION 53

When All My Five and Country Senses See

Dylan Thomas, 1914–53

When all my five and country senses see,
The fingers will forget green thumbs and mark
How, through the halfmoon's vegetable eye,
Husk of young stars and handful zodiac,
Love in the frost is pared and wintered by.
The whispering ears will watch love drummed away
Down breeze and shell to a discordant beach,
And, lashed to syllables, the lynx tongue cry
That her fond wounds are mended bitterly,
My nostrils see her breath burn like a bush.
My one and noble heart has witnesses
In all love's countries, that will grope awake:
And when blind sleep drops on the spying senses,
The heart is sensual, though five eyes break.

The language of Dylan Thomas is so unusual as to seem baffling at first reading. How can "fingers forget green thumbs" and what is the half-moon's "vegetable eye"? Certainly the poet is not talking with simple directness; his words do not "mean" with a single, unchanging meaning, but seem to move in several directions at once. Suppose we try to paraphrase in this fashion: "If all my five natural senses could perceive clearly, see—like my eyes—then even the sense of touch, that helped love grow, would 'see' with the passage of time how love grows old and is laid by, like fruit after harvest; the sense of hearing would 'see' love finished, driven away, ending in discord; the tongue, which is both taste and talk, would 'see' love's pains reluctantly ended; the sense of smell would 'see' love consumed as in a fire. But my heart has other means of perception of love, and these will go on beyond the decaying senses, so that my heart will still know love."

LITERARY SELECTION 54

Helen

George Seferis, 1900–71

The first Greek to win the Nobel Prize for literature (1963), Seferis is renowned for introducing modernist forms and techniques into Greek writing. Much of his own writing has been based on ancient Greek myths and history and critics have compared his philosophy, ethics, and sense of justice with those of Anaximander and Aeschylus. This selection is translated by Edmund Keeley and Philip Sherrard.

TEUCER: . . . *in sea-girt Cyprus, where it was decreed by Apollo that I should live, giving the city the name of Salamis in memory of my island home.*

·   ·   ·   ·   ·

HELEN: *I never went to Troy; it was a phantom.*

·   ·   ·   ·   ·

SERVANT: *What? You mean it was only for a cloud that we struggled so much?*

HELEN by Euripides[2]

"The nightingales won't let you sleep in Platres."[3]

Shy nightingale, in the breathing of the leaves,
you who bestow the forest's musical coolness
on the parted bodies, on the souls
of those who know they will not return.
Blind voice, you who grope in the darkness of memory
for footsteps and gestures—I wouldn't dare say kisses—
and the bitter raging of the slavewoman grown wild.

"The nightingales won't let you sleep in Platres."

Platres: where is Platres? And this island: who knows
       it?   10
I've lived my life hearing names I've never heard before:
new countries, new idiocies of men
or of the gods;
my fate, which wavers
between the last sword of some Ajax
and another Salamis,[4]
brought me here to this shore.
The moon
rose from the sea like Aphrodite,
covered the Archer's stars, now moves to find   20
the heart of Scorpio, and changes everything.
Truth, where's the truth?

I too was an archer in the war;
my fate: that of a man who missed his target.

Lyric nightingale,
on a night like this, by the shore of Proteus,
the Spartan slave girls heard you and began their lament,
and among them—who would have believed it?—Helen!
She whom we hunted so many years by the banks of
       the Scamander.
She was there, at the desert's lip; I touched her; she
       spoke to me: 30
"It isn't true, it isn't true," she cried.
"I didn't board the blue-bowed ship.
I never went to valiant Troy."

High-girdled, the sun in her hair, and that stature
shadows and smiles everywhere,
on shoulders, thighs, and knees;
the skin alive, and her eyes
with the large eyelids,
she was there, on the banks of a Delta.
And at Troy?   40
At Troy, nothing: just a phantom image.
The gods wanted it so.
And Paris, Paris lay with a shadow as though it were a
       solid being;
and for ten whole years we slaughtered ourselves for
       Helen.

Great suffering descended on Greece.
So many bodies thrown
into the jaws of the sea, the jaws of the earth
so many souls
fed to the millstones like grain.
And the rivers swelling, blood in their silt,   50
all for a linen undulation, a bit of cloud,
a butterfly flicker, a swan's down,
an empty tunic—all for a Helen.
And my brother?
Nightingale, nightingale, nightingale,
what is a god? What is not a god? And what is there
       between them?

"The nightingales won't let you sleep in Platres."

Tearful bird,
on sea-kissed Cyprus
consecrated to remind me of my country,   60
I moored alone with this fable,
if it's true that it is a fable,
if it's true that mortals will not again take up
the old deceit of the gods;
if it's true
that in future years some other Teucer,
or some Ajax or Priam or Hecuba,

---

2. Euripides' play assumes that only a phantom of Helen went with Paris to Troy. Helen herself was carried by Hermes to the Egyptian court of Proteus, where she was eventually reunited with her husband Menelaos long after the Trojan war ended.
3. Platres is a summer resort on the slopes of Mt. Troödos in Cyprus.
4. Where the Greeks defeated the Persian fleet in 480 BC.

or someone unknown and nameless who nevertheless
   saw
a Scamander overflow with corpses,
isn't fated to hear 70
newsbearers coming to tell him
that so much suffering, so much life,
went into the abyss
all for an empty tunic, for a Helen.

STUDY QUESTIONS

1. Describe the poet's feeling about war, any war. Is there anger here? Remember that Italy and Germany invaded Greece in World War II and that there was a brutal civil war after the Allies drove the Germans out. Communists kidnapped thousands of Greek children, who were never seen again.
2. What does the nightingale symbolize? Why won't it let you sleep in a summer resort?

DRAMA

Realistic Theatre

Modern drama is called "realistic" when its theatrical conventions generally reflect or represent the world in which we live. Actors look, act, and talk like people that any of us might know. The sets usually give the illusion of actual rooms, lawns, or gardens. No one on stage speaks in rhymed couplets; the medium is prose, not poetry. Actors do not regularly talk to ghosts, play to the audience, or meditate in blank verse on an empty stage. The characters are, in the main, men and women in all walks of life rather than kings and queens, knights and fair ladies.

Some realistic elements appeared in theatre shortly after the Renaissance, but the main development came after the middle of the nineteenth century. Realist dramatists (and representative plays) include Henrik Ibsen (1828–1906), *Hedda Gabler*; George Bernard Shaw (1856–1950), *Pygmalion*; Anton Chekhov (1864–1904), *The Cherry Orchard*; and, later, Arthur Miller (b. 1915), *Death of a Salesman*. The emergence of realistic drama paralleled a comparable development in the painting of Daumier, Courbet, and Winslow Homer (see figs. 25.14–16).

Theatre of the Absurd

The other major kind of modern theatre is generally called, for want of a better term, "unrealistic drama." Of the several varieties of "unreality" the most significant is Theatre of the Absurd, a movement that grew in response to existentialism as it affected, and was affected by, the status of

society following World War II. Absurdist playwrights do not necessarily subscribe totally to the philosophy of existentialism, but they do share certain existential ideas: human life appears to have no meaning or purpose; we invent ourselves as we live our lives; our actions are either erratic or they respond to rules that make no sense; all we have in common with anyone else is certain death. Human existence is seen, therefore, as absurd.

The originator of Theatre of the Absurd was Samuel Beckett (1906–89; 1969 Nobel Prize for literature). A Protestant Irishman who once served as James Joyce's secretary (and as a spy for the French underground during World War II), Beckett preferred to live in Paris and compose his novels and plays in French. His play *Endgame* sums up human life with a blind, paralyzed protagonist who has bottled up his parents in a trash can. In *Krapp's Last Tape* a single actor sits at a tape recorder playing back a tape of a long-ago love affair. *Happy Days* stars a married couple—with the wife babbling incessantly about her possessions. She is buried up to the waist in the first act and up to her neck in the second act.

Beckett's first performed play, *Waiting for Godot*[5] (1953), remains one of the finest—and best known—of all absurdist dramas. Displaying what have become the most familiar qualities of absurdist theatre, the drama takes place, not in sequential time, but in a timeless present. Two main characters, who may or may not be two different aspects of the same person, are waiting for Godot, who never comes, but who may or may not already be on stage as one of the players. All is ambiguity. Such drama substitutes "tension" for the "conflict" of traditional plot, but the tension is in the mind and emotions of the spectator. Since the tension is usually left unresolved, in marked distinction to the logical endings of conventional plays, the spectator is left with questions that he or she alone can resolve. Theatre that, in itself, appears to be unrealistic and illogical turns out to pose the greatest intellectual questions precisely where they should be raised—in the mind of the beholder. A questioning remains rather than the **catharsis** of the Aristotelian definition of tragedy. Indeed, Euripides anticipated this type of drama in the choral speeches with which he completes both *The Bacchae* and *Alcestis*:

Gods manifest themselves in many forms,
Bring many matters to surprising ends;
The things we thought would happen do not happen;
The unexpected, god makes possible:
And that is what has happened here today.

5. At this time, the copyright holder does not allow this play to be anthologized, which explains its absence from this chapter. Reading it in its authorized version is strongly recommended.

MODERN PROSE FICTION

Everything that has been said about modern literature applies also to the novel and short story. As in poetry and drama, prose writers are concerned with new forms, fresh methods of penetrating into the truths of human experience. Black humor and science fiction are two forms that writers have explored in considerable depth and with a great range of subject matter.

Black Humor

Catch-22 by Joseph Heller is perhaps the best known and one of the finest examples of black humor. Black humor *is* funny, but with a bitterness that stings. Basically it is satire, an attack on established ways of thought and action, but a satire that uses surrealistic techniques to achieve its purposes. The typical novel of this sort uses scenes that are sharply etched, with almost photographic naturalism. Yet the scenes and events exist in a bizarre juxtaposition—as in a Dali painting—so that all ordinary sense is lost, and a mind accustomed to logical relationships is utterly confounded. The reader is left with the sense of living through a comical nightmare in which time is compressed or expanded, in which space is purely relative and which may change without warning. A novel such as *Catch-22* reveals a crazy world that would amuse only the insane—and then the reverse: maybe the world of the novel is sane and we, with our conventional, Aristotelian minds, are the crazy ones.

A brief discussion of *Catch-22* (the novel, not the movie) can illustrate the nature of black humor. The central object of ridicule throughout the novel is rational thought that goes around in a circle until it ends in total absurdity. The novel takes place during World War II on an Air Force base off the coast of Italy. It seems to satirize military life, but a closer scrutiny reveals that it is an attack on much of twentieth-century society and its values. The "catch" is first unveiled when Yossarian, a bombardier and the protagonist of the novel, objects to flying more missions and pleads insanity with the medical officer in the expectation of a medical discharge (Section 8). The doctor explains that anyone who expresses fear in a dangerous situation is obviously sane and cannot be discharged. Yossarian asks about the men who are flying missions without protest. The doctor's explanation is simple: those men are insane, but since they aren't asking to be relieved of duty he can't send them home. If they asked, they, like Yossarian, would demonstrate they were sane and be immediately returned to duty. This is "Catch-22": perfectly logical, totally absurd, allowing no hope. Repeated use of this circular logic confirms the novel's hopeless, helpless mood.

Heller satirizes other fallacies of our way of life, such as our dependency on paperwork rather than facts in making judgments. Indeed, ex-P.F.C. Wintergreen, a mail clerk, handles and scrambles messages, directing military actions more completely than the generals. Another case in point is the suicidal mission to bomb the city of Bologna, when Yossarian sneaks down to the central map at headquarters and moves the ribbon showing the Allied ground position above the city. Word flies from one level of command to the next: Bologna has been taken and the bombing mission is scrubbed. Finally, inevitably, the truth is known and the mission rescheduled.

Free enterprise and the profit system are attacked unmercifully in the person of supply officer Milo Minderbinder and his M and M Enterprises. Starting with simple trading for supplies, he finally deals with both the enemy and his own side; at one point he directs the enemy bombing of his own airbase, at another he arranges a total battle, having charge of both sides. He reaps enormous profits, of course, though he constantly reminds each investor that he "has a share" in M and M Enterprises. "Having a share" is one of the great double-meanings of the book.

The first two-thirds of the book are timeless, shifting from one incident to another with no regard for chronology. For Yossarian, however, the central incident is the fate of his crewmate, Snowden. Yossarian attempts to treat the wounded gunner but, when he zips open the flak suit, Snowden's guts spill out on the floor of the plane. Yossarian suddenly realizes that the world, friend or enemy, is really divided into two groups, the killers and the victims, and that he, as bombardier, is a killer. He refuses this role and for a time goes naked (even when the general is pinning a medal on him) rather than wear the uniform. Referred to throughout the early part of the novel, the Snowden incident is not fully explained until two-thirds of the way through, at which point the story moves on in chronological time. The Snowden incident leads to the first explanation of "Catch-22" and the hopelessness of the situation.

One pilot, Yossarian's tentmate, Orr, has seemed crazier than all the others. His planes keep having engine trouble or are shot down over the sea. Orr ditches his bombers in the water from which everyone is always rescued. The last time Orr ditches his plane his crew is rescued but he is never found. It appears that he has drowned.

The novel ends with a hospital scene with Yossarian and other officers complaining that there is no hope at all. When they hear that Orr has successfully paddled his life raft to neutral Sweden (from the Mediterranean!) the mood changes. Yossarian flees to Rome, intending, somehow, to reach Sweden. The other men, bound by various obligations, will not run for it, but now there is some hope. Man may not conquer, but he can refuse to be conquered. In spite of "Catch-22," the individual can assert himself.

Science Fiction

Science fiction is not really new, for most utopian literature shares in its fantasy and Jules Verne and H. G. Wells wrote science fiction in the past century. What is new is its renewed status as a serious genre; what had degenerated into comic-strip stuff in the 1930s is now widely accepted. The difference lies in the reasons for writing science fiction. Utopians used it to show that things could be better; Jules Verne wrote literate, highly popular adventure tales containing some amazingly accurate predictions about the future. At the present time numerous writers are jolting our minds from ordinary channels and enlarging our concepts of what is possible, or what is not impossible. As we are transported through space, time, or time-warps we begin to inhabit a world in which A may not be A; in which not-A can very well be A. Writers have to work to stay ahead of developments in science and technology; advanced technology has already made some of the ideas and devices of earlier science fiction come true and there are more wonders certain to come.

Flourishing Literary Arts

In an age when print media are eyeing the relentless onslaught of computer technology, more books (poetry, short stories, novels, biographies, drama, essays) are being published than at any time in history. No one can reasonably predict what the coming century holds, but the literary arts are currently flourishing as perhaps never before. Momentous changes, however, are even now waiting impatiently in the wings:

> We are coming to the end of the culture of the book. Books are still produced and read in prodigious numbers, and they will continue to be as far into the future as one can imagine. However, they do not command the center of the cultural stage. Modern culture is taking shapes that are more various and more complicated than the book-centered culture it is succeeding.[6]

Many of us have difficulty facing up to the waning centrality of the printed book; it has been, after all, basic to Western civilization for five centuries. On the other hand, what is a mere five centuries in the thousands of years of human history? We must remember that the incredible pace of computer evolution is still accelerating. If, for example, "the cost of transportation had fallen as dramatically since 1950 as the cost of computing power, today's traveler would be able to buy a round-trip ticket to Mars for $12.50."[7]

6. O. B. Hardison, Jr. *Disappearing Through the Skylight: Culture and Technology in the Twentieth Century* (New York: Viking Penguin, 1989), p. 264.
7. *Ibid.*, p. 270.

LITERARY SELECTION 55

The Other Wife

Sidonie Gabrielle Colette, 1873–1954

One of the outstanding French writers of the century, Colette is known for her insight into human psychology, especially her vivid portrayals of a wide variety of women. Her novels include *Chéri, The Last of Chéri, The Cat,* and *Gigi.* In this very short story notice how adroitly she communicates key information with a remarkable economy of means; the translation is by Margaret Crosland.

"For two? This way, Monsieur and Madame, there's still a table by the bay window, if Madame and Monsieur would like to enjoy the view?"

Alice followed the *maître d'hôtel.*

"Oh, yes, come on Marc, we'll feel we're having lunch on a boat at sea . . . ."

Her husband restrained her, passing his arm through hers.

"We'll be more comfortable there."

"There? In the middle of all those people? I'd much prefer . . ." 10

"Please, Alice."

He tightened his grip in so emphatic a way that she turned round.

"What's the matter with you?"

He said "sh" very quietly, looking at her intently, and drew her towards the table in the middle.

"What is it Marc?"

"I'll tell you, darling. Let me order lunch. Would you like shrimps? Or eggs in aspic?" 20

"Whatever you like, as you know."

They smiled at each other, wasting the precious moments of an overworked, perspiring *maître d'hôtel* who stood near to them, suffering from a kind of St. Vitus's dance.

"Shrimps," ordered Marc. "And then eggs and bacon. And cold chicken with cos lettuce salad. Cream cheese? *Spécialité de la maison?* We'll settle for the *spécialité.* Two very strong coffees. Please give lunch to my chauffeur, we'll be leaving again at two o'clock. 30 Cider? I don't trust it . . . . Dry champagne."

He sighed as though he had been moving a wardrobe, gazed at the pale noonday sea, the nearly white sky, then at his wife, finding her pretty in her little Mercury-type hat with its long veil.

"You're looking well, darling. And all this sea-blue colour gives you green eyes, just imagine! And you put on weight when you travel . . . It's nice, up to a point, but only up to a point!"

Her rounded bosom swelled proudly as she leant 40 over the table.

"Why did you stop me taking that place by the bay window?"

It did not occur to Marc Séguy to tell a lie.

"Because you'd have sat next to someone I know."

"And whom I don't know?"

"My ex-wife."

She could not find a word to say and opened her blue eyes wider.

"What of it, darling? It'll happen again. It's not important." 50

Alice found her tongue again and asked the inevitable questions in their logical sequence.

"Did she see you? Did she know that you'd seen her? Point her out to me."

"Don't turn round at once, I beg you, she must be looking at us. A lady with dark hair, without a hat, she must be staying at this hotel . . . On her own, behind those children in red . . . "

"Yes, I see . . ." 60

Sheltered behind broad-brimmed seaside hats Alice was able to look at the woman who fifteen months earlier had still been her husband's wife. "Incompatibility," Marc told her. "Oh, it was total incompatibility! We divorced like well-brought-up people, almost like friends, quietly and quickly. And I began to love you, and you were able to be happy with me. How lucky we are that in our happiness there haven't been any guilty parties or victims!"

The woman in white, with her smooth, lustrous hair 70 over which the seaside light played in blue patches, was smoking a cigarette, her eyes half-closed. Alice turned back to her husband, took some shrimps and butter and ate composedly.

"Why didn't you ever tell me," she said after a moment's silence, "that she had blue eyes too?"

"But I'd never thought about it!"

He kissed the hand that she stretched out to the bread basket and she blushed with pleasure. Dark skinned and plump, she might have seemed slightly 80 earthy, but the changing blue of her eyes, and her wavy golden hair, disguised her as a fragile and soulful blonde. She showed overwhelming gratitude to her husband. She was immodest without knowing it and her entire person revealed overconspicuous signs of extreme happiness.

They ate and drank with good appetite and each thought that the other had forgotten the woman in white. However, Alice sometimes laughed too loudly and Marc was careful of his posture, putting his shoulders 90 back and holding his head up. They waited some time for coffee, in silence. An incandescent stream, a narrow reflection of the high and invisible sun, moved slowly over the sea and shone with unbearable brilliance.

"She's still there, you know," Alice whispered suddenly.

"Does she embarrass you? Would you like to have coffee somewhere else?"

"Not at all! It's she who ought to be embarrassed! And she doesn't look as though she's having a madly 100 gay time, if you could see her . . . "

"It's not necessary. I know that look of hers."

"Oh, was she like that?"

He breathed smoke through his nostrils and wrinkled his brows.

"Was she like that? No. To be frank, she wasn't happy with me."

"Well, my goodness."

"You're delightfully generous, darling, madly generous. . . . You're an angel, you're. . . . You love me 110 . . . I'm so proud, when I see that look in your eyes . . . yes, the look you have now. . . . She. . . . No doubt I didn't succeed in making her happy. That's all there is to it, I didn't succeed."

"She's hard to please—"

Alice fanned herself irritably, and cast brief glances at the woman in white who was smoking, her head leaning against the back of the cane chair, her eyes closed with an expression of satisfied lassitude.

Marc shrugged his shoulders modestly. 120

"That's it," he admitted. "What can one do? We have to be sorry for people who are never happy. As for us, we're so happy. . . . Aren't we, darling?"

She didn't reply. She was looking with furtive attention at her husband's face, with its good colour and regular shape, at his thick hair, with its occasional thread of white silk, at his small, well-cared-for hands. She felt dubious for the first time and asked herself: "What more did she want, then?"

And until they left, while Marc was paying the bill, 130 asking about the chauffeur and the route, she continued to watch, with envious curiosity, the lady in white, that discontented, hard-to-please, superior woman.

STUDY QUESTIONS

1. How does Colette use light to create feelings of ambiguity?
2. What is implied in the physical description of Marc and the fact that he has a chauffeur?
3. What is implied by a "woman in white"?
4. Explain how Alice's feelings for Marc change from beginning to end.

LITERARY SELECTION 56

The Disinterested Killer Bill Harrigan

Jorge Luis Borges, 1899–1986

The great Argentine master of short prose-forms is represented by a selection from his collection of essays called *A Universal History of Infamy* (1930s), here in a translation by Norman Thomas di Giovanni. This is a partly fictional story of Billy the Kid written in what Borges called "baroque," in which his writing "borders on its own parody." The style is deliberately cinematic and the ending becomes a playful parody on the tendency of writers to mythologize criminals and readers to venerate them—from a safe distance.

An image of the desert wilds of Arizona, first and foremost, an image of the desert wilds of Arizona and New Mexico—a country famous for its silver and gold camps, a country of breathtaking open spaces, a country of monumental mesas and soft colors, a country of bleached skeletons picked clean by buzzards. Over this whole country, another image—that of Billy the Kid, the hard rider firm on his horse, the young man with the relentless six-shooters, sending out invisible bullets which (like magic) kill at a distance.   10

The desert veined with precious metals, arid and blinding-bright. The near child who on dying at the age of twenty-one owed to the justice of grown men twenty-one deaths—"not counting Mexicans."

The Larval Stage

Along about 1859, the man who would become known to terror and glory as Billy the Kid was born in a cellar room of a New York City tenement. It is said that he was spawned by a tired-out Irish womb but was brought up among Negroes. In this tumult of lowly smells and wooly heads, he enjoyed a superiority that stemmed   20
from having freckles and a mop of red hair. He took pride in being white; he was also scrawny, wild, and coarse. At the age of twelve, he fought in the gang of the Swamp Angels, that branch of divinities who operated among the neighborhood sewers. On nights redolent of burnt fog, they would clamber out of the foul-smelling labyrinth, trail some German sailor, do him in with a knock on the head, strip him to his underwear, and afterward sneak back to the filth of their starting place. Their leader was a gray-haired Negro, Gas House Jonas,   30
who was also celebrated as a poisoner of horses.

Sometimes, from the upper window of a waterfront dive, a woman would dump a bucket of ashes upon the head of a prospective victim. As he gasped and choked, Swamp Angels would swarm him, rush him into a cellar, and plunder him.

Such were the apprentice years of Billy Harrigan, the future Billy the Kid. Nor did he scorn the offerings of Bowery playhouses, enjoying in particular (perhaps without an inkling that they were signs and symbols of   40
his destiny) cowboy melodramas.

Go West!

If the jammed Bowery theatres (whose top-gallery riffraff shouted "Hoist that rag!" when the curtain failed to rise promptly on schedule) abounded in these blood and thunder productions, the simple explanation is that America was then experiencing the lure of the Far West. Beyond the sunset lay the goldfields of Nevada and California. Beyond the sunset were the redwoods, going down before the ax; the buffalo's huge Babylonian face; Brigham Young's beaver hat and plural bed; the red   50

man's ceremonies and his rampages; the clear air of the deserts; endless-stretching range land; and the earth itself, whose nearness quickens the heart like the nearness of the sea. The West beckoned. A slow, steady rumor populated those years—that of thousands of Americans taking possession of the West. On that march, around 1872, was Bill Harrigan, treacherous as a bull rattler, in flight from a rectangular cell.

The Demolition of a Mexican

History (which, like certain film directors, proceeds by a series of abrupt images) now puts forward the image of   60
a danger-filled saloon, located—as if on the high seas— out in the heart of the all-powerful desert. The time, a blustery night of the year 1873; the place, the Staked Plains of New Mexico. All around, the land is almost uncannily flat and bare, but the sky, with its storm-piled clouds and moon, is full of fissured cavities and mountains. There are a cow's skull, the howl and the eyes of coyotes in the shadows, trim horses, and from the saloon an elongated patch of light. Inside, leaning over the bar, a group of strapping but tired men drink a   70
liquor that warms them for a fight; at the same time, they make a great show of large silver coins bearing a serpent and an eagle. A drunk croons to himself, poker-faced. Among the men are several who speak a language with many s's, which must be Spanish, for those who speak it are looked down on. Bill Harrigan, the red-topped tenement rat, stands among the drinkers. He has downed a couple of *aguardientes* and thinks of asking for one more, maybe because he hasn't a cent left. He is somewhat overwhelmed by these men of the   80
desert. He sees them as imposing, boisterous, happy, and hatefully wise in the handling of wild cattle and big horses. All at once there is dead silence, ignored only by the voice of the drunk, singing out of tune. Someone has come in—a big, burly Mexican, with the face of an old Indian squaw. He is endowed with an immense sombrero and with a pair of six-guns at his side. In awkward English, he wishes a good evening to all the gringo sons of bitches who are drinking. Nobody takes up the challenge. Bill asks who he is, and they whisper   90
to him, in fear, that the Dago—that is the Diego—is Belisario Villagrán, from Chihuahua. At once there is a resounding blast. Sheltered by that wall of tall men, Bill has fired at the intruder. The glass drops from Villagrán's hand; then the man himself drops. He does not need another bullet. Without deigning to glance at the showy dead man, Bill picks up his end of the conversation. "Is that so?" he drawled. "Well, I'm Billy the Kid, from New York." The drunk goes on singing unheeded.

One may easily guess the apotheosis. Bill gives out   100
handshakes all around and accepts praises, cheers, and whiskies. Someone notices that there are no notches on the handle of his revolver and offers to cut one to stand for Villagrán's death. Billy the Kid keeps this someone's razor, though he says that "It's hardly worthwhile noting down Mexicans." This, perhaps, is not quite enough. That night, Bill lays out his blanket beside the corpse and—with great show—sleeps till daybreak.

Deaths for Deaths' Sake

Out of that lucky blast (at the age of fourteen), Billy the Kid the hero was born, and the furtive Bill Harrigan died. 110
The boy of the sewer and the knock on the head rose to become a man of the frontier. He made a horseman of himself, learning to ride straight in the saddle—Wyoming- or Texas-style—and not with his body thrown back, the way they rode in Oregon and California. He never completely matched his legend, but he kept getting closer and closer to it. Something of the New York hooligan lived on in the cowboy; he transferred to Mexicans the hate that had previously been inspired in him by Negroes, but the last words he ever spoke were 120
(swear) words in Spanish. He learned the art of the cowpuncher's life. He learned another, more difficult art—how to lead men. Both helped to make him a good cattle rustler. From time to time, Old Mexico's guitars and whorehouses pulled on him.

With the haunting lucidity of insomnia, he organized populous orgies that often lasted four days and four nights. In the end, glutted, he settled accounts with bullets. While his trigger finger was unfailing, he was the most feared man (and perhaps the most anonymous and 130
most lonely) of that whole frontier. Pat Garrett, his friend, the sheriff who later killed him, once told him, "I've had a lot of practice with the rifle shooting buffalo."

"I've had plenty with the six-shooter," Billy replied modestly. "Shooting tin cans and men."

The details can never be recovered, but it is known that he was credited with up to twenty-one killings—"not counting Mexicans." For seven desperate years, he practiced the extravagance of utter recklessness.

The night of the twenty-fifth of July 1880, Billy the Kid 140
came galloping on his piebald down the main, or only, street of Fort Sumner. The heat was oppressive and the lamps had not been lighted; Sheriff Garrett, seated on a porch in a rocking chair, drew his revolver and sent a bullet through the Kid's belly. The horse kept on; the rider tumbled into the dust of the road. Garrett got off a second shot. The townspeople (knowing the wounded man was Billy the Kid) locked their window shutters tight. The agony was long and blasphemous. In the morning, the sun by then high overhead, they began 150
drawing near, and they disarmed him. The man was gone. They could see in his face the used-up look of the dead.

He was shaved, sheathed in ready-made clothes, and displayed to awe and ridicule in the window of Fort Sumner's biggest store. Men on horseback and in buckboards gathered for miles and miles around. On the third day, they had to use make-up on him. On the fourth day, he was buried with rejoicing.

STUDY QUESTIONS

1. How does the meaning of "disinterested" differ from that of "uninterested"? Does the style of the writing agree with the meaning of the text? How is this accomplished?
2. Borges consistently evokes "images," which are a major factor in his cinematic style. Does the style seem less or more serious than that of a standard biography? What does this style allow him to do that more ordinary biographies cannot accomplish?
3. What did the author accomplish by fictionalizing the display and disposal of the outlaw's body?
4. As related by Borges, does this disinterested killer possess any virtues? What did he value and what was of little or no interest? Listing these items should provide a rounded picture of Billy the Kid that was accomplished by a gifted writer in a few pungent paragraphs.

LITERARY SELECTION 57

The Bean Eaters

Gwendolyn Brooks, b. 1917

Brooks uses everyday language somewhat like Wordsworth, but her economic use of words and her vivid images mark her as one of the most effective of today's poets.

They eat beans mostly, this old yellow pair.
Dinner is a casual affair.
Plain chipware on a plain and creaking wood,
Tin flatware.

Two who are Mostly Good.
Two who have lived their day,
But keep on putting on their clothes
And putting things away.

And remembering . . .
Remembering, with twinklings and twinges,
As they lean over the beans in their rented back room
     that is full of beads and receipts and dolls and
     cloths, tobacco crumbs, vases and fringes.

STUDY QUESTIONS

1. What is this couple living on and why aren't their children helping them?
2. Are they living on something special in addition to food and money? What might that be?

We Real Cool

The Pool Players
Seven at the Golden Shovel

Gwendolyn Brooks

We real cool. We
Left school. We

Lurk late. We
Strike straight. We

Sing sin. We
Thin gin. We

Jazz June. We
Die soon.

LITERARY SELECTION 58

Jews in the Land of Israel

Yehuda Amichai, b. 1924

Perhaps the best known contemporary Israeli poet, Amichai was born in Germany and emigrated to Israel in 1936. He has long struggled with the horrendous Jewish past and the problems of identity in what remains a strange and sunlit land. The translation here is by Assia Gutmann and Harold Schimmer.

We forget where we came from. Our Jewish
Names from the exile reveal us,
Bring up the memory of flower and fruit, medieval cities,
Metals, knights that became stone, roses mostly,
Spices whose smells dispersed, precious stones,
    much red,
Trades gone from the world.
(The hands, gone too.)

The circumcision does it to us,
Like in the Bible story of Shechem and the sons
    of Jacob,
With pain all our life.   10

What are we doing here on our return with this pain?
The longings dried up with the swampland,
The desert flowers for us and our children are lovely.
Even fragments of ships, that sunk on the way,
Reached this shore,
Even winds reached. Not all the sails.

What are we doing
In this dark land that casts
Yellow shadows, cutting at the eyes?
(Sometimes, one says even after forty   20
Years or fifty: "The sun is killing me.")

What are we doing with souls of mist, with the names,
With forest eyes, with our lovely children, with
    swift blood?

Spilt blood isn't roots of trees,
But it's the closest to them
That man has.

LITERARY SELECTION 59

Two Songs

Adrienne Rich, b. 1929

In the following poem, reminiscent of the enthusiastic attitude of the ancient Greeks, Adrienne Rich speaks of lust that "too is a jewel."

1
Sex, as they harshly call it,
I fell into this morning
at ten o'clock, a drizzling hour
of traffic and wet newspapers.
I thought of him who yesterday
clearly didn't
turn me to a hot field
ready for plowing,
and longing for that young man
pierced me to the roots   10
bathing every vein, etc.
All day he appears to me
touchingly desirable,
a prize one could wreck one's peace for.
I'd call it love if love
didn't take so many years
but lust too is a jewel
a sweet flower and what
pure happiness to know
all our high-toned questions   20
breed in a lively animal.

2
That "old last act"!
And yet sometimes
all seems post coitum triste
and I a mere bystander.
Somebody else is going off,
getting shot to the moon.
Or, a moon-race!
Split seconds after
my opposite number lands   30
I make it—
we lie fainting together
at a crater-edge
heavy as mercury in our moonsuits
till he speaks—
in a different language
yet one I've picked up
through cultural exchanges . . .
we murmur the first moonwords:
Spasibo. Thanks. O.K.   40

THE LITERATURE OF MOVING IMAGES

Motion pictures were developed long before anyone realized their artistic or, especially, commercial possibilities. In 1824 Peter Mark Roget, an English scholar, published a paper entitled "The Persistence of Vision with Regard to Moving Objects." The thesis is that the human eye retains an image slightly longer than the image is actually present. Specifically, if sixteen pictures are made of one second of movement, the persistence of vision puts them together to give the illusion of movement. This is the basis of all motion pictures.

Generally considered the dominant medium of this century, motion pictures display interesting paradoxes inherent in the medium. Film uses machines to record images of reality and it combines still photographs to give the illusion of continuous motion. It therefore seems to present images of life itself but it is also used to portray unrealities unapproached even by anyone's wildest dreams.

Film can and should be studied as an art form, but it is a medium that must be experienced, preferably in a theatre with an audience. With very few exceptions movies are made to make money in public showings before a mass audience. "Motion picture industry" is the term generally used to describe corporate enterprises that use a large number of highly skilled people: screenwriter, director, actors, cinematographer, film editor, film scorer, set and costume designers, and many others. Unlike a novel, a film cannot be credited to a single creator. Critics tend to lavish credit on the director as the person in charge but this is only a convention that tends to slight everyone else. One cannot, for example, think of director Elia Kazan's *On the Waterfront* without recalling Marlon Brando's masterful performance. In the final analysis no film is better than its literary base, the screenplay itself, for this is where virtually all movies begin.

Movies are a prime mass-entertainment medium the world over and, as commercial enterprises, about 99 percent of them are eminently forgettable. But from the beginning of motion pictures, there have been exceptions, movies that have made an artistic impact and that have withstood the test of time. Usually referred to as film classics, these are works of art that effectively synthesized the efforts of many creators. Following is a list of movies that are generally regarded as true classics. Some, perhaps, are not to everyone's taste, but all are notable works of art and all should be seen, preferably more than once. They are among the best of a new literature that began in this century. Following the standard procedure, credit for the movies is assigned to the directors but, in every case, the viewer should give due credit to all participants, both on and off camera.

Antonioni, Michelangelo. *L'Avventura*. Italy, 1959.
Bergman, Ingmar. *The Seventh Seal*. Sweden, 1956.
———.*Wild Strawberries*. Sweden, 1957.
———.*Fanny and Alexander*. Sweden, 1985.
Buñuel, Luis. *Belle de Jour*. France, 1968.
Chaplin, Charles. *The Gold Rush*. U.S., 1925.
Cocteau, Jean. *Beauty and the Beast*. France, 1947.
DeSica, Vittorio. *The Bicycle Thief*. Italy, 1948.
Eisenstein, Serge. *Potemkin*. Russia, 1925.
Fellini, Federico. *La Strada*. Italy, 1954.
———.*La Dolce Vita*. Italy, 1959.
Gance, Abel. *Napoleon*. France, 1925, 1982.
Griffith, David W. *Intolerance*. U.S., 1916.
Hitchcock, Alfred. *Vertigo*. U.S., 1958.
Kazan, Elia. *On the Waterfront*. U.S., 1954.
Kurosawa, Akira. *Roshomon*. Japan, 1950.
———.*Ikiru*. Japan, 1952.
———.*Seven Samurai*. Japan, 1954.
———.*Ran*. Japan, 1986.
Lang, Fritz. *M*. Germany, 1931.
Penn, Arthur. *Bonnie and Clyde*. U.S., 1967.
Renoir, Jean. *La Grande Illusion*. France, 1938.
———.*Rules of the Game*. France, 1939, 1965.
Truffaut, François. *The 400 Blows*. France, 1959.
———.*Jules and Jim*. France, 1961.
Welles, Orson. *Citizen Kane*. U.S., 1941.
Wiene, Robert. *The Cabinet of Dr. Caligari*. Germany, 1919.
Wilder, Billy. *Some Like It Hot*. U.S., 1959.

SUMMARY

The time chart for the twentieth century on page 454 provides an overview of our bewildering century of violence and invention. The century has been one of interminable warfare, including the two most destructive wars in human history, but there have also been remarkable technological developments. Consider transportation, for example. The Wright brothers flew the first heavier-than-air flying machine in 1903. Thirty-one years later the jet engine was invented and, eighteen years after that, commercial jets were making the world much smaller. Goddard invented the liquid-fuel rocket in 1926, the Russians put Sputnik into orbit thirty-one years later and, twelve years after that, an American astronaut walked on the moon, just sixty-six years after the Wright brothers' flying machine.

Communications technology also developed in a rush. Twelve years after the beginning of commercial television transcontinental television became a reality; a decade later communication satellites were starting to beam television to the entire world. We do indeed live in a Global Community with the possibility, no matter how faint, of evolving into a peaceful community in which human values will be more important than material possessions and national rivalries. High-tech makes this possible, but only human beings can make it a reality.

CULTURE AND HUMAN VALUES

Does literature really matter? Further, are those who read and write morally or ethically superior to those who neither read nor write?

Literature has been manifestly important in every literate culture known to humankind; but whether or not literature makes anyone superior in any way seems to be an arbitrary, even artificial, issue. Non-literate societies are not necessarily morally or ethically inferior to any other culture regardless of the literacy rate.

If literature does not make us better human beings, then what does it do? Does it, as so often stated, conserve the past? The literature of past cultures is, of course, our heritage; but, as is amply demonstrated in this chapter, literature consumes the past as it seeks its own ways to expose and confront the foibles, vanities, and shenanigans of humankind.

The plays of Shakespeare, for example, were subversive; in effect they were dangerous to every aspect of English civilization that had a formal existence: government, religion, societal conventions, and so on. *Waiting for Godot,* in turn, is clearly hostile to every Shakespearean dramatic convention: chronology, character development, and logical plot construction. *Godot* is absurd because it violates all accepted dramatic conventions and, most importantly, because it directly confronts the absurdities seemingly inherent in the human condition.

Catch-22 attacks traditional attitudes about the necessity of warfare. Those who see war as insane can logically refuse to become involved. Anyone, however, who recognizes the insanity of war can still be ordered to fight because he is sane enough to know that warfare is madness—and *that* is Catch-22. Joseph Heller's novel is subversive literature; it challenges the whole concept of war as a necessary and proper instrument of national policy.

Most of the literary selections in this unit have targeted war, bigotry, and chauvinism, but what of the rest? Consider again the remarks on page 519 about modern art reflecting the twentieth century. The same statement can be made about modern literature and, to one extent or another, about all the arts.

Artists seem to be more sensitive and articulate (in their medium) than the average person and, one way or another, their era is reflected in their creative output. Though all art is concerned with truth as perceived by the artist, that truth is not always nor necessarily the ugliness of bigotry or war. Literature—and the other arts—can be concerned with such themes as beauty, love, faith, and justice. Our society may be neither better nor worse than a non-literate culture, but our literature certainly helps make it more articulate and much more interesting.

APPENDIX

Music Listening and Notation

Music listening is always enriched by a basic knowledge of how it is constructed. This appendix aims to provide such knowledge. It should, ideally, be studied for content and used, along with the glossary, as often as necessary in conjunction with the material on music.

CHARACTERISTICS OF MUSICAL SOUNDS

Musical tones are sounds of definite pitch and duration, as distinct from noises and other less identifiable sounds. Musical tones have the four characteristics of pitch, intensity, tone color, and duration, which may be described as follows:

Pitch   The location of musical sound from low to high or high to low.
Intensity   Relative degree of softness or loudness.
Tone color   The quality of a sound that distinguishes it from other musical sounds of the same pitch and intensity; for example, the different tone quality of a flute as contrasted with a clarinet. Also called timbre.
Duration   The length of time a tone is audible.

THE FOUR ELEMENTS OF MUSIC

Rhythm, melody, harmony, and tone color are the essential elements of music. Composers and performers are concerned with each, while for the listener, they are experienced as a web of sound that often makes it difficult to single out any one element. Each can, however, be considered in isolation as a guide to understanding.

Rhythm

There is rhythm in the universe: our heartbeat, the alternation of day and night, the progression of the seasons, waves crashing on a beach. Artificially produced rhythm can be heard in train wheels clicking on rails, a ping-pong game, or the clacking castanets of a Spanish dancer. Although little is known about prehistoric music, the earliest music was probably the beating out of rhythms long before the existence of either melody or speech.

Essentially, rhythm is the organization of musical time—that is, everything that takes place in terms of sound and silence, accent and non-accent, tension and relaxation. Rhythm can also be defined as the "melody of a monotone"; music can

often be recognized just by hearing its rhythm. For example, tapping out the rhythmic patterns of "Dixie" can bring that familiar melody to mind.

Rhythm is not to be confused with beat, which results from a certain regularity of the rhythmic patterns. Beat, or pulse, can be compared with the heartbeat or the pulse rate. The beat will usually be steady, but it may temporarily speed up or slow down. It may be explicit (the uniform thump of a bass drum in a marching band) or implicit (resulting from combinations of rhythmic patterns). As soon as one note follows another, there will be rhythm but not necessarily beat. Certain types of music (such as Gregorian chant) do not produce the regular pulsation called beat.

When beats are produced by the music in a repeating pattern of accents, the result is meter. Metered music is measured music, with groupings of two, three, or four beats (or combinations of these) in each measure, or bar.

Time Signatures

When there is a regular pattern of accented and unaccented beats, it is customary to use a time signature. This looks like a fraction, in which the upper figure indicates the number of beats in a measure and the lower figure the unit of beat; that is, the note value the composer has selected to symbolize one beat. For example:

2/4   =   two beats per measure (duple meter)
       =   ♩ unit of beat (quarter note receives one beat)

3/8   =   three beats per measure (triple meter)
       =   ♪ unit of beat (eighth note receives one beat)

Melody and Harmony

A melody is a horizontal organization of pitches or, simply, a succession of musical tones. Harmony is a vertical organization of pitches in which two or more tones are sounded together. The following example illustrates melody on the upper staff and harmony on the lower staff.

"Old Folks at Home"

Tone Color

Sometimes called timbre (TAM-ber), tone color is to music what color is to the painter. It is tone color that enables us to distinguish between a flute, a clarinet, and an oboe. A soprano voice differs from a bass voice not only by its higher pitch, but also by its different tone color. Through experience, people learn to recognize the unique colors of many instruments. Further study leads to finer discriminations between similar instruments such as violin and viola, oboe and English horn, and so on. Composers select instruments for expressive purposes based largely on their coloration, whether singly or in combination. The full sound of a Beethoven symphony differs from a work by Richard Strauss, for example, because Strauss uses a wider range of instrumental colors.

MUSICAL LITERACY

The most abstract of the arts, music is sound moving in time. Factual information about music certainly helps the listener, but all the facts in the world can only assist the listening process; information can never replace the sound of music. One extremely useful method of learning to understand music is to study major themes and ideas in musical notation while listening to the music itself.

A practical approach to intelligent listening must include some instruction in musical literacy sufficient to read a single line of music. This is a simple process that can be quickly learned by young children and can be taught to an adult in a few minutes. The strangely prevalent attitude that musical notation is "too hard" or "too technical" has no foundation in fact, and probably refers to reading music as a performer—a very different matter that need not concern us here. As basic to music as the ABC's of written language, musical notation is an indispensable guide for music listeners.

Learning to pick out musical themes will turn abstract sounds into intelligible tunes, thus giving oneself an opportunity to anticipate the themes as they emerge in the music. Equally valuable is the repetition of themes after the listening experience. To summarize, picking out melodies on the piano is an aid to understanding, a helpful preview of music to be listened to, and a reminder of music already heard.

Try to approach the following material not with apprehension but with anticipation. Master the principles of musical notation with the positive attitude that this not only will materially assist in a better understanding of the music in this text but also lead, in time, to a lifetime of pleasurable listening.

MUSICAL NOTATION

Pitch

The essential elements of our notational system were devised some ten centuries ago and subsequently altered and augmented to become a reasonably efficient means of communicating the composer's intentions to a performer. The system is based on the first seven letters of the alphabet and can best be illustrated on a piano keyboard. The pitches range from low to high, from A through G in a repeating A–G pattern.

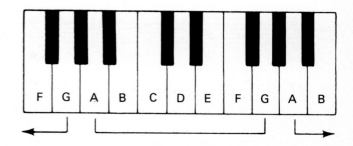

In order to know which of the eight A's available on the piano is the intended note, you will need to do the following:

1. Use a musical staff of five lines and four spaces.
2. Use a symbol for a musical pitch, i.e., a note.

3. Place the notes on the lines or in the spaces of the staff.

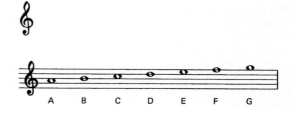

4. Indicate by means of a clef sign the names of the notes.

The word "clef" (French, "key") implies that the key to precise placement of the notes is the establishment of the letter name of one of the lines or spaces of the staff. There are two clefs in common use. Both are ornamental symbols, one derived from the letter G and one from F. The solid lines below are the present clef signs and the dotted lines their original form:

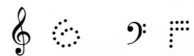

The clefs are placed on the staff to indicate the location of the letters they represent. The spiral portion of the G clef curls around the second line to fix the location of G; the two dots of the F clef are placed above and below the fourth line to show that this is the F line.

Once the five-line staff has received its pitch designation of G or F, the staff is subsequently identified as a treble or a bass staff.

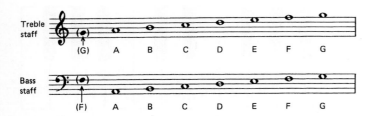

Not all melodies are composed so that they can be played on the white notes only of the piano. Sometimes another key, or different set of pitches, is used, as demonstrated in the following examples:

"Joy to the World"   Handel (1685–1759)

Key of C

In the second version, below, the key signature indicates that all the F's and C's have been raised a half step to the next closest note—on a piano the adjacent black keys to the right. A symbol called a sharp (#) indicates raised notes.

"Joy to the World"   Handel

Key of D

The other common symbol that changes a note is the flat (♭), which lowers a note a half step to the next closest note. Following is the same melody written in the key of B♭. As indicated by the key signature, all the B's and E's have been lowered to B♭ and E♭. Key signatures can include up to seven sharps or flats.

"Joy to the World"   Handel

Key of B♭

You will see that the staff just given has an added short line, a ledger line, used to accommodate the last two notes.

On a piano keyboard the black keys are grouped in alternating sets of two and three. The white note, or key, immediately to the left of the two black keys is always C. There are eight C's; the C closest to the center is called middle C. It is from this C that you can locate the notes of the themes.

Below is a guide to the chromatic scale, which includes all the black and white keys, twelve in all, in one octave.

Duration

The notation of the length of time of musical sounds (and silences) was developed, more or less, in conjunction with the notation of pitch. The modern note-value system consists of fractional parts of a whole unit, or whole note (𝅝), expressed in mathematical terms as 1/1. A half note (𝅗𝅥) is one-half the whole unit, or 1/2; a quarter note (♩) is one-quarter the unit, or 1/4; and so on.

The name of the note value indicates the number of notes in the whole-note unit. There are four quarter notes (4 × 1/4 = 1/1), eight eighth notes (8 × 1/8 = 1/1), etc.

With note values smaller than the whole note, the relationships remain constant. There are two quarter notes in a half note (2 × 1/4 = 1/2), two eighth notes in a quarter note (2 × 1/8 = 1/4), etc.

Rhythmic notation is both relative and fixed. The duration of a whole note is dependent on the tempo (speed) and notation of music. It may have a duration of one second, eight seconds, or something in between. The interior relationships, however, never vary.

A whole note has the same duration as two half notes, four quarter notes, and so forth. The mathematical relationship is fixed and precise. See table A.1 for an outline of the system.

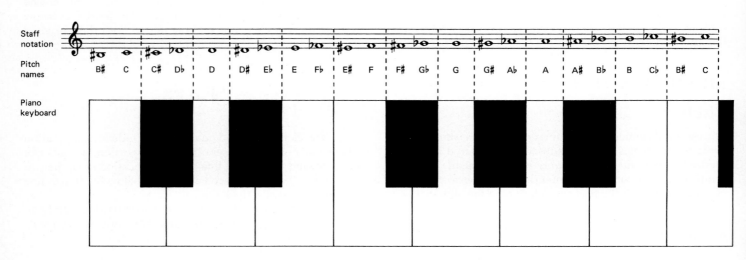

VOICES AND INSTRUMENTS

Choral ensembles are usually divided into four voice parts ranging from high to low: soprano and alto (women) and tenor and bass (men).

TABLE A.1 NOTE AND REST VALUES

Note value	Symbol
Whole note (basic unit)	𝅝
Half note	𝅗𝅥
Quarter note	𝅘𝅥
Eighth note	𝅘𝅥𝅮
Sixteenth note	𝅘𝅥𝅯

Rest value	Symbol
Whole (note) rest	▬
Half rest	▬
Quarter rest	𝄽
Eighth rest	𝄾
Sixteenth rest	𝄿

Instruments of the symphony orchestra and other ensembles are grouped by family, from highest pitch to lowest:

Strings	Woodwinds	Brass	Percussion
violin	piccolo	trumpet (and cornet)	snare drum
viola	flute	French horn	timpani
cello	oboe	trombone	bass drum
bass	clarinet	tuba	cymbals
	bassoon		(many others)

Keyboard instruments include piano, harpsichord, and organ. The piano, originally called *pianoforte* (It., "soft" "loud"), is based on the principle of hammers striking the strings; the harpsichord has a mechanism that plucks the strings. Organs are built with two or more keyboards called manuals. The traditional organ uses forced air to activate the pipes; some modern organs use an electronic reproduction of sound.

MUSICAL TEXTURE

The words for the three kinds of musical texture are derived from Greek and are virtually self-explanatory:

monophonic (one sound)
homophonic (same sound)
polyphonic (many sounds)

Monophonic music has a single unaccompanied melodic line. Much of the world's music—including Chinese and Hindu music and, in Western civilization, Gregorian chant and troubadour songs—is monophonic. Homophonic music has a principal melodic line accompanied by harmony, sometimes referred to as chordal accompaniment. Although homophony is relatively unknown outside Western culture, it comprises the bulk of our music, including nearly all popular music. Polyphonic music has two or more melodies sounding simultaneously. Familiar rounds such as "Three Blind Mice" and "Row, Row, Row Your Boat" are polyphonic, as is most Renaissance music. The music of Baroque composers such as Bach, Handel, and others is basically polyphonic too.

MUSICAL FORM

Briefly stated, form in music is a balance of unity and variety. Too much unity becomes boring, whereas excessive variety leads to fragmentation and even chaos. Understanding form in music is essential to its appreciation. As German composer Robert Schumann remarked, "Only when the form is quite clear to you will the spirit become clear to you."

The smallest unit of form is the motive. This is a recurring combination of at least two notes with an identifiable rhythmic pattern. The principal motive in the first movement of Beethoven's Fifth Symphony has two different pitches in a four-note rhythmic pattern:

Symphony No. 5,   **Beethoven**
First movement   **(1770–1827)**

A musical phrase is a coherent group of notes roughly comparable to a literary phrase and having about the same function. Two related phrases form a period, analogous to a sentence. In the period illustrated below, the first phrase has a transitional ending called a half cadence, and the second phrase ends solidly with a full cadence. Note also the extreme unity; the first three measures of each phrase are identical.

"Ode to Joy"   **Beethoven**

In large works the musical periods are used in various combinations to expand the material into sections comparable to paragraphs, and these are then combined to make still larger units.

Musical structure can be comprehended only after the music has arrived at wherever the composer intends it to go. Look again at "Ode to Joy" (from Beethoven's Ninth Symphony). You can "see" its form only because the music is notated, which is why learning some notation is so important. When the music is played, your ear follows the line to the half cadence, which is then heard as a statement that demands completion. As the second phrase begins, there is aural recognition of its relationship to the first phrase. When the second phrase concludes with a gratifying full cadence, there is a kind of flashback to the memory of the first phrase. In other words, the conclusion of the second phrase is satisfying because it completes the thought of the still-remembered first phrase. The music conforms to its own inner logic; that is, the second phrase is a logical consequence of the first.

As a general rule, most music is constructed around two different but logically related musical ideas. We can call one idea A and the other B. One common musical form is two-part (binary), or simply AB. An even more common form is three-part (ternary), or ABA. In two-part form the composer makes a musical statement (A), which is followed by a new section (B), which is sufficiently different to provide variety but not so different as to destroy the balance. The following hymn tune is a complete composition in two-part form, with two phrases in each section. Section B has the same rhythm as Section A, but the melody is a kind of inversion of the melody in A. The inner logic is maintained through the similarities.

"St. Anne"

The following complete hymn tune has a form related to two-part form: AA'B, called A, A prime, B. Part A is followed by another A that is varied going into the cadence. Part B is properly different but related to A and A' by the similarity of measures 2, 6, and 10. In terms of measures, the structure of the piece can be diagrammed as:

```
     A        A'        B
   2 + 2     2 + 2     2 + 2
```

"Regent Square"

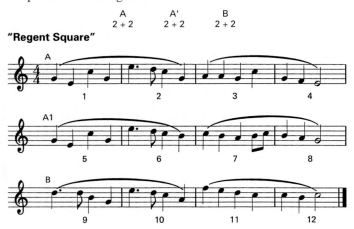

Three-part form operates on the principle of closing with the melody that began the piece, a rounding off of the material: ABA. The following example can be analyzed as AA'BA' and diagrammed as:

```
   A        A'        B        A'
 4 + 4     4 + 4     4 + 4     4 + 4
```

This is the thirty-two-measure form most commonly used for popular songs.

"In the Gloaming"

There are, of course, other variants of AB and ABA forms, as well as several other structures. However, the examples given illustrate the principle of a balance between unity and variety, of which unity is paramount. Perhaps because of its fluid nature, music, more than any other art, emphasizes repetition, restating the material again and again, but mixing it with enough variety to maintain interest. The forms illustrated can also be heard in the larger context of longer compositions. For example, "In the Gloaming" has thirty-two measures in a basic ABA form; a large symphonic work could have, say, 200 measures and be diagrammed as follows:

```
  A    B    A         A    B    A'        A    B    A'
 aba  aba  aba   or  aba' aba a'ba'  or  aa'ba aba aa'ba'
```

THE LISTENING EXPERIENCE

Listening to music begins with the question, *What do you hear?* This is an objective question that has nothing whatever to do with a story you may imagine the music is telling, random associations the music happens to trigger, or any meaning that may be attributed to the music. The idea, rather, is to objectively identify the sounds to determine how the sounds are produced, and to try to determine how the sounds are organized.

Composers do not pour out notes as if emptying a can of beans on a tabletop. They arrange their sounds in a sort of container in a manner that molds the receptacle to the material it holds. Learning to comprehend the musical structure leads to the ability to anticipate the next melody, cadence, section, or other development. Being able to anticipate what is to happen next means that you are tuned in to the web of sound, listening along with the pace of the music. Almost everyone has already acquired the ability to follow the progress of popular music and to anticipate what comes next in favorite recordings. The larger world of classical music lies only a step beyond this level of listening ability. It is an inspiring and enriching stride into one of the greatest achievements of Western civilization.

Glossary

Pronunciation: Approximations are given where necessary. The syllables are to be read as English words and with the capital letters accented.

Abbreviations: Lat., Latin; Fr., French; Ger., German; Gk., Greek; It., Italian; Sp., Spanish.

Asterisks: An asterisk preceding a word or phrase indicates that a definition and/or illustration can be found under that heading.

A

Abacus   The flat slab on top of a *capital.

Abstract Art   Term covers many kinds of non-representational art, e.g., action painting, works by Kandinsky, the Cycladic sculptures.

Academy   Originally derived from the *Akademeia*, the grove in which Plato taught his seminars.

Acanthus   A plant whose thick leaves are reproduced in stylized form on *Corinthian *capitals (see fig. 9.7).

A cappella (ah ka-PELL-ah; Lat.)   Originally unaccompanied music sung "in the chapel." Term now applies to choral music without instrumental accompaniment.

Acoustics   The science of sound.

Aerial perspective   See *perspective.

Aesthetic   Concerned with a sensitivity to the pleasurable and the beautiful; the opposite of anaesthetic.

Aesthetics   The study or philosophy of beauty; theory of the fine arts and human responses.

Agnosticism (Gk., *agnostos*, "unknowing")   The impossibility of obtaining knowledge of certain subjects; assertion that people cannot obtain knowledge of God.

Agora   In ancient Greece, a marketplace or public square.

Allegory   A literary mode with a literal level of meanings plus a set of meanings above and beyond themselves. This second level may be religious, social, political, or philosophical, e.g., *The Faerie Queen* by Spenser is an allegory about Christian virtues.

Alleluia   Latinization of the Hebrew *Halleluyah* ("Praise ye the Lord"). Third item of the Proper of the *Mass.

Altarpiece   A painted (or sculptured) panel placed behind an altar.

Ambulatory   A passageway around the *apse of a church (see fig. 14.19).

Amphora   Greek vase, usually quite large, with two handles, used to store food staples (see fig. 7.7).

Apocalypse   Prophetic revelation given through a symbolic vision of the future. Apocalyptic literature concerns the final period of world history and depicts the final confrontation between God and the powers of evil, as described, for example, in the Book of Revelation in the New Testament.

A posteriori (a-pos-TEER-e-or-e; Lat., "following after")   Reasoning from observed facts to conclusions; inductive; empirical.

A priori (a-pree-OAR-e; Lat., "coming before")   Reasoning from general propositions to particular conclusions; deductive; nonempirical.

Apse   A recess, usually semicircular, in the east wall of a Christian church or, in a Roman *basilica, at the wall opposite to the general entrance way.

Arabesque   Literally Arab-like. Elaborate designs of intertwined flowers, foliage, and geometric patterns used in Islamic architecture.

Arcade   A series of connected *arches resting on *columns (see fig. 9.8).

Arch   A curved structure (semicircular or pointed) spanning a space, usually made of wedge-shaped blocks. Known to the Greeks, who preferred a *post and lintel system, but exploited by the Romans.

Archetype (Gk., *arche*, "first"; *typos*, "form")   The original pattern of forms of which things in this world are copies.

Architrave   The lowest part of an *entablature, a horizontal beam or *lintel directly above the *capital (see fig. 7.24).

Archivolt   In architectural sculpture, the decorative molding carried around an arched wall opening.

Aria (It., AHR-eeah, "air")   Solo song (sometimes duet) in *operas, *oratorios, *cantatas.

Ars antiqua (Lat., "old art")   Music of the late twelfth and thirteenth centuries.

Ars nova (Lat., "new art")   Music of the fourteenth century. Outstanding composers were Machaut (France) and Landini (Italy).

Art Nouveau   A style of architecture, crafts, and design of the 1890s and a bit later characterized by curvilinear patterns. Examples include Tiffany lamps and the work of Beardsley and Klimt.

Art song   Song intending an artistic combination of words and music, as distinct from popular song or folk song.

Astrolabe   An instrument formerly used to determine positions of heavenly bodies. It had a suspended disk with degrees marked on the circumference and a movable pointer at the center. It was succeeded in the eighteenth century by the sextant.

Atheism (Gk., *a*, "no"; *theos*, "god")   The belief that there is no God; also means "not theistic" when applied to those who do not believe in a personal God.

Atonal   Music that has no tonal center, in which all notes are of relatively equal importance. In a composition in C major, on the other hand, C is the most important note. Almost all popular music is written in keys such as C major, D major and so on. Most compositions by Schoenberg are atonal.

Atrium   The court of a Roman house, roofless, and near the entrance (see fig. 9.5). Also the open, colonnaded court attached to the front of early Christian churches.

Augustinian   Roman Catholic monastic order that uses the old rule of St. Augustine.

Aulos (OW-los)   A shrill-sounding oboelike instrument associated with the Dionysian rites of the ancient Greeks. Double-reed instrument normally played in pairs by one performer (see fig. 7.46).

Aureole   A circle of light or radiance surrounding the head or body of a representation of a deity or holy person; a halo.

Avant-garde (a-vahn-gard)   A French term meaning, literally, "advanced guard," used to designate innovators and experimentalists in the various arts.

B

Babylonian Captivity   The exile of the Jews, 586–538 BC; also the Church of Rome in Avignon rather than in Rome, 1305–78.

Baldacchino (ball-da-KEEN-o)   A canopy over a tomb or altar of which the most famous is that over the tomb of St. Peter in St. Peter's in Rome designed by Bernini.

Ballad (Lat., *ballare*, "to dance")   Originally a dancing song. A narrative song, usually folk song, but also applied to popular songs.

Ballade   Medieval *trouvère song. In the nineteenth and twentieth centuries dramatic piano pieces, frequently inspired by Romantic poetry.

Balustrade   A railing plus a supporting row of posts.

Banjo   Instrument of the *guitar family, probably introduced into Africa by Arab traders and brought to America on the slave ships. The body consists of a shallow, hollow metal drum with a drumhead on top and open at the bottom. It has four or more strings and is played with fingers or plectrum.

Baptistery   Originally a separate building, later a part of the church containing the baptismal font.

Barrel vault   See *vault.

Basilica   In Roman architecture, a rectangular public building used for business or as a tribunal. Christian churches that use a *cruciform plan are patterned after Roman basilicas. Though basilica denotes an architectural style, the Church of Rome designates a church a basilica if it contains the bones of a saint.

Bas-relief   A sculptural term (low relief) used to describe an object with a design slightly projecting from the surface. The opposite of high relief in which the design appears to be almost wholly detached.

Bay   In Romanesque and Gothic churches the area between the *columns (see fig. 14.19).

Behaviorism   School of psychology that restricts both animal and human psychology to the study of behavior; stresses the role of the environment and conditioned responses to exterior stimuli.

Black-figure technique   Greek vase painting in which the subject is incised in black on a light, usually orange, background. In what is essentially silhouette painting, the effect can be very powerful and compelling. Exekias (active 545–525 BC) is the foremost Greek painter of the black-figure technique.

Blank verse   Unrhymed *iambic pentameter* (see *meter) in the English language, much used in Elizabethan drama.

Bourgeoisie   The middle class; in Marxist theory, the capitalist class, which is opposed to the proletariat, the lower or industrial working class.

Branle   (bruhn-l; Fr., *branler*, "to sway") Originally, in the Middle Ages, a step in the Basse Danse.

Buttress   Exterior support used to counter the lateral thrust of an *arch or *vault. A *pier buttress* is a solid mass of masonry added to the wall; a *flying buttress* is typically a pier standing away from the wall from which an arch "flies" from the pier to connect with the wall at the point of outward thrust (see fig. 14.18).

C

Cadence   Term in music applied to the concluding portion of a phrase (temporary cadence) or composition (permanent cadence).

Cameo   In jewelry, a technique of engraving in relief on a gem or other stone, especially with layers of different hues, leaving the raised design with one color and the background with another.

Campanile   Italian for bell tower, usually freestanding. The Leaning Tower of Pisa is a campanile (see fig. 14.12).

Canon   (Gk., "law, rule")   1. A body of principles, rules, standards, or norms. 2. In art and architecture, a criterion for establishing proportion, measure, or scale. 3. In music, in which a melody is imitated strictly and in its entirety by another voice. Canons that have no specified way to end but keep going around are called "rounds," for example, "Three Blind Mice."

Cantata   (It., *cantare*, "to sing")   A "sung" piece as opposed to a "sound" (instrumental) piece, for example, *sonata. The term is now generally used for secular or sacred choral works with orchestral accompaniment, which are on a smaller scale than *oratorios.

Cantilever   A self-supporting projection that needs no exterior bracing; e.g., a balcony or porch can be cantilevered.

Cantus firmus   (Lat., "fixed song")   A preexisting melody used as the foundation for a *polyphonic composition. *Plainsong melodies were used for this purpose, but other sources included secular songs, Lutheran *chorales, and *scales. Any preexisting melody may serve as a cantus firmus.

Capital   The top or crown of a *column (see fig. 7.24).

Cartoon   A full-size preliminary drawing for a pictorial work, usually a large work such as a *mural, *fresco, or tapestry. Also a humorous drawing.

Caryatid   (karry-AT-id)   A female figure that functions as a supporting *column; male figures that function in a like manner are called *atlantes* (at-LAN-tees; plural of Atlas; see fig. 7.30).

Catacombs   Subterranean Christian cemeteries, e.g. those in the outskirts of Rome, Naples, and Syracuse.

Catharsis   (Gk., "purge, purify")   Purification, purging of emotions effected by tragedy (Aristotle).

Cella   The enclosed chamber in a classical temple that contained the cult statue of the god or goddess after whom the temple was named.

Chamber music   Term now restricted to instrumental music written for a limited number of players in which there is only one player to each part, as opposed to orchestral music, which has two or more players to some parts, e.g., sixteen or more players on the first violin part. True chamber music emphasizes ensemble rather than solo playing.

Chanson   (Fr., "song")   A major part of the *troubadour-*trouvère tradition, dating from the eleventh through the fourteenth centuries. Also a generic term for a song with a French text.

Chanson de geste   A genre of Old French epic poems celebrating deeds of heroic or historical figures.

Chevet   (sheh-vay; Fr., "pillow")   The eastern end of a church, including *choir, *ambulatory, and *apse.

Chiaroscuro   (kee-AR-oh-SKOOR-oh; It., "light-dark")   In the visual arts the use of gradations of light and dark to represent natural light and shadows.

Chinoiserie   (she-nwaz-eh-ree; Fr.) Chinese motifs as decorative elements for craft objects, screens, wallpaper, and furniture; prominent in eighteenth-century rococo style.

Choir   That part of the church where the singers and clergy are normally accommodated; usually between the *transept and the *apse; also called chancel (see fig. 14.19).

Chorale   A *hymn tune of the German Protestant (Lutheran) church.

Chord   In music the simultaneous sounding of two or more tones.

Chromatic   (Gk., *chroma*, "color")   The use of notes that are foreign to the musical *scale and have to be indicated by a sharp, flat, natural, etc. The *chromatic* scale is involved in these alterations. It consists of twelve tones to an octave, each a semitone apart.

Cire perdue   (seer pair-due; Fr., "lost wax")   A metal-casting method in which the original figure is modeled in wax and encased in a mold; as the mold is baked the wax melts and runs out, after which the molten metal is poured into the mold.

Clavichord   The earliest type of stringed keyboard instrument (twelfth century). Probably developed from the *monochord. It is an oblong box, 24 by 48 inches (61 x 132 cm) with a keyboard of about three octaves. The strings run parallel to the keyboard, as opposed to harpsichords and pianos, in which the strings run at right angles to the keyboard. The keys are struck from below by metal tangents fastened to the opposite ends of elongated keys. The tone is light and delicate but very expressive because the performer can control the loudness of each note. It was sometimes called a "table *clavier" because it was portable.

Clavier   Generic term for any instrument of the stringed keyboard family: *clavichord, harpsichord, and piano.

Clef   (Fr., "key")   In music a symbol placed on the staff to indicate the pitches of the lines and spaces. There are three clefs in use today: G, F, and C. The G clef is used to indicate that the note on the second line is G (treble clef). The F clef is usually used to indicate that F is on the fourth line (bass clef). (See Appendix.)

Clerestory   In a *basilica or church, the section of an interior wall that rises above the roof of the side aisles and which has numerous windows.

Cloisonné   Enamel used for artistic purposes and painted on metal bases. Thin wires of gold, silver, or copper are soldered onto a base plate of the same metal. After these *cloises* (compartments) are filled with powdered glass, the object is baked in an oven until the glass fuses. Additional powdered glass or metal may be enameled for subsequent firings.

Cloister   (Lat. *claustrum*, "hidden").   An inner court bounded by covered walks; a standard feature of monastery architecture.

Collage (Fr., "pasting") Paper and other materials pasted on a two-dimensional surface.

Colonnade A series of spaced *columns, usually connected by *lintels (see fig. 7.21).

Column A vertical support, usually circular, which has a base (except in *Doric style), shaft, and *capital (see fig. 7.24).

Comedy A play or other literary work in which all ends well, properly, or happily. Opposite of *tragedy.

Comitatus Early Anglo-Saxon society was organized in families and clans and centered on the warrior and a system of reciprocity (mutual loyalty) called *comitatus*.

Concerto (con-CHAIR-toe) A musical work for one or two solo instruments with orchestral accompaniment.

Concerto grosso A musical work for a small group of instruments (usually three or four) with orchestral accompaniment.

Corinthian The most ornate style of Greek architecture, little used by the Greeks but preferred by the Romans; tall, slender, channeled *columns topped by an elaborate *capital decorated with stylized *acanthus leaves (see fig. 9.7).

Cornice The horizontal, projecting member crowning an *entablature.

Cosmology Philosophic study of the origin and nature of the universe.

Counterpoint In music, the art of combining melodies.

Couplet In poetry two successive rhymed lines in the same meter.

Covenant A legal concept often used in the Bible as a metaphor describing the relationship between God and humankind. This idea lies at the heart of the Bible and explains the selection of the word "testament," a synonym for covenant, in naming the two parts of the Bible.

Crocket In Gothic architecture, an ornamental device shaped like a curling leaf and placed on the outer angles of *gables and pinnacles (see fig. 14.35).

Crossing In a church, the space formed by the interception of the *nave and the *transepts.

Cruciform The floor plan of a church in the shape of a *Latin cross (see fig. 14.19).

Cuneiform A writing system of ancient Mesopotamia consisting of wedge shapes.

Cupola A rounded roof or ceiling; a small *dome.

D

Daguerrotype Photograph made on a silver-coated glass plate; after L. J. M. Daguerre (1789–1851), the inventor.

Determinism (Lat., *de*, "from," *terminus*, "end") The doctrine that all events are conditioned by their causes and that people are mechanical expressions of heredity and environment; in short, we are at the mercy of blind, unknowing natural laws in an indifferent universe.

Deus ex machina (DAY-oos ex ma-KEE-na;

Lat.) In Greek and Roman drama a deity who was brought in by stage machinery to resolve a difficult situation; hence, any unexpected or bizarre device or event introduced to untangle a plot.

Dialectic Associated with Plato as the art of debate by question and answer. Also dialectical reasoning using *syllogisms (Aristotle) or, according to Hegel, the distinctive characteristic of speculative thought.

Didactic Intended to instruct or teach.

Diorite A dense igneous rock, ranked in hardness between gabbro and granite.

Dome A hemispherical *vault; may be viewed as an *arch rotated on its vertical axis.

Doric The oldest of Greek temple styles, characterized by sturdy *columns with no base and an unornamented cushionlike *capital (see fig. 7.24).

Dormer A window set vertically in a small gable projecting from a sloping roof.

Drum The circular sections that make up the shaft of a *column; also the circular wall on which a *dome is placed.

Drums Percussion musical instruments having a skin stretched over one or both ends of a frame.

Dualism In *metaphysics, a theory that admits two independent substances, e.g., Plato's dualism of the sensible and intelligible worlds, Cartesian dualism of thinking and extended subjects, Kant's dualism of the noumenal and the phenomenal.

Duple meter In music, two beats per measure. Most marches and ragtime music are in duple meter.

Dynamics In music, the degrees of loudness and softness.

E

Echinus The highest part of the shaft of a Greek *column immediately below the *abacus. It is wider at the top and narrower at the bottom and contains whatever decorative elements the column may have.

Elegy A meditative poem dealing with the idea of death.

Elevation The vertical arrangements of the elements of an architectural design; a vertical projection.

Embossing In metalworking, the adding of decorative relief designs.

Empiricism The view that the sole source of knowledge is experience, that no knowledge is possible independent of experience.

Enamel A vitreous, usually opaque, protective or decorative coating baked on metal, glass, or ceramic ware. A paint that dries to a hard, glossy surface. Any glossy, hard coating resembling enamel, such as nail enamel.

Engaged column A non-functional form projecting from the surface of a wall; used for visual articulation (see fig. 9.6).

Engraving The process of using a sharp instrument to cut a design into a metal plate, usually copper; also the print that is made from the plate after ink has been

added.

Entablature The part of a building of *post and lintel construction between the *capitals and the roof. In classical architecture this includes the *architrave, *frieze, and *cornice (see fig. 7.24).

Entasis (EN-ta-sis) A slight convex swelling in the shaft of a *column.

Epic A lengthy narrative poem dealing with protagonists of heroic proportions and issues of universal significance, e.g., Homer's *Iliad*.

Epicurean One who believes that pleasure, especially that of the mind, is the highest good.

Epistemology A branch of philosophy that studies the origin, validity, and processes of knowledge.

Eschatology (Gk., *eschata*, "death") That part of theology dealing with last things: death, judgment, heaven, hell.

Estampie (es-tahm-pea) A dance form popular during the twelfth to fourteenth centuries. Consists of a series of repeated sections, for example, aa, bb, cc, etc.

Etching A kind of *engraving in which the design is incised into a wax-covered metal plate, after which the exposed metal is etched by a corrosive acid; the print made from the plate is also called an etching.

Ethos In ancient Greek music, the "ethical" character attributed to the various modes. The Dorian was considered strong and manly; the Phrygian, ecstatic and passionate; the Lydian, feminine, decadent, and lascivious; the Mixolydian, mournful and gloomy. (See p. 86.)

Eucharist (Gk., *eucharistia*, "thanksgiving") The *sacrament of Communion, the taking of Christ's body and blood, that Christ instituted at the Last Supper.

Euphemism An innocuous term substituted for one considered to be offensive or socially unacceptable, e.g., "passing away" for "dying."

F

Facade In architecture the face of a building; one or more of the exterior walls of a building, especially the one containing the main entrance.

Fenestration The arrangement of windows or other openings in the walls of a building.

Feudalism A medieval contractual arrangement by which a lord granted land to his vassal in return for military service. Feudalism was further characterized by the localization of political and economic power in the hands of lords and their vassals.

Fiddle Colloquialism for the violin. Also used to designate the bowed ancestors of the violin, particularly the medieval instrument used to accompany dances.

Finial In Gothic architecture an ornament fitted to the peak of an *arch; any ornamental terminating point, such as the screw-top of a lamp.

Flamboyant Late Gothic architecture of the fifteenth or sixteenth centuries, which featured wavy lines and flamelike forms.

Flèche (flesh; Fr., "arrow") In architecture

a slender exterior spire above the intersection of the *nave and *transepts (see fig. 14.18).

Flute   A woodwind instrument made of wood (originally), silver, gold, or preferably platinum. It is essentially a straight pipe with keys, is held horizontally and played by blowing across a mouthpiece.

Fluting   The vertical grooves, usually semicircular, in the shaft of a *column or *pilaster.

Foot   A metrical unit in poetry such as the iamb (˘—) (see *meter).

Foreshortening   Creating the illusion in painting or drawing that the subject is projecting out of or into the frontal plane of a two-dimensional surface.

Forum   The public square and/or marketplace of an ancient Roman city.

Free verse   Verse that uses parallelism and sound effects rather than *meter and rhyme.

Fresco (It., "fresh")   Painting on plaster, usually wet plaster, into which the colors sink as the plaster dries so that the fresco becomes part of the wall.

Frieze   In architecture, a decorated horizontal band, often embellished with carved figures and molding; the portion of an *entablature between the *architrave and the *cornice above (see fig. 7.24).

Fugue   *Polyphonic musical composition in which a single theme is developed by the different musical voices in succession. A favorite style of Baroque composers such as Bach and Handel.

G

Gable   In architecture, the triangular section at the end of a pitched roof, frequently with a window below.

Genre (zhan-re)   In the pictorial arts, a depiction of scenes of everyday life. In literature, the type of work—epic, novel, and so on.

Gesso   White chalky pigment bound in a water and glue medium, used as a ground on wood and other supports in painting and gilding.

Gnosticism   The doctrines of certain early Christian cults (particularly in Egypt) that valued inquiry into spiritual truth above faith.

Goliards   Wandering scholars of the tenth through the thirteenth centuries: students, young ecclesiastics, dreamers, and the disenchanted.

Gospels   In the Bible, New Testament accounts (Matthew, Mark, Luke, and John) of the life and teachings of Christ.

Gouache (goo-ahsh; Fr.)   Watercolor made opaque by adding zinc white.

Graphic arts   Visual arts that are linear in character: drawing, engraving, printing, printmaking, typographic, and advertising design.

Great Schism   Separation of Eastern Orthodox Churches from the church of Rome in 1054; rival popes of the Church of Rome in Rome, Avignon, and Pisa, 1378–1417.

Greek cross   A cross in which the four arms are of equal length.

Gregorian chant   See *plainsong.

Groin   In architecture the edge (groin) formed by the intersection of two *vaults (see fig. 14.10).

Guild   An association of persons of the same trade, pursuits, or interests, formed for their mutual aid and protection and the maintenance of standards; in the Middle Ages a society of merchants or artisans.

Guitar   A plucked string instrument with a flat body and six strings (modern guitar). Brought into Europe during the Middle Ages by the Moorish conquest of Spain.

H

Harmony   In music the simultaneous combination of notes in a chord.

Harp   Musical instrument consisting of upright, open triangular frame with forty-six strings of graduated length.

Harpsichord   Actually a harp turned on its side and played by means of quills or leather tongues operated by a keyboard. It was the most common keyboard instrument of the sixteenth to eighteenth centuries and is again being built today in increasing numbers.

Hatching   A series of closely spaced parallel lines in a drawing or print giving the effect of shading.

Hedonism   The doctrine that pleasure or pleasant consciousness are intrinsically good; that pleasure is the proper—and the actual—motive for every choice.

Heroic couplet   Two successive lines of rhymed iambic pentameter, used, e.g., in Pope's *Essay on Man*.

Hieratic (hye-uh-RAT-ik)   Of or used by priests; priestly.

Hieroglyphics   Symbols or pictures giving written form to syllables or sounds; writing system of ancient Egyptians.

Holy Roman Empire   Political body embracing most of central Europe from 962 to 1806. "Roman" because it claimed succession to imperial Rome. "Holy" because it originally claimed supremacy over Christendom.

Homophonic (Gk., "same sound")   Music in which a single melodic line is supported by chords or other subordinate material (percussion instruments).

Horn   Wind instrument made of brass.

Hubris (HU-bris)   Tragic flaw, i.e., excessive pride or arrogance that harms other people and brings about the downfall of the person with the flaw.

Hue   The attribute of a color. The chief colors of the spectrum are: red, yellow, blue (primary); green, orange, violet (secondary).

Humanism   "Man is the measure of all things" (Protagoras) and "Many are the wonders of the world, and none so wonderful as man" (Sophocles) give the essence of humanism. The Greeks conceived their gods as perfect human beings, free from infirmities and immortal, but subject to human passions and ambitions. The Renaissance conception of man as the potential master of all things arose out of the awakening to the glories of Greece and Rome.

Hydraulis   Ancient Greek pipe *organ, probably invented in the Middle East 300–200 BC. Air for the pipes was provided by hydraulic pressure and the pipes activated by a keyboard. Originally the tone was delicate and clear, but the Romans converted it into a noisy outdoor instrument by a large increase in air pressure.

Hydria   Greek vase designed to hold water (see fig. 7.6).

Hymn   A poem of praise, usually, but not necessarily, sacred. The music accompanying a hymn is called the hymn tune.

I

Icon (EYE-kon; Gk., "image")   Two-dimensional representation of a holy person; in the Greek church a panel painting of a sacred personage (see fig. 11.7).

Iconography   Visual imagery used to convey concepts in the visual arts; the study of symbolic meanings in the pictorial arts.

Illumination   Decorative illustrations or designs, associated primarily with medieval illuminated manuscripts (see fig. 14.1).

Impasto (It., "paste")   A painting style in which the pigment is laid on thickly, as in many of van Gogh's paintings.

Incarnation   Denotes the embodiment of a deity in human form, a frequent idea in mythology. Vishnu is believed by Hindus to have had nine incarnations. For Christians the incarnation is a central dogma referring to the belief that the Son of God, the second of the Trinity, became man in the person of Jesus Christ.

Inductive method   The process of arriving at a general conclusion from a set of particular facts.

Intaglio (in-TAL-yo)   A graphic technique in which the design is incised; used on seals, gems, and dies for coins and also for the kinds of printing and printmaking that have a depressed ink-bearing surface.

Ionic   A style of Greek classical architecture using slender, *fluted *columns and *capitals decorated with scrolls and *volutes (see fig. 7.24).

Isocephaly (I-so-SEPH-uh-ly)   In the visual arts a convention that arranges figures so that the heads are at the same height (see fig. 7.19).

J

Jamb figure   Sculpted figure flanking the portal of a Gothic church (see fig. 14.21).

Jihad   Muslim holy war; a Muslim crusade against unbelievers.

Jongleurs (zhō-gleur)   French professional musicians (minstrels) of the twelfth and thirteenth centuries who served the *troubadours and *trouvères.

K

Keystone   The central wedge-shaped stone in an *arch; the last stone put in place, it makes the arch stable.

Kibla   The point toward which Muslims turn when praying, toward Mecca.

Kithara (KITH-a-ra)   The principal stringed instrument of the ancient Greeks. Essentially a larger version of the *lyre, it has a U-shaped form and usually seven to eleven strings running vertically from the cross-arm down to the sound-box at the base of the instrument. The legendary instrument of Apollo.

Kore   Archaic Greek sculpture of a standing, clothed female figure (see fig. 7.9).

Kouros   Archaic Greek sculpture of a standing, usually nude, male figure (see fig. 7.10).

L

Lancet arch   In architecture, a narrow arch pointed at the top like a spear.

Lancet window   In architecture a tall, narrow window set in lancet arch.

Lantern   In architecture, a small decorative structure that crowns a *dome or roof.

Lapis lazuli   Long valued as a deep blue ornamental gem and the source of ultramarine pigment, lapis lazuli is a contact metamorphic rock that varies in composition and physical property. It is distinguished from jasper by tiny flecks of gold and the absence of the colorless quartz crystals present in jasper.

Latin cross   A cross in which the vertical member is longer than the horizontal arm it bisects.

Libretto (It., "little book")   The text or words of an *opera, *oratorio, or other extended vocal work.

Lied, Lieder   (Ger., leet, LEE-der; "song, songs"). Term usually applied to the German Romantic *art songs of Schubert, Schumann, Brahms, Wolf, and others.

Lintel   In architecture, a horizontal crosspiece over an open space, which carries the weight of some of the superstructure (see fig. 7.21).

Lithography   A printmaking process that uses a polished stone (or metal plate) on which the design is drawn with a crayon or greasy ink. Ink is chemically attracted only to the lines of the drawing, with a print made by applying paper to the inked stone.

Liturgical   Pertaining to public worship, specifically to the organized worship patterns of Christian churches.

Liturgical drama   Twelfth- and thirteenth-century enactments of biblical stories, frequently with music. Developed into the "mystery plays" of the fourteenth through sixteenth centuries.

Lituus (Lat.)   Bronze *trumpet used by the Roman armies. Shaped like the letter *J*.

Logos (Gk., *logos*, "speech, word, reason")   Cosmic reason, considered in Greek philosophy as the source of world intelligibility and order.

Lost-wax process   See *cire perdue.

Lunette   In architecture, a crescent-shaped or semicircular space, usually over a door or a window.

Lute   Plucked string instrument with a pear-shaped body and a fingerboard with frets. It had eleven strings tuned to six notes (five sets of double strings plus a single string for the highest note). It was the most popular instrument during the Middle Ages and Renaissance.

Lyre (or Lyra)   Ancient Greek instrument, a simpler form of the *kithara. The sound-box was often made of a tortoise shell. Used mainly by amateurs. The larger kithara was used by professional musicians (see fig. 7.45).

Lyric   Poetry sung to the accompaniment of a *lyre (Greek); *troubadour and *trouvère poetry intended to be sung; short poems with musical elements.

M

Madrigal   Name of uncertain origin that refers to fourteenth-century vocal music or, more usually, to the popular sixteenth-century type. Renaissance madrigals were free-form vocal pieces (usually set to love lyrics) in a *polyphonic style with intermixed *homophonic sections. Flemish, Italian, and English composers brought the madrigal to a high level of expressiveness in word painting and imagery. Madrigals were sometimes accompanied but mostly *a cappella.

Magi   The Magi (singular Magus) were the priestly hierarchy of Zoroastrianism. Like the Brahmans of India, they were keepers of the cult and of sacrificial power and exercised considerable political influence when Zoroastrianism was the Persian state religion. Christians honor them as the first Gentiles to believe in Christ and celebrate their visit to Bethlehem, as told in the Bible, by the feast of the Epiphany.

Manifest Destiny   The belief that the United States was destined to extend from sea to sea so that it could bring the blessings of liberty to the entire continent. The westward expansion was also seen as a moral obligation to enlarge the area of freedom, thereby keeping the lands from falling to a tyrant.

Manorialism   The economic, social, and administrative system that prevailed in medieval Europe. Originating in the fourth century, it peaked in the twelfth century and then began a long decline that ended only in modern times.

Mass   The central service of public worship of some Christian churches, principally the Church of Rome.

Materialism   The doctrine that the only reality is matter; that the universe is not governed by intelligence or purpose but only by mechanical cause and effect.

Meander   The Greek fret or key pattern used in art or architecture. From a winding, turning course, like a river.

Measure   In music, the metrical unit between two bars on the *staff; a bar.

Melisma   A melodic unit sung to one syllable; *plainsong has frequent *melismatic* passages.

Metaphor   A form of figurative language that compares dissimilar objects (e.g., publicity is a two-edged sword; the moon is blue).

Metaphysics   Philosophic inquiry into the ultimate and fundamental reality; "the science of being as such."

Meter   In music, a grouping of beats into patterns of two, three, or four beats or combinations thereof; in English poetry the basic rhythmic pattern of stressed (—) and unstressed (˘) syllables. Metrical patterns include: *iambic* (˘ —), *trochaic* (— ˘), *anapestic* (˘ ˘ —), and *dactylic* (— ˘ ˘).

Metope (MET-o-pay)   In classical architecture the panel between two *triglyphs in a *Doric *frieze; may be plain or carved. The Parthenon metopes are all carved (see fig. 7.28).

Mihrab   A niche inserted in the wall of a mosque indicating the direction of Mecca so that all worshipers may face Mecca.

Minaret   A tall, slender tower attached to a Muslim mosque from which a muezzin calls the faithful to prayer (see fig. 11.15).

Minibar   The high pulpit from which the Islamic preacher delivers the sermon. Originally used by judges administering the law.

Modes, rhythmic   A thirteenth-century system of music rhythmic notation based on the patterns of poetic meter. Rhythmic modes give the characteristic flavor to thirteenth-century *organum and *motets because of the constant repetition of the same rhythmic patterns. All modes were performed in so-called "perfect" *meter, that is, triple.

Monism (Gk., *mones*, "single")   The philosophical position that there is but one fundamental reality. The classical advocate of extreme monism was Parmenides of Elea; Spinoza is a modern exponent.

Monochord   A device consisting of a single string stretched over a soundboard with a movable bridge. Used to demonstrate the laws of acoustics, especially the relationships between intervals and string lengths and the tuning of *scales (see fig. 15.2).

Monophonic (Gk., "one sound")   A single line of music without accompaniment or additional parts, as in *plainsong, *troubadour-*trouvère-minnesinger songs, and some folk songs.

Monotheism   The religious conception of a single, transcendent god. It contrasts with polytheism (belief in many gods) and pantheism (belief in God as synonymous with the universe). Judaism, Christianity, and Islam are the principal monotheistic religions.

Montage (mon-tahzh)   A composition made of existing photographs, paintings, or drawings; in cinematography the effects achieved by superimposing images or using rapid sequences.

Moor   The term Moor (Sp., *moro*) is derived from "Mauretania," the Roman name for present-day Morocco and Algeria. As the Islamic tide swept across

Africa it was joined by the Berbers of this region, who invaded Spain in 711, where they remained in power for eight centuries.

Mosaic   The technique of embedding bits of stone, colored glass, or marble in wet concrete to make designs or pictures for walls or floors. To achieve a complex interplay of light and shadows, the bits are set in the holding material with minute differences in the angles, as in the mosaics of San Vitale in Ravenna (see figs. 11.13 and 11.14).

Mosque   A place of public worship in the Islamic religion. The term is from the Arabic *masjid*, "a place to prostrate one's self [in front of God]."

Motet (from Fr., *mot*, "word")   The most important form of early *polyphonic music (ca. thirteenth to seventeenth centuries). *Medieval motet* (thirteenth to fourteenth centuries). Usually three parts (triplum, motetus, *tenor). The tenor "holds" to a *cantus firmus and the upper two voices sing different texts (sacred and/or secular).

Mullion   A vertical member that divides a window into sections; also used to support the glass in stained glass windows.

Mural   A painting on a wall; a *fresco is a type of mural.

Mythology   Collections of stories explaining natural phenomena, customs, institutions, religious beliefs, and so forth of a people. Usually concerned with the supernatural, gods, goddesses, heroic exploits, and the like.

N

Narthex   A porch or vestibule of a church through which one passes to enter the *nave (see fig. 14.19).

Naturalism   The view that the universe requires no supernatural cause or government, that it is self-existent, self-explanatory, self-operating, and self-directing, and that it is purposeless, deterministic, and only incidentally productive of humanity. In relation to literature sometimes defined as "realism on all fours." The dominant traits of literary naturalism are biological determinism (people are what they must be because of their genes) and environmental determinism (people are what they are because of how they are brought up.)

Nave   The main central space of a church running from the entrance to the *crossing of the *transepts; typically flanked by one or two side aisles. Name derived from *naval* because the barrel *vault ceiling has the appearance of the inside hull of a ship (see fig. 14.19).

Neoplatonists   The Florentine Neoplatonists derived some of their ideas from Plotinus, the founder of Neoplatonism, from Plato, and from Christian mysticism.

Neume (From Gk., *pneuma*, "breath")   Sign used in notation of medieval *plainsong.

Nimbus   In Christian iconography, a device symbolizing sanctity, usually a radiance or a bright circle.

Notre Dame school   The composers of the twelfth- and thirteenth-century cathedral school at Notre Dame de Paris, most notably Léonin and Pérotin. The Notre Dame school invented rhythmic notation for *polyphonic music.

O

Obbligato   In music, an essential instrumental part, second in importance only to the principal melody.

Oboe (From Fr., *haut bois*, "high wind," that is, high-pitched instrument)   A double-reed, soprano-range instrument with a conical bore (slightly expanding diameter from reed to bell). It has a nasal, but mellow and poignant, tone.

Octave   In music, the interval of eight diatonic degrees between tones, one of which has twice as many vibrations per second as the other.

Odalisque   (oh-da-leesk) French word for a harem slave or concubine but used more broadly to refer to a reclining female figure, a favorite subject of such painters as Ingres and Matisse.

Ode   A formal lyric on a usually dignified theme, in exalted language, e.g., works by Horace.

Office hours   In the Church of Rome, the services (usually observed only in monastic churches) that take place eight times a day (every three hours): Matins, Lauds, Prime, Terce, Sext, None, Vespers, and Compline. Musically the important services are Matins, Vespers, and Compline.

Oligarchy (Gk., "rule by the few")   A form of government in which a small group of people holds the ruling power. Some political theorists believe that even democratic governments can end up in the hands of an oligarchy ("iron law of oligarchy").

Onomatopoeia   A word that sounds like its referent, e.g., the bee buzzes.

Ontology (Gk., *on*, "being," *logos*, "logic")   Philosophic inquiry into the ultimate nature of things, what it means to be.

Open score   In music, one voice part per *staff.

Opera (From It., *opera in musica*, "works in music")   A play in which the text is generally sung throughout to the accompaniment of an orchestra. Modern opera had its beginnings in Florence in the late sixteenth century when some musicians, poets, and scholars attempted a revival of Greek drama, which they assumed to have been sung throughout.

Oratorio   A musical setting of a religious or epic theme for performance by soloists, chorus, and orchestra in a church or concert hall. Originally (early seventeenth century) it was similar to an *opera (sacred opera) with staging, costumes, and scenery. It is now usually presented in concert form, for example, *Messiah* by G. F. Handel.

Orchestra (From Gk., *orcheisthai*, "to dance")   In ancient Greek theatres the circular or semicircular space in front of the stage used by the chorus; group of instrumentalists performing ensemble music, e.g., symphony orchestra.

Organ, pipe organ   An instrument (see *Hydraulis) of ancient origin consisting of from two to seven keyboards (manuals) and a set of pedals (usually thirty-two notes) for the feet.

Organum (OR-ga-num; Lat.)   The name given to the earliest types of *polyphonic music.

Ornamentation   In music, the added trills and turns that make lines, usually the melodic lines, more elaborate.

P

Pantheism (Gk., *pan*, "all," *theos*, "god")   As a religious concept, the doctrine that God is immanent in all things.

Patrician   Member of the hereditary aristocratic class of ancient Rome and entitled to privileges denied other citizens. By the third century BC the plebeians substantially diminished the patricians' privileged position. The distinction between the two classes became blurred during the empire and "patrician" eventually became an honorific title.

Pax Romana   The period from the rule of Caesar Augustus through Marcus Aurelius (27 BC–AD 180) in which there were no major wars anywhere in the Roman Empire.

Pediment   In classical architecture, a triangular space at the end of a building framed by the *cornice and the ends of the sloping roof (*raking cornices). (See fig. 7.24.)

Pendentive   In architecture, a concave triangular piece of masonry, four of which form a transition from a square base to support the circular rim of a *dome (see fig. 11.12).

Pentateuch   The first five books of the Bible, the so-called "Books of Moses": Genesis, Exodus, Leviticus, Numbers, and Deuteronomy.

Percussion   Instruments that are played by striking, shaking, scraping, etc.

Peristyle   A series of *columns that surround the exterior of a building or the interior of a court, e.g., the Parthenon has a peristyle (see fig. 7.26).

Perspective   The illusion of a three-dimensional world on a two-dimensional surface. *Linear perspective* uses lines of projection converging on a *vanishing point, with objects appearing smaller the further from the viewer. *Aerial (atmospheric) perspective* uses diminished color intensity and blurred contours for objects apparently deeper in space.

Pier   A mass of masonry, usually large, used to support *arches or *lintels; more massive than a *column and with a shape other than circular.

Pietà (pyay-TA; It., "pity, compassion")   Representations of the Virgin mourning the body of her Son.

Pilaster   A flat *column projecting from the wall of a building; usually furnished with a base and *capital in the manner of an *engaged column, which is rounded rather than rectangular like the pilaster.

Plainsong The term generally used for the large body of nonmetrical, *monophonic, *liturgical music of the Church of Rome; also called Gregorian chant.

Polyphony (po-LIF-o-nee) *Polyphonic* (pol-ly-PHON-ik), that is, "many-voiced" music having melodic interest in two or more simultaneous melodic lines. Examples of polyphonic music would be *canons and *rounds.

Polytheism The belief in and worship of many gods.

Portico A porch or walkway with a roof supported by *columns.

Positivism Philosophic inquiry limited to problems open to scientific investigation. Traditional subjects such as *aesthetics and *metaphysics are dismissed as "meaningless" because their content cannot be subjected to verification.

Post and lintel A structural system in which vertical supports or *columns support horizontal beams. The *lintel can span only a relatively short space because the weight of the superstructure centers on the mid-point of the horizontal beam. In a structural system using *arches the thrust is distributed to the columns supporting the bases of the arches, thus allowing for a greater span. The lintel is also called an *architrave. (See fig. 7.21.)

Pragmatism (Gk., *pragma*, "things done") Philosophic doctrine that the meaning of a proposition or course of action lies in its observable consequences and that its meaning is the sum of its consequences. In everyday life the favoring of practical means over theory; if something works, it's good; if not, it's bad.

Primary colors The *hues of red, yellow, and blue with which the colors of the spectrum can be produced. Primary colors cannot be produced by mixing.

Program music Music intended to depict ideas, scenes, or other extramusical concepts.

Proscenium (Gk., *pro*, "before," *skene*, "stage") In traditional theatres the framework of the stage opening.

Psalm A sacred song, poem, or *hymn; the songs in the Old Testament book of Psalms.

Psalter Vernacular name for the book of Psalms.

Psaltery Ancient or medieval instrument consisting of a flat soundboard over which a number of strings are stretched. A psaltery is plucked with the fingers. The *harpsichord is a keyed psaltery.

Purgatory In the teaching of the Church of Rome, the state after death in which the soul destined for heaven is purged of all taint of unpunished or unrepented minor sins.

Q

Quadrivium The higher division of the *seven liberal arts in the Middle Ages: arithmetic, astronomy, geometry, and music.

Quatrain A stanza of four lines, either rhymed or unrhymed.

R

Raking cornice The end *cornice on the sloping sides of a triangular *pediment.

Rayonnant (Fr., "radiant") The ultimate phase of High Gothic architecture that emphasizes soaring lines and vast expanses of stained glass walls (see fig. 14.26).

Rebec A small, bowed medieval string instrument adapted from the Arabian *rehab*. One of the instruments from which the violin developed during the sixteenth century (see fig. 15.3).

Recorder A straight, end-blown *flute, as distinct from the modern side-blown (transverse) flute. It was used from the Middle Ages until the eighteenth century and has been revived in the twentieth century.

Red-figure style Incised, shaded orange figures against a jet black background. The technique was capable of infinite subtleties. Euphronios (fl. 520–505 BC) was probably the greatest painter in the style, though many artists were noteworthy.

Refrain Recurring section of text (and usually music), e.g., verse-refrain.

Register In music, the range of an instrument or voice, described as high, middle, or low.

Relief In sculpture, carvings projecting from a background that is a part of the whole. Reliefs may be high (almost disengaged from the background) or low (*bas-relief*, slightly raised above the background).

Reliquary (Fr., "remains") A receptacle for storing or displaying holy relics.

Round In music a commonly used name for a circle *canon. At the conclusion of a melody the singer returns to the beginning, repeating the melody as often as desired. Examples: "Brother James," "Three Blind Mice," and "Row, Row, Row Your Boat."

S

Sacrament In Christianity, one of certain ceremonial observances held to be instituted by Christ when on earth.

Sahn A ritual pool in mosque courtyards in which the faithful make their ablutions.

Salon The French equivalent and precursor of the Royal Academy exhibitions. It derived its name from the *Salon d'Apollon* in the Louvre. It became a biennial feature in 1737 and annual after the Revolution. In the nineteenth century the admissions system was so exclusive that the *Salon des Refusés* arose as a short-lived alternative.

Salon d'Automne In Paris, the annual fall exhibition of contemporary art.

Sanctuary A sacred or holy place set aside for the worship of a god or gods; a place of refuge or protection.

Sarcophagus A stone coffin.

Satire An indictment of human foibles using humor as a weapon, e.g., the relatively mild satires of Horace and the bitter ones of Juvenal and Jonathan Swift.

Scale (Lat., "ladder") The tonal material of music arranged in a series of rising or falling pitches. Because of the variety in the world's music there are many different scales. The basic scale of European music is the diatonic scale (C-D-E-F-G-A-B-C), i.e., the white keys of the piano. This arrangement of tones is also called a major scale, in the example given, a C major scale. (See Appendix.)

Scherzo In music, a lively symphonic movement, usually in 3/4 time.

Scholasticism The philosophy and method of medieval theologians in which speculation was separated from observation and practice, revelation was regarded as both the norm and an aid to reason, reason respected authority, and scientific inquiry was controlled by theology.

Secondary colors Those *hues located between the *primary colors on a traditional color wheel: orange, green, and violet.

Sequence A type of chant developed in the Early Middle Ages in which a freely poetic text was added to the long *melisma at the end of the *Alleluias. Subsequently separated from the Alleluias, the sequences became independent syllabic chants. The composition of many original sequences finally led to the banning of all but five sequences by the Council of Trent (1545–63).

Seven liberal arts Term originally used to mean studies suited to freemen and consisting of *trivium (grammar, logic, rhetoric) and *quadrivium (arithmetic, geometry, astronomy, music).

Sfumato (foo-MAH-toe) A hazy, smoky blending of color tones in a painting to create ambiguities of line and shape, as in Leonardo's *Mona Lisa*.

Silkscreen Stencil process. Closely woven silk is tacked tightly over a frame; areas on the silk not to be printed are "stopped out" before paint is squeezed through the silk mesh onto cloth or paper underneath.

Simile A comparison between two quite different things, usually using "like" or "as."

Skene (SKAY-nuh) The Greek stage building, originally of wood, at the rear of the orchestra.

Sonata (From It., *sonare*, "to sound") A musical composition, usually in three or four movements (sections) for a piano or *organ or a solo instrument (*violin, *trumpet, etc.) with keyboard accompaniment.

Sonnet A fourteen-line poem in iambic pentameter (see *meter). Petrarch, the fourteenth-century Italian poet, used a rhyming scheme of *abbaabba* followed by *cde cde* or variants thereof. Shakespeare used a rhyming scheme of *abab cdcd efef gg*, or four *quatrains followed by a rhymed couplet.

Sphinx A creature in Egyptian mythology that combined the body of an animal (usually a lion) with the head of a man. In the story of Oedipus the sphinx became a winged monster with the body of a lion and the head of a woman.

Squinch   In architecture, a device to effect a transition from a polygonal base to a circular *dome (see fig. 11.12).

Staff   In music, the set of horizontal lines and spaces on which notes are written or printed. (See Appendix.)

Stele   (STEE-lee) A carved slab of stone or pillar used especially by the Greeks as a grave marker (see fig. 7.19).

Still life   In pictorial arts, inanimate objects used as subject matter.

Stucco   A durable finish for exterior walls, applied wet and usually composed of cement, sand, and lime.

Stylobate   The third of three steps of a Greek temple on which the *columns rest; essentially the platform on which the *cella and *peristyle are erected (see fig. 7.24).

Syllogism   A form of deductive reasoning consisting of a major premise, a minor premise, and a conclusion. Example: all men are mortal; Socrates is a man; therefore Socrates is mortal.

Symphony   A long composition for orchestra, consisting of related movements, usually four in number.

T

Teleology (Gk., *telos*, "end, completion") The theory of purpose, ends, goals, final cause; opposite of materialism.

Tempera   A painting technique using pigment suspended in egg yolk.

Tenor (Lat., *tenere*, "to hold") 1. Originally the part that "held" the melody on which early sacred *polyphonic music was based. 2. The highest male voice (S A T B). 3. Prefix to the name of an instrument, e.g., tenor saxophone.

Terra-cotta (It., "baked earth") A baked clay used in ceramics and sculptures; a reddish color.

Tesserae (TESS-er-ee) Bits of stone and colored glass used in *mosaics.

Theatre (From Gk. *theasthai*, "to view, to see") This is not only a structure or "seeing place" but the sum of all the arts required for the production of dramas.

Theocracy (Gk., "rule by God") A form of government in which divine authority is paramount or in which religious leaders play the leading role. The term was first used by the Jewish historian, Josephus, who applied it to the politics of ancient Israel.

Thrust   The outward force caused by the weight and design of an *arch or *vault, a thrust that must be countered by a *buttress (see fig. 14.18).

Timbre   The quality of a sound that distinguishes it from other sounds of the same pitch and volume; especially the distinctive tone color of a musical instrument or voice.

Time signature   In music a symbol, commonly a numerical fraction, placed on a staff to indicate the *meter. (See Appendix.)

Torah (Hebrew, "instruction") Applied in particular to the written Mosaic law contained in the first five books of the Bible—Genesis, Exodus, Leviticus, Numbers, and Deuteronomy—also called the *Pentateuch.

Toreutics   Hammering metals to make various shapes.

Tracery   In architecture, the lacy open-stone work in Gothic windows; from trace, "to draw."

Tragedy   A serious play or other literary work with an unhappy or disastrous ending caused, in Greek drama, by *hubris on the part of the protagonist.

Transcendental   Beyond the realm of the senses; rising above common thought or ideas; exalted.

Transept   That part of a *cruciform-plan church whose axis intersects at right angles the long axis of the cross running from the entrance through the *nave to the *apse; the cross-arm of the cross.

Triforium   In a Gothic cathedral, the gallery between the *nave arcades and the *clerestory; the triforium gallery opens on the *nave with an *arcade (see fig. 14.23).

Triglyph   Projecting block with vertical channels that alternates with *metopes in a *Doric *frieze of a Greek temple. The ends of the marble beams are stylized versions of the wooden beams used in early temples.

Trilogy   A grouping of three, usually applied to the three related tragedies that Greek dramatists submitted every year to the judges. The most famous trilogy is the *Oresteia* by Aeschylus.

Trinity   In Christian belief, the union of three divine figures, the Father, Son, and Holy Spirit, in one Godhead.

Trivium   The lower division of the *seven liberal arts in the Middle Ages: grammar, logic, and rhetoric, including literature.

Trompe-l'oeil (trohmp luh-yuh; Fr.) Illusionistic painting designed to convince the observer that what is seen is an actual three-dimensional object rather than a two-dimensional surface; literally, "eye fooling."

Trope   Additional text and/or music added to a preexisting *plainsong. The earliest tropes were *sequences. Troping became so widespread that it was banned by the Council of Trent. *Liturgical drama was a direct outgrowth of the trope.

Troubadours   Poet-musicians, mostly men and women of aristocratic birth, of southern France (Provence) who, during the period ca. 1100–1300, cultivated the arts of poetry and music in chivalrous service to romantic love. Their music was *monophonic in style and popular in flavor but exerted considerable influence on the development of *polyphonic music.

Trouvères   Poet-musicians of central and northern France from ca. 1150 to 1300. Their music developed from the *troubadours and showed the same general characteristics except for the change in language from that of the south (Provençal) to the medieval forerunner of modern French.

Trumpet   Soprano brass-wind instrument consisting of long metal tube looped once and ending in a flared bell.

Truss roof   In architecture, a framework of wooden beams or metal bars, often arranged in triangles, and used to support a roof.

Tuscan order   Simplified form of the Doric order.

Tympanum   The space, usually elaborately carved, enclosed by the *lintel and *arch of a doorway; also, the space within the horizontal and *raking cornices of a *pediment (see fig. 14.11).

V

Vanishing point   In linear *perspective the point at which parallel lines converge on the horizon.

Vault   A masonry ceiling constructed on the principle of the *arch. A *barrel vault* is an uninterrupted series of arches amounting to a very deep arch.

Viol   Any of a family of string instruments, chiefly in the sixteenth and seventeenth centuries.

Virelai   Any of several medieval French verse and song forms.

Virginal   A harpsichord used mainly in England and supposedly played by young ladies.

Volute   The spiral scrolls of an *Ionic *capital.

Voussoir (voo-SWAHR; Fr.) The wedge-shaped blocks of stone used to construct *arches and *vaults.

W

Woodcut   A wood block that has been carved so that the design stands out slightly from the block, comparable to printing type.

Z

Ziggurat   A temple tower of the ancient Mesopotamians (see p. 8).

Annotated Bibliography

Prologue   An Introduction to Integrated Humanities

Boorstein, Daniel J. *The Discoverers: A History of Man's Search to Know His World and Himself.* New York: Random House, 1983. An exciting introduction to cultural and intellectual history. Very highly recommended.

Toynbee, Arnold. *A Study of History.* In several editions (preferably the one-volume abridgement). This classic study articulates and documents one of the most impressive culture-epoch theories of the rise and fall of civilizations.

1   The Emergence of Early Culture

Amiet, Pierre. *Art of the Ancient Near East.* Trans. John Shepley and Claude Choquet. New York: Harry N. Abrams, 1980. Probably the best illustrated text on this subject now available.

Kostof, Spiro. *A History of Architecture: Settings and Rituals.* New York: Oxford University Press, 1985. From the first prehistoric environments on record to the most recent examples of architecture and urban design. A splendid one-volume survey.

Translations of Original Material

Herodotos of Halicarnassus. *The Persian Wars (Histories* in some translations). Trans. Aubrey de Selincourt. Baltimore: Penguin, 1972. The "Father of History" is more than a historian; he is an enthusiastic and fascinating storyteller. The first five of the nine books recount the growth of the Persian Empire and the beginnings of oriental aggression, following which he glowingly relates the Greek triumphs over the Persian invader.

Pritchard, James B., ed. *The Ancient Near East: An Anthology of Texts and Pictures.* Princeton: Princeton University Press, 1958. A wide-ranging collection that includes *The Epic of Gilgamesh.*

2   Egypt: Land of the Pharaohs

Aldred, Cyril. *The Egyptians.* New York: Thames & Hudson, 1984. An overview of cultural and political history.

Edwards, I. E. S. *The Pyramids of Egypt.* Baltimore: Penguin, 1975. The development of the pyramids with speculation on their meaning.

Osman, Ahmed. *Stranger in the Valley of the Kings: Solving the Mystery of an Ancient Egyptian Mummy.* San Francisco: Harper & Row, 1987. A well-documented thesis that the biblical Joseph was the father-in-law of Amenhotep III and grandfather of Akhenaton, thus implying that the latter's monotheism was derived from the Hebrew religion.

Translation of Original Material

Erman, A., ed. *The Ancient Egyptians: A Sourcebook of Their Writings.* New York: Harper Torchbooks, 1966. Fine collection.

See also the Bibliography (Translations of Original Material) for chapter 1.

3   The Aegean Heritage

Campbell, Joseph, and Charles Muses, eds. *In All Her Names: Four Explorations of the Feminine in Divinity.* San Francisco: Harper & Row, 1991.

Eisler, Riane. *The Chalice and the Blade: Our History, Our Future.* San Francisco: Harper & Row, 1987. The thesis that male dominance is not a natural situation, that more viable societies with balanced gender participation existed in Old Europe, and that similar partnership societies are the best hope for the modern world.

Frymer-Kensky, Tikva. *In the Wake of the Goddesses; Women, Culture, and the Biblical Transformation of Pagan Myth.* New York: Free Press, 1992. Author contends that the modern conception of the Bible as misogynistic is more appropriately attributed to the Hellenistic period. She shows that, when it has been cleared of misconceptions, the stark ideal of monotheism, in which humanity must bear full responsibility for its actions in a singular relationship to God, can offer us more today than a return to the gender-based world view of an earlier time.

Gimbutas, Marija. *Goddesses and Gods of Old Europe.* Berkeley: University of California Press, 1982. Peaceful, indigenous Neolithic societies in southeastern Europe, the Aegean, and the Adriatic islands in which agriculture developed nearly as early as in Mesopotamia.

———. *The Language of the Goddess.* San Francisco: Harper & Row, 1989. Goddesses in art and religion.

Goodrich, Norma Lorre. *Priestesses.* New York: HarperCollins, 1990.

Higgins, Reynold. *Minoan and Mycenaean Art.* World of Arts series. New York: Oxford University Press, 1981. A finely illustrated survey.

Fiction

Renault, Mary. *The Bull from the Sea.* New York: Random House, 1962. Fine historical fiction that brings ancient Crete to life.

———. *The King Must Die.* New York: Bantam, 1964.

4   Early Greece: Preparation for the Good Life

Burn, A. R. *Persia and the Greeks: The Defense of the West.* Stanford, Calif.: Stanford University Press, 1984. A stirring account of the heroic battles that set the stage for the Greek Golden Age.

Creasy, E., and J. P. Mitchell, *Twenty Decisive Battles of the World.* New York: Macmillan, 1964. Colonel Mitchell added five battles to Creasy's 1851 classic.

Vivante, Paolo. *Homer.* New Haven: Yale University Press, 1985. An enthusiastic introduction for the general reader.

Warner, Rex. *The Stories of the Greeks.* New York: Farrar, Straus, & Giroux, 1961. Fascinating accounts of heroes and gods.

General Studies of Greek Culture

These works cover the whole period through the Hellenistic age and will not be listed again.

Barr, Stringfellow. *The Will of Zeus; A History of Greece from the Origins of Hellenic Culture to the Death of Alexander.* Philadelphia: J. B. Lippincott, 1961. Whenever possible Barr lets the Greeks tell their own tale. No one can tell it better.

Bulfinch, Thomas. *Bulfinch's Mythology.* New York: HarperCollins, 1991. The age of fable, the age of chivalry, legends of Charlemagne. The recognized standard work, originally published in three separate volumes.

Bury, J. B. *History of Greece.* New York: St. Martin's Press, 1975. Still the standard history and for all the right reasons.

Chamoux, François. *The Civilization of Greece.* New York: Simon & Schuster, 1965. A handsome cultural history with fine illustrations.

Eliot, Alexander. *The Horizon Concise History of Greece.* New York: Horizon Press, 1973. Packed with information; fascinating reading.

Finley, M. I., *The Legacy of Greece: A New Appraisal.* New York: Oxford University Press, 1981. After a lifetime of study a noted classicist offers his mature assessment of the Greek achievement.

Translations of Original Material

Fitzgerald, Robert. *The Iliad of Homer.* Garden City, N.Y.: Doubleday, 1975. *The Odyssey of Homer.* Garden City, N.Y.: Doubleday, 1961. Each generation should have its own translation of Homer, and these are superb.

Hogan, James C. *A Guide to the Iliad; based on the translation by Robert Fitzgerald.* Garden City, N.Y.: Doubleday, 1979.

NOTE: The latest archeological evidence about Aegean civilizations can be found in periodicals such as: *National Geographic, Smithsonian, Science News, Archeology, Nature.*

5   Hellenic Athens: The Fulfillment of the Good Life

Fantham, Elaine, et al. *Women in the Classical World.* New York: Oxford University Press, 1994.

Hill, Donald. *A History of Engineering in Classical and Medieval Times.* La Salle, Ill.: Open Court Publishing, 1984. Includes an important reevaluation of the role of technology in ancient Greece.

Knox, Bernard. *The Oldest Dead White European Males and Other Reflections on the Classics.* New York: W. W. Norton, 1993. Despite all the sound and fury about not being "politically correct," the title of this latest book by a noted classicist states what cannot be denied: this is where, for the most part, Western civilization came from.

Pomeroy, Sarah. *Goddesses, Whores, Wives and Slaves: Women in Classical Antiquity.* New York: Schocken, 1975. Valuable study.

Rose, H. J. *A Handbook of Greek Literature from Homer to the age of Lucian.* New York: Dutton, 1960. London: Methuen, 1948. A standard reference work in the field.

Sagan, Eli. *The Honey and the Hemlock; Democracy and Paranoia in Ancient Athens and Modern America.* New York: Basic Books of HarperCollins, 1991. Remarkable insights into the parallels between ancient and modern democracies.

Scarisbrick, Diana, et al. *Jewellery: Makers, Motifs, History, Techniques.* London: Thames & Hudson, 1989. Possibly the best one-volume history of this ancient craft.

Taplin, Oliver. *Greek Fire: The Influence of Ancient Greece on the Modern World.* New York: Atheneum, 1990. Fascinating. Very highly recommended. The opening line foretells the contents: "Not back to the Greeks, but forward with the Greeks."

Thucydides. *History of the Peloponnesian War.* Trans. Richard Crawley. New York: Random House, 1981. Objective, thorough, a highly readable book by one of the most distinguished of the ancient Greek historians.

Translations and Studies of Greek Drama

Bates, William N. *Euripides: A Student of Human Nature.* New York: Russell & Russell, 1969. The dramatist as a realist.

Cook, Albert. *Oedipus Rex: A Mirror for Greek Drama.* Belmont, Calif.: Wadsworth, 1964. A broad, general approach to Greek drama and highly recommended.

Fitts, Dudley, and Robert Fitzgerald. *The Oedipus Cycle.* New York: Harcourt, Brace, Jovanovich, 1967. Brilliant translations that are both faithful and poetic.

Grene, David, and Richard Lattimore. *Greek Tragedies.* 3 vols. Chicago: University of Chicago Press, 1960. Excellent modern translations of the more important plays of Aeschylus, Sophocles, and Euripides.

McLeish, Kenneth. *The Theatre of Aristophanes.* New York: Taplinger, 1980. Fascinating discussion of style and content.

6 Greece: From Hellenic to Hellenistic World

General Studies of the Hellenistic World

Burn, Andrew R. *Alexander the Great and the Hellenistic World.* New York: Macmillan, 1974. Alexander's role in spreading Greek culture.

Bury, J. B. *The Hellenistic Age.* New York: W. W. Norton, 1970. A fine treatment by the eminent Greek historian.

Grant, Michael. *From Alexander to Cleopatra: The Hellenistic World.* New York: Charles Scribner's Sons, 1982. Comprehensive overview.

Hamilton, J. R. *Alexander the Great.* Pittsburgh: University of Pittsburgh Press, 1974. Excellent biographical study.

Philosophy and Social Issues

Else, Gerald F. *Greek Homosexuality.* New York: Random House, 1980. Behavior

and attitudes as revealed in vase paintings, poetry, Plato, lawcourt speeches, and the comedies of Aristophanes.

Taylor, A. E. *Plato: The Man and His Work.* New York: World Publishing, 1966. Outstanding and comprehensive.

Waithe, Mary Ellen, ed. *A History of Women Philosophers: Volume 1, Ancient Women Philosophers, 600 BC–AD 500.* Boston: Martinus Nijhoff, 1987.

Translations of Original Material

Aristotle. *Aristotle: Selections from Seven Books.* Ed. Philip Wheelwright. Indianapolis: Odyssey Press, 1951. Significant selections.

———. *Aristotle's Poetics.* Trans. James Hutton. New York: W. W. Norton, 1982. Includes helpful introduction and notes.

———. *The Ethics of Aristotle: The Nichomachean Ethics.* Ed. Hugh Tredinnick, trans. J. A. Thompson. Baltimore: Penguin, 1977. The discussion of happiness is particularly accessible.

Plato. *Great Dialogues of Plato.* Trans. W. H. D. Rouse. New York: New American Library, 1956. The standard one-volume work.

Fiction

Renault, Mary. *Fire from Heaven.* New York: Pantheon, 1970. The first in her Alexandrian trilogy: *Alexander's Youth. The Persian Boy* (1972) recounts his life from age twenty-six to his death. *Funeral Games: The Combat of Alexander's Heirs* (1981) concludes the trilogy.

———. *The Mask of Apollo.* New York: Bantam, 1974. A lively picture of Plato's times.

7 The Greek Arts

Art and Architecture

Lawrence, A. W. *Greek Architecture.* Rev. ed. New York: Viking, 1984. A comprehensive study.

Lullies, Reinhard, and Max Hirmer. *Greek Sculpture.* New York: Harry N. Abrams, 1960. Includes 282 magnificent photographs by Hirmer.

Richter, Gisela M. A. *Handbook of Greek Art.* 7th ed. New York: Dutton, 1980. Concise and well illustrated. Includes minor arts.

Dance and Music

Georgiades, Thrasybulos. *Greek Music, Verse, and Dance.* Reprint. New York: Da Capo Press, 1973. The interrelationships in Greek culture.

Sorell, Walter. *Dance in Its Time.* Garden City, N.Y.: Doubleday, 1981. Dance in its cultural contexts throughout history.

Poetry

Bowra, C. M. *Greek Lyric Poetry.* 2nd ed. New York: Oxford University Press, 1961. Written by a noted classicist, this is regarded as the standard discussion of the topic.

Duban, Jeffrey M. *Ancient and Modern Images of Sappho: Translations and Studies in Archaic Greek Love Lyrics.* Lanham, Md.: University Press of America, 1984. An illuminating focus on the great poet.

8 A Thousand Years of Rome

Auguet, Roland. *Cruelty and Civilization: The Roman Games.* London: Allen & Unwin,

1972. Excellent survey of a subject both fascinating and repulsive.

Brantlinger, Patrick. *Bread and Circuses: Theories of Mass Culture as Social Decay.* Ithaca: Cornell University Press, 1985. The "decline and fall" motif from Greece and Rome to the present day.

Cary, Max, and H. H. Scullard, *A History of Rome.* New York: St. Martin's Press, 1975. One of the finest short histories.

Casson, Lionel. *The Horizon Book of Daily Life in Ancient Rome.* New York: American Heritage, 1975. Outstanding series that also includes Ancient Egypt, the Middle Ages, the Renaissance, and Victorian England.

Gardiner, E. N. *Athletics in the Ancient World.* Chicago: University of Chicago Press, 1978. The single most useful source on the interrelationship of athletics and religion in Greece and Rome.

Petit, Paul. *Pax Romana.* Trans. James Willis. Berkeley: University of California Press, 1976. Excellent study of the Roman world order.

Rostovzeff, Mikhail. *Social and Economic History of the Roman Empire.* New York: Oxford University Press, 1957. The standard work.

Translations and Interpretations of Original Material

Translations of all Roman authors are available in the Loeb Classical Library series published by Harvard University Press. Excellent translations of standard works are also published by the Indiana University Press, Bloomington, Indiana. The following works are also recommended:

Davenport, Basil, ed. *The Portable Roman Reader.* New York: Viking, 1959. The best cross section of Roman literature in a single volume.

Graves, Robert. *Suetonius: The Lives of the Twelve Caesars.* Baltimore: Penguin, 1957. The author of *I, Claudius* is also a superb translator.

Hammond, N. G., and H. H. Scullard, *Oxford Classical Dictionary.* Oxford: Clarendon Press, 1970. The definitive reference work for Greek and Roman culture.

Mulls, Barriss. *Epigrams from Martial: A Verse Translation.* Lafayette: Purdue University Press, 1969. Skillful contemporary translation.

Sesar, Carl. *Selected Poems of Catullus.* New York: Mason & Lipscomb, 1974. Idiomatic, profane, erotic, and scatalogical and, thus, very close to the style and spirit of the original.

Turner, Paul. *Plutarch's Lives.* Carbondale: Southern Illinois University Press, 1963. Good translation of a standard work.

9 Roman Art and Architecture: The Arts of Megalopolis

Grant, Michael. *The Art and Life of Pompeii and Herculaneum.* New York: Newsweek, 1979. A popular and picturesque account.

Henig, Martin, ed. *A Handbook of Roman Art: A Comprehensive Survey of All the Arts of the Roman World.* Ithaca: Cornell University Press, 1983.

Sear, Frank. *Roman Architecture.* Ithaca: Cornell University Press, 1983. Comprehensive overview of 1,000 years of Rome.

10   The Star and the Cross

Judaism: General History and Culture
Albright, William F. *From the Stone Age to Christianity.* Baltimore: Johns Hopkins University Press, 1957. A standard work that traces the rise of monotheism.

Bright, John. *A History of Israel.* Philadelphia: Westminister Press, 1972. Excellent survey by a noted biblical scholar.

Christianity: General History and Culture
Johnson, Paul. *A History of Christianity.* New York: Atheneum, 1976. A detailed survey from the apostolic and patriarchal ages to the present.

Pelikan, Jaroslav. *Jesus Through the Centuries: His Place in the History of Culture.* New Haven: Yale University Press, 1985. A stimulating, informative, and illustrated study of the changing role of Christ in cultural movements of Western civilization.

Wilken, Robert L. *The Christians as the Romans Saw Them.* New Haven: Yale University Press, 1985. A fascinating account of the Christian movement from a non-Christian perspective.

Translations and Expositions of the Bible
Fiorenza, Elizabeth Schussler. *In Memory of Her—A Feminist Theological Reconstruction of Christian Origins.* New York: Crossword Publishing Company, 1989.

Friedman, Richard Elliot. *Who Wrote the Bible?* New York: Summit, 1987. A noted biblical scholar documents the Pentateuch as written by four different authors and combined into one narrative by an editor. He also identifies significant contradictions between the creation stories in Genesis 1 and Genesis 2.

Frye, Northrop. *The Great Code: The Bible and Literature.* New York: Harcourt, Brace, Jovanovich, 1982. A renowned critic examines the continuing significance of the Bible as the single most important influence in the imaginative tradition of Western art and literature.

Gastor, Theodor H. *The Dead Sea Scrolls.* Garden City, N.Y.: Anchor, 1976. Assesses the significance for biblical studies of this modern find of ancient manuscripts.

Kraemer, Ross Shepard. *Her Share of the Blessings—Women's Religions Among Pagans, Jews and Christians in the Greco-Roman World.* New York: Oxford University Press, 1992.

Pritchard, J. B., ed. *Ancient Near Eastern Texts Relating to the Old Testament.* Princeton: Princeton University Press, 1955. Mesopotamian and Egyptian documents that exhibit provocative parallels with biblical texts.

Stendahl, K. *The Bible and the Role of Women.* Philadelphia: Fortress Press, 1966.

11   The Beginnings of Christian Art

Beckwith, John. *Early Christian and Byzantine Art.* Pelican History of Art Series. New York: Penguin, 1980. A good introduction in a fine series.

Hulme, F. Howard. *Symbolism in Christian Art.* Atlantic Highlands, N.J.: Humanities Press, 1971. A classic study of the subject.

Mango, Cyril. *Art of the Byzantine Empire.* Englewood Cliffs, N.J.: Prentice Hall, 1972. A wide-ranging survey.

———. *Byzantine Architecture.* History of World Architecture Series. New York: Harry N. Abrams, 1976. Excellent study in a consistently good series.

12   Building Medieval Walls

General
Bishop, Morris. *The Middle Ages.* Magnolia, Mass.: Peter Smith, 1983. A graceful and witty account of the 1,000 years between Rome and the Renaissance.

Gies, Joseph, and Frances Gies. *Life in a Medieval Castle.* New York: Harper & Row, 1979. Everyday life in a castle.

Peterson, Karen, and J. J. Wilson. *Women Artists—Recognition and Reappraisal, From the Early Middle Ages to the Twentieth Century.* New York: Harper & Row, 1976.

Literature
Rexroth, Kenneth, and Ling Chung. *The Orchid Boat—Women Poets of China.* New York: McGraw Hill, 1973.

Terry, Patricia. *The Song of Roland.* Indianapolis: Bobbs-Merrill Educational Publishing, 1965. Considered the best available translation and the one used in this chapter.

Trapp, J. B., ed. *Medieval English Literature.* New York: Oxford University Press, 1973. Fine anthology which includes *Beowulf, Sir Gawain and the Green Knight*, Chaucer, and other classics.

13   The Late Middle Ages: Expansion and Synthesis

Barber, Richard. *The Knight and Chivalry.* New York: Harper & Row, 1982. An overview of a fascinating subject.

Durrell, Lawrence. *Pope Joan.* New York: Penguin, 1974. The persistent legend of the Joan who became Pope John, engagingly retold by a renowned novelist.

Gies, Frances. *Joan of Arc: The Legend and the Reality.* New York: Harper & Row, 1981.

———. and Joseph Gies. *Life in a Medieval City.* New York: Harper & Row, 1981. An engaging popular account with a focus on thirteenth-century Troyes.

Gies, Joseph, and Frances Gies. *Women in the Middle Ages.* New York: Barnes & Noble, 1980. The status and roles of women.

Gimpel, Jean. *The Medieval Machine: The Industrial Revolution of the Middle Ages.* New York: Penguin, 1977. Significant technological developments in late medieval times.

Heller, Julek, and Deirdre Headon. *Knights.* New York: Schocken, 1982. Rich illustrations capture the romance of legendary knights: Lancelot, Galahad, Tristan, Roland.

Hildegard of Bingen. *Scivias.* Trans. Columba Hart and Jane Bishop. New York: Paulist Press, 1990.

Howarth, David. *1066: The Year of Conquest.* New York: Penguin, 1981. Exciting re-creation of the Norman invasion of England.

Mayer, Hans Eberhard. *The Crusades.* Trans. John Gillingham. New York: Oxford University Press, 1972. The idealism, realism, and barbarism of the Crusades in what is acclaimed as the best one-volume survey.

Translations and Studies of Original Material
Kibler, William, ed. and trans. *Chrétien de Troyes: Lancelot, or the Knight of the Cart.* New York: Garland Publishing, 1981. A superb translation of one of the finest medieval romances.

Loomis, Laura H., and Roger S. Loomis, eds. *Medieval Romances.* New York: Random House, 1965. The best of the genre.

Power, Eileen. *Medieval Women.* Cambridge, U.K.: Cambridge University Press, 1975.

Radice, Betty, trans. *The Letters of Abelard and Heloïse.* New York: Penguin, 1976. The correspondence from the most famous love affair of the Middle Ages.

Richards, Earl Jeffrey, trans. *The Book of the City of Ladies by Christine de Pizan.* New York: Persea Books, 1982. First published in 1405, this is a delightful book by a gifted writer.

Wilhelm, James J., and Laila Zamuelis Gross, eds. *The Romance of Arthur: An Anthology.* Arthurian material in modern translation.

Yenal, Edith. *Christine de Pisan; A Bibliography of Writings by Her and About Her.* Metuchen, N.J.: Scarecrow Press, 1982.

14   The Medieval Synthesis in Art

Brown, Peter, ed. *The Book of Kells: A Selection from the Irish Medieval Manuscripts.* New York: Alfred A. Knopf, 1980. Reproductions from one of the world's most beautiful books.

Calkins, Robert. *Illuminated Books of the Middle Ages.* Ithaca, N.Y.: Cornell University Press, 1983. Includes exquisite color plates.

Simson, Otto von. *The Gothic Cathedral.* New York: Harper & Row, 1964. Classic coverage of the origins and philosophy of the Gothic cathedral.

15   Medieval Music and Dance: Sacred and Secular

Collins, Fletcher, Jr. *The Production of Medieval Church Music-drama.* Charlottesville: University of Virginia Press, 1972. Both historical and practical.

Drinker, Sophie. *Music and Women: The Story of Women in Their Relation to Music.* New York: Coward McCann, 1948, reprinted 1980. Influential women in music, art, poetry, and politics from the ancient world to the modern era.

Harksen, Sibylle. *Women in the Middle Ages.* New York: Abner Schram, 1975. From anonymous women in everyday life to those in art, music, professions, and positions of power.

Whigham, Peter, ed. *The Music of the Troubadours.* Santa Barbara: Ross-Erikson, 1979. Good collection of words and music.

Wilhelm, James J. *Seven Troubadours: The Creators of Modern Verse.* University Park: Pennsylvania State University Press, 1970. Engaging study of some fascinating troubadours.

16 A New Way of Looking at the World

Bainton, Roland H. *Here I Stand: A Life of Martin Luther.* Nashville: Abingdon Press, 1978. Acclaimed as the best introductory biography in English.
———. *Women of the Reformation: In Germany and Italy.* Minneapolis: Augsburg Publishing, 1971. Explores a dimension too often neglected.
Burckhardt, Jacob C. *The Civilization of the Renaissance in Italy.* In any edition. The 19th-century classic that formulated, in part, the modern view of a golden age.
Dickens, A. G. *The Counter-Reformation.* New York: W. W. Norton, 1969. The Roman Catholic response to the Reformation.
Grimm, Harold J. *The Reformation Era: 1500–1650.* New York: Macmillan, 1973. Fine overview.
Morison, Samuel E. *Christopher Columbus, Mariner.* New York: New American Library, 1983. A fine, shorter version of this superb storyteller's definitive *Admiral of the Open Sea.*
Rachum, Ilan. *The Renaissance: An Illustrated Encyclopedia.* New York: W. W. Smith, 1980. Exceptionally useful.
Weber, Max. *The Protestant Ethic and the Spirit of Capitalism.* New York: Charles Scribner's Sons, 1977. The classic study arguing that Calvinism led to the triumph of capitalism.

17 Renaissance Art: A New Golden Age

Ackerman, James S. *Palladio.* New York: Penguin, 1977. Fine study of a very influential architect.
Andres, Glenn, and others. *The Art of Florence.* 2 vols. New York: Abbeville, 1989. Florence from 1200 to 1600 is given a social and historical context in an excellent new study.
Berenson, Bernard. *The Italian Painters of the Renaissance.* Ithaca: Cornell University Press, 1980. A classic study, still influential.
Bramly, Serge, trans. Sian Reynolds. *Discovering the Life of Leonardo da Vinci.* New York: HarperCollins, 1991. An excellent new study.
Coulas, Ivan. *The Borgias.* New York: Franklin Watts, 1989. A readable scholarly study of an infamous but fascinating family.
De Tolnay, Charles. *Michelangelo: Sculptor, Painter, Architect.* Princeton: Princeton University Press, 1982. A condensation of the author's magisterial six-volume study.
Fine, Elsa Honig. *Women and Art; A History of Women Painters and Sculptors from the Renaissance to the 20th Century.* Montclair/London: Allanheld & Schram/Prior, 1978.
Fuller, Edmund, ed. *Vasari's Lives of the Painters, Sculptors, and Architects.* New York: Dell Publishing, 1963. The most pertinent selections from the Renaissance classic.
MacCurdy, Edward, trans. *The Notebooks of Leonardo da Vinci.* 2 vols. London: Chatto Bodley Jonathan, 1978. Only in the notebooks can one begin to appreciate the range and richness of one of the greatest minds in history.
Panofsky, Erwin. *The Life and Art of Albrecht Dürer.* Princeton: Princeton University Press, 1955. Probably the finest single work in English on the German genius.

Snyder, James. *Northern Renaissance Art.* New York: Abrams, 1985. Excellent coverage.

18 Renaissance Music: Court and Church

Dolmetsch, Mabel. *Dances of England and France from 1450–1600: With Their Music and Authentic Manner of Performance.* New York: Da Capo Press, 1975.
Lincoln, Harry B., ed. *Madrigal Collection L'amorosa Ero* (Brescia, 1588). Albany, N.Y.: State University of New York Press, 1968.
Scott, Charles K., ed. *Madrigal Singing.* Westport, Conn: Greenwood, n.d.

19 Shadow and Substance: Literary Insights into the Renaissance

Chute, Marchette. *Shakespeare of London.* New York: E. P. Dutton, 1950. One of the best popular biographies.
Montaigne, Michel de. *Essays.* Trans. J. M. Cohen. New York: Penguin, 1959. Recommended translation of fascinating essays by the inventor of the form.
More, Thomas. *UTOPIA and Other Writings.* James Green and John Dolan, eds. New York: New American Library, 1984. Excellent edition.
Phillips, Margaret M. *Erasmus and the Northern Renaissance.* New York: Rowman, 1981. Explores the central role of Erasmus.
Rabelais, François. *Gargantua and Pantagruel.* Trans. John M. Cohen. New York: Penguin, 1955. Excellent translation of the ribald classic.
Ross, James Bruce, and Mary Martin McLaughlin, eds. *The Portable Renaissance Reader.* New York: Viking, 1968. Excellent collection of writings of acknowledged masters.

20 Science, Reason, and Absolutism

Historical Background
Lefebvre, Georges. *The French Revolution: Vol. I From Its Origins to 1793.* Trans. John H. Stewart. New York: Columbia University Press, 1962. By the greatest modern scholar of the French revolt.
Stone, Laurence. *The Causes of the English Revolution, 1529–1642.* New York: Harper & Row, 1972. How clashes between Puritans and monarchs led to the Cromwell commonwealth experiment.

Cultural Developments
Bennet, Jonathan. *Locke, Berkeley, Hume: Central Themes.* New York: Oxford University Press, 1971. Three of the most influential thinkers of the time.
Burke, Peter. *Popular Culture in Early Modern Europe.* New York: New York University Press, 1978. A fascinating account of the period 1500–1800.
Gay, Peter. *The Enlightenment: An Interpretation.* 2 vols. New York: W. W. Norton, 1977. A remarkable work by a noted authority.
Hall, A. Rupert. *The Revolution in Science: 1500–1750.* New York: Longman, 1983. From Copernicus and Galileo to Newton

and the foundation of the modern scientific outlook.
Santillana, Giorgio de. *The Crime of Galileo.* New York: Time Inc., 1962. A devastating analysis of what a powerful institution can do to an innocent victim.

Original Materials
Montesquieu, Charles de. *The Spirit of the Laws.* Ed. David W. Carrithers. Berkeley: University of California Press, 1978. Influential in several revolutions.
Peterson, Merrill D., ed. *The Portable Thomas Jefferson.* New York: Penguin, 1979. Ample collection of writings by the Yankee genius, including correspondence with prominent people.

21 Art: Baroque, Rococo, and Neoclassic

Bazin, Germain. *The Baroque: Principles, Styles, Modes, Themes.* New York: W. W. Norton, 1978. A comprehensive analysis of general features.
Clark, Kenneth. *An Introduction to Rembrandt.* New York: Harper & Row, 1978. A fine art historian on one of the most famous painters.
Wright, Christopher. *The Dutch Painters: One Hundred Seventeenth-Century Masters.* Woodbury, N.Y.: Barron, 1978.

22 Music: Baroque, Rococo, and Classical

Pauly, Reinhard. *Music in the Classic Period.* Englewood Cliffs, N.J.: Prentice Hall, 1965. Survey of the style with a minimum of technical obstacles.
Rosen, Charles. *The Classical Style: Haydn, Mozart, Beethoven.* New York: W. W. Norton, 1972. Winner of the 1972 National Book Award for Arts and Letters.

23 Revolution, Romanticism, Realism

Historical Background
Arendt, Hannah. *On Revolution.* New York: Penguin, 1977. A noted political analyst examines what the American and French revolutions mean to people living today.
Burchell, Samuel C. *The Age of Progress.* New York: Time-Life Books, 1966. Excellent.
Fieldhouse, D. K. *Colonialism, 1870–1945: An Introduction.* New York: St. Martin's Press, 1981. Today's world, especially the Third World, cannot be fully understood without constant reference to colonialism and its aftermath.
Tuchman, Barbara. *The Guns of August.* New York: Macmillan, 1962. A vivid account of the Great War's outbreak. Her *The Proud Tower* is an equally riveting study of the two decades leading to the war.

Cultural Developments
Eiseley, Loren C. *Darwin's Century: Evolution and the Men Who Discovered It.* Garden City, N.Y.: Doubleday, 1958. A beautifully written account.
———. *The Immense Journey.* New York: Random House, 1957. A classic account of evolution and the story of humankind.

Literature and Criticism
Bloom, Harold, and Lionel Trilling, eds. *Romantic Prose and Poetry.* New York: Oxford University Press, 1973. An

excellent anthology.

Trilling, Lionel, and Harold Bloom, eds. *Victorian Prose and Poetry.* New York: Oxford University Press, 1973. A fine companion volume to their anthology of Romantic works.

Videotape

Burns, Ken. *The Civil War.* First aired in 1990 on PBS, this is a stunning 13-hour series. Richmond, Va., Time-Life Video.

24 Romanticism in Music

Dannreuther, E. *The Romantic Period.* New York: Cooper Square, 1973. Quite a thorough exposition of the varieties of Romantic expression.

Holoman, D. Kern. *Berlioz: A Musical Biography of the Creative Genius of the Romantic Era.* Cambridge, Mass.: Harvard University Press, 1990. By far the most intellectual of the great composers, Berlioz is also honored in French literature as a writer and a critic.

Plantinga, Leon. *Romantic Music.* New York: W. W. Norton, 1982. Introductory text.

25 Nineteenth-Century Art: Conflict and Diversity

Herbert, Robert L. *Impressionism.* New Haven: Yale University Press, 1988. A major new interpretation of the style in its social/cultural context. Strongly recommended.

Prather, Marla, and Charles F. Stuckey, eds. *Gauguin: A Retrospective.* New York: Hugh Lauter Levin Associates, 1987. Outstanding text and illustrations.

Rewald, John. *The History of Impressionism.* New York: New York Graphic Society Books, 1980. Any book by Rewald on Impressionism or Postimpressionism is highly recommended.

———. *Post-Impressionism: From van Gogh to Gauguin.* New York: New York Graphic Society Books, 1979.

Shapiro, Meyer. *Van Gogh.* New York: Abrams, 1984. One of the few objective studies. Highly recommended.

Simpson, Marc, and others. *Winslow Homer: Paintings of the Civil War.* Fine Arts Museum of San Francisco and Bedford Arts Publications, 1988. A unique visual overview of the conflict. Poignant.

26 Things Fall Apart: The Center Cannot Hold

Historical Background

Galbraith, John Kenneth. *The Great Crash, 1929.* Boston: Houghton Mifflin, 1979. The celebrated economist on the catastrophe that ushered in the Great Depression.

Mitchell, Broadus. *Depression Decade: From New Era through New Deal, 1929–1941.* Arnmonk, N.Y.: M. E. Sharpe, 1977. New York: Newsweek Books, 1970. Fine review of significant developments.

Taylor, A. J. P. *The Origins of the Second World War.* New York: Atheneum, 1983. A respected historian reviews the evidence.

Cultural and Scientific Developments

Calder, Nigel. *Einstein's Universe.* New York: Greenwich House, 1982. Einstein explained for the general reader.

Dawkins, Richard. *The Blind Watchmaker: Why the Evidence of Evolution Reveals a Universe Without Design.* New York:

W. W. Norton, 1986. The author's thesis is that the Darwinian worldview could, in principle, help solve the mystery of our existence.

Edelson, Marshall. *Hypothesis and Evidence in Psychoanalysis.* Chicago: University of Chicago Press, 1984.

Gell-Mann, Murray. *The Quark and the Jaguar: Adventures in the Simple and Complex.* New York: W. H. Freeman, 1994.

Gleick, James. *Chaos: Making a New Science.* New York: Viking, 1887. As a physicist put it, "relativity eliminated the Newtonian illusion of absolute space and time; quantum theory eliminated the Newtonian dream of a controllable measurement process; and chaos eliminated the Laplacian fantasy of deterministic predictability."

Grünbaum, Adolf. *The Foundations of Psychoanalysis: A Philosophical Critique.* Berkeley: University of California Press, 1984.

Hitler, Adolf. *Mein Kampf.* Boston: Houghton Mifflin, 1962. Hitler's self-serving autobiography of 1925 with his version of history and vision of the future.

Lewin, Roger. *Complexity: Life at the Edge of Chaos.* New York: Macmillan, 1992.

Noakes, Jeremy, and Geoffrey Pridham, eds. *Documents on Nazism, 1919–1945.* New York: Viking, 1975. A revealing collection, to say the least.

Pipes, Richard. *The Russian Revolution.* New York: Knopf, 1990. The thesis that the February Revolution was a military rebellion (not a workers' revolt) and the Bolshevik takeover in October a *coup d'état.* Further, that when Stalin came to power in 1924 Lenin had all the totalitarian controls firmly in place.

Waldrop, M. Mitchell. *Complexity: The Emerging Science at the Edge of Chaos.* New York: Simon & Schuster, 1992.

Historical Fiction

Pasternak, Boris. *Dr. Zhivago.* New York: Ballantine Books, 1981. The Nobel Laureate's portrait of the Russian Revolution and its aftermath as seen from the inside.

Steinbeck, John. *The Grapes of Wrath.* New York: Penguin, 1977. An indelible picture of the Great Depression as experienced by the Joad family from Oklahoma.

27 Ideas and Conflicts that Motivate the Twentieth Century

Historical Background

Capute, Philip. *A Rumor of War.* New York: Ballantine Books, 1978. Acclaimed the best memoir of the American experience in Vietnam.

Hilberg, Raul. *The Destruction of European Jews.* New York: Harper & Row, 1979. A study of Nazi genocide.

Johnson, Paul. *Modern Times: The World from the Twenties to the Eighties.* New York: Harper & Row, 1983. Highly recommended.

Knox, Bernard. *The Oldest Dead White European Males and Other Reflections on the Classics.* New York: W. W. Norton, 1993. Despite all the sound and fury about being "politically correct," the title of this latest book by a noted classicist states what cannot be denied: this is where, for the most part, Western civilization came from.

Lerner, Gerda. *Women and History.* Volume

One: The Creation of Patrimony. New York: Oxford University Press, 1986. Excellent.

Wiesel, Elie. *Night.* Trans. Stella Rodway. New York: Bantam Books, 1982. The celebrated writer and Nobel Laureate describes his experiences in Hitler's death camps.

Taplin, Oliver. *Greek Fire: The Influence of Ancient Greece on the Modern World.* New York: Atheneum, 1990. Fascinating. The opening line foretells the contents: "Not back to the Greeks, but forward with the Greeks."

Cultural Developments

Baruch, Grace, Rosalind Barnett, and Caryl Rivers. *Life Prints: New Patterns of Love and Work for Today's Women.* New York: McGraw-Hill, 1983. Important study.

Blashfield, Jean F. *Hellraisers, Heroines, and Holy Women: Women's Most Remarkable Contributions to History.* New York: St. Martin's Press, 1981. Just about everything from the "Astronomer to Classify the Most Stars" (Annie Jump Cannon) to the "First Woman to be Kicked Out of Harvard" (Harriet Hunt, 1859).

Greer, Germaine. *Sex and Destiny: The Politics of Human Fertility.* New York: Harper & Row, 1984. An analysis of gender relations in contemporary society.

Herbert, Nick. *Quantum Reality: Beyond the New Physics.* Garden City, N.Y.: Anchor Press/Doubleday, 1985. A popular exposition of six emergent models of the ultimate nature of atomic reality based on post–Einsteinian physics.

Littwin, Susan. *The Postponed Generation: Why American Youth Are Growing Up Later.* New York: William Morrow and Company, 1986. An intriguing analysis of diminished expectations.

Mosse, George L. *Nazi Culture.* New York: Schocken Books, 1981. A noted historian analyzes the vulgarity of Hitler's Germany.

28 Art in the Twentieth Century: Shock Waves and Reactions

Arnason, H. Hovard. *History of Modern Art: Painting, Sculpture, and Architecture.* New York: Abrams, 1986. Excellent general study with an exhaustive bibliography.

Bearden, Romare, and Harry Henderson. *A History of African-American Artists: From 1792 to the Present.* New York: Pantheon, 1993.

Billington, David P. *The Tower and the Bridge: The New Art of Structural Engineering.* New York: Basic Books, Publishers, 1983. The efficiency, economy, and elegance of structural engineering.

Broude, Norma, and Mary D. Garrard, eds. *Feminism and Art History: Questioning the Litany.* New York: Harper & Row, 1982. Essays toward revising the history of art.

Chipp, Herschel. *Picasso's Guernica: History, Transformations, Meanings.* Berkeley: University of California Press, 1988.

Connor, Steven. *Postmodernist Culture: An Introduction to Theories of the Contemporary.* New York: Blackwell, 1990.

Fine, Elsa Honig. *The Afro-American Artist: A Search for Identity.* Reprint. New York: Hacker, 1982. Twenty important artists.

Goodman, Cynthia. *Digital Visions:*

Computers and Art. New York: Abrams, 1987. Computer-generated art.

Huffington, Arianna Stassinopoulos, "Picasso: Creator and Destroyer." *The Atlantic*, June 1988, Vol. 261, No. 6, pp. 37–78. Controversial and highly critical biography of Picasso the man.

Hughes, Robert. *The Shock of the New: Art and the Century of Change.* New York: Knopf, 2nd ed., 1990. This fascinating work grew out of the TV series for BBC and, later, PBS.

Hutcheon, Linda. *A Poetics of Postmodernism: History, Theory, Fiction.* New York: Routledge, 1990. Primary focus on literature.

Jencks, Charles. *Architecture Today.* New York: Abrams, 1988. Significant trends in Late-Modern and Postmodern architecture.

Newhall, Beaumont. *The History of Photography: From 1839 to the Present.* Completely revised and enlarged edition. New York: The Museum of Modern Art, 1982. Hailed as a classic work on the subject.

Normand-Romain, Antoinette Le. *Sculpture: The Adventure of Modern Sculpture in the Nineteenth and Twentieth Centuries.* New York: Rizzoli, 1986. Fine overview and beautifully illustrated.

Parker, Rozsica, and Griselda Pollock. *Old Mistresses: Women, Art, and Ideology.* New York: Pantheon, 1982. A reexamination not merely of women artists, but of art history in general.

Quirarte, Jacinto. *Mexican American Artists.* Austin: University of Texas Press, 1973. A good overview with an extensive bibliography.

Rosen, Randy, and Catherine Brewer. *Making Their Mark: Women Artists Move into the Mainstream.* New York: Abbeville, 1989. The prominent role of women: 1970–85.

Rubinstein, Charlotte Streifer. *American Women Artists: From Early Indian Times to the Present.* Boston: G. K. Hall, 1982. The first comprehensive survey of American women artists.

Russell, John. *The Meaning of Modern Art.* New York: Harper & Row, 1981. Outstanding interpretation. Invaluable.

Slatkin, Wendy. *Women Artists in History: From Antiquity to the 20th Century.* Englewood Cliffs, N.J.: Prentice Hall, 2nd ed., 1990. Good overview. Recorded names of women artists dating back to the 3rd century BC (updated 31 July, 1992).

Toulmin, Stephen. *Cosmopolis: The Hidden Agenda of Modernity.* New York: Free Press, 1990. Primary focus on philosophy.

29   Modern Music

Classical Music

Hamm, Charles. *Music in the New World.* New York: W. W. Norton, 1983. Good overview of American music.

Morgan, Robert P. *Twentieth-Century Music.* New York: W. W. Norton, 1987. From the Norton Introduction to Music Series.

Zaimont, Judith Lang, and Karen Famera, eds. *Contemporary Concert Music by Women: A Directory of the Composers and Their Works.* Westport, Conn.: Greenwood, 1981.

Jazz

Berendt, Joachim. *The Jazz Book: From Ragtime to Fusion and Beyond.* Westport, Conn.: Hill, Lawrence, 1982. Excellent work by a recognized authority.

Booth, Mark W. *American Popular Music: A Reference Guide.* Westport, Conn.: Greenwood, 1983. Valuable resource for ragtime, jazz, Tin Pan Alley, Broadway, Hollywood, Nashville, and so on.

Oliver, Paul. *The Meaning of the Blues.* New York: Macmillan, 1963. Probably the best single book on the blues.

Placksin, Sally. *American Women in Jazz: 1900 to the Present.* New York: Seaview Books, 1982. Overdue recognition of some fine jazz musicians.

Tanner, Paul, et al. *Jazz.* 6th ed. Dubuque, Ia.: Wm. C. Brown, 1988. Good general text.

Credits

Index